W9-AFS-887

American History through Literature
1820–1870

American History through Literature
1820–1870

VOLUME **2** **HARPERS FERRY** to **QUAKERS**

JANET GABLER-HOVER & ROBERT SATTELMEYER
Editors in Chief

CHARLES SCRIBNER'S SONS
An imprint of Thomson Gale, a part of The Thomson Corporation

THOMSON
GALE

Detroit • New York • San Francisco • San Diego • New Haven, Conn. • Waterville, Maine • London • Munich

THOMSON

GALE

American History through Literature, 1820–1870

Janet Gabler-Hover and Robert Sattelmeyer, Editors in Chief

© 2006 Thomson Gale, a part of The Thomson Corporation

Thomson and Star logo are trademarks and Gale and Charles Scribner's Sons are registered trademarks used herein under license.

For more information, contact
Thomson Gale
27500 Drake Road
Farmington Hills, MI 48331-3535
Or visit our Internet site at
http://www.gale.com

Permissions Department
Thomson Gale
27500 Drake Road
Farmington Hills, MI 48331-3535
Permissions hotline:
248-699-8006 or 800-877-4253, ext. 8006
Fax: 248-688-8074 or 800-762-4058

LIBRARY OF CONGRESS CATALOGING-IN-PUBLICATION DATA

American History through Literature, 1820–1870 / Janet Gabler-Hover and Robert Sattelmeyer, editors-in-chief.
   p. cm.
  Includes bibliographical references and index.
  ISBN 0-684-31460-6 (set hardcover : alk. paper) — ISBN 0-684-31461-4 (v. 1) — ISBN 0-684-31462-2 (v. 2) — ISBN 0-684-31463-0 (v. 3) — ISBN 0-684-31492-4 (e-book)
   1. American literature—19th century—Encyclopedias. 2. Literature and history—United States—History—19th century—Encyclopedias. 3. United States—History—19th century—Historiography—Encyclopedias. 4. History in literature—Encyclopedias. I. Gabler-Hover, Janet II. Sattelmeyer, Robert.
PS217 .H57A84 2005
810. 9'358'09034—dc22
                                          2005023615

This title is also available as an e-book
ISBN 0-684-31492-4
And may be purchased with its companion set,
American History through Literature, 1870–1920
ISBN 0-684-31468-1 (6-vol. print set)
Contact your Thomson Gale sales representative for ordering information

Printed in the United States of America
10 9 8 7 6 5 4 3 2 1

Contents

Volume 2

Y

HARPERS FERRY

The Potomac drains the eastern slopes of the Allegheny Mountains and flows southeast until, at Harpers Ferry, it confronts the Shenandoah, flowing north out of the Virginia Blue Ridge. The rivers converge, proceed through a mountain pass, and flow past Washington, D.C., into the Chesapeake Bay. In 1859 Harpers Ferry, Virginia, was a prosperous town, strategically situated at this river junction, on two rail lines, and almost midway along a canal that carried freight from the Chesapeake to Pennsylvania. The town, with a population of almost three thousand, had a military economy: it was home to a U.S. armory, a federal arsenal, and Hall's Rifle Works.

THE RAID ON HARPERS FERRY

During the night of 16 October 1859, nineteen men walked into Harpers Ferry, captured the armory, and then commandeered the thousands of rifles stored at the arsenal. Three others waited outside town to provide a rear guard. Most members of this "multiracial alliance" were free-soil veterans of the Kansas civil war and were trained in guerrilla tactics. Their apparent plan was to capture the weapons and to quickly move them into improvised natural fortifications located at regular intervals along the Appalachian and Allegheny Mountains. There the alliance would free slaves, arming some with pikes or rifles, and open a defendable route of ridgeline escape and logistical resupply from Alabama to Canada. Despite a last-minute shortage of volunteers and poor planning for food, ammunition, and transport, the raid quickly met its initial goal of capturing the weapons. But before the raiders could make a quiet escape, the mission's objectives were redrawn to include the capture of several prominent hostages and the theft of some symbolically charged weapons that had once belonged to George Washington.

John "Osawatomie" Brown (1800–1859), a fifty-nine-year-old radical abolitionist, led the raid. His growing reputation in the Kansas civil war had earned him enthusiastic support in preceding years as he lectured northerners on the need for armed resistance to slavery—although his audiences had probably assumed he meant further action in Kansas. Brown had met and corresponded with important literary figures, including Henry David Thoreau, Ralph Waldo Emerson, Amos Bronson Alcott, and Thomas Wentworth Higginson. But in addition to the raiding party, his close conspirators included Frederick Douglass (1818–1895), Harriet Tubman (c. 1820–1913), some influential and financial backers who have become known as the "Secret Six," his fifteen-year-old daughter, Annie Brown, and his daughter-in-law, Martha Brown.

In the early morning hours of 17 October, Brown awaited the return of the hostage-taking detachment he had sent five miles away to capture Lewis Washington and some Washington family heirlooms. But on two occasions sporadic shooting broke out in the town. The hostage detail finally returned to Harpers Ferry around 5:00 A.M., but lingering agitation over the inadvertent murder of a free black resident of Harpers Ferry delayed Brown from making a timely exit. By sunrise, with church bells pealing, the town's residents were becoming aware of the disturbance.

Harper's Ferry Insurrection. Newspaper illustration of federal troops capturing Brown's men, October 1859. © CORBIS

Inconceivably, Brown and his men dawdled as units of the Virginia militia in nearby towns were notified. Forgoing his last clear chance of escaping with the captured rifles, Brown released a previously halted B&O passenger train, which then proceeded toward Baltimore without him as the townspeople began to put up a fledgling defense. Erratic gunfire kept Brown and his men engaged through the morning. By noon the raiders were pinned down with their hostages in a fire-engine garage under growing threat from units of the Virginia militia. By nightfall, Brown and five of the raiders defended the engine house against several hundred militiamen. The other raiders had been killed or wounded or had escaped into the nearby mountains.

Colonel Robert E. Lee (1807–1870), in temporary command of ninety marines, entered the fracas before midnight and ordered federal troops to form a perimeter around Brown and his demoralized raiders. Early the next morning, Lee offered to accept an unconditional surrender from Brown. During the ensuing negotiations over the terms of surrender, twelve marines stormed the building. Within three minutes, a seriously wounded Brown, along with four of his followers, had been captured alive.

THE NATIONAL REACTION

Rumors of abolitionist conspiracies and slave insurrections spread throughout the slave states during the rest of the winter. Democratic and southern newspapers blamed the Republicans and abolitionists for the attack, accusing them of encouraging slaves to murder defenseless families. Even northern and Republican newspapers expressed shock and horror over the raid. Republican leaders reacted to the news by distancing themselves from Brown and his methods. William Lloyd Garrison (1805–1879), the editor of *The Liberator,* called the raid "misguided, wild, and apparently insane." Accurately concerned that the nation's moral outrage could result in their own arrest, many of Brown's coconspirators fled the country, entered an asylum, or otherwise avoided the public gaze. A few of the more courageous or defiant refused to flee.

THE LEGEND: "MANIAC" TO "MARTYR"

Early support for John Brown and for his violent raid began in a surprising yet familiar place, Concord, Massachusetts, a town that "instigated the first American 'insurrection,'" according to James

Redpath, a journalist who had befriended Brown during the Kansas war. One Concord resident, Henry David Thoreau (1817–1862), learned of the Harpers Ferry incident a day after the engine house had been stormed. Thoreau was misinformed that Brown had been killed; in his journal entry that day he ranted for an unprecedented eleven pages against the federal government, the newspapers, Republicans, his neighbors, and humankind. Almost daily until 8 December Thoreau's journal dwelt upon Brown, and much of this invective was excerpted for lectures and later essays. Over the next several weeks, he gave fiery speeches in Concord, Boston, and Worcester that were culled from these journal entries. Later, Thoreau compiled these speeches into an essay that he titled "A Plea for Captain John Brown."

Meanwhile, a slowly healing Brown was charged with murder and treason and quickly put on trial. Throughout the very public and internationally reported proceedings, a passionate letter and lecture campaign blossomed. Lydia Maria Child (1802–1880), a prolific abolitionist author, wrote to the governor of Virginia requesting permission to visit Brown and to act as his prison nurse. The governor used the opportunity of a public reply to belittle northern sympathy for Brown and his violence. To raise funds for Brown's legal defense and for his family's ongoing support, the

Boston abolitionist Wendell Phillips (1811–1884) made a powerful speech in Brooklyn on 1 November. Six days later, Ralph Waldo Emerson (1803–1882) spoke at a well-attended and sympathetic Boston fund-raiser. To mixed applause, Emerson compared the prospect of Brown's execution on the gallows to the death of Jesus on the cross.

Others writers contributed essays, letters, and poems and were quoted in support of Brown in important newspapers. Victor Hugo (1802–1885) published a letter referring to Brown as "the liberator, the champion of Christ." On 2 December, the day of Brown's hanging near Charles Town, Virginia, sympathizers attended memorial services that were held throughout the North. The Concord event included readings, hymns, prayers, and eulogies. Thoreau, Emerson, Amos Bronson Alcott (1799–1888), and Louisa May Alcott (1832–1888) participated. In another part of Concord, however, Brown was hanged in effigy. Popular sentiment across the nation was beginning to shift. From the day of Brown's execution, a regional divergence of public opinion developed as to the meaning of the raid. Northerners began to view the assault as a pious and heroic—if desperate—effort by a martyr in the cause of liberty; southerners blasted it as an insane act of terrorism against innocent citizens of Virginia.

Within months, James Redpath published a volume of poems, letters, and essays honoring Brown the martyr. Included in this collection were poems by Louisa May Alcott, John Greenleaf Whittier, Lydia Maria Child, and William Dean Howells. Less than five months after Brown's hanging, the Democratic Party split into regional factions over its slavery platform. During the ensuing Civil War, Brown's legend grew with Union victories and benefited from the spirit of home-front sacrifice. Many Union soldiers marched to "John Brown's Body"—a rousing song with multiple versions—that inspired Julia Ward Howe to write "The Battle Hymn of the Republic" to the same tune.

After the war, lengthy biographies of Brown, written by devotees such as Richard Hinton and Franklin Sanborn, helped to preserve the John Brown legend. Borrowing a metaphor from Thoreau, both Herman Melville (1819–1891) and Walt Whitman (1819–1892) paid tribute to Brown the "meteor" in several poems about the war. In 1882 the American historian George Washington Williams (1849–1891) recognized that the view of John Brown as a "madman" had been corrected.

Like West Virginia itself, which had abandoned its allegiance to Virginia at the outbreak of the Civil War,

---

While much of the country reacted with shock and outrage to news of John Brown's raid, early justification for the radical action was voiced by Henry David Thoreau. Within a month of the raid, Thoreau's speeches in Boston, Concord, and Worcester, carried by the national press, compared Brown's heroic acts at Harpers Ferry to the horrific violence preserving slavery in the South.

There sits a tyrant holding fettered four millions of slaves; here comes their heroic liberator. This most hypocritical and diabolical government looks up from its seat on the gasping four millions, and inquires with an assumption of innocence, "What do you assault me for? Am I not an honest man? Cease agitation on this subject, or I will make a slave of you, too, or else hang you."

Henry David Thoreau, "A Plea for Captain John Brown," in *Henry David Thoreau: Reform Papers,* edited by Wendell Glick (Princeton, N.J.: Princeton University Press, 1973), p. 129.

Harpers Ferry had also jettisoned the stigma it had gained as a site of violence. The town became an abolitionist shrine, a symbol of liberty in the national literary imagination. Seen within the context of the Civil War, the violence of the raid seemed less shocking and more justifiable. By 1900 the historical facts of John Brown's abortive raid, his indecisive leadership, his resort to violence, and his failure to incite an immediate slave insurrection had faded in importance and in meaning, while the almost-sacred ruins of the once-prosperous town had come to represent the continuing struggle for African American rights.

See also Abolitionist Writing; *Battle-Pieces;* Civil War; Transcendentalism

BIBLIOGRAPHY
Primary Works
Emerson, Ralph Waldo. *Emerson's Antislavery Writings.* Edited by Len Gougeon and Joel Myerson. New Haven, Conn.: Yale University Press, 1995.

Hinton, Richard J. *John Brown and His Men.* 1894. New York: Arno Press, 1968.

Redpath, James. *Echoes of Harper's Ferry.* 1860. New York: Arno Press, 1969.

Sanborn, F. B., ed. *The Life and Letters of John Brown, Liberator of Kansas and Martyr of Virginia.* 1885. New York: Negro Universities Press, 1969.

Thoreau, Henry David. *The Essays of Henry D. Thoreau.* Edited by Lewis Hyde. New York: North Point Press, 2002.

Secondary Works
Boyer, Richard O. *The Legend of John Brown: A Biography and a History.* New York: Knopf, 1973.

Finkelman, Paul, ed. *His Soul Goes Marching On: Responses to John Brown and the Harpers Ferry Raid.* Charlottesville: University Press of Virginia, 1995.

Geier, Clarence R., Jr., and Susan E. Winter, eds. *Look to the Earth: Historical Archaeology and the American Civil War.* Knoxville: University of Tennessee Press, 1994.

Karcher, Carolyn L. *The First Woman in the Republic: A Cultural Biography of Lydia Maria Child.* Durham, N.C.: Duke University Press, 1994.

Oates, Stephen B. *To Purge This Land with Blood: A Biography of John Brown.* New York: Harper and Row, 1970.

Peterson, Merrill D. *John Brown: The Legend Revisited.* Charlottesville: University of Virginia Press, 2002.

Quarles, Benjamin. *Allies for Freedom and Blacks on John Brown.* 1972. Chicago: Da Capo Press, 1974.

Richardson, Robert D., Jr., *Henry Thoreau: A Life of the Mind.* Berkeley: University of California Press, 1986.

Stauffer, John. *The Black Hearts of Men: Radical Abolitionists and the Transformation of Race.* Cambridge, Mass: Harvard University Press, 2002.

Thoreau, Henry David. *The Journal of Henry D. Thoreau.* Vols. 12–13. 1906. Edited by Bradford Torrey and Francis H. Allen. New York: Dover, 1962.

Joseph M. Petrulionis

HARPER'S NEW MONTHLY MAGAZINE

What do Mathew Brady, Santa Claus, Little Dorrit, Wild Bill Hickok, Winslow Homer, Elizabeth Stuart Phelps, Mark Twain, and Boss Tweed hold in common? All debuted before a national audience in monthly or weekly magazines published by Harper & Brothers between 1850 and 1870. Beyond such firsts, the firm's magazines themselves stand as landmarks in American mass media history. By closely associating word and image, *Harper's New Monthly Magazine* (1850) and its spin-off, *Harper's Weekly* (1857), set the course for general magazines for generations to come. In so doing, they fundamentally, if unintentionally, fostered American literature.

"A TENDER TO OUR BUSINESS"

Quickly growing from its 1817 foundation in New York City to become the nation's top book publisher, Harper & Brothers brought to its magazines much organizational experience. By each specializing in executive, financial, operational, and editorial functions, the four brothers—James, John, Joseph Wesley, and Fletcher—developed a quasi-modern managerial system that easily adopted innovations like steam-powered presses, stereotyping, and integrated factory production. The productive capacity readily found far-flung outlets via transportation lines increasingly linking New York to the nation. This nexus of production and distribution yielded an immense business—by January 1854 Harper counted 1,549 "works on hand . . . in editions varying from five hundred to fifty thousand" ("A Word of Apology," p. 147).

The firm's success with books gave rise in June 1850 to *Harper's New Monthly Magazine,* later described by Fletcher Harper (1806–1877), the chief editor of Harper and the youngest of the four brothers, as "a tender to our business" (p. 85)—that is, a promotional sampler. Indeed the magazine advertised only Harper imprints and frequently excerpted them. The contents of the magazine more subtly

Engraving of the Harpers building on Franklin Square, New York. From *Harper's New Monthly Magazine,* December 1865. CLEMENTS LIBRARY, UNIVERSITY OF MICHIGAN

reflected the firm's book business too. Diffusing risks by juggling biographical, historical, reference, scientific, theological, and travel titles as well belles lettres and textbooks, Harper & Brothers had ample editorial resources for a general magazine. The firm's many schoolbook and family library series provided precedents for marshaling miscellaneous material to maintain reader interest. In pursuing this, the brothers learned that illustrations sold books; their first-rate artists soon served the magazine so well that it became known for its illustrations. Finally, Harper had prospered by reprinting British works unprotected by international copyright. The magazine naturally followed house tradition in serializing British best-sellers.

"SIMPLY STEALING"?

Harper's transatlantic orientation sparked controversy in a time of literary nationalism. Some observers accused the firm of piracy, of "simply stealing" foreign work, as it was stated in the July 1852 *American Whig Review* (p. 16) and thus not funding native talent. True, the magazine published British superstars such as Edward Bulwer-Lytton, Charles Dickens,

Mary Russell Mitford, Agnes Strickland, and William Makepeace Thackeray. However, the Harpers did at times buy from them advance sheets—Dickens's *Bleak House* (April 1852–October 1853) cost them $1,728— to scoop local rivals pirating the eventual British edition.

Whether *Harper's* discouraged American writers is also unclear. In the 1850s most articles were anonymous, making nationality claims hard to assess. Still, some prominent Yankee contributors' names, like those of Jacob and John Abbott, did commonly appear. The magazine even occasionally publicized American literati in passing. For instance, the February 1856 introduction to Dickens's *Little Dorrit* (January 1856–July 1857) summoned Nathaniel Hawthorne's "P's Correspondence" (1845), about a lunatic envisioning alternate histories, to ponder the cultural impoverishment that would have ensued had Boz—the pen name Dickens (1812–1870) used—died before finishing *The Pickwick Papers,* which had been published serially in 1836–1837.

More substantively, by the late fifties *Harper's* paid at least five dollars a page for all American work, thus furthering professionalism. Herman Melville

(1819–1891) was one writer who turned magazinist via *Harper's,* where he published several stories, including "The Paradise of Bachelors and the Tartarus of Maids" (April 1855). Despite Melville's conformance to the house style of "nonpartisan sentiment" (Post-Lauria, p. 167), in this story a paper mill serves as a grim synecdoche for the very industrialization the Harper factory represented—some indication of the forbearance granted local talent. The national presence increased over time, for by December 1861, when nearly all authors were being identified, all but two were Americans, including notable women like Louise Chandler Moulton and Elizabeth Stoddard. The trend continued throughout the 1860s, even for novices. For example, in January 1864 came "A Sacrifice Consumed" by the nineteen-year-old Elizabeth Stuart Phelps (1844–1911) who would publish the best-selling *The Gates Ajar* in 1868, while the December 1866 issue contained "Forty-three Days in an Open Boat" by Mark Twain (1835–1910; Twain's name was mistakenly printed as Mark Swain), who was at that point in his career a complete unknown. In short, *Harper's New Monthly Magazine* not only launched and sustained many careers; it also stimulated a national market for current literature.

INTO THE FAMILY CIRCLE

At the outset *Harper's Monthly* predicted that it would "make its way into the hands or the family circle of every intelligent citizen" ("A Word at the Start," p. 2), and it soon seemed progressing toward that goal. Priced reasonably at twenty-five cents an issue or three dollars annually, the magazine had after six months a circulation of 50,000 and by 1860 about 200,000—almost seventeen times more than the average monthly. Like other magazines, *Harper's* benefited from 1852 federal regulations that shifted postage fees from receiver to sender, while dramatically lowering them. Unlike competitors, however, *Harper's* had the advantage of a brand name, sumptuous pictures of exotic places, rare access to British literary lions, a steady stable of writers, and above all deep pockets to survive economic downturns.

These elements might not have jelled without the brothers' truly national aspirations, shaped by their Methodist ethic of getting the word out to everywhere and everyone through inoffensive and informative entertainment. Indeed in *The House of Harper* (1912), J. Henry Harper credits his grandfather Fletcher Harper's weekly dinners with prominent ministerial raconteurs returning from the road as the source for the magazine's humorous and highly popular "Editor's Drawer" (p. 34). Borrowing and secularizing that

entertaining oral sensibility throughout their magazine, the Harpers made it an ideal vehicle for the common social practice of reading aloud.

Who actually read the magazine remains uncertain because of circumstantial and fragmentary evidence. Scholars have variably seen *Harper's* expressing upper- or middle-class interests, but such terms scarcely encompass the complex mid-century social formations from which it drew readers. Correspondence and diaries show the magazine being read nationwide by laborers and the leisured alike, with wide availability through libraries and informal lending. Still, the magazine's tone bespoke refinement, reflected in coffee-table-book pictorialism that culminated in the January 1857 founding of *Harper's Weekly.* It would be a chronicle for the times, whereas the nonpartisan monthly stood for the ages; together they opened Americans' eyes to a new visual universe.

"THE MOST STRIKING PICTURES FOR MANY YEARS"

The extent and quality of illustrations uniquely characterized Harper magazines. The monthly had "the most striking pictures for many years," especially of exotic places, and thus faced "no competition" until the 1870s, according to the firm's historian J. Henry Harper (p. 88), while the weekly (itself with circulations over 100,000) far outpaced its two serious rivals, *Frank Leslie's Illustrated Newspaper* and the derivative *New York Illustrated News.* In an era before cheap photomechanical reproduction would make the glossy magazine commonplace, *Harper's* ably served a reading public hungry for visual imagery.

In obliging its audience, *Harper's* spared no expense for illustrations. While in its earliest issues the magazine sported few but diverse images of authors (or their homes), fashions, wondrous locales, and scientific processes, decorations for poetry and fiction, and cartoons, it slowly multiplied the number. As of December 1865 the magazine boasted printing over ten thousand wood engravings, the average of which cost about thirty dollars—then an extraordinary figure. It is no wonder, for the process was long and complex and involved an array of artists. A field sketch, photograph, or studio drawing was often copied, even altered, by a chief artist before being transferred to the polished surfaces of boxwood blocks. These were then carefully cut by engravers, set on a page along with type, and by 1865, electrotyped onto metal plates ready for the press. What the engravers did not chisel away, namely the drawing's lines, absorbed ink and appeared black when printed, while carved areas yielded white. During the Civil War the staff of *Harper's Weekly* labored around the clock to translate images rushed from the battlefront into printed illustrations. For less timely subjects the magazine was not averse to requisitioning woodblocks from its book department and copying illustrations from other publications.

Harper's magazine illustrations advanced the reputations of many artists and popularized visual renditions of celebrated, notorious, and fictitious figures. The magazine's numerous Mathew Brady (1823–1896) portraits whetted rather than sated appreciation of the celebrated New York photographer's artistry. The popularity of the Civil War sketches and drawings of everyday scenes that Winslow Homer (1836–1910) did for the magazine presaged his later renown as a painter. So faithful was his depiction of the positions of Union forces in *First Days' Firing at Yorktown* that cautious generals censored its publication. Scathing caricatures of "Boss" Tweed (William Marcy Tweed, 1823–1878) as the bloated kingpin of the corrupt Tweed Ring (1866–1871) that debased New York City politics secured both his timeless infamy and the reputation of the cartoonist Thomas Nast (1840–1902), who repeatedly depicted Tweed and his nefarious doings in *Harper's* and other periodicals. Nast also conjured up beloved characters in 1860s issues, including the quintessential Santa Claus: portly, jolly, and hoary bearded. The magazine's February 1867 engravings of the flowing haired, mustachioed, gun-toting Wild Bill Hickok (James Butler Hickok, 1837–1876), when coupled with a thirteen-page derring-do adventure, helped fashion a national folk legend from a regional curiosity.

Competition from *Scribner's Monthly* around 1870 only spurred *Harper's* on to greater heights in the number and quality of its graven images, which became increasingly refined, even ethereal. However, the era of fine wood engraving was nearing its end as inexpensive photographic processes supplanted the costly and laborious procedure while satisfying the taste for greater realism. *Harper's* legacy, however, remains wedded to the heyday of wood engraving, when it won the hearts of an audience who not only read but also beheld and imagined what was rarely seen.

See also Book Publishing; Editors; English Literature; Literary Marketplace; Literary Nationalism; Periodicals; Photography; Publishers

BIBLIOGRAPHY

Primary Works

Guernsey, Alfred H. "Making the Magazine." *Harper's New Monthly Magazine,* December 1865, pp. 1–31.

"A Letter to the Proprietors of *Harper's Magazine*." *American Whig Review* 16 (July 1852): 12–21.

"A Word at the Start." *Harper's New Monthly Magazine,* June 1850, pp. 1–2.

"A Word of Apology." *Harper's New Monthly Magazine,* January 1854, pp. 145–158.

Secondary Works

Allen, Frederick Lewis. *"Harper's Magazine," 1850–1950: A Centenary Address.* New York: Newcomen Society in North America, 1950.

Barnhurst, Kevin G., and John C. Nerone. *The Form of News: A History.* New York: Guilford Press, 2001.

Beam, Philip C. *Winslow Homer's Magazine Engravings.* New York: Harper and Row, 1979.

Belk, Russell W. "Materialism and the Making of the Modern American Christmas." In *Unwrapping Christmas,* edited by Daniel Miller, pp. 75–104. New York: Oxford University Press, 1993.

Brodhead, Richard H. *Cultures of Letters: Scenes of Reading and Writing in Nineteenth-Century America.* Chicago: University of Chicago Press, 1993.

Exman, Eugene. *The Brothers Harper: A Unique Publishing Partnership and Its Impact upon the Cultural Life of America from 1817 to 1853.* New York: Harper and Row, 1965.

Exman, Eugene. *The House of Harper: One Hundred and Fifty Years of Publishing.* New York: Harper and Row, 1967.

Harper, Joseph Henry. *The House of Harper: A Century of Publishing in Franklin Square.* New York: Harper & Brothers, 1912.

Keller, Morton. *The Art and Politics of Thomas Nast.* New York: Oxford University Press, 1968.

Meredith, Roy. *Mr. Lincoln's Camera Man: Mathew B. Brady.* New York: Charles Scribner's Sons. 1946. Rev. ed. New York: Dover, 1974.

Miller, Perry. *The Raven and the Whale: The War of Words and Wits in the Era of Poe and Melville.* New York: Harcourt, Brace, 1956.

Mott, Frank Luther. *A History of American Magazines.* Vol. 2, *1850–1865.* Cambridge, Mass.: Harvard University Press, 1938.

Pearson, Andrea G. "*Frank Leslie's Illustrated Newspaper* and *Harper's Weekly:* Innovation and Imitation in Nineteenth-Century American Pictorial Reporting." *Journal of Popular Culture* 23 (1990): 81–111.

Post-Lauria, Sheila. *Correspondent Colorings: Melville in the Marketplace.* Amherst: University of Massachusetts Press, 1996.

Zboray, Ronald J. *A Fictive People: Antebellum Economic Development and the American Reading Public.* New York: Oxford University Press, 1993.

Zboray, Ronald J., and Mary Saracino Zboray. *Everyday Ideas: Socio-Literary Experience in Antebellum New England.* Knoxville: University of Tennessee Press, forthcoming.

Ronald J. Zboray
Mary Saracino Zboray

HARPER'S WEEKLY

See Book and Periodical Illustration; Periodicals; Pictorial Weeklies

"HAWTHORNE AND HIS MOSSES"

On Monday, 5 August 1850, several writers and their editors gathered together in the Berkshire Mountains for what turned out to be a historic meeting: Nathaniel Hawthorne (1804–1864), author of the acclaimed *The Scarlet Letter,* published just five months earlier (and the only novel Hawthorne acknowledged having written) was introduced to Herman Melville (1819–1891), himself the author of five books, including his best-selling *Typee: A Peep at Polynesian Life* (1846), which Hawthorne had reviewed. Both writers were then living in the Berkshire Mountains—Melville in Pittsfield, Hawthorne in a small cottage in Lenox—but had not yet encountered one another. They did, however, share a friendship with the editor, publisher, and bibliophile Evert Augustus Duyckinck (1816–1878), who indirectly brought the two men together.

Exercising the literary arm of the Young America movement, Duyckinck had issued Melville's *Typee* as one of Wiley and Putnam's Library of American Books, a series that intended to promote national authors in affordable editions and thereby compete with the cheap British books flooding the American market. That there was no international copyright law vexed the literary members of the Young America movement, who made copyright reform one of their chief issues. First in the series was Hawthorne's edition of the *Journal of an African Cruiser* (1845), written by his college friend Horatio Bridge, and soon after Duyckinck published Hawthorne's second collection of stories, *Mosses from an Old Manse* (1846).

Four years later, while Duyckinck and the essayist Cornelius Mathews (c. 1817–1889) were visiting the Melvilles in Pittsfield, James T. Fields (1817–1881), the Boston publisher of *The Scarlet Letter,* and his wife were scheduled to stop by the Hawthornes' house. A Berkshire neighbor, learning of the coincidence, arranged an outing for a group that also included the poet and essayist Oliver Wendell Holmes (1809–1894) and the Young American historian Joel Headley (1813–1897). On 5 August the party gathered to climb Monument Mountain and enjoy a hilarious day of rainstorms, champagne, and good conversation about, among other things, the importance of an American literature.

The topic had bothered American writers for almost half a century and certainly ever since the journalist Sydney Smith (1771–1845), in the pages of the *Edinburgh Review* in 1820, had condescendingly wondered, "In the four quarters of the globe, who reads an American book?" Authors as various as the novelist John Neal (1793–1876) and Ralph Waldo Emerson (1803–1882) had risen to the challenge. Neal replied that people want American, not English, books from America. In 1836, in *Nature,* Emerson enjoined American writers to enjoy an original relation to nature, by which he meant to depend on themselves, not European models, for inspiration. By that time, Hawthorne had already been in search of local materials for his stories in early histories of New England, such as Cotton Mather's (1663–1728) *Magnalia Christi Americana* (1702) and William Sewell's (1653–1720) *History of the Quakers* (1728).

Although Melville had already been given a copy of Hawthorne's *Mosses from an Old Manse,* it is not certain whether he had begun reading it before he met Hawthorne. Nor is it certain when exactly he began to review it. But when Duyckinck returned to New York City the week of 12 August, he carried with him the first installment of Melville's essay "Hawthorne and His Mosses," which he immediately printed in his journal, the *Literary World.* Shortly thereafter, Melville supplied the second installment of the essay, and the two sections, published on 17 and 24 August, still constitute one of the most probing commentaries on Hawthorne ever written.

Pretending to be a Virginian on summer vacation in Vermont, Melville claimed to have just read Hawthorne's *Mosses* while lying outdoors in the open air. It was an ecstatic experience. "His wild, witch voice rings through me," Melville declared ("Hawthorne and His Mosses," p. 239). "Already I feel that this Hawthorne has dropped germinous seeds into my soul," Melville resumed in distinctly erotic prose. "He expands and deepens down, the more I contemplate him; and further and further, shoots his strong New-England roots into the hot soil of my Southern soul" (p. 250).

So unmistakable is Melville's ebullient eroticism that some scholars consider it a sign of Melville's uncategorizable sexuality (at least as evinced in his novels), his likely homosexual experiences, and his obvious infatuation with the handsome Hawthorne, his senior by fifteen years. No evidence, however, suggests that Melville's homoerotic response to Hawthorne translated into action; nor do Hawthorne or Melville seem troubled by it. Admissions of love, between men or between women, were not yet taboo or titillating, either culturally or medically. Whatever his erotic motivation, Melville's shrewd analysis and unconditional support of Hawthorne's work were gratefully appreciated by the elder author.

Despite the success of *The Scarlet Letter* and his reputation as a writer of unerring elegance, Hawthorne long considered himself "for a good many years, the obscurest man of letters in America" ("Preface," p. 1150). In fact, just five years earlier, in 1845, Duyckinck himself had proposed that the government establish a literary pension fund for such indigent, neglected writers as Hawthorne, and just two years later, in 1847, Edgar Allan Poe hailed Hawthorne as "the example, par excellence, in this country, of the privately admired and publicly under-appreciated man of genius" (p. 242). Now here was Melville, a published author willing and capable of seeing that under Hawthorne's "mild moonlight of contemplative humor" lay "a great, deep intellect, which drops down into the universe like a plummet" ("Hawthorne and his Mosses," pp. 241, 242). For in "spite of all the Indian-summer sunlight on the hither side of Hawthorne's soul," wrote Melville, "the other side—like the dark half of the physical sphere—is shrouded in a blackness, ten times black" (p. 243).

"Certain it is," Melville continued in his now-famous formulation,

> that this great power of blackness in him derives its force from its appeals to that Calvinistic sense of Innate Depravity and Original Sin, from whose visitations, in some shape or other, no deeply thinking mind is always and wholly free. For, in certain moods, no man can weigh this world without throwing in something, somehow like Original Sin, to strike the uneven balance. (P. 243)

This formulation influenced early Hawthorne biographers, such as Newton Arvin, who emphasized his Puritan inheritance and somber estimation of human perfectibility, as well as literary critics, such as F. O. Matthiessen, whose *American Renaissance* (1941) largely shaped canonical thinking about Hawthorne and Melville for several decades.

Yet according to Melville, not everyone reading Hawthorne comprehends him, "for it is, mostly, insinuated to those who may best understand it, and account for it" (p. 245). Actually many of Hawthorne's

IN TOKEN

OF MY ADMIRATION FOR HIS GENIUS,

This Book is Inscribed

TO

NATHANIEL HAWTHORNE.

Dedication page of the first edition of *Moby-Dick*, 1851. SPECIAL COLLECTIONS LIBRARY, UNIVERSITY OF MICHIGAN

champions had preferred more insubstantial sketches, such "Buds and Bird-Voices," to the somberness and ambiguity of "Young Goodman Brown." "It is the least part of genius that attracts admiration," Melville explained (p. 242). Consoling Hawthorne on his obscurity and poor sales, Melville acknowledged that "few men have time, or patience, or palate, for the spiritual truth" (p. 245).

In "Hawthorne and His Mosses," Melville recognized in Hawthorne the same outsized literary ambition he himself harbored—and the same frustrations. "In this world of lies," Melville averred, "Truth is forced to fly like a scared white doe in the woodlands; and only by cunning glimpses will she reveal herself, as in Shakespeare and other great masters of the great Art of Telling the Truth—even though it be covertly and by snatches" (p. 255). The public wants entertainment, not truth, and even Shakespeare, according to Melville, could but insinuate "the things, which we feel to be so terrifically true, that it were all but madness for any good man, in his own proper character, to utter, or even hint of them" (p. 244).

The comparison of Hawthorne and Shakespeare was meant to startle Melville's readers, particularly those, as Melville said, whose "absolute and unconditional adoration of Shakespeare has grown to be part of our Anglo Saxon superstitions" (p. 245). Such blind hero worship is distinctly unrepublican—un-American; "men not very much inferior to Shakespeare are this day being born on the banks of the Ohio," exclaimed Melville (p. 245). Stumping for an American literature in the manner of the nationalistic Young American and sounding much like Emerson—"the world is as young today, as when it was created" (p. 246)—Melville enjoined his reader to "contemn all imitation . . . and foster all originality" (p. 248), to take risks, speak without bounds, and to support American authors. That is, declaiming that the American must seize the moment, write in and of the present, not sound like anyone else, not play lackey to what Emerson called the courtly muses of Europe, and scrap all "leaven of literary flunkeyism towards England," Melville was staking out his own literary territory in the expansionist terms of Young America: "We are rapidly preparing for that political supremacy among the nations, which prophetically awaits us at the close of the present century" (p. 248).

By presenting himself as a southerner linked indissolubly to Hawthorne the New Englander, Melville also suggests that an American literature contains multitudes, as Walt Whitman would say. Surely they contain Melville, for he believed he found a quality of genius in Hawthorne that both men shared. "I somehow cling to the strange fancy," Melville wrote near the conclusion of his essay, "that, in all men, hiddenly reside certain wondrous, occult properties—as in some plants and minerals—which by some happy but very rare accident . . . may chance to be called forth here on earth" (p. 253). "For genius, all over the world, stands hand in hand," Melville affirmed, "and one shock of recognition runs the whole circle round" (p. 249).

Yet more and more, Melville was apparently feeling that he could not write as he wished and remain the solvent, popular author of *Typee;* the book had catapulted him to dubious fame as the man who had lived among cannibals. "What I feel most moved to write, that is banned,—it will not pay," he would regretfully confide in Hawthorne while finishing *Moby-Dick* (1851). "Yet, altogether, write the *other* way I cannot" (*Correspondence,* p. 192).

Because Melville wrote few reviews and scant criticism and because a very limited correspondence survives, his "Hawthorne and His Mosses" has become a window into Melville's literary intentions, particularly regarding his next novel and masterpiece, *Moby-Dick,* which he dedicated to Hawthorne. There, in magniloquent prose, Melville merged adventure story with metaphysical quest, history of whaling with philosophical meditation. But *Moby-Dick* confounded reviewers, some of whom considered it blasphemous or baffling. Still, Melville believed his brooding insights could be approached only through indirection; and so he aspired to utter the "madness of vital truth"—albeit covertly and in snatches—much as his character Pip, a black cabin boy, does.

Evert Duyckinck, Melville's friend and publisher, responded so tepidly to the book that Hawthorne chastised him. But if Hawthorne suggested he himself review *Moby-Dick,* Melville rejected the offer, and Hawthorne took him at his word. Yet much to Melville's delight, Hawthorne had appreciated *Moby-Dick* so much that, as Melville wrote to Hawthorne, he believed that Hawthorne's "heart beat in my ribs and mine in yours, and both in God's" (*Correspondence,* p. 212). Unfortunately, Hawthorne's letter of praise for *Moby-Dick* has never been discovered, and the correspondence between the two dwindled after the Hawthornes returned to eastern Massachusetts. Hawthorne was then appointed American consul in Liverpool, England, by his college friend, Franklin Pierce (1804–1869), recently elected president of the United States, and left America for seven years.

The friendship between Hawthorne and Melville subsequently cooled, although Hawthorne clearly perceived, both in *Moby-Dick* and Melville himself, a penchant for a restless, yearning inquiry into the nature of things. Hawthorne shared it. And later, when the two men were briefly reunited in England, Hawthorne with his own eloquent acumen described his unhappy friend as one who "can neither believe, nor be comfortable in his unbelief; and he is too honest and courageous not to try to do one or the other" (*English Notebooks,* p. 163).

See also Calvinism; English Literature; Literary Criticism; Literary Marketplace; Literary Nationalism; *Moby-Dick;* Same-Sex Love; Young America

BIBLIOGRAPHY
Primary Works
Hawthorne, Nathaniel. *English Notebooks.* 1870. Edited by Thomas Woodson and Bill Ellis. Columbus: Ohio State University Press, 1997.

Hawthorne, Nathaniel. "Preface to *Twice-Told Tales.*" In *Tales and Sketches,* edited by Roy Harvey Pearce. New York: Library of America, 1996.

Melville, Herman. *Correspondence.* Edited by Harrison Hayford. Northwestern-Newberry Edition of the Writings of Herman Melville, vol. 14. Evanston, Ill.: Northwestern University Press, 1993.

Melville, Herman. "Hawthorne and His Mosses." 1850. In *The Piazza Tales and Other Prose Pieces, 1839–1860,* edited by Harrison Hayford, Alma A. MacDougall, and G. Thomas Tanselle. Northwestern-Newberry Edition of the Writings of Herman Melville, vol. 9. Evanston, Ill.: Northwestern University Press, 1987.

Poe, Edgar Allan. "Tale-Writing—Nathaniel Hawthorne." *Godey's Magazine and Lady's Book* 35 (November 1847).

Secondary Works
Parker, Hershel. *Herman Melville, A Biography: 1819–1851.* Vol. 1. Baltimore: John Hopkins University Press, 1996.

Wineapple, Brenda. *Hawthorne: A Life.* New York: Alfred A. Knopf, 2003.

Brenda Wineapple

HEALTH AND MEDICINE

It is impossible to discuss health in the period 1820–1870 without discussing disease. Consistent good health was the possession of only a small percentage of a population rapidly approaching ten million. Lacking a germ theory of disease, people ate contaminated food, drank contaminated water, and lived amid animal and human waste without blinking. Lacking knowledge of good nutrition, people suffered from chronic indigestion (or dyspepsia), fatigue, anemia, food poisoning, and other digestive ailments. The unchecked spread of bacteria, viruses, and insects resulted in epidemics of "ague" (malaria), cholera, diphtheria, dysentery, polio, smallpox, and typhoid, crippling or abbreviating many lives. Tuberculosis, commonly known as consumption, was the leading cause of death in the nineteenth century. Chronic bouts of influenza, pneumonia, and other endemic maladies further reduced not only life's quantity but its quality. Life expectancy in this era was somewhere between thirty and forty years, nearly half of all children died before their tenth birthdays, and countless women died in childbirth.

WOMEN'S HEALTH
Females who survived into adulthood were not exactly robust. Victorian ideals of womanhood encoded a form of embodiment that mimicked diseased states.

Middle-class white women were expected to be frail, delicate, nervous, emotional, and moody. The term "hysteria" derived from the Greek *hyster,* or womb, and the disease itself, which reached near-epidemic proportions as the century advanced, was said to be caused by the uterus's ties to the nervous system as well as its potential to float untethered in the body, wreaking havoc. Hysterics fainted, raved, wept, choked, threw fits, entered trances, tore out their hair, behaved frenetically. Though the disease was rampant in the nineteenth century, hysteria lives on in the early twenty-first century only as a pejorative term, leading some historians to speculate that it allowed nineteenth-century middle-class white women to enact their rage against confining gender roles, to perform femininity with a vengeance.

A slew of medical advice books directed at the female invalid only further established her as a type and as a widespread cultural concern. In perhaps the most famous lay advice book of the 1850s, *Letters to the People on Health and Happiness* (1855), the educator and reformer Catharine Beecher (1800–1878) sounds the alarm about the "terrible decay" in health among Anglo-Americans since the time of their ancestors. She especially laments the state of women's health, claiming in one letter that for all her travels among and conversations with married women she could number less than ten whom she would consider vigorously healthy. Beecher identifies upbringing, fashion, poor hygiene, and the lack of both exercise and fresh air as culprits, but she also points a blaming finger at women's inherently frail and delicate nature. She is as wont to chastise women for overstimulating their more easily taxable brains as she is to chastise the culture for failing to provide women with stimulating occupations.

When it came to etiology, the medical establishment tended to come down heavily on the side of nature rather than culture. According to prevailing medical doctrine, women were inherently and recurrently susceptible to disease, if only because they were afflicted by such avowedly pathological cyclical processes as menstruation, reproduction, and menopause. Many doctors believed their female patients to be governed by their wombs, and according to theories of bodily energy as circulating within a closed system, this was the healthiest regime, for if energy were to be diverted away to another vital organ—say, the brain, through studying or reading—the resulting depletion in the uterus would "unsex" the body, shriveling its breasts and ovaries, stimulating hair growth, and rendering the perpetrator sterile and unfit for her crowning destiny: wife- and motherhood. Those who achieved (or

Residence	Strong and perfectly healthy	Delicate or diseased	Habitual invalids
Hudson, Michigan	2	4	4
Castleton, Vermont	0	9	1
Bridgeport, Vermont	4	4	2
Dorset, Vermont	0	1	9
South Royalston, Massachusetts	4	2	4
Townsend, Vermont	4	3	3
Greenbush, New York	2	5	3
Southington, Connecticut	3	5	2
Newark, New Jersey	2	3	5
New York City	2	4	4
Oneida, New York	3	2	5
Milwaukee, Wisconsin	1	3	6
Rochester, New York	2	6	2
Plainfield, New Jersey	2	4	4
New York City	3	6	1
Lennox, Massachusetts	4	3	3
Union Vale, New York	2	5	3
Albany, New York	2	3	5
Hartford, Connecticut	1	5	4
Cincinnati, Ohio	1	4	5
Andover, Massachusetts	2	5	3
Brunswick, Maine	2	5	3
Southington, Connecticut	3	5	2
Rochester, New York	2	6	2
Albany, New York	2	4	4
Milwaukee, Wisconsin	1	3	6
Plainfield, New Jersey	2	4	4
New York City	3	6	1
New York City	2	4	4
Worcester, Massachusetts	1	6	2
Newark, New Jersey	2	3	5
Bonhomme, Missouri	3	5	2
Painted Post, New York	1	3	6
Wilkins, New York	2	3	5
Johnsburg, New York	3	6	1
Burdett, New York	4	3	3
Horse Heads, New York	3	2	5
Pompey, New York	4	4	2
Tioga, Pennsylvania	3	4	3
Lodi, New York	2	5	3
Seymour, Connecticut	3	7	0
Williamsville, New York	4	2	4
Herkimer, New York	3	2	5
Hudson, Michigan	2	4	4
Kalamazoo, Michigan	3	6	1

SOURCE: Beecher, *Letters to the People*, pp. 127–128.

"The following were furnished by ladies who simply arranged the names of the ten married ladies best known to them in the place of their residence, in three classes, as marked over the several columns."

desired) neither goal faced warnings of more diseases and a shorter, stunted life.

The fact that the majority of the nation's women were held to no such standards and labored by the sweat of their brows without falling into hysterical fits did little to dissuade many physicians and ideologues that women were by nature shrinking violets, pedestal-bound. Of course, women across the socioeconomic spectrum did contract real illnesses, resulting

from improper nutrition and sanitation, from overwork and restrictive fashions, from infection and from childbirth.

Complications associated with childbirth, chief among these puerperal fever—infection following childbirth—were a leading cause of death in women from this period, so that with each pregnancy the expectant mother had to face her own mortality. Birth-control methods and abortifacients were discreetly advertised in the newspapers and whispered between friends. Those whose pregnancies went full term were usually attended throughout their travail by female family members or a local midwife (also typically female).

In the early decades of the nineteenth century, as the birthrate still hovered around seven births per married woman (a statistic that held within it the makings of a potentially lucrative medical practice) physicians began sounding the alarm about the safety of female midwifery, even while conceding that modesty made this lay healer a logical choice. As William Ray Arney has noted, the medical profession saw the midwife as a "social, political and economic impediment to the development of obstetrics along the lines members of the profession wished to pursue, and the profession implemented a political program to solve the 'midwife problem'" (p. 3). An example of this program can be seen in the remarks of a Harvard doctor who in 1820 questioned women's moral suitability to the practice, finding their inherent passivity and their excessive sympathy a dangerous mix in the birthing chamber. Although midwives continued to deliver more than half of all babies well up until 1910, their authority was routinely challenged by members of the emergent field of obstetrics.

THE PROFESSION OF MEDICINE

For most of the nineteenth century, practicing medicine rarely proved lucrative. Paul Starr reports that New England doctors typically made $500 or less a year, charging fees per service or per case, a sum that also included bartering and credit arrangements. Nor did medical practitioners earn much in the way of respect, as conventional medicine in this period was routinely criticized for its "heroic" methods. The invasive, aggressive therapeutics practiced by nineteenth-century doctors was advanced by such notables as the Philadelphia physician Benjamin Rush (1745–1813), who himself learned them from his teacher William Cullen of Edinburgh. "Bleed, blister, and purge" were the mainstays of the heroic practitioner's repertoire, though "puking" patients through emetics was another core practice. The use of toxic drugs such as

That Mothers Might Live. Illustration by Dean Cornwell from his *Pioneers of American Medicine* series (1939–1943). Oliver Wendell Holmes is shown reading his essay "The Contagiousness of Puerperal Fever" to members of the Boston Society for Medical Improvement. Holmes was a physician and professor of anatomy at Harvard before gaining fame as an author, and in his 1843 essay he correctly hypothesized the souce of postpartum infections. GETTY IMAGES

calomel, which contained mercury, violated the physician's oath to first do no harm. About the only remedies in a regular doctor's arsenal that had any therapeutic effect were digitalis (for heart problems or "dropsy"), lime juice (to treat scurvy), and quinine for malaria.

Of course doctors also routinely performed more useful, less invasive interventions, such as prescribing diets and bed rest, setting bones, removing growths, and draining abscesses. The success of these more benign remedies and the failure of more aggressive interventions helped to turn the tide against heroic methodologies, which were on the wane by the 1860s and more or less obsolete by the 1870s. Not only were they by this point proven ineffective when compared to nature's healing powers and recent scientific advances, but they had been challenged all along by homeopaths and other alternative or "irregular" practitioners.

Along with the desire for more income, power, and status, these challenges—which only increased "regular" doctor's concern over the exponential rise in "quackery"—became a major impetus behind attempts to organize and regulate the medical profession. J. Marion Sims (1813–1883), who began his term as president of the American Medical Association in 1875, reflected in his autobiography on the status of his profession earlier in the century, confessing that "the practice of that time . . . was murderous. I knew nothing about medicine, but I had sense enough to see that doctors were killing their patients, that medicine was not an exact science, that . . . it would be better to trust entirely to Nature than to the hazardous skill of the doctors" (p. 150).

Faced with widespread public distrust of the profession's attempts to assert its expertise, along with a mounting crisis over lax medical education and licensing, a National Medical Convention was held in

The first page of Dr. Benjamin Rush's chapter "Defence of Blood-Letting" in his Medical Inquiries and Observations (1805) defends the medical practice of "bleeding":

Blood-letting, as a remedy for fevers, and certain other diseases, having lately been the subject of much discussion, and many objections having been made to it, which appear to be founded in error and fear, I have considered that a defence of it, by removing those objections, might render it more generally useful, in every part of the United States.

Rush, Medical Inquiries and Observations, 4:285.

New York in 1846, out of which the American Medical Association—whose first meeting was held in Philadelphia in 1847—was born. By the time the country entered its Gilded Age, the medical profession had gained much in legitimacy and clout. Still, it was actually only in the first decades of the twentieth century that medical practitioners finally achieved what Starr terms "professional sovereignty," boosted by genuine end-of-the-century advances in technology and therapeutics, especially in the fields of bacteriology and germ therapy.

In the same year that the National Medical Convention was held, the first modern woman doctor, Elizabeth Blackwell (1821–1910), was applying to medical schools, and the country's first medical school for women only—Boston Female Medical School—was but two years from opening. The historian Regina Morantz-Sanchez contends that American medicine was defined from the outset via a dialectic between "sympathy" and "science," and that, in the main, male practitioners identified (or were identified) more with the scientific definition of their profession, while female practitioners proclaimed (or were acclaimed for) their sympathetic capacities. While heroic techniques like frequent bloodletting and heavy dosing remained popular among those who considered themselves scientists, a number of those who defined themselves as sympathetic healers argued for the scientific merits and benefits of more moderate remedies.

The groundswell of support at mid-century for women's admittance into the medical establishment stemmed in part from a belief that women's inherently empathic natures, when partnered with science, would make for better doctors and, consequently, better patients. As Angenette A. Hunt insisted in 1851, "It is certain that the health of the world, depends on the women of the world and at least, some of the qualities needed in the medical profession—as gentleness, patience, quick perceptions, natural instinct which is often surer than science, deep sympathy . . . all these belong to the [female] sex in an eminent degree" (Morantz-Sanchez, p. 28). The very capacity for sympathy, for feeling, that made women so susceptible to disease in one lexicon in yet another proved their capacities as healers.

ALTERNATIVE MEDICINE

Enlisting the aid of a female healer may have been one option for those disgruntled with their regular male practitioners. But in the days before the medical profession had earned the public's trust, a number of alternative routes to health were pursued. Starr identifies three spheres of medical practice and rates them of roughly equal importance: in addition to physicians there were also lay healers (such as midwives) and "the medicine of the domestic household" (p. 32). The home was where most of the sick were attended to, where herbs, charms, and potions were administered as remedies for ailing family members and where the mother figure or an older female relative usually presided over the sickbed. Many households relied for guidance on William Buchan's Domestic Medicine, the most popular and most reprinted (some thirty editions) of such manuals throughout the early 1800s, until it was replaced in popularity by John C. Gunn's Domestic Medicine, published in 1830. While these manuals promoted naturalistic interpretations of disease, there were those who still interpreted illness through a moral valence, seeing in each malady the hand of God punishing sinners. Sufferers swayed by such moral interpretations often entrusted their care to God's or their preacher's hands.

Though many a domestic healer brewed her own medicines at her own hearth, a number purchased the patent medicines and gadgets advertised in the papers and hawked by snake-oil salesmen. Lydia Pinkham's vegetable compound was by far the most popular of these nostrums. Remedies were also available for purchase from the unregulated sectarians whose popularity and organizational force increased as aversion to conventional medicine's aggressions mounted.

The skeptical rebellion against "regular" (i.e., licensed and schooled) physicians in the early decades of the nineteenth century was led by the Thomsonian sect. The New Hampshire farmer Samuel Thomson (1769–1843) proposed his botanical method of healing—learned in part from a female herbalist—as a democratic challenge to the establishment (a particularly effective strategy in the anti-elitist Jacksonian era). His motto would become "every man his own physician." Thomson claimed to have spent thirty years studying and experimenting with medicinal herbs and to have developed a safer system than that of conventional medical practice. Identifying heat with life and cold with death, he sought to provide the fuel through food and medicines to keep people alive rather than to poison them, as he accused regular physicians of doing. He generated this vital heat in his patients by peppering, steaming, and puking them. During the early decades of the century, after obtaining a patent in 1813, his agents sold "family rights" to his practice for twenty dollars. Thomsonians and other herbalists believed their botanical cures to be both lifesaving and money-saving, especially when compared to being "doctored to death" by the allopaths.

Thomsonianism dominated the alternative sects from about the 1810s to the 1840s. Those who remained true to Thomsonian methods thereafter typically joined forces with the eclectics, doctors who resisted heroic methods and frequently dispensed botanic medicine, hoping to combine the best of the various schools. They were outnumbered by the homeopaths, devotees of a therapeutics developed by the German physician Samuel Hahnemann and imported to the United States around 1825, with resounding success. Homeopaths held to two central tenets: they believed that the substances that would produce disease in the healthy would cure the sick (the law of similars), and they also believed that medicine becomes more effective as the dosage is decreased (the law of infinitesimals—a law that also suggests homeopathy's governing faith in nature's healing powers). The popularity of homeopathy surged by the time of the Civil War, with hundreds of thousands of devotees—roughly two-thirds of whom were women—who willingly opted for the benign interventions that stood in such stark contrast to the physician's heroic therapeutics.

A number of other sects appealed to those in search of alternative treatment. Of these, perhaps the most popular and least harmful was hydropathy, yet another sect popularized in the United States in the early decades of the nineteenth century and distinguished by its rejection of drugs altogether. Hydropathic therapies, often administered at facilities that functioned as retreats, relied solely on water—used in multiple ways including baths, douches, and wraps—combined with fresh air, exercise, and diet. Other health reformers championed diet, dress reform—the abandonment of corsets and other constrictive fashions and the adoption of such health-promoting costumes as "bloomers"—and attention to proper hygiene. Advocates took to the lecture circuit to inform the populace of their recommendations, providing not only information and entertainment but often conflicting guidance to a citizenry in pursuit of health.

PUBLIC AND MENTAL HEALTH

A crucial force that may have been more responsible than any other for fighting contagion during the nineteenth century was the rising public health movement and the establishment of municipal health, housing, and sanitation departments. The unprecedented growth of urban centers and the outbreak of the Civil War only quickened the spread of disease and the pace of public health reforms. The cramped and unsanitary tenement districts in these cities became breeding grounds for disease, and calls for some sort of structural intervention were answered by those within the burgeoning public health movement. Health reform got a jump start during the war, as some six million sick and injured soldiers were tended (before the days of antiseptic surgery) in newly established hospitals by some 750,000 volunteers, including members of the U.S. Sanitary Commission.

The carnage of war may have ended in 1865, but the aftereffects lingered on. Even during the war, doctors, including S. Weir Mitchell (1829–1914), were recording and studying its effects on not just the body but the mind. Mitchell and other neurologists, including George M. Beard (1839–1883), went on to make careers out of diagnosing and treating "neurasthenia," a term Beard coined in 1869 for a constellation of symptoms, most prominent among them mental and physical exhaustion, resulting from the depletion of nervous energy. An equal-opportunity disease, neurasthenia afflicted not only what Beard called "the comfortable classes" but lower-class laborers and farmers. It was a diagnosis offered more readily to men than to women, perhaps because women were so essentially, etymologically linked to that other prevalent nervous disorder, hysteria. Beard was to conclude that neurasthenia was the price one paid for the pace and progress endemic to American civilization. U.S. citizens in 1870 may not have been appreciably healthier than they were in 1820, but they were—in Beard's sense—more civilized.

LITERARY TREATMENTS

Given health's status as national obsession and disease's identification as civilization's price, it is little wonder that both were seized upon as literary subjects. What is curious about these fictional representations is that illness is rarely discussed overtly or treated literally. Or perhaps not so curious: a culture so intimately acquainted with disease and death would value literature that offered the possibility of escape. Where authors did discuss the sick and dying, they tended to make the familiar not strange but meaningful—that is, to render illness as metaphor and to offer metaphor as solace.

The most pervasive such trope pervading antebellum literature was that of the female invalid, who was usually very young, very good, and very ill. While a number of authors sketched this figure, a few exemplary characters continue even in the early twenty-first century to capture the hearts and minds of readers. The beautiful, angelic, dying girl child remains best personified by both Harriet Beecher Stowe's (1811–1896) Little Eva and Louisa May Alcott's (1832–1888) Beth. Eva, the angelic, consumptive child heroine of Stowe's *Uncle Tom's Cabin* (1852), wastes away in the certain knowledge of slavery's evil and heaven's release. Eva's disease is treated evasively, though most contemporary readers would have recognized her tubercular symptoms; Stowe suggests strongly that slavery is the blight on her soul, eating away at her insides. In this one sees God's hand at work, though here Eva is not a sinner being punished but a martyr for the nation's sins, for its sickening inclination to treat human beings as things.

Alcott's Beth, the saintly March sister in the classic *Little Women* (1868–1869), was, like Eva, never long for this world. Surviving a brush with illness in the first book, she succumbs in the second. Beth dies, but her death represents not simply the end of life but the end of pain; Beth's face in death is "full of painless peace," and death itself is described as "the long sleep that pain would never mar again" (p. 514). Death here is no grim reaper but pain's antidote, providing release and bringing peace not only to Beth herself but, in some small measure, to mourning readers.

This emphasis on pain's surcease could derive from Alcott's attempt to explore within the safety net of fiction the seemingly inevitable outcome of her own illness. Several years prior to *Little Women*'s publication, the author had served for six weeks as a hospital nurse and contracted typhoid pneumonia while tending to the wounded amid the unsanitary conditions of the Union Hotel Hospital in the Georgetown area of Washington, D.C. Her previously rugged constitution was ravaged in the short term by the fever and in the long term by the mercury in the medication she received. In her account of her wartime activities, *Hospital Sketches* (1863), drafted shortly after leaving her nursing post, Alcott breezes over her own suffering.

She makes a virtue of "not complaining" (p. 55) about pain—devoting only one and a half out of roughly one hundred pages to her illness. Alcott's reluctance to elaborate upon the nurse's pain hints at a belief—a desire, never to be realized—that her recently contracted illness would prove both transitory and insignificant. Although Alcott would test numerous remedies—ranging from water to "mind" cures, from morphine to massage, from homeopathy to a nursing home—she was never again to regain her formerly robust health.

Yet another writer who attended the bedsides of Union wounded was Walt Whitman (1819–1892), already famous (or infamous) for his *Leaves of Grass*. Called to the hospital on behalf of his injured brother George, Whitman stayed to comfort other "poor boys," the recipients of his copious sympathies. His book of war poems, *Drum-Taps* (1865), encompasses the war from its earliest, most fervent and patriotic beginnings through the myriad horrors of the battlefield and hospital, closing with his beautiful elegy for the assassinated president. Whitman is one of the few writers to graphically represent pain and suffering on the page. In his poem "The Dresser," for instance, Whitman describes the pails overflowing with bloody rags, the putrefaction of gangrene, the bullet wounds, the amputated limbs. But he details these calamities with a compassionate rather than objective eye, a "soothing" if "impassive" hand, and a breast aflame with fellow-feeling.

At one point in this poem Whitman rhapsodizes about the merciful advent of "beautiful death." His fellow poet Edgar Allan Poe (1809–1949) also associated death and beauty but for very different reasons. In "The Philosophy of Composition," Poe argues that beauty (which he declares the provenance of poetry) moves one most deeply when the subject is sad and that therefore the "soul" of poetry is that most melancholy of topics, the death of a beautiful woman. The poem he anatomizes in this essay, "The Raven," evokes a beautiful woman's death via her lover's remorse; it reiterates his melancholic desire, abetted by the Raven's repetitions, to relive the anguish of their parting. Throughout Poe's corpus, death often figures as more titillating than terrifying. Dead or dying women populate Poe's works, from "Annabel Lee" to "Ligeia" to "The Fall of the House of Usher," and his recurrent device of resurrecting these lost loves uncannily evokes many readers' sense of the thin, permeable line dividing the living from the dead.

Whereas Poe's beautiful female protagonists are, as Diane Price Herndl attests, exceptional for being "the most unrelentingly sickly" (p. 91),

Nathaniel Hawthorne's (1894–1864) female characters are often at least initially robust: indeed, the more robust they are the greater seem the odds of their early demise. Beatrice in "Rappaccini's Daughter" (1844), Georgiana in "The Birth-mark" (1846), and Zenobia in *The Blithedale Romance* (1852) all possess vigorous health at the outset but wind up dead by the close. A woman's illness may have threatened her own life, but Hawthorne's stories suggest that a woman's health may threaten others, including the men around her as well as the patriarchal order to which these men subscribe.

One sees this same logic operating in a quirky doctor-authored novel published on the eve of the Civil War. Oliver Wendell Holmes (1809–1894) was at once a Harvard professor of anatomy and physiology, a founding member of the American Medical Association, the beloved "Autocrat of the Breakfast Table," a poet and essayist who coined the term "Brahmin" for Boston's elite, and a regular contributor to the *Atlantic Monthly*. In 1859 he began serializing in that journal his first attempt at a novel, *Elsie Venner* (published in book form in 1861). It is, as he argues in his preface, an attempt to substitute a naturalistic interpretation of disease for a moralizing one; his protagonist is not to blame for her actions, determined as they were in utero, when a snake bit Elsie's pregnant mother. Elsie may be serpentine, but she is also healthy—that is, until she comes under the supervision of not one but three doctors.

Holmes's first novel can be read as an attempt to assert the power of the clinical gaze at a time when that assertion would have been met with the raising of many a skeptical eyebrow. In the days before the medical profession had achieved authoritative status, this doctor-authored novel sharply differentiates a medical and pathological way of seeing. Elsie's "mesmerizing," passionate eyes signal her disease to the novel's three clinical observers, who coolly observe and diagnose but offer no remedy. Better, it seems, for Elsie's poisoned and poisonous femininity to self-destruct than to allow it to continue to cause dis-ease in those around her. It cannot be entirely coincidental, during this bumpy period in American medical history, that the narrative asserts the power of medical vision rather than intervention, of diagnosis rather than cure, strategically grounding its authority in the former at a time when the latter's success could not be guaranteed and, if enacted, might undermine the observer's objectivity and credibility.

Where disease was treated, then, few verifiable cures were offered, either in life or in literature. Suffering was commonplace, alleviation scarce.

Nature ran its course, and sometimes that course led the sufferer back down the road to health. Where it did not, hope still lingered that not only the life—however truncated—but the disease—however painful—possessed some greater meaning.

See also Death; Domestic Fiction; *Leaves of Grass;* Mental Health; Mourning; Popular Science; Psychology; Science; Sexuality and the Body; Urbanization

BIBLIOGRAPHY

Primary Works

Alcott, Louisa M. *Hospital Sketches.* 1863. In *Civil War Nursing: Hospital Sketches; Memoirs of Emily Elizabeth Parsons; History of American Nursing,* edited by Susan Reverby. New York: Garland, 1984.

Alcott, Louisa M. *Little Women.* 1868–1869. New York: Modern Library, 1983.

Beard, George M. *A Practical Treatise on Nervous Exhaustion (Neurasthenia): Its Symptoms, Nature, Sequences, Treatment.* 2nd ed. New York: W. Wood, 1880.

Beecher, Catharine. *Letters to the People on Health and Happiness.* New York: Harper & Brothers, 1855.

Channing, Walter. *Remarks on the Employment of Females as Practitioners in Midwifery: By a Physician.* 1820. Excerpted in *Major Problems in the History of American Medicine and Public Health: Documents and Essays,* edited by John Harley Warner and Janet A. Tighe, pp. 67–69. Boston: Houghton Mifflin, 2001.

Hawthorne, Nathaniel. *Complete Short Stories of Nathaniel Hawthorne.* New York: Doubleday, 1959.

Holmes, Oliver Wendell. *Elsie Venner: A Romance of Destiny.* Boston: Houghton Mifflin, 1891.

Poe, Edgar Allan. *Complete Stories and Poems of Edgar Allan Poe.* New York: Doubleday, 1966.

Rush, Benjamin. *Medical Inquiries and Observations.* 4 vols. Philadelphia: Published by Johnson and Warner, Matthew Carey et al., 1809.

Sims, J. Marion. *The Story of My Life.* New York: Appleton, 1884.

Stowe, Harriet Beecher. *Uncle Tom's Cabin.* 1852. Rev. ed. Edited by Elizabeth Ammons. New York: Norton, 1994.

Secondary Works

Apple, Rima D. *Women, Health, and Medicine in America: A Historical Handbook.* New York: Garland, 1990.

Arney, William Ray. *Power and the Profession of Obstetrics.* Chicago: University of Chicago Press, 1982.

Berman, Alex. "The Heroic Approach in 19th-Century Therapeutics." In *Sickness and Health in America: Readings in the History of Medicine and Public Health,* edited by Judith Walzer Leavitt and Ronald L. Numbers, pp. 77–86. Madison: University of Wisconsin Press, 1978.

Davis, Cynthia J. *Bodily and Narrative Forms: The Influence of Medicine on American Literature, 1845–1915.* Palo Alto, Calif.: Stanford University Press, 2000.

Ehrenreich, Barbara, and Deirdre English. *For Her Own Good: 150 Years of the Experts' Advice to Women.* New York: Anchor-Doubleday, 1989.

Herndl, Diane Price. *Invalid Women: Figuring Feminine Illness in American Fiction and Culture, 1840–1940.* Chapel Hill: University of North Carolina Press, 1993.

Leavitt, Judith Walzer, and Ronald L. Numbers, eds. *Sickness and Health in America: Readings in the History of Medicine and Public Health.* Madison: University of Wisconsin Press, 1978.

Morantz-Sanchez, Regina. *Sympathy and Science: Women Physicians and American Medicine.* New York: Oxford University Press, 1985.

Numbers, Ronald L. "Do-It-Yourself the Sectarian Way." In *Sickness and Health in America: Readings in the History of Medicine and Public Health,* edited by Judith Walzer Leavitt and Ronald L. Numbers, pp. 87–96. Madison: University of Wisconsin Press, 1978.

Sicherman, Barbara. "The Uses of a Diagnosis: Doctors, Patients, and Neurasthenia." In *Sickness and Health in America: Readings in the History of Medicine and Public Health,* edited by Judith Walker Leavitt and Ronald L. Numbers, pp. 25–38. Madison: University of Wisconsin Press, 1978.

Smith-Rosenberg, Carroll. *Disorderly Conduct: Visions of Gender in Victorian America.* New York: Oxford University Press, 1986.

Starr, Paul. *The Social Transformation of American Medicine.* New York: Basic, 1982.

Stevens, Rosemary. *American Medicine and the Public Interest: A Sociological Analysis.* New Haven, Conn.: Yale University Press, 1971.

Warner, John Harley, and Janet A. Tighe, eds. *Major Problems in the History of American Medicine and Public Health.* Boston: Houghton Mifflin, 2001.

Cynthia J. Davis

THE HIDDEN HAND

Capitola Le Noir, also known as Cap Black, is undoubtedly the most engaging young heroine ever to escape from the busy pen of E. D. E. N (Emma Dorothy Eliza Nevitte) Southworth (1819–1899), prolific author of adventure and romance novels whose career from the mid- to the late nineteenth century spanned over forty-four years. A displaced wife turned writer, Southworth, by her own admission, wrote not just for the growing number of women readers who were drawn to her strong female characters and ambitious plots but for a heterogeneous "multitude" that included college professors, preachers, government leaders, "street gamins," adolescents—the refined and the not-so-refined. In Cap Black, Southworth found a feisty street gamine to give voice to the author's shoot-from-the-hip critique of middle-class presumptions and to throw open to question the issue of gender role expectations in nineteenth-century America.

Scrappy Capitola Black, "the Bowery b'hoy," was well beloved by several generations of *New York Ledger* readers, who followed her exploits in three serializations under the title of *The Hidden Hand*—1859, 1868–1869, and 1883—after which the *Ledger*'s editor, Robert Bonner, purchased the copyright for $1,000. It was published in book form in 1888 and often reprinted in two volumes, *The Hidden Hand* and *Capitola's Perils* (modern editions appeared in 1988 and 1997). More than forty dramatic adaptations of *The Hidden Hand* played to sold-out audiences at major theaters all over the United States, giving Cap Black genuine icon status. Women wore Capitola clothes, Capitola hats, and Capitola boots. People could even go to the Capitola Hotel or travel to the town of Capitola, California. As the saucy prototype of an assembly line of tomboy characters that persists to this day in American fiction, Capitola Black the Bowery b'hoy presented a defiant challenge to the gender constraints that existed in Victorian America.

CAP BLACK, BOWERY B'HOYS, AND THE IDEOLOGIES OF MANHOOD

Drawing on the working-class, popular culture image of the scrappy Bowery b'hoy—the rowdy, pugnacious young street ruffian who prowled the streets of the Bowery in Manhattan, especially during the 1840s and 1850s—Southworth challenges the complex and competing ideologies of manhood that were fermenting in mid-nineteenth-century America. The disquieting question of the nature of manhood was the result of a fluid and dynamic American society in transition from the dominance of an agrarian, quasi-aristocratic economy—especially in Virginia, where most of the novel is set—to a competitive market economy where self-starter capitalist adventurers clashed with wage laborers. During the decades prior to the Civil War, America was a nation moving toward rapid urbanization. In 1820 only a handful of cities in the Northeast had

E. D. E. N. Southworth.

populations above twenty-five thousand. By 1850, twenty-six cities had more than twenty-five thousand residents, and more than sixty cities had at least ten thousand residents. More and more people, primarily men, left farms to join the rising working class, doing wage work in factories, offices, or out on the street in some capacity.

A struggling wage laborer who never loses touch with her working-class role, Capitola the Bowery b'hoy acts, quite literally, as a foil for the conflicting notions of what it means to be an honorable man in the 1840s. But she does this in the body of a teenage woman. Though readers learn of her mystery-shrouded birth in Virginia in the opening chapters, they actually meet Cap Black for the first time as an insouciant, cross-dressing preadolescent of thirteen trying to survive in the streets of New York by peddling the penny press (cheap newspapers full of crime reports and human interest stories) and performing whatever manual labor she can to put food in her belly. Cap sleeps in broken-down public transportation vehicles, under ghetto brownstone steps, and behind discarded boxes out on the street, forced to masquerade as a boy to avoid being pursued by rapacious males. To Cap being a female means starvation and exploitation, so

to avoid a lascivious and deadly environment, when other preadolescent young girls are reading guidebooks on how to behave like submissive young ladies, Cap assumes the role of a young man.

Real-life b'hoys, many of whom were Irish, were often violent, engaging in barroom brawls and picking territorial fights with other b'hoy gangs. Their swaggering presence and antiaristocratic bravado offered radical new possibilities for an alternative masculine ideal because, as a grassroots figure of the transforming industrial society, the b'hoy was an active participant in the bootstrap, individualist pragmatism toward which society was leaning. Like George Foster in *New York By Gas-light* (1850), Fanny Fern in *Ruth Hall* (1854), and Walt Whitman in "Song of Myself" (1855), Southworth rescues the violent Bowery b'hoy image and rehabilitates it in the compassionate Capitola. Southworth's reconfiguration of this image into a young female between childhood and womanhood has a twofold function. First, by using a familiar image from popular culture, she targets a receptive readership and elicits an already positive response to her radical heroine. Second, by quickly returning her b'hoy figure to her true place as female, she offers women readers the opportunity to witness a female character whose masquerade demonstrates that male and female deportment is not "natural"—derived as it is from an inherent grid of behaviors—but instead is in fact role-playing.

TRANSGRESSING THE CATEGORIES

In Capitola one sees a transgressive female survivor of boy and girl twins born on a blustery Halloween eve into a world of masks and disguises. Capitola's evil uncle, in an effort to steal his brother's (Capitola's father's) estate, murders him and arranges to kidnap Capitola's mother as she is about to give birth. The uncle's plan is to get rid of the baby, thereby putting himself in line for the inheritance. However, Capitola's mother delivers two babies, one a stillborn male and the other, of course, Capitola. After delivering the babies, a blindfolded midwife hides Capitola in the folds of her shawl and gives the kidnappers the dead male baby, whose death makes Capitola's survival possible. Having absorbed the energy of her fated twin brother, Capitola, by her very existence, flies in the face of patrician, patriarchal institutions that rigidify society's expectations of female behavior. Moreover, Capitola's clandestine transformation from displaced plantation heiress into independent Bowery b'hoy laborer is emblematic of the manifest change in population resulting from the rapid growth of larger cities such as New York during the 1830s and 1840s.

The working class became a visible and threatening presence, and the Bowery b'hoy was a phenomenon of this complicated tangle of gender role definitions, which challenged the politics of gender categories by turning on issues of financial and class position. Southworth, herself not a stranger to financial hardship after her husband's abandonment four years after their 1840 marriage left her to fend for herself with two small children, gives the image her own spin by posing the question of how gender and status impact on one's ability to survive.

In the novel, for instance, the discovery of Capitola's masquerade and subsequent arrest by the police is attributed to the loss of part of her "ragged boy" costume: "the wind blowed off my cap and the policeman blowed on me!" (p. 41). When Major Warfield, who does not know who Capitola is, realizes that a thirteen-year-old girl is about to be sent to a juvenile detention hall for selling newspapers in boy's clothing, he intercedes on her behalf, spiriting her off to his plantation in Virginia, where he demands that "the creature" appear "in its proper dress." Used to the tension of the streets, Capitola does not enjoy her "rescued" life of a Virginia belle. Using Bowery slang, Capitola complains about the sheer boredom of being resigned to a spiritless life of sewing and managing personal servants and wishes she were back in the Bowery, where there were fires and gang fights—something to get her adrenaline pumping. To Cap, a return to the Virginia mountains is like "decomposing above ground," while role-playing as a boy on Broadway empowers her.

Cap's dismay is understandable, because the culture of young males during the antebellum period existed as a social sphere unto itself—separate from the public domain of men and the domestic scene of women, small children, and girls. In this liminal, or threshold, space, positioned between the irresponsibility of childhood and the maturity of adulthood, boys were accountable to neither parlor authority nor business and commercial demands. Back in Virginia, Capitola, though no longer dressing in rags and patches, still enjoys flouting the rules that keep her from maintaining her independence and rather enjoys taunting her guardian, Major Warfield, called "Old Hurricane," who continuously dares her to disobey him by issuing threats of dire consequences. In the never-never land of boys, the dare is an ever-present springboard to dangerous bravado, and Capitola cannot resist responding to Old Hurricane's attempts to constrain her by performing ever more dangerous stunts. For example, while speaking to a man who is really the infamous bandit Black Donald in disguise, Capitola admits that she would love to see this Black Donald in

the flesh because she enjoys the thrill that heightened fear evokes. Black Donald warns her against wishing for something rash because she just might get that wish; however, Capitola comes back at him chanting three times, "I wish it." In true Halloween magic fashion, Capitola's incantation makes it so, as Black Donald unmasks and shows himself to her. After a brief moment of admiration and awe, she suddenly jumps on him "like a bundle of sin on the back of a Christian" in an effort to capture him all by her tomboy self. For a brief time she is literally his cross to bear, a foreshadowing of his redemption at her hands and an indication of Southworth's vision of herself as a moralist.

BLACK DONALD AS DOUBLE

Of the many doubles linked with Capitola, "Cap'n" Black Donald is a worthy opponent for Cap Black as he too resorts to disguise to accommodate his evil purposes, often presenting the precise image that his victims expect to see in order to exploit them. Described as "stately," Black Donald is a towering figure standing at six feet, eight inches with "fine aquiline features" and "strong, steady dark eyes," looks that would have broken the hearts of society debs or "made his own fortune in any city of America as a French Count or a German baron" (p. 147). His handsome and imposing appearance links him with a sophisticated, wealthy, and influential socioeconomic class that manipulates and relies upon appearances to sustain its power. Black Donald uses his looks, his intelligence, his command of the language, and his manipulative skills to take advantage of those, such as Mrs. Condiment, Old Hurricane's revival-attending maid, who are too unworldly to detect con artistry. Clearly he is no Virginia country hayseed gone wrong. Another clue to Black Donald's association with classist values is the description of his outlaws' lair. Ironically, even though the men of Black Donald's posse have evil names like "Stealthy" Steve and "Demon" Dick," their operations room where they plan their evil doings is a kitchen parlor—a space associated more with domesticity than with rowdyism. In giving the gangster Black Donald an elitist appearance and a domestic thieves' den, Southworth provides another level at which Capitola, as antiaristocratic b'hoy, is his antithesis. Even the language Black Donald uses to rouse his gang—"Your castle is stormed. The enemy is at your throats with drawn swords"—alludes to royalty defending itself against certain death. He goes on to include references to the potential fall of an industrial empire: "The ship's sinking; the cars have run off the track, the boiler's burst" (p. 188). These images represent economic progress—the manufacture and transportation of goods—run amok. Without the skills of the working class in the manufacturing and transportation arenas, the owner class will lose all. Black Donald's fight with Capitola, therefore, illustrates the antagonism between the classes and also suggests the threat of a working-class reclamation of power in the figure of Capitola.

Cap's primary task is to match wits with Black Donald to combat his daunting physicality and his overpowering personality, and she does so with more role-playing. In a climactic scene, Black Donald, attracted to her while also badly underestimating her, menacingly invades her bedroom at Hurricane Hall. Cap realizes that Black Donald's preconception of her "womanly ways" is part of what attracts him to her and that she must outwit him if she is to escape from his attack. If Black Donald is, as Alfred Habegger suggests, "the most untamed and virile man of all," Capitola must be "man" enough to escape from his clutches while playing his own game against him. Giving herself a pep talk, Capitola tells herself, as Black Donald advances rapaciously toward her, to "be a man" but then corrects herself by saying "be a woman"—or even "the devil and Doctor Faust, if necessary" (p. 345). In the face of dangerous manhood, the only recourse is to manipulate appearances and come in for the kill; "nearly all girls are clever imitators," Southworth reminds readers (p. 276). Flirting coyly, Capitola pretends first to be a femme fatale to emotionally disarm him and to feed his ego and second to be a moral reformer in order to prevail on his better nature. However, neither of these roles daunt Black Donald because these are the behaviors he expects from a woman. It is not until Capitola takes on the role of a nongendered, superior, almost godlike being that she is able to thwart his lustful designs. She calls him simply "Man" and tells him to take pity on himself, offering him one last chance to walk away from his sin. Southworth reiterates in this exchange that Black Donald is just a man, a fallen man, and in a theatrically appropriate metaphor, Capitola releases the trapdoor under the carpet in her bedroom, and he falls into the black hole he deserves. He goes to prison, and Cap, feeling sorry for him, tries to get him released legally. Failing that, she helps him escape to become a better, redeemed man.

PERFORMING GENDER

Role-playing defines Capitola's interaction with many of the characters in the novel and is instrumental in saving not only herself but also another of her foils, Clara Day, daughter of the good Dr. Day and the kidnapped bride-victim of Craven Le Noir, Capitola's evil uncle. Clara is the typical heroine figure that nineteenth-century readers would recognize but that Capitola's character is, in effect, rewriting. After teaching Clara to throw her head back and swagger like a Bowery b'hoy to evade discovery by Craven Le Noir's household, Capitola successfully impersonates Clara as the sobbing, helpless, abductee during the marriage ceremony. Just as the disguised Capitola is required to say "I do," she throws off her disguise and mockingly calls attention to the charade before the confused assembly and introduces herself as the "principal performer," enjoying her curtain calls "amid the applause of the audience" (pp. 282–283). Lifting the curtain and striking the sets, Capitola returns to her Bowery b'hoy persona once more. She subsequently receives the highest praise Old Hurricane can muster for saving Clara: he tells her she should have been a man. Thus, by being a girl behaving like a boy pretending to be a girl, Capitola becomes a man, which is to say an adult, with all an adult's rights and privileges.

Capitola's performance as b'hoy recalls the subversive nature of the minstrel performer. Her sly humor and predisposal to pranks, along with her early history of finding sanctuary with a mulatto woman, links her with the blacked-up figures that traipsed across the stage of the Bowery theater. An avid playgoer, Southworth may have seen a two-act burletta titled *The Two B'hoys; or, The Beulah Spa* by Charles Dance, which was performed in theaters in major cities such as Philadelphia and New York in 1832. One of the four main characters in the cast that performed at Mitchell's Olympic Theater in New York was played by Frank Chanfrau, the actor who became the literal personification of Mose, the Bowery b'hoy in Benjamin Baker's production *A Glance at New York* (1848). This minor comedy also features a woman dressed as a male minstrel singer. In this production, however, Chanfrau did not play a rowdy but rather a dandy who initiates a duel under false pretenses while attending a party at a resortlike plantation. Although the meaning of the term "b'hoys" is more ironic than apparent in the reading of the play, one can only assume that the physical appearance of the particular actors provided a clue to the play's topsy-turvy confusion of identities. In other words, who are the eponymous "b'hoys" if they are removed from their Bowery context, and does a b'hoy have to be a boy? Southworth thought not. Ironically the term "Bowery," which in the 1840s referred to a section of New York City where all ethnicities of working-class citizens came together, is, according to the *Oxford English Dictionary,* an adaptation of the Dutch word *Bouwery,* which means barn or plantation. It is impossible to know if Southworth knew of the rural origin of the word; however, the irony of Capitola the Bowery b'hoy returning to a Virginia *Bouwery,* a move that solidifies her identity and conflates her performance with her birthright as heiress of "forests and fields, iron and coal mines, water power, steam mills, furnaces and foundries" (p. 185) is difficult to miss. It is not a coincidence that the penultimate chapter of *The Hidden Hand* is titled "Capitola, a Capitalist."

By novel's end, southern elitist culture has been outstripped by egalitarian, working-class culture, so much so that Cap's entry into middle-class life, although inevitable, through her marriage to the tender and quiet Herbert Greyson seems almost contrived. Even Southworth suggests, tongue in cheek, that the happily-ever-after theme is as much a myth image as those of the sharp-tongued shrewish wife and the tyrannized husband, roles that Southworth intimates the couple will assume.

Southworth's depiction of Capitola, actress and champion of the exploited who never relinquishes her Bowery personality, calls into question gender borders and performance, class expectations, and cultural sociopolitics in mid-nineteenth-century American society. It is not surprising that *The Hidden Hand* has risen to the surface of a sea of women's popular novels published during that era. Its sly humor and outrageous plotlines continue to seduce new readers, who cannot help but laugh with and root for Cap, American literature's first and cleverest tomboy.

See also Childhood; Crime and Punishment; Cross-Dressing; Female Authorship; Feminism; Gothic Fiction; Humor; Irish; Labor; *Ruth Hall;* Sensational Fiction; Theater; Urbanization

BIBLIOGRAPHY
Primary Work
Southworth, E. D. E. N. *The Hidden Hand; or, Capitola the Madcap.* 1859. Introduction by Nina Baym. Oxford: Oxford University Press, 1997.

Secondary Works
Carpenter, Lynette. "Double Talk: The Power and Glory of Paradox in E. D. E. N. Southworth's *The Hidden Hand.*" *Legacy* 10, no. 1 (1993): 17–30.

Dobson, Joanne. Introduction to *The Hidden Hand; or, Capitola the Madcap.* Edited by Joanne Dobson. New Brunswick, N.J.: Rutgers University Press, 1988.

Foster, George. *New York by Gas-light and Other Urban Sketches.* Edited by Stuart Blumin. Berkeley: University of California Press, 1990.

Habegger, Alfred. "A Well Hidden Hand." *Novel* 14 (1981): 208.

Huddleston, Sarah M. "Mrs. E. D. E. N. Southworth and Her Cottage." *Records of the Columbia Historical Society* 23 (1920): 59–77.

Hudock, Amy. "Challenging the Definition of Heroism in E. D. E. N. Southworth's *The Hidden Hand.*" *ATQ* 9, no. 1 (1995): 5–20.

Kasson, John. *Rudeness and Civility: Manners in Nineteenth-Century Urban America.* New York: Hill and Wang, 1990.

Leverenze, David. *Manhood and the American Renaissance.* Ithaca, N.Y.: Cornell University Press, 1989.

Okker, Patricia, and Jeffrey Williams. "'Reassuring Sounds': Minstrelsy and *The Hidden Hand.*" *ATQ* 12, no. 2 (1998): 133–144.

Papashivily, Helen. *All the Happy Endings.* New York: Harper, 1956.

Reynolds, David. *Beneath the American Renaissance: The Subversive Imagination in the Age of Emerson and Melville.* Cambridge, Mass.: Harvard University Press, 1988.

Rotundo, E. Anthony. *American Manhood: Transformations in Masculinity from the Revolution to the Modern Era.* New York: Basic, 1993.

Rotundo, E. Anthony. "Boy Culture: Middle-Class Boyhood in Nineteenth-Century America." In *Meanings for Manhood: Constructions of Masculinity in Victorian America,* edited by Mark C. Carnes and Clyde Griffen, pp. 15–22. Chicago: University of Chicago Press, 1990.

Carole Policy

HISTORY

History was crucial to American attempts at self-definition, as members of the revolutionary generation and their antebellum descendants themselves recognized. History could provide models and guidance for citizens of the new nation, they believed, while simultaneously creating a sense of shared experience that could strengthen tenuous national bonds. Thus emphasizing the functional character of history, these historians embraced the traditional view of history as, in Henry St. John Bolingbroke's famous words, "philosophy teaching by example." For these historians, the purpose of history was to instill virtue in their readers by providing them with moral examples to imitate or avoid.

Revealing the popularity and importance of history in the early nineteenth century, the number of historical works that were published in this period rose from 26 in the first decade of the century to 158 in the 1830s. The creation of institutions devoted to the preservation of history in this period also reflected and furthered the growing interest in history. The Massachusetts Historical Society, founded in 1791, was the first historical society established in the United States, and by 1860, 111 historical societies had been established throughout the nation. Recognizing the importance of primary documents to the writing of history, these societies collected and preserved historical manuscripts. In their concern with preserving and publishing primary documents, historians revealed their allegiance to the critical methods of scholarship that were then developing in Germany, which emphasized the importance of truth and accuracy and based truth on a critical analysis of primary sources.

Even while Americans used history to promote nationalism, the writing of history became increasingly sectionalized in this period, as New England historians came to dominate the field. Forty-eight percent of the historians writing in the period between 1800 and 1860 came from New England, and half of these historians were from Massachusetts. As part of what has been termed the "Brahmin" elite, these historians offered a vision of America and its past that represented the interests of the New England elite. Writing before history had become a professionalized discipline, these historians believed that history was supposed to be the vocation of gentlemen amateurs. Thus most of them did not make a living from historical writing; they were either independently wealthy or supported themselves by pursuing other occupations in addition to history.

As David Levin has demonstrated, historians in this period viewed history as Romantic art. Influenced by Sir Walter Scott (1771–1832), the leading Romantic historians in this period—William Hickling Prescott, George Bancroft, John Lothrop Motley, and Francis Parkman—saw themselves as literary artists and sought to convey a sense of drama and immediacy in their historical works just as Scott had in his historical novels. Using metaphors of painting and portraiture to describe their work, they believed the historian's goal was to enable readers to visualize the past as though it were a painting rather than simply cataloging facts. For this reason they employed a vivid descriptive style that re-created historical scenes and events in graphic detail. Such an approach required the exercise of the imagination by the historian and demanded an emotional investment in his or her topic. Only in this way could the historian engage the emotions of readers and transport them back in time, enabling them to relive the vital experience of the past. And so nineteenth-century American historians assigned to history varied and sometimes conflicting purposes,

at once emphasizing the social function of history and displaying a genuine concern with truth and at the same time viewing history as both philosophy and art.

JARED SPARKS

The appointment of Jared Sparks (1789–1866) to the McLean Chair in Ancient and Modern History at Harvard—the first chair in modern nonecclesiastical history in the United States—in 1839 revealed both the growing importance of history in this period and Sparks's stature within the field. Thus he revealed the complex relationship between the nationalist purposes of antebellum historians and their concern with truth and accuracy. From humble origins, Sparks began his career as a Unitarian minister, leaving the ministry in 1823 to pursue his literary and historical interests. In 1834 Sparks published the first volume of his *Library of American Biography* (1834–1848), a series of popular biographies about prominent figures in American history, edited by him. In addition to Sparks himself, contributors to this series included well-known intellectual and political figures in his time, such as Francis Bowen and John Gorham Palfrey. In the preface to the first volume, Sparks affirmed his belief in the moral function of history, declaring that the office of biography was to combine "entertainment with instruction" (1:iv). To Sparks, the didactic function of biography was inseparable from its nationalist function, for, by providing his readers with moral examples to imitate or avoid, he hoped these biographies would instill the kind of civic virtue and concern for the public good necessary for the preservation of the Republic.

Sparks also published and edited the writings of Revolutionary-era figures such as Benjamin Franklin and Gouverneur Morris, the best known of which was his *Writings of George Washington* (1834–1837)—a multivolume collection of Washington's papers that also included a biography of Washington by Sparks. In his emphasis on biography, Sparks revealed the importance and popularity of biography as a genre of history in this period. And in his concern with collecting and publishing primary sources, Sparks revealed his commitment to critical methods of scholarship. Yet in his treatment of Washington's writings, Sparks revealed how his nationalist purposes limited his scholarly integrity, as he changed or omitted passages in Washington's letters to preserve his dignity. In addition to correcting grammatical errors, he changed slang expressions used by Washington, such as "Old Put" to "General Putnam" and "but a flea-bite at present" to "totally inadequate to our demands at

George Bancroft. THE LIBRARY OF CONGRESS

this time," to make Washington seem more dignified (Stevens, p. 308).

GEORGE BANCROFT AND AMERICAN EXCEPTIONALISM

Sharing Sparks's belief in the nationalist function of history, George Bancroft (1800–1891) brought together these nationalist purposes with a Romantic conception of history as a form of literary art. Born in Massachusetts, Bancroft was one of the first Americans to do graduate work in Germany, and he brought back the influence of both German idealism and German critical scholarship to the United States. In 1831 the publication of an article supporting President Andrew Jackson's attack on the Bank of the United States brought Bancroft to political prominence and marked the beginning of his career as a leading figure in the Massachusetts Democratic Party.

Bancroft's rise to political eminence coincided with his emergence as a historian. With the publication of the first volume of his *History of the United States* in 1834, Bancroft immediately established his reputation as one of the nation's leading historians.

Bancroft followed this volume with nine other volumes at irregular intervals, with the last volume appearing in 1874. The most comprehensive account of American history to that point, Bancroft's work achieved a commanding influence over nineteenth-century American historical writing. Bancroft's history was so popular and influential because of its ability to articulate and crystallize the basic assumptions of American exceptionalist ideology, namely the belief that the United States had a special destiny to embody and carry out democratic principles. While for this reason modern scholars have often attributed to him a mythic and uncritically celebratory view of the nation's past, Bancroft was actually a more sophisticated historian than these scholars have acknowledged, and his work combined a fervent nationalism with a cosmopolitan perspective. Very much aware of the international context for American developments, Bancroft's extensive research included both colonial and European archival sources, and he in fact devoted much of his discussion to European events.

Bancroft could take such a broad view of American history because he embraced a teleological perspective that treated the colonial past and indeed all of human history as having a design and purpose leading inexorably up to the Revolution. In Bancroft's words, "prepared by glorious forerunners," the Revolution "grew naturally and necessarily out of the series of past events by the formative principle of a living belief" (7:23). Bancroft believed the Revolution was inevitable because it had been decreed by the "grand design of Providence" (7:23). In his belief that America's historical development fulfilled a divine purpose and his belief that the Revolution represented a turning point in human history, Bancroft articulated two of the central assumptions of American exceptionalism. The Revolution was, for Bancroft, a turning point because it had brought about the realization of America's destiny to advance the cause of liberty. Structuring his analysis around the development of liberty in America, Bancroft dated this development back to the Reformation and began his history with the colonial era. Bancroft emphasized the role of the New England Puritans in developing and transplanting the principles of democracy and liberty to America, for, as he put it, Puritanism was "religion struggling for the People" (1:500).

This account of the origins of liberty served political and social purposes. An ardent Jacksonian, Bancroft gave historical legitimacy to the democratic principles he espoused by tracing their roots in the past. Bancroft's emphasis on the Puritan contribution to democracy reflected his own sectional loyalties: by locating the roots of democracy in New England,

Bancroft asserted the primacy of his own region in American development and defined the nation in terms of New England. At the same time Bancroft's history also served nationalist purposes. Recognizing that Puritanism was just one of the many strands that contributed to American independence, Bancroft gave credit to victims of Puritan persecution, like Roger Williams, and to William Penn and the settlers of Virginia for instituting the principles of liberty in their respective regions. Bancroft thus sought to instill national unity by giving each section a role in the advance of democracy. The other major theme of Bancroft's history was the development of union in America.

With the Revolution, Bancroft believed, America had embarked on a process of continual progress. While the principles of the Revolution did not require a dramatic change in the nation's social or political system, the vitality of the principles themselves made them a source of continual renovation and reform for Bancroft. In his belief that the nation could remain indefinitely in a state of revolution without undergoing fundamental change, Bancroft summed up the exceptionalist vision of America as a nation that was exempt from the normal processes of historical change and decay. In this vision, by virtue of its closeness to nature, the United States could remain in a state of perpetual innocence and simplicity, untouched by the social forces that had corrupted the Old World.

WILLIAM HICKLING PRESCOTT

While their nationalist purposes made U.S. history a natural subject of study for antebellum historians, they also took an interest in other areas of history. One of the leading Romantic historians, William Hickling Prescott (1796–1859), for example, focused on the history of Spain and its conquest of the New World. Born into a wealthy Boston family, Prescott published his first historical work, *History of the Reign of Ferdinand and Isabella the Catholic,* in 1837. This history immediately achieved critical and popular acclaim, and Prescott's reputation would only grow with his subsequent books—*History of the Conquest of Mexico* (1843) and *History of the Conquest of Peru* (1847). While the subject matter for his histories differed from that of Bancroft and Sparks, Prescott shared many of their assumptions about the nature and purpose of history. Thus in his most highly regarded work, the *Conquest of Mexico,* Prescott took Bancroft's view of history as the inevitable march of progress into his interpretation of the Spanish conquest of the Aztecs. For Prescott, the historian could fulfill his or her moral purpose only by identifying the larger principles of progress at work in the events he or she described, for these principles would provide the standards by which to judge historical actors. Identifying these principles was important for the historian's aesthetic purposes as well. Firmly committed to the Romantic view of history as literary art, Prescott viewed his *Conquest of Mexico* as an "epic in prose" (Levin, p. 164). He thus sought to give dramatic unity to his history by structuring his narrative around the conflict between the "civilization" of the Spanish conquerors and the "semi-civilization" of the Aztecs, culminating in the inevitable defeat of the Aztecs by the Spanish. For Prescott, the contrast between the leaders of these two groups—the decisive and resolute Hernán Cortés and the weak and vacillating Montezuma—embodied the differences between the Spanish and the Aztecs and revealed why the Spanish victory was inevitable and necessary for progress.

JOHN LOTHROP MOTLEY

Prescott in turn influenced the other major Romantic historian of this period, John Lothrop Motley (1814–1877), and with Prescott's death in 1859, Motley became the nation's leading historian of Europe. But whereas Prescott had focused on Spanish history, Motley turned his attention to Dutch history. With the publication of *The Rise of the Dutch Republic* in 1856, Motley immediately achieved wide popular and critical acclaim, and he followed this work with other studies of Dutch history—*The History of the United Netherlands* (1860–1867) and *The Life and Death of John of Barneveld* (1874). Highly praised by American and European historians in his time, *The Rise of the Dutch Republic* was Motley's most influential work and became a best-seller in both the United States and Britain. Like Prescott, Motley structured his narrative around the struggle between the forces of progress and their opponents. Taking for his subject the Dutch rebellion against Philip II of Spain, Motley, however, identified the Dutch with progress and the Spanish with decline and reaction. More specifically, because Motley, like Bancroft, equated progress with the advancement of liberty, he depicted the conflict between the Spanish and the Dutch as one between liberty and tyranny. And like Bancroft, Motley emphasized the role of Providence in the advance of progress, portraying progress as the inevitable realization of divine will. While this work did not possess the same dramatic unity as Prescott's, Motley in his own way sought to achieve the ideal of history as Romantic art through the excitement and emotion of his prose and through his ability to create vivid and dramatic characters.

WOMEN AND THE WRITING OF HISTORY: ELIZABETH ELLET

Although women were for the most part excluded from this circle of historians, women did engage in the writing of history in this period. As Nina Baym has demonstrated, women wrote about history in many different genres, including conventional narrative histories, historical novels, travel writings, plays, and poetry. Probably the best-known female historian from this period was Elizabeth Ellet (c. 1812–1877). A prolific author who wrote on a wide variety of topics, ranging from American history to original poetry and literary criticism, Ellet published her first major historical work, *Women of the American Revolution,* a three-volume collective biography of women in the Revolution, between 1848 and 1850. At a time when the ideology of domesticity excluded women from the public world of historical writing and politics, Ellet challenged conventional assumptions about women's domestic roles not only by writing history herself but also by showing women's contributions to the public realm during the Revolution. Ellet's *Domestic History of the American Revolution* (1850) went further and challenged conventional definitions of history, which emphasized political and military events, by arguing for the importance of studying the history of everyday social life—in which women played a major part—during the Revolution. Yet Ellet would only go so far in subverting conventional gender roles. Even while urging the need to recognize women's contributions to political events like the Revolution, Ellet still reinforced the association of women with the domestic sphere by emphasizing the domestic character of those contributions and identifying women with the realm of sentiment and emotion.

CHALLENGES TO ROMANTIC HISTORY: RICHARD HILDRETH

Although the Romantic nationalism of Bancroft and Motley prevailed in the nineteenth century, this style of history did not go unchallenged. One of the best-known dissenters from the Romantic style of history was Richard Hildreth (1807–1865). From the same cultural milieu as his fellow New England historians, Hildreth combined historical writing with a career as an antislavery reformer and philosopher. Hildreth published the first three volumes of his *History of the United States* in 1849, followed by three more volumes in 1851 and 1852, which continued the *History* up to 1821. In contrast to the Romantic style of his contemporaries, Hildreth wrote in a dry, colorless style that listed facts and events in an unemotional way, occasionally relieved by the ironic humor and vivid prose of his caustic declamations against human bigotry

and hypocrisy. Hildreth expressed his desire to challenge patriotic myths about American history in his preface, where he declared that his purpose was "to present for once, on the historic stage, the founders of our American nation unbedaubed with patriotic rouge" (1:iii). Hence Hildreth ridiculed the conventional patriotic view of the Puritans as exponents of liberty, arguing instead that bigotry and intolerance defined Puritanism. In Hildreth's view, rather than a direct outgrowth of Puritanism as Bancroft had claimed, liberty was primarily the product of forces in conflict with Puritan ideals, and the struggle and eventual triumph of these forces against a powerful Puritan theocracy served as major organizing themes for the first two volumes of his history. Hildreth's critical perspective on the Puritans reflected his skepticism about religion more generally. Influenced by utilitarian philosophy, Hildreth interpreted human history in purely secular terms and rejected the providential interpretation embraced by most of his contemporaries.

Hildreth was equally unconventional in his interpretation of the Revolution as an economic struggle to free the colonies from British commercial restrictions, for this interpretation challenged the patriotic view of the Revolution as a struggle for the abstract principle of liberty. And rather than celebrating the Revolution as a turning point in history, Hildreth pointed to its limits, criticizing the Revolution for its failure to realize the democratic principles it proclaimed, particularly with regard to slavery. While Hildreth's history did not achieve much popular success, this work was important as a precursor to the scientific ideal of objective truth that would develop later in the nineteenth century.

THE ART AND SCIENCE OF HISTORY: FRANCIS PARKMAN

Romantic and scientific history were not mutually exclusive, as Francis Parkman (1823–1893) revealed. Part of the Boston Brahmin elite like his Romantic predecessors, Parkman came from a wealthy and privileged background. Fascinated with the "wilderness," Parkman expressed his enthusiasm for the outdoors and for vigorous physical activity through his many hiking trips to remote wilderness regions. In these travels Parkman went to many of the places he discussed in his histories, enabling him to base his descriptions on firsthand experience. In 1846 Parkman traveled west in an expedition on the Oregon Trail, and his chronicle of this trip provided the basis for his first book, *The California and Oregon Trail,* published in 1849. Parkman's love of outdoor activity made the health problems he began to suffer in 1843 all the more of a constraint on his way of life. Suffering from

Francis Parkman. © BETTMANN/CORBIS

headaches, insomnia, indigestion, arthritis, and partial blindness, Parkman often had to lie down in a darkened room without moving for days at a time. Despite his illness, Parkman managed to continue his work on history by having others read his sources aloud to him, by dictating his narrative to one of his assistants, and by setting up a wire mechanism to guide his pencil, which enabled him to do some writing in the dark.

As a result of these efforts, Parkman published his *Pioneers of France in the New World,* the first part of his seven-part study of the French and English conflict in North America, now known as *France and England in North America,* in 1865. Parkman completed this

series in 1892 with the publication of his *A Half Century of Conflict.* The best known and most highly regarded volume in this series was Parkman's *Montcalm and Wolfe,* published in 1884, which brought the imperial conflict between France and England to a close by examining the French and Indian War and its outcome—the establishment of British colonial supremacy in North America. Like his predecessors, Parkman viewed himself as a literary artist and sought to make the past come to life for the reader through the use of the imagination. At the same time Parkman's extensive primary source research was consistent with the scientific ideal of objective truth that was emerging in his time. Parkman saw no conflict between his artistic purposes and his commitment to truth and scholarship. On the contrary, through extensive quotations from his primary sources and the accumulation of details drawn from these sources, Parkman was able to make the events he described seem more vivid and immediate to his audiences. Writing in a direct, vigorous style, Parkman sought to create a sense of drama in *Montcalm and Wolfe* by structuring his narrative around a series of oppositions—between England and France, old and new France, nature and civilization, effeminacy and manhood, and his two central characters, the Marquis de Montcalm and General James Wolfe. Associating nature with freedom and savagery, Parkman believed the English were ultimately able to prevail over the French because of their ability to balance the vigor of nature with the order of civilization. If for Parkman the French represented overrefined civilization, Native Americans at the other extreme embodied the chaotic savagery of nature. Rather than idealizing Native Americans as "noble savages," Parkman portrayed them as cruel and irrational barbarians who were doomed to be destroyed by the advance of civilization.

Yet if Parkman embraced Romantic ideals in his style of writing, his interpretation of history was darker and more pessimistic than that of his Romantic predecessors. Reflecting his own skepticism about religion, Parkman rejected his predecessors' belief in a providential design for history, barely mentioning Providence in his histories. So while he shared the Romantic fascination with nature, he did not see nature as a realm where the individual could commune with the divine as Romantic thinkers did. Instead, reflecting the influence of the evolutionist Charles Darwin, Parkman described nature as a realm defined by the struggle for existence. Parkman's view of nature as an amoral force, governed by fixed laws and indifferent to the fate of humanity, was part of a larger theory of causation that downplayed the individual's ability to control historical events. Parkman instead emphasized the power of larger forces beyond individual control and pointed to the role of petty and trivial occurrences in bringing about events of momentous significance. Thus Parkman did not think progress was inevitable. Deeply critical of the materialistic and democratic tendencies of his time, Parkman feared that, far from improving on their ancestors, his contemporaries had fallen away from the spirit of vigor and heroism that their predecessors had displayed in the colonial struggle against France. In this way Parkman's work at once represented the culmination of Romantic history and pointed to its demise. By the time of Parkman's death in 1893, American historians had increasingly turned away from the Romantic view of history as a literary art in favor of what they considered the more scientific ideal of objectivity, which equated truth with an unbiased account of the facts, detached from any social or political purpose.

See also History of the Conquest of Mexico; The Oregon Trail; Philosophy; Romanticism

BIBLIOGRAPHY
Primary Works
Bancroft, George. *History of the United States, from the Discovery of the American Continent.* Vol. 1. Boston: Charles Bowen, 1834.

Bancroft, George. *History of the United States, from the Discovery of the American Continent.* Vol. 7. Boston: Little, Brown, 1858.

Hildreth, Richard. *The History of the United States of America, from the Discovery of the Continent to the Organization of Government under the Federal Constitution.* 3 vols. New York: Harper & Brothers, 1849.

Sparks, Jared, ed. *Library of American Biography.* 25 vols. 1834. New York: Harper & Brothers, 1839–1851.

Secondary Works
Baym, Nina. *American Women Writers and the Work of History, 1790–1860.* New Brunswick, N.J.: Rutgers University Press, 1995.

Bercovitch, Sacvan. *The Rites of Assent: Transformations in the Symbolic Construction of America.* New York: Routledge, 1993.

Callcott, George. *History in the United States, 1800–1860: Its Practice and Purpose.* Baltimore: Johns Hopkins University Press, 1970.

Casper, Scott. *Constructing American Lives: Biography and Culture in Nineteenth-Century America.* Chapel Hill: University of North Carolina Press, 1999.

Handlin, Lilian. *George Bancroft: The Intellectual as Democrat.* New York: Harper and Row, 1984.

Kraus, Michael, and Davis D. Joyce. *The Writing of American History.* Rev. ed. Norman: University of Oklahoma Press, 1985.

Levin, David. *History as Romantic Art: Bancroft, Prescott, Motley, and Parkman.* Stanford, Calif.: Stanford University Press, 1959.

Noble, David. *Historians against History: The Frontier Thesis and the National Covenant in American Historical Writing since 1830.* Minneapolis: University of Minnesota Press, 1965.

Ross, Dorothy. "Historical Consciousness in Nineteenth-Century America." *American Historical Review* 89 (October 1984): 909–928.

Stevens, Michael. "Jared Sparks." In *American Historians, 1607–1865*, vol. 30 of *Dictionary of Literary Biography*, edited by Clyde N. Wilson, p. 308. Detroit: Gale, 1984.

Van Tassel, David D. *Recording America's Past: An Interpretation of the Development of Historical Studies in America, 1607–1884*. Chicago: University of Chicago Press, 1960.

Vitzthum, Richard C. *The American Compromise: Theme and Method in the Histories of Bancroft, Parkman, and Adams*. Norman: University of Oklahoma Press, 1974.

Wilson, Clyde N., ed. *American Historians, 1607–1865*. Vol. 30 of *Dictionary of Literary Biography*. Detroit: Gale, 1984.

Wish, Harvey. *The American Historian: A Social-Intellectual History of the Writing of the American Past*. New York: Oxford University Press, 1960.

Eileen Ka-May Cheng

HISTORY OF THE CONQUEST OF MEXICO

William H. Prescott's (1796–1859) *History of the Conquest of Mexico* (1843) is an often cited (though seldom read) example of the work of Romantic historians in America, a group of distinguished men of letters that includes George Bancroft (1800–1891), John Lothrop Motley (1814–1877), and Francis Parkman (1823–1893). These authors brought new rigor and flair to American historical writing, and their work complemented the projects of novelists and poets of their day. But to call Prescott an American Romantic historian obscures the contexts and purposes of his bravura rendition of Hernán Cortés's (1485–1547) conquest of Mexico. Beneath the terms "Romantic" and "American" lie a complex range of meanings.

THE CONQUEST OF MEXICO AS ROMANCE?

Prescott presents the conquest of Mexico between 1519 and 1521 as a drama in five acts, or books: "The subversion of a great empire by a handful of adventurers, taken with all its strange and picturesque accompaniments, has the air of romance rather than of sober history." However, Prescott's aim is not to romanticize a historical subject but to treat a Romantic subject rigorously as history: "I have conscientiously endeavoured to distinguish fact from fiction, and to establish the narrative on as broad a basis as possible of contemporary evidence" (1:ix–x). Prescott parted company with novelists like Sir Walter Scott and James Fenimore Cooper, who argued that details might be altered or scenes invented so long as the writer

represented the true spirit of the past. Not that Prescott avoided the conventions of Romantic fiction—he was fond of portraying dramatic action against spectacular backdrops—but he always required documentary evidence to substantiate his scenic displays. The famous Noche Triste (Melancholy Night) during which Cortés's forces were nearly destroyed, really did take place on a dark and stormy night.

However, *The History of the Conquest of Mexico* comes to us in seven books, not five. Prescott framed the drama with two other very different books—the first, a "philosophical" description of Aztec society before Spanish conquest; the last, an account of Cortés's career after his triumph in Mexico. The disquisition on the Aztecs followed in the tradition of German Romantic scholarship pioneered by J. G. von Herder, who argued that the innate characteristics of racially defined nations are the chief forces in historical development and who saw the purpose of history as the evolution of nation-states in which the geniuses of particular peoples found their embodiment. In an earlier work, *The Reign of Ferdinand and Isabella* (1837), Prescott had provided such an analysis of the Spanish nation. *The Conquest of Mexico* therefore begins with a comparable account of Aztec society that allows his subsequent narrative to depict a clash between two conflicting peoples. But Prescott takes care to delineate the internal tensions of Aztec civilization. Montezuma appears as the leader of a conglomeration of smaller kingdoms, hedged in by other polities such as Tlascala and Cholula that resist Aztec authority and by other Nahua peoples resentful of Aztec demands for sacrificial victims. Prescott describes the rise of Aztec religious practices, including human sacrifice and cannibalism, as recent innovations on earlier Olmec and Toltec civilizations. His use of Romantic ideas about historical development is thus neither monolithic nor simplistic, and he accords Aztec society the same level of complexity with which he had depicted Spain.

Prescott's account of Cortés's later career challenges another Romantic convention, the concept of the Representative Man. As developed by Thomas Carlyle and Ralph Waldo Emerson, the Representative Man was the natural outgrowth of Herder's Romantic nationalism: a heroic figure who embodies the qualities of a people. Cortés was an obvious candidate for such a role, and Prescott could have chosen to end his tale with his victory over Mexico. "Indeed, the history of the Conquest . . . is necessarily that of Cortés, who is . . . not merely the soul, but the body, of the enterprise" (3:352). Instead, Prescott's account of Cortés's later years complicates this image. Cortés leads a rigorous but inconclusive expedition to Honduras and

These three excerpts from Prescott's History of the Conquest of Mexico *represent characteristic aspects of his work. The first two offer portraits of key individuals, Montezuma and Cortés. Montezuma is offered as a Romantic figure—the Aztec "Representative Man"—and also displays Prescott's use of orientalist images. The last two excerpts offer examples of Prescott's Romanticism—especially the latter, in which his use of settings and conventions of dramatic fiction writing are most obvious.*

Prescott on Montezuma

In his younger days, he had tempered the fierce habits of the soldier with the milder profession of religion. In later life, he had withdrawn himself still more from the brutalizing occupations of war and his manners acquired a refinement tinctured, it may be added, with an effeminacy, unknown to his martial predecessors.

The condition of the empire, too, under his reign, was favorable to this change. The dismemberment of the Tezcucan kingdom, on the death of the great Nezahualpilli, had left the Aztec monarchy without a rival; and it soon spread its colossal arms over the furthest limits of Anahuac. The aspiring mind of Montezuma rose with the acquisition of wealth and power; and he displayed the consciousness of new importance by the assumption of unprecedented state. He affected a reserve unknown to his predecessors; withdrew his person from the vulgar eye, and fenced himself round with an elaborate and courtly etiquette. When he went abroad, it was in state, on some public occasion, usually to a great temple, to take part in the religious services; and as he passed along, he exacted from his people, as we have seen, the homage of an adulation worthy of an Oriental despot. His haughty demeanour touched the pride of his more potent vassals, particularly those who, at a distance, felt themselves nearly independent of his authority. His exactions, demanded by the profuse expenditure of his palace, scattered broad-cast the seeds of discontent; and, while the empire seemed towering in its most palmy and prosperous state, the canker had eaten deepest into its heart.

Prescott on Cortés

Before marching, the general spoke a few words of encouragement to his own men. He told them, they were now to embark, in earnest, on an enterprise which had been the great object of their desires; and that the blessed Saviour would carry them victorious through every battle with their enemies. "Indeed," he added, "this assurance must be our stay, for every other refuge is now cut off, but that afforded by the Providence of God, and your own stout hearts." He ended by comparing their achievements to those of the ancient Romans, "in phrases of honeyed eloquence far beyond any thing I can repeat," says the brave and simple-hearted chronicler who heard them [Bernal Diaz]. Cortés was, indeed, master of that eloquence which went to the soldiers' hearts. For their sympathies were his, and he shared in the romantic spirit of adventure which belonged to them. "We are ready to obey you," they cried as with one voice. "Our fortunes, for better or worse, are cast with yours." Taking leave, therefore, of their hospitable Indian friends, the little army, buoyant with high hopes and lofty plans of conquest, set forward on the march to Mexico.

Prescott on the Noche Triste (Melancholy Night), 1 July 1520

The night was cloudy, and a drizzling rain, which fell without intermission, added to the obscurity. The great square before the palace was deserted, as, indeed, it had been since the fall of Montezuma. Steadily, and as noiselessly as possible, the Spaniards held their way along the great street of Tlacopan, which so lately had resounded to the tumult of battle. All was now hushed in silence; and they were only reminded of the past by the occasional presence of some solitary corpse, or a dark heap of the slain, which too plainly told where the strife had been hottest. As they passed along the lanes and alleys which opened into the great street, or looked down the canals, whose polished surface gleamed with a sort of ebon luster through the obscurity of night, they easily fancied that they discerned the shadowy forms of their foe lurking in ambush, and ready to spring on them. But it was only fancy; and the city slept undisturbed even by the prolonged echoes of the tramp of the horses, and hoarse rumbling of the artillery and baggage trains. At length, a lighter space beyond the dusky line of buildings showed the van of the army that it was emerging on the open causeway. They might well have congratulated themselves on having thus escaped the dangers of an assault in the city itself, and that a brief time would place them in comparative safety on the opposite shore.—But the Mexicans were not all asleep.

Prescott, *History of the Conquest of Mexico,* 1:130–131, 1:392–393, 2:361–362.

receives honors and riches from the Spanish government, but he also becomes victimized by the Byzantine politics of the Spanish court. These events complicate any easy identification of Cortés's career with Spain's historical destiny, and Prescott identifies Cortés's genius in his power over a wide variety of men: "differing in race, in language, and in interests, with scarcely anything in common among them . . . compelled to bend to the will of one man, . . . to breathe . . . one spirit, and to move on a common principle of action!" (3:355). If Cortés is representative, he embodies an almost accidental force that coheres in a peculiar moment rather than a unified people moving toward its Manifest Destiny.

THE CONQUEST OF MEXICO AS AMERICAN HISTORY?

Prescott is often grouped with Parkman, Motley, and other contemporaries as "American" historians, even though their subject was not the United States. Their works are deemed "American" because they imply that the United States represented the providential destiny of the Americas' settlement, for which the histories of imperial Spain, France, Britain, and the Netherlands were flawed forerunners. This generalization captures the underlying moralism in the works of the Romantic historians but obscures the complexity of their identity as American authors. It would be more accurate to think of Prescott as a Boston Federalist striving to come to terms with his city's place in the nation's conflicts. To be a Boston writer was to be at once provincial and cosmopolitan. As the son of a wealthy lawyer and delegate to the Hartford Convention that contemplated New England's secession from the United States in 1814, Prescott grew up in a tradition that did not assume that the United States fulfilled a providential design for human progress. The willingness of Jeffersonian administrations to sacrifice New England's commercial interests for the sake of territorial expansion made the American Republic

An 1821 engraving of the meeting of Hernán Cortés and Montezuma. © CORBIS

seem inhospitable to those of Prescott's persuasion. At the same time, Boston's commercial interests made the city unusually cosmopolitan, a trait reflected by Prescott's contemporaries who sought to overcome their provincial upbringing by seeking education and travel in Europe. Boston's mercantile connections with Latin America encouraged Prescott and his peers to view this region as an independent partner in trade rather than a potential new area for U.S. colonization.

When Prescott published *The Conquest of Mexico* in 1843, the Texas question lay at the center of national politics. Prescott was bitterly opposed: "the craving for foreign acquisitions has ever been a most fatal symptom in the history of republics," and the annexation of Texas was "the most serious shock yet given to the stability of our glorious institutions" (*Miscellanies*, p. 305 n). *The Conquest of Mexico* can be read as an object lesson in the dangers of military adventurism—admonitory rather than celebratory American history. In a telling passage, Prescott begins book 2 with an overview of early-sixteenth-century Spain, borrowing phrases directly from the U.S. Constitution: "The [Spanish] nation at large could boast as great a degree of constitutional freedom as any other, at that time, in Christendom. Under a system of salutary laws and an equitable administration, domestic tranquility was secured, public credit established" (1:211–212). The parallels between Spain's emergence as a united monarchy out of "the numerous states, into which she had been so long divided" (1:211) and the nascent American republic are obvious, and the meaning of Cortés's conquest is clear—the short-term riches and power that military expansion brought to Spain were in the long run disastrous, not only for Mexico but for Spain as well. If Spain's salutary laws, domestic tranquility, and public credit could be ruined by the war spirit, so too could the American republic. In his review of Bancroft's *History of the United States,* written while he was completing *Conquest of Mexico,* Prescott claimed that "until the period has elapsed which shall have fairly tried the strength of our institutions, through peace and through war, . . . the time will not have come to write the history of the Union" (*Miscellanies*, p. 305). If the American continent was the stage on which the world's destiny would be played out, the United States was not necessarily the chosen vehicle to carry the designs of providence forward.

ORIENTALISM AND *THE CONQUEST OF MEXICO*

Then how did Prescott understand the historical contest that was unfolding in the New World? The answer that emerges throughout Prescott's prose epic is one that pits the West against the East, as the latest in a long sequence of conflicts going back to the ancient Greeks and Persians. In his account of Aztec civilization, Prescott often makes Orientalist comparisons in order to explain the existence of a complex New World society and rank it on a scale of human development. Egypt is the most common point of comparison, but others abound, as a few examples will demonstrate. On luxury, "The Spaniards might well have fancied themselves in the voluptuous precincts of an Eastern harem, instead of treading the halls of a wild barbaric chief in the Western World" (2:86). On religion, "[The Aztecs] invested their deities with attributes, savoring much more of the grotesque conceptions of the eastern nations in the Old World, than of the lighter fictions of Greek mythology" (1:56). On despotism, "The Tezcucan monarchs, like those of Asia, and ancient Egypt, had the control of immense masses of men, and would sometimes turn the whole population of a conquered city, including the women, into the public works" (1:180). Prescott argues in a lengthy appendix, "Origin of the Mexican Civilization," that the ancient peoples of Mexico must have had their roots in Asia as well (3:371–418).

Framing these comparisons is Prescott's conviction that there is a "wide difference" in the "inventive power" among nations: "Some nations seem to have no power beyond that of imitation," and the dividing line runs between East and West. "Such, for example, are the Chinese." By contrast, "Far from looking back, and forming itself slavishly on the past, it is characteristic of the European intellect to be ever on the advance" (1:131–132). In this sense, the conflict between the Spanish conquistadors and the armies of Montezuma "was, in short, the combat of the ancient Greeks and Persians over again" (1:445). For Prescott, Aztec soldiers were a force of nature, powerful through their sheer numbers, animal strength, and physical courage. But the Spaniards' victory "established the superiority of science and discipline over mere physical courage and numbers" (1:447). Embedded in these comparisons are standard Orientalist oppositions: Christian versus infidel, civility versus barbarism, science versus superstition, representative government versus despotism, masculine vigor versus feminine passivity, and an underlying racial distinction between white Europeans and colored Asiatics.

Prescott's use of racial stereotypes about Native Americans is contained within his Orientalism. A telling example comes in his description of Guatemozin, Montezuma's successor as Aztec emperor, who fought nobly against Cortés through the final siege of Tenochtitlan. Unlike Montezuma, who was marked by passivity and indecision—"an effeminacy, unknown to his martial predecessors," similar to "Alexander, after he was infected by the manners of the Persians" (2:130, 131 n)—Guatemozin is a "fierce young monarch" with a "haughty spirit" (3:191–193). Not surprisingly, Prescott suggests that Guatemozin's "complexion [was] fairer than those of his bronze-colored nation" (3:205). However, Prescott does not create a complete binary opposition between Spaniards and Aztecs. He offers a more subtle, if no less pernicious, suggestion that what undermines the success of Cortés is the degree to which Spain itself was orientalized by its former domination under Arab rule and its consequent tendency to embrace despotic forms of government and religion. If, under Ferdinand and Isabella, Spain had made progress toward constitutional liberties, this was ruined by their successor, Charles V, and by the creation of the Spanish Inquisition. The career of Cortés recapitulated this evolution. As a military leader Cortés always relied on the consent of his men. But after his final conquest of the Aztecs, his attempt to rebuild the Mexican empire brought out a despotic streak: "All within the immediate control of Cortés were pressed into the service. . . . Reconstruction went forward with a rapidity like that shown by an Asiatic despot, who concentrates the population of an empire on the erection of a favorite capital" (3:240). Prescott's comparison of the Spanish Inquisition with Aztec human sacrifice also advances the image of Spanish despotism. "Human sacrifice, however cruel, has nothing in it degrading to its victim. It may rather be said to ennoble him by devoting him to the gods. . . . The Inquisition, on the other hand, branded its victims with infamy in this world, and consigned them to everlasting perdition in the next" (1:84). Prescott's rendering of Spain and its empire as tainted by oriental qualities has been described by Richard L. Kagan as "Hispanism."

The Conquest of Mexico offers readers a Romantic chapter in the ongoing history of West versus East. Its orientalist stereotypes might suggest that Prescott saw this as a struggle between white Protestant Europeans and various ranks of lesser peoples. But the distinctions Prescott makes among races and nations are never absolute. Within any society—Spain, Mexico, or, for that matter, the United States—Prescott finds varying mixtures of the qualities he associates with progress or decline. Among the native peoples of Mexico, he praises the kingdom of Tezcuco as "the Athens of the Western World" (1:173) and describes "its superiority, in all the great features of civilization, over the rest of Anahuac" in words reminiscent of a proud Bostonian extolling his city's virtues over the crass materialism of New York: "The best histories, the best poems, the best code of laws, the purest dialect, were all allowed to be Tezcucan. The Aztecs rivaled their neighbors in splendor of living, . . . but this was the development of the material, rather than the intellectual principle" (1:204–205).

Ultimately *The Conquest of Mexico* casts doubt on the notion that the forces of progress are racial or national characteristics. For Prescott, virtuous actions and the development of wise institutions determine human progress, and these can be found, to some measure, in any society. Prescott argues that the Aztec empire could never have been conquered by Cortés and the conquistadors alone.

> The Aztec monarchy fell by the hands of its own subjects, under the direction of European sagacity and science. Had it been united, it might have bidden defiance to the invaders. . . . Its fate may serve as a striking proof, that a government, which does not rest on the sympathies of its subjects, cannot long abide; that human institutions, when not connected with human prosperity and progress, must fall. (3:222–223)

If Prescott believed that the United States was a superior embodiment of progressive virtues, his provincial chauvinism ran still deeper, for he saw New England as the superior part of the United States. *The Conquest of Mexico* was also a cautionary tale to his fellow citizens, warning them against assuming too readily, as Cortés had done, that providence was on their side, and reminding them of the dangers faced by a government in which people differed violently over whether its institutions supported human prosperity and progress.

See also History; Orientalism; Romanticism

BIBLIOGRAPHY
Primary Works
Prescott, William Hickling. "Bancroft's United States." In his *Biographical and Critical Miscellanies*, pp. 294–305. New York: Harper & Brothers, 1845.

Prescott, William Hickling. *History of the Conquest of Mexico.* 3 vols. New York: Harper & Brothers, 1843.

Prescott, William Hickling. *History of the Reign of Ferdinand and Isabella, the Catholic.* 3 vols. Boston: American Stationers Company, 1837.

Secondary Works
Ernest, John. "Reading the Romantic Past: William H. Prescott's *History of the Conquest of Mexico*." *American Literary History* 5, no. 2 (1993): 231–249.

Gardiner, C. Harvey. *William Hickling Prescott: A Biography.* Austin: University of Texas Press, 1969.

Kagan, Richard L., ed. *Spain in America: The Origins of Hispanism in the United States.* Urbana: University of Illinois Press, 2002.

Levin, David. *History as Romantic Art: Bancroft, Prescott, Motley, and Parkman.* Stanford, Calif.: Stanford University Press, 1959.

McWilliams, John P., Jr. *The American Epic: Transforming a Genre, 1770–1860.* Cambridge, U.K.: Cambridge University Press, 1989.

Ringe, Donald A. "The Function of Landscape in Prescott's *The Conquest of Mexico.*" *New England Quarterly* 56, no. 4 (1983): 569–577.

Mark A. Peterson

HONOR

The tradition of honor has largely disappeared from modern discourse with the exception of military life. In that world, separated from civilian conventions, this ancient, once practically universal, code of behavior still reigns. No army, past or present, has long survived without a disciplined sense of hierarchy under orders, an ideal of valor under battle stress, and an intense bonding of warriors under arms. For those at war, faith in the ethic helps to reduce a sense of vulnerable isolation and fear of dying alone and unmourned. With all its qualities of discipline and heroic bearing, though, honor's relationship to violence is undeniable. Thanks in part to films including *Gone with the Wind,* the popularity of Civil War reenactments, and neo-conservative Rebel flag waving, nostalgia for the romance of heroism and cavalier manners persists in public memory. Honor also has long had a merciless side, however, that is not always recognized. As the sociologist Orlando Patterson asserts, all slave societies from prehistory to the modern era have required an adherence to that ethic. The slaveholding South was no exception.

ORIGINS OF HONOR IN THE SOUTHERN UNITED STATES

From the beginning of regional settlement, traditions of honor served as the basis for conventions in the relative absence of institutional, mediating structures. The ethic embraced the whole spectrum of living, from the famous practice of dueling as an assertion of power to romantic literary representations. Equally important for understanding its scope is honor's centrality to the relationship between men and women and to a reliance upon family and exclusive community. A biological ranking placed male over female, age over youth, rich over poor, strength over frailty, and, above all, white over black. It was a world of stark moral contrast—good vs. evil, honorableness vs. disgrace. For some men, honor was a reward above all

others. Richard II in Shakespeare's play of the same name cries out, "Take honor from me, and my life is done." Less eloquently Senator James Henry Hammond of South Carolina confessed, "Life without honor is the deepest damnation. Not to do your duty is dishonor" (McDonnell, p. 123). Yet, the transatlantic community has always known that traditional honor relies upon public opinion and is a capricious monarch. To borrow again from Shakespeare, this time from *Troilus and Cressida,* outward shows of honors— "place, riches, and favour, / Prizes of accident"— sometimes weigh more than integrity. For white antebellum Southerners like Hammond, honor embodied the independency of the individual, the white family, and the property holder whose eternal rights included "*laisser asservir*"—the white man's right to hold human beings as possessions (Fisher, p. 412).

Whereas males might take different roads toward the goal of respect, women were defined by their ineligibility for reaching that prize by similarly aggressive means. The convention for them took on a negative character: modesty, not outspokenness; chastity, not license; submissiveness, not assertiveness; domesticity, not public notice. A woman's obligation was not merely to obey men but also to rear sons valorously dedicated to the protection of dependent family members. The mother of Sam Houston of Tennessee, founder of the Texas Republic, once handed her young son a musket and reminded him that it would be better for her sons to "fill one honorable grave, than one of them should turn his back to save his life" (Wyatt-Brown, p. 51). Although increasing religious conversions and an emerging commercial climate were well underway by the advent of secession and civil war, Southerners learned to combine old ways with the newly adopted. As a result, the venerable code survived the transatlantic changes that set the Northern industrializing states on a different, secular, and progressive path.

RATIONALES FOR HONOR

Projected aggressively outward, honor permitted its adherents few inner doubts. Its psychology and its opposite, shame, have always differed from the ethic of conscience and guilt. In the latter case, a sense of remorse arises from interior, often religious sources, rather than from threats of public exposure. To illustrate, consider a planter who kept his slave mistress at a distance from his residence. His male friends would know and, as he walked by, slyly joke about his upcoming rendezvous. Affably he would acknowledge their smiles. But if his wife were to find out and be openly pitied, and if both men and women together gossiped

"THE CODE OF HONOR; OR, RULES FOR THE GOVERNMENT OF PRINCIPALS AND SECONDS IN DUELLING"

John Lyde Wilson's (1784–1849) dueling manual, published in 1838, was the only such set of instructions published in America. It did, however, resemble "The Irish Code of Honor," a manual that Wilson attached to a later edition of his brief pamphlet. In the preface to his text, Wilson, a lawyer then senator and governor of South Carolina, stoutly defended the practice of dueling against its critics. He asks where could one ever hope to find a "tribunal to do justice to an oppressed and deeply wronged individual?" Gentlemen should not "be subjected to a tame submission to insult and disgrace," he asserted (Williams, p. 88). If nations resorted to arms and bloodletting to protect liberty, happiness, and reputation, it followed that men of honor were justified in doing likewise.

THE PERSON INSULTED, BEFORE CHALLENGE SENT

1. Whenever you believe you are insulted, if the insult be in public, and by words or behavior, never resent it there, if you have self-command enough to avoid noticing it. If resented there, you offer an indignity to the company, which you should not.

2. If the insult be by blows or any personal indignity, it may be resented at the moment, for the insult to the company did not originate with you. But although resented at the moment, yet you are bound still to have satisfaction, and must therefore make the demand.

3. When you believe yourself aggrieved, be silent on the subject, speaking to no one about the matter, and see your friend who is to act for you, as soon as possible.

4. Never send a challenge in the first instance, for that precludes all negotiation. Let your note be in the language of a gentleman, and let the subject matter of complaint be truly and fairly set forth, cautiously avoiding attributing to the adverse party any improper motive.

5. When your second is in full possession of the facts, leave the whole matter to his judgment, and avoid any consultation with him unless he seeks it. He has the custody of your honor, and by obeying him you cannot be compromised.

John Lyde Wilson, "The Code of Honor; or, Rules for the Government of Principals and Seconds on Duelling" (1838), in Williams, *Duelling*, pp. 88–103.

about it, the adulterer would only then lose his honorable standing and be disgraced. Appearance of virtue, not the real thing, mattered most.

The major duty of the man of honor was to uphold his own and his family's reputation and to protect the purity of the bloodline. In a chronically distrustful world, he was expected to guard the chastity of female relatives. They, in turn, could seek no autonomy. A case of black amalgamation–black male with white female—was the most horrifying possibility imaginable. In early 1861 John S. Preston, secession commissioner from South Carolina, informed the Virginia convention debating disunion that abolitionists would force white women to cohabit with blacks. "No community of laws, no community of language, of religion, can amalgamate . . . people whose severance is proclaimed by the most rigid requisitions of universal necessity," he warned (Reese 1:90). Such Protestant clergymen as Benjamin Morgan Palmer and John Fletcher asserted that in Genesis 9 God cursed Ham's sexual sin of alleged miscegenation, bringing divine castigation upon the black race. That ancient incident had suppos-

edly undermined the natural order that the Creator had fashioned at the world's beginning.

In addition to protecting families from dishonor, sexual and otherwise, the Southern male was expected to react forcefully to insult or to anticipate humiliation. This was the underlying principle of the duel. Members of a community expected that violent retribution, sometimes by the gentlemen's ritualized encounter on the field of honor, should be the manly vindication of an insulted party. The duel was ordinarily confined to those admitted to a circle of gentlemen. The principals were required to be approximately the same in age, rank, and public standing.

DUELS

Contrary to general understanding, the duel was uncommon in America until the French and English officer corps introduced it during the French and Indian War (1756–1763). When national parties developed after the Constitution was ratified, Revolutionary veterans, as militia officers and political leaders, displayed their willingness to die for the honor of their faction by dueling with partisan foes. Thus, they demonstrated a murderous loyalty to their followers and thereby bound them to their leader. Often these supporters, mostly young attorneys, junior militia officers, and editors, would likewise serve their patrons, hoping to advance in power. To solidify their separate and feuding factions' constancy, Alexander Hamilton (1755–1804) and Jeffersonian vice president Aaron Burr's (1756–1836) meeting at Weehawken in 1804 followed the patron-client pattern. Northern outrage against the practice erupted, however, when Hamilton fell. Few Yankees thereafter met an opponent on the ground. In the South, however, a connection between the duel and the exhibition of manly leadership continued up to the Civil War.

Southern states did pass weak laws against the practice. Occasionally the clergy criticized it. Yet, confident of public acquiescence, apologists defied the scowls of church and state. Justifying a duel with Thomas L. Clingman of North Carolina, William L. Yancey of Alabama proclaimed that God's order, state laws, and even a father and husband's duty to family "yield, as they have ever done," in the past—and the present—to the imperative of the duel or be humiliated (Wyatt-Brown, p. 51).

HONOR AS SOCIAL DISCOURSE

In public affairs, the honor code was supposed to guide men toward mutual regard of each other, if reputations so warranted. Honor therefore offered little in the way of personal privacy or deviancy from accepted rules. The presentation of the self as honorable had to be accepted by the local public or else the claimant to regard was disdained or worse. He had to take such a loss of face as part of his own personality. This mode of deciding who belonged and who did not was largely a consequence of the agrarian character of the Old South and the limited number residing in any community, where everyone knew everyone else's business. Indeed, in such face-to-face locales, strangers were unwelcome and suspected of malicious intentions. To win favor, they had quickly to establish some connection to known parties, demonstrate an admired skill, or exhibit an easy manner. Moreover, honor also enlisted violent community means to suppress some alleged outrage. Whippings, the applications of tar and feathers, and possibly lynch law might replace ordinary judicial processes. After the terrifying ritual of shaming or execution, participants congratulated themselves for having purified the moral environment.

Needless to say, however, not all Southerners participated in such celebrations. Instead, in elite circles, the most elevated form of honor often guided manners and appearances. They sought to meet the ideals of noblesse oblige, magnanimity, and gentle manners, an aspect of ancient concepts of Stoic dignity. Steven Shapin comments that in seventeenth-century England "a series of classical and pagan virtues—fortitude, fidelity, valor—were expressed in the notion of a gentleman's *word*" (p. 68). In his class notes after a lecture by the German American political scientist Francis Lieber, James Henry Hammond at South Carolina College in Columbia, jotted down this sentiment: "Honor is that principle of nature which teaches us to respect ourselves, in order that we may gain the esteem of others" (Wyatt-Brown, p. 103). Like Thomas Jefferson years earlier, Southern gentlemen of an elevated spirit considered the pursuit of honor to be praiseworthy only if the claimant understood that he had to treat others, if deserving, with respect—even slaves. That spirit endured into the late nineteenth century. In 1891 the Confederate general Wade Hampton, a defeated, old-style South Carolina governor, explained that holding elective office "is only honorable as an evidence of the good will, the esteem, the confidence of those who bestow it" (Holden, p. 72). With his gravitas, Christian bearing, and refined sense of honor, Robert E. Lee epitomized that widely praised Southern gentlemanly tradition. Long after the Civil War he served as the South's prime exemplar.

POLITICAL MANIFESTATIONS OF HONOR

In light of this code—in both its truculently primal and its genteel forms—the South regarded the growing controversy with the free states as a form of dueling. Heated insults rang through the congressional corridors. They appeared in print, pulpit, and public speeches as well. An upsurge of Southern anger was scarcely a wonder. The relentlessness with which Northern politicians, preachers, and reformers had voiced their antislavery sentiments throughout the years before the war was bound to prompt almost hysterical responses, particularly in the lower South. The density of its slave population, rural character, and relative isolation from Northern influences set the region apart, even from the other slave states closer to the Northern juggernaut. Southern whites were so proud of their religious devotion, suppression of deviant ideas, agrarian prosperity, and honorable motives that they considered secession a God-given choice. To many of them, as Susan Keitt of Charleston, wife of a leading Fire-Eater, put the matter, the Northern enemy was just "a motley throng of . . . Infidels and Free Lovers, interspersed by Bloomer women, fugitive slaves and amalgamationists" (Marchant, p. 348). In politics, every Yankee advance seemed to threaten the

Southern way of life. Economically and socially dependent upon their slaves, white Southerners could not imagine what other way of life there could be.

As sectional differences became ever more bitter, Southerners proclaimed themselves a culture apart from the rest of the nation. The fast growth and ethnic diversity of the Northern population was eroding the underpopulated South's political strength in the Congress and endangering slaveholding control of the national government. The idea of a social order based upon the "cavalier" followers of the Stuart monarchy appealed to the Southern slaveholding elite. In 1861 Samuel Phillips Day, an English journalist, observed that the struggle harkened to earlier times when "Cavalier and Roundhead" took to warfare. The descendants of "Plymouth Rock" and the Virginia colonists had become no less bloodthirsty than the Puritans and Cromwellians of old.

HONOR IN LITERATURE

In the development of a distinctive antebellum Southern literature, the traditions of honor were bound to appear. William Gilmore Simms (1806–1870) of South Carolina, one of the first American authors to make a living from fiction writing, depicted stereotypical heroes, handsome and virile. They were Southern through and through. Novelists like Simms followed such contemporary conventions as depicting cousinly wedding ties that for decades had been a regional means to hold property within family boundaries and find partners compatible in habits and aims. Unlike such contemporary Northern writers as Nathaniel Hawthorne (1804–1864), they did not examine the deepest feelings of their characters. Instead, the artist relied on the given verities—the success or failure of their heroes and heroines to meet lofty standards. A culture steeped in honor sets a wall of reticence around the inner life. Moreover, Simms, Nathaniel Beverley Tucker (1784–1851) of Virginia, and others held that the artist's duty was to offer examples of moral achievement and dishonorable perversity. In the grandiloquent rhetoric that Southern novelists treasured, Tucker, author of *The Partisan Leader* (1836), has the hero, George Balcombe of Virginia, admonish a friend for belittling good bloodlines. Given all other claims, Balcombe crows, "is it not a higher honour to spring from a race of men without fear and without reproach—the ancient cavaliers of Virginia?" Such gentlemen as he could never tarnish their honor. Rather, Tucker writes, Balcombe and company would spill "their blood like water," and sacrifice "their wealth like chaff" if honor so demanded (Taylor, pp. 320–321). It never occurred to the Southern belletrists to criticize their society for its anti-intellectualism, blind adherence to outworn ideas, racism, and, above all, dedication to slavery. To do so would have violated a sacred social compact, in which the precepts of honor and community loyalty were paramount.

Although Edgar Allan Poe's (1809–1849) poetry and fiction are not generally associated with his native Virginia, he, too, embraced the ideals of Southern honor and even more, a dread of shame. Alcoholic and quite possibly affected by bipolar disorder, he recognized his social and moral inadequacy by the criteria of respectability. He displayed a self-destructiveness in his many quarrels and frequently severed connections with literary colleagues. Poe's gothic stories often involved a sadist, who, after almost senseless acts of rage and malice, recognizes his unworthiness for normal acceptance. In remorse, he confesses his crime to some official or else comes to a self-inflicted death. An orphan reared by an unloving Richmond merchant and his melancholy wife, Poe placed his well-hidden resentments and sense of doom in such tales as "The Cask of Amontillado."

HONOR IN SOUTHERN POETRY

Likewise, Southern poetry was largely steeped in the various aspects of the honor code. An example was the Kentuckian Theodore O'Hara's (1820–1867) poem "The Bivouac of the Dead" (1848). It was composed to memorialize veterans killed in the Mexican-American War and stressed the immortal glory of heroes:

> Nor shall your glory be forgot
> While Fame her record keeps,
> Or Honor points the hallowed spot
> Where Valor proudly sleeps.
> *(Hughes and Ware, p. 58)*

The battles in Mexico were a prelude to bloodier encounters not many years later. The concept of military honor was no less pronounced in the Civil War. In 1861 the Reverend George L. Lee, a Baptist of Alabama, lectured a battalion on the eve of departure from home. "I want you to do noble . . . deeds that will bring glory to God, honor to Christ, happiness to man, confusion to devils, and to all of old Abe's fanatics, and eternal credit and honor to yourselves" (Flynt, p. 114). In the mind of a well-read soldier, war, honor, and literature were easily combined. "I am blessing old Sir Walter Scott daily," wrote a South Carolinian officer early in the fight, "for teaching me, when young, how to rate knightly honour, & our noble ancestry for giving me such a State to fight for" (McPherson, *For Cause and Comrades*, p. 27). One was unlikely to locate the same Cavalier sensibility among the Northern "Roundheads," the historian

James McPherson observes. As the Carolinian implied, adherence to honor plunged its devotees into the ruin of civil war—and defeat.

Indeed, Southerners so venerated Scott that the language of his romances had arisen earlier in political debate. Just before resigning, Congressman Lawrence Keitt of South Carolina put his own hostility toward Northern Unionists into Scott's rhetoric. He was prepared, he thundered, to face the Yankee foe "with helmet on, with visor down, and lance couched" (Walther, p. 186). With the Southern duel in mind, he welcomed a war soon to be fought on "the field" of honor. Walter Scott's *Ivanhoe* (1819) and other historical novels appealed to the planter class because in them they found their own basic ideals and values reified. That sense of romance continued well into the war but gradually faded as reality offered a different perspective.

HONOR ON THE BATTLEFIELD

In the war itself, however, the concept of a heroic cavalier spirit for a time helped to disguise the sights and smells of death, injury, and devastation. Unsurprisingly, solders' letters home often spoke of honor. A new enlistee from North Carolina pledged to "give up my life in defence of my Home and Kindred. I had rather be dead than see the Yanks rule this country" (McPherson, *Battle Cry of Freedom*, p. 310). He and so many others would meet that very prospect. Intermixed with pledges to honor was a fear of shaming their units by a seizure of panic or an impulse for cowardly flight. Some feigned illness. Others, truly sick, joined their comrades, "determined," an Alabama lieutenant wrote his wife, "to not have it said that our Comp[any] was in a fight and I not with them" (McPherson, *For Cause and Comrades*, p. 79).

Not all, however, were convinced. Honor seemed an empty vessel as the war lengthened and specters of failure loomed. The poet Henry Timrod (1828–1867) of Charleston had won popularity with his cheerleading verses. Yet, as early as the aftermath of First Manassas, fought on 21 July 1861, Timrod sang mournfully of "meadows beaten into bloody clay," banners "drooping in the rain," and of "whispers round the body of the dead!" (Rubin, p. 205). These lines did not inspire nor were they meant to.

As Timrod and others ultimately recognized, courage and a devotion to the principles of honor could not win a war for the doomed rebel cause. After the destructiveness of Sherman's march, after Lee's surrender, after slavery's fall, Southerners were bound to mourn. They looked upon the carnage and the bravery and whispered soulfully and proudly "We have lost all save honor."

DISTURBING LEGACIES

In fact, honor was still restorative enough to inspire the launching of a guerrilla war with vigilante groups and the Ku Klux Klan, whose night riders spread near-anarchy. The paramilitary units and the Democratic "Redeemers" were determined to wrest political control from the Republicans, preserve white dominion, and resist by every means "social equality"—not only the intermingling of races but also all signs of freed people's advancement. From 1865 to the 1870s the hard-pressed Republicans in the South, both white and black, tried to create a new order of biracial, two-party democracy. They failed as Northerners grew weary of trying and Southern resistance mounted. The era of lynch law under Redeemer state governments held the emancipated race in a new grip. It took nearly a century to undo, at least partially, the enormous moral and social damage that a virulent spirit of honor, tragically, had helped to generate.

See also Civil War; English Literature; Individualism and Community; Manhood; Proslavery Writing; Slavery

BIBLIOGRAPHY
Primary Works
Day, Samuel Phillips. *Down South; or, An Englishman's Experience at the Seat of the American War.* London: Hurst and Blackett, 1862.

Reese, George H., ed. *Proceedings of the Virginia State Convention of 1861, February 13–May 1.* 4 vols. Richmond: Richmond State Library (Historical Publications Divisions), 1965.

Secondary Works
Brown, William Garrott. *The Lower South in American History.* 1902. New York: Haskell House Publishers, 1968.

Donald, David Herbert. *Charles Sumner and the Coming of the Civil War.* New York: Knopf, 1960.

Fisher, David Hackett. *Albion's Seed: Four British Folkways in America.* New York: Oxford University Press, 1989.

Flynt, Wayne. *Alabama Baptists: Southern Baptists in the Heart of Dixie.* Tuscaloosa: University of Alabama Press, 1998.

Haynes, Stephen R. *Noah's Curse: The Biblical Justification of American Slavery.* New York: Oxford University Press, 2002.

Holden, Charles J. "'Is Our Love for Wade Hampton Foolishness?' South Carolina and the Lost Cause." In *The Myth of the Lost Cause and Civil War History,* edited by Gary W. Gallagher and Alan T. Nolan. Bloomington: Indiana University Press, 2000.

Hughes, Nathaniel Cheairs, Jr., and Thomas Clayton Ware. *Theodore O'Hara: Poet-Soldier of the Old South.* Knoxville: University of Tennessee Press, 1998.

McDonnell, Lawrence T. "Struggle against Suicide: James Henry Hammond and the Secession of South Carolina." *Southern Studies* 22 (summer 1983): 109–137.

McPherson, James M. *For Cause and Comrades: Why Men Fought in the Civil War.* New York: Oxford University Press, 1997.

McPherson, James M., *Battle Cry of Freedom: The Civil War Era.* New York: Oxford University Press, 1988.

Marchant, John H. "Lawrence M. Keitt, South Carolina Fire-Eater." Ph.D. diss., University of Virginia, 1976.

Patterson, Orlando. *Slavery and Social Death: A Comparative Study.* Cambridge, Mass.: Harvard University Press, 1982.

Rubin, Louis D., Jr. *The Edge of the Swamp: A Study in the Literature and Society of the Old South.* Baton Rouge: Louisiana State University Press, 1989.

Shapin, Steven. *A Social History of Truth: Civility and Science in Seventeenth-Century England.* Chicago: University of Chicago Press, 1994.

Taylor, William Robert. *Cavalier and Yankee: The Old South and American National Character.* New York: Braziller, 1961.

Walther, Eric H. *The Fire-Eaters.* Baton Rouge: Louisiana State University Press, 1992.

Williams, Jack Kenny. *Dueling in the Old South: Vignettes of Social History.* College Station: Texas A & M University Press, 1980.

Wyatt-Brown, Bertram. *Southern Honor: Ethics and Behavior in the Old South.* New York: Oxford University Press, 1982.

Bertram Wyatt-Brown

HOPE LESLIE

Hope Leslie; or, Early Times in the Massachusetts (1827) is the third novel of Catharine Maria Sedgwick (1789–1867), following her early domestic novels *A New-England Tale* (1822) and *Redwood* (1824). A writer of juvenile fiction, moral tales, and domestic literature as well as numerous novels, Sedgwick was a well-respected literary figure in New England before the appearance of *Hope Leslie*. But this novel is important to any critical assessment of her work because of its skillful use of historical materials and its ability to offer cultural criticism about the United States in the 1820s through the literary medium of revisionary history. Although the novel was only a modest commercial and critical success, it did help Sedgwick's literary career, and it did further legitimate the role of the professional woman writer in America.

PURITANISM AND THE PLOT OF *HOPE LESLIE*

Hope Leslie is a historical novel about Puritan New England that manages to address important social and cultural issues facing early-nineteenth-century America. Sedgwick turned to Puritan history during a period of great cultural interest in colonial history. During the 1820s, after all, New Englanders were celebrating the bicentennial commemorations of the founding of Plymouth and Massachusetts Bay Colonies. Sedgwick makes use of Puritan and early national histories as well as cultural myths of the period (for example, the heroic Puritan founding of New England and the Pocahontas legend) to reconstruct the meaning of New England's colonial past for contemporary American readers. *Hope Leslie* is thus a novel highly self-conscious about the nature—and politics—of historical truth.

The plot of *Hope Leslie* is characteristically complex for early American historical novels that were influenced by the literary models provided by Sir Walter Scott (discussed below). The novel begins by putting Puritanism in a transatlantic context, exposing the mixture of religious and worldly motives behind the Puritan migration in the character of William Fletcher, who loses both his financial inheritance and his chance for true love in leaving England for the Massachusetts Bay Colony. Once there, he soon escapes to the Massachusetts frontier and establishes a homestead aptly named (after the biblical Israelites) "Bethel." Set in this locale during the 1630s and 1640s, the rest of the novel creates an entangled romance plot that involves Fletcher's son, Everell, with three young women: Hope Leslie, Magawisca, and another Puritan girl (more pristine and dutiful than Hope) named Esther Downing. This complicated romance plot is set within the historical context of the violent conflict between English settlers and Algonquian Indians. In the novel, this culminates with Magawisca's own eyewitness account—a revisionary history of sorts—of the infamous Pequot War (1637), in which Puritan forces annihilated two Native American settlements in Connecticut. The Native American reprisal for this act sets the plot into motion: it leads to Everell's captivity, Magawisca's effort to free him (where she loses her arm), and the captivity of Hope's sister Faith, who becomes culturally assimilated and marries a Pequot warrior.

Part 2 sustains the novel's general pattern of cultural crossing, masculine violence, and captivity. However, Sedgwick complicates the plot even further by introducing the villain Sir Philip Gardiner (a character based upon a real person mentioned in the Puritan historian William Bradford's *Of Plymouth Plantation*).

Catharine Maria Sedgwick, c. 1832. Engraving from a painting by Charles Ingham.
THE LIBRARY OF CONGRESS

Gardiner is a closet Catholic, a sexual rake, and a political conspirator against the Bay Colony; he is accompanied by his "page"—a concubine disguised in male dress. The novel later describes Magawisca's furtive reentry into Puritan settlements, her help in enabling Hope to see her "captive" sister, Magawisca's subsequent imprisonment and trial by the Puritan authorities, Hope's successful liberation of Magawisca, the failed kidnapping of Hope, and the exposure of Gardiner's duplicity. Throughout, Sedgwick employs the Shakespearean convention of disguises and mistaken identities—mainly to call into question the essential nature of women and men—as well as such

features of popular romantic fiction as secret plots, chase scenes, and explosions. The romance plot is consummated by the betrothal of Hope and Everell, while Esther Downing decides upon the life of a single woman and Magawisca relinquishes her affections for Everell and retreats into the American wilderness. So the novel both predictably and strangely concludes.

Hope Leslie makes use of such established literary genres as historical romance, frontier romance, and the Indian captivity narrative. Indeed its overall plot is structured according to the importance—and transgression—of "borders" in these three literary genres: between English and Native American racial identities, between "civilization" and "savagery," between the norms for masculine and feminine behavior, and between Old World and New World societies. The novel is structured upon repeating cycles of captivity and liberation in order to question these borders—those, the novel suggests, that all forms of patriarchal social and political authority are founded upon. The novel's emphasis on female heroism ultimately asks its readers to consider important questions about the social and political identities of women and the political consequences of women acting out the virtue of benevolent feeling in both private and public settings.

THE HISTORICAL NOVEL AND THE SUBJECT OF NATIVE AMERICANS

Beginning in the 1820s, American novelists like Sedgwick and James Fenimore Cooper (1789–1851) borrowed from the model for historical fiction that Sir Walter Scott (1771–1832) had popularized for Anglo-American audiences in novels like *Waverly* (1814). This model was based on eighteenth-century theories about the nature of social and historical progress. It fictively dramatized the central conflict between supposedly traditional and modern societies—in Scott's case, Scottish Highlanders and the English nation. The protagonist (like Hope, Everell, or Magawisca) typically "wavers" between these two competing allegiances until the forces of progress ultimately prevail. Scott's formula contains important literary and ideological features that American writers like Sedgwick adapted to their own purposes and design: characters embody and symbolize larger historical forces; they maintain "romantic," or larger-than-life, stature as they move upon a historical stage; the novel itself rationalizes the historical process and the dominance of the modern nation-state; and the marriage plot becomes the literary convention of romance that enables and symbolizes the reconciliation of these conflicting historical forces—that is, marriage signals the absorption of tradition into progress associated with nationalism and modernity.

Scott's formula for historical fiction was both an attractive and a limited one for Sedgwick. Written during a time when the federal government was considering the removal of many Native American tribes to lands west of the Mississippi River (a policy that would culminate during the ensuing presidency of Andrew Jackson), *Hope Leslie* takes up the "Indian Question" as a way of addressing contemporary dilemmas about racial difference in the United States. On the one hand, the model was complex and flexible enough to produce the kind of nostalgic and senti-mental feeling for what in the 1820s and 1830s Americans were calling "the vanishing American." This kind of feeling was crucial to the literary medium of historical fiction. On the other, Scott's model insufficiently characterized the historical conflict between Puritans and Native Americans. While Sedgwick's Puritans represent the beginnings of the progressive and enlightened American nation—a view that many Americans held in the 1820s—the novel just as vigorously exposes their repressive and barbaric qualities. During one scene, for example, Sedgwick shows that the Puritan authorities were offering money for Native American scalps. One of the major themes of *Hope Leslie* concerns the moral terms of community as the Puritans define it and as Hope and Magawisca defy it.

Historical novels like *Hope Leslie* and Lydia Maria Child's *Hobomok* (1824) adapted British literary models to original designs. Women's historical fiction about Puritan New England thus developed its own literary conventions—the tyrannical father figure, the rebellious daughter, the possibility of interracial love, and the idealized, progressive marriage, like the one between Hope Leslie and Everell Fletcher, that signals the enlightened escape from Puritan authoritarian control. The thematic emphasis in *Hope Leslie* is upon the moral and political value of feeling as a new kind of authority for contemporary America. In this sense, then, *Hope Leslie*'s tendency to show the political efficacy of feeling, as characters follow their benevolent impulses rather than the dictates of patriarchal authority, is typical of a great deal of women's antebellum fiction. Thus "Puritanism" in *Hope Leslie* is more of an ideological abstraction than a historical "reality." The novel asks its readers to reconsider colonial history as a way of distancing themselves from what Sedgwick perceives to be a heroic and yet dangerously intolerant worldview. Moreover, if the final union of Hope and Everell represents the promise of the early American Republic, the failure of that promise—the fact of Indian removal in the 1820s, racial slavery, and the political disenfranchisement of American women—provides the novel's implicit cultural critique.

THE MOTIF OF CAPTIVITY

The more overt representations of this critique occur largely through the motif of captivity. *Hope Leslie* shows important literary and historical connections between the Indian captivity narrative and the early American novel. The captivity narrative dates back to early modern writers like Álvar Núñez Cabeza de Vaca (c. 1490–c. 1560) and John Smith (c. 1580–1631), and it flourished in Puritan New England as a preeminent genre that combined elements of spiritual autobiography and cultural ethnography. (Mary Rowlandson is only the most famous exemplar of this literary form in colonial American literature). During the late eighteenth century, however, the captivity narrative became increasingly secular, sensationalist, violent, and overtly racist. *Hope Leslie* both reveals and resists this trend. Sedgwick obviously employed captivity as a way of enhancing the popular appeal of frontier romance. Yet Everell's captivity among the Pequot allows Sedgwick to redeploy the legendary rescue of John Smith by the Native American girl Pocahontas that originally came from John Smith. Magawisca's sacrifice of her arm while saving Everell suggests the viability of cross-cultural acts of benevolence—though skeptical readers may see it as perpetuating the myth of Indian sacrifice for the sake of American civilization. Similarly, the captivity of Faith Leslie and her romance with Oneco, the Native American warrior and son of the Pequot sachem Mononoto, represent a strong argument for the reality of cultural—rather than simply racial—formation of identity.

The motif of captivity, however, unfolds on multiple levels in the novel. One of its striking characteristics is its inversion of the very premises of the Indian captivity narrative. It dramatizes, for example, the Puritan captivity of Native Americans—notably Nelema (accused of witchcraft by the superstitious Puritans while she was saving the life of Cradock) and Magawisca (put in jail on Gardiner's testimony that she is guilty of conspiracy against the colony). These instances of Puritan captivity suggest how the patriarchal commonwealth keeps all of its female "citizens" in a kind of social and political bondage. One can push this idea even further and say that *Hope Leslie* reveals the pervasiveness of captivity in this kind of social and political organization. That is, all, men and women alike, are asked to suppress what the novel calls the "natural" feelings of sympathy and benevolence in the name of community, the rule of law, or even "God." Hence Hope liberates both herself and imprisoned Native American women when she follows through on her best impulses and helps them escape from Puritan prison, which (as in Nathaniel Hawthorne's *The Scarlet Letter*) is one of the most poignant symbols of Puritan authority, or perhaps of any authority bent upon utopian dreams.

THE POWER OF FEELING

The thematic premium the novel places on benevolence, however, creates striking moments of dissonance between its racial and gendered projects. For much of *Hope Leslie,* the forms of feeling that connect Hope and Magawisca dominate the novel. Since Hope and Magawisca are each motivated by benevolence and since each wields that virtue to defy patriarchal law, the two characters significantly are "doubled." Much of the novel suggests that sympathy can overcome racial difference—a form of difference that the novel represents ambiguously—and that new communities of feeling can form out of this virtue. Yet the novel's treatment of the romance plot severely complicates its idealistic endorsement of a form of human sympathy that crosses racial and cultural boundaries. This becomes most apparent during the scene where Magawisca arranges to have Hope see her sister. While the very fact of Faith's cultural assimilation—one of the main anxieties of both the captivity narrative and the frontier romance novel—would seem to belie racial categories, the revulsion Hope feels at this moment probably reflects that of most early national readers. What this subplot achieves, then, is the novel's ambivalence toward "miscegenation"—the interracial mixing that produces new kinds of identity. Although this term is somewhat anachronistic (it actually was not coined until the Civil War as part of a Democratic satire on supposedly Republican beliefs), *Hope Leslie* runs into difficult moments where its racial and gendered themes tend to produce inconsistent meanings of "difference." This was true of many nineteenth-century novels, especially those that directly confronted the proper relations between Anglo-Americans and such groups as Native Americans and African Americans. But in *Hope Leslie* the power of sympathy—which theoretically dissolves difference—finally cannot overcome other kinds of "difference," be they racial or cultural.

This thematic ambivalence finally comes to a head during the resolution of the romance plot. Whereas Cooper, for example, in *The Last of the Mohicans* (1826) kills off Uncas and Cora Munro, Sedgwick has her Native American heroine renounce her feelings for Everell. This is significant because for much of the novel Sedgwick allows this love plot between the two to become a fictional possibility. The union of English and Algonquian peoples would suggest a more radical solution for colonial America and, by implication, the modern American nation. Yet at this moment Magawisca transforms from the benevolent child of nature to the natural inheritor of vengeance. When she tells Hope and Everell that the two are naturally meant for each other and that vengeance is written on the Native American heart, the novel effectively recoils from the radical political and racial solutions it has been pursuing, albeit inconsistently, for hundreds of pages. Put another way, Sedgwick must withdraw her investment in Native American sympathy in order to signal the birth of the nation in purely

Anglo-American terms. The marriage between Everell and Hope not only has a transatlantic dimension but a generational one as well: by following their "nature" they succeed where their parents back in England had failed. As many critics have noted, the novel fictively performs its own kind of "removal" of Native Americans that parallels—and supports—the political logic of Indian removal. In the end, Magawisca retreats to the western wilderness; the marriage between Faith and Oneco remains real but thematically decontextualized and all but invisible.

OTHER QUESTIONS

Hope Leslie is culturally and biographically significant in other ways as well. As a native of Stockbridge, Sedgwick was completely familiar with that part of western Massachusetts in which the novel takes place. By the 1820s, this area was no longer inhabited by many Native American tribes—indeed recent scholarship suggests that Sedgwick's eighteenth-century ancestors were directly involved in the removal of Native Americans from the Stockbridge area. The colonial setting of the Massachusetts frontier easily facilitated the novel's ongoing description of the natural landscape. The novel displays these rather painterly and philosophical landscapes sometimes as narrative digressions and sometimes as integral parts of the dramatic action—during Everell's captivity, for example. They serve the dual (and sometimes contradictory) purposes of charting historical "progress" in America while celebrating the moral and symbolic value of wild and uncultivated landscape. They "Americanize" the novel in terms of "Nature" long before Ralph Waldo Emerson and Henry David Thoreau, for example, were writing on this Romantic subject.

The novel also inscribes its author's personal ambivalence toward both marriage and the larger cultural role for American women that has been dubbed the nineteenth-century "cult of true womanhood." If the marriage between Hope and Everell consummates the novel's national and gendered themes, *Hope Leslie* still gives the last word, so to speak, to Esther Downing, who decides to remain unmarried the rest of her life. For American women at this time, to marry was to become a *femme coverte*—a woman "covered" by her husband's legal, political, and civil identity. As the novel's narrator finally asserts, "marriage is not essential to the contentment, the dignity, or the happiness of woman" (p. 350). If this represents a more radical departure from social and literary conventions, it also describes the life of Catharine Sedgwick, who refused to (in the words of *Hope Leslie*) "Give to a party what was meant for mankind" (p. 350). Thus

the novel's final message resonates autobiographically for Sedgwick. She spent much of her adult life shuttling between western Massachusetts and New York City, devoting her energies to her writing as well as to her beloved brothers and their families.

Sedgwick's refusal to marry does not necessarily radicalize *Hope Leslie*'s messages about gender ideology and the social and political position of women in the early American Republic. But it does suggest the author's ambivalence, if not complete hostility, toward the codes of "true womanhood," which emphasized the ideals of domesticity, chastity, piety, and submission. As many historians of nineteenth-century women now argue, these norms may not have been a historical reality for all American women (especially those from the urban working classes or women of color), but they did put significant cultural pressure on the behavior of white bourgeois and upper-class women. *Hope Leslie* pushes at the boundaries of cultural norms and gender roles without completely (or consistently) breaking them. The novel shows how most early American women writers, if they expected to maintain the respect of their audiences, needed to work subtly within accepted cultural conventions in order to change them.

See also Captivity Narratives; Cross-Dressing; Domestic Fiction; English Literature; Ethnology; History; Indians; Indian Wars and Dispossession; Marriage; Miscegenation

BIBLIOGRAPHY

Primary Work

Sedgwick, Catharine Maria. *Hope Leslie; or, Early Times in the Massachusetts*. 1827. Edited by Mary Kelley. New Brunswick, N.J.: Rutgers University Press, 1987.

Secondary Works

Baym, Nina. *American Women Writers and the Work of History, 1790–1860*. New Brunswick, N.J.: Rutgers University Press, 1995.

Bell, Michael Davitt. *Hawthorne and the Historical Romance of New England*. Princeton, N.J.: Princeton University Press, 1971.

Buell, Lawrence. *New England Literary Culture: From Revolution through Renaissance*. Cambridge, U.K., and New York: Cambridge University Press, 1986.

Castiglia, Christopher. *Bound and Determined: Captivity, Culture-Crossing, and White Womanhood from Mary Rowlandson to Patty Hearst*. Chicago: University of Chicago Press, 1996.

Fetterley, Judith. "'My Sister! My Sister!': The Rhetoric of Catharine Sedgwick's *Hope Leslie*." *American Literature* 70 (1998): 491–516.

Foster, Edward Halsey. *Catharine Maria Sedgwick.* New York: Twayne, 1974.

Garvey, T. Gregory. "Risking Reprisal: Catharine Sedgwick's *Hope Leslie* and the Legitimation of Public Action by Women." *American Transcendental Quarterly* 8 (1994): 287–298.

Gould, Philip. *Covenant and Republic: Historical Romance and the Politics of Puritanism.* Cambridge, U.K., and New York: Cambridge University Press, 1996.

Insko, Jeffrey. "Anachronistic Imaginings: *Hope Leslie's* Challenge to Historicism." *American Literary History* 16 (2004): 179–207.

Kelley, Mary, ed. *The Power of Her Sympathy: The Autobiography and Journal of Catharine Maria Sedgwick.* Boston: Massachusetts Historical Society, 1993.

Maddox, Lucy. *Removals: Nineteenth-Century American Literature and the Politics of Indian Affairs.* New York: Oxford University Press, 1991.

Nelson, Dana D. *The Word in Black and White: Reading "Race" in American Literature, 1638–1867.* New York: Oxford University Press, 1992.

Tawil, Ezra. "Domestic Frontier Romance; or, How the Sentimental Heroine Became White." *Novel* 32 (1999): 99–124.

Weierman, Karen Woods. "Reading and Writing *Hope Leslie:* Catharine Maria Sedgwick's Indian 'Connections.'" *New England Quarterly* 85 (2002): 415–443.

Zagarell, Sandra A. "Expanding 'America': Lydia Sigourney's *Sketch of Connecticut,* Catharine Sedgwick's *Hope Leslie.*" *Tulsa Studies in Women's Literature* 6 (1987): 225–245.

Philip Gould

THE HOUSE OF THE SEVEN GABLES

Following the admonishment by his publisher James T. Fields to eschew the type of dreary tone of *The Scarlet Letter* (1850), Nathaniel Hawthorne (1804–1864) wrote *The House of the Seven Gables* (1851), a book that Hawthorne described as more difficult to write than *The Scarlet Letter* but one more in keeping with his own temperament. Writing to Fields on 3 November 1850, Hawthorne states, "I find the book [*House*] requires more care and thought than the 'Scarlet Letter';—also, I have to wait oftener for a mood. The Scarlet Letter being all in one tone, I had only to get my pitch and could then go on interminably" (*Letters, 1843–1853,* p. 371). Later (27 January 1851) Hawthorne noted that he "prefers" *The House of the Seven Gables* to *The Scarlet Letter* (*Letters, 1843–1853,* p. 386) and on 22 July 1851 conceded to his friend Horatio Bridge that *The*

House of the Seven Gables "is a work more characteristic of my mind, and more proper and natural for me to write, than the Scarlet Letter" (*Letters, 1843–1853,* p. 461).

Whether Hawthorne's self-assessment as a writer whose mood is more happy than brooding is disingenuous or sincere, Hawthorne did recognize a natural proclivity toward melancholy as he forced himself to write a happy ending to the novel: "It darkens damnably towards the close, but I shall try hard to pour some setting sunshine over it," he wrote to Fields on 29 November 1850 (*Letters, 1843–1853,* p. 376). It is debatable whether the formulaic ending typical of sentimental women's novels, the marriage between Phoebe and Holgrave, is filled with "sunshine," as the reader witnesses a contemplative and "half-melancholy" Holgrave, who realizes that the radical dreams of his youth are about to be over and who finds himself a conservative, longing for the permanence of a house of stone rather than the temporality of a house of wood. In resigning himself to a marriage with Phoebe, he also aligns himself with the avaricious nature of the evil progenitor, Colonel Pyncheon, and his capitalist heir, Judge Pyncheon. Holgrave moves, as tenant, from one Pyncheon household, the House of the Seven Gables, to another, now as owner, of "the elegant country-seat of the late Judge Pyncheon" (p. 314)—and in becoming gentrified will no doubt share the same oppressive attitudes as his erstwhile Pyncheon rivals. Hawthorne's final vision of the status quo seems burdensome compared to Holgrave's earlier dreams of social amelioration. As Neill Matheson asserts, "The conception of history dramatized in *The House of the Seven Gables* is ultimately a melancholic one, in which the subject unknowingly carried within itself a determinative piece of history" (p. 1). Hawthorne is always concerned with how the past impinges upon the present—and how difficult it is to escape the influence of the past.

REALISM AND THE ROMANCE

When Hawthorne penned *The House of the Seven Gables,* he was writing in a genre he had already defined in "The Custom-House" introduction of *The Scarlet Letter*—what he called the "romance" form. Like other Romantics, Hawthorne believed that the realm of the imagination was more important than rationality, and thus the form he adopts as his genre, the romance, makes the most of poetic license. Hawthorne's accursed characters, like Judge Pyncheon, prefer the head to the heart, whereas the sympathetic characters (like Phoebe) are empowered by the heart. However, as Hawthorne recognizes, there are many passages in *The House of the Seven Gables* that are fraught with "the minuteness of a Dutch picture," as he writes on 3 November 1850 to J. T. Fields (*Letters, 1843–1853*, p. 371)—and hence his affiliation with the school of realists as well as with the Romantics. In his preface to the novel, Hawthorne differentiates clearly between the forms of the romance and the novel, insisting that the romance writer can claim a "certain latitude" (p. 1) not permitted the novelist.

The art form of the daguerreotype, the early form of photography, with its blurry, imprecise, almost otherworldly, renditions of reality, characterizes the tone of the novel. In his preface to *The House,* Hawthorne describes his artistic style using the language of daguerreotypy (and perhaps unwittingly identifying himself with his protagonist, the daguerreotypist Holgrave): "he may so manage his atmospherical medium as to bring out or mellow the lights and deepen and enrich the shadows of the picture" (p. 1). Critics like Carol Shloss and Susan Williams have noted Hawthorne's use of the daguerreotype (with its duality of light and dark and the duality of realism and magic) as a metaphor for his own art. Hawthorne's preface explains that his style involves "bringing his fancy-pictures almost into positive contact with the realities of the moment" (p. 3). As in *The Scarlet Letter,* moonlight is important; it is the medium Holgrave uses to tell Phoebe the story of "Alice's Posies," and he admits the power of moonlight to change one's perspective—and even to ameliorate society: "Moonlight, and the sentiment in man's heart, responsive to it, is the greatest of renovators and reformers" (p. 214).

THE BURDEN OF HISTORY AND THE GOTHIC FRAMEWORK OF *THE HOUSE*

There is no doubt that Hawthorne felt the burden of history as he delved into his own family past. His Puritan great-grandfather had presided over the Salem witch trials, and as if to wash himself of the family sin, Hawthorne had changed his name from "Hathorne" to "Hawthorne" around the time of his graduation from Bowdoin College in 1825. In "The Custom-House" of *The Scarlet Letter,* Hawthorne professed himself to be "a citizen of somewhere else" (p. 44), but it is debatable whether Hawthorne could ever remove himself from his ancestral and childhood past in Salem. Even after his move from Salem to Lenox, Massachusetts, he was still involved in scenes of his ancestral home as he wrote *The House of the Seven Gables.* Hawthorne may have been inspired to write *The House of the Seven Gables* by his earlier visits to the actual

House of the Seven Gables (the Turner-Ingersoll House in Salem), inhabited by a second cousin, the reclusive Susannah Ingersoll, who told him many legends about the house and who, through her eccentricity, might have provided the inspiration for Hepzibah's character. The house itself becomes a dominant personality in the romance.

Though Holgrave initially preaches the need for each generation to build its own houses, he finally accepts the traditional country estate of the persecuting Judge Pyncheon as his final abode. Hawthorne intuitively realized that one re-creates one's ancestral home even if one tries to move away from it. He equates houses with the evil of the past: "The evil of these departed years would naturally have sprung up again, in such rank weeds (symbolic of the transmitted vices of society) as are always prone to root themselves about human dwellings" (p. 86). In his historical fiction, Hawthorne often tries to come to terms with a national past that is dark and personally humiliating. For him, the fallen Eden was already etched deep in America's past.

The conflict that precipitates the feud between the Maules and the Pyncheons is not really a landownership debate between the white European settlers. The original crime is the dispossession of Indian lands—both the Maules and Pyncheons participated in this usurpation of Indian territory. Though Maule feels wronged when Pyncheon claims his land, the only rightful owner of the Pyncheon-Maule land is the Native American. Though the mystery of the missing Indian deed is solved at the end of the novel when Holgrave discovers it (p. 316), the sense of entitlement is spurious, according to Timothy B. Powell, who points out that the Indian deed being ultimately "worthless" reflects the "legal debate about white entitlement which erupted during Hawthorne's lifetime" (p. 35), a conflict that finally showed whites, to their dismay, that they were "colonizers" (p. 36). Brook Thomas discusses Hawthorne's indirect indictment of the Maules, as he emphasizes their similarities to the Pyncheons: "To be sure, Hawthorne never explicitly accuses the Maules of stealing the land from the Indians," but he does show that the "Maules' claim to the land is based on a fictional foundation, an imagined moment outside of history" (p. 73).

Discussion of the Maules or Pyncheons as legal claimants is presented by other historicist critics such as Walter Benn Michaels and Milette Shamir, who, along with Thomas, address the contemporary national debate about property rights. Michaels suggests that there is "a parallel between romance and the property

The House of the Seven Gables, antique as it now looks, was not the first habitation erected by civilized man, on precisely the same spot of ground. Pyncheon-street [*sic*] formerly bore the humbler appellation of Maule's Lane, from the name of the original occupant of the soil, before whose cottage-door it was a cow-path. A natural spring of soft and pleasant water—a rare treasure on the sea-girt peninsula, where the Puritan settlement was made—had early induced Matthew Maule to build a hut, shaggy with thatch, at the point, although somewhat too remote from what was then the centre of the village.

Hawthorne, *The House of the Seven Gables*, pp. 6–7.

rights of impoverished aristocrats" (p. 93). In the 1840s and 1850s, says Michaels, the national debate was raging about legal possession of land and "the land for the landless" campaign that eventually resulted in the Homestead Act of 1862—which contended that "the land should belong to those who worked it and not to the banks and speculators" (p. 94). Although Brook Thomas suggests that Hawthorne's approach seems democratic in allowing the natural right of the land to go to the plebian Maules (who worked the land) instead of to the aristocratic Pyncheons (who claimed the land), he shows the fallacy of the law: "the Indians, not the Maules, were the original owners of the soil" (p. 70). Shamir focuses on the middle-class right to privacy as market relations destroyed the notion of individuality and ownership. Artistic ownership is akin to property ownership, and the novel makes an inquest into both types of legality.

In *The House of the Seven Gables*, various protagonists are wrongly accused and persecuted—the progenitor Matthew Maule, who gets cheated out of his land by Colonel Pyncheon (who accuses him of wizardry), and later, the Pyncheon descendant, Clifford Pyncheon, who is falsely imprisoned (for allegedly killing his Uncle Pyncheon). The grandson of the wizard Matthew Maule, the carpenter Matthew Maule, tries to vindicate the wrongs done to the Maule line by humiliating the most delicate of the Pyncheons, Alice Pyncheon, who later dies as a result of his "experiment." This Maule, a mesmerist, abuses his power by putting her into a trance and afterward controlling her every move. Hawthorne shows how easy it is for the oppressed to become the oppressor: "He [Maule] had meant to humble Alice, not to kill her;—but he had taken a woman's delicate soul into his rude grip to play with;—and she was dead" (p. 210). The book seeks retribution for the feuding families, who have both become tainted through their lust for power. If the reconciliation does not occur, their ancestors will become grotesque images of what once was—the Pyncheon line has already disintegrated to the point where they are like the misshapen, degenerate chickens in the garden who cannot breed properly.

As an avid reader of such gothic writers as Horace Walpole and Sir Walter Scott, Hawthorne might have borrowed various literary conventions from gothic novels: the idea of the feuding families, the search for a home, magical occurrences (the "bewitched" water of Maule's Well, the Pyncheon family disease), the theme of class conflict between the aristocracy and the emerging middle class (and with that, the working class), and the motif of the "sins of the fathers." His historical romance illustrates the claim he makes in his preface "that the wrong-doing of one generation lives into successive ones, and, divesting itself of every temporary advantage, becomes a pure and uncontrollable mischief" (p. 2). His "moral" is to teach the reader the consequences of greed, the cupidity represented by such characters as the Ur-Pyncheon, Colonel Pyncheon, and the contemporary Judge Pyncheon—to "convince mankind (or, indeed, any one man) of the folly of tumbling down an avalanche of ill-gotten gold, or real estate, on the heads of an unfortunate posterity, thereby to maim and crush them" (p. 2). The curse of the fathers is made manifest through a magical phenomenon—the death of the power-hungry Pyncheon is caused by the mysterious ailment apoplexy, which has the condemned party choke on his own blood. As the original wizard Maule prophesied, "God will give him blood to drink!" (p. 8). As is often the case in gothic novels, a reconciliation between the feuding families is made in Hawthorne's story through the marriage of the more enlightened offspring, that is, between Holgrave (Maule) and Phoebe (Pyncheon).

ELEMENTS OF CONTEMPORARY HISTORY

Elizabeth Palmer Peabody, Hawthorne's famous sister-in-law, who promoted Hawthorne's work early in his career, aptly described Hawthorne's notion of history when she, an avid abolitionist, tried to excuse his political conservatism. In a letter of 4 June 1887 she suggested that Hawthorne was more aware of the distant past than of the present: "It was perfectly true what he often said—that he knew nothing about contemporaneous history, that he could not understand history until it was at least a *hundred years old!*" (Peabody, p. 445). Hawthorne did realize that in *The House of the Seven Gables* he had come closer to the historical present. And, it is true, the current history seemed to make him more uneasy—with the fictional latitude of the writer removed. As he wrote to his publisher Fields on 27 January 1851, "It [*The House*] has undoubtedly one disadvantage, in being brought so close to the present time; whereby its romantic improbabilities become more glaring" (*Letters, 1843–1853*, p. 386). Implicit in this self-critique is that the present, in literary material, is too glaringly real—and that renditions of the historical present are less nuanced because of a myopic perspective. He adamantly wished his audience to accept the disclaimer to historical accuracy offered in his preface: "The personages of the Tale—though they give themselves out to be of ancient stability and considerable prominence—are really of the Author's own making, or, at all events, of his own mixing" (p. 3).

For all of Hawthorne's shyness or disingenuousness about discussing contemporary history, the characters he creates in *The House of the Seven Gables* show a deep awareness of serious social and political issues of the mid-nineteenth century. Holgrave himself is representative of many social reform movements of his time. He is a mesmerist, a social utopian (or Fourierist, who associates with "reformers, temperance-lecturers, and all manner of cross-looking philanthropists," p. 84), a daguerreotypist, and a writer of women's fiction. Hepzibah's mistrust about Holgrave's surreptitious activities also reflects Hawthorne's basic suspicions about the reformer type, whom he will critique again in his next novel, *The Blithedale Romance* (1852), through the character of Hollingsworth. However, Hawthorne also approves of Holgrave, because he "has a law of his own" (p. 85). One is reminded of the self-reliant Hester Prynne, whose very existence makes a mockery of the conformist society judging her.

Holgrave's lawlessness may be construed as negative because it is linked to the "vagrant and lawless plants" thriving in the decaying soil in the garden of the House of the Seven Gables (p. 86). The upstanding Phoebe Pyncheon recognizes an innate evil and recoils from Holgrave initially: "She rebelled . . . against a certain magnetic element in the artist's nature, which he exercised towards her, possibly without being conscious of it" (p. 94). Holgrave has inherited the powers of the first Matthew Maule's wizardry and the second Matthew Maule's mesmerism, but he uses his power with "reverence for another's individuality" (p. 212). Mesmerism, developed by the German Franz Mesmer (1734–1815), became fashionable for mid-nineteenth-century intellectuals suffering from incurable ailments. When his fiancée, Sophia Peabody, wrote Hawthorne about her intent to visit a mesmerist to cure her headache, Hawthorne was alarmed and advised her to "take no part" in "these magnetic miracles," warning her instead of the possible violation by the mesmerist into her soul (*Letters, 1813–1843*, p. 588). Holgrave is redeemed by not using his mesmeric power against Phoebe in the garden at Maule's Well.

Perhaps, rather than magic, Hawthorne suggests, Holgrave possesses the somnambulistic qualities of a bad storyteller who writes for the women's periodicals. Hawthorne may be parodying his own work as a writer when he describes Holgrave's effect on his female listener—and as he equates mesmerism with art. Samuel Coale has written persuasively on the similarities between Holgrave the mesmerist and Hawthorne the writer. Though Holgrave has bragged that he has published for popular journals, he ultimately engages in self-mockery, as he exclaims, "My poor story, it is but too evident, will never do for *Godey* or *Graham!* Only think of your falling asleep, at what I hoped the newspaper critics would pronounce a most brilliant, powerful, imaginative, pathetic, and original winding up!" (p. 212). This criticism could explain Hawthorne's intent to provide a sunny ending, one that the female readers would prefer. Holgrave's legend of "Alice's Posies" ends with the humiliation and destruction of Alice, hardly a proper ending for the pages of sentimental women's fiction.

The character who serves as the redemptive force of the romance, Phoebe Pyncheon, represents the nineteenth-century ideal known as the Cult of True Womanhood, as described by conservative writers such as Catharine Beecher in *A Treatise on Domestic Economy* (1841). As a quintessential True Woman, Phoebe has a preternatural ability to bring order and joy to the gloomy Pyncheon household: her housekeeping is "a kind of natural magic" (p. 71) and "homely witchcraft" (p. 72), which allies her with the magical powers of Holgrave. And like Holgrave, she has had a middle-class, rather than aristocratic, upbringing; she announces to Hepzibah, "I mean to earn my bread. You know, I have not been brought up a Pyncheon. A girl learns many things in a New England village" (p. 74). Because Phoebe has done the shopping errands for her family, she is confidently aware that she is "as nice a little saleswoman" as she is "a housewife" (p. 78). Phoebe has common sense and can manage the cent-shop (and turn a profit) as adroitly as she cooks, cleans the house, and manages the garden, domestic aspects that have fallen into shambles under Hepzibah's lack of housekeeping, culinary, and gardening skills. Phoebe has the makings of a good mother—children are drawn to her in the cent-shop; she has taught grammar school in her village; and she feels "an odd kind of motherly sentiment" (p. 216) toward her cousins, Hepzibah and Clifford. Phoebe is cast in terms that paint her as the "angel of the household" (another metaphor associated with the True Woman), and though not born a lady, she is gentrified though her domestic abilities. Joel Pfister maintains that Hawthorne uses Phoebe as a way to display "the cultural uses of and need for a distinctively middle-class femininity" (p. 149).

Hawthorne's feminism in his second romance is more problematic than in *The Scarlet Letter,* in which Hester Prynne embodies the best traits of the self-reliant nineteenth-century woman, as expressed in Margaret Fuller's *Woman in the Nineteenth Century* (1845). Hawthorne is aware of woman's emerging role in the public sphere, especially with such events as the 1848 Seneca Falls Convention, where Elizabeth Cady Stanton and Lucretia Mott advocated a Declaration of Sentiments written as a revisionist Declaration of Independence for women. Property laws were also passed throughout the 1840s, permitting married women to own their own property; Hepzibah, though single, is basically fighting about her property rights to the house. The grotesque old maid, she appears to be a manifestation of what Hawthorne fears and believes the new type of woman, the emancipated bluestocking, will resemble. She represents the new options open to women—working in the marketplace—but her femininity and "ladylike" qualities, for Hawthorne, disintegrate in the process. Hawthorne saw Hepzibah as the horror of the new labor that meant corporeality and "subjection to a mesmeric power that hystericizes the individual body" (Brown, p. 82).

SOCIAL ISSUES: SLAVERY AND POVERTY

Although Hawthorne does not bring up the topic of slavery per se, the master-slave relationship between Matthew Maule and Alice Pyncheon—and its ramifications for the present-day Maules and

Pyncheons—resonates throughout the text. But the early Maule-Pyncheon relationship is not the only unhealthy relationship between the sexes. The original Pyncheon, Colonel Pyncheon, "had worn out three wives" and "by . . . the hardness of his character in the conjugal relation, had sent them, one after another, broken hearted, to their graves" (p. 123). Judge Pyncheon, though only married once, lost his wife in the "third or fourth year of marriage," but it was rumored that "the lady got her death-blow in the honeymoon" and "never smiled again" as her husband forced her to serve him as if he were "her liege-lord and master" (p. 123).

African American slavery is not foregrounded in the novel, though it is definitely in the picture with the presence of Scipio, the black servant of Gervayse Pyncheon (father to Alice Pyncheon). As the property of the Pyncheon household, Scipio shares the family's same condescending attitude to Maule, the "low carpenter-man" (p. 188) who would try to be equal to Alice Pyncheon. Hawthorne may use Scipio as a stock comic-relief device, but Scipio is haunted by the Pyncheon past as profoundly as are the inhabitants of the House of the Seven Gables: "The house is a berry good house, and old Colonel Pyncheon think so too, I reckon; else why the old man haunt it so, and frighten a poor nigger, as he does?" (p. 187). Just as Gervayse Pyncheon's household was built upon slave labor, so too does the current Gables owner depend upon the institution of slavery, at least symbolically.

Hepzibah's first business transaction involves selling a Jim Crow image in the form of a gingerbread cookie to the young boy Ned. This suggests that the economy of the Pyncheon household resides upon the selling of the "Jim Crow" effigy—or that the economy depends upon slavery to thrive. Young Ned Higgins demands a Jim Crow cookie that did not "have a broken foot" (p. 50). Though this is not the actual slave trade, it resonates in a grotesque manner with such a slave sale. The young boy devours the Jim Crow cookie and demands yet another, but Hepzibah, who had given the boy his first cookie for free, demands a cent in return. As Robert Martin points out, "The exchange of money gives her a 'copper stain,' the indelible mark of participation in the slave economy"; the transaction "reveals the hidden source of northern wealth" (p. 134). Jim Crow represented the stereotypical good-natured black minstrel, the infantilized product of the white imagination, and the business transaction made by Hepzibah allies her with the larger national slave-based economy. Even before Hepzibah opens the cent-shop, she thinks nostalgically about the Pyncheons who have migrated to the

South and made a fortune from their plantation life: she remembers hearing about "a Pyncheon who had emigrated to Virginia in some past generation, and become a great planter there" (p. 65) and fantasizes about the fortune that the apocryphal Virginian Pyncheon would send her.

Hawthorne, aware of the imposing presence of the Salem Almshouse, is concerned with the local and national problem of poverty in his depiction of Uncle Venner and of Hepzibah. The town pauper, Uncle Venner, has gained a modicum of freedom and respectability from his "privileges of age and humble familiarity" (p. 63); "at least a score of families" (p. 61) allow him to do odd jobs around the house in return for scraps of food. Uncle Venner sees the almshouse as a utopian place of retirement, and Hepzibah even entertains the possibility of moving there with him if her cent-shop fails (p. 63). As the self-reliant Venner misconstrues it, he thinks of retiring to his "farm"—"That's yonder—the great brick house, you know—the work-house, most folks call it; but I mean to do my work first, and go there to be idle and enjoy myself" (p. 62). Hawthorne shows his preference for communal charity, a throwback to the Puritan idea of charity, over institutionalized charity, represented by the almshouse.

In accordance with the historical reality of the burgeoning middle class, Hepzibah is transformed from "patrician lady" to "plebeian woman" (p. 38): "Poverty, treading closely at her heels for a lifetime, has come up with her at last. She must earn her own food, or starve!" (p. 38). Whereas she had felt a false sense of charity for the poor, Hepzibah now has a feeling of scorn for the wealthy. As a finely dressed and "beautifully slippered" lady passes through the street, Hepzibah rightly asks, "For what good end, in the wisdom of Providence, does that woman live! Must the whole world toil, that the palms of her hands may be kept white and delicate?" (p. 55). Hawthorne thus critiques the false consumer needs incited by a capitalist economy and the unequal system of profit and productivity.

Hawthorne's solution to the problem of poverty, at the end of the novel, is a bit far-fetched—the stuff of sentimentality, Victorian novel coincidences, and fairy tales. The only son of Judge Pyncheon, the ostensible heir to the Pyncheon fortune, dies of cholera in a foreign land before embarking at sea for home. Clifford and Hepzibah inherit the Pyncheon legacy, and Phoebe's share will go to Holgrave, through marriage. They decide to take Uncle Venner along with them to the Pyncheon estate in the country, where, Phoebe says, he will live in a cottage of his own, a "sweetest-looking place . . . as if it were made of gingerbread" (p. 317). The allusion to gingerbread is suspicious, as one is reminded of the slavery represented earlier by the Jim Crow gingerbread. Clifford means to keep Venner as his company, or perhaps better put, a servant, within a "five minutes' saunter of [his] chair" (p. 317), thus keeping the privileged aristocracy, now in the guise of the newly empowered capitalists, intact.

ARTISTIC INTEGRITY IN THE MARKETPLACE

Driving the characters and producing the conflict in this novel is the invisible hand of capitalism. When Hepzibah leaves her position as fallen aristocrat to become part of the marketplace world of capitalism, by opening her cent-shop, the narrator even makes reference to the eighteenth-century economist Adam Smith's notion of "the invisible hand": "It might have been fancied . . . that she expected to minister to the wants of the community, unseen, like a disembodied divinity, or enchantress, holding forth her bargains to the reverential and awestricken purchaser, in an invisible hand" (p. 40). She engages inadvertently in the same money structure that demonizes and finally kills Judge Pyncheon, thereby reflecting the realm of realism, but she also serves to introduce the realm of the magical world (as "enchantress") of the romance mode, which allies her with the supernatural aspects attributed to both Holgrave and Phoebe early on in the book. Holgrave, by marrying Phoebe, also becomes a conservative capitalist and sells out to the realist world. At the end of *The House of the Seven Gables,* then, all hands are sullied, and so it is debatable whether there is a release from the past—even though one could point to the ascension of Alice's spirit in the kaleidoscopic final images from Maule's well as a positive sign.

Whether the ending is deemed positive or negative depends upon whether one reads through the lens of the romance or (in the mode of realism) the novel. Alan Trachtenberg maintains that Hawthorne "endows the ending with the redemptive power of 'Romance'"; this is achieved, he says, with "a lost vision of entrepreneurial, petit bourgeois social relations elevated into a historical impossibility, the dream of a restored 'circle'" (p. 47). Richard Brodhead feels that "having reached this condition of understanding and perception the characters have no more need of romance" (p. 88). Brodhead believes that Hawthorne "makes a strong commitment" to both "fictions of realism and fictions of romance" but finally "resists an ultimate commitment to either" (p. 90).

Does the novel end with a statement about commerce or art, or is Hawthorne caught between both realms? Michael T. Gilmore asserts that Hawthorne, like Holgrave, finally was forced to compromise. He had to placate his editor, Fields, and the public: Holgrave's truth, like Hawthorne's art, is "private and unsalable" (p. 109). Holgrave's final decision, which renders him a conservative, is similar to "Hawthorne's contrivance of a happy ending at the expense of narrative consistency" (p. 109). The "invisible hand" of capitalism also has its grip on the world of publishing and marketing. *The House of the Seven Gables* shows an inclination to remain true to the calling of an artist, even with the compromises demanded from the marketplace world of publishing.

See also The Blithedale Romance; "The Custom-House"; Domestic Fiction; Feminism; History; The Romance; Slavery; *The Scarlet Letter*

BIBLIOGRAPHY

Primary Works

Hawthorne, Nathaniel. *The House of the Seven Gables.* 1851. Centenary edition, vol 2. Columbus: Ohio State University Press, 1965.

Hawthorne, Nathaniel. *The Letters, 1813–1843.* Centenary edition, vol. 15. Edited by Thomas Woodson et al. Columbus: Ohio State University Press, 1984.

Hawthorne, Nathaniel. *The Letters, 1843–1853.* Centenary edition, vol 16. Edited by Thomas Woodson et al. Columbus: Ohio State University Press, 1985.

Hawthorne, Nathaniel. *The Scarlet Letter, 1850.* Centenary edition, vol. 1. Columbus: Ohio State University Press, 1962.

Peabody, Elizabeth Palmer. *Letters of Elizabeth Palmer Peabody, American Renaissance Woman.* Edited by Bruce A. Ronda. Middletown, Conn.: Wesleyan University Press, 1984.

Secondary Works

Brodhead, Richard H. "Double Exposure: *The House of the Seven Gables.*" In his *Hawthorne, Melville, and the Novel,* pp. 69–90. Chicago: University of Chicago Press, 1976.

Brown, Gillian. "Women's Work and Bodies in *The House of the Seven Gables.*" In her *Domestic Individualism: Imagining Self in Nineteenth-Century America,* pp. 63–95. Berkeley: University of California Press, 1990.

Coale, Samuel Chase. "Mysteries of Mesmerism: Hawthorne's Haunted House." In *A Historical Guide to Nathaniel Hawthorne,* edited by Larry J. Reynolds, pp. 49–77. New York: Oxford University Press, 2001.

Elbert, Monika M. "Hawthorne's Reformulation of Transcendentalist Charity." *American Transcendental Quarterly* 11, no. 3 (1997): 213–232.

Gilmore, Michael T. "The Artist and the Marketplace in *The House of the Seven Gables.*" In his *American Romanticism and the Marketplace,* pp. 96–112. Chicago: University of Chicago Press, 1985.

Goodwin, Lorinda B. R. "Salem's House of Seven Gables as Historic Site." In *Salem: Place, Myth, and Memory,* edited by Dane Anthony Morrison and Nancy Lustignan Schultz, pp. 299–314. Boston: Northeastern University Press, 2004.

Martin, Robert K. "Haunted Jim Crow: Gothic Fictions by Hawthorne and Faulkner." In *American Gothic: New Interventions in a National Narrative,* edited by Robert K. Martin and Eric Savoy, pp. 129–142. Iowa City: University of Iowa Press, 1998.

Matheson, Neill. "Melancholy History in *The House of the Seven Gables.*" In *Literature and Psychology* 48, no. 3 (2002): 1–37.

Michaels, Walter Benn. "Romance and Real Estate." In his *The Gold Standard and the Logic of Naturalism: American Literature at the Turn of the Century,* pp. 87–112. Berkeley: University of California Press, 1987.

Moore, Margaret B. *The Salem World of Nathaniel Hawthorne.* Columbia: University of Missouri Press, 1998.

Pfister, Joel. "Cleaning House: From the Gothic to the Middle-Class World Order." In his *The Production of Personal Life: Class, Gender, and the Psychological in Hawthorne's Fiction,* pp. 144–161. Stanford, Calif.: Stanford University Press, 1991.

Powell, Timothy B. "Nathaniel Hawthorne: History Imagined 'Historically Awry.'" In his *Ruthless Democracy: A Multicultural Interpretation of the American Renaissance,* pp. 30–48. Princeton, N.J.: Princeton University Press, 2000.

Shamir, Milette. "Hawthorne's Romance and the Right to Privacy." *American Quarterly* 49, no. 4 (1997): 746–779.

Shloss, Carol. "Nathaniel Hawthorne and Daguerreotypy: Distinterested Vision." In her *Invisible Light: Photography and the American Writer: 1840–1940,* pp. 25–54. New York: Oxford University Press, 1987.

Thomas, Brook. *Cross-Examinations of Law and Literature: Cooper, Hawthorne, Stowe, and Melville.* New York: Cambridge University Press, 1987. See pp. 45–90.

Trachtenberg, Alan. "Seeing and Believing: Hawthorne's Reflections on the Daguerreotype in *The House of the Seven Gables.*" In *National Imaginaries, American Identities: The Cultural Work of American Iconography,* edited by Larry J. Reynolds and Gordon Hutner, pp. 31–51. Princeton, N.J.: Princeton University Press, 2000.

Williams, Susan S. "Hawthorne, Daguerreotypy, and *The House of the Seven Gables.*" In her *Counfounding Images: Photography and Portraiture in Antebellum American Fiction*, pp. 96–119. Philadelphia: University of Pennsylvania Press, 1997.

Monika Elbert

HUMOR

American humor of the nineteenth century is characterized by egalitarian values. A reflection of the changes in America's social and cultural landscape as the Republic moved toward greater democratization, the humor is discernibly native, its inception growing out of a decline in the hierarchical social structure that gave way to more attention and voice for marginalized peoples, usually rural or backwoods types. Regional customs, modes of behavior, peculiarities, eccentricities, and anti-intellectuality were reflected in the subject matter as well as in the characterization. As Walter Blair noted in *Native American Humor*, "American humor . . . [became] a graspable phenomenon" (p. 39).

WASHINGTON IRVING

In the 1820s Washington Irving (1783–1859) was America's best-known and most influential humorist, especially reflected in his two classic tales "The Legend of Sleepy Hollow" and "Rip Van Winkle," both published in *The Sketch Book* (1819–1820), Irving's first significant work. Though the language of Irving's narrator, Geoffrey Crayon, is formal and ornate, these tales feature and privilege the rustic—Brom Bones and Rip Van Winkle, respectively, who represent stability and harmony and who are admired by the community, even though neither character is particularly exemplary or given significant voice in the narratives. The humor in "Sleepy Hollow" derives from the clash of cultures: the genteel and cultivated as represented in the idealistic, enterprising, and gullible Connecticut schoolmaster Ichabod Crane, an intruder in the rural hamlet of Sleepy Hollow and a harbinger of disruptive change, and Brom Bones, a rambunctious, affable, free-spirited ring-tailed roarer and instigator of practical jokes and pranks, who frightens Ichabod, forcing him to leave, and who in so doing restores communal harmony. Like Brom, Rip Van Winkle is another congenial backwoods type who avoids work, hunts, plays with children, tells stories, and evades civilization, withdrawing to the wilderness for twenty years and escaping time, thereby never having to grow up and live responsibly. In addition to introducing native character types, Irving created scenarios that would be widely used by American humorists in the decades immediately following, especially some antebellum southern frontier humorists who would likewise refashion similar scripts endorsing the triumph of the common person and rural, frontier values over newness and inevitable transformation.

DOWN EAST HUMOR

By 1830 America's native humor had been significantly shaped by a type that had become widely associated with the United States, the comic Yankee, a New England rustic who had been prominently featured in Royall Tyler's 1787 play *The Contrast*. While Tyler and others helped to popularize the comic Yankee, the election to the presidency in 1828 of Andrew Jackson—a war hero and man without pedigree or high social status who did not favor eastern banking interests and was suspicious of European influences, which he believed threatened American values—was a major stimulus in prompting the development of Down East humor.

Down East humor was initially published in newspapers and magazines, and its practitioners used conventional literary modes, such as mock letters, essays, and poems. Voice was given to common folk characters, who spoke their sentiments in a colloquial idiom and, although lacking the advantages of formal education and cosmopolitan outlook, depended on common sense, traditional values, and practical experience to guide their judgments and observations. Walter Blair and Hamlin Hill define this brand of humor as "reputable," one that "tended to exalt traditional values . . . , upheld order over disorder, decorum over unbridled license . . . , and championed a moral and predictable universe" (p. 163).

In 1830 Seba Smith (1792–1868), the editor of the *Portland* (Maine) *Daily Courier*, created the most popular and influential of these unsophisticated rustic Yankees with his Jack Downing, a cracker-barrel philosopher who wrote comic letters in the colloquial mode to his relatives back in the country about current events he observed in the city. (Smith did not invent this comic type: George W. Arnold, the creator of the Vermonter Joe Strickland, did that in 1825.) Smith created his amiable country naïf and wise fool for reasons of expediency: to rejuvenate his failing independent newspaper. Jack's letters initially focused on his simplistic observations to his relatives and friends in Downingville, his rural home, about the politically balanced but ineffectual state legislature in Portland, where political affiliations created a ridiculous impasse. Smith felt these dialect letters would

serve as an effective vehicle for satire and would entertain his readers, thereby boosting subscriptions to his
newspaper. The letters were actually more popular
than Smith had anticipated and were reprinted in
newspapers throughout the country. The enthusiastic
and national reception of the letters encouraged
Smith to continue to write them for twenty-nine
years, expanding the correspondents to include some
of Jack's Downingville relatives—Uncle Joshua, Aunt
Keziah, Cousin Ephraim, and Cousin Nabby. Many
of the Downing letters were collected and published
in two popular books, *The Life and Writings of Major
Jack Downing* (1833)and *My Thirty Years out of the
Senate* (1859). Typically the humor in the early letters depends on Jack's innocent manner of pointing
out foibles of the political process that he only half
understands because of his literal-minded, shallow
perceptions about the state legislature. In a letter
from Portland (18 January 1830) to his cousin
Ephraim, Jack naively renders the confrontation
between pro-Jackson Democratic-Republicans and the
anti-Jackson National Republicans, who have about
the same number of representatives, as being like two
boys playing on a seesaw. At another point, when
opponents protest the seating of a new representative
who has apparently been elected unfairly, Jack doesn't
quite follow the problem and sympathetically observes,
"for they wan't crowded, and there was a number of
seats empty." After treating the political scene in
Portland, Maine, Jack goes to Washington, D.C., as an
adviser to President Jackson and a member of his
Kitchen Cabinet, and his letters shift their focus to
national issues, such as Manifest Destiny, the nullification controversy, the abuses of the spoils system, and
weaknesses in national leaders, such as Presidents
Jackson and James K. Polk, Daniel Webster, and General
Winfield Scott. Smith's humorous satire is double-
edged, not only belittling political parties and their devi-
ous ways but also exposing Jack's naïveté and cynicism.

The rich lode featuring the rustic Yankee wise fool
that Seba Smith first popularized in the Downing letters
was also adapted by other Down East humorists. Charles
Augustus Davis (1795–1867), the principal Downing
imitator, wrote a series of comic letters, published initially in the *New York Daily Advertiser*. He subsequently
reprinted more than two dozen of them in *Letters of J.
Downing, Major, Downingville Militia, Second Brigade,
to His Old Friend, Mr. Dwight, of the "New York Daily
Advertiser"* (1834). A writer with a clear-cut political
agenda, Davis used Downing as a vehicle to attempt to
sway public feeling against Jackson's efforts to destroy
the Bank of the United States.

In the 1830s the Canadian Thomas Chandler
Haliburton (1796–1865), regarded by his fellow

Major Jack Downing. Lithograph from a painting by
Joseph T. Harris, 1833. Seba Smith's fictional commentator is shown writing, with a picture of Andrew Jackson
pinned to the wall behind him. THE LIBRARY OF CONGRESS

Nova Scotians as the "Jack Downing of British North
America," created Sam Slick, a rustic clock maker and
shrewdly enterprising peddler from Slickville,
Connecticut, whose "go ahead" spirit reflected progressive American attitudes of the time. Haliburton
published his Sam Slick pieces, mainly in monologue
form, in the *Halifax Nova Scotian* beginning in
September 1835, giving Sam voice to showcase his
homespun, aphoristic wit in amusing anecdotes.
Between 1836 and 1844 Haliburton wrote several
widely popular books, including *The Clockmaker; or,
The Sayings and Doings of Samuel Slick, of Slickville*,
which appeared in three series in 1836, 1838, and 1840;
and *The Attaché; or, Sam Slick in England*, which
appeared in two series in 1843 and 1844. Sam is a
Yankee outsider with a cracker-barrel wit, keen insight
into human weaknesses, and an equally keen understanding of how to use flattery to serve his personal
financial advantage. Haliburton employs him to address
slavery, marriage, and English travelers as well as to
ridicule Nova Scotians, who waste much of their time
raising horses, building expensive houses rather than
barns, and bickering over politics rather than moving
toward constructive change. Like Sam Slick, Jonathan
Slick, his fictive brother and the comic rustic persona of
the journalist and prolific author of sentimental novels

Ann Stephens (1810–1886), is a likable and unsophisticated outsider from an onion farm in Weathersfield, Connecticut, and an aspiring writer who combines feeling and honesty with common sense and morality. The Jonathan Slick letters, which treat such topics as theater, fashion, parties, and social manners, were first published in the *New York Express* in 1839; Stephens collected and reprinted them in *High Life in New York by Jonathan Slick, Esq.* (1843). Like his comic Yankee predecessors, Jonathan Slick employs vernacular discourse. The spelling reflects the spoken word of an uneducated rustic, and the word choice and imagery reflect reference points familiar to the rural world from which Jonathan has come. Stephens has Jonathan chronicle his experiences in the city, where he faces new customs and modes of social behavior that result in a humorous juxtaposition between the world of New York City and Jonathan's rural Connecticut background. Like Smith before her, Stephens employs double-edged satire: Jonathan functions as both the vehicle and the object of ridicule, who unwittingly exposes urban falsity and pretentiousness and at the same time displays ignorance and an absence of sophistication.

Frances Miriam Whitcher (1814–1890) and B. P. Shillaber (1814–1890) were the first Down East humorists to give Yankee comic women extensive treatment and voice. Whitcher focused on rural home life reflective of a woman's culture, creating several memorable comic characters—Widow Spriggins, Aunt Maguire, and the Widow Bedott—who were featured in the *Albany Argus, Neal's Saturday Gazette,* and *Godey's Lady's Book.* Shillaber created Mrs. Partington, whose comic sayings and monologues appeared in the 1840s in the *Boston Post* and the *Carpet-Bag,* the latter of which he edited. Mrs. Partington, a character in the mold of Benjamin Franklin's Silence Dogood, is a narrow-minded literalist and user of malapropisms (words that sound like the one intended but are comically misused) whose monologues and witty sayings voice the sentiments of the common people regarding the sociocultural environment of Boston. Whitcher's comic women, like Stephens's Jonathan Slick, are vehicles used to mock shortcomings such as narrow-mindedness, pretense, gossip, and the vulgar provincial tastes of New York village culture as well as to serve as objects of self-deprecating ridicule. The more popular book-length collections featuring these comic women are Shillaber's *Life and Sayings of Mrs. Partington and Others of the Family* (1854) and Whitcher's *The Widow Bedott Papers* (1855) and *Widow Spriggins, Mary Elmer, and Other Sketches* (1867).

James Russell Lowell's (1819–1891) chief contribution to Down East humor is his first series of *The Biglow Papers* (1848), an anti–Mexican-American War satire in the form of versified letters in untutored New England dialect. Disturbed by the federal government's decision to bring the country into an unnecessary war that he feared would also extend slave territory into the West, Lowell, who had strong faith in the judgment of the common person, employed as his principal mouthpiece Hosea Biglow, a conservative, moralistic Yankee farmer whose satiric letters in humorous verse convey Lowell's condemnation. Parson Homer Wilbur, verbose and pedantic as well as vain and likable, is another source of amusement who functions as counterpoint to Hosea and to the despicable, disreputable, bogus superpatriot Birdofredum Sawin ("bird of freedom soaring"), who goes to war for his own self-aggrandizement but becomes disillusioned. Lowell subsequently revived these characters for a second series of *The Biglow Papers* (1862–1867) to support the stance of the North in the Civil War. Through his caricaturing of Birdofredum, who migrates to the South and settles on a plantation, Lowell derides the worse aspects of southern culture.

HUMOR OF THE OLD SOUTHWEST

The humor of the Old Southwest (encompassing North and South Carolina, Georgia, Alabama, Louisiana, Mississippi, Arkansas, Missouri, and Tennessee) is also known as frontier or backwoods humor and the humor of the Old South. This form of humor, which flourished between the mid-1830s and the Civil War and reflects many of the concerns of antebellum southern culture, developed concurrently with Down East humor and shares some of the same characteristics. Like its Yankee counterpart, antebellum southern humor features regional types and eccentric local characters, particularly the tall-talking braggart or ring-tailed roarer; vernacular dialect; extravagant and extraordinary situations and activities; and exaggerated, outlandish descriptions. Moreover, it celebrates rural and frontier lifestyles and culture, concentrating on the moment during "flush times" when the civilized and the primitive clash and agrarian and frontier values are being threatened with replacement by a higher standard of life that would foster materialistic and social progress. In contrast to most of the Down East humorists, the humorists of the Old Southwest were amateurs and only writers by avocation. Moreover, all these humorists were white men and professionals—newspaper editors, doctors, judges, lawyers, planters, ministers, officials in local or state government, actors and theatrical managers, and soldiers—who typically wrote to instruct but more often to amuse other men of their class and status, an agenda that is not unusual given the earthy, sometimes

THE ORIGIN OF SOUTHWESTERN HUMOR

In addition to the influence of Down East humor, the origins and analogues of the humor of the Old Southwest are found in diverse literary and subliterary forms and draw on a rich legacy of literary conventions and prior discourses. These include, but are not limited to, the extravagant boasts of mythological heroes who exchanged attenuated insults with each other; the oral tradition of storytelling associated with traditional folk cultures; the popular and widespread influence of the German Rudolph Raspe's Baron Munchausen tall tales, first published in *Baron Munchausen's Narrative of His Marvellous Travels and Campaigns* (1785); the braggart soldier figure of the commedia dell'arte tradition; the essays of the eighteenth-century British writers Joseph Addison and Richard Steele; the picaresque tradition in the eighteenth novel; early-nineteenth-century British sporting periodicals such as the *London Sporting Magazine* and *Bell's Life in London,* which featured sketches and reports on horse races, hunting excursions, and travel adventures; William Byrd II's *History of the Dividing Line,* which records his observations about the topography, scenes, activities, and inhabitants of the area near the dividing line of the colonies of Virginia and North Carolina in 1728; Ebenezer Cooke's satiric burlesque of the clash of urbane and civilized culture with the primitive society of Maryland planters; the comic eclogues of the southern poet William Henry Timrod; Washington Irving's widely popular American comic tales "Rip Van Winkle" and "The Legend of Sleepy Hollow (especially the influence of the latter, which was appropriated and imitated by such southwestern humorists as Augustus Baldwin Longstreet, William Tappan Thompson, Joseph B. Cobb, Orlando Benedict Mayer, Frances James Robinson, and William Gilmore Simms); and the Jack Tales of the southern Appalachians.

Henry Clay Lewis (Madison Tensas), Joseph Glover Baldwin, George Washington Harris (Mr. Free; Sugartail), Davy Crockett, Alexander G. McNutt (the Turkey Runner), Solomon Franklin Smith, James Kirke Paulding, Mason Locke Weems, Henry Junius Nott (Thomas Singularity), George Wilkins Kendall, Christopher Mason Haile (Pardon Jones), Joseph M. Field (Everpoint), Charles F. M. Noland (N. of Arkansas and Pete Whetstone), Hardin E. Taliaferro (Skitt), Matthew C. Field (Phazma), John S. Robb (Solitaire), Phillip B. January (Obe Oilstone), William Gilmore Simms, Thomas Kirkman (Mr. Snooks), William C. Hall (Yazoo), Francis James Robinson, John Gorman Barr, William Penn Brannon, Orlando Benedict Mayer (Haggis), Adam G. Summer (Vesper Brackett), J. Ross Browne, Marcus Lafayette Bryn (David Rattlehead), Joseph B. Cobb, Joseph Gault, William Elliott, Charles Napoleon Bonaparte Evans, Hamilton C. Jones, Bartow Lloyd, Kittrell J. Warren, James Edward Henry, and others who wrote anonymously or pseudonymously and have not been identified. Unlike Down East humor, where the emphasis was on the comic Yankee, the humorists of the Old Southwest focused on a broad range of topics reflective of the interests and the way of life of a culture still largely rural and on the fringes of a frontier threatened with extinction. Fights (between men or between men and animals), horse races, militia drills, hunting excursions, camp meetings, sermons, gambling, primitive medical practices, drunkenness, con artistry and roguery, pranks and practical jokes, courting, dances, dandies and foreigners, horse trading, the rural rube in the city, legal procedure and courtroom activities, and similar subjects are featured in their work, which makes this brand of humor the first flowering of realism in American literature.

The popularity and wide dissemination of Down East humor, with its comic rustics, vernacular discourse, and emphasis on common sense and traditional values, may have provided the most immediate impetus for the humor of the Old Southwest. And like Down East humor, the humor of the Old South had its precursors. *The Drunkard's Looking Glass* (1812) by Mason Locke Weems, a book peddler and preacher, is a collection of humorous observations, anecdotes, and replications of vernacular speech that he had accumulated during his travels on the southern frontier. James Kirke Paulding's *Letters from the South* (1817) comprises epistles recording the humorous manners and customs of Virginia backwoodsmen, while his *The Lion of the West* (1830) features a tall-talking Kentucky frontiersman. The opening section of Henry Junius Nott's *Novellettes of a Traveler* (1834) depicts the comical misadventures of Thomas Singularity, whose

raucous subject matter and character types featured in their comedy.

The practitioners of southwestern humor include Augustus Baldwin Longstreet, William Tappan Thompson (Major Jones), Johnson Jones Hooper, Thomas Bangs Thorpe (the Bee Hunter; P. O. F.),

knavery anticipates that of Johnson Jones Hooper's rogue Simon Suggs. These represent the trailblazing efforts of the writers who first experimented with themes, subject matter, and character types that became staples in southern antebellum humor. Davy Crockett's autobiography *Narrative of the Life of David Crockett of the State of Tennessee* (1834), possibly edited by Thomas Chilton and featuring humorous anecdotes about Crockett's hunting adventures and skirmishes with the Indians, also anticipates the kinds of materials that later and more significant southwestern humorists would similarly exploit.

Yet it is the widely popular *Georgia Scenes* (1835) by Augustus Baldwin Longstreet (1790–1870) that can be considered the first book of southwestern humor. This collection of eighteen sketches and tales, which he had previously published pseudonymously in 1833 and 1834 in the *Milledgeville* (Georgia) *Southern Recorder* and the *Augusta States Rights Sentinel,* provided the major stimulus and generated widespread appeal for the southern brand of frontier comedy. Edgar Allan Poe, who reviewed *Georgia Scenes* for the *Southern Literary Messenger* in March 1836, confidently predicted that Longstreet's book was "a sure omen of better days of the literature of the South" (Poe, p. 29). Among the most amusing tales in the collection are "Georgia Theatrics," "The Fight," "The Dance," and "The Horse Swap," which combine two levels of discourse—the formal and standard language of the educated and refined gentleman and the frontier vernacular of the uninhibited yeomen and backwoodsmen—in which the reserved and genteel behavior and judgmental attitudes of the former humorously clash with the unrestrained actions and sometime amoral values of the latter.

This clash of civilized and backwoods cultures, which Longstreet prominently featured in *Georgia Scenes* and which would be variously adapted, modified, and rejected by other southern humorists of the period, depended on contrived structural control: the frame device was used as a means of separating and distinguishing between the rural folk and the dignified gentleman-outsider, who spoke in formal discourse, establishing the circumstances that occasioned the tale before shifting the emphasis to the colloquial-speaking rustics. The gentleman-outsider, as a moral arbiter, would sometimes interject his judgment on what has transpired and would close the tale. Kenneth Lynn, in *Mark Twain and Southwestern Humor* (1959), who used Longstreet's *Georgia Scenes* as a focal point and who viewed southern antebellum humor generally as a criticism of Jacksonian democracy, claimed that the "morally irreproachable Gentleman" of Southwest sketches and tales formed a cordon sanitaire around himself, placing him "outside and above the comic action" (p. 64). In doing so, Lynn further observed, the "Self-controlled Gentleman" was able to restrict and to condemn satirically the excesses of the yeoman characters. Lynn's thesis, an affirmation of the Whig ideal of an order in which the wealthy, educated, moderate, and genteel were at the top of the social ladder, has subsequently been challenged because it is not widely applicable to the large and diverse body of southwestern humor that has emerged through later studies. What Lynn failed to note is that most of the humorists willingly chose to live in the Southwest, primitive, deficient, or lacking in culture as it may have been. Moreover, in many southwestern humorous texts, backwoods vernacular characters are apportioned major space and emphasis and granted extensive, mostly uncensored voice. Rarely in southwestern humorous texts do the authors consciously disparage or belittle yeomen; instead, they often make their rustics appealing, thereby affording readers the opportunity for a temporary vicarious release from order, formality, and responsibility so that they can laugh comfortably with the yeomen.

Among the texts that create these circumstances most favorably are the letters of an untutored rustic, Major Joseph Jones, authored by and initially published in 1842 in Georgia newspapers by William Tappan Thompson (1812–1882) and subsequently reprinted in *Major Jones's Courtship* (1843); and the letters of Pardon Jones, authored by the journalist Christopher Mason Haile (1814–1849), who published the majority of them in the *New Orleans Picayune* between 1840 and 1848. Both Joseph Jones and Pardon Jones are fashioned in the mold of Seba Smith's Jack Downing, and their letters exclusively feature dialect-speaking rustics. Other texts in which the vernacular voice dominates are the humorous tall tales recounted by Surry County, North Carolina, storytellers and the comical dialect folk sermons of the Reverend Charles Gentry, an African American slave preacher—all of whom the author Hardin E. Taliaferro (1811–1875) portrays approvingly in his book *Fisher's River (North Carolina) Scenes and Characters* (1859). An even better example of authorial indulgence of a yeoman are the sketches and tales featuring George Washington Harris's (1798–1882) Sut Lovingood, the fun-loving, conscienceless, sensually oriented East Tennessee mountaineer who recounts—with little or no interruption from the authorial narrator George—his encounters and scrapes with and triumphs over doctors, preachers, sheriffs, adulterers, and other frauds and hypocrites deserving of his pranks.

The most famous tale of southern frontier humor is "The Big Bear of Arkansas" by Thomas Bangs Thorpe (1815–1878), which William Trotter Porter, the editor of the *New York Spirit of the Times,* published on 27 March 1841, calling it "the best sketch of backwoods life that we have seen in a long while." A hunting tale that has been compared to Herman Melville's *Moby-Dick* and William Faulkner's "The Bear," both of which, like Thorpe's tale, give the hunt a ritualistic and mythical dimension, "The Big Bear" is the masterwork in southwestern humor. It employs the key ingredients of the genre, the frame device, vernacular dialect, exaggerated figurative comparisons reaching tall tale proportions, and contrasts the civilized audience of auditors with an enthralling backwoods raconteur, Jim Doggett. In the story within the story, Jim hyperbolically describes crops and game in Arkansas of incredible size. His litany of whoppers culminates in an engaging, imaginatively embellished yarn of his unceasing hunt for and eventual killing of an "unhuntable" bear, an event most Thorpe critics perceive as representing the sad fate of the vanishing American wilderness.

In addition to the frame-tale format, the southwestern humorists employed other forms: sketches; tall tales; turf reports; almanac pieces; essays on outdoor sports such as horse racing, hunting, and fishing; profiles of local characters; mock sermons; letters; burlesques; and mock historical accounts. Southwest humor also featured a wide gallery of characters, the most memorable and entertaining being storytellers (Uncle Davy Lane, Larkin Snow, and Oliver Stanley in Taliaferro's Surry County sketches and tales; Simms's Bill Bauldy in "Bald-Head Bill Baudy"; and Jim Doggett in Thorpe's "The Big Bear of Arkansas"); hunters and adventurers (Mikhoo-tah in Henry Clay Lewis's "The Indefatigable Bear Hunter" and the mythologized Davy Crockett in the *Crockett Almanacs*); half-horse, half-alligator types, otherwise known as screamers and roarers (Nimrod Wildfire in James Kirke Paulding's *The Lion of the West*, the keelboatman Mike Fink, and the "shemales" Lotty Ritchers and Sal Fink in the *Crockett Almanacs*); and con artists, pranksters, and rogues (Ned Brace in Longstreet's "The Character of a Native Georgian," Simon Suggs in Hooper's "The Captain Attends a Camp-Meeting," Sut Lovingood in "Parson John Bullen's Lizards," and Ovid Bolus in Joseph Glover Baldwin's "Ovid Bolus, Esq.").

As an exclusively male enterprise, the humor of the Old South was expectedly a patriarchal genre restricted by gender and racial politics. Therefore, in these humorous works it is understandable why women and African Americans typically did not play major roles or rarely transcended their marginalized status. Several of the humorists, however, did challenge the conventional attitudes and assumptions toward race. The best texts exhibiting these transgressions include James Edward Henry's "My Man Dick," John S. Robb's "The Pre-Emption Right," Taliaferro's folk sermons "The Origin of Whites" and "Jonah and the Whale," and Francis James Robinson's "Old Jack' C—." Others transgressed the barrier of gender, notably Thompson's "Supposing a Case" and "A Runaway Match," Orlando Benedict Mayer's "The Corn Cob Pipe," Harris's "Dick Harlan's Tennessee Frolic" and "Blown Up with Soda," Solomon Franklin Smith's "The Consolate Widow," and Lewis's "The Curious Widow" and "A Tight Race Considerin'." Humorists of both groups, though not radically subversive in defying minority stereotyping, nevertheless encouraged the inclusion and a less-constricted representation of African Americans and women, empowering them by liberating their voices and expanding their race- or gender-circumscribed roles. The diversionary tactics these humorists employed created a safe ambivalence: the comedy provided a noncontroversial means for legitimating increased freedom for women and African Americans through greater emphasis, more complex characterization, and more verbal freedom than minorities customarily enjoyed in canonical texts authored by men during the antebellum period.

The humor of the Old Southwest was mainly a newspaper enterprise. While many of these materials were published in small-town newspapers, such as the *Greenville (South Carolina) Mountaineer,* the *Columbia South Carolinian,* and the *Lafayette East Alabamian,* others were printed in big-city dailies, such as the *New Orleans Picayune,* the *St. Louis Reveille,* and the *Cincinnati News,* and occasionally in literary magazines, such as the *Southern Literary Messenger,* the *Magnolia,* and the *Southern Literary Journal.* The most important outlet for Southwest humor, however, was the *New York Spirit of the Times,* edited by William Porter, who, during his twenty-five-year editorship, encouraged numerous correspondents from the South to contribute humorous materials to his paper. Among *Spirit*'s southern contributors were Joseph M. Field, Matthew C. Field, Haile, Harris, Hooper, Phillip B. January, Hamilton C. Jones, George Wilkins Kendall, Thomas Kirkman, Lewis, Alexander G. McNutt, Robb, Sol Smith, Adam Summer, Thompson, Thorpe, and Charles F. M. Noland (who contributed over two hundred sporting papers and humorous letters, making him the *Spirit*'s most prolific contributor). Because Porter's *Spirit* enjoyed wide circulation, his paper gave these humorists greater exposure than they might have ordinarily expected. Porter subsequently collected some of the better pieces previously printed in the *Spirit* and published them in *The Big Bear of Arkansas, and Other Sketches* (1845) and *A Quarter Race in Kentucky, and Other Tales* (1847).

A number of other southwestern humorists collected and reprinted their comic sketches and tales. These collections include Hooper's *Some Adventures of Captain Simon Suggs* (1845) and *A Ride with Old Kit Kuncker* (1849), Joseph Gault's *Reports of Decisions in Justice's Courts, in the State of Georgia, from the Year of Our Lord 1820 to 1846* (1846), Thorpe's *Mysteries of the Backwoods* (1847), Robb's *Streaks of Squatter Life and Far-West Scenes* (1847), Joseph M. Field's *The Drama in Pokerville* (1847), Thompson's *The Chronicles of Pineville* (1845) and *Major Jones's Sketches of Travel* (1848), Lewis's *Odd Leaves from the Life of a Louisiana "Swamp Doctor"* (1850), Joseph B. Cobb's *Mississippi Scenes; or, Sketches of Southern and Western Life and Adventure* (1851), Baldwin's *Flush Times of Alabama and Mississippi* (1853), Robinson's *Kups of Kauphy* (1853), Kittrell J. Warren's *Ups and Downs of Wife Hunting* (1861) and *Life and Public Services of an Army Straggler* (1865), and Sol Smith's *Theatrical Management in the West and South for Thirty Years* (1868).

FANNY FERN

The satirist and proto-feminist Sara Payson Willis Parton (1811–1872), who wrote under the pseudonym Fanny Fern, represented a new departure from the Down East and southern frontier brands of humor. Her humorous sketches, critiques on social manners and conventions, particularly patriarchal attitudes resulting in the oppression of women, were Fern's assertive and ironic responses to erroneous or absurd public claims. Though many of these sketches first appeared in her weekly newspaper columns in the *Boston True Flag* and in the *New York Ledger*, she reprinted some of the best of them in *Fern Leaves from Fanny's Portfolio* (1853). Fern's derisive barbs are bluntly disparaging and outspoken; her persona speaks in formal English rather than in dialect and displays a demeanor that is neither self-effacing nor respectable, thus distinguishing her humor from that of her female predecessors, Frances Whitcher and Ann Stephens. In representative sketches—"Aunt Hetty on Matrimony" and "Hints to Young Wives"—Fern forthrightly attacks the inequities of married life, warning young women to beware of male duplicity and ridiculing wives who sacrifice their identities by foolishly catering to their husbands' whims and desires.

LITERARY COMEDIANS

The humor of the Old Southwest, like Down East humor, proved that native American comedy was marketable and paved the way for the emergence of the nation's first professional humorists—the literary comedians or "phunny phellows"—and Mark Twain.

The major humorists of this school—Charles Farrar Browne (Artemus Ward), Henry Wheeler Shaw (Josh Billings), David Ross Locke (Petroleum Vesuvius Nasby), George Horatio Derby (John Phoenix; Squibob), Robert H. Newell (Orpheus C. Kerr), Edgar W. Nye (Bill Nye), and Charles H. Smith (Bill Arp)—initially published their work in local newspapers and gained even greater public exposure when their work was reprinted through the newspaper exchange system and in books, such as Browne's *Artemus Ward: His Book* (1862), Smith's *Bill Arp, So-Called: A Side Show of the Southern Side of the War* (1866), and Locke's *Swingin Round the Cirkle* (1867). In addition, most of the literary comedians turned to the lecture circuit, discovering that the public humorous performance was financially lucrative. The multiple outlets for their work brought their humor to a larger, more diverse audience than their predecessors had enjoyed, "permeating," as Jesse Bier observes in *The Rise and Fall of American Humor*, "the national mind as never before" (p. 77).

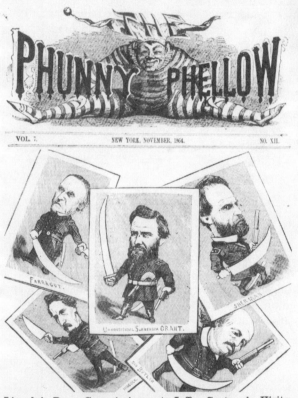

Cover of the humor magazine *The Phunny Phellow*, November 1864. Published from 1859 to 1876, *The Phunny Phellow* featured contributions from noted humorists such as Bret Harte and Josh Billings (often reprinted without their permission), and cartoons by Thomas Nast. BROWN UNIVERSITY LIBRARY

The literary comedians, or "phunny phellows," of the nineteenth century used a variety of verbal eccentricities, devices, and strategies to achieve their brand of popular humor. A sampling follows.

Anticlimax

I see in the papers last nite that the Government hez institooted a draft, and that in a few weeks sum hundreds uv thousands uv peeceable citizens will be dragged to the tented field. I know not wat uthers may do, but ez for me, I cant go.

*(David Ross Locke [Petroleum V. Nasby],
"[Nasby] Shows Why He Should Not Be
Drafted," in Blair, Native American Humor,
p. 410)*

Tears are unavailing! I once more become a private citizen, clothed only with the right to read such postal cards as may be addressed to me, and to curse the inefficiency of the postal department. I believe the voting class to be divided into two parties; viz., those who are in the postal service, and those who are mad because they cannot receive a registered letter every fifteen minutes of each day, including Sunday.

*(Edgar Wilson Nye [Bill Nye], "'A Resign' from
an 1883 letter to the president of the United
States, tendering his resignation as postmaster of
the Laramie, Wyoming, post office," in Blair,
Native American Humor, p. 454)*

The symphonie opens upon the wide and boundless plains, in longitude 115° W., latitude 35° 21' 03" N., and about sixty miles from the west bank of the Pitt River.

*(George Horatio Derby [John Phoenix], from
"Musical Review Extraordinary," in Blair,
Native American Humor, p. 395)*

Orthographic Wit

I'm in a far more respectful bisniss nor what pollertics is. I wouldn't giv two cents to be a Congresser. The wuss insult I ever received was when sertin citizens of Baldinsville axed me to run for the Legislater. Sez I, My frends, dostest think I'd stoop to that there? They turned as white as a sheet. I spoke in my most orfullest tones, & they knowed I wasn't to be trifled with. They slunked out of site to onct.

*(William Farrar Browne [Artemus Ward],
"Interview with President Lincoln," in Blair,
Native American Humor, p. 401)*

Mr Linkhorn, sur, priviately speakin, I'm afeerd I'll git in a tite place here among these bloods, and have to slope out of it, and I would like to have your Skotch cap and kloak that you travelled in to Washington. I suppose you wouldn't be likely use the same disgize agin, when you left, and therefore I would propose a swap. I am five feet five, and could git my plow breeches and coat to you in eight or ten days if you can wait that long. I want you to write to me immeditly about things generally, and let us know whereabouts you intend to do your fitin.

*(Charles Henry Smith [Bill Arp], "Bill Arp to
Abe Linkhorn," in Blair, Native American
Humor, pp. 421–422)*

Antiproverbisms

"Large bodys move slo," this ere proverb don't apply tu lies, for the bigger tha ar, the faster tha go.

It is tru that welth won't maik a man vartuous, but i notis there ain't ennyboddy who wants tew be poor jist for the purpiss ov being good.

*(Henry Wheeler Shaw [Josh Billings],
in Bier, The Rise and Fall of American
Humor, p. 104)*

Though the literary comedians employed some of the same forms as the Down East and southwestern humorists—letters, dramatic monologues, and anecdotes—the conscious intent of their humor, Walter Blair has noted in *Native American Humor,* was on "continuous amusement," with comic ingredients contained in every sentence and generated by using ludicrous verbal discourse and techniques. In the preface to his first and most popular book, *Doesticks: What He Says* (1855), Mortimer Neal Thomson

(1831–1875), one of the pioneers in employing verbal humor, described his basic strategy for enlivening his language for a comic effect, stating that he "dressed up" his thoughts "in a lingual garb . . . quaint, eccentric, fantastic, or extravagant," fabricating in the process a "trick of phrase, [an] affectation of a newfound style" (p. vi). In his meshing of words and phrases into amusingly clever, figurative syntactical configurations, Thomson clearly anticipated the mode of humorous wit employed by Browne and other literary comedians. Their humor is the comedy of phrase and sentence, a burlesque of the spoken word and the consequence of the deliberate defiance of grammatical and syntactical correctness and logic, as manifested in misspelling (a quasi-phonetic spelling), mixed metaphors, misquotations, anti-proverbs, neologisms, puns, non sequiturs, malapropisms, anticlimaxes. Because their comic materials mirrored the social and historical concerns of their times and because of the fractured grammar, malapropisms, eccentric sentences, dominance of dialect discourse, and other distorted verbal concoctions, the humor of the literary comedians creates difficulty for contemporary readers who do not regard it as particularly amusing. Also, because of the oral qualities of this humor, it seems to have been better suited to performance on the lecture platform.

As comic lecturers, Browne and other literary comedians found a new venue for their comedy. Adopting the poses of their homespun, semi-illiterate personae as their mouthpieces, they successfully transferred to the stage the amusing "lingual garb" they had first tried out in print. As performers they amused large audiences, assuming a dim-witted demeanor and exhibiting a dead earnestness as they slowly meandered through their droll, digressive, and ludicrously absurd routines.

MARK TWAIN

Samuel L. Clemens (1835–1910), who adopted the pen name Mark Twain and who became America's most famous humorist, was the principal beneficiary of the brand of humor popularized by the humorists of the Old Southwest and the literary comedians, a dual legacy that would reach the pinnacle of artistic achievement in *Adventures of Huckleberry Finn* (1885). Recognizing the potential of the humorous story as a distinctive American art form, one reflective of his preferred improvisational manner of storytelling, Twain wrote in "How to Tell a Story" (1895) that "the humorous story is told gravely; the teller does his best to conceal the fact that . . . there is anything funny about it. . . . To string incongruities and absurdities together in a wandering and sometimes purposeless way and seem innocently unaware that they are absurdities is the basis of the American art" (*Selected Shorter Writings*, pp. 239, 241).

Knowledgeable of the work of his predecessors who exploited the vernacular and prominently featured rustic, semiliterate characters, Twain, in some of his own early humorous pieces, drew freely from the comic devices they had popularized. Twain's first sketch, "The Dandy Frightening the Squatter"

(1852), published in Shillaber's *The Carpet-Bag*, re-creates the familiar plot of the clash of civilized and backwoods cultures and the triumph of the backwoodsman. Twain likewise drew on the conventions of southwest humor in three humorous letters he published under the pseudonym Thomas Jefferson Snodgrass in the *Keokuk Post* on 1 and 29 November 1856 and 10 April 1857 while working as a journeyman printer. Snodgrass, an innocent, dialect-speaking country bumpkin, like Thompson's Major Joseph Jones, is duped during his adventures in the city. Several other of Twain's apprenticeship pieces—including his letter to Annie Taylor (25 May 1856), featuring a "great mass meeting" of bugs, and "A Washoe Joke" (1862), an account of a petrified man found in the West and a mockery of serious scientific papers reporting incredible findings—reflect his assimilation and application of the tall tale genre widely used by antebellum southern humorists.

Published on 18 November 1865 in the *New York Saturday Press,* "Jim Smiley and His Jumping Frog" (subsequently published as "The Celebrated Jumping Frog of Calaveras County") masterfully merges some of the conventions of southern frontier humor and the narrative strategies of the literary comedians. A frame story juxtaposing a naive, genteel easterner, who is also the frame narrator, and an affable westerner, an old miner named Simon Wheeler who feigns earnestness and recounts in the vernacular an amusing, rambling, outlandish narrative, the "Jumping Frog" tale features Jim Smiley, a compulsive bettor who becomes the victim of a stranger's deception as Wheeler's eastern auditor becomes the dupe of the old miner's fanciful narrative ruse. Actually the easterner, who retrospectively introduces and closes Simon Wheeler's story, employs a deadpan pose too, both in his ironic comment about Wheeler's "monotonous narrative" and his pretended boredom and abrupt departure after Wheeler, who is momentarily interrupted, returns to continue his story. This sudden ending, which is not a resolution at all but rather an unexpected comic reversal, illustrates Twain's application of anticlimax, a favorite device of Artemus Ward and other literary comedians.

Mark Twain extended his humorous repertoire to encompass the experience of American travelers in Europe and the Holy Land in a series of letters he wrote principally for the *San Francisco Alta California* during a five-month cruise he took in 1867 aboard the steamship *Quaker City;* he then revised and expanded the letters for inclusion in his first book, *The Innocents Abroad* (1869). Combining humor and burlesque, Twain ridicules American provincialism, cultural inferiority, chauvinism, and barbaric manners (the latter exemplified when American tourists, desirous of bringing home souvenirs, vandalize revered monuments). An equal-opportunity satirist, Twain likewise debunks European snobbery, exploitation of dubious relics for commercial purposes, irritating guides, and even the conventions and rhetoric of travel books, particularly those deceptively describing venerable places in the Holy Land.

Roughing It (1872), Twain's second book, which like *The Innocents Abroad* is fictionalized autobiography, is based on the five and a half years Twain spent in the Far West and Hawaii during the early 1860s. In a manner similar to much of his earlier humor, in *Roughing It,* Twain employs verbal and physical exaggeration of details, formal and vernacular discourses, and the frame device to juxtapose different cultures, represented by a naive young man who retrospectively recounts his amusing experiences in his encounters with western life. The familiar script in "Bemis's Buffalo Hunt," "Jim Blaine and His Grandfather's Old Ram," "The Genuine Mexican Plug," and "Lost in the Snow"—the most amusing pieces in the book—involves the misadventures of a young greenhorn whose inexperience and naïveté make him look ridiculous. For instance, in "Jim Blaine and His Grandfather's Old Ram," the narrator, who is deceived into believing that, when drunk, Jim would recount the story of his grandfather's ram, never actually hears this tale but instead hears a shaggy dog story, a string of rambling irrelevant digressions about a cast of unusually amusing characters.

CONCLUSION

The brand of comedy that emerged between 1820 and 1870, the golden age of American humor, celebrates the subject matter of the evolving democratic nation, features a memorable gallery of rustic characters, and employs a colloquial vernacular that mimics the oral speech of the uneducated and semiliterate. This tradition, especially the humor of the Old Southwest, left a rich legacy to Mark Twain and to some of Twain's contemporaries, female local humorists such as Mary Noailles Murfree, Idora McClellan Moore, Sherwood Bonner, and Ruth McEnery Stuart. This same style of humor has also had its inheritors among moderns—William Faulkner, Flannery O'Connor, Eudora Welty, Fred Chappell, Ishmael Reed, and numerous others from both literary and popular culture—all of whom in their comedy have drawn on some of the properties of nineteenth-century native American humorous traditions, reconfiguring and giving them a renewed vitality.

See also "The Big Bear of Arkansas"; "The Celebrated Jumping Frog of Calaveras County"; Dialect; Satire, Burlesque, and Parody; Short Story; *Some Adventures of Captain Simon Suggs*

BIBLIOGRAPHY

Primary Works

Derby, George Horatio [John Phoenix]. "Musical Review Extraordinary." In *Native American Humor,* by Walter Blair, pp. 393–399. San Francisco: Chandler, 1960.

Doesticks, Q. K. Philander [Mortimer N. Thomson]. *Doesticks: What He Says.* 1855. Delmar, N.Y.: Scholars' Facsimile and Reprints, 1986.

Locke, David Ross [Petroleum V. Nasby]. "Shows Why He Should Not Be Drafted." In *Native American Humor,* by Walter Blair, pp. 410–411. San Francisco: Chandler, 1960.

Nye, Edgar Wilson [Bill Nye]. "A Resign." In *Native American Humor,* by Walter Blair, pp. 453–458. San Francisco: Chandler, 1960.

Rachels, David, ed. *Augustus Baldwin Longstreet's Georgia Scenes Completed.* Athens: University of Georgia Press, 1998.

Smith, Charles H. [Bill Arp]. "Bill Arp to Abe Linkhorn." In *Native American Humor,* by Walter Blair, pp. 421–422. San Francisco: Chandler, 1960.

[Taliaferro, H. E.]. *Fisher's River (North Carolina) Scenes and Characters, by "Skitt," "Who Was Raised Thar."* New York: Harper, 1859.

Thorpe, Thomas Bangs. 1841. "The Big Bear of Arkansas." In *Humor of the Old Southwest,* edited by Hennig Cohen and William B. Dillingham, pp. 336–347 Athens: University of Georgia Press, 1994.

Twain, Mark. *Selected Shorter Writings of Mark Twain.* Edited by Walter Blair. Boston: Houghton Mifflin, 1962.

Secondary Works

Bier, Jesse. *The Rise and Fall of American Humor.* New York: Octagon Books, 1981.

Blair, Walter. *Horse Sense in American Humor: From Benjamin Franklin to Ogden Nash.* Chicago: University of Chicago Press, 1942.

Blair, Walter. *Native American Humor.* San Francisco: Chandler, 1960.

Blair, Walter, and Hamlin Hill. *America's Humor: From Poor Richard to Doonesbury.* New York: Oxford University Press, 1978.

Cohen, Hennig, and William B. Dillingham. "Introduction." In *The Humor of the Old Southwest,* edited by Hennig Cohen and William B. Dillingham, 3rd ed., pp. xv–xl. Athens: University of Georgia Press, 1994.

Covici, Pascal, Jr. "Mark Twain and the Humor of the Old Southwest." In *The Frontier Humorists: Critical Views,* edited by M. Thomas Inge, pp. 233–258. Hamden, Conn.: Archon, 1975.

Cox, James M. "Humor of the Old Southwest." In *The Comic Imagination in American Literature,* edited by Louis D. Rubin Jr., pp. 101–112. New Brunswick, N.J.: Rutgers University Press, 1973.

Cox, James M. *Mark Twain: The Fate of Humor.* Princeton, N.J.: Princeton University Press, 1966.

Dresner, Zita Z. "Sentiment and Humor: A Double-Pronged Attack on Women's Place in Nineteenth-Century America." *Studies in American Humor* 4, nos. 1–2 (1985): 18–29.

Eby, Cecil D. "Yankee Humor." In *The Comic Imagination in American Literature,* edited by Louis D. Rubin Jr., pp. 77–84. New Brunswick, N.J.: Rutgers University Press, 1973.

Grammer, John M. "Southwestern Humor." In *A Companion to the Literature and Culture of the American South,* edited by Richard Gray and Owen Robinson, pp. 370–387. Oxford: Blackwell, 2004.

Inge, M. Thomas. *The Frontier Humorists: Critical Views.* Hamden, Conn.: Archon, 1975.

Justus, James H. *Fetching the Old Southwest: Humorous Writing from Longstreet to Twain.* Columbia: University of Missouri Press, 2004.

Kesterson, David. B. "Those Literary Comedians." In *Critical Essays on American Humor,* edited by William Bedford Clark and W. Craig Turner, pp. 167–183. Boston: G. K. Hall, 1984.

Lemay, J. A. Leo. "The Origins of the Humor of the Old South." In *The Humor of the Old South,* edited by M. Thomas Inge and Edward J. Piacentino, pp. 13–21. Lexington: University Press of Kentucky, 2001.

Lenz, William E. *Fast Talk and Flush Times: The Confidence Man as a Literary Convention.* Columbia: University of Missouri Press, 1985.

Lenz, William E. "The Function of Women in Old Southwestern Humor: Rereading Porter's Big Bear and Quarter Race Collections." In *The Humor of the Old South,* edited by M. Thomas Inge and Edward J. Piacentino, pp. 36–51. Lexington: University Press of Kentucky, 2001.

Lynn, Kenneth S. *Mark Twain and Southwestern Humor.* Boston: Little, Brown, 1959.

Morris, Linda A. *Women Vernacular Humorists in Nineteenth-Century America: Ann Stephens, Frances Whitcher, and Marietta Holley.* New York: Garland, 1988.

Nickels, Cameron L. *New England Humor from the Revolutionary War to the Civil War.* Knoxville: University of Tennessee Press, 1993.

Piacentino, Ed. "Contesting the Boundaries of Race and Gender in Old Southwestern Humor." In *The Humor of the Old South,* edited by M. Thomas Inge and Edward J. Piacentino, pp. 52–71. Lexington: University Press of Kentucky, 2001.

Poe, Edgar Allan. "Georgia Scenes." In *Humor of the Old Southwest,* edited by Hennig Cohen and William B. Dillingham. Athens: University of Georgia Press, 1994.

Pullen, John J. *Comic Relief: The Life and Laughter of Artemus Ward, 1834–1867.* Hamden, Conn.: Archon, 1983.

Romine, Scott. "Darkness Visible: Race and Pollution in Southwestern Humor." In *The Humor of the Old South,* edited by M. Thomas Inge and Edward J. Piacentino, pp. 72–83. Lexington: University Press of Kentucky, 2001.

Rourke, Constance. *American Humor: A Study of the National Character.* New York: Harcourt Brace, 1931.

Walker, Nancy. "Wit, Sentimentality, and the Image of Women in the Nineteenth Century." *American Studies* 22, no. 2 (1981): 5–22.

Weber, Brom. "The Misspellers." In *The Comic Imagination in American Literature,* edited by Louis D. Rubin Jr., pp. 127–137. New Brunswick, N.J.: Rutgers University Press, 1973.

Wimsatt, Mary Ann, and Robert L. Phillips. "Antebellum Humor." In *The History of Southern Literature,* edited by Louis D. Rubin, pp. 136–156. Baton Rouge: Louisiana State University Press, 1985.

Wonham, Henry B. *Mark Twain and the Art of the Tall Tale.* New York: Oxford University Press, 1993.

Yates, Norris W. *William T. Porter and the "Spirit of the Times": A Study in the Big Bear School of Humor.* Baton Rouge: Louisiana State University Press, 1957.

Ed Piacentino

IMMIGRATION

Immigration became a major factor in American life in the antebellum period, and the influence of the many cultures represented by the growing tide of newcomers changed American culture itself. During the period from the American Revolution through the Napoleonic Wars in Europe (1776–1815), immigration from Europe to America had fallen to low levels. This began to change in the period around 1820. Restrictions upon emigration from Europe were lessened with the end of the Napoleonic Wars; American expansion after the War of 1812, fought with Great Britain, promised land and jobs to the immigrants.

ECONOMIC AND SOCIAL CAUSES

The general forces driving immigration to the United States during the period 1820–1870 are seen in the interactions between social and economic conditions in Europe and those in the United States. Europe saw unprecedented population growth during the nineteenth century. This created pressure upon the existing land, and young people unable to inherit land were obliged to move away. At the same time, the Industrial Revolution, begun in the British Isles in the eighteenth century, was now being felt elsewhere in western Europe. The rise of the factories began to drive the old-fashioned artisans and craftspeople out of business. The movement of European population was therefore out of the countryside and small towns and toward the industrial cities and foreign places. America was by far the favored goal of the nineteenth-century European migrants.

America held out attractive possibilities to newcomers. There land was available much more cheaply than in Europe. Labor also brought greater rewards in America. Both the rapid expansion of the country to the west and the development of the new factory system created a demand for labor. All that was needed to stimulate migration was information about American conditions. A growing list of guidebooks and travelers' accounts told of the opportunities offered by migration, and letters from immigrants in America to friends and relatives in the old country spread the news about the New World.

The flow of migrants responded to these conditions. Deterred somewhat by a depressed economy in the United States after the panic of 1819, migration increased steadily from about six thousand in 1823 to about seventy-nine thousand in 1837. The panic of 1837 set off another decline, but immigration revived again in the early 1840s, reaching 154,000 in 1846. Then began one of the largest waves of migration in American history, lasting until 1854, in which year 428,000 immigrants arrived. After that wartime conditions in Europe and a slow economy in the United States slowed the flow of migrants. Immigration remained below 200,000 annually during the upheaval of the Civil War (1861–1865), then began to revive once more as postwar expansion opened new areas to settlement and the Industrial Revolution began to reach its peak. In 1870 about 387,000 immigrants arrived, and the census of that year showed that 5.5 million people (about 14.4 percent of the U.S. population) were foreign-born.

Region of birth of foreign-born population of the United States, 1870–1920

Region	1870		1880		1890		1900		1910		1920	
Europe	4,941,049	(88.8)	5,751,823	(86.2)	8,030,347	(86.9)	8,881,548	(86.0)	11,810,115	(87.4)	11,916,048	(85.7)
Asia	64,565	(1.2)	107,630	(1.6)	113,383	(1.2)	120,248	(1.2)	191,484	(1.4)	237,950	(1.7)
Africa	2,657	(0.1)	2,204	(–)	2,207	(–)	2,538	(–)	3,992	(–)	16,126	(–)
Oceania	4,028	(0.1)	6,859	(0.1)	9,353	(0.1)	8,820	(0.1)	11,450	(0.1)	14,626	(0.1)
Latin America	57,871	(1.0)	90,073	(1.3)	107,307	(1.2)	137,458	(1.3)	279,514	(2.1)	588,843	(4.2)
Northern America	493,467	(8.9)	717,286	(10.7)	980,938	(10.6)	1,179,922	(11.4)	1,209,717	(9.0)	1,138,174	(8.2)
Not reported	3,592		4,068		6,012		10,742		9,614		8,925	
Total foreign-born population	5,567,229		6,679,943		9,249,547		10,341,276		13,515,886		13,920,692	

Note: Numbers in parentheses represent percentage of total foreign-born residents with region of origin reported; (–) rounds to zero.

SOURCE: U.S. Bureau of the Census.

The largest components of the immigrant flow during this half century were from Ireland, Germany, and England (including Scotland and Wales), in that order. These were followed by smaller groups from the Scandinavian countries, from French Canada, and from other mostly western European countries. The gold rush in California beginning in 1849 brought America its first sizable influx of Chinese; they came as temporary workers, but many of them stayed to form the core of future Asian settlements. While the same general conditions involving land, labor, and population growth were at work among all of these groups, each had its own particular story.

IMMIGRANTS FROM IRELAND

Ireland in the early years of the nineteenth century had experienced a rapid growth of population, but the country had little in the way of industry to draw off the surplus population. Much of the land was held by tenants of larger landlords, and the typical plots of land were very small, so that a drought or famine might create immediate havoc. This became most evident in the years of the Great Famine following the failure of the potato crop in 1845. Over the next decade about 1.3 million Irish fled to the United States. Driven by near-starvation, they reached America by the cheapest way possible, often in empty lumber ships. The trip in sailing ships normally took five to six weeks but might take three months in adverse weather. Many of these immigrants left the ships penniless and had to find jobs immediately. The pre-famine Irish had already become the primary source of common labor in America, being frequently recruited to dig the canals, build the railroads, and tend the infrastructure of the growing cities. Irish women were the most readily available domestic servants; women with families often became the stereotypical

"Irish washerwoman" or turned their houses into boardinghouses to eke out some additional income for the family. The largely working-class Irish were dependent on two main sources for cohesion: the church and the saloon. The predominantly Catholic population, stiffened by their long experience struggling against a hostile Protestant England, rallied around their priests and based much of their social organization in the church. In the saloons the Irish also learned the value of forming a united political bloc, led by immigrant politicians who urged them to become naturalized as quickly as possible and consistently delivered Irish votes for the Democratic Party. That political power would eventually earn them political office and patronage. The Irish became perhaps the most successful ethnic group in American politics. The Irish were the foreign-born element most frequently encountered by most Americans; they were spread out across the ever-extending transportation network and concentrated in the cities and towns.

IMMIGRANTS FROM GERMANY

By 1870 the German-born segment of the population (about 1.7 million) was about 90 percent of the total Irish-born (about 1.85 million). The Irish had produced more immigrants during the years from 1820 through the Great Famine, but after 1855 the Germans tended to come in greater numbers. The German immigrants had a more complex social structure than did the Irish, because their background in Europe was much more varied. Most immigrants of the early nineteenth century came from the western parts of Germany, which at the time was still a patchwork of small states and principalities. The country was not united until 1871. It was in the western regions that both the conditions of land scarcity and the effects of the Industrial Revolution were first being felt.

Later in the nineteenth century eastern Germany would be affected by the same conditions. Young Germans began to feel the lack of opportunity when they could not inherit sufficient land or find any employment outside the factory towns. Others who tried their hand at industrial employment decided their skills would be more profitable in America. The pressures to leave became particularly strong when crop failures raised the price of food, harming producers and consumers alike. Political conditions in the German states were not always stable; the failed republican revolutions in both 1830 and 1848 propelled many out of the region. These included refugees who took part in the revolutions but also others who simply hoped for a more stable society in the United States.

Many factors contributed to the great diversity of the German immigrants. Their varying provincial backgrounds in Germany and Austria meant much to them. Religion, which was a unifying factor among the Irish, was a divisive factor among the Germans. They were divided roughly equally among Catholics, Lutherans, and Calvinists, with some Jews and a significant number of "freethinkers" as well. Friction among the various religious persuasions made it difficult to get Germans together on political or social issues. Fewer Germans were of the working class than was true of the Irish; many more were middle class and arrived with some degree of monetary resources. Some, such as businesspeople, lawyers, journalists, and other professionals, were better positioned to offer political leadership. The Germans took up farming much more often than did the Irish; some came to America with the proceeds from land sold in Germany, which would buy larger quantities of land in the expanding West. The ironic result of this diversity among the group was that the Germans, with a greater array of talent and resources, ended up wielding much less political power than did the Irish because of their inability to unite as a bloc. Germans gravitated toward the cities along the East Coast and toward the Ohio and Mississippi Valleys. New York had the largest number of German-born, but other cities, such as Cincinnati and Baltimore, had a larger proportion of Germans in their populations. Philadelphia, St. Louis, and Pittsburgh also attracted German immigrants, and by 1850 Milwaukee, Chicago, and Cleveland became destinations. More Germans than Irish achieved their goal of acquiring land, forming German communities in the farmlands of Ohio, Indiana, Illinois, Wisconsin, and Iowa. After 1850 railroads began to obtain government land grants for their construction and used those properties to develop immigrant communities along their lines. The rural communities were relatively homogeneous compared to the varied and diverse communities of Germans in the cities.

In this passage from his American Notes, *Charles Dickens, visiting New York City in 1842, meets two Irish brothers.*

Let us see what kind of men those are . . . those two laborers in holiday clothes, of whom one carries in his hand a crumpled scrap of paper from which he tries to spell out a hard name, while the other looks about for it on all the doors and windows.

Irishmen both! You might know them, if they were masked, by their long-tailed blue coats and bright buttons, and their drab trousers, which they wear like men well used to working dresses, who are easy in no others. It would be hard to keep your model republics going, without the countrymen and countrywomen of those two labourers. For who else would dig, and delve, and drudge, and do domestic work, and make canals and roads, and execute great lines of Internal Improvement! Irishmen both, and sorely puzzled too, to find out what they seek. . . .

Their way lies yonder, but what business takes them there? They carry savings: to hoard up? No. They are brothers, those men. One crossed the sea alone, and working very hard for one half year, and living harder, saved funds enough to bring the other out. That done, they worked together side by side, contentedly sharing hard labour and hard living for another term, and then their sisters came, and then another brother, and lastly, their old mother. And what now? Why, the poor old crone is restless in a strange land, and yearns to lay her bones, she says, among her people in the old graveyard back home: and so they go to pay her passage back: and God help her and them, and every simple heart, and all who turn to the Jerusalem of their younger days, and have an altar fire upon the cold hearth of their fathers.

Charles Dickens, *American Notes* (London: Oxford University Press, 1957), pp. 81–82.

OTHER EUROPEAN IMMIGRANTS

Another element, less noticeable in the American social fabric, was the migration from England, Scotland, and Wales. Britain had been in the forefront of the Industrial Revolution in the late eighteenth century, and British technology was well advanced by 1820, when the American industrial expansion was in its infancy. Emigrants included the usual groups of artisans such as weavers, whose skills had been rendered less useful by the machinery of the textile mills. They also included factory workers in England who hoped for better conditions of employment in America. Among them was a small but important group who knew the more advanced technology of English industry well enough to replicate it in the United States. And they included as well the landless farmers seeking employment and the landed farmers seeking to trade their holdings for better lands in America. In a survey of 1851 English immigrants, about a quarter were farmers by occupation, another quarter were laborers, and the remaining half were spread among the crafts, industry, commerce, and the professions. British migrants reached a peak in the early 1850s, averaging around fifty thousand yearly, then declined through the Civil War. At the end of the war the numbers of migrants increased sharply, reaching a new peak of 104,000 in the year 1870. The census of that year showed over half a million English-born within the United States. In the early nineteenth century Britons settled more often in the urban areas of the Middle Atlantic states and New England, but the farmers and others followed the opening of new land in the Midwest and were found particularly in regions adjacent to the Great Lakes. The similarities of language and culture between Britain and America helped these immigrants merge more quickly into American society and assimilate more easily than other immigrants.

Most of the other immigrants before 1870 came from northwestern Europe, but their numbers seem small when compared to the Irish, Germans, and English. Migration from Scandinavia occurred at low levels after 1820 but began to rise in the 1850s and 1860s with the exception of the Civil War years. By 1870 the census found 114,000 Norwegians, 97,000 Swedes, and 30,000 Danes among the American population. Most of these had come from rural regions in their native lands and sought out farms in the upper Midwest. The same census counted 116,000 from France, 75,000 from Switzerland, and about 65,000 from the Netherlands, Belgium, and Luxembourg.

PEAK YEARS OF IMMIGRATION

During the large wave of immigration of 1846–1854, nearly three million new immigrants reached American shores. European problems such as the Irish famine and other crop failures, revolutions, and political unrest combined with an American economy rising to boom proportions to draw many across the Atlantic. Some of the boom was caused by the California gold rush of 1849, which pumped new wealth into the economy and drew both American-born and foreign-born gold seekers into the state. The gold rush also was the lure that drew many Chinese across the Pacific, the vanguard of the country's first sizable Asian migration. Many came to "Gold Mountain" (the Chinese name for California) with borrowed money and owed much of their earnings to Chinese lenders. Most came as sojourners, most of them male; many stayed on, if not as miners then as construction workers or farm laborers. By 1870 there were sixty-three thousand Chinese-born in the United States, the majority of them in California.

IMMIGRANTS AND AMERICAN POLITICS

As newcomers, the immigrants conditioned their political attachments largely on the basis of "friends" and "enemies." As the Jacksonian Democratic Party formed during the 1820s and 1830s, it cultivated the immigrants' support, warning them of the hostile forces within the opposition party, later known as the Whigs. That opposition included various reformers who attacked the immigrant culture with ideas like temperance and Sabbatarianism (enforcement of strict Sunday observance). These reforms of course clashed with the customs of drinking and Sunday celebration practiced by many immigrants from Europe. The reformers also included nativists—those openly opposing the presence of the foreign-born in the society. Drawing on English Protestant traditions dating back to the English Reformation, nativists particularly targeted Catholic immigrants, especially the Irish. The nativist movement grew as immigration grew from 1830 to the 1850s, sometimes taking on aspects of violence, like the bloody Philadelphia riots of 1844.

Fear of nativism, along with continuing patronage from the Democratic Party, kept most immigrants tied to that party until the early 1850s, when the nativist movement began to take organized political shape in the "American" or "Know-Nothing" Party. But about the same time the issue of the expansion of slavery into the West began to disturb existing political alignments. During the 1850s a considerable portion of the Germans, often led by new leaders who were refugees of the 1848 revolution, began to attach themselves to the "free-soil" movement, opposing the further extension of slavery into the West, which took concrete shape in the new Republican Party. By the election of Abraham Lincoln in 1860, perhaps half the Germans were Republicans, but the rest of the Germans

Newly arrived immigrants being recruited to serve in the Union Army during the Civil War. From the *Illustrated London News,* 17 September 1864. Castle Garden was the reception station for immigrants in New York City from 1855 to 1892. ©CORBIS

and nearly all the Irish retained their Democratic allegiances.

CIVIL WAR ERA

The Civil War years brought great changes in the lives of American immigrants, as with other Americans. Young immigrants responded to the call for arms, sometimes in special ethnic regiments with their own officers. Other new immigrants were recruited directly off the immigrant ships. Others, however, resisted involvement in the war and especially opposed the call for a draft. The draft law passed in 1863 brought about immigrant protests, the most serious of which were the New York draft riots, which particularly involved Irish workers. Working-class immigrants particularly feared the implications of the abolition of slavery and the competition from the labor of freed slaves that might follow in consequence of abolition. The war years also tore many immigrants away from their ethnic communities and thus sped the assimilation of many. Immigrants served in the Confederate forces as well as the Union forces. In the years after the war the tide of immigration renewed, and many immigrants, including some of the second generation, were moving toward the western frontier regions now being opened up by the railroads.

IMMIGRANT CULTURE AND LITERATURE

The immigrants brought their own cultures with them, including traditions of music, theater, and literature. Although the Irish immigrants to America were in the majority illiterate, nevertheless they had their journalists and novelists and poets. The prolific Philadelphia publisher Matthew Carey wrote his own defenses of the Irish and published the work of many others. The editor and poet Thomas D'Arcy McGee championed other Irish American writers and wrote the first history of Irish American immigration (1850). By the 1850s novels on themes of Irish nationalism and migration were common in the literary marketplace.

The Germans, with a much higher literacy rate, supported a much more developed culture, including music, theater, literature, and a prolific system of German-language newspapers (estimated at 144 in 1860). The advent of German intellectuals and activists following the revolutions of 1848 greatly enlivened the German cultural scene and introduced much ideological controversy. The famed German Turner societies sponsored not only gymnastics but also libraries and literary societies. Both German-language materials and literature translated from other languages were commonly found in German libraries. German newspapers and literary journals published serialized fiction, and in the 1850s there was a craze of *Geheimnisse* (secrecy)

novels, usually revealing dark mysteries of the urban environment.

American treatments of the immigrant were much dominated in the 1830s and 1840s by negative stereotypes in the nativist literature. These tracts and sensational novels characterized the Irish as priest-ridden, brutish, ignorant, prone to violent brawls and heavy drinking, and politically servile. The Germans were also caricatured as given to wild celebration, addicted to beer, clannish, possibly inclined to radicalism, and resistant to assimilation. The stereotypical nativist portrayals were carried over in a usually milder form into the popular literature of the day. The early-nineteenth-century theater was already developing the "stage Irishman" and the "stage German." The German and Scandinavian stereotypes were generally less disparaging than those portraying the Irish. The Chinese stereotype was still that of the immoral "coolie," as the movement to forbid by law all Chinese immigration continued to gain strength in the years following the Civil War. Literary representations, while often recognizing the immigrants for their hard work and desire to succeed, nevertheless usually consigned them implicitly to a lower rank in American society.

By the last quarter of the nineteenth century immigrants had become an inescapable factor in American life. In every region except the more remote parts of the Southeast, Americans regularly encountered different ethnic cultures. Despite many frictions among American cultural groups, immigrants, especially the second generation, increasingly adopted new American ways of life. And American cultural ways themselves began to change under the influence of the many immigrant cultures.

See also Agrarianism; California Gold Rush; Catholics; Chinese; Civil War; Ethnology; Foreigners; Irish; Labor; Political Parties

BIBLIOGRAPHY

Secondary Works

Billington, Ray Allen. *The Protestant Crusade, 1800–1860: A Study of the Origins of American Nativism.* 1938. Gloucester, Mass.: Peter Smith, 1963.

Coleman, Terry. *Going to America.* New York: Pantheon, 1972.

Conzen, Kathleen. *Immigrant Milwaukee, 1836–1860: Accommodation and Community in a Frontier City.* Cambridge, Mass.: Harvard University Press, 1976.

Daniels, Roger. *Coming to America: A History of Immigration and Ethnicity in American Life.* 2nd ed. New York: Perennial, 2002.

Fanning, Charles. *The Irish Voice in America: 250 Years of Irish-American Fiction.* 2nd ed. Lexington: University Press of Kentucky, 2000.

Kamphoefner, Walter D., Wolfgang Helbich, and Ulrike Sommer, eds. *News from the Land of Freedom: German Immigrants Write Home.* Translated by Susan Carter Vogel. Ithaca, N.Y.: Cornell University Press, 1991.

Knobel, Dale T. *Paddy and the Republic: Ethnicity and Nationality in Antebellum America.* Middletown, Conn.: Wesleyan University Press, 1986.

Miller, Kerby A. *Emigrants and Exiles: Ireland and the Irish Exodus to North America.* New York: Oxford University Press, 1985.

Möller, Herbert, ed. *Population Movements in Modern European History.* New York: Macmillan, 1964.

Trommler, Frank, and Joseph McVeigh, eds. *America and the Germans: An Assessment of a Three-Hundred-Year History.* Vol. 1, *Immigration, Language, Ethnicity.* Philadelphia: University of Pennsylvania Press, 1985.

Van Vugt, William E. *Britain to America: Mid-Nineteenth-Century Immigrants to the United States.* Urbana: University of Illinois Press, 1999.

Walker, Mack. *Germany and the Emigration, 1816–1885.* Cambridge, Mass.: Harvard University Press, 1964.

James M. Bergquist

THE IMPENDING CRISIS OF THE SOUTH

In 1920 a book lover pondered Hinton Rowan Helper's *The Impending Crisis of the South: How to Meet It* (1857). "That a work should be once so popular," he mused, "and now altogether forgotten, may occasion surprise" (Sargent, p. 594). If by 1920 the general public cared little about *The Impending Crisis,* historians already regarded it as one of the most significant contributions to the acrimonious debate over slavery that preceded the Civil War. It stood out from other assaults on the South's "peculiar institution" because of Helper's style of argument, his call for southerners themselves to end slavery, and the controversy it generated. In 1968 the scholar George M. Frederickson called it "the most important single book, in terms of its political impact, that has ever been published in the United States" (Helper, *The Impending Crisis,* p. ix).

"Popular" might not be the right word to describe *The Impending Crisis.* When it first appeared it received both lavish praise and angry denunciations in speeches, articles, and books, even provoking attacks in both houses of Congress. For defenders of slavery, "Helperism" signified an especially dangerous variety of fanaticism. From the cooler perspective of history, *The Impending Crisis* looks much less original and radical than it did in its day but also far more interesting for what it reveals about sectional tensions on the eve of the Civil War, divisions among white southerners, and the relationship between democracy and racism.

BEFORE *THE CRISIS*

Neither the author nor the book were obvious candidates for literary and political notoriety. Although little is known about Helper's early years, his origins were part of what made *The Impending Crisis* so disturbing to its critics. Helper (1829–1909) was born in Hinton (later Davie) County, North Carolina, the youngest of eight children. His father died before he was a year old, but the family had enough resources to provide Hinton with a good education at a local private academy. He therefore wrote both with erudition and as a native southerner, not as an ill-informed Yankee abolitionist.

As a young man Helper worked as a clerk in Salisbury, North Carolina, a commercial hub for the area. Ever restless, he left North Carolina in 1851 to seek his fortune in California's goldfields. His nearly three years there were disappointing, disillusioning, and the subject of his first book, *The Land of Gold* (1855). It was not successful, but it helped hone Helper's mastery of harsh language and foreshadowed *The Impending Crisis* in other intriguing ways. His unflattering portraits of racial minorities in California were a preview of his later white supremacist diatribes. *The Land of Gold* also told a story similar to the second book when it argued that, rather than producing wealth, gold mining created a crass, ignorant, blighted society. Two years later Helper said much the same about slavery and the South.

By then, however, he had resettled in Baltimore, joined the young Republican Party, and begun an attack on slavery that went far beyond the position of most of his new political allies. They maintained that slavery should be left alone where it existed but not be allowed to expand into new territories. He argued passionately that it must end immediately.

HELPER'S CASE AGAINST SLAVERY

The Impending Crisis was an unlikely best-seller in 1857. It was lengthy, repetitive, and unoriginal in many respects. Like numerous abolitionists before him, Helper reprinted lengthy antislavery quotations from famous Americans, foreigners, religious leaders, and the Bible. More original was Helper's extensive use of statistics and tables based on U.S. census data. Other abolitionists mobilized numbers to show the harmful effects of slavery, but none so exhaustively. Among Helper's goals in using statistics was to refute the notion that cotton was "king" of the American economy. "The truth is," he proclaimed, "that the cotton crop is of little value to the South" (p. 54). Helper showed that the North and South were roughly equal in every major respect at the time of the Revolution, but since then the former had far outstripped the latter in all positive ways. Unsparing in his attack, Helper did not stop with economic indicators such as the value of manufactures, agricultural products, and imports and exports. He also gave statistics on public schools, "libraries other than private," newspapers and periodicals, and illiteracy among whites, all calculated to show that the South trailed the North in everything that made a society civilized and a nation great. Many northern reviewers agreed with the *Binghamton* (New York) *Standard* that "the author marshals to his aid an array of statistics absolutely overwhelming in demonstrating the fatality and madness of slavery" ("Impending Crisis," p. 118). Helper was less persuasive in convincing southerners that "slavery lies at the root of all the shame, poverty, ignorance, tyranny, and imbecility of the South" (p. 153).

Whatever its net effect, Helper's barrage of numbers enabled him to shift the terms of the debate over slavery. Prior to 1857, most abolitionists' fundamental objections to the institution were moral, not economic. It was a sin, not bad business. Five years before *The Impending Crisis*, Harriet Beecher Stowe embodied that view in the most popular American novel of the nineteenth century, *Uncle Tom's Cabin* (1852). Helper acknowledged that he had little to say about slavery's "humanitarian or religious aspects." With Stowe doubtless in mind, he added that "it is all well enough for women to give the fictions of slavery; men should give the facts" (n.p.). Appealing to "the science of statistics," he said of his tables, "their language is more eloquent than any possible combination of Roman vowels and consonants" (p. 142).

Helper's claim to have a rational, scientific case was at odds with his overwrought prose. He called slaveholders "detestable" and "more criminal than common murderers." Their religion was "satanic piety" and an especially degraded one "sucked in the corrupt milk of slavery from the breasts of his father's sable concubines" (pp. 147, 140, 258, 169). Helper's rhetoric even troubled favorable reviewers, one of whom deplored his "application of harsh adjectives to slaveholders" while acknowledging that "These may be richly deserved" ("Impending Crisis," p. 118).

When Helper moved from bitter denunciations of slavery to prescribing its demise, he was at his most

Recapitulation of actual crops per acre on the average—1850

Free states	
Wheat	12 bushels per acre
Oats	27 bushels per acre
Rye	18 bushels per acre
Indian corn	31 bushels per acre
Irish potatoes	125 bushels per acre
Slave states	
Wheat	9 bushels per acre
Oats	17 bushels per acre
Rye	11 bushels per acre
Indian corn	20 bushels per acre
Irish potatoes	113 bushels per acre

SOURCE: Helper, *The Impending Crisis of the South*, p. 70

"What an obvious contrast between the vigor of Liberty and the impotence of Slavery! What an unanswerable argument in favor of free labor! Add up the two columns of figures above, and what is the result? Two hundred and thirteen bushels as the products of five acres in the North, and only one hundred and seventy bushels as the products of five acres in the South. Look at each item separately, and you will find that the average crop per acre of every article enumerated is greater in the free States than it is in the slave States."

original. Other abolitionists saw the end coming with individual moral repentance or through northern repudiation of the institution. Some imagined that it might take a bloody slave uprising. Few believed, as Helper argued, that non-slaveholding white southerners held the key to abolitionism. *The Impending Crisis* presented an eleven-point platform for ending slavery, the first and most crucial plank of which called for them to engage in "Thorough Organization and Independent Political Action" (pp. 155–156). The majority of the remaining proposals were primarily designed to break the political and economic power of slaveholders through boycotts, elections, and taxation.

Helper insisted that his plan was supremely practical, but it is not apparent how realistic his call for a political uprising by white non-slaveholders was. Given southern censorship of abolitionist propaganda, there was no guarantee that his primary constituency would ever hear what he had to say. Some of his most vitriolic language, moreover, aimed at the very people he called upon to end slavery. Non-slaveholding whites, he declared, were "bowed down in the deepest depths of degradation" (pp. 152–153). If so, Helper was placing his hope for overthrowing slavery on an unpromising group of would-be rebels.

No matter how improbable Helper's proposals might have been, defenders of slavery saw them as a serious threat. Slaveholders were a declining minority in the South. In 1850 about 31 percent of southern whites lived in slaveholding families. That figure dropped to 26 percent in 1860. It was already clear by 1857 that the trend since 1830 was downward. "Numerically considered," Helper wrote, "it will be perceived that the slaveholders are, in reality, a very insignificant class" (p. 142). Their political power—hence the security of the institution—rested on the votes of non-slaveholders. If they turned against slavery, it was doomed.

When imagining the United States without slavery, Helper's vision was very un-southern. Proslavery writers commonly insisted upon the superiority of an agrarian way of life over an urban, commercial, and industrial one; in other words, the superiority of the South over the North. Helper, however, embraced the northern model and drove the point home in uncompromising prose. "Without commerce," he warned southern readers, "we can have no great cities, and without great cities we can have no reliable tenure of distinct nationality. Commerce is the forerunner of wealth and population" (p. 348). Emancipation, he believed, would attract immigrants to the South, produce a more urban and industrial society, encourage the arts to flourish, and make his native region more like the North. He was no tradition-minded spokesman for independent white farmers—as some scholars later viewed him—but rather a promoter of economic change.

There was, however, an ugly twist to Helper's vision of American slavery. The nation would be more unified, dynamic, and democratic, but for whites only. As he put it in another book, he spoke not just for non-slaveholders but also for "*the Heaven-descended and incomparably Superior White Races of Mankind*" (*Nojoque*, n.p.). He endorsed the conclusions of writers who used dubious "scientific" methods to assert the superiority of white people (and of men over women). Like the more extreme of them, he denied "the unity of the races," maintaining that whites and blacks were created separately and that the latter were biologically subhuman. Black people had, he believed, no place in a civilized nation, and he yearned for the day when they "shall have entirely receded from their uncongenial homes in America" (p. 299). One plank in Helper's platform to end slavery proposed a sixty dollar tax on slaveholders to provide money to send former slaves to Africa and elsewhere.

The racism in *The Impending Crisis* was among the things that set Helper apart from other abolitionists, although he applied the term to himself. For most white southerners and many northerners as well, "abolitionists" were a small minority of extremists, men and women, black and white, whose views on slavery and many other issues were wild and dangerous. Slaveholders believed they and their ideas had no place in the South. It was indeed true that by 1831 new, more radical groups of abolitionists had emerged in the North, insisting that slavery must end immediately and without compensation for slaveholders, points Helper similarly made. From their perspective, he was an unexpected southern ally who chose weapons—economic arguments and statistical methods—they seldom used but did not disdain. Yet the great majority of northern abolitionists repudiated Helper's "colonizationist" argument that African Americans should be expelled from the United States. Moreover, while racism certainly existed among abolitionists, most envisioned a biracial society after freedom, and there was a high degree of cooperation between African American and white abolitionists. Helper's racism made for a starkly different vision of post-emancipation America. His book was a mixed blessing for his would-be abolitionist allies.

THE CONTROVERSY INTENSIFIES

In spite of the strong responses it provoked, *The Impending Crisis* might have been just another polemic against slavery if Helper's flair for self-promotion had not converged with a sharp turn in American politics. Hoping to increase the circulation of his ideas and further the Republican Party cause, he set out to produce a shorter, cheaper, and less offensive version of *The Impending Crisis*. The result was a *Compendium* edition in which he toned down some of his harsh language and removed five of the most extreme proposals in his plan to end slavery (including one on the expulsion of African Americans). In seeking support for the project, he elicited endorsements from Republican Party leaders, among them Congressman John Sherman of Ohio.

While Helper was promoting his *Compendium* in the fall of 1859 he suddenly achieved even greater notoriety thanks to a dramatic and unanticipated event. In October, John Brown and a small band of white and black followers raided the federal arsenal at Harpers Ferry, Virginia, hoping to seize weapons and stir a slave uprising. Here was every slaveholder's nightmare: a black insurrection encouraged by fanatical abolitionists. Helper's critics wrongly saw this as "Helperism" in action.

Harpers Ferry was in everyone's mind when, soon afterward, the House of Representatives reconvened in Washington, faced with the difficult task of choosing a new Speaker. The Republican Party had a plurality, but not a majority. Electing a Republican Speaker would require votes from Democrats or from Know-Nothings, members of a declining anti-immigrant party. At one point the most likely candidate to prevail was John Sherman. Then, a Democratic representative from Missouri, with Brown's raid in mind, introduced a resolution declaring *The Impending Crisis* to be "insurrectionary and hostile to the domestic peace and tranquility of the country." It asserted "that no Member of this House who has indorsed and recommended it, or the compend from it, is fit to be Speaker of this House" (Sherman 1:169). Sherman was unsure whether or not he had endorsed the *Compendium* but certain that he had not read it. The political damage, nonetheless, was done, and he withdrew his candidacy. Although *The Impending Crisis* was controversial from the moment of its publication, the firestorm over the *Compendium* gave Helper his greatest measure of fame.

AFTER *THE CRISIS*

Helper's life thereafter was a sad tale of great expectations and disappointing realities. He sought a political reward from the Republicans and received it in 1861 with his appointment as U.S. consul in Buenos Aires, a post he fulfilled diligently until 1866. He devoted the rest of his life to various public projects, including promotion of an intercontinental railroad to connect all of North and South America, another expression of his vision of an expansionist, commercial economic future. He also tried his hand at encouraging white workingmen to engage in independent political action—a replay of what he urged non-slaveholders to do in *The Impending Crisis*. During Reconstruction, Helper's racism deepened as his own party enfranchised African American men and numbered them among its southern officeholders. It emerged unchecked in his later publications, notably an 1867 book, *Nojoque: A Question for the Continent*. Fredrickson suggests that it "may be the most virulent racist diatribe ever published in the United States" (Helper, *The Impending Crisis*, p. xlix). Helper's slow downward spiral into poverty, obscurity, and mental instability ended by his own hand on 8 March 1909.

Exaggerated claims for *The Impending Crisis* abound. The pro-southern author Thomas Dixon, for example, wrote in 1905 that it "precipitated the Civil War, and was once received in the North as a verbally inspired revelation from God" ("The Bookman's Letter Box," p. 409). Yet there is no way to gauge its direct impact on public opinion or politics, beyond costing Sherman the Speakership of the House. The significance of the book lies in other areas. It was a bold attempt to transform how Americans argued about slavery. It also provides a reminder that white southerners did not speak with one voice about the institution or the relative merits of agrarian and commercial societies. Finally, Helper's views represent a dark, enduring strand in American political thought, one that preaches democracy and equality but for white people only.

See also Abolitionist Writing; Harpers Ferry; Labor; Proslavery Writing; Slavery

BIBLIOGRAPHY
Primary Works

Helper, Hinton Rowan. *Compendium of the Impending Crisis of the South*. New York: A. B. Burdick, 1859.

Helper, Hinton Rowan. *The Impending Crisis of the South: How to Meet It*. 1857. Edited by George M. Fredrickson. John Harvard Library. Cambridge, Mass.: Harvard University Press, 1968.

Helper, Hinton Rowan. *The Land of Gold: Reality versus Fiction*. Baltimore: H. Taylor, 1855.

Helper, Hinton Rowan. *Nojoque: A Question for the Continent*. New York: George W. Carleton, 1867.

"The Impending Crisis of the South." *National Era* (Washington, D.C.), 23 July 1857, p. 118.

Sherman, John. *John Sherman's Recollections of Forty Years in the House, Senate and Congress*. 2 vols. Chicago, New York, London, and Berlin: Werner Company, 1895.

Secondary Works

Bailey, Hugh C. *Hinton Rowan Helper: Abolitionist-Racist*. University: University of Alabama Press, 1965.

"The Bookman's Letter Box." *The Bookman: A Review of Books and Life* 21, no. 2 (1905): 407–411.

Brown, David. "Attacking Slavery from Within: The Making of *The Impending Crisis of the South*." *Journal of Southern History* 70, no. 3 (2004): 541–576.

Sargent, George H. "The Problem of the Plugs." *The Bookman: A Review of Books and Life* 50, no. 6 (1920): 594–598.

Ronald G. Walters

INCIDENTS IN THE LIFE OF A SLAVE GIRL

Harriet Ann Jacobs (1813–1897) completed the manuscript for *Incidents in the Life of a Slave Girl, Written by Herself* in 1858. Jean Fagan Yellin and others have discussed the uphill struggle Jacobs faced in securing publication of her narrative. After its editor, Lydia Maria Child (1802–1880), failed to persuade the American Anti-Slavery Society to publish *Incidents*, the Boston publishers Thayer and Eldridge agreed to

Harriet Jacobs. Portrait from the frontispiece to *Incidents in the Life of a Slave Girl,* 1861.

publish it, only to succumb to bankruptcy before they could complete the transaction. *Incidents* was finally published "for the author," in 1861 in Boston and in 1862 by William Tweedie in London, as *The Deeper Wrong: Incidents in the Life of a Slave Girl, Written by Herself.*

When *Incidents* initially appeared, it garnered a number of endorsements, and several of these are contained in Nellie Y. McKay and Frances Smith Foster's coedited Norton critical edition of the narrative. The black antislavery activist William C. Nell, in a 21 July 1861 letter to William Lloyd Garrison, the white editor of the antislavery periodical *The Liberator,* described *Incidents* as a "handsome volume of 306 pages" that "presents features more attractive than many of its predecessors purporting to be histories of slave life in America" (p. 161). He added in his glowing endorsement of Jacobs's work that her words "shine by the luster of their own truthfulness—a rhetoric which always commends itself to the wise

head and honest heart" (p. 161). Nell concluded with the hope that the narrative would "find its way into every family, where all, especially mothers and daughters, may learn yet more of the barbarism of American slavery and the character of its victims" (pp. 161–162). In a 4 April 1861 letter to the poet and antislavery advocate John Greenleaf Whittier (1807–1892), Lydia Maria Child expressed joy that the former enjoyed reading the narrative; unsigned letters in the 9 February 1861 *Anti-Slavery Bugle* and the 11 January 1862 *Christian Recorder* also endorsed *Incidents* (see McKay and Foster, pp. 162–165).

Yellin's research into the narrative's background proved that "Linda Brent" was indeed Harriet Jacobs (or Hatty), formerly of Edenton, North Carolina. Yellin published her scholarly edition of *Incidents* in 1987, and it includes photographs and portraits of some of the people associated with the text including one thought to be that of Dr. James Norcom (Jacobs's chief persecutor). The volume also includes a copy of a codicil to Margaret Horniblow's will (dated 3 July 1825) leaving Harriet to her three-year-old niece, Mary Matilda Norcom. Other documents include the notice posting a one-hundred-dollar reward for Harriet Jacobs's capture and return, Hannah Pritchard's 10 April 1828 petition for the emancipation of Jacobs's grandmother Molly Horniblow, and letters, maps, and a drawing of the crawl space Jacobs lived in for almost seven years.

INCIDENTS AND THE SLAVE NARRATIVE TRADITION

Incidents deals primarily with the period of Jacobs's life from her early teens in Edenton through her late twenties when she arrived in Philadelphia. The body of the narrative is composed of forty-one chapters whose titles range from "Childhood" to "Free at Last." Appearing in print the year that marked the beginning of the Civil War, *Incidents* (and its author) had fallen into obscurity by the twentieth century. As Yellin notes, the book's reappearance around 1973 (largely a result of the efforts of mid-century civil rights activism) generated scholarly debate about the narrative's authenticity and validity. Part of the skepticism can be attributed to Jacobs's novelization of her life story and her use of the pseudonymous narrator Linda Brent. In composing *Incidents,* Jacobs borrowed conventions and narrative strategies from two popular nineteenth-century literary forms: the women's domestic sentimental novel and the autobiographical narrative of a journey from slavery to freedom (the slave, or freedom, narrative). Jacobs's story fits easily into the freedom narrative subgenre of African American literature, and as such its serves also as a political document that indicts the American justice system for its complicity in the many deprivations and abuses associated with chattel slavery. In addition, the narrative serves as an historical document that contains numerous references to actual historic landmarks, events, and persons. It has become a staple of courses in literature, gender studies, and history.

The major difference between *Incidents* and other autobiographical narratives about slavery, especially male-authored narratives, is its consistent, sustained engagement with the issue of sexual and reproductive exploitation. While other narrators, such as Elizabeth Keckley in *Behind the Scenes* (1868) and Frederick Douglass in *Narrative of the Life of Frederick Douglass* (1845), broached the subject of sexual and reproductive exploitation under slavery, Jacobs stands alone in her almost total dedication of *Incidents* to the issue and the manner in which it fostered black family disruption. Indeed, the narrative's "plot" turns on this central issue. Jacobs wrote and published *Incidents* during an era when the (white and middle-class) "true woman" was expected to exhibit ideals of domesticity, piety, submissiveness, and chastity. Jacobs used *Incidents* to critique true womanhood ideology and to proffer a revised definition of womanhood within the constraints of the domestic novel form. Claudia Tate has explored Jacobs's manipulation of the domestic sentimental novel form to tell a story peculiar to the social (and domestic) concerns of enslaved black women. Jacobs represents Linda as a resistant heroine expressing feminine virtues through her acts of courage, cunning, and self-determination. In the end, notes Tate, Jacobs manipulates the conventions of both the women's domestic sentimental novel *and* the African American freedom narrative by telling a gendered story peculiar to an enslaved black woman. Jacobs's casting of her heroine as a seducer actually subverts a convention of the women's domestic novel, and while marriage usually represented the ultimate happiness for the heroine of the domestic sentimental novel, Linda expresses instead a desire for a domicile, or home, for herself and her children.

Because it is first and foremost an antebellum freedom narrative, *Incidents* comes with an accompanying set of authenticating documents that certify it as genuine, as having been written by the author, and as containing a true account of the narrator's experiences. Such documents (often, but not always, written by prominent white citizens) include letters, prefaces, introductions, or simple statements preceding or appended to the body of a freedom narrative. Jacobs wrote her own preface for *Incidents,* and it precedes the introduction by the white abolitionist editor Lydia Maria Child. Completing the authenticating machinery is an appended letter from the well-known white antislavery feminist (and former Quaker) Amy Post and a short statement signed by another antislavery advocate, George W. Lowther.

Jacobs explains in the first paragraph of her preface that she changed the names of people and places in *Incidents* because she "deemed it kind and considerate towards others to pursue this course" (p. 1). She refers to her children, Louisa Matilda and Joseph Jacobs, as Ellen and Benny. Jacobs's grandmother, Molly Horniblow, and brother John S. Jacobs become Aunt Marthy (or grandmother) and William, respectively. The aptly named Mr. and Mrs. Flint were James Norcom and Mary Matilda Horniblow Norcom, and Mr. Sands (Linda's white lover) was, in reality, Samuel Tredwell Sawyer. The Bruces were Nathaniel Parker Willis (1806–1867), a well-known American writer, and his first and second wives, Mary Stace Willis and Cornelia Grinnell Willis; Jacobs performed domestic work in their home.

The body of *Incidents* comports with the structure typical to antebellum freedom narratives, which Frances Smith Foster outlines in *Witnessing Slavery.* The freedom narrative begins with a summary of Linda Brent's childhood and culminates in her awareness around the age of six that she was chattel. Next follows a carefully crafted depiction of American chattel slavery as an evil institution that reduced human beings to the status of property by stripping them of natural and other rights routinely enjoyed by their oppressors. In this task Jacobs/Brent follows to some degree Frederick Douglass's rhetorical strategy in his *Narrative,* recounting numerous deprivations of tangible and intangible property, horrendous physical abuses, and general life- and self-destroying practices that were part and parcel of the everyday operations of the evil institution. She includes information about her sexual persecution as well as her sexual agency, and she recalls the events leading to her decision finally to take flight, a decision that is tied to the central issue of family disruption under slavery. She continues by sharing the story of her subsequent escape (which includes almost seven years hiding in a crawl space over her grandmother's porch), and, finally, she expresses her feelings about having arrived in the North, the promised land.

Closer scrutiny of the narrative reveals that after being orphaned in early adolescence (Jacobs's mother, Delilah, and father, Daniel, died in 1819 and 1826 respectively) and left by her "kindly" mistress (Margaret Horniblow, who died in 1825) to a three-year-old daughter of the Flints, Linda began serving the elder Flints. Later, Dr. Flint began his sexual stalking of her. Jacobs represents Flint as the personification of

A number of historical figures and organizations are associated with Incidents in the Life of a Slave Girl, *ranging from people in Jacobs's life who are pseudonymously represented in the narrative to antislavery advocates who played important roles in the book's publication and dissemination.*

Lydia Maria Child (1802–1880): Born Lydia Maria Francis in Medford, Massachusetts, Child became a well-known author and antislavery activist. Her published fiction and nonfiction works include *Hobomok* (1824), *The Frugal Housewife* (1829), *The Mother's Book* (1831), *The Little Girl's Own Book* (1831), *An Appeal in Favor of That Class of Americans Called Africans* (1833), *Authentic Anecdotes of American Slavery* (1835), *Anti-Slavery Catechism* (1836), *The Family Nurse* (1837), *Philothea* (1836), *Letters from New York* (1843–1845), *Flowers for Children* (1844–1847), *Fact and Fiction* (1846), *The Progress of Religious Ideas* (1855), a biography of the Quaker Isaac T. Hopper, and several other volumes. Child served on the executive committee of the American Anti-Slavery Society, and her husband, David, edited the *National Anti-Slavery Standard* between 1841 and 1844.

American Anti-Slavery Society (1833–1870): Both Jacobs and her brother John S. Jacobs were affiliated with the society. Great Britain abolished slavery in 1833 with the Abolition of Slavery Act, and that same year, William Lloyd Garrison and others formed the largest organization of antislavery activists in the United States, the American Anti-Slavery League, which became the American Anti-Slavery Society. The organization spawned some 2,000 auxiliary societies, its membership soaring to between 150,000 and 200,000 before it was officially disbanded in 1870. Sponsoring a variety of antislavery activities including lectures, meetings, journals, and petitions to Congress, the society was a well-organized and consistent collective voice calling for an immediate end to slavery in the decades leading to the Civil War.

George W. Lowther (1822–1898): One of Jacobs's northern antislavery activist friends, Lowther had grown up in Edenton, North Carolina. He was emancipated as a young man and moved to Massachusetts, where he was elected to the state house of representatives in the 1870s.

John S. Jacobs (1815–1875): The brother Jacobs refers to as William in *Incidents* became a well-known antislavery activist and published an autobiographical account of his life in *A True Tale of Slavery.*

Samuel Tredwell Sawyer (1800–1865): Samuel Tredwell Sawyer, referred to as Mr. Sands in *Incidents,* was a U.S. representative from North Carolina born in Edenton, North Carolina, in 1800. He attended both Edenton Academy and the University of North Carolina at Chapel Hill. Sawyer fathered Harriet Ann Jacobs's two children, Joseph (in 1829) and Louisa Matilda (in 1833). A lawyer by trade, he served in the state legislature between 1829 and 1834. As Jacobs notes in her narrative, he was elected to Congress on the Whig ticket; he served from 1837 to 1839, chairing the Committee on Expenditures on Public Buildings. Failing in his bid for reelection, Sawyer moved to Virginia and resumed his law practice; during the Civil War, he served as a major in the Confederate service and died in New Jersey in 1865.

the moral hypocrisy inherent in the so-called Christian slaveholder, and he serves as a vehicle through which Jacobs critiques the slaveholder's perversion of true Christianity—again, in a manner similar to that of Douglass in his 1845 narrative. When Linda develops a romantic interest in a free man of color, Flint strongly condemns and forbids the relationship; Linda also realizes that a liaison with the black man would mean that by law their children would be considered slaves. Flint reminds her that he owns her and can do with her as he wishes; despite her resistance, he continues to demand her complete submission to his will. When Linda learns that Flint is building a concubine's cottage for her, she initiates an affair with a single white neighbor, Mr. Sands. Aware that slavery precludes bondwomen from aspiring to the ideals of true womanhood by forcing them to be sexual in one way or the other, the narrator tells her readers that it was preferable to choose Sands rather than be compelled to submit to Flint. Ultimately motherhood and a mother's desire to protect her children by removing them from slavery's grip serve as the impetus for

Linda's decision to take flight. She escapes with the help of friends and neighbors, both black and white. Sands purchases Linda's (and his) children (though he does not immediately manumit them), and, after overcoming logistical and other obstacles, mother and children are reunited in the North. There Brent becomes part of the antislavery community, gaining the support of antislavery activists and subsequently being persuaded to write her story.

HISTORICAL REFERENCES: THE BLACK CHURCH AND NAT TURNER'S REVOLT

In chapter 31, "Incidents in Philadelphia," Brent recalls that upon arriving at the North, she was introduced to the Reverend Jeremiah Durham of the Bethel Church. Here she uses the real name of an antislavery activist minister who was affiliated with Bethel African Methodist Episcopal Church at the time. The historical reference serves as a site of memory in Jacobs's narrative, a landmark pointing not only to the historic black Church (in terms of a continuous religious and spiritual tradition) in America but also to one of the oldest black churches in America. Founded by Richard Allen and a delegation of formerly enslaved persons in 1794 in response to their growing impatience and outrage with the racism they experienced in the white-dominated Methodist Church in Philadelphia, the church's first and subsequent structures were built at Sixth and Lombard, the property serving as the oldest property in the United States continuously owned by African Americans. (The current structure was built in 1889–1890.) Bethel served during the antebellum period as part of the Underground Railroad network. In addition to Richard Allen, who went on to become the first ordained black Methodist bishop in the United States, a number of other famous Americans, including Frederick Douglass, the Underground Railroad conductor William Still, the black female preacher Jarena Lee, and the white feminist activist Lucretia Mott, have been affiliated with the church. In 1830 Bethel served as the site for the first national convention of black Americans. Jacobs's insertion of Bethel Church into her personal story as a major historic landmark, her depiction of her grandmother as a devout Christian and her personal touchstone for morality, and the discourse on religion and spirituality (particularly in the chapter titled "The Church and Slavery") that permeates her narrative all underscore the seminal roles of the church and religious practice in individual and collective African American experience.

Interestingly, the chapter immediately preceding "The Church and Slavery" is titled "Fear of Insurrection" and begins with the following statement: "Not far from this time Nat Turner's insurrection broke out;

and the news threw our town into great commotion" (p. 63). The narrator explains that the usual yearly "muster" (a procession of musketed white men, gentry and peasant alike, in full military regalia or plain clothes) had already passed when Nat Turner's Southampton County, Virginia, rebellion occurred in late August 1831. Turner and his followers, numbering some sixty in all, managed to kill fifty-five whites (beginning with Turner's owner's family) before the rebellion was suppressed. In response to the Turner-led rebellion, hundreds of black Americans in the areas near the rebellion site were massacred. Though Nat Turner initially avoided capture, he was subsequently arrested on 31 October 1831, tried on 5 November, and executed on 11 November. Brent tells us that because Edenton was only about sixty miles south of the rebellion site, the event occasioned another muster that year. She recalls the mobilization: "Far as my eye could reach, it rested on a motley crowd of soldiers. Drums and fifes were discoursing martial music. The men were divided into companies of sixteen, each headed by a captain. Orders were given, and the wild scouts rushed in every direction, wherever a colored face was to be found" (pp. 63–64). Brent describes a climate of fear in which black dwellings were entered and searched, oftentimes with "low whites" appropriating items of property and inflicting abuses on men, women, and children, who were "whipped till the blood stood in puddles at their feet" (p. 64). The local meetinghouse that served as the black church was destroyed, and blacks who wanted to attend church were forced to sit in the galleries of white churches. In the chapter that follows, "The Church and Slavery," the narrator continues with a discussion of the impact that the Turner rebellion had on religious instruction of enslaved persons, with masters and ministers working in concert to instill blacks with principles of obedience and docile acceptance of their status as slaves. Jacobs thus provides in these two chapters an eyewitness account of events surrounding the aftermath of a major historic event that had widespread social and legal implications for slavery's beneficiaries and victims alike.

SLAVERY AND AMERICAN LAW

Like other formerly enslaved narrators, Jacobs also focuses on the manner in which American law worked to keep slavery (and racial discrimination) in place. She immediately offers a discourse on the expropriations that were part of the system of slavery. While she clearly advances the idea that human beings should be paid for their labor and that they are entitled to whatever tangible property they earn through their own efforts, she also gives equal consideration to intangible property in the control over her sexuality and the general well-being of herself and her children. She continues her engagement with American law, particularly its complicity in the sexual and reproductive lives of enslaved women, by expressing her disdain for laws that make human beings the property of slaveholders. For Linda Brent this means saying no to Flint's claim of ownership of her mind, body, and offspring. Included in Flint's legally sanctioned claim is, among other things, the right to own Linda's sexuality, but as Jacobs reveals, it is not merely a matter of sexual submission. Linda felt deprived of her "light heart" by Flint's shadowing of her (p. 28) and of her "pride of character" and virtue by Flint's persecution of her (p. 31). She knew that Flint "was well aware" of how much she "prized her refuge by the side" of her old aunt, and "he determined to *dispossess*" her of that refuge (p. 33; emphasis added). Flint also deprives Linda of the right to choose her own lover with his threat concerning the free black man she wants to marry. In short, as representative slave master, he robs her of general well-being and peace of mind, and thus Jacobs uses her narrative to document the less easily seen psychological abuses of slavery along with the more visible physical abuses and deprivations. Indeed, it serves as eyewitness testimony and analysis of specific aspects of America's past. *Incidents,* clearly addressed to other (primarily white, northern) women, depicts Linda Brent's pragmatic and deft negotiation of the impossible space within which slavery forced her and other bondwomen to exist and operate. Harriet Jacobs's determination to resist the laws supporting slavery is captured in Brent's reversal of the language of the famous *Dred Scott* decision of 1857; she states that she regarded laws making her and her children chattel as "the regulations of robbers, who had no rights that" she "was bound to respect" (p. 187).

Though we tend to date Jim Crow segregation laws as beginning in the late 1800s, near the end of chapter 31 Brent describes a trip on a segregated public conveyance. The experience takes place shortly after her arrival in Philadelphia in 1842. She muses that it was "the first chill" to her "enthusiasm about the Free States. Colored people were allowed to ride in a filthy box, behind white people, at the south, but there they were not required to pay for the privilege. It made me sad to find how the north aped the customs of slavery" (pp. 162–163). Most noticeably in regard to American law, she delivers through her own story a resounding indictment of the U.S. government for passing the 1850 Fugitive Slave Law. Jacobs titles chapter 40 "The Fugitive Slave Law" and uses that space to reflect on the injustice of the law. After her arrival in the North, her struggle continues because under the law she could be captured and returned to slavery. Jacobs writes that she and her brother spent most of their time together talking of the

> distress brought on our oppressed people by the passage of this iniquitous law . . . What a disgrace to a city calling itself free, that inhabitants, guiltless of offence, and seeking to perform their duties conscientiously, should be condemned to live in such incessant fear, and have nowhere to turn for protection." (P. 191)

Her employer Cornelia Grinnell Willis purchased Harriet Jacobs from the Norcom family in 1852, ending Jacobs's fear of being captured and returned to slavery but leaving her with a sense of duty to Willis and anguish about the pecuniary means by which her freedom had been gained.

Though Harriet Ann Jacobs began her life in North Carolina slavery, she is now a member of the North Carolina Literary Hall of Fame. In 2004 Yellin published the biography *Harriet Jacobs: A Life,* which documents, among other things, Jacobs's decision process in regard to the form her narrative would take. Yellin presents and expands on the life represented in *Incidents* in three parts: "Hatty: Private Dreams of Freedom and a Home"; "Linda: Public Dreams of Freedom and a Home"; and "Mrs. Jacobs: Public Demands for Freedom and Homes." The first part focuses on Jacobs's life in North Carolina; the second part focuses on *Incidents,* the public document; and the third part represents Jacobs the author and activist in her personal, social, and political milieus beyond slavery and the Civil War. *Harriet Jacobs: A Life* thus expands richly on our portrait of Harriet Jacobs—both in her southern and northern milieus—and *Incidents* has become a staple text not only for courses in African American literature but also for courses in gender and women's studies and American history.

See also Autobiography; Compromise of 1850 and Fugitive Slave Law; Domestic Fiction; Female Authorship; Feminism; *Narrative of the Life of Frederick Douglass;* Slave Narratives; Slave Rebellions; Slavery

BIBLIOGRAPHY

Primary Works

Douglass, Frederick. *Narrative of the Life of Frederick Douglass, an American Slave, Written by Himself.* Boston: Anti-Slavery Office, 1845.

Jacobs, Harriet Ann. *Incidents in the Life of a Slave Girl, Written by Herself.* 1861. Edited by Jean Fagan Yellin. Cambridge, Mass.: Harvard University Press, 1987. All quotations in the text refer to this edition.

Jacobs, Harriet Ann. *Incidents in the Life of a Slave Girl, Written by Herself.* 1861. Norton critical edition. Edited by Nellie Y. McKay and Frances Smith Foster. New York: Norton, 2001.

Secondary Works

Carby, Hazel V. " 'Hear My Voice, Ye Careless Daughters': Narratives of Slave and Free Women before Emancipation." In her *Reconstructing Womanhood*, pp. 40–61. New York and Oxford: Oxford University Press, 1987.

Clinton, Catherine. "'With a Whip in His Hand': Rape, Memory, and African American Women." In *History and Memory in African-American Culture,* edited by Geneviève Fabre and Robert O'Meally, pp. 205–218. New York and Oxford: Oxford University Press, 1994.

Foster, Frances Smith. *Witnessing Slavery: The Development of Ante-Bellum Slave Narratives.* Madison: University Press of Wisconsin, 1994.

Foster, Frances Smith. *Written by Herself: Literary Production by African American Women, 1746–1892.* Bloomington: Indiana University Press, 1993.

Garfield, Deborah M., and Rafia Zafar, eds. *Harriet Jacobs and* Incidents in the Life of a Slave Girl. Cambridge, U.K.: Cambridge University Press, 1996.

Greenberg, Kenneth S., ed. *Nat Turner: A Slave Rebellion in History and Memory.* New York and Oxford: Oxford University Press, 2003.

Kaplan, Carla. "Recuperating Agents: Narrative Contracts, Emancipatory Readers, and *Incidents in the Life of a Slave Girl.*" In *Provoking Agents: Gender and Agency in Theory and Practice,* edited by Judith Kegan Gardiner, pp. 280–301. Urbana: University of Illinois Press, 1995.

Lincoln, C. Eric, and Lawrence H. Mamiya. *The Black Church in the African-American Experience.* Durham, N.C.: Duke University Press, 1990.

Mitchell, Henry H. *Black Church Beginnings: The Long-Hidden Realities of the First Years.* Grand Rapids, Mich.: William B. Eerdman, 2004.

Peterson, Carla L. *"Doers of the Word": African American Women Speakers and Writers in the North (1830–1880).* New York: Oxford University Press, 1995.

Smith, Valerie. "'Loopholes of Retreat': Architecture and Ideology in Harriet Jacobs's *Incidents in the Life of a Slave Girl.*" In *Reading Black, Reading Feminist: A Critical Anthology,* edited by Henry Louis Gates Jr., pp. 212–226. New York: Meridian, 1990.

Smith, Valerie. *Self-Discovery and Authority in Afro-American Narrative.* Cambridge, Mass.: Harvard University Press, 1987.

Tate, Claudia. *Domestic Allegories of Political Desire.* New York and Oxford: Oxford University Press, 1992.

Yellin, Jean Fagan. *Harriet Jacobs: A Life.* New York: Basic Books, 2004.

Lovalerie King

INDIANS

The pre–Civil War period of American history confirmed the determination of the American people to deprive Indians of their land regardless of treaty obligations, civil law, and humanity. Removal was the great fact of this period and the great political issue of the 1830s, given irresistible momentum by Andrew Jackson's election to the presidency in 1828, an event followed by the government's adoption of a policy to relocate the remaining eastern Indians across the Mississippi. Over and over a sad drama was enacted in which a tribe pleaded to be spared this deracination while the government urged willing compliance upon it. When that failed, the Indians would be forcibly removed with great suffering and loss of life. In major Indian wars of the period, Black Hawk War in Illinois and contiguous states (1832) and the Seminole Wars in Florida (1817–1818, 1835–1842, 1855–1858), Indian allies fought and died with government troops, thinking that their service would spare them from removal. They were treated no better than the defeated enemy. The Potawatomi chief who predicted ruin to tribes who warred against whites might have expanded his prophecy to include those who did not go to war as well. Hostile or peaceful, all were required to vacate the lands east of the Mississippi. As Helen Hunt Jackson (1830–1885) wrote of this history in her landmark study, *A Century of Dishonor* (1881), "Every year has its dark stain. The story of one tribe is the story of all, varied only by differences of time and place" (p. 337).

THE TRAIL OF TEARS

The most flagrant example was the removal of the Cherokees from Alabama and Georgia. Early in the century this Indian nation had made a conscious decision to adopt every aspect of white American culture. The Cherokees became successful farmers (and slaveholders), converted to Christianity, and developed a written language. Soon they had a high rate of literacy. Their newspaper, the *Phoenix,* printed on their own press, was the first to appear in both English and a Native American language (1828). The usual racist arguments that the Cherokees were incapable of living as whites lived fell before such evidence, yet the states insisted that the Cherokees must go. While they tried to protect their land and possessions from impatient marauders, the Cherokees sought every remedy to avoid dispossession, including the courts, but when the Supreme Court ruled in their favor on 3 March 1832, President Jackson (1767–1845) refused to enforce the decision, falsely maintaining to the Indians that the federal government had no authority to prevent depredations against them. Jackson was more responsive to ultimatums made to him by the southern states and to the logic of population. Without federal protection, the 22,000 Cherokees could not resist the will of more than 300,000 Alabama and Georgia whites. Jackson's reelection by a large margin in 1832 ratified on the national level this will to implement the expulsion, which was then carried out under military supervision. Although other southern tribes had already been transferred under conditions of extreme hardship, no effort was made to avoid the same mistakes during the Cherokee migration, known to history as the Trail of Tears (1838–1839). As a consequence, 4,000 Cherokees died.

The Trail of Tears was simply the culminating episode in a familiar pattern. All Indians were strongly attached to their homelands; they had to be deceived, pressured, or coerced into moving—giving the lie to the promise of the Indian Removal Act (1830) that force would not be used to effect their departure. Inevitably they were moved, unable to oppose the surging white population that had the power to carry out its designs.

In his surrender speech after the Black Hawk War, Chief Black Hawk (1767–1838), a Sauk Indian, noted bitterly that "an Indian who is as bad as the white men could not live in our nation; he would be put to death, and eaten up by the wolves" (McLuhan, p. 141). In truth, Indians were poorly prepared to engage such a formidable enemy as white America. Accustomed to living in small communities, they could never make common cause to the extent necessary to mount an effective resistance. Whites exploited tribal enmities, divided tribes into factions, and introduced vices that weakened the Indians' resolve and the fabric of their societies. Alcohol, in particular, reduced Indians to helplessness and tractability. Whether or not whites employed more reprehensible tactics, such as deliberately bringing smallpox and other epidemic diseases into Indian villages, as has so often been asserted, many hated Indians enough to be indifferent to the means used to clear the coveted land of their presence.

VIOLENCE

By the 1840s, with Indians now a negligible presence in the eastern United States, the tide of westward settlement beyond the Mississippi began to exert pressure on Indians farther west. Here occurred what was

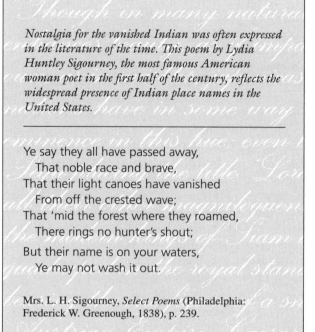

Nostalgia for the vanished Indian was often expressed in the literature of the time. This poem by Lydia Huntley Sigourney, the most famous American woman poet in the first half of the century, reflects the widespread presence of Indian place names in the United States.

Ye say they all have passed away,
   That noble race and brave,
That their light canoes have vanished
   From off the crested wave;
That 'mid the forest where they roamed,
   There rings no hunter's shout;
But their name is on your waters,
   Ye may not wash it out.

Mrs. L. H. Sigourney, *Select Poems* (Philadelphia: Frederick W. Greenough, 1838), p. 239.

arguably the greatest atrocity, the Massacre of Sand Creek in Colorado Territory (1864). Volunteers under the command of an ambitious zealot, Colonel John Chivington (1821–1894), attacked a peaceful band of southern Cheyenne camped close to Fort Lyon by the authority of the military. When Chivington's men withdrew, more than two hundred Indians, mostly women and children, had been killed, many revoltingly mutilated. Indian anger over this outrage sparked reprisal raids, but the federal government could not fully address the suffering of the settlers until the war ended. At Medicine Lodge, Kansas, a huge gathering of five southern Plains tribes met government representatives in the fall of 1867. In return for relocating on reservations, the Indians were promised various goods, including badly needed food, but a typical cultural misunderstanding resulted in a continuing state of hostilities rather than peace: while the treaty made its slow way through the political process, the Indians, having expected to receive the promised items immediately, felt angry and betrayed. They began attacking and burning settlements. In response, the army sent a former Civil War hero, George Armstrong Custer (1839–1876), against a Cheyenne winter encampment on the Washita River. A well-known advocate for peace, Chief Black Kettle (b. 1807) was among those killed in the ensuing battle (1868). Custer would later be best remembered for the Battle of the Little Bighorn (1876), at which he and five companies of his regiment were killed by Lakota Sioux and allied tribes.

To the north the Sioux, led by the militant Oglala chief Red Cloud (c. 1822–1909), enjoyed the greatest success against white immigration. Red Cloud's repeated attacks on the Bozeman Trail, including an ambush that killed eighty soldiers from Fort Phil Kearney, Wyoming Territory, led the government to agree to abandon the three forts it had placed along the trail (1868). Like the Battle of the Little Bighorn in 1876, Red Cloud's War was only a momentary victory for the Indians. It was in this western theater of Indian-white conflict that a remark made by General Philip Sheridan (1831–1888) became instantly popular as a serious statement: "The only good Indian is a dead Indian." Repeated waves of immigration released by the end of the Civil War in 1865 created the same conditions that had dispossessed and destroyed eastern Indians: in the decade after 1860 a million white settlers had crossed the Mississippi; in the decade after 1870 some two and a half million joined them. The major western Plains tribes—the Apache, Kiowa, Comanche, Cheyenne, Lakota Sioux, and Arapaho—would all be subdued by force or hunger.

RACISM

Although racism played a part in the removal of Indians, the country tolerated other nonwhite races confined to inferior positions. Two factors made its relations with Indians different. First and foremost was the desire for Indian land: the growing nation, which Jefferson had envisioned existing between the Atlantic Ocean and the Appalachian Mountains, ultimately comprehended a continental expanse. This set the stage for the final thrust of Manifest Destiny that would place all Indian tribes on out-of-the-way reservations and permanently end their threat to the

The Last of the Race, 1847. Painting by Tompkins Harrison Matteson. COLLECTION OF THE NEW YORK HISTORICAL SOCIETY

United States. Second, whereas other racial communities aspired to better terms of inclusion in American society, Indians remained radically unassimilated, preferring their own cultures to those of the settlers.

It was rare for either party to bridge cultural and linguistic gulfs in a systematic or meaningful way. The white world officially prohibited all forms of miscegenation, although it tacitly tolerated a fair number of white men having relationships with Indian women in the fluid space of the frontier. Indians seldom thrived in the communities of the dominant culture; some white men, however, were strongly attracted to the Indian way of life.

Given the rapid disappearance of Indians from the United States proper, Americans could readily believe that the continent's indigenous inhabitants were a vanishing race, withering away before the superior whites. An emerging "scientific" racism bolstered such views, which would gain momentum as the century progressed. Proponents argued that Indians were genetically incapable of civilization: whatever improvements occurred were due to interbreeding with whites. Samuel Morton's influential *Crania Americana* (1839) used his measurement of skulls to assert that the Indians (like other nonwhites) belonged to an inferior race. His compilation of cranial data convinced the eminent scientist Louis Agassiz that this conclusion had been empirically established. Josiah Nott and George Gliddon reiterated the denigration of the Indian in their huge and widely read compendium, *Types of Mankind* (1854). The views of scientific racism were also transmitted by historians such as Francis Parkman (*The Conspiracy of Pontiac,* 1851) and Lewis Henry Morgan (*The League of the Iroquois,* 1851) and by the writers of a new kind of American fiction.

INDIANS IN FICTION

Reduced to a powerless remnant in reality, Indians would now become part of a nationalistic branch of Romantic literature that saw their displacement as a critical episode in the settlement of the New World. Ironically, while they were fictionalized as figures of power, either as noble or ignoble savages, eastern Indians increasingly lived the marginalized and hand-to-mouth lives of a poverty-stricken minority. Their circumstances would spread westward along with the arrival of white settlers.

The first work to capitalize on Indians as a Romantic subject was *Yamoyden, A Tale of the Wars of King Philip: in Six Cantos* (1820), a narrative poem written by James Wallis Eastburn (1797–1819) and Robert Sands (1799–1832). One of the country's most influential critics, John G. Palfrey (1796–1881),

hailed *Yamoyden* as fulfilling nationalistic aspirations to use early American history in the manner of Sir Walter Scott, whose novels were enormously popular in the United States. Palfrey, who elsewhere had denigrated the Wampanoag leader King Philip as ignorant and barbarous, objected to the presentation of Indians as noble savages in *Yamoyden,* although the poem imposes the standard conclusion of racial conflict by killing its Indian protagonist, Yamoyden, along with his white wife. Like many "good Indians" in the novels that followed this epic poem, Yamoyden gives his life to save a white person.

The novels with Indian characters that began to appear in the 1820s often borrowed a narrative framework from earlier nonfictional accounts of Indian captivity. These had found large audiences from the late seventeenth century when Mary White Rowlandson's story of her captivity (1682) became the first American best-seller. During the eighteenth century, however, the captivity became stylized and reified, with obligatory episodes and conventions. Many purportedly true histories were, if not outright inventions, undoubtedly heightened for greater effect. By the time of its appropriation by nineteenth-century novelists, the captivity narrative needed the revitalization that the freer treatment of acknowledged fiction could give it.

James Fenimore Cooper (1789–1851) perfected the form of the frontier romance in his Leatherstocking Tales (1823–1841), a popular series of fictions built around a frontiersman protagonist, Natty Bumppo, and his noble Indian companion, Chingachgook. The cast of characters included a white hero and heroine and assorted villains, both red and white. Many of the novels' "good" characters were captured by "bad" Indians, who were usually extravagantly described as blood-drinking devils. The action of *The Last of the Mohicans* (1826), the most ambitious of these tales, is driven by serial captivity married to a Romantic plot that requires the union of hero and heroine as well as the defeat of the enemy Indians.

Later in the century western settlers often blamed Cooper, as the foremost of a large group of contemporary writers, for a romanticized image of Indians that they found to be inaccurate to frontier experience. But this widely held view was unfair: the Romantic tradition in which Cooper wrote dominated American literature until the Civil War. Moreover, whether friend or foe, his Indians were always decisively portrayed as inferior. Like most of his countrymen at the time, Cooper stresses what he regards as differences between Indians and whites rather than a common humanity. Each race has its "gifts" or special abilities: Indians are proficient in wilderness skills, for example, whereas whites are masters of technology. Not surprisingly, because Cooper was a white author writing for white readers, his Indians can never fully acquire white habits and abilities and thus are doomed to extinction, but white characters can best the Indian on his home ground. Cooper has survived where so many of his contemporaries in the genre are unknown today because he transcends his predictable plots and racial stereotypes with a poetic sensitivity to the vanishing wilderness.

Two other writers of notable frontier romances, Lydia Maria Child (1802–1880) and Catharine Maria Sedgwick (1789–1867), have been rehabilitated by the work of feminist recuperation. In Child's *Hobomok* (1824) a white woman whose fiancé appears to have been lost at sea proposes marriage to a noble Indian, the title character. The novel treats this union as anomalous from its bizarre beginning in the heroine's superstitious ritual to its end when the missing hero reappears and (re)claims her. Although Hobomok and his wife have had a child, he willingly relinquishes his family and simply disappears. His son is educated at Harvard and Cambridge, retaining—one can assume—no trace of his Indian heritage. Child's substitution of assimilation for genocide was extraordinary for her time. Although she became better known as an abolitionist, Child retained an interest in Indians, criticizing their treatment by the Puritans in *The First Settlers of New-England* (1828) and returning to the subject late in life with *An Appeal for the Indians* (1868). Sedgwick's popular novel *Hope Leslie* (1827) is even more exceptional in allowing a white woman, the victim of captivity, to marry an Indian and reject white civilization, yet not die. She and her husband are the only interracial couple in the frontier romance to be granted a happy ending, although their union produces no new generation, perhaps because of the prevailing view that the offspring of mixed-race unions combined the worst of both races. In any case this woman is not the novel's white heroine. Sedgwick's treatment of Magawisca, the good Indian maiden, is more conventional. She loves the white hero but understands that their different races must keep them apart.

If in the frontier romance both good and bad Indians generally die at the end—in keeping with the popular assumption that whatever their individual qualities, they belonged to a dying race—in one subgroup of this fiction a protagonist dedicates himself to tracking down and killing Indians. This single-minded devotion to genocide is explained as the result of a family trauma inflicted by Indians, at times the killing of parents and siblings, at others of wife and children. Such works as Robert Montgomery Bird's *Nick of the Woods* (1837) and James Hall's account of the historical

Colonel John Moredock in *Sketches of the West* (1835), the source of Herman Melville's Indian hater episode in *The Confidence-Man* (1857), represent a central figure who lives like an Indian in order to hunt Indians. In keeping with the overriding superiority of whites, the Indian hater surpasses his quarry in seeking revenge, stalking, and killing—as well as in "wilderness skills"—and in so doing, relinquishes some of his acculturation as a white man. Driven by a compulsion to kill Indians that only ends with his death, the Indian hater cannot be contained within his own frontier society. Nevertheless, he embodies its feelings and values: he acts on the communal belief system about Indians that has produced him.

Outside the frontier romance, there were literary figures of stature whose attitude toward Indians was sympathetic. Among writers of fiction, Melville (1819–1891) is preeminent in portraying Indians as worthy of respect, whereas Nathaniel Hawthorne (1804–1864) often represents them as victims of Puritan intolerance. Henry David Thoreau (1817–1862) had a lifelong fascination with Indians, and Washington Irving (1783–1859) wrote an impassioned defense of King Philip as a warrior whose heroic qualities and achievements merited the respectful treatment of poets and historians. But Irving also realized that a truthful account of New World settlement, one that emphasized the "dark story" of wrongs done to Indians, would challenge the investment of white readers in the desirability of a settled Christian people supplanting nomadic heathens and in the greatness of the country's pioneer forebears.

Henry Wadsworth Longfellow (1807–1882) created the most popular version of the American Indian as noble savage with his long poem *The Song of Hiawatha* (1855), modeled on the Finnish epic *Kalevala*. Longfellow adapted legends and myths from the pioneering work of Henry Rowe Schoolcraft, published in various volumes of *Algic Researches*. Longfellow's Hiawatha exists in prehistory; when the white man appears in his country, he gracefully withdraws, in keeping with the widely held American belief that Indians would simply die out.

INDIAN WRITERS

Belonging to oral cultures, Indians left little trace as writers during this time, but their eloquence as speakers was often preserved in school textbooks. American children were especially familiar with the poignant farewell address of Chief Logan, who lamented with stark simplicity the massacre of his entire family. One exceptional case deserves mention: in a five-year period, a Pequot Indian named William Apess (1798–1839) published five works, including an autobiography, *A Son of the Forest* (1829), and a eulogy on King Philip (1836) that compares the Indian leader to George Washington. Apess liberated himself from servitude and parlayed his scanty education into a career as a Methodist minister, a writer, and an activist instrumental in securing the right of self-government to the Mashpee Pequots. The rest of Apess's life has left no historical trace. Scholarly interest in recuperating minority experience may unearth more evidence of Apess and bring to light nineteenth-century texts written by other Indian writers (a few exist in manuscript).

See also Captivity Narratives; Cherokee Memorials; Ethnology; *Hope Leslie;* Indian Wars and Dispossession; "An Indian's Looking-Glass for the White Man"; Leatherstocking Tales; Native American Literature; *The Song of Hiawatha;* Trail of Tears

BIBLIOGRAPHY

Primary Works

Apess, William. *On Our Own Ground: The Complete Writings of William Apess, a Pequot.* Edited and with an introduction by Barry O'Connell. Amherst: University of Massachusetts Press, 1992.

Child, Lydia Maria. *Hobomok and Other Writings on Indians.* 1824. Edited and with an introduction by Carolyn L. Karcher. New Brunswick, N.J.: Rutgers University Press, 1986.

Cooper, James Fenimore. *The Last of the Mohicans.* 1826. Albany: State University of New York Press, 1983.

Jackson, Helen Hunt. *A Century of Dishonor.* 1881. St. Clair Shores, Mich.: Scholarly Press, 1964.

Sedgwick, Catharine Maria. *Hope Leslie.* 1827. Edited by Mary Kelley. New Brunswick, N.J.: Rutgers University Press, 1987.

Secondary Works

Barnett, Louise K. *The Ignoble Savage: American Literary Racism, 1790–1890.* Westport, Conn.: Greenwood, 1975.

Berkhofer, Robert F., Jr. *The White Man's Indian: Images of the American Indian from Columbus to the Present.* New York: Alfred A. Knopf, 1978.

Dippie, Brian W. *The Vanishing American: White Attitudes and U.S. Indian Policy.* Middletown, Conn.: Wesleyan University Press, 1982.

Horsman, Reginald. *Race and Manifest Destiny: The Origins of American Racial Anglo-Saxonism.* Cambridge, Mass.: Harvard University Press, 1981.

Jaskoski, Helen, ed. *Early Native American Writing: New Critical Essays.* Cambridge and New York: Cambridge University Press, 1996.

Krupat, Arnold. "Native American Autobiography and the Synecdochic Self." In *American Autobiography: Retrospect and Prospect,* edited by Paul John Eakin, pp. 171–194. Madison: University of Wisconsin Press, 1991.

McLuhan, T. C., ed. *Touch the Earth: A Self-Portrait of Indian Existence.* New York: Outerbridge and Dienstrey, 1971.

Rogin, Michael Paul. *Fathers and Children: Andrew Jackson and the Subjugation of the American Indian.* New York: Vintage Books, 1976.

Trachtenberg, Alan. *Shades of Hiawatha: Staging Indians, Making Americans, 1880–1930.* New York: Hill and Wang, 2004.

Louise Barnett

"AN INDIAN'S LOOKING-GLASS FOR THE WHITE MAN"

Almost forgotten until the late 1970s, the writing of William Apess—"Apess" has become standard although the name is also sometimes spelled "Apes"—a Pequot, exists today in a volume of complete works and in a growing body of critical work. His extraordinary essay "An Indian's Looking-Glass for the White Man" (1833) is a powerful indictment of what Apess called color prejudice and what would today be called racism.

William Apess was born in 1798 in the small town of Colrain, Massachusetts, some distance from North Stonington and Ledyard, Connecticut, where his people, the Pequots, mostly resided on two small reservations. Early in his life his parents moved back to Connecticut and unfortunately entrusted his care to his alcoholic grandparents who beat him severely and then sold him as an indentured laborer when he was only four or five years old. Apess eventually ran off from his master's house and, later, although still a very young man, participated in the unsuccessful American attack on Montreal in the War of 1812. He had taken up drinking in the army, and after leaving it in 1815 he wandered about and held a number of odd jobs. In 1813 he had had a religious experience, and he turned to evangelical Methodism to help him regain control of his life. He was baptized into the church in 1818 and was ordained a minister in 1829. Apess died in New York in 1839, apparently of alcoholism.

Apess's first publication was a full-scale autobiography, *A Son of the Forest: The Experience of William Apes, a Native of the Forest* (1829), the first such text to be written entirely by a Native American person. (An earlier, eighteenth-century autobiographical text by a Mohican, the Reverend Samson Occom, was only

William Apess. Portrait engraving from the frontispiece to *A Son of the Forest*, 1829.

a sketch of several pages, and for some time Native American autobiographies would, for the most part, be dictations to one or another white person.) Apess followed this with an abbreviated version of his life story along with short biographies of his wife and four other native converts to Christianity in *The Experiences of Five Christian Indians of the Pequ'd Tribe* (1833). As the conclusion to this book, Apess published "An Indian's Looking-Glass." (He did not reprint it when the *Experiences* was reissued in 1837.) In 1836 Apess published the last of his works, the eulogy for Metacom, or King Philip, a leader of the Wampanoag nation in the seventeenth century, claiming Philip as a distant ancestor and calling him "the greatest man that ever lived upon the American shores" (p. 290).

RHETORICAL STRATEGIES IN "THE INDIAN'S LOOKING-GLASS"

Careful attention to "An Indian's Looking-Glass" will note the ways it works against the dominant society's racialist construction of Indians as an inferior race and employs a still-powerful religious discourse to insist

that native people and people of color generally are equal to whites in the sight of God.

Although "An Indian's Looking-Glass" was not delivered orally by Apess, its oratorical style is immediately apparent. The regular use of direct address—although the address is always to the "reader"—and the number of insistent interrogatives—"Now I ask," "Now I would ask," and so on—all suggest a situation in which a speaker stands before an audience, sometimes sharply pointing a finger. It is tempting to assign this tactic to the influence upon Apess of some form of traditional Native American oral performance, but he nowhere writes of Pequot or any other native oral performances. (He says almost nothing, in any of his work, about New England native cultures.) Thus, without entirely ruling out the possibility that native oral performance of one sort or another might possibly have influenced Apess, it seems reasonable to point out that he lived in a time when the lecture hall—which might feature Ralph Waldo Emerson, Henry David Thoreau, or Frederick Douglass—and the pulpit provided abundant examples of the powers of oratory.

Well aware that Indian peoples in popular discourse had regularly been consigned to passivity (because they are inferior to the more active whites) and to the past (they are a last remnant, a doomed and dying race), Apess opens with words that insist upon the active presence and equality of at least one Indian person, the author himself: "Having a desire to place a few things before my fellow creatures. . . ." By opening with the participial "Having," and the characterization of his audience as his "fellow creatures," Apess asserts the activity, contemporaneity, and equality of the Indian writer. This is reinforced by his second sentence: "*Now* I ask if degradation has not been heaped long enough upon the Indians?" (p. 155, emphasis added). Apess will go on to pose many troubling questions to his readers.

He will also stir their thoughts and emotions with his wordplay. In his third paragraph, for example, Apess writes of the white neighbors of the Indians that they are people "who have no principle" (p. 156), and in the second sentence of his fourth paragraph he asks whether Indians are not "said to be men of talents" (p. 156). Principles and talents are, of course, moral and intellectual or cultural qualities. But both these words also reference the economic and financial: principle and interest, this is to say, are words that have to do with money, and "talents" appear in the Bible as monetary units. Apess will develop the notion that the materially well-off whites are not at all superior to the Indians from a religious and moral perspective because they are unprincipled—bankrupt—when it comes to dealing with those of a different skin color. Indeed, his fourth paragraph has no fewer than five uses of the word "principle" or a variant, and in every case this is to establish the *un*principled actions of white men in regard to red men (p. 156).

Apess uses "black" as an adjective metaphorically to describe morals—principles—that have become corrupted by an aversion to literally black or colored skin. He writes of "the impure black principle . . . as corrupt and unholy as it can be" (p. 156), of color prejudice, leading to his notation of the "black inconsistency that you place before me," the extremely bad "principle" of considering "skins of color—more disgraceful than all the skins that Jehovah ever made" (p. 157). Not only is this bad, but it is absurd, for if "black or red skins or any other skin of color" were disgraceful in God's eye, "it appears that he has disgraced himself a great deal—for he has made fifteen colored people to one white and placed them here upon this earth" (p. 157).

All of this is, obviously enough, delivered with a full freight of irony, and Apess's use of irony as a rhetorical device is something we might have noted earlier. His first strong irony, for example, appears in only the seventh paragraph of his text, where he writes, "But, reader, I acknowledge that this is a confused world, and I am not seeking for office, but merely [!] placing before you the *black* inconsistency that you place before me—which is ten times *blacker* than any skin that you will find in the universe" (p. 157, emphasis added). Apess will use ironic discourse again and again to induce the sort of shame in his audience that might produce a revolution in moral feeling.

It is in his eighth paragraph that Apess launches his bitter and powerful indictment of the white man's crimes and a strong challenge to his presumptive racial superiority. Echoing the strategy with which he began, he poses a rhetorical question: "Now let me ask you, white man. . . ." He then offers the truly horrifying possibility that if all the world's "different skins were put together, and each skin had its national crimes written upon it—which skin do you think would have the greatest?" (p. 157). We have noted earlier that Apess links his outrage at the mistreatment of Indians to the mistreatment of blacks. In this particular paragraph, Apess's charge against the white citizens of the United States is not only that they have robbed "a *nation* almost of their whole continent, and murder[ed] their women and children" but as well that they have robbed "another *nation* to till their grounds and welter out their days under the lash with hunger and fatigue under the scorching rays of a burning sun" (p. 157, emphasis added). The verb choice—

"welter"—is interesting in that Apess knows well that "the lash" raises "welts" on the backs of black men and women, *writing,* as it were, on their skin.

Perhaps most extraordinary in this indictment of the United States is Apess's repeated use of the word "nation" and his complete avoidance of the word "race." Racialist thought was abundant in Apess's time, and it would soon become the dominant discourse for the expression of difference. The word "race," this is to say, was in common usage in a great deal of American writing by 1833 (it would become even more common later in the century), but it does not appear even once in "An Indian's Looking-Glass." (Apess does occasionally use it in other of his writings.) It is surely no accident that Apess here refers to Indians and Africans not as races but as nations, a potent political term.

CHRISTIANITY

Apess's counter-discourse, as we have noted, grounds itself in religious doctrine. Thus Apess can rhetorically ask, "Is not religion the same now under a colored skin as it ever was? If so, I would ask, why is not a man of color respected?" (p. 158). He goes on to adduce biblical support for these arguments, noting that "Jesus and his Apostles never looked at the outward appearances. Jesus in particular looked at the hearts, . . . and his Apostles . . . looked at their fruit without any regard to the skin, color, or nation" (p. 158). Directly addressing his audience, he throws out the challenge, "But you may ask: Who are the children of God? Perhaps you may say, none but white. If so, the word of the Lord is not true" (p. 159). At this point Apess boldly engages what he knows may be for some the unacknowledged heart of these matters: "Perhaps you will say that if we admit you to all of these privileges you will want more. I expect I can guess what that is—Why, say you, there would be intermarriages" (p. 159). This "would be nothing strange or new to me," Apess writes. He then virtually taunts his audience, noting, "I do not wonder that you blush, many of you, while you read," becoming thus as *red* as those against whom those "many" discriminate. He continues in this vein of irony, assuring the reader that he is "not looking for a wife, having one of the finest cast" (p. 160).

Apess's penultimate paragraph repeats what has been central to his argument thus far, as the author again addresses the reader directly: "By what you read, you may learn how deep your principles are. I should say they were skin deep" (p. 160). He assures the reader that many "men of fame" advocate the cause of the Indians, among them such luminaries of the period as Daniel Webster, Edward Everett, and William Wirt. He takes pains to conclude on a positive note, exhorting his readers to be hopeful:

> Do not get tired, ye noble-hearted—only think how many poor Indians want their wounds done up daily; the Lord will reward you, and pray you stop not till this tree of distinction be leveled, and the mantle of prejudice torn from every American heart—then shall peace pervade the Union. (Pp. 160–161)

William Apess would continue to speak out against race prejudice, most particularly in his "Eulogy on King Philip" in 1836, raising a powerful voice in favor of equal rights and justice for all.

See also Crime and Punishment; Evangelicals; Indian Wars and Dispossession; Indians; Methodists; Native American Literature; Oratory; Rhetoric

BIBLIOGRAPHY

Primary Work

Apess, William. *On Our Own Ground: The Complete Writings of William Apess, a Pequot.* Edited by Barry O'Connell. Amherst: University of Massachusetts Press, 1992.

Secondary Works

Donaldson, Laura. "Son of the Forest, Child of God: William Apess and the Scene of Postcolonial Nativity." In *Postcolonial America,* edited by C. Richard King. Urbana: University of Illinois Press, 2000.

Krupat, Arnold. "Monologue and Dialogue in Native American Autobiography." In his *The Voice in the Margin: Native American Literature and the Canon.* Berkeley: University of California Press, 1989.

Murray, David. "Christian Indians: Samson Occom and William Apes." In his *Forked Tongues: Speech, Writing, and Representation in North American Indian Texts.* Bloomington: University of Indiana Press, 1991.

Walker, Cheryl. "The Irony and Mimicry of William Apess." In her *Indian Nation: Native American Literature and Nineteenth-Century Nationalisms.* Durham, N.C.: Duke University Press, 1997.

Arnold Krupat

INDIAN WARS AND DISPOSSESSION

In Colorado Territory in 1864, Colonel John Chivington, a Civil War veteran, led a band of Colorado militia against an encampment of Cheyenne and Arapaho Indians at Sand Creek. "I have come to kill Indians, and believe it is right and honorable . . . to kill Indians," Chivington is reported to have said before the attack (quoted in Brown, p. 85). His raid killed 105 Indian women and children and 28 Indian men. Black Kettle, leader of the Cheyenne, was holding an American flag attached to a pole as Chivington's riders bore down. The local paper, the *Daily Rocky Mountain News,* quoted Chivington's own description of the raid as "a victory unparallelled in the history of Indian warfare" (quoted in Coward, p. 112). Later one of Chivington's men wrote, "In going over the battle-ground the next day I did not see a body of a man, woman, or child but was scalped, and in many instances their bodies were mutilated in the most horrrible manner" (quoted in Brown, p. 89). Nothing of this was reported at the time.

The disparity between newspaper accounts of Indian fights in this period and the actual facts of the matter leads John Coward to some sober conclusions. "Indian war reporters," he writes, "approached the West with a set of ideas about Indians. . . . there was no 'Indian side' to the Indian wars . . . because Indians had no legitimate standing in the public conception of the West" (p. 132). If there was no "Indian side" to the "Indian wars" in the press, how was the history of Indian removal and dispossession represented in the literature of the period? Did the nineteenth-century literary author, any more than the nineteenth-century journalist, propose an "Indian side" to the story of Euro-American–Native American relations?

For the most part, the answer is no. Too many powerful sets "of ideas about Indians" got in the way. Even for us to see an "Indian side" to the story today requires, as the historian Francis Jennings puts it, some "painful revision of the pleasant myths we all learned in grade school" about the "winning of the west." The central myth—what others have called the myth of the frontier—offers a narrative of decent folk "setting out with their families to conquer the wilderness and create civilization . . . these sturdy, God-fearing folk endure all the hazards and toil of their mission, standing constantly at arms to fend off attacks by savage denizens of the wilderness." This myth of the ever-advancing frontier of civilization, Jennings writes, is "nationalist and racist propaganda to justify conquest of *persons* who happen to be Indians, and their dispossession" (p. 312).

There were a great many novels, histories, biographies and autobiographies, poems, plays, burlesques, and even operas in this period that took Indians as their subject matter. Few of the authors who wrote them are among those we consider important today, but all, major and minor figures alike, believed that native people, even those who were their contemporaries, were essentially relics of the past, last remnants of a dying race. The belief that human beings were divided into distinct "races" and that some "races" were inferior to others became widespread in the United States by the 1830s. This belief held that Indian "savages" were "fated" to vanish before the superior "race" of "civilized" Anglo-Saxons or "Caucasians," and there was no changing fate.

Even the writers who later came to be considered the major literary authors of the period, some of whom were decidedly sympathetic to the Indians, for the most part believed that Indians were destined or fated to "vanish." We will examine the representation of Indians in the work of these authors because it is a very important, if often neglected, aspect of their work. However, it needs to be said, in fairness, that to judge these authors solely from this perspective would be to flatten out and simplify their work. Only the Reverend William Apess, a Pequot, succeeds in fully dramatizing an "Indian side" to America's history, the progress of "civilization," as it were, from the point of view of its victims.

INDIAN REMOVAL OR DISPOSSESSION

From a historical perspective, the year 1820 may be viewed as marking the two hundredth anniversary of European settlers' invasion of Native America, a period during which native tribal nations were substantially reduced in their numbers and lands by force of germs and force of arms. In 1620 the *Mayflower* pilgrims landed in Provincetown Bay, making their way farther up Cape Cod, eventually to found Plymouth Plantation on Indian lands. In 1630 a fleet of Puritans from England arrived, and soon Massachusetts Bay Colony was established, also on lands occupied by indigenous—native—people. Indians mostly sided with the British during the Revolutionary War and, having chosen the losing side, were forced to make the best deal they could with the citizens of the new United States. Native people again sided with the British in the War of 1812, with assurances that this time the king would not lay down the tomahawk until Indian rights and claims were fairly met. Nonetheless, at the war's end in 1815 England left its Indian allies no better off than they had been before.

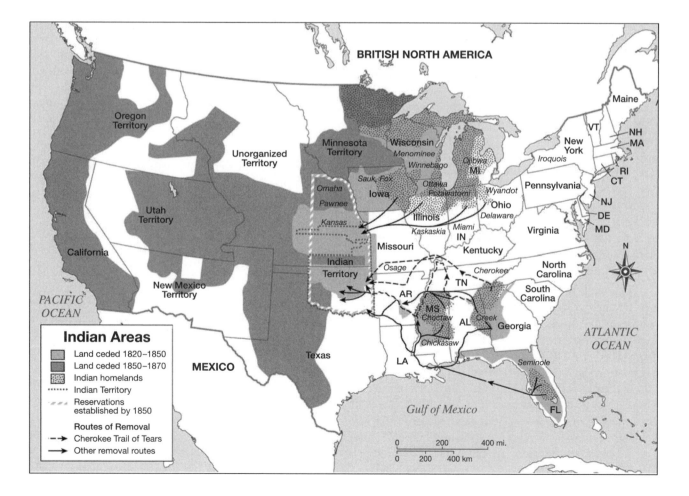

In the next half century, from 1820 to 1870, Americans continued to displace tribal nations from the Southeast, Southwest, and the eastern plains, violently reducing the number of California Indians by some two-thirds. Andrew Jackson, who had defeated the Creeks of southern Georgia in 1814, forcing them to cede no fewer than twenty million acres of land to the United States, was elected president in 1828. An important part of Jackson's program was "Indian Removal," the relocation of southeastern tribes to lands (already occupied by other native peoples) west of the Mississippi.

The Cherokees of Georgia were a major target for removal. By the time of Jackson's election the Cherokees had a written language, a constitution modeled after that of the United States, and the first newspaper (the Cherokee *Phoenix*, established in 1828) to publish in an indigenous language and in English. Many Cherokee people had converted to Christianity and had extensive agricultural plantings. Large Cherokee landholders also owned slaves. In response to Jackson's removal policy, the Cherokees sent a number of "memorials"—documents roughly having the status of petitions—to Congress arguing their sovereignty (that is, their legal status as domestic *independent* nations). They also published these in their newspaper and encouraged papers in the East sympathetic to the Cherokees' plight to reprint the memorials.

Nonetheless, in 1830 the Indian Removal Act, granting the president the authority to enter into treaties with the eastern tribes for their removal west of the Mississippi, was passed by Congress. Jackson immediately worked for the removal of the Cherokees and also of the other four so-called Five Civilized Tribes, the Choctaws, Chickasaws, Creeks, and Seminoles. Cherokee removal by federal troops under General Winfield Scott in 1838 gave rise to the Trail of Tears, the bitter trek in winter to Indian Territory, present-day Oklahoma, a forced march in which some four thousand persons out of a population of thirteen thousand died.

Less well known is the suffering of some of the midwestern tribes. The Winnebagos, for example, whose home was in the area of the Wisconsin River, ceded land no fewer than seven times in the period from 1829 to 1866, moving some six times, their population declining by 50 percent. As a result of the Black Hawk War of 1832, the last Indian war fought (mostly) east of the Mississippi, Chief Black Hawk's Sauk people of Iowa were seriously restricted. As we shall also note below in regard to King Philip's War in the seventeenth century, to call what happened to Black Hawk's people a "war," Herman Viola believes,

"stretches all credulity, for at most 70 whites lost their lives, whereas nearly all of the Indian group of 500 men, women and children perished" (quoted in Kennedy, "Margaret Fuller," p. 7).

Following the Mexican-American War of 1848, American victory led not only to massive land acquisitions—Arizona, New Mexico, and southern California—but to conflict with Navajo and Apache people in those areas. The California gold rush of 1849 brought a great number of prospectors to the territory, many of whom regarded the local Indians as less than human, often shooting them on sight. As the U.S. commissioner of Indian Affairs, Adam Johnson, himself acknowledged, "The majority of [California] tribes are kept in constant fear on account of the indiscriminate and inhuman massacre of their people" (quoted in Jennings, p. 366).

In 1862, while the attention of the northern states was primarily focused on the Civil War with the South, Indians once more required attention. In Minnesota, crowded by the advancing Euro-Americans, upset by the delay in payments agreed to by the U.S. government in exchange for their lands, and with many of their people starving, a large number of Santee Sioux along with some Wahpeton and Sisseton Sioux attacked settlements in Minnesota, killing some five hundred settlers and soldiers. When the uprising was put down, in addition to those Indians killed, wounded, and imprisoned, 303 Santees were sentenced to be hanged. Notified of the sentences, President Abraham Lincoln (who as a young man had fought against Black Hawk's Indians) asked to review the trial records. A report to the president concluded that those records showed a failure to differentiate between Indian people guilty of capital crimes and those guilty of far lesser infractions. In the interest of justice Lincoln commuted the sentences of all but thirty-eight of the condemned Indians. Yet by May 1863 the remaining Santee nonetheless began to be shipped out of the state to the Crow Creek reservation on the Missouri River in Dakota Territory.

About this time in the Southwest, Kit Carson was enlisted by the government to help pacify the Navajo. Carson's policy of destroying their crops, livestock, and peach orchards forced the Navajo to submit, leading in 1864 to the Long Walk in winter from Fort Canby and Fort Wingate to Fort Sumner in New Mexico. Many Navajo people did not survive the journey or the captivity.

We have already mentioned Chivington's 1864 raid in Colorado Territory against the peaceful encampment of Black Kettle and his people at Sand Creek.

Indian Battles, 1846–1870

With the end of the Civil War in 1865, former Union troops became available for duty on the plains and in the Southwest. Thus it was that in 1868 the Civil War general George Armstrong Custer, soon to achieve legendary status for his "last stand" against the Cheyenne and Lakota (Sioux) on the Little Bighorn River in 1876, managed to do what Chivington had not: to kill Black Kettle, who was this time camped with his people on the Washita River. Custer and his men killed 103 Cheyennes, only 11 of them men of fighting age.

By the time the Bureau of the Census declared the "frontier" closed in 1890, most of the country's Indian nations had been reduced in numbers, penned on reservation lands, or both, and American destiny, as the nineteenth century approached its end, could be seen to have manifested itself in the achievement of domination "from sea to shining sea."

INDIAN DISPOSSESSION AND THE CANONICAL AUTHORS

For Nathaniel Hawthorne (1804–1864), Indians are most often savages in league with the devil. Their expertise in the use of medicinal herbs is useful to the malevolent Chillingworth in *The Scarlet Letter* (1850), and Chillingworth may also have learned the pleasures of revenge from the Indians. Near the novel's conclusion, when there seems yet a possibility that Hester Prynne and the Reverend Arthur Dimmesdale, the father of her child, may go off together, leaving the constraints of Puritanism in seventeenth-century

SELECTED WORKS WITH INDIAN SUBJECTS, 1820–1870

The works listed below are intended to give some idea of the extent and variety of writing that dealt substantially with Native Americans in the period 1820–1870. Many of the works included are literary in the current sense of the word—novels, poems, plays, tales, romances, and autobiographies. Others testify to a change in our understanding of the category of literature. In this period, for example, captivity narratives—stories, most of them true, but some fictitious—about persons captured and held by Indians qualified as literature. Even some of the titles labeled "history" are written in a style and a manner that today looks more nearly literary than strictly historical. Melodramas and burlesques then were probably literature, although today we would add the qualifying adjectives "popular," or even "bad." The reader will notice the degree to which most of those whom we now consider to be the major authors of the period are not represented on this list. Also to be noted are the writings of some few, but important, Native American authors.

1820: James W. Eastburn and Robert Sands, *Yamoyden, a Tale of the Wars of King Philip: In Six Cantos.*

Washington Irving, *Sketch Book of Geoffrey Crayon, Gent.* (Reprints "Philip of Pokanoket" and "Traits of Indian Character.")

1821: Joseph Doddridge, *Logan, the Last of the Race of Shikellemus, Chief of the Cayuga Nation.* (Play.)

1822: John Neal, *Logan.* (Sensational fiction.)

1823: Elias Boudinot (Buck Watie, Cherokee), *Poor Sarah; or, Religion Exemplified in the Life and Death of an Indian Woman.* (Religious tract attributed to Boudinot, who may not have written it but did translate it into Cherokee.)

Lewis Cass, *Inquiries, Respecting the History, Traditions, Languages, Manners, Customs, Religion, &c. of the Indians, Living in the United States.* (This was an official survey by Cass, governor of Minnesota Territory.)

James Fenimore Cooper, *The Pioneers; or, The Sources of the Susquehanna: A Descriptive Tale.*

John Dunn Hunter, *Memoirs of a Captivity among the Indians of North America.*

1824: Lydia Maria Child, *Hobomok: A Tale of Early Times.* (Novel.)

James E. Seaver, ed., *A Narrative of the Life of Mrs. Mary Jemison, Who Was Taken by Indians in the Year 1755.* (Captivity narrative.)

1825: Rufus B. Anderson, ed., *Memoir of Catharine Brown, a Christian Indian of the Cherokee Nation.* (Biography and collected letters.)

1826: Elias Boudinot (Buck Watie, Cherokee), *An Address to the Whites. Delivered in the First Presbyterian Church* [probably Philadelphia] *on the 26th of May 1826.* (Argument that Indians are capable of becoming as "civilized" as whites.)

James Fenimore Cooper, *The Last of the Mohicans; or, A Narrative of 1757.*

1827: James Fenimore Cooper, *The Prairie: A Tale.*

David Cusick (Tuscarora), *Sketches of Ancient History of the Six Nations.*

Catharine Maria Sedgwick, *Hope Leslie; or, Early Times in the Massachusetts.* (Novel.)

1828: Lydia Maria Child, *The First Settlers of New-England; or, Conquest of the Pequods, Narragansets, and Pokanokets: As Related by a Mother to Her Children, and Designed for the Instruction of Youth.*

1829: William Apess (Pequot), *A Son of the Forest.* (Autobiography.)

James Fenimore Cooper, *The Wept of Wish-ton-wish.* (Novel.)

1830: John Augustus Stone, *Metamora; or, The Last of the Wampanoags.* (Play, first performance.)

John Tanner, *A Narrative of the Captivity and Adventures of John Tanner,* ed. Edwin James.

1831: Richard Peters, *The Case of the Cherokee Nation against the State of Georgia.*

Henry Whiting, *Sannillac, a Poem, by Henry Whiting. With Notes by Lewis Cass and Henry Rowe Schoolcraft, Esqs.*

1832: Samuel G. Drake, *Biography and History of the Indians of North America.*

James Hall, *Legends of the West.*

B. B. Thatcher, *Indian Biography; or, An Historical Account of Those Individuals Who Have Been Distinguished among the North American Natives, as Orators, Warriors, Statesmen, and Other Remarkable Characters.* (This went through many editions over many years.)

1833: William Apess (Pequot), *The Experiences of Five Christian Indians of the Pequ'd Tribe.* (Autobiography and biography; concludes with "An Indian's Looking-Glass for the White Man.")

Black Hawk (Sauk), *Life of Ma-ka-tai-me-she-kia-kiak or Black Hawk,* ed. J. B. Patterson. (Autobiography.)

1834: Richard Emmons, *Tecumseh.* (Play, first performance.)

1835: William Apess, *Indian Nullification of the Unconstitutional Laws of Massachusetts Relative to the Marshpee Tribe; or, The Pretended Riot Explained.* (Account of Apess work among the Mashpee to obtain an extension of their rights.)

James Hall, *Sketches of History, Life, and Manners in the West.* (Contains the sketch "The Indian Hater.")

Washington Irving, *A Tour of the Prairies.*

William Gilmore Simms, *The Yemassee, a Romance of Carolina.*

1836: William Apess (Pequot), "Eulogy on King Philip."

1837: Robert Bird, *Nick of the Woods; or, The Jibbenainosay: A Tale of Kentucky.* (Novel.)

1838: Benjamin Drake, *The Life and Adventures of Black Hawk: With Sketches of Keokuk, the Sac and Fox Indians, and the Late Blackhawk War.*

1839: Samuel G. Drake, *Tragedies of the Wilderness . . . .* (Captivity narratives.)

1840: James Fenimore Cooper, *The Pathfinder; or, The Inland Sea.* (Novel.)

1841: George Catlin, *Letters and Notes on the Manners, Customs, and Condition of the North American Indians, by George Catlin. Written during Eight Years' Travel amongst the Wildest Tribes of Indians in North America. In 1832, 33, 34, 35, 36, 37, 38, and 39, with Four Hundred Illustrations Engraved from His Original Paintings.* (Also published in London and reprinted many times with varying numbers of engravings of the paintings.)

James Fenimore Cooper, *The Deerslayer; or, The First War-Path: A Tale.*

Benjamin Drake, *Life of Tecumseh, and of His Brother the Prophet; with a Historical Sketch of the Shawanoe Indians.*

1842: William L. Stone, *Uncas and Miantonomah: A Historical Discourse Delivered at Norwich* (Connecticut) *on the Fourth Day of July, 1842, on the Occasion of the Erection of a Monument to the Memory of Uncas, the White Man's Friend, and First Chief of the Mohegans.* (This book is 209 pages long, so presumably Stone did not "deliver" all of it on the Fourth of July.)

1844: Margaret Fuller, *Summer on the Lakes, in 1843.* (Travel account with references to Black Hawk and the Black Hawk War.)

1845: Henry Rowe Schoolcraft, *Onéota; or, The Red Race of America.* (Popular version of his collection of Indian myths and legends.)

1846: Henry Rowe Schoolcraft, *Notes on the Iroquois.* (Report to the government on the possibility of "civilizing" the Iroquois.)

1847: John Brougham, *Metamora; or, The Last of the Pollywogs.* (Burlesque.)

George Copway (Ojibwe), *The Life, History, and Travels of Kah-ge-ga-gah-bowh (George Copway).*

Henry Rowe Schoolcraft, *Historical and Statistical Information Respecting the History, Condition, and Prospects of the Indian Tribes of the United States . . . Prepared for the Bureau of Indian Affairs.* (Further volumes of this massive work were issued from 1851 to 1857.)

1848: George Henry (Maungwudaus, Ojibwe), *An Account of the Ojibway Indians.*

1849: Mary Henderson Eastman, *Dahcotah: or, Life and Legends of the Sioux around Fort Snelling.*

Elbert H. Smith, *Ma-ka-tai-me-she-kia-kiak; or, Black Hawk, and Scenes in the West: A National Poem in Six Cantos.*

Francis Parkman, *The California and Oregon Trail: Being Sketches of Prairie and Rocky Mountain Life.*

1850: Lewis H. Garrard, *Wah-to-yah and the Taos Trail; or, Prairie Travel and Scalp Dances with a Look at Los Rancheros from Muleback and the Rocky Mountain Camp-fire.* (An extraordinary account by a seventeen-year-old from Cleveland who was part of a militia that helped retake Taos after the uprising of 1847.)

1851: George Copway (Ojibwe), *The Traditional History and Characteristic Sketches of the Ojibway Nation.*

Lewis Henry Morgan, *League of the Ho-do-no-sau-nee or Iroquois.* (Full-scale study of the Iroquois.)

Henry Rowe Schoolcraft, *Personal Memoirs of a Residence of Thirty Years with the Indian Tribes on the American Frontiers 1812–42.*

1852: John A. McClung, *Sketches of Western Adventure.* (Includes many captivity narratives.)

1853: Mary Henderson Eastman, *The Romance of Indian Life.* (Poems, tales, and chromolithographs.)

1854: John Rollin Ridge (Yellow Bird, Cherokee), *The Life and Adventures of Joaquín Murieta, the Celebrated California Bandit.* (Novel.)

1855: Henry Wadsworth Longfellow, *The Song of Hiawatha.* (Epic poem.)

John Brougham, *An Original Aboriginal Erratic Operatic Semi-Civilized and Demi-Savage Extravaganza, Being a Per-Version of ye Trewe and Wonderfulle Hystorie of ye Renownned Princesse Pocahontas; or, The Gentle Savage.*

1856: Henry Rowe Schoolcraft, *The Myth of Hiawatha, and Other Oral Legends, Mythologic and Allegoric of the North American Indians.*

Charles M. Walcot, *Hiawatha; or, Ardent Spirits and Laughing Water, a Musical Extravaganza.*

1857: Royal B. Stratton, *Captivity of the Oatman Girls: Being an Interesting Narrative of Life among the Apache and Mojave Indians.*

1858: Sylvester Crakes, *Five Years a Captive among the Black-Feet Indians . . . Endured by John Dixon.* (Fictitious captivity narrative.)

1859: William Gilmore Simms, *The Cassique of Kiawah: A Colonial Romance.*

1861: Peter Jones (Ojibwe), *History of the Ojibway Indians.* (Published posthumously by his English wife.)

1864: Ann Coleson, *Miss Coleson's Narrative of Her Captivity among the Sioux Indians . . . a Victim of the Late Indian Outrages in Minnesota.*

1868: Lydia Maria Child, "An Appeal for the Indians."

John Rollin Ridge (Yellow Bird, Cherokee), *Poems.*

1870: Thomas L. McKenney and James Hall, *History of the Indian Tribes of North America.*

Francis Parkman, *The Conspiracy of Pontiac; and the Indian War after the Conquest of Canada.* (History.)

America, Chillingworth, her lawful husband, is seen with some Indians, "wild . . . painted barbarians," but more particularly, with some who are even wilder, "swarthy-cheeked sailors" whom Hawthorne calls "the wild men of the ocean, as the Indians were of the land" (quoted in Maddox, p. 122). Lucy Maddox notes that the sailors' eyes have an "animal ferocity," matching, perhaps, the Indians' "snake-like black eyes" (p. 122). For Hester to join the company of such sailors may once again be to put herself in danger of sin.

Just as Hawthorne had written of the institution of slavery that it was "one of those evils which divine Providence does not leave to be remedied by human contrivances," so too did he believe that Providence would assure that soon only "a few Indian arrowheads shall be treasured up as memorials of a vanished race" (quoted in Arac, p. 254). Divine Providence would, in due time, put an end to slavery, but until then the actions of men and women could produce no "remedy." So too would Providence see to it that native people would vanish, nor could the actions of men and women alter the workings of Providence.

Herman Melville (1819–1891), in his epic novel *Moby-Dick* (1851), names the whaling ship the *Pequod,* which, the narrator, Ishmael says, "you will no doubt remember, was the name of a celebrated tribe of Massachusetts Indians, now extinct as the ancient Medes" (p. 67). It is true that the tribe's numbers had declined considerably by the time Melville wrote, but they were by no means "extinct." Indeed, Melville almost surely knew of the Pequot William Apess, whose last publication appeared in 1836.

But why does Melville compare the Pequots to "the ancient *Medes*" rather than, for example, to the ancient *Greeks,* more familiar to his audience and also "extinct?" The answer would seem to be that the ancient Greeks, founders of classical "civilization," are *our* "racial" ancestors. Pequots cannot be like them even in the matter of extinction; rather, Pequots are only comparable to "ancient Medes," that is, Persians, of who knows what "race," certainly not "ours." (The Pequots continue to exist today and run one of the richest casinos in the world, Foxwoods Resort and Casino in Mashantucket, Connecticut.)

Even living, breathing Indians right before Ishmael's eyes are best comprehended as relics of the past. Ishmael introduces "Tashtego, an unmixed Indian [i.e., pureblood] from Gay Head, the most westerly promontory of Martha's Vineyard, where there still exists the last remnant of a village of red men" (p. 107). Tashtego is described strikingly:

> Tashtego's long, lean, sable hair, his high cheekbones and black rounding eyes—for an Indian, Oriental in their largeness, but Antarctic in their glittering expression—all this sufficiently proclaimed him an inheritor of the unvitiated blood of those proud warrior hunters, who, in quest of the great New England moose, had scoured, bow in hand, the aboriginal forests of the main. (P. 107)

It is obvious that Melville has made Tashtego's people, the Gay Head Indians, a "last remnant," soon perhaps to be as "extinct" as the Pequots. Yet Melville's description of Tashtego seems uneasy. Tashtego's hair may be long and black but it cannot be "lean." Only his frame or physique can be "lean."

Next, Melville guesses accurately the origins of Indian peoples of the North American continent in an age when some still argued that the Indians were descended from the Lost Tribes of Israel. The leading scientific hypothesis today is that Indian peoples did indeed come from the East, through the Arctic regions, crossing, perhaps some fifteen thousand years ago, over what then existed as a land bridge across the Bering Strait to the North American continent. Tashtego, "an unmixed Indian," has inherited the "unvitiated blood of . . . proud warrior hunters." Ishmael's description of Tashtego continues: "To look at the tawny brawn of his lithe snaky limbs, you would almost have credited the superstitions of some of the earlier Puritans, and half believed this wild Indian to be a son of the Prince of the Powers of the Air" (p. 107). That is to say, a son of the devil. Looking at Tashtego's "tawny brawn," Ishmael perhaps finds himself tempted, as Eve was tempted by the snake. Although Puritan beliefs that Indians were sons of the devil are called "superstitions," Ishmael nonetheless invokes them to warn himself that Tashtego's alluring "tawny brawn" includes "snaky limbs" and that both the snake and the son of the devil are to be resisted. Having racialized Tashtego—references to his "blood" and his "tawny" color—Ishmael can only conclude that this descendant of "proud warrior hunters" is, nonetheless, part of a "last remnant." (The Gay Head Indians continue to exist today as a federally recognized tribe on Martha's Vineyard.)

It would not be fair to Melville to leave this very brief account without acknowledging the degree to which, again and again in *Moby-Dick* (and in other work), he relativizes or calls into question the matter of savagery and civilization. In *Moby-Dick,* Captain Ahab and the whale hunters, for example, are referred to as the real savages of the day, and Queequeg, the South Seas islander, descendant of cannibal royalty, and Ishmael's friend, is again and again celebrated for his civility. It is also curious to note that Melville may have taken the name of the sympathetic Queequeg from a Narragansett Indian mentioned in accounts of King Philip's War, Queequegununt.

Melville's novel *The Confidence-Man: His Masquerade* (1857) has almost four short chapters dealing with "The Metaphysics of Indian Hating." Although Melville wrote before Chivington's raid at Sand Creek, Melville's Indian hater, Colonel John Moredock, like Chivington, is one who believes that killing Indians is both right and just. Moredock's story, as its narrator makes clear, derives from James Hall's sketch "The Indian Hater" (1835). Moredock is the son of a woman whose three successive husbands were killed by Indians on the frontier before she herself, along with her nine children, succumbed to Indian attack. Only Moredock survived, and he has devoted his life to hunting down and killing the guilty Indians, and later to murder any Indian he encounters.

The Confidence-Man is a complex, unsettling, even strange book. Some critics have read Melville's chapters on Moredock as an allegory concerning Christianity, or any blind faith, trust, monomania, or "confidence" in general. Others have—quite incredibly, it seems now—read them as sanctioning the single-minded crusade against evil or "savagery" as these are represented by "the Indian." More likely is the suggestion that Melville's portrait of Moredock is meant to comment on the progress of American civilization generally. "Indian-hating still exists," Melville's narrator affirms, "and, no doubt will continue to exist, so long as Indians do" (p. 124). The portrait of the Indian-hating Colonel Moredock is not a pretty picture, but it is one we must acknowledge as relevant to us all.

In his eulogy for Henry David Thoreau (d. 1862), Ralph Waldo Emerson remarked that "every circumstance touching the Indian [was] important in his eyes" ("Thoreau," p. 1243) At his death Thoreau left behind notebooks focused on every aspect of Indian history and culture—some 2,800 handwritten pages. Robert Sayre, in his book *Thoreau and the American Indians,* concludes that Thoreau's "savagism, naturalism, and classicism were all related" (p. 35). Thoreau's intense interest in nature and natural history inevitably drew him to an awareness of and admiration for Indian people who were already identified—often detrimentally, we must recall—with "nature." Thoreau's general acceptance of the savagist view of Indians as precivilized persons—persons of an earlier time, for all that many of them were living and breathing before him—led him to identify them with our earlier and more robust ancestors the Greeks. In this regard Thoreau's savagism seems to have operated independently of the racialism typical of his time. As all his writings show, Thoreau did not think very highly of America's "civilization," nor was he certain that the Christianity he knew contributed to a life of principle more than a life of self-interest.

On the Fourth of July 1845 Thoreau moved into the cabin he had built in the Walden woods. Whatever else he intended, he was surely engaged in playing Indian, exploiting his positive conception of "Indians" for his own purposes. This use of Indians continued to the end of his life. Yet as he grew older—Thoreau was only forty-five when he died—he was able to keep an open mind about what he "knew," even to the point of depicting one living Indian, Joe Polis, an Abnaki guide to Thoreau on one of his three trips to Maine, as very much a complex *contemporary*. Sayre is probably right to note that "Joe Polis is the most realistic and attractive Native American" (p. 172) character portrayed by any non-native writer in the nineteenth century. But not even from Thoreau can we hope to get the "Indian side" of the story of Indian-white relations in the 1800s.

Ralph Waldo Emerson made public a letter he composed in April 1838 to President Martin Van Buren protesting the removal of the eastern Cherokees to Indian Territory. (There is evidence that Thoreau's mother, Cynthia Dunbar Thoreau, was one of the people who urged him to write it.) But even as he sympathizes, he uses the racialized discourse of Indian inferiority typical of the period. His plea on behalf of the Cherokees notes that "we have witnessed with sympathy the painful labors of these red men to redeem their own race from the doom of eternal inferiority, and to borrow and domesticate in the tribe the art and customs of the Caucasian race" (p. 303). But inasmuch as the Cherokees *had* managed to write, to plant, to govern themselves, and even to pray in much the same way as "the Caucasian race," it is difficult to see how their "inferiority" could be "eternal."

Virginia Kennedy has examined what is perhaps Emerson's most influential work, the extended essay published as *Nature* (1836), for references to the native people of this continent, and we will look at only a few of these. In chapter 3, "Beauty," Kennedy notes Emerson's imaginative reconstruction of Columbus' arrival to "the shore of America" (quoted

in "Ralph Waldo Emerson," p. 3). Columbus never reached the North American mainland; his first landing was Guanahani, in the West Indies (an island he renamed San Salvador), where he sees "the beach lined with savages" (quoted in "Ralph Waldo Emerson," p. 3). She remarks Emerson's assertion in chapter 4, "Language," that "children and savages use only nouns or names of things, which they convert into verbs" (quoted in "Ralph Waldo Emerson," p. 10). This is an extraordinary generalization considering the fact that there were hundreds of Indian languages, that Emerson had no knowledge of any of them, and that Navajo (for example) has many more verb forms than English.

Some years later Emerson's attitude toward the Sioux—they seem to stand generally for the "wild" Indians of the plains—would indicate no change of heart about the Indian's lack of brains. In a late volume of verse called *May-Day and Other Pieces* (1867) there is a poem called "The Adirondacs." On a hiking trip in 1858, Emerson and some Boston friends meet someone who informs them that the transatlantic cable has been completed. Emerson is fascinated at the notion of transatlantic communication, even as he appreciates his rural surroundings. He writes,

> We praise the guide, we praise the forest life:
> But will we sacrifice our dear-bought lore
> Of books and arts and trained experiment,
> Or count the Sioux a match for Agassiz?
> O no, not we!
>
> (P. 193)

Louis Agassiz, professor of natural history at Harvard, Emerson's alma mater (and Thoreau's), was a believer in innate racial differences; in 1850 he had written of "the submissive, obsequious negro" and "the indomitable, courageous, proud Indian" (quoted in Dippie, p. 92)—proud, perhaps, but no match for Emerson's civilized company. Thus Emerson again contributes to the triumphal narrative of American progress, here, the progress of arts and science. The Sioux have not achieved the "dear-bought lore" of civilization, nor could they possibly achieve it, racially inferior as they are to Emerson and his fellow Euro-Americans; they are no "match for Agassiz."

THE FATE OF THE INDIANS IN OTHER WRITERS OF THE PERIOD

Washington Irving's essays "Philip of Pokanoket" and "Traits of Indian Character" were originally published earlier than the period of our concern, but he reprinted both in *The Sketch Book of Geoffrey Crayon, Gent.* (1819–1820). In "Traits of Indian Character," Irving (1783–1859) announces that Indians "will vanish like a vapour from the face of the earth; their very history will be lost in forgetfulness" (pp. 248–249). Of King Philip he says, "He was an evil that walked in darkness, whose coming none could foresee, and against which none knew when to be on the alert" (p. 258). In *Astoria,* Irving's 1836 celebration of the entrepeneur John Jacob Astor, he notes that contrary to the energetic Astor, Indians are people whose lives are "little better than a prolonged and all-besetting death"; indeed, "in a little while scarcely any traces [of the Indians] will be left" (quoted in Maddox, p. 73).

This seems also the point of view of Henry Wadsworth Longfellow (1807–1882), whose *Song of Hiawatha* (1855) sold out its first printing of four thousand copies on the day of its publication and completed its first year in print with sales of thirty-eight thousand copies, extraordinary numbers for the time. Longfellow's poem, Helen Carr has written, "anaesthetised American anxieties over their treatment of the Indian; it created a moment of self-indulgent melancholy that could appease the liberal conscience and make further action unnecessary" (p. 141).

Thus Longfellow did not write about the Indians of his own day; instead he worked from Native American stories and legends published by Henry Rowe Schoolcraft, a government researcher whose wife, Jane Johnston Schoolcraft, was part Ojibwe. Schoolcraft's *Algic Researches* (1839) was the source for many of the characters and events in *Hiawatha.* But Longfellow got a good deal of Schoolcraft's material wrong. Longfellow's "song" deals with Algonquian peoples of the Great Lakes area, but their leader, Hiawatha, is a Mohawk from northern New York. Nor did Longfellow manage to distinguish between Hiawatha, a historical personage of the late fourteenth century who established the Iroquois League of Peace, and Manabozho, a mythic trickster figure of the Algonquians.

For his meter, Longfellow did not look to any of Schoolcraft's experiments in translating native song. Instead he chose for his poem a singsong meter that he took from the Finnish epic *Kalevala,* first published in its entirety in 1849. Although Longfellow had studied Finnish, he worked from the German translation of *Kalevala* by Anton Schiefner (1852). (The first English translation appeared in 1888.) The point is that Longfellow spent some time with Schoolcraft (although not enough time to understand the material) and considerable time with a Finnish epic in German translation, but the poem denies its relation to such sources. Consider the following lines from the introduction to *Hiawatha:*

> Should you ask me, whence these stories?
> Whence these legends and traditions,

> With the odors of the forest,
> With the dew and damp of meadows,
> With the curling smoke of wigwams,
> With the rushing of great rivers,
> . . . .
> I should answer, I should tell you,
> "From the forests and the prairies,
> From the great lakes of the Northland,
> From the land of the Ojibways,
> From the land of the Dacotahs,
> From the mountains, moors and fen-lands,
> Where the heron, the Shuh-shuh-gah
> Feeds among the reeds and rushes. . . ."

(P. 15)

Indian stories, legends, and traditions thus do not arise from cultural and intellectual work; rather, they arise from the land, the mountains, moors, and fen-lands. Indian "culture" is simply "nature," springing as it does both from the land—forests, prairies, lakes, mountains, moors and fen-lands—and its fauna (the heron, or Shuh-shuh-gah).

And just as nature must submit to cultivation, so too must the Indian, nature's creature, also submit to "civilization." Longfellow dramatizes the general attitude of eastern progressive thought about Indians by having Hiawatha counsel his people to abandon the old ways, naturally charming as they may have been, and prepare themselves to "vanish" before the inevitable progress of "civilization."

James Fenimore Cooper's five Leatherstocking novels (1823, 1826, 1827, 1840, 1841) also deal with earlier periods of Indian–Euro-American relations. Although Cooper (1789–1851) sometimes regretted the "inevitable" demise of the Indians, he was quite clear that there could be no future for them. Typically for the period, Cooper racializes the sociohistorical encounter between white and red on this continent. He can grant a certain "nobility" to the "savage" but finds no future for him; Cooper's Indians must give way to a "higher" race. As Cooper wrote in *Notions of the Americans* (1828), "As a rule, the red man disappears before the superior moral and physical influence of the white" (quoted in Pearce, p. 201). While the "superior moral[s]" of "the white" remain an open question, there was no doubt about the superior "physical" force of "the white" to which the Indians did indeed succumb, although they did not quite "disappear."

Lydia Maria Child's novel *Hobomok* (1824) took its inspiration from James Wallis Eastburn and Robert Sands's narrative poem *Yamoyden,* or at least from a review of it she read in the influential *North American Review.* Making what was then an almost inevitable reference to the historical novels of Sir Walter Scott representing an earlier period on the

Scottish border, the reviewer had suggested that American writers could find the equivalent of Scott's settings and characters in the American Indians. But the young Lydia Maria Child (1802–1880) set her novel not among the Indians of her own time but of an earlier period, the time of the so-called King Philip's War (1675–1676). King Philip's name was Metacom, and he was not a king, although he was one of the principal leaders of the Wampanoag nation of Massachusetts. The Wampanoags were attacked by New Plymouth, Massachusetts Bay Colony, and Connecticut, leading to a war frowned upon by England, still the mother country of the American colonists. The colonists named Philip, bestowed upon him his rank, and called the war they had instigated his, implying thereby that the victim had been the aggressor, an implication that would again operate just over a half-century later in the naming of the Black Hawk War.

Child's novel suggested that intermarriage between whites and Indians and Indian assimilation into the dominant society might be alternatives to "fate." More than forty years later, in Child's 1868 *An Appeal for the Indians,* she writes, "The plain truth is, our relations with the red and black members of the human family have been one almost unvaried history of violence and fraud" (p. 84). She continues, "Yet, while we are perpetually robbing them, and driving them 'from post to pillar,' we go on repeating with the most impudent coolness, 'They are *destined* to disappear before the white man'" (p. 94).

With Lydia Maria Child we can remark the intersection of concern for women's rights, the abolition of slavery, and Indian rights. In some regards these concerns run parallel to one another, and in other regards the attempt to see them as parallel leads to confusions. Child, for example, sacrificed the popularity her earlier publications had brought her when, in 1833, in *An Appeal in Favor of That Class of Americans Called Africans,* she advocated, as Carolyn Karcher summarizes it, "immediate emancipation, an end to all forms of racial discrimination, and the abrogation of laws prohibiting 'marriages between persons of different color'" (p. xiii).

Child's "Appeal for the Indians" has both the strengths and the weaknesses of her abolitionist position. It argues for justice for both native and African American people and asserts that both "races" can attain the heights of white "civilization" given time and opportunity. Thus Child bravely argues against even the progressive view of the time that Indian cultures—not necessarily Indians—be wiped out as quickly as possible so that "civilization" may take their

place. She has very little sense—few in the period did—of the value of those cultures, but she does not equivocate in her judgment, as we have seen, that Americans have treated Indians with "violence and fraud" all the while insisting that it is destiny that requires their disappearance.

Very likely inspired by Child's *Hobomok,* Catharine Maria Sedgwick's *Hope Leslie* (1827) is also set in the colonial period. Karcher points out that Sedgwick, too, proposes the possibility of Indian-white marriage (although not on the part of the novel's title character) and, even more strongly, "an alliance between white women and Indians" (p. xxxv). Once more, these are issues important to her time, although they are not raised in contemporary terms. It has been suggested that in *The Wept of Wish-ton-wish* (1829), James Fenimore Cooper returned to Indian material with the intention of opposing Sedgwick's vision of Indian-white marriage and alliance. Cooper's insistence in *The Wept* on the incompatibility—again, largely racial in nature—between native "savages" and "civilized" whites comes at a portentous moment. For it was only a year before the publication of Cooper's novel, as we have noted, that Andrew Jackson, famed as an Indian fighter, was elected president and set in motion the policy of Indian removal.

Another champion of women's rights (she was somewhat wary of the abolitionists), Margaret Fuller (1810–1850) also briefly wrote about Indians in her short life (she died in a shipwreck), in *Summer on the Lakes, in 1843* (1844) and to a lesser extent in journalism of the same period for the *New-York Daily Tribune.* Although Fuller occasionally wrestles with the dominant discourse of "the unfortunately vanishing Indian"—Fuller's words—she ultimately embraces it. She writes that in regard to the Indian "the power of fate is with the white man" (quoted in Kennedy, "Margaret Fuller," p. 11), and later, shifting the "power" of fate elsewhere, she remarks that "nature seems . . . to declare that this race [Indians] is fated to perish" (quoted in Kennedy, "Margaret Fuller," p. 16). Whether "fate" manifests itself as being "with the white man" or whether it is "nature" that is responsible for "fate," there is no question that the Indian must vanish.

In 1845 Fuller wrote a review of Henry Rowe Schoolcraft's book *Onéota; or, The Red Race of America* (1845) for the *Tribune.* Fuller opens with the standard observation that "the Red Race" has "well nigh melted from our sight" (quoted in Kennedy, "Margaret Fuller," p. 32). She endorses Schoolcraft's notion that Indian society might have been "reorganized"—except, of course, as Fuller writes, "it is too late for act . . . nothing remains but to write their epitaph with some respect to truth" (quoted in Kennedy, "Margaret Fuller," p. 33). As we have again and again noted, "sympathy" for the Indians' plight goes hand in hand with the racialized discourse of their inevitable disappearance.

Although his major work appeared after 1870, Mark Twain (1835–1910) deserves a brief word. In the 1960s the critic Leslie Fiedler concluded that Twain was "obsessed by a hatred of Indians from the very beginning of his literary career" (quoted in McNutt, p. 224) This is certainly accurate in regard to Twain's early journalism. In an 1868 piece for the *New York Tribune,* for example, he wrote, "Inflict soap and a spelling-book on every Indian that ravages the Plains, and let them die" (quoted in McNutt, p. 227). There are a very great many other quotations one could offer as evidence of Twain's antipathy toward Indians. Nonetheless, in a career that continued into the early twentieth century, Twain did eventually modify such rabid and uninformed views.

Our survey thus far indicates that the aim of this encyclopedia, to offer "a comprehensive overview of American history through a literary lens," cannot be fulfilled when it comes to Native Americans and the major or even the minor literary authors of the period. All of them reference Indians historically or symbolically with some frequency, but they rarely engage with them as contemporary, historical, cultural, and social beings—and when they do, as we have noted even with Melville and Thoreau, it is still to see them as living anachronisms or last remnants.

INDIAN DISPOSSESSION AND NATIVE AMERICAN WRITERS

If this is the case for authors from the dominant Euro-American culture, what can be said of Native American authors of the period? Quantitatively they are not many, and of those few, fewer still wrote in genres currently recognized as even approximately literary. William Apess (1798–1839), a Pequot, published a full-scale autobiography, the first such text by a Native American, in 1829 and followed this with an abbreviated version of his life story along with brief biographies of his wife and four other native converts to Christianity, *The Experiences of Five Christian Indians of the Pequ'd Tribe* (1833). The original edition of this book concluded with an extraordinary essay called "An Indian's Looking-Glass for the White Man," a powerful indictment of what Apess called color prejudice and what we would call racism. (He did not reprint this essay in the 1837 edition of *The Experiences*). Apess also published an account of his

activism, as we would call it now, on behalf of the Mashpee Indians of Massachusetts, helping them to achieve a greater degree of self-government from the Massachusetts board of overseers and publishing the arguments for this in his *Indian Nullification of the Unconstitutional Laws of Massachusetts Relative to the Marshpee Tribe; or, The Pretended Riot Explained* (1835). In 1836 Apess published the last of his works, a eulogy to Metacom, or King Philip, whom he claims as a distant ancestor and denominates "the greatest man that was ever in America" (p. 308) Apess's work powerfully documents many of the wrongs and injustices done to his people in the past and laments the current sad state, as he has personally experienced it, of native people in and around Connecticut and Massachusetts.

The Cherokee author John Rollin Ridge (Yellow Bird, or Chees-quat-a-law-ny, 1827–1867), was quite prolific but left only a single novel, *The Life and Adventures of Joaquín Murieta, the Celebrated California Bandit* (1854), and a poetry volume, *Poems* (1868), as his literary testament. Curiously Ridge's novel does not deal with the history of Cherokee dispossession that he suffered personally. Ridge, whose father, John Ridge, was assassinated as a consequence of his acquiescence to Cherokee removal, went off to California and took, as the subject of his only novel, the adventures of a Mexican bandit. Like others of the writers we have so briefly noted, his work only indirectly bears on the history of his period.

See also Indians; "An Indian's Looking-Glass for the White Man"; Leatherstocking Tales; Miscegenation; *Moby-Dick;* Native American Literature; Romanticism; *The Song of Hiawatha;* Transcendentalism; Trail of Tears

BIBLIOGRAPHY
Primary Works
Apess, William. "Eulogy on King Philip." 1836. In *On Our Own Ground: The Complete Writings of William Apess, a Pequot.* Edited by Barry O'Connell. Amherst: University of Massachusetts Press, 1992.

Apess, William. "An Indian's Looking-Glass for the White Man." 1833. In *On Our Own Ground: The Complete Writings of William Apess, a Pequot.* Edited by Barry O'Connell. Amherst: University of Massachusetts Press, 1992.

Child, Lydia Maria. *An Appeal for the Indians.* 1868. In *Hobomok and Other Writings on Indians.* Edited by Carolyn Karcher. New Brunswick, N.J.: Rutgers University Press, 1986.

Emerson, Ralph Waldo. "Letter to President Martin Van Buren." 1838. In *The Letters of Ralph Waldo Emerson,* vol. 7, *1807–1844,* edited by Eleanor M. Tilton. New York: Columbia University Press, 1990.

Emerson, Ralph Waldo. "The Adirondacs." 1867. In *Poems by Ralph Waldo Emerson,* vol. 9, pp. 182–195. New York: William Wise, 1929.

Emerson, Ralph Waldo. "Thoreau." 1862. In *The Norton Anthology of American Literature.* Vol. B. 6th ed. New York: Norton, 2003.

Irving, Washington. *Sketch Book of Geoffrey Crayon, Gent.* 1819–1820. Edited by Susan Manning. New York: Oxford University Press, 1996.

Longfellow, Henry Wadsworth. *The Song of Hiawatha.* 1855. Indianapolis, Ind.: Bobbs Merrill, 1906.

Melville, Herman. *The Confidence-Man: His Masquerade.* 1857. Edited by Hershel Parker. New York: Norton, 1971.

Melville, Herman. *Moby-Dick.* 1851. Edited by Harrison Hayford and Hershel Parker. New York: Norton, 1967.

Secondary Works

Arac, Jonathan. "The Politics of The Scarlet Letter." In *Ideology and Classic American Literature,* edited by Sacvan Bercovitch and Myra Jehlen, pp. 247–266. Cambridge, U.K.: Cambridge University Press, 1986.

Bergland, Renée. *The National Uncanny: Indian Ghosts and American Subjects.* Hanover, N.H.: University Press of New England, 2000.

Brown, Dee. *Bury My Heart at Wounded Knee: An Indian History of the American West.* New York: Bantam, 1978.

Carr, Helen. *Inventing the American Primitive: Politics, Gender, and the Representation of Native American Literary Traditions, 1789–1936.* New York: New York University Press, 1996.

Coward, John M. *The Newspaper Indian: Native American Identity in the Press, 1820–90.* Urbana: University of Illinois Press, 1999.

Dippie, Brian. *The Vanishing American: White Attitudes and United States Indian Policy.* Middletown, Conn.: Wesleyan University Press, 1982.

Jennings, Francis. *The Founders of America.* New York: Norton, 1993.

Karcher, Carolyn. "Introduction." In *Hobomok and Other Writings on Indians.* New Brunswick, N.J.: Rutgers University Press, 1986.

Kennedy, Virginia. "Margaret Fuller and Nineteenth-Century Literary Indian Removal." Master's thesis, Montclair State University, 2001.

Kennedy, Virginia. "Ralph Waldo Emerson, William Apess, and the Native American Identity." Unpublished paper, 9 May 2000.

Maddox, Lucy. *Removals: Nineteenth-Century American Literature and the Politics of Indian Affairs.* New York: Oxford University Press, 1991.

McNutt, James. "Mark Twain and the American Indian: Earthly Realism and Heavenly Idealism." *American Indian Quarterly* 4 (1978): 223–242.

Pearce, Roy Harvey. *Savagism and Civilization: A Study of the Indian and the American Mind.* Berkeley: University of California Press, 1988.

Sayre, Robert. *Thoreau and the American Indians.* Princeton, N.J.: Princeton University Press, 1977.

Arnold Krupat

INDIVIDUALISM AND COMMUNITY

The terms "individualism" and "community" are open to shifting, sometimes contradictory interpretations. Henry David Thoreau's (1817–1862) individualism, for example, is at odds with the dominant economic individualism of his period, just as the individualism of Herman Melville's (1819–1891) Captain Ahab is different from Ishmael's in *Moby-Dick* (1851). Thoreau's and Ishmael's oppositional versions are attractive, but most Americans nonetheless recognize the central importance of the practices and values of economic individualism or possessive individualism. It may be difficult to reconcile these often-divisive values and practices, which include private ownership, capitalist enterprise, and the division of labor, with the cooperation, cohesion, and inevitable conflict usually associated with the ideal of community.

Alternatively, however, in American usage the "and" in "individualism and community" often means "versus," reflecting a sense that far from being a positive ideal, communal involvement will stifle or absorb or homogenize that which is most uniquely individual, a view animating the transcendentalist individualism of Thoreau and Ralph Waldo Emerson (1803–1882). Community, a sense of shared values and practices linking people together, can also be achieved at the expense of devalued Others—blacks, Jews, gays—whose culturally sanctioned inferiority constitutes a contrasting community of the righteous united by their shared sense of racial, sexual, or religious superiority. In a more neutral sense, "community" can refer to a more or less compatible group, ranging from the village communities of the early nineteenth century to constructs like "the black community." Within this range of possibilities, in the immediacy of their fiction, essays, and poems, mid-nineteenth-century writers bring alive the historically grounded energies of American individualism and community.

MELVILLE'S *MOBY-DICK*

In *Moby-Dick* (1851), Melville goes deep into American culture and returns with conflicting and challenging insights. He creates that ungodly, godlike man, Captain Ahab, whose version of American individualism has the same implacable energy as his merchant contemporaries but directed toward metaphysical, not material, goals. In *The Protestant Temperament* (1977), Philip Greven has shown that evangelical Protestants, for all their subordination to God's will, can also act fearlessly, independently, and ruthlessly in the face of all the powers of the earth. Greven, that is, has shown that the evangelical discipline of the self, the punitive suppression of a person's will and desire, generates anger and hatred. This suppressed anger and hatred are often turned outward against enemies and demonized Others—Indians, foreigners, the unrighteous, all of the White Whales of American culture—antagonists who are then ferociously attacked and punished. As Melville's Father Mapple puts it less pejoratively, "delight is to him, who gives no quarter in the truth, and kills, burns, and destroys all sin though he pluck it out from under the robes of Senators and Judges" (p. 54).

In Father Mapple's account of the the self, empowered but subordinated to God, the anger and hatred are concealed. For Ahab, however, they are central and openly acknowledged. Ahab has directed against the White Whale all of the anger and hatred he himself has experienced, most immediately from the emasculating loss of his leg. Instead of recognizing and accepting the loss as a painful personal tragedy, however, Ahab elevates his experience into a metaphysical drama. For him the White Whale embodies all the torments and dilemmas,

> all the subtle demonisms of life and thought; all evil, to crazy Ahab, were visibly personified, and made practically assailable in Moby-Dick. He piled upon the whale's white hump the sum of all the general rage and hate felt by his whole race from Adam down; and then, as if his chest had been a mortar, he burst his hot heart's shell upon it. (P. 156)

In Melville's remarkable metaphor, the heart, the seat of the cohesive emotions of love and sympathy, becomes instead an instrument of hate, rage, and military violence. Ahab as titanic individual, in his eyes the representative of his redeemer nation and of all mankind, assaults "all evil" in an archetypal attack that illuminates whole swaths of American culture, including American foreign policy.

Closer to home, Melville uses Ahab to expose the danger of tyranny latent in American political culture. For Ahab there is room for only one individual. He defies the powers above even as he "sometimes think[s] there's naught beyond" (p. 140). Just as he would "strike the sun if it insulted me," he uses the authority of his office combined with the force of his personality and will to dominate those below him (p. 140). In a ship populated by "isolatos" and reminiscent of an immigrant culture lacking the cohesion of established traditions, Ahab supplies the unifying, emotionally charged rituals—the black rites on the quarterdeck—and the compelling, underground motive—revenge on Moby-Dick—a motive that goes deeper even than the lure of cash. Ahab is the unifying "long central keel" that makes the fragmentary crew into something like a community (p. 415).

Drawing energy from and illuminating the contradictory tendencies of evangelical Protestantism, Ahab's overpowering individualism fills the need for community with an authoritarian dominance. Like others in his tradition, he oscillates between a sense that he is nothing and that he is everything, that he is totally insignificant and all-powerful, that he is an instrument of Fate in a predetermined drama and the willful power who determines action and compels obedience. In either mode, as subordinated or expanded self, Ahab reveals that the unstable individualism of evangelical Protestantism bears on authoritarian politics in America. As insignificant subordinate—"I am the Fates' lieutenant" (p. 418)—he reveals a counterintuitive American propensity to be dominated and to follow orders. As the controlling force, where the boundary between Ahab and God disappears—"is it I, God, or who, that lifts this arm?" (p. 406)—Ahab reveals the authoritarian consequences of a God-empowered individual in command of the levers of official power.

Through Ahab and his assault on the White Whale, Melville has created an archetypal narrative that, inseparable from its metaphysical and epistemological probing, illuminates the complex uses of the antagonist coded as "evil" as well as the related potential for tyranny in America. The fear of tyranny has recurred periodically in U.S. history. At the very outset of the nation Patrick Henry (1736–1799) and Melancton Smith (1744–1798), articulate antifederalists, opposed adopting the Constitution because they believed that despotism could too easily result from giving the president control of the military as commander in chief. During the Civil War, Lincoln reactivated these concerns when he silenced the opposition press and abolished the right of habeas corpus. In 2004, critics such as Chalmers Johnson and Chris Hedges drew a link between a White Whale war on evil and the accompanying threat of an American dictatorship. As with Ahab, here are individualism and community in their most disturbing and distorted forms.

More persistent and recognizable is the American economic individualism Melville powerfully satirizes, nowhere more effectively than in Fleece's inverted Sermon on the Mount. Melville has the negro cook, Fleece, expose the gap between the values of "love thy neighbor" and the practices of a sharkish capitalism in which the strongest sharks do not help "de small fry ob sharks" but instead fill their own bellies to the full (p. 238). For Fleece, civility is impossible in this individualistic world of shark against shark. In contrast to theories establishing the supportive link between capitalism and Protestant religion, Melville uses Fleece to expose the realities of economic individualism as totally at odds with the values of Christianity. "Cussed fellow-critters," Fleece concludes in a despairing indictment Melville shares, "kick up de damndest row as ever you can; fill your dam' bellies till dey bust— and den die" (p. 239).

In opposition to both Ahab and the economic individualism of Fleece's sermon, Melville's narrator, Ishmael, comes to embody another recognizably American form of individualism: open, independent, freethinking, and challenging of orthodoxy. Ishmael has all of Ahab's philosophic depth and intensity but, unlike Ahab, he has the ability to sustain uncertainty without pressing for an absolute resolution. As a pioneering cultural anthropologist, moreover, Ishmael gradually goes against the grain of dominant American views about sexuality, religion, and race. Ishmael forms an intimate relation with Queequeg, a South Sea "savage" who takes Ishmael beyond the limits of American culture. His "stiff prejudices" loosened by a night in bed with this "comely looking," multicolored "cannibal," Ishmael experiences the "strange feelings" and the "melting in me" that link him to Queequeg and redeem Ishmael's "splintered heart" (pp. 58, 36, 56). The love between Ishmael and Queequeg is in part a tribute to Ishmael's individualism, which allows him to participate in Queequeg's non-Christian religious ceremonies, to marry Queequeg in a ritual that is a custom of Queequeg's country, and to come to an unprecedented insight about race, namely that black, not white, is the normative color, "as though a white man were anything more dignified than a whitewashed Negro" (p. 62).

Their unsublimated, culturally taboo sexuality gives their love added significance. The love between Ishamel and Queequeg does not constitute a community, but it does suggest the cohesive ties that are a necessary if not sufficient condition for a genuine community. The relation between Ishmael and Queequeg also dramatizes the sexual, religious, and racial barriers to community in America. In contrast to the mutuality between Ishmael and Queequeg, Melville further renders these barriers in his treatment of Ahab and Fedallah's relation of ambiguous domination and subordination. His handling of this relation also reinforces rather than subverts American racial and religious biases, in the case of Fedallah, deep biases against the "the tiger-yellow," demonic, non-Christian "Oriental" (pp. 181, 191). Combined with Ahab's force and Fleece's exposure of the divisive power of economic individualism, from Melville's perspective the barriers to community in America are daunting.

In *Whiteness of a Different Color*, Matthew Jacobson regards the racial antagonisms Melville both criticized and reinforced as central to the constitution of Irish, Polish, Slavic, Jewish, and Italian immigrants as Americans. From Jacobson's point of view, that is, these immigrant Americans achieved their sense of community as Americans by defining themselves as "white" against "dark" or "yellow" denigrated Others. In contrast to the Ishmael-Queequeg relation, the early-twenty-first-century appeal to homophobia functions to make gays the reviled Other, constituting by their despised difference the dominant community of the righteous.

DOUGLASS'S *NARRATIVE*

In his *Narrative of the Life of Frederick Douglass, an American Slave* (1845), Frederick Douglass (1818–1895), like Melville, brings alive a sense of American individualism, highlights the racial and religious obstacles to community, and goes beyond the confines of America to convey a sense of community. At the center of his narrative Douglass celebrates the power of love, "the loving hearts" and the special feeling he and his fellow slaves had for each other. "We were linked and interlinked with each other," he stresses. "I loved them with a love stronger than any thing I have experienced since." Not only "would we have died for each other" but also, further specifying the qualities of community, Douglass goes on to emphasize that "we never undertook to do any thing, of any importance, without a mutual consultation. We never moved separately. We were one, and as much so by our tempers and dispositions, as by the mutual hardships to which we were necessarily subjected by our condition as slaves" (p. 89).

In calling attention to "our tempers and dispositions" as distinct from the oppression of slavery, Douglass is saying he and his fellows were by nature loving and cooperative. He shares but inverts the racial essentialism of his period. For those who reject this essentialism, Douglass allows his readers to realize that the values and practices of African tribal, agrarian culture are the source of the ties he responds to. On this view Douglass fuses African practices and values with the Christian language of love to convey a unique blend, an African American slave culture as a positive model for the New World.

In his account of his crucial fight with the slave breaker Covey, Douglass achieves the same blend of the African and Christian but with redemptive violence substituting for the loving hearts of the African American slave community. As a Christian who believes that in a previous episode God has directly intervened to protect him, Douglass is reserved about the power of the root a conjure man has given him to ward off Covey's attacks. Douglass nonetheless strongly implies that the spirit that inspires him to fight back comes from the root, which is to say, from the world of African religious values and practices. This spirit reinforces and is reinforced by the imperatives of American manhood and American individualism. To live up to the prescribed code, American men must assert themselves violently against those they believe have wronged them. In Douglass's case, his action transforms him from "a brute" and "revived within me a sense of my own manhood" (p. 80). He breaks radically with his mentor, the abolitionist William Lloyd Garrison (1805–1879), who was committed to nonviolence, just as Douglass rejects the opportunity to "turn the other cheek." Douglass instead stresses that "he only can understand the deep satisfaction I experienced, who has himself repelled by force the bloody arm of slavery. I felt as I had never felt before. It was a glorious resurrection from the tomb of slavery, to the heaven of freedom" (p. 81). Douglass draws on the Christian narrative of resurrection and rebirth but not here on the values of meekness and love. He combines this militant Christianity with the animating spirit of the African root and the vitalizing energy of American individualism to create a compelling and to some a threatening theology of liberation. The threat is not only the militant Christianity but also that a black man should assert his manhood through a violence typically reserved for white men.

THOREAU, TRANSCENDENTALISM, AND "RESISTANCE TO CIVIL GOVERNMENT"

From the perspective of a white New Englander who articulates the best of the values and assumptions of transcendentalist individualism, in "Civil Disobedience" or "Resistance to Civil Government" (1849), Thoreau gives his radical, nonviolent response to slavery and the related Mexican-American War. The transcendentalist movement Thoreau epitomizes was not a tightly organized group, but during the 1830s and 1840s it did bring like-minded New Englanders together,

beginning in 1836 around Emerson and Frederic Henry Hedge (1805–1890) in the Transcendental Club and later around *The Dial* (1840–1844), which Margaret Fuller (1810–1850) and then Emerson edited. *The Dial* gave writers as different as George Ripley (1802–1880), Amos Bronson Alcott (1799–1888), and Christopher Pearse Cranch (1813–1892) an outlet and audience, however limited—it had three hundred subscribers. Most of those loosely associated with the movement were Harvard-trained, many of them at the Divinity School, and were in rebellion against the decorum and intellectual and emotional restraints of a Unitarianism they wanted to transform into a more spiritually and emotionally vital force. Like Emerson, they had to balance their criticism of American economic individualism and materialism with their own reliance not only on God but also on the economic system that supported them, however meagerly in the cases of, for example, Jones Very (1813–1880) and Amos Bronson Alcott. Their version of a divinely animated individualism led Emerson and Thoreau to keep at arm's length the communal Brook Farm experiment George Ripley conducted between 1842 and 1847 as an alternative to the economic individualism of the pre–Civil War period. For our purposes of illuminating individualism and community in mid-century America, Thoreau's "Resistance to Civil Government" and Orestes Augustus Brownson's (1803–1876) neglected "The Laboring Classes" (1840) show the movement at its most revealing and provocative.

As he explains in "Resistance to Civil Government," Thoreau withdraws his allegiance to the state and refuses to pay taxes to support a Constitution that enshrines slavery and a government that has found excuses to wage the Mexican-American War to extend slavery. He acts on his principles by going to jail and then, even more significantly, by dramatizing and deepening his protest through the play of mind, language, and values in "Resistance to Civil Government." For Thoreau, who reverses commonsense views of freedom, the prison house is "the only house in a slave State in which a free man can abide with honor" (p. 235). Thoreau celebrates "the individual as a higher and independent power" (p. 245) than the state. Along with Emerson and other transcendentalists, Thoreau assumes that "it is not so important that many should be as good as you, as there be some absolute goodness somewhere; for that will leaven the whole lump" (p. 230). He also assumes that through principled action, the individual can bring alive in the world versions of this transcendental "absolute goodness."

Behind Thoreau's ethical language of "goodness," "principle," and "right," he assumes that a transcendental divinity runs like a life-giving stream through every person and through all of existence. This divine principle is the source of and is inseparable from the ethical principle he articulates when he declares that

> action from principle, the perception and the performance of right, changes things and relations; it is essentially revolutionary, and does not consist wholly with any thing which was. It not only divides states and churches, it divides families; aye, it divides the *individual*, separating the diabolical in him from the divine. (Pp. 232–233)

"It is essentially revolutionary" because through the act of the inspired individual the divine—the essential—enters into and transforms both the individual and the world of ordinary affairs. On this view, moreover, the individual can defy community consensus and the numerical majority and constitute "a majority of one" because divinity is morally and spiritually greater than the "mass of men" who only become fully human, fully "men," when they are in touch with the divinity within (pp. 234, 228). Although not doctrinally Protestant, Thoreau and other transcendentalists nonetheless reveal the familiar paradox of Protestant individualism—for them, too, the radical independence of the inspired individual is inseparable from reliance on divinity.

Although his transcendentalist version of individualism leads him in practice and theory to be wary of the group involvement associated with community, Thoreau recognizes and is the beneficiary of his grounding in the small, relatively cohesive community of Concord, Massachusetts. He relies heavily on the value-charged word "neighbor" as a check on arbitrary, inhumane action and as imposing on the Thoreauvian individual the duty to treat others in the community "as a neighbor and well-disposed man," a duty and set of obligations not easy to fulfill (p. 234). If they fulfill these obligations, however, Thoreau argues for the right of a few to live apart from society as responsible, morally and spiritually questing individuals. At the same time, Thoreau, like Melville, satirizes the economic individualism that prevails in his society of merchants and landowners. Thoreau uses his wit and eye for the telling detail and phrase to expose the contradiction between the moral, religious, and democratic values he shares with his contemporaries and the values and practices of the possessive individualism that leads people to ignore the wounds to their conscience and to "postpone the question of freedom to the question of free trade, and quietly read the prices-current along with the latest advices from Mexico, after dinner, and, it may be, fall asleep over them both" (p. 230).

ORESTES BROWNSON'S "THE LABORING CLASSES"

Although works like "Resistance to Civil Government," *Walden,* and Emerson's essays are famous for awakening the reader, Orestes Brownson's lesser-known "The Laboring Classes" is the most politically radical statement of the American transcendental movement. Brownson stays true to his origins on a poverty-stricken Vermont farm, or as he puts it, he was "born and reared in the class of proletaries; and . . . [has] merely given utterance to their views and feelings" (p. 443). In a transcendentalist discourse that knows about money, merchants, and farmers but avoids class, Brownson's class awareness is as remarkable as his speaking from the inside, for those who do the hard manual work of society. He sees society as a system in impending crisis, a society unequally divided between, in his words, owners and operatives, between businessmen and labor, between "Merchants and Manufacturers,—landed capital and commercial capital" and "labor" (p. 437).

For Brownson, class struggle—the "struggle between the operative and his employer, between wealth and labor"—is inevitable in the system of possessive individualism. Brownson is clear that reform will not work, that the "evil we speak of is inherent in all our social arrangements, and cannot be cured without a radical change of those arrangements" (p. 439). In what he calls the prevailing "system," "the whole class of simple laborers are poor, and in general unable to procure anything beyond the bare necessities of life" (p. 438). Changing managers, he points out, will not change the system. Addressing the usual argument of American individualism, that the talented individual will rise on his own, Brownson admits it but stresses that, although individual laborers can rise above their fellows, the laboring class as a whole will continue to exist, the inadequate price of labor will continue to be set by the employers, and the resulting inequality will continue to thwart "that equality between man and man, which God has established between the rights of one and those of another" (p. 438).

He calls specifically for legislation "which shall free government, whether State or Federal, from the control of the Banks" because the banks always favor "the business community" and "are the natural enemies of the laboring class" (p. 441). Brownson also insists on getting rid of "the hereditary descent of property" to correct the anomaly that some are born rich and some poor (p. 441). Whereas other transcendentalists eventually came to support the emancipation of the slave, Brownson is committed "to emancipate the proletaries" (p. 439). Although he "recoils with horror" at the prospect, he recognizes that this emancipation will not come peacefully, that "the rich, the business community, will never voluntarily consent to it," and that "it will be effected only by the strong arm of physical force" (p. 442). No wonder Brownson's "The Laboring Classes" has been marginalized.

WHITMAN'S "SONG OF MYSELF"

Instead of focusing on divisive class conflict, the threat of violent change, and the economic inequity built into the system of possessive individualism, in his signature poem, "Song of Myself" (1855), Walt Whitman (1819–1892) celebrates the individual—"I celebrate myself"—and brings alive a democratic America and a vital universe (p. 675). For Whitman, the "I" of his poem embodies possibilities that may be shared and realized by all who are liberated by his free-verse rhythms and his vision of a diverse America and an expanding universe. Like Thoreau and Emerson, Whitman believes in an energizing spirit running through individuals and all of existence. Unlike Thoreau and Emerson, however, for Whitman what resolves the paradox of the one and the many and establishes that "there was never any more inception than there is now, . . . And will never be any more perfection that there is now, Nor any more heaven or hell than there is now"—the guarantee is the "urge and urge and urge, / Always the procreant urge of the world," the animating, sexualized energy that is both like and shockingly unlike the unifying spirit premised by his great contemporaries (p. 676).

For the Whitman of "Song of Myself," it is not logic or even Thoreau's "action from principle" but instead the existential experience of sexual communion that validates his belief that there is "Always a knit of identity . . . always distinction . . . always a breed of life," such that the individual is at once distinct and merged, the "knit of identity" experienced in sexual consummation (p. 676). To develop the insight, Whitman presents a strikingly rendered love scene, probably between two men, on the summer grass, a scene during which

> You settled your head athwart my hips and gently
> turned over upon me,
> And parted the shirt from my bosom-bone, and
> plunged your tongue to my barestript heart,
> And reached till you felt my beard, and reached
> till you held my feet.

At the climax, "swiftly arose and spread around me the peace and joy and knowledge that pass all the art and argument of the earth" (p. 678). The experience leads Whitman to affirm that for him an unsublimated love is the central unifying keel of existence, connecting him as brother and lover to all the men and women ever born (p. 679). This is a unique version of

American individualism, a culturally radical celebration of the individual connected to the rest of humanity. Whitman's unorthodox vision of cohesion is a crucial alternative to the loneliness and isolation often resulting from America's unfettered individualism, a view Jay Grossman extends to Whitman's 1860 "Calamus" poems.

In the more public, less personal sections of "Song of Myself," Whitman celebrates the ordinary people and activities of preindustrial America. His generally egalitarian America of small landowners, fur traders, carpenters, journeymen, sailors, fancymen, and housewives is not marked by the class conflict Brownson highlights, by the conflicts about race and slavery Douglass addresses, or by the regional, economic, and racial conflicts of the impending Civil War. Whitman instead draws on and brings America to the test of its egalitarian ideals and the democratic possibilities available in his period. Implicitly and explicitly he calls on the reader to bring alive what he sees as the real America. He recognizes but rejects the tight, competitive individualism of those who "feed the greed of the belly" in a process of "many sweating and ploughing and thrashing, and then the chaff for payment receiving, / A few idly owning, and they the wheat continually claiming" (p. 725). In contrast, for Whitman "whoever walks a furlong without sympathy walks to his own funeral, dressed in his shroud" (p. 734).

For Whitman a degree of economic and social inequality exists but it is not systemic. He more often uses parallel structure to give a grammatical basis to his belief in an underlying equality, to his view that, as in one of his many remarkable sequences, the bride, the opium eater, the prostitute, and the president are of equal value (p. 689). This sequence and others like it play on and subvert the conventional social hierarchy in the service of Whitman's egalitarian vision. If anything, Whitman inclines to the ordinarily rejected and despised, to "the democracy" in the old sense of the unwashed and the ungrammatical:

> I speak the password primeval. . . . I give the sign
> of democracy;
> By God! I will accept nothing which all cannot
> have their counterpart of on the same terms.
> Through me many long dumb voices, . . .
> Voices of the diseased and despairing, and of
> thieves and dwarfs, . . .
> And of the rights of them the others are
> down upon,
> Of the trivial and flat and foolish and despised,
> Of fog in the air and beetles rolling balls of dung.
> *(P. 699)*

Although his panoramas and catalogues are often based on nineteenth-century genre paintings and are both vivid and nonthreatening, as he does with the prostitute and the balls of dung, Whitman also enacts a defiant nonconformity that repeatedly offends conventional religious, sexual, and social orthodoxy. Cumulatively in the course of "Song of Myself," as in lines like "You sea, . . . / Cushion me soft . . . rock me in billowy drowse, / Dash me with amorous wet. . . . I can repay you" or "Thruster holding me tight and that I hold tight! / We hurt each other as the bridegroom and the bride hurt each other," Whitman succeeds in conveying an unintimidated individualism in touch with ordinarily repressed sexuality, frequently conventionally suspect male-to-male sexuality (p. 696). He does the same with bodily processes typically excluded from polite discourse and major poetry, as in such controversial passages as

> I keep as delicate around the bowels as around
>   the head and heart,
> . . . Divine am I inside and out, and I make holy
>   whatever I touch or am touched from;
> The scent of these arm-pits is aroma finer
>   than prayer,
> This head is more than churches or bibles
>   or creeds.
>
> *(P. 699)*

Although his defiant individualism can be disruptive, in the absence of acknowledged or rendered institutional ties, in the world of "Song of Myself," as bard, as the creator of the narratives and images that unify the nation, the "I" of the poem also holds together the diverse individuals, activities, occupations, and regions Whitman lovingly, precisely records. They flow into him and out to the abundance, subtlety, and extremity of the poem. Whitman appeals to the reader to complete the poem and to bring into full existence the vibrant self, country, and universe he presents. His legacy is the energy, the unchastened individualism, and the unifying power he attributes to the cohesive, unorthodox, sexualized love at the center of "Song of Myself."

See also Democracy; Labor; *Moby-Dick; Narrative of the Life of Frederick Douglass;* Reform; "Resistance to Civil Government"; "Song of Myself"; Transcendentalism

BIBLIOGRAPHY

Primary Works

Brownson, Orestes A. "The Laboring Classes." 1840. In *The Transcendentalists: An Anthology,* edited by Perry Miller, pp. 436–446. Cambridge, Mass.: Harvard University Press, 1950. See also Miller's introduction and headnotes for insight into the transcendentalist movement.

Douglass, Frederick. *Narrative of the Life of Frederick Douglass, an American Slave, Written by Himself.* 1845. New York: Signet, 1997.

Melville, Herman. *Moby-Dick.* 1851. Edited by Hershel Parker and Harrison Hayford. 2nd ed. New York: Norton, 2002.

Thoreau, Henry David. "Resistance to Civil Government." 1849. In *Walden and Resistance to Civil Government: Authoritative texts, Thoreau's Journal, Reviews, and Essays in Criticism.* 2nd ed. Edited by William Rossi, pp. 226–245. New York: Norton, 1992.

Whitman, Walt. "Song of Myself." 1855. In *The Complete Poems.* Edited by Francis Murphy, pp. 675–738. New York: Penguin, 1977. Quotations are from the original untitled 1855 version of the poem Whitman later revised, somewhat tamed, and titled "Song of Myself."

Secondary Works

Abrahams, Roger D. *Singing the Master: The Emergence of African American Culture in the Plantation South.* New York: Pantheon, 1992. On communal agrarian practices in Africa.

Carey, Patrick W. Introduction to *The Early Works of Orestes A. Brownson: The Transcendentalist Years, 1836–1838,* vol. 3, pp. 1–40. Milwaukee, Wis.: Marquette University Press, 2002.

Dimock, Wai-Chee. *Empire for Liberty: Melville and the Poetics of Individualism.* Princeton, N.J.: Princeton University Press, 1989.

Duban, James. "Conscience and Consciousness: The Liberal Christian Context of Thoreau's Political Ethics." *New England Quarterly* 60, no. 2 (1987): 208–222.

Erkkila, Betsy. *Whitman the Political Poet.* New York: Oxford University Press, 1989.

Greven, Philip. *The Protestant Temperament: Patterns of Child-Rearing, Religious Experience, and the Self in Early America.* New York: Knopf, 1977.

Grossman, Jay. "'The Evangel-Poem of Comrades and of Love': Revising Whitman's Republicanism." *American Transcendental Quarterly* 4 (September 1990): 201–218.

Hedges, Chris. "On War." *New York Review of Books,* 16 December 2004, pp. 8–14.

Herbert, T. Walter, Jr. *Moby-Dick and Calvinism: A World Dismantled.* New Brunswick, N.J.: Rutgers University Press, 1977.

Jacobson, Matthew Frye. *Whiteness of a Different Color: European Immigrants and the Alchemy of Race.* Cambridge, Mass.: Harvard University Press, 1998.

Johnson, Chalmers. *The Sorrows of Empire: Militarism, Secrecy, and the End of the Republic.* New York: Metropolitan Books, 2004.

Macpherson, C. B. *The Political Theory of Possessive Individualism: Hobbes to Locke.* Oxford, U.K.: Oxford University Press, 1962.

Martin, Robert K. *Hero, Captain, and Stranger: Male Friendship, Social Critique, and Literary Form in the*

Sea Novels of Herman Melville. Chapel Hill: University of North Carolina Press, 1986.

Meyer, Michael. *Several More Lives to Live: Thoreau's Political Reputation in America*. Westport, Conn.: Greenwood Press, 1977.

Moon, Michael. *Disseminating Whitman: Revision and Corporeality in Leaves of Grass*. Cambridge, Mass.: Harvard University Press, 1991.

Porte, Joel. *Consciousness and Culture: Emerson and Thoreau Reviewed*. New Haven, Conn.: Yale University Press, 2004.

Shulman, Robert. *Social Criticism and Nineteenth-Century American Fictions*. Columbia: University of Missouri Press, 1987.

Sundquist, Eric J., ed. *Frederick Douglass: New Literary and Historical Essays*. Cambridge, U.K., and New York: Cambridge University Press, 1990.

Wood, Ellen Meiksins. *Mind and Politics: An Approach to the Meaning of Liberal and Socialist Individualism*. Berkeley: University of California Press, 1972.

Robert Shulman

THE INNOCENTS ABROAD

The Innocents Abroad (1869) by Mark Twain (Samuel L. Clemens, 1835–1910) has lasted as the book of travel written by an American that is the most widely read. Nearly 70,000 copies sold in the United States during its first year after publication, and by 1872 the honest count had passed 100,000 without including sales in Great Britain. There it became the most pirated of Mark Twain's books because the publisher had not protected the copyright. It "sells right along like the Bible" Twain would gloat to a friend (Howells, p. 8), partly because it turned into a guidebook; General Ulysses S. Grant, reporters told the home audience, carried it into Palestine on his closely followed travels of 1879. Twain, ever alert to marketing, several times considered reprising the title somehow in his later writings. In gratitude for its success he first decided to name the house where he would die "Innocence at Home." By 1910 *The Innocents Abroad* had still outsold his Tom-Huck novels. It has stayed in print with a widening choice of editions since the copyright expired.

Starting out, *The Innocents Abroad* benefited from the marketability of travel books, particularly about—in the most popular phrase—the Holy Land. American interest in the personages and scenes featured in the Bible was driven by Protestant ministers and educators, by their Sunday schools, sermons, and favorite parables. Twain's account of Palestine has only Christian

Illustration of Mark Twain dressed as an American Indian. From the first edition of *Innocents Abroad*, 1869. This drawing was later used in advertisements for the book. SPECIAL COLLECTIONS LIBRARY, UNIVERSITY OF MICHIGAN

relevance, blind to the economics and political pressure shaping the present natives he encountered marginally. Still, with the Civil War settled, Americans were thinking more broadly about foreign relations, so they also appreciated his early chapters on Europe, especially France and Italy. While a transatlantic tour cost far too much for most people, they nevertheless liked his emphasis on practical details such as adjusting to hotels, ordering foreign foods, and handling the insistent guides as well as beggars. However, even the travel books that centered on the famous objects and sights gave glimpses of day-to-day problems. *The Innocents Abroad* was and is uniquely popular because the literary persona of Mark Twain emerged at full height and depth, projecting his unique character. The passages most quoted deploy his greatest talent, his sense of humor. But readers were—and are—ultimately responding to a spirit vibrating between empathy and aggression, between warmth and icy disdain, between irreverence on principle and earthiness, between all of humankind's polarities.

COMPOSITION

Though any broad fact about Twain needs refining footnotes, the origins of *The Innocents Abroad* grow clear from a mass of documents—his notebooks, the installments of the commentary that was earning his passage, and the journalistic reports of at least nine other tourists aboard the *Quaker City* as well as private records and his own personal letters. Those letters prove that he had been yearning to move up from freelance articles to book form. Just before the *Quaker City* set out, *The Celebrated Jumping Frog of Calaveras County, and Other Sketches* (1867) had issued with faint success. But he had been projecting some more substantial book such as a reworking of his letters from the Sandwich (now Hawaiian) Islands for the *Sacramento Union* or his letters in early 1867 from the East Coast to the San Francisco *Alta California*. When the American Publishing Company of Hartford, Connecticut, approached him soon after the *Quaker City* came home, he was primed to negotiate. That the feeler came from a "subscription" firm suited his ambition to rake in big royalties, which would compensate for being peddled door to door by agents for advance orders. He would later exult over having gambled on a royalty of 5 percent (the edition commonly ordered cost $3.50) rather than a flat payout of $10,000.

The questions of when and where Twain put together the text of *The Innocents Abroad* are settled. Those facts help judge how severely his shipmate Mrs. Mary Mason Fairbanks had restrained his impulses during the trip and later (very little, actually) or how primly his fiancée, Olivia Langdon, with whom he vetted the proof sheets, censored his western roughness (still less, evidently). Those background facts also clarify the effect of the controversies among the tourists after settling in back home and the interplay between Twain's book and "The American Vandal Abroad," his lecture during the 1868–1869 season. Overall, knowing precisely when and where proves how effectively Twain could work under shifting and distracting circumstances or—less admirably—shows that *The Innocents Abroad* grew at a tempo that may have intensified its breathless tone.

Having signed a contract in late January 1868, Twain immediately set to work on the opening chapters while supporting himself with dispatches from Washington, D.C., for western newspapers and with freelance sketches, mostly political. Then, to settle the copyright on his letters about the trip for which the *Alta California* had paid $1,250 in greenbacks (and had added $500 in gold for onshore expenses), he trekked to San Francisco, where in May and June he completed the basic manuscript while lecturing occasionally for income. He headed back east—by a still roundabout, enervating route—in early July. By October 1868 he submitted his manuscript. After a winter of more freelancing, lecturing, and fervently courting Olivia Langdon, he revised during February 1869, started with the proof sheets on 12 March, and fondled bound copies in mid-July.

More than Twain at first intended, probably, *The Innocents Abroad* recycled his fifty letters (by the most accepted count) to the *Alta California*, adding some material from his six letters to the *New York Herald* but little from four minor pieces in the *New York Tribune*. For a national readership he minimized slang, inside jokes, and western references. Though not able, fortunately, to repress himself for long stretches, he toned down his irreverence, especially about biblical Christianity, and his trademark irascibility as the humorist and even "moralist" of the "Pacific Slope." At the level of craftsmanship he had to turn commentary created on the move, while grabbing at ideas, into what would read like an integrated book. He wove in continuities and a firmer sequence for the itinerary, inserting about 35,000 words into and around his printed yet now diligently revised letters. The Mark Twain persona functioned more clearly and more frequently as "I" and as a raconteur. Yet throughout, Twain stuck with the pattern that had worked for him so far, alternating seriousness and entertainment while trying, however, to pitch the humor at a more cerebral level than his routines in Nevada and San Francisco. Driving for a hefty book (it would issue with 651 pages) he produced too much manuscript. When Bret Harte, whom Twain still looked up to, agreed to cut sub-par passages and even chapters, Twain accepted his editing docilely, gratefully. Otherwise, he felt so assertive as to take active interest in choosing the 254 illustrations that the sales prospectus puffed. (Though Twain used "New Pilgrim's Progress" [singular] in the subtitle, the publisher, whether carelessly or deliberately, made the plural "Pilgrims'" the form commonly used today.)

THE INNOCENTS ABROAD AS TRAVELOGUE

While *The Innocents Abroad* dazzles contemporary readers as a solitary beacon, the book of travels has a long pedigree; it grew right along with printing itself. Also, it soon developed a shaky reputation; early travelers tended to imagine marvels that outdid the rarest realities. During the nineteenth century a sounder species evolved. Most specifically, the Americans who began going abroad to study sciences, languages, or the fine arts sometimes published their impressions; the sightseeing travelers who went next attracted a larger if still serious readership. Every stay-at-home who kept informed knew about the experiences of Bayard Taylor, George W. Curtis, and Margaret Fuller. Twain's preface assumed a familiar model when it promised to avoid "the usual style of travel-writing" and "to suggest to the reader how *he* would be likely to see Europe and the East if he looked at them with his own eyes instead of the eyes of those who traveled in those countries before him." Actually Twain's promise to probe beyond stereotypes was already close to a cliché. More distinctively, he avoided promising to edify or educate. His preface started forthrightly: "This book is a record of a pleasure-trip." True, the final chapter, based on his letter published the morning after the *Quaker City* got back, dismissed its trip as a "funeral excursion without a corpse" (p. 644). But the recurring effect of his book would be comic and exuberant, in tune with the "picnic on a gigantic scale" that he had pretended to expect (p. 19).

Comparativist perspectives show that *The Innocents Abroad* represented a tourist's rather than a traveler's experiences. The ideal traveler aims to engage another society on its own terms, to interact with another people minding their local affairs. The "programme" for the *Quaker City* promised an "Excursion to the Holy Land, Egypt, the Crimea, Greece, and Intermediate Points of Interest" (p. 20). Those points took in the Azores, Gibraltar, Morocco, Spain, France, Italy, and Turkey. All that in five months—minus about six weeks at sea. As for living abroad, the party's regular hotel was the ship itself, stocked with American cuisine. The sixty-six paying passengers usually went ashore as a group or in cliques. Twain had few adventures of his own worth mentioning. Guides who bickered over this next flock of sheep to be fleeced knew what services, sights, and illusions they wanted. *The Innocents Abroad* kept the touring aspect central, reporting on fees and prices, changing hygienes, misunderstandings, and street scenes. Twain's aggressive curiosity, delight in the bizarre, habitual impatience, and tremors of enthusiasm made the *Quaker City* excursion seem as rushed as tours that now dip into still another European metropolis each day.

Paradoxically, Twain's cross-grained spontaneity left some readers satisfied to do their touring by proxy. At least when Twain felt fatigued, bored, harassed, cheated, or surfeited, they felt better about not affording the trip themselves. Too many of the *Quaker City*'s passengers, leaning toward old age and pompously conventional, turned out to be dull or downright prickly companions, more fun to smile at than travel

with. Nor did most sights turn out to be worth so much expense and effort, especially in the Holy Land—the crowning goal of the trip. Besides the heat and the dirt, Palestine was so benighted, Twain joked, that the Second Advent was unlikely: Christ would not care to return. Maybe the smartest move was to settle down with Twain's book in the family circle. While running the gamut of entertainment, it gave the blunt, self-respecting, and quizzical lowdown about the famous places—the Cathedral of Notre Dame, Versailles, Pompeii, Vesuvius, the Catacombs, the canals of Venice, the Mosque of St. Sophia, the Church of the Holy Sepulcher, and the pyramids. Twain's readers could finish up believing that they comprehended the Old World more realistically than either its inhabitants or his awed, earnest companions (excepting his own clique).

Some readers of *The Innocents Abroad* enjoyed Twain's landscapes; "scene painting" was a must for travel-tourist literature that he met with pleasure. More as a duty, he grew eloquently solemn at the most venerable sites such as the Acropolis; in Jerusalem he apologized for not shouting louder hosannas. But modern analysts, like a few reviewers in 1869–1870, have fretted over the book's appeal to a less defensible part of the audience (or to a different side of it). *The Innocents Abroad* sounded the chauvinistic bugle, assuming that the United States, attuned to the present and future rather than a hierarchical past, exemplified progress, powered by its practical know-how. Likewise, Twain as American was supposedly showing how to combat highbrow taste or social practices (except when meeting the tsar of Russia). *The Innocents Abroad* went far beyond discovering that there's no place like home. Erratically, yet insistently, it flared up into New World swagger, combative alertness to not being taken in ("sold"), iconoclasm toward classical painting, and eagle-eyed readiness to pounce on the gap between pretense and reality, even at the Church of the Nativity.

Less gratifying, consciously, for a readership that supported Protestant Christianity as the quasi-official morality was Twain's irreverence. For these readers his anti-Catholic sermons helped to sanitize his more impious tendencies. But the subtitle of his breezy book alluded to John Bunyan's revered allegory, and several passages came close to parodying the Bible, generally heard as the literal word from Heaven. Uneasy about the reviewers, Twain decided that his irreverence had proved a "tip-top good feature," financially at least (*Letters* 3:329). Bracketing his impieties with solemn homilies may have further lulled the literalists. Yet crypto-agnostics, old deists, and budding freethinkers could take confirmatory pleasure from *The Innocents Abroad.* Deplorably, the nativist constituency left over from the Know-Nothing Party must have enjoyed a tangential irreverence: Twain's savagery toward the "savages," that is, the Semitic natives descended from Jesus' people. If the "I" narrator berated the commoners of the Azores, Italy, and Greece as feckless, he heated up to accusatory contempt in Palestine: "Squalor and poverty are the pride of Tiberias" (p. 505).

THE MARK TWAIN PERSONA

Surely, humane readers winced at Twain's berating of the poor and luckless, however boldly his publisher featured the book's "mirth" and the consensus among reviewers praised its geniality. That consensus overlooked or excused many traits of its narrating personality. Besides Twain's anti-compassionate politics for export and his slurs on foreign humanity as backward, supine, and gullible, he approached sounding arrogant, even vindictive, declaring his pleasure in taking "satisfied revenge" (p. 459) no matter how petty. Easily irritated, he lashed back—in retrospect—with ridicule, justifying those Hobbesian analysts who find superiority or hostility at the core of humor.

Sometimes Twain as American pilgrim seemed to approve of hardly anyone, including his flawed self. Bret Harte's review was generous in calling him "irascible." His jaunty irreverence kept descending into joking about dyspepsia, dung, disfigurement, diseases, and ungainly deaths. Appropriately, his favorite habits made him expert at gambling and at ordering cocktails. Alert to attractive women, he gauged their availability. Not all of his masculine freewheeling was tolerable as Western since the persona mostly claimed a national identity. Not even the sales-centered publisher recommended *The Innocents Abroad* for Sunday schools.

Nevertheless, those glitches of character faded when the persona turned on his charm. His humor helped crucially, honed by years of practice in the moves of the literary comedians and, recently, by admiring analysis of Artemus Ward's technique. "Is he dead?" became an international tagline for teasing routinized behavior rather than baiting a guide who was practicing a useful skill. Weeping at the supposed tomb of Adam raised gut hilarity rather than a suspicion of being satirized. The persona also earned much indulgence through honesty about himself, confessing his blunders (famously, his buying gloves at Gibraltar) or his ignorance about the paintings brashly belittled ("we [I] do not know much about art" (p. 423). In switching without apology from the beauty of Genoese women to local tobacco his verve made his free dissociation a virtue, exhilarating rather than disorienting. Defying the rules of either stable character or orderly prose rounded out to an encompassing spirit of play, of delight in feeling, doing, and saying the unexpected. The reader began to discount and then to enjoy Twain's harsh criticisms and even threats as mock violence, as part of a game. Yet, concurrently, Twain was establishing a presence as one of the shrewdest passengers on the *Quaker City* and, within his clique, a leader of the "boys." Of all his books, *The Innocents Abroad* most irresistibly overruns any pattern or abstract system that critics propose for it.

Eventually, the critic trying to understand *The Innocents Abroad* as an integrated construct has to argue that it achieves unity through literary finesse. The opening chapters create an ironic, tolerantly cynical voice that soon adds both verve and worldliness. As the tour moves along, the persona also shows the resilience of getting over his blunders. Though deepening in acerbity he never rages for long or pontificates without his humor poised to interrupt. His self-awareness makes a virtue of his vehemence by declaring that "I like no half-way things" (p. 239). Though oscillating between send-ups and conventionalities—and deadpanning in the middle so craftily that readers have to stay alert—he comes across as basically self-determined. A forceful, colorful, yet easy-jointed prose bonds the diversifying elements. Despite the upsurges of anarchic spontaneity the ultimate effect is like the Washoe Zephyr, which *Roughing It* would admire for carrying everything and everybody in the direction it wanted to go. While apparently honoring authenticity, Twain invents dialogue, even incident, and develops a crew of supporting characters to help fill his sails. Some critics emphasize his introspective consciousness or a search for inner identity as a master theme. But readers are primarily swept along by an attitude, brilliantly articulated for a personality who reacts and pro-acts impulsively, comfortable with his forceful inconsistency in a complex world.

AFTER 1869

The Innocents Abroad established Mark Twain financially and professionally. His publisher, who concentrated on a few books, promoted it diligently. Newspapers paid unpaid attention because Twain did credit to their world as a reporter-columnist who made his mark (the inevitable pun). Unexpectedly, the sedate *Atlantic Monthly* carried a long, favorable review, unsigned (from a young William Dean Howells). Twain had upgraded from a freelancer to a writer of books, even of literature, exemplified in the publisher's later prospectuses by the threnody on the Sphynx, "so sad, so earnest, so longing, so patient" (p. 629). Revising in

1872 for a new British edition, Twain showed a rising sense of what he had accomplished and how he rated in turn. By 1879, when *The Innocents Abroad* joined the Tauchnitz editions solidly respected across Europe, he felt gratified but not surprised. It would stay prominent during his lifetime, leading off in the collected edition of his works that finally got on track in 1899.

By 1886, after a string of books, Twain could look at *The Innocents Abroad* quizzically, echoing its irreverence by pairing it with how God must have felt later about the world He created: "The fact is, there is a trifle too much water in both" (DeVoto, p. 764). But he appreciated how much the writing it and how much the experiences behind it had taught him. On the *Quaker City* he had mixed, for the first prolonged time, with middle- and upper-middle-class people—including Olivia Langdon's brother, who would introduce Twain to his family. While still wary afterward of highbrow culture, he did try harder to see paintings and choose music its way. Less hearteningly, touring Palestine, especially in continued retrospect, must have shaken any lingering Sunday-school legends and any faith in the Bible as substantive history. Literarily, *The Innocents Abroad* led to the first stage of mastery of his prose style and of his persona as he aimed to captivate a national readership and its guardians.

See also Americans Abroad; "The Celebrated Jumping Frog of Calaveras County"; Humor; Satire, Burlesque, and Parody

BIBLIOGRAPHY
Primary Works
DeVoto, Bernard, ed. *The Portable Mark Twain.* New York: Viking, 1946.

Twain, Mark. *The Innocents Abroad; or, The New Pilgrims' Progress.* 1869. Edited by Shelley Fisher Fishkin, afterword by David E. E. Sloane. New York: Oxford University Press, 1996. A facsimile reprint of the first edition. Page numbers refer to this text.

Twain, Mark. *Mark Twain's Letters.* Vol. 2, *1867–1868.* Edited by Harriet Elinor Smith and Richard Bucci. Berkeley: University of California Press, 1990.

Twain, Mark. *Mark Twain's Letters.* Vol. 3, *1869.* Edited by Victor Fischer and Michael B. Frank. Berkeley: University of California Press, 1992.

Secondary Works
Bridgman, Richard. *Traveling in Mark Twain.* Berkeley: University of California Press, 1987.

Budd, Louis J., ed. *Mark Twain: The Contemporary Reviews.* New York: Cambridge University Press, 1999.

Cox, James M. *Mark Twain: The Fate of Humor.* Princeton, N.J.: Princeton University Press, 1966.

David, Beverly R. *Mark Twain and His Illustrators.* Vol. 1, *1869–1875.* Troy, N.Y.: Whitston, 1986.

Ganzel, Dewey. *Mark Twain Abroad: The Cruise of the "Quaker City."* Chicago: University of Chicago Press, 1968.

Hill, Hamlin L. *Mark Twain and Elisha Bliss.* Columbia: University of Missouri Press, 1964.

Howells, W. D. *My Mark Twain: Reminiscences and Criticisms.* New York: Harper, 1910.

McKeithan, Daniel Morley. *Traveling with the Innocents Abroad: Mark Twain's Original Reports from Europe and the Holy Land.* Norman: University of Oklahoma Press, 1958.

Melton, Jeffrey Alan. *Mark Twain, Travel Books, and Tourism: The Tide of a Great Popular Movement.* Tuscaloosa: University of Alabama Press, 2002.

Obenzinger, Hilton. *American Palestine: Melville, Twain, and the Holy Land Mania.* Princeton, N.J.: Princeton University Press, 1999.

Quirk, Tom. "Introduction." In *The Innocents Abroad,* edited by Tom Quirk. New York: Penguin Books, 2002.

Smith, Henry Nash. *Mark Twain: The Development of a Writer.* Cambridge, Mass.: Harvard University Press, 1962.

Ziff, Larzer. *Return Passages: Great American Travel Writing, 1780–1910.* New Haven, Conn.: Yale University Press, 2000.

Louis J. Budd

IRISH

Since 1169 Ireland has been occupied by an English army: the history of the Irish, like the history of many oppressed, colonized people, has had great influence on the character of the Irish in Ireland and abroad. Penal laws were instituted by the British beginning in 1695 to force the Irish to adopt both the Protestant faith and the capitalist ethic of the industrializing English nation. The adopting of such external values offered the Irish a way out of poverty to economic security, but leaving the Catholic Church required a rejection of one's self, family, community, and history. The Penal Code restricted all but the converted Irish from any mobility (including education and landownership), took away their language, and attempted to take their religion.

IMMIGRATION TO AMERICA
Protestant Irish had been immigrating to North America since the 1700s, and in 1815 and 1816 twenty thousand mostly Protestant Irishmen from Ulster arrived in the United States. But it was not until

the mid-1820s that poorer Catholic Irish, self-identified as laborers, began to immigrate in significant numbers. By the late 1830s the majority of immigrants from Ireland were Catholic, rural, and poor. Large-scale Irish immigration to the United States began after the period from 1845 to 1849 known as the Irish potato famine, also called the Great Hunger, when a series of potato crop failures, the sole crop for most Irish farmers, led to extreme poverty and starvation, leading to over a million deaths in Ireland and as many emigrants leaving Ireland. Between 1845 and 1870, 2.5 million Irish immigrated to the United States.

Emigration for the famine generation Irish was not seen as a way to strike it rich in the New World but rather as a forced, involuntary exile. Before a family member was about to leave, an "American wake" was held, a ceremony bemoaning the necessity to emigrate. Of course, there were those Irish who chose willingly to go, particularly women—who were doubly oppressed—and anglicized Irish. But on the whole, continuing religious persecution from the British combined with extreme poverty were the motivating factors to undertake the arduous and often dangerous crossing of the Atlantic: in 1847 (known as "Black '47") 20 percent of Irish passengers on the sea died either during or shortly after the voyage, a total of over forty-two thousand people.

Famine generation Irish immigrants often did not have the support network available to those arriving afterward and were vulnerable to experiences of homesickness, unemployment, and cultural dislocation. Although some went out west and a few became millionaires during the California gold rush of 1848 and 1849, most often these predominantly rural Irish immigrants (who refused to return to farming, defeated by the potato blight) settled in the burgeoning metropolitan areas, adapting to urban life just as urban life was beginning to burst. Slums and ghettos developed, and a shantytown in the upper west side of New York City's Central Park was established by those who were either evicted from the slums or who refused to live in them.

The immigrants quickly discovered that their treatment in America was no different than it had been in Ireland by the British. Anti-Catholicism had been a feature of American society since colonial times, and it became increasingly virulent as more Irish and German Catholics entered the United States from the 1820s onward. The Catholic Church was seen as bowing to a foreign power, with priests and nuns portrayed in the popular press as immoral and unsavory. Antagonism between Catholics and Protestants also followed the immigrants from Ireland: in 1837 a mob

of Protestant workmen in Boston burned a Catholic convent; in the 1840s it was not uncommon for riots to evolve out of the fighting between Protestants and Irish Catholics, and several Catholic churches were burned in Philadelphia. In the 1850s the antiforeign and anti-Catholic American Party, commonly called the Know-Nothing Party, advocated national unity, the exclusion of foreign-born people from voting or holding public office, and anti-Catholic legislation.

Conflicts between Irish Americans and African Americans began in the 1830s and 1840s when Irish immigrants were recruited to work on the canals of upstate New York, thus displacing other unskilled workers, including free blacks: "To many Irish, abolitionism was a nativist and anti-Catholic movement that represented a profound threat to their livelihoods: the freeing of four million enslaved Americans would compete with them" for jobs, suggests Maureen Dezell (p. 147). Despite such feelings, Irish immigrants enlisted in the Union Army during the Civil War in high numbers, often for the pay. Yet when the federal government passed a draft law in 1863 allowing rich draftees to pay their way out of the war, many poor Irish immigrants responded angrily. The Civil War draft riots, says Dezell, were "the largest and bloodiest insurrection that has ever taken place in the United States. Blacks had been used as strikebreakers in New York and were exempt from the draft, and Irish laborers turned on African Americans" (p. 147). The burning and looting of buildings, including the draft board building and the Negro Orphan Asylum, went on for four days, ultimately confirming the negative stereotypes of Irish immigrants.

AMERICANIZING THE IRISH AMERICAN: FAMILY, POLITICS, AND THE CHURCH

Despite the conflicts that the famine generation of immigrants faced, Irish arriving in the United States were relatively successful in assimilating due to three pillars: the family, politics, and the church. All three institutions helped to protect Irish immigrants from anti-Irish Catholic prejudice yet at the same time encouraged assimilation.

Unlike Protestant Irish immigrants, who often discouraged family members from following them to the United States, Irish Catholic immigrants, perhaps because of the starvation faced by family members during the potato famine era, often sacrificed themselves to save enough money to bring family members to the United States. Although such attention to family ties may have impeded economic success in the United States, close family relationships provided psychological support for immigrants on their own in a new country.

"NO IRISH NEED APPLY"

"No Irish Need Apply" was a popular song among Irish Americans in the 1860s. This version was written by John Poole.

I am a dacint Irishman, just come from Ballyfad;
Oh I want a situation and I want it mighty bad.
A position I saw advertised. 'Tis the thing for me,
    says I;
But the dirty spalpeen ended with: No Irish need apply.
Whoa! Says I; but that's an insult—but to get this
    place I'll try.
So, I went to see the blaguard with: No Irish need
    apply.
Well some may think it a misfortune; To be chris-
    tened Pat or Dan
But to me it is an honor; To be born an Irishman.
Well I started out to find this chap, I found him
    mighty soon;
He was seated in the corner, he was reading the
    TRIBUNE.
When I told him what I came for, he in a rage did fly.
And he says, you are a Paddy, and no Irish need
    apply!
Then I felt me dander rising, that I'd like to black his
    eye
To tell a dacint gentleman: No Irish need apply!
Well, I couldn't stand his nonsense so ahold of him
    I took
And I gave him such a batin' as he'd get in
    Donnybrook

And he hollered "mile murder" and to get away did try
And he swore he'd never write again: No Irish need
    apply.
He made a big apology; I bid him then goodbye
Sayin' when next you want a batin' write: No Irish
    need apply.
Well, I've heard that in America it always is the plan
That an Irishman is just as good as any other man;
A home and hospitality they never will deny
To strangers here, or ever write: No Irish
    need apply.
Ah but some black sheep are in the flock: a dirty lot
    says I;
A dacint man will never write: No Irish need apply!
Now old Ireland on the battle field a lasting fame
    has made;
You all have heard of Meagher's men and Corcoran's
    brigade
Though fools may flout and bigots rave, fanatics
    they may cry,
But when they want good fightin' men the Irish may
    apply.
And when for freedom and for right they raise the
    battle cry
Those rebel ranks will surely think: No Irish need
    apply!

Moloney, *Far from the Shamrock Shore*, p. 16.

Yet economic effects in the United States also had a transforming impact on Irish American family structure, particularly in terms of gender roles. In Ireland, family duties, social events, and even church attendance were all sex- and age-segregated. Although a wife might occasionally work in the fields during harvest time, the spheres of influences for both sexes were clearly delineated: women controlled the house, men the farm. Men were in control of economic and marriage decisions. As Irish families established themselves in the United States, however, new family structures emerged that gave rise to the stereotype of the controlling, bossy Irish matriarch. The immigrant husband would work long hours, often far away from home, giving the wife total control over family life, including money management and the raising of the children. Also, in times of high unemployment, Irish women, married or not, were often more employable than men. Although most married women did not work outside the home, some had to, and virtually all Irish women worked before marriage. The effects of this change in gender roles were not entirely negative: children of such mothers were usually pushed to succeed economically, helping the Irish to assimilate in terms of social and economic class within a single generation.

Experience in politics learned in Ireland also worked in the favor of the Irish immigrants: between

Anti-Catholic cartoon by Thomas Nast, 1867. Inspired by a St. Patrick's Day riot in New York City in 1867, Nast created this derogatory depiction of Irish Catholics. THE GRANGER COLLECTION, NEW YORK

1820 and 1880, the Irish worked together to create political allegiances that reached an apex in the influence they wielded within the Democratic Party organization of Tammany Hall in 1880s New York City. Irish immigrants used existing structures such as local parishes and saloons in order to organize, quickly electing fellow Irishmen as leaders within the Democratic Party and achieving power within the political systems of most urban areas. Voter loyalty was maintained through patronage: in cities such as New York, Chicago and Boston, the Irish quickly held leadership posts in police and fire departments and in sanitation and public works jobs. Most Irish Americans were upwardly mobile economically by the late nineteenth century.

The Catholic Church in the United States was also essential in the Americanization of the Irish immigrants. With the sheer numbers of Irish immigrants, Irish clergy easily gained control of the church in the United States. Before the 1830s, the leadership of the Catholic Church in the United States was mostly French or French-trained, but by 1860 the church had become an immigrant church. Although most pre-famine Catholic immigrants were non-churchgoing, the leadership of the Irish-born bishop John Hughes (1797–1864) in gathering Irish immigrants into the church family was effective. By 1870 the parish church became the center of the immigrant community: priests were directly involved in Irish American family life, and Irish families returned the favor by contributing money to build churches and parochial schools and to support more priests from Ireland.

THE IRISH IN AMERICAN LITERATURE

The Irish American literary tradition began with the first wave of Protestant Irish immigrants in the eighteenth century and has continued into the twenty-first century, making it "the most extended continuous corpus of literature by members of a single American ethnic group available to us," writes Charles Fanning in the introduction to his anthology *The Exiles of Erin* (p. 1). Unlike the famine generation writers who followed, the first Irish immigrants to the United States were generally received with indifference more than hostility, and because there were so few of them, they were able to assimilate more quickly. Granted, the British had exported an anti-Irishness that was seen in American newspapers and magazines even before the arrival of mostly Irish Catholic immigrants in the form of Irish stereotypes: the alcoholic, baboon-like figure who cries in his beer while singing a ditty, for example. But early Irish-born writers in America, usually educated and middle class themselves, used satire and parody to combat these stereotypes.

Henry David Thoreau (1817–1862) was unusual in the thoughtfulness of his references to the Irish immigrants in *Walden* (1854) and in his journal: he criticizes the Irish at first for their poor living conditions, yet at the same time he praises those Irish immigrants in Concord, Massachusetts, whom he considered hard working and frugal. One might notice a small irony in the fact that Thoreau built his cabin at Walden Pond from the wood of an Irishman's shanty. In his journal for 1851, Thoreau writes about several Irish immigrants as individuals who impress him, including a young Johnny Riordan who walks to school during the Massachusetts winter without shoes or coat. As Herbert Joseph Smith notes in his impressive study of the Irish in American fiction: "Thoreau's observations constitute the fullest record of a major American writer's personal reflections on his encounters with the Irish during this period" (p. 179). Most non-Irish writers of the time either referred to the Irish immigrants stereotypically or not at all.

In *Exiles of Erin,* Fanning notes that works by Irish immigrant writers before the 1840s illustrate a return to the eighteenth-century use of self-satire as a response to immigration and to the Irish immigrant position in the United States. For example, *The Life and Travels of Father Quipes, Otherwise Dominick O'Blarney* (1820) and *The Life of Paddy O'Flarrity* (1834), each ostensibly an autobiographical narrative "written by Himself," are anonymously produced satires of the Irish immigrant dream of success in the United States. *Six Months in the House of Correction; or, The Narrative of Dorah Mahoney* (1835), by another anonymous Irish writer, mocks the anti-Catholic fiction of the period. John McDermott Moore's *The Adventures of Tom Stapleton* (1842) mocks Irish American and American "social, political, and literary life, while parodying a range of New York dialects and the conventions of popular, sentimental fiction" (Fanning, *Exiles,* p. 23). One of the earliest Irish American novels is by an Ulster Protestant immigrant, James McHenry: *The Wilderness* (1823) is the story of Ulster immigrants to western Pennsylvania.

Fanning argues that McHenry's novels "are pioneering attempts to define Irishness for an American audience" (*Exiles,* p. 23).

By the time Irish Catholics arrived in the United States from Ireland, they chose to address their fiction to their own kind, other Irish immigrants, dismissing satire as just too cruel for a people so constantly humiliated. The fiction turned serious and didactic, providing pragmatic advice for the newcomers on how to survive their hostile reception in Protestant America.

The themes of this didactic fiction, often in the form of domestic novels, included the struggle between good and evil in the New World; how to become economically secure without losing your faith; the power of the church; the power of the Irish mother; and nostalgia for Ireland. Some of the titles emphasize these themes, as well as the dualistic worldview inherent in them: examples include *The Cross and the Shamrock; or, How to Defend the Faith* (1853) by Father Hugh Quigley; and *The Lost Rosary; or, Our Irish Girls, Their Trials, Temptations, and Triumphs* (1870) by Peter McCorry. Writers such as Mary Anne Sadlier and Father John Roddan reassured Irish immigrants that they too could partake in the American dream of prosperity without giving up their Irish culture and Catholic religion, yet only if they could overcome the many obstacles in their path. The hero of Roddan's novel *John O'Brien; or, The Orphan of Boston* (1850) nearly loses his faith in the process of working for a series of Protestant employers. Although he ends up in a reformatory, he eventually returns to the Catholic Church and at the end is rewarded with economic prosperity.

Fiction by Irish American writers in the late nineteenth century often focused on this conflict: the desire for middle-class respectability in the face of ongoing poverty versus the fear of losing one's sense of Irish identity. The Irish American press played an important role in immigrant literature by printing an abundance of short fiction written by Irish Americans in this period. Periodicals such as the Boston *Pilot,* a popular Catholic magazine that had a national circulation as early as the 1840s, sought to counteract stereotypes and promote Irish nationalism in its Irish American readers. Yet, like the fiction of the time, such magazines published stories that rarely showed tenement life or working conditions—despite the fact that many Irish were still in the ghettoes as late as the 1870s. Instead they emphasized success stories about Irish immigrants who became Americanized without losing their ethnic identity. For the most part the Irish American press printed stories that, although unrealistic, provided early positive images of Irish Americans who worked hard but stayed Catholic in the process of assimilation.

MARY ANNE SADLIER: BARD OF THE IRISH AMERICANS

One of the most popular women writers of this period was Mary Anne (Madden) Sadlier (1820–1903), who in 1846 had married James Sadlier of the publishing firm of D. and J. Sadlier and Company, a prominent member of the Roman Catholic press based in Montreal and New York. She wrote dozens of novels, all best-sellers within the Irish immigrant community. Her literary fame in America began when her first immigrant novel, *Willy Burke; or, The Irish Orphan in America*, was published in the *Pilot* in 1850 and then later that same year published as a book. In her preface to *Willy Burke* she identifies the didactic goal of her immigrant fiction: it was "written for the express purpose of being useful to the young sons of my native land, in their arduous struggle with the tempter" (p. 3). The novel sold seven thousand copies within a few weeks of publication. At the end of the optimistic novel, the hero Willy not only achieves economic success, but he successfully gets two Protestant characters to convert to Catholicism.

Sadlier shrewdly marketed her books with an eye to reaching an audience of Catholic working-class immigrants. The scholar Michele Lacombe notes that Sadlier bears comparison with her contemporary Harriet Beecher Stowe (1811–1896), in that she "claimed to be working not for fame but for God and country—in this case the Catholic faith and the Irish nation in America"—but she was rewarded with fame nonetheless (p. 101).

The Blakes and the Flanagans: A Tale, Illustrative of Irish Life in the United States (first published serially in 1850), Sadlier's most popular novel, depicts one of the central issues in Irish American politics in 1850: the "schools question." Catholics objected to the Protestant-controlled public school system and set out to create a separate system of Catholic schools. The idealized, "good" Catholic Flanagans in Sadlier's novel find success in America as a result of their piety: their children are not corrupted by the public school system. The Blakes, however, are depicted as fallen Catholics, worse than Protestants, and are justly punished for their betrayal of Catholicism. In Sadlier's works, loyalty to the Catholic Church supersedes all. Irish Catholic tradition (as well as the ideal of the Victorian American woman) expected women to be both submissive to their husbands and also moral and religious guardians. It is not surprising then that Sadlier's women characters like Mrs. Blake are the first

In The Blakes and the Flanagans (1850), *Mary Anne Sadlier illustrates the conflict over identity faced by the Irish in America, and she advocates the values of those characters who maintain their sense of Irishness. When Miles Blake warns that "men can't be Irishmen and Americans at the same time; they must be either one or the other," his nephew Ned Flanagan answers:*

I myself am a living proof that your position is a false one. I was brought up, as you well know, under Catholic—nay, more, under Irish training; I am Irish in heart—Catholic, I hope, in faith and practice, and yet I am fully prepared to stand by this great Republic, the land of my birth, even to shedding the last drop of my blood, were that necessary. I love America; it is, as it were, the land of my adoption, as well as of my birth, but I cannot, or will not, forget Ireland.

Fanning, *The Irish Voice in America*, p. 124.

to recognize any encroachment on their religion: it is Mrs. Blake, and not her husband, who first realizes the not-so-hidden agenda of the public schools.

The novel also explicitly notes that the virtue of working did not mean, for good Catholics, that money was the sole object. Mr. Blake is criticized for spending more time earning money than watching over his family. Sadlier particularly feared that social mobility in America threatened what she saw as indivisible safety nets for Irish immigrants: religion, family, and ethnicity. The Blake children learn to reject both Catholicism and all things Irish while in public school—this, in turn, destroys family ties between generations. By maintaining ethnic and religious ties, the Flanagan family stays intact: they earn a comfortable living at a family-run business.

Although Sadlier only implies the real-life social problems of Irish immigrants in her early novels (perhaps to avoid focusing on ethnic stereotypes), by the time she wrote *Bessy Conway* (1861) she highlights them: alcoholism, poverty, and spousal abuse exist within the Irish community, and not just as punishment for lapsed Catholics and Protestants. Here Sadlier takes the more American stance of blaming the individual rather than the circumstances. The novel depicts the tale of hard-working Bessy, who refuses to convert to Protestantism in order to save her job and who is rewarded at the end with a return to Ireland, bringing pockets full of money but warning her neighbors: "Keep your girls at home!" (p. 296). The rest of the novel's characters do not fare as well as Bessy: one cousin becomes an alcoholic and wife beater; his sister-in-law marries a fool who leaves her alone with a crippled daughter. Another character is eventually killed by her abusive husband, and their son is adopted by Protestants who turn him against Catholicism. Meanwhile, pious Bessy returns in time to save her family from eviction and so impresses the landlord's son that he converts to marry her: the self-sacrificing, religious woman who manages to avoid the negative effects of immigration is rewarded at the end, in this world and the next. With this novel, Sadlier effectively moved from being an Irish-American writer to being an American writer, foreshadowing themes in the works of later Irish writers in America where character becomes more important than ethnic circumstances.

See also Blacks; Catholics; Domestic Fiction; Immigration; Labor; Political Parties; Religion; Satire, Burlesque, and Parody

BIBLIOGRAPHY

Primary Works

Fanning, Charles, ed. *The Exiles of Erin: Nineteenth-Century Irish-American Fiction*. Notre Dame, Ind.: University of Notre Dame Press, 1987. Many of the nineteenth-century works mentioned in this essay are reprinted in part in this anthology.

Roddan, John. *John O'Brien; or, The Orphan of Boston*. Boston: Donahoe, 1850.

Sadlier, Mary Anne. *Alice Riordan: The Blind Man's Daughter*. Boston: Donahoe, 1851.

Sadlier, Mary Anne. *Bessy Conway; or, The Irish Girl in America*. New York: Sadlier, 1861.

Sadlier, Mary Anne. *The Blakes and the Flanagans: A Tale Illustrative of Irish Life in the United States*. New York: P. J. Kennedy, 1855. First published serially in 1850.

Sadlier, Mary Anne. *Con O'Regan; or, Emigrant Life in the New World*. New York: Sadlier, 1864.

Sadlier, Mary Anne. *Elinor Preston; or, Scenes at Home and Abroad*. New York: Sadlier, 1861.

Sadlier, Mary Anne. *New Lights; or, Life in Galway*. New York: Sadlier, 1853.

Sadlier, Mary Anne. *Old and New; or, Taste Versus Fashion*. New York: Sadlier, 1862.

Sadlier, Mary Anne. *Willy Burke; or, The Irish Orphan in America*. Boston: Donahoe, 1850.

Thoreau, Henry David. *The Annotated Walden: Walden, or, Life in the Woods*. Edited by Philip Van Doren Stern. New York: Barnes and Noble, 1992.

Thoreau, Henry David. *Journal*. 8 vols. to date. Edited by Elizabeth Hall Witherell et al. Princeton, N.J.: Princeton University Press, 1981– .

Secondary Works

Biddle, Ellen Horgan. "The American Catholic Irish Family." In *Ethnic Families in America: Patterns and Variations*, edited by Charles H. Mindel and Robert W. Habenstein, pp. 89–123. New York: Elsevier, 1976.

Daniels, Roger. *Coming to America: A History of Immigration and Ethnicity in American Life*. New York: HarperCollins, 1990.

Dezell, Maureen. *Irish America: Coming into Clover*. New York: Doubleday, 2000.

Diner, Hasia R. *Erin's Daughters in America: Irish Immigrant Women in the Nineteenth Century*. Baltimore: Johns Hopkins University Press, 1983.

Fanning, Charles. *The Irish Voice in America: 250 Years of Irish-American Fiction*. 2nd ed. Lexington: University Press of Kentucky, 2000.

Jensen, Richard. "'No Irish Need Apply': A Myth of Victimization." *Journal of Social History* 36, no. 2 (2002): 405–429.

Lacombe, Michele. "Frying Pans and Deadlier Weapons: The Immigrant Novels of Mary Anne Sadlier." *Essays on Canadian Writing* 29 (summer 1984): 96–116.

McDannell, Colleen. *The Christian Home in Victorian America, 1840–1900*. Bloomington: Indiana University Press, 1986.

McDannell, Colleen. "The Devil Was the First Protestant": Gender and Intolerance in Catholic Fiction." *U.S. Catholic Historian* 8 (winter/spring 1989): 51–65.

Miller, Kerby A. *Emigrants and Exiles: Ireland and the Irish Exodus to North America*. New York: Oxford University Press, 1985.

Moloney, Mick. *Far from the Shamrock Shore: The Story of Irish-American Immigration through Song*. New York: Crown, 2002.

Olson, James S. *The Ethnic Dimension in American History*. 3rd ed. St. James, N.Y.: Brandywine Press, 1999.

Rose, Anne C. *Voices of the Marketplace: American Thought and Culture, 1830–1860*. New York: Twayne, 1995.

Smith, Herbert Joseph. "From Stereotype to Acculturation: The Irish-American's Fictional Heritage from Brackenridge to Farrell." Ph.D. diss., Kent State University, 1980.

Takaki, Ronald. *A Different Mirror: A History of Multicultural America*. Boston: Little, Brown, 1993.

Walsh, Francis. "Lace Curtain Literature: Changing Perspectives of Irish American Success." *Journal of American Culture* 2, no. 1 (1979): 139–146.

Stacey Lee Donohue

JEWS

Although they constituted a small percentage of the population prior to 1870, Jews occupied a significant place in the American imagination from the time of the founding of the New England colonies. This can largely be attributed to the centrality of Hebrew scripture to seventeenth-century Puritan colonists, an importance reflected by the choice of a translation of biblical psalms from Hebrew as the first book to be published in New England. On a more abstract and enduring level, the discourse of Puritans suggested identification between themselves and biblical Israelites. Typical of this analogy is an assertion in John Winthrop's sermon "A Model of Christian Charity" (1630) that if fellow colonists act properly, "We shall find that the God of Israel is among us." This sense of identification recurs in subsequent literature, such as Timothy Dwight's epic poem of the American Revolution, *The Conquest of Canaan* (1785), which features George Washington as an American version of the biblical Joshua. Herman Melville would later observe in *White-Jacket* (1850) more equivocally, "we Americans are the peculiar, chosen people—the Israel of our time; we bear the ark of the liberties of the world" (p. 506). Such symbolic resonance between biblical Jews and antebellum Americans rarely seems to have been affected by interactions with contemporary Jews.

JEWISH LIFE BEFORE 1870

Jews had lived in the colonies from the seventeenth century onward, yet by 1820 there were fewer than three thousand American Jews, most of whom traced their ancestry to Spain and Portugal. These Sephardic Jews would soon become a minority within the Jewish community as increasing numbers of Jews from northern and central Europe arrived despite the prevalent attitude in their native countries that the United States was a place where traditional Jewish religious customs, study, and institutions were minimal. By 1850 the American Jewish population was approximately fifty thousand, and by 1870 it approached a quarter of a million, still less than 1 percent of the overall population. American Jewish practices differed markedly from European observances as new arrivals settled in a variety of areas and established their own institutions. Many of these institutions were less religious in nature than they were community oriented, such as B'nai B'rith, or religious in a nontraditional manner, as was the case with congregations that adhered to the tenets of Reform Judaism. The range of Jewish life in the United States forms the basis of *Three Years in America, 1859–1862* (1862; English translation, 1956), an account of travels in the United States by a German-Jewish writer, Israel Joseph Benjamin (1818–1864).

The American response to the Jewish presence was complex. Legal restrictions against Jews holding office and voting were maintained in a few states and Christian missionary societies devoted to proselytizing among Jews reflected a degree of intolerance. Yet in general the civil and economic rights enjoyed by Jews surpassed conditions they encountered in Europe, where state-sponsored discriminatory practices were common and organized violence against Jews recurred. Moreover, the political successes of some Jews in both the North and the South, which included election to seats in Congress, attests to a level of acceptance. Historians have argued that the relative freedoms of the United States were a major appeal to young immigrants, yet the consensus is that economic opportunity, which was often associated at the time with prospects for marriage, was the primary attraction. This explanation accounts for the continued growth of Jewish immigration even after 1870, a period of increased racial and ethnic tension throughout the nation, when restrictions against Jews expanded.

Antebellum Jews produced a range of journalistic pieces, essays, letters, and other occasional works, but few Jews devoted themselves to more sustained literary projects. Mordecai Manuel Noah (1785–1851), the most prominent American Jewish personage of his era, built a reputation as a politician, diplomat, playwright, and essayist, although he is largely remembered for his unsuccessful attempt in 1825 to create a Jewish colony called Ararat near Buffalo, New York. Another notable Jewish figure whose influence was more enduring, Isaac Leeser (1806–1868), disseminated translations and textbooks on religion and in 1843 founded *The Occident*, an important periodical that gave voice to traditional religious attitudes. A weekly newspaper devoted to Reform Judaism, *The Israelite*, was established in 1854 by Isaac Mayer Wise

(1819–1900), who also wrote novels, plays, and poetry. Other Jewish newspapers and periodicals of the era attest to the spread of the Jewish population from northeastern cities as far west and south as California and Florida. In addition to these publications, poetry by such Sephardic women writers as Penina Moïse (1797–1880) and the actress Adah Isaacs Menken (c. 1835–1868) attained a degree of popularity, albeit not as great as that later achieved by Emma Lazarus (1849–1887), the most famous nineteenth-century American Jewish poet.

JEWS AND NINETEENTH-CENTURY AMERICAN LITERATURE

The association between Jews and biblical writings remained strong within the literature of the period. Passing references may be found in works by James Fenimore Cooper, such as *The Oak Openings; or, The Bee-Hunter* (1848), and others alluding to the legend that Native Americans were descended from the ten lost tribes of Israelites, a connection that had been pursued through comparative analysis of Hebrew and Indian languages by the eighteenth-century theologian Jonathan Edwards. Biblical settings were also a staple of the religious novel, a popular genre throughout the nineteenth century that presented Jews in remote, romanticized settings. The most successful writer of religious novels during this era, Joseph Holt Ingraham (1809–1860), depicted biblical Jews with some degree of sympathy, although his enormously popular *The Prince of the House of David* (1855) was dedicated to the hope that American Jews would convert to Christianity.

The most forceful evocation of biblical Judaism, however, may be found in abolitionist writings, which often referred to biblical episodes or reflected the ominous rhetoric of the prophetic books. For example, the staunchly abolitionist poet John Greenleaf Whittier in "The Cities of the Plain" (1831) used a biblical tale of God's wrath to warn that "vengeance shall gather the harvest of crime!" (p. 76), and the prophetic tone permeating the closing chapter of Harriet Beecher Stowe's *Uncle Tom's Cabin* (1852) likewise foretells disaster as a result of slavery. Frederick Douglass's "The Meaning of July Fourth to the Negro" (1852), which castigates Northerners for tolerating slavery, most explicitly relates the cause of abolition to the emancipation of biblical Israelites from Egypt, a thematic association found in the lyrics of some spirituals.

Treatments of contemporary Jews tended toward the stereotypical, particularly in the popular literature of the period. Some positive images of exotic Jewish

Uriah Phillips Levy (1792–1862), who rose to the naval rank of commodore, is perhaps best remembered for purchasing Jefferson's home and donating it to the United States, although he was especially proud of his efforts to abolish the naval practice of flogging. In 1857 he reflected on his identity and career:

My parents were Israelites, and I was nurtured in the faith of my ancestors. In deciding to adhere to it, I have but exercised a right, guaranteed to me by the Constitutions of my native State, and of the United States—a right given to all men by their Maker—a right more precious to each of us than life itself. But, while claiming and exercising this freedom of conscience, I have never failed to acknowledge and respect the like freedom in others. I might safely defy the citation of a single act, in the whole course of my official career, injurious to the religious rights of any other person.

A Documentary History of the Jews of the United States, 1654–1875, edited by Morris U. Schappes (New York: Schocken, 1971), p. 376.

women or benevolent Jewish men may be found, but negative associations between Jews and money prevailed. The enduring influence of Shakespeare's *The Merchant of Venice,* which features the merciless usurer Shylock, is indicated by the fact that it was among the most frequently performed plays in the United States before 1900. George Lippard's *The Quaker City* (1845), a sensationalistic novel of urban corruption, alludes to Shylock with the villainous Gabriel Von Gelt. Von Gelt, whose name incorporates the Yiddish word *gelt* (money), is a humpbacked southern forger who speaks with a heavy accent and is introduced with the phrase, "'Jew' was written on his face clearly and distinctly" (p. 175). Depiction of the stereotypical money-mongering and physically distinct Jew would recur in Lippard's novels and elsewhere. For example, John Beauchamp Jones, author of novels about life on the frontier, would depict Jews as unscrupulous in their business dealings in *The Western Merchant* (1849) and in *The Winkles* (1855).

More positive images of contemporary Jews, however, may also be found in antebellum literature. The novelist Charles Brockden Brown presented in *Arthur Mervyn* (1799–1800) a wealthy young Jewish widow who is sufficiently decorous to seem a suitable mate for the virtuous title character. Brown's approving characterization lacks nuance, which is not the case for the protagonist of Nathaniel Hawthorne's *The Marble Faun* (1860), Miriam. An exotic character with Jewish ancestry who carries a burden of guilt, Miriam also conveys an awareness of moral obligation, evidence of a more highly developed consciousness than that present, according to Hawthorne, among the Jews of the Rome ghetto, who are described in subhuman terms. Hawthorne also refers to Jews occasionally in terms of the Christian legend of the Wandering Jew, a figure of guilt who appears in the short story "Ethan Brand" (1850). Ambiguity is likewise conveyed in Henry Wadsworth Longfellow's "The Jewish Cemetery at Newport" (1852), a curiously elegiac poem that recalls ancient glory and "the grand dialect the Prophets spake" before concluding, "the dead nations never rise again" (pp. 61–62). All of these works suggest the authors had little if any familiarity with living Jews.

The most exceptional treatment of Jews may be found in Melville's book-length poem *Clarel* (1876). Based on Melville's 1856–1857 journey to the Levant, the poem portrays a young American divinity student's search for religious knowledge. Melville depicts the hardships faced by Jews living in Palestine as well as their customs, but what is most striking is the range of Jewish characters, for they do not conform to existing stereotypes. Instead both major and minor characters create a sense of Jewish humanity unique to the period. Although *Clarel* would remain relatively obscure, it presaged the more complex treatments of Jews that would follow in later American literature.

See also Abolitionist Writing; The Bible; Catholics; Immigration; Urbanization

BIBLIOGRAPHY

Primary Works

Benjamin, Israel Joseph. *Three Years in America, 1859–1862.* 2 vols. Translated by Charles Reznikoff. Philadelphia: Jewish Publication Society of America, 1956.

Hawthorne, Nathaniel. *Novels: Fanshawe, The Scarlet Letter, The House of the Seven Gables, The Blithedale Romance, The Marble Faun.* New York: Literary Classics of America, 1983.

Lippard, George. *The Quaker City; or, The Monks of Monk Hall: A Romance of Philadelpha Life, Mystery, and Crime.* 1845. Edited by David S. Reynolds. Amherst: University of Massachusetts Press, 1995.

Longfellow, Henry Wadsworth. "The Jewish Cemetery at Newport." 1850. In *Nineteenth-Century American Poetry,* edited by William C. Spengemann, pp. 60–62. New York: Penguin, 1996.

Melville, Herman. *Clarel: A Poem and Pilgrimage in the Holy Land.* 1876. Evanston, Ill.: Northwestern University Press and the Newberry Library, 1991.

Melville, Herman. *Redburn, His First Voyage; White-Jacket; or, The World in a Man-of-War; Moby-Dick, or, The Whale.* New York: Literary Classics of America, 1983.

Whittier, John Greenleaf. "The Cities of the Plain." 1831. In *Nineteenth-Century American Poetry,* edited by William C. Spengemann, pp. 76–77. New York: Penguin, 1996.

Secondary Works

Borden, Morton. *Jews, Turks, and Infidels.* Chapel Hill: University of North Carolina Press, 1984.

Diner, Hasia R. *A Time for Gathering: The Second Migration, 1820–1880.* Baltimore: Johns Hopkins University Press, 1992.

Harap, Louis. *The Image of the Jew in American Literature: From Early Republic to Mass Immigration.* Philadelphia: Jewish Publication Society, 1974.

Marcus, Jacob Rader. *United States Jewry, 1776–1985.* 4 vols. Detroit: Wayne State University Press, 1989–1993.

Mayo, Louise A. *The Ambivalent Image: Nineteenth-Century America's Perception of the Jew.* Rutherford, N.J.: Fairleigh Dickinson University Press, 1988.

Sarna, Jonathan D. *American Judaism: A History.* New Haven, Conn.: Yale University Press, 2004.

Joseph Alkana

JOURNALS AND DIARIES

Journals and diaries, accounts of everyday events, are among the most prevalent forms of literature written by common people, prominent figures, and celebrated authors alike. Dating back to the fifteenth century in Europe (and earlier elsewhere), diary keeping was well established by the time the first settlers arrived in British North America during the 1600s and 1700s. At that time diaries and journals served miscellaneous purposes, both practical and imaginative. They were cherished as spiritual and intellectual anchors during turbulent times precipitated by, for example, long journeys or war; or they charted the soul's progress, revealed God's divine plan, and proffered, in the case of the Puritans, evidence of "election," or predestined salvation. By the 1820s diaries and journals, along with the new nation, had become more sizable, complex, and eclectic, and they continued to develop along those lines until the 1870s. They provided a forum for negotiating change and upheaval acutely experienced by westward pioneers, sojourning politicians, Civil War civilians and soldiers, and even professional authors pondering the national spirit of growth, movement, and dislocation. As white women achieved higher levels of schooling, they, along with some free African American women, increasingly turned to diaries as self-reflective and expressive outlets. So esteemed was diary writing as a mark of intellectual attainment that many people practiced it for its own sake, sometimes maintaining the routine for decades. Each one a unique artifact that reveals through its author's eyes how life was mentally constructed in another era, the diary surpasses other records of the past for its sense of social and cultural immediacy. In talented hands, certainly those of eminent authors, the nineteenth-century journal achieved an elevated, literary quality. As multivalent productions, diaries and journals justly hold a notable place in American literary history.

DEFINITIONS AND TYPES

Specialists strain to define precisely the "diary" or "journal," but a consensus might form around the following: both are dated, timely records of everyday incidents, often written on a daily basis. The two terms are usually considered synonymous, but some prefer to draw distinctions. While the generic term "diary" may encompass all "journals," the latter word is occasionally reserved for records of work, such as farming or business; it may, conversely, signify an ideational, inwardly reflective record rather than one (namely, a diary) describing exoteric occurrences. Given that most nineteenth-century diaries are at least partially contemplative or work oriented and most journals are relatively descriptive, elusive distinctions between the two etymologically related words are usually abandoned.

In format and style, nineteenth-century diaries varied considerably. Dated entries might be penned or penciled on loose sheets of paper, in hand-sewn pamphlets, manufactured predated "pocketbooks," almanacs, cloth-covered blank books, or expensive leather-bound volumes. Despite good intentions, diarists seldom wrote every day or over long periods of time. They neglected their journals because illness, work, or indifference precluded writing. Conscientious backsliders, however, filled in gaps of days, weeks, or even years with a generalized, retrospective entry. By transforming diaries, or parts of them, into scrapbooks of news clippings or albums of original essays and poems, diarists breached standard forms of journal keeping. Some even jotted down lists of books they read or lent out to neighbors. Such transgressions

This excerpt from the first entry in Harriett Low's travel diary reveals the public nature of such writings and their agency in relieving stress.

1829 Sunday May 24th Embarked on board Ship Sumatra bound to Manilla from thence to Macao where I shall probably take up my residence for the next 4 years and for you my Dear Sister [Mary Ann Low] shall this journal be kept. I left home at 5 o'clock with feeling not to be *described,* nor *imagined,* but by those who have been placed in a similar situation. We were *escorted* out, as far as Baker's Island by a few friends from Salem which made it rather pleasanter for me though I cannot say that I enjoyed any thing that took place that day.

Low, *Lights and Shadows of a Macao Life: The Journal of Harriett Low, Travelling Spinster, Part One: 1829–1832,* p. 19.

mark out diaries as creative, rather than hackneyed, endeavors.

Contrary to what one might expect, diaries were generally public rather than private ventures. Epistolary diaries, written as letters with dated entries and sent to a correspondent, necessarily eluded privacy as they were meant to be read by one or perhaps more recipients. Indeed most diaries addressed an audience: a specific, contemporary one such as a spouse or child; future generations; or even imagined readers that informed the writer's tone and style. Few people in the nineteenth century could have envisioned the modern, clandestine mode of diary keeping. Instead diaries were commonly read aloud to family or friends, loaned, copied, and emulated. Needless to say, diarists sometimes censored themselves and discreetly rendered intimate matters.

General incentives, such as self-improvement and a desire to memorialize passing days, gave diaries their universal appeal. Diaries instilled discipline, honed writing skills, and activated thought. They additionally captured, in pen and ink, evanescent episodes easily forgotten. More specific motivations for beginning, continuing, or terminating a diary, however, imply discrete types: the situational, the life, and the spiritual diary.

Situational diaries, commenced at important junctures in life, were the largest group. Milestone events such as a new marriage, courtship, the death of a family member, an expedition, or a voyage were all likely impetuses for starting this type of journal, as were nationally significant phenomena, including the Civil War, western migration, and the California gold rush. People coped with these stressful life transformations by confiding to a journal. The very act of daily writing stabilized unsettled emotions and helped illuminate patterns within the seemingly chaotic flow of events. Predictably, with the catalyzing condition's cessation, such as a sojourn's end, came the diary's abandonment. Sometimes, however, they survived for years longer. If so, they became life diaries.

Life diaries, more thematically complex and longer than situational diaries, nonetheless emerged from them. Although they usually were begun at a crucial life moment, life diaries inevitably strayed from their original thematic purpose. They conveyed no single purpose or topical focus and instead seemingly adjusted themselves to life's ever-vacillating phases. Life diaries written during the 1850s, 1860s, and 1870s were more likely to highlight periods of travel than earlier ones. They also acquired a more intimate tone as the century progressed. Nonetheless, for life diarists writing itself became a habitual, worthy exercise. Because changing conditions little affected the diarists' tenacity, they often wrote over decades in several volumes. Some families—such as that of President John Adams, his son John Quincy, and grandson Charles Francis—sustained a multigenerational diary.

The New England Puritan spiritual diary that flourished during the seventeenth century still attracted a few practitioners in the early 1800s. Instead of evidencing "election," the later ones simply demonstrated piety in a secularized era. Quakers dutifully composed them to exhibit faith publicly; these were always conceived for others to read for testimony of the diarists' religiosity. Even though the spiritual diary had all but vanished by 1820, its influence could still be discerned in transcendentalist diaries that located spiritual design in natural phenomena. Ralph Waldo Emerson (1803–1882), for one, perceived unity in nature's disparate elements while studying and reflecting upon his journal.

DIARIES AND LITERATURE

A self-conscious literary enhancement of observations distinguishes nineteenth-century diaries from earlier ones. Inspired by Romantics drawn to imagination and intuition, contemplation of nature, and a spirit of rebellious individualism, diarists frequently embellished their entries with stylistic flourishes, metaphorical language, and fanciful descriptions that roused introspective meditations. Some injected diaries with novelistic suspense, even melodrama, or treated acquaintances populating everyday life scenes as if they were fictive characters. It is no wonder that numerous authors kept journals to develop distinctive writing styles. Outstanding literary diarists include the historian Francis Parkman, President John Quincy Adams, and the novelist Eliza Francis Andrews.

Often ranked with the finest literary accomplishments, authors' diaries in turn illustrated the process of literary production. Besides honing style, diaries yielded material, in the form of direct passages or drafts, for publications. Henry David Thoreau's (1817–1862) journal, thought by many to be his major work, was the wellspring of lectures and publications including *A Week on the Concord and Merrimack Rivers* (1849) and *Walden* (1854). In his "Notebooks," Nathaniel Hawthorne (1804–1864) developed ideas and characters for *The Blithedale Romance* (1852), *The Marble Faun* (1860), and *Our Old Home* (1863). Likewise, Ralph Waldo Emerson and Washington Irving (1783–1859) distilled publications from their diaries, yet they eschewed printing the diaries themselves.

By printing exceptional and curious diaries, or memoirs and biographies typically saturated with journal excerpts, publishers gratified American readers' craving for a glimpse of other people's lives. Heavily edited journals were published as volumes, while others were excerpted in popular periodicals and in historical societies' proceedings catering to genealogists. Contemporary exploration and travel accounts such as Henry R. Schoolcraft's *Journal of a Tour into the Interior of Missouri and Arkansas* (1821) and John C. Fremont's *Report of the Exploring Expedition to the Rocky Mountains* (1845) sated the demand for adventure. The Missouri journalist Edwin Bryant's exploration journal, *What I Saw in California* (1848), peppered with western folk legends, historical allusions, and witty digressions, appeared with the appended sensational record of a California-bound Donner party member who witnessed his starving companions' cannibalism. Not so sensational but equally marketable as veritable success stories, spiritual guides, heroic fables, or villainous downfalls were the Boston industrialist Amos Lawrence's *Extracts* (1855), the missionary David Brainerd's *Memoirs* (1822), President George Washington's *Diary* (1860), the antislavery actress Frances Anne "Fanny" Kemble's *Journal* (1863), and the duelist-traitor Aaron Burr's *Private Journal* (1838). Among a spate of Civil War diaries by Confederate war clerks, Union officers, chaplains, prisoners of war, and army surgeons published after 1865, the editor Thomas Wentworth Higginson's *Army Life in a Black Regiment* (1870) stands out for its dignified portrait of African American soldiers. Although there was no shortage of publishable native diaries, lax copyright laws allowed American publishers to pirate popular European editions of Samuel Pepys's *Diary* and John Gibson Lockhart's *Life,* about the Scottish novelist Sir Walter Scott, among others. Diaries, like novels, allured readers who would vicariously live another life. It is no wonder that diary fiction was so popular.

Diary fiction—satire, novels, or short stories that employed the diary form to weave a first-person, present-tense narrative—simulated actual diaries. Most were not intentional hoaxes, but they could fool the unwary. In diary fiction, events appear to be unfolding in timely fashion as the fictive narrator, namely the diarist, ostensibly writes entries in real time, not knowing what will happen the next day. In some pieces a third-person voice, the diary's supposed publisher or discoverer, for instance, prefaces or periodically comments upon the text, thereby conjuring an illusion of the manuscript's authenticity. American authors looked to published sea, travel, and spiritual diaries for inspiration but also British and European literary precedents, including Joseph Addison's "Journal of a Sober Citizen" (1712), a satire about self-improvement diaries, Samuel Richardson's *Pamela* (1740), a letter-journal novel, and Johann Wolfgang von Goethe's *The Sorrows of Young Werther* (1774), the first true diary novel. Edgar Allan Poe's (1809–1849) "Ms. Found in a Bottle" (1833), an early American diary story, weaves a horrifying tale of a doomed voyager who writes even as a violent whirlpool sinks his ship; as the title suggests, the journal, safely tucked in a bottle, later washes up on shore. Poe's "Journal of Julius Rodman" (1840), supposedly left by the "first" explorer to cross the Rocky Mountains in 1792, was so convincing that it was mentioned, as if authentic, in the U.S. Senate documents (26th Congress, 1839–1840). The prolific cheap-fiction author Joseph Holt Ingraham employed the genre in *The Diary of a Hackney Coachman* (1844), a novelette about the mysterious death of an affable coach driver whose diary, when discovered, inculpates his murderer. Other examples include Lucius Manlius Sargent's *Diary of Rev. Solomon Spittle* (1847), John Greenleaf Whittier's *Leaves from Margaret Smith's Journal* (1849), and Caroline H. Woods's *The Diary of a Milliner* (1867).

Nineteenth-century readers could readily see their own diary-keeping habits mirrored in a wide array of publications. It is not surprising then that they used diaries for making transcriptions of and comments on published literature. These diaries resembled commonplace books, storehouses of citations, but the former melded mundane observations

This passage from Edgar Allan Poe's "Ms. Found in a Bottle" (1833) demonstrates the diary fiction writer's art. Here the diarist-narrator locates his writing implements and devises a method for preserving his journal.

It is long since I first trod the deck of this terrible ship, and the rays of my destiny are, I think, gathering to a focus. Incomprehensible men! Wrapped up in meditations of a kind which I cannot divine, they pass me by unnoticed. Concealment is utter folly on my part, for the people *will not* see. It was but just now that I passed directly before the eyes of the mate—it was no long while ago that I ventured into the captain's own private cabin, and took thence the materials with which I write, and have written. I shall from time to time continue this journal. It is true that I may not find an opportunity of transmitting it to the world, but I will not fail to make the endeavour. At the last moment I will enclose the MS. in a bottle, and cast it within the sea.

Edgar Allan Poe, "Ms. Found in a Bottle," in *The Complete Works of Edgar Allan Poe*, vol. 2, edited by James A. Harrison (New York: AMS Press, 1965), pp. 9–10.

with literary ones. Not only did authors such as Emerson and Thoreau liberally sprinkle their journals with quotations or ideas culled from books they read, so too did ordinary diarists who valued the printed word. Whereas biblical references abounded, allusions to other religious and secular literature were also numerous. Responses to reading materials ranging from short declarations of satisfaction or disappointment to lengthy digressions that interweave book review–type comments with the diarist's personal cogitations are found in journals, especially those by highly literate New Englanders. However, a diverse set of mill workers, housewives, retirees, and students from that region periodically engaged even transcendentalist literature, notwithstanding its enigmatic language. Much of it was casually encountered, through periodicals like the *Atlantic Monthly* or at the public lyceum, where auditors took copious mental notes for their diaries. Diaries thus inventively interwove literature into pages otherwise devoted to everyday affairs.

RACE, ETHNICITY, AND GENDER

By the early nineteenth century some African Americans, immigrants, laborers or lower-class people and many more white women than before took up the practice of diary keeping. Hampered by laws prohibiting slave literacy, most enslaved African Americans could not (or dared not) write. Extant written retrospectives or autobiography told to white amanuenses, such as slave narratives or freed people's (emancipated slaves) reminiscences, have received more scholarly attention than diaries maintained by several free African Americans. James A. Healy, son of an Irish Georgia plantation owner and an African American slave, left a fascinating academic diary (1849–1850), still housed at College of the Holy Cross in Worcester, Massachusetts, where he was a Catholic seminarian. William Johnson, a wealthy Natchez, Mississippi, landowner, proprietor, and moneylender, born into slavery but freed in 1821, kept a highly detailed record (1835–1851) of his business affairs, leisure activities, and southern high society. Like their white literate counterparts, African American Union soldiers, chaplains, and orderlies on the Civil War battlefield immortalized their heroic acts in diaries, but many of these have been only recently published.

Extraordinary for its high literary caliber, narrative propulsion (diaries can seem aimless), and outspoken sense of racial identity, the diary of Charlotte Forten Grimké (1837–1914), a schoolteacher and published author, has become one of the most important of American diaries. Grimké began it in 1854 upon moving from Philadelphia to Salem, Massachusetts, to attend grammar school; after graduating in 1855 she continued it while teaching in the same town and later in the Sea Islands off South Carolina, where she taught freed people during the Civil War. A distinctly erudite sensibility pervades the diary, chock-full of meditations upon lyceum lectures, poetry, history, and travel books. Equally imbued with emotional outpourings, it discloses Grimké's painful grappling with bigotry and slavery's legality within a democracy.

Very few diaries of first- and second-generation literate immigrants, notably Germans and the Irish, who arrived in great numbers after 1840, survived, but those that did candidly portray the hardships of dislocation and resettlement or bitingly criticize American culture, society, and politics. The Bavarian immigrant and devout Jew Abraham Kohn began his German-language diary prior to embarking for New York in 1842 and continued it until 1843, while peddling goods under much tribulation in New England. His longings for home seem only to magnify his woe over his precarious occupation and abject poverty. The three-volume published work *My Diary* (1862–1866), by the Polish emigré and

U.S. State Department translator Adam Gurowski, elicited notices in the influential *North American Review* (January 1863, April 1864) and *Continental Monthly* (April 1864) rebuking his unflattering wartime observations. Travelers or other observers sometimes wrote about the immigrant experience. Thomas Cather detailed his tumultuous 1836 voyage from Limavady, Ireland, to New York, the city's shockingly fast pace, and encounters with what he called "yankeefied" Irish, seemingly bent on moneymaking.

Due to their rising literacy rates, more women produced diaries in the early 1800s than in either of the two previous centuries. Though similar in many ways to men's, women's diaries have some distinguishing characteristics. In that they mainly recount household rhythms, they reflect gender prescriptions limiting women to domestic work. They also reveal a greater consciousness of family, community, and generational ties. Women used diaries instrumentally, as outlets for self-affirmative reflection under disempowering conditions, such as abusive marriages, long and risky trips, or warfare. The case of pioneer women stands out. They expressed fears about their journey's ultimate success of which menfolk, conversely, stoically assured themselves. These women also saw Indians' gestures through a lens of cooperation rather than combat. All in all, diaries gave women a sense of efficacy at a time when they were granted but little independence.

Gender differences broke down regarding the preferred form of diary. Women sometimes penned entries in pocket diaries that were widely available in America after 1850. These small, printed, and predated books that fit conveniently into the pocket were designed for businessmen and professionals as well as for women. Alongside printed pages devoted to interest tables and other statistics or useful information for investors, women tersely jotted down their domestic activities, social calls, and reading in the small spaces allotted for each day. Women who kept records of spending on food or sewing items used these diaries' "cash accounts" section for quite different purposes than men, who might record business-related spending.

Although most nineteenth-century women's diaries are inherently valuable windows on historic domestic and community life, several qualitatively surpass the mean for their literariness and shrewd insight. The sojourner Harriett Low's (1809–1877) witty and self-reflective journal (1829–1834), kept for her sister in Salem, Massachusetts, offers singular, scathing portrayals of life among international merchants trading with China; her copious entries about assorted books illuminate middle-class women's reading tastes. Helen McCowen Carpenter's diary of her Kansas-to-California journey (1857) is remarkable for its spirited, vivid details, skillfully woven narrative, and novel-like structure. The southerner Mary Boykin Chesnut's diary (1861–1865), striking for its well-crafted expository writing, is also outstanding for its shrewd portrayal of civilians' wartime experience and contemporary attitudes toward slavery. Aware of her diary's value as a cultural and social document, Chesnut revised and augmented her original entries for publication.

Although only a few of them ever published their work, nineteenth-century diarists usually wrote with other readers in mind. Diaries were, then, less a mirror image of the self than a window on the world. Over time, as they became increasingly private, they became more candidly revealing of the writer's everyday activities and internal states of mind. Precisely because they acted as confidants, diaries throughout much of the twentieth century often came equipped with lock and key. In the early twenty-first century, on Internet "weblogs," "bloggers" have forgone privacy to publish their daily thoughts and activities. Links between bloggers create an electronic community that allows them to converse among themselves. This revival of the social diary, oddly enough, also links bloggers with the nineteenth century and places them within the historically situated community of diarists who wrote, reflected, and most of all shared their life stories with others.

See also Autobiography; Blacks; Civil War; Exploration and Discovery; Female Authorship; Immigration; Irish; Jews; Literacy; Transcendentalism; Travel Writing

BIBLIOGRAPHY

Primary Works

Cather, Thomas. *Voyage to America: The Journals of Thomas Cather.* Edited by Thomas Yoseloff. New York and London: Thomas Yoseloff, 1961.

Kohn, Abraham. "A Jewish Peddler's Diary." Edited by Abram Vossen Goodman. In *Critical Studies in American Jewish History,* edited by Jacob R. Marcus, pp. 45–73. Cincinnati, Ohio: American Jewish Archives, 1971.

Low, Harriett. *Lights and Shadows of a Macao Life: The Journal of Harriett Low, Travelling Spinster.* 2 vols. Edited by Nan P. Hodges and Arthur W. Hummel. Woodinville, Wash.: History Bank, 2002.

Secondary Works

Bunkers, Suzanne L. "Introduction." In *Diaries of Girls and Women: A Midwestern American Sampler,* edited by Suzanne L. Bunkers, pp. 3–40. Madison: University of Wisconsin, 2001.

Bunkers, Suzanne L., and Cynthia A. Huff. "Issues in Studying Women's Diaries: A Theoretical and Critical Introduction." In *Inscribing the Daily: Critical Essays on Women's Diaries,* edited by Suzanne L. Bunkers and Cynthia A. Huff, pp. 1–20. Amherst: University of Massachusetts Press, 1996.

Cobb-Moore, Geneva. "When Meanings Meet: The Journals of Charlotte Forten Grimké." In *Inscribing the Daily: Critical Essays on Women's Diaries,* edited by Suzanne L. Bunkers and Cynthia A. Huff, pp. 139–155. Amherst: University of Massachusetts Press, 1996.

Culley, Margo, ed. *A Day at a Time: The Diary Literature of American Women from 1764 to the Present.* New York: Feminist Press, 1985.

Hoobler, Dorothy, and Thomas Hoobler. *The Irish American Family Album.* New York: Oxford University Press, 1995.

Jackson, Blyden. *A History of Afro-American Literature.* Vol. 1, *The Long Beginning, 1746–1895.* Baton Rouge: Louisiana State University Press, 1989.

Kagle, Stephen E. *Early-Nineteenth-Century American Diary Literature.* Boston: Twayne, 1986.

Kagle, Stephen E. *Late-Nineteenth-Century American Diary Literature.* Boston: Twayne, 1988.

Martens, Lorna. *The Diary Novel.* Cambridge, U.K., and New York: Cambridge University Press, 1985.

Matthews, William. "Preface." In *American Diaries: An Annotated Bibliography of American Diaries Written Prior to the Year 1861,* compiled by William Matthews, pp. vii–xii. Berkeley: University of California Press, 1945.

McCarthy, Molly. "A Pocketful of Days: Pocket Diaries and Daily Record Keeping among Nineteenth-Century New England Women." *New England Quarterly* 73 (2000): 274–296.

Pollin, Burton R. "Introduction." In The Journal of Julius Rodman." In *Collected Writings of Edgar Allan Poe,* vol. 1, *The Imaginary Voyages,* edited by Burton R. Pollin, pp. 508–515. Boston: Twayne, 1981.

Sattelmeyer, Robert. "Historical Introduction." In *The Writings of Henry D. Thoreau,* vol. 2, *Journal, 1842–1848,* edited by Robert Sattelmeyer, pp. 445–466. Princeton, N.J.: Princeton University Press, 1984.

Sattelmeyer, Robert. "The Remaking of *Walden.*" In *Writing the American Classics,* edited by James Barbour and Tom Quirk, pp. 53–78. Chapel Hill: University of North Carolina Press, 1990.

Schlissel, Lillian. *Women's Diaries of the Westward Journey.* New York: Schocken, 1982.

Wink, Amy L. *She Left Nothing in Particular: The Autobiographical Legacy of Nineteenth-Century Women's Diaries.* Knoxville: University of Tennessee Press, 2001.

Zboray, Ronald J., and Mary Saracino Zboray. *Everyday Ideas: Socio-Literary Experience among Antebellum New Englanders.* Knoxville: University of Tennessee Press, forthcoming.

Zboray, Ronald J., and Mary Saracino Zboray. "Transcendentalism in Print: Production, Dissemination, and Common Reception." In *Transient and Permanent: The Transcendentalist Movement and Its Contexts,* edited by Charles Capper and Conrad Edick Wright, pp. 310–381. Boston: Massachusetts Historical Society, 1999.

Ronald J. Zboray
Mary Saracino Zboray

"JUMPING FROG"

See "The Celebrated Jumping Frog of Calaveras County"

KNICKERBOCKER WRITERS

For many literary historians early nineteenth-century American literature is synonymous with the outburst of creative thought and experimentation that F. O. Matthiessen (1902–1950) called the "American Renaissance," reflected in groundbreaking works by Herman Melville (1819–1891), Nathaniel Hawthorne (1804–1864), Ralph Waldo Emerson (1803–1882), Henry David Thoreau (1817–1862), and Walt Whitman (1819–1892). Among the bold experiments of these writers were Whitman's challenge to traditional prosody, Melville's joining of metaphysical speculation to maritime narrative, and Thoreau's invention of a new genre of "poetic natural history." A set of more conservative impulses lay behind a group of nineteenth-century writers who celebrated New York's past and its local traditions. While businesspeople and entrepreneurs championed the commercial prospects of America's largest urban centers, Washington Irving (1783–1859) led a group of New York authors whose satires, histories, and sketches chronicled the city, its past, and its environs.

THE SCHOOL OF IRVING

When he was in his early twenties, Irving had already spent two years in Europe. An inveterate traveler, he stockpiled stories associated with sites in England and the Continent. As he developed his observations of Europe into a colorful form of descriptive writing, his perspective sharpened his attachment to continuity between Old World values and American culture. Irving's early works reflected the influence of the witty, gossipy style of the classic British essayists of the former century. His early literary efforts were also collaborative

Washington Irving. THE LIBRARY OF CONGRESS

ventures, establishing the sociable and cordial tone of subsequent New York writers for whom Irving became a model. With his brother William Irving and the young James Kirke Paulding (1778–1860), Irving produced *Salmagundi* (1807–1808), an occasional periodical in which the collaborators posed as club members who discussed politics, manners, and the life of the town. Other works were similarly infused with the town spirit of Old New York: Dr. Samuel Latham Mitchill's *The Picture of New-York* (1807) recalled the glory days of the burgher aristocracy, and *The Croaker Papers* (1819) of Fitz-Greene Halleck (1790–1867) and Joseph Rodman Drake (1795–1820) constituted a *Salmagundi* in poetic form.

For his own burlesque *A History of New York, from the Beginning of the World to the End of the Dutch Dynasty* (1809), Irving chose the pseudonym Diedrich Knickerbocker, an amateur historian who delves into the past in a spirit of lighthearted celebration. Irving announced one of his central purposes in a preface that he eventually added to the volume: "to clothe home scenes and places and familiar names with those imaginative associations so seldom met with in our own country, but which live like charms and old spells about the cities of the old world" (p. 13). On the rare

occasion that parts of this clever history are anthologized, Irving's later chapters on Peter Stuyvesant or his rather obvious satire on Thomas Jefferson are usually chosen, but the *History* pokes fun at the presumptuousness and pretenses of American and European historians alike. This volume, which has been overshadowed by *The Sketch Book of Geoffrey Crayon, Gent.* (1819–1820), established the tone for the Knickerbocker group of writers, who would dominate New York's cultural scene until well after the Civil War.

In "The Author's Account of Himself" for *The Sketch Book,* Irving introduced Geoffrey Crayon, a roving bachelor who sought out the picturesque corners and grand monuments of Europe. The "author" Crayon used Diedrich Knickerbocker to frame his two most celebrated narratives, "Rip Van Winkle" and "The Legend of Sleepy Hollow." Rip and the inhabitants of Sleepy Hollow are overtaken by the inevitable progress and bustling commerce that was sweeping through New York, just as the saturnine Dutchmen in Knickerbocker's *History* are displaced by invading and acquisitive Yankees. As a young New Yorker, Irving had visited his friend Paulding at Tarrytown on the banks of the Hudson and absorbed legends and superstitions that he would incorporate into his most famous volume. Irving's travels to England had served to reinforce his attraction to gothic ruins and buildings, and his sojourn in Germany fortified his appetite for tales of ghosts, inexplicable happenings, and hidden mysteries. All these features influenced the mood of *The Sketch Book* and *Bracebridge Hall* (1822), set in an old manor house where customs and values forgotten in urban venues survived in the countryside. These early works established the central themes of much Knickerbocker literature that followed: the collision between tradition and progress in the new nation and the subtle interconnections between European and American culture.

Knickerbocker writers, steeped in the neoclassical traditions of wit and satire, were also attracted to figures who were leaders of the Romantic movement in Great Britain: Sir Walter Scott, Lord Byron, Thomas Moore, and Thomas Campbell. Several Knickerbocker writers were New Englanders by birth—William Cullen Bryant (1794–1878), Halleck, Nathaniel Parker Willis (1806–1867), and Samuel Woodworth (1785–1842)—but their literary careers reached maturity in New York, as did that of Richard Henry Dana (1787–1879), who arrived in the city in 1821 to commence publication of *The Idle Man,* a periodical modeled after *The Sketch Book.* Among other writers sometimes associated with Knickerbocker culture—Charles Fenno Hoffman, William Leggett, and Park Benjamin—the shadow of Irving was all but inescapable, whether his narrative voice and strategies were exploited, burlesqued, or imitated outright.

CLUBS, THE THEATER, AND JOURNALISM

The Knickerbocker school of writers was loosely organized, but many of them socialized in private clubs. Throughout the early part of the nineteenth century, numerous private clubs and voluntary organizations had sprung up, and they helped to define and shape cultural activity. The "club-mania" of the era, as one periodical defined it, brought together individuals of similar intellectual interests and tastes. Perhaps the most famous literary organization in New York was the Bread and Cheese Club, founded by James Fenimore Cooper (1789–1851) in 1822. Irving became an honorary member in 1826, and some of the club's members gravitated toward the Sketch Club, many participants in which were painters. The Literary Confederacy, founded in 1817 by Bryant and Gulian Verplanck, was a book club that encouraged its members to write for periodicals. Halleck became poet laureate of the Ugly Club, a social fraternity of the city's most handsome men. Others found fellowship in the Book Club or the Union Club, precursors either to emerging professional societies or to a host of organizations that imitated the urban sophistication of English clubs. Several Knickerbockers were merchants or businesspeople, and for respite from the commercial culture of New York, they sought out the relaxed atmosphere of taverns and cafés or the polite atmosphere of private literary salons, where musicians, artists, and poets gathered in a spirit of informal social exchange. The writer Anne Lynch presided as a hostess at many of these prominent literary soirees in the 1840s.

Many Knickerbockers were devotees of the theater, and William Dunlap (1766–1839), as manager of the Park Theatre, was instrumental in bringing serious drama to New York. Dunlap, an authority on scenic design, favored American plays, but he also introduced German and French plays to American audiences. "There is no place of public amusement of which I am so fond as the Theatre," wrote Irving, introducing a pseudonymous piece, in 1802 (*Letters of Jonathan Oldstyle*, p. 10). By the early 1820s he was a silent partner in dramatic collaborations with John Howard Payne (1791–1852), an experienced dramatist and actor who had appeared on the London stage. In addition to Payne, Paulding, Willis, and Woodworth, New Yorkers who had plays produced before 1840 included Samuel Judah, Anna Mowatt Ritchie, Mordecai M. Noah, George Pope Morris, and Cornelius Mathews.

Just as the club atmosphere of the period stimulated informal literary and social interchange, the theater offered Knickerbocker writers access to the lively world of playwrights, actors, and artists. The vastly expanding newspaper and magazine trade offered further opportunities for writers who supported themselves by editing or contributing to periodicals. Irving's early education in and affection for the theater was formed in his *Letters of Jonathan Oldstyle, Gent.* (1824), written for the *Morning Chronicle*, a daily paper edited by his brother Peter Irving. Payne's interest in theatrical matters was manifested in the *Thespian Mirror,* a weekly review that began in 1805. Woodworth wrote successfully for the theater, and after brief editorial stints with periodicals in New England, he and George Pope Morris began the *New-York Mirror* in 1823. This periodical, which was devoted to life in the city in all its cultural variety, survived changes of nearly two decades. Morris served as its primary editor until 1842.

Knickerbocker journalism was never impersonal, and Lewis Gaylord Clark (1808–1873) dominated the content and tone of the *Knickerbocker* when he became its editor in 1834. The magazine took its name from Irving's Knickerbocker *History,* and it served as the primary organ for the dissemination of the literary and cultural values among this group of writers. Infused with Irving's amiable or genial humor, contributors to the *Knickerbocker* stressed tone and atmosphere rather than the intricacies of plot. Prose works were highly descriptive, and many early stories were strongly influenced by Irving's framing devices and his tale-within-a-tale techniques. A typical issue might include fiction, sketches, verse, humor, and reviews. Travel writing was also a staple of the magazine: Irving's "Sketches in Paris in 1825," for example, appeared in the magazine in November and December 1840.

Wholesome subject matter was standard fare, reflecting the temperamental conservatism of the editor, who shunned any material that might be offensive to literary taste or his genteel sensibility. Any writing that smacked of foreign corruption was scorned—the works of Edward Bulwer-Lytton seemed to Clark to convey a tone of decadence, and the *Knickerbocker* struck a generally patriotic tone in its early years. Despite this moderately nationalistic flavor, the English essay tradition of Joseph Addison, Sir Richard Steele, William Hazlitt, and Leigh Hunt was a strong stylistic influence on Clark and contributed an urbane and cosmopolitan quality to the magazine. If for clarity of style Clark preferred the transparency of the English essay tradition to the vagueness of the transcendentalists, a British counterpart to Irving was Charles Lamb (1775–1834), whose genial, playful, and compassionate tone was celebrated by Clark and other *Knickerbocker* contributors.

In an essay on humor written for the magazine, Frederick S. Cozzens (1818–1869), reflecting the influence of Lamb, distinguished the intellectual appeal of wit from the warmth and pathos employed by the humorist. Cozzens, who wrote for the *Knickerbocker* throughout Clark's editorship, adapted these principles in *The Sparrowgrass Papers* (1856), sketches of New Yorkers who experiment with living in the country on the banks of the Hudson. The sketches of Cozzens and Frederick W. Shelton, whose *Up the River* (1853) had its origin in the *Knickerbocker*, offered the attraction of rural life to the growing urban readership of the magazine. The appeal was to New York suburbanites who might venture outside the city on tours or vacations.

LATTER-DAY KNICKERBOCKERS

The Knickerbocker Gallery (1855), a collection of stories, poems, and essays by friends of the editor, paid homage to Clark. The magazine survived until the 1860s, but even before that time much of its writing took on a predictably sentimental cast, infused with an Irving-esque afterglow. If the values championed by Irving and Clark survived, they surfaced in works like Cozzens's *The Sayings of Dr. Bushwhacker, and Other Learned Men* (1867) in which a bushy-headed old Knickerbocker offers strong opinions on inoffensive topics. Many Knickerbocker writers—Halleck, Cozzens, Richard Burleigh Kimball—divided their time between business and literary pursuits, and by the 1870s, their passion for the past, overtaken by New York's rampant commercialism, was reduced to pure nostalgia. Many of them wrote memoirs of English or American literary figures that were central to the fashioning of a Knickerbocker literary tradition. Others resorted to Irving's technique of burlesque, but many of these strategies appeared derivative or reliant on targets that had lost their currency. The jesting, genial tone of Knickerbocker writing—buoyed by the economic and social forces that shaped New York's emerging literary culture in the early part of the century—did not outlast the conditions that engendered it. After the Civil War a few Knickerbocker writers still won ready acceptance from reviewers and magazine editors even if pioneers such as Irving and Cooper had passed from the literary scene. A respectful but nostalgic tone colors such works as James Grant Wilson's *Bryant, and His Friends: Some Reminiscences of the Knickerbocker Writers* (1886); Abram C. Dayton's *Last Days of Knickerbocker Life in New York* (1882); and Hamilton Wright Mabie's *The Writers of Knickerbocker New York* (1912). In Edith Wharton's stories of Old New York, the Knickerbocker Club receives passing mention as a once-vital aspect of a vanished social scene.

Irving was the first American author to be hailed in England, and his *Sketch Book* did much to transform foreign attitudes toward American writing. Clark's editorial hand served to reinforce the Anglo-American lineage by welcoming British authors in the pages of the *Knickerbocker*. Although Knickerbocker writers were not pioneers in literary practice, they stand at the forefront of what Malcolm Bradbury calls a "transatlantic" dimension in American letters.

See also New York; Young America

BIBLIOGRAPHY

Primary Works

Irving, Washington. "The Author's Apology." In *A History of New York*, author's rev. ed. New York: G. P. Putnam's Sons, 1848.

Irving, Washington. *Letters of Jonathan Oldstyle*. 1802. In *History, Tales, and Sketches*. New York: Library of America, 1983.

Secondary Works

Bradbury, Malcolm. *Dangerous Pilgrimages: Transatlantic Mythologies and the Novel*. New York: Viking, 1996. See pp. 53–83.

Brooks, Van Wyck. *The World of Washington Irving*. New York: E. P. Dutton, 1944.

Callow, James T. *Kindred Spirits: Knickerbocker Writers and American Artists 1807–1855*. Chapel Hill: University of North Carolina Press, 1967.

Taft, Kendall B. *Minor Knickerbockers: Representative Selections*. With introduction, bibliography, and notes. New York: American Book Company, 1947.

Kent P. Ljungquist

LABOR

In the antebellum United States, labor and literature were so entangled with each other that one cannot be understood without consideration of the other. These were the years of America's celebrated "literary declaration of independence" from the European past, of that extraordinary outburst of creativity known later as the American "renaissance." Yet, these were also the years when Thomas Jefferson's dream of an America populated by independent yeoman farmers yielded to the inexorable pressures of industrialization, to its concomitant divisions of labor, and to the drawing of sharp class distinctions based on the different kinds of labor men and women performed. Industrialism not only threatened some of the traditional republican values espoused by Jefferson and many others but called into question the work ethic itself: After all, if industrialism was transforming the work many Americans performed into mindless drudgery, how could these Americans be persuaded that hard work was a critical constituent of their moral personhood?

Nor were working-class men and women the only ones to feel the changes wrought by industrialism and the spread of a market economy. The widening separation of middle-class men's and women's "spheres" increasingly made work both a signifier and a creator of gender identity. Not only were certain kinds of work deemed suitable or unsuitable depending on one's gender, but one's very success in being a man or woman depended more and more on successful performance of gender-appropriate work.

These challenges to the nature and organization of work had profoundly unsettling consequences. Americans in the antebellum years were forced to rethink their understanding of labor and to reassess which kinds of labor had value, and for whom, and why. Writers found themselves fully engaged in this process of reevaluation. Indeed, they did not merely observe their society's deep uneasiness about the ways the nature and shape of work seemed to be changing; nor did they merely represent the labor they witnessed in the world around them. Highly self-conscious about the social status, political consequences, and gender implications of their own work of writing, they understood that it was not just a medium for representing labor but a kind of labor itself. Literature was not just about labor. Literature itself was labor.

IMPACT OF INDUSTRIALISM

When industrial mills began to spread throughout eastern Rhode Island and Massachusetts in the second and third decades of the century, neither owners nor operatives (as the factory hands were called) foresaw the extent to which they would change the way men and women worked. Until that time the farm had been the primary unit of economic organization in the colonies and in the newly created nation; likewise, the individual family working a farm was the prevalent unit of organized labor. The work performed by the farmer and his family was regarded as a noble calling—indeed as the life most suited to a republican society with a republican form of government. The independence of the farmer—an independence secured by his ownership of his property and his possession of all the knowledge and skills required to farm that property—was thought to be the indispensable foundation of republican citizenship. In theory, the independent farmer's vote could not be bought or sold; nor could economic pressure render him subservient to political factions and other concentrations of power.

The work of the independent farmer was also thought to produce moral qualities along with these political virtues. These qualities sprang in part from the farmer's close ties to the soil and the landscape, from the fact that the rhythms of farmwork were in harmony with the seasonal rhythms of nature itself. Farmwork also produced a model family working together in a spirit of cooperation under the benevolent and protective eye of the paterfamilias. While men and women performed many separate tasks on farms, they also shared a good deal; the rigid distinction between work suitable for men and work suitable for women had not yet been established. Children grew up learning work from both of their parents and living in a world in which work and life were largely coextensive. Work was not an activity carved out as a separate domain of life, taking place only in certain hours and at particular locations; work was woven into the patterns of everyday life, and life itself was inextricably connected with work.

Before the arrival of the factory system, the work of many artisans—shoemakers, printers, carpenters, and the like—was likewise characterized by personal independence and patriarchal family structure. Master artisans were the lords and masters of their workshops and were able to exert a good deal of control over the scope and pace of the work performed therein. Their rhythms of work were established by custom, not regulated by the impersonal mechanism of the clock. The master and his journeymen and apprentices usually took their meals together, and the master's role was modeled on that of a father; the master was held responsible for the training and the general well-being (including the moral rectitude) of his workers. Moreover, there was also a considerable degree of social mobility built into the artisanal organization of labor. In theory, at least, an apprentice would become a journeyman after he had served his years of indenture; eventually, a hardworking and skillful journeyman could set himself up as an independent artisan in his own workshop. Artisans could also control much of the production process. They bought their raw materials, they designed their products, and they oversaw the production process from start to finish—from sheets of hide to finished shoes, from iron ore to horseshoes and nails.

The combination of authority and independence that made farm and artisanal labor perfectly congruent with the principles of republicanism was immediately jeopardized by the new factory system. Industrialism's production process could be undertaken with little regard for the seasons, and work rhythms were strictly governed by an abstract sense of time measured out by clocks. Operatives in the factory exercised very little control over the production process; instead, they had to adapt their labor to the requirements of the factory's machinery. This loss of control was exacerbated by industrialism's division of labor, which split the production process into separate units, each performed by individuals working repetitively and exclusively on their one part of the whole. Whereas the village blacksmith had overseen his work from design to finished product, the factory operative merely worked on one part of patterns others had designed; he or she had little responsibility for the finished product and proportionately less pride in it. Work was transformed into drudgery.

As these changes in the nature and scope of work became known, they sparked an intense debate in which writers and intellectuals figured prominently. Advocates of industrialism hailed the efficiency of the new factories, whereas critics deplored what they saw as an alarming dehumanization of work. A wide range of writers, including Ralph Waldo Emerson (1803–1882), Henry David Thoreau (1814–1862), Herman Melville (1819–1891), and Rebecca Harding Davis (1831–1910) took the side of the critics. In "The American Scholar," Emerson complained that the original unity of man "has been so minutely subdivided and peddled out, that it is spilled into drops and cannot be gathered. The state of society is one in which the members have suffered amputation from the trunk, and strut about so many walking monsters,—a good finger, a neck, a stomach, an elbow, but never a man. Man is thus metamorphosed into a thing, into many things" (p. 54). In *Walden* (1854), Thoreau asks: "Where is this division of labor to end? and what object does it finally serve?" (p. 44). Melville's story "The Paradise of Bachelors and the Tartarus of Maids" is a scathingly satirical depiction of the way factory labor usurps human sexuality, and Davis's *Life in the Iron Mills* (1861) bitterly condemns its extirpation of man's creative energies.

But not every writer's response to industrialism was so unequivocally hostile. While Walt Whitman (1819–1892) celebrated artisanal labor and the independence it fostered, he was surprisingly untroubled by the factory system and in "Song of the Exposition" (first written in 1871 and later revised in 1876 and 1881) sang its praises:

Mark the spirit of invention everywhere, thy rapid
    patents,
Thy continual workshops, foundries, risen or rising,
    See, from their chimneys how the tall flame-fires
    stream.

(P. 349)

The *Lowell Offering,* a magazine purportedly written wholly "by factory operatives," included in its 1842 edition a "Song of the Spinners" with the lyrics "And now we sing, with gladsome hearts / The theme of the spinner's song / That labor to leisure a zest imparts / unknown to the idle throng." Yet one wonders whether this song genuinely expressed the feelings of the factory operatives: Just a few years earlier, in 1836, striking female mill workers in Lowell, Massachusetts, had sung a quite different tune.

> Oh! Isn't it a pity, such a pretty girl as I
> Should be sent to the factory to pine away and die?
> Oh! I cannot be a slave, I will not be a slave,
> For I'm so fond of liberty,
> That I cannot be a slave.

As the industrial manufacturing process increasingly separated skilled from unskilled labor, labor itself was increasingly understood in terms of a sharp distinction between manual and mental activities. To many observers it seemed obvious that some men and women worked with their hands only while others worked with their minds. Because this distinction rested on deeper dualisms in which mind and spirit were favored over body and matter, manual labor was soon represented as being utterly devoid of meaning and unworthy of the respect it had once enjoyed. For example, when Edward Everett (1794–1865), formerly a distinguished professor of literature at Harvard and the editor of the *North American Review,* discouraged working men from organizing themselves into a political party and urged them to accept a subordinate position in society, he based his argument on a presumed superiority of spirit over matter. It is surely "the reasoning soul" which "makes man superior to the beasts that perish," he said, "so it is this, which, in its moral and intellectual endowments, is the sole foundation for the only distinctions between man and man, which have any real value" (p. 31). Similarly, the political economist Theodore Sedgwick (1811–1859) could bluntly assert that "the more a man labours with his mind, which is mental labour, the higher he is in the scale of labourers; all must agree to that" (p. 272).

Sedgwick's "must" was doubtless aimed at the laborers and labor advocates who at that very moment were trying to reclaim for the factory workers some of the autonomy and social respect they had formerly enjoyed as independent artisans. The tactics of these advocates varied. Some claimed that factory labor was not itself incompatible with mental and spiritual qualities. The literary productions of the Lowell mill girls was implicitly such a claim, and more explicitly so when they titled one of their volumes *Mind among the Spindles.* More typically, though, attempts to claim rights for factory workers took the more radical step of

asserting the value of manual labor in terms of the value of the body, thereby running directly counter to their culture's long-standing belief that the mind and spirit had more intrinsic worth than the body and matter. The Philadelphia shoemaker and labor advocate William Heighton, for example, argued that the "fountain" of a nation's wealth "consists of the *marrow and the bones, the blood and muscles of the Industrious classes* . . ." (p. 10) and that by contrast, the "Trading class . . . are UNPRODUCERS; with their own hands they *shape* no materials, *erect* no property, create no wealth" (p. 11).

Situated in this debate over the relative worth of manual and mental labor, writers at the time were pulled in two directions. On the one hand, because the presumed mentality and spirituality of their own work was what gave it much of its social value and respect, they were reluctant to call that principle into question. On the other hand, they tended to recoil from the antidemocratic, or inegalitarian, consequences entailed by that principle. Their most characteristic response, therefore, was to collapse the distinction between body and mind and to figure their work as being both mental and corporeal.

This effort found expression in many ways and reached a fever pitch in the late 1830s and 1840s. In 1840 Orestes Brownson published "The Laboring Classes" in *The Boston Quarterly Review.* In April 1841 Theodore Parker published his essay "Thoughts on Labor" in *The Dial,* arguing that "Things will never come to their proper level, so long as Thought with the Head and Work with the Hands are considered incompatible" (p. 515). That month also saw the establishment of the Brook Farm community, described by its founder George Ripley as an attempt "to combine manual and mental labor," or to "unite the thinker and worker as far as possible in the same individual" (quoted in Frothingham, p. 307). One visitor to Brook Farm was Horace Greeley, the founding editor of the New York *Herald Tribune.* Strongly sympathetic to Ripley's project, Greeley was also an investor in a Fourierist community in Red Bank, New Jersey, called the North American Phalanx. With his eye on all these developments, in 1852 Charles Eliot Norton went so far as to suggest that "the distinguishing characteristic of the literature of the present age is the attention it bestows to that portion of society which is generally called 'the lower classes'" (p. 464).

Precisely because the split between manual and mental labor rested on assumed ontological distinctions between body and mind, and matter and spirit, writers who sought to undo that split often did so with no explicit reference to the lower classes, or to the factory system, or to the division of labor. Take, for example, the last words of the long, elaborately wrought first sentence of *Walden:* "and lived by the labor of my hands only" (p. 3). At first glance one might think that Thoreau is referring here merely to his labor of hoeing beans and chopping wood; but when his words are placed next to Sedgwick's and Heighton's one can see that he is also intervening in the argument between them. His sentence can be read as subtly asserting that the spiritual quest he undertakes by the shores of the pond is perfectly compatible with the manual labor he performed there. Furthermore, he might even be suggesting that his work as a writer is in crucial ways the labor of the "hands" and the body, not just of the mind and spirit. If so, *Walden* can be read as Thoreau's solitary and idiosyncratic response to the Brook Farm experiment and as an indirect but powerful contribution to a vigorous cultural debate of which Thoreau was well aware. *Walden* is far from unique in this respect. The tension between a traditional commitment to the spirituality of artistic and literary labor and a new interest in the corporeal aspects of their labor informs the work of many antebellum writers. This tension appears also in a number of slave narratives, in which embodiment is understood both as a source of one's oppression and as the foundation of one's community.

PROFESSIONALIZATION AND THE SEPARATION OF SPHERES

Antebellum cultural anxieties about work triggered by industrialism were intensified by two other sources of unease. One was the professionalization of forms of middle-class work that had traditionally been considered vocational, including literature and the ministry. William Charvat and Michael Gilmore, among others, have shown how the emergence of a mass reading audience transformed literature into a commodity and subjected writers to the new and often discomfiting pressures of a literary marketplace. Likewise, the rise of professionalism in this period, along with competition from Evangelical denominations, transformed the traditional New England ministry from a genteel calling into an increasingly competitive struggle for survival. To be a man of letters now was to be a professional and thus a worker.

The separation of men's and women's "spheres" was another cause of anxiety about work—an anxiety that created a booming market for advice manuals and textbooks, especially works that instructed women in how to be wives, mothers, and domestic managers. Catharine Beecher's *Treatise on Domestic Economy* (1841) was perhaps the best known of these. Other works included Lydia Maria Child's *The Mother's Book* (1831), Maria J. McIntosh's *Woman in America: Her Work and Her Reward* (1850), and Mrs. A. J. Graves's

Woman in America: Being an Examination into the Moral and Intellectual Condition of American Female Society (1847). Even as these books sought to train women to "regulate" their homes with maximum efficiency, they were also disciplining the women themselves, explicitly exhorting them to conform to emerging standards of "true womanhood."

This discourse on domesticity was intimately connected with other kinds of literary production. Harriet Beecher Stowe (1811–1896) was Catharine Beecher's sister; she assisted Catharine in the composition and revisions of the *Treatise,* she later wrote her own popular advice columns (later collected as *Household Papers and Stories,* 1876), and she incorporated her beliefs about the value of domestic labor in her fiction, most notably perhaps in *Uncle Tom's Cabin* (1851–1852). Lydia Maria Child (1802–1880) was also an accomplished author of fiction and poetry and an abolitionist best known today for her preface to Harriet Jacobs's *Incidents in the Life of a Slave Girl* (1861). Concerns about the nature and worth of women's domestic work also permeated the popular fiction written by what Nathaniel Hawthorne notoriously called "that damned mob of scribbling women." *The Wide, Wide World* (1850) by Susan Warner (1819–1885) is just one of many novels that trace the fortunes of a motherless girl who must learn for herself what being a good wife and mother entails. The confluence of literary and domestic labor was no accident. As the historian Mary Kelley has argued, women authors wrote about private, domestic life in part because their choice of this subject legitimated their commitment to the public work of an author, work that was supposed to be the province of men: "The literary domestics could enter man's world because they had not left behind women's work" (p. 287).

Conversely, a number of male writers in the antebellum period worried that their own work of authorship was not sufficiently masculine because it was performed within the sanctuary of the home and spared the harsher work environment deemed suitable for men. Several of Emerson's lectures and essays, for example, and some of Hawthorne's and even Melville's fiction, voice insecurity about the gender dimension of literary labor. And Thoreau's claim to have lived by the labor of his "hands only" and Whitman's bold assertion of his identity as a working man, or "one of the roughs," take on new meaning when viewed against the backdrop of this intense cultural investment in work as a crucial determinant of one's femininity or masculinity.

As all of these examples suggest, antebellum anxieties about work crossed class lines and troubled middle-class proprietors and professionals as much as working-class men and women and their spokespersons. Antebellum works of literature reveal how complex these anxieties were and how deeply they reached into the values and outlook of the period. Certainly antebellum writers were keenly aware that their interventions in the debates about work and labor were partisan, not neutral; they understood that what was at stake was not just the cultural value of the work being performed by factory hands, bankers, artisans, mothers, and so on, but the worth of the work being performed in their own studies, at their own desks, by their own hands guiding a pen across a sheet of paper.

See also Banking, Finance, Panics, and Depressions; Factories; Immigration; *Life in the Iron Mills; Lowell Offering*

BIBLIOGRAPHY

Primary Works
Emerson, Ralph Waldo. *Ralph Waldo Emerson: Essays and Lectures.* New York: Library of America, 1983.

Everett, Edward. *A Lecture on the Working Men's Party.* Boston: Gray and Bowen, 1830.

Frothingham, O. B. *George Ripley.* Boston: Houghton Mifflin, 1882.

Heighton, William. *An Address to the Members of Trade Societies, and to the Working Classes Generally.* Philadelphia, 1827.

Norton, Charles Eliot. "Dwellings and Schools for the Poor." *North American Review* 74, no. 105 (1852): 464–490.

Parker, Theodore. "Thoughts on Labor." *The Dial* 1, no. 4 (1841): 497–519.

Sedgwick, Theodore. *Public and Private Economy.* New York: Harper & Brothers, 1836.

Thoreau, Henry David. *Walden and Other Writings.* 1854. Edited by Brooks Atkinson. New York: Modern Library, 2000.

Whitman, Walt. "Song of the Exposition." In *Poetry and Prose.* New York: Library of America, 1982.

Secondary Works
Augst, Thomas. *The Clerk's Tale: Young Men and Moral Life in Nineteenth-Century America.* Chicago: University of Chicago Press, 2004.

Bromell, Nicholas K. *By the Sweat of the Brow: Literature and Labor in Antebellum America.* Chicago: University of Chicago Press, 1993.

Charvat, William. *The Profession of Authorship in America, 1800–1870.* Columbus: Ohio State University Press, 1968.

Cott, Nancy F. *The Bonds of Womanhood: "Woman's Sphere" in New England, 1780–1835.* New Haven, Conn.: Yale University Press, 1977.

Dawley, Alan. *Class and Community.* Cambridge, Mass.: Harvard University Press, 1976.

Dublin, Thomas. *Women at Work: The Transformation of Work and Community in Lowell, Massachusetts, 1826–1860.* New York: Columbia University Press, 1979.

Gilmore, Michael T. *American Romanticism and the Marketplace.* Chicago: University of Chicago Press, 1985.

Kelley, Mary. *Private Woman, Public Stage: Literary Domesticity in Nineteenth-Century America.* New York: Oxford University Press, 1984.

Laurie, Bruce. *Artisans into Workers: Labor in Nineteenth-Century America.* New York: Hill and Wang, 1989.

Maibor, Carolyn R. *Labor Pains: Emerson, Hawthorne, and Alcott on Work and the Woman Question.* New York: Routledge, 2004.

Rodgers, Daniel T. *The Work Ethic in Industrial America, 1850–1920.* Princeton, N.J.: Princeton University Press, 1978.

Ryan, Mary P. *The Empire of the Mother: American Writing about Domesticity, 1830–1860.* New York: Oxford University Press, 1982.

Nick Bromell

LANDSCAPE ARCHITECTURE

As Perry Miller persuasively argued in *Nature's Nation,* Americans have long considered themselves as inhabiting a space that has been defined by its relationship with nature. The relationship between Americans and American nature has been long-standing, but the terms of that relationship have changed as the nation has grown. The "howling wilderness" from which William Bradford (1663–1752) recoiled when he first viewed it from the deck of the *Mayflower* in 1620 had become by 1820 a prized emblem of both the new nation's past and its future promise. With the publication of James Fenimore Cooper's (1789–1851) *The Pioneers* (1823), the wilderness had become one of the principal locales for an emerging national literature. Ironically, in this novel, in which Cooper introduces his frontier hero, Natty Bumppo, and his Indian friend, Chingachgook (Indian John in this novel), the wilderness is under assault by the forces of settlement and civilization. In fact, *The Pioneers,* with its scenes depicting the slaughter of the passenger pigeon flock and the devastation of the forest, can be called the first ecological novel in American literature.

Five years later in *Notions of the Americans* (1828), Cooper would explore the European view of American space. In this work, a "Count," loosely based on Lafayette, the French ally of the American revolutionaries, writes letters home about what he observes in America. As Wayne Franklin points out, the Count perceives the distinctions between "settled field and wild forest," but he attempts to make these contrasting scenes "coalesce visually, reducing their difference to a mere contrast of hue—the very finesse of which gives the tamely artful land dominance over the wild" (p. 215). Franklin reminds us that "Cooper's . . . practice as a novelist was to stress and intensify" this contrast (p. 215).

Rather early on, then, in American life and letters distinctions were drawn between the wild and the tame landscape. Just as there were Americans who celebrated the wilderness, by the 1820s there were also those who advocated a tamer, more domestic nature. By the end of the first two decades of the nineteenth century, parts of America had been settled long enough for their inhabitants to think about how nature could be incorporated within their private and public spaces. While Cooper was introducing readers to the American wilderness as a threatened site of national drama, he and other landowners in New York and elsewhere in the more settled eastern parts of the nation were beginning to take an interest in English and European concepts of landscape gardening.

EARLY DEVELOPMENT OF LANDSCAPE GARDENING IN THE UNITED STATES

In his study of the early history of horticulture in the United States, Ulysses Hedrick observes that "in the first half of the nineteenth century the fever to improve grounds was increased by every visitor to England" (p. 226). James Fenimore Cooper quickly caught the gardening fever. His daughter, Susan (1813–1894), who would later write *Rural Hours* (1850), wrote in her journal of the avidity with which her father sought to improve the grounds of Angevine, the family residence from 1817 to 1822. Americans were visiting England and coming back with ideas for their gardens, and Englishmen were also coming to America and bringing with them their gardening concepts. When William Cobbett (1763–1835), later to become famous as an English political reformer, took up residence on North Hempstead, Long Island, in 1817, he remarked on the lack of variety found in the American kitchen garden. In 1818 Cobbett recounted his experiences on Long Island in *A Year's Residence in the United States of America*. He later reworked some of the material from this book into *The American Gardener* (1819). In his preface to this work, Cobbett tartly observed that the vastness of America and the relative cheapness of the land militated against careful gardening. Cobbett noted that "where land is abundant, attachment and even attention to *small spots* wears away" (p. xxiv).

English gardens and gardeners were a decided influence on American landscape design, but, according to Hedrick, it was André Parmentier (1780–1830), who arrived in America from France in 1824,

who first achieved success as a "professional landscape gardener" in the United States (p. 227). Although he lived only until 1830, Parmentier had a profound impact on the growth of landscape architecture in America. Upon his arrival in America, he established a botanical garden near present-day Brooklyn that provided him with the nursery stock he needed to implement his gardening designs.

Parmentier enunciated his theories on gardens in "Landscape and Picturesque Gardens," an essay that appeared in Thomas Green Fessenden's (1771–1837) *The New American Gardener* (1828). Parmentier argued that "gardens should be treated like landscapes, whose charms are not to be improved by rules of art" (p. 184). For Parmentier, naturalness, with its surprises, pleased more than artifice. A proponent of curving and winding vistas, he asked how any person of sensibility and taste "would not prefer to walk in a plantation irregular and picturesque, rather than those straight and monotonous alleys, bordered with mournful box?" (p. 185). According to Hedrick, Parmentier's theories influenced the later work of Andrew Jackson Downing (1815–1852), whose *Treatise on the Theory and Practice of Landscape Gardening* (1841) was the most influential work on landscape gardening in America in the mid-nineteenth century.

Parmentier's publisher, Thomas Green Fessenden—a lawyer, political satirist, Hudibrastic (mock-verse) poet, and horticultural author—was another force in the growth of landscape gardening in America. In 1822 Fessenden moved from Brattleborough, Vermont, to Boston and started *The New England Farmer,* to which he contributed until his death in 1837. He also edited *The Horticultural Register* and *The Silk Manual.* Fessenden was well enough known that Nathaniel Hawthorne (1804–1864) wrote an essay on him, later reprinted in *Fanshawe and Other Pieces* (1876). Hawthorne praised *The New England Farmer* as an original venture, claiming that "Numerous papers on the same plan sprung up in various parts of the country, but none attained the standard of their prototype" (p. 580).

Among Fessenden's contemporaries who were also important figures in the history of landscape architecture in America were Bernard M'Mahan (c. 1775–1816) and William Prince (1766–1842). In 1802 M'Mahan published the *American Gardener's Calendar,* which was among the first works to provide planting dates that corresponded with the climate of the eastern United States. Prince's contribution to the growing body of literature on the topic was a *Short Treatise on Horticulture* (1828). Robert Squibb published *The Gardener's Calendar for the States of North-Carolina, South Carolina, and Georgia* in 1809.

Illustration of a picturesque landscape from Andrew Jackson Downing's *Landscape Gardening*, 1841. In this seminal work, Downing differentiated between two desirable forms of landscaping: the beautiful, characterized by "simple and flowing forms," and the picturesque, "expressed by striking, irregular, spirited forms." This illustration represents the latter. GRADUATE LIBRARY, UNIVERSITY OF MICHIGAN

THE LITERARY RESPONSE TO CHANGING PERCEPTIONS OF LANDSCAPE

By the 1830s American attitudes toward nature and landscape had changed so profoundly that essayists were educating the American public on how to view what they had previously either ignored or taken for granted. With the publication of Ralph Waldo Emerson's *Nature* in 1836, Americans were introduced to not only how to "read" the landscape but also how to draw spiritual sustenance from it. In this important essay, Emerson (1803–1882) laid claim to the land that others only imagined they held. He observed that "Miller owns this field, Locke that, and Manning the woodland beyond. But none of them owns the landscape" (p. 9). In terms that reveal his debt to English Romanticism and its extolling of the primacy of the child's vision, Emerson declared that

"few adult persons can see nature" (p. 10). Only those people who have "retained the spirit of infancy even into the era of manhood," are, according to Emerson, capable of truly appreciating nature (p. 10). For Emerson, those who can truly perceive the underlying forms inherent in nature are poets.

In "The Poet" (1844), Emerson develops his platonic theory of how the poet apprehends the forms residing in nature. To the poet, "Nature offers all her creatures . . . as a picture language" (p. 452). Emerson's ideal poet is one who needs no stimulants to spur his imagination. The poet's "cheerfulness should be the gift of the sunlight; the air should suffice for his inspiration, and he should be tipsy with water" (p. 461). It is not in wealth, or in the seats of power that the poet must seek inspiration but in nature.

Nature alone is noble: "new nobility is conferred in groves and pastures, and not in castles, or by the sword-blade, any longer" (p. 467).

What America had to offer that made it a special place was not like the castles and grand ruins that had so affected the imaginations of European painters and poets; what America offered was space in which to dream. When Margaret Fuller (1810–1850), the editor of *The Dial*—the journal of the transcendentalist movement—recounted her travels in Illinois and Wisconsin, it was the spaciousness of the landscape that most impressed her. In *Summer on the Lakes* (1844), she wrote that, on the prairies "a man need not take a small slice from the landscape, and fence it in from the obtrusions of an uncongenial neighbor, and there cut down his fancies to miniature improvements which a chicken could run over in ten minutes" (p. 26).

As Annette Kolodny informs the reader in *The Land before Her*, although they were not often acknowledged in their own time or later, women were central figures in the process of settling and domesticating spaces such as the prairies. Among the authors Fuller read before she embarked on her journey to the Midwest was Caroline Kirkland (1801–1864), who, in *A New Home—Who'll Follow?* (1839), offered an unblinking look at the reality of trying to reproduce Eden on the American prairies. As Kolodny points out, Kirkland's narrative persona, Mary Clavers, grants that the new Adams and Eves in the Midwest might create a new Eden but it would be a New World garden. Although there might be "tall oaks near the cottage," the rest of the setting would lack the "rocky . . . glenny . . . streamy" landscape so dear to the heart of European Romantics (Kolodny, p. 145).

If the Midwest and the open spaces even farther west were uncongenial to Emerson's ideal, perhaps a life connected to nature could be worked out closer to home—indeed, almost in Emerson's backyard. No one took Emerson's advice so seriously and tried to enact it so fervently as did Henry David Thoreau (1817–1862). Emerson schooled his fellow citizens on what to look for in nature and how to live in harmony with nature. Henry David Thoreau reported to them on his experiment in living according to those precepts Emerson had laid down. In *Walden* (1854), Thoreau recorded the results of his attempts at living life "deliberately." For Thoreau it was not space itself but the spaciousness of the imagination that counted. "Though the view from my door was . . . contracted, I did not feel crowded or confined in the least. There was pasture enough for my imagination. The low shrub oak plateau to which the opposite shore arose, stretched as far as the prairies of the West and the steppes of Tartary" (p. 83).

The following is an excerpt from "The Piazza," the title story of Herman Melville's The Piazza Tales *(1856):*

When I removed into the country, it was to occupy an old-fashioned farm-house, which had no piazza—a deficiency the more regretted, because not only did I like piazzas, as somehow combining the coziness of in-doors with the freedom of out-doors, and it is so pleasant to inspect your thermometer there, but the country round about was such a picture, that in berry time no boy climbs hill or crosses vale without coming upon easels planted in every nook, and sun-burnt painters painting there. A very paradise of painters. The circle of the stars cut by the circle of the mountains. At least, so looks it from the house; though, once upon the mountains, no circle of them can you see. Had the site been chosen five rods off, this charmed ring would not have been.

Melville, *The Piazza Tales*, p. 621.

Although Nathaniel Hawthorne never experimented with life on the level of Thoreau's experiment at Walden Pond, he did participate in a utopian experiment at Brook Farm in Massachusetts; later, he used his experiences at Brook Farm as the basis for *The Blithedale Romance* (1852). Hawthorne also had a personal connection to Emerson, as he lived in the Old Manse at Concord. The Old Manse, formerly the minister's home, was the home in which Emerson lived in his youth. Hawthorne rented the Old Manse from 1842 to 1845 and recounted his time there and his impressions of the grounds in his *American Notebooks* (1804–1864) and *Mosses from an Old Manse* (1846). When Hawthorne and his new bride, Sophia Peabody, moved into the Old Manse, Thoreau planted a garden for them as a wedding present.

When Hawthorne later moved to Pittsfield in the Berkshire mountains, his new friend and fellow author Herman Melville (1819–1891) moved there also. Melville moved into a farm nearby that he named Arrowhead after the quantity of Indian artifacts he uncovered in the farm's fields. In the title story of *The Piazza Tales* (1856), Melville described the one deficiency in his new old home. "Now, for a house, so situated in such a country, to have no piazza for the convenience of those who might desire to feast upon

The Old Manse. Engraving, 1881. This house, where Nathaniel Hawthorne lived from 1842 to 1845, and its sur-rounding landscape provided inspiration for Hawthorne's story collection *Mosses from an Old Manse* and sketches in his *American Notebooks.* THE LIBRARY OF CONGRESS

the view, and take their time and ease about it, seemed as much of an omission as if a picture-gallery should have no bench" (pp. 621–622).

COTTAGE AND ESTATE: DESIGNS FOR LIVING

Hawthorne, Melville, and other literary figures were not alone in their search for rural tranquility. Even those who did not desire to nurse a muse felt the need to create a way of living that allowed them to feel less constrained. Andrew Jackson Downing, who designed the National Mall in Washington, D.C., and whose *Treatise on the Theory and Practice of Landscape Gardening, adapted to North America* (1841) was the most important work on American landscape design in the first half of the nineteenth century, felt that not only the wealthy but also the working classes deserved living spaces that connected them to nature. In *The Architecture of Country Houses* (1850), Downing argues that the United States should eschew becoming "a nation, whose rural population is content to live in

mean huts and miserable hovels" (p. v). If the country were to tolerate such mean living dwellings for its rural inhabitants, it would find itself "behind its neighbors in education, the arts, and all that makes up the external signs of progress" (p. v). Downing felt that if rural Americans followed his precepts about home and garden design, they could avert the "gross blunders in taste" that he observed elsewhere (p. 205).

Country Houses offered the public not only plans for villas and country houses but also designs for cottages and farmhouses. Downing addressed the designs of rural residencies more directly in *Cottage Residences* (1842). His ideas on cottage design would survive into the early twentieth century. Many of the prefabricated houses sold by mail-order firms such as Sears and Roebuck were based on designs that can be traced back to Downing's pioneering work in this field. In addition to writing on home and landscape design, Downing founded the *Horticulturalist* (1846), a magazine dedicated to advancing the practice of

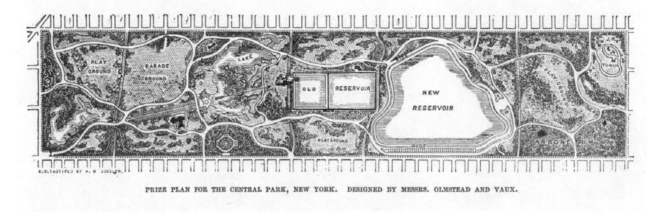

PLAY GROUND PARADE GROUND LAKE OLD RESERVOIR NEW RESERVOIR PLAYGROUND PLAYGROUND ARBORETUM TOWER

ELECTROTYPES OF A. H. JOCELYN.

PRIZE PLAN FOR THE CENTRAL PARK, NEW YORK. DESIGNED BY MESSRS. OLMSTEAD AND VAUX.

The Greensward Plan for New York's Central Park. Drawn by Frederick Law Olmsted and Calvert Vaux, 1858.
THE GRANGER COLLECTION, NEW YORK

gardening in the United States. Most of Downing's editorials for the *Horticulturalist* were published posthumously in *Rural Essays* (1853).

Downing was not alone in his interest in the design of cottages and gardens. Walter Elder published *The Cottage Garden of America* (1849) and Lewis Falley Allen wrote on *Rural Architecture* (1852). In 1850 Susan Fenimore Cooper published *Rural Hours,* in which she encouraged rural landowners to consider how to shape and maintain their woodlots with an eye to creating a pleasing vista. The language of flowers was also a topic that received literary attention. In 1830 Sarah Josepha Hale (1788–1879) published *Flora's Interpreter.* In 1852 Frederick Law Olmsted (1822–1903) published *Walks and Talks of an American Farmer in England.*

If Downing was the most important figure in American landscape architecture in the first half of the nineteenth century, Olmsted was the most important American landscape architect in the second half of the nineteenth century. Perhaps best remembered for his work on public spaces and parks such as New York's Central Park, Brooklyn's Prospect Park, and Buffalo's Chapin Parkway, Olmsted also worked with his partner, Calvert Vaux (1824–1895), in laying out the plan for Riverside, a Chicago suburb that combined proximity to the city with the spaciousness and green space of a country setting.

As John G. Mitchell notes in "Frederick Law Olmsted's Passion for Parks," it was Olmstead's connections with literary figures such as Washington Irving and William Cullen Bryant that helped him secure the position of superintendent of what would become New York's Central Park. Olmsted's association

with public spaces and streetcar suburbs signified a shift in the American vision of landscape architecture. Although there would still be efforts to construct country retreats on the grand scale of European chateaus (Olmsted himself would later work on the Biltmore Estate in North Carolina), the projects taken on by Olmsted and other landscape architects during the latter half of the nineteenth century reflected the urbanization of America and the need to provide green spaces for city dwellers.

In *A Writer's America,* Alfred Kazin describes Olmsted's plan for Central Park as a reaction to the monotony of the city's urban gridlines. "For his park he wanted a rural unkemptness, picturesque roads. In the vast planting to replace the old swamp wasteland he emphasized wild plants, random tufts, a thick growth of low brambles, ferns, asters, gentians, irregularly spaced trees" (p. 168). If the city dweller could not escape to the country, Olmsted would bring the country to the city. Although Walt Whitman (1819–1892) voiced his objections to the plan because the miles of carriageways obviously catered to the wealthier classes, he did concede that Olmsted's grand plan "represented at least a trial marriage of art and enlightened enterprise, nature and life in the city" (Kazin, p. 171).

As Lee Clark Mitchell points out, "Olmsted's vision extended well beyond city limits" (p. 49). Olmsted campaigned for restricting the commercialization of Niagara Falls and when he moved to California in 1863 he worked to preserve the Yosemite Valley and the Big Tree Grove in Mariposa (pp. 49–50). In 1865 he wrote a report on the Yosemite Valley for the California Yosemite Commission. Olmsted's efforts were instrumental in removing Yosemite from

The following is an excerpt from Charles Dudley Warner's My Summer in a Garden *(1870):*

Broad acres are a patent of nobility; and no man but feels more of a man in the world if he have a bit of ground that he can call his own. However small it is on the surface, it is four thousand miles deep; and that is a handsome property. And there is a great pleasure in working in the soil, apart from the ownership of it. The man who has planted a garden feels he has done something for the good of the world.

Warner, *My Summer in a Garden*, p. 6.

private control and placing it in the hands of the government. Twenty-five years after Olmsted's report, John Muir (1838–1914) and others were finally able to move Congress to enact Olmsted's plan to preserve the Yosemite Valley (Mitchell, p. 50). In this instance, it was Olmsted, the landscape architect and designer, who showed the way for environmental writers such as Muir.

Muir, who would write *The Mountains of California* (1894), *Our National Parks* (1901), *My First Summer in the Sierra* (1911), and *The Yosemite* (1912), among other works, is perhaps the best known of the preservationists who came of age in the late nineteenth century. However, as Mitchell notes, it was George Perkins Marsh (1801–1882), author of *Man and Nature* (1864), who defined the science of ecology at a time when the term itself had not yet come into use (p. 59). Marsh argued that through "careful control and intelligent planning" the nation might be able to preserve its natural legacy (quoted in L. C. Mitchell, p. 60).

In the 1870s and continuing into the 1880s and 1890s America awakened to the need to preserve its natural wonders. The movement to create and preserve national parks was and remains a laudable endeavor. It was, however, equally important for writers to remind Americans, as Thoreau had done almost a quarter of a century earlier, of the pleasures to be found closer to home. In a modest work of less than a hundred pages, Charles Dudley Warner (1829–1900) did just that. Warner is best remembered for being both Harriet Beecher Stowe's and Mark Twain's neighbor in Hartford, and perhaps best forgotten for being the author of some truly turgid prose published

in *Harper's New Monthly Magazine*. But in *My Summer in a Garden* (1870), Warner takes off his stiff workday collar, rolls up his shirtsleeves, and celebrates the elemental passion for dirt. "The love of dirt is among the earliest of passions, as it is the latest. Mud-pies gratify one of our first and best instincts. So long as we are dirty, we are pure" (p. 6).

Whether the nineteenth-century American's desire to commune with nature took the form of Thoreau's impulse to thrust himself headfirst into the soil or Warner's more pedestrian wish to get his hands dirty in his garden, the nineteenth century witnessed America coming to terms with the disappearance of the frontier wilderness and the need to preserve what was still wild and amend what was tame. Literary figures and landscape designers each participated in the project of celebrating, preserving, and recreating the American landscape.

See also Agrarianism; Americans Abroad; English Literature; Foreigners; *Nature;* Taste; Transcendentalism; Urbanization; *Walden;* Wilderness

BIBLIOGRAPHY
Primary Works
Cobbett, William. *The American Gardener.* 1819. New York: Modern Library, 2003.

Cooper, James Fenimore. *Notions of the Americans.* 1828. Historical introduction and textual notes by Gary Williams. Albany: State University of New York Press, 1991.

Cooper, James Fenimore. *The Pioneers.* 1823. New York: New American Library, 1964.

Cooper, Susan Fenimore. *Rural Hours.* 1850. Edited by Rochelle Johnson and Daniel Patterson. Athens: University of Georgia Press, 1998.

Downing, Andrew Jackson. *The Architecture of Country Houses; including designs for cottages, farmhouses, and villas, with remarks on interiors, furniture, and the best modes of warming and ventilating.* New York: D. Appleton and Co., 1850.

Downing, Andrew Jackson. *Cottage Residences; or, A series of designs for rural cottages and cottage villas, and their gardens and grounds, adapted to North America.* 1842. 4th ed. New York: Wiley and Halsted, 1856.

Downing, Andrew Jackson. *A Treatise on the Theory and Practice of Landscape Gardening, adapted to North America.* New York, London, Wiley and Putnam; Boston: C. C. Little and Co., 1841.

Emerson, Ralph Waldo. *Essays and Lectures.* Edited by Joel Porte. New York: Library of America, 1983.

Fessenden, Thomas Green. *The New American Gardener.* Boston: J. B. Russell, 1828.

Fuller, Margaret. *Summer on the Lakes, in 1843.* 1844. Urbana: University of Illinois Press, 1991.

Hawthorne, Nathaniel. *Mosses from an Old Manse.* 1846. Reprinted in *Tales and Sketches.* New York: Literary Classics of the United States, 1982.

Kirkland, Caroline. *A New Home—Who'll Follow? or, Glimpses of Western Life.* 1839. Edited by William S. Osborne. Schenectady, N.Y.: College and University Press, 1965.

Melville, Herman. *The Piazza Tales.* 1856. Edited by Egbert S. Oliver. New York: Hendricks House, 1948.

Olmsted, Frederick Law. *The Papers of Frederick Law Olmsted.* Vol. 1, *The Formative Years, 1822–1852.* Edited by Charles Capen McLaughlin. Baltimore: Johns Hopkins University Press, 1977.

Thoreau, Henry David. *Walden and Other Writings.* New York: Modern Library, 2000.

Warner, Charles Dudley. *My Summer in a Garden.* 1870. Introduction by Allan Gurganus. New York: Modern Library, 2002.

Secondary Works

Dean, Sharon L. *Constance Fenimore Woolson and Edith Wharton: Perspectives on Landscape and Art.* Knoxville: University of Tennessee Press, 2002.

Franklin, Wayne. *The New World of James Fenimore Cooper.* Chicago: University of Chicago Press, 1982.

Hedrick, Ulysses P. *A History of Horticulture in America to 1860.* New York: Oxford University Press, 1950.

Kazin, Alfred. *A Writer's America: Landscape in Literature.* New York: Knopf, 1988.

Kolodny, Annette. *The Land Before Her: Fantasy and Experience of the American Frontiers, 1630–1860.* Chapel Hill: University of North Carolina Press, 1984.

Leighton, Ann. *American Gardens of the Nineteenth Century: "For Comfort and Affluence."* Amherst: University of Massachusetts Press, 1987.

Miller, Perry. *Nature's Nation.* Cambridge, Mass.: Belknap Press of Harvard University Press, 1967.

Mitchell, John G. "Frederick Law Olmsted's Passion for Parks." *National Geographic* 207, no. 3 (2005): 32–51.

Mitchell, Lee Clark. *Witnesses to a Vanishing America: The Nineteenth-Century Response.* Princeton, N.J.: Princeton University Press, 1981.

Thacker, Robert. *The Great Prairie Fact and Literary Imagination.* Albuquerque: University of New Mexico Press, 1989.

Wolschke-Buhlman, Joachim, and Jack Becker, eds. *American Garden Literature in the Dumbarton Oaks Collection (1785–1900).* Washington, D.C.: Dumbarton Oaks, 1998.

James J. Schramer

THE LAST OF THE MOHICANS

See Leatherstocking Tales

LEATHERSTOCKING TALES

James Fenimore Cooper's (1789–1851) Leatherstocking Tales were the first American stories to capture the imagination of readers around the world, and they began the tradition of the American novel. Named after the garment worn by their central character, Natty Bumppo, the Leatherstocking Tales consist of *The Pioneers* (1823), *The Last of the Mohicans* (1826), *The Prairie* (1827), *The Pathfinder* (1840), and *The Deerslayer* (1841). Bumppo appears in all the novels: as an aging marksman in *The Pioneers;* as Hawkeye, named for his prowess with a rifle, in *The Last of the Mohicans;* as "the trapper," an old man, in *The Prairie;* as a young "scout" during wartime in *The Pathfinder;* and as a young hunter in *The Deerslayer.* Cooper and the public were loyal to Natty throughout his many incarnations, and he may have reminded some Americans of frontiersmen such as Daniel Boone (1734–1820). To the French novelist Honoré de Balzac, Bumppo was a unique combination of savagery and civilization "who will live as long as literatures last" (p. 2).

COOPER AND THE EARLY REPUBLIC

The key word for the inception of both the Leatherstocking Tales and the United States is "experiment." The Founding Fathers knew that republican government is the most difficult form of government to establish and preserve, and most educated Europeans still consider the United States an experiment in government and in multicultural living. Cooper, toying with the idea of becoming a novelist, plunged into writing with the same energy he had expended previously on agricultural studies, whaling, and the navy.

As Cooper wrote in a preface to *The Spy* (1821), his first attempt at an American novel, the nation was "passing from the gristle into the bone" (p. 21). He was uniquely positioned to identify with the founding because he was born the year the Constitution took effect and had been moved in infancy to the frontier that would become Cooperstown, New York. Not only was his father a judge and congressman but the family also knew the founders and many of the heroes of the American Revolution. The story that would become *The Spy* in fact grew from an anecdote told to him by John Jay (1745–1829), the first chief justice of the Supreme Court and one of the founders of the nation. When the book was pirated and turned out to be popular not only in England but also in France, Germany, Russia, Poland, Denmark, Sweden, and Italy, America had its first major novelist. From that time on, newspapers in the states prefaced reviews of Cooper's early works by reprinting the taunt of the English critic Sydney Smith (1771–1845), who had sneered in *The Edinburgh Review* (January 1820): "In the four corners of the globe, who reads an American book?"

Much of the popularity of *The Spy* can be explained by its subject. By 1820 the American Revolution seemed to be succeeding, unlike the French experiment that had ended in the Reign of Terror. Cooper was uniquely qualified to write such a history since he added to his family's connections with the founders his own 1811 marriage to Susan De Lancey. This gave him access to the papers and some of the property of one of the most prominent Tory families in our first civil war. He was living in a cottage he and Susan had built in 1817 on the "neutral ground" that is the scene of much of the action in the novel.

The amount of fiction and history that Cooper wrote during his lifetime attests to his love of writing, and once he found that he could write for profit he reassessed his position. Saying that he had written to please others, including his wife (who had read the proofs for the first volume of *The Spy* while he was busy elsewhere), he said that he was writing *The Pioneers* to please himself. No one at the time had any indication that this would turn out to be the first of the Leatherstocking Tales, but the debut of the series was notable because *The Pioneers* sold 3,500 copies on the morning of its publication in 1823.

THE PIONEERS

Readers complain that *The Pioneers* starts slowly, although in the first chapter the founder of the village, Judge Temple, shoots at a deer and instead hits and wounds a mysterious young man who lives in a cabin with Natty Bumppo, a white hunter, and a Delaware Indian whose Christian name is John Mohegan. Cooper the historian takes over as he tells about Judge Temple's acquisition of the land and his pre-Revolutionary friendship with the Effingham family who, having fought as Loyalists, had lost their prop-

James Fenimore Cooper. Portrait engraving by J. W. Jarvis after a painting by E. Scriven. GETTY IMAGES

erty after the war and had returned to England. All this is necessary for the reader's later understanding of the behavior of the young man and of many of Natty Bumppo's statements.

In the third chapter, a party in the judge's sleigh halts at the top of a mountain and admires the vista. Nestled in the valley below are the village and lake that will be the scene of much of the action. The judge's daughter, Elizabeth, gets her first glimpse of the home she left four years earlier to finish her schooling. A second sleigh arrives driven by the judge's cousin, Richard Jones, who fancies himself an expert at everything and proves to be a menace. The characters introduced include an old German, Major Hartmann, a descendant of the Palatine settlers, who has arrived for his Christmas visit; a Frenchman, Le Quoi, a political refugee from Martinique who is running a store in the village but longs to return to France; an Episcopal minister, Mr. Grant; and Agamemnon, a black indentured to Richard Jones, who is no Quaker like the judge and can own a temporary slave.

When the narrative reaches the judge's home, Cooper introduces Benjamin Penguillan, a native of Cornwall and a former British sailor now employed as a majordomo by Jones; Remarkable Pettibone, a snuff-taking Puritan with all the unlovely characteristics

Cooper attributed to members of that group; and a self-appointed "doctor" named Todd, who has read books and practiced medicine in order to be accepted as a physician.

It is Christmas Eve, and many of the characters attend a church service in a building that serves as both school and church, its exact denomination being unsettled as the congregation of settlers is made up of "half the nations in the north of Europe" (p. 124). After a lengthy discussion of the various forms of worship contending for supremacy, most of the principal males retire to a tavern kept by the Irish Hollisters (who are Methodists), two characters Cooper's readers would remember from *The Spy*. As the customers assemble, the best seats are taken by "Dr." Todd and one of the town's two lawyers. When others arrive and they drink from mugs they pass around, tensions and different values emerge. The lawyer tries to stir up support for a lawsuit against the judge for wounding someone the lawyer alleges is "the son of Leatherstocking" (p. 150). One Hiram Doolittle, whose unwarranted self-assurance prompts him to speak out on all subjects and who gets a job later as justice of the peace, thinks it may be a prison matter. As the judge arrives, the lawyer "slunk from the room" (p. 157). His comfortable seat is taken by Richard Jones.

In the ensuing discussion, some of the themes of the book emerge as the judge learns that one settler has cashed in his cleared land instead of staying to farm it and has temporarily opened a school until spring when he may go into trade or move to a region "they say" is booming. (Rumors are so important in the village that They Say almost becomes a character.) Meanwhile, Natty and John Mohegan have arrived and after a few drinks the Indian, obviously drunk, starts bragging of his victories only to be interrupted by Natty, who says, "Why do you sing of your battles, Chingachgook, . . . when the worst enemy of all is near you and keeps the Young Eagle from his rights?" (p. 165). To Natty, the judge is the worst enemy and the wounded man is the Young Eagle whose land the judge now possesses. Natty is speaking the Delaware language, however, and the reader is dependent on Cooper's translation for the sense of this provocative statement. By the end of the tavern scene most of the latent problems of forming a settled society out of such disparate peoples are clear.

To the motley crew assembled so far, Cooper shortly adds a woodchopper, Billy Kirby, who hates trees as a symbol of upper-class estates in the Old World and makes a living collecting syrup from them as well as cutting them down. (The need to conserve and build on the natural resources of the country,

represented by the judge, will be seconded later in the novel by Natty Bumppo, after the famous scene in which thousands of pigeons are needlessly wiped out; Natty constantly complains of the "wasty ways" [p. 248] of the settlers.) More characters appear Christmas morning as a free black brings a collection of fowl that he sells as prizes in the annual holiday turkey shoot. Abraham Freeborn, a superior showman, uses his race to his advantage insisting that the people paying for a chance to shoot at the head of one of his fowls "gib a nigger fair play" (p. 193).

As the novel proceeds and Natty is accused of killing a deer out of season, the judge correctly upholds the rule of law and insists that Natty stand trial but attempts privately to aid the culprit when he gives Elizabeth money to give Natty so he can pay his fine. In spite of such minor offenses, however, Natty ultimately emerges as admirable because he proves to have cared for old Major Effingham, his former employer, since the Revolution and because he befriends Chingachgook. Natty insists that baptism as a Christian is no fair exchange for the loss of the Indians' lands and the curse of alcohol that the whites have brought to them. At Chingachgook's death as the book ends, the sober Indian reverts to his true culture. The French writer George Sand (1804–1876) wrote that by making Chingachgook an ally of the whites and a "sort of" convert, Cooper could plead for the Indian without hurting the pride of the country. Yet she insisted that he was also lamenting "a noble people exterminated" and "a serene natural world laid waste" (pp. 281–282).

THE LAST OF THE MOHICANS

The second book in the series, *The Last of the Mohicans*, is subtitled "A Narrative of 1757," which is the date of a famous massacre at Fort William Henry during the French and Indian war. Along with the French infraction of the Laws of War (which were internationally recognized long before the Geneva Accords), responsibility for the massacre lay with the Abenaki Indians, who hated the British for reasons of their own. For his own purposes Cooper makes these animosities personal rather than tribal, and he introduces a motivation for Indian hatred that Mark Twain would adopt for Injun Joe in *The Adventures of Tom Sawyer*: an Indian never forgets an injury. This explains the villain, Magua, a renegade Indian who has been flogged by Colonel Munro, the Scottish commander of Fort William Henry. Magua gets his chance for revenge when he volunteers to guide Munro's daughters and their escort, Major Duncan Heyward, to the fort. Fortunately for them, in the forest they encounter Natty, Chingachgook, and Chingachgook's son, Uncas. This trio alerts Heyward to the danger, but when they try to capture Magua he escapes, only to return later at the head of a band of hostile Indians.

From then on the book is a series of captures, pursuits, disguises, and deceptions. Magua wants to even the score with Munro by enslaving and abusing his eldest daughter, Cora, with everyone knowing he could kill her at any time. Cora and Uncas, as the action unfolds, are mutually attracted. Alice, the other daughter, is a blond fainting type typical of the Cooper female and other heroines of the time. Only Duncan Heyward is interested in her, but when he asks Colonel Munro for her hand, the father brings up the subject of race, which has been lurking in the novel ever since Cora admired the Indians and insisted on being fair to the people of dark skin. Munro says that while he was on duty in the West Indies he married the daughter of a gentleman whose wife was "descended, remotely, from that unfortunate class who are so basely enslaved to administer to the wants of a luxurious people" (p. 159). Cora's mother having died, the colonel, enriched by the marriage, had returned to Scotland and married the woman who would be the mother of Alice. In *The Pioneers*, Elizabeth Temple had taken the part of the Indians and said that she grieved to see old Mohegan walking on the land like the ghost of one of its ancient possessors and feel how small was her own right to possess it. Elizabeth had also aided Natty and Chingachgook at the risk of her own life. Cora is equally resourceful, and she aids Natty (and herself and Alice) by following his instructions and marking a trail that Natty and the Indians can follow.

In this, the most operatic of the Leatherstocking Tales, flight and recapture and disguises and deceits occur at a breathless pace until the final scenes in the camp of the Delawares. Here the famous chief Tamenund presides over an Indian court that reluctantly awards Cora to Magua as his legitimate prisoner but at the same time reveals that Uncas, whose chest is marked by a totemic turtle, is the last of the most noble line of chiefs of the Delawares. One more flight-and-fight sequence follows, ending in the deaths of both Cora and Uncas and with Natty shooting Magua. At the funeral ceremony for Cora and Uncas, the Indians predict that they will be together in the next world, but Natty disagrees even while he is pledging his undying loyalty to Chingachgook. Tamenund has the last word, however, declaring that the palefaces are the masters of the earth and that the "time of the red men has not yet come again" (p. 350).

For the nation's Bicentennial in 1976, the Wilmington, Delaware, Opera Society commissioned an opera of *The Last of the Mohicans*. In the accompanying booklet, Gladys Tantaquidgeon, a Mohegan, said that the last hereditary chief named Uncas died in 1769. While appropriating Mohegan lands, the whites also appropriated the name of Tamenund. After the Revolution, Tammany societies in New York, Philadelphia, and elsewhere (but not New England) were formed in honor of this famous chief. The one in New York lasted the longest and eventually degenerated into the "boss" system of corrupt politics. More than a dozen films have been made of this novel, which confirms Cooper's belief that "There is little reluctance to mingle the white and red blood. . . . I think an amalgamation of the two races would in time occur. Those families of America who are thought to have any of the Indian blood, are rather proud of their descent" (*Notions of the Americans*, p. 490). As Jeffrey Walker has written, "to match Uncas with the fair-haired Alice, as Hollywood filmmakers continue to do, is to misunderstand the very essence of Cooper's theme in *The Last of the Mohicans*" (p. 182).

A FRESH VIEW OF NORTH AMERICAN HISTORY

With the solemn and ceremonial ending of *The Last of the Mohicans*, Cooper broke new ground by insisting that the continent had a history predating the arrival of the white man. Some people in New England had long portrayed the region as a territory without a past prior to their arrival. James Russell Lowell (1819–1891) described the operative view in *The Biglow Papers* (1848), writing, "O Strange New World, thet yit wast never young, / Whose youth from thee by gripin' need was wrung." By ignoring the Indians they had killed off or sold into slavery, New Englanders had claimed to have settled a land without a history. (Not for nothing did Herman Melville name the doomed ship in *Moby-Dick*, which was owned by sharp Yankee traders who did business out of a wigwam made of whalebone, the *Pequod*—a reference to the Massachusetts Indian tribe all but extermintated by the Puritans.)

The pledge that Natty makes to Chingachgook in *The Last of the Mohicans* had already been carried out, in a minor way, in *The Pioneers*, and the reader sees practically nothing of Chingachgook until the last of the Leatherstocking Tales, in which Natty's commitment is central. According to Cooper and his daughter Susan, Chingachgook, Uncas, and Hard-Heart (the Pawnee Natty will adopt in the next tale) were based on two chiefs—Ongpatonga and Petalesharo—who were honored guests in New York during the winter of 1821–1822. The former was a famous orator and the latter had become a hero for risking his life to save a girl from becoming a sacrifice in a ritual of her

Half title from the 1872 edition of *The Last of the Mohicans*. Illustration by Felix Octavius Carr Darley.
© BETTMANN/CORBIS

captors, as James Franklin Beard has noted in his introduction to *The Last of the Mohicans.*

THE PRAIRIE

For his next tale, *The Prairie,* Cooper departed from prehistory and transferred Natty Bumppo to the history being made more currently by way of the expedition of Meriwether Lewis and William Clark. He also used Major Stephen Long's report of his journey to the Rocky Mountains in 1819–1820. Cooper added to these explorations a heroine snatched from the Louisiana Territory, purchased from France by Thomas Jefferson.

Cooper had begun writing *The Prairie* immediately after finishing *Mohicans,* but the new novel was only half-written when he moved his family to France in June 1826. Preparing for a lengthy stay in the Old World, Cooper realized that in Natty he had created a character that was one answer to a major question of the time: What is an American? Without family, money, or possessions that he has not obtained by his own efforts, the illiterate Natty has only one advantage. He has been exposed to the religious views of the Moravians, who were important missionaries to the Indians. To the Catholic Moravians Natty credits his

Christian morality and his (lowercase "c") catholic tolerance for differences in people. He was a very possible American for the new republic to produce; even his famous shooting ability was only slightly exaggerated, if at all. Yet such was the soundness of his morality, particularly when compared to the sordid jealousies and petty actions of his contemporaries in *The Pioneers,* that even modern readers might agree with the Boston reader who said he longed to go with him when Natty whistles to his hounds, shoulders his gun, and departs into the forest at the end of the book.

Cooper ages the old hunter still more for *The Prairie,* and the famous first scene makes him appear larger than life when seen by other migrants on the frontier in the light of the setting sun. The travelers are the clan of Ishmael Bush, who, like Natty, is illiterate, and who has also fallen afoul of the laws of the settled parts of the country. To the casual observer, the two men seem much alike, but the book will dramatize the differences as well as explain, if not condone, the actions of various Indians, women, and other white men. The aged Natty, lonely and garrulous, is reduced to making his living by trapping rather than hunting, but he is still able to return the "grasp of any extended hand" (p. 15). He is the only character who can literally speak everyone else's language and is consequently pivotal in the action. The setting is important because the prairie, having no boundaries, is a neutral ground where one has to create one's own society. In addition to representing the political and ideological openness of America, the prairie may also be a symbol of the ruined landscape of the American future.

The novel offers—besides warring Indians and a pedantic "scientist" who represents Cooper's attempt at a comic character—a spectrum of females. An orphan, Ellen Wade, is a well-bred girl who must depend on her aunt Esther, who is Ishmael's mannish wife. Esther's daughters are as crude as their father and brothers. A captive of the clan is a Catholic girl of Spanish blood kidnapped on her wedding day by Esther Bush's brother and being held for ransom. Even more helpless and pitiful than Spanish Inez is Tachechana, the wife of the Sioux chief Mahtoree.

Cooper's speculation about future assimilation of dissimilar peoples comes with his prediction of a happy marriage for Inez and Captain Duncan Uncas Middleton, the grandson of Duncan Heyward and Alice Munro of *The Last of the Mohicans.*

> In such a novel intermixture . . . of men born and
> nurtured in freedom, and the compliant minions
> of absolute power, the catholic and the protestant,
> the active and the indolent, some little time was
> necessary to blend the discrepant elements of society. In attaining so desirable an end, woman was

The following scene from The Prairie *(1827), which elicits "superstitious awe" (p. 15) in the boorish family of Ishmael Bush, fittingly introduces the aged Natty Bumppo.*

The sun had fallen below the crest of the nearest wave of the prairie, leaving the usual rich and glowing train on its track. In the centre of this flood of fiery light a human form appeared, drawn against the gilded background, as distinctly and seemingly as palpable, as though it would come within the grasp of any extended hand. The figure was colossal; the attitude musing and melancholy, and the situation directly in the route of the travellers. But imbedded, as it was, in its setting of garish light, it was impossible to distinguish its just proportions or true character.

Cooper, The Prairie, pp. 14–15.

made to perform her accustomed and grateful office. The barriers of Prejudice and religion were broken through by the irresistible power of the Master Passion, and family unions, ere long, began to cement the political tie which had made a forced conjunction, between people so opposite in their habits, their educations, and their opinions. (P. 156)

This marriage, connecting Natty to the two previous Leatherstocking Tales, prepares for the final scene in which Natty dies in a Pawnee village. He sends his rifle, pouch, and horn back to the Effinghams in Templeton and gives his traps and his blessing to his adopted Pawnee son, Hard-Heart. He asks Middleton to bury him with the skin of his dead dog Hector at his side. Middleton also promises him to erect above this Indian-style burial a white man's gravestone. Through the book Natty has predicted that, in spite of the various names he has been called through life, "I shall be able to answer to any of mine in a loud and manly voice" (p. 385). At sunset Natty dies after saying one word, a loud and clear "Here!" (This had also been his answer to the judge in The Pioneers.) By contrast with this memorable tableau, at the end of the book the teams and herds of the squatter Ishmael are "blended among a thousand others. Though some of the numerous descendants of this peculiar pair were reclaimed from their lawless and semi-barbarous lives," Ishmael and his virago of a wife "were never heard of more" (p. 364).

NATTY BUMPPO REDIVIVUS: THE PATHFINDER AND THE DEERSLAYER

Having buried Natty at the end of The Prairie in 1827, Cooper acknowledged in his 1851 preface to The Pathfinder that bringing him back to life after he had been "consigned to his grave" was a "hazardous experiment." The resurrected Natty is about the same age he was in Last of the Mohicans and is once again involved in the French and Indian War of 1754–1760 but in a different part of the frontier as the British and French fight for possession of North America. A year after publishing The Pathfinder, Cooper produced The Deerslayer, which is the first nickname Natty acquires and shows Natty and Chingachgook at the beginning of their careers. The direction of the Leatherstocking Tales thus goes from old age in The Pioneers to youth in the The Deerslayer except for The Prairie. D. H. Lawrence declared that this was the "true myth" of America: the name Chingachgook (which means "great serpent" and is pronounced king-ach-gook) may have been what led Lawrence to say that America "starts old, wrinkled and writhing in an old skin. And there is a gradual sloughing of the old skin, towards a new youth" (p. 54).

After writing The Prairie, Cooper had invented the sea novel with the publication of The Pilot (1823) and Red Rover (1824). He had also written novels set in Europe and travel books about Europe and had lent his pen to Lafayette in a French controversy over the comparative costs of monarchy and democracy. His long residence in Europe and his involvement in French affairs, coupled with his criticism of American society on his return home, led to attacks by the American media. Attempting to recapture his American readers, and being largely dependent on British and other foreign royalties, Cooper responded to his British publisher's request for a "naval story on your own inland Seas" (the Great Lakes). Cooper's answer described the work in progress as "a nautico-lake-savage romance" (Letters and Journals, p. 370) that he first called "Inland Sea." He later referred to "Pathfinder" as a working title. Once in possession of his, and the public's, favorite hero, Cooper worked steadily.

The French and Indian War put the colonials in a difficult position because they disliked the French but had mixed feelings about the English. The loyalties of the Indian tribes were similarly confused, and the book is a snarl of betrayals that contrast with the Pathfinder's fidelity. The book opens with four people, two of each sex, on a pile of trees overlooking a forest that the heroine compares to the ocean. Two of the four are Indians; the male Indian proves to be a traitor while the female Indian's loyalties are tragically divided between obedience to her husband and her liking for the white heroine, Mabel. Mabel is a docile daughter who consents to marry Natty, who is her father's friend, even though she loves another character, Jasper. Natty recognizes the threat to his career and his character, saying, "I sometimes tell the sergeant, that he and his daughter will be the spoiling of one of the best and most experienced scouts on the lines" (p. 190). When he magnanimously relinquishes Mabel to Jasper, he says, "I have indeed, been on a false trail since we met!" (p. 272). He promises to see the couple whenever he can look upon Mabel "as a sister . . . or a child," and Cooper tells the reader that they never met again (p. 467).

In no other Leatherstocking tale is there so much talk about God's Providence and about the wilderness as a religious sanctuary. Natty's repeated references to Providence were usual for the time, and Cooper's readers might be aware that George Washington (1732–1799), fighting in the same French and Indian War, had said that only God's Providence had saved him when he had bullet holes in his clothing and two horses shot out from under him. Natty's morality, more than his prowess as a hunter or guide, comes through in this book as he says, "The 'arth is the temple of the Lord, and I wait on him hourly, daily, without ceasing, I humbly hope" (p. 433–434). Cooper's own judgment had been put in the mouth of Eve Effingham in his *Home as Found* (1838); she describes him as a "renowned hunter; a man who had the simplicity of a woodsman, the heroism of a savage, the faith of a Christian, and the feelings of a poet" (p. 196).

While Natty has always been willing to aid others, not until *The Pathfinder* has he made a personal sacrifice that increases his moral stature. The basis for such a character is predicted in the opening of *The Deerslayer*, where he is introduced as one of "two men who had lost their way, and were searching in different directions for their path" (p. 17). The other man, Harry March, is younger and better-looking than Natty. Their different characters are immediately suggested when Harry shoots at a deer and the echo seems to "object." By contrast, when Natty kills his first man, an Indian who is firing at him from ambush, nature attests to the fairness of the act as the hills return a single echo for the two shots. This Indian, dying, gives him the name Hawkeye. Harry has come to the lake to see a woman he is courting while Natty is there to meet Chingachgook and help him retrieve his betrothed, Hist-oh!-Hist, who has been kidnapped by another Indian.

Scalping was introduced by Europeans and the British and French are paying well for scalps. For the first time in the Leatherstocking Tales scalping is important as a test of character. Natty does not oppose scalping by Indians, but he never takes a scalp. By contrast, Harry and the old pirate Thomas Hutter, who is hiding out on the lake, go after scalps for the cash. (Harry also considers Indians animals, as some of Cooper's critics did.)

Again, the moral hierarchy the book offers is mixed. One girl, Hetty, is dangerously pious and literally too good for this world. Natty does not respond to the blandishments of the beautiful but tarnished Judith in spite of her imaginative effort to save him from torture by the Indians. Rivenoak, the chief of the enemy Hurons, comes through as a likable character as he tries to provide for his tribe (including the widow of the man Natty has killed) and is unable to deny them the vengeance they demand in return for their losses. At the end of the action, Natty leaves with Chingachgook and Hist, only to return with Chingachgook and Uncas fifteen years later. Finding a ribbon in the ruins, which recalls Judith's "beauty" and "failings" (p. 547), Natty knots it on the stock of Killdeer, the rifle she had given him.

Some have seen in the lifelong friendship of Natty and Chingachgook the beginning of a pattern of interracial masculine loyalty that would be repeated in Melville's Ishmael and Queequeg, Twain's Huck and Jim, and in television's Lone Ranger and Tonto. Although Twain famously burlesques Cooper's style and plotting in "Fenimore Cooper's Literary Offenses," his borrowings from Cooper were plentiful, as Sacvan Bercovitch and others have noticed, and the usages he said he found in *The Deerslayer* are not there. Added to Twain's funny spoof is the judgment of Max Rudin, publisher of the Library of America, who said "Cooper's greatness never rested on a literary style that could become outmoded; it lay in the founding of a literature that will forever oscillate between the desolation of promise betrayed and the immense longing for another fresh start."

See also Borders; Exploration and Discovery; Indians; Manhood; Nature; Nautical Literature; Romanticism

BIBLIOGRAPHY

Primary Works

Balzac, Honoré de. *Revue Parisienne*. 1840. In *Leatherstocking and the Critics*, translated by Warren S. Walker. Chicago: Scott, Foresman, 1965.

Cooper, James Fenimore, *The Deerslayer*. 1841. Albany: State University of New York Press, 1987.

Cooper, James Fenimore. *Home as Found*. 1838. New York: Putnam, Pathfinder Edition, n.d.

Cooper, James Fenimore. *The Last of the Mohicans.* 1826. Albany: State University of New York Press, 1983.

Cooper, James Fenimore. *Letters and Journals.* Vol. 3. Cambridge, Mass.: Belknap Press of Harvard Univeristy Press, 1964.

Cooper, James Fenimore. *Notions of the Americans.* 1828. Albany: State University of New York Press, 1991.

Cooper, James Fenimore. *The Pathfinder.* 1840. Albany: State University of New York Press, 1981.

Cooper, James Fenimore. *The Pioneers.* 1823. Albany: State University of New York Press, 1980.

Cooper, James Fenimore. *The Prairie.* 1827. Albany: State University of New York Press, 1985.

Cooper, James Fenimore. *The Spy.* 1821. Brooklyn, N.Y.: AMS Press, 2002.

Secondary Works

Berkovitch, Sacvan. "Huckleberry Bumppo: A Comparison of *Tom Sawyer* and *The Pioneers.*" *Mark Twain Journal* 14, no. 2 (1968): 1–4.

Dyer, Alan F. *James Fenimore Cooper: An Annotated Bibliography of Criticism.* New York: Greenwood Press, 1991.

Lawrence, D. H. *Studies in Classic American Literature.* 1923. New York: Viking Press, 1964.

Ringe, Donald A. *The Pictorial Mode: Space and Time in the Art of Bryant, Irving, and Cooper.* Lexington: University Press of Kentucky, 1971.

Rudin, Max. "Editorial Extra from The Library of America." Remarks delivered (on the publication of the Leatherstocking novels and two Cooper sea tales) at the Museum of the American Indian in New York City, April 1999.

Sand, George. *Autour de la Table.* 1865. As quoted in translation by D. B. Wood in *Fenimore Cooper: The Critical Heritage,* edited by George Dekker and John P. McWilliams. London and Boston: Routledge and Kegan Paul, 1973.

Twain, Mark. "Fenimore Cooper's Literary Offences." *North American Review* (July 1895): 1–12.

Walker, Jeffrey. "Deconstructing an American Myth." In *Hollywood's Indian: The Portrayal of the Native American in Film,* edited by Peter C. Rollins and John E. O'Connor. Lexington: University Press of Kentucky, 1998.

Kay Seymour House

LEAVES OF GRASS

"Walt Whitman, an American, one of the roughs, a kosmos" is how the poet identifies himself in the first edition of *Leaves of Grass* (1855). In one of the boldest acts of autopoeisis in American literature, Whitman (1819–1892) foregoes the name he used as a New York journalist in the 1840s, "Walter Whitman," which appears only on the copyright notice of his book, and uses a nickname rather than the formal trinominal typical of an age dominated by Ralph Waldo Emerson (1803–1882) in the high culture and the likes of William Cullen Bryant (1794–1878) and Henry Wadsworth Longfellow (1807–1882) among the most popular poets. The poet's name does not appear at all on the title page—only his picture, a daguerreotype of a handsome man with a short beard, in shirtsleeves, open collar, and wide-brimmed hat, workingman's garb. The virtually self-made, radically democratic, and aggressively informal poet erupts on the scene in the first edition of *Leaves of Grass,* a thin quarto with green binding decorated with gold vegetation, vines and leaves twining among the letters of the title to signify the organic identities everywhere proclaimed in the method and textual practices of the book.

The collection's long preface rambles in a loosely Emersonian manner on the topic of what poetry should become in a great democracy in the open air of an unspoiled continent full of promise. What America needs, says the preface, is "poets of the kosmos" who represent the "gangs of kosmos," the common people of the United States. The poet should show the people the path between reality and their souls, he says, and should be "absorbed" lovingly by the country. The twelve untitled poems that follow set out to make good on its promises in a stunning display of poetic experimentation. Whitman took the Romantic premises of democratic poetry and the organic theory of art that he inherited from William Wordsworth (1770–1850) and Emerson to extremes never imagined by his predecessors. He brought new discourses into the province of poetry, ranging from scientific language to street talk, used extravagant figures of speech, treated topics usually considered outside the scope of poetry, including "low" topics dealing with sexuality and procreation, and experimented more widely and diversely with free verse than any English-language poet before him; free verse was an analogue to the freedom of people he espoused and the freedom of speech that he pursued in becoming "the poet of the body and the poet of the soul."

Over the next four decades, as if to enact the organic theory, *Leaves of Grass* grew. Enlarged and revised editions appeared in 1856, 1860, 1867, 1871, and 1881 along with separate issues containing annexes and inserts in 1876 and in the so-called deathbed edition of 1891–1892, on which most

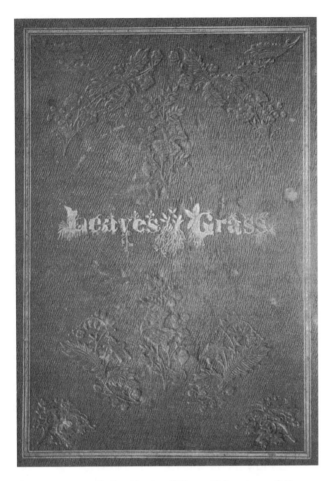

Front cover of the first edition of *Leaves of Grass*, 1855. THE PIERPONT MORGAN LIBRARY/ART RESOURCE, NY

present-day editions of the book depend (such as the comprehensive reader's edition). With the help of the extensive and authoritative online Walt Whitman Archive, readers can now follow the progress of the editions' exfoliations over the course of Whitman's lifetime and can see what scholars with privileged access to the best libraries and private collections have witnessed over the years: *Leaves of Grass* stands as an extraordinary poetic record of life in the mid-nineteenth century. With the Civil War at its center and the theme of "merging"—of poetic union and democracy—at its foundation, Whitman's book embodies the struggles of a nation confronted with the processes of modernization, the experiences of total war, westward expansion, urbanization, industrialization, incorporation, technology on the grand scale, and finally globalization. From farm to city, from nature to culture, from war to peace, from childhood to maturity, from person to nation and nation to kosmos, *Leaves of Grass* follows the movements of the American people.

1855: LANGUAGE EXPERIMENT

The 1855 *Leaves* provides what scholars agree is the most radically innovative, longest, and most widely celebrated of Whitman's poems. Best known under its final title as "Song of Myself," it appears first and takes up almost half the space allotted to the twelve poems in the first edition. Like the rest, it is untitled in 1855 and goes through a number of title changes and revisions in subsequent editions. It ranges far and wide in theme, touching on all the major topics of the book as a whole, offering an unsparing treatment of Whitman's concept of selfhood in relation to his representation of mid-century America as an ascendant force for democracy. The persona of "myself" speaks in the name of Walt Whitman but also claims to embody the voices of others, including the underrepresented voices of the lower classes, the workers, the poor, women, slaves, prostitutes, immigrants, the mentally ill and deficient. The poem tells stories both personal and historical, fictional (such as the anecdote of the lady, the "twenty-ninth bather," behind the curtains of the fancy house, watching longingly the young men swimming in the surf) and nonfictional (such as the tale of the young men massacred in the Mexican-American War or the great sea fights from the wars with the British); it urges the reader to join the poet in an intensive program of self-realization and self-reliance on the Emersonian model; it models the marriage of body and soul; and it celebrates life in all of its variety, refusing to ignore the material realities of sex and death and poverty and even evil but keeping health and heartiness always in the forefront. It strives to give a sense of the present-day, the modern, the historical moment as the culmination of centuries and ages of preparation and thus represents one of the fullest poetic celebrations of progress and the emerging concept of evolution in English-language poetry.

With the exception of two poems previously published in periodicals—"Europe, the 72nd and 73rd Years of These States," a poem affirming America's solidarity with the European spirit of 1848, and "A Boston Ballad," an antislavery lyric, both of which differ stylistically from "Song of Myself"—the other poems appear to be spin-offs both in style and theme. They all use the breathlessly long lines, unrhymed and metrically irregular, depending for their poetic effect and cohesion upon a wide range of devices for repetition—such as alliteration, assonance, and anaphora—often recalling the oratorical techniques commonly used in the day and unfolding the characteristic enumerative style, Whitman's famous "catalogs" of anecdotes and images. The poem that would ultimately become "I Sing the Body Electric" develops the themes of sexual energy and the sacredness of bodily existence, protesting the selling of human beings in the twin evils of slavery and prostitution and drawing upon natural history and eclectic medical science for language and for authority. The poem finally known as "The Sleepers" focuses on the health of the mind, with the shamanistic figure of the poet leading the reader on a fantastic journey into the thoughts and dreams of fellow citizens sleeping in their variously troubled and contented psychological conditions.

Other poems look forward to future developments in *Leaves* even as they pick up key themes in the 1855 book. The theme of childhood experience and its formative influence upon adult life takes center stage in the mildly autobiographical lyric of reflection "There Was a Child Went Forth," which adds a key dimension to the treatment of selfhood and looks forward to "Out of the Cradle Endlessly Rocking." "A Song for Occupations" develops the celebration of the working class and anticipates "Crossing Brooklyn Ferry" in its direct approach to readers in the present and the future. "To Think of Time" sets the stage for later philosophical musings such as "Chanting the Square Deific."

Leaves of Grass was all but ignored by the publishing establishment despite Whitman's connections on the journalistic and literary scene in New York. The reviews that did take notice—other than those written anonymously by Whitman himself in the kind of self-promotion in which he would indulge throughout his career—tended to dismiss the volume on either moral or artistic grounds. Reviewers saw the poems as either obscene or decidedly unpoetic, not really qualifying as poetry at all.

It made the biggest splash in Boston. Whitman sent a copy to Emerson, who not only shared the book with Henry David Thoreau (1817–1862) and Amos Bronson Alcott (1799–1888), both of whom visited New York to meet the author of such a work, but also penned what has become perhaps the most famous letter among literary figures in America. No doubt recognizing his own influence, Emerson praised the originality and power of the book and wondered about its "long foreground." Whitman took heart from this letter, which propelled him forward into a flurry of creativity to match, if not surpass, the inspired state that produced the first edition.

1856: THE FIRST EXPANSION

The greatly expanded second edition appeared a year later, setting the standard for the future growth of the book. The 1856 *Leaves* is often remembered for the poet's attempt to build upon his connections in the literary world, some would say tastelessly if not

shamelessly. On the spine of the green book with its squat little format (a new pocket-sized volume in the minds of Whitman and his publishers), Whitman had a sentence stamped in gold letters from Emerson's private letter of 1855, along with a blurb-like attribution—"I greet you at the beginning of a great career—R. W. Emerson"; and the letter itself was included in the book's front matter, used without permission and followed by a long response from Whitman, virtually a new preface, addressed to his "dear friend and Master." Although Emerson remained cordial to Whitman thereafter, his ardor for *Leaves of Grass* cooled significantly after he was made unwittingly to endorse the new edition, the expansion of which significantly increased the number of lines dealing directly with matters of sex and the body, themes with which Emerson was never comfortable and which he urged Whitman to subdue in later editions.

Whitman's boldness as the self-proclaimed poet of the body may have gathered steam in 1856 from another connection, the sponsorship of a new publisher—the phrenological firm of Fowler and Wells, a group also known for a forthright, if otherwise conservative, treatment of sexual issues in its publications on health and society. Whitman, who was writing features for the firm's weekly publication, *Life Illustrated,* in the mid-1850s, could not sustain the relationship with his publishers beyond the one edition, however; ironically, it may have been the issue of his sexual candor, the "libidinousness" that one of the few reviewers denounced as "foul" and "impious," that led to the break, although poor sales could just as easily have been to blame. The awkward attempt of the self-conscious outsider to push his way into the literary mainstream appears even in the new titles given the poems in the second edition. As if in response to those critics who wondered whether these works could rightly be called poetry at all, Whitman included the word "Poem" in every title. Thus what finally become "Song of Myself" appeared as "Poem of Walt Whitman, an American" in 1856; "I Sing the Body Electric" went by "Poem of the Body"; and perhaps worst of all, the new poem ultimately named "A Song of the Rolling Earth" was called "Poem of the Sayers of the Words of the Earth."

In the view of many critics, the 1856 *Leaves* absorbed rather too heavy a dose of the social-scientific spirit characteristic of Whitman's phrenologist sponsors and other reformers in the "feminine fifties." The influence is especially clear in his approach to such issues as the social position of women. The appeal to a new kind of woman, vigorous and equal in power to the ideal workingmen of Whitman's vision, takes a particularly disconcerting turn in "A Woman Waits for

Me," which appeared as "Poem of Procreation" in 1856 and which has proved one of Whitman's most controversial works among not only readers of his own time (including Emerson) but also feminist critics, largely because the sexual forthrightness suggests an element of brutality, a reduction of women to the function of maternity, and a step toward accepting the kind of eugenicist program later associated with racial exclusionists and Social Darwinism. The anatomical catalog of body parts and functions added in 1856 to "I Sing the Body Electric" has been criticized along similar lines as an aesthetically ill-advised appeal to the scientific temper of the times. Even the more widely admired "Unfolded out of the Folds," which uses the female genitalia as a figure for poetic creativity, seems to embrace the eugenic theme.

The ugliness of the volume, Whitman's personal shortcomings in handling promotional considerations, and even his occasional shift into a programmatic mode that slights aesthetic concerns should not, however, detract from the considerable accomplishments of the 1856 *Leaves*. The new poems were pouring forth at a rate and with a quality that remains a wonder in the history of poetic productivity. Among the more successful was the provocative "Spontaneous Me," which walks the fine line between the merely shocking and the purposeful unsettling of an audience too comfortable in their habits of reading. By modeling poetic inspiration and mystical enlightenment with masturbatory imagery and by asserting the creativity of all people by suggesting that the "real poems" of life are the parts and practices of physical regeneration, "Spontaneous Me" urges a reconception of the hierarchical relationships assumed in his culture. The body's relation to the larger processes of degeneration and renewal forms the topic of another new poem, "This Compost," perhaps the most ecologically powerful poem in nineteenth-century American literature, which dramatizes at once the human tendency to recoil from the threat of the earth, embodied in disgust over death and sickness, and the sublime realization of the earth's power to absorb and refine corrupt materials and regenerate the air, water, and soil that nourish and renew life. The continuity of life across the distances of space and time forms the key theme of perhaps the greatest 1856 poem, "Crossing Brooklyn Ferry," which sees in the amassing of people and activities in the urban environments the culmination of the past and the promise of the future, both material and spiritual.

For all its accomplishments, the book did not sell and failed to catapult the author into the arms of an adoring public. In the late 1850s, Whitman found himself admired by a limited circle of New York Bohemians and Boston transcendentalists but ignored by the masses he desperately wanted to reach. He lost his publisher and found his personal life in disarray. The nation whose unity and power he had celebrated was on the brink of war. And yet, from these troubles, he managed to create a new kind of poetic vision, something darker and more elegiac than the epic and celebratory poetry of the 1855 and 1856 poems. *Leaves of Grass* continued to grow and now diversified, sending its roots deeper into the resources of the human spirit, thereby extending its range and appeal.

1860: THE NEW BIBLE

By the time he contracted with a venturesome and enthusiastic new publishing firm, Thayer and Eldridge of Boston, Whitman had dozens of new poems ready to go. The 1860 *Leaves of Grass* would be the first edition to have so many poems that Whitman felt the need to arrange some of them into what he called "clusters," a practice he would follow in all subsequent editions. The poems on the love of man for woman, for example, would be all the more noticeable in this edition for having their own cluster, *Enfans d'Adam,* later *Children of Adam,* which complemented a cluster of new poems called *Calamus.*

Calamus, which celebrated the love of man for man as the heart of democracy and the "base of all metaphysics," appears to have begun as something like a free-verse sonnet sequence in a manuscript originally titled "Live Oak, with Moss" after the key poem "I Saw in Louisiana a Live-Oak Growing." The sequence contains a rough narrative of a relationship with another man, following it through joyful beginnings to a tragic break. The narrative is submerged in *Calamus* as it was finally published in 1860, the individual poems redistributed and joined with other short poems celebrating a more general love of humankind. But the homoeroticism, the feelings of loneliness and alienation from the mass of men and women, and the near-sexual intensity of the original group would remain. While critics have acknowledged the debt of the sentiment in *Calamus* to the Romantic friendship tradition, which always seems to edge over into homosexuality to modern readers more publicly attuned to the possibility of sex among men than were readers of Whitman's day, most have concluded that *Calamus* arises from and celebrates homosexual experience and thus stands at the beginning of a gay tradition in American letters. The cluster took on a new notoriety at the end of the century, especially among English readers like John Addington Symonds (1840–1893) who, in the context of the "sexual science" of writers like Havelock Ellis (1859–1939) and the historical shifts in consciousness occasioned by events like the trial of Oscar Wilde, began to see homoeroticism at the center of Whitman's book, with *Calamus* as the focal point. When Symonds questioned Whitman directly about the possibility of homosexuality in *Calamus,* the poet vigorously denied any such intention. Despite the denial and the cautious indirection of the poems themselves, the "paths untrodden" invoked in the cluster hint strongly at a relationship among men that goes beyond the constraints of a dominantly heterosexual culture.

The confinement of the poems on love into the two clusters tends to add emphasis to the poetry of the body in the 1860 *Leaves.* And yet, a note from the late 1850s as well as the avowed intention of the new overture poem "Starting from Paumanok" (called "Proto-Leaf" in 1860) suggests that Whitman hoped to bolster the poetry of the soul in this edition. The note referred to the forthcoming volume as the New Bible. The poems best fulfilling this ambition were later located in a cluster called *Sea Drift,* two of which—"As I Ebb'd with the Ocean of Life" and "Out of the Cradle Endlessly Rocking"—deserve special mention as products of Whitman's return to the seashore of his childhood home on Long Island in search of his inspiration, a linking of landscape and spirituality in a revival of the kind of natural mysticism first developed in the 1855 "Song of Myself." "As I Ebb'd with the Ocean of Life" forms a record of his depression in the late 1850s, a kind of rural, ebb-tide counterweight to the celebratory affirmation of the urban flood tide in "Crossing Brooklyn Ferry." "Out of the Cradle" dramatizes the middle-aged man's return to the source of his inspiration by narrating the story of the boy-poet's vicarious encounter with loss and death through his observation of a mockingbird singing for its lost mate. In both of these poems, as well as in *Calamus,* the poet suggests that he was able to come to terms with his poetic vocation only after nearly abandoning it. He recoils from his earlier poems, leaves the city that has provided his central themes and subject matter, throws himself on the mercy of nature (the ocean figured as an old crone whispering "death," for example, in "Out of the Cradle"), and working through his suffering and alienation, recovers the spiritual connection with the kosmos that seemed to have come so easily in poems like "Song of Myself" and "Crossing Brooklyn Ferry."

The tragic depth and added psycho-spiritual dimension of these new poems has made the 1860 edition the favorite of many readers. Still at the height of his poetic experimentation with language and verse form, Whitman attained in this volume a richness and range that he would sometimes equal but never surpass.

1867: THE WAR COMES TO *LEAVES OF GRASS*

The young publishers of the 1860 *Leaves* were forced to close operations with the onset of the Civil War, so once again, the book was a financial failure, although the number of copies in circulation greatly increased. Whitman was gradually becoming known as a public figure and the object of controversy, the author of a notorious book. During the Civil War years, his fame grew and the public perception of his work shifted to some degree. He relocated to Washington, D.C., and became acquainted with other writers such as William Douglas O'Connor (1832–1889), who helped Whitman get a government job and defended him with a famous pamphlet, *The Good Gray Poet,* when he lost the job, ostensibly because he had written an immoral book. Again with the help of O'Connor, Whitman found an appreciative audience in England, led by William Michael Rossetti (1829–1919) who brought out a selection of Whitman's poems in 1867 and introduced a generation of enthusiastic English readers to *Leaves of Grass.*

Whitman first came to Washington, D.C., on a family errand in search of his wounded younger brother, who was serving in the Union cause at Fredericksburg. After visiting with his brother in camp, Whitman was compelled to stay close to the war and redefine his poetic mission accordingly. While working part-time as a clerk in the government offices, he volunteered as a companion to sick and injured soldiers in the many war hospitals set up in the capital— an experience that changed his life forever and moved him to write a new collection of poems, *Drum-Taps,* published with a late sequel added in 1865–1866. The sequel contained his great elegy to Abraham Lincoln, "When Lilacs Last in the Dooryard Bloom'd."

When he first conceived of *Drum-Taps,* Whitman thought it superior to *Leaves of Grass* as a book because of its epic theme of war and because of its artistic unity. (Yet in addition to the war poems it contained other performances of the period, many only marginally connected with the war, such as "Give Me the Splendid Silent Sun" on the tension between city and country, "When I Heard the Learn'd Astronomer" on the tension between the ways hard science and Romantic mysticism approach nature, and "Pioneers! O Pioneers!" on the topic that would consume him in the 1870s, westward expansion.) Finally, however, *Leaves of Grass* absorbed the wartime poems into its growth, with new clusters entitled *Drum-Taps* and *Memories of President Lincoln,* and new places for the poems not directly related to war. In the 1867 *Leaves,* often called the workshop edition, *Drum-Taps* and the *Sequel* were roughly stitched into the covers at the end. These rough sequels account for the largest expansion of the volume. The poetic energy that did not go into the war poems was expended primarily on revision of the earlier poems, painstakingly worked out in Whitman's famous Blue Book copy of the 1860 *Leaves*. By the time the 1871–1872 *Leaves of Grass* was published, the war clusters had begun to settle into the structure of the book proper, although they were not arranged into their final clusters until the 1881–1882 edition.

The poems composed for *Drum-Taps* and the *Sequel* build upon preexisting trends in *Leaves of Grass* and also extend the book's range. "When Lilacs Last in the Dooryard Bloom'd" as well as shorter lyrics about Lincoln and about death on the battlefield, such as the remarkable "Vigil Strange I Kept on the Field One Night," establish Whitman as one of the leading authors of the English elegy, taking the dark themes of personal experience from the 1860 poems and applying them to the mournful mood of the postwar nation. Nature lyrics such as "When I Heard the Learn'd Astronomer" extend the ecopoetical canon of Whitman's writing, adding new perspectives to older poems like "Song of Myself" and "This Compost" and anticipating such shorter lyrics as "A Noiseless Patient Spider" as well as the delightful prose vignettes of retreat to nature in *Specimen Days*. In such poems as "Cavalry Crossing a Ford" and "Bivouac on a Mountain Side," Whitman experiments with a new genre, a kind of proto-modern imagistic lyric that anticipates the poetics of Ezra Pound, William Carlos Williams, and other twentieth-century artists working under the influence of photographic technology.

In all, Whitman's wartime experience greatly enriched *Leaves of Grass* even as it may have destroyed the poet's health. The war restored his lagging sense of purpose as a poet but broke him physically and may have signaled the waning of his powers.

1871 AND AFTER: DECLINE AND FINALE

The dominant critical tradition in Whitman studies suggests that the poems composed and published after the Civil War suffer a significant loss of artistic power, reflecting the poet's aging and the increasingly uncertain condition of his health. The critics divide sharply over where to set the line of demarcation—after the 1860 edition, or after "When Lilacs Last in the Dooryard Bloom'd," or even later—but there is general agreement that the original energy of the 1850s is in decline by the 1870s and 1880s. During this time Whitman published his best-known prose works, *Democratic Vistas* and *Specimen Days*, and continued to add poems to *Leaves of Grass*, but the later poems

were not as daringly unconventional either in subject matter or in poetic form. In subject matter, he largely avoided the sexual topics that had stirred such controversy (with a few notable exceptions, such as "The Dalliance of the Eagles") and focused instead on democratic political theory, nature, war reminiscences, westward expansion, technological progress, and spiritual matters. In poetic form, his drift back toward conventional forms began as early as 1856, when he abandoned the odd, oratorically suggestive use of multiple periods in varying numbers that he employed as punctuation in 1855. By 1860 the poet who had vigorously rejected "poems distilled from other poems" had begun to include more frequent echoes and borrowings, drawing upon Emerson, Edgar Allan Poe, and even Alfred Tennyson in "Out of the Cradle," for example. Whitman's elegies grew more conventional in diction and topic by the time of "Lilacs" and other poems from the *Drum-Taps* era. One of the Lincoln poems, "O Captain! My Captain!" which became (somewhat to the poet's chagrin) perhaps his all-time most popular poem, featured regular stanzas and even rhymed. By the 1870s, Whitman was less inclined to employ the wild tropes and experimental language of the earlier poems and more inclined to use shorter, more regular lines and conventional poetic diction, even "thee" and "thou" (which could have come from his Quaker heritage but which were never used in the best-known earlier poems) as well as personifications of abstractions and figures from classical mythology.

The turn to convention suggests that the poet had wearied of working as a kind of one-man avant-garde. The war strengthened his desire to be regarded as the national poet, which in turn led him to make some concessions to conventional taste. His nationalism also prompted him to cultivate a kind of globalist, some would say imperialist, attitude about the place of the United States in world affairs. The 1871 "Passage to India" begins with a celebration of the technologies that opened the different cultures to both influences and intrusions from other peoples—the Suez Canal, the transoceanic cables, and the transcontinental railroad—and finishes with a spiritual flourish that urges the soul outward to new possibilities. The poetic linking of spiritual growth to cultural imperialism proves disturbing for many critics, as does the decidedly preconservationist sentiment of a poem like "Song of the Redwood-Tree," which made its way into the 1881–1882 edition of *Leaves* and in which the poet gives voice to the song of natural spirits departing from the old forests, willingly abandoning the field to the new race of human beings with their axes and city plans. Poems on Christopher Columbus and on

Custer's Last Stand ("From Far Dakota's Cañons") contribute to the view of Whitman as primarily the white man's poet of westward expansion, although a more sympathetic view would also notice the tragic note of such poems: the too-heavy insistence on the promise of the future as the compensatory celebration of an old poet who feels that time has passed him by, like the war hero George Armstrong Custer, the aged old mariner wrecked on the shore in "Prayer of Columbus," or the spirits of the redwood trees departing before the coming generation of pioneers.

Moreover, the late editions still offer much to admire. The organization of the book as a whole, with well-crafted clusters and strings of individual "Songs," 293 poems in all, took on its final shape in the 1881 *Leaves,* a significant advance over the organization of the 1867 and 1871 editions. In the deathbed edition of 1891–1892, Whitman added "annexes" rather than disturbing the order of the 1881 *Leaves.* The first annex, "Sands at Seventy," serves as kind of reprise for the treatment of nature throughout the book. In particular Whitman revives an interest in his native shoreline, offering several fine examples of the short nature lyric, including the much-admired series "Fancies at Navesink." The second annex, "Good-bye My Fancy," includes among other accomplishments the outstanding lyric "To the Sun-set Breeze." While echoing sources in the Romantic and transcendentalist traditions with a celebration of a cool wind that comes at the end of a hot summer day and stirs the spirit of the sick old man, inspiring a vision of remembered landscapes to the north, the poem remains characteristically Whitmanian with its attention to the condition of the body and the full experience of all the senses, with a special emphasis reserved for the tactile. To the end, Whitman would leave his mark as the poet of the body, never neglecting the soul but showing the way there by loving attention to the intensities of material life.

See also "Crossing Brooklyn Ferry"; Democracy; Individualism and Community; "Out of the Cradle Endlessly Rocking"; "The Poet"; Romanticism; Sexuality and the Body; "Song of Myself"; Urbanization; "When Lilacs Last in the Dooryard Bloom'd"

BIBLIOGRAPHY
Primary Works
Whitman, Walt. *Drum-Taps (1865) and Sequel to Drum-Taps (1865–6): A Facsimile Reproduction.* Edited by F. DeWolfe Miller. Gainesville, Fla.: Scholars' Facsimiles and Reprints, 1959.

Whitman, Walt. *Leaves of Grass: Comprehensive Reader's Edition.* Edited by Sculley Bradley and Harold W. Blodgett. New York: New York University Press, 1965.

Whitman, Walt. The Walt Whitman Archive. Edited by Kenneth M. Price and Ed Folsom. http://www.whitmanarchive.org.

Whitman, Walt. *Walt Whitman's Blue Book: The 1860–61 "Leaves of Grass" Containing His Manuscript Additions and Revisions.* 2 vols. Edited by Arthur Golden. New York: New York Public Library, 1968.

Secondary Works
Killingsworth, M. Jimmie. *The Growth of Leaves of Grass: The Organic Tradition in Whitman Studies.* Columbia, S.C.: Camden House, 1993.

LeMaster, J. R., and Donald D. Kummings, eds. *Walt Whitman: An Encyclopedia.* New York: Garland, 1998.

Loving, Jerome. *Walt Whitman: The Song of Himself.* Berkeley: University of California Press, 1999.

M. Jimmie Killingsworth

LECTURES

See Lyceums; Oratory

"THE LEGEND OF SLEEPY HOLLOW"

Washington Irving (1783–1859) had been living in England for five years when he finished *The Sketch Book of Geoffrey Crayon, Gent.* (1819–1820), a collection of tales, essays, and sketches that would come to be counted as the first internationally successful work by an American author. A New Yorker, the son of a hardware merchant, Irving had dabbled in writing before, most notably producing the satirical *A History of New York by Diedrich Knickerbocker* (1809). Americans of the early national period yearned for evidence of cultural independence, but questions abounded regarding the proper form and content for an American literature, and authors would continue to doubt the literary potential of a country that seemed so shallowly new. *The Sketch Book* reflects these cultural insecurities: most of the sketches deal with English scenes, and the book's narratorial persona, Geoffrey Crayon, suffers acute bouts of Anglophilia. But a handful of selections turn to American settings and subjects, among them "The Legend of Sleepy Hollow."

"The Legend of Sleepy Hollow" is presented by Crayon as having come from the papers of Diedrich

Knickerbocker, Irving's fictive historian, the "source" for many of his New York–area tales. Set in a precinct of Tarrytown (about twenty-five miles north of New York City), the tale centers on Ichabod Crane, a Connecticut Yankee who came to predominantly Dutch Sleepy Hollow not long after the Revolution. A devourer of supernatural lore, the lanky schoolteacher spends much of his time swapping spooky tales with the Dutch housewives, especially tales of the "headless horseman"—a Hessian trooper who lost his head in a battle nearby. Ichabod also falls for the neighborhood belle, Katrina Van Tassel. But the courtship raises the ire of a rival suitor, the broad-shouldered Dutch local wag, Brom Bones. This, along with Ichabod's addiction to ghost stories, proves his undoing in Sleepy Hollow. Riding home one night after a party, he is joined on the road by an shadowy rider, whom he perceives to be headless. The terrified Ichabod finally makes it to the bridge where the horseman is said to disappear, but instead the figure hurls his "head" at Ichabod, and it is Ichabod who vanishes, running off from the village for good. The reader is left with hints—in the shattered pumpkin, in Brom Bones's knowing laugh—that perhaps Ichabod's pursuer was less than spectral. But only perhaps.

LITERARY AND CULTURAL INFLUENCES

Clearly readable in the lines of "The Legend of Sleepy Hollow" are influences of late-eighteenth and early-nineteenth-century European cultural movements: a gothic literature featuring supernatural apparitions and a broader Romantic movement characterized by an emphasis on imagination over reason, an attraction to the marvelous, and a longing for the legendary past. Despite claims that U.S. culture should be founded in commonsense rationalism, liberated from Old Worldly superstition, these movements had infiltrated American tastes by the beginning of the nineteenth century. And though initially influenced by urbane British neoclassical writers, Irving to no small degree shared Geoffrey Crayon's Romantic antiquarianism and fascination with supernatural lore. These leanings were drawn out by Irving's immersion in the British literary scene in the 1810s and by the tutelage of

***Crane and Horseman,* c. 1835.** Painting attributed to William John Wilgus. "The Legend of Sleepy Hollow" provided vivid material for visual artists, and its frequent reinterpretation in paintings and popular prints both reflected and promoted the tale's extreme popularity. THE GRANGER COLLECTION, NEW YORK

Sir Walter Scott, who had incorporated folkloristic materials into his fictions of the Scottish border. "The Legend of Sleepy Hollow" also owes a particular debt to Romantic interest in German legends: the story's climactic scene (right down to the pumpkin) was borrowed from a story recorded in Johann Karl August Musäus's *Volksmärchen der Deutschen* (parts of which had been translated into English in 1791 as *Popular Tales of the Germans*).

But it would be a mistake to see this story solely as an application of European Romanticism or a grafting of German lore to an American setting. First of all, it is not what might be called a straight ghost story. Indeed, most readers probably find the tale more humorous than horrifying. Irving maintains a suspicion of the imagination and an ironic distance from the ghostly, which has led critics to label his approach to gothic materials as "sportive" or "inconclusive." Without fully disavowing the ghosts, "The Legend of Sleepy Hollow" suggests the possibility of rational explanation, inviting readers to join in a practical joke on Ichabod Crane in a way that indulged Romantic tastes while also catering to American self-proclaimed pragmatism. Second, while "The Legend of Sleepy Hollow" owes something to European models, it also draws from domestic sources. Irving had traveled a good deal in the Hudson Valley (including Tarrytown), and he clearly had at least some knowledge of the Dutch, Native American, African, and British vernacular cultures that contributed to the region's cultural inheritance. Although it is now difficult to trace direct localized sources for "The Legend of Sleepy Hollow," scholars have located analogs in regional folklore for material in Irving's tales as well as real-life models for Ichabod Crane and Brom Bones.

HISTORICAL BACKGROUNDS AND SOCIAL COMMENTS

"The Legend of Sleepy Hollow" also is redeemed from derivativeness by its ties to specific historical backgrounds and to contemporary social and political issues. The story is founded in regional history, most prominently building on the fact that New York was initially a Dutch colony and retained Dutch influences through the nineteenth century. Irving utilizes the "ancient" and "peculiar" Dutch (p. 272) to add apparent depth to American history and to stand as a sort of American folk. Irving also tethers the tale to local events of the Revolutionary War, setting it within what was the "neutral ground"—a segment of the Hudson Valley caught between the British and American armies for most of the war and plagued with violent infighting among residents. Within this infamous territory—which also featured in the second

success of American literature, James Fenimore Cooper's *The Spy* (1821)—Tarrytown was particularly notorious as the place where John André, the British officer subsequently executed as a spy for his dealings with the traitorous Benedict Arnold, was captured. The "unfortunate André" (p. 292) was a troublingly sympathetic figure who epitomized ambivalences lurking in Revolutionary memory.

Even as the story cultivates a sense that the United States had worthwhile, usable history and folk traditions, Irving still recognizes that tales of haunting can also reflect a disconnection from the past. This double-edged sense of haunting is epitomized by the headless horseman. The ghost is linked to historical fact (Hessian mercenaries fought for the British during the Revolutionary War), yet it also signals a sense of historical obscurity and uncertainty—a headless and thus unidentifiable figure killed in a "nameless" battle, surrounded by "floating facts" (p. 273), who, after all, seems little related to either the Dutch or the Yankee protagonist currently inhabiting the area. The haunting at the core of "The Legend of Sleepy Hollow" is directly connected to social and historical dislocations attendant upon a contemporary phenomenon that at first would seem antithetical to ghost stories: a "great torrent of migration and improvement" (p. 274) that had particular salience in the New York area. Ichabod Crane represents a tidal wave of New Englanders pouring into New York, causing the state population to quadruple between 1790 and 1820 and transforming the social, economic, and cultural dimensions of the region. And though Irving jokes about the foreshortening of historical memory he associates with this torrent, he also paints Ichabod as essentially a devourer—a potentially community-destroying force implicitly associated with capitalistic progress. Ichabod's attraction to Katrina Van Tassel is really based on his hungry-eyed appraisal of her father's farm; at one point he envisions selling it off for cash and then moving on to conquer new frontiers.

But here is the twist. Ichabod—the representative of the race of hardheaded, restless pioneers who have the capacity to overrun local custom and history—is essential in activating the ghost story. In part this is because Ichabod is not really all that hardheaded. He "potently believe[s]" in Cotton Mather's witchlore, and his "appetite for the marvellous" is only matched by his extraordinary "powers of digesting it" (pp. 276–277). Also, his susceptibility to perceiving the uncanny in his surroundings is increased by his fundamental unfamiliarity with the neighborhood and the neighbors. The Dutch are comfortable in this place in ways the itinerant Ichabod is not. Specifically, because they know that Brom Bones is given to midnight trickery, they might have reason to be suspicious of ghostly intervention, whereas Ichabod is disposed, both by what he knows (spooky stories from New England and New York) and by what as a stranger he does not know, to see ghosts in the Sleepy Hollow shadows.

One can easily see Ichabod's "odd mixture of small shrewdness and simple credulity" (p. 277) as a two-pronged attack on Yankee—and by extension, American—character, lamenting the disruptive tendencies of profit-driven capitalism while also belying conceits of superior rationality. One might also see in the representation of Ichabod a gentle mocking of individuals overly devoted to imagination—a self-satirization, perhaps, on Irving's part, as well as a register of his own doubts about the possibility of being a "man of letters" (p. 276) in an American context. Ichabod's imaginative endeavors tend to align him with the feminine in the story, the women "spinning" by the fire (p. 277), especially in contrast to the brawny Brom Bones. And the story explicitly exposes strains of anti-intellectualism in American culture: after Ichabod's disappearance his books are burned by the farmer he last boarded with, who also declines to send his children to school anymore because "he never knew any good come of . . . reading and writing" (p. 295).

Perhaps more seriously, Ichabod's gullibility also opens into a political comment. Irving leaned toward what might be called a Federalist ideal of a benignly hierarchal society, rooted in grounding traditions and respect for established authority. This ideal was confronted in Irving's time by the democratic ferment which would lead to the "Jacksonian revolution" and the expanded suffrage of the 1830s. In this light "The Legend of Sleepy Hollow" can be seen to reflect concerns that also color the work of Charles Brockden Brown and James Fenimore Cooper, about the potential within a transient democratic society for people to be swayed by charismatic voices, by stories that may or may not be true. Though outright references to politics are few in "The Legend of Sleepy Hollow," politically loaded questions of authority and authenticity surface throughout the tale, especially in the way the story is framed, coming through a series of intermediating narrators, each of questionable reliability. Knickerbocker, one learns in the postscript, heard the story at a city meeting from an unidentified teller who may merely be trying to entertain in order to earn his wine; this teller himself confesses, in the story's last line, that he does not "believe one half of it myself" (p. 297). It is even unclear who is the author of the story as the reader receives it: If the postscript explicitly was "Found in the Handwriting of Mr. Knickerbocker" (p. 296), then whose hand wrote the foregoing tale? Irving establishes a whole machinery of provenance and authentication—giving the tale the semblance of a historical document—only to undercut it at every turn. In the end, the reader, like Ichabod Crane, cannot be sure of anything. Thus on one level "The Legend of Sleepy Hollow" represents an attempt to invest the American countryside with cultural foundations of legends; on another level the story uses issues of authenticity common to ghost stories to raise doubts about American social and political stability.

LEGACY

Though Irving fell into critical disfavor in the early twentieth century, his tales have received appreciative reappraisals by later generations, who have recognized "The Legend of Sleepy Hollow" as a pioneering work in numerous ways. In addition to showing that American materials could be worked into successful literary form, even in a predominantly Romantic cultural moment, "The Legend of Sleepy Hollow," along with "Rip Van Winkle," has been credited with inventing the short-story form. Its humor has been described as anticipating the "tall tale" genre that surfaced most famously in the work of Mark Twain (Ichabod's hands "dangled a mile out of his sleeves," while his feet "might have served for shovels" [p. 274]). Its innovative plays on gothic materials have been seen as prefiguring works by Edgar Allan Poe, Nathaniel Hawthorne, and Henry James, and the questions of narratorial reliability it raises resonate with postmodern critical approaches.

But the story's place in literary history is only part of its cultural legacy. "The Legend of Sleepy Hollow" was also a pioneering work of American popular culture. Not only has it been widely read, but the sketch has also been so thoroughly adopted as bona fide American folklore that many know the story of Ichabod Crane and the headless horseman without having any idea that it comes from a story written by Washington Irving. There is something marvelously ironic—one might say sly—about this: commenting on the potential for restless Americans to be sold unreliable stories, Irving produced a story that would come to stand as authentic American lore, something he also wholeheartedly encouraged.

See also Folklore; Gothic Fiction; Humor; Literary
    Nationalism; "Rip Van Winkle"; Romanticism;
    Satire, Burlesque, and Parody; Short Story;
    Tall Tales

BIBLIOGRAPHY

Primary Work

Irving, Washington. *The Sketch Book of Geoffrey Crayon, Gent.* 1819–1820. Edited by Haskell Springer. Boston: Twayne, 1978.

Secondary Works

Fox, Dixon Ryan. *Yankees and Yorkers.* New York: New York University Press, 1940.

Myers, Andrew B., ed. *A Century of Commentary on the Works of Washington Irving, 1860–1974.* Tarrytown, N.Y.: Sleepy Hollow Restorations, 1976.

Pochmann, Henry A. "Irving's German Sources in *The Sketch Book.*" *Studies in Philology* 27 (1930): 477–507.

Richardson, Judith. *Possessions: The History and Uses of Haunting in the Hudson Valley.* Cambridge, Mass.: Harvard University Press, 2003.

Ringe, Donald A. *American Gothic: Imagination and Reason in Nineteenth-Century Fiction.* Lexington: University Press of Kentucky, 1982.

Rubin-Dorsky, Jeffrey. *Adrift in the Old World: The Psychological Pilgrimage of Washington Irving.* Chicago: University of Chicago Press, 1988.

Thompson, G. R. "Washington Irving and the American Ghost Story." In *The Haunted Dusk: American Supernatural Fiction 1820–1920,* edited by John W. Crowley, Charles L. Crow, and Howard Kerr, pp. 11–36. Athens: University of Georgia Press, 1983.

Williams, Stanley T. *The Life of Washington Irving.* 2 vols. New York: Oxford University Press, 1935.

Judith Richardson

LEISURE

Between 1820 and 1870 changes in the nature and structure of American labor simultaneously transformed the practice and the concept of leisure in the United States. At the beginning of the antebellum period, when the majority of Americans still lived on farms or in small towns, leisure activities were predominantly rural, communal, and improvisatory, and the line separating leisure from work was often blurred. Over the next half-century, however, as more Americans moved to cities and as wage-centered industrial employment with its omnipresent time clock displaced both rural and artisanal work rhythms, labor and leisure became increasingly separate realms. Although the pace of change differed by region, the nature of leisure shifted as well, becoming, like labor, more routinized, specialized, and commodified. There were benefits to these changes: for the first time, new forms of commercial leisure and spectator entertainments were within the reach of working-class Americans. But there were drawbacks as well. Fault lines in the wider culture separating genders, classes, and ethnic groups often formed in the world of leisure, resulting in exclusions and hierarchies. In the South, at least until the 1860s, the leisure activities of an entire class depended on the forced labor of black slaves.

Under the pressure of these changes, disagreements over the "proper" use of leisure, which had been common since the colonial period, became more vocal and sometimes violent. Injunctions against idleness and profligacy appeared with renewed vigor, particularly early in the period, and many middle- and upper-class Americans sought to stamp out or reform what they considered disreputable or even dangerous amusements. At the same time, the monotony and tediousness of industrial labor, fast becoming an inescapable reality for many in the United States, helped steer a profoundly work-oriented culture toward a halting but ultimately affirmative embrace of play. Class-based debates over leisure did not wholly abate; but alongside such disputes there emerged a growing appreciation for the restorative, character-building, and even morally uplifting dimension of time productively spent away from work. This trend, which would evolve into an even more emphatic "gospel of play" by the end of the century—propelled in part by mid-century health reform movements and the spread of active outdoor sports—was one of the most important of the era.

American writers participated in these revaluations of work and play in myriad ways. Not only did literary texts frequently depict and comment on scenes of leisure, but reading itself, through the dramatic expansion of affordable newspaper, journal, and book publishing, also became a prominent—and to some minds, freshly dangerous—leisure activity. Nineteenth-century American literary works thus inculcated new ideals of play, challenged existing or emerging ideologies of leisure, and probed the cultural divisions exacerbated or initiated by new forms of, or new ideas about, recreation and amusement.

A brief note on terminology: although during this period the terms "leisure," "play," "recreation," "sport," and "amusement" were sometimes used interchangeably, each also developed its own nuances of meaning. "Leisure" tended to refer to free time most broadly, "play" to the activities of children, "recreation" to actions that refreshed or rejuvenated, "sport" to organized games or events, and "amusement" to paid entertainments.

THE DIVERSITY OF LEISURE ACTIVITIES

Although foreign visitors to the United States in the early nineteenth century often complained that Americans were too consumed by business to take leisure seriously, anyone traveling widely through the country in the early 1820s would have been witness to a diverse range of leisure activities. Often varying by region, these activities also differed in purpose, scale, and level of participation. On the western frontier of Illinois or Michigan, for example, one would likely have encountered preindustrial forms of recreation, including barn raisings, corn huskings, quilting bees, and other communal activities that introduced an element of fun into the large-scale tasks often necessary in farming societies. One might also have found ample attention paid, particularly among men, to such blood sports as cockfighting, which were popular not just in rural areas but in towns and cities around the country as well. Rat baiting, in which spectators typically wagered on the number of rats a dog could kill within a given period of time, became a popular leisure activity among working-class men in New York City, among other places, in the 1830s.

Other spectator sports operated on a grander scale. In 1823 perhaps as many as seventy thousand people—including northerners, southerners, whites, blacks, and men and women from all classes—gathered at Union Course, Long Island, to watch the northern thoroughbred, Eclipse, defeat its southern challenger, Sir Henry, in a twenty-thousand-dollar match race. Although such huge crowds remained rare in the largely preprofessional antebellum era, prominent bare-knuckle prizefights, rowing matches, and even walking races (known as "peds," short for "pedestrian" races) at times drew similarly large audiences and wagers.

Americans also pursued more private recreations. In towns and cities, voluntary societies, such as those founded by immigrant groups to preserve cultural and linguistic ties, often sponsored musical, theatrical, or athletic gatherings for their members. Many Americans seeking to connect anew with the natural world were drawn to such field sports as hunting and fishing, which, especially in nonrural areas, had only recently become recreational rather than subsistence activities. Along the East Coast in particular, inspiration for such pursuits might have come indirectly from the Romantic poetry of writers such as William Cullen Bryant or, a bit later, from reflections on nature's regenerative spiritual power by such transcendentalists as Ralph Waldo Emerson, Margaret Fuller, and Henry David Thoreau.

More broadly, though in equally diverse ways, rhetorics of leisure, recreation, and sport often played significant roles in the works of many of the most popular early-nineteenth-century American authors. In "Rip Van Winkle" (1819–1820), a story by Washington Irving (1783–1859), for example, although the easy-going Rip will uncomplainingly help his neighbors complete even the most arduous of tasks (and is always prominent at work frolics and bees), he scrupulously avoids all activity that resembles profitable labor. Rip is not punished for his dilatory ramble into the Kaatskill Mountains, when an afternoon of leisurely squirrel hunting turns into a twenty-year nap—he even snoozes through the American Revolution—but is instead rewarded with an old man's immunity from responsible work. Other writers, particularly those who set their fiction on the frontier, also championed an ethic of play over busyness. The best-selling Leatherstocking novels (1823–1841) by James Fenimore Cooper (1789–1851) are a case in point. Drawing on the already mythologized image of the wilderness hunter epitomized by Daniel Boone (1734–1820), Cooper's novels not only depict frequent scenes of frontier sport (as well as unsporting frontier waste, as proto-industrial modes of mechanized slaughter mock the sportsman's code of honor and restraint), but they also transform his character Natty Bumppo—also known as Deerslayer, Pathfinder, and Hawkeye—into a nearly mythic figure of sporting fair play.

Related yet distinct literary traditions buttressed regional notions of leisure and play. Southwestern humorists, for example, countered Cooper's heroic sporting myth with the outlaw figure of the backwoods gamesman, whose role was to outwit an unsuspecting genteel opponent—or better yet, another backwoods con man. Among the plantation romancers of the American South, by contrast, the respectable leisure and spirited play of the landed class was offered as proof of the superiority of southern culture. *Swallow Barn* (1832), a novel by John Pendleton Kennedy (1795–1870), though in certain ways ambivalent about planter class values, helped link the genre of plantation fiction to the idea of the distinctiveness of southern, predominantly male, leisure. These traditions also had their own implicit and explicit critics. In her 1839 novel of the Michigan frontier, *A New Home—Who'll Follow?*, for example, Caroline Kirkland (1801–1864) challenged many of the classic motifs of the frontier sporting tradition with a deflating irony. *Recollections of a Southern Matron* (1837), by Caroline Howard Gilman (1794–1888), minimizes masculine honor and sporting culture in favor of domestic attentiveness and feminine compassion. Southern black autobiographers such as Frederick

Douglass (1818–1895) depicted the powerful communal bonds forged among slaves during moments of temporary relaxation from toil while simultaneously critiquing the planter's common contrivance of providing intermittent leisure to bondsmen and bondswomen, particularly at Christmastime, to defuse the threat of revolt.

Americans seeking to read about diverse leisure activities could look to journalism as well as literature. The first national sporting magazines appeared in the 1810s and multiplied in each of the next five decades. Among the most influential was *Spirit of the Times,* launched in 1831 by William T. Porter (1809–1858) and marketed to sporting gentlemen. Reaching a national circulation of over 40,000, Porter's paper provided not merely sporting but also theatrical news and humorous sketches. Those who could not afford the ten-dollar annual subscription fee to *Spirit of the Times* could turn instead to the penny press, which offered, in addition to sports news, salacious reporting on crime and scandal. Women readers had their own leisure magazines, most prominently *Godey's Lady's Book,* first published in 1830 and reaching as many as 150,000 subscribers at its peak before the Civil War. An illustrated national monthly best known for printing sentimental literature, advice columns, and watercolor engravings of women's fashions, *Godey's* provided its readers with a dynamic mix of information and entertainment, as well as spiritual, moral, and aesthetic uplift.

REFORMERS TAKE AIM

Nowhere were the changes taking place in American leisure more visible or controversial than in U.S. cities. To many middle- and upper-class moralists—weaned on a nineteenth-century evangelicalism that judged idleness and intemperance even more censoriously than had their Puritan forebears—the persistence of blood sports, the pervasiveness of gambling, and the proliferation of working-class dance halls, theaters, and saloons were all signs of irredeemable spiritual and social degradation. Where possible, reformers tried to control working-class leisure. Using moral suasion and regulation, they succeeded, for example, in placing modest constraints on liquor sales. Attempts to shape workers' free time more drastically, however, met with opposition or indifference from workers themselves, who continued to patronize "Bowery" entertainments (typically the only affordable alternatives for working-class men and women) or simply ignored genteel injunctions against, for example, alcohol consumption and boisterous play in such new leisure venues as urban parks.

Literary responses to the rise of reformist energies varied. Capitalizing on both the reformers' zeal for condemning the misuse of leisure and the public's thirst for titillating narratives, popular novels that grimly illuminated the depths to which the unsuspecting leisure abuser might fall often became massive best-sellers. These included George Lippard's *The Quaker City; or, The Monks of Monk Hall* (1845) and Timothy Shay Arthur's *Ten Nights in a Bar-Room* (1854). Respectable national magazines such as *Harper's Weekly* periodically satirized such popular urban pleasure grounds as Jones's Woods on the east side of Manhattan, which featured bowling alleys, dancing stands, and beer halls, as well as space for picnics, sporting events, and festivals. Accompanying one such editorial from 1859 was an engraved illustration showing a densely packed exurban scene, at the center of which appeared an anxious young mother. In the near background leer bearded, heavy-jowled men; on the right margin an eager young man—identified in the editorial as the woman's husband—takes aim at targets in a shooting gallery, forgetful of his family (indeed, according to the editorial, he will soon be swindled by gamblers who con him into wagering on his next shots); on the far left two men, one of them an aproned African American, perhaps taking a break from work, quaff beer. In the top right corner of the engraving, above the forgetful husband's head, three apprehensive figures momentarily defy gravity on the vertiginous upswing of a ballistic ride, while above the whole scene teeters an insouciant high-wire performer, his face plastered with an inane grin.

Literary critics have differed in their assessment of the degree to which American writers partook of the reformist, or conversely, the resistant, attitude toward mid-century attempts to control leisure. Some have argued that in his writings, with the exception of *The Scarlet Letter* (1850), Nathaniel Hawthorne (1804–1864) stages the repeated defeat of play at the hands of sin and death. Others discern in Hawthorne's work a deep ambivalence toward contemporary reform culture and its susceptibility to the very immoralities it professed to correct. In the case of Thoreau (1817–1862), scholars generally agree that his major works, particularly *Walden* (1854), offer the paradoxical ideal of earnest play as life's most important work. But some have also noted that Thoreau's ideal pointedly excludes from its otherwise capacious imaginings such new Americans as the Irish immigrants crowding Walden's shores in the middle of the century. According to some critics, Herman Melville's work subverts reform ideology; for others it is suffused with, and enriched by, a dark reformist rhetoric. The fact that Melville (1819–1891), along with Irving, signed the inflammatory elite petition that helped trigger the Astor Place Opera House riot of 1849—in which the city's militia, anxious to protect the upper-class Opera House from working-class

SUNDAY AT JONES'S WOODS, IN NEW YORK.

Sunday at Jones's Woods, in New York. An example of the mid-century middle-class critique of poorly spent leisure, this engraving mocks the inability of a popular New York City pleasure ground to provide true enjoyment or respectable recreation for its Sabbath-breaking patrons. "Jones's Woods are not Elysian fields," intones a caustic editorial accompanying the engraving. "It is the business of pleasure that prevails—the labor of entertainment, the hard work of enjoyment. Of a Sunday morning you will find there hundreds upon hundreds of straggling wanderers, toiling earnestly to experience amusement; laying themselves out with unflinching determination to acquire gratification at all hazards; often pervaded with firmest convictions that their purpose is in course of accomplishment, and that only a few more struggles are needed to perch them upon a tolerably lofty elevation of bliss." GRADUATE LIBRARY, UNIVERSITY OF MICHIGAN

demonstrators protesting elite support for a despised British actor, shot into a crowd of thousands, killing at least twenty-two—highlights how deeply mid-century conflicts over leisure touched many Americans, famous and obscure.

A NEW SPIRIT OF PLAY

Beginning around 1850, a few formerly rabid critics of leisure broke ranks to speak out on behalf of beneficial play and repose. The Reverend Henry Ward Beecher (1813–1887), Harriet Beecher Stowe's younger brother, was one such figure. Barely ten years after Beecher had published his fiery sermons against idleness, *Seven Lectures to Young Men* (1844), which would remain one of the best-selling American advice books for at least another generation, the influential minister unexpectedly shifted his position and offered praise for the restorative effects of rest and relaxation.

Part of the impetus behind this shift was Beecher's own move to Brooklyn from Indianapolis. Away from the relative deprivations of the Midwest, Beecher gradually embraced the new ideology of repose taking shape in thriving middle-class suburbs such as Brooklyn. Surplus and rest, well used, might bring joy rather than dissipation, Beecher argued. He also found himself influenced by the new mid-century reform emphasis on health and exercise. Alarmed by the pale, sickly bodies of overworked Americans, some Christian reformers embraced physical improvement as a necessary part of mental and spiritual uplift. In his important 1858 essay, "Saints, and Their Bodies," Reverend Thomas Wentworth Higginson (1823–1911)—later a Civil War colonel and also an interlocutor of Emily Dickinson—argued that only a more "muscular" Christianity would be "manly" enough to confront the multiple dangers of the age.

Under the influence of spiritual and intellectual leaders such as Beecher and Higginson, the idea that leisure, sport, and recreation—rightly managed—might actually build character rather than destroy it, slowly took hold. This timely ideological shift not only validated the new middle-class practice of taking planned vacations from work; it also encouraged the expansion of nascent, male-dominated outdoor sports such as baseball, cricket, and rowing while simultaneously rehabilitating older, less reputable indoor pastimes such as tenpin bowling and billiards. In the proper setting, almost any formerly vicious pursuit could be rendered wholesome. Other activities and recreations that instilled or rewarded Victorians' sense of healthful discipline, order, and self-control, such as calisthenics and gymnastics (a staple program of many German immigrant fraternal organizations), found new participants, not only in cities but eventually on college campuses and in the schools. By 1870 many of the bureaucratic and organizational structures that would underlie modern sports and recreation were firmly in place, including the first professional baseball associations, city and regional athletic clubs, and both the Young Men's and Young Women's Christian Associations. Less formal and more social recreational activities, including ice skating, sledding, croquet, and an entire class of private "home entertainments," thrived during this period as well and encouraged mixed-sex play. Although this new ideology of leisure was theoretically available to all, and while its broad cultural success eventually helped suppress some of the working-class activities most objectionable to middle-class reformers, in the last decades of this era most leisure activities, especially commercial pursuits, were deeply stratified by economic status. In addition, women's participation in the new leisure culture, while expansive in many ways, was limited in others, particularly as male-oriented sports drew an ever-larger share of cultural attention. And while the importance of the freedom conferred by emancipation on black Americans cannot be underestimated—for the first time, most blacks ostensibly controlled their work and leisure time—a postwar color line frequently prevented full participation in America's new sporting ethic.

American writers continued to shape and critique the new ideas about play emerging after 1850. In *Leaves of Grass* (first published in 1855), for example, Walt Whitman (1819–1892) seems fully to share the reformers' newfound respect for productive relaxation and a healthy body, repeatedly celebrating the freedom and exhilaration of a vigorous "manhood." In *Ragged Dick* (1867), the first of Horatio Alger Jr.'s massively successful serial novels, Alger (1832–1899) imagines a working-class bootblack addicted to low pleasures and commercial entertainments who is pulled out of the Bowery and into the middle class by his own newly awakened desire for respectability in both work and play. Conversely, Herman Melville's "The Paradise of Bachelors and the Tartarus of Maids" (1855) and Rebecca Harding Davis's (1831–1910) *Life in the Iron Mills* (1861) both provide dark portraits of the class and gender stratifications that continued to structure labor and leisure despite the presence of these new ideas, whereas domestic satirists such as Fanny Fern (Sara Payson Willis Parton, 1811–1872) called attention to the particular labors of working women, a class largely overlooked by leisure reform. Finally, African American activists and writers such as Sojourner Truth (c. 1797–1883) and Frances Ellen Watkins Harper (1825–1911), through their speeches, poems, and stories, similarly critiqued the seemingly endless toil of black workers who all too frequently had no margin for rest, relaxation, or play. After 1870, although free time and disposable income would finally begin to increase for most American workers, regardless of class, region, race, or gender, the larger questions attending leisure not only failed to disappear—they grew, if anything, thornier and more vexed.

See also Circuses and Spectacles; Health and Medicine; Labor; Manhood; Reform; Urbanization

BIBLIOGRAPHY

Primary Works

Alger, Horatio. *Ragged Dick; or, Street Life in New York with the Boot-Blacks.* 1867. Introduction by David K. Shipler. New York: Modern Library, 2005.

Davis, Rebecca Harding. *Life in the Iron Mills and Other Stories.* Rev. ed., edited by Tillie Olsen. Old Westbury, N.Y.: Feminist Press, 1985.

Douglass, Frederick. *Narrative of the Life of an American Slave.* Boston: Anti-Slavery Office, 1845.

Irving, Washington. "Rip Van Winkle." In *The Complete Tales of Washington Irving,* edited by Charles Neider. Garden City, N.Y.: Doubleday, 1975.

Kennedy, John Pendleton. *Swallow Barn; or, A Sojourn in the Old Dominion.* Edited by Lucinda H. MacKethan. Baton Rouge: Louisiana State University Press, 1986.

Kirkland, Caroline M. *A New Home, Who'll Follow? or, Glimpses of Western Life in the West.* 1839. Edited by Sandra A. Zagarell. New Brunswick, N.J., and London: Rutgers University Press, 1990.

Thoreau, Henry David. *Walden* and *Resistance to Civil Government.* Norton critical edition. Edited by William Rossi. New York: Norton, 1992.

Whitman, Walt. *Leaves of Grass: Comprehensive Reader's Edition.* Edited by Sculley Bradley and Harold W. Blodgett. New York: New York University Press, 1973.

Secondary Works

Braden, Donna R. *Leisure and Entertainment in America.* Dearborn, Mich.: Henry Ford Museum and Greenfield Village, 1988.

Butsch, Richard, ed. *For Fun and Profit: The Transformation of Leisure into Consumption.* Philadelphia: Temple University Press, 1990.

Click, Patricia C. *The Spirit of the Times: Amusements in Nineteenth-Century Baltimore, Norfolk, and Richmond.* Charlottesville: University Press of Virginia, 1989.

Dawson, Melanie. *Laboring to Play: Home Entertainment and the Spectacle of Middle-Class Cultural Life, 1850–1920.* Tuscaloosa: University of Alabama Press, 2005.

Gleason, William A. *The Leisure Ethic: Work and Play in American Literature, 1840–1940.* Stanford, Calif.: Stanford University Press, 1999.

Gorn, Elliott J., and Warren Goldstein. *A Brief History of American Sports.* Urbana: University of Illinois Press, 2004.

Grover, Kathryn, ed. *Hard at Play: Leisure in America, 1840–1940.* Amherst: University of Massachusetts Press, 1992.

Lehuu, Isabelle. *Carnival on the Page: Popular Print Media in Antebellum America.* Chapel Hill: University of North Carolina Press, 2000.

Oriard, Michael. *Sporting with the Gods: The Rhetoric of Play and Game in American Culture.* New York: Cambridge University Press, 1991.

Reynolds, David S. *Beneath the American Renaissance: The Subversive Imagination in the Age of Emerson and Melville.* Cambridge, Mass.: Harvard University Press, 1989.

Rogers, Daniel T. *The Work Ethic in Industrial America, 1850–1920.* Chicago: University of Chicago Press, 1974.

Spears, Betty, and Richard A. Swanson. *History of Sport and Physical Activity in the United States.* 3rd ed. Edited by Elaine T. Smith. Dubuque, Iowa: Wm. C. Brown Publishers, 1988.

William Gleason

LETTERS

Nineteenth-century letters may be defined as handwritten messages, usually inscribed with pencil or ink on paper and sent to specific persons or audiences. Through them, correspondents conducted commercial, political, and academic business or, conversely, transacted personal matters. These familiar letters, typically invested with more literary sensibility than matter-of-fact business correspondence, attended the era's signal geographical mobility prompted by marriage, employment, fortune seeking, or westward expansion. By 1860 over one-third of the citizenry had moved from their birthplaces. The Civil War's (1861–1865) mobilization of regiments spurred copious correspondence, with an estimated 180,000 letters each day flowing between the battlefield and the home front. For whatever reasons they found themselves separated from friends and kinfolk, ordinary and eminent people alike declared love, facilitated courtship, announced births, offered condolences, extended thanks, and most often simply kept in touch from afar through letters. Before the era of widespread rapid telecommunication, letters were lifelines of communication over time and space. Even illiterate people dictated messages to scribes.

CONTENT AND FORM

Although each one was a unique artifact bearing singular features, letters shared common themes related to estrangement: the expanse of space between correspondents, loneliness, and hope of reunion, if only after death. Because epistolary text replaced face-to-face interaction, attempts to replicate conversation were duly noted; yet in the struggle to sustain intimate bonds, correspondents inevitably felt defeated when conveying visual imagery, palpable events, or emotional states. Slaves or freed people torn from enslaved families encountered the limitations of epistolary expression perhaps more than did their white contemporaries. For example, Hannah Valentine, an Abingdon, Virginia, slave, desperately sought reunion via letter with her husband, Michael, at Richmond with his master, the state's newly elected governor.

This excerpt from a letter dated 30 January 1838, from Hannah Valentine to her husband Michael Valentine, reveals the deep anxiety people felt when their correspondence went unanswered; even word-of-mouth news was a poor substitute for a letter.

My dear husband

I begin to feel so anxious to hear from you and my children, and indeed from all the family that I have concluded to write to you altho you have treated me badly in not answering my last letter. I heard through Mr Gibson last week that you were all well, but hearing from you in that way does not satisfy me. I want a letter to tell me what you are doing and all about yourself and Eliza & David.

Starobin, ed., *Blacks in Bondage: Letters of American Slaves*, pp. 69–70.

For emigrants to Liberia, Africa, reporting home about their new but difficult conditions, written words poorly substituted for spoken dialogue.

Unlike lively, spontaneous conversation, letters followed formulas derived from either epistolary manuals or custom, both of which potentially engendered stilted writing. To elude humdrum scribbling, some letter writers subverted conventions such as opening greetings, sign-off partings, and postscripts with comic parody that amused recipients. Fearing reproof or, worse yet, the correspondents' termination of letter exchange, writers ritually begged pardon for garrulous, shallow, or dilatory missives. Sometimes they enhanced a letter's interest by versifying instead of writing prose, enclosing objects of affection (such as dried flowers, hair ringlets, or bookmarks), adorning margins with sketches, or inserting clippings from the latest news.

Despite the challenges endemic to writing, letters often sparked lively intellectual discourse. In the highly literate Boston region, for example, many correspondents, especially women, zealously wrote about the latest literature. "Have you read . . . ?" was a ubiquitous query that invited reviewer-like repartee. This discourse not only fed the literary marketplace, it lubricated epistolary conversation. By writing to other sympathetic female souls about literature, both the formally educated and the self-taught correspondents transgressed proscriptions against women's intellec-

tual attainment. Letter writing in this sense advanced female education.

Beyond the text itself, correspondents valued the letter's tangible qualities—ink and paper, handwriting, envelope and stamps, enclosures—because they represented material traces of the letter writer. Letters were cherished and carefully stored away to be admired, repeatedly read, or studied for any slight variations in chirography that disclosed changes in the writer's health, well-being, or mentality. Writers consequently took pains with penmanship, the high caliber of which not only reflected deliberation in committing thoughts to paper but also character, gentility, and refinement. To ensure fine script, well-to-do writers and some poorer folk purchased quality ink and, to absorb it evenly, high rag-content paper (versus cheap pulp). After mid-century, manufactured steel or gold pens that could glide over paper supplanted cheap quills that required cutting and mending. Before envelopes were patented in 1849, correspondents usually mailed stationery sheets, folded blank side out and secured with colorful sealing wax. Customized seals for stamping wax personalized letters and concealed their contents. So engaging were signets that the popular author Elizabeth Oakes Prince Smith, in her poem "The Twice-Told Seal" (1845), immortalized one that figuratively thawed a business letter's icy text.

TRANSMISSION

Letters were sent in various ways: via telegraph, courier, and postal system. First laid by Samuel B. Morse as a line between Washington, D.C., and Baltimore in 1843 and augmented by Western Union and other firms as a more far-reaching communication network after the Civil War, the electric telegraph quickly transmitted business messages and the latest news. But because it was expensive, most correspondents depended on other means. Although the federal postal system developed rapidly during the nineteenth century, with over fourteen thousand offices by 1845 and twice as many by 1860, correspondents still asked overland travelers and voyagers to "page" for them, that is, carry letters as a favor. Unlike volunteers, postal carriers provided regular service, making mailing more expeditious but certainly not cheaper than paging. Until 1845 a single sheet cost upward of six cents to mail depending on how far it traveled; a twenty-five-cent charge, then a considerable sum, was not uncommon. Forty-niners' eastern kin paid a whopping forty cents per California-bound letter. The thrifty illicitly scribbled on newspapers, much cheaper to mail than letters; if detected, however, they exacted letter postage. Mailing letters became economical after 1851, when

Elizabeth Oakes Prince Smith's poem "The Twice-Told Seal" (1845), the first stanza of which is shown here, is an homage to decorative signets commonly used for stamping the sealing wax that secured letters.

The letter was a common one,
A business letter too,
Announcing some commission done,
And thence its words were few.
I read it idly, tossed it by,
And then a pretty seal
And kindly motto met my eye,
That gave my heart to feel.

Elizabeth Oakes Prince Smith, *The Poetical Writings of Elizabeth Oakes Smith* (New York: J. S. Redfield, 1845), pp. 194–195.

rates dropped to three cents per single letter conveyed within three thousand miles, but newspaper exchange still had its adherents.

The postal service's relative efficiency notwithstanding, many letters never reached their destinations for various reasons, such as misdirection, the death of the receiver, or a change of address, and wound up in the dead letter office, established in 1825 as mail volume expanded along with the population and national boundaries. There, miscarried letters with valuable enclosures like wedding rings, gems, or money were opened with the intent of notifying the sender; unclaimed goods were auctioned and unretrieved letters burned. The department's dolorous mission inspired fiction, such as Herman Melville's short story "Bartleby, the Scrivener" (1853) and Metta Fuller Victor's (1831–1885) book *The Dead Letter* (1866), the first full-length American detective novel. In both, the office, a synecdoche for communication breakdown, plays a key role in delineating the protagonists' characters and indeed the human condition.

LETTERS AND LITERATURE

Because familiar letter writing essentially is an imaginative act involving creative self-representation, some believe it is automatically imbued with literariness. In form, content, and purpose, the correspondence of aspiring or published authors and prominent figures generally simulated that of ordinary writers, but the former exemplified creative facility of language, style, and thought, and because such writers often anticipated future publication, a self-conscious presentation

of self. The historian and critic Henry Brooks Adams (1838–1918), for one, composed letters with their future publicity in mind. Nonetheless, for Adams, corresponding, a warmly human activity, counterpoised publishing for an anonymous mass reading audience. Some authors predictably elevated writing over speaking. Throughout his early life, the transcendentalist author Ralph Waldo Emerson (1803–1882) preferred epistolary discussion to conversation, a predilection perhaps cultivated by his erudite aunt Mary Moody Emerson; so prized were her letters that Emerson transcribed excerpts in his journals. His epistles to fellow transcendentalists, especially Caroline Sturgis Tappan, exhibited artfulness within the rigid form. *Nature* (1836), among other publications and lectures, extracted ideas from correspondence and captured its more familiar tone. Like Emerson, the poet Emily Dickinson (1830–1886) inventively exploited letters for literary ends, to an extent probably greater than contemporary professional counterparts ventured; indeed, classifying her works as either letters or poems often becomes impossible.

The epistolary act, so commonplace to readers, inspired authors' belletristic productions for the literary marketplace. It was thematically highlighted in sundry poems and became an element essential to the plot or characters' development in novels and short stories. Dickinson, an enthusiastic correspondent, devoted twelve poems to epistolary exchange, including "This Is My Letter to the World" and "The Way I Read a Letter's—This." In the latter, Dickinson envisioned sealed letters as secret treasures, locked up safe from snoopers' eyes and awaiting liberation. The poet Mary Eliza Tucker Lambert's poems about Civil War battlefront letters, "No Letter" (1867) and "The Mail Has Come" (1867), pondered civilian correspondents' emotional bind: eagerly awaited mail possibly bore bad news, while no letters at all portended tragedy. The aforementioned novel by Metta Fuller Victor not only situated its opening chapter in a post office, it wove its plot around a baffling "dead letter" that proffered clues in a murder case. Similarly Edgar Allan Poe (1809–1849) in his "The Purloined Letter" (1844) fashioned a riveting detective story around a stolen letter, recovered by amateur psychology rather than professional investigation. Both psychologically nuanced pieces addressed contemporaries' anxieties about lost or intercepted letters. Literary letter-writing cameos unveiled tensions and frustrations. Perhaps the most famous appears in Harriet Beecher Stowe's (1811–1896) best-seller, *Uncle Tom's Cabin* (1852): the elderly slave, Uncle Tom, recalling long-forgotten writing lessons, warily drafts a letter to his estranged wife and children under the watchful eye of Eva, his master's daughter. Though sentimentalized, the scene simulated actual impediments to slave family communication and symbolized, for white audiences, their own family disruptions.

In epistolary fiction, as opposed to fiction with letter-writing themes or vignettes, a series of letters, mimetic of actual correspondence, drives rather than informs the narrative. Although its European heyday had passed before the turn of the nineteenth century, the genre—apotheosized by Samuel Richardson's novels *Pamela; or, Virtue Rewarded* (1740) and *Clarissa Harlow* (1747–1748)—attracted several American authors writing between 1820 and 1870. Following upon William Hill Brown's *The Power of Sympathy* (1789) and Charles Brockden Brown's *Clara Howard* (1801) and *Jane Talbot* (1801), the authors John Neal (*Randolph*, 1823), Theodore Sedgwick (*Hints to My Countrymen*, 1826), and John Gardiner Calkins Brainard (*Letters Found in the Ruins of Fort Braddock*, 1834) all invested the fading genre with contemporary appeal. The period's most noteworthy epistolary novels—the Unitarian minister William Ware's historical trilogy, *Letters from Lucius M. Piso [pseud.] from Palmyra* (1837), *Probus; or, Rome in the Third Century* (1838), and *Julian; or, Scenes in Judea* (1841), and the prolific, cheap-fiction writer Joseph Holt Ingraham's biblical tomes *Prince of the House of David* (1855), *Pillar of Fire* (1859), and *Throne of David* (1860)—previewed Lewis Wallace's *Ben Hur* (1880). Toward century's end epistolary fiction writers abandoned sentimentality for greater verisimilitude. Accordingly a review in the April 1871 issue of *Atlantic Monthly* praised Abby Morton Diaz's humorous *William Henry Letters* (1870) for its naturalistic rendering of a boarding schoolboy's letters home.

Epistolary fiction naturally evolved from "letter-writers," instructive guides for novice correspondents that in England date back to the sixteenth century. Manuals characteristically featured templates, or model letters, for diverse writing occasions and became increasingly didactic and literary in that they portrayed well-drawn characters and wove entertaining narratives. By the early nineteenth century reading letter-writers had become a form of entertainment as well as instruction. Indeed, Irwin P. Beadle of dime-novel fame tapped this market with *Beadle's Dime Letter-Writer* (1860). Most authors of these guides carefully guarded their anonymity, perhaps because the titles often promised more than the books could deliver. "R. Turner's" popular *Parlour Letter-Writer* (1835) dubiously sported model letters "On Every Occurrence in Life." Other books barraged readers with a hodgepodge of wisdom: besides writing lessons, one offered instruction in *How to Behave, How to Talk, How to Do Business* (1869); yet another contained *The Very Best Directions for Making All Kinds of Ice Creams* (1855). The levity no doubt eased correspondents' anxieties about writing. Publishers brought forth at least sixty original editions between 1837 and 1857 alone, but the market for these guides flourished well beyond the Civil War.

In the early twenty-first century, when most communication between separated people is conducted via telephone or e-mail, it becomes difficult fully to appreciate the impact of ostensibly silly guidebooks, sentimentally fraught epistolary fiction, macabre dead letter offices, and now-rarified stationery items upon nineteenth-century literate populations for whom the culture of letter writing was vital. While that culture was one of deceleration rather than acceleration of communication—letters after all took time to write, send, read, and respond to—it nonetheless amply nourished relationships that might otherwise have unraveled under the stress of dislocation. For that reason alone, nineteenth-century letters may be counted among the nation's most treasured cultural—and literary—artifacts.

See also Civil War; Death; Dime Novels; English Literature; Female Authorship; Friendship; Humor; Poems of Emily Dickinson; Slavery; *Uncle Tom's Cabin*

BIBLIOGRAPHY

Primary Work

Victor, Metta Victoria Fuller. *The Dead Letter Office and the Figure Eight*. 1866. Durham, N.C.: Duke University Press, 2003.

Secondary Works

Bowyer, Mathew J. *They Carried the Mail: A Survey of Postal History and Hobbies*. Washington, D.C.: Robert B. Luce, 1972.

Decker, William Merrill. *Epistolary Practices: Letter Writing in America before Telecommunications*. Chapel Hill: University of North Carolina Press, 1998. Chapters on Ralph Waldo Emerson, Emily Dickinson, and Henry Adams.

Guillén, Claudio. "On the Edge of Literariness: The Writing of Letters." *Comparative Literature Studies* 31 (1994): 1–24.

John, Richard. "The Politics of Innovation." *Daedalus* 127 (1998): 187–214.

Kelley, Mary. "Reading Women/Women Reading: The Making of Learned Women in Antebellum America." *Journal of American History* 83 (1996): 401–424.

Kielbowicz, Richard B. *News in the Mail: The Press, Post Office, and Public Information, 1700–1860s*. New York: Greenwood Press, 1989.

Peters, John Durham. *Speaking into the Air: A History of the Idea of Communication.* Chicago: University of Chicago Press, 1999.

Silber, Nina, and Mary Beth Sievens, eds. *Introduction to Yankee Correspondence: Civil War Letters between New England Soldiers and the Home Front.* Charlottesville: University Press of Virginia, 1996. See pp. 1–24.

Singer, Godfrey Frank. *The Epistolary Novel: Its Origin, Development, Decline, and Residuary Influence.* Philadelphia: University of Pennsylvania Press, 1933.

Starobin, Robert S., ed. *Blacks in Bondage: Letters of American Slaves.* New York: New Viewpoints, 1974.

Thornton, Tamara Plakins. *Handwriting in America: A Cultural History.* New Haven, Conn.: Yale University Press, 1996.

Zboray, Ronald J. *A Fictive People: Antebellum Economic Development and the American Reading Public.* New York: Oxford University Press, 1993.

Zboray, Ronald J., and Mary Saracino Zboray. *Everyday Ideas: Socio-Literary Experience among Antebellum New Englanders.* Knoxville: University of Tennessee Press, forthcoming.

Zboray, Ronald J., and Mary Saracino Zboray. "'Have You Read . . . ?' Real Readers and Their Responses in Antebellum Boston and Its Region." *Nineteenth-Century Literature* 52 (1997): 139–170.

Ronald J. Zboray
Mary Saracino Zboray

LETTERS ON THE EQUALITY OF THE SEXES

The 1830s proved to be among the most explosive decades in American history. Racial tensions had reached unprecedented levels of intensity, abolitionists and their critics alike were discovering new ways of getting their voices heard, and riots erupted with increasing frequency across the country's major cities. The epicenter of this furor was Boston and its environs; there William Lloyd Garrison (1805–1879) and his supporters orchestrated a national campaign to end slavery—not gradually, not in good time, but immediately. Although small in number and poor in resources, the abolitionists attracted the attention of a broad range of reform interests, including moral crusaders, pacifists, free speech proponents, and early women's rights activists. Such a diverse and combustible mixture of cultural energies could not but struggle to retain its focus, and soon enough the movement found itself battling not only external opposition but internal strife as well. By decade's end, abolitionism itself came to wear an altogether new aspect.

BACKGROUND: THE ABOLITIONIST–WOMEN'S RIGHTS NEXUS

Among the chief catalysts for this transformation was Sarah Moore Grimké (1792–1873). Daughter of a prominent South Carolina jurist and slaveholder, older sister of Angelina Grimké (1805–1879), Sarah had left her native South to join a Quaker sect in Philadelphia while still a young woman. The early years of her self-imposed exile from slavery were spent in deeply spiritual, sometimes mystical, reflections on the state of her soul and the world. By the mid-1830s Sarah came to realize that the salvation of both were intertwined, and she resolved with Angelina to join the antislavery host. Together they would lift up their voices and testify as few could against the benighted system. In the process Sarah and Angelina harnessed the forces unleashed by abolitionism to revolutionize the prospects of women's rights.

Abolition leaders in New York and Boston were quick to recognize the unique possibilities presented by Sarah and her sister. They knew slavery as others did not, knew it firsthand, had grown up under its wing. At the encouragement of Theodore Dwight Weld (1803–1895) and others, the Grimkés underwent training in New York City, where they practiced the antislavery message before small, largely female audiences. By the late spring of 1837 the sisters were judged ready for larger things and were called to a series of lectures in the greater Boston area. Before crowds ranging from several hundred to well over a thousand, the Grimkés traveled from town to town, in all addressing more than forty thousand curious, supportive, and sometimes hostile listeners. Inevitably, perhaps, with such fame must come infamy, and by midsummer of 1837 the forces of opposition were ready to put a stop to the spectacle. And little wonder: what had started out as a protest against slavery appeared now to justify women's claim that they, too, had a public role to play in the affairs of the nation.

The Reverend Nehemiah Adams (1806–1878) was not an unreasonable man by most standards. But he, like many other New England clerics, was becoming ever more exasperated by the abolitionists and their ways. The religious leaders were not in principle antiabolition, and certainly they were not proslavery. But they were above all men of the cloth, whose office it was to minister the Word to the faithful in buildings constructed for that purpose and that purpose only. To have their churches set upon by antislavery agitators, their doors opened and halls filled by crowds stirring up social unrest, to have the flock exposed to the

Sarah Grimké. THE LIBRARY OF CONGRESS

sight of women speaking in public was more than they could tolerate. It fell to Reverend Adams, accordingly, to publish on 28 June 1837 "A Pastoral Letter of the General Association to the Congregational Churches under Their Care." In tightly composed and uncompromising language, the "Pastoral Letter" set forth the case of the clergy and admonished its readers on three main points. First, such controversial subjects as abolitionism were not to be imposed on the faithful as fit matter for debate. Second, the letter warned ministers to avoid talking to or otherwise accommodating those who would so impose upon the good offices of the church. And finally, it attacked in no uncertain terms the involvement of women—especially women speakers—in matters of public controversy. The "Pastoral Letter" was in turn followed by two "Clerical Appeals," which specifically targeted Garrison and the unseemly actions of women who took it upon themselves to operate outside their divinely appointed spheres of influence.

LETTERS

The stage was thus set. The Grimké sisters had heard much of this before publication of the "Pastoral Letter"; indeed such opposition had hounded them throughout their New England tour. By early July Sarah decided to respond. In a series of fifteen letters,

written between 11 July and 20 October 1837 and published in the *New England Spectator* (and reprinted in Garrison's *Liberator*), Grimké trained her formidable powers of argument against those seeking to silence women's role in abolition specifically and the work of public moral reform generally. The result was a stunning display of rhetorical ingenuity and moral force. "Sarah sought to reevaluate the very root of Christianity's devaluation of woman," writes one historian of the period, and in doing so, "she rewrote woman's role in cosmic history" (Abzug, p. 215).

Sarah Grimké was no match for her sister as an orator; she was not as widely engaged by other social issues and political problems as were some of her fellow women writers, such as Lydia Maria Child (1802–1880); nor was she an organizer along the lines of Mary S. Parker, president of the Boston Female Anti-Slavery Society, to whom the *Letters* were nominally addressed. But she was without peer as a student of biblical scripture and the meaning it held for women's status as individuals and as citizens. This erudition, combined with a direct, forceful, and often elegant prose style, is evident throughout the series. The missives are topically arranged in the following chronological order:

  I. The Original Equality of Woman
 II. Woman Subject Only to God
III. The Pastoral Letter of the General Association of Congregational Ministers of Massachusetts
 IV. Social Intercourse of the Sexes
  V. Condition in Asia and Africa
 VI. Women in Asia and Africa
VII. Condition in Some Parts of Europe and America
VIII. On the Condition of Women in the United States
 IX. Heroism of Women—Women in Authority
  X. Intellect of Woman
 XI. Dress of Women
XII. Legal Disabilities of Women
XIII. Relation of Husband and Wife
XIV. Ministry of Women
 XV. Man Equally Guilty with Woman in the Fall

Together, the letters constitute a comprehensive critique of women's subjugation, especially as it was justified by conventional appropriations of Holy Scripture. Broadly rendered, Grimké's arguments may be grouped as they appeal respectively to (1) Holy Writ; (2) geographical history; and (3) law. Notably Grimké criticizes not only patriarchal practices, although that is her focus, but also certain practices among women themselves, particularly with respect to their complicity in long-standing conventions of dress and marriage relations. Underwriting all these observations is an insistent appeal to the meaning and portent of the Bible, from which she draws virtually all her interpretive authority, many of her examples, and her rhetorical inspiration. The following provides a brief exposition of the three argumentative appeals.

At the heart of Grimké's reading of scripture is the conviction that man and woman were created equal. Interpretations to the contrary, she argues, are a result not of biblical evidence but of translations rendered by men for purposes advantageous to men. This stress on the corruption to which the Bible has been subjected and the attendant need to reinterpret its meaning represents a radical and early effort that will bear additional fruit later in the century with Elizabeth Cady Stanton's (1815–1902) *Woman's Bible* (1895, 1898). Grimké's insight eliminates any rationale for women's inferiority as scripturally given. "God created us equal," she insists, "he created us free agents; he is our Lawgiver, our King, and our Judge, and to him alone is woman bound to be in subjection, and to him alone is she accountable for the use of those talents with which her Heavenly Father has entrusted her" (*Letters on the Equality of the Sexes,* p. 34). To the extent that women are subjected, it is because of men and men only. Still, Grimké concludes: "I ask no favors for my sex. I surrender not our claim to equality. All I ask of our brethren, is that they will take their feet from off our necks, and permit us to stand upright on that ground which God designed us to occupy" (*Letters on the Equality of the Sexes,* p. 35).

Having established her scriptural premises, Grimké then undertakes a survey of the condition of women from a historical and global point of view. In this she was materially assisted by the previous work of Lydia Maria Child, whose *History of the Condition of Women, in Various Ages and Nations* (1835) similarly sought to examine the question from what might now be called a multicultural perspective. Although Grimké finds exceptions to the general rule, she reports a disturbing familiarity in the relationship between the sexes across time and space. Casting her eye over Asia and Africa, for example, Grimké finds that "men, in the exercise of their usurped dominion over woman, have almost invariably done one of two things. They have either made slaves of the creatures whom God designed to be their companions and their coadjucators in every moral and intellectual improvement, or they have dressed them like dolls, and used them as toys to amuse their hours of recreation" (Grimké, *Letters on the Equality of the Sexes,* p. 44). And what of woman's condition in America? Only the same, a fact made more poignant and painful in view of her own country's vaunted ideals of human equality.

Grimké's treatment of women's legal disabilities is particularly interesting for several reasons. Daughter to the famed South Carolina jurist John F. Grimké, Sarah frequently sat with her father in his study and discussed the law; indeed Sarah had been told by him that if she were a son, she would have made a great lawyer herself. Her sharp eye for legal issues did not dim in adulthood, as the *Letters* make clear; if anything, she developed a particularly well-informed and subtle analysis of women's subjugation before the law. It is worth observing in this regard that her argument in the *Letters* antedates many similar points made more than a decade later at the Seneca Falls Convention (1848). Although Grimké does not explicitly call for woman suffrage, she attacks directly the legal conditions that in effect prevent women from being genuine citizens. "Woman has no political existence," Grimké declares. "With the single exception of presenting a petition to the legislative body, she is a cipher in the nation" (*Letters on the Equality of the Sexes,* p. 72). Drawing from William Blackstone (1723–1780) and a number of legal authorities and precedents, Grimké exposes the effect that law has on women generally, married women, property, labor, and religion. The result, she writes, is to debase women to the status of slaves, and until "such laws are annulled, woman can never occupy that exalted station for which she was intended by her Maker" (*Letters on the Equality of the Sexes,* p. 77).

The combined forces of history, patriarchy, geography, and law thus collaborate in the systematic subjugation of women. Grimké's *Letters* include a great many additional targets not addressed here. It is important to note, however, that Grimké's efforts are not entirely devoted to negative critique, nor does she at any point give way to despair or cynicism. The rhetorical strategy at work in the *Letters* is rather designed to first expose the problem and then summon her readers to solve it. The final letter accordingly takes up the "Duties of Women." Here Grimké is not concerned to itemize a list but to examine the conditions under which the imperative to act for the common good may be realized. Among the barriers to action is the attitude expressed by the "Pastoral Letter" enjoining women from public ministry. The call to duty, she argues, overrides any and all such false contrivances. "Now to me it is perfectly clear, that WHATSOEVER IT IS MORALLY RIGHT FOR A MAN TO DO, IT IS MORALLY RIGHT FOR A WOMAN TO DO; and that confusion must exist in the moral world, until woman takes her stand on the same platform with man, and feels that she is clothed by her Maker with the *same rights,* and, of course, that upon her devolve the *same duties*" (*Letters on the Equality of the Sexes,* p. 100).

CONCLUSION

Taken together, the fifteen letters represent a major contribution to the early women's movement. Written at a moment of unprecedented excitement and alarm over the role of women in public moral reform, the *Letters* may be seen as a testament to Grimké's overall point; that is, they are a perfect example of what women were capable of doing once they acknowledged their agency as free moral beings. To be sure, with action comes risk, and it must be said that the *Letters* helped to put at risk the prospects of abolitionism and women's reform by fanning the fires of opposition. But it was a risk worth taking, as Grimké and many others realized; and indeed the two sisters continued to speak before large audiences, provoke yet more resistance, and galvanize supporters for decades to come. For this reason, Grimké's *Letters* must be accorded a prominent and unique place in the story of women's march toward freedom.

See also Abolitionist Writing; The Bible; Boston; Feminism; History; Letters; Quakers; Rhetoric; Seneca Falls Convention; Suffrage

BIBLIOGRAPHY
Primary Works
Grimké, Sarah. *Letters on the Equality of the Sexes, and Other Essays.* 1838. Edited by Elizabeth Ann Bartlett. New Haven, Conn.: Yale University Press, 1988.

Grimké, Sarah. *The Feminist Thought of Sarah Grimké.* Edited by Gerda Lerner. New York: Oxford University Press, 1998.

Secondary Works
Abzug, Robert H. *Cosmos Crumbling: American Reform and the Religious Imagination.* New York: Oxford University Press, 1994.

Lerner, Gerda. *The Grimké Sisters from South Carolina: Pioneers for Women's Rights and Abolition.* Chapel Hill: University of North Carolina Press, 2004.

Stephen Howard Browne

THE LIBERATOR

On the first of January 1831, the inaugural issue of *The Liberator* was published in Boston. Edited by William Lloyd Garrison (1805–1879), this four-page newspaper became America's longest-running radical abolitionist periodical, appearing weekly through the end of December 1865, after a bitter Civil War had definitively ended slavery in the United States. Drawing on the evangelical and revolutionary traditions in early America, Garrison promoted his message in a strident, denunciatory manner, yet he embraced a philosophy of nonviolent resistance, believing that "moral suasion" could effect slavery's demise. Garrison's timing was auspicious. Thanks to many factors,

primarily an increasingly literate population and cheaper methods of distribution, the mid-nineteenth century witnessed an explosion in periodical readership; when *The Liberator* commenced, over one thousand daily newspapers were avidly read in America.

ROLE IN THE ABOLITIONIST MOVEMENT

At the time *The Liberator* commenced, American slavery had been outlawed in all northern states for more than a decade. Over two million slaves, however, were still held as legal chattel in a dozen southern states. Prior to Garrison, American antislavery efforts had largely centered on religious objections. Some had called for gradually emancipating slaves, the method followed in most northern states, while others proposed relocating freed slaves to the African nation of Liberia (founded in 1830), a practice known as "colonization." Garrison rejected these proposals and demanded immediate emancipation for slaves. Even more extreme, he insisted that blacks be fully integrated into American society as the social and political equals of whites. In 1832 Garrison helped found the New England Anti-Slavery Society, followed by the American Anti-Slavery Society in 1833. Both organizations adhered to a platform of "immediatism."

In the 1830s anti-abolition sentiment dominated the U.S. political climate, North as well as South. White readers objected vehemently to Garrison's zealous tone, but free blacks avidly read the paper, thrilled by its extremism. From advertisements for runaway slaves to lurid articles depicting slave auctions, *The Liberator* forced northerners to confront naked human beings bartered and bred like livestock and children sold from their families, all for monetary profit. Within five years of the newspaper's shaky beginning, hundreds of state and local antislavery societies had organized, and *The Liberator* significantly expanded its size and circulation.

Garrison delighted in responding to his enemies publicly. In 1835 he derided the popular Unitarian minister William Ellery Channing for his lukewarm antislavery stand; in 1850 he condemned Massachusetts senator Daniel Webster as "lick spittle" to the slave power. Not surprisingly, southerners responded furiously to *The Liberator;* simply possessing a copy of it would lead to arrest in some southern states. Garrison relished the hostility, regularly publishing editorials branding him a fanatic. This fury intensified when, eight months after the paper's debut, the Virginia slave Nat Turner led a bloody revolt that left more than fifty whites (including women and children) dead. Enraged legislators set a $5,000 price on Garrison's head, but the editor denied inciting Turner—*The Liberator* was not

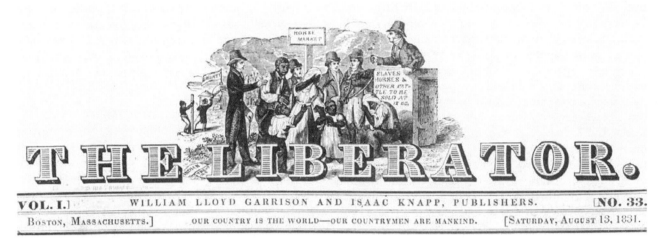

Masthead of the 13 August 1831 issue of *The Liberator.* THE LIBRARY OF CONGRESS

distributed in the South, and Turner had likely never heard of it. Still, Garrison had excerpted David Walker's incendiary pamphlet *Walker's Appeal, in Four Articles, Together with a Preamble, to the Coloured Citizens of the World* (1829), which urged slaves to violent resistance; moreover, although Garrison abhorred the violence of Turner's melee, his editorials equated the slaves' right to revolt with that of the American Revolution's patriots. Further, in addition to his southern enemies, Garrison denounced northern foes of abolition.

INFLUENCE ON LITERARY PRODUCTION

The Liberator provided a forum for writers in several genres. It regularly published political coverage, sentimental verse and fiction, antislavery sermons and speeches, travel literature, slave narratives, epistolary repartee, and debates on women's rights, temperance, and religion. Antislavery poems ran on the last page of every issue, featuring verses by William Cullen Bryant, Oliver Wendell Holmes, and most often John Greenleaf Whittier, whose poignant verses particularly evoked the suffering of slave families. Heartrending stanzas by Lydia Maria Child, Frances E. W. Harper, Frances Osgood, and Felicia Hemans also reflected Garrison's strategy of emotional appeals that specifically targeted a female audience.

Although British and European authors, including Hemans, Elizabeth Barrett Browning, Harriet Martineau, and Victor Hugo, appeared in *The Liberator,* its literary content derived primarily from American writers, including well-known figures such as Walt Whitman, Louisa May Alcott, James Russell Lowell, Henry David Thoreau, and Ralph Waldo Emerson as well as little-known abolitionists and former slaves such as John Rankin, Charles Lenox

Remond, William Cooper Nell, Theodore Weld, and Maria Stewart. Even the southerner Edgar Allan Poe's "The Raven" appeared in February 1845.

The epistolary genre comprised a large segment of every *Liberator*. Letters from fugitive slaves announced their arrival in Canada via the Underground Railroad; correspondence from anti-abolitionists (northern and southern) ranted against Garrison while that of abolitionists deliberated various political issues. In October 1841 *The Liberator* published a letter from Cinque, the hero of the *Amistad* slave mutiny, bidding farewell to his American supporters. Additionally, fervent letters from antislavery lecturers (referred to as "agents") shared their progress in spreading the gospel to the unenlightened, correspondence that also contributed to the popular genre of travel writing. While on lecture tours, Garrison sent missives relaying details of stage travel and scenery, companions met along the way, the quality of accommodations—and always, the reception of his mission. When he encountered hostility, a common occurrence, those responsible found themselves publicly rebuked: "The orthodox clergyman here is Samuel Lee, who pretends to be an abolitionist, but whose *support* of our cause is a thousand times more detrimental to it than the most violent *opposition*. . . . He is a conceited spiritual rabbi, on a Lilliputian scale" (3:251–252).

The Liberator fostered debate on a variety of politically charged topics. Controversies over women's rights, temperance, nonresistance, and religion were deliberated in its columns. When abolitionists split into two groups in the late 1830s, Garrison led those arguing for women's full participation. In antebellum America gender roles typically were structured according to the doctrine known as "separate spheres." While

printing the most scathing letters received over the controversy.

Joining Garrison for a time was another central abolitionist figure of the nineteenth century, Frederick Douglass (1818–1895). The two men met in 1841 and soon embarked on the lecture circuit together, the editor eagerly enlisting the former slave's fiery oratory in the abolitionist struggle. In 1845 *The Liberator's* printing office published the first of Douglass's three autobiographies, *Narrative of the Life of Frederick Douglass,* for which Garrison wrote a preface authenticating Douglass's story. Although at the time Douglass may or may not have desired the purported benefit of Garrison's words, this preface nevertheless reinscribed the black man's "need" for a white voice to authorize the slave's own text. For a variety of reasons, including Douglass's resentment of what he considered Garrison's paternalism, the two men became estranged by 1847. Thereafter Douglass appeared in *The Liberator* mainly as the recipient of Garrison's anger.

Despite this fallout, Douglass's *Narrative* tremendously enlarged the market for authentic stories of slave life. As first-person accounts of bondage and hairbreadth escape, slave narratives delivered a credibility that prevailed over Garrison's best editorials. Through the decades, *The Liberator* enthusiastically promoted the narratives of William Wells Brown (1849), Henry Bibb (1849), Henry Box Brown (1851), and Josiah Henson (1849), among others, helping to popularize the genre and to secure its spot in the literary marketplace. Although usually positive, *The Liberator's* reviews of antislavery literature evaluated works through a Garrisonian perspective. For example, when Garrison assessed the best-selling *Uncle Tom's Cabin* (1852), by his friend Harriet Beecher Stowe (1811–1896), he praised the author's "descriptive powers" as well as Tom's "religious" character. Yet the editor disparaged Tom's groveling submission, and he censured Stowe for promoting colonization at the novel's conclusion (*The Liberator,* 26 March 1852).

One of the most frequent female contributors to *The Liberator* was Lydia Maria Child (1802–1880). Christened "the first woman in the republic" by Garrison, Child had enjoyed a successful literary career, publishing juvenile fiction, romantic novels such as *Hobomok* (1824), and popular women's advice manuals, including *The Frugal Housewife* (1829) and *The Mother's Book* (1831). Her impressive career suffered, however, when she turned to political writing with *An Appeal in Favor of That Class of Americans Called Africans* (1833). This in-depth analysis of slavery echoed Garrison's call for both immediate emancipation and complete social integration of the races; the radical

---

> *The radical abolitionist William Lloyd Garrison did not apologize for the harshness of his antislavery rhetoric. The front page of* The Liberator's *first issue thundered the uncompromising, insistent stance for which he and his newspaper were known for thirty-five years. Southerners and northerners alike, he promised, would "tremble" when they read his paper.*
>
> ---
>
> I am aware, that many object to the severity of my language; but is there not cause for severity; I will be as harsh as truth, and as uncompromising as justice. On this subject I do not wish to think, or speak, or write, with moderation. No! no! Tell a man whose house is on fire, to give a moderate alarm; tell him to moderately rescue his wife from the hands of the ravisher; tell the mother to gradually extricate her babe from the fire into which it has fallen;—but urge me not to use moderation in a cause like the present. I am in earnest—I will not equivocate—I will not excuse—I will not retreat a single inch—and I will be heard.
>
> William Lloyd Garrison, "To the Public," *The Liberator,* 1 January 1831, p. 1.

men handled the political and social work of governance and commerce, women reigned as moral custodians, empowered through their domestic roles as wives and mothers but usually out of the public eye. Given Garrison's belief that abolitionism was above all a moral crusade, he naturally argued that women should enter the public fray—as lecturers, agitators, and voting delegates at conventions. Thus early on *The Liberator* championed the feminist cause alongside abolition.

In addition to regularly reporting on women's rights, *The Liberator* intensified the heated debate between the abolitionist Angelina Grimké (1805–1879) and the women's advice author Catharine Beecher (1800–1878). Daughters of a South Carolina slave owner, Grimké and her sister had moved north and adopted Quakerism; together they caused a sensation, addressing mixed audiences on the volatile topic of slavery. In 1836 Grimké published *An Appeal to the Christian Women of the South,* to which the anti-abolitionist Beecher responded with *Essay on Slavery and Abolitionism* (1837), a lengthy dispute of Grimké's claims that women in particular should join the abolitionists. For thirteen weeks, one letter at a time, *The Liberator* carried Grimké's *Letters to Catharine E. Beecher,* unleashing a furor that Garrison fed by

activist Thomas Wentworth Higginson credited it with converting him to abolitionism. Despite having a gentler tone than Garrison, Child angered many friends and publishers with her frank discussion of slavery and race relations. From this time on she continued to write fiction but primarily directed her talents to antislavery writing and editing, which were familiar presences in *The Liberator*. Garrison honored their long association by running Child's poem "Through the Red Sea into the Wilderness" on the front page of the paper's final issue.

Garrison also enjoyed close ties to the literary figures connected with the transcendentalist circle. The radical ministers Theodore Parker and Thomas Wentworth Higginson as well as the literati centered in Concord, Massachusetts—Ralph Waldo Emerson, Henry Thoreau, Amos Bronson Alcott—counted Garrison as a friend. Despite Emerson's discomfort with Garrison's denunciatory tone, by 1850 the sage of Concord had put aside his distrust of collective reform movements and embraced radical abolitionism. *The Liberator* regularly published Emerson's and Thoreau's antislavery speeches, sometimes on the front page, as with Emerson's 1844 address on West Indian emancipation.

In 1854, in the aftermath of the fugitive Anthony Burns's return to slavery, Henry David Thoreau (1817–1862) shared a lecture podium with Garrison at an antislavery rally. His remarks soon appeared in *The Liberator* with the title "Slavery in Massachusetts." This address revealed Thoreau's increasing identification with abolitionism; he denounced Massachusetts officials and confessed "thoughts" that were "murder to the state." Five years later, Garrison publicized Thoreau's militant address praising John Brown's violent raid on Harpers Ferry, a speech later expanded and published as "A Plea for Captain John Brown"; likewise, a few months later *The Liberator* published Thoreau's eulogy "The Last Days of John Brown." Although Garrison had called Harpers Ferry a "misguided, wild, and apparently insane" mission, he tempered his censure when it became apparent that Brown's martyrdom would work to the abolitionists' advantage. As civil war loomed, Garrison maintained his long-standing pacifism but also acknowledged that bloodshed in the struggle to end slavery now seemed inevitable. When war did break out, *The Liberator* covered troop movements and debated battle strategies; Garrison particularly enjoyed printing letters from black soldiers serving in the Union army's "colored" units. Finally, on 1 January 1863 *The Liberator* achieved its paramount objective: front-page headlines emblazoned the triumphant message "Three Million of Slaves Set Free! Glory Hallelujah!"

For more than three decades *The Liberator* delivered Garrison's aggressive abolitionist tirade. Its pages reflect the extent to which early-nineteenth-century writers successfully engaged with social and political reform while also catering to the market's taste for sentiment and satire. In addition, the newspaper's graphic portrayals of slavery and related political debates—delivered week after week for thirty-five years—helped to transform antebellum literary taste. Readers of *The Liberator* were more than prepared to usher in the era of realism that would dominate the literary marketplace after the Civil War.

See also Abolitionist Writing; *An Appeal in Favor of That Class of Americans Called Africans; The Confessions of Nat Turner;* Feminism; Harpers Ferry; Letters; Slave Narratives; Slavery; Transcendentalism; Underground Railroad; *Walker's Appeal*

BIBLIOGRAPHY

Primary Works

Garrison, William Lloyd. *The Letters of William Lloyd Garrison*. Edited by Walter M. Merrill and Louis Ruchames. 6 vols. Cambridge, Mass.: Belknap Press of Harvard University Press, 1971–1979.

Garrison, Wendell Phillips, and Francis Jackson Garrison. *William Lloyd Garrison 1805–1879: The Story of His Life Told by His Children.* 1885. 4 vols. New York: Negro Universities Press, 1969.

Moran, John Michael, Jr., ed. *Collected Poems of Franklin Benjamin Sanborn of Transcendental Concord Edited with Indices and a Checklist of Literary Contributions to the "Liberator" by Sanborn, Emerson, Thoreau, Bryant, Whittier, Lowell, Longfellow, and Others.* Hartford, Conn.: Transcendental Books, 1964.

Nelson, Truman, ed. *Documents of Upheaval: Selections from William Lloyd Garrison's the "Liberator," 1831–1865.* New York: Hill and Wang, 1966.

Secondary Works

Bacon, Jacqueline. "The *Liberator's* 'Ladies' Department,' 1832–37: Freedom or Fetters?" In *Sexual Rhetoric: Media Perspectives on Sexuality, Gender, and Identity,* edited by Meta G. Carstarphen and Susan C. Zavoina, pp. 3–19. Westport, Conn.: Greenwood Press, 1999.

Blassingame, John, and Mae G. Henderson, eds. *Antislavery Newspapers and Periodicals.* 5 vols. Boston: G. K. Hall, 1980–1984.

Cain, William E., ed. *William Lloyd Garrison and the Fight against Slavery: Selections from the "Liberator."* Boston: Bedford Books, 1995.

Mayer, Henry. *All on Fire: William Lloyd Garrison and the Abolition of Slavery.* New York: St. Martin's Press, 1998.

Rohrbach, Augusta. "'Truth Stronger and Stranger than Fiction': Reexamining William Lloyd Garrison's

Liberator." *American Literature* 73 (December 2001): 727–755.

Stewart, James Brewer. *William Lloyd Garrison and the Challenge of Emancipation.* Arlington Heights, Ill.: Harlan Davidson, 1992.

Thomas, John L. *The Liberator: William Lloyd Garrison.* Boston: Little, Brown, 1963.

Sandra Harbert Petrulionis

THE LIFE AND ADVENTURES OF JOAQUÍN MURIETA

The title page to John Rollin Ridge's 1854 novel *The Life and Adventures of Joaquín Murieta, the Celebrated California Bandit* introduces two stories. The novel's title indicates the novel's focus, Ridge's telling of Joaquín Murieta's (c. 1829–1850) exploits as a legendary bandit in southern California. The second story, evoked in the byline, "by Yellow Bird," concerns Ridge's Cherokee heritage. A mixed-blood Cherokee, Ridge (1827–1867) registers as author his tribal name instead of his anglicized name. The byline draws attention to Ridge's Cherokee ancestry, a turbulent history that includes the Cherokee Nation's removal from Georgia and the deaths of over eight thousand people on the forced march west that came to be known as the Trail of Tears. At first glance, the stories of Murieta and Ridge appear unrelated: Murieta's crime stories, set during California's booming gold rush, seem a long way from Ridge's Cherokee past. Yet when read side by side, compelling parallels evolve that not only link the two stories but also help explain Ridge's somewhat sympathetic depiction of Murieta's criminal life.

Ridge's Murieta is inescapably transformed by violence. Murieta, a dignified citizen, becomes corrupt because he is a victim of racially motivated violence, an aggression stemming from cultural conditions shaping a newly annexed California. Consequently, Ridge's narrative regards Murieta's crimes not as innate but as a response to violence, a reaction motivated by revenge. Ridge himself understood this vengeance. The son of Cherokee leaders, Ridge watched family elders suffer through events akin to the violent assaults he describes as being committed against Murieta. Themes of violence and vengeance shape both stories, and the similarities have likewise influenced much of the scholarship examining the first Native American–authored novel. Scholars have concentrated largely on two threads: much scholarship reads *The Life and Adventures of Joaquín Murieta,* first, as a reflection of the author's own violent Cherokee past and, second, as a story exploring how the violent conditions surrounding the California gold rush shaped Murieta's life for the worse and simultaneously gave birth to an exclusive national identity.

1835–1849: CHEROKEE VIOLENCE

In 1835 Ridge's grandfather (Major Ridge), father (John Ridge), and cousin (Elias Boudinot) signed the Treaty of New Echota on behalf of the Cherokee Nation. The treaty authorized the removal of the Cherokee people from Georgia in exchange for western lands, $4.5 million, and funds for establishing schools within the nation. After signing the treaty, Ridge's grandfather is alleged to have said, "I have signed my death warrant." Ridge's relatives penned and signed the treaty because they considered removal inevitable: the discovery of gold only increased the already high value of Cherokee farmlands in Georgia, and President Andrew Jackson had not only outlined his detailed plan for Indian removal but also rejected Supreme Court decisions protecting Cherokee homes and rights in Georgia. As expected, many Cherokee, led by their chief John Ross, condemned the treaty and censured the Ridge family for their endorsement. The Ridges' relationship with the Cherokee grew further estranged when they, with the help of slaves, moved west peacefully, while sixteen thousand Cherokee—including the Ross family—suffered on the 1838 Trail of Tears.

Once in Oklahoma, the Ross faction designed plans for increasing their power within the nation, and key was eliminating the men responsible for signing the treaty. After proclaiming the treaty signers guilty of treason, on 22 June 1839, in three coordinated incidents, men murdered Ridge's grandfather, father, and cousin. While riding to Arkansas, Major Ridge was captured and shot to death; Boudinot died when attackers repeatedly hit him in the head with an ax and stabbed him with a knife. Ridge's father was snatched from his home, stabbed twenty-nine times, slashed in the jugular vein, thrown into the air, and then trampled by his assailants—all in front of his twelve-year-old son John, who eventually left Oklahoma because of the hostilities.

In 1847 John Ridge returned to Cherokee territory in Arkansas. Having gained his education at a Massachusetts boarding school and started a family, Ridge concentrated on Cherokee affairs. As a journalist, he wrote anti-Ross literature, but any desire he might have had to revenge his father's violent death was expressed only in muted prose. Then in an 1849 argument concerning a horse that had been stolen from him, Ridge killed David Kell, a pro-Ross neighbor Ridge believed partly responsible for the assassinations. James Parins, a Ridge scholar, posits the horse stealing was part of a plan designed by the Ross faction to provoke Ridge into fighting and to create a pretext for killing him. Again hostilities intensified, and Ridge left in search of safety.

1849–1854: VIOLENCE IN CALIFORNIA'S GOLD RUSH

On 24 January 1848 James Marshall discovered gold on the American River in California. At first a distinctly California enterprise, gold mining soon motivated people from all over the world: Chinese, Native Americans, African Americans, Irish, French, Germans, and Mexicans all migrated to California with hopes of prospering financially. Instead of riches, most settlers found gold mining on the California frontier harsh and beset with gambling, drinking, vigilantism, and violence. Widespread resentment of immigrants compounded the problem of lawlessness further, and the Foreign Miners' Tax Law ultimately identified immigrant settlers as outsiders and limited their mining rights. The law, Joseph Henry Jackson notes in his introduction to the 1955 edition of *The Life and Adventures of Joaquín Murieta*, could not have developed a better method for promoting both intolerance and vice.

Among the thousands of people moving to California in 1849 was Ridge, who went to seek his fortune and escape violence in the Cherokee Nation. Ironically, instead of riches, he found a culture as violent as the one he left. After failing as a miner, Ridge turned to writing poetry and reporting news from gold rush towns for local newspapers. In those settlements he observed California's culture of corruption and obsession with differentiating "Americans" from "foreigners." He witnessed how laws defined Native Americans as inferior and encouraged derogatory epithets like "digger." Ridge perceived how immigrants, especially Mexicans, were similarly identified as subordinate and not "American." Moreover, he comprehended how laws marking immigrants as second class gave rise to a vigilante violence that accentuated difference. In a culture of violence that targeted immigrant miners, Ridge also heard stories of a Mexican bandit—an ostensibly ubiquitous yet anonymous figure known only as "Joaquín"—who became notorious for random crimes that terrorized mining communities.

In 1852 and 1853 the frequency of newspaper reports detailing accounts of robbery and horse stealing increased. Stories of gangs appeared, and legends arose about the omnipresent "Joaquín," reputedly able to be in two places at once. Five men sharing the name "Joaquín" were all considered as possible suspects in the crimes. During the spring of 1853 the California legislature responded to the panic of its constituents by commissioning a company of Mexican-American War veterans under the Texan captain Harry Love to search for the shadowy perpetrator. Historians have documented extensively the soldiers' search, which ended in the death of a criminal named Joaquín, but they are less certain about that suspect's actual identity. Love maintained that his company had executed the "real" Joaquín, whom they had determined to be the rogue Joaquín Murieta. To substantiate his claim, Love displayed in a bottle the head of the captured man, along with the hand of a man who was infamous as Joaquín's principal collaborator, known as Three-Fingered Jack; they also made available documents asserting the head belonged to Murieta, a case that did little to assuage the public's skepticism that the soldiers' undertaking had been successful. While published arguments questioned both Love's credibility and the head's identity as the "true" Joaquín, tales of Murieta's criminal life gained in popularity, inspiring Ridge to compose the first California novel.

RIDGE'S MURIETA: A VIOLENT BUT NOBLE HERO

Ridge begins his narrative with a qualification: the story's extreme violence is neither superfluous nor meant to please debased readers. Instead, the violence is historically significant, essential to understanding the crucial role a burgeoning California played in transforming Murieta. Thus Ridge's title character is not the feared criminal Californians knew but rather a likable, handsome, and honest eighteen year old. Having found success as gold miner, Murieta achieved fairly the dream of all miners: in addition to gold, Murieta enjoys civic respect, a lovely companion named Rosita, and a home country he loves—America. He credits America for offering such opportunity and feels deep affection for people known as "Americans." Such affection went unreciprocated, for Murieta's success stirred feelings of resentment from whites "who bore the name Americans but failed to support the honor and dignity of that title" and who held "a class of contempt for any and all Mexicans" (p. 9).

Prejudice quickly gives way to violence in the text as Murieta falls victim to brutalities resembling those that Ridge experienced in the Cherokee Nation. Vigilantes first bind Murieta and force him to watch men assault Rosita. Next, after leaving mining to farm, Murieta is again attacked by vigilantes, and he is forced to move. Finally, after a third relocation, Murieta is accused of stealing a horse. Refusing to hear Murieta's explanation for how his half brother acquired the horse, a mob of Americans whips Murieta and then lynches his relative. Thrice scarred from violence

Poster advertising the exhibition of the head of Joaquín Murieta. From *The Life and Adventures of Joaquín Murieta,* by (Yellow Bird) John Rollin Ridge. COURTESY OF UNIVERSITY OF OKLAHOMA PRESS, NORMAN

triggered by discrimination, Murieta pledges revenge and turns to violence as a sufferer "shut . . . away forever from his peace of mind and purity of heart" (p. 14).

Whenever Murieta fulfills his vow of revenge against all Americans, Ridge reminds readers that Murieta's violence is not inborn. He further emphasizes this point by contrasting Murieta with his favored accomplice, Three-Fingered Jack. Murieta commits violence for vengeance or self-defense. When Murieta slashes the throat of a local sheriff, he murders because the sheriff is near discovering him. The bloodthirsty monster Three-Fingered Jack, on the other hand, savors violence. For instance, as General Bean chases

Murieta, Jack surprises and kills the general with his knife. Seeing the general's corpse only energizes Jack more; he kicks his boot many times into the corpse's face and, when finished kicking, shoots two bullets into the mangled head. About killing Chinese, Jack boasts: "I can't help it; but, somehow or other, I love to smell the blood of a Chinaman. Besides, it's such easy work to kill them. It's a kind of luxury to cut their throats" (p. 64). Fortunate are those people, Ridge tells readers, who confront Murieta instead of Jack.

Though Murieta commits crimes—none as excessively violent as Jack's—Ridge distinguishes Murieta from other bandits by pointing out Murieta's decency.

Ridge notes, "Murieta in his worst days had yet a remnant of the noble spirit which had been his original nature" (p. 65). Consequently, he saves a poor ferryman from Jack, rescues a young woman kidnapped by a member of his gang, and spares the life of a young man from Arkansas who has impressed him with his bravery. He is described by Ridge as a "hero" and "angel"—terms not typically used to describe feared criminals. In Murieta, Ridge saw parallels that helped explain his own need for vengeance, and scholars have spent much time examining these similarities.

Researchers have also studied how Ridge's Murieta account connects to the historical issue of nation building following the Mexican-American War (1846–1848). Of specific interest is Murieta's plan to obtain, through robbery, an abundance of resources—particularly money, horses, and weapons—to clear southern California of settlers. Only then, Murieta deems, will he finish his mission and be able to retire securely in the Sonoran mountains: "When I do this, I shall wind up my career. My brothers, we will then be revenged for our wrongs, and some little, too, for the wrongs of our poor, bleeding country. We will divide our substance and spend the rest of our days in peace" (p. 75). Through violence, Murieta gains both revenge and peace as he builds a "nation" out of his land and people. Again, the parallels linking Ridge's experiences to Murieta's loss of nation and desire for peace are evident.

To read Ridge's book as the simple story of a bandit's crimes would be to misread it. As he concludes the book, Ridge highlights the lesson of Murieta's story: "There is nothing so dangerous in its consequences as *injustice to individuals* . . . that a wrong done to one man is a wrong to society and the world" (p. 158). Ridge, a victim of many wrongs, appreciated his source material. While similar to Murieta in many ways, Ridge, instead of resorting to mass violence like the lead character, took pen to paper to compose his vengeance, a commentary on violence that extends to his Cherokee home and stands as the first Native American–authored novel.

See also California Gold Rush; Indian Wars and Dispossessions; Native American Literature; Trail of Tears

BIBLIOGRAPHY

Primary Work

Ridge, John Rollin. *The Life and Adventures of Joaquín Murieta, the Celebrated California Bandit.* 1854. Reprinted as *The Life and Adventures of Joaquín Murieta,* with an introduction by Joseph Henry Jackson. Norman: University of Oklahoma Press, 1955.

Secondary Works

Christensen, Peter G. "Minority Interaction in John Rollin Ridge's *The Life and Adventures of Joaquín Murieta, the Celebrated California Bandit.*" *MELUS* 17, no. 2 (1991–1992): 61–72.

Johnson, Susan Lee. *Roaring Camp: The Social World of the California Gold Rush.* New York: Norton, 2000.

Lowe, John. "'I am Joaquín': Space and Freedom in Yellow Bird's *The Life and Adventures of Joaquín Murieta, the Celebrated California Bandit.*" In *Early Native American Writing: New Critical Essays,* edited by Helen Jaskoski, pp. 104–121. Cambridge, U.K.: Cambridge University Press, 1996.

Parins, James W. *John Rollin Ridge: His Life and Works.* Lincoln: University of Nebraska Press, 2004.

Rowe, John Carlos. "Highway Robbery: 'Indian Removal,' the Mexican-American War, and American Identity in *The Life and Adventures of Joaquín Murieta.*" *Novel* 31, no. 2 (1998): 149–173.

In a paragraph appearing at the end of the novel, Ridge eulogizes Murieta. Rather than highlighting the protagonist's crimes, he characterizes Murieta as an "extraordinary" man with heroic qualities. His tone reveals the respect Ridge held for Murieta, a respect grounded in his understanding of the effects of violence. The paragraph also reveals the story as more than a crime novel; Ridge's narrative is meant to offer a lesson essential to understanding the history of California specifically and the nature of violence more generally.

The story is told. Briefly and without ornament, the life and character of Joaquín Murieta have been sketched. His career was short, for he died in the twenty-second year; but, in the few years which were allowed him, he displayed qualities of mind and heart which marked him as an extraordinary man, and leaving his name impressed upon the early history of this State. He also leaves behind him the important lesson that there is nothing so dangerous in its consequences as *injustice to individuals*—whether it arise from prejudice of color or from any other source; that a wrong done to one man is a wrong to society and to the world.

Ridge, *The Life and Adventures of Joaquín Murieta*, p. 158.

Streeby, Shelley. *American Sensations: Class, Empire, and the Production of Popular Culture.* Berkeley: University of California Press, 2002.

Varley, James. *The Legend of Joaquín Murieta: California's Gold Rush Bandit.* Twin Falls, Idaho: Big Lost River Press, 1995.

Walker, Cheryl. *Indian Nation: Native American Literature and Nineteenth-Century Nationalisms.* Durham, N.C.: Duke University Press, 1997.

Wilkins, Thurman. *Cherokee Tragedy: The Ridge Family and the Decimation of a People.* 2nd ed., rev. Norman: University of Oklahoma Press, 1986.

Ronald L. Pitcock

LIFE IN THE IRON MILLS

Published anonymously in the well-respected *Atlantic Monthly* under the editorship of James T. Fields in 1861 at the outbreak of the Civil War, *Life in the Iron Mills,* by Rebecca Harding Davis (1831–1910), ushered in American literary realism and at the same time launched a pathbreaking exposé of the effects of capitalism and industrialization, including the physical, spiritual, and intellectual starvation of immigrant wage earners. In fact, the novel is recognized as being the first literary work in America to focus on the relationships among industrial work, poverty, and the exploitation of immigrants within a capitalistic economy. It also contains elements of naturalism likened to that of later works by the French writer Émile Zola and the American writer Frank Norris.

Life in the Iron Mills departs from the popular domestic women's fiction of the 1850s, known as the "feminine fifties" and dominated by authors like Harriet Beecher Stowe, Catharine Sedgwick, Fanny Fern, E. D. E. N. Southworth, and Mary Jane Holmes, among others. Meant for middle- and upper-class readers, domestic fiction typically focused on virtuous heroines ("true women") who, despite trials and tribulations or competition from vain, shallow, fashionable coquettes out to snare wealthy husbands, find love and marriage and create happy homes as ideal wives and mothers. Some domestic novels, however, like Catharine Sedgwick's *Married or Single?* (1857), introduced feminist themes by questioning whether marriage and motherhood should be the goal of all women. Instead, greatly inspired by the moral darkness and dilemmas of Nathaniel Hawthorne's tales, Davis chose to focus on the commonplace and common folk: the working class, slaves, freed slaves, and women. Indeed, Davis's realistic depiction of the gritty, hellish mills and the impoverished workers' lives is far removed from the material advantages of the upper classes often portrayed in domestic fiction. She also uses the vernacular and dialect skillfully to depict realistically her uneducated immigrant characters and to emphasize their lower-class status. Davis counteracts positive images of healthy, wholesome mill girls and mills as ideal places of work. *Life in the Iron Mills* challenges the optimism of transcendentalism by showing how industrialism fueled by greedy capitalists destroys the natural environment and the human spirit.

After *Life in the Iron Mills* was first published in the *Atlantic Monthly,* both Emily Dickinson and Nathaniel Hawthorne praised the work. Elizabeth Stuart Phelps was also greatly influenced by Davis's *Life in the Iron Mills* and in 1868 published in the *Atlantic Monthly* "The Tenth of January," based on the 1860 fire at the Pemberton Mills in Lawrence, Massachusetts.

DAVIS'S LIFE AND CAREER

Davis was born Rebecca Blaine Harding in Washington, Pennsylvania, to genteel parents, Rachel Leet Wilson and Englishman Richard Harding, who had immigrated to America. Her family lived briefly in Big Springs, Alabama, before moving in 1837 to Wheeling, Virginia (now West Virginia), on the Ohio River. Its iron mills and immigrant populations inspired the setting of *Life in the Iron Mills.* Rebecca Harding was educated at Washington Female Seminary in Washington, Pennsylvania, where she studied religion, heard the speeches of abolitionists (among them Horace Greeley), and graduated valedictorian in 1848, the same year the American feminists Elizabeth Cady Stanton, Susan B. Anthony, Lucretia Mott, and other agitators met at Seneca Falls. Thus, during her adolescent years, religious, abolitionist, and feminist reform was prominent.

Harding began her career as a writer for the *Wheeling Intelligencer,* in which she published reviews, editorials, stories, and poems. In December 1860 she submitted her manuscript of *Life in the Iron Mills* to the *Atlantic Monthly* and received acceptance of it in January. In 1863, at the age of thirty-one, Rebecca Harding married the abolitionist L. Clarke Davis, and they had three children, Richard Harding, Charles Belmont, and Nora. Like other prominent female authors, including Harriet Beecher Stowe and Elizabeth Oakes Smith, Davis learned how to combine the roles of wife, mother, and author. Her body of work—much of it treating issues of race, class, and gender—comprises more than five hundred publications, including short stories; satirical, realistic, and

In "The Paradise of Bachelors and the Tartarus of Maids" (1855), to which Life in the Iron Mills is often compared, Herman Melville offers a critique of industrial America through his allegorical depiction of a paper mill, where long hours of monotonous, grueling labor render single young women sickly and old and therefore unsuitable for the traditional roles of marriage and motherhood.

In one corner stood some huge frame of ponderous iron, with a vertical thing like a piston periodically rising and falling upon a heavy wooden block. Before it—its tame minister—stood a tall girl, feeding the iron animal with half-quires of rose-hued note paper. . . .

Seated before a long apparatus, strung with long, slender strings like any harp, another girl was feeding it with foolscap sheets, which, so soon as they curiously traveled from her on the cords, were withdrawn at the opposite end of the machine by a second girl. They came to the first girl blank; they went to the second girl ruled.

I looked upon the first girl's brow, and saw it was young and fair; I looked upon the second girl's brow, and saw it was ruled and wrinkled. Then . . . the two—for some small variety to the monotony—changed places; and where had stood the young, fair brow, now stood the ruled and wrinkled one. . . .

Not a syllable was breathed. Nothing was heard but the low, steady, overruling hum of the iron animals. The human voice was banished from the spot. Machinery—that vaunted slave of humanity—here stood menially served by human beings, who served mutely and cringingly as the slave serves the Sultan. The girls did not so much seem accessory wheels to the general machinery as mere cogs to the wheels.

Herman Melville, "The Paradise of Bachelors and the Tartarus of Maids," in *The Norton Anthology of American Literature 1820–1865*, 6th ed., vol. B, edited by Nina Baym (New York: Norton, 2003), p. 2366.

social protest novels; essays; juvenile fiction; and local color sketches. In 1904 Houghton, Mifflin and Company published *Bits of Gossip*, Davis's memoirs and last book. But despite a prolific writing career, her contributions to American literature were overshadowed by the achievements of her husband, who edited the *Philadelphia Inquirer* and *Public Ledger*, and of her son, Richard Harding Davis, who was lauded as a journalist and short story writer, even though his mother's writing abilities surpassed his. As a result, *Life in the Iron Mills* received little scholarly attention before it was resurrected in 1972 by Tillie Olson and published by the Feminist Press.

HISTORICAL AND LITERARY CONTEXTS

The story of the Wolfes that the narrator of *Life in the Iron Mills* tells takes place in the 1830s, a time when the Industrial Revolution was well underway. Until the 1840s well-to-do entrepreneurs established new mills and factories through their own finances because banks usually did not invest in industry or make loans to manufacturers. Industry thrived until the panic of 1837, originating in Britain, affected investments in the United States, resulting in the bankruptcies of both British and American manufacturers and extensive unemployment. The American economy fell into a depression from which it did not emerge until 1843. By the 1850s iron manufacturing was doing especially well, and by 1860 it was the nation's leading industry. Cotton production was another major industry. Investors profited significantly at the expense of workers.

Industry depended greatly on immigrant laborers. Approximately four million Irish, German, and British immigrants moved to the United States between 1820 and 1860. Most of them were unskilled peasants, laborers, and farmers who found employment in factories, on construction sites, at warehouses and docks, and in private homes. As depicted in *Life in the Iron Mills*, the living conditions for many immigrants were poor, indeed not much better than what they had experienced in Europe. Lacking enough money to buy food, many suffered from malnutrition and from diseases like cholera, smallpox, and consumption (tuberculosis), with which the main character, Hugh Wolfe, is afflicted.

As Davis shows, the Industrial Revolution also brought with it class distinctions clearly exhibited by the material wealth of capitalists and industrialists who possessed the means to build lavish homes with elaborate architecture. In contrast, factory workers and other unskilled laborers often lived in crowded boardinghouses and small apartments. Because they lived in such deplorable and disorderly conditions, held such lower-class status, and faced the stress and uncertainty of work, many wage earners indulged in alcohol consumption. Davis effectively captures these problems in *Life in the Iron Mills*.

In the decades prior to the 1861 publication of *Life*, several reform movements were established, and they were still flourishing when Davis wrote her story. Beginning in the 1830s, the Quakers Angelina Grimké and Sarah Grimké agitated for both women's rights and antislavery. During the 1840s and 1850s, educational reform provided opportunities for women to be educated as teachers. In the 1840s the woman's rights movement gained prominence. Members of the business elite and middle class, many with Congregationalist or Presbyterian connections, formed benevolent and moral reform societies in an attempt to establish social order and discipline in the lives of common farmers, laborers, and factory workers. In her story, Davis raises the possibility of religious reform and benevolence to improve the lives of the working class.

SYNOPSIS AND MAJOR THEMES

Treated as either a long short story or a novella in the genre of local regionalism, *Life in the Iron Mills* begins with an epigraph composed of lines from Alfred, Lord Tennyson's popular poem "In Memoriam A. H. H." (1850), clearly signaling the bleakness of the story:

> Is this the end?
> O Life, as futile, then as frail!
> What hope of answer or redress?

The narrator, whose gender is never clearly identified although many scholars assume the narrative voice is female, draws in the reader with the question, "A cloudy day: do you know what that is in a town of iron-works?" (p. 11). From a window of her residence she describes the sights, sounds, and smells of the polluted industrial atmosphere of the setting based on Davis's hometown of Wheeling, Virginia: "drunken Irishmen . . . puffing Lynchburg tobacco in their pipes" (p. 11); smoke rolling "sullenly in slow folds from the great chimneys of the iron-foundries, and [settling] down in black, slimy pools on the muddy streets" (p. 11). In a passage reminiscent of Henry David Thoreau's observation of masses of Concord men leading lives of quiet desperation in *Walden* (1854), the narrator observes

> masses of men, with dull, besotted faces bent to the ground, sharpened here and there by pain or cunning; skin and muscle and flesh begrimed with smoke and ashes; stooping all night over boiling caldrons of metal, laired by day in dens of drunkenness and infamy; breathing from infancy to death air saturated with fog and grease and soot, vileness for soul and body. (P. 12)

This stifling setting and the social ills associated with it clearly establish the movement away from an agrarian economy and idyllic lifestyle often exalted in Romantic literature toward an increasingly industrial-based economy and the deadening lifestyle it inflicts upon its workers. The narrator also notes in her room a dirty caged canary, a reminder of the use of caged birds in mines to alert miners to danger—if the birds died, the air was toxic—and signifying the caged existence of mill workers whose lives can also be sniffed out by poisonous industrial toxins.

After establishing the slimy, stagnant setting absent of "green fields and sunshine" (p. 12) and devoid of beauty, the narrator invites the reader—whom she labels an amateur psychologist and an "Egoist, or Pantheist, or Arminian" (p. 14), thereby suggesting self-aggrandizement, and whom she views as being a member of a higher social class—to hear the story of Hugh Wolfe. The narrator now inhabits the house where Hugh and his family lived thirty years ago. She predicts hope for the future and suggests the possibility of "a secret, underlying sympathy between that story and this day" (p. 14).

Hugh Wolfe, along with his father, a Welsh immigrant, and cousin Deborah, live in two cellar rooms of the house, rented to six families. Hugh and his father are puddlers, working for low earnings at Kirby & John's mill making iron for the railroad, while Deborah works as a picker in a cotton mill for a lower wage. The story centers on Hugh and Deborah and their impoverished existence, which represents the lives of all downtrodden mill workers. Concealing her unrequited love for Hugh, Deb, "almost a hunchback" (p. 17), delivers to him every night a supper of bread, salt pork, and ale. Her most basic needs not being met, Deb's deformed body hungers for food, but more importantly, her soul starves for love and spiritual sustenance. Not physically beautiful as are most heroines of popular domestic fiction and feeling unworthy to attract a suitor, Deb believes that Hugh abhors her appearance and that he yearns for beauty and purity. She is convinced of his attraction to the much more appealing Little Janey, a young Irish girl who lives with the Wolfes while her father is in jail.

At Kirby & John's mill, the monstrous furnaces that Hugh tends are like the pits of hell or Dante's Inferno. The work has caused him to lose his manly strength and vigor and to become feminized: "his muscles were thin, his nerves weak, his face (a meek, woman's face) haggard, yellow with consumption" (p. 24). Many a nineteenth-century heroine, including Edgar Allan Poe's Ligeia, succumbed to this disease. Considering Hugh a girl-man, the other mill workers have named him Molly Wolfe. Unlike the other workers, Hugh has received some education. What really sets him apart from the other mill workers, however, is his longing for beauty and his artistic talent. Out of the korl, the refuse from the ore, "a light, porous substance, of a delicate, waxen, flesh-colored tinge,"

Lackawanna Valley, **1855.** Painting by George Inness. Inness was hired by the Lackawanna Railroad Company to paint an idyllic scene of the railroad blending into the natural landscape, perhaps to assuage those who feared that industrial technology would corrupt the landscape and undermine hope associated with the American pastoral ideal. *Life in the Iron Mills,* on the other hand, directly contradicts the notion that technology and nature can coexist harmoniously. THE GRANGER COLLECTION, NEW YORK

Hugh sculpts figures—"hideous, fantastic enough, but sometimes strangely beautiful" (p. 24). Thus Hugh serves as an artist figure whose art could allow him a means of emotional, intellectual, and economic escape if he can recognize and develop his talent and create in an environment conducive to creativity.

Several visitors arrive at the mill and, noticing a korl statue of Hugh's in the shape of a woman, discuss the plight and exploitation of the immigrant workers. The visitors include the overseer, Clark; the son of the mill owner Kirby; Dr. May, one of the town's physicians; a reporter writing a review of leading manufacturers; and Mitchell, one of Kirby's brothers-in-law, who, not being familiar with the city, is "spending a couple of months in the borders of a Slave State, to study the institutions of the South" (p. 29).

Class difference creates a notable division between the impoverished, powerless workers and the powerful, well-to-do businesspeople and professionals. Young Kirby admits that his father coerces his mill workers to vote for certain political candidates, indicating that the immigrants are exploited not only as laborers but also as voting citizens. Wolfe notices the well-bred manners, dress, and speech of the men, especially Mitchell. His observations are described in words suggestive of the artist. As Mitchell "knocked the ashes from his cigar, Wolfe caught with a quick pleasure the contour of the white hand, the blood-glow of a red ring he wore. His voice, too, and that of Kirby's, touched him like music,—low, even, with chording cadences" (p. 29). "More and more like a dumb, hopeless animal," Wolfe listens to Kirby, May, and Mitchell and observes their refinement, compared to his "filthy body, his more stained soul" (p. 30). He realizes the huge gulf that lies between them.

Mitchell suddenly starts at the sight of Wolfe's korl statue, "a woman, white, of giant proportions, crouching on the ground, her arms flung out in some wild gesture of warning" (p. 31), a self-portrait of its creator whose manhood and art are called into question.

Recognizing the statue as a working woman, Dr. May assumes she desires food, but correcting him, Wolfe says she hungers not for meat but for something to make her live. Mitchell asserts that the korl woman asks questions of God, indicating spiritual deprivation and crisis. When May suggests that Kirby should nurture Wolfe's talent, Kirby refuses, claiming that the Lord will take care of the workers and that in America opportunities to climb the social ladder are open to all. Lacking any moral conscience, Kirby is not concerned with any social problems—"slavery, caste, white or black" (p. 35). Mitchell and May debate whether the "degraded souls" (p. 39) of the mill workers can be reformed and redeemed. After the men discuss whether money is the answer to improving the lives of the working-class poor, Kirby throws Deborah some money. Doing good for the community is not a priority for these men, suggesting that benevolent reform is waning.

Believing money to be the answer to their problems, Deb gives Hugh money she stole out of Mitchell's pocket. Tempted to keep the stolen money, Hugh attends a church meant for the upper classes and hears a Christian reformer's sermon. Davis is suggesting that perhaps Christian salvation is the answer to the social ills of the common workers, but the preacher, having used exalted language meant for cultured and well-educated church members, fails to reach Hugh, who is later arrested and sentenced to nineteen years in prison for grand larceny. Deb is sentenced to three years as his accomplice.

Shackled at the ankles because of two attempted escapes, Hugh still tries to flee, but he is weak and bleeding at the lungs from consumption. From his cell, Hugh watches people—whites and blacks—shopping on market day and enjoying the freedom to walk the streets. He recognizes that even a dog or slave or servant woman has more freedom. Believing he will never be free and in his caged state unable to connect spiritually with anyone on the outside, not even the lamplighter Joe, Hugh slashes his wrists ironically with "a dull bit of tin, not fit to cut korl with" (p. 57). At the end he lies dying with arms extended, suggesting a Christlike stance and his role as a martyr for the working class, his death allowing for Deb's redemption and rebirth.

But in his death, not all have forsaken Hugh. A Quaker woman acting as a Good Samaritan arrives to retrieve Hugh's body for burial in the hills where she lives. She invites Deb to come live there with her. Years later, as the narrator tells the reader, Deb has found Christ's love and a place among the Quakers, a community of Friends who truly and actively practice Christian reform and agitate for human rights for all. Both Deb and Hugh are freed from the confining and corrupt urban and industrial environment.

Kept hidden behind a curtain, Hugh's korl woman statue remains, now in the possession of the narrator. Her arm reaches out beseechingly and her pale lips appear to question, "Is this the end?" (p. 64). Perhaps this question is answered when the narrator notices a cool gray light pointing to the Far East, the East serving as a metaphor for Christ, where "God has set the promise of the Dawn" (p. 65). The narrator mentions another art object in her room, "a little broken figure of an angel pointing upward from the mantel-shelf; but even its wings are covered with smoke, clotted and black" (p. 12). Thus, while the angel has not triumphed over despair, perhaps the korl woman, symbolic of working-class souls, will be awarded salvation. The korl woman's "wild gesture of warning" (p. 31) may also prophesy a possible revolution by the working classes, as indicated by Hugh's statement that "the money was his by rights, and that all the world had gone wrong" (p. 51).

CRITICAL INTERPRETATION AND DEBATE

Primary areas of scholarly debate concern the role and identity of the narrator and the meaning of the ending of *Life in the Iron Mills*. Most scholars assume the narrator is female because of support for the cause of benevolence. In opposition to this assumption, another scholar argues that nineteenth-century readers probably believed the narrator to be male and that Mitchell is the narrator. Critics have also noted the narrator's deliberately antagonistic stance toward the story's audience, the function of which is to both repel readers and draw them in.

The principle controversy surrounds the purpose and meaning of the ending. Does Davis offer a solution for alleviating the capitalistic exploitation and oppression of immigrant industrial laborers, whose condition, Davis may be suggesting, is worse than that of chattel slaves? If so, what is the solution? Some critics interpret the ending as instilling hope and argue that it probably satisfied James T. Fields, the editor of the *Atlantic Monthly,* and its readers, who would have supported Christian benevolence and charity. Furthermore, a Quaker woman as the Good Samaritan motivates her readers to lobby for change on behalf of the oppressed and exploited working class. Since Quakerism sanctions social causes like abolitionism and prison reform, the unnamed Quaker woman is a logical role model for Davis's readers to emulate. But one privileged person alone cannot agitate for reform. Individuals of the upper classes must unite and actively practice a Christian ethic to initiate reform. Passive Christianity is not the answer to the problem of America's working-class poor, and as suggested by the broken wings of the angel figure, which preclude flight, the ending also dismisses transcendence as the solution for escaping oppression and poverty. Opposing more optimistic interpretations, other critics conclude that the narrator fails to answer the question posed by the korl woman statue because, like the "true woman" of sentimental fiction, she is confined by her domestic space, her gender, and her middle-class status.

While *Life in the Iron Mills* did not have the same degree of impact for inciting reform as Stowe's anti-slavery novel *Uncle Tom's Cabin* (1852), it nonetheless alerted readers to the devastating effects of industrialization on working-class immigrants and on the environment. It also debunked the myth of the American Dream, that opportunity for success awaits all. Most importantly, it introduced American literary realism and at the same time provided the first scathing critique of industrial capitalism by showing the price a nation pays for depending on technology in the name of progress.

See also Factories; Immigration; Labor; Manhood; Quakers; Reform; Technology

BIBLIOGRAPHY

Primary Works

Davis, Rebecca Harding. *Bits of Gossip.* Boston: Houghton Mifflin, 1904.

Davis, Rebecca Harding. *Life in the Iron Mills and Other Stories.* 1972. Rev. ed., edited by Tillie Olsen. Old Westbury, N.Y.: Feminist Press, 1985.

Secondary Works

Doriani, Beth Maclay. "New England Calvinism and the Problem of the Poor in Rebecca Harding Davis's *Life in the Iron Mills.*" In *Studies in Puritan American Spirituality: Literary Calvinism and Nineteenth-Century American Women Authors,* edited by Michael Schuldiner, pp. 179–224. Lewiston, N.Y.: Edwin Mellen Press, 1997.

Harris, Sharon M. *Rebecca Harding Davis and American Realism.* Philadelphia: University of Pennsylvania Press, 1991.

Harris, Sharon M. "Rebecca Harding Davis: From Romanticism to Realism." *American Literary Realism, 1870–1910* 21, no. 2 (1989): 4–20.

Henwood, Dawn. "Slaveries 'In the Borders': Rebecca Harding Davis's *Life in the Iron Mills* in Its Southern Context." *Mississippi Quarterly* 52 (1999): 567–592.

Hesford, Walter. "Literary Contexts of *Life in the Iron Mills.*" *American Literature* 49, no. 2 (1977): 70–85.

Hood, Richard. "Framing a *Life in the Iron Mills.*" *Studies in American Fiction* 23, no. 1 (1995): 73–84.

Hughes, Sheila Hassell. "Between Bodies of Knowledge There Is a Great Gulf Fixed: A Liberationist Reading of Class and Gender in *Life in the Iron Mills.*" *American Quarterly* 49, no. 1 (1997): 113–137.

Lang, Amy Schrager. "Class and Strategies of Sympathy." In *The Culture of Sentiment: Race, Gender, and Sentimentality in Nineteenth-Century America,* edited by Shirley Samuels, pp. 128–142. New York: Oxford University Press, 1992.

Lasseter, Janice Milner. "Hawthorne's Legacy to Rebecca Harding Davis." In *Hawthorne and Women: Engendering and Expanding the Hawthorne Tradition,* edited by John L. Idol Jr. and Melinda M. Ponder, pp. 168–178. Amherst: University of Massachusetts Press, 1999.

Morrison, Lucy. "The Search for the Artist in Man and Fulfillment in Life—Rebecca Harding Davis's *Life in the Iron Mills.*" *Studies in Short Fiction* 33 (1996): 245–253.

Rose, Jane Atteridge. *Rebecca Harding Davis.* New York: Twayne, 1993.

Seltzer, Mark. "The Still Life." *American Literary History* 3 (fall 1991): 455–486.

Shocket, Eric. "'Discovering Some New Race': Rebecca Harding Davis's *Life in the Iron Mills* and the Literary Emergence of Working-Class Whiteness." *PMLA* 115, no. 1 (2000): 46–59.

Shurr, William. "*Life in the Iron Mills:* A Nineteenth-Century Conversion Narrative." *American Transcendental Quarterly* 5 (1991): 245–257.

Jane E. Rose

LITERACY

Nineteenth-century Americans imagined themselves as a nation of readers. Federal census returns affirmed that by 1840 more than 90 percent of white adults could read and write, while reports of the skyrocketing volume of newspapers, books, and mailed letters suggested they were avidly doing so. Public schools received credit for generating this literacy as proof of national civic achievement. The Hutchinson Family Singers' *Uncle Sam's Farm* (1848) boasted:

> Yes! we're bound to lead the nations for our
>   motto's "Go ahead,"
> And we'll tell the foreign paupers that our people
>   are well fed;
> For the nations must remember that Uncle Sam is
>   not a fool,
> For the people do the voting and the children go
>   to school.
>
> *(Hutchinson, p. 4)*

Intrepidity, prosperity, sagacity, and democracy were thus linked to schooling. If the "strength of a people" relied, as Richard D. Brown has observed, on "an informed citizenry" (p. i), Americans had through public education seemingly attained a literacy rate commensurate with their strident national ambitions.

THE EXTENT OF LITERACY

Once thought to be a competency uniform in all times and places with similar effects, literacy is now understood as a wide variety of practices, contingent upon prevailing geographical, social, and historical influences. Such "situated literacies" (Barton, Hamilton, and Ivanic, p. xiv), that is, ones located within specific contexts, elucidate the social meaning of reading and writing in the mid-nineteenth century United States: the "nation of readers" ("Nationality in Literature," p. 264) is revealed as being but a hopeful notion of them.

Precisely because censuses measured illiteracy to demonstrate national progress, their figures are unreliable. In 1850, for example, the literacy question was so self-incriminating—it immediately preceded one on disability, insanity, poverty, and criminality—that it elicited under-reporting of illiteracy. Moreover, through 1860 census takers asked whether adults could read and write; doing either, even reading but a tavern sign, generated a "yes." When the 1870 census finally distinguished reading from writing, it discovered a quarter more "readers" than writers. Since writing is a surer test of literacy, previous censuses had clearly overstated its extent.

The rate falls further when illiterates are compared not to aggregate populations including children but to all adults. If only North Carolinian whites over nineteen in 1850 are considered, for instance, the state's illiteracy rate rises from 14.52 percent to just fewer than one in three. When adult slaves are added, it can be said that half of North Carolinian adults were illiterate in 1850—far from the one-in-seven ratio Hinton Rowan Helper (1829–1909) abstracted from the census in his *The Impending Crisis of the South* (1857).

As this example suggests, literacy differed dramatically among regions, with the Southeast, Southwest, and Old Northwest having widespread illiteracy and the Northeast (Delaware excepted) having relatively little. These disparities emerged in colonial times, when New England reached near-universal adult male literacy (over 90 percent) and would never lose it. Religious motivations are commonly given to explain this achievement, but as William J. Gilmore found for a later time, reading there more likely became a "necessity of life" (even for women whose literacy grew to equal men's in the late eighteenth century and early nineteenth century) in locales of heightened market activity, thus signaling more secular influences. Although it remains unclear whether universal literacy was an effect, cause, or mere by-product of commercialization, by 1840 adult literacy in New England reached over 99 percent. Even the arrival in the 1840s and 1850s of numerous illiterate immigrants, especially victims of the Irish potato famine, resulted in only a slight regional downturn.

AGENTS OF LITERACY

The educational history of New England and, to a lesser extent, the Middle Atlantic States challenges another "notion of readers": that public schooling directly led to mass literacy. The surge in rates predated the mid-century public school movement and rather resulted from informal instruction in families, neighborhoods, and on the job. Sunday schools, local proprietary "Dame" schools, and the often poorly funded, short-session district schools merely supplemented informal learning. Only long after state school boards in Massachusetts and Connecticut were founded in the late 1830s would free public schooling reverse conditions: the home became the reinforcer of literacy and the school its primary generator.

The relatively high antebellum illiteracy rate in western states (about 9 percent) underscores the importance of informal instruction. Many settlers came from literate northeastern states, but western conditions frustrated reproducing similar levels in the next generation: particularly, open-country farming reduced both population densities and, consequently, opportunities for neighborhood and on-the-job instruction. Unable fully to revive traditional eastern-style local literacy, western states rushed to launch school systems to stem the seeming social degeneration.

Whether in the Northeast or West, then, public schools expressed commitment to sustaining already fairly extensive literacy acquired under informal conditions, not the main means of achieving it. Yet although the advent of public schools promoted greater meritocracy that moderated class bias in literacy, this little benefited people of color and other outsiders stymied by prejudice. For whites, even after mid-century, illiteracy itself was not a bar to economic mobility—a "literacy myth," according to Harvey Graff (p. 17). Being white helped more than being literate.

LITERACY CAMPAIGNS

To turn a notion of readers into a nation of them, mid-nineteenth-century literacy reformers pursued several agendas, not all of them benign. Philosophically, the Enlightenment had bequeathed widespread belief in the perfectibility of humankind through education. Politically, the widening franchise pressured voters to learn to read and write in order to participate in national political discourse as "republican machines," the term coined in 1798 by Benjamin Rush (1745–1813) in "Of the Mode of Education Proper in a Republic" (Rush, p. 14). Socially, literacy promised to help remedy the emerging pluralistic threat to national unity by providing the skill that gave outsiders access to a common cultural heritage in print. Middle-class reformers particularly waged literacy campaigns against poorer immigrants and native racial minorities. Protestant evangelicals pushed Bible reading against both irreligion and Catholicism—to them, illiteracy along with indolence, intemperance, and unchastity were but symptoms of sinfulness. To counter illiteracy, the American Bible Society (1816), American Sunday-School Union (1824), and American Tract Society (1825), among other evangelical publishing organizations, pioneered the mass production of inexpensive imprints (non-Protestants would respond via their own publication programs). In the economic realm, industrialism increasingly required a docile workforce able to read and follow basic rules yet one sophisticated enough to manipulate "the grammar of the machine" (Stevens, p. iii).

All these agendas eventually converged upon public education as a panacea, resulting in the most concentrated literacy campaign in the nation's history: the antebellum common school movement. Its reformers shared, according to Carl Kaestle, goals that included "more schooling for each child, more state involvement, more uniformity, and a more pervasive public purpose for schooling" (p. 105). The systems created by reformers like Horace Mann and Henry Barnard forged the still-persistent link between schooling and literacy—in most cases, a standardized imposition from above of a narrowly defined literacy as an unalloyed skill. Little room was left for local community contexts for literacy. The resulting shortcomings starkly emerged in the instance of Northern-directed schooling of freed people during and after the Civil War: reformers could not grasp why black students and parents preferred black teachers to middle-class Northern whites, for if literacy was simply a skill, why should the trainer's race or ethnicity matter? Rather than reexamine their assumptions, white reformers blamed the freed people for being uneducable, only to abandon them eventually in the 1870s.

LITERACY AND READERSHIP

In this supposed nation of readers, the audience for printed materials hardly approximated the adult population, but it was nevertheless vast. This is partly

An elderly black man reads the news of the Emancipation Proclamation, c. 1863. Watercolor by Henry Louis Stephens. Stephens's picture captures the grim irony of the enslavement of human beings who possess the same potential for thinking, feeling, and learning as others. THE LIBRARY OF CONGRESS

because reading printed material aloud within groups was at least as common as reading it silently alone, thus yielding an audience far exceeding the numbers of actual readers, let alone those who purchased books or periodicals. How, then, does one figure the audience for the 300,000 copies of Harriet Beecher Stowe's (1811–1896) *Uncle Tom's Cabin* (1852) sold in its first year? Judged by sales alone, the book reached only about 1.3 percent of the population, but if there were at least three listeners for every copy read aloud and each copy went to two households, the percentage rises to nearly 8 percent. It is, after all, one thing to say that mature women read the book but quite another to say they heard it read while sewing at night among groups that included men, children, the elderly, and even servants. And all of these people might take turns reading aloud.

If sales figures cannot gauge literacy's impact upon readership, what can? Diaries and correspondence provide the richest information, for they reveal not only the who, what, when, and where of reading but also bespeak its significance within the writer's life course. A comprehensive diary kept by a Boston locomotive factory clerk and his wife, for example, which identifies 1,198 titles read from 1839 through 1861, also suggests larger principles guiding their selection: natural and family cycles (e.g., more reading in winter and more fiction as newlyweds), religious and political commitments such as Unitarianism or abolitionism, and ephemeral events like a comet in the sky, an exhibition, or a high-profile murder trial. Such accounts also reveal writers' own literacy levels, which in New England often approached that of published authors but elsewhere fell shorter.

Whatever the level, the desire to join the nation of readers spurred ever more literacy. After all, literacy was an admission ticket to a cultural nationality increasingly transacted through print. If one did not read the papers, quote poets, converse about novels, dispute pamphlets, and in short, engage the universe of print, one was not quite fully a citizen. Nor could people keep contact easily with distant loved ones strewn about by early industrial capitalism unless they could express themselves well with pen and paper.

READING, GENDER, AND RACE

The resistance of oppressed groups against marginalization from the literary franchise testifies to the power of the printed word in nineteenth-century America. Women had to struggle both against traditions that limited their influence to biological mothering and emergent conceptions of woman's sphere that, although granting them basic literacy to enable cultural reproduction, would narrowly confine their intellectual horizon to domesticity and benevolent volunteerism. Although women at times used domestic ideologies to justify their intellectual achievements, it is a tribute to their efforts that by mid-century the schoolmarm symbolized basic literacy, learned women like astronomer Maria Mitchell stood for advanced learning, and the "scribbling women" derided by the novelist Nathaniel Hawthorne represented professional authorship (Kelley, p. 345 n 2). A literary woman was neither an oxymoron nor at all unusual.

Race and literacy played very differently, of course. Racial minorities had to strive not only to overcome prejudice but also to maintain autonomy and distinctiveness. One notable attempt at balancing literacy and autonomy was Sequoyah's 1821 invention of a Cherokee national language syllabary, which gained such acceptance that it spawned a newspaper, the *Cherokee Phoenix* (1828), written using it. More common, however, was the experience of the Pequot writer William Apess (1798–1839) in his *Son of the Forest* (1829). His schooling began when as a four-year-old

he was bound out to a white neighbor after being "dreadfully beaten" by an intoxicated grandmother (p. 6). "I learned to read and write, though not so well as I could have wished," he rued (p. 7), and his sentiment was echoed by people of color receiving inferior and incomplete instruction. On hearing his master forbid his mistress from continuing her reading lessons—because "if you learn him now to read, he'll want to know how to write; and, this accomplished, he'll be running away with himself" (Douglass, p. 146)—Frederick Douglass (1818–1895) drew a key lesson in his *My Bondage and My Freedom* (1855): "from that moment I understood the direct pathway from slavery to freedom" (p. 147). Indeed, literacy acquisition became a focal point of many slave narratives as they elicited "Talking Books" to speak in a black voice, for doing so in the face of physical punishment and legal proscription meant gaining mental if not corporeal emancipation. Through these African Americans' notions of reading and by those of other groups pushed out of the circle of literacy, an unimagined nation of readers was indeed in the offing.

See also Curricula; Female Authorship; Immigration; Native American Literature; Reform; Slavery

BIBLIOGRAPHY
Primary Works
Apess, William. *Son of the Forest and Other Writings*. 1829. Edited with an introduction by Barry O'Connell. Amherst: University of Massachusetts Press, 1997.

Douglass, Frederick. *My Bondage and My Freedom*. New York: Miller, Orton, and Mulligan, 1855.

Hutchinson, Jesse, Jr. *Uncle Sam's Farm*. Portland, Maine: Augustus Robinson, 1850.

"Nationality in Literature." *U.S. Democratic Review* 20 (March 1847): 264–272.

Rush, Benjamin. *Essays: Literary, Moral, and Philosophical*. Philadelphia: Thomas and Samuel Bradford, 1798.

Secondary Works
Barton, David, Mary Hamilton, and Roz Ivanic. *Situated Literacies: Reading and Writing in Context*. London: Routledge, 2000.

Baym, Nina. American *Women of Letters and the Nineteenth-Century Sciences: Styles of Affiliation*. New Brunswick, N.J.: Rutgers University Press, 2002.

Brown, Richard D. *The Strength of a People: The Idea of an Informed Citizenry in America, 1650–1870*. Chapel Hill: University of North Carolina Press, 1996.

Cohen, Patricia Cline. *A Calculating People: The Spread of Numeracy in Early America*. Chicago: University of Chicago Press, 1982.

Collins, William J., and Robert A. Margo. "Historical Perspectives on Racial Difference in Schooling in the United States." Vanderbilt University Department of Economics Working Paper, no. 9770, June 2003.

Cornelius, Janet Duitsman. *"When I Can Read My Title Clear": Literacy, Slavery, and Religion in the Antebellum South.* Columbia: University of South Carolina Press, 1991.

Davis, Charles T., and Henry Louis Gates Jr. *The Slave's Narrative.* New York: Oxford University Press, 1985.

Gates, Henry Louis, Jr. "James Gronniosaw and the Trope of the Talking Book." In *Studies in Autobiography,* edited by James Olney, pp. 51–72. New York: Oxford University Press, 1988.

Gilmore, William J. "Elementary Literacy on the Eve of the Industrial Revolution: Trends in Rural New England, 1760–1830." *Proceedings of the American Antiquarian Society* 92, no. 1 (1982): 87–178.

Gilmore, William J. *Reading Becomes a Necessity of Life: Material and Cultural Life in Rural New England, 1780–1835.* Knoxville: University of Tennessee Press, 1989.

Graff, Harvey J. *The Legacies of Literacy: Continuities and Contradictions in Western Culture and Society.* Bloomington: Indiana University Press, 1987.

Graff, Harvey J. *The Literacy Myth: Literacy and Social Structure in the Nineteenth-Century City.* New York: Academic Press, 1979.

Hobbs, Catherine, ed. *Nineteenth-Century Women Learn to Write.* Charlottesville: University Press of Virginia, 1995.

Kaestle, Carl F. *Pillars of the Republic: Common Schools and American Society, 1780–1860.* New York: Hill and Wang, 1983.

Kelley, Mary. *Private Woman, Public Stage: Literary Domesticity in Nineteenth-Century America.* New York: Oxford University Press, 1984.

Lockridge, Kenneth A. *Literacy in Colonial New England: An Enquiry into the Social Context of Literacy in the Early Modern West.* New York: Norton, 1974.

Morris, Robert Charles. *Reading, 'Riting, and Reconstruction: The Education of Freedmen in the South, 1861–1870.* Chicago: University of Chicago Press, 1981.

Murray, David. *Forked Tongues: Speech, Writing, and Representation in North American Indian Texts.* Bloomington: Indiana University Press, 1991.

Soltow, Lee, and Edward Stevens. *The Rise of Literacy and the Common School in the United States: A Socioeconomic Analysis to 1870.* Chicago: University of Chicago Press, 1981.

Stevens, Edward W., Jr. "The Anatomy of Mass Literacy in the Nineteenth-Century United States." In *National Literacy Campaigns: Historical and Comparative Perspectives,* edited by Robert F. Arnove and Harvey J. Graff, pp. 99–122. New York: Plenum Press, 1987.

Stevens, Edward W. *The Grammar of the Machine: Technical Literacy and Early Industrial Expansion in the United States.* New Haven, Conn.: Yale University Press, 1995.

University of Virginia Geospatial and Statistical Data Center. Historical Census Browser. University of Virginia. http://fisher.lib.virginia.edu/census/.

Zboray, Ronald J., and Mary Saracino Zboray. *Everyday Ideas: Socioliterary Experience among Antebellum New Englanders.* Knoxville: University of Tennessee Press, forthcoming.

Zboray, Ronald J., and Mary Saracino Zboray. "Reading and Everyday Life in Antebellum Boston: The Diary of Daniel F. and Mary D. Child." *Libraries and Culture* 32, no. 3 (1997): 285–323.

Ronald J. Zboray
Mary Saracino Zboray

LITERARY CRITICISM

Reviewing the Pennsylvanian Adam Seybert's (1773–1825) *Annals of the United States* in the January 1820 issue of Scotland's venerable *Edinburgh Review,* the English critic, clergyman, and author Sydney Smith (1771–1845) asked a question that would ring in the ears of American writers for over a generation: "In the four quarters of the globe, who reads an American book? Or goes to an American play? Or looks at an American picture or statue?" Several decades after the Declaration of Independence and the successfully waged Revolution, most knowledgeable observers felt that it was still too soon to identify a distinctively American way of writing, much less a coherent body of literary criticism produced on the American scene. A mere half century later, however, a vibrant, compelling, and durable body of American literature had been produced, and criticism had begun to take stock of the young nation's literary efforts.

The most important American literary criticism of the antebellum period was not written in university settings by professional academics but instead was produced by public intellectuals who typically were also active themselves as writers in such genres as poetry, fiction, essays, and religious sermons. The rise of major research universities in the United States, which began in earnest only in the late nineteenth century, would eventually spawn legions of highly trained academic critics wielding advanced degrees and diverse critical theories, but before the Civil War, literary criticism developed much more sporadically and with far less institutional support than in later years. Nevertheless, the criticism produced during this period has been extremely influential, particularly since some of the most indelibly important literary artists of the period—Walt Whitman (1819–1892), Herman Melville (1819–1891), Edgar Allan Poe (1809–1849), Margaret Fuller (1810–1850), and Ralph Waldo Emerson (1803–1882)—also made major contributions to American literary criticism.

PERIODICALS AND THE RISE OF AMERICAN CRITICISM

Literary tastes were shaped largely by essays and reviews published in a range of newspapers and, especially, American magazines like the *Christian Examiner, Biblical Repertory, United States Magazine and Democratic Review, American Whig Review, The Dial, North American Review, Boston Quarterly Review, Southern Literary Messenger, Putnam's Monthly Magazine, Atlantic Monthly,* and *Catholic World.* Periodicals flourished in the United States, but American readers, most of whom read prose and poetry by both British and American writers, also continued to rely as well upon British critical opinion found in periodicals such as *Blackwood's Magazine* and *Edinburgh Review* in order to cultivate their own ideas about literature. Indeed, many American periodicals did not serve to produce distinctively "American" writing and criticism but instead followed the more conservative aesthetic tendency to favor the British Enlightenment tradition of neoclassical prose styles and oratory rather than the Romanticism, Democratic nationalism, and vernacular styles that eventually came to dominate the literary production of the major nineteenth-century American writers. Of particular note, the *North American Review,* an eminent Boston magazine founded in 1815, served as a venue for major publications in the areas of history, literature (especially poetry), and literary criticism. For instance, more than any other American magazine of the period, the *North American Review* was created along the lines of nineteenth-century English literary quarterlies—issues included not only literary criticism but also scholarly articles and reviews in an eclectic range of other intellectual fields, such as history, science, and theology—and maintained very strong ties with the scholarly worlds of Harvard and the Boston Unitarian establishment. So important were British publications for the development of American criticism that the young Maine novelist John Neal (1793–1876), an early advocate of American literature, actually had some of his greatest influence during 1824–1827, when he lived in England and became the first

American to write for the major British reviews, including a series of critical essays on American writers for *Blackwood's Magazine.*

DOCUMENTING THE "AMERICAN RENAISSANCE"

At approximately mid-century, an important exception to the dominance of periodicals in the field of antebellum literary criticism was produced just at the moment of America's most profound literary activity; just a few of the major works published during 1850–1855 include Emerson's *Representative Men* (1850), Harriet Beecher Stowe's *Uncle Tom's Cabin* (1852), Thoreau's *Walden* (1854), Whitman's *Leaves of Grass* (1855), Melville's *Moby-Dick* (1851), and Nathaniel Hawthorne's *The Scarlet Letter* (1850). The first major book to reckon comprehensively and critically with the American literary tradition arrived in the form of the large (ten pounds spread over two volumes) and lavishly illustrated *Cyclopedia of American Literature* (1855), produced by Evert Augustus Duyckinck (1816–1878) and George L. Duyckinck (1823–1863), two prominent New York editors and contributors to the *Literary World,* the leading weekly literary review of the period. Destined to become a standard reference work for American literary history, the *Cyclopedia* trumpeted innovative fiction by Duyckinck's close friends Nathaniel Hawthorne (1804–1864) and Melville in particular as representative of the best in American writing while reserving lesser praise for more popular (and more traditional) writers like the poets Nathaniel Parker Willis (1806–1867), James Russell Lowell (1819–1891), and Henry Wadsworth Longfellow (1807–1882).

Although he is remembered primarily for his short fiction and poetry, during the frenetic two decades before his death in 1849, Edgar Allan Poe was one of the more active book reviewers and literary critics of his generation. Having acquired some literary repute for his popular poem "The Raven" (1845), Poe proceeded soon after to detail his method and principles for composing verse in "The Philosophy of Composition" (1846), published in *Graham's Magazine* (1826–1858). It is here that Poe famously announced his intersecting aesthetic principles of brevity and the macabre. First, "If any literary work is too long to be read at one sitting, we must be content to dispense with the immensely important effect derivable from unity of impression. . . . What we term a long poem is, in fact, merely a succession of brief ones" (p. 1375). Second, and more notoriously, Poe insisted on the production of beautiful lyrical effects, the most critical being that of poetry's ideal subject. Consequently, he would write "Beauty . . .

Evert Augustus Duyckinck.

incites the sensitive soul to tears. Melancholy is thus the most legitimate of all poetical tones" (p. 1377) and, citing the theme of his most famous poem, "The death, then, of a beautiful woman is, unquestionably, the most poetical topic in the world" (p. 1379). Poe refined his ideas on poetry—his own and that of British and American contemporaries like Percy Bysshe Shelley, Lord Byron, Alfred, Lord Tennyson, Willis, and Longfellow—in a popular lecture titled "The Poetic Principle" delivered in various cities during 1848–1849. That talented public speakers like Poe, Emerson, and others could deliver lectures on poetry to large urban audiences during the nineteenth century suggests the extent to which literary criticism was a matter not only for printed texts but also for popular oratory on the lyceum circuit.

The fullest expression of Poe's theory of prosody and poetic technique arrived in final form in the pages of the *Southern Literary Messenger* with the publication of "The Rationale of Verse" (1848). Based in Richmond, Virginia, the *Southern Literary Messenger* (1834–1864) became one of the earliest American

vehicles for southern literary criticism and book reviews. Its most prominent contributor, Poe, took over the editorship for the period 1835–1837, during which time he became notorious for his hard-hitting reviews and attacks on other writers. The *Southern Literary Messenger* quickly waned in its literary influence in the 1840s and especially as the Civil War approached, and the magazine's pages came to be filled with discussions of military and naval affairs.

"YOUNG AMERICA" AND NATIONALIST CRITICISM

For the early decades of the nineteenth century, most American writers continued to look to Europe, and especially to England, for their ideas about literature. But the theme of American literary identity steadily came to dominate the new nation's literary criticism during the antebellum period. As the century progressed, American writers increasingly spoke of the need for a distinctively American literature: one that would boldly express the new nation's difference from Europe while setting forth its own distinctive cultural, political, and moral sensibility. Based in New York City in the decades before the Civil War, the "Young America" literary movement, led by critics such as Evert Augustus Duyckinck, Cornelius Mathews, Bayard Taylor, Rufus Wilmot Griswold, and William Gilmore Simms, was perhaps the most vocal of all American groups advocating a resistance to European literary influences in favor of an authentic and innovative American way of writing. The antebellum Young America movement, which was active in both political and literary discourses, took a good deal of its energy from the jingoistic political concept of American "Manifest Destiny," a term first published in 1845 by John L. O'Sullivan (1813–1895) in New York City's *United States Magazine and Democratic Review.*

The fervor associated with the Young America movement can be traced through much literary criticism of the antebellum period, but the matter of American literary achievement found its watershed precisely in the summer of 1850 with the publication of Melville's lengthy essay-review of his friend Hawthorne's *Mosses from an Old Manse* (1846) in the influential New York magazine the *Literary World.* Identifying himself only as "a Virginian Spending July in Vermont," Melville in his review took the bold step of comparing Hawthorne's genius to that of William Shakespeare, whose plays had become a highly popular staple of the antebellum American stage. The tragic sensibility of Shakespeare, wrote Melville, could be discerned in Hawthorne's great historical fictions of early America, in which readers could discover a "great power of blackness in him [that] derives its force from its appeals to that Calvinistic sense of Innate Depravity and Original Sin, from whose visitations, in some shape or other, no deeply thinking mind is always and wholly free" (p. 243). At the same time Melville, who would not publish his masterwork *Moby-Dick* (1851) until the following year, would leave room for a new American writer (perhaps himself) who might surpass Shakespeare and Hawthorne in both genius and national sensibility:

> But it is not meant that all American writers should studiously cleave to nationality in their writings; only this, no American writer should write like an Englishman, or a Frenchman; let him write like a man, for then he will be sure to write like an American. Let us away with this leaven of literary flunkeyism [*sic*] towards England. If either we must play the flunkey [*sic*] in this thing, let England do it, not us. While we are rapidly preparing for that political supremacy among the nations, which prophetically awaits us at the close of the present century; in a literary point of view, we are deplorably unprepared for it; and we seem studious to remain so. (P. 248)

LITERARY TRANSCENDENTALISM: ETHICS AND AESTHETICS

Before the Young America movement took firm hold at mid-century and signaled the shift of intellectual and critical preeminence from Boston to New York City, the most innovative currents of American literary criticism drew their sustenance from European Romanticism. Foremost among the groups of writers influenced by Romanticism were the New England transcendentalists, led by Ralph Waldo Emerson and including such writers and critics as Amos Bronson Alcott, Theodore Parker, Sarah Margaret Fuller, George Ripley, Orestes Augustus Brownson, Elizabeth Palmer Peabody, Thoreau, Hawthorne, Jones Very, and others. The critical principles of Romanticism came to these writers from numerous European sources, but a watershed event for many of them was James Marsh's (1794–1842) American edition of Samuel Taylor Coleridge's *Aids to Reflection* (1829). It was Coleridge's Neoplatonic distinction between ordinary cognition (Understanding) and the spiritual activity of the mind's eye (Reason) that led Emerson to a number of crucial pronouncements about poetry in his most important essays.

The Dial (1840–1844), a seminal but short-lived Boston journal devoted to literature, philosophy, and religion, served in many respects as an organ of the New England transcendentalist movement and was a major vehicle for important critics of the day.

Although its circulation was small and its content disparaged by the mainstream press at the time, *The Dial*—edited by the brilliant feminist critic Margaret Fuller, who was assisted by George Ripley (1802–1880)—presented a learned and eclectic mixture of literary criticism, much of it grounded firmly in the traditions of European Romanticism. Its essays included, for example, Fuller's "Goethe" and the Unitarian minister Theodore Parker's (1810–1860) "German Literature," among many others. While it never adopted a clear editorial position or cultivated a single critical model, its pages nevertheless reflected the continuing influence of European thinkers on the development of an American literature. Emerson succeeded Fuller as editor of *The Dial* in 1842.

Emerson's literary theory is at once the most rigorously stated and the most subtly complex of the antebellum period. Beginning with the eight brief chapters of his anonymously published *Nature* (1836) and continuing with his first edition of collected *Essays* (1841), Emerson set forth the main principles of his distinctive brand of Romantic intuitionism and laid the groundwork for Henry David Thoreau's (1817–1862) profound analysis of the correspondence between language and nature in *Walden* (1854). For instance, from Emerson's assertion, in *Nature*, that "words are signs of natural facts" (p. 20) grows much of Thoreau's interest in the relation between thinking, writing, and the natural world.

WHITMAN: TOWARD A NEW AMERICAN POETICS

Walt Whitman (1819–1892), whose preface to his 1855 edition of *Leaves of Grass* stands with, and probably above, Emerson's essays as the major statement of American literary theory for the nineteenth century, is at once a major theorist and an unprecedented innovator in the field of American poetry. Although their ideas about American literature are not identical, there are profound links between Emerson's transcendental intuitionism and the younger Walt Whitman's own critical ideas and the innovative poetry that he produced between 1855 and 1891. As Whitman himself readily admitted, Emerson's literary theory—expounded not only in *Nature* but also in "The Poet," "The American Scholar," and "Self-Reliance"—was transformative for Whitman's sense of himself as America's greatest poet. "I was simmering, simmering, simmering; Emerson brought me to a boil" (Trowbridge, p. 166), Whitman was said to have written of the influence of Emerson's thought, thus confirming the intellectual linkage between the most crucial American poet and essayist, respectively, of the nineteenth century.

In his essay "The Poet" (1844), which was so important for Whitman's intellectual development, Emerson had outlined a concept of the poet as an heir to intertwined traditions of Christianity and Romanticism. As a former Unitarian minister trained at Harvard, Emerson saw in the greatest poets a prophetic dimension that infused an aesthetic of Romantic self-expression with the moral force of religion. Consequently, he could say with supreme confidence that "the poet is the sayer, the namer, and represents beauty" and, moreover, that "the world is not painted or adorned, but is from the beginning beautiful; and God has not made some beautiful things, but Beauty is the creator of the universe. Therefore the poet is not any permissive potentate, but is emperor in his own right" (p. 449).

Less a literary critic than a founder of a new type of poetics in his untitled preface to *Leaves of Grass,* Whitman is nevertheless of major importance as a theorist concerned with new forms of writing that would be appropriate to the American nation. In that crucial preface, Whitman declares that the ideal poet must be a complete lover of the universe, one who draws the materials of his composition from nature while prophetically serving as America's representative of the common people. The preface also makes specific assertions about a new poetry that will proceed organically, will be free of all unnecessary ornament, and will entirely avoid conventional rhyme and meter. When it came to the formal requirements of the new American poetry, Whitman insisted boldly,

> the rhyme and uniformity of perfect poems show the free growth of metrical laws and bud from them as unerringly and loosely as lilacs or roses on a bush, and take shapes as compact as the shapes of chestnuts and oranges and melons and pears, and shed the perfume impalpable to form. (P. 11)

In addition to his prescription for poetry freed of the traditional rules of rhyme and meter, though, Whitman's largest critical project is woven into his political sympathies and nationalist preferences for the concept of "America." Thus, he opens his preface to *Leaves of Grass* with a prose hymn to America, thereby signifying that his revolutionary poetics are inseparable from an implicit critique of all that is not American: "The Americans of all nations at any time upon the earth have probably the fullest poetical nature. The United States themselves are essentially the greatest poem" (p. 5). The elitism and cultural imperialism that such statements apparently engender, though, are modified by Whitman's abiding concern for democratic

arrangements and a populist sense of preference for the ordinary human being, so that "the poet sees for a certainty how one not a great artist may be just as sacred and perfect as the greatest artist" (p. 9). Echoing the New York advocates of Young America who preceded him, Whitman would insist further in his preface to *Leaves of Grass* that "of all nations the United States with veins full of poetical stuff most need poets and will doubtless have the greatest and use them the greatest" (p. 5)—the problem of literary criticism in America would remain for much of the nineteenth century inseparable from the problem of national politics. And only by enduring the trauma of the Civil War would criticism in America finally make the enormous adjustments required to see the complexities of American literary ambition through a cultural lens shaped profoundly by issues of race, class, and gender as well as by the earlier desire to create a literature of distinction that could claim artistic independence from Europe.

See also The Dial; "Hawthorne and His Mosses"; Literary Nationalism; Periodicals; "The Philosophy of Composition"; "The Poet"; Transcendentalism; Young America

BIBLIOGRAPHY

Primary Works

Emerson, Ralph Waldo. *Nature.* 1836. In *Essays and Poems,* pp. 7–49. New York: Library of America, 1996.

Emerson, Ralph Waldo. "The Poet." 1844. In *Essays and Poems,* pp. 445–468. New York: Library of America, 1996.

Melville, Herman. "Hawthorne and His Mosses." 1850. In *The Writings of Herman Melville,* vol. 9, *The Piazza Tales and Other Prose Pieces,* edited by Harrison Hayford et al., pp. 239–253. Evanston, Ill.: Northwestern University Press, 1987.

Poe, Edgar Allan. "The Philosophy of Composition." 1846. In *Poetry, Tales, and Selected Essays,* pp. 1373–1385. New York: Library of America, 1996.

Whitman, Walt. *Leaves of Grass.* 1855. In *Poetry and Prose.* New York: Library of America, 1996.

Trowbridge, John Townsend. "Reminiscences of Walt Whitman." *Atlantic Monthly,* February 1902, pp. 163–175.

Secondary Works

Green, Martin. *The Problem of Boston: Some Readings in Cultural History.* London: Longmans, 1966.

Grey, Robin. *The Complicity of Imagination: The American Renaissance, Contests of Authority, and Seventeenth-Century English Culture.* Cambridge, U.K, and New York: Cambridge University Press, 1997.

Matthiessen, F. O. *American Renaissance: Art and Expression in the Age of Emerson and Whitman.* London and New York: Oxford University Press, 1941.

Miller, Perry. *The Raven and the Whale: The War of Words and Wits in the Era of Poe and Melville.* New York: Harcourt, Brace, 1956.

Reynolds, David S. *Beneath the American Renaissance: The Subversive Imagination in the Age of Emerson and Melville.* 1988. Cambridge, Mass.: Harvard University Press, 1989.

Spiller, Robert E., Willard Thorp, Thomas H. Johnson, and Henry Seidel Canby, eds. *Literary History of the United States.* 3 vols. 3rd ed., rev. New York: Macmillan, 1963–1972.

Widmer, Edward L. *Young America: The Flowering of Democracy in New York City.* New York: Oxford University Press, 1999.

Zboray, Ronald J. *A Fictive People: Antebellum Economic Development and the American Reading Public.* New York: Oxford University Press, 1993.

James Emmett Ryan

LITERARY MARKETPLACE

Between 1820 and 1870 a new kind of culture was forming in America. For simplicity's sake, scholars often speak of the outcome of this transformation as the creation of America's literary marketplace—a gradual yet sweeping change that saw the printed matter of books, magazines, and newspapers displace local networks of oral communication and thereby become the nation's essential means of mass communication and its dominant source of cultural activity. It is true, as Cathy Davidson and others have demonstrated, that this new culture first began to take shape during the decades immediately following the American Revolution, when there were dramatic increases in levels of popular literacy and education, as well as in the sheer number of books available for circulation. Yet books and more widespread popular literacy, while necessary for the development of the mid-nineteenth-century American literary marketplace, were not sufficient causes for that development.

INNOVATIONS IN THE BOOK TRADE

In the early nineteenth century, technological innovations such as the cylinder rotary press, stereotyping, and electrotyping sped up the printing process by mechanizing operations that previously had been performed by hand, thereby allowing for the production of books at lower prices and in larger editions than ever before. In 1855 one prominent American publisher estimated that an average of fifty-two books had been published annually in the United States between 1830 and 1842. By contrast, in 1853, the year before Henry David Thoreau's (1817–1862) *Walden* appeared, 733 works had been printed—an increase of 800 percent in less than twenty years. The growth in numbers printed in first editions of mid-nineteenth-century books was greater still: initial press runs of 10,000 were not uncommon by the mid-century, and some first editions went as high as 100,000 copies.

Together with this dramatic increase in the overall supply of books, publishers began to market a variety of new kinds of books. Some designed volumes intended to add prestige to the mere possession of a book. The antebellum period was the heyday of richly bound ornamental books known as literary annuals (compendiums of excerpts taken from already published books of poetry and prose) and "gift books" (collections of various kinds of articles, fictional forms and poetry). Other publishers began the practice of printing individual books in series that were designed to popularize the latest literary products and scientific discoveries of the day. Among the most successful of these was the Family Library produced from 1830 on by J. & J. Harper, with titles that included biographies, histories, natural science books, and travel literature. The New York publishing house of Wiley and Putnam also made use of the series format in its efforts to promote an indigenous high literary culture. In 1845 under the editorship of Evert Duyckinck (1816–1878), it launched the Library of American Books, which was brought out in parallel with the Library of Choice Reading an already successful series of well-established English classics.

Ticknor and Fields, however, was the publisher that during the 1850s and 1860s brought Duyckinck's project to fruition and in the process became the first great publisher-patron of American authors. Under the leadership of James T. Fields (1817–1881), the Boston publishing house not only built a stronger list than Wiley and Putnam—by 1860 its writers included Ralph Waldo Emerson, Nathaniel Hawthorne, Oliver Wendell Holmes, Henry Wadsworth Longfellow, James Russell Lowell, Harriet Beecher Stowe, and Thoreau—it also pioneered new ways of marketing American literature. Fields began the practice of advertising beyond local markets. He also used a nationwide network of friendly ties with editors of newspapers and magazines in which he advertised his books to prompt favorable reviews, in some cases even publishing reviews he had written himself.

NEWSPAPERS IN MID-NINETEENTH-CENTURY AMERICA

"For who are the readers and thinkers of 1854? Owing to the silent revolution which the newspaper has wrought, this class has come in this country to take in all classes. Look into the morning trains which, from every suburb, carry the business men into the city to their shops, counting-rooms, work-yards, and warehouses. With them enters the car—the newsboy, that humble priest of politics, finance, philosophy, and religion. He unfolds his magical sheets—twopence a head his bread of knowledge costs—and instantly the entire rectangular assembly, fresh from their breakfast, are bending as one man to their second breakfast. There is, no doubt, chaff enough in what he brings; but there is fact, thought, and wisdom in the crude mass, from all regions of the world."

Ralph Waldo Emerson, "The Fugitive Slave Law" (1854), in *Selected Writings of Emerson*, edited by Donald McQuade (New York: The Modern Library, Random House, 1981), pp. 753–754.

MAGAZINES AND NEWSPAPERS

The historical emergence of the American literary marketplace during the mid-nineteenth century can also be traced by examining data on the growth of magazines and newspapers. The periodical press came into its own between 1820 and 1870. In 1825 there had been fewer than 125 American magazines; by 1870 there were somewhat more than 1,200. Most of these new periodicals appealed to local or special interests. The early decades of the nineteenth century were prolific in the founding of religious magazines and weekly newspapers, and as late as 1850 religious periodicals still outnumbered the new genre of popular literary magazines. None of them, however, ever managed to attain the national circulation and influence of their secular counterparts, which in time came to constitute an eclectic literary genre with contents that included fiction and verse, biographical and historical essays, and travel sketches and illustrations. By the end of the 1850s, leading monthlies such as *Godey's Lady's Book* (1830–1898), *Peterson's Ladies' National Magazine* (1842–1898), and *Harper's New Monthly Magazine* (1850–) all claimed to have more than 100,000 paid subscribers. The circulation of other more short-lived ventures such as *Graham's Magazine*

(1841–1858), *Putnam's Monthly Magazine* (1853–1870), the *United States Magazine and Democratic Review* (1837–1859), and *Sartain's Union Magazine of Literature and Art* (1847–1852) was also substantial, ranging from 20,000 to 70,000.

The commercial success of these new American literary magazines also served to raise the rates at which well-known writers were paid for their articles. During the 1840s *Graham's* and *Godey's* were the leaders in increasing payments for magazine writing, with rates ranging from four to twelve dollars a page for prose, and ten to fifty dollars a poem. *Putnam's* normal price of three dollars per page was probably the average among other general literary periodicals. Rates leveled off during the 1850s, but by the end of that decade the standard set by the *Atlantic Monthly*— six dollars a page—compared favorably to that of leading British literary magazines.

Perhaps most important and spectacular of all the developments that signaled the emergence of the literary marketplace, however, was the proliferation of daily and weekly newspapers, which quickly came to be seen as uniquely powerful American institutions. Emerson called newspapers the nation's "second breakfast." American newspapers almost tripled in number—from 1,200 to 3,000—during the 1840s and 1850s, and came to exist in far greater variety and numbers than in any European country at the time. With newspaper postage fixed by law at one cent per copy up to one hundred miles, and after 1845 free up to thirty miles, newspapers came to make up 90 percent of the mail while providing only one-ninth of postal revenues. Almost every American town of moderate size had a daily paper. Most large cities had several, and even remote frontier settlements issued their own weeklies. The majority of dailies had circulations of a few thousand, and the great mass of weeklies only a few hundred.

During the 1840s, however, a new generation of "penny press" newspapers based in northern cities acquired dramatic increases in circulation, which in turn gave them increasingly prominent roles in shaping cultural and political attitudes in their local communities. Horace Greeley's (1811–1872) *New York Tribune* remains the best known of these newspapers. Thanks to the success of a weekly edition designed for national circulation, it also established itself as America's largest and most influential newspaper. Yet the daily edition of Greeley's newspaper, which had a circulation of 77,000 at the end of 1860, had several powerful rivals in its ability to influence local opinion. In 1860 in New York, the *Herald* also claimed a circulation of 77,000, and the *Sun* 59,000; both the

Boston Herald and the *Philadelphia Inquirer* averaged 65,000 in 1862. Although such numbers hardly signaled that nineteenth-century newspapers were seen as reliable agents of public information, they do describe the most palpable change in the reading matter of ordinary Americans as the nation moved gradually from an era of scarcity to that of abundance.

As with books, the dramatic increase in the overall supply of magazines and newspapers brought with it a rich and diverse bill of fare that added to the glut of printed information. Some periodicals were themselves little more than books in disguise, providing anthologies of various kinds of articles and fiction. The absence of an international copyright law also allowed for the pirated reprinting of articles from leading British and French magazines, and periodicals such as *Littell's Living Age* (1844–1941) and *The Eclectic Magazine* (1844–1907) for several decades earned their livelihood from this practice. Notices and reviews of books were ubiquitous, and the steady growth in the size of magazines was attributable, in part, to efforts their editors made to keep track of what many perceived as an ongoing bibliographical deluge.

The vast majority of antebellum newspapers were mouthpieces of political parties, but when the electioneering season ended, they also provided an extraordinary variety of information. Together with reports on local, national, and international news, newspapers printed compilations of agricultural and commercial data and reports on recent developments in science. Their pages also included advertisements for new products and new business opportunities and at the same time provided the publicity that oiled the new national lecture system of the 1840s and 1850s. In fact, as Donald Scott has shown, newspapers helped to make lectures significant cultural events by printing advertisements about which speakers were lecturing where and when, as well as stories about particular lectures, and editorials proclaiming the importance of the lecture as a new cultural institution. Some key metropolitan newspapers, especially the New York *Tribune* and the *Boston Herald,* also played central roles in nationalizing the reputations of leading figures in the popular lecture circuit—a group that included Emerson and, from time to time, Thoreau.

FROM ORAL TO PRINT CULTURE

All this is now well known to specialists when they consider changes in the literary culture of nineteenth-century America. Yet the question of how this unprecedented abundance of print altered the working of that culture has been posed and approached in different ways. Literary historians usually argue that the most

HORACE GREELEY, RALPH WALDO EMERSON, AND THE WORKINGS OF THE LITERARY MARKETPLACE

Reviews and notices of Emerson's writings, as well as notices of his activities as a lecturer, were regular features of Greeley's newspapers during the 1840s and 1850s.

At a time when popular demand for the sorts of reviews and books in which Emerson's writings could be found remained relatively small, Greeley saw his main duties as an American "newspaperman" to include the promotion of a new generation of American writers. As a result, beginning in the early 1840s, Greeley-edited publications, starting with *The New Yorker,* and continuing with daily and weekly editions of the *New York Tribune,* provided a steady stream of reviews and notices that in effect served to nationalize Emerson's reputation well before his publications gained any significant commercial success. Greeley was in no position to dictate any national consensus regarding Emerson, but he did hold institutional power that provided the continuing publicity needed to make and keep Emerson's name visible in American culture at large.

striking development during this period was an unprecedented growth in the production and consumption of novels. The numbers that appear to support this view are striking. During the 1820s, 128 American novels were published, a figure that was almost 40 more than had been published in the previous fifty years, and five times the number published during the previous decade—and yet more than double that number appeared in the 1830s; and the total more than doubled again in the 1840s, to nearly 800. In 1826 James Fenimore Cooper's (1789–1851) *The Last of the Mohicans* qualified as a best-seller with 5,750 copies in circulation. In contrast, between 1846 and 1851, George Lippard's (1822–1854) *The Quaker City* sold some 210,000 copies, making it the country's best-selling novel before the appearance of Harriet Beecher Stowe's (1811–1896) *Uncle Tom's Cabin* in 1852. In that year alone, the sales of Stowe's antislavery saga outdid Lippard's earlier aggregate figure, and estimates of total copies purchased before the Civil War range as high as 5 million. While no other antebellum novel even approached these figures, there were several others that enjoyed remarkable commercial success during the 1850s—particularly

Fetridge & Co. periodical arcade, Boston. Illustration from *Gleason's Pictorial Drawing Room Companion,* 31 July 1852, showing the large number of publications available. Middle- and upper-class women constituted a large segment of the readership for both books and magazines. THE LIBRARY OF CONGRESS

Fanny Fern's (Sara Payson Willis Parton, 1811–1872) *Ruth Hall* (1855), logging sales of 55,000, and Maria S. Cummins's (1827–1866) *The Lamplighter* (1854), surpassing 40,000 within eight weeks.

Regardless of whether America gained or suffered from this unprecedented growth of popular interest in fiction, it is important to observe that most scholars who concentrate their efforts on interpreting mid-nineteenth-century fiction appear to be guided by two closely related assumptions. The first is that the three decades prior to the Civil War should be seen as a time when a dramatic increase in the productive power of American publishing served to make book publishing into a major industry that catered to the demands of a new mass reading public. The other is that in this new setting, where the preferences of a mass readership supposedly came to govern the workings of the literary marketplace, all writers of poetry and prose now were compelled to come to terms with an altogether new

culture in which literature had been reduced to the status of a commodity, and where success for writers now meant appealing to an anonymous, distant, and unknown audience. These assumptions have served to support the familiar view that during the middle decades of the nineteenth century the emergence of the literary marketplace served to open the split between "mass" and "high" culture.

A number of cultural historians have called this approach into question for various reasons and thereby laid the groundwork for somewhat different approaches. One group, led by Donald Scott, retains the view that print did indeed become the central force for change in antebellum culture, but he argues that the dynamics of America's emerging literary marketplace cannot be understood in isolation from forms of oral communication that continued to characterize the culture of both elite and ordinary Americans. Scott has shown that the spread of the popular lecture system was one of the most important by-products of the new world of print, since many of its prominent figures included editors, journalists, and writers. Not surprisingly, the most frequent topics of discussion within lyceums—biography, history, natural science, and travel—also mirrored those found in books, magazines, and newspapers. But the national lecture system was at the same time an institution that helped to sort out and assimilate the huge supply of facts and opinions created by a new culture of abundant print. And in this respect, Scott has argued persuasively, the lecture system itself, during its heyday—which included the years immediately following the Civil War—was perhaps America's first truly national cultural marketplace.

Other historians have followed Scott in stressing that oratory was as ubiquitous as print, although they speak of its practical implications in slightly different terms. Lawrence Levine has argued, for instance, that the frequent and prominent staging of Shakespeare's plays during the decades before the Civil War reveals the existence of a "shared public culture" in which the spoken word remained a central part of American life, and in which Shakespeare thus had little difficulty finding a central place. Equally important, the enormous popularity of Shakespeare's drama also brings into question the practice of seeing mid-nineteenth-century culture on a vertical plane that can be neatly divided into a hierarchy of inclusive adjectival categories such as "high," "low," "pop," "mass," "folk," and the like. The continuing use of such terms, Levine argues convincingly, only serves to obscure the dynamic complexity of American culture during the middle decades of the nineteenth century.

Richard Brown has shown that the cultural interests of America were large and diverse in ways that our standard literary histories have tended to underestimate. Yet where Levine sees the continuing existence of a "shared popular culture," Brown argues that in a society where both print and public speech were ubiquitous, a comprehensive culture became ever more remote and eventually no longer an ideal. By the start of the Civil War, he observes, America had gone from being a society in which public information had been scarce—and largely under the control of the learned and wealthy few—to one in which a new abundance of public information found its way to a diverse variety of consumers by way of specialized printing, public speech, and specialized information. Patterns of information diffusion that before the mid-nineteenth century had reinforced cultural cohesion now became the foundation of cultural fragmentation and diversity.

Perhaps most significant of all, the familiar view that improvements in the technology of publishing quickly served to put books within the physical and financial reach of ordinary Americans also is not holding up under close empirical investigation. There can be no question that the long-term trend was a steady increase in the number of book titles and especially of novels. Yet the numbers themselves, while suggesting that writing books for publication became increasingly common, do not support the view that, before the mid-1850s at the earliest, the reading habits of America's extraordinarily literate public ought to be understood primarily in terms of the books they bought. At the outset, the dramatic increase in the number of books available was not accompanied by a comparable increase in the velocity and extent of their circulation. Although subscription libraries and reading societies certainly grew in numbers, most Americans could not as yet afford to join them. Books also remained very difficult to distribute for sale before 1850, when railroads first began to link up different regions of the country and provide northern publishing houses with access to the American interior. Before the mid-century, only the Bible—not surprisingly, the first book printed with stereotyped plates in America—was nationally distributed, thanks to the efforts of the American Bible Society's traveling agents and local auxiliaries.

Robert Gross has shown that the problems involved in creating a national marketplace for books were political as well as economic and geographic. While the Postal Act of 1790 allowed American newspapers to circulate throughout the country at cheap rates (with editors exchanging papers for free), it also banned books from mailbags. Beginning in July 1839 books did for a time move through the mail in great quantities, aided by enterprising papers such as *Brother Jonathan* (1839–1843) and *New World* (1839–1844), which seized upon a loophole in the postal laws to issue pirated reprintings of popular British novels in huge "story-paper" formats. But America's first paperback revolution not only turned out to be relatively short-lived—in April 1843 the Post Office changed its policy and began charging book postage on cheap reprints—it also did considerable economic damage to both American book publishers and writers at the time it occurred. The Post Office's new ruling eventually served to kill off the leading serial reprinters but not before a widespread competition in cheap reprints had led to price-cutting that glutted the market and severely reduced revenues of regular publishers who also had brought out cheap reprints of their own. In 1843 retail prices of books were driven so low that it became extremely difficult for publishers to make money off the sales of new books by American authors, and it was not until the late 1840s that prices again rose to levels where some profits were possible.

Dealing in books remained risky for yet another reason. For example, something of an Anglo-American market for books came into existence during the first half of the nineteenth century, with many leading American publishers then establishing their own agents in London. Yet here too distribution costs were often discouragingly expensive. Mail service was not only costly but also notoriously slow and unreliable. High exchange rates also meant that imported British books sometimes became too expensive for the American market, and freight and duty charges only added further to the cost of books. Perhaps most damaging of all, however, was the absence of an international copyright law. This not only made it difficult for publishers and writers to benefit financially from even modestly successful ventures, it made the practice of literary piracy commonplace on both sides of the Atlantic until the passage of the International Copyright Law in 1891.

Finally, Ronald J. Zboray has pieced together a somewhat different pattern of evidence to argue against the notion that books—with only a few well-known exceptions—ever became the object of mass consumption before the Civil War. Despite the glowing accounts of growth in production and readership provided by antebellum American publishers, the earliest innovations in nineteenth-century print technology served to create new markets for books whose lavish illustrations and elaborate bindings made them luxury items well beyond the reach of most Americans. Technological innovations and the expansion of the book market did cut the average price of hardcover books to between $0.75 and $1.25—which was roughly half the cost in the late eighteenth century. (The first editions of both sets of Emerson's *Essays* and of Thoreau's *Walden* were priced at $1.00.) However, as Zboray has pointed out, in an economic setting where skilled white male workers made only about a dollar a day, and white women workers usually only a quarter of that, the one-dollar price of most books represented a full one-sixth of a male's weekly wages and well over half of the woman's wages, equivalent today to anywhere between fifty and one hundred dollars. It also is worth noting here that most of the "story-papers" of the early 1840s appear to have stood out of the reach of ordinary Americans. Only a handful of these papers sold for as low as twelve-and-a-half cents; the most common price was fifty cents. Moreover, while it may be reasonable to consider these supplements as "mass-market" items in their own time, publishers could make a profit on a sale of five thousand copies, and even the most successful issues of the story-papers rarely sold more than thirty thousand.

Finally, and perhaps most important, those few books that could be bought cheaply by Americans during the 1840s and 1850s typically were novels by French and British authors, whose writings were as yet unprotected by an international copyright law, and whose popularity revealed America's continuing cultural dependency. By contrast, few American novels appeared in very inexpensive editions before the mid-1850s, and the continuing high prices for American-authored books suggests that technological innovations in printing had yet to bring American literature to the masses in book form.

AN OPEN AND PLURALISTIC CULTURE

All this scholarship has deepened our understanding of the workings of American culture between 1820 and 1870. Yet it also has made it difficult to find a straightforward historical generalization that captures all the diverse and sometimes contradictory developments that characterized American culture during these decades. In the end, then, it may be somewhat misleading to speak of *the* American literary marketplace. Research has not revealed the existence of a single literary marketplace in which professional writers for the first time came to confront a new mass audience of readers. Rather, an open and pluralistic culture emerged in which the new forms of print remained closely bound up with other more traditional forms of cultural activity and sought to gain attention of diverse audiences of individuals who still wanted to look and hear, as well as to read.

One should keep in mind, too, that other cultural entrepreneurs, operating out of the same urban centers where editors and publishers presided over the world of print, took advantage of new technologies and the general rise of personal wealth to expand the production and consumption of the fine arts, music, and theater. Joined with the huge amount and variety of fact and opinion available in print, this babble of voices that competed to instruct and entertain nineteenth-century Americans served to create what Donald Scott has described aptly as "a vast cultural bazaar" ("Print and the Public Lecture System," p. 292).

To say all this is not to ignore the fact that the evidence still points toward a fundamental transformation from an oral to a print culture. This transition must at the same time be described as a historical change that was still in the early stages of development in 1870, and in which the creation of mass culture remained only one among many possible outcomes. Viewed from this angle, it also seems fair to say that while the assertion that mid-nineteenth-century America was a nation of novel readers correctly describes the aspirations of novelists and their publishers, it does not serve as an accurate description of the dominant cultural activity that took place during this period. There was no one dominant activity.

See also Book Publishing; Gift Books and Annuals; Literacy; Periodicals; Publishers

BIBLIOGRAPHY

Secondary Works

Brown, Richard D. *Knowledge Is Power: The Diffusion of Information in Early America, 1700–1865.* New York: Oxford University Press, 1989.

Charvat, William. *Literary Publishing in America, 1790–1850.* Philadelphia: University of Pennsylvania Press, 1959.

Davidson, Cathy N. *Revolution and the Word: The Rise of the Novel in America.* New York: Oxford University Press, 1986.

Gilmore, Michael T. *American Romanticism and the Marketplace.* Chicago: University of Chicago Press, 1985.

Gilmore, Michael T. "The Book Marketplace I." In *The Columbia History of the American Novel,* edited by Emory Elliott. New York: Columbia University Press, 1991.

Gross, Robert A. "Printing, Politics, and the People" *Proceedings of the American Antiquarian Society* 99, part 2 (1989): 375–397.

Levine, Lawrence W. *Highbrow/Lowbrow: The Emergence of Cultural Hierarchy in America.* Cambridge, Mass.: Harvard University Press, 1988.

Mott, Frank Luther. *American Journalism: A History, 1690–1960.* New York: Macmillan, 1962.

Mott, Frank Luther. *A History of American Magazines, 1741–1850.* New York, London: D. Appleton, 1930.

Mott, Frank Luther. *A History of American Magazines, 1850–65.* New York: D. Appleton, 1930.

Scott, Donald. "The Popular Lecture and the Creation of a Public in Mid-Nineteenth-Century America," *Journal of American History* 66, no. 4 (1980): 791–809.

Scott, Donald. "Print and the Public Lecture System." In *Printing and Society in Early America,* edited by William Joyce, David D. Hall, Richard D. Brown, and John B. Hench. Worcester, Mass.: American Antiquarian Society, 1983.

Tebbel, John. *A History of Book Publishing in the United States.* Vol. 1, *The Creation of an Industry, 1630–1865.* New York: R. R. Bowker Co., 1972.

Teichgraeber, Richard F. III. *Sublime Thoughts/Penny Wisdom: Situating Emerson and Thoreau in the American Market.* Baltimore: Johns Hopkins University Press, 1995.

Zboray, Ronald J. *A Fictive People: Antebellum Economic Development and the American Reading Public.* New York: Oxford University Press, 1993.

Richard F. Teichgraeber III

LITERARY NATIONALISM

For most of the latter half of the twentieth century, mid-nineteenth-century American literary nationalism appeared to be a straightforward subject. Early Americanists such as F.O. Matthiessen (1902–1950) and Richard Volney Chase (1914–1962) mapped out what Matthiessen labeled an "American Renaissance," centered on the New England and New York writers Ralph Waldo Emerson (1803–1882), Henry David Thoreau (1817–1862), Nathaniel Hawthorne (1804–1864), Herman Melville (1819–1891), and Walt Whitman (1819–1892). These authors were perceived to have adopted the main tenets of European Romanticism and to have adapted them to the demands and possibilities of what was still a new nation. Thus, while James Fenimore Cooper (1789–1851) could claim in *Notions of the Americans* (1828) that there was "not much to be said" about American authorship, and that it is "obvious that . . . the literature of England and that of America must be fashioned after the same models" (pp. 647–648), by 1855 all of the above writers had contributed to the creation of what came to be seen as a distinctively national canon.

Critics have identified other national narratives, told by Americans who did not belong to the northern male literary elite, and have challenged this account. Long-neglected writings by women and by African Americans have been rediscovered and reclaimed, along with the stories told by Native Americans and immigrants, and it is now generally recognized that American literary nationalism is a complex and multivoiced genre. Although Matthiessen's subjects were (and remain) integral to the emergence of a national voice, American literature was not merely constructed as a discourse concerned with distancing itself from English texts written in a shared language. Instead, as the writings of women, African Americans, and other once-marginalized groups illustrate, the American identity was multiple, contested, and unsettled in the years preceding the Civil War.

THE AMERICAN RENAISSANCE

The philosopher and poet Ralph Waldo Emerson is the pivotal figure in the emergence of the American Renaissance. In differing ways, all the other writers identified by Matthiessen can be said to have responded to Emerson's calls for a national literature. In essays such as *Nature* (1836), "The American Scholar" (1837), and "Self-Reliance" (1841), Emerson both defines what he sees as the principal characteristics of American identity, and calls for authors to represent them. Thus, in "The American Scholar," he announces that "our long apprenticeship to the learning of other lands, draws to a close" (p. 83) and demands that American writers follow his lead and "embrace the common . . . the familiar, the low" (p. 102). Despite the learned nature of his own prose, Emerson stresses the need for a literature that can celebrate the individualism, democracy, and equality that he identifies at the heart of American life.

Emerson's transcendentalism can also be seen to symbolize a particular nationalist ideology. He imagines the self to expand and to incorporate the universe at a time when the United States was adopting a policy of westward expansion and the ideology of Manifest Destiny (a term coined in 1845 by the *New York Post* editor and journalist John L. O'Sullivan to help justify the annexation of Texas). Emerson's quest for spiritual occupation of the continent echoes political nationalism's understanding of the relationship between Americans and what was assumed to be their land.

But Emerson is also writing at a moment of crisis: he begins *Nature* by stating, "Our age is retrospective," and calls for his generation to "enjoy an original relation to the universe" and "a poetry and philosophy of insight and not of tradition" rather than "grop[ing] among the dry bones of the past." For Emerson, the dependence on a European tradition and on history rather than self-reliance is distinctly un-American, and he makes a nationalistic demand for the "new lands, new men, new thoughts" to shape "our own works and laws and worship" (p. 35)

The succeeding generation of American writers, as identified by Matthiessen, address this sense of crisis in a variety of different ways, but each fosters his own brand of literary nationalism. Henry David Thoreau is perhaps closest to Emerson in his understanding of the importance of nature to the construction of individual and national selfhood, but Thoreau also extends Emerson's transcendentalist philosophy in two significant directions. First, where Emerson tends to deal in sweeping generalizations, Thoreau's writings are constructed around attention to detail, whether in listing his provisions during his stay at Walden Pond or in his measurements of the pond itself. Thoreau attempts to demonstrate an idealized version of the "simplicity" advocated by Emerson and juxtaposes this with what he sees as the overly complicated, economically driven lives led by his contemporaries. Second, Thoreau is unafraid to engage directly with political causes in a manner that is absent from Emerson's most famous early writings. Thus, in "Resistance to Civil Government" (1849), Thoreau explains that his refusal to pay his poll tax and subsequent imprisonment for one night is based (at least in part) on a principled opposition to slavery and to the war with Mexico and

on the belief that the problems of the United States are the result of the abandonment of the Bible and the Constitution and the "purer sources of truth" (p. 411) from which they stem. For Thoreau, the very concept of government is anathema to American identity based upon individualist action from principle.

For Walt Whitman, the process is as much to do with form as with content. Thus, while much of the subject matter of the first edition of *Leaves of Grass* (1855) echoes Emerson's ideas about the relationship of the self to the natural world and to the nation—as well as extending them to include celebration of the increasingly urban and industrialized society of which Emerson was deeply suspicious—the structures of poems such as "Song of Myself" are also important. Whitman's free-verse efforts to unite the nation at a moment when it was being pulled apart in the build up to the Civil War function in a variety of ways. First, the differences in layout of various sections mirror the diversity of peoples and environments within the United States. His claim that "I am large . . . I contain multitudes" (p. 85) is as much a commentary on his verse form as on the relationship between the poetic "I" and the nation. As subsequent revisions of *Leaves of Grass* illustrate, Whitman's poetry allows for expansion and incorporation of new ideas and peoples, just like the expanding nation. Unlike traditional formal poetry, Whitman's verse is always capable of being stretched to include celebrations of new aspects of an ever-changing and growing national identity. And like the nation pushing across the continent, the individual lines of Whitman's poems continue until their image or meaning is complete, rather than being curtailed by the lack of space of the old (European) world and its rigid poetic structures.

Like Whitman, Nathaniel Hawthorne is concerned with how Americans should write as well as with what they should say. Thus, while his romances engage with ideological and historical conceptions of what the nation should be as a fundamental component of their narratives, they also (both implicitly and explicitly) argue for a particularly American way of writing. Alongside engagement with issues such as self-reliance, class, the legacy of Puritanism, and the relationship of the self to the community, his fictions also contain a metanarrative considering the appropriate way to tell the national story. Unlike Emerson, Hawthorne feels that contemporary America can only be understood in relation to its past. Thus, many of his tales (including, most notably, *The Scarlet Letter*, 1850) utilize their staging in seventeenth-century Puritan New England as a means of allegorizing events taking place in the mid-nineteenth century. The point is made in two ways: in "The Custom-House" introduction to *The Scarlet Letter,* Hawthorne uses the indolence of his coworkers as an example of the lethargy he believes has replaced the zeal of his ancestors. Although Hawthorne finds much to fault in the Puritans, he believes that their energy—if not their lack of imagination and subsequent failure to tolerate other opinions—offers a positive alternative to the decaying society he sees around him. Hawthorne justifies his turn to the past as subject matter for his fiction because the world he represents in "The Custom-House" is dull and unimaginative.

For this reason, Hawthorne argues that the dominant European form of storytelling—the realist novel—is unsuitable to American needs. While the realism of Honoré de Balzac (1799–1850) and Charles Dickens (1812–1870) depended upon the complexities of class relations, urban geography, and political and legal intrigue based on hundreds of years of history, the relatively new and egalitarian nation, which lacked such surface complexities, demanded a different form. In the preface to *The House of the Seven Gables* (1851), Hawthorne explains that the writer of a romance should "claim a certain latitude, both as to its fashion and material" (p. 1) not available to the novelist. To discover the truths of the "new" nation, Hawthorne felt that it was necessary to look beneath the surface and to apply the powers of the imagination to the bare bones of historical detail. Unlike in the old world, where the surfaces presented the realities of individual and social identity, Hawthorne argued that in the United States the potential of the nation—the self-reliance that he called the "truth of the human heart" (p. 1)—could only be discovered elliptically, through the use of symbolism and allegory.

In many ways, Herman Melville is the most problematic of Matthiessen's authors. What are now considered to be his major novels (*Moby-Dick, Pierre, The Confidence-Man*) were largely unread during his lifetime, and those critics who did comment on his work, such as George Washington Peck (1817–1859), thought that Melville was more effective when writing about "savages" than when attacking white American society. Indeed, in response to the publication of *Moby-Dick* (1851), many critics felt that Melville had lost his mind.

Much of Melville's rediscovery in the twentieth century by the leading Americanists of the cold war, such as Richard Volney Chase, is due to their reading of *Moby-Dick*'s Ishmael as the embodiment of an American freedom juxtaposed with the totalitarianism of Captain Ahab. Nevertheless, such readings are highly problematic: rather than celebrating this freedom, Melville's writing echoes Emerson's in their

shared sense of national crisis. *Moby-Dick* and *Pierre* (1852), like shorter pieces including "Bartleby, the Scrivener" (1853) and "Benito Cereno" (1855), suggest that the politicians and people of the northern states are self-interested proto-imperialists obsessed with financial gain, and are complicit with (rather than opposed to) southern racial practice. For Melville, as for Thoreau, it is evident that the nation has deviated from the ideals established in the Constitution, and the fates of his non-conformists, such as Bartleby and Pierre, illustrate his sense of despair about modern America. Thus, while Melville's writing is nationalistic in its adherence to a particular set of principles laid out in one of the nation's founding documents, he sees little in his own culture that resembles those ideals.

OTHER VOICES

The notion that a select group of writers from New England and New York could speak for the American people remained largely uncontested until the 1970s. With a general critical consensus accepting transcendentalism as the benchmark of American cultural identity, even the most popular white male writers of the early to mid-nineteenth century, such as Washington Irving (1783–1859), James Fenimore Cooper, and the poets Henry Wadsworth Longfellow (1807–1882), James Russell Lowell (1819–1891), and John Greenleaf Whittier (1807–1892), were largely forgotten, their national narratives condemned for their adherence to European forms despite Longfellow's celebration of Native American legends and Lowell and Whittier's support for the abolitionist cause.

As popular a writer as Edgar Allan Poe (1809–1849) did not warrant a mention from Matthiessen, perhaps because his southern upbringing and sympathies generated a discourse that refused to participate in American cultural life in the manner of Thoreau, Whitman, or Melville. In line with his southern sympathies, Poe appears to have been not only proslavery but also very different from his New England contemporaries in his understanding of the writer as an aristocratic, rather than democratic, figure and in his attitude toward women. In addition, most of Poe's fictions deal with American national identity obliquely, in narratives set in a timeless European past, rather than in the open fashion of Thoreau, Whitman, and Melville. As a result—and also perhaps because of the unease with which most critics confront his political position—Poe has tended to be read as a modernist and removed from his specific historical circumstances. The defeat of the South in 1865 and the canonization of transcendentalism as the embodiment of American literary nationalism have led many critics to forget the extent to which the debate over what constituted American literature was contested at the time.

WOMEN AND LITERARY NATIONALISM

The exclusion of women from the nationalist canon was a product of the belief that women's lives were confined to the domestic sphere and that their selves were defined accordingly. In some ways, the writers of the American Renaissance underwrote the process: following the death of the leading transcendentalist Margaret Fuller (1810–1850), Emerson spent many years subtly undermining her reputation; likewise, Hawthorne and Melville resented and ridiculed the success of their much more commercially successful female contemporaries, condemned by Hawthorne in a letter to his publisher as a "damned mob of scribbling women." Later, a generation of critics that accepted implicitly the primacy of the public, political world assumed, almost by definition, that writing by women would be inferior and unimportant.

More recently, this dichotomy has been reassessed in various ways: critics such as Jane Tompkins have argued that the sentimental fiction of writers including Harriet Beecher Stowe (1811–1896), Susan Warner (1819–1885), and Fanny Fern (Sarah Payson Willis Parton, 1811–1872) performed essential cultural work and is as important as the works of Hawthorne and Melville in the construction of an American literature. Thus, most famously in the case of Stowe's *Uncle Tom's Cabin* (1852), sentimental narratives function as jeremiads showing their American readership how the country is straying from its proper course, warning of the consequences if matters are not rectified, and promising national and spiritual salvation if, as Stowe puts it, people's feelings "are in harmony with the sympathies of Christ" (p. 624). *Uncle Tom's Cabin* is largely addressed to wives and mothers and is an attempt not only to imagine the nation from a female perspective but also to use that perspective to change the nation's cultural identity. Thus, unlike the individual self-reliance of Emerson, Thoreau, and Hawthorne, it posits national identity collectively. The book serves as one example of what Amy Kaplan and others have pointed out—that is, the extent to which women were not merely confined to the domestic sphere (counter to earlier critical belief) but participated in the public debate over national identity, in the call for suffrage and abolition, and in political debates over Indian removal and Manifest Destiny.

The multitude of recent studies of Emily Dickinson (1830–1886) has also illustrated the degree to which this "private" poet both challenges and reshapes our sense of literary nationalism. Although Dickinson tends to be contrasted with Whitman— they had differing attitudes to American public and private life and opposing verse forms—such bracketing is unnecessarily restrictive. Dickinson's privacy in itself serves as an ironic commentary on nationalist narratives of individual self-reliance, from the perspective of a writer whose options were limited because she was a woman. In her verse, Dickinson turns such narratives inward, experiencing processes of self-discovery through internal journeys, and through the act of writing, rather than through the travels across public space that characterize the works of Whitman and Melville.

In the form of her verse, Dickinson also challenges the equation of a national voice with limitless space. Her ideas are condensed into short poems, constantly disrupted by her use of dashes, and her subject matter is equally fragmented. Where Whitman seeks symbolic harmony between the "multitudes" he "contains," Dickinson's verse epitomizes the divided nature of the United States at the time, both in its form and in her refusal to reach tidy, unifying conclusions. Perhaps more than any other writer of her time, Dickinson illustrates the irresolvable conflicts that were tearing the nation apart.

MULTICULTURAL LITERARY NATIONALISM

A further product of the construction of an American literary canon comprised of white New England and New York writers involved in adapting (and distancing themselves from) the European Romantic tradition was the marginalization of other racial voices. Much recent criticism has demonstrated that fugitive slave narratives can be seen to construct a very different kind of national literary identity that both embraces and subverts dominant narratives of individualism and self-reliance. In addition, scholars such as Eric J. Sundquist and John Carlos Rowe have extended the critical studies of African American literature conducted in the 1960s and 1970s in order to illustrate the presence of African folklore alongside strategies of affirmation developed to deal with centuries of oppression, not only in slave narratives but also in the work of white writers such as Melville. Sundquist sees a reciprocal process of exchange between the traditions of European American and African American literatures, and Rowe shows how the explicitly political works of Frederick Douglass (1818–1895) and Harriet Jacobs (c. 1813–1897) engage more directly with national identity than do many texts by Emerson, Whitman, and Melville. It is clear not only that there are important independent traditions inherent to women, and to African Americans (as well as to other groups whose narratives had less effective political or literary impact at the time, such as Native Americans), but also that there is an ongoing dialogue across and among these groups and the figures once assumed to define American literary nationalism.

See also "The American Scholar"; *Leaves of Grass;* Literary Criticism; Manifest Destiny; Transcendentalism; Young America

BIBLIOGRAPHY
Primary Works
Cooper, James Fenimore. *Notions of the Americans.* 1828. In *The Norton Anthology of American Literature,* vol. 1, edited by Ronald Gottesman, Laurence B. Holland, David Kalstone, Francis Murphy, Hershel Parker and William H. Pritchard, pp. 643–671. New York: Norton, 1979.

Emerson, Ralph Waldo. "The American Scholar." 1837. In *Selected Essays,* edited with an introduction by Larzer Ziff, pp. 83–105. New York: Penguin, 1982.

Emerson, Ralph Waldo. *Nature.* 1836. In *Selected Essays,* edited with an introduction by Larzer Ziff, pp. 35–82. New York: Penguin, 1982.

Hawthorne, Nathaniel. *The House of the Seven Gables.* 1851. Oxford and New York: Oxford University Press, 1991.

Stowe, Harriet Beecher. *Uncle Tom's Cabin.* 1852. New York: Penguin, 1981.

Thoreau, Henry David. "Resistance to Civil Government." 1849. In *Walden and Civil Disobedience,* edited with an introduction by Michael Meyer, pp. 385–413. New York: Penguin, 1983.

Whitman, Walt. *Leaves of Grass.* 1855. New York: Penguin, 1986.

Secondary Works
Bercovitch, Sacvan, ed. *The Cambridge History of American Literature,* vol. 2, *Prose Writing 1820–1865.* Cambridge and New York: Cambridge University Press, 1995.

Bercovitch, Sacvan, and Myra Jehlen, eds. *Ideology and Classic American Literature.* Cambridge and New York: Cambridge University Press, 1986.

Chase, Richard Volney. *The American Novel and Its Tradition.* New York: Doubleday, 1957.

Giles, Paul. *Transatlantic Insurrections: British Culture and the Formation of American Literature, 1730–1860.* Philadelphia: University of Pennsylvania Press, 2001.

Kaplan, Amy. *The Anarchy of Empire in the Making of U.S. Culture.* Cambridge, Mass.: Harvard University Press, 2002.

Lewis, R. W. B. *The American Adam: Innocence, Tragedy, and Tradition in the Nineteenth Century.* Chicago: University of Chicago Press, 1955.

Marx, Leo. *The Machine in the Garden: Technology and the Pastoral Ideal in America.* New York: Oxford University Press, 1964.

Matthiessen, F.O. *American Renaissance: Art and Expression in the Age of Emerson and Whitman.* London and New York: Oxford University Press, 1941.

Pease, Donald E. *Visionary Compacts: American Renaissance Writings in Cultural Context.* Madison: University of Wisconsin Press, 1987.

Reising, Russell J. *The Unusable Past: Theory and the Study of American Literature.* London: Routledge, 1986.

Reynolds, David S. *Beneath the American Renaissance: The Subversive Imagination in the Age of Emerson and Melville.* New York: Knopf, 1988.

Rowe, John Carlos. *At Emerson's Tomb: The Politics of Classic American Literature.* New York: Columbia University Press, 1997.

Sundquist, Eric J. *To Wake the Nations: Race in the Making of American Literature.* Cambridge, Mass.: Harvard University Press, 1993.

Tompkins, Jane. *Sensational Designs: The Cultural Work of American Fiction, 1790–1860.* New York: Oxford University Press, 1985.

Christopher Gair

LITTLE WOMEN

The novel *Little Women* (1868–1869), by Louisa May Alcott (1832–1888), tells the story of Meg, Jo, Beth, and Amy March, four sisters in a New England family whose father is serving as a chaplain for the Union during the Civil War. The first volume follows the family through the events of a single year; in the second volume, the story commences three years later, as the sisters transition into adulthood and come to terms with their ambitions and responsibilities.

TEXTUAL HISTORY
Louisa May Alcott, the second daughter of the educator and transcendentalist Amos Bronson Alcott and Abba May Alcott, was editing a children's magazine, *Merry's Museum,* when she was asked in September 1867 by Thomas Niles, an editor at the Boston publishing house Roberts Brothers, to write a novel for girls that might approximate some of the success experienced by the contemporary writers Horatio Alger and William T. Adams ("Oliver Optic") in their series books for boys. Initially scoffing at the request, Alcott noted that she did not know many girls or care much

Illustration of Jo and Beth for the first edition of *Little Women,* **1868.** Drawing by May Alcott, Louisa's sister. © BETTMANN/CORBIS

instance, "The Witch's Curse," the melodrama enacted by the March sisters on Christmas Day, alludes to characters and plots from the theatricals written and performed by Alcott and her elder sister, Anna, during their adolescence (published in 1893 with Anna Alcott Pratt under the title *Comic Tragedies*). The book of fairy stories written by Jo and burned by Amy in *Little Women* is reminiscent of *Flower Fables,* a collection of fantasy tales and poems dedicated to Ralph Waldo Emerson's daughter Ellen and published by Alcott in 1855. "The Masked Marriage," a romantic story excerpted and attributed to Meg in the Pickwick Club newspaper published by the March sisters in *Little Women,* was written by Alcott and published in 1852 in *Dodge's Literary Museum.* Jo's first published story, "The Rival Painters," shares its title with Alcott's first published story, which appeared in a Boston periodical, the *Olive Branch,* in 1852. An 1856 short story published in the *Saturday Evening Gazette,* "The Sisters' Trial," dealt with the artistic trials and romantic tribulations of four sisters: there, as in *Little Women,* one aspired to be an actress, another a writer, a third a musician, and a fourth a painter. Inspired by Anna Alcott's marriage to John Bridge Pratt, the story "A Modern Cinderella," which Alcott originally published in the *Atlantic Monthly* in 1860, depicts the courtship of Nan and John, forerunners of Meg and John Brooke in *Little Women.* The thriller stories published by Jo in New York City in part two of the novel are reminiscent of the blood-and-thunder stories that Alcott published—sometimes anonymously, sometimes under the pseudonym A. M. Barnard, or, occasionally, under her own name—in such publications as the *American Union, Frank Leslie's Lady's Magazine,* and the *Flag of Our Union* throughout the 1860s. The critical response Jo receives when her first novel is published is drawn from Alcott's own experiences upon the publication of her adult novel *Moods* in 1864.

Although she did not begin to write *Little Women* in earnest until May 1868, Alcott had finished the manuscript of the first volume by mid-July. Her youngest sister, (Abby) May Alcott, provided illustrations for the volume, and Roberts Brothers released it at the beginning of October to an overwhelming positive response. Prompted not only by the novel's considerable financial success but also by the thousands of letters Alcott received from eager young readers who wanted to know more about the characters, she began to write a sequel on 1 November. Finished by 1 January 1869, it was published in April 1869. Part two, also known as *Good Wives,* was illustrated by Hammatt Billings (who also illustrated, among other works, Harriet Beecher Stowe's *Uncle Tom's Cabin*).

for the ones she had encountered, other than her own three sisters, but, driven by her family's continual poverty, she agreed to try. Early in 1868 she began to experiment in *Merry's Museum* with characterizations and episodes that foreshadowed the content of the novel. In the editorial column "Merry's Monthly Chat" for January 1868, she sketched a brief story about four girls who give up their breakfast to help less fortunate neighbors—a prototype for the *Little Women* episode in which the March girls give up their breakfast to help the poverty-stricken Hummels. Alcott's short story in the same issue, "Tilly's Christmas," depicted a poor mother and daughter who are the recipients of a rich neighbor's generosity. In the rich neighbor, readers can see a model for *Little Women*'s kind, wealthy Mr. Laurence.

Familiarity with Alcott's earlier work, however, would show that in some ways she had been writing or preparing to write *Little Women* all her life. For

Volumes one and two were published in separate volumes for several years, although beginning in 1870 they were available in a set. In 1880 Roberts Brothers published a revised, 586-page single-volume edition with over two hundred new illustrations by Frank T. Merrill, which Alcott enthusiastically praised. The following year, as part of an eight-volume set of Alcott's works, Roberts Brothers issued what is known as the regular edition of *Little Women*, a smaller, 532-page edition without the Merrill illustrations. Neither Alcott nor Niles appears to have made the revisions that materialize in the 1881 text, although neither seemed to have objected to their being made; Niles commented in an 1883 letter to Alcott that the changes in style seemed to have resulted in additional sales. Among the textual changes, punctuation was modernized, spelling was modified, and instances of slang were deleted or changed. Characters were made more attractive and more fashionable: Laurie is taller, less ethnic (his "long nose" in the first edition becomes a "handsome nose" in the revised text), and more attractive; Marmee becomes a "noble-looking" woman; Meg's violet silk requires twenty-five yards of fabric, rather than twenty; and Professor Bhaer is described as more of a gentleman. The character of Jo in particular is altered so that she becomes less tomboyish, less colloquial, and more conventional.

Throughout the next century, the regular edition would be the version made available to most readers. It was not until the 1980s that the first edition was reprinted and studied. The changes in the novel and its textual history are the subject of ongoing scholarship.

LITERARY INFLUENCES AND ATTRIBUTES
In writing *Little Women*, Alcott alluded overtly in numerous instances to John Bunyan's *The Pilgrim's Progress* (published in two parts in 1678 and 1684), a Christian allegory that was among her father Bronson Alcott's favorite stories and one of the most well-known texts of the nineteenth century. The preface to *Little Women* is an adapted quotation from the second part of Bunyan's work, which, like *Little Women*, depicts a mother guiding and inspiring her four children as they journey through life toward a heavenly reward. Early in the novel, Marmee encourages her daughters to take up their burdens and travel toward the "Celestial City" as they did when they were children with the goal of overcoming their personal shortcomings and finding confidence and moral strength as they transition into adulthood. Chapter titles in the first volume emphasize Alcott's association of her characters with scenes and situations from *The Pilgrim's Progress*—for example, "Beth Finds the Palace Beautiful," "Amy's Valley of Humiliation," "Meg Goes to Vanity Fair," and "Jo Meets Apollyon," among others. Because of these allusions, many readers have assumed that the books Marmee gives her daughters on Christmas are individual copies of *The Pilgrim's Progress*. Other critics, however, have argued convincingly that Marmee gives each of her daughters her own copy of the New Testament. Nonetheless, the novel is inarguably structured on and inspired by Bunyan's Puritan allegory, although Alcott does translate Christian's journey into a more realistic nineteenth-century American female experience. Meg's "Vanity Fair" involves her weakness for French fashions and wealthy, if shallow, friends, while Jo's "Apollyon," rather than being an actual fiend, is her own temper, which she must learn to keep if she is to become an acceptable nineteenth-century American woman. Amy's "Valley of Humiliation" provides Alcott with an opportunity to point out the flaws in nineteenth-century American educational systems, and Beth's "Palace Beautiful," the Laurence mansion, features the artistic and aesthetic accoutrements of upper-class American culture.

Alcott's realism also draws from more contemporary American literary traditions. An important influence on *Little Women* is Susan B. Warner's (1819–1895) *The Wide, Wide World* (1850), in which the protagonist Ellen Montgomery must leave her ailing mother and go to live with a distant relative in New England. Like the March sisters, Ellen embraces *The Pilgrim's Progress* as a guidebook. She also struggles to fulfill her domestic responsibilities and resents her lack of economic and social status. Where the March family is befriended by the Laurences, Ellen is the beneficiary of moral, spiritual, and economic support from her neighbors John and Alice Humphreys. *The Wide, Wide World* follows Ellen from childhood into young womanhood, concluding with the promise of her marriage to John Humphreys. Though Ellen's experiences are more conventionally Christian than the March sisters', the realism of Warner's novel, with its folksy New England setting and occasional, rustic entertainments, would have been a model for Alcott's own work.

Another of *Little Women*'s nineteenth-century American forerunners is Harriet Beecher Stowe's (1811–1896) *Uncle Tom's Cabin* (1852), with its insistence on the sanctity of the family and its rejection of the institution of slavery. Set during the Civil War, *Little Women* depicts a realistic home front, in which the March sisters and their mother sew and knit in support of the soldiers, forgo extras in order to contribute to the war effort, and tell each other stories about others who are sacrificing everything they have in support of the Union cause. Father March becomes ill and Marmee must travel to a Washington hospital to nurse him, and John Brooke serves in the Union Army and receives an honorable discharge. (Both Warner's and Stowe's novels are directly alluded to in *Little Women*.)

Alcott's realism extends beyond setting and plot, however, into her compelling characterizations. Meg, Jo, Beth, and Amy, and their neighbor Theodore "Laurie" Laurence, strive for self-improvement, but in nearly every chapter they are doing something unusual, imaginative, and playful. They write and stage theatricals and found a Pickwick Club in tribute to the characters of Charles Dickens's 1836–1837 novel *Pickwick Papers,* who report to each other about their experiences as they travel around England; in the roles of Samuel Pickwick, Augustus Snodgrass, Tracy Tupman, and Nathaniel Winkle, Meg, Jo, Beth, and Amy write and publish a family newspaper very similar

to one the Alcott sisters produced in the late 1840s and early 1850s. The March sisters also establish a neighborhood post office, go on picnics, and are each devoted to a branch of the arts. They squabble, demonstrate jealousy and pettiness, are grammatically incorrect, and are lazy. Alcott depicts their activities with humor and sympathy—Jo's disastrous dinner party, Beth's dilapidated doll family, Amy's tendency to use the wrong words, Meg's romantic dreams. Because of the sisters' vibrant, appealing, realistic characterizations, readers have felt a strong connection to them since their first appearance in print. In comparison with another well-known nineteenth-century book for girls, also published in 1868, in which Martha Finley's (1828–1909) saintly title character, Elsie Dinsmore, dedicates her childhood to converting her father to Christianity, *Little Women* is surprisingly secular, playful, and real.

In the following excerpt from Little Women, *the sisters rehearse their Christmas theatrical. In it, we see the older sisters' affinity for acting and writing, Jo's desire to take on male roles (in art if not in life), personality clashes between Amy and Jo, and in general the sisters' ability to entertain themselves, despite their economic and social restraints.*

"I don't mean to act any more after this time; I'm getting too old for such things," observed Meg, who was as much a child as ever about "dressing up" frolics.

"You won't stop, I know, as long as you can trail round in a white gown with your hair down, and wear gold-paper jewelry. You are the best actress we've got, and there'll be an end of everything if you quit the boards," said Jo. "We ought to rehearse tonight; come here, Amy, and do the fainting scene, for you are as stiff as a poker in that."

"I can't help it; I never saw any one faint, and I don't choose to make myself all black and blue, tumbling flat as you do. If I can go down easily, I'll drop; if I can't, I shall fall into a chair and be graceful; I don't care if Hugo does come at me with a pistol," returned Amy, who was not gifted with dramatic power, but was chosen because she was small enough to be borne out shrieking by the hero of the piece.

"Do it this way; clasp your hands so, and stagger across the room, crying frantically, 'Roderigo! save me! save me!'" and away went Jo, with a melodramatic scream which was truly thrilling.

Amy followed, but she poked her hands out stiffly before her, and jerked herself along as if she went by machinery; and her "Ow!" was more suggestion of pins being run into her than of fear and anguish. Jo gave a despairing groan, and Meg laughed outright, while Beth let her bread burn as she watched the fun, with interest.

"It's no use! do the best you can when the time comes, and if the audience shout, don't blame me. Come on, Meg."

Then things went smoothly, for Don Pedro defied the world in a speech of two pages without a single break; Hagar, the witch, chanted an awful incantation over her kettleful of simmering toads, with weird effect; Roderigo rent his chains asunder manfully, and Hugo died in agonies of remorse and arsenic, with a wild "Ha! ha!"

"It's the best we've had yet," said Meg, as the dead villain sat up and rubbed his elbows.

"I don't see how you can write and act such splendid things, Jo. You're a regular Shakespeare!" exclaimed Beth.

Alcott, *Little Women*, pp. 14–15.

Particularly in the second volume, the characters of *Little Women* encounter more substantive personal disappointments and setbacks; they also struggle to maintain their moral and ethical beliefs as they leave home and venture out from under Marmee's careful supervision. Although Beth succumbs in the second volume to the aftereffects of the scarlet fever she contracted from the Hummels in the first volume, each of the surviving sisters finds male mentors with similar values who influence their choices and behaviors. Jo experiments with publishing thrillers before she recognizes, with Professor Bhaer's guidance, that she would be embarrassed to have her family know what she has been doing. Amy is determined to marry for money and status, yet when she is offered the opportunity to wed the Englishman Fred Vaughn, she ultimately cannot go through with her plan, in part because of Laurie's wise counsel. Meg is tempted by her desire for the kind of lifestyle her wealthy friend Sallie Moffat has, but an honest conversation with her husband deters her. In each case, Alcott contrasts "fashionable" or upper-class mores with the simple values originally established in the March family home. In addition, each character comes to appreciate the importance of relationships in connection with artistic achievement: Jo finds her greatest authorial success when she begins to write for her family; Amy recognizes in Rome that her talent, while evident, is not genius, and directs her talents to depicting her family and close friends; and Laurie, who originally wanted to be a famous composer, discovers that going into business is not the dreaded future it once seemed because it brings him closer to his grandfather. Although critics have complained that the characters seem to give up their artistic ambitions, Jo and Amy and Laurie are still practicing their respective arts—writing and sculpture and musical composition—at the end of the novel.

One of the most continuously successful American novels of all time, *Little Women* is perhaps the most significant depiction in literature of American girlhood. It offers readers a relevant, enduring depiction of the complex relationships of sisters. It also features a compelling, substantive depiction of male-female friendship. Jo and Laurie, whom Alcott refused to marry to one another merely to please her readers, have an intense, attractive, intimate relationship—one to which readers continue to react passionately.

RECEPTION

Since its first appearance in print, *Little Women* has attracted millions of enthusiastic readers, among them such famous figures as Theodore Roosevelt and Simone de Beauvoir. From the novel's first publication, Alcott became a celebrity. She published two sequels to *Little Women*—*Little Men* (1871) and *Jo's Boys* (1886)—in addition to other novels for young readers as well as a number of short story collections and sketches collected in six volumes under the title *Aunt Jo's Scrap-Bag* (1872–1882). Although highbrow authors such as Henry James and Edith Wharton disparaged her work and her talents, many authors of children's and adolescent literature have alluded to the influence of *Little Women,* among them L. M. Montgomery (author of the 1908 classic *Anne of Green Gables*), Jean Webster (whose orphan protagonist in the 1912 novel *Daddy-Long-Legs,* Judy Abbott, discovers that every other girl in the college she is attending has been raised on *Little Women*), Laura Ingalls Wilder (whose series of Little House books began in 1932), Beverly Cleary (whose series featuring the character Ramona first appeared in the 1950s), and many others. In 1893 *Little Women* was listed as one of the top forty best books in America, and in response to a poll sponsored by *Current Literature* in 1927 asking "What book has interested you most?" high school students chose *Little Women* as their first choice, followed by the Bible and *Pilgrim's Progress.* As of 1968 *Little Women* was one of the two most circulated books in the New York Public Library.

Little Women has been the subject of two silent films (in 1917 and 1918), three major motion pictures (1933, 1949, and 1994), and two made-for-television films (1970 and 1978), in addition to multiple theatrical productions, including a 1998 opera by Mark Adamo. In addition, it has inspired postage stamps, comic strips, cookbooks, dolls, and a 1997 episode of the television program *Friends.*

Although the novel was rarely the subject of serious critical consideration before the 1960s, it has become one of the most often analyzed American novels of the nineteenth century, particularly following the discovery and republication of Alcott's thrillers by the Alcott scholars Leona Rostenberg and Madeleine B. Stern. Critics have applied a wealth of critical approaches to the novel, including feminist, psychoanalytic, historical, New Historical, Marxist, and queer readings, with intriguing results. A bestselling popular novel, it has raised important critical questions about the connections between canonical and noncanonical works. A substantive, allusive, and compelling text, *Little Women* continues to appeal to professional and recreational readers alike.

See also Childhood; Children's and Adolescent Literature; Civil War; Domestic Fiction; Fashion; Female Authorship; *The Wide, Wide World*

BIBLIOGRAPHY

Primary Works

Alcott, Louisa May. *The Journals of Louisa May Alcott.* Edited by Joel Myerson, Daniel Shealy, and Madeleine B. Stern. Boston: Little, Brown, 1989.

Alcott, Louisa May. *Little Women.* 1868–1869. Edited by Anne K. Phillips and Gregory Eiselein. New York: Norton, 2004.

Alcott, Louisa May. *The Selected Letters of Louisa May Alcott.* Edited by Joel Myerson, Daniel Shealy, and Madeleine B. Stern. Boston: Little, Brown, 1987.

Secondary Works

Alberghene, Janice M., and Beverly Lyon Clark, eds. *"Little Women" and the Feminist Imagination: Criticism, Controversy, Personal Essays.* New York: Garland, 1999.

Clark, Beverly Lyon, ed. *Louisa May Alcott: The Contemporary Reviews.* Cambridge, U.K.: Cambridge University Press, 2004.

Delamar, Gloria T. *Louisa May Alcott and "Little Women": Biography, Critique, Publications, Poems, Songs, and Contemporary Relevance.* Jefferson, N.C.: McFarland, 1990.

Elbert, Sarah. *A Hunger for Home: Louisa May Alcott's Place in American Culture.* New Brunswick, N.J.: Rutgers University Press, 1987.

Keyser, Elizabeth Lennox. *Whispers in the Dark: The Fiction of Louisa May Alcott.* Knoxville: University of Tennessee Press, 1993.

Stern, Madeleine B. *Louisa May Alcott: A Biography.* 1950. Boston: Northeastern University Press, 1999.

Stern, Madeleine B., ed. *Critical Essays on Louisa May Alcott.* Boston: G. K. Hall, 1984.

Anne K. Phillips

LOWELL OFFERING

The *Lowell Offering,* a literary magazine written and edited by factory workers in the cotton mills of Lowell, Massachusetts, from 1840 to 1845, stands at the intersection of early industrial capitalism in the United States and changing modes of authorship, literary production, and gender identity. In the mid-1800s, Lowell, Massachusetts, developed into an urban center with large cotton mills operated by a group called the Boston Associates. The transition from rural life and labor in the region of Lowell to an early urban-industrial order was accompanied by a reconception of young womanhood. Daughters, rather than working on local farms or staying in rural communities, left home to become wage earners in vast industrial enterprises. The *Lowell Offering,* both as a general proposition and in its specific contents, used the idea of literary work to ease the cultural tensions associated with the movement of rural women from the family to the factory.

Young women were not the only laborers to move into factories in this early stage of America's industrialization, but their presence in this mode of production raised particular sorts of gendered problems. Factory labor removed women from the supervision of their families during young adulthood, at a moment when conventional patterns of courtship and marriage stood on the near horizon; it separated these wage earners from the economic unit of the family and their dependence on it; factory work also threatened to turn young women into "wage slaves," a class of chronically poor and abused industrial laborers that critics insisted was already visible in England's urban industrial economy. The mills at Lowell and the money earned at them provided potentially unpalatable personal freedoms to young women, even as they simultaneously threatened to compromise the femininity of those who came to be called "mill girls" by pushing grueling and unprecedented kinds of commercially driven work upon them.

LITERARY CULTIVATION AND "THE PLEASURES OF FACTORY LIFE"

In order to recruit their workforce for the mills in Lowell, the Boston Associates presented their enterprise less as the organization of young women into a potentially defeminized or proletarianized workforce and more as the congenial extension of the home life the factory girls had already been leading. The strategy was multi-pronged. The Boston Associates built boardinghouses, instituted codes of moral behavior that applied in and out of work, and paid supervisors of the residences to watch over the activities of the "factory girls." In addition, they sponsored a variety of social and cultural activities, including lectures, readings, and other events designed to uplift and educate their operatives in ways that could only be seen as desirable. Finally, the Boston Associates financed the publication of the *Lowell Offering,* a publication, as its title page reported, "written exclusively by females employed in the mills."

While scholars generally agree that the contents of the journal were, indeed, written by workers in the factory—usually under pen names, without clear attribution, or only signed by initials—the controlling, or at least influential, hand of those who owned and managed the mills is readily apparent. The *Offering* typically portrayed the girls and women working at the factory as inextricably bound to the rural families they had left behind, as workers who earned wages primarily so that they could bring or send them home to their families. Other stories highlighted the cultural activities and responsible supervision of the girls provided by management.

From 1840 to 1845 in the pages of the *Offering* the town of Lowell and the mills burgeoning along the river running through it became places for young women to have the paradoxically idyllic experience of independence monitored and constrained by a paternalistic company that stood in for rural parents. Workers at the mills' machines packed the earliest issues of the *Offering* with poetic, fictional, and autobiographical accounts of coming to Lowell and finding splendid opportunities for exposure to culture's finer forms in lectures, reading groups, and performances sponsored by the Boston Associates. Sarah Bagley, one of the most prominent contributors to the *Offering*, put it this way in her revealingly titled "The Pleasures of Factory Life":

> Let no one suppose that the 'factory girls' are without guardian. We are placed in the care of overseers who feel under moral obligations to look after our interests. . . . In Lowell, we enjoy abundant means of information, especially in the way of public lectures. . . . And last though not least, is the pleasure of being associated with the institutions of religion. . . . Most of us, when at home, live in the country, and therefore cannot enjoy these privileges to the same extent; and many of us not at all. (*Offering*, December 1840, pp. 25–26)

The mill town, here, far from taking daughters spiritually away from home, replicates home and its values in urban-industrial space, adding possibilities for education and increased attention to piety that are unavailable in the hinterlands.

LITERARY AND INDUSTRIAL CONFLICTS

At the same time, the *Offering* tended overwhelmingly to avoid accounts of the long and grueling days that operatives spent in drearily repetitive work at machines, but, during the years of the *Offering's* publication, operatives regularly worked twelve-hour days six days a week. The *Offering* also seldom hinted at any problems of adjustment with the move from rural rhythms and customs to those of a relatively small but booming industrial city. If, however, one turns away from the *Offering* and toward other publications and personal correspondence, one finds powerful, very direct evidence of dissatisfaction among the mill girls with the demands of factory and even urban life.

By the last years of its run, as mill operatives increasingly favored a reduction to ten-hour workdays, even the *Offering* acknowledged, sometimes only quietly, conflicts between management and the

---

THE FACTORY GIRLS DEFEND THEIR WOMANHOOD

An opinion extensively prevails, not merely beyond the limits of Massachusetts, that the manufacturing city of Lowell is a nucleus of depravity and ignorance.

Confessedly, wherever there exists *any* depravity or ignorance, there is *too much* of it. We have this to testify, however, that they who know least of the people of Lowell, including the Factory Operatives, entertain the most unworthy and unjust opinions of them. Close personal observation has satisfied us, that in respect of morality and intelligence, they will not suffer in comparison with the inhabitants of any part of moral and enlightened New England. We shall have occasion to speak of this subject at considerable length hereafter. We shall note the unsurpassed (if not unequalled) advantages of education enjoyed by our population; and the extensive means of information and piety furnished by popular lectures and religious institutions. We shall note the absence of theatres and kindred abominations; the care taken to exclude unworthy persons from the Corporations, &c.

("*Editorial Corner*," Lowell Offering,
October 1840, p. 16)

"She has worked in a factory, *is sufficient to damn to infamy the most worthy and virtuous girl.*" So says Mr. Orestes A. Brownson [editor of the *Boston Quarterly Review*]; and either this horrible assertion is true, or Mr. Brownson is a slanderer. I assert that it is *not* true, and Mr B. may consider himself called upon to prove his words, if he can. . . . And whom has Mr. Brownson slandered? A class of girls who in this city alone are numbered by the thousands. . . . girls who generally come from quiet country homes, where their minds and manners have been formed under the eyes of the worthy sons of the Pilgrims.

("*Factory Girls*," *signed* "*A Factory Girl.*"
Lowell Offering, *December 1840, p. 17*)

---

so-called factory girls and the generally difficult working conditions that prevailed. In 1844 one writer, describing her first experience of working at a mill in a series of published letters, noted the tremendous din of the factory. The noise of the machines affected her hearing and, after leaving the building, "it seemed as though cotton-wool was in my ears." At first, the racket bothered her, but "now I do not mind it at all. You know that people learn to sleep with the thunder of Niagra in their ears and the cotton mill is no worse." She added that "it makes my feet ache and swell to stand so much, but I suppose I shall get accustomed to that too" (*Offering,* June 1844, p. 170). Perhaps even more troublingly for the mill owners, the *Offering,* which in 1842 stated that "with wages, board, &c, we have nothing to do," by 1845 included an editorial in support of the ten-hour workday. Also in 1845 Sarah Bagley, who had earlier elaborated for readers on "The Pleasures of Factory Life," declared in the July issue of the pro-labor *Voice of Industry* that the *Offering* was effectively censored, or, in her words, "controlled by corporation influences" (quoted in Foner, p. 61). Not surprisingly, with these conflicts becoming more and more visible, the *Offering* ceased publication in 1845 and the *Voice of Industry,* a far more explicitly politicized periodical that received no support from the Boston Associates, became the main vehicle for the literary expression of factory workers.

This short history of the *Offering* suggests some of the more apparent reasons that historians and literary scholars have found it a noteworthy publication, despite its brief life and the absence of any individually canonized literary voices in its pages. The *Offering* makes clear some of the ways that corporate owners and managers sought to present the shifts to urban industrial life as palatable, and even desirable, to a growing industrial workforce unsure of early industrialism's virtues. It also shows the extent to which the laborers themselves could be brought into the process of imagining their work in ways that made it consistent with a preexisting sense of selfhood. Finally, with the publication's demise in 1845, the *Offering* also suggests that even in a publication so originally and apparently in sympathy with the advent of industrial labor and production, it is possible to look for ambivalent resistance to the process and for the persistent presence of rhetorical and material conflict between laborers and owners.

Even more intriguing from the perspective of those interested primarily in the history of literature and authorship in the United States, the *Offering* displays some of the important meanings attached to cultural activities such as reading and writing in the mid-1800s, particularly for women. Authors in the *Offering* did not typically imagine themselves as literary geniuses and on many occasions said so specifically. They wrote, for the most part, in very imitative

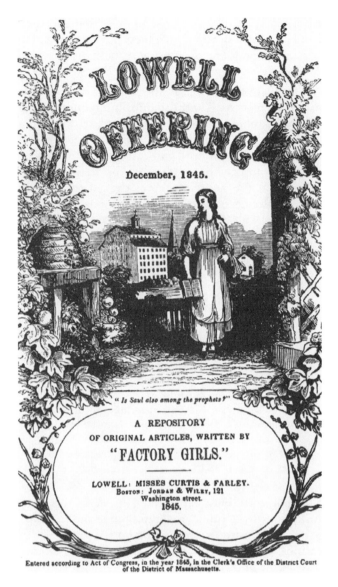

Title page of the *Lowell Offering*, December 1845.
© BETTMANN ARCHIVE/NEWSPHOTOS, INC./CORBIS

modes, echoing the language of feeling so central to the sentimental fiction and poetry of the period while making no claims to powerful originality. They wrote (at least in the early years) in ways that self-consciously reinforced a model of femininity grounded in feeling, in piety, in what some historians have called a "cult of true womanhood" and tried to reconcile this vision of the pure and angelic woman with the factory labor they performed. It was largely through their professedly modest engagement with the literary and their attendance at events such as educational lectures that these young, female industrial workers were imagined as beings higher and more spiritualized, more appropriately feminine, than would otherwise have been possible. The *Offering* and literary work, in other words, rhetorically removed the factory girls from the ranks of a proletarianized working class. It made them feminine; it aligned them with an idea that privileged literary cultivation over industrial production; it preserved the notion of attachment to rural families and moral codes over young women's moneymaking and potential independence from family.

The irony, of course, is that this use of the literary relied precisely upon and did nothing to contest a fundamental cultural polarization between the literary and the industrial. The *Offering* changed little about the perception of industrial work itself but served as a kind of beautifying garnish intended to dress up the object of anxiety that industrial work had become. This persistent polarization of the literary and the industrial shone through in the *Offering* again and again and sometimes highlighted by implication the drudgery of industrial work even as it sought to elevate the operatives who performed it. The *Offering*, for example, had as its epigraph on title pages a passage from Thomas Grey's "Elegy in a Country Churchyard" (1751):

> Full many a gem of purest ray serene
> The dark unfathomed caves of ocean bear;
> Full many a flower is born to blush unseen,
> And waste its sweetness on the desert air.

The passage undoubtedly points to the literariness of the factory girls. They know and quote Thomas Grey, and, thus, must not be debased industrial workers. In addition, the passage seems to position the operatives themselves as "gems" and "flowers" in possession of literary light and blossoms. In both of these ways, the engagement with the literary separates the operatives from ordinary industrial workers. But this passage also suggests that the mills themselves are dark caves and deserts seeking to obscure the expressive powers, the finer yearnings, of the operatives working in them. In order for the language of literary elevation to work, it must implicitly be contrasted with the drudgery of industrial labor that the girls engage in twelve hours a day in cavelike factories.

The final point about the *Offering*, then, is not that it collapsed when the material interests of the workers and the Boston Associates came too much into conflict, although that is a crucial part of the *Offering*'s history. Equally important is that built into the very idea of the *Offering* was the notion that industrial and literary labors opposed one another, that literary work was a higher, more spiritual, more appropriately feminine calling, especially when done in an imitative, sentimental mode. Given such a starting point, no one should have been surprised that the long-term showcasing of the mill girls' "literary" talent would be untenable as a defense of the factory floor and industrialization. Such a use of authorship assumed from the beginning that factory work was, in its nature, debasing.

See also Agrarianism; Factories; Female Authorship; History; Labor; Urbanization

BIBLIOGRAPHY
Primary Works
Eisler, Benita, ed. *The Lowell Offering: Writings by New England Mill Women (1840–1845)*. Philadelphia: Lippincott, 1977.

Foner, Philip S., ed. *The Factory Girls*. Urbana: University of Illinois Press, 1977.

Robinson, Harriet Jane Hanson. *Loom and Spindle: or, Life among the Early Mill Girls*. 1898. Rev. ed. with an introduction by Jane Wilkins Pultz. Kailua, Hawaii: Press Pacifica, 1976.

Secondary Works
Alves, Susan. "Lowell's Female Factory Workers, Poetic Voice, and the Periodical." In *The Only Efficient Instrument: American Women Writers and the Periodical, 1837–1916*, edited by Aleta Feinsod Cane and Susan Alves, pp. 149–164. Iowa City: University of Iowa Press, 2001.

Dublin, Thomas. *Women at Work: The Transformation of Work and Community in Lowell, Massachusetts, 1826–1860*. New York: Columbia University Press, 1979.

Husband, Julie. "'The White Slave of the North': Lowell Mill Women and the Reproduction of 'Free' Labor." *Legacy: A Journal of American Women Writers* 16, no. 1 (1999): 11–21.

Michael Newbury

LYCEUMS

After delivering a series of lectures at the Andersonian University in Glasgow in 1800–1801, George Birkbeck (1776–1841) helped to establish the London Institution for the Diffusion of Science, Literature, and Arts. In the early 1820s a group of mechanics in attendance at Birkbeck's lectures formed the Glasgow Mechanics' Institute. Within a decade the British mechanics' institute movement had gathered momentum via courses of lectures on chemistry, geometry, and hydrostatics with practical applications to the arts, astronomy, and electricity. In France, Baron Charles Dupin attempted to adapt the British movement to the needs of his country. The founders of these European institutions worked to procure lecture rooms and scientific apparatus, but the central feature of this new form of education was the public lecture, which would become a hallmark of nineteenth-century American culture. Experiments and demonstrations often accompanied public lectures, but the main purpose of these presentations was the scientific education of workers, which became the central objective of the American lyceum movement when it began in 1826.

DEVELOPMENT OF THE LYCEUM IN AMERICA

Josiah Holbrook (1788–1854), a Connecticut native and a graduate of Yale College, published his manifesto for a Society for Mutual Education in the *American Journal of Education* in 1826. Holbrook's first goal was to offer practical and useful information to young workingmen. A secondary objective was to apply the sciences to the domestic sphere or, more generally, to the common purposes of life. Holbrook suspected that he had a receptive audience for his plan in Worcester County, Massachusetts, where a mixed economy of manufacturing and agriculture furnished jobs for a population of mill workers, mechanics, tradesmen, clerks, and farmers. Shortly after submitting his article to the *American Journal of Education,* the first branch of the American Lyceum had begun in Millbury, Massachusetts. Within a few years, the lyceum had spread to the towns and cities of New England and then to other parts of the country.

The early lyceums seemed to come at a time of relative consensus about the need to improve education, to offer a context for learning, and to provide a setting for public debate. The growth of local lyceums coincided with the proliferation of a range of voluntary groups: agricultural societies, charitable organizations, corporations, library associations, and committees for the promotion of the arts. The lyceum may have stimulated reform of the country's common or district schools with its practices of assembling and distributing books and accumulating scientific apparatus. The simple requirements of a lyceum program included a small amount of money for start-up operations, a convenient public venue, and a series of small admission fees for a course of lectures. Despite such modest features, the lyceum movement also established an atmosphere for subsequent forms of adult learning as well as tax-supported public education. In Massachusetts, Horace Mann (1796–1859), secretary of the Board of Education, traveled throughout the state in the 1830s and 1840s to promote the cause of popular education.

Many proponents of the lyceum professed that it was open to all classes and social groups. As did other speakers, the popular travel writer and lecturer Bayard Taylor (1825–1878) counted merchants, stable keepers, mechanics, and day laborers among the members of his audiences. When he lectured in the West, miners in his audience took regular breaks to consume the alcoholic beverages they had brought for the occasion.

Lyceum lecture by James Pollard Espy, meteorologist, at Clinton Hall, New York, 1841. Unsigned drawing. Espy's primary contribution was the development of a theory concerning the formation of rain clouds, a subject of wide popular interest. THE GRANGER COLLECTION, NEW YORK

In the West, Taylor also observed a greater social diversity in audiences representative of new immigrant groups, including Scandinavians and Germans. In marked contrast, when the young lawyer Emory Washburn (1800–1877) delivered his "Lecture, Read before the Worcester Lyceum" on 30 March 1831, he could not be persuaded of any foundation for discussing distinctions in ranks and classifications of people. Among other institutions, Washburn argued, the lyceum could be a force for social cohesion that discouraged reformers and workingmen from creating jealousies or tensions among classes. The lyceum system could serve to develop a harmonious society in which leaders could gather to discuss and to advance matters of public interest.

EDUCATION AND ENTERTAINMENT

In its first phase, the lyceum movement stressed mutual instruction and random lectures. By its second phase in the 1840s and 1850s, citizens in large cities might be able to choose from dozens of different courses of lectures, paid for via individual presentation or subscription. Local lectures had expanded so significantly that nearly four thousand communities contained organizations sponsoring public lectures. Aided by the growth of railroads and newspapers, the lyceum grew regionally and on such a scale that an intricate national circuit had developed that extended to the Midwest, the Middle Atlantic States, and the South. The popular lecture itself remained the centerpiece of this system, and many itinerant speakers achieved the status of national celebrities for their presentations. For those with speaking skills, the lyceum was a source of steady or supplementary income. Some lecturers charged for the individual appearance—typically $25 or $50 for a presentation. The lecturer Thomas Starr King (1824–1864) articulated his primary reason for performing: "FAME—Fifty and My Expenses." King's lecture "Substance and Show," which distinguished the force of ideas from the value of material things, became a staple of the lyceum circuit. Taylor styled himself essentially a poet and novelist, but he could not resist the income from speaking, and he sometimes gave over two hundred lectures per season, which would last from the fall to early spring. He might also take pains to arrange a full-scale lecture tour that might net him as much as $5,000 for three months' work. To meet the demands of such a regimen, lecturers might have to endure uncertain train schedules, inclement weather, constant movement, poor accommodations, bad food, and lack of sleep. Taylor resolved to give up the lyceum several times, but despite such unwelcome conditions, lecturing remained a mainstay of his income.

The public lecturer, with obligations to a local lyceum, committee, or other official body, fulfilled a socially defined and carefully bounded role, which precluded partisan or sectarian discourse. In "American Audiences" (1905), Thomas Wentworth Higginson (1823–1911) describes the lyceum lecturer as being under "strict surveillance" and likely to be "tested by an audience altogether hospitable, but merciless in its criticism" (pp. 77–78). The conventions of the lyceum were designed to immunize lecturers from the commercial marketplace, although several commentators distinguished the respectable public lecturer from the itinerant humbug or charlatan who peddled his stores of knowledge. Lecturers were discouraged from dealing with controversial topics, although Frances Wright (1795–1852) delivered her views on women's rights, free education, birth control, and so-called free union, which were presented in New York and were contained in her *Course of Popular Lectures* (1829).

Lecturers typically gravitated toward safer subjects: travel, history, biography, foreign affairs, and the art of living. Dressed in Oriental garb, Bayard Taylor might deliver a lecture on "The Arabs." For purposes of contrast, he would then speak in the same city on "Life in the Polar Zone," ultimately completing his lecture course with a more general offering on "The Philosophy of Travel." Even more popular than Starr King's "Substance and Show," Wendell Phillips's (1811–1884) "The Lost Arts," first delivered in 1838, challenged the notion that nineteenth-century developments in the practical sciences had outshone the wisdom of the ancients. Higginson's lecture on "Physical Education," also called "Physical Training for Americans," reflected his notion that fitness was an important aspect of human development as well as the lyceum's emphasis on personal improvement. Other recurrent topics were natural history, individual education, religious sentiment, and the cultivation and uses of the imagination.

As the Civil War approached, more controversial topics alternated with popular topics. Antislavery views were prominently displayed, and in 1845 Ralph Waldo Emerson and Henry David Thoreau challenged conservative town officials by inviting the fiery Phillips to speak before the Concord Lyceum. Mann, Edward Everett Hale (1822–1909), William Lloyd Garrison (1805–1879), Theodore Parker (1810–1860), and Horace Greeley (1811–1872) also mounted the lecture platform to denounce laws that sanctioned slavery. These lecturers sought to promote specific social values and to effect social reform, although the general thrust of the lyceum was alteration of people's attitudes rather than enactment of new laws.

Scientific lecturers tended to eschew complicated technical terminology and abstruse theoretical issues in favor of providing Americans with tangible practical information. Ormsby MacKnight Mitchel (1809–1862), a professor from Cincinnati, attempted, in language members of his audience could understand, to enlighten them about astronomy. His objective was to broaden popular understanding of science by exciting an eager interest in the subject of astronomy. Mitchel earmarked the income he derived from lecturing to fund the development of astronomical observatories in Ohio and elsewhere. In an attempt to advance primitive American farming practices so that they could compete with those of Europe, James Jay Mapes (1806–1866) lectured widely on agricultural science, primarily to farmers in the Northeast. Reflecting the fluidity of a an emerging professional world in which public intellectuals wore a number of different hats, Mapes turned from consulting work in analytical chemistry and activities as an expert witness in chemical patent cases to the promotion of new forms of agriculture on the lecture platform and in his periodical the *Working Farmer*. Working farmers turned to Mapes for possible answers to the problems of soil depletion. Although much of his scientific knowledge may have been derivative, Mapes is reported to have delivered more than 150 lectures in a five-year span in the 1850s.

If Mapes's lectures stressed the practical benefits of new practices for working farmers, other scientific lecturers turned to less-concrete topics. Orson Fowler (1809–1887) used the lecture platform to promote knowledge of phrenology, and his presentations often included professional delineations of the character of selected audience members. He also offered advice about health, raising children, and the institution of marriage. Fowler's promotion of the scientific study of phrenology was clearly consistent with the lyceum's goal of individual reform. Higginson took the subjects of religion and science in a speculative direction when he lectured on spiritualism in New York City in 1858 and 1859. Higginson believed that spiritualism rested on a set of facts that warranted verification, and the ideas from his lectures were eventually set forth in two pamphlets on the subject. Even those individuals who did not fashion themselves experts turned to more speculative aspects of science, as did Edgar Allan Poe (1809–1849) when he lectured in New York on "The Universe," eventually published as *Eureka* (1848).

Although Higginson recorded the advice of Wendell Phillips that "the two departments of literature and oratory were essentially distinct, and could not be well combined in the same person" ("On the Outskirts," p. 328), he and other literary figures did not slavishly follow such prescriptions. Many of Emerson's essays had their origins on the lecture platform, and the lyceum, his secular pulpit, afforded him and others a venue to try out ideas before they were refined and polished into published form. Works like Thoreau's "Life without Principle" and "A Plea for Captain John Brown" most often appear in standard anthologies, but a proper context for their genesis was their delivery as lectures to live audiences. As a lyceum performer Thoreau garnered mixed reviews, although some New England audiences savored the Yankee wit and clever wordplay in his lectures on "Cape Cod." Even the opening chapters of *Walden* (1854) take on greater resonance if one knows their origin as lectures in the late 1840s before local lyceums in Concord and other locations in New England.

The lyceum was not the most hospitable setting for the cause of belles lettres, although Henry Norman Hudson (1814–1886) championed Shakespeare's works to American audiences in a series of popular lectures. Nor was poetry the usual fare on the lecture circuit, as evidenced by the hostile reaction afforded Poe when he read his lengthy philosophical poem "Al Aaraaf" before the Boston Lyceum in 1845. John G. Saxe's (1816–1887) satirical verse fared better, and Park Benjamin (1809–1864) often recited his "Age of Gold," written in the wake of the California gold rush. Literary criticism fared more poorly than poetry, as evidenced by indifferent or hostile reactions to Poe. He was attacked in Boston for ridiculing didactic verse, and his lectures on "American Poetry" (1843), "The Poets and Poetry of America" (1848) and "The Poetic Principle" (1848–1849) stimulated mixed responses at best. He earned greater praise when he recited his popular poem "The Raven."

At the outset of the lyceum, most lecturers, predominantly male, came from the ranks of the clergy and the law. Higginson dates the financial high point of this phase of popular lecturing as the period soon after the Civil War, when Henry Ward Beecher (1813–1887) could command a speaking fee of $200 per appearance. The temperance advocate John B. Gough (1817–1886) and the Universalist clergyman E. H. Chapin (1814–1880) followed close behind. Charles Sumner (1811–1874), George William Curtis (1824–1892), Oliver Wendell Holmes (1809–1894), Anna Dickinson (1842–1932), Edwin P. Whipple (1819–1886), and Frederick Douglass (1818–1895) achieved slightly lower grades of popularity. In "A Plea for Culture" (1867; *Atlantic Essays*, 1871), however, Higginson noted an overall decline in the quality of public address. By the 1880s some veteran lecturers like Curtis, Higginson, and Josiah G. Holland (1819–1881) praised the antebellum lyceum but derided its postwar counterpart, which had devolved into a setting that stressed entertainment rather than education. The lecture system had become more commercialized, and managers from central booking agencies like those owned by James Redpath and Major J. B. Pond replaced the informal practices and modest speaking fees of local committees with a system that emphasized "Star Courses," lucrative contractual arrangements, and profits for promoters. Nevertheless, the lecture made somewhat of a comeback with its reemergence, albeit in altered form, in the Chautauqua tent. If the public lecture had once opened the doors to the pursuit of culture to a hungry population that wanted its benefits, the economic prosperity in cities and emerging manufacturing towns widened the gap between the populations in these growing centers and the poorer inhabitants in villages outside them. In *Ethan Frome* (1911) Edith Wharton's (1862–1937) title character sought refuge from his cultural impoverishment and intellectual starvation in rural western Massachusetts by traveling to bigger "towns, where there were lectures and big libraries and 'fellows doing things.'"

See also Abolitionist Writing; Education; Literacy; Oratory; Transcendentalism

BIBLIOGRAPHY

Primary Works

Higginson, Thomas Wentworth. "American Audiences." In *Part of a Man's Life,* pp. 73–92. Boston and New York: Houghton Mifflin, 1905.

Higginson, Thomas Wentworth. "On the Outskirts of Public Life." In *Cheerful Yesterdays,* pp. 326–361. Boston: Houghton Mifflin, 1898.

Taylor, Bayard. *Selected Letters of Bayard Taylor.* Edited by Paul C. Wermuth. Lewisburg, Pa.: Bucknell University Press, 1997.

Secondary Works

Bode, Carl. *The American Lyceum: Town Meeting of the Mind.* New York: Oxford University Press, 1956.

Buell, Lawrence. "New England Oratory from Everett to Emerson." In *New England Literary Culture: From Revolution through Renaissance,* pp. 137–165. Cambridge, U.K.: Cambridge University Press, 1986.

Kett, Joseph F. *The Pursuit of Knowledge under Difficulties: From Self-Improvement to Adult Education in America, 1750–1990.* Stanford, Calif.: Stanford University Press, 1994.

Mead, David. *Yankee Eloquence in the Middle West: The Ohio Lyceum, 1850–1870.* East Lansing: Michigan State College Press, 1951.

Scott, Donald M. "The Popular Lecture and the Creation of the Public in Mid-Nineteenth-Century America."
Journal of American History 66 (March 1980): 791–809.

Scott, Donald M. "The Professon That Vanished: Public Lecturing in Mid-Nineteenth-Century America." In *Professions and Professional Ideologies in America,* edited by Gerald L. Geison, pp. 12–28. Chapel Hill: University of North Carolina Press, 1983.

Kent P. Ljungquist

LYRIC POETRY

The poets most associated with nineteenth-century American writing are Emily Dickinson (1830–1886) and Walt Whitman (1819–1892), but in their time they had not yet risen above the crowd. Emily Dickinson was barely known and published only a few poems in her lifetime; Walt Whitman was well-published and his name was recognized, but he was not at the peak of his eventual popularity. Perhaps the most popular poets of the time were the Fireside Poets, so called because of their sensibility to heart and hearth: William Cullen Bryant, Oliver Wendell Holmes, Henry Wadsworth Longfellow, James Russell Lowell, and John Greenleaf Whittier. Other writers who are well known for their prose also wrote poetry: Ralph Waldo Emerson, Herman Melville, Henry David Thoreau, and Edgar Allan Poe. They shared the poetry pages of books, magazines, and newspapers with others who were successful but whose names are not generally known: Jones Very, Frederick Goddard Tuckerman, Lydia Huntley Sigourney, Sarah Josepha Hale, and George Moses Horton. There were other poets, too, who, for the most part, were lost to posterity until they were rediscovered one hundred years later, in the 1960s and 1970s, when the canon of literature written primarily by European American males was opened to include the voices of the past that had been edited out of literary history, notably the voices of women and African Americans.

SETTING THE NATIONAL CHARACTER

Poets writing in the middle of the nineteenth century shared with the rest of the country the task of forging its national character and ideals. The war with Great Britain was over and, although its literature and the literature of Europe were still popular, the new country was ready for its own literary tradition, one commensurate with its ethnically diverse and burgeoning population, its vast territory, and the challenges and blessings of the technological revolution.

At the same time that the United States was stepping out of the shadow of England and Europe, it was letting go of the infrastructure of realism, the

"FEMALE EDUCATION"

Lydia Huntley Sigourney (1791–1865) published more than 46 books and 2,000 articles in her lifetime. Her poetry addressed pressing issues such as abolition and women's rights, and also contemplated personal issues of loss and suffering common to the period. Although her first book, Moral Pieces, in Prose and Verse *(1815), was published under her own name, she subsequently published under a pseudonym. In 1830 when her husband's business failed, she resumed publishing under her own name and supported the family with her writing income. Although her writing has been criticized for being sentimental, she was included in an 1849 series that also published Henry Wadsworth Longfellow (1807–1882) and William Cullen Bryant (1794–1878). This poem was probably addressed to Sor Juana Ines de la Cruz (1652–1695), a South American poet who promoted the education of women.*

Thou, of the living lyrd,
Thou, of the lavish clime,
Whose mountains mix their lightning-fire
With the storm-cloud sublime,
We, of thy sister-land
The empire of the free,
Joy as those patriot-breasts expand
With genial Liberty.

Thy flowers their fragrant breast
Unfold to catch its ray,
And Nature's velvet-tissued vest
With brighter tint is gay,
More blest thy rivers roll
Full tribute to the Sea,
And even Woman's cloister'd soul
Walks forth among the free.

Aid with thy tuneful strain
Her bold, adventurous way,
Bid the long-prisoned mind attain
A sphere of dazzling day,
Bid her unpinion'd foot
The cliffs of knowledge climb,
And search for Wisdom's sacred root
That mocks the blight of time.

Sigourney, *Zinzendorff*, p. 66.

Romanticism emerged with its emphasis on nature, personal experience, and imagination as guides for thought and action.

This trend was not unique to America, it took place throughout the Western world, but in America it was particularly suited to the emergent character and ideals of a nation that was still inventing itself and the zeal that accompanied its efforts. That zeal was manifest in several ways. First, perhaps, was the sanctification of democratic opportunity in the broadest sense, meaning freedom from classist roles set at birth. This trend also was not unique to America, revolutions were occurring elsewhere, but rather than forcing change in preexisting institutions, it helped give shape to the United States' emerging institutions. With it came the beginnings of the women's movement and increased dialogue on the immorality of slavery, the former leading to the first women's rights gathering, the 1848 Seneca Falls Convention (Gray, p. xvii), and the latter to the Civil War (1861–1865).

Religious fervor accompanied the drive for a democratic common denominator and carried in it a mission for the country: America was to be the best example of democracy and would serve as a model for all the world. Reiterating a belief expressed frequently in the documents of the Continental Congress, Thomas Jefferson said, we "acted not for ourselves alone, but for the whole human race" (Nye, p. 12).

THE RANGE AND SCOPE OF LYRIC POETRY

The lyric poetry of 1820 to 1870 in America was as rich and diverse and contradictory as the decades themselves. Jones Very (1813–1880) in "The Hand and Foot" expresses the contradiction of the commanding but invisible presence of God and compounds it with the contradiction of inaction resulting in action.

The hand and foot that stir not, they shall find
Sooner than all the rightful place to go;
Now in their motion free as roving wind,
Though first no snail more limited and slow;
I mark them full of labor all the day,
Each active motion made in perfect rest;
They cannot from their path mistaken stray,
Though 'tis not theirs, yet in it they are blest;
The bird has not their hidden track found out,
Nor cunning fox though full of art he be;
It is the way unseen, the certain route,
Where ever bound, yet thou art ever free;
The path of Him, whose perfect law of love
Bids spheres and atoms in just order move.

(P. 193)

dominant philosophical stance of the eighteenth century that relied on reason and intellect in the search for truth and understanding. In its place American

The theme is reiterated in other poems including "The Silent" in which God speaks in the oxymoron of a silent voice:

There is a sighing in the wood,
A murmur in the beating wave;
The heart has never understood
To tell in words the thoughts they gave.

Yet oft it feels an answering tone,
When wandering on the lonely shore;
And could the lips its voice make known,
'Twould sound as does the ocean's roar.

And oft beneath the wind swept pine,
Some chord is struck the strain to swell;
Nor sounds nor language can define,
'Tis not for words or sounds to tell.

'Tis all unheard; that Silent Voice,
Whose goings forth unknown to all,
Bids bending reed and bird rejoice,
And fills with music nature's hall.

And in the speechless human heart
It speaks, where'er man's feet have trod;
Beyond the lips' deceitful art,
To tell of Him, the Unseen God.

(P. 202)

The simple title is a complexity unto itself, for there are three possibilities for who or what is "The Silent." God speaks with a silent voice and so is silent. Humans are unable to articulate that which God speaks, so they are silent: "Nor sounds nor language can define, / 'Tis not for words or sounds to tell." Even nature appears to be silent except in its iteration of God's voice and will: "Bids bending reed and bird rejoice / and fills with music Nature's hall."

Very was born in Massachusetts and attended Harvard. There he was influenced by Ralph Waldo Emerson (1803–1882), who said in an address to the Divinity School senior class, "God incarnates himself in man" (Bain, p. 135). This is a tenet of the informal transcendental movement and is clearly seen in Very's poems: God speaks in the human heart, as he does in the wind, and his "perfect law of love" directs the movement not only of planets but of the atoms that make up the larger world including human life.

Although Very wrote forward into the transcendental movement, he became identified with it after the fact of his writing and is not so much a product of the movement as he is emblematic of the change in thinking that took place in the early nineteenth century. The form and style of his poems reflect a bridge to the past as much as their content reflects a bridge to the future. "The Hand and Foot" is a sonnet, a poetic form that dates back to the thirteenth century. "The Silent" is also rhymed and metered, a poetic convention that would only begin to lose its grip on poetry toward the end of the nineteenth and into the twentieth century. The retention of form in poetry not only acknowledged the heritage of the new poems but also offered some measure of order in a world that was changing swiftly. Readers of the poetry of the time seemed to prefer this familiar comfort to the transformed writing of Dickinson and Whitman who defined their own forms and also defined their own subject matter, for both of them more a matter of consciousness and the unconscious workings of the mind than the workings of the world.

As Very was influenced at Harvard by Emerson, so was Frederick Goddard Tuckerman (1821–1873) influenced by Very, also while at Harvard. Very was Tuckerman's tutor in Greek, a common element in the nineteenth-century university curriculum. Tuckerman was born in Boston and spent some time in England. Most of his poems are sonnets, but the one that sets him apart is the 131-line "The Cricket" (c. 1870). Written in five sections, it would not have been considered unduly long. It is a mix of rhymed and metered lines coupled with blank and free verse. Section 1 starts conventionally with "The humming bee purrs softly o'er his flower; / From lawn and thicket / The dogday locust singeth in the sun / From hour to hour" (p. 69), but in section 2 the steady lines give way to play with sound and sense, the rhymes coming not in regular order, but in a tumble that echoes the statement of the section:

There let the dull hop be,
Let bloom, with poppy's dark refreshing flower:
Let the dead fragrance round our temples beat,
Stunning the sense to slumber, whilst between
The falling water and fluttering wind
     Mingle and meet,
     Murmur and mix,
No few faint pipings from the glades behind,
     Or alder-thicks:
But louder as the day declines,
From tingling tassel, blade, and sheath,
Rising from nets of river vines,
     Winrows and ricks,
     Above, beneath,
     At every breath,
At hand, around, illimitably
Rising and falling like the sea,
     Acres of cricks!

(Pp. 69–70)

Section 3 of the poem introduces a subject common to nineteenth-century poetics: the struggle to comprehend and live with loss and grief. Tuckerman lost an infant daughter and then his wife. In the poem, the singing of the cricket stirs dual and contradictory emotions: happy memory and sorrowful remembrance:

Thou bringest too, dim accents from the grave
To him who walketh when the day is dim,

Dreaming of those who dream no more of him,
With edged remembrances of joy and pain;
And heyday looks and laughter come again:
Forms that in happy sunshine lie and leap,
with faces where but now a gap must be,
Renunciations, and partitions deep
And perfect tears, and crowning vacancy!
And to thy poet at the twilight's hush,
No chirping touch of lips with laugh and blush,
But wringing arms, hearts wild with love and woe,
Closed eyes, and kisses that would not let go.

(Ll. 50–62)

The draw to death as a subject is understandable in an era before the discovery of penicillin and other benefits of twentieth-century medicine. A measure of the depth of loss was the occasional practice of not naming a child before the age of one lest it not live through those vulnerable years.

The poem "Death of an Infant" by Lydia Huntley Sigourney (1791–1865) models the sentimental poem of the early nineteenth century, marked by a glossing-over of the darker elements of loss: "But there beamed a smile, / So fixed, so holy, from that cherub brow, / Death gazed, and left it there. He dared not steal / The signet ring of Heaven" (*Select Poems*, p. 31). Poems such as this were especially popular among women, but twentieth-century rereadings of women's writing of the nineteenth century have revealed a robust literature that seriously addresses compelling issues, including death. "The Stars," by Sigourney, was well-known. This first stanza addresses stars in general. Subsequent stanzas address specific constellations and reveal Sigourney's knowledge of classic mythologies.

The Stars
Make friendship with the stars.
Go forth at night,
And talk with Aldebaran, where he flames
In the cold forehead of the wintry sky.
Turn to the sister Pleiades, and ask
If there be death in Heaven? A blight to fall
Upon the brightness of unfrosted hair?
A severing of fond hearts? A place of graves?
Our sympathies are with you, stricken stars,
Clustering so closely round the lost one's place.
Too well we know the hopeless toil to hide
The chasm in love's fond circle. The lone seat
Where the meek grandsire, with his silver locks,
Reclined so happily; the fireside chair
Whence the fond mother fled; the cradle turn'd
Against the wall, and empty; well we know
The untold anguish, when some dear one falls.
How oft the life-blood trickling from our hearts,
Reveals a kindred spirit torn away!
Tears are our birth-right, gentle sister train,
And more we love you, if like us ye mourn.

(Select Poems, pp. 21–22)

PUBLIC TRAGEDIES

Besides struggling with personal loss, citizens of the fitful new country also had to come to terms with the public tragedies of slavery, the Civil War, the assassination of President Abraham Lincoln (14 April 1865), and the desperate situation of the American Indians. The 1830 Removal Act allowed relocation of eastern Native Americans to western land and culminated in the 1838–1839 Cherokee Trail of Tears, a forced migration that resulted in the deaths of more than four thousand Cherokee people. More concerned with affairs outside the home than was generally recognized in literary criticism, which held that women were restricted to sentimental writing by virtue of their gender, Sigourney empathized, in "Indian Names" (1834), with the Native Americans and their situation:

Wachuset hides its lingering voice
Within its rocky heart,
And Alleghany graves its tone
Throughout his lofty chart:
Monadnock on his forehead hoar
Doth seal the sacred trust;
Your mountains build their monument,
Though ye destroy their dust.

(Select Poems, pp. 259–260)

Sigourney, born in Connecticut, was one of the most successful women writers in the mid-nineteenth century. She supported her family with her publications after her husband's finances collapsed. *Godey's Lady's Book*, the most popular women's magazine of the era, paid her $500 annually just to list her name as an editor. The literary editor of *Godey's* was another successful woman writer, Sarah Josepha Hale (1788–1879), who was born in New Hampshire. Although her most well-known poem is the sentimental children's nursery rhyme "Mary Had a Little Lamb," Hale, widowed with five children, supported her family with her writing, publishing, and editing, including her publication of anthologies of writing by women. Hale's passion for her work is revealed in a passage from "First Hour" (1848), a section of her longer work "Three Hours; or, The Vigil of Love":

A blessing on the printer's art!
Books are the Mentors of the heart.
The burning soul, the burdened mind,
In books alone companions find.
We never speak our deepest feelings;
Our holiest hopes have no revealings,
Save in the gleams that light the face,
Or fancies that the pen may trace:
And hence to books the heart must turn,
When with unspoken thoughts we yearn;
And gather from the silent page
The just reproof, the counsel sage,

The consolation kind and true
That soothes and heals the wounded heart,
As on the broken plant the dew
Calls forth fresh leaves and buds to view,
More lovely as the old depart.

(Three Hours, *pp. 19–20*)

Publishing also afforded opportunity to African Americans, who were otherwise generally disenfranchised from business ventures. George Moses Horton (c. 1798–c. 1880) probably born in North Carolina was regarded to be the first professional African American poet and was published when he was still a slave. In the 1840s he successfully published his collected poems through subscription, a common means of publishing in the eighteenth century. In "The Art of a Poet" (1865), Horton wrote about the intellectual endeavor of writing poetry. He contemplates the process, ending with acknowledgment of the prize:

A bard must traverse o'er the world,
Where things concealed must rise unfurled,
And tread the foot of yore;
Tho' he may sweetly harp and sing,
But strictly prune the mental wing,
Before the mind can soar.

(Naked Genius, *p. 98*)

Horton also wrote about slavery, and about the Civil War. In "The Spectator of the Battle of Belmont, November 6, 1863," he articulates the unspeakable impact of battle—"What mortal, the fate of this combat shall tell?"—certain that a human cannot fully tell the tale: "The dark dirge of destiny, sung by a spirit, / Alone can the scene of the combat display" (p. 50). He also wrote about Lincoln's assassination and, in "Lincoln Is Dead" (1865), found compensation in the loss: "He is gone out of glory to glory, / A smile with the tear may be shed; / O, then let us tell the sweet story, / Triumphantly, Lincoln is dead" (p. 31).

Herman Melville (1819–1891), born in New York City, who is best known for *Moby-Dick* and other novels, also wrote about Lincoln's assassination. In "The Martyr" (1866) he closed with a bitter triumph: "There is sobbing of the strong, / And a pall upon the land; / But the People in their weeping / Bare the iron hand; / Beware the People weeping / When they bare the iron hand" (p. 122).

Prior to the Civil War, abolition was a common poetic theme often couched in the issue of the integrity of the new nation. John Greenleaf Whittier (1807–1892) was especially well known for his abolitionist stance, as was Melville, who predicted war as the inevitable outcome of the hanging of John Brown (1800–1859), an abolitionist who became a martyr to the cause. At the time, "weird" meant having the power to direct fate, and meteors were believed to portend significant human events. In Melville's poem "The Portent" (1859, 1866), the image of Brown's signature flowing beard is conflated with the image of a streaming meteor.

Hanging from the beam,
slowly swaying (such the law),
Gaunt the shadow on your green,
Shenandoah!
The cut is on the crown
(Lo, John Brown),
And the stabs shall heal no more.
Hidden in the cap
Is the anguish none can draw;
So your future veils its face,
Shenandoah!
But the streaming beard is shown
(Weird John Brown),
The meteor of the war.

(P. 53)

In 1851 Very also enjoined the argument, believing that slavery enslaved the country that condoned it:

Slavery
Not by the railing tongues of angry men,
Who have not learned their passions to control;
Not by the scornful words of press and pen,
That now ill-omened fly from pole to pole;
Not by fierce party cries; nor e'en by blood,
Can this our Country's guilt be washed away;
In vain for this would flow the crimson flood,
In vain for this would man his brother slay.
Not by such means; but by the power of prayer;
Of faith in God, joined with a sense of sin;
These, these alone can save us from despair,
And o'er the mighty wrong a victory win;
These, these alone make us free from all
That doth ourselves, our Country still inthral.

(P. 265)

Women also wrote about slavery. Sigourney's "To the First Slave Ship" (c. 1827) imagines the situation for the slaves who live with the injustice: "The fetter'd chieftain's burning tear,— / The parted lover's mute despair,— / The childless mother's pang severe,— / The orphan's misery, are there" (*Poems*, p. 176).

THE FRONTIER OF THE MIND

The exigencies of the body and its earthly state easily commanded the attention of poets. Edgar Allan Poe (1809–1849) was known both for his sensational and thoughtful short stories, and poems such as "The Raven" and "Annabel Lee." He was especially adept at parsing the dark side of the human condition, and he generally did not temper his vision with comforting thoughts of triumph in death. "The Conqueror Worm" (1843) ends without benefit of hope:

> Out—out are the lights—out all!
> And, over each quivering form,
> The curtain, a funeral pall,
> Comes down with the rush of a storm,
> And the angels, all pallid and wan,
> Uprising, unveiling, affirm
> That the play is the tragedy, "Man,"
> And its hero, the Conqueror Worm.
>
> *(Pp. 78–79)*

The little comfort that Poe is able to muster comes not from the potential of the future but from the fact of the past:

> *To Helen*
> Helen, thy beauty is to me
> Like those Nicéan barks of yore,
> That gently, o'er a perfumed sea,
> The weary, way-worn wanderer bore
> To his own native shore.
>
> On desperate seas long wont to roam,
> Thy hyacinth hair, thy classic face,
> Thy Naiad airs have brought me home
> To the glory that was Greece,
> And the grandeur that was Rome.
>
> Lo! in yon brilliant window-niche
> How statue-like I see thee stand,
> The agate lamp within thy hand!
> Ah, Psyche, from the regions which
> Are Holy-Land!
>
> *(P. 62)*

Poe used conventional forms in this and other poems, and called upon traditional mythologies outside of the American experience, but the wild nature of the stories he tells in both the poems and fiction breaks new ground for writers. Although not aligned with the transcendentalists, he shares with them, and with Whitman and Dickinson, the territory of the unconscious as proper subject for poetic treatment.

Ralph Waldo Emerson (1803–1882) and Henry David Thoreau (1817–1862) are the standard-bearers of the transcendental movement. Although both are primarily recognized for their essays, both wrote poetry that echoed the sentiments of the prose: it is not necessary to wait for the afterlife to attain union with God and the perfection and peace that attend that union. For the transcendentalist, God exists everywhere and is accessible through experience on earth, especially by way of contemplation, by yielding to nature, and through the work of the imagination. In this way, the soul can transcend the limitations of the body. Emerson's fifty-line, single-stanza "Each

and All" (1839) walks the reader through a pastoral scene and concludes:

> Pine-cones and acorns lay on the ground,
> Over me soared the eternal sky,
> Full of light and deity;
> Again I saw, again I heard,
> The rolling river, the morning bird;—
> Beauty through my senses stole;
> I yielded myself to the perfect whole.
>
> *(P. 10)*

Thoreau, too, excels at elucidating the pastoral, as in "A Winter and Spring Scene" which he brings to rest in a transcendent moment:

> The catkins green
> Cast o'er the scene
> A summer sheen,
> A genial glow.
>
> *(P. 583)*

The transcendental promise offered a new means of relief for ever-present loss. Instead of pining for peace in heaven, it can be gained through surrender to the presence of God in the present time and space. This expansion of the mental landscape echoed the geographic opening of the west and its opportunity without boundary.

THE PRAIRIES

From 1820 to 1870 fifteen states were admitted to the Union, from Maine to California and Minnesota to Texas. Three of them, Kansas, West Virginia, and Nevada, were admitted during the Civil War. Immigration expanded from 60,000 a year in 1820 to a peak of 427,833 a year in 1854.

The expansion into the West, which in the early 1800s referred to today's Midwest, was fueled by the doctrine of Manifest Destiny, a belief that the United States not only had the right to incorporate all of North America into its borders but also had an obligation to do so. This was consistent with the ideals of the country: that America was destined to lead the world in progress and achievement, and in democracy grounded in freedom.

The immigrant experience was often nurtured in hope and experienced in dismay. The potential wealth of the land had to be freed from its wildness—woods cleared, roads made, sod broken into soil for farming. The physical task was daunting, and although men and women both yielded to the necessity, many longed for the comforts left behind. In Sigourney's "The Western Emigrant" (1836), a husband is saddened by his wife's tears:

> "Wife! did I see thee brush away a tear?
> 'Twas even so. Thy heart was with the halls
> Of thy nativity. Their sparkling lights,

Carpets, and sofas, and admiring guests,
Befit thee better than these rugged walls
Of shapeless logs, and this lone, hermit home."
(Select Poems, p. 65)

Then, in sleep, he gives in to his own longing:

Up rose the thronging mart
Of his own native city,—roof and spire,
All glittering bright, in fancy's frost-work ray.
The steed his boyhood nurtur'd proudly neigh'd,
The favorite dog came frisking round his feet,
With shrill and joyous bark,—familiar doors
Flew open,—greeting hands with his were link'd
In friendship's grasp,—he heard the keen debate
From congregated haunts, where mind with mind
Doth blend and brighten,—and till morning rov'd
'Mid the loved scenery of his native land.
(Pp. 65–66)

Yearning and loss of place were also elements of poems that recognized the devastating experiences of the American Indians, dispossessed of their homes not by will but by mandate. Sigourney spoke to this in "Indian Names," and others also memorialized the loss, as did Micah Flint in "The Mounds of Cahokia" (1826):

Farewell; and may you still in peace repose.
Still o'er you may the flowers, untrodden, bloom.
And gently wave to every wind, that blows,
Breathing their fragrance o'er each lonely tomb,
Where earthward mouldering, in the same dark
     womb,
Ye mingle with the dust from whence ye rose.
(Olson, pp. 60–61)

However, the more common approach to the western experience was sentimental (Bain, p. xxvii). In his study *The Prairie in Nineteenth Century American Poetry,* Steven Olson notes examples of the romanticized experience, even regarding death, as in William Leggett's (1801–1839) "Lines Written on Leaving Illinois, Aug. 29, 1822":

Beneath the prairie turf they lie,
And sweetest wild-flow'rs deck the sod;
Their spirits soar beyond the sky
In sweet communion with their God.
(Olson, p. 60)

J. K. Mitchell, in "The Song of the Prairie" (1848, 1874), represents the land in sonorous and benign terms reminiscent of familiar and sentimental descriptions of oceans:

O! Fly to the prairie, sweet maiden, with me,
'Tis as green and as wide and as wild as the sea:
O'er its soft silken bosom the summer winds glide,
And wave that wild grass in billowy pride.
(Olson, pp. 62–63)

Poems like this one were especially popular in newspapers and magazines that were sold to a public hungry for news of the promising West.

THE TECHNOLOGY FRONTIER

The other promise at hand came with advances in industry and transportation. The incursion of roads and railroads proceeded steadily westward, the steam engine transformed river traffic, and the invention of the telegraph united the nation in time, as did the great media industry that sprang from advances in printing technology. Steam presses, advances in typography, and improved distribution systems cohered into an unprecedented publishing force that was unconstrained by copyright. The first such law was not passed in the United States until 1891 and reprints were produced without regard to ownership of the material. An increasingly literate reading public and improved oil lamps to read by at night fostered a ready market. From 1820 to 1860 publishing revenues increased eightfold, and an authors' list long dominated by Europeans became dominated by Americans.

Americans were not surprised. Progress was part of the national agenda and carried the imprimatur of the divine, as noted by Very in 1858:

The First Atlantic Telegraph
With outward signs, as well as inward life,
The world is hastening onward to its end!
With higher purposes our Age is rife,
Than those to which with grovelling minds
     we tend.
For lo! beneath the Atlantic's stormy breast
Is laid, from shore to shore, the Electric Wire;
And words, with speed of thought, from east
     to west
Dart to and fro on wings that never tire.
May never man, to higher objects blind,
Forget by whom this miracle was wrought;
But worship and adore the Eternal Mind,
Which gave at length to man the wondrous
     thought;
And on wise-hearted men bestowed the skill
His Providential Purpose to fulfill.
(Pp. 311–312)

POETRY'S PLACE

Poetry was an integral cultural element of the nineteenth century. It was used to instruct and inform, to promote social change and to entertain. The freewheeling development of a mass media provided opportunity for new voices to be heard: the market needed verse and poets profited from the need. Although not all poetry written was great, it was greatly needed: it helped articulate the experiences and values of the adolescent country and kept it in touch with the serious business of the soul. The refrain in Sigourney's "Poetry" (1836) warns "'Oh, speak no ill of poetry, / For 'tis a holy thing'" (*Select Poems,* p. 232). Melville, writing in 1891, defined the process:

> *Art*
> In placid hours well-pleased we dream
> Of many a brave unbodied scheme.
> But form to lend, pulsed life create,
> What unlike things must meet and mate:
> A flame to melt—a wind to freeze;
> Sad patience—joyous energies;
> Humility—yet pride and scorn;
> Instinct and study; love and hate;
> Audacity—reverence. These must mate,
> And fuse with Jacob's mystic heart,
> To wrestle with the angel—Art.
>
> (P. 322)

See also Fireside Poets; Poems of Emily Dickinson; Popular Poetry; Taste

BIBLIOGRAPHY
Primary Works
Emerson, Ralph Waldo. *Collected Poems and Translations.* New York: Library of America, 1994.

Griswold, Rufus. *The Poets and Poetry of America.* Carefully rev., much enl. New York: J. Miller, 1873.

Hale, Sarah Josepha. *Poems for Our Children.* Boston: R. W. Hale, 1830.

Hale, Sarah Josepha. *Three Hours; or, The Vigil of Love; and Other Poems.* Philadelphia: Carey and Hart, 1848.

Horton, George Moses. *The Poetical Works for George M. Horton, the Colored Bard of North Carolina.* Hillsborough, N.C.: D. Heartt, 1845.

Horton, George Moses. *Naked Genius.* Raleigh, N.C.: Wm. B. Smith and Co., 1865.

Melville, Herman. *The Poems of Herman Melville.* Edited by Douglas Robillard. Rev. ed. Kent, Ohio: Kent State University Press, 2000.

Poe, Edgar Allan. *Poetry and Tales.* New York: Library of America, 1984.

Sigourney, Lydia Huntley. *Select Poems.* Philadelphia: Parry and McMillan, 1856.

Sigourney, Lydia Huntley. *Zinzendorff.* New York: Leavitt, Lord and Co., 1836.

Thoreau, Henry David. *Collected Essays and Poems.* New York: Library of America, 2001.

Tuckerman, Frederick Goddard. *Complete Poems.* Edited by N. Scott Momaday. New York: Oxford University Press, 1965.

Very, Jones. *The Complete Poems.* Edited by Helen R. Deese. Athens: University of Georgia Press, 1993.

Secondary Works
Bain, Robert, ed. *Whitman's & Dickinson's Contemporaries: An Anthology of Their Verse.* Carbondale: Southern Illinois University Press, 1996.

Coultrap-McQuin, Susan. *Doing Literary Business: American Women Writers in the Nineteenth Century.* Chapel Hill: University of North Carolina Press, 1990.

Gray, Janet, ed. *She Wields a Pen: American Women Poets of the Nineteenth Century.* Iowa City: University of Iowa Press, 1997.

Kizer, Carolyn, ed. *100 Great Poems by Women: A Golden Ecco Anthology.* Hopewell, N.J.: Ecco Press, 1995.

McGill, Meredith L. *American Literature and the Culture of Reprinting 1834–1853.* Philadelphia: University of Pennsylvania Press, 2003.

Nye, Russel Blaine. *Society and Culture in America, 1830–1860.* New York: Harper and Row, 1974.

Olson, Steven. *The Prairie in Nineteenth-Century American Poetry.* Norman: University of Oklahoma Press, 1994.

Spengemann, William C., ed., with Jessica F. Roberts. *Nineteenth-Century American Poetry.* New York: Penguin Books, 1996.

Walker, Cheryl, ed. *American Women Poets of the Nineteenth Century: An Anthology.* New Brunswick, N.J.: Rutgers University Press, 1992.

Wilson, R. Jackson. *Figures of Speech: American Writers and the Literary Marketplace, from Benjamin Franklin to Emily Dickinson.* New York: Knopf, 1989.

Wolff, Cynthia Griffin. *Emily Dickinson.* New York: Knopf, 1986.

Susan Carol Hauser

MANHOOD

John Wayne embodies a powerful myth of American manhood, a towering and graceful figure bearing a rifle. Potential rivals instinctively defer to his centered and invulnerable self-reliance or choose the suicidal path of resistance. He is a white man, and he rules over men of color with the natural ease with which he rules over women. To its devotees, this myth seems an eternal truth, simple and self-evident; but it came to the center of American culture during the 1820s under specific historical circumstances, and by the end of the Civil War its complexities had been explored in powerful works of literature. Major writers celebrated this emerging style of manhood but also exposed its destructive potential and came to challenge its dominance, envisioning a rich democratic culture that recognizes a range of valid masculinities rather than granting a monopoly to any single model.

A classic exemplar of the dominant ideal was created in 1823 when James Fenimore Cooper (1789–1851) published *The Pioneers,* featuring Natty Bumppo—nicknamed Leatherstocking—who lives in a shack outside a rapidly growing frontier town in upstate New York. Bumppo so fascinated readers that Cooper wrote four more novels about him in the series now famous as the Leatherstocking Tales.

In *The Pioneers,* Bumppo is an aging frontiersman who lives on his own in the woods, having arrived long before the town began to grow. He is disgusted by the waste and destructiveness of the new settlers, who befoul the woodlands by clogging streams, unnecessarily hewing down trees, and by slaughtering wildlife far in excess of their need for food. The settlers kill passenger pigeons for fun, using long poles to knock them down, as well as rifles, pistols, and small cannon. Leatherstocking sees this as a wicked and shocking sacrilege against God's creation, and he also despises the settlers because they cannot shoot well enough to bring down single birds. His own sharpshooting—through all the novels about him—is uncannily accurate. Bumppo's communion with nature includes a sacred bond to his rifle.

Judge Marmaduke Temple, the patriarch of the town, establishes game laws in order to protect the wildlife, and it soon happens that Bumppo, needing meat for the table, goes hunting out of season. When a deputy arrives to arrest Bumppo for poaching, the enraged old man kicks him down the hill, and a charge of resisting arrest is added to his indictment. Cooper thus deftly unfolds the drama that defines Bumppo's character and the tradition of manhood he inaugurates.

Leatherstocking is a man of natural piety and absolute self-command. If all men were like him there would be no need for game laws or indeed any laws at all. Without him there would be no frontier town, because he scouted the wilderness and made possible the settlement that followed. Yet he cannot live within the lawful community and soon must leave for unsettled territory westward. "He had gone far towards the setting sun," Cooper says of his departure, "the foremost in that band of pioneers who are opening the way for the march of the nation across the continent" (p. 436).

A state of lawlessness, seen as prior to social order, is Bumppo's natural habitat. Bumppo enacts the classic

***Leatherstocking Meets the Law,* 1832.** The artist John Quidor was inspired by chapter 30 of James Fenimore Cooper's *The Pioneers,* in which the manly Leatherstocking hurls Hiram Doolittle, the meddlesome representative of the law, almost into the lake. FENIMORE ART MUSEUM, COOPERSTOWN, NY

American drama of "regeneration through violence," as described by Richard Slotkin, in which the male hero facing bewildering social complexities makes a sharp discrimination between good and evil and, taking the law into his own hands, rescues the good and vanquishes the evil. D. H. Lawrence (1885–1930) provides a classic statement of the internal psychology that matches Bumppo's social role: he represents the "essential American soul," Lawrence says: "hard, isolate, stoic, and a killer" (quoted in Slotkin, p. 466).

Many conventions of masculinity flourished across North America when *The Pioneers* was written. Zuni and Navajo cultures in the Southwest celebrated male heroes in pairs, as primordial "hero twins," and Native American communities elsewhere initiated growing boys in widely diverse cultural traditions. The imported folkways of British culture, David Hackett Fischer has shown, sponsored four distinct traditions of gender and family life, with a distinct version of masculinity belonging to each. The traditions of masculinity brought by African slaves resisted the crushing pressure of violent subordination that enforced their enslavement to whites, and waves of immigration from Ireland and the continent of Europe brought their own versions and styles.

Despite such alternatives, the manhood dramatized in Leatherstocking soon became dominant within the national culture, partly because it informed the mythology through which westward expansion was celebrated. When *The Pioneers* was published, only the states of Missouri and Louisiana lay west of the Mississippi; all the remaining territories were added in the next four decades, in a sweeping conquest that was officially proclaimed as the nation's "Manifest Destiny." The legendary heroes of that conquest—Daniel Boone, Davy Crockett, Sam Houston, Kit Carson—were seen to possess the manly virtues of Leatherstocking.

SELF-RELIANT MANHOOD IN URBAN AMERICA

Cooper's imagined frontier corresponds poorly to actual frontier conditions, and frontier settlers did not provide much of a market for novels. Instead, Leatherstocking found his devotees in the metropolitan centers that burgeoned in the Northeast, in cities like Boston, New York, and Philadelphia, where an emerging culture of middle-class economic competition was swiftly becoming dominant. Dana Nelson has traced the contours of the urban white male fraternity that laid claim to the Leatherstocking virtues of solitary self-reliance, from which African American men and Native American men as well as women were excluded. This style of manhood, serving a leadership class of elite males, was fused with the national character itself, claiming an exclusive title to be called "American."

Powerful new conditions shaped the social environment of the 1820s for white men of the emerging middle class. The small-scale networks of community life that drew Americans together in rural hamlets and market towns were broken up by new opportunities for trade and manufacture along the eastern seaboard by increasing waves of immigration and by prospects for taking up new land in the West. Men who came to the cities to make their fortunes found themselves in "a world of strangers," the anonymous downtowns where making a favorable first impression became an essential survival skill. Herman Melville's (1819–1891) *The Confidence-Man* (1857) bitterly satirizes the systematic deception that came to pervade commercial relations in this era.

Before this transformation gained momentum, David Leverenz has shown, there were three well-recognized forms of Anglo masculinity: "patricians" maintained a style suited to their birthright of wealth and public leadership, while "artisans" found manliness in skills as master craftsmen and in their management of household enterprises like shoemaking, blacksmithing, cooperage, printing, and family farming. But the rapidly enlarging urban centers favored the development of a third style, that of "entrepreneurs" who incessantly pursued opportunities for profit, seeking new markets and new ways to finance and manage business enterprises.

As face-to-face communities of status and obligation were swept aside, entrepreneurs struggled against fierce competitors, relying on their own shrewdness and unstinting efforts. They cultivated a sacred bond to their own brave and self-sufficient proficiency, like that of Natty Bumppo with his unerring long rifle. And they envisioned "nature" and "the wilderness" as the environment best suited to their gifts, conceiving the inevitable obstructions to their self-directed ambition—arising from family obligations, religious traditions, legal requirements, and government regulation—as the noxious entanglements of "society." This powerful myth obscured the realities of privilege, making it virtually impossible to recognize that "self-reliance" is an option reserved for the fortunate. Men handicapped by race or other misfortune were held personally answerable for failure, scorned by "self-made men" as lazy, shiftless, and irresponsible.

The new capitalist economy was turbulent, and the business cycle was ill understood, so that periods of rapid economic expansion were followed in 1818–1819 and 1837–1838 by shattering collapses that brought bewilderment as well as ruin to the unfortunate. Nor did the new economic order equally reward the hardworking and self-disciplined. A study of the men most successful during this era shows that a large percentage of them were well-off at birth, yet unlike their fathers these men were not exempted from the constant struggle. Alexis de Tocqueville commented on the paradox of men enjoying unprecedented economic abundance yet haunted by melancholy, and he traced it to ceaseless competition among the affluent and insecure.

The ideal of manly self-reliance shone like a beacon over these troubled and confusing waters. Middle-class white men yearning to maintain their self-respect and their chances for success could hardly do better than embrace the manhood enshrined in Natty Bumppo, whose piety attached itself not to social institutions but to a god of nature beyond them, whose self-possession was never shaken by emergencies, and whose combat proficiency enabled him to survive in a trackless wilderness. Thus the frontier dream was taken to heart, as it is still taken to heart, by American men vexed by the difficulties facing them in a complex urban society.

THE TRANSCENDENTAL QUEST FOR SPIRITUAL INTEGRITY

Ralph Waldo Emerson (1803–1882) organized his philosophy of transcendentalism around the sharp dichotomy between "nature" and "society" found in Bumppo's view of the world. In *Nature,* the 1836 essay inaugurating his career as a major American writer, Emerson scolds those who take their bearings from the history and social relations into which they are born, announcing that each man should establish his own unique and direct relationship to the universe. Compared to the eternal essences of nature, Emerson taught, the historical and social textures of human existence are trivial. True manliness is impaired by conformity to social requirements; a proper communion with nature, by contrast, enables a man to place an absolute trust in himself and to build his own world by ordering his life to match the vision of truth in his mind.

The competitive moneymaking scramble of the 1830s disgusted Emerson. He himself was descended from a Boston social elite whose economic position was increasingly precarious, and he came to believe that fundamental human self-respect was threatened in the world of profit and sale. "Men are become of no account," he remarked: "men in the world of today, are bugs, are spawn, and are called 'the mass' and 'the herd'" (p. 75). Rather than distracting himself with the latest commercial innovations and the vicissitudes of an ever-changing market economy, a man should commune with the sacred integrity of his own mind, as it is renewed and refreshed by nature.

Yet even as he denounced the incessant scrimmage of self-reliant striving, Emerson became a classic spokesman for its guiding ideology. The self-trust of the self-reliant man prepares the ground for profit and social acclaim: "If the single man plant himself indomitably on his instincts, and there abide," Emerson declares, "the huge world will come round to him" (p. 79).

Henry David Thoreau (1817–1862) likewise sought spiritual integrity, in defiance of the competitive struggle for financial well-being that forced men to lead a denatured life remote from their own true selves. Men lead "mean and sneaking lives," he remarked, "trying to get into business and trying to get out of debt . . . always promising to pay, promising to pay . . . seeking to curry favor, to get custom" (pp. 3–4). Escape from the enslavement scarcely seemed imaginable for most, so that "the mass of men lead lives of quiet desperation," victims of "a stereotyped but unconscious despair" (p. 4).

Thoreau's quest for a solution lay out of doors, in his hut on the shore of Walden Pond outside the town of Concord, like Natty Bumppo in his shack. There Thoreau lived alone in communion with nature, seeking to determine what was truly necessary to a self-respecting life and what could be set aside. But the turbulent new economy generated a more conventional solution to the spiritual desolation inflicted upon men, namely the middle-class home. A new ideal of domesticity became conventional during the 1840s and 1850s which assigned to women the task of providing men spiritual redemption by performing new roles as wife and mother.

THE WORLDLY WARRIOR AT HOME
Nathaniel Hawthorne (1804–1864) felt obligated to fulfill the obligations of self-sufficient manhood, and in "The Custom-House" introduction to *The Scarlet Letter* (1850) he fears that receiving a government salary will sap his soul of its "courage and consistency . . . its self-reliance, and all that gives the emphasis to manly character" (p. 39). Yet he was also haunted by the spiritual degradation resulting from the greedy struggles of the world, and he celebrated his marriage to Sophia

MANHOOD AND SELF-RELIANCE

"The mass of men lead lives of quiet desperation." With this famous observation, Thoreau located a turbulence at the heart of America's dominant tradition of manhood, and he built his cabin at Walden Pond in order to live with dignity and full self-reliance. The ruling American ideal of manhood demands that men be self-reliant in an economic and political order of relentless competition in which true self-reliance is impossible. But it is necessary to remain quiet about the resultant desperation, because confessing to it would appear "unmanly," a competitive disadvantage. Powerful mythologies of manhood in America have sought to manage this turbulence, to envision ways of being masculine in which dignity becomes possible.

Hawthorne as a sanctuary where his own true existence could be sustained through her selfless love. In *The House of the Seven Gables* (1851), the love and marriage of Holgrave and Phoebe Pyncheon dramatize the salvation that the domestic angel works upon the soul of the self-made man. Holgrave is a paragon of Emersonian self-reliance, who has jauntily pursued a series of ad hoc enterprises—as schoolmaster, salesman, newspaper editor, peddler, and now as daguerreotypist. He "had never violated the innermost man," Hawthorne tells us, in "putting off one exterior, and snatching up another, to be soon shifted for a third" (p. 177). But at the crisis of the novel Holgrave's self-certainty collapses, his world becomes a nightmare of unrealities, and he turns to Phoebe to save his soul.

Phoebe possesses redemptive power by virtue of her divine purity. She was "a Religion in herself," Hawthorne declares,

> like a prayer, offered up in the homeliest beauty of one's mother-tongue. Fresh was Phoebe, moreover, and airy and sweet in her apparel; as if nothing she wore—neither her gown, nor her small straw bonnet, nor her little kerchief, any more than her snowy stockings—had ever been put on, before; or, if worn, were all the fresher for it, and with a fragrance as if they had lain among the rosebuds. (P. 168)

Essential to Phoebe's redemptive power is her body, which is magically free of sweat or menstrual discharges. She possesses a physical presence so intensely pure that it cleanses her garments from within.

Hawthorne does not say that Phoebe is sexually pure: she embodies a divine purity that could only be defiled by the mention of sexuality.

THE SEXUAL ANXIETIES OF SELF-MADE MEN

The sexual purity demanded of the domestic angel mirrors sexual anxieties that became endemic to the lives of self-made men in the new social order. Men now left the home in order to make a living, rather than managing an economic enterprise centered in the family. Large numbers of children, once an asset because they could be put to work at an early age, now became an economic liability. The stoical self-reliant masculinity that was required for survival in the competitive floundering worldly turmoil was not laid aside when the man escaped his disconcerting relations to other men and came home to his wife. On the contrary, his domestic existence was arranged so as to reinforce the necessary worldly virtues, not least because the failure to exercise these virtues at home could destroy the family's prospect of entering the middle class or of remaining within it. Middle-class couples perforce became "prudent procreators" in Mary Ryan's memorable phrase, because having too many children could overwhelm a family's finances (p. 180). In the absence of reliable contraceptive techniques, marital abstinence became the only reliable strategy for limiting the number of births.

A number of cultural developments testify to the upsurge in male sexual anxiety. The novels of George Lippard and John Neal exemplify the new genre of pornographic fiction, which stressed the ravages of male lust amid a murky atmosphere of guilty fascination. A rapidly proliferating literature of "male hygiene" enjoined vigorous exercise, cold showers, and a bland diet as strategies for maintaining male purity, and a similarly vital new anti-masturbation literature issued fearful warnings against the mental and moral debilitation that were sure to follow from indulgence in the "secret vice."

Women recruited into the task of allaying male sexual anxieties had to confront the "whore-angel dichotomy," the choice between stainless purity and the life of a "fallen woman," stained by sexual sin. Hawthorne's *The Scarlet Letter* is centered on exactly such a woman, Hester Prynne, around whom the male characters form a pattern that probes deeply into male sexual dilemmas. Hester's husband is Roger Chillingworth, whose sexuality has been repressed by his fierce adherence to the ideal of manly self-possession and now takes the form of sadistic vengeance against Arthur Dimmesdale, her remorseful lover. Arthur only fitfully attains self-command, and his life is ravaged by emotional impulses and sexual impulses that humiliate and exhaust him.

The core ideal of self-contained and self-controlling masculinity threatens to split into incompatible components under the pressure of sexual desire, which like hunger and drowsiness chronically resists conscious control. Roger and Arthur dramatize this dichotomy, itself gendered "masculine" and "feminine." Roger is an emotionless, self-contained, hypermasculine moralist; Arthur is effeminate and artistic. The two men are inseparably paired in the novel: they spend more time with each other than either spends with Hester; they live together, and they die together.

Hester offers a challenge to this self-alienated masculinity not only by reason of her sexual vitality but also because of her powerful desire to attain moral and financial independence. *The Scarlet Letter* was published two years after the Seneca Falls Convention of 1848, at which women gathered to declare the democratic principle that all men and women are created equal and to demand that systems of male dominance be dismantled. Another powerful influence upon Hawthorne's presentation of Hester came from Margaret Fuller (1810–1850), whose *Woman in the Nineteenth Century* (1845) challenged men to learn a new masculinity grounded on recognition of women's moral and intellectual autonomy rather than requiring subordination to men. Though Hester broods deeply over these liberatory visions and dreams of becoming a prophetess to proclaim them, Hawthorne arranges the conclusion of the novel to vindicate the domestic ideal. Hester decides that she is too "stained with sin" to take a public role, and redemption is allocated once again to a "pure" womanhood. Hawthorne insists that the psychic and social torments suffered in the name of self-reliant manhood can only be assuaged within the middle-class home, where "sacred love" is dispensed by domestic angels (p. 263).

WOUNDED MANHOOD AND CHARISMATIC REVENGE

Herman Melville (1819–1891) treats the maladies of self-reliant manhood as they take form in the world of men. *Typee* (1846) and *Omoo* (1847) depict the beachcomber life of male rovers in Polynesia; *Redburn* (1849) concerns a voyage to mercantile Liverpool; *White-Jacket* (1850) takes place on an American warship; and *Moby-Dick* (1851) explores the inner meanings of masculinity amid the complex world of nineteenth-century whaling, an enterprise combining exotic travel, military reconnaissance, merchant shipping, and industrial production.

Like Natty Bumppo, Captain Ahab is a famous hunter who pursues his quarry into a world outside society, into "the stillness and seclusion of many long night-watches in the remotest waters, and beneath constellations never seen here at the north," where he has received "all nature's sweet or savage impressions fresh from her own virgin, voluntary and confiding breast" (p. 71). Yet communion with nature has not permitted Ahab to attain Bumppo's spiritual serenity or the worldly distinction that Emerson promised. Instead, Ahab is full of rage at the manifold worldly violations of an "immaculate manliness" (p. 104) that he claims as an inalienable right and whose source and guarantor, Melville declares, is "the great democratic God" (p. 105).

Ahab's resentment resembles that of Hester Prynne; it results from an awareness of inherent rights violated and abused. The ideal of masculine self-reliance was restricted to middle-class white males like Captain Ahab, but as Thoreau recognized, even such fortunate free men end up living like slaves, driven by the relentless competitive pressures of the workplace. Hawthorne, Thoreau, and Melville all focus on the vexations that men suffered as the American nation, founded with proclamations of democratic equality, developed a bourgeois society in the early nineteenth century in which class, gender, and race oppression were perpetuated and even middle-class men felt themselves subtly and pervasively enslaved.

When Ahab's leg is torn off by Moby-Dick, his stifled misery crystallizes into vengeful rage: he envisions the whale as the "monomaniac incarnation" of "all his intellectual and spiritual exasperations" (p. 160). The whale "unmans" Ahab: felt as a castration, the loss of his leg serves as a culmination of the myriad traducements and assaults that have affronted his masculine dignity. Ahab's subordinates—the mates and crew of the *Pequod*—are likewise consumed by unfocused resentment at the mischances and injustices of their lot. Ahab's visibly wounded manhood becomes an emblem of the wounded manhood in each of them; they are stirred by his rage and soon identify themselves with his insane quest for vengeance. Ahab becomes a charismatic demagogue leading his community against the forces of "evil"—a figure for regeneration through violence gone completely mad—and the result is death and destruction for the ship and crew together.

Ahab solicits and exploits Ishmael's loyalty as well. Ishmael too suffers from the bafflements of an abortive manhood and for a time projects all his miseries onto the hated whale. But Ishmael also explores an alternative masculinity not addicted to solitary and competitive self-reliance. Readers meet him as a penniless young man walking the streets of New Bedford in hopes of finding a place among the multiracial and economically exploited "mongrel renegades and castaways" (p. 162) that make up the crews of whaling vessels. For Ishmael, the dignity grounded in the great democratic God is not restricted to privileged white males but also appears in the workingman's self-respect. He sees it "shining in the arm that wields a pick or drives a spike" (p. 104) and in the spiritual serenity of the Polynesian islander Queequeg, with whom he forms an intense loving relationship.

Natty Bumppo had lived comfortably with a non-white companion, an elderly Native American named John Mohegan. Yet between Cooper's pioneers in 1823 and *Moby-Dick* in 1851, the culture of self-made masculinity had developed a phobic abhorrence of same-sex desire. Personal intimacy between men awakened the anxieties evident in the anti-masturbation mania as well as being stigmatized because it could lead to competitive disadvantage in an environment of incessant rivalry. Melville's adventures aboard ship and in Polynesia had introduced him to male cultures in which the Christian prohibition against sodomy was absent or ignored. But the "bosom" friendship that flowers between Ishmael and Queequeg, like the "Squeeze of the Hand" chapter, mocks the sexual phobias that had arisen to police the newly dominant style of masculinity. Ishmael survives the wreck of the *Pequod* to tell the tale, in a form suggesting that the democratic ideal should support multiple masculinities rather than being monopolized by white heterosexual men proclaiming the virtues of competitive self-reliance.

ENLARGING THE CHARTER OF DEMOCRACY

Hester Prynne speaks for a tradition in the early nineteenth century that invoked the democratic principle of equality in claiming new legal entitlements and social options for women. Walt Whitman (1819–1892) and Frederick Douglass (1818–1895) were male writers who likewise worked to enlarge the democratic charter on behalf of new possibilities for men. For Whitman the "sign of democracy" was a primary motive force of his entire poetic project, and it entailed seeking to articulate the "many long dumb voices," those rendered voiceless by antidemocratic systems of social and economic oppression: "Voices of the interminable generations of prisoners and slaves . . . and of the rights of them the others are down upon." Whitman spoke also on behalf of himself, as a man animated by sexual attraction to other men and determined to affirm his desire as healthy and right:

> Through me forbidden voices,
> Voices of sexes and lusts, voices veil'd and I
> remove the veil,
> Voices indecent by me clarified and transfigured.
>
> (P. 44)

The poems of same-sex love that he published in *Calamus* and the *Children of Adam* cost Whitman the friendship and strategic support that Emerson had offered and consigned him to a long career in the shadows of public disapproval. By the end of his life Whitman lived out a painful paradox, the champion of the common man now celebrated by a tiny handful of enthusiastic sophisticates. Yet Whitman's example emerged as a source of inspiration in the mid-twentieth century as a major influence on the poet Allen Ginsberg and on the broad evolution in the gay community that entered a new period of self-confidence in the 1960s and continues to work for democratic reforms.

Frederick Douglass's *Narrative* (1845) of his escape from slavery likewise emphasizes "manhood" as a condition from which African American men are wrongfully excluded. He outlines the strategies by which southern slave masters kept him in subjection through the denial of literacy and through seeking to persuade him that slavery is right. He correspondingly learns to read and write and learns to see through the moral and religious deceptions justifying slavery. The central drama arrives when he confronts the slaveholders' use of direct force. "You have seen how a man was made a slave," Douglass remarks; "you shall see how a slave was made a man" (p. 97).

Douglass attains this manhood before he attains his freedom. He is sent to Mr. Covey, a "slavebreaker" who augments his income by taking rebellious and disobedient slaves under his control and brutalizing them until they capitulate. Thus "broken" to submissiveness, the slave could be returned to his owner, presumably to live out his days in peaceful obedience. Douglass resists the beatings inflicted by Covey and fights him to a draw when the two of them finally battle it out, whereupon Covey ceases to abuse him. "This battle with Mr. Covey was the turning point in my career as a slave. It rekindled the few expiring embers of freedom, and revived within me a sense of my own manhood" (pp. 104–105).

Douglass's experience forms an instructive contrast against the convention of "regeneration through violence" that informs the dominant tradition of white masculinity. Douglass does not enjoy a mystical ascendancy resulting from his communion with nature, nor are his fighting skills supernaturally awesome. He does not defeat Covey outright, and the stalemate he achieves does not regenerate the social order: Covey remains a free white slave owner and Douglass an enslaved black man.

Douglass points out, in fact, that successful physical resistance was not the master key to his victory, since Covey could easily have had him punished by the constable. What gives Douglass the victory is Covey's need to preserve the reputation as a "slave-breaker" that would have been lost had he sent Douglass, then a boy of about sixteen, to the public whipping post.

Douglass's achievement of manhood does not depend on the power of "nature" to equip a man to control "society." It is the story of a man enmeshed in social relations, born into slavery yet emboldened to seek his freedom, who comes to the crucial turning point of his quest when he is able to play a slave breaker's reputation against him. Douglass represents a manhood rooted in tangible immediate needs and options, not ratified by an antisocial ideology of "nature" that restricts masculine dignity to a leadership class within the elite. For this reason, however, Douglass's achievement of manhood is all the more formidable and inspiring and fills Douglass himself with profound respect for himself and with contempt for "cruel but cowardly" (p. 83) slaveholder males who masquerade as nature's gentlemen, performing gestures of a presumptively God-given command while lacking the inner qualities that deserve respect.

Douglass's example is a reminder that certain traditional virtues of the dominant ideal descending from Cooper's Leatherstocking are indeed virtues, even as the literary explorations of 1820–1870 aid one in recognizing this ideal's power to guide American men, and the nation as a whole, into calamitous self-defeating folly and to search for more constructive and more democratic possibilities.

See also Honor; Individualism and Community; Leatherstocking Tales; *Leaves of Grass; Moby-Dick; Narrative of the Life of Frederick Douglass;* Same-Sex Love; *The Scarlet Letter;* "Self-Reliance"; Sexuality and the Body; Slavery; Transcendentalism; Wilderness

BIBLIOGRAPHY

Primary Works

Cooper, James Fenimore. *The Pioneers; or, The Sources of the Susquehanna.* 1823. Afterword by Robert E. Spiller. New York: New American Library, 1964.

Douglass, Frederick. *Narrative of the Life of Frederick Douglass.* 1845. Edited by Benjamin Quarles. Cambridge, Mass.: Harvard University Press, 1960.

Emerson, Ralph Waldo. "The American Scholar." 1837. In *Selections from Ralph Waldo Emerson: An Organic Anthology,* edited by Stephen H. Whicher. Boston: Houghton Mifflin, 1957.

Hawthorne, Nathaniel. *The House of the Seven Gables.* 1851. Edited by Fredson Bowers, Matthew J. Bruccoli, and L. Neal Smith. The Centenary Edition of the Works of Nathaniel Hawthorne, volume 3. Columbus: Ohio State University Press, 1965.

Hawthorne, Nathaniel. *The Scarlet Letter*. 1850. Edited by Fredson Bowers and Matthew J. Bruccoli. The Centenary Edition of the Works of Nathaniel Hawthorne, volume 1. Columbus: Ohio State University Press, 1962.

Melville, Herman. *Moby-Dick*. 1851. Edited by Harrison Hayford and Herschel Parker. Norton critical edition. New York: Norton, 1967.

Thoreau, Henry David. *Walden and Civil Disobedience*. 1854, 1849. Edited by Sherman Paul. Boston: Houghton Mifflin, 1957.

Whitman, Walt. "Song of Myself." In *Leaves of Grass and Selected Prose*. Edited by Lawrence Buell. New York: Modern Library, 1981.

Secondary Works

Appleby, Joyce. *Inheriting the Revolution: The First Generation of Americans*. Cambridge, Mass.: Harvard University Press, 2000.

Barker-Benfield, G. J. *The Horrors of the Half-Known Life: Male Attitudes toward Women and Sexuality in Nineteenth-Century America*. 1976. New York: Routledge, 2000.

Fischer, David Hackett. *Albion's Seed: Four British Folkways in America*. New York: Oxford University Press, 1989.

Greven, Philip. *The Protestant Temperament: Patterns of Child-Rearing, Religious Experience, and the Self in Early America*. New York: Knopf, 1977.

Halltunen, Karen. *Confidence Men and Painted Women: A Study of Middle-Class Culture in America, 1830–1870*. New Haven, Conn.: Yale University Press, 1982.

Herbert, T. Walter. *Dearest Beloved: The Hawthornes and the Making of the Middle-Class Family*. Berkeley: University of California Press, 1993.

Herbert, T. Walter. *Sexual Violence and American Manhood*. Cambridge, Mass.: Harvard University Press, 2002.

Leverenz, David. *Manhood and the American Renaissance*. Ithaca, N.Y.: Cornell University Press, 1989.

Lofland, Lyn H. *A World of Strangers: Order and Action in Urban Public Space*. New York: Basic Books, 1973.

Nelson, Dana D. *National Manhood: Capitalist Citizenship and the Imagined Fraternity of White Men*. Durham, N.C.: Duke University Press, 1998.

Nissenbaum, Stephen. *Sex, Diet, and Debility in Jacksonian America: Sylvester Graham and Health Reform*. Westport, Conn: Greenwood Press, 1980.

Ryan, Mary. *Cradle of the Middle Class: The Family in Oneida County, New York, 1790–1865*. Cambridge, U.K.: Cambridge University Press, 1981.

Sellers, Charles. *The Market Revolution: Jacksonian America, 1815–1846*. New York: Oxford University Press, 1991.

Slotkin, Richard. *Regeneration through Violence: The Mythology of the American Frontier, 1600–1860*. Middletown, Conn.: Wesleyan University Press, 1973.

Wiebe, Robert H. *The Opening of American Society: From the Adoption of the Constitution to the Eve of Disunion*. New York: Vintage, 1984.

Wills, Garry. *John Wayne's America: The Politics of Celebrity*. New York: Simon and Schuster, 1997.

Wyllie, Irvin G. *The Self-Made Man in America: The Myth of Rags to Riches*. New Brunswick, N.J.: Rutgers University Press, 1954.

T. Walter Herbert

MANIFEST DESTINY

In an essay on "Annexation" published in the *United States Magazine and Democratic Review* in the summer of 1845, John L. O'Sullivan (1813–1895) proclaimed that it was the "manifest destiny of the United States to overspread the continent allotted by Providence for the free development of our yearly multiplying millions" (p. 5). Here was the first use of a phrase that would come to loom large in antebellum America and subsequently. Better than any other slogan, Manifest Destiny expressed the powerful expansionist drive of the 1840s. In a mere four years, the expansionist movement—led by the Democratic administration of James K. Polk (1795–1849)—achieved its goal of making the United States a continental power. American territory approximately doubled as a result of Texas annexation (1845), the settlement of the Oregon boundary dispute with Britain (1846), and the Mexican cessation (1848). The continental United States as it exists today came into being. That expansionist drive, however, was not dead: Alaska was purchased in 1867. Following the war with Spain in 1898, the United States came to control Cuba, Hawaii, Puerto Rico, and the Philippines, becoming a global power.

A large body of scholarship has been devoted to uncovering and revealing the multiple meanings and contradictions of Manifest Destiny, a phrase that brilliantly conflates matters of national self-interest—here territorial acquisition—with a divine mission for America to lead and serve other nations. The ideas that form the basis of Manifest Destiny go back to a time even before British settlement on the continent, and, as reflected in President George W. Bush's second inaugural address on 20 January 2005, persist even in the early twenty-first century.

MANIFEST DESTINY BEFORE 1776

"Any genealogy" of the term Manifest Destiny, the historian Anders Stephanson argues, must begin with the "biblical notions . . . of the predestined, redemptive role of God's chosen people in the Promised Land:

MELVILLE ON MANIFEST DESTINY

And we Americans are the peculiar, chosen people—the Israel of our time; we bear the ark of the liberties of the world. Seventy years ago we escaped from thrall; and, besides our first birthright—embracing one continent of earth—God has given to us, for a future inheritance, the broad domains of the political pagans, that shall yet come and lie down under the shade of our ark. . . . God has predestinated, mankind expects, great things from our race. . . . The rest of the nations must soon be in our rear. We are the pioneers of the world; the advance-guard, sent on through the wilderness of untried things, to break a new path in the New World that is ours. . . . And let us always remember that with ourselves, almost for the first time. . . . national selfishness is unbounded philanthropy; for we can not do a good to America but we give alms to the world.

Melville, *White-Jacket*, p. 151.

providential destiny revealed" (p. 5). John Winthrop's (1588–1649) sermon "A Model of Christian Charity," evidently written on board the ship *Arbella* in 1630, cast the Puritans as the New Israel, the people so manifestly destined to be a light unto the nations that the claim needed no proof: "We shall find that the God of Israel is among us . . . when He shall make us a praise and glory that men shall say of succeeding plantations, the Lord make it like that of New England. For we must consider that we shall be as a city on a hill. The eyes of all people are upon us" (p. 225). The test for the not-yet-created nation is that others come to emulate its behavior. To quote from the narrator's summary of Arthur Dimmesdale's Election Day sermon in Nathaniel Hawthorne's *The Scarlet Letter* (1850), the Puritans quickly came to believe that "a high and glorious destiny" awaited "the newly gathered people of the Lord" in "the New England which they were here planting in the wilderness" (pp. 332–333).

Slightly earlier, in the 1610 *A True Declaration of the Estate of the Colonie of Virginia*, the Virginia Company invoked a set of related ideas to promote migration, asserting that the same God who had joined England, Scotland, and Ireland "wil not be wanting to add a fourth" nation in North America. "In this call to renew the effort of English colonization at Jamestown," Eric Cheyfitz points out, we can locate the beginnings of the translation of the *translatio imperii* into the nineteenth-century idea of Manifest Destiny" (p. 111). The phrase *translatio imperii et studii* refers to the destined transfer westward not only of power and rule but of knowledge and discovery. Yet, such visions had to contend with the reality that the American continent already was occupied. The first book printed in English about the New World, Thomas Hariot's (1560–1621) *A Briefe and True Report of the New Found Land of Virginia* (1588), acknowledges an Indian presence that "renders the conquest of America something other than the unilateral unfolding of a manifest destiny. It is a contest, a collision," as Myra Jehlen has put it (p. 62). With the introduction of slaves of African origin at Jamestown in 1619, the white settlers added a tragic complication to the myth that the unoccupied North American continent had been destined solely for those in the vanguard of the Anglo-Saxon movement westward.

Still, the growing prosperity of British North America and the seemingly unstoppable spread of white settlers westward seemed to provide confirmation that on this continent God's purpose was being realized. Even Jonathan Edwards (1703–1758), the great American exponent of Calvinism, spoke in visionary terms of the American destiny. As Perry Miller summarized Edwards's position, the New World, "though it does not escape the brotherhood of sin . . . is nevertheless the hope of the world, if there is hope anywhere. In America alone is the spirit of God poured forth upon the common people, in plain New England churches" (p. 326). Just as America was supplying the Old World with material resources, so too, Edwards predicted, "the course of things in spiritual respects will be in like manner turned" (Miller, p. 326). Edwards's reference to the "common people" reflects an important new dimension of Manifest Destiny: that America had been selected to bring a democratic social order to the world.

CONTINENTAL DREAMS AND MANIFEST DESTINY AFTER INDEPENDENCE

A number of poets active at the time of the American Revolution, including John Trumbull (1750–1831), Philip Morin Freneau (1752–1832), and Timothy Dwight (1752–1817), took up the related themes of Manifest Destiny and *translatio imperii et studii*. As John McWilliams puts it, these poets deployed "a form variously called the prospect poem, the vision poem, or the rising glory poem," enabling them to speak with "an authority both secular and spiritual." They "ascrib(ed) the American Revolution to the progressive protestant spirit of the forefathers, showing how the *translatio studii* has brought the forces of empire to the New World, and ending with a prospect in which various forms of republicanism, peace, and empire, spread from the United States of America across the Western Hemisphere, and often over the globe." Here one finds the "protective and progressive assumptions that were to be crucial to the Monroe Doctrine, Manifest Destiny, the Homestead Act, and the imperialism of the 1890s." As reflected in the national seal, the Founding Fathers envisaged the nation as ushering in nothing less than a "*novus ordo seclorum*," a "new order of the ages" (pp. 160–161).

For such leaders as Thomas Jefferson (1743–1826) and John Quincy Adams (1767–1848), the achievement of independence meant that it was time to give substance to the concept of *translatio imperii et studii*. Through the Louisiana Purchase in 1803 Jefferson doubled the nation's size, an expansion that he conceived in racial terms. In *Race and Manifest Destiny*, Reginald Horsman quotes Jefferson as asserting that Anglo-Saxons were destined to "cover the whole northern, if not the southern continent, with a people speaking the same language, governed in similar forms, and by similar laws; nor can we contemplate with satisfaction either blot or mixture on that surface." In doing so, Horsman comments, Jefferson "stepped lightly over the question of what would happen to the numerous peoples in North and South America if there was to be no 'blot or mixture' in that vast area" (p. 93). Acting as secretary of state in the Monroe administration, Adams in 1819 acquired Florida from Spain and convinced President James Monroe (1758–1831) to assert in his 1823 annual message the principles that came to be known as the Monroe Doctrine. Yet, as a member of the U.S. House of Representatives until his death in 1848, Adams would oppose the Mexican-American War as an attempt to spread slavery.

Unprecedented growth during the first half of the nineteenth century strengthened the belief in America's providential mission. In November 1839, John L. O'Sullivan proclaimed America as "The Great Nation of Futurity," claiming that

> the far-reaching, the boundless future will be the era of American greatness. In its magnificent domain of space and time, the nation of many nations is destined to manifest to mankind the excellence of divine principles; to establish on earth the noblest temple ever dedicated to the worship of the Most High—the Sacred and the True. (P. 427)

Similarly, in "The Young American" (1844), Ralph Waldo Emerson (1803–1882) seemed to echo O'Sullivan's visionary rhetoric, declaring that America "is the country of the Future," the country that best embodies that "sublime and friendly Destiny by which the human race is guided." Like other proponents of Manifest Destiny, Emerson makes the remote future palpably real: "To men legislating for the vast area betwixt two oceans, between the snows and the tropics, somewhat of the gravity and grandeur of nature will infuse itself into the [American] code" (p. 217).

Such assertions of America's manifestly high destiny had become so familiar that when O'Sullivan first used the phrase in connection with Texas annexation, it attracted little attention. However, when on 27 December 1845, in an editorial on "The True Title" in *New York Morning News*, O'Sullivan again used the phrase, it became the focus of national debate. At issue was the dispute with Great Britain over the Oregon boundary; some expansionists pushed for a boundary at 54°40′ north latitude—all the way up to Alaska. A staunch Democrat with close ties to the Polk administration, O'Sullivan dismissed all legal quibbling in asserting America's claims:

> We have a still better title than any than any that can ever be constructed out of all these antiquated materials of old black-letter international law. Away, away with all these cobweb tissues of rights of discoveries, settlement, continuity, etc. . . . And that claim is by the right of our manifest destiny to overspread and to possess the whole of the continent which Providence has given us for the development of the great experiment of liberty and federative self-government entrusted to us. (Quoted in Weinberg, pp. 144–145).

O'Sullivan's unilateralism in foreign policy became a lightning rod for Whig critics. Speaking in the House of Representatives on 16 January 1846, Charles Goodyear of New York scornfully characterized "manifest destiny" as the sort of claim that "has ever been used to justify every act of wholesale violence and rapine that ever disgraced the history of the world. It is the robber's title" (quoted in Graebner, p. 110). Representative Robert C. Winthrop of Massachusetts, speaking in the House on 3 January of the same year, had condemned claims made by "right of our Manifest Destiny! . . . I suppose that the right of a manifest destiny to spread will not be admitted to exist in any nation except the universal Yankee nation!" (quoted in Graebner, p. 118). Such attacks brought the phrase into the national discourse. In the event, Polk settled the boundary dispute peacefully at 49° north latitude and within the conventions of international law.

MANIFEST DESTINY AND THE MEXICAN-AMERICAN WAR

Determined to acquire California and the large New Mexican territory, Polk sent an emissary, John Slidell

John L. O'Sullivan. THE GRANGER COLLECTION, NEW YORK

(1793–1871), to Mexico City to offer terms of purchase. When it became clear that the Mexican government would not accede to American demands, Polk ordered American troops under Zachary Taylor (1784–1850) into the region between the Neuces and Rio Grande. The Mexicans responded by killing some sixteen American soldiers and capturing others. Claiming that the Mexicans had "shed American blood on American soil," Polk pushed a war resolution through Congress, passed on 13 May 1846. So politically skillful was Polk—and so widely shared were the ideas of Manifest Destiny—that critics of "Mr. Polk's War" failed to mount a forceful challenge (Heidler and Heidler, pp. 141–163). Frederick Douglass (1818–1895) observed on 21 January, 1848 that

> Mexico seems a doomed victim to Anglo-Saxon cupidity and love of dominion. The determination of our slaveholding President to prosecute the war, and the probability of his success in wringing from the people men and money to carry it on, is made evident, rather than doubtful, by the puny opposition arrayed against him. No politician of any considerable distinction or eminence, seems willing to hazard his popularity, or stem the fierce current of executive influence, by an open and unqualified disapprobation of the war. (Quoted in Graebner, p. 235)

With the defeat of the Mexican armies and the signing of Treaty of Guadalupe Hidalgo in 1848, America achieved its territorial aims. The *Oxford Companion to American History* concludes that "in a small way, America had become an imperialist nation, the control of the South in national politics was reinforced, and the slavery issues were revived in deadly earnest" (Johnson, p. 527). But one might see the Mexican-American War as neither a "small" nor a new step in the nation's history.

With few exceptions, such as Douglass and James Russell Lowell (1819–1891) in *The Biglow Papers* (1848), American writers failed to mount a concerted attack on Polk's war. In a diary entry made most likely in March 1844, about the time that he delivered his "The Young American" lecture in Boston, Emerson writes that he was prepared to accept even questionable "methods" so long as territorial aims of the American race were realized:

> It is very certain that the strong British race which have now overrun so much of this continent, must also overrun [Texas] & Mexico & Oregon also, and it will in the course of ages be of small import by what particular occasions & methods it was done. It is a secular question. It is quite necessary & true to our New England character that we should consider the question in its local and temporary bearings, and resist the annexation tooth and nail. (*Journals,* p. 74)

But the currents of Manifest Destiny were so strong that no such "tooth and nail" resistance developed. On the contrary, Walt Whitman (1819–1892) echoed O'Sullivan in an editorial on 2 December 1847 in the *Brooklyn Eagle:* "It is for the interest of mankind that [American] power and territory should be extended. . . . We claim those lands . . . by a law superior to parchment and dry diplomatic rules" (p. 370). Although Henry David Thoreau (1817–1862) famously spent a night in jail in 1846, there is no evidence that he did so to protest the Mexican-American War. But he strongly felt the westward pull, as he wrote in the posthumously published "Walking" (1862): "I must walk toward Oregon, and not toward Europe. And that way the nation is moving, and I may say that mankind progress from east to west" (p. 234).

MANIFEST DESTINY GOES MARCHING ON

Even before the establishment of America as an independent nation, such leaders as John Winthrop and Jonathan Edwards spoke of the nation's destiny in messianic terms: as a light unto the nations. At the same time, America's destiny was conflated with national self-interest, notably the need to expand across the continent. Following World War I, President Woodrow Wilson gave new emphasis to the redeemer nation concept, proclaiming that it was America's destiny to help bring freedom, democracy, and prosperity to the nations of the globe. Over the course of the twentieth century and into the twenty first, Americans have continued to search for ways to reconcile the sometimes conflicting meanings of Manifest Destiny.

See also Borders; Exploration and Discovery; Mexican-American War; Political Parties; Puritanism; Religion; Transcendentalism

BIBLIOGRAPHY

Primary Works

Emerson, Ralph Waldo. *The Journals and Miscellaneous Notebooks.* Edited by William H. Gilman et al. Vol. 10. Cambridge, Mass.: Harvard University Press, 1960–1970.

Emerson, Ralph Waldo. "The Young American." In his *Essays and Lectures,* pp. 213–230. New York: Library of America, 1983.

Hariot, Thomas. *A Briefe and True Report of the New Found Land of Virginia.* 1588. New York: Dover, 1972.

Hawthorne, Nathaniel. *The Scarlet Letter.* 1850. In *Collected Novels.* New York: Library of America, 1983.

Lowell, James Russell. *The Biglow Papers.* 1848. Edited by Thomas Wortham. DeKalb: Northern Illinois University Press, 1977.

Melville, Herman. *White-Jacket.* 1850. Evanston, Ill.: Northwestern University Press, 2000.

O'Sullivan, John L. "Annexation." *United States Magazine and Democratic Review* 17 (July–August 1845): 5–10.

O'Sullivan, John L. "The Great Nation of Futurity." *United States Magazine and Democratic Review* 6 (November 1839): 426–430.

O'Sullivan, John L. "The True Title." *New York Morning News,* 27 December 1845.

Thoreau, Henry David. *Collected Essays and Poems.* Edited by Elizabeth Hall Witherell. New York: Library of America, 2001.

Whitman, Walt. *The Journalism.* Vol. 2. Edited by Herbert Bergman et al. New York: Peter Lang, 2003.

Winthrop, John. "A Model of Christian Charity." In *Norton Anthology of American Literature,* vol. 1, 5th ed., edited by Nina Baym. New York: Norton, 1998.

Secondary Works

Cheyfitz, Eric. *The Poetics of Imperialism: Translation and Colonization from* The Tempest *to* Tarzan. Expanded ed. Philadelphia: University of Pennsylvania Press, 1997.

Graebner, Norman A., ed., *Manifest Destiny.* Indianapolis: Bobbs-Merrill, 1968.

Heidler, David S., and Jeanne T. Heidler. *Manifest Destiny.* Westport, Conn.: Greenwood Press, 2003.

Horsman, Reginald. *Race and Manifest Destiny: The Origins of American Racial Anglo-Saxonism.* Cambridge, Mass.: Harvard University Press, 1981.

Jehlen, Myra. "The Literature of Colonization." In *Cambridge History of American Literature,* vol. 1, *1590–1820,* edited by Sacvan Bercovitch. Cambridge, U.K., and New York: Cambridge University Press, 1994.

Johnson, Thomas H. *Oxford Companion to American History.* New York: Oxford University Press, 1966.

McWilliams, John. "Poetry in the Early Republic." In *Columbia Literary History of the United States,* edited by Emory Elliott et al. New York: Columbia University Press, 1988.

Miller, Perry. *Jonathan Edwards.* 1949. New York: Meridian, 1959.

Stephanson, Anders. *Manifest Destiny: American Expansionism and the Empire of Right.* New York: Hill and Wang, 1995.

Weinberg, Albert K. *Manifest Destiny.* Baltimore: Johns Hopkins Press, 1935.

Robert J. Scholnick

MARITIME COMMERCE

It is an unfortunate truth that voyages of discovery and engagements of great naval fleets too often have at base a commercial motive. In a sense, then, literature of the sea is fundamentally based on commerce—its setting, characters, and plots molded to match particular maritime trades. Even yachting is the most conspicuous reward of successful commercial enterprise.

At the beginning of the nineteenth century, maritime commerce undertaken by English-speaking peoples was still largely a function of the British Empire. The worldwide commercial empire predicted for Portugal by the poet Luis Vas de Camoëns in *The Lusiad* (1572) had been achieved by the British in the eighteenth century—and had been celebrated by William Julius Mickle (1735–1788) in the 150-page introduction to his translation of the Portuguese epic. The superiority and uncorruptibility of the British Empire was as obvious to Mickle in 1776 as it was diabolical to certain other English-speaking maritime communities on the eastern seaboard of North America. The Boston Tea Party (1773) was only the best known of their responses to British commercial policy. Although revolution and independence did not automatically establish a vast international trade for the fledgling United States, freedom from trade restrictions imposed on the colonies by the mother country did result in an explosive growth in merchant shipping to the "loose fish" (originally an unsecured

Deprived of a large navy and with most of their ports blockaded, during the Civil War (1861–1865) the Confederacy turned to commerce raiding—a form of warfare in which fast, lightly armed vessels specialize in destroying unarmed enemy commercial vessels. The Confederate raiders were few in number but huge in influence: they struck such fear into Northern merchants that insurance rates became prohibitive and vessels often languished in port or were reregistered under foreign flags. After the war, because of a technicality in American maritime law, the latter vessels were not allowed to resume their registry as American vessels. From this "flight from the flag" the American merchant marine never recovered.

    The most famous of the Confederate raiders was the CSS Alabama, *commanded by the flamboyant Raphael Semmes. A gifted writer as well as warrior, Semmes produced the best naval book to come out of the war,* Memoirs of Service Afloat *(1869).*

The ship which was now running down for us was, as I have said, a picture, with her masts yielding and swaying to a cloud of sail, her tapering poles shooting skyward, even above her royals, and her well-turned, *flaring* bows—the latter a distinctive feature of New York–built ships. She came on, rolling gracefully to the sea, and with the largest kind of a "bone in her mouth." She must have suspected something, from our very equivocal attitude in such weather, and in such a place; but she made no change in her course, and was soon under our guns. A blank cartridge brought her to the wind. If the scene was beautiful before, it was still more so now. If she had been a ship of war, full of men, and with hands stationed at sheets, halliards, and braces, she could not have shortened sail much more rapidly, or have rounded more promptly and gracefully to the wind, with her main topsail aback. Her cloud of canvas seemed to shrivel and disappear, as though it had been a scroll rolled up by an invisible hand. It is true, nothing had been furled, and her light sails were all flying in the wind, confined to the yards only by their clew-lines, but the ship lay snugly and conveniently for boarding, as I could desire. I frequently had occasion, during my cruises, to admire the seamanship of my enemies. . . .

    The prize, upon being boarded, proved to be the *Lafayette,* from New York, laden with grain, chiefly for Irish ports. We learned from newspapers captured on board of her, that news of our capture of the *Brilliant* and *Emily Farnum* off the Banks of Newfoundland, had reached the United States, and, as was to be expected, I found, when I came to examine the papers of the *Lafayette,* plenty of certificates to cover her cargo. In fact, from this time onward, I rarely got hold of an enemy's ship, whose cargo was not certificated all over—oaths for this purpose being apparently as cheap, as the much-derided custom-house oaths, that every ship-master is expected to take, without the least regard to the state of the facts. Upon examination of these certificates, I pronounced them fraudulent, and burned the ship.

Semmes, *Memoirs of Service Afloat,* pp. 481–482.

---

whale, but applied by Herman Melville humorously to nations ready for exploitation) of the Far East, a trade interrupted by Thomas Jefferson's Embargo (or legal cessation of international trade) of 1807 and later by the War of 1812. But the growing markets of the interior of the continent, the accessibility of materials for shipbuilding, and at least nominally free trade ensured the growth of an American merchant marine. The first "Flowering of New England" (in the words of literary historian Van Wyck Brooks) may, in fact, have been commercial and maritime.

    The first major maritime work of the period, David Porter's (1780–1843) *Journal of a Cruise made to the Pacific Ocean* (1815; heavily revised and expanded, 1822), recounts the adventures of the commerce-raider *Essex,* the first American flag vessel to wage war in the Pacific. Porter's work subsequently inspired, and was plundered by, writers of major sea fiction including James Fenimore Cooper (1789–1851) and Herman Melville (1819–1891). American writers of the sea, however, have usually made a thematic distinction between warfare and exploration on one hand and trade and fisheries on the other. The nature of the latter commercial activities shapes about half of American literature of the sea.

COOPER

If Cooper invented the sea novel in 1824 with *The Pilot,* it was his third sea novel, *The Water-Witch* (1830), that first matched plot and vessel to a specifically commercial venture—smuggling around New York harbor. He returned to this theme in each phase of his literary career, with *The Wing-and-Wing* (1842) and *Jack Tier* (1845). In the two first romances, each book takes its title from the name of the sleek vessel on board of which most of the action takes place—in the former a brigantine, in the latter a felucca. In the more darkly realistic *Jack Tier*, remarkable among Cooper's sea novels for its contemporary setting, arms smuggling during the Mexican-American War juxtaposes a noble Mexican with the degenerate Captain Spike of the tired brig *Molly Swash*, named, as is the book, after Spike's long-lost sweetheart—now a dumpy transvestite sailor.

Cooper's middle years were powerfully influenced by the reappearance of a boyhood shipmate, the alcoholic Ned Myers. Myers's career may be taken to represent the average seaman's life in the first half of the nineteenth century. Unlike Richard Henry Dana Jr. (1815–1882), whose *Two Years before the Mast* (1840) exposed the demeaning life of a common sailor in the California hide trade, Myers had no Boston family to return to. The biography of him that Cooper published

in 1843 was subtitled "A Life before the Mast," and most of that life was spent bouncing from one vessel to another in most kinds of maritime trade in which America was engaged. Cooper cut the biography short, saving both Ned's narrative voice and the variety of his maritime experiences for the double novel *Afloat and Ashore* (1844). Notably supplemented by accounts from Washington Irving's (1783–1859) *Astoria* (1836) and the recent conclusion of the controversial U.S. Exploring Expedition (1838–1842), Cooper's work mimics and expands on previous summaries of commercial adventure exemplified by Edmund Fanning's *Voyages round the World* (1833) and Benjamin Morrell's *Narrative of Four Voyages to the South Sea* (1832), the latter of which also provided an important source for Edgar Allan Poe's gothic tale *Narrative of Arthur Gordon Pym of Nantucket* (1838).

Cooper began and ended his career in maritime fiction with tales of the fisheries. In *The Pilot*, one of the episodes illustrating the three types of literary conflict at sea—man against man, man against the sea, man against the beast of the sea—the latter category is represented by a didactic but thrilling (only Cooper,

---

The following excerpt is from chapter 13 of Richard Henry Dana Jr.'s Two Years before the Mast:

The next day, the cargo having been entered in due form, we began trading. The trade room was fitted up in the steerage, and furnished out with the lighter goods, and with specimens of the rest of the cargo; and Mellus, a young man who came out from Boston with us before the mast, was taken out of the forecastle, and made supercargo's clerk. He was well qualified for the business, having been clerk in a counting-house in Boston; but he had been troubled for some time with the rheumatism, which unfitted him for the wet and exposed duty of a sailor on the coast. For a week or ten days all was life on board. The people came off to look and to buy—men, women, and children; and we were continually going in the boats, carrying goods and passengers, for they have no boats of their own. Everything must dress itself and come aboard and see the new vessel, if it were only to buy a paper of pins. The agent and his clerk managed the sales, while we were busy in the hold or in the boats. Our cargo was an assorted one; that is, it consisted of everything under the sun. We had spirits of all kinds (sold by the

cask), teas, coffee, sugars, spices, raisins, molasses, hardware, crockeryware, tinware, cutlery, clothing of all kinds, boots and shoes from Lynn, calicoes and cottons from Lowell, crepes, silks; also, shawls, scarfs, necklaces, jewelry, and combs for the ladies; furniture; and, in fact, everything that can be imagined, from Chinese fireworks to English cart wheels—of which we had a dozen pairs with their iron tires on.

The Californians are an idle, thriftless people, and can make nothing for themselves. . . . Things sell, on an average, at an advance of nearly 300 per cent upon the Boston prices. This is partly owing to the heavy duties which the government, in their wisdom, with the intent, no doubt, of keeping the silver in the country, has laid upon imports. These duties, and the enormous expenses of so long a voyage, keep all merchants but those of heavy capital from engaging in the trade. . . .

This kind of business was new to us, and we liked it very well for a few days, though we were hard at work every minute from daylight to dark, and sometimes even later.

Richard Henry Dana Jr., *Two Years before the Mast* (New York: Signet, 2000), pp. 67–68.

---

perhaps, could combine the two) chapter on hunting the sperm whale, written in response to Sir Walter Scott's description of an attack on a stranded right whale in *The Pirate* (1821). In 1849 Cooper published *The Sea Lions,* in which the sealing industry of New England and Antarctica forms the background for a tale of religious conversion. This novel, reviewed by Melville in the *Literary World* (April 1849), capitalized on the sublime landscape of the polar continent, quite opposed to the sunny Mediterranean of *The Wing-and-Wing,* which also had ended in a conversion.

MELVILLE

Herman Melville's literary career may have begun when he ran away from a whaler, but his actual sea service began, as Cooper's did, in the transatlantic trade. *Redburn* (1849), based on a round-trip voyage the young Melville made to Liverpool, thematically addresses questions of class while exploring inhuman treatment of sailors and passengers alike, a theme partially addressed by Dana not only in *Two Years before the Mast,* but also in his second work, *The Seaman's Friend* (1841) basically a guidebook to the rights and responsibilities of sailors and a work from which Melville borrowed heavily for *Redburn.*

Melville may have thought he had covered the whaling industry as much as it merited in his first three books—*Typee* (1846), *Omoo* (1847), and the largely forgotten *Mardi* (1849). But to a suggestion from Dana that he treat whaling as he had the merchant service (in *Redburn*) and the navy (in *White-Jacket* [1850], a work also prompted by a letter from Dana, whom Melville then regarded as a sort of soulmate), the younger author responded—perhaps less testily than he felt—that he was halfway in the work already. Nearly the next day he borrowed a set of William Scoresby's *Account of the Arctic Regions* (1820) and ordered a copy of Thomas Beale's *Natural History of the Sperm Whale* (1839), from each of which he adapted freely for the systematic account of the whale fishery that forms the center of *Moby-Dick* (1851) and its comprehensive exploration of cetology.

When Melville asked in *Moby-Dick* the philosophical question, "Who ain't a slave?" three million Americans would not have seen the question as rhetorical. Although the slave trade had been abolished in England and the United States as early as the first decade of the nineteenth century, slavery at sea remained a real as well as a literary issue. While Thomas Clarkson's *History of the Rise, Progress, and Accomplishment of the Abolition of the African Slave Trade by the British Parliament* (1808) contributed the most lasting visual image of slaves crammed into subhuman spaces in the 'tween decks of slavers, Melville transformed Amasa Delano's account of the *Tryall* in *A Narrative of Voyages and Travels in the Northern and Southern Hemispheres* (1817) into his chilling account of slave revolt in "Benito Cereno" (1855). And although the *Amistad* incident (1839) is better known, another episode, in which more than seventy-five slaves from Washington, D.C., sought their freedom—unsuccessfully—on the small schooner *Pearl* in 1848, found a moving literary treatment in Harriet Beecher Stowe's *Key to Uncle Tom's Cabin* (1853).

DEMISE

Remarkably, American authors did not seem to respond to the greatest achievement of maritime commerce of the era—the rise and fall of the clipper ship, built and designed by such marine architects as Donald McKay, whose portrait forms the frontispiece to F. O. Matthiessen's classic of literary history, *The American Renaissance: Art and Expression in the Age of Emerson and Whitman* (1941). The Civil War ended the golden age of American maritime commerce, as the havoc created by the CSS *Alabama* and her sister commerce-raiders drove insurance rates skyward and vessels to seek immunity under foreign flags. Raphael Semmes's *Memoirs of Service Afloat, during the War between the States* (1869) closed the literary age as Porter had opened it, with the record of burning whaleships foreshadowing the end of commercial supremacy at sea.

See also "Benito Cereno"; Exploration and Discovery; Foreigners; *Moby-Dick;* Nautical Literature; Slave Rebellions; *Two Years before the Mast; Typee*

BIBLIOGRAPHY

Primary Works
Cooper, James Fenimore. *Afloat and Ashore.* 1844. New York: AMS Press, 2004.

Dana, Richard Henry, Jr. *The Seaman's Friend.* 1841. Mineola, N.Y.: Dover, 1997.

Porter, David. *Journal of a Cruise.* 1815. Annapolis: Naval Institute Press, 1986.

Samuels, Samuel. *From the Forecastle to the Cabin.* 1887. London: Macdonald and Jane's, 1974.

Semmes, Raphael. *Memoirs of Service Afloat.* 1869. Baton Rouge: Louisiana State University Press, 1996.

Secondary Works
Albion, Robert Greenhalgh. *Rise of New York Port.* New York: Scribners, 1939.

Albion, Robert Greenhalgh, William A. Baker, and Benjamin W. Labaree. *New England and the Sea.* Middletown, Conn.: Wesleyan University Press for the Marine Historical Association, 1972.

Morison, Samuel Eliot. *Maritime History of Massachusetts, 1783–1860.* 1921. Boston: Houghton Mifflin, 1941.

Philbrick, Thomas. *James Fenimore Cooper and the Development of American Sea Fiction.* Cambridge, Mass.: Harvard University Press, 1961.

Springer, Haskell, ed. *America and the Sea: A Literary History.* Athens: University of Georgia Press, 1995.

R. D. Madison

MARRIAGE

The marriage contract occupied the minds and hearts of writers and readers in the nineteenth century. It signaled the newly conceived possibilities of the Republic and of the political alliances to be formed among families and factions. As Nancy Cott has argued in *Public Vows: A History of Marriage and the Nation*, marriage represented religious, civil, and political investments in sexual and gender identities and in the social control of the new populace. Marriage became a way to define the population—both citizens and aliens—in terms of monogamy and voluntary union or consent, with "marriage and the form of government mirroring each other" (p. 10). Moreover, the doctrine of coverture governed the legal relation between men and women, wherein women would surrender their legal status to husbands, who were full citizens. Women could exercise influence in marriage but had no legal power, could not vote, and in many states could not own property. (Married Women's Property Acts were in place by the 1860s.)

LITERARY CRITICISMS OF MARRIAGE

Women's resistance to coverture, and indeed to the stifling influences of patriarchal control, helped to shape much of the literature of this period. Such poems as "The Dying Wife" (1834), "The Bride" (1837), and Fanny Gage's "The Maniac Wife" (1866) describe in stark terms the miserable conditions for women under the control of willful husbands in what one critic describes as "voluntary incarceration" (Bennett, pp. 122–123). Emily Dickinson (1830–1866) compares marriage to submission:

> I'm "wife"—I've finished that—
> That other state—
> I'm czar—I'm "Woman" now—
> It's safer so.

Marriage is ostensibly "safer" because it affords women some measure of protection. One of the cleverest indictments of marriage is in a coded letter, "Atkinson's Casket," in an 1832 magazine, which reveals the author's real views of marriage if one reads every other line of the letter:

> I tell you my dear
> husband is one of the most amiable of men,
> I have been married seven weeks, and
> have never found the least reason to
> repent the day that joined us, my husband is
> in person and manners far from resembling
> ugly, crass, old, disagreeable, and jealous
> monsters, who think by confining to secure
> (Lanser, pp. 679–680)

Such reading between the lines represents the overt censoring and covert repression of women's critical voices.

Rebecca Rush's (1779–c. 1850) 1812 novel *Kelroy* gives readers a glimpse into the expectations for white women's marriages. Rush's plot characterizes marriages in the early Republic insofar as her characters are pitted against each other in terms of political alliances. The widowed mother of two girls, Mrs. Hammond wants to marry them off into wealthy families, thereby securing her future and, incidentally, theirs. Mrs. Hammond and her accomplice Mr. Marney believe in filial obedience (influenced by Federalist policy) and want to arrange the daughters' marriages based on calculated self-interest. The first daughter, Lucy, marries into British aristocracy, but it is a loveless union, and Lucy is a coldhearted mother. The sentimentalists, represented in the novel by the second daughter Emily and her lover, the impoverished poet Kelroy, assert the Jeffersonian value of sincerity and affiliation through love, not rational self-advancement. The mother foils the marriage but not without breaking her daughter's heart and ruining her own reputation. Thus, in Rush's world, the Federalist version of marriage and obedience cannot coexist with the newer generation's Jeffersonian model of consent and individual self-control. Thus, the seduction plot, which heretofore fueled myriad novels—most famously, Hannah Webster Foster's (1759–1840) *The Coquette* (1797) and Susanna Rowson's (1762–1824) *Charlotte Temple* (1794)—disappeared, while the new conflict between political models of affiliation informed courtship and marriage plots.

New, more sentimental models of marriage began to appear in novels and plays, but even these were no less politicized as a form of union. Catharine Maria Sedgwick's (1789–1867) *Hope Leslie* (1827) features intermarriage between a white woman taken captive as a child and an Indian man, as does Lydia Maria Child's (1802–1880) *Hobomok* (1824). Both Sedgwick and Child, as well as James Fenimore Cooper, used marriage

A couple poses for a wedding photograph, c. 1870. GETTY IMAGES

as a way to test cultural politics of citizenship: Could whites intermarry with Native Americans and preserve a sense of cultural superiority? Did cultural superiority matter in a potentially hybrid culture?

Walt Whitman (1819–1992) later represented just such a marriage in "Song of Myself": "I saw the marriage of the trapper in the open air in the far west, the bride was a red girl" (1881 edition, l. 185). As a preoccupation among the middle and upper classes, marriage signifies not just class standing but also racial superiority, as the legal rights of marriage were restricted solely to whites until African Americans were granted, after emancipation, the right to wed. As Ann duCille writes, African Americans desired the "coupling convention" that had been denied to enslaved blacks. Indeed, marriage in African American culture was politicized from the very beginning. Slaveholders' failure to recognize marriages between slaves tested the Christian notion of marriage, although the assumed sexual licentiousness of the slaves was seen as much as a threat to the nation as were Mormonism and divorces.

Even before the debate about slavery ended, bondage was an important way of representing marriage.

In "The Great Lawsuit" (1843), later expanded into *Woman in the Nineteenth Century* (1845), Margaret Fuller (1810–1850) indicates the rhetorical connection between chattel slavery and marital enslavement:

> It is not surprising that it should be the Anti-Slavery party that pleads for woman, when we consider merely that she does not hold property on equal terms with men; so that, if a husband dies without a will, the wife, instead of stepping at once into his place as head of the family, inherits only a part of his fortune, as if she were a child, or ward only, not an equal partner. (P. 1627)

Instead of the "ravishing harmony" that Fuller desires between married men and women, women are denied equity.

Perhaps no novelist put the situation as well as did Fanny Fern (Sara Payson Willis Parton, 1822–1891) in *Ruth Hall* (1855), a best-seller that dramatizes the plight of a mother left destitute when her childlike husband dies and leaves her to the mercy of his parents and her own unsympathetic brother. Ruth Hall saves herself by writing columns filled with common sense and humor about the plight of womanhood. In 1871

Elizabeth Stuart Phelps (1844–1911) focused on the same theme—the impossibility of being a "silent partner" in a marriage—insofar as both of her heroines refuse marriage proposals (middle-class and working-class versions) in favor of embracing benevolent practices. Fern and Phelps, among many others, raise the question of whether marriage was a companionate or an economic union, whether it is more fully realized on spiritual, psychological, and social terms, or whether its true implications result from an economic or commercial union. One of Phelps's later novels, *The Story of Avis* (1877), chronicles how a demanding marriage and husband doom a woman's ambition as an artist. Like her mother, a novelist of the same name, in "The Angel over the Right Shoulder" (1852), the daughter pits women's duties against her desires. By the end of the century, marriage advice and manual writers would proclaim with not a little irony that marriage was to be endured, not celebrated. In 1886 one such manual— *How to Be Happy Though Married, Being a Handbook to Marriage,* written by "A Graduate in the University of Matrimony"—addresses itself "to those brave men and women who have ventured, or who intend to venture, into that state which is a blessing to a few, a curse to many, and a great uncertainty to all" and is dedicated to "their courage" (acknowledgment page) in attempting such unions. The age of innocence—blessed unions and political marriages—was indeed over.

ANXIETIES ABOUT MARRIAGE IN THE WORK OF HAWTHORNE AND MELVILLE

Perhaps the most famous novel in nineteenth-century American literature is the story of a marriage gone wrong and the disastrous consequences, Nathaniel Hawthorne's (1804–1864) *The Scarlet Letter* (1850). Its focus on adultery puts it in company with Gustave Flaubert's *Madame Bovary* and Leo Tolstoy's *Anna Karenina.* These novels take as their defining position that the way marriages fail reveals not only the deepest psychological implications of characters but also the dominant cultural anxieties of their milieux. *The Scarlet Letter* is so well known that it may be summarized briefly. A man uses his position as doctor to marry a younger, vulnerable woman, but when she has grounds to presume that he is dead, she turns to her minister for sexual comfort. Leslie Fiedler argues that the wilderness scene in which Hester Prynne enjoins the Reverend Arthur Dimmesdale's sympathy actually replicates an earlier scene that the reader never gets to see: her original seduction of the cleric. Whether the novel is considered a marriage novel or not, it displays one side of Hawthorne's vision of marriage as an institution. The novel could not have the potency it has had for generations unless it also expressed a deeply

held American sense of marriage as a profoundly viable civic institution, one that can give stature to even the furthest outcasts from American society.

In *The House of the Seven Gables* (1851), Hawthorne explores several dimensions by which American history is shaped by the pursuit of happy marriages. When Matthew Maule sees Alice Pyncheon and assumes that the class differences that keep her from him can never be surmounted, he joins her intolerant father in a shared policy of domestic devastation. His curse on the Pyncheons is the resentment of a marriage that cannot be, whereas the novel closes with a vision of a happier union once the class barriers have been rendered insubstantial. *The Blithedale Romance* (1852), on the other hand, treats marriage as secondary to the cultivation of intimacy and by doing so helps to secure the life of intense personal relations as the American social value that will ultimately surpass marriage as a defining cultural good. Miles Coverdale's contorted tale of his own bachelorhood is a prototype for the bachelor fictions that predominated in the 1850s: his desperate protest of love for Priscilla, hollow as many readers have found it, testifies both to his incomprehension of the proceedings and to his equally helpless vision of romantic, heterosexual love as the adequate counterbalance to the social ills the novel has chronicled.

Hawthorne's short stories also play out the duality of marriage, not to mention Hawthorne's ambivalences, which the novels portray. On the one hand, Hawthorne creates a series of bachelor protagonists who find marriage suffocating. Such characters might be typified in "Wakefield" (1835), in which the protagonist abandons his wife for twenty years, living around the corner from her and observing her during his absence. In large part, this story functions as Hawthorne's critique of encroaching urbanism and the soulless anonymity of city life. That dominant reading, however, ought not overshadow the implicit critique of marriage as the primary source of consolation in an increasingly alienated culture. On the other hand, Hawthorne creates another series of protagonists for whom the prospect of marriage is potentially redemptive. One such character is Owen Warland in "The Artist of the Beautiful" (1844), who pits his craft in service of this ideal. Beyond such artist figures, however, are the better-known malevolent villains like Aylmer of "The Birth-mark" (1843), who in the name of searching for the perfect wife systematically goes about destroying the very human woman who loves him. Perhaps Hawthorne's best-known short story, "Young Goodman Brown" (1835), circulates these anxieties about marriage in the protagonist's vision of his wife's imagined infidelity with the devil and his attendant loss of his aptly named wife, Faith.

Nina Baym's famous formulation of "melodramas of beset manhood" best captures the sense of fear and anxiety nineteenth-century male characters (and some writers) felt about the stifling dynamics of middle-class marriage. Herman Melville's (1819–1891) famous diptych of 1855, "The Paradise of Bachelors and the Tartarus of Maids," gave the lie to the number of sentimental portrayals of national monogamy, for his bachelors prefer their own company and his maids are servants to their millwork. Melville's bachelors call wives and children "twinges of their consciences" likely to give men "anxious thoughts" (p. 2361). Then again, there's *Pierre* (1852), Melville's novel about a man engaged to one woman but passionate about his half sister, one of the many nineteenth-century plots verging on incest, such as E. D. E. N. Southworth's 1869 novel, *The Fatal Marriage*.

IDEALIZATION AND COMPLICATIONS

Hawthorne's and Melville's writings notwithstanding, marriage was promoted as a civic ideal, serving as a social glue: Marmee in Louisa May Alcott's (1832–1888) *Little Women* (1868–1869) professes marriage as the highest ideal and noblest goal for women: after Mr. March leaves for the war, Marmee declares that she "gave my best to the country I love, and kept my tears till he was gone. Why should I complain, when we both have merely done our duty, and will surely be the happier for it in the end?" (p. 103). Such "maternal pedagogy," as Elizabeth Freeman calls it, was to prepare her girls for submission to the greater power of "national manhood" and provide a buffer against capitalist and commercial interests (p. 41). Conduct literature and advice books were popular, providing young men and women with codes for proper married living. The debate about marriage rested on the assumptions about companionate affiliation versus economic partnership.

By the 1850s, "free-love" communities were on the rise, and the argument for sexual emancipation took many forms. "Complex marriages" occurred at Oneida, Putney, and Wallingford because they secured the notion that every member would be married to everyone else (Freeman, p. 107). In fact, the founder of the Oneida Community, John Humphrey Noyes (1811–1886), argued that sexual activity could be distinct from reproduction. The Shakers prevented marriage altogether since they found it to encourage privatization (Freeman, p. 129). One of the most outspoken voices against sexual repression was Angela Fiducia Tilton Heywood (1840–1935), who spoke out for her imprisoned husband, Ezra Hervey Heywood (1829–1893), in their newspaper, the *Word*. Angela Heywood argued for free expression

between husband and wife: "Animals rise on the back, mount from behind; the arrival of human intelligence appears in face to face meeting, coition front-wise. . . . In creative sex-power resides the *central matter-of-fact* of social endeavor. It is insipid *falsehood* for woman to pretend to man that the sex-fact is not as much to her, as it is to him." The Heywoods advanced provocative arguments for women's equal sex expression in marriage.

Nevertheless, many women writers argued for the protective benefits for women in sentimental affiliation, whereas others lamented women's lack of power in marital relations. Harriet Beecher Stowe's (1811–1896) *Pink and White Tyranny* (1871) satirized women's sex power in marriage. The novel details the disastrous marriage of John Seymour, a country businessman, to a frothy young woman, Lillie Ellis, whose career as a belle started when she was eight and who "used to sell her kisses through the slats of the fence for papers of candy, and thus early acquired the idea that her charms were a capital to be employed in trading for the good things of life" (p. 46). Thoroughly steeped in American materialism, Lillie rejects her husband's benevolence and idealism for fashionable life. Throughout the novel, she employs her sex power—flirting and kissing and crying—to undermine his plans of moral uplift for her. Such fashionable training in womanhood, Stowe argues, destroys the sacredness of married life. Stowe comments on the situation of marriage in America: "We have heard much talk, of late, concerning the husband's ownership of the wife. But, dear ladies, is that any more pronounced a fact than every wife's ownership of her husband?—an ownership so intense and pervading that it may be said to be the controlling nerve of womanhood" (p. 66). Lillie Ellis, like Louisa May Alcott's Jean Muir from *Behind a Mask* (1866) and later Edith Wharton's Lily Bart from *The House of Mirth* (1905), uses sex power to arrange for an advantageous marriage.

The challenges marriage faced came not only in the domestic sphere but also in what were seen as threats to national stability. The crisis of Mormonism was focused on polygamy, which was criminalized in 1862, before slavery was outlawed. For instance, Maria Ward's 1855 best-seller, *Female Life among the Mormons*, detailed the "Sacrifices, Sorrows, and Sufferings" of a woman forced to go to Salt Lake City with her Mormon husband. Such sensational literature focused attention on antirepublicanism and on women's legal dependence in marriage (Merish, p. 165). In 1843 the Mormon prophet Joseph Smith (1805–1844) declared "Celestial marriage" a divine revelation and duty for Mormon men. Although its existence in the Mormon community was kept quiet until the 1850s, plural marriage provoked great debate, and approximately sixty anti-Mormon novels were published in the nineteenth century, denouncing the lust and sensuality of the Mormon "harem," a dangerous relation to the Eastern sheik and his collection of women. Mormonism galvanized many discussions about marriage and monogamy's legitimate relation to the nation, since plural marriage challenged the sanctity and order of the Christian home. Other novels, such as Metta Victoria Fuller Victor's *Mormon Wives* (1856), used sentimental rhetorical strategies to attack the defilers of Christian monogamy.

It was feared that both widespread miscegenation and Mormonism would produce an adverse effect on national morality. As DuCille argues in *The Coupling Convention*, the marriage plot and the novel structure were useful tools for African American writers to explore race, sexuality, and female subjectivity (p. 4). Harriet Jacobs's *Incidents in the Life of a Slave Girl* (1861) and Harriet E. Wilson's *Our Nig* (1859) both make impassioned arguments for black women's "freedom to desire" and freedom from white patriarchal power. Marriage was also a test of black people's fitness for citizenship. Stowe's *Uncle Tom's Cabin* (1852) expresses the ideal relationship between George Harris, an escaped slave, and his family; Harris claims that his identity—as a free man—is predicated on his relationship (often in terms of purchasing) his wife and child. (No such marital ownership occurs in Jacobs's or Wilson's stories.) As he explains to his wife Eliza, "Don't you know a slave can't be married? There is no law in this country for that; I can't hold you for my wife, if [the slaveholder] chooses to part us" (p. 82). After the Civil War, all men would be owners of their households, a wife and child theirs by right.

These debates occasioned a concomitant rise in divorces; more women than men sought an end to marriage. In turn, advocates marshaled for stricter control on marriage, including raising the age of consent and instituting eugenic requirements, all in an effort to promote "formal monogamy," as Cott puts it, and later to control reproduction of immigrants (p. 110). Fears of Catholicism and Jewish marriages also dominated reform movements because it was believed that these foreign alliances did not promote egalitarian marriages but tribalism and foreign allegiances. Adah Isaacs Menken (c. 1835–1868), the popular stage actress and author of Jewish poems and essays, for example, married six times. This gave opponents of immigrant marriage a case to pursue.

Marriage in the nineteenth century was the social barometer for the transition from bondage and coverture to contract relations. These contract negotiations had both domestic and national meanings: in the home, contract regulated the division of labor, whereas in the nation the contract between husband and wife was the moral register of American exceptionalism, progress, and privacy.

See also Bachelors and Spinsters; Courtship; Free Love; *Ruth Hall;* Sex Education

BIBLIOGRAPHY

Primary Works

Alcott, Louisa May. *Little Women.* 1868–1869. New York: Modern Library, 1983.

Dickinson, Emily. "I'm 'wife'—I've finished that." In *Norton Anthology of American Literature,* 6th ed., pp. 2503–2539. New York: Norton, 2003.

Fern, Fanny [Sarah Payson Willis Parton]. *Ruth Hall.* 1855. New Brunswick, N.J.: Rutgers University Press, 1990.

Fuller, Margaret. "The Great Lawsuit." 1843. In *Norton Anthology of American Literature,* 6th ed., pp. 1620–1654. New York: Norton, 2003.

A Graduate in the University of Matrimony. *How to Be Happy Though Married, Being a Handbook to Marriage.* New York: Scribners, 1886.

Hawthorne, Nathaniel. *The Blithedale Romance.* 1852. New York: Oxford University Press, 1991.

Hawthorne, Nathaniel. *The House of the Seven Gables.* 1851. New York: Oxford University Press, 1992.

Hawthorne, Nathaniel. *The Scarlet Letter.* 1850. New York: Penguin Classics, 1986.

Heywood, Angela Fiducia Tilton. "Sex Service—Ethics of Trust." *Word,* October 1889.

Melville, Herman. "The Paradise of Bachelors and the Tartarus of Maids." 1855. In *Norton Anthology of American Literature,* 6th ed., pp. 2355–2371. New York: Norton, 2003.

Phelps, Elizabeth Stuart. *The Silent Partner.* 1871. New York: Feminist Press, 1983.

Phelps, Elizabeth Stuart. *The Story of Avis.* 1877. New Brunswick, N.J.: Rutgers University Press, 1988.

Rush, Rebecca. *Kelroy.* 1812. New York: Oxford University Press, 1992.

Stowe, Harriet Beecher. *Pink and White Tyranny: A Society Novel.* 1871. New York: New American Library, 1988.

Stowe, Harriet Beecher. *Uncle Tom's Cabin.* 1852. New York: Penguin Books, 1981.

Whitman, Walt. "Song of Myself." In *Norton Anthology of American Literature,* 6th ed., pp. 2147–2189. New York: Norton, 2003.

Secondary Works

Baym, Nina. "Melodramas of Beset Manhood." In *Feminism and American Literary History: Essays.* New Brunswick, N.J.: Rutgers University Press, 1992.

Bennett, Paula Bernat. *Poets in the Public Sphere: The Emancipatory Project of American Women's Poetry, 1800–1900.* Princeton, N.J.: Princeton University Press, 2003.

Cott, Nancy F. *Public Vows: A History of Marriage and the Nation.* Cambridge, Mass.: Harvard University Press, 2000.

DuCille, Ann. *The Coupling Convention: Sex, Text, and Tradition in Black Women's Fiction.* New York: Oxford University Press, 1993.

Freeman, Elizabeth. *The Wedding Complex: Forms of Belonging in Modern American Culture.* Durham, N.C.: Duke University Press, 2002.

Lanser, Susan S. "Toward a Feminist Narratology." In *Feminisms: An Anthology of Literary Theory and Criticism,* edited by Robyn R. Warhol and Diane Price Herndl, pp. 674–693. New Brunswick, N.J.: Rutgers University Press, 1991.

Merish, Lori. *Sentimental Materialism: Gender, Commodity Culture, and Nineteenth-Century American Literature.* Durham, N.C.: Duke University Press, 2000.

Stanley, Amy Dru. *From Bondage to Contract: Wage Labor, Marriage, and the Market in the Age of Slave Emancipation.* Cambridge, U.K., and New York: Cambridge University Press, 1998.

Dale M. Bauer

MENTAL HEALTH

A popular contemporary joke says that anyone ahead of you driving slower than you want to go is an idiot and that anyone who passes you is a maniac. If someone disagrees with one's point of view, one might ask, "Are you crazy?" One might describe a chaotic classroom as like bedlam. People freely, even humorously, use the terms of mental health to define not only others but also themselves. The literary critic Shoshana Felman, in her study *Writing and Madness,* says, "To talk about madness is always, in fact, to deny it. However one represents madness to oneself or others [for example, a novelist to his or her readers], to represent madness is always, consciously or unconsciously, to play out the scene of the denial of one's own madness" (p. 252). Fictional representations of mentally disordered characters appear in the earliest works of American literature. The novel *Wieland* (1798), by the first professional belletristic writer in America, Charles Brockden Brown (1771–1810), is narrated by a confessed madwoman, Clara Wieland. Clara's brother, Theodore Wieland, thinks that God has spoken directly to him and commanded him to kill his family, but he has been tricked by a ventriloquist. His sister

Clara analyzes her own feelings as she tells this tale of disturbing psychological imbalance.

A number of other classic American novels from the nineteenth century present characters with mental disorders. A mentally unhinged singing master, David Gamut, in James Fenimore Cooper's *The Last of the Mohicans* (1826), moves freely amid the murderous Magua and his band of Hurons because lunatics received reverential treatment. Nathaniel Hawthorne's (1804–1864) masterpiece *The Scarlet Letter* (1850) presents the demoniacally insane character of Roger Chillingworth, whose obsessive desire for revenge against his unfaithful wife, Hester Prynne, and her lover, the Reverend Arthur Dimmesdale, propels the novel's plot. Rather than acknowledge his situation in a stable fashion, Chillingworth—himself a physician with an understanding of medicinal herbs—displays neurotic behavior that seeks to rectify his feelings of betrayal by cunningly inflicting misery on others. The literary reputation of Hawthorne's friend and neighbor Herman Melville (1819–1991) rests with general readers largely on the basis of one novel: *Moby-Dick* (1851). Melville's character Captain Ahab is most often described by critics as being megalomaniacal (desiring omnipotence) or monomaniacal (pathologically obsessed with one idea) because of his single-minded purpose of using his ship and its crew to get revenge on the white whale that physically harmed him by biting off his leg; Ahab is unable to grasp the extent to which Moby-Dick caused him psychological harm.

Readers of literature typically want to see characters who resemble themselves but who also differ in some degree—better looking, wiser, more adventurous. Readers' interest also extends to characters who are psychotic, conflicted, emotionally disturbed, especially those who advance the story by means of deviously constructed schemes growing out of some form of mental derangement. In the early twenty-first century one refers to people with various mental disorders with compassion, but not so long ago in America individuals with mental illness were routinely called lunatic, maniac, mad, evil-possessed, deranged, and the like. Manifestations of odd behavior that both amuse and unsettle one have become a staple of American literature, whether in the form of minor characters such as Cooper's David Gamut or central characters in twentieth-century novels such as Frederick Exley's *A Fan's Notes* (1968) and Ken Kesey's *One Flew over the Cuckoo's Nest* (1962), both of which are principally set in psychiatric hospitals.

MENTAL HEALTH IN COLONIAL TIMES

The earliest settlers in America clustered for mutual protection and support in villages and towns along the eastern seaboard, so society was "urban" in the sense that people lived in close proximity. Aberrant behavior was readily apparent in these close-knit settlements that grew progressively into towns and cities. The citizen majority who consider themselves sane determine which individuals are not sane. Forms of insanity have always existed in American community life, and novelists and poets reflect these aberrancies in their writings. In literature, corruption, crime, or mental instability typically occur in cities, while the bucolic, scarcely populated countryside represents purity and normalcy. In colonial times, mentally handicapped people in American urban communities were kept by their families in private homes, but some towns housed the violently insane in jails with common criminals or in almshouses with the poor. As communities grew, they began developing institutions for the mentally ill as early as the middle of the eighteenth century.

The first mental hospitals arose in or near major cities—Philadelphia, Williamsburg, New York, Boston, Hartford, Lexington. The establishment of these specialized hospitals during colonial times was consistent with the egalitarian attitude that America could cure all its societal ills in its quest to improve upon the European culture from which it sought to dissociate itself. With characteristic optimism, Americans thought that if something was wrong, a solution lay in setting about to correct it. If some individuals were insane, then insane asylums would solve the problem. In 1751, when the first general hospital in the British North American colonies was founded in Philadelphia, Benjamin Franklin urged that it include facilities for the treatment of the mentally ill. In 1766 Governor Francis Fauquier of Williamsburg argued in the Virginia House of Burgesses for the establishment of a mental hospital. Norman Dain notes that Fauquier called attention to "a poor unhappy set of People who are deprived of their Senses and wander about the country, terrifying the Rest of their Fellow Creatures" (p. 7). He called the insane "miserable Objects who cannot help themselves" and called upon the colony to "endeavor to restore them to their lost Reason" (p. 7).

As state mental hospitals appeared, families often relinquished the care and treatment of the mentally ill from the home to the institution. Families were not only relieved of the burden of caring for a loved one in the home but also comforted by the developing medical specialty that treated the mentally afflicted. They did not send relatives away to be chained in a dungeon but to be cared for by trained professionals whose abilities surpassed that of family members. Communities actively sought to establish these facilities as a mark of their cultural progression and civic pride in caring for their citizenry. Nor were these hospitals simply madhouses where pandemonium reigned. Benjamin Reiss writes that the doctors at the New York State Lunatic Asylum at Utica, founded in January 1843, practiced medical intervention with their patients, but they became known for their innovative treatment of insanity as the result of a psychological or moral cause. In a nurturing environment, they closely monitored their patients and engaged them in useful and enriching activities such as reading, writing, performing plays, worshipping at chapel, and learning marketable skills.

MENTAL HEALTH AND SLAVERY

As the nation grew and as hospitals for the insane became widespread, a special problem arose. Before the Civil War, most asylums in the United States, both North and South, either refused admission to blacks or gave them inferior treatment and facilities. Indeed, common knowledge among both medical professionals and lay people held that blacks and whites were so different in every way that they could not even suffer the same forms of mental illness. Peter McCandless writes that South Carolinians admitted slaves to their state mental hospital in 1848 but not necessarily out of a sense of altruism. Politically, the admission of blacks blunted some abolitionists' criticism of the generally harsh treatment of slaves in the South.

The novelist and poet William Gilmore Simms (1806–1870), one of the most talented writers in the South and a native of Charleston, South Carolina, published his first novel, *Martin Faber,* a psychological study of a criminal, in 1833. He also spoke out on the issue of slavery and mental illness. Simms argued in an essay titled "The Morals of Slavery" (1838) that the slave system actually encouraged mental stability because the slaves had no concerns about the future, no worries about supporting themselves or their children, and no anxiety about being cared for in old age. Simms's views carried great weight in the South because of his influential position as editor of the proslavery *Southern Quarterly Review* (1849–1856), a widely circulated periodical with a strong regional slant that published stories, poems, book reviews, and essays. Others in the antebellum South dismissively thought that distinctive mental disorders occurred in blacks because of their belief in witchcraft, conjuring, spells, and potions—the deeply rooted cultural beliefs that originated in Africa and the Caribbean and were brought to America by the slaves. The African American writer Charles W. Chesnutt (1858–1932) uses conjuring as a psycho-physiological motif in his short story "The Goophered Grapevine," first published in 1887 but set in the antebellum South. The story depicts a slave whose physical appearance changes with the seasons of the year because of his belief in the power of a conjuring or spell cast on him.

A New Orleans physician, Samuel Cartwright (1793–1863), believed that slaves sometimes suffered from a peculiar form of mental illness that he termed drapetomania, the abnormality that caused slaves to run away, from *drapeto,* meaning "to flee," and "mania," "an obsession." Clearly, however, Cartwright had subjective motives for his peculiar example. Harriet Beecher Stowe (1811–1896), in a very different sense, employed the motif of the runaway slave in her widely influential novel *Uncle Tom's Cabin,* first published serially in the magazine the *National Era* in 1851 and 1852. Uncle Tom does not run away because his deep religious faith allows him to transcend his servitude; he will receive his freedom in heaven. But in one of the most memorable scenes in the novel, the slave Eliza Harris, holding her young son Harry, leaps from one ice floe to the other over the Ohio River in her successful escape from Kentucky to Ohio. Her husband, George, later runs away and is united with his wife and child. One of the ironies apparent to modern readers concerning an attempt to invent a medical term for the act of a slave's running away is that the institution of slavery itself represented a sort of regional insane asylum, a vast madhouse populated with slaves as unwilling inmates. To want to escape from a place of madness must surely be a form of sanity, not insanity.

QUACKERY

Because mental illness manifests itself in such a variety of individual ways, no single method of treatment or panacea drug is likely to be discovered. Certainly the modern day pharmacopoeia can bring about dramatic improvement in patients suffering from depression, schizophrenia, and other neuroses. In the early to mid-nineteenth century, psychiatry was an unknown term. Patients suffering from mental illness received treatment for their symptoms, not the underlying causes of the symptoms. If patients were violent, they were restrained. If they spouted nonsense and could not communicate, they were isolated from those who could talk sensibly. During this period in American history, some of the cures advocated by respectable physicians seem ridiculous in the early twenty-first century: shaving the patient's head and washing it with vinegar, making the patient stand under a waterfall, or pouring cold water on his or her head. The reasoning behind these practices held that if the patient is "out of his or her head," the problem must lie within the head itself; therefore, the application of physical therapies to the part of the body that is disordered must be the correct medical approach. Other cures called for a regimen of exercise, fresh air, games, special diets, bleedings, purges of the bowels, cold baths, the administration of various tonics, excursion trips to exotic locales, and the imbibing of alcohol.

One can see that the imprecise understanding of mental illness invited all sorts of quackery. Among them, as is now known, was the practice of phrenology (from the Greek *phren,* "the mind"; hence the word "frenzy"). Commonly misunderstood as simply feeling the bumps of one's skull, a phrenological reading was, in fact, analogous to the palpations of a modern clinician who feels and thumps not simply the exterior of a patient's body but also, and more importantly, the organs within; their sizes, shapes, and sounds can tell a skilled practitioner much about the patient's condition. Similarly, the skull and its bumps are not as crucial as the form of the enclosed brain. A trained phrenologist was believed to be able to read the bumps that reveal the shape of the brain beneath them. These shapes were said to indicate a person's behavioral qualities such as combativeness, wonder, cautiousness, ideality, and benevolence. Once diagnosed, the patients were encouraged to modify their behavior to suppress bad tendencies and endeavor to adhere to the good tendencies.

Enjoying its greatest respectability from the 1820s through the 1840s, phrenology, in its early stages, was a serious attempt at discovering the origins of human behavior. This quasi-scientific field of inquiry now belongs to the netherworld of palmistry, soothsaying, and snake-oil elixir treatments. In an era when devices such as sonograms, computed tomography imaging (CT scanning), magnetic resonance imaging, and X-rays were still yet to be imagined, a group of the most esteemed medical doctors in Philadelphia proposed testing the validity of phrenological theory by measuring and examining the brains of selected individuals who were known achievers, so the first phrenological society was established there in 1822. The German neurologist Johann Gaspar Spurzheim taught a course in phrenology at Harvard Medical School in 1832, increasing the discipline's following among physicians and the public in general. In 1839 George Combe, a Scottish phrenologist, delivered a series of lectures at the Philadelphia Museum. Edgar Allan Poe studied Combe's *Lectures on Phrenology* (1839) for assistance in writing his 1839 short story "The Fall of the House of Usher."

The second edition of Walt Whitman's *Leaves of Grass* was published in 1856 by Fowler and Wells, a company whose officers were, in fact, phrenologists. The brothers Orson Squire Fowler (a classmate of Henry Ward Beecher at Amherst College) and Lorenzo Niles Fowler along with Samuel R. Wells operated their phrenological cabinet in New York City following the success of their operation in Philadelphia. Lorenzo Fowler examined Whitman's cranium in July 1849, and it is possible to match, as scholars have done, all the qualities of Fowler's reading with selections

New York Lunatic Asylum. Colored engraving, 1868. Built in 1839 on Blackwell's Island, now Roosevelt Island, in the East River, the New York Lunatic Asylum was typical of such institutions of the period, inadequately housing patients and dispensing treatments that were generally ineffective and sometimes lethal. THE GRANGER COLLECTION, NEW YORK

from *Leaves of Grass* because Whitman consciously inserted phrases and imagery that would complement the reading. Although Whitman retained some references to phrenology until his masterwork's final edition in 1892, he gradually distanced himself from practitioners of the pseudoscience when they were supplanted by sincere, progressive alienists—the original term for psychiatrist.

Without completely embracing phrenology, most of the principals in the transcendentalist movement showed interest. Amos Bronson Alcott, the leader of the transcendentalists at his commune Fruitlands, gave little credence to phrenology, although he willingly sat for at least four readings in the 1830s, including one reading by Lorenzo Niles Fowler.

Initially fascinated with the promise of phrenology to decipher character, Ralph Waldo Emerson (1803–1882) later rejected phrenology. Perry Miller

quotes Emerson as saying, "Phrenology laid a rough hand on the mysteries of animal and spiritual nature, dragging down every sacred secret to a street show" (p. 499). Even as he condemned its coarser aspects, Emerson credited phrenology with having "a certain truth to it; it felt connection where the professors denied it" (p. 499).

Margaret Fuller, who had a phrenological reading, was more enthusiastic than most of her transcendentalist friends, believing that any effort to understand the mind a worthwhile study; the parallels between idea and nature were central to transcendentalist thought. Theodore Parker, whose keen mind Emerson admired, credited the phrenologists with weakening old ways of thinking and inviting progress in understanding the nature of humankind. The transcendentalists' reaction to phrenology varied, and it never became integral to their movement; they viewed it as they would any scientific inquiry into the mind, and as phrenology's general appeal faded, so did their interest.

A REPRESENTATIVE WRITER

Of all American writers in the mid-nineteenth century, Edgar Allan Poe (1809–1849) is most often associated with madness or instability. A possible exception to this claim may be made for Jones Very (1813–1880), a minor poet and tutor in Greek at Harvard who insisted that his sonnets were communicated to him by the Holy Ghost. Very voluntarily committed himself to an insane asylum. Poe's legendary alcoholism and other unusual behavior such as his marriage to his thirteen-year-old cousin suggest an unstable individual. Lorenzo Niles Fowler conducted a phrenological reading of Poe (the date is not certain) and published his reading in the *Illustrated Phrenological Almanac for 1851* (1851). The reading wove phrenological theory with the circumstances of Poe's life, such as his mother's career as an actress, his being orphaned at a young age, and his alienation from his foster father, to account for his personal behavior as well as his highly psychoanalytical writings.

Poe is foremost in American literature for using psychological abnormality in poetry and fiction. His poem "The Haunted Palace" (1839) symbolizes a deranged mind, and his most famous poem, "The Raven" (1845), presents a tormented narrator mourning the loss of his lover and imagining a dialogue with a fantasy bird. Among tales in which Poe uses insanity as a theme are "The Cask of Amontillado" (1846), "The Fall of the House of Usher" (1839), "The Black Cat" (1843), and "The Tell-Tale Heart" (1843). Without knowing the modern-day terminology for depression, Poe's unnamed narrator in "The Fall of the House of Usher" describes his friend Roderick Usher as "alternately vivacious and sullen" (p. 721), a clear example of bipolar disorder. As Roderick's mental state deteriorated, he "rocked from side to side with a gentle yet constant and uniform sway" (p. 729). Modern psychotherapists would view this action as part of the rapid cycling that signals the onset of a complete breakdown.

The narrator of "The Tell-Tale Heart" talks to investigating police after he has committed a senseless murder of an old man. He challenges the police: "How then am I mad? Hearken! and observe how healthily, how calmly, I can tell you the whole story" (p. 731). The narrator tells the police that "what you mistake for madness is but over-acuteness of the senses" (p. 731). The more he attempts to appear calm during the interrogation, the more excitable he becomes, especially as he thinks he hears the incessant beating of the heart of his victim lying beneath the boards of the floor. The

only way the narrator can expiate himself of his intolerable guilt is to confess. The role of the police in this story is similar to that of a modern-day psychoanalyst. By allowing the narrator to tell his tale, to talk it out, the disturbed person arrives at his own cure: confession.

Because mental health—or mental illness, depending upon one's point of view—is part of the shared human experience, literature and madness have been intertwined since the earliest forms of storytelling, enriching generations of listeners and readers. In legends, folklore, mythology, and the Bible, evidence abounds that readers and writers have a continuing fascination with the abnormal and the inexplicable, a psychic belief in the supernatural, a fascination with the grotesque, and a respectful awe of the fearful aspects of the human psyche.

See also "The Fall of the House of Usher"; *Leaves of Grass; Moby-Dick;* Philosophy; Proslavery Writing; Psychology; "The Raven"; *The Scarlet Letter;* Science; Slavery

BIBLIOGRAPHY
Primary Works
Miller, Perry, ed. *The Transcendentalists: An Anthology.* Cambridge, Mass.: Harvard University Press, 1950.

Poe, Edgar Allan. "The Fall of the House of Usher." 1839. In *The Norton Anthology of American Literature,* edited by Nina Baym, shorter 5th ed. New York: Norton, 1999.

Poe, Edgar Allan. "The Tell-Tale Heart." 1843. In *The Norton Anthology of American Literature,* edited by Nina Baym, shorter 5th ed. New York: Norton, 1999.

Secondary Works
Dain, Norman. *Disordered Minds: The First Century of Eastern State Hospital in Williamsburg, Virginia, 1766–1866.* Williamsburg, Va.: Colonial Williamsburg Foundation, 1971.

Davies, John D. *Phrenology: Fad and Science: A Nineteenth-Century American Crusade.* New Haven, Conn.: Yale University Press, 1955.

Feder, Lillian. *Madness in Literature.* Princeton, N.J.: Princeton University Press, 1980.

Felman, Shoshana. *Writing and Madness.* Ithaca, N.Y.: Cornell University Press, 1985.

Hemenway, Robert. "Brockden Brown's Twice Told Insanity Tale." *American Literature* 40 (1968): 211–215.

Hungerford, Edward. "Poe and Phrenology." *American Literature* 2 (1930–1931): 209–231.

Hungerford, Edward. "Walt Whitman and His Chart of Bumps." *American Literature* 2 (1930–1931): 350–384.

McCandless, Peter. *Moonlight, Magnolias, and Madness: Insanity in South Carolina from the Colonel Period to the Progressive Era*. Chapel Hill: University of North Carolina Press, 1996.

Myerson, Joel. "Mary Gove Nichols' *Mary Lyndon*: A Forgotten Reform Novel." *American Literature* 58 (1986): 523–539.

Reiss, Benjamin. "Letters from Asylumia: The Opal and the Cultural Work of the Lunatic Asylum, 1851–1960." *American Literary History* 16 (2004): 1–28.

Reynolds, David S. *Walt Whitman's America: A Cultural Biography*. New York: Knopf, 1995.

Russo, James R. "'The Chimeras of the Brain': Clara's Narrative in *Wieland*." *Early American Literature* 16, no. 1 (1981): 60–88.

Scull, Andrew, ed. *Madhouses, Mad-Doctors, and Madmen: The Social History of Psychiatry in the Victorian Era*. Philadelphia: University of Pennsylvania Press, 1981.

Stern, Madeleine B. "Poe: 'The Mental Temperament' for Phrenologists." *American Literature* 40 (1968–1969): 155–163.

Shepard, Odell. *Pedlar's Progress: The Life of Bronson Alcott*. Boston: Little, Brown, 1937.

Trautmann, Joanne, ed. *Healing Arts in Dialogue: Medicine and Literature*. Carbondale: Southern Illinois University Press, 1981.

Philip W. Leon

METHODISTS

Contrary to the expectations of its founder, the Anglican priest John Wesley (1703–1791), Methodism developed into the most successful and most influential religious movement of nineteenth-century America. By 1820 a host of itinerant and local preachers—most notably Francis Asbury (1745–1816; "The Father of American Methodism"), Richard Allen (1760–1831), and "Crazy" Lorenzo Dow (1777–1834)—had converted some 250,000 individuals to the Methodist faith. Only twenty years later, Methodist membership totaled 900,000 and surged to roughly 1,500,000 in the mid-1850s when the various branches of the Methodist Church had consolidated their position as the fastest growing and largest religious denomination in the United States. Under the auspices of official Methodist presses such as the Methodist Book Concerns in Philadelphia (1789), New York (1804), Cincinnati (1820), and Nashville (1854) as well as the New York Methodist Tract Society (1817) and a number of independent publishers, this diverse and prolific community of believers produced religious letters, itinerant journals, tracts, church histories, sermons, hymnbooks, diaries, minutes, autobiographical conversion and slave narratives, magazines, and newspapers on an unprecedented scale. The seamless circulation of these increasingly political publications not only helped the Methodist Church as a whole to further fortify its religious stronghold but also gradually pulled an originally "otherworldly" and apolitical institution onto political turf. At the closing of the 1860s the Methodist Church had become so entrenched in worldly affairs that Ulysses S. Grant, eighteenth president of the United States, said in 1868 that he considered it one of the three great political parties (Hatch and Wigger, p. 309).

There are four reasons why the American Methodist Church rose to such popularity in a comparatively short period of time. On the political level, Methodism benefited from the First Amendment's "Establishment Clause," which barred Congress from promoting or prohibiting the exercise of religion and yielded greater tolerance of denominationalism. On the economic level, Methodism reaped the fruits of the industrial and market revolutions (1820–1860), which opened up new markets for devotional literatures in the American backcountry, enhanced mass printing, spurred urbanization, and magnified class differences. Methodism's all-inclusiveness appealed to the underprivileged and uneducated classes. Unlike their Calvinist competitors, who believed in the preordained salvation of an "elect" few, the Methodist Church stressed universal salvation, accessible to all regardless of sex, ethnicity, or social standing. In accordance with their egalitarian "doctrine" (the theoretical guide to the faith's principal beliefs), Methodist itinerants, or "circuit riders" (preachers who toured the country on horseback or on foot), traveled long distances to preach to those who lacked the means or desire to attend church. The gospel they preached was plain, accessible to the unschooled and unchurched, and lenient enough to be enjoyable rather than taxing. The fourth feature of Methodism during its formative years was seeming consistency between the church's principles and actions. Until the 1830s, Methodist institutions employed the socially marginalized as lay preachers and exhorters: the African American Richard Allen (1760–1831), author of *The Life, Experience, and Gospel Labours of Rev. Richard Allen* (1833); the Pequot Indian William Apess (1798–1839), whose autobiographical conversion narrative, *A Son of the Forest*, appeared in 1829; the African American itinerants "Mrs. Cook" and "Sister Tilgham" (Juliann Jane Tilmann) of whom Jarena Lee, an African American exhorter, makes mention in her narrative of *Life and Religious Experience of Jarena Lee, A Coloured Lady* (1836); Zilpha Elaw (c. 1790–?), who published her *Memoirs of the Life, Religious Experience, Ministerial Travels and Labours* in 1846; Sarah Hinton of North Carolina, one of the earliest converts to Methodism (1780), who later

Methodist camp meeting, c. 1850. Lithograph by Kellogg and Comstock. Throughout the nineteenth century, Methodist religious leaders often held outdoor meetings to draw converts and spread doctrines in less populated areas. © BETTMANN/CORBIS

helped establish a Methodist church in Washington, Beaufort County, North Carolina; and the New England native Nancy Towle (1796–1876), who published her diaries and letters in the *Vicissitudes Illustrated, in the Experience of Nancy Towle, in Europe and America* (1832).

DOCTRINE AND DISCIPLINE OF THE METHODIST CHURCH

Co-opting the belief that any individual has the power and intellectual ability to choose or reject salvation freely, Methodist doctrine offered ethical regeneration to those who were willing to experience conversion. The conversion experience comprised three stages of salvation: "repentance," a stage in which believers acknowledged their sinfulness; "justification," which assured individuals that Christ had died to atone for their sins; and "sanctification," in which new converts gained certainty of their spiritual perfection.

Individual stages of this three-part model varied in form and intensity. Methodist spiritual autobiographies of later writers—including Augustus R. Green's

The Life of the Rev. Dandridge F. Davis, of the African M.E. Church (1850), Harriet Jacobs's *Incidents in the Life of a Slave Girl* (1861), or Julia Foote's *A Brand Plucked from the Fire: An Autobiographical Sketch* (1879)—tended to describe the conversion experience as mere moments of joy. Conversion narratives written during Methodism's formative period, however, equated their writers' conversions with the loss of chains and shackles and the gain of "perfect freedom"—that is, the achievement of both spiritual and social equality among believers.

Methodism, while totally egalitarian in theory, proved less so in practice. Methodist leaders such as Francis Asbury, James O. Andrew, Lovick Pierce, Allen Turner, Augustus Longstreet, William J. Parks, W. J. Sasnett, and Samuel Anthony were initially willing to bend the rather rigid laws of their discipline to propagate the gospel in America. Suffering from a distressing shortage of qualified ministers, they temporarily employed African American and Native American men and women as "exhorters." Exhorting, unlike preaching, was a private and informal gathering of groups of seekers during which an exhorter would relate personal stories with a moral in order to motivate listeners to do good. Uncle Tom, the shining example of Methodist virtue in Harriet Beecher Stowe's *Uncle Tom's Cabin* (1852), occasionally acts as one such exhorter. Only in exceptionally rare cases and during a relatively short period of time were minorities and women—such as Nancy Towle or Jarena Lee—promoted to the position of preacher within the Methodist Episcopal Church (MEC) or the African Methodist Episcopal Church (AME).

Following Francis Asbury's death in 1816 and the redirection of Methodism's missionary zeal toward the emerging conservative middle class, the church's apparent egalitarian fervor abated. After a series of struggles against the "spiritual despotism" of church authorities, African Methodists under the leadership of Richard Allen, Daniel Coker, and James Champion submitted their resignation to preclude public expulsion from the MEC. In 1816 the African Methodist Episcopal Church (AME) was founded in Philadelphia and Richard Allen was ordained as its first African American bishop. One year later the AME published its *Doctrine and Discipline of the African Methodist Episcopal Church* (1817). In 1822 the African Methodist Episcopal Zion congregation (AME Zion) in New York followed the example set by the AME six years earlier; they segregated from the MEC and nominated James Varick as their bishop.

Yet not only slaves and free blacks deliberately left the MEC over the question of social equality. After he was denied ordination by the MEC in 1829, the Methodist exhorter and prayer leader William Apess joined the Protestant Methodist Church, a unified body of New England Methodist splinter groups that agreed to ordain him the very same year. Similarly at odds with egalitarian American Methodist doctrine was the treatment of Nancy Towle, who, despite Lorenzo Dow's open advocacy of equal rights for females in his preface to her autobiography, was barred from the pulpit in 1836. In 1842 Orange Scott (1800–1847), a northern abolitionist who bemoaned the backwardness of the MEC toward slavery, split with the church and established a religious periodical, the *True Wesleyan* (1843), to accentuate the institution's double standards. Much of the mid-nineteenth-century literature written by, for, or about Methodists can be read as a disillusioned response to the growing awareness of the discrepancy between MEC doctrine and discipline. William Apess was one of the first to hint at the disparity between Methodist doctrine and its discipline or "course of conduct" in *A Son of the Forest* (1829). Only three years later, Jarena Lee (1783–?) joined him in his criticism as she differentiated between good Christians and

those "wicked" ones who supported slavery. In a similar vein, Frederick Douglass's *Narrative* (1845) contrasts Christianity "proper" with the Christianity of the United States. From his description American Christianity emerges as southern barbarity cloaked in the "religion" of the South, in which "Negro-breakers" serve as Methodist class leaders. Douglass (1818–1895) directed his criticism directly at the South because the MEC discipline of the southern states differed from that of the northern states and Virginia in one important point: the former included an article that favored slavery and the latter did not. Echoing Douglass, Harriet Jacobs's *Incidents* condemns the sophistry of the South, which allowed white southern Methodists to be both slaveholders and class leaders who snickered at the plight of their human "property." In the end, Jacobs (1813–1897) inverts the traditional spiritual hierarchy by accusing American Christians of being heathens themselves. Herman Melville (1819–1891) made this very point first in his anti-flogging narrative *White-Jacket* (1850) and, one year later, in his most celebrated novel, *Moby-Dick* (1851). "After all," Melville's White-Jacket muses, reflecting on the missionary efforts of American Christianity, "all those maxims which . . . we busily teach the heathen, we Christians ourselves disregard" (p. 324). Or, as *Moby-Dick*'s famous Father Mapple, whom Melville modeled after the Methodist minister Father Taylor from Boston, warns us, "woe to him who . . . while preaching to others is himself a castaway" (p. 53).

DENOMINATIONAL PRESS AND SECTIONAL ALIENATION

While many were disillusioned and sought to attack or reform MEC discipline, others agreed with and even advocated its righteousness and egalitarian nature. The most heated, enduring, and politically decisive debate that erupted between the two camps (reformers and defenders of southern Methodist discipline) filled the pages of more than thirty denominational magazines and newspapers in mid-nineteenth-century America. Despite its dislike for controversy and its presumptive political neutrality, the *Methodist Review* (1818–1828)—later titled the *Methodist Magazine and Quarterly Review* (1830–1840), the *Methodist Quarterly Review* (1841–1884), and the *Methodist Review* (1885–)—inadvertently sided with the North as it defended the principles of "free will" and all-inclusive, "unconditional election" that the southern version of the MEC discipline sought to redefine. The journal's egalitarian attitude and opposition to slavery was voiced most clearly between 1856 and 1884, under the editorial leadership of Daniel D. Whedon (1808–1885). Whedon was a staunch opponent of slavery who saw the *Methodist Quarterly Review,* which sold roughly one million copies annually in its peak years, as an "anti-slavery organ of an anti-slavery church based on an anti-slavery discipline" (Sweet, p. 301).

Whedon's antislavery activism was surpassed by Boston's *Zion's Herald* (1823) and by perhaps its most militant contributor, the Vermont preacher Orange Scott. Scott, an avid reader of William Lloyd Garrison's abolitionist paper *The Liberator,* who called for the immediate release of all slaves and separated from the Methodist Episcopal Church in 1842. He later edited the *American Wesleyan Observer,* an antislavery newspaper based in Lowell, Massachusetts. A number of smaller Methodist journals supported Whedon's and Scott's cause, including the *Wesleyan Repository* (1821), founded by the New Jersey layman William S. Stockton, and the *Richmond Christian Advocate* (1832).

After the MEC's breakup over the question of "discipline" in the Methodist Episcopal Church, North (MEC), and the Methodist Episcopal Church, South (MECS), in 1844, southern responses to critics and reformers of their discipline grew increasingly hostile. In reaction to Scott's attacks on slavery and the Methodist discipline of the southern states, Nathan Bangs (1778–1862), a church elder, editor of the *Christian Advocate and Journal* (1827), and future editor of the *Methodist Quarterly Review,* initially did little more than close his journal to the discussion of abolition. A few years later, however, William Wightman, editor of the *Southern Christian Advocate* (1837) at Charleston, openly condemned northern activism and the antislavery movement after the schism of 1844. Indicative of his agenda, Wightman offered to print the proslavery and pro–southern discipline "Letters on the Epistle of Paul to Philemon" written by Augustus Longstreet (1790–1870), a conservative Methodist church elder, in 1845. After that, the journal continued to back the southern cause. Similarly supportive of MECS creeds was the *Southern Review* (1867–1879), an intellectual and literary journal edited by Albert Taylor Bledsoe (1809–1877) and William Hand Browne (1828–1912) that intended to defend the position of the MECS by explaining its theology. Yet the journal's personal attacks on Daniel D. Whedon hindered rather than advanced its cause. The *Methodist Advocate of Atlanta;* the *Army and Navy Herald,* founded by the Macon Methodist J. R. Harp; and the radical *Texas Christian Advocate* (which went as far as to justify the 1860 Texas lynching of the Reverend Anthony Bewley) presented local sounding boards for MECS views.

Clearly, white Americans dominated periodical production in the antebellum period and the mid-

1860s. In the years following the Civil War, however, it was the African American press that thrived. The rapidly growing AME founded several church journals including the *New Orleans Advocate,* later the *Southwestern Christian Advocate* at New Orleans (1866); the *Living Epistle* (1876); the *Christian Standard and Home Journal* (1867); the *Free Methodist Journal* (1868); and the *A.M.E. Church Review* (1884). The African Zion Church, which quadrupled the number of its adherents between 1866 and 1868 from 42,000 to over 164,000, issued its first congregational periodical, the *Star of Zion,* in 1867. It was not until mid-March of 1870 that L. C. Matlack in the *Central Christian Advocate* called for the reconciliation of the reformists and defenders, whose ardent struggle over the meaning of spiritual and social equality had not only exposed the covert conservatism of church authorities but also led to the diversification and democratization of Methodist faiths.

See also Abolitionist Writing; Calvinism; Evangelicals; Protestantism; Religion; Religious Magazines

BIBLIOGRAPHY
Primary Works
Apess, William. *A Son of the Forest and Other Writings.* 1829. Edited by Barry O'Connell. Amherst: University of Massachusetts Press, 1997.

Douglass, Frederick. *Narrative of the Life of Frederick Douglass.* 1845. New York: Dover, 1995.

Jacobs, Harriet A. *Incidents in the Life of a Slave Girl.* 1861. Edited by Lydia Maria Child. Cambridge, Mass.: Harvard University Press, 1987.

Melville, Herman. *Moby-Dick.* 1851. Edited by Hershel Parker and Harrison Hayford. New York: Norton, 2002.

Melville, Herman. *White-Jacket; or, The World in a Man-of-War.* 1850. Evanston, Ill.: Northwestern University Press, 1970.

Stowe, Harriet Beecher. *Uncle Tom's Cabin.* 1852. Edited by Elizabeth Ammons. New York: Norton, 1994.

Towle, Nancy. *Vicissitudes Illustrated, in the Experience of Nancy Towle, in Europe and America.* Charleston, S.C.: J. L. Burges, 1832.

Secondary Works
Andrews, Dee E. *The Methodists and Revolutionary America, 1760–1800: The Shaping of an Evangelical Culture.* Princeton, N.J.: Princeton University Press, 2000.

Andrews, William L., ed. *Sisters of the Spirit: Three Black Women's Autobiographies of the Nineteenth Century.* Bloomington: Indiana University Press, 1986.

Hatch, Nathan O. *The Democratization of American Christianity.* New Haven, Conn.: Yale University Press, 1989.

Hatch, Nathan O., and John H. Wigger, eds. *Methodism and the Shaping of American Culture.* Nashville, Tenn.: Kingswood, 2001.

Heyrman, Christine Leigh. *Southern Cross: The Beginnings of the Bible Belt.* New York: Knopf, 1997.

Lambert, Frank. *"Pedlar in Divinity": George Whitefield and the Transatlantic Revivals, 1737–1770.* Princeton, N.J.: Princeton University Press, 1994.

Mathews, Donald G. *Religion in the Old South.* Chicago: University of Chicago Press, 1977.

Mott, Frank Luther. *A History of American Magazines.* 5 vols. Cambridge, Mass.: Harvard University Press, 1938–1968.

Noll, Mark A. *America's God: From Jonathan Edwards to Abraham Lincoln.* Oxford and New York: Oxford University Press, 2002.

Owen, Christopher H., ed. *The Sacred Flame of Love: Methodism and Society in Nineteenth-Century Georgia.* Athens: University of Georgia Press, 1998.

Sweet, William Warren. *Methodism in American History.* Nashville, Tenn.: Abingdon Press, 1953.

Merit Kaschig

MEXICAN-AMERICAN WAR

After Texas entered the Union as a state in December 1845, rather than accepting the Nueces River as the United States's southernmost border (as the Republic of Texas had formerly agreed to do), in February 1846, President James K. Polk ordered General Zachary Taylor to lead what Polk called an "observatory force" to assert a U.S. boundary at the Rio Grande. Mariano Paredes y Arrillaga, the president of Mexico, immediately declared a defensive war to defend his nation's border. After two years of bloody combat, in the spring of 1848 the United States and Mexico cosigned the Treaty of Guadalupe Hidalgo. According to the terms of this treaty, Mexico recognized the Rio Grande as the border of Texas, and the United States assumed $5 million of the unpaid claims that Mexico owed to U.S. citizens. For an additional $15 million, Mexico ceded over a half million square miles of northern California to the United States (retaining the area that is now the Mexican state of Baja California). The U.S. territory was then divided into the provinces of New Mexico and California, which later become the states of New Mexico, Utah, Nevada, and California.

A PATRIOTIC IDEAL

At the time of the war's inception in 1846, the patriotic ideals in whose name the Mexican-American War was fought commanded all of the resources and symbols of U.S. patriotism. It was the first military campaign in which soldiers marched to the tempo of "The Star-Spangled Banner" as the national anthem, and it was the first war that was fought under the "stars and stripes" as the national flag. The Mexican-American War was also the first military campaign in which war correspondents were employed to report from the field. So many newspapermen were embedded in the ranks of the early volunteers that they were able to found newspapers of their own—popularly known as the "Anglo-Saxon press"—in Mexico's occupied cities.

By 1846 most of the key figures from the American revolutionary generation were either dead or dying. Upon representing each military success in Mexico as a vivid reminder of the nation's revolutionary beginnings, war reporters encouraged the troops to model their actions in the field after the example of the revolutionary heroes. The press thereby propagated the fiction that the war was the collective expression of the sons and daughters of the revolution, who were ready to sacrifice their lives and the nation's treasure on behalf of the independence of the Mexican people. Through its depiction of the war as a collective ordeal that forged a sacred link with the Founding Fathers' generation, the press also empowered its readers to imagine themselves as participants in the foundational event of the national community.

There were few U.S. residents who did not have a family member or some friend involved in the fighting. In his *Pictorial History of Mexico and the Mexican War* (1848), John Frost, the war's unofficial historian, portrayed the actions that took place in Mexico as part of a providential design that elevated the United States itself into an heroic protagonist. Frost's popular history of the war legitimated the doctrine of Manifest Destiny that designated the United States as God's favored nation and that characterized the inhabitants of its territory as God's chosen people.

The soldiers who took part in the Mexican-American War and the citizens who supported it alike believed that this national ordeal would fulfill the ideals of the nation's Founding Fathers. In *To the Halls of the Montezumas: The Mexican War in the American Imagination*, Robert W. Johannsen has described how deeply this fantasy penetrated into the psyche of the U.S. peoples. It "was a war," Johannsen writes,

> that was experienced more intimately, with greater immediacy and closer involvement than any major event in the nation's history. It was the first American war to rest on a truly popular base, the first that grasped the interest of the population, and the first people were exposed to on an almost daily basis. (P. 16)

The Mexican-American War, 1846–1848

- U.S. territory, 1846
- Mexican territory, 1846
- Mexican cession, 1848
- Disputed territory

Soldiers identified so powerfully with figures from the revolutionary past that they imagined themselves as supplying them with their flesh and blood as they headed off to do battle. Even though George Washington had been dead for nearly fifty years, General Zachary Taylor conjured up his spectral presence at the Battle of Buena Vista on 22 February 1847. After General Taylor reminded his troops that this was the date of their founder's birth, Taylor asked each soldier under his command to imagine his body taken up by the spirit of Washington's valor. As Washington's name resounded through their ranks, Taylor's men turned back a Mexican armed force that was five times greater in size. Taylor would subsequently call his troops' identification with Washington as the decisive factor in the victory that John Frost describes as the turning point in the war.

Soldiers in the field drew comparably remarkable inspiration from William Hickling Prescott's epic *History of the Conquest of Mexico* (1843). Upon reading Prescott's account of the Spanish conquest, U.S.

soldiers propagated the belief that the Prescott epic foretold their second conquest of Mexico. As they envisioned the empires of Montezuma II (1466–1520) and Hernán Cortes (1485–1547) giving way to the irresistible force of the "empire of liberty" they were bringing to the Mexican people, the troops associated this contemporary struggle with events from the past of civilization itself.

In addition to Prescott's history of the Spanish conquest, the Texas-Mexican borderland furnished the cultural context into which the literature inspired by the Mexican-American War was placed. In the editorials he published in the *Brooklyn Daily Eagle* from 1846 to 1848, Walt Whitman (1819–1892) evoked the memories of famous battles of the so-called Texas Revolution to establish a norm of dominance whereby the United States represented the hemisphere itself as a national entitlement. In relocating the origins of the Mexican-American War in the massacres that took place at the Alamo and in Goliad, Whitman described the entirety of Mexico as the site of a war crime: "The

A Texas Ranger. Illustration from John Frost's *Pictorial History of Mexico and the Mexican War*, 1848. THE LIBRARY OF CONGRESS

massacre at the Alamo, the bloody business at Goliad, the red butcheries which the cowardly Mexicans effected whenever they got the people of Texas in their power during the course of the sanguinary contest, should be avenged more signally than ever outrage was avenged before" (p. 347).

But insofar as it reflected the soldier's willingness to make sacrifices in the interest of the country, the Mexican-American War was likewise crucial to the dissemination of the ideology of republicanism. The terms that writers invoked to celebrate the soldiers' heroism— the sacrifice of interest in the self for love of country— also corroborated republican virtue. Soldiers in turn construed the battlefield as a fabulous space that recalled them to the ideals of honor and duty. The capacious expanse of republican ideology allowed its proponents to adopt utterly opposed attitudes toward the Mexican-American War without experiencing them as irresolvable contradictions. Those who supported the war in the name of republican ideals argued that it was the nation's moral responsibility to liberate Mexico from the chains of monarchical tyranny. Those who opposed the war invoked the very same ideals to argue that if American freedom was grounded in the consent of the people, the American people could not acquiesce to the exercise of military force over an unwilling people.

LITERARY CELEBRATION AND OPPOSITION

U.S. canonical writers exemplified republicanism's ambivalence in their variegated responses to the war. In his essay on the grounds for his civil disobedience, Henry David Thoreau (1817–1862) gave expression to the conviction he shared with Ralph Waldo Emerson (1803–1882), Margaret Fuller (1810–1850), and Herman Melville (1819–1891) that territories acquired by military force and administered without the consent of the governed were incompatible with the ideals of a constitutional democracy. In his novel *Jack Tier; or, The Florida Reef* (1848), James Fenimore Cooper (1789–1851) was also openly critical of President Polk's decision to use a predominately volunteer army, which Cooper viewed as responsible for an untoward cost in dollars and casualties. However in the campaign biography that he composed for Franklin Pierce in 1852, Nathaniel Hawthorne (1804–1864) favorably portrayed the Mexican battlefields as the training grounds upon which Pierce developed the civic virtues of prudence and self-sacrifice that prepared him to lead the country. And Walt Whitman celebrated the Mexican-American War as an overturning of tyranny that inspired the revolutionary actions taking place throughout Europe in 1848. Despite their antithetical stances on the war, Cooper, Thoreau, Emerson, Fuller, and Melville based their opposition to it upon the same presupposition that led Hawthorne and Whitman to support it: that the United States was the guardian over the ideals of liberty that it was commissioned to propagate throughout the world.

But William Gilmore Simms's (1806–1870) reaction to the war was representative of a cadre of Southern writers who differed from their contemporaries from the North in that they did not attempt to reconcile the war with the United States' adherence to democratic institutions. Simms turned to an imagined Middle Ages to give romantic shape to this "nineteenth century crusade," which he believed essential to maintain the security of southern institutions. In his 1848 collection of verse *Lays of the Palmetto: A Tribute to the South Carolina Regiment, in the War with Mexico*, Simms connected the South Carolina volunteers' chivalric valor with the southern code of paternalism, honor, and duty through which the South also justified the institution of slavery.

But U.S. abolitionists invoked its complicity with the slave power to justify their unanimous condemnation of the war. Frederick Douglass (1818–1895) denounced the war as a violation of the democratically achieved rights of the all-but-defenseless Mexican people. William Lloyd Garrison (1805–1879) described the war as a conspiracy to expand the domain of the slave power. And John Greenleaf Whittier (1807–1892) singled out Mexico's abolition of slavery as one of the unstated the causes of the war. After exposing the ways in which the American people's patriotic sentiments had been manipulated to expand slavery's dominion, Whittier wrote a series of poems that he designed to dissociate the Mexican-American War from the nation's revolutionary ideals. In "Yorktown," the representative poem in this series, Whittier drew out vivid parallels between the Mexican people and the patriotic revolutionaries who opposed the slave power of the British Empire.

RACIAL IDENTITY

The historian Reginald Horsman suggests that these debates about the conduct of the war provoked the first widespread embrace of the Anglo-Saxon race as prototypical of the U.S. national identity. The U.S. literary figure James Russell Lowell (1819–1891) exemplified this trend when, after supporting the abolitionists' opposition to the war in *The Biglow Papers* (1848), Lowell also mitigated this criticism with the observation that it was "the manifest destiny of the English race to occupy this whole continent and to display there that practical understanding in matters of government and colonization that no other race has given such proof of possessing since the Romans" (Johannsen, p. 218).

Their promotion of Anglo-Saxon liberty led politicians as well as writers to racialize the Mexican population as nonwhite. In *Our Army at Monterey* (1847), the southwestern humorist Thomas Bangs Thorpe (1815–1878) characterized the Mexican soldier as the degraded biological product of different races "where the evil qualities of each . . . [are] alone retained" (p. 95). Thorpe invoked these racist stereotypes to explain why the conquest of Mexico should be understood as an expression of Anglo-Saxon liberty. In his prowar novel *The Volunteer* (1847), Ned Buntline (Edward Zane Carroll Judson, 1823–1886) invented a protagonist who lent support to the proslavery and white racist values to which President Polk had appealed when he characterized the racial heterogeneity of the Mexican people as the factor that made him chiefly wary of incorporating Mexico into the United States.

When the U.S. writers racialized Mexicans as non-white, they also racialized Mexican land and Mexican labor in ways that were intended to diminish the class and racial anxieties of the laborers who read about the war in the industrial cities of the North. In *American Sensations: Class, Empire and the Production of Popular Culture*, Shelley Streeby has persuasively demonstrated how class and racial hierarchies in northeastern cities were inextricably tied up with the scenes of empire building in Mexico. According to Streeby, popular sensational novelists who wrote about working-class culture redeployed this racial idiom when they wrote about Mexico. Viewed through the eyes of the white laborer from El Norte, the Mexicans ways of occupying lands and performing seemed unproductive and wasteful.

But whereas the abolitionists and transcendentalists appealed to tenets of republican ideology to discuss the war with the middle classes, the dime novelists promoted a form of nativism that drew upon working-class fears of foreign laborers, slave rebellions, rival empires, and papist conspiracies. The discourse of nativism assigned assumptions about race and gender that served as the idiom of working-class cultures. Insofar as nativism presupposed social hierarchies that reenforced commercial interests, nativism was inassimilable to republican ideology. But it was its very inassimilability to republican ideology that foregrounded nativism as U.S. republicanism's seamy underside.

In 1847 George Lippard (1822–1854), America's most widely read novelist, collaborated with the working class's ideology of nativism in his popular novel *Legends of Mexico*. After racializing the class division between the Mexicans and the working-class soldiers in the volunteer army, Lippard forged an imperial solution to the problems of industrial capitalism. In *Legends of Mexico*, he described Taylor's troops as an army of industrial workers, and then he identified these militant proletariats as the true agents of revolutionary social change in Mexico. In so doing Lippard used the racist idiom sedimented within the workers' nativism to place Mexicans in the spaces that had formerly been occupied by Irish, Italian, Bavarian, and other workers from ethnic minorities so as to advocate the incorporation of these particular immigrant laborers into an "American race."

HISTORICAL ASSESSMENT

Overall, the Mexican-American War powerfully influenced the ways in which the major issues of the nineteenth century—immigration, race relations, free soil versus slavery, interhemispheric geopolitics, the question as to whether the United States was a republic or an empire—were represented, discussed, analyzed, and evaluated. As the greatest of the American wars before the Civil War, the Mexican-American War might as a consequence have been expected to occupy a lofty place in U.S. history. But events from a nation's past only remain useful to its historians as long as they reflect and reinforce their generally shared assumptions. As a war of aggression that gave expression to expansionist ambitions, the Mexican-American War could not be integrated within the grand narrative of U.S. history that unequivocally commemorated U.S. purposes as altruistic, noble, and innocent. While it was considered a fulfillment of revolutionary ideals as it was taking place, this "forgotten war," as it is sometimes called, was eclipsed by the Civil War that drastically reduced its historical standing to the status of one of its tributary causes.

From the time of the war's conclusion in 1848, Mexican historians have joined with the Spanish-speaking artists, writers, poets, and denizens of the borderlands between the United States and Mexico in a collective effort to challenge historians' accounts of the war. But the assumptions that have driven and defined the historical scholarship about the Mexican-American War have made it extremely difficult for these alternative historiographical frameworks and analytic narratives to find a reputable place in the discussion of the war. Indeed, for many years the U.S. historians who analyzed the war did not merely fail to represent the Mexican writers' different accounts; because these omissions were consistent with the assumptions of U.S. historiography, historians did not even notice their absence.

But the reemergence of the question of empire and the interrogation of the strategies whereby U.S. historians had ignored that question has led to widespread questioning of the assumptions that formerly enabled U.S. historians to forget about the Mexican-American War. Although scholars conventionally located the origins of U.S. imperialism at the end of the nineteenth century, the reexamination of the Mexican-American war has led to the uncovering of a much longer history of empire in the Americas. Scholars in Chicano/a studies of the standing of Rosaura Sánchez, José David Saldívar, and Carl Gutiérrez-Jones (to name only a few) have uncovered a vast archive of *testimonios* from the 1840s that represent the history of U.S. interaction with Mexico in terms that promise to supply the representations of the Mexican-American War with a very different shape in the future.

See also Borders; Manifest Destiny; Slavery; Spanish Speakers and Early "Latino" Expression

BIBLIOGRAPHY

Primary Works

Alcaraz, Ramon, et al. *The Other Side; or, Notes for the History of the War between Mexico and the United States.* 1850. Translated by Albert C. Ramsey. New York: Burt Franklin, 1970.

Buntline, Ned. *The Volunteer; or, The Maid of Monterey: A Tale of the Mexican War.* Boston: F. Gleason, 1847.

Cooper, James Fenimore. *Jack Tier; or, The Florida Reef.* New York: Burgess, Stringer, and Co., 1848.

Frost, John. *Pictorial History of Mexico and the Mexican War.* Richmond, Va.: Harrold and Murray, 1848.

Hawthorne, Nathaniel. *The Life of Franklin Pierce.* Boston: Ticknor, Reed, and Fields, 1852.

Lippard, George. *Legends of Mexico.* Philadelphia: T. B. Peterson 1847.

Lowell, James Russell. *The Letters of James Russell Lowell.* Vol. 1. Edited by Charles Eliot Norton. New York: Harper & Brothers, 1894.

Prescott, William Hickling. *History of the Conquest of Mexico.* 3 vols. New York: Harper & Brothers, 1843.

Simms, William Gilmore. *Lays of the Palmetto: A Tribute to the South Carolina Regiment, in the War with Mexico.* Charleston, S.C.: John Russell, 1848.

Thorpe, Thomas Bangs. *Our Army at Monterey.* Philadelphia: Carey and Hart, 1847.

Whitman, Walt. *The Collected Writings of Walt Whitman: The Journalism.* Vol. 1, *1834–1846.* Edited by Herbert Bergman. New York: Peter Lang, 1998.

Secondary Works

Brack, Gene. *Mexico Views Manifest Destiny, 1821–1846: An Essay on the Origins of the Mexican War.* Albuquerque: University of New Mexico Press, 1975.

Brown Charles H. *Agents of Manifest Destiny: The Lives and Times of the Filibusters.* Chapel Hill: University of North Carolina Press, 1980.

Chávez, John R. *The Lost Land: The Chicano Image of the Southwest.* Albuquerque: University of New Mexico Press, 1984.

Gruesz, Kirsten. *Ambassadors of Culture: The Transamerican Origins of Latino Writing.* Princeton, N.J.: Princeton University Press, 2001.

Gutiérrez-Jones, Carl Scott. *Rethinking the Borderlands: Between Chicano Culture and Legal Discourse.* Berkeley: University of California Press, 1995.

Hietala, Thomas. *Manifest Design: Anxious Aggrandizement in Late Jacksonian America.* Ithaca, N.Y.: Cornell University Press, 1985.

Hogan, Michael. *The Irish Soldiers of Mexico.* Guadalajara, Mexico: Fondo Editorial Universitario, 1997.

Horsman, Reginald. *Race and Manifest Destiny: The Origins of American Racial Anglo-Saxonism.* Cambridge, Mass.: Harvard University Press, 1981.

Johannsen, Robert W. *To the Halls of the Montezumas: The Mexican War in the American Imagination.* New York: Oxford University Press, 1985.

Pagden, Anthony. *Spanish Imperialism and the Political Imagination.* New Haven, Conn.: Yale University Press, 1990.

Paredes, Américo. *Folklore and Culture on the Texas-Mexican Border.* Edited by Richard Bauman. Austin, Tex.: Center for Mexican American Studies, 1993.

Saldívar, José David. *Border Matters: Remapping American Cultural Studies.* Berkeley: University of California Press, 1997.

Saldívar, Ramón. *Chicano Narrative: The Dialectics of Difference.* Madison: University of Wisconsin Press, 1990.

Sánchez, Rosaura. *Telling Identities: The Californio Testimonios.* Minneapolis: University of Minnesota Press, 1995.

Streeby, Shelley. *American Sensations: Class, Empire, and the Production of Popular Culture.* Berkeley: University of California Press, 2002.

Donald E. Pease

MISCEGENATION

Relative to the cultural phenomenon it names, the word "miscegenation" is a recent invention, dating only as far back as the U.S. Civil War. From the beginning of their colonial expansion into the Americas, Europeans expressed curiosity about sexual unions between men and women belonging to different racial categories (a point exhaustively demonstrated in 1997 by Werner Sollors in *Neither Black Nor White Yet Both: Thematic Explorations of Interracial Literature*). Even before a racial vocabulary had fully emerged, observers were commenting on sexual relations between Europeans and Native Americans or Africans living in America. The earliest additions to this racial vocabulary were primarily descriptors of the products of those sexual unions. While by the mid-sixteenth century "mongrel" could be used pejoratively, "mulatto" and "mestizo"—two terms borrowed from Spanish and Portuguese to describe the offspring of Europeans and either Africans or Native Americans—were often used merely to identify parentage. The emergence of increasingly refined categories, such as "quadroon" and "octoroon," indicates an obsessive interest in calculating the degree to which a person could be considered mixed. Other terms, such as "hybrid" and "half breed," focus on the fact of interracial union rather than on any specific genetic combination. The diversity of this racial discourse reflects how attitudes toward interracial unions could vary according to regional differences, changes over time, and the particular ways that a particular combination cut across race and class lines. In the United States it was not until the nine-teenth century that words emerged to express—and often condemn—the desires driving these unions.

Nineteenth-century American literature reflects this complex linguistic and ideological heritage. While the word "miscegenation" was coined in the intense turmoil of Civil War fervor for the purpose of satirizing and condemning the sexual union of Euro-Americans and African Americans, the racist attitude that underlies it is the cumulative product of at least 250 years of talk about interracial sex in America. To understand "miscegenation" as both a cultural and literary phenomenon, it is first necessary to understand how racial thinking evolved over time and shaped nineteenth-century American attitudes toward sex, love, and marriage.

THE POCAHONTAS MYTH, CAPTIVITY NARRATIVES, AND FRONTIER ROMANCES

By 1820 stories of interracial sexual unions between Europeans and Native Americans had long titillated readers. One of the most durable of these stories was the legend of Pocahontas. In the popular melodrama *The Indian Princess; or, La Belle Sauvage* (1808), James Nelson Barker (1784–1858) depicted a mature and noble Pocahontas. Her dialogue with her English lover, Lieutenant Rolfe, articulates the Euro-American fantasy of Native American submission to, and even love for, a superior European culture that will rescue her from "the path of savage error" (p. 149). This romantic fantasy, however, is doubled in the play's comic plot, in which the clownish Robin overcomes his fears of native savagery to steal off into the woods with his "little dusky divinity," Nima (p. 148). Their banter knowingly winks at the sexual realities underlying the play's sanitized allegorical resolution of European and Native American cultural differences through the marriage of noble racial representatives. Throughout the nineteenth century, variations on this theme of interracial love in the woods were acted out on stages across the United States.

As the double plot of *The Indian Princess* indicates, Americans held a variety of attitudes toward sexual relationships between European men and Native American women. Although by the 1820s seven states prohibited marriage between Euro-Americans and Native Americans, the rhetoric of noble savagery typified by the Pocahontas myth, as well as the material realities of frontier life, led some Americans to tolerate and even encourage Indian-white marriages. Such relative tolerance must be understood, however, against the anxiety that surrounded sexual relationships between Euro-American women and Native American men. One of the primary sites for the expression of this fear was the Indian captivity narrative. These narratives, first popularized in the seventeenth century, were still widely read

The Marriage of Pocahontas. Nineteenth-century lithograph. The story of the love affair and marriage of the Native American Pocahontas and the Englishman John Rolfe, a popular subject in nineteenth-century American literature, reflects the Euro-American fantasy of Native American submission to, and even love for, a superior European culture.
THE LIBRARY OF CONGRESS

in the nineteenth, both in the form of eyewitness accounts and as stylized potboilers. Many of these narratives stressed the valiant resistance of white women against their Indian captors' savage lusts. Some, however, detailed the lives of captured girls and women who, having been adopted into Native American communities, married Indian men and raised mixed-race children. For example, the best-selling *A Narrative of the Life of Mrs. Mary Jemison* (1824) relates the story of a woman who had been taken captive at age fifteen and gradually adapted to living among Native Americans. Far from sensationalizing taboo sexual relations, Jemison's narrative factually recounts her two marriages to Native American men (the second lasting some fifty years) and justifies her decision to remain among her adopted culture by documenting an extensive family network that included eight children and dozens of descendants. Jemison's experience was not unique, but her telling of it was; far more of these accounts included stock elements that came to typify captivity narratives: sudden violent attacks, frail white women, lascivious

savages, heroic and harrowing escapes. The threat of rape or forced marriage was a frequent motif, even if only to deny their occurrence.

The strenuousness with which these narratives reinforced racist attitudes betrays the desire of nineteenth-century Euro-Americans to deny the interracial mixing that, whether by force or by choice, was taking place in all corners of the United States and its territories. In addition to the coupling between Euro-American settlers and Native Americans on the western frontier, black slaves mixed (often by choice) with white indentured servants and (often by force) with white slave owners. In the Southeast, escaped black slaves joined and married into Native American communities. In addition, as the United States acquired territories previously held by France and Spain, it absorbed significant mixed-race populations.

Recognizing the tension between the democratic ideals of the United States and its racism, the novelists Lydia Maria Child (1802–1880), James Fenimore

Cooper (1789–1851), and Catharine Maria Sedgwick (1789–1867) plotted historical romances featuring interracial unions. In Child's *Hobomok, A Tale of Early Times* (1824), Mary Conant, the daughter of New England Puritans, marries and bears the son of a Wampanoag Indian, Hobomok. Despite the daring depiction of marriage between a white woman and a Native American man, the novel essentially reinforces racist attitudes. When Child writes that Mary herself "knew that her own nation looked upon her as lost and degraded; and, what was far worse, her own heart echoed back the charge," she effectively endorses the social values of her time (p. 135). Two years later, Cooper's *The Last of the Mohicans* (1826) took an even more oblique approach toward interracial unions. At times the novel plays on Euro-Americans' worst fears of Indian savagery, as when the malevolent Magua threatens to take Cora Munro to "live in his wigwam forever" (p. 119). And yet it also traces the blossoming romance between Cora and the heroic Uncas, a romance cut short by their deaths but consummated symbolically through an Indian funeral chant that envisions their partnership in the afterworld. With respect to interracial union, however, even this happy prospect is undermined by the reader's awareness that, although she is praised by the Indians as having "blood purer and richer than the rest of her nation," she is in fact "descended . . . remotely" from African slaves (pp. 386, 180). The novel's ideology of racial purity is further affirmed by the chaste friendship of its protagonist, Hawkeye, and his stoic Native American sidekick, Chingachgook. The racial group to which Mohicans like Chingachgook belonged was the Lenni Lenape, which as Cooper explains in his preface to the first edition of the novel signifies "unmixed people" (p. 4). In contrast, Magua's guile is represented as characteristic of one who was born a Huron but who has learned to affiliate himself with other nations (i.e., the Mohawks and the French). The most frequent proponent of racial purity, however, is Hawkeye himself; he repeatedly makes assertions to the effect that he "has no cross in his blood, although he may have lived with the red skins long enough to be suspected!" (pp. 39, 42). Through Hawkeye, Cooper displaces the Pocahontas myth by presenting a hero who embodies both European and Native American traits, but who simultaneously rejects the interracial logic upon which the earlier myth was predicated.

A year after the publication of *Mohicans*, Catharine Maria Sedgwick published her own story of interracial romance and marriage, *Hope Leslie; or, Early Times in the Massachusetts* (1827). Although Sedgwick allowed her characters to cross the racial dividing line to a greater extent than Cooper, the manner in which she constructed her multiple love plots undermines the appearance of supporting interracial unions. She fashioned the primary love plot out of elements from the Pocahontas story. The bold and passionate Indian maiden Magawisca protects her Euro-American lover from the wrath of her vengeful father. In the process of shielding him from execution, however, her arm is violently severed. As a consequence of Magawisca's disfigurement, the culturally mixed (but racially pure) Puritan girl Hope Leslie takes her place as primary love object. The novel's other interracial romance plot borrows from the captivity narrative tradition. Hope's younger sister, Faith, having been taken captive as a child, marries into the family of her captors. Although her decision to remain with her husband, even after she has been restored to her white family, appears to endorse the viability of interracial love, the childlike simplicity of her attachment and the absence of any offspring from the union suggest that such love is necessarily stunted and doomed. Ultimately the firmness with which the novel rejects such unions is expressed by Hope Leslie herself, who in response to the news of her sister's marriage exclaims, "God forbid! . . . My sister married to an Indian!" (p. 196).

In addition to the consciously literary efforts of Child, Cooper, and Sedgwick, publishers churned out fictionalized pulp versions of captivity narratives in an attempt to capitalize on their popularity. In the anonymously written *Gertrude Morgan; or, Life and Adventures among the Indians of the Far West* (1866), the eponymous heroine describes her encounter with one of the chiefs of the Pawnee who have taken her captive. Summoning her to his lodge, "The Yellow Face" warns, "Don't be afeard, Missus, I'ze not agwine to hurt you. Yah! Yah! I jes want you to come and be my wife; now won't you?" (p. 404). As his name and caricatured dialect indicate, this chief is not Native American but rather an escaped mulatto slave. That a fugitive slave would appear in such a narrative is not particularly remarkable; those who could not make it to the North could often find refuge by merging into Indian communities. However, "The Yellow Face's" motiveless sexual aggression, in contrast to Magua's vengefulness, exemplifies how representations of black-white sexual unions focused less on allegories of national unification than on the perceived dirty consequences of desires that many Americans believed were both unnatural and immoral.

THE MULATTO AS IDOL AND TARGET

As the persistence of the Pocahontas myth suggests, Americans could at least tolerate the idea of sexual relations between Euro-American men and Native American women. Part of this tolerant attitude stemmed from the belief (held by Thomas Jefferson and others) that the mixture of native and European peoples would result in a new people entitled to the emerging continental empire. Others viewed the inter-marriage of whites and Indians as a humane approach to civilizing and preserving a people that would other-wise be extinguished by westward expansion. The atti-tude toward sexual relations between whites and blacks, however, was decidedly less favorable. As early as the 1660s, as Winthrop Jordan has documented, Virginia and Maryland passed laws prohibiting sexual relations and marriages between whites and blacks (pp. 78–80). Such laws were instrumental in consolidating the status of Africans as inherently inferior and there-fore permissible to enslave. They also codified a racial distinction between people of European and African descent that increasingly differentiated between inden-tured servitude and permanent slavery. Preserved and reinforced by slavery, such laws continued to exist into the nineteenth century (and in many locations, into the twentieth). By the 1820s, Elise Lemire notes, eighteen of the twenty-three states then in existence prohibited black-white marriages. In contrast, only seven states prohibited Indian-white marriages (p. 47).

Legal statutes, though important, reveal only one part of the complicated matrix of social and cultural attitudes toward interracial sexual relationships. Both abolitionists and defenders of slavery used interracial sex to promote their positions. Abolitionists decried the inherent injustice of laws prohibiting interracial mar-riage, noting that such laws violated Christian principles of brotherhood and equality. Lydia Maria Child, a fol-lower of the antislavery advocate William Lloyd Garrison, argued in her *Appeal in Favor of That Class of Americans Called Africans* (1833) that the government was powerless to regulate affections and that "A man has at least as good a right to choose his wife, as he has to choose his religion" (p. 187). With the exception of a few radicals, however, few went so far as to promote intermarriage. Indeed, to make their arguments more palatable to moderate audiences, many abolitionists reinforced racist attitudes by arguing that slavery actu-ally promoted racial mixing. Such arguments were intended to shock audiences by exposing a sexual degeneracy southerners wanted to hide; in the process, however, they also portrayed sexual relationships between blacks and whites as immoral and unnatural. For example, when Frederick Douglass (1818–1895) flatly states in his *Narrative of the Life of Frederick Douglass* (1845) that "My father was a white man. . . . The opinion was also whispered that my master was my father," he reveals slavery's cruelty and hypocrisy (p. 48). The coy depiction of his master's attentions toward his Aunt Hester, culminating in Douglass's voyeuristic description of his aunt being stripped and whipped, fur-ther paints such relationships as immoral and perverse.

Defenders of slavery denied that such sexual abuses occurred. They did, however, use a similarly structured argument about the perversity and immorality of inter-racial sex to attack abolitionism. As Lemire has docu-mented, in 1834 New York City was engulfed by widespread rioting following newspaper reports claim-ing that the abolitionists supported "amalgamation" between blacks and whites. By borrowing this term from metallurgy to describe genetic mixing, anti-aboli-tionists effectively encoded racial preference (and repul-sion) as governed by the laws of nature. The year after the riots, Jerome B. Holgate anonymously published *A Sojourn in the City of Amalgamation in the Year of Our Lord 19—by Oliver Bolokitten—Esq.* (1835). In it, Holgate describes a northern city of the future in which whites and blacks have intermarried out of a sense of moral and political obligation contrary to their natural inclinations. The marriages themselves are universally loveless; the resulting offspring are ugly.

Depicted by defenders of slavery, mixed-race chil-dren were the misshapen fruit of unnatural and immoral unions. Some abolitionist writers inverted this portrait by making biracial characters into sympathetic models of virtue and righteous suffering. Despite their intentions, these portraits eventually consolidated into a stereotype that was as unrealistic in its idealism and sentimentality as the anti-abolitionists' caricatures were ridiculous: the tragic mulatto. Judith Berzon surveys the propagandistic utility of the tragic mulatto in anti-slavery novels. In their natural goodness, such charac-ters belied racist stereotypes of African inferiority. Through their tribulations, biracial characters who looked white and acted with Christian virtue demon-strated the patent injustice of a system that enslaved individuals according to their parentage. White readers could also identify with them more closely than char-acters that were phenotypically and culturally black. In some texts, white-seeming characters unaware of their mixed racial heritage dramatically (and tragi-cally) discovered the truth of their status, often too late to prevent falling into the clutches of an evil slave-holder—giving white readers a graphic illustration of the precariousness with which they held their place in the racial hierarchy (Berzon, pp. 54–58, 99–101). Ultimately the moral and logical appeal of tragic mulatto stories rested in their inherent endorsement of white supremacy. What makes the tragic mulatto's life so tragic is that he or she inevitably must be denied the benefits of whiteness that he or she clearly merits or to which he or she has become accustomed.

Novels featuring light-skinned mulattoes passing for white and circulating through white communities and white bedrooms held another appeal for readers, regardless of race or politics. With this conceit, such novels could purport to reveal the truth behind the whispered rumors and emphatic denials of the slave-holding South. In addition, the possibility that one could unwittingly break such a strong taboo titillated some and frightened others. In Richard Hildreth's (1807–1865) antislavery novel *The Slave; or, Memoirs of Archy Moore* (1836; republished in 1856 as *Archy Moore, the White Slave; or, Memoirs of a Fugitive*), Archy Moore, the son of a Virginia aristocrat and his female mulatto slave, becomes so disgusted with the indignity of being enslaved by his own father that he escapes to Britain where he passes for white. Unrecognized when he returns to the United States, Moore is free to gossip about the rumored interracial trysts of Jefferson and Martin Van Buren. While the novel plays on the thrilling power of hiding behind a secret identity, it also hints at its dangers by suggesting not only that offspring of unknown or unacknowledged parentage would inevitably result in incestuous pairings but also that the appeal of interracial sex existed at least partially in that very possibility.

The mulatto's firsthand experience of both the power of whiteness and the suffering of enslavement was figured by abolitionist writers at times as an unbearable internal conflict that must eventually lead to a tragic demise. In Child's short story "The Quadroons" (1842; revised 1846) for example, it is precisely the white-inflected beauty of the mulatto that makes her so attractive, and precisely the pride inherent in that whiteness that prevents her from accepting her white lover's inevitable rejection. Harriet Beecher Stowe (1811–1896) used similar plot elements in her two great abolitionist novels, *Uncle Tom's Cabin; or, Life among the Lowly* (published serially in 1851 and 1852) and *Dred; or, A Tale of the Great Dismal Swamp* (1856). In *Uncle Tom's Cabin* the beautiful and proud Cassy becomes a helpless, isolated victim in a system of sexual exploitation, willing to murder her own mixed-race children rather than permit them to suffer enslavement. Cora Gordon faces an equally hopeless situation in *Dred*. Pampered because of her beauty, exploited because of her background, it is only through her intelligence and strong character—what her brother Harry describes as her "blood [coming] up"—that she nurses her lover/master out of illness and saves his plantation (p. 63). She is rewarded with emancipation and marriage but, in an echo of Hildreth's incest motif, upon his death becomes vulnerable to the legal and sexual predations of her white half-brother, Tom. If in these female characters biraciality is represented as a pair of isolating negations, such that one is neither white nor black, in Stowe's male characters, mixed racial identity manifests itself as a violent internal struggle of contending impulses. In *Uncle Tom's Cabin* the "high, indomitable spirit" that George Harris

has inherited from his white father manifests itself as a bristling and bitter rebelliousness (p. 182). When in *Dred* Harry Gordon exclaims that he is "Colonel Gordon's oldest son"—just as white as, and a good deal wiser than, his half-brother, Tom—he sets in motion a chain of rebellious acts that unfold with prophetic inevitability (p. 386).

In the hands of well-meaning white abolitionists, the tragic mulatto figure functioned as a logical and emotional icon; white injustice and black suffering were embodied in a single tortured body and psyche. The popular theater seized on the melodramatic appeal of the tragic mulatto. Watching the 1852 stage version of *Uncle Tom's Cabin* by George L. Aiken (1830–1876), one of many based on Stowe's novel, audiences could see George and Eliza Harris's white skin and hear their crisp white diction. Audiences could similarly sympathize with the plight of Zoe, the mulatto heroine of Dion Boucicault's (1820–1890) *The Octoroon* (1859), which concludes with her drinking poison onstage rather than continuing to live as a slave. Nevertheless, these dramas and other popular amusements tended to skirt the political controversy and psychological complexity that mulatto characters could generate. In comparison, biracial authors imagined a greater range of motivations and reactions for their mixed-race characters, perhaps as a consequence of their own experiences as children of interracial unions. When William Wells Brown (c. 1814–1884), himself the child of mixed parentage, adapted Child's "The Quadroon" for use in *Clotel; or, The President's Daughter: A Narrative of Slave Life in the United States* (1853), he placed his vignettes of interracial union within a larger and richer network of social forces. As a result, the tragic consequences of these outcomes seem less predetermined by inherent conflicts within the characters than externally generated by economics and politics.

An even stronger example of this phenomenon is Harriet Jacobs's (1813–1897) *Incidents in the Life of a Slave Girl* (1861). Writing as "Linda Brent," Jacobs stresses that, although her power to control her own fate is limited by slavery and further compromised by her biraciality, she is not circumscribed by a stereotypically tragic script. Rather than suffer endlessly at the hands of her cruel master, Dr. Flint, she elects (though it is a choice made under duress) to attach herself to another (white) man, in part because their mixed-race children might enjoy greater protection than any born exclusively under her master's legal authority. By humbly repenting her sexuality and explaining it as a rational response to a sexually exploitative economy, she contradicts racist portrayals of black licentiousness. Through the conclusion of the narrative, in which Jacobs secures freedom and a safe home for herself and her family, she revises the propagandistic, melodramatic portrayals of Child and Stowe to show that a mulatta can overcome an oppressive system to find personal happiness.

THE INVENTION OF A PECULIAR AMERICANISM

While abolitionists deployed the tragic mulatto figure as a rhetorical weapon in the war of words preceding the Civil War, supporters of slavery continued to make racist appeals by claiming that the inevitable outcome of abolition would be racial amalgamation. In the process they made a lasting contribution to the American lexicon: "miscegenation." A brief overview of the word's origins forms a useful lesson in the difficulty of discussing interracial sexual relationships without resorting to an inherently racist vocabulary. Sidney Kaplan traces the origins of the word to the presidential election of 1864 and two enterprising newspaper reporters. In December 1863 David Goodman Croly (1829–1889) and George Wakeman (1841–1870), writers for the Democratic New York *World*, anonymously published a seventy-two page pamphlet titled *Miscegenation: The Theory of the Blending of the Races, Applied to the American White Man and the Negro*. In it, the authors explain that the word "miscegenation" is derived from the Latin *miscere* (to mix) and *genus* (race or kind). Adopting a tone of cool scientific detachment, the authors explain that the inevitable outcome of abolition and a second Lincoln presidency will be a miscegenated U.S. populace, a vision calculated to inflame political opposition. Croly and Wakeman sent copies of their pamphlet to leading abolitionists, several of whom replied with praise tempered by concern that the pamphlet's enthusiasm for such a controversial social policy would jeopardize the immediate aim of abolition. Meanwhile, the anti-Lincoln papers treated the authors' mishmash of pseudoscientific reasoning and provocative vision of a future United States in which "the most perfect and highest type of manhood will not be white or black, but brown" as an authentic statement of the abolitionist position. Opposition to miscegenation was so hostile and so popular that even most advocates of emancipating African Americans rejected the possibility of marrying one.

Although the Civil War emancipated African Americans from chattel slavery, the miscegenation controversy helped shape the widespread acceptance of racial segregation in the United States for the next hundred years. In American literature the theme of interracial sex, detached from debates about abolition, focused less on the tragic fates of mulatto characters exploited by a heartless legal system than on the personal choices individuals would make in a politically reconstructed, yet socially segregated, United States. Once again,

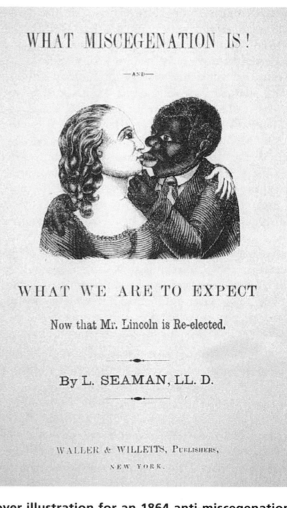

Cover illustration for an 1864 anti-miscegenation treatise. By claiming that abolitionists were proponents of miscegenation, Democrats attempted to turn public opinion against the antislavery Republican Party. THE LIBRARY OF CONGRESS

Child's would be a leading voice. In *A Romance of the Republic* (1867), she traces a complicated web of interracial relationships beset by the kinds of tricks and tragedies characteristic of antebellum abolitionist fiction. However, it also presents biracial progeny as more than mere victims. The novel's profusion of racial pairings results in a large, happy, prosperous, multihued family. The conclusion, featuring a star-spangled pageant of patriotic songs and Negro spirituals, celebrates the Union's victory and optimistically portends Croly and Wakeman's facetiously conceived miscegenated American future. In a different manner, optimism also characterizes the resolution of "The Foster-Brothers" (1869), a short story written by President Lincoln's private secretary, John Hay (1838–1905). Hay permits the union of a southern white aristocrat and the white-looking daughter of his father's former slave, but only because her true racial identity is kept secret. In the story's cataclysmic conclusion, the two fathers kill each other, suggesting that the future of interracial love in the postbellum United States was necessarily predicated on the violent repression of the nation's racist past.

See also Abolitionist Writing; Blacks; Captivity Narratives; *Hope Leslie;* Indians; Leatherstocking Tales; Marriage; Slave Narratives; *Uncle Tom's Cabin*

BIBLIOGRAPHY

Primary Works

Aiken, George L. *Uncle Tom's Cabin; or, Life among the Lowly.* 1852. In *Early American Drama,* edited by Jeffrey H. Richards. New York: Penguin Books, 1997.

Barker, James Nelson. *The Indian Princess; or, La Belle Sauvage.* 1808. In *Early American Drama,* edited by Jeffrey H. Richards. New York: Penguin, 1997.

Boucicault, Dion. *The Octoroon; or, Life in Louisiana.* 1859. In *Early American Drama,* edited by Jeffrey H. Richards. New York: Penguin, 1997.

Brown, William Wells. *Clotel; or, The President's Daughter: A Narrative of Slave Life in the United States.* 1853. Boston: Bedford/St. Martin's, 2000.

Child, Lydia Maria. *An Appeal in Favor of That Class of Americans Called Africans.* 1833. Amherst: University of Massachusetts Press, 1996.

Child, Lydia Maria. *Hobomok.* 1824. In *Hobomok and Other Writings on Indians.* Edited by Carolyn L. Karcher. New Brunswick, N.J., and London: Rutgers University Press, 1986.

Child, Lydia Maria. "The Quadroons." 1842, 1846. In *An Anthology of Interracial Literature: Black-White Contacts in the Old World and the New,* edited by Werner Sollors. New York and London: New York University Press, 2004.

Child, Lydia Maria. *A Romance of the Republic.* 1867. Lexington: University Press of Kentucky, 1997.

Cooper, James Fenimore. *The Last of the Mohicans.* 1826. New York: Oxford University Press, 1994.

[Croly, David Goodman, and George Wakeman.] *Miscegenation: The Theory of the Blending of the Races, Applied to the American White Man and the Negro.* 1863–1864. Upper Saddle River, N.J.: Literature House, 1970.

Douglass, Frederick. *Narrative of the Life of Frederick Douglass.* 1845. New York: Penguin, 1986.

Gertrude Morgan; or, Life and Adventures among the Indians of the Far West. 1866. In *American Captivity Narratives,* edited by Gordon M. Sayre. Boston: Houghton Mifflin, 2000.

Hay, John. "The Foster-Brothers." *Harper's New Monthly Magazine* 39 (1869): 535–544.

Hildreth, Richard. *The Slave; or, Memoirs of Archy Moore.* 1836. Upper Saddle River, N.J.: Gregg Press, 1968.

[Holgate, Jerome B.] *A Sojourn in the City of Amalgamation in the Year of Our Lord 19— by Oliver Bolokitten—Esq.* New York, 1835.

Jacobs, Harriet. *Incidents in the Life of a Slave Girl.* 1861. Cambridge, Mass.: Harvard University Press, 1987.

Seaver, James E. *A Narrative of the Life of Mrs. Mary Jemison.* 1824. In *Women's Indian Captivity Narratives,* edited by Kathryn Zabelle Derounian-Stodola. New York: Penguin, 1998.

Sedgwick, Catharine Maria. *Hope Leslie; or, Early Times in the Massachusetts.* 1827. New York: Penguin, 1998.

Stowe, Harriet Beecher. *Dred; A Tale of the Great Dismal Swamp.* 1856. New York: Penguin, 2000.

Stowe, Harriet Beecher. *Uncle Tom's Cabin.* 1851–1852. New York: Penguin, 1981.

Secondary Works

Berzon, Judith. *Neither White Nor Black: The Mulatto Character in American Fiction.* New York: New York University Press, 1978.

Jordan, Winthrop D. *White over Black: American Attitudes toward the Negro, 1550–1812.* Chapel Hill: University of North Carolina Press, 1968.

Kaplan, Sidney. "The Miscegenation Issue in the Election of 1864." *Journal of Negro History* 34 (1949): 274–343.

Kinney, James. *Amalgamation!: Race, Sex, and Rhetoric in the Nineteenth-Century American Novel.* Westport, Conn.: Greenwood Press, 1985.

Lemire, Elise. *"Miscegenation": Making Race in America.* Philadelphia: University of Pennsylvania Press, 2002.

Sollors, Werner. *Neither Black Nor White Yet Both: Thematic Explorations of Interracial Literature.* New York: Oxford University Press, 1997.

Sollors, Werner, ed. *Interracialism: Black-White Intermarriage in American History, Literature, and Law.* New York: Oxford University Press, 2000.

Tilton, Robert S. *Pocahontas: The Evolution of an American Narrative.* New York: Cambridge University Press, 1994.

Michael Householder

MISS RAVENEL'S CONVERSION FROM SECESSION TO LOYALTY

A landmark in the rise of realism in American literature, *Miss Ravenel's Conversion from Secession to Loyalty* (1867) remains one of the best novels ever written about the American Civil War. The author, John W. De Forest (1826–1906), had been a captain in the Twelfth Connecticut Regimental Volunteers, had joined in the battles of Georgia Landing and Bisland and in the siege of Port Hudson in Louisiana in 1862–1863, and saw action in Philip Henry Sheridan's Shenandoah Valley campaign in Virginia in 1864. When De Forest returned to his Connecticut home at the end of the war, as he later reminisced,

> I found myself in possession of new material, for I had studied men under fire and in all sorts of places, and knew a good deal more about life than when I went in. When I was discharged, my mind turned easily to writing again, and I wrote "Miss Ravenel's Conversion from Secession to Loyalty," a book out of my own experience. . . . In that book for the first time in my life I came to know the value of personal knowledge of one's subject and the art of drawing upon life for one's characters. (Oviatt, p. 856)

SENTIMENTAL ROMANCE

Issued by Harper & Brothers on 25 May 1867, *Miss Ravenel's Conversion* carefully develops two distinct story lines. On the one hand, De Forest tells a love story governed by the conventions of nineteenth-century sentimental romance. Lillie Ravenel belongs to a popular tradition of heroines who make disastrous marriages, such as Mary Harvey in Sarah Josepha Hale's *My Cousin Mary; or, The Inebriate* (1839), Amelia Sedley in William Makepeace Thackeray's *Vanity Fair* (1848), and Ellen Montgomery in Susan B. Warner's *The Wide, Wide World* (1850). While she was "very fair, with lively blue eyes and exceedingly handsome hair" (p. 12), the narrator allows that "there were different opinions" on the question of whether she was "lovely" (p. 13). She marries the good-natured but rakish Colonel Carter, who later has an affair with the coquettish shrew Madame Larue, speculates with government money, and dies in battle before his scheme is exposed and his reputation besmirched. In truth, Carter and the dark siren Larue, who prattles on about the *sainte passion* (p. 377) and *divin sens* (p. 379), are more complex characters than either Lillie Ravenel or Captain Edward Colburne, a noble and heroic captain in the Union Army who also loves Lillie. When she learns of Carter's infidelity, for example, Lillie swoons according to the conventions of nineteenth-century melodrama. Nor is her "conversion to loyalty" rendered in psychologically realistic terms. It seems little more than a conceit for the gradual triumph of the Northern armies in the Civil War. In a tableau near the end of the novel, Colburne finally confesses his love for Lillie, and they embrace in a conventional set piece "with her head on his shoulder, sobbing, trembling, but full of joy" (pp. 514–515). The Union captain, tempered by the fire of war, has matured

into a virile and self-reliant citizen. The Southern belle Lillie, chastened by sacrifice and humiliation, has blossomed morally and intellectually. Figuratively, their union reconciles the regions they represent—a plot device invented by De Forest and subsequently used by such writers as Albion Tourgée in *A Fool's Errand* (1879) and Owen Wister in *The Virginian* (1902). As for the reason he "always had boy and girl in love in my books," De Forest once explained to an interviewer that "it was the only kind of plot a writer could get the public interested in" (Oviatt, p. 856). Some 75 to 80 percent of all books and magazines during this period were bought by women.

DEPICTIONS OF WAR

The battle scenes in the novel are written in an entirely different timbre than the love scenes. De Forest proved his reportorial skill at depicting men at war, from the tedium before combat to the grisly butchery of the field hospital. While under rebel fire in chapter 20, Colburne cites army regulations to justify his decision not to assist soldiers wounded in the field until the enemy has withdrawn or the battle decided. De Forest often reworked passages from his own Civil War diary into the narrative. In the midst of the Union attack on Port Hudson on 14 June 1863, for example, Captain De Forest felt trapped in "a ridiculous situation," according to his diary, with the Confederate fort shrouded in dense fog and rifle balls "spatting furiously" around him. He lost "several men in this blind, useless skirmish" before he knew in which direction he should advance (*Volunteer's Adventures,* p. 136). In the battle described in chapter 20, similarly, Captain Colburne seems lost in a maze: he does not know "the whereabouts of the Major" (p. 284) or "how many of his soldiers had been hit" (p. 287), whether there are other Federal forces in the vicinity, or whether to advance or retreat. De Forest also noted in his diary that a body retrieved many hours after the battle "was a horrible spectacle, swollen and perfectly black with putrefaction, so rapid was that shocking change under the heat of the Louisiana May" (*Volunteer's Adventures,* p. 132). He worked this detail into chapter 21 of his novel, when an officer dies and "before night he was black with putrefaction, so rapid was that shocking change under the heat of a Louisiana May" (p. 294). Although De Forest based his depiction of the battles of Georgia Landing and the siege of Port Hudson in the first part of the novel on his own experiences, he recreated the battles of Fort Winthrop (or Fort Butler in the novel) and Cane River in the later chapters from oral accounts and newspaper reports months after the events. Just as some war movies since the late twentieth century have revised the conventional Hollywood war movie with its sanitized combat, *Miss Ravenel's Conversion* transformed the genre of war novels epitomized by James Fenimore Cooper's *The Last of the Mohicans* (1826) and Sir Walter Scott's *Rob Roy* (1817) with their chivalric heroes, false bravado, and easy moral distinctions.

THE ISSUE OF SLAVERY

Though De Forest payed lip service in the novel to the rights of free blacks, in truth he was not very advanced on the race question. The Civil War, according to De Forest both in his own voice and in the novel, was waged to preserve the Union, only incidentally to free the slaves in the South. The physician Dr. Ravenel, Lillie's father, concedes as early as chapter 4 that the war was a Manichaean struggle between the angels of commercial progress and enlightened civilization on the one hand and the legions of ignorance and arrogance on the other. The "slaveholding Sodom," he asserts,

> will perish for the lack of five just men, or a single just idea. It must be razed and got out of the way, just like any other obstacle to the progress of humanity. It must make room for something more consonant with the railroad, electric-telegraph, printing-press, inductive philosophy, and practical Christianity. (Pp. 58–59)

A moderate Republican opposed to slavery but no abolitionist, De Forest tries to imagine the amelioration of the "peculiar institution" in chapter 18, when Dr. Ravenel "commences the reorganization of Southern labor" (p. 247), that is, free black labor, a social experiment undertaken at several abandoned Louisiana plantations between 1862 and 1865. The manumitted slaves "did more work that summer" under Ravenel's direction than the deposed planters "had ever got from double their number by the agency of a white overseer, drivers, whips, and paddles" (p. 265). The doctor even assigns Lillie the task of teaching "all these poor people to read" (p. 257) arguing that they should never again suffer the indignities of illiteracy: "Negro children are just as intelligent as white children until they find out that they are black. Now we will never tell them that that they are black; we will never hint to them that they are born our inferiors" (p. 257).

For all the reform and antislavery talk in the novel, however, De Forest's black characters never transcend racial stereotypes. In chapter 12, Colburne visits a Creole family named Meurice in whose New Orleans home he meets "New Englanders, New Yorkers, and even stray Marylanders and Kentuckians" (p. 185). Colburne defends "the mixed race," specifically "their intelligence, education, good breeding, respectability of character, and exceptional patriotism in a community of rebels" (p. 186) presumably inherited from their white ancestors. Similarly, in chapter 19 Colburne in a letter to Dr. Ravenel writes condescendingly about his "boy Henry," his young black servant, who "dances and gambles all night and then wants to sleep all day" (p. 273). Colburne must spend "hours every day in shouting for Henry" (p. 273). He disparages freedmen as "lazy bumpkins" and is unconvinced that emancipation will succeed, as he explains to the doctor: "I am as much an abolitionist as ever, but not so much of a 'nigger-worshipper.' I don't know but that I shall yet become an advocate of slavery" (p. 273). For the record, De Forest expressed similar sentiments in letters home from Louisiana. He referred derisively to his servant, a "little yellow vagrant named Harry," whom he had dismissed "for never being on hand when wanted" (*Volunteer's Adventures*, p. 77).

CRITICAL RECEPTION

Miss Ravenel's Conversion was not a commercial success, at least initially. Sales of the first edition were miserable, with 1,608 of the press run of 5,000 copies still unsold in 1884. Despite the love story, the realism of its war chapters apparently repelled nineteenth-century readers inured to undistilled sentimentality and domestic romance. While it failed to sell in large numbers, the novel was nonetheless a modest critical success. To be sure, most reviewers for Southern publications reviled it. According to the critic for the *Charleston Courier*, perhaps William Gilmore Simms, the novel epitomized "all the brutal malignity Northern writers have conceived . . . to the slander of the South." Similarly, *De Bow's Review*, edited in Nashville, scorned most of De Forest's characters as "caricatures" and averred that "the fights and skirmishes he brings into the plot will be laughed at by old campaigners on either side." After a British edition of the novel appeared in May 1868, the London *Athenæum* recommended that De Forest "expend no more of his time and industry on an art for which he has no special qualification" (6 June 1868, p. 795).

More commonly, however, the novel was praised by reviewers, particularly for the realism of its battle scenes. The *American Literary Gazette* hailed it as "a most brilliant and charming book" with "some scenes of fighting and hospital life" that "no one could have written who had not taken part in that deadly struggle" (1 June 1867, pp. 71–72, 77). *Peterson's* regarded it as "one of the best American novels that has appeared in years" (September 1867, p. 234). The New York *Round Table* lauded "De Forest's battle-pieces, and, indeed, all his sketches of military affairs" for their "faithful and effective" details (20 June 1867, pp. 40–41). According to the *New York Citizen*, it was "the best war which has yet been written" with its "truthfully written episodes of battle" (1 June 1867, p. 5). Henry James even commended it in the *Nation* for its "excellent description of campaigning in the terrible swamps and forests of Louisiana and in the trenches at Port Hudson" (20 June 1867, pp. 491–492). William Dean Howells, the dean of American letters and the foremost American theorist of realism, championed the novel throughout his career. Howells declared in the *Atlantic Monthly* for August 1874 that "so far [De Forest] is really the only American novelist" (p. 229), high praise indeed from the friend and patron of Henry James and Mark Twain. Howells believed *Miss Ravenel's Conversion* represented something of a turning point in American fiction. It exhibited "an advanced realism before realism was known by that name" and was "one of the best American novels" ever written (*My Literary Passions,* p. 223). In 1887 Howells suggested that *Miss Ravenel* did not pale in comparison even to Leo Tolstoy's *War and Peace* (1869): "it is an admirable novel and spacious enough for the vast drama glimpsed in it" (*Harper's Monthly,* September 1887, p. 639). As late as 1900 Howells insisted the novel "paints war as it is, with Tolstoyan fidelity" (*North American Review,* December 1900, p. 947). Although *The Red Badge of Courage* (1895) replaced *Miss Ravenel's Conversion* in the canon of American literature as ostensibly the best novel about the American Civil War, De Forest's canvas was larger than Stephen Crane's and his realism more stark and mordant. De Forest, not Crane, inaugurated the American tradition of realistic war writing that includes novels by Ernest Hemingway, Norman Mailer, James Jones, and Tim O'Brien.

See also Civil War

BIBLIOGRAPHY
Primary Works
De Forest, John W. *Miss Ravenel's Conversion from Secession to Loyalty.* New York: Harper & Brothers, 1867.

De Forest, John W. *A Volunteer's Adventures: A Union Captain's Record of the Civil War.* New Haven, Conn.: Yale University Press, 1946.

Secondary Works
American Literary Gazette and Publishers' Circular (1 June 1867): 71–72, 77.

Antoni, Robert William. "*Miss Ravenel's Conversion*: A Neglected American Novel," *Southern Quarterly* 24, no. 3 (1986): 58–63.

Cecil, L. Moffitt. "*Miss Ravenel's Conversion* and *Pilgrim's Progress.*" *College English* 23 (February 1962): 352–357.

Fick, Thomas H. "Genre Wars and the Rhetoric of Manhood in *Miss Ravenel's Conversion from Secession to Loyalty.*" *Nineteenth Century Literature* 46 (March 1992): 473–494.

Gargano, James W., ed. *Critical Essays on John William De Forest.* Boston: G. K. Hall, 1981.

Howells, William Dean. "Editor's Study." *Harper's Monthly* 75 (September 1887): 639.

Howells, William Dean. *My Literary Passions.* New York: Harper, 1895.

Howells, William Dean. "The New Historical Romances." *North American Review* 171 (December 1900): 947.

Howells, William Dean. "Recent Literature." *Atlantic Monthly* 34 (August 1874): 229.

James, Henry. "Miss Ravenel's Conversion." *Nation* (20 June 1867): 491–492.

Light, James F. *John William De Forest.* New York: Twayne, 1965.

Oviatt, Edwin. "J. W. De Forest in New Haven." *New York Times Saturday Review,* 17 December 1898, p. 856.

Simpson, Claude M. "John W. De Forest's *Miss Ravenel's Conversion.*" In *The American Novel from James Fenimore Cooper to William Faulkner,* edited by Wallace Stegner, pp. 35–46. New York: Basic Books, 1965.

Solomon, Eric. "The Novelist as Soldier: Cooke and De Forest." *American Literary Realism, 1870–1910* 19, no. 3 (1987): 80–88.

Gary Scharnhorst

MOBY-DICK

Students or general readers confronting *Moby-Dick* for the first time often feel as terror-stricken as sailors at the sight of the legendary white whale heading for them "with open jaws, and a lashing tail" (p. 558). Those undaunted by the book's vast bulk and towering reputation find themselves frustrated by what appear to be continual digressions from its ostensible plot—the story of Captain Ahab's vengeful hunt for the Leviathan that chewed off his limb. To appreciate *Moby-Dick,* one must heed the cue its subtitle, "The Whale," furnishes: the book's subject is not just the monster Captain Ahab tries in vain to slay but "the whale" as a species; hence, the cetology chapters, far from being intrusive padding, are integral to the larger story the narrator Ishmael relates, of whaling as a commercial enterprise and of his own unfulfilled quest to "know" the whale, a creature whose "living contour" can only be glimpsed at the "risk of being eternally stove and sunk by him" (p. 264).

Readers' enjoyment of *Moby-Dick* will also be greatly enhanced if they realize how often Ishmael is teasing them when he seems to be straying from the

Herman Melville, c. 1860s. THE LIBRARY OF CONGRESS

plot or feeding them dry natural history. A vein of irreverent, bawdy humor runs through the novel, from the rollicking comedy of the scenes that describe Ishmael and the cannibal Queequeg in bed together to the sexual jokes and roguish parody that enliven the cetology chapters, poking fun at the nineteenth century's religious, philosophical, scientific, social, and racial assumptions. Humor erupts as well in wild tonal shifts, both within and between chapters, which playfully upset reader expectations. These tonal shifts, along with the remarkable range of styles *Moby-Dick* exhibits—poetic, meditative, colloquial, punning, oratorical, scientific, legalistic, nautical, tragic, comic—call attention to the book's experimental form. Defying critics' efforts to fit it into a single genre, *Moby-Dick* mixes novel, romance, epic, drama, farce, travel narrative, anatomy, and scientific treatise. It also flouts the novelistic convention of maintaining a consistent narrative point of view. Ishmael disappears for long stretches, giving way sometimes to a third-person omniscient narrator, sometimes to stage directions, soliloquys, and full-cast theatrical performances. Through such experiments with form, *Moby-Dick* extends the project of challenging tradition to the domain of literature itself.

BIOGRAPHICAL AND HISTORICAL CONTEXTS

"If I shall ever deserve any real repute in that small but high hushed world" of great literature, writes Ishmael in the chapter "The Advocate," speaking for his creator Herman Melville (1819–1891), "I prospectively ascribe all the honor and the glory to whaling; for a whale-ship was my Yale College and my Harvard" (pp. 111–112). A whale-ship was likewise the crucible of Melville's literary imagination. Embarking aboard the whaler *Acushnet* on 3 January 1841 (ten days after his fictional persona's Christmas 1840 departure aboard the *Pequod*), Melville spent three and a half years at sea, during which he made three whaling voyages before returning home on a man-of-war. He based his first five novels—*Typee* (1846), *Omoo* (1847), *Mardi* (1849), *Redburn* (1849), and *White-Jacket* (1850)—on his adventures as a sailor, indicating the extent to which they molded him into the writer he became. Not until his art reached maturity in *Moby-Dick*, however, did he attempt the feat of rendering "blubber" into "poetry," as he put it in a letter of 1 May 1850 to the fellow sea-novelist Richard Henry Dana Jr. (1815–1882).

Moby-Dick took Melville uncharacteristically long to complete. Its composition stretched over some eighteen months and its design expanded to accommodate chapters that kept accreting even as the manuscript was going through the press in the summer of 1851, more than a year after Melville had told Dana it was half finished. "God keep me from ever completing anything. This whole book is but a draught—nay, but the draught of a draught," exclaims Melville through Ishmael, as if to account for his unending revisions (p. 145). During the writing process, Melville not only consulted books about whaling, which he cited in the "Extracts" prefacing the novel, but studied Milton's *Paradise Lost* and Shakespeare's tragedies (especially *King Lear* and *Macbeth*), which together shaped his conception of his own satanic tragic hero, Ahab. In August 1850 Melville also met Nathaniel Hawthorne, whom he hailed in the review essay "Hawthorne and His Mosses" as an American Shakespeare, and to whom he dedicated *Moby-Dick* as a "token of . . . admiration for his genius." This formative encounter, some critics have speculated, may have led Melville to recast *Moby-Dick* from a whaling chronicle on the same model as his earlier autobiographical narratives into the ambitious symbolic work we now have. Whether or not one accepts the "Two *Moby-Dick*s" hypothesis, one will find that a close reading reveals elaborate patterns interweaving the various filaments of the book.

While digesting new literary influences and wrestling with the problems of composition, Melville confronted the main political issues of his time: slavery,

Indian dispossession, expansionist wars, environmental despoliation, exploitative labor conditions, class conflict, and the specters of slave insurrection at home and revolution abroad. By 1850 the United States seemed to be staking its national existence on maintaining slavery indefinitely. Instead of decreasing, the slave population was exponentially increasing and had reached upward of four million. Instead of following the example of northern states after the Revolution and passing gradual emancipation laws, the southern states demanded the right to export slavery even into territories from which earlier ordinances had barred it. Because plantation agriculture quickly exhausted the soil, the slave system could not survive unless planters could either move to fertile land farther west or sell their surplus slaves on the interstate market. The necessity for continual expansion in turn generated pressure for more wars—against the Creeks in Alabama, against the Sac and Fox in Illinois, against the Seminoles in Florida, and eventually against Mexico, from which the United States annexed Texas in 1845 and seized the area encompassing the present states of Colorado, Utah, Arizona, Nevada, New Mexico, and California in 1848. Meanwhile, the slave states were calling for more and more draconian federal regulations to protect their peculiar institution. They were also threatening to secede from the Union if their demands were not met.

The constitutional crisis that resulted in the Compromise of 1850, with its infamous law requiring all U.S. citizens to collaborate in catching fugitive slaves, burst literally over Melville's household as he was writing *Moby-Dick*. In April 1851 Melville's own father-in-law, Lemuel Shaw (1781–1861), chief justice of the Massachusetts Supreme Court, became the first northern judge to implement the law by sending a fugitive slave back to his master in chains. Coinciding with the nation's domestic travails, the years 1848–1851, as Michael Paul Rogin has pointed out, spanned the outbreak and suppression of revolutions throughout Europe, reminding Americans of the doom that awaited them if they did not abolish slavery before it destroyed the very essence of their democracy, subverted the liberty of all citizens, and provoked either a massive slave uprising or a bloody civil war.

Moby-Dick comments on these events both directly and obliquely. The relevant passages have been cited by a long line of critics from Charles H. Foster and Alan Heimert onward. For example, alluding to the role that the Massachusetts senator Daniel Webster (1782–1852) and Judge Shaw played in authoring and executing the Compromise of 1850, the famous sermon by Father Mapple on the story of Jonah exhorts the godly to "pluck" "sin . . . from under the robes of Senators and Judges" (p. 48). Not only does Mapple himself speak in

the accents of the abolitionist Theodore Parker (1810–1860), who had compared Shaw to King Ahab, but the entire plot resounds with echoes of contemporary political rhetoric, in which biblical analogies and metaphors such as the ship of state, the Leviathan, and storms at sea figured prominently. In addition, the novel features a number of significant black characters: a nameless "Angel of Doom" in a "negro church," who preaches about "the blackness of darkness, and the weeping and wailing and teeth-gnashing there" (pp. 9–10); the cabin boy Pip, who goes mad after being abandoned for hours in mid-ocean when he disobeys the order not to jump out of the whale boat during the chase because "a whale would sell for thirty times what [he] would . . . in Alabama" (p. 413); the arthritic old cook Fleece, who repays his demeaning treatment by the second mate, Stubb, with a curse that fulfills itself: "Wish, by gor! whale eat him" (p. 297); and the harpooneer Daggoo, "a gigantic, coal-black negro-savage, with a lion-like tread—an Ahasuerus to behold" (p. 120)—who exemplifies the spirit of the native African never subjected to white enslavement.

References to America's history of Indian wars also abound. The *Pequod* is named for the Connecticut tribe all but exterminated by the Puritans in 1637. The ship's owners, Captains Peleg and Bildad, recruit sailors under a "wigwam" on the quarter-deck, at the apex of which waves a "tufted point . . . like the top-knot on some old Pottowottamie Sachem's head" (p. 70). Among the *Pequod*'s harpooneers is Tashtego, an "unmixed Indian from Gay Head," on Martha's Vineyard, "where there still exists the last remnant of a village of red men" (p. 120). Another Gayheader, the "old squaw Tistig," foresees that Captain Ahab's ill-omened name will "somehow prove prophetic" (p. 79). "Aboriginal whalemen" from the neighboring island of Nantucket, Ishmael notes, gave "chase to the Leviathan" long before whites (p. 8). Suggesting that the nation built on the dispossession and genocide of its native peoples may inherit their fate, the *Pequod*, constructed of American wood, goes down with Tashtego hammering a red flag to the mast, wrapped around a sky-hawk representing the American Eagle, accidentally caught in its folds. The red flag, as Larry J. Reynolds has argued, also evokes the banner of Europe's 1848 revolutions and thus links the nemeses of Old World and New.

If Melville embeds his reflections on Indian genocide, slavery, and expansionist warfare in coded symbols, he graphically depicts both the brutal working conditions whalers face and the ravages whaling inflicts on the environment. The *Pequod*'s first mate, Starbuck, notwithstanding his reputation for prudence, insists on pursuing a whale in the teeth of a white squall that swamps his boat and imperils his crew. During the chase the sailors are routinely "enveloped in whale-lines," whose "complicated toils, twisting and writhing around" (p. 280–281) them, risk bowstringing them as the harpoon flies out and the wounded whale thrashes the sea into gigantic waves. On one occasion, Ishmael and Queequeg's boat is "jammed between" (p. 390) whales in the middle of an enormous herd from which they barely escape. As harpooneer, one of Queequeg's tasks is to supervise the stripping of the whale's blubber while its slippery body revolves beneath his feet like a treadmill; in the meantime, "rabid" (p. 321) sharks snap at the bloody mass, and his fellow harpooneers defend him with keen-edged whale spades that are as likely to amputate a foot as to behead a shark. In the blubber room "toes are scarce" because sailors must chop up sheets of blubber "as the ship pitches and lurches about" (p. 418). After cleaning up the decks "by the combined and simultaneous industry of almost the entire ship's company" (pp. 428–429), the exhausted crew frequently gets no chance to rest before being summoned to pursue another whale. No wonder, then, that nearly every ship can report "a death by a whale" (p. 206), and many the loss of a whole boat's crew. "For God's sake, be economical with your lamps and candles!" Ishmael exhorts *Moby-Dick*'s comfortable middle- and upper-class readers: "not a gallon you burn, but at least one drop of man's blood was spilled for it" (p. 206).

Besides lamps and candles, whale oil supplied lubricants for machinery until supplanted by petroleum in the late 1860s. The world's first oil industry, as well as the first international capitalist enterprise to be dominated by the United States, whaling both raked in super-profits and recklessly plundered the environment. "Nowhere in all America will you find more patrician-like houses; parks and gardens more opulent, than in New Bedford," Ishmael underscores (p. 32). With "reservoirs of oil in every house," New Bedford's elites make no effort to conserve the resources they have "harpooned and dragged up hither from the bottom of the sea" (p. 32). Their wasteful consumption drives the whaling industry to ever greater excesses, Ishmael shows. In one stomach-churning scene, the *Pequod*'s boats converge on a blind, crippled old whale, "choking" (p. 355) through his spout and suffering from an ulcerous wound. The creature is "horribly pitiable to see," remarks Ishmael. "But pity there was none" (p. 357). The sailors regard the old whale only as a swimming "bank" worth "three thousand dollars" (p. 354). Despite his age and decrepitude, he must be "murdered, in order to light the gay bridals and other merry-makings of men, and also to illuminate the solemn churches that preach unconditional inoffensiveness by all to all" (p. 357). His killing, moreover, turns out to be useless, because his carcass sinks before it can be rifled of its blubber and spermacetti.

Later chapters raise the prospect that the whaling industry may be hunting the entire species into extinction. Sperm whales have been slaughtered on such a scale, observes Ishmael, that they no longer swim in small groups but in "extensive herds," as if "for mutual assistance and protection" (p. 382). When the *Pequod* happens on such a herd, with nursing mother and infant whales at its center, the sailors try to "wing" as many as possible, "so that they can be afterwards killed at . . . leisure" (p. 386). How long can Leviathan "endure so wide a chase, and so remorseless a havoc" (p. 460) Ishmael asks, wondering whether whales will dwindle like the "buffalo, which, not forty years ago, overspread by tens of thousands the prairies of Illinois and Missouri" (p. 460). Although he wrongly concludes that the sea affords the whale better chances of survival than does the prairie the buffalo, he at least contemplates the threat of the whales' annihilation. In sum, all of the issues *Moby-Dick* addresses—from the pillage of natural resources and the superexploitation of workers to slavery, Indian genocide, and expansionist warfare—portend disaster for America and the world.

BIBLICAL PROPHECY AND PAGAN MYTH

Melville's fear that his country was headed for shipwreck led him naturally to one of the chief unifying devices around which he structured *Moby-Dick*: the apocalyptic prophecies of the Bible. These prophecies of a day of wrath on which the world would go up in flames and evildoers would be condemned to eternal damnation laced the rhetoric of nineteenth-century American preachers and reformers. Indeed, less than a decade before the publication of *Moby-Dick*, the followers of the evangelist William Miller (1782–1849) had prepared for the end of the world on 22 October 1844. In invoking such prophecies, Melville thus draws on a widespread religious belief system.

Omens of apocalyptic destruction punctuate *Moby-Dick*. As early as the second chapter, Ishmael hears a message of doom in an African American church, where he stumbles into an ash-box that reminds him of Gomorrah (p. 9), one of the Old Testament cities reduced to ashes for its sinfulness and often cited as a prototype of the judgment to come. Subsequently, when Ishmael takes Queequeg to enroll in the crew of the *Pequod*, Captain Bildad hands the cannibal a tract titled "The Latter Day Coming; or No Time to Lose" (p. 89). On the heels of this warning of apocalyptic judgment, a crazy stranger named Elijah, after the prophet who rebuked King Ahab and who is supposed to return "before the coming of the great and dreadful

Frontispiece to Thomas Beale's *Natural History of the Sperm Whale*, 1839. Beale was an English physician who wrote his *Natural History* after serving aboard a whaling vessel. His work has been cited as an influence in *Moby-Dick*.
GETTY IMAGES

day of the LORD" (Malachi 4:5), admonishes Ishmael and Queequeg against embarking on the *Pequod*. Another crazy prophet on board the ship *Jeroboam,* a Shaker who takes himself for the angel Gabriel, "announc[es] the speedy opening of the seventh vial" (the last plague poured over the earth in the book of Revelation), which he claims to carry in his vest pocket (p. 314). Gabriel also identifies Moby Dick as "the Shaker God incarnated" and predicts that "sacrilegious assailants of his divinity" will meet "speedy doom" (p. 316). True, all of these prophets are comic figures, in keeping with the satire on religion that pervades *Moby-Dick;* nevertheless, the foundering of the *Pequod* with its multiracial crew fulfills the biblical warnings of apocalyptic judgment overtaking an unrepentant world.

The biblical text most central to *Moby-Dick* is the book of Jonah, which tells how the Assyrian city of Nineveh averts apocalyptic destruction by repenting. Father Mapple's sermon emphasizes the aspect of the Jonah story relevant to Ishmael, who is almost swallowed by a whale, as was the biblical prophet, but survives to warn an American Nineveh to repent. At the same time, Father Mapple's retelling of the story invites the reader to view Ahab as a Jonah who persists in his disobedience and pays the price: refusing either to heed God's message or to spare others from sharing his fate, Ahab is not rescued from a whale but towed to death tied to one, involving his entire crew in the debacle of his futile quest for vengeance.

Notwithstanding his use of the Bible to structure *Moby-Dick,* Melville subverts rather than endorses its absolutist truth claims as a sacred text that literally inscribes the Word of God. Throughout the novel pagan myths compete with the Bible to provide alternative unifying frameworks. As H. Bruce Franklin has demonstrated, the story of Ahab's epic battle with Moby Dick closely follows the Egyptian myth recounting the sun god Osiris's murder and dismemberment by his brother Set, or Typhon, a sea monster comparative mythologists have associated with the biblical Leviathan. Like Osiris, who is slain in the winter and resurrected in the spring, personifying the seasonal death and rebirth of nature, Ahab loses his leg to Moby Dick in the winter, suffers another symbolic dismemberment when his ivory leg pierces his groin just before the *Pequod* sails on Christmas Day, remains out of sight for weeks as if "the dead wintry bleakness of the sea" were keeping him "secluded" (p. 124), and only begins to stay on deck in warm weather (see chapters 28, 41, and 106).

The Osiris myth also applies to Queequeg, who embodies life-affirming values opposed to Ahab's and thus better approximates Osiris's role as a savior. Not only does Queequeg rescue two men from drowning—first, a "bumpkin" (p. 61) who has earlier insulted him and second, Tashtego, whom he "deliver[s]" (p. 344) from entrapment in a sinking whale's head—but he too undergoes a symbolic death and resurrection. Descending into the hold to stop a leak in a cask of sperm (a symbol of life that recalls Osiris's origins as a fertility god), Queequeg catches a chill that nearly kills him. As he lies near death, he asks the ship's carpenter to make him a coffin and lay him in it—an allusion to another part of the Osiris myth, in which Set locks his brother in a coffin-like chest. At the eleventh hour, Queequeg "change[s] his mind about dying" (p. 480) because he remembers a duty he has left undone. His coffin, which he orders turned into a life buoy, ultimately saves Ishmael from the wreck of the *Pequod*, thereby fulfilling both Osiris's redemptive mission and Queequeg's pledge to "die for [Ishmael], if need should be" (p. 51).

Queequeg's god Yojo, a hunchbacked "Congo idol" of "polished ebony" (p. 22) uncannily resembling images of the West African trickster god Esu-Elegbara, offers yet another alternative to the Bible as a means of structuring *Moby-Dick*. "A rather good sort of god, who perhaps meant well enough upon the whole, but in all cases did not succeed in his benevolent designs" (p. 68), Yojo instructs Queequeg to let Ishmael choose the ship on which they are to sail—a ship Yojo has already preselected but which Ishmael, if left to himself, will "infallibly light upon," as though "by chance" (p. 68). Meanwhile, Queequeg spends the day closeted with Yojo in a ritual of "fasting, humiliation, and prayer" (p. 69) that apparently serves to ensure Ishmael's salvation. The outcome of their fateful voyage on the *Pequod* hence owes as much to the intervention of an African trickster god and the propitiation of a Polynesian cannibal as to the providential design revealed in the Bible's prophecies.

Queequeg himself incarnates the spirit of human brotherhood, transcending barriers of religion and race. With his Polynesian tattooing, "Congo idol," and Indian tomahawk/peace pipe, he combines the attributes of three races victimized by white colonialism. Queequeg's hybridity, betokening the oneness of humankind, even causes Ishmael to take him initially for a white man tattooed by cannibals and later to notice his resemblance to George Washington. Through his

conduct, Queequeg models an alternative to religious and racial conflict. "Melting" Ishmael's heart and "redeem[ing]" (p. 51) him from misanthropy and prejudice, Queequeg smokes a peace pipe with him, divides his possessions equally between them, makes him a present of thirty dollars in silver—the sum for which Judas betrayed Jesus—and teaches Ishmael that true worship consists not in upholding one creed over another but in "do[ing] to my fellow man what I would have my fellow man to do to me" (p. 52). The "marriage" the two celebrate in the landlord's conjugal bed (chapter 4)—flouting taboos against interracial as well as same-sex unions—exemplifies a loving partnership of equals. As such, it suggests the ideal toward which white Americans should aspire in seeking to resolve the problems of slavery and perpetual warfare with Indians. Within the microcosm of the *Pequod*, Queequeg and Ishmael's "marriage," broadened into an ethic of solidarity that embraces the entire crew, represents the antithesis of the unity Ahab forges among the sailors when he conscripts them into his "fiery hunt" (p. 195)—a unity forged in combat against an external foe.

INTERPRETING AHAB'S "FIERY HUNT"

How are we to interpet Ahab's "fiery hunt"? Is it a heroic battle against evil or a mad revolt against nature? Is Ahab a liberator seeking to free human beings from the tyranny of the gods, or is he a tyrant in his own right, driving his conscripts to their deaths in a war he has manipulated them into joining? The answers to these questions, which critics continue to debate, will determine how readers understand the novel.

Ahab openly admits that his prime motive for pursuing Moby Dick is vengeance: "It was Moby Dick that dismasted me; Moby Dick that brought me to this dead stump I stand on now. . . . It was that accursed white whale that razeed me; made a poor pegging lubber of me for ever and a day!" (p. 163). Yet Ahab rationalizes his lust for vengeance on a "dumb brute"—a lust Starbuck calls "blasphemous"—by identifying the white whale with "an inscrutable malice" lurking beneath the surface of the world (pp. 163, 164). As Ishmael theorizes, Ahab has projected onto Moby Dick all his personal woes—bodily, intellectual, and spiritual—and "all the general rage and hate felt by his whole race from Adam down" (p. 184). By turning Moby Dick into a concrete embodiment of everything he hates and fears, Ahab has given himself the illusion of being able to eradicate the source of his tribulations. He has made "all evil" seem "visibly personified, and . . . practically assailable" (p. 184) in a single target.

To enlist the sailors in his crusade against evil, Ahab must arouse their "unconscious" fears of a "great demon" that glides through the "seas of life" (p. 187), and he must appeal to their fighting instincts. He does so in a ritual that begins by whipping up their passion for the hunt and climaxes by literally intoxicating them with a liquor "hot as Satan's hoof" (p. 165)—a veritable devil's communion. Ahab supplements ritual with financial incentive, promising a gold doubloon worth sixteen dollars—a large sum for an ordinary seaman—to the crew member who first sights Moby Dick. He paralyzes opposition from Starbuck by exploiting the first mate's sense of racial superiority to isolate him from the "Turkish" infidels and "Pagan leopards" he officers (p. 164). As omens of disaster accumulate and murmurs of rebellion grow louder, Ahab awes the sailors with his command of technology, remagnetizing the inverted ship's compass. Finally, he resorts to undisguised brutality: "Down, men! the first thing that but offers to jump from this boat I stand in, that thing I harpoon" (p. 568).

Throughout the chase, Ahab insists that neither he nor his crew is free to change course, no matter how bleak the prospects of achieving their goal. "All your oaths to hunt the White Whale are as binding as mine; and heart, soul, and body, lungs and life, old Ahab is bound," he emphasizes (p. 508). When Starbuck attempts one last time to dissuade him, Ahab replies: "This whole act's immutably decreed. . . . I am the Fates' lieutenant; I act under orders. Look thou, underling! that thou obeyest mine" (p. 561). Ahab's belief in predestination absolves him of responsibility for leading his men to destruction and denies them any agency in shaping their own fate. Yet the question *Moby-Dick* raises, as Joyce Adler has argued, is precisely "whether man will continue to be directed to destruction by the 'death-dealing' spirit of war or will be saved by the spirit of life-preserving brotherhood" (Adler, p. 58).

Ishmael's gradual detachment from Ahab's quest and his survival on Queequeg's coffin proffer a tentative answer to that question. Despite his bond with Queequeg, Ishmael at first succumbs to the mass frenzy Ahab has incited. As he confesses: "I, Ishmael, was one of that crew; my shouts had gone up with the rest; my oath had been welded with theirs; and stronger I shouted, and more did I hammer and clinch my oath, because of the dread in my soul" (p. 179). In short, Ishmael has caught the contagion of terror and joined the collective demon chase to master his fear.

The metaphysical terror Moby Dick arouses in Ishmael, however, differs in kind from the fear experienced by his unphilosophical comrades. "It was the whiteness of the whale that above all things appalled me," he explains (p. 188). In one of literature's greatest virtuoso performances, Ishmael proceeds to dismantle the association of whiteness with "whatever is sweet, and honorable, and sublime" (p. 189), which lies at the basis of his culture's ideology of white supremacy. This association, Ishmael spells out, endows whiteness with a "pre-eminence" (p. 189) displayed in symbols of royalty throughout the world, from Burma to Austria—a "pre-eminence" that "applies to the human race itself, giving the white man ideal mastership over every dusky tribe" (p. 189). Nevertheless, in a two-page series of subordinate clauses that grammatically subvert the principle of hierarchy and equate the symbols of nonwhite, non-Christian peoples with those of white Christians, Ishmael undermines the alleged "mastership" of white over nonwhite, exposing it precisely as "ideal" rather than real, an "idea" rather than a fact (p. 189). His main clause ends up overturning the very foundations of white supremacist ideology by associating whiteness with terror rather than holiness: "there yet lurks an elusive something in the innermost idea of this hue, which strikes more of panic to the soul than that redness which affrights in blood" (p. 189). To account for the terror it arouses in him, Ishmael speculates that as the "visible absence of color, and at the same time the concrete of all colors," whiteness may conjure up the "colorless, all-color of atheism" (p. 195). The atheist sees the universe in the light of scientific theory, which holds that color is only an illusion, like the rouge of a harlot, "whose allurements cover nothing but the charnel-house within" (p. 195). But far from enabling him to see more truthfully, the atheist's refusal to wear the "colored and coloring glasses" (p. 195) needed to protect his eyes against intense light blinds him as he gazes at a universe shrouded in the whiteness of death, until he sees nothing at all. It is the terror Ishmael associates with whiteness—death, atheism, nihilism—that the white whale symbolizes for him, he concludes, and it is to overcome this terror that he has joined Ahab's "fiery hunt," even though he knows it may well prove fatal.

Two pivotal experiences eventually enable Ishmael to turn away from Ahab's deadly pursuit of evil and rediscover the loving fellowship of equals toward which Queequeg had earlier directed him. First, in a scene Ishmael portrays as both a baptism and a homoerotic orgy, the task of squeezing lumps of spermacetti back into fluid allows him to wash his hands and his heart of his oath to kill Moby Dick, free himself from "malice," and revel in "an abounding, affectionate, friendly, loving feeling" for his coworkers (p. 416). Second, after an evening of staring into the flames of the try-works, in which the whale's blubber is being rendered into oil, Ishmael falls asleep at the tiller and has a hellish vision of his comrades as fiends and of the *Pequod* as "the material counterpart of her

CHAPTER 42, "THE WHITENESS OF THE WHALE"

Though in many natural objects, whiteness refiningly enhances beauty, as if imparting some special virtue of its own, as in marbles, japonicas, and pearls; and though various nations have in some way recognised a certain royal pre-eminence in this hue; even the barbaric, grand old kings of Pegu placing the title 'Lord of the White Elephants' above all their other magniloquent ascriptions of dominion; and the modern kings of Siam unfurling the same snow-white quadruped in the royal standard; and the Hanoverian flag bearing the one figure of a snow-white charger; and the great Austrian Empire, Caesarian heir to overlording Rome, having for the imperial color the same imperial hue; and though this pre-eminence in it applies to the human race itself, giving the white man ideal mastership over every dusky tribe; and though, besides all this, whiteness has been even made significant of gladness, for among the Romans a white stone marked a joyful day; and though in other mortal sympathies and symbolizings, this same hue is made the emblem of many touching, noble things— the innocence of brides, the benignity of age; though among the Red Men of America the giving of the white belt of wampum was the deepest pledge of honor; though in many climes, whiteness typifies the majesty of Justice in the ermine of the Judge, and contributes to the daily state of kings and queens drawn by milk-white steeds; though even in the higher mysteries of the most august religions it has been made the symbol of the divine spotlessness and power; by the Persian fire worshippers, the white forked flame being held the holiest on the altar; and in the Greek mythologies, Great Jove himself being made incarnate in a snow-white bull; and though to the noble Iroquois, the midwinter sacrifice of the sacred White Dog was by far the holiest festival of their theology, that spotless, faithful creature being held the purest envoy they could send to the Great Spirit with the annual tidings of their own fidelity; and though directly from the Latin word for white, all Christian priests derive the name of one part of their sacred vesture, the alb or tunic, worn beneath the cassock; and though among the holy pomps of the Romish faith, white is specially employed in the celebration of the Passion of our Lord; though in the Vision of St. John, white robes are given to the redeemed, and the four-and-twenty elders stand clothed in white before the great white throne, and the Holy One that sitteth there white like wool; yet for all these accumulated associations, with whatever is sweet, and honorable, and sublime, there yet lurks an elusive something in the innermost idea of this hue, which strikes more of panic to the soul than that redness which affrights in blood.

Melville, *Moby-Dick*, pp. 188–189.

monomaniac commander's soul" (p. 423). Awakening just in time to prevent the ship from capsizing, he realizes that succumbing to Ahab's fixation on evil can only destroy him and everyone else on board.

As the sole survivor of the *Pequod*'s wreck, Ishmael's mission is to share the wisdom he has learned from his voyage. Through the story of Ahab's vendetta against Moby Dick, he reveals the lethal consequences of seeking to cure the ills of the world by personifying them in an "evil" and "practically assailable" foe (p. 184)—an impulse deeply rooted in his Puritan culture. And through the story of his redemptive "marriage" with Queequeg, Ishmael conjures up the dream of a future in which the spirit of human brotherhood will encircle the globe, empowering diverse peoples to live in harmony as equals.

REREADING *MOBY-DICK*

The seemingly disparate strands of *Moby-Dick*— Ahab's epic monster hunt and Ishmael and Queequeg's comic romance, cetology and whaling lore, biblical prophecy and pagan myth, religious satire and political commentary—turn out on repeated rereadings to be intricately intertwined. Recognizing the structural patterns that connect themes and chapters to each other, and understanding the purpose of the formal experimentation, yield access to some of the greatest pleasures the book affords. A few examples must suffice. Take the relationship between Father Mapple's sermon on the book of Jonah in chapter 9 and Ishmael's hilarious disquisition on "Jonah Historically Regarded" in chapter 83. While Father Mapple expounds the "lesson that the book of Jonah teaches" (p. 47), Ishmael parodies biblical exegetists who go to ridiculous lengths to prove the literal truth of the text, in the process missing its point. The gap between the two modes of reading challenges us to figure out how to read *Moby-Dick*.

Or take the interrelationships among chapters 24 ("The Advocate"), 81 ("The *Pequod* Meets the Virgin"), 82 ("The Honor and Glory of Whaling"), and 87 ("The Grand Armada"). In "The Advocate," which lays the groundwork for portraying whaling as an epic enterprise and Ahab as a tragic hero, Ishmael combats snobbish disdain for his trade as "unpoetical and disreputable" (p. 108). Whaling is as worthy of epic treatment, he contends, as war, the subject par excellence of the epic. The one is no more a "butchering sort of business" than the other (p. 108). In chapters 81 and 87, however, which describe the killing of the blind old whale and the winging of countless others, Ishmael exposes whaling as indeed both wanton butchery and war against a kindred species—the implication of his title "The Grand Armada." This butchery, in turn, casts an ironic light on Ishmael's effort in chapter 82 to establish "The Honor and Glory of Whaling" (to which he had credited his art in "The Advocate") by claiming Perseus, St. George, Hercules, Jonah, and Vishnu as archetypal whalemen. At the same time, the juxtaposition of a Christian saint and a biblical prophet with Greek demigods and a Hindu god once again asserts the equal validity—or fishiness—of all religions.

Melville explicitly draws attention to the book's complex structure. "There are some enterprises in which a careful disorderliness is the true method," Ishmael announces in "Honor and Glory" (p. 361). "Out of the trunk, the branches grow; out of them, the twigs. So, in productive subjects, grow the chapters," he instructs us in "The Crotch" (p. 289). Such self-conscious reflections on his literary "method" invite us to ask why Melville frustrates the reader's desire for a linear plot, refuses to stick to first-person narration, and opts to mix genres.

Consider the anticlimactic placement of the chapter "Cetology" just after Ahab has called up to the mast-head and issued his first order to look out for a white whale. Ready for action, the reader is in no mood at this juncture for a treatise on cetology. The reading habit formed by plots organized around the exploits of epic heroes primes us to join rather than resist Ahab's hunt. Hence, Melville must thwart this impulse if he is to liberate the reader from Ahab's worldview. That is, Melville must teach alternative ways of reading. "Cetology" accomplishes that aim by satirizing learned authorities and the arbitrary systems of classification they have erected, whether biological taxonomies or literary genres. Ishmael's no less arbitrary division of whales and

books by size instead of by internal characteristics casts doubt on the legitimacy of any classification system. In addition, it prepares the reader for Melville's violations of narrative rules and genre distinctions in the sequence that opens three chapters later with "The Mast-Head" and closes with "Midnight, Forecastle."

"The Mast-Head" picks up the narrative thread from the moment when Ahab shouts "Mast-head, there! Look sharp" (p. 132), just before Ishmael decides it is time for a cetology lesson. Although he has resumed the job of narration, Ishmael continues to resist Ahab's call. "With the problem of the universe revolving in me," he admits, "I kept but sorry guard" (p. 158). Describing his "reverie" at the mast-head, he shifts from first to third to second person and thus mimes the dissolution of his "identity" at the end of the chapter, as his mystical fusion with nature culminates in an imaginary fall from his perch that drowns him in the ocean. Appropriately, he now disappears as narrator for the next few chapters, giving way to a five-act play dominated by Ahab. In this play Ishmael's voice no longer mediates between the reader and the other characters, for he has become one with the crew swept away by Ahab's rhetoric.

And so has the reader, because dramatic form removes the mediating presence of a narrator and confronts the reader directly with the actors. Clearly Melville chose to switch genres for that very reason, so that the reader could experience Ahab's power as if on board the *Pequod*.

No single genre or point of view, Melville realized, could accommodate the many stories he wanted to tell, let alone succeed in transforming readers' consciousness—his ultimate goal. Nor can any single reading (in the sense of both perusal and interpretation) do justice to a novel as impossible to encompass as the whale of which Ishmael writes: "Dissect him how I may, then, I but go skin deep; I know him not, and never will" (p. 379).

Melville's readers of the 1850s rebelled against the demands his magnum opus made of them. Not until the 1920s, three decades after his death in 1891 and seven decades after the novel's publication in 1851, did *Moby-Dick* begin to secure its reputation as a literary classic. In the twenty-first century, however, faced with the grim legacies of slavery, genocide, religious absolutism, expansionist warfare, environmental depredation, and the threat of literal world annihilation, *Moby-Dick* has more lessons to teach the reader than ever.

See also "Bartleby, the Scrivener"; *Battle-Pieces;*
    Democracy; The Romance; Romanticism;
    Sexuality and the Body; Slavery; *Typee*

BIBLIOGRAPHY

Primary Works

Melville, Herman. *Correspondence*. Edited by Lynn Horth. Vol. 14 of *The Writings of Herman Melville*. Evanston, Ill., and Chicago: Northwestern University Press and Newberry Library, 1993.

Melville, Herman. "Hawthorne and His Mosses." 1850. In *"The Piazza Tales" and Other Prose Pieces, 1839–1860*, edited by Harrison Hayford et al., pp. 239–253. Vol. 9 of *The Writings of Herman Melville*. Evanston, Ill., and Chicago: Northwestern University Press and Newberry Library, 1987.

Melville, Herman. *Moby-Dick; or, The Whale*. 1851. Vol. 6 of *The Writings of Herman Melville*. Edited by Harrison Hayford, Hershel Parker, and G. Thomas Tanselle. Evanston, Ill., and Chicago: Northwestern University Press and Newberry Library, 1988.

Secondary Works

Adler, Joyce Sparer. *War in Melville's Imagination*. New York: New York University Press, 1981.

Bickman, Martin, ed. *Approaches to Teaching Melville's "Moby Dick."* New York: Modern Language Association of America, 1985.

Brodhead, Richard, H. ed. *New Essays on "Moby-Dick."* New York: Cambridge University Press, 1986.

Eldridge, Herbert G. "'Careful Disorder': The Structure of *Moby-Dick*." *American Literature* 39 (1967): 145–162.

Foster, Charles H. "Something in Emblems: A Reinterpretation of *Moby-Dick*." *New England Quarterly* 34, no. 1 (1961): 3–35.

Franklin, H. Bruce. *The Wake of the Gods: Melville's Mythology*. Stanford, Calif.: Stanford University Press, 1963.

Gilmore, Michael T. "Melville's Apocalypse: American Millennialism and *Moby-Dick*." *ESQ* 21, no. 3 (1975): 154–161.

Heimert, Alan. "*Moby-Dick* and American Political Symbolism." *American Quarterly* 15 (1963): 498–534.

Karcher, Carolyn L. *Shadow over the Promised Land: Slavery, Race, and Violence in Melville's America*. Baton Rouge: Louisiana State University Press, 1980.

Otter, Samuel. *Melville's Anatomies*. Berkeley: University of California Press, 1999.

Parker, Hershel. *Herman Melville: A Biography*. Vol. 1, *1819–1851*. Baltimore: Johns Hopkins University Press, 1996.

Reynolds, Larry J. *European Revolutions and the American Literary Renaissance*. New Haven, Conn.: Yale University Press, 1988.

Robertson-Lorant, Laurie. *Melville: A Biography*. New York: Clarkson Potter, 1996.

Rogin, Michael Paul. *Subversive Genealogy: The Politics and Art of Herman Melville*. New York: Knopf, 1983.

Shulman, Robert. "The Serious Functions of Melville's Phallic Jokes." *American Literature* 33 (May 1961): 179–194.

Spark, Clare L. *Hunting Captain Ahab: Psychological Warfare and the Melville Revival*. Kent, Ohio: Kent State University Press, 2001.

Sten, Christopher. *Sounding the Whale: "Moby-Dick" as Epic Novel*. Kent, Ohio: Kent State University Press, 1996.

Stewart, George R. "The Two *Moby-Dick*s." *American Literature* 25 (January 1954): 417–448.

Carolyn L. Karcher

THE MORGESONS

"I confess to secular habits entirely," proclaimed Elizabeth Stoddard (1823–1902) in one of the semimonthly "Lady Correspondent" columns she wrote for San Francisco's *Daily Alta California* (20 January 1855). Virtually unique in the published writing of nineteenth-century American women, her secularism informs her work. Like Ralph Waldo Emerson, Herman Melville, and Emily Dickinson, she emphasizes individuals' responsibility to live without benefit of religious or other doctrine and with self-awareness, courage, and integrity. Yet Stoddard contrasts with most of her contemporaries because she brings this exacting philosophy to bear on the domestic realm, considered in her day the most comforting and protected area of human life. In her powerful first novel, *The Morgesons* (1862), as in *Two Men* (1865) and *Temple House* (1867), it is home that is precarious, not, say, the quest of an obsessed captain. The most consequential realities—philosophical and ethical, economic, psychological and sexual—take their starkest form there. Stoddard's fiction thus disputes the antebellum ideology of separate spheres, which cast the home, associated with women, as a refuge from the public realm of men. Indeed, she casts men's participation in commerce and other aspects of public life and women's preoccupation with piety or domestic routine as escapes from the existential pressures that mark home life.

NARRATIVE DESIGN AS PHILOSOPHICAL CHALLENGE

Like life as Stoddard viewed it, *The Morgesons* is intense and exacting and comes without reliable guidelines. The novel seems to immerse readers in the experiences of its protagonist, Cassandra Morgeson, as they unfold. That Cassandra is also the novel's narrator is essential to this

Elizabeth Stoddard. Portrait engraving, c. 1870. GETTY IMAGES

effect: she tells her story without overt explanation or assessment. Unaided by a directive narrator like those favored by the best-selling domestic fiction—the mode of contemporary writing that most commonly featured female protagonists—readers must constantly find their bearings by taking the measure of Cassandra as narrator as well as of her narrative. The novel's design also contributes to the effect of immersion without guidelines. The very form of domestic fiction, that of the bildungsroman (novel of development) served to orient readers. Following a clear trajectory characterized by the literary historian Nina Baym as one of trials and triumph, novels like Susan Warner's *The Wide, Wide World* (1851) and Maria Cummins's *The Lamplighter* (1854) keep pace with their heroines' childhood ordeals (including separation from family or orphanhood) and the difficulties and temptations encountered in the course of the figurative and literal road to a mature adulthood. The journey is rewarded by marriage. Recursive rather than developmental, *The Morgesons* focuses on Cassandra's fortitude and consciousness as she leaves and returns to her family home in the village of Surrey, at the base of Cape Cod. Process, not progress, is the operative concept, with staples of domestic fiction like dramatic action and entertaining characterization of less importance

than Cassandra's observations, thoughts, and feelings and, to a lesser extent, those of her eccentric younger sister, Veronica.

As a child in Surrey, Cassandra is already the alert, willful, impetuous person she will remain. Neither her affable, conventional father, Locke, nor her pious but withdrawn mother, Mary, gives her much guidance. Eventually they send her to nearby Barmouth to live with her stern maternal grandfather and attend a school for the daughters of the town's elite. There her incipient sense of alienation from her world is consolidated, as her snobbish classmates educate her effectively in her social inferiority and the Puritan-like patriarchal asceticism of Grand'ther Warren's house confirms her atheism.

Cassandra also becomes strikingly beautiful, and shortly after she returns to Surrey, her irreverence and looks attract a chance visitor and distant cousin, Charles Morgeson. He invites her to his home in relatively cosmopolitan Rosville to acquire social "finish" and study at its widely respected academy, open to women as well as men. Her Rosville experiences include such conventional novelistic fare as the formation of several friendships and her acquiring of social polish and formal education, but their epicenter is Cassandra's emergent sexuality. Sustained evocation of her awareness of her own sexual appeal and her strong attraction to the married Charles, uninflected by moral comment, seems designed to urge readers' acknowledgment of sexuality not just as a powerful force but as one that can occur outside marriage. Just as radically, at a time when literature subsumed respectable women's sexual feelings within romantic love, *The Morgesons* shows that Cassandra is paralyzed by an inability to distinguish between the two. She dislikes Charles, but she can only conceive her attraction to him as romantic, a "bond" (p. 123); only after he dies in a carriage accident in which she herself is injured does she feel able to leave Rosville.

After returning home, Cassandra continues to "advance by experience" (p. 150) rather than progress through trials toward triumph. She observes the nuances of her family's dynamics and the limits of Surrey life with new clarity, but like most women of her class and era, she can do little to change her external circumstances. When her Rosville friend Ben Somers visits Surrey and becomes engaged to Veronica, Cassandra is invited to leave again, this time as ambassador of the undistinguished Morgesons to Ben's aristocratic family in Belem (modeled on Salem, Massachusetts, known for its wealthy elite as well as for its infamous witch trials). This visit is another inconclusive encounter with uncharted experiences. Cassandra faces down Ben's formidable, hostile mother; she learns to conduct herself well with the elite;

and fusing love and desire, she and Ben's alcoholic older brother, Desmond, fall in love. But her life coheres no more than it had. She returns to Surrey, where a series of unrelated events cast life's peril and unpredictability into high relief. Upon reaching home, she discovers her mother dead "in [her] chair" (p. 206); shortly thereafter her father declares bankruptcy. Ben and Veronica marry; Cassandra's father precipitates Cassandra's estrangement from him by marrying Charles's widow, Alice. Cassandra's sense of self fluctuates as unpredictably as her circumstances, shifting from despondency to powerful self-affirmation to a determination to subordinate herself to her family's needs. Finally she comes to terms with living independently; eventually Desmond appears, his alcoholism conquered, and they marry. The novel ends inconclusively. Cassandra's marriage receives virtually no attention, and the book's final pages return to the lives of all the Morgesons—Cassandra's continued alienation from Locke's new family, Ben's death as the result of alcoholism, Veronica's psychological collapse. It closes with Desmond's ambiguous religious explanation for catastrophes like Ben's death—"God is the Ruler. . . . Otherwise let this mad world crush us now" (p. 253)—and the contrasting image of Cassandra "in her chamber" in the old Morgeson house continuing to struggle with "this mad world" (p. 252) by writing *The Morgesons.*

REPRESENTATION OF DOMESTIC LIFE

As in domestic fiction, depictions of commonplace domesticity constitute much of *The Morgesons.* Unlike writers such as Warner and Harriet Beecher Stowe, though, Stoddard does not shape these depictions to tutor readers in religion or conduct. Her compressed style and sparing use of conventions that guide readers, such as scene setting or the clear identification of speakers, contribute to her representation of domestic life as charged and unpredictable. Here is a typical passage, a conversation Cassandra witnesses among her mother, her mother's sister Mercy, the Morgesons' longtime servant Temperance, and Fanny, an impoverished girl Mrs. Morgeson has recently taken in, as they inspect the bedroom Cassandra has redecorated after returning from Rosville:

> "Do you like my covered doors?" I inquired.
>
> "I vow," Temperance exclaimed, "the nails are put in crooked! And I stood over Dexter the whole time. He said . . . that you must be awfully spoiled to want such a thing. 'You get your pay, Dexter,' says I. . . . I do believe the man is a cheat and a rascal. . . . But they are all so."
>
> "In my young days," Aunt Merce remarked, "young girls were not allowed to have fires in their chambers."

> "In our young days, Mercy," mother replied, "*we* were not allowed to have much of anything."
>
> "Fires are not wholesome to sleep by," Temperance added.
>
> "Miss Veronica never has a fire," piped Fanny, who had remained, occasionally making a stir with the tongs.
>
> "But she ought to have!" Temperance exclaimed vehemently. "I do wonder, Mis' Morgeson, that you do not insist upon it, though it's none of my business" (P. 144)

Speakers' concern with their status and feelings of grievance thicken the air in this perfectly mundane scene. Everything Temperance says affirms her standing as a quasi-family member, superior to manual laborers and to Fanny; her indirection and show of deference to Mrs. Morgeson also acknowledge her lesser position as "help" while allowing her to reproach Mary Morgeson for inadequately mothering Veronica. Fanny justifies her presence by appearing to work but tries to sow discord between the sisters and to needle Cassandra for a luxurious life dependent on others' labor. The references to Veronica also register the often slipshod, sometimes destructive child-rearing practices that are commonplace in *The Morgesons;* so too does the household's stunning lack of reflection about why Cassandra might want so opulent a room.

Dynamics like those evident in this scene recur in *The Morgesons* so frequently that they can be said to have narrative heft, yet they do not cohere into distinct themes or subjects. Rather, Stoddard's representations of domestic life seem almost like unedited transcripts. This was an artistic choice and one she did not make for the more conventional short fiction she penned to sell to magazines like *Harper's.* A consequence of this artistry is that readers must scrutinize dialogue and sequence with a care they may normally not extend to domestic practices, whether in fiction or their own lives, to catch the overtones and comprehend the nuances of everyday domestic life.

The Morgesons solicits the same kind of attention to domesticity's center of gravity, the family. In antebellum ideology, the white, middle-class family constituted a cultural, social, and political treasure: a haven in a harsh world and the source of members' moral values, religious conviction, and education. Domestic fiction criticized individual families for failing to live up to the ideal, but it venerated "the family" writ large. Precisely because the family perpetuated social norms, Ralph Waldo Emerson, America's foremost cultural commentator, sometimes cast it as stifling and mediocre, urging self-reliant men to shun it. For *The Morgesons,* the family cannot be evaded: it is a condition of human life, characterized by the vagaries and tragedies that characterize all life. Indeed, the novel's representation of families anticipates the famous first sentence of Leo Tolstoy's *Anna Karenina* (1876), "All happy families are alike; every unhappy family is unhappy in its own way," with the caveat that "happy family" is an oxymoron.

Many commentators have responded to *The Morgesons*' depiction of family life by concentrating on defects of particular families or on the damage caused by specific historical matters like antebellum definitions of gender. Yet each family in the novel is troubled, the variety of ways attesting to life's variability. Every child in the natal family of Cassandra's mother is marred by Gran'ther Warren's Calvinist, patriarchal authoritarianism. The Somers' home life is toxic—"a devil's household," Desmond terms it (p. 191). Bellevue Pickersgil Somers, through whom the family wealth and aristocratic status have descended, is an economic and emotional tyrant: her sons are alcoholic and her daughters incapable of affection. The conventionalism of the family of Charles and Alice Morgeson is disastrous. They assume their marriage is normal and happy. Charles takes pleasure in his domestic authority and his business, Alice is "almost exclusively preoccupied" with her children (p. 75); only their interests in social status and luxurious living unite them. This traditional arrangement allows Charles to make Cassandra the subject of his desires and Alice to fail to notice until Cassandra tells her after his death.

In this context, the fault lines, flaws, and mutual disappointment in Cassandra's own family seem commonplace. The novel highlights the yearning Cassandra and Veronica feel for a mother who is often tantalizingly remote, the sisters' rivalries and hostilities, the perniciousness of the family's faithfulness to sanctioned ideas about gender. But it also emphasizes family members' intense love for each other, even as it belies the contemporary faith in love as a universal solvent, able to dissipate problems. The Morgesons love each other, and they are self-absorbed, partly incompatible, and often discontented with each other. The interests and temperaments of Locke and Mary Morgeson are so different that their lives diverge despite their love. Although they love their children, neither can give them adequate guidance or emotional sustenance. (When the eighteen-year-old Cassandra, uncertain about what she should do with her life, asks her mother, the reply is "mechanical": "Read the Bible, and sew more" [p. 64]). Despite family members' commitments to each other, moreover, the Morgesons are as vulnerable to disaster and uncertainty as other families. By the novel's end, all of them have died or founded new families; the latter, of course, are, or are likely to be, unhappy in their own ways.

STODDARD'S LIFE AND LITERARY REPUTATION

Although *The Morgesons* is a work of fiction, its challenging artistry reflects the drive and iconoclasm of its author. Born and raised in Mattapoisett, Massachusetts, Elizabeth Stoddard was hungry for broader experience of the world. On a visit to New York City in 1851, she attended a literary soiree, where she met the poet Richard Henry Stoddard. The two married in 1853 and thenceforth made their home in New York City, though Elizabeth continued to visit Mattapoisett. The Stoddard marriage was apparently happy, but success, even luck, eluded them. Only one of their three children, Lorimer, lived to adulthood, and he too predeceased his parents: he died in 1901, just as his career as a playwright was taking off. The family was always beset by financial difficulty: Richard's earnings as a poet were meager (unsurprisingly, given the mediocre quality of his verse) and were insufficiently augmented by his labors as a magazine editor. For a while the fiction Elizabeth began to write shortly before her marriage and the poetry she took up just after it were favorably received, and she had high hopes for *The Morgesons*. But the book's idiosyncrasy, along with the outbreak of the Civil War, made for poor sales in spite of positive reviews.

Disappointing sales were especially difficult for Stoddard because readers' interest inspired her creativity. Her first published writing, the "Lady Correspondent" columns (1854 to 1858), plays to readers' appreciation. Declaring "I own I am an egoist," she clearly expected her readers to relish her thoughts as much as she did (17 February 1856), and she flaunted her maverick opinions on subjects ranging from women's rights, recent literature, and gossip to life in New York City. Although the short fiction she wrote for the cash she and Richard needed so badly does superficially adhere to conventions about love and marriage, even this work smuggles in her desire to appeal on the grounds of non-conformist views about both. Even though her later novels are stylistically and structurally more accessible than *The Morgesons*, they too brandish their own singularity—and they too failed to command the wide readership she craved.

By the 1870s, lack of recognition so discouraged Stoddard that her writing tapered off. Aside from *Lolly Dinks' Doings* (1874), a quirky book for children based on tales she told Lorimer when he was a boy, she produced mainly regionalist sketches, memoirs about the antebellum New England of her youth, and a few poems in her last decades. When she died in 1902 few people knew her work or that of Richard, who died the next year. Only in the mid-1980s, with the republication of writing by nineteenth-century American women and feminist literary historians' devising of frameworks for reading it, did readers begin to respond to *The Morgesons*. For a time, commentators sought to align it with domestic fiction and other genres favored by contemporary women, but they are recognizing its unusual psychological dimensions as well as Stoddard's generic, stylistic, and philosophic iconoclasm. In consequence, interest in her literary journalism, her short fiction, and her novels continues to grow. Both *The Morgesons* and some of her other writing are now available in modern editions.

See also Calvinism; Childhood; Courtship; Domestic Fiction; Female Authorship; Marriage; Philosophy; Romanticism; Sexuality and the Body; *The Wide, Wide World*

BIBLIOGRAPHY

Primary Works

Stoddard, Elizabeth Drew Barstow. *"The Morgesons" and Other Writings, Published and Unpublished.* Edited by Lawrence Buell and Sandra A. Zagarell. Philadelphia: University of Pennsylvania Press, 1984.

Stoddard, Elizabeth Drew Barstow. *Stories.* Edited by Susanne Opfermann and Yvonne Roth. Boston: Northeastern University Press, 2003.

Stoddard, Elizabeth Drew Barstow. *Temple House.* 1867. Rev. ed. Philadelphia: H. T. Coates, 1901. Reprint, New York: Johnson Reprint Corporation, 1971.

Stoddard, Elizabeth Drew Barstow. *Two Men.* 1865. Rev. ed. Philadelphia: H. T. Coates, 1901. Reprint, New York: Johnson Reprint Corporation, 1971.

Secondary Works

Baym, Nina. *Woman's Fiction. A Guide to Novels by and about Women in America, 1820–1870.* 2nd ed. Urbana: University of Illinois Press, 1993.

Buell, Lawrence. *New England Literary Culture from Revolution through Renaissance.* Cambridge, U.K.: Cambridge University Press, 1986.

Harris, Susan K. *19th Century American Women's Novels: Interpretive Strategies.* Cambridge, U.K.: Cambridge University Press, 1990.

Henwood, Dawn. "First-Person Storytelling in Elizabeth Stoddard's *Morgesons*." *ESQ: A Journal of the American Renaissance* 41, no. 1 (1995): 41–63.

Smith, Robert McClure, and Ellen Weinauer, eds. *American Culture, Canons, and the Case of Elizabeth Stoddard.* Tuscaloosa: University of Alabama Press, 2003.

Zagarell, Sandra A. "Strenuous Artistry: Elizabeth Stoddard's *The Morgesons*." In *The Cambridge Companion to Nineteenth-Century American Women's Writing,* edited by Dale M. Bauer and Philip Gould, pp. 284–307. Cambridge, U.K.: Cambridge University Press, 2001.

Sandra A. Zagarell

MORMONS

Mormonism was one of many religious movements that emerged in antebellum America during the ferment known as the Second Great Awakening. In 1820 a youthful Joseph Smith (1805–1844) told his family and skeptical neighbors that he had been visited by Jesus Christ in response to his prayerful request for guidance in choosing a true religion. All Christian denominations had gone astray, the personage told him. Smith created little subsequent stir on the religious stage until ten years later, when he produced the Book of Mormon, a lengthy narrative purportedly written by ancient American prophets of Israelite origins and revealed to him by the angel Moroni. It detailed three migrations to the Western Hemisphere from the Old World but focused on the clan history of one group in particular— the Nephites—from their arrival until their demise (c. 600 B.C.E.–400 C.E.), narrating their wars, their belief in a coming Messiah, and his eventual visitation to the New World after his Jerusalem crucifixion.

Almost immediately after publication of the record, Smith assumed the role of prophet, seer, and revelator and organized the Church of Christ (subsequently designated the Church of Jesus Christ of Latter-day Saints), conceived as a full restoration of ancient priesthood authority and gospel truth. Mormon claims of new scripture, modern prophets, and angelic visitations offended prevailing religious sensibilities. Rapid growth of the sect, cultural differences, and the Mormon practice of gathering into cohesive, self-dependent communities created tensions and upset the local political balance of power, leading to violent confrontation and expulsion from successive areas of Missouri settlement in the 1830s. Most inflammatory of all was the rumored Mormon practice of plural marriage, which created disaffection within and attacks from without, culminating in the murder of Smith and the expulsion of Mormons from Illinois in the mid-1840s. Resettling in the Salt Lake Basin under the leadership of Brigham Young (1801–1877) in 1847, Mormons publicly announced their devotion to plural marriage in 1852 and thereby provoked public outrage and a moral crusade that would involve literary, military, political, and judicial responses over the next four decades.

Consumed with the challenge of surviving in a harsh, arid environment, and characterized by a predominantly puritan morality (polygamy aside), Latter-day Saints devoted little time and energy to literary pursuits in their early Utah period. The Book of Mormon was consistently distributed in those years but has historically served more as a palpable manifestation of Smith's prophetic status than as a text receiving attention or investigation in its own right. Although a

"Lizzie Monroe in her prison—Brigham Young Making Insulting Proposals." Illustration from Orvilla S. Belisle, *The Prophets; or, Mormonism Unveiled,* 1855. A common theme among authors was the abduction of "gentile" women for the "harems" of Mormon leaders. Women who resisted were tortured or killed; those who acquiesced frequently went insane and took their own lives. COURTESY OF TERRYL GIVENS

Baptist Herald editor admitted in 1840 that "we have never seen a copy of the book of Mormon," he felt confident in declaring the Book of Mormon "a bungling and stupid production. . . . We have no hesitation in saying the whole system is erroneous" (Givens, *By the Hand of Mormon,* p. 86). Such prima facie dismissal has been typical of public response to the book. However, the Book of Mormon is in fact a text of remarkable structural complexity, incorporating multiple layers of narrative, a cast of hundreds, approximately one thousand references to geography and chronology, and numerous generic forms—from psalm to midrash to epic to sermon. Mormon apologists stress the miracle of the book's ninety-day production by a process of spontaneous dictation corroborated by several witnesses; point to the book's pervasive Hebraic patterns and resonances, especially its many intricate instances of chiasmus, or inverted parallelism; and note its parallels with Old World ritual and cultural elements.

Skeptics draw attention to the unlikelihood of detailed pre-Christian references to Christ and his earthly ministry, apparent anachronisms (such as references to horses and steel), and assert a number of parallels with elements of nineteenth-century culture and religion.

With well over 120 million copies in print, the Book of Mormon is easily the most widely published book ever produced by an American. However, given the supernaturalistic elements surrounding its appearance and the challenges raised by the few archaeologists and evangelicals who have looked at it, convincing secular scholars to examine the book is no easy task. However, religious scholars and historians are increasingly noting the undeniable cultural significance of the book, especially as Mormonism appears poised on a trajectory to become a world religion.

The book's primary value to Mormons, however, has been as a sign of Smith's prophetic status, and it became an object of serious theological investigation only in the late twentieth century. And although Mormon scholars have been engaged in serious textual study of the Book of Mormon for apologetic purposes since the 1950s, few of them have plumbed the book's literary features or value.

Other than lending its name to the new movement, then, the Book of Mormon did little to shape public perceptions of early Mormonism. Neither did the Mormons find any significant voice in the secular press or publishing industry to promote their cause or shape their own image. Into this void stepped critics, crusaders, and pulp fiction writers happy to appropriate the latest cultural villain to their own moral and literary agendas. In the process, fiction writers reveal more about the peculiar anxieties Mormonism provoked than any culturally or historically authentic features of Mormonism. At least two patterns of representation emerge from several dozen novels and stories of the era. First, is a conspicuous tendency to Orientalize or otherwise exoticize Mormonism. Such portrayals—beyond simply exploiting the shared sensuous appeal of Eastern harems and Mormon polygamy—had the advantage of recasting religious intolerance in patriotic terms. Reconstructing an unpopular but homegrown Christian sect as a variant of Islam, which E. D. Howe did as early as 1834 (*History of Mormonism*), made it possible to parallel the anti-Catholic practice of making the target church an enemy of republicanism, domestic values, and American womanhood. That tendency would become most pronounced in the decades after the Civil War.

More striking in the prewar representations of Mormonism were themes of coercion and bondage. The sensationalistic appeal of a system of virtual white slavery evoked by polygamy is obvious. But the first generation of novels suggests more is at work here. The first anti-Mormon work of fiction, *The Mormoness* (1853), by John Russell (1793–1863), does not even address plural marriage. It does depict Mormonism as a system of "fatal snares" (p. 42) and "ingenious sophistry" (p. 53). The kindly protagonists—both male and female—are "deluded," guilty of only "too much . . . gentleness and goodness" (p. 42). In Maria Ward's *Female Life among the Mormons* (1855), Smith is a "serpent-charmer" (p. 9) who learned to mesmerize his victims of both sexes with skills acquired from a German peddler. Similarly, Theodore Winthrop's *John Brent* (1862) is "compelled" to listen by the Mormon leader's "unwholesome fascination" (p. 92). In Orvilla S. Belisle's *The Prophets; or, Mormonism Unveiled* (1855); Alfreda Bell's *Boadicea, the Mormon Wife: Life-Scenes in Utah* (1855); and Metta Victoria Fuller Victor's *Mormon Wives* (1856), women are more blatantly coerced into harems through kidnapping and violence

(as they are in the most famous, but British, treatment of Mormonism, Arthur Conan Doyle's 1888 *Study in Scarlet*). In every single case, the common feature of these early works is Mormonism's erasure of the will to resist. "Choosing" Mormonism is not conceivable in this universe, where deliberate embrace of the religion is rendered unthinkable, as if the literary imagination were not expansive enough to comprehend the spiritual yearnings that the appearance of a new prophet and new Christian scripture fulfilled for so many seekers.

See also Protestantism; Religion; Utopian Communities

BIBLIOGRAPHY
Primary Works
Russell, John. *The Mormoness; or, The Trials of Mary Maverick*. Alton, Ill.: Courier Stream Press, 1853.

[Standish, Burt L.] "Frank Merriwell among the Mormons; or, The Lost Tribes of Israel." *Tip Top Weekly*, 19 June 1897.

Ward, Maria. *Female Life among the Mormons: A Narrative of Many Years' Experience among the Mormons*. London: Routledge, 1855.

Winthrop, Theodore. *John Brent*. New York: Lovell, 1862.

Secondary Works
Arrington, Leonard J., and Rebecca Foster Cornwall. "Perpetuation of a Myth: Mormon Danites in Five Western Novels, 1840–90." *BYU Studies* 23, no. 2 (1983): 147–165.

Arrington, Leonard J., and Jon Haupt. "Intolerable Zion: The Image of Mormonism in Nineteenth Century American Literature." *Western Humanities Review* 22 (summer 1968): 243–260.

Givens, Terryl L. *By the Hand of Mormon: The American Scripture that Launched a New World Religion*. Oxford and New York: Oxford University Press, 2002.

Givens, Terryl L. *The Viper on the Hearth: Mormons, Myths, and the Construction of Heresy*. New York: Oxford University Press, 1997.

Lambert, Neil. "Saints, Sinners, and Scribes: A Look at Mormons in Fiction." *Utah Historical Quarterly* 36 (winter 1968): 63–76.

Terryl Givens

MOURNING

"The sorrow for the dead," mused Washington Irving (1783–1859) in *The Sketch Book of Geoffrey Crayon* (1819–1820), "is the only sorrow from which we refuse to be divorced" (p. 153). The nineteenth-century literary preoccupation with mourning does indeed suggest a culture wedded to its sorrow over the dead. Depictions of mourning, much like those of marriage, reveal its dual function as a means of social ordering and as an index of emotional, or affective, and psychic topographies. The Puritan emphasis on the moment of death as a theologically instructive event gave way during the eighteenth and early nineteenth centuries to an intense concentration on the emotional aftermath of loss. This shift dramatically altered the social meaning of death. Literary representations of mourning in this changed context foreground both an increasing interest in interiority and an investment in the development of proper affective relations to the past.

Twentieth- and twenty-first-century critics have often viewed with suspicion the elaborate culture of mourning developed in the nineteenth century, assessing it as a mode of sentimentalized false consciousness covering an inability to deal with the grim reality of death. But many cultural and ideological factors beyond the fear of death need to be considered when assessing past bereavement practices. In nineteenth-century culture, mourning designated both a set of conventions designed to order the borderline period between the loss of an intimate and the bereaved person's reintegration into ordinary social life, and an ongoing emotional activity suggesting the tenacity of ties to the departed. The spiritual significance of mourning was linked to the emotional value assigned by Romantic and sentimental writers to grief's refining effect on the personal integrity of the survivor. Literary manifestations of mourning depict a new relationship between feeling, (social) space, and (historical) time suggested by the aesthetics of memorial; a regulation of expressions of grief that addressed both the universality of sorrow and the racial, cultural, and gender specificity of mourning behavior; and the connections between the solicitation of feeling around mourning and appeals for social reform.

THE VALUE OF SORROW

Readers steeped in the post-Freudian understanding of mourning as a psychological process must recall that in the nineteenth century the term "mourning" indicated first of all a set of social conventions. The formal mourning period was highly ritualized: proscriptions on social events and communication, the draping of the home of the bereaved, and mourning clothes and veils all formed part of an elaborate system marking both the degree of kinship between the mourner and the departed and the time elapsed since death. While adherence to these conventions was understood primarily as a mark of respect for the dead, a refusal to observe formal mourning also suggested a lack of concern for communal norms. In the mid-century best-seller *The Wide, Wide World* (1851), by Susan Warner (1819–1885), for instance,

the protagonist Ellen Montgomery, sent to live with her hard-hearted Aunt Fortune while her parents travel in Europe, learns of her mother's death through the scandalized gossip of neighbors who fault Fortune for not having dressed the girl in mourning. Paying too much attention to social conventions, however, was viewed as potentially more injurious than paying too little, for such attention implied that the departed could be replaced by the commodities of condolence. In her novel *Hope Leslie* (1827), Catharine Maria Sedgwick (1789–1867) disparages the embrace of fashionable mourning in a scene in which the protagonist's good-natured but foolish aunt, Mrs. Grafton, cheerfully explains how her friend Lady Penyvére managed to console herself for the disastrous loss of an entire family by ordering mourning clothes: "That is the great use of wearing mourning, as she said: it takes the mind off from trouble." Hope responds by gently upbraiding her aunt for confusing consumption with consolation; having recently survived a dangerous situation, she reminds her aunt, "If . . . I had lost my life the other day, all the mourning in the king's realm would not have turned your thoughts from trouble" (p. 268).

An insistence on the importance of feeling, rather than mere adherence to social form, dominated nineteenth-century literary depictions of mourning. A deep emotional relationship to the dead not only provided testimony to the merits of the departed but was also understood as a means of self-improvement for the mourner. As Irving's Geoffrey Crayon insists, "the natural effect of sorrow over the dead is to refine and elevate the mind" (p. 149). Crayon compares the emptiness of the contemporary urban funeral to the banality of modern-day poetry, which, he contends, lacks the natural pathos of Shakespeare. Both failures, he asserts, result from the modern attention to form over content, a preference that has not yet infiltrated the charming customs of rural memorial: "There is certainly something more affecting in these prompt and spontaneous offerings of nature, than in the most costly monuments of art" (p. 150). The spontaneous memorial speaks more passionately than the artificial monument because the former testifies to a sincere emotional connection between the mourner and the departed, the kind of sincerity that constitutes the heart of the truly "poetical," as opposed to the "polite" alienation of modern life (p. 151). The quasi-spiritual significance assigned by romantics such as Crayon to the mourner's feelings turned emotion into a conduit for meaningful relations between past and present, relations that might regenerate the affective impoverishment of the modern world even as individual grief forced mourners to confront their own defects in character.

Wreath of Flowers, 1866. Painting by John La Farge. The wreath was a symbol of victory for the ancient Greeks. It was later adopted by Christians as a mourning symbol to emphasize Christian redemption in death. La Farge's placement of Greek text reading "as summer was just beginning" beneath the wreath implies the mourning of a particularly tragic loss and may have been inspired by the illness and death of his infant son.

SMITHSONIAN AMERICAN ART MUSEUM, WASHINGTON, DC/ART RESOURCE, NY

Such romanticized assumptions about the affective pedagogy of mourning shaped the aesthetics of memorial in the nineteenth century. The new "rural cemeteries" that appeared in the second quarter of the century were intended to produce the kind of contemplative relationship to the dead that Irving's Crayon lauds. The design of these park-like burial grounds, strewn with trees and ponds and sectioned by hills and winding paths, emphasized a Romantic approach to consolation,

insisting on the spiritually regenerative capacity of nature while providing mourners with a measure of privacy for the indulgence of sorrow over the dead. The dominant motifs of nineteenth-century mourning art (classically robed mourners with heads bowed over graves, weeping willows, trees and urns symbolizing the eternity of the spirit) similarly suggested a dual connection to the eternal spirit of the departed and the earthly sorrow of the bereaved. The mourner in this new configuration was charged with the duty of carrying a personal connection to the past forward in time.

Guided by these convictions, literary scenes of bereavement deployed mourning itself as a form of consolation for loss, suggesting that mourning was not simply a mark of the value of the departed but itself a valuable and improving activity. This understanding permeated the literary forms and conventions most congenial to mourning: deathbed scenes and sentimental elegies. Initially popularized in evangelical tracts as episodes of spiritual pedagogy, deathbed scenes in nineteenth-century fiction supplemented the original focus on the religious authority of the dying person with an increased emphasis on the emotional testimony of the witnesses/mourners; such testimony spoke to the bonds grief created among survivors. In perhaps the best-known deathbed scene of nineteenth-century American fiction, the death of young Eva St. Clare in Harriet Beecher Stowe's *Uncle Tom's Cabin* (1852) is closely followed by an exchange between the distraught slave girl Topsy, who laments that Eva was the only person to ever treat her kindly, and Miss Ophelia, Eva's northern aunt, who, touched by the child's distress, resolves to imitate Eva's behavior, sealing the pact by weeping along with Topsy.

The nineteenth-century poetic elegy also insisted on the value of mourning. Even as it bewailed the irrevocable loss of the irreplaceable dead, its focus on the painful feelings of the speaker/mourner became a form of consolation. In his elegy for Nathaniel Hawthorne, for instance, a bereft Henry Wadsworth Longfellow (1807–1882) laments the silencing of his friend's pen, but the poem's attention to the pain of mourning as an opening to the speaker's dreamlike recollection of the past compensates in part for the impossibility of reversing time. In "When Lilacs Last in the Dooryard Bloom'd" (1867), an intimate elegy to Abraham Lincoln, Walt Whitman (1819–1892) also uses sorrow over the dead as a means of gaining an alternative perspective on the passage of time. The poet-speaker's grief over the departed, which returns each spring on the anniversary of the assassination, accompanies the regenerative blooming of the natural world. But suffering, the poem contends, is something from which the dead are exempted; it is rather for those who remain behind and is thus to be embraced as part of nature, both as a sign of loss and as a sign of life.

A NATION OF MOURNERS

In the final chapter of *The Last of the Mohicans* (1826), by James Fenimore Cooper (1789–1851), the frenetic adventure that dominates the novel gives way to a leisurely depiction of the funeral rites for the young Mohican sachem Uncas. Uncas's death is commemorated by an elaborate ceremony that Cooper adapted, with a number of Romantic flourishes, from John Heckewelder's ethnographic account of a Lenni Lenape funeral. Recounting the ornate formality of these rites, from the long, solemn period of near-motionless waiting with which the service opens to the elaborate song of lament contributed by a group of female mourners and finally to the ritual upbraiding of the young chief for abandoning his tribe by the grief-stricken survivors, Cooper emphasizes the touching emotional undercurrent that runs throughout, coupling an insistence on the exotic nature of Indian ritual with an appeal to the universality of true feeling.

The nineteenth-century investment in the value of sorrow enabled mourning to be understood as a unifying force. The deep feeling associated with true mourning was seen not simply as creating authentic channels of historical transmission and avenues for self-improvement but as contributing as well to the establishment of affective social bonds between otherwise alienated strangers. Condolence rituals formalized the human capacity for sympathy that the eighteenth-century British philosopher Adam Smith analyzed as the foundation of democratic self-regulation, establishing a kind of fellowship of the bereaved (*Theory of the Moral Sentiments,* 1759). Accounts of such bonds—whether in Cooper's fictionalized account of the passing of Uncas, which transformed the Delaware into a "nation of mourners," or in the outpouring of writing that followed the assassination of President Lincoln in 1865—used the language of private feeling to emphasize their sincerity. Public figures became not simply revered but cherished and loved, as mourner-citizens participated in a spontaneous, affective coming together more durable than acts of collective democratic decision making such as voting. Public mourning, in this sense, provided nationalism with a spiritual dimension.

The multiple modes of productivity attached to mourning in the nineteenth century, however, required an observance of religious, cultural, and behavioral norms in the expression of grief in order to ensure that it functioned properly. Cooper's depiction of the Delaware funeral in *The Last of the Mohicans* is not intended for imitation; its melancholy may appeal to the reader but the "creed" the Delaware embrace is, the novel suggests, unacceptable to a civilized Christian culture. Accordingly, the chapter juxtaposes the Delaware rites and the simultaneous funeral of Cora Munro, a young Englishwoman. Although Cora is also attended by Delaware women and buried in the woods, her service, conducted by the colonial psalmodist David Gamut, consists of a simple hymn and prayer. The Christian burial ritual allows the novel at once to embrace the natural spirituality of true feeling and to assert the superiority of civilized Christian cultures over the Delaware culture, which, it implies, will soon follow the young sachem to the grave. The touching spectacle of Indian mourning serves, in effect, as an elegy for Native American culture as a whole.

The restrained norms of Christian bereavement were reflected in the increased attention given to the emotional dimension of mourning throughout the nineteenth century. Condolence manuals and sentimental literature alike insisted that, however heartfelt, mourning should never remain untempered by spiritual awareness. While grief was expected as a mark of attachment to the dead and was embraced as an opportunity for refinement on the part of the living, excessive indulgence in mourning was seen as a mark of disrespect for both the living and the dead. In *The Wide, Wide World,* for instance, Ellen Montgomery's prolonged grief for her mother is rebuked by her "adopted" brother John Humphreys, who reminds her of her duty to be consoled by pointing out that her mother, a Christian, would have wanted nothing less. Unrestrained mourning also had dangerous social implications, as comparative accounts of the denial and the refusal of consolation in *Uncle Tom's Cabin* suggest. Prue, a much-abused slave, is deprived of the opportunity to mourn her infant child by a harsh mistress. Unable to cope with her sorrow, she takes to drinking and dies a horrific, solitary death. Prue's fate is implicitly juxtaposed to that of Marie St. Clare, mistress of the St. Clare plantation and the mother of Eva. Marie's melodramatic fits of grief in the wake of her daughter's death fail to bring about any improvement in her character; moreover, they have a profoundly negative effect on the other members of the household, who are denied time for their own mourning because of the demands created by her hysteria. Even as well-composed mourning was understood to produce both interior refinement and external cohesion, abuses of grief were held to damage both the psychic and the social realms.

The prevalence of female mourners in didactic examples of unrestrained grief suggests a gendered division of labor in the culture of mourning. Yet, while the conventional allegorical figuration of the mourner as a woman has led many to assume that mourning in the nineteenth century was women's work, condolence manuals and sentimental literature suggested that men grieved as profoundly as women. But while men were indeed expected to mourn, they were under additional pressure to moderate expressions of feeling, particularly in public. True manliness consisted of an ability to feel deeply and, at the same time, to restrain the physical manifestations of feeling. In the final scene of Cooper's *The Pioneers* (1823), for instance, the grizzled frontiersman Natty Bumppo weeps before the grave of his lifelong companion, the Mohican sachem Chingachgook, but when his friends Oliver and Elizabeth Effingham approach, he hastily wipes away his tears. And Oliver also reacts with manfully restrained sorrow to the death of Chingachgook, who had adopted him as a son, and to the departure of Natty for the western wilderness. Women, in contrast, were expected to display grief openly, if not to excess; accordingly, Elizabeth, Oliver's wife, weeps unashamedly throughout the touching scene. In this sense, the part played by women in the cult of the mourner was in many ways comparable to the American social critic Thorstein Veblen's account, at the turn of the century, of their function in the culture of consumption (*The Theory of the Leisure Class*, 1899): women give ceremonial expression to values embraced by the culture as a whole.

MOURNING AND CRITIQUE

The nineteenth-century belief in the moral elevation of the mourner lent itself to the depiction of scenes of mourning as a call for social reform. This kind of appeal resounds throughout the pages of Stowe's *Uncle Tom's Cabin*, as the narrator repeatedly pleads with her readers to sympathize with the suffering of slaves by comparing their sorrows to the grief common to all who have mourned the loss of a loved one. But cultural differences in the experience of grief were also treated as evidence of the need for social change. The matter-of-fact description, in the *Narrative of the Life of Frederick Douglass, an American Slave* (1845), of the author's lack of emotional response to his mother's death—"Never having enjoyed, to any considerable extent, her soothing presence, her tender and watchful care, I received the tidings of her death with much the same emotions I should probably have felt at the death of a stranger" (p. 16)—might have struck readers steeped in the culture of mourning as shocking. Frederick Douglass (1818–1895), however, makes clear in his narrative that his startling failure to feel the loss of his mother is an effect of slavery's destruction of the very connections most valorized in the culture of mourning, namely, the deep emotional bonds that made familial

affect the cornerstone of the social. Ten years later, in *My Bondage and My Freedom* (1855), Douglass amplified this reflection, adding that he maintains a "life-long, standing grief" not over his mother's death itself but over the loss of connection to her enforced by the slave system (p. 155).

While some nineteenth-century writers used mourning as a means of foregrounding the need for social reforms, others critically interrogated the assumptions surrounding the culture of mourning itself. In his short story "The Minister's Black Veil" (1836), Nathaniel Hawthorne (1804–1864) questions the tendency to make moral distinctions between types of sorrow. In the story, the residents of a New England village are disturbed when their minister, Reverend Hooper, suddenly and without explanation dons a black veil. This conventional sign of bereavement, unmoored from familiar social coordinates, becomes deeply unsettling, and the villagers anxiously debate whether the veil signifies ordinary mourning, the "type of an innocent sorrow," or a mark of penance for secret sin (p. 46). Hooper, however, refuses to choose between the two motives assigned to his veil, remarking only that both are common to all humanity. His refusal undermines the habitual assumption that grief is redemptive, while shame is simply corrosive. Finally, on his deathbed, Hooper announces that the veil reflects the habit of concealment itself. His insistence that all mortals hide both their sins and their deepest feelings from one another further troubles the tendency to depict grief as morally refining.

An even deeper critique of the assumptions surrounding the culture of mourning is conveyed by Ralph Waldo Emerson (1803–1882) in his essay "Experience" (1844). Emerson notes that while people tend to seek truth in grief, it does not reveal itself there; reflecting on the death of his own son, he argues that such calamities "leave me as [they] found me,—neither better nor worse" (p. 29). Yet while Emerson challenges the productivity assigned to sorrow over the dead in the nineteenth century, his essay reproduces the desire for this productivity, the longing for authentic emotional experience as compensation for human "evanescence." Emerson's mournful renunciation of this fantasy—"I grieve that grief can teach me nothing, nor carry me one step into real nature" (p. 29)—might be read as an elegiac reflection on the culture of mourning as a whole.

See also The Gates Ajar; Indians; Individualism and Community; Landscape Architecture; Leatherstocking Tales; Lyric Poetry; Manhood; Reform; Romanticism; Slavery; *Uncle Tom's Cabin; The Wide, Wide World*

BIBLIOGRAPHY

Primary Works

Cooper, James Fenimore. *The Last of the Mohicans: A Narrative of the Year 1757.* 1826. New York: Penguin, 1986.

Cooper, James Fenimore. *The Pioneers.* 1823. New York: Penguin, 1988.

Douglass, Frederick. *Autobiographies.* New York: Library of America, 1994.

Emerson, Ralph Waldo. "Experience." 1844. In *The Collected Works of Ralph Waldo Emerson,* vol. 3, pp. 25–49. Cambridge, Mass.: Harvard University Press, 1983.

Hawthorne, Nathaniel. "The Minister's Black Veil: A Parable." 1836. *Twice-Told Tales,* edited by William Charvat et al., pp. 37–53. In The Centenary Edition of the Works of Nathaniel Hawthorne, volume 9. Columbus: Ohio State University Press, 1974.

Heckewelder, John. *History, Manners, and Customs of the Indian Nations Who Once Inhabited Pennsylvania and the Neighbouring States.* 1819. Philadelphia: Historical Society of Pennsylvania, 1876.

Irving, Washington. "Rural Funerals." 1819–1820. In *The Sketch-Book of Geoffrey Crayon,* pp. 144–157. Reading, Pa.: Dutton, 1936.

"A Lady." *The Mourner's Book.* Boston: Benjamin B. Mussey, 1850.

Longfellow, Henry Wadsworth. "Hawthorne." 1866. In *Poems and Other Writings,* pp. 474–475. New York: Library of America, 2000.

Sedgwick, Catharine Maria. *Hope Leslie; or, Early Times in the Massachusetts.* 1827. Edited by Mary Kelley. New Brunswick: Rutgers University Press, 1987.

Syme, J. B., ed. *The Mourner's Friend; or, Sighs of Sympathy for Those Who Sorrow.* Worcester: William Allen, 1852.

Stowe, Harriet Beecher. *Uncle Tom's Cabin; or, Life among the Lowly.* 1852. Edited by Ann Douglas. New York: Penguin, 1981.

Whitman, Walt. "When Lilacs Last in the Dooryard Bloom'd." 1867. In *Complete Poetry and Collected Prose,* pp. 459–467. New York: Library of America, 1982.

Warner, Susan. *The Wide, Wide World.* 1851. New York: Feminist Press, 1987.

Secondary Works

Ariès, Philippe. *The Hour of Our Death.* Translated by Helen Weaver. New York: Oxford University Press, 1991.

Farrell, James J. *Inventing the American Way of Death, 1830–1920.* Philadelphia: Temple University Press, 1980.

Halttunen, Karen. "Mourning the Dead: A Study in Sentimental Ritual." In her *Confidence Men and Painted Women: A Study of Middle-Class Culture in America, 1830–1870,* pp. 124–152. New Haven, Conn.: Yale University Press, 1982.

Kete, Mary Louise. *Sentimental Collaborations: Mourning and Middle-Class Identity in Nineteenth-Century America.* Durham, N.C.: Duke University Press, 2000.

Pike, Martha V., and Janice Gray Armstrong. *A Time to Mourn: Expressions of Grief in Nineteenth-Century America.* Stony Brook, N.Y.: The Museums at Stony Brook, 1980.

Schorsch, Anita. *Mourning becomes America: Mourning Art in the New Nation.* Clinton N.J.: Main Street Press, 1976.

Sloane, David Charles. *The Last Great Necessity: Cemeteries in American History.* Baltimore: Johns Hopkins University Press, 1991.

Dana Luciano

MUSIC

Music composition, publication, and performance in the United States during the antebellum period developed and expanded from localized practices to a recognized and influential national culture, aided by the rise of new technologies in printing, manufacturing, and commercial distribution. Following the wars for independence from Britain, individual states retained their strongly differentiated ethnic and religious populations, but by the end of the Civil War—despite the divide between North and South—recognizably "American" forms of music not only spanned geographic expanses but also had even begun to represent the United States abroad.

Music was always heard live, and was thus ephemeral. Other than the barrel organ and music box, no sound machines existed until late in the century (Thomas Edison patented his "talking machine" in 1877). For most Americans music was ubiquitous and casual, performed or encountered in the homes of their family and friends, at school, and in public venues and commercial establishments. Musicians and patrons employed music for different reasons in those spheres—for entertainment, moral training, and solace within the home, or as an essential component of the curricula of female seminaries intended to mold middle-class mothers, for example. Vocal and piano skills were highly prized and families brought music teachers into their homes to train their daughters. Music was more than household entertainment. It was a medium for instilling social and ethical values.

In all its genres, music reflected the issues to which American writers were also responding and musicians drew on literature as a source of text and merged the two arts to create public and private performances. At the same time, writers—especially poets and journalists—responded to the sounds around them. Walt Whitman (1819–1892) most famously echoed the rough voices of everyday life in "I Hear America Singing" (1860), and no other American poet's works have been set to music more often by later songwriters who are attracted by his American imagery as well as his "rhythmic elasticity" (Sullivan, p. 97). Whitman was opera critic for the *Brooklyn Daily Eagle* in the 1840s and 1850s and his poems abound with musical references. His *Drum-Taps* (1865) "bridges the gap between written and aural modes of representation" (Picker, p. 2). Edgar Allan Poe (1809–1849) employed musical sounds, not only in his poems but also as evocative imagery in his stories. His 1846 essay "The Philosophy of Composition," was a manifesto for authors and contemporary American composers.

Only since the 1970s have scholars turned their attention to the music of this era, in contrast to the relatively abundant scholarship on novels, poetry, short stories, and other forms of literature. Whereas the writings of Poe and of Harriet Beecher Stowe (1811–1896), for example, have prompted symposia, monographs, and articles from all perspectives, very few studies exist for comparable figures in music. One reason is that until the 1990s few libraries catalogued their collections of antebellum music and fewer still have assembled accessible archival collections.

From the beginning of European settlement in North America, music was a useful art, and the first book published in the English-speaking colonies was the *Bay Psalm Book* (1640) for singing sacred texts. In 1789 the new constitution established the legal concept of copyright that included music as a form of literature, and music publications were an important if small sector of the nation's early publications. When Congress reestablished its library after the War of 1812 by purchasing Thomas Jefferson's collection in 1815, it acquired not only his books but also his music, undoubtedly the largest private library of music scores in the country.

As Alexis de Tocqueville famously noted in *Democracy in America,* America lacked institutions. In 1820 there were few ongoing groups dedicated to presenting music to the public. But there was no shortage of musicians, and America presented a new market, especially for Europe's concert and theatrical composers and performers. Music traveled quickly with the touring musicians, and its styles and texts came to unify the nation to some extent. Some of those touring musicians adopted American ideals into their repertories and carried them abroad, representing America in other parts of the world, particularly the port cities of Europe and Asia frequented by travelers. In the 1840s minstrel performers began taking their shows to London and Glasgow and sheet-music imprints show that the songs caught on quickly there. Popular songs, especially those by Stephen Foster (1826–1864), were carried abroad where they were heard as something new, familiar inasmuch as they retained elements from Old World practices, but original and distinctly American.

SONGS

Oral literature in the unwritten traditions of immigrant cultures was known to all ethnic and economic classes of Americans, but because of its ad hoc nature it went largely unremarked and left almost no documented descriptions. Published music, however, constitutes the largest genre of printed literature extant from the period. Twenty-four percent of all copyright deposits in the nineteenth century (more than 400,000 items) were music.

Vocal music was practiced in both the sacred and secular realms of American society. Protestant hymnody, which had dominated eighteenth-century American composers' output, flourished anew, fed on the one hand by the rural camp-meeting revivalist movement that simplified and intensified the redemptory imagery of Isaac Watts's hymns, and on the other by reform impulses in the established urban churches. American hymnody in the 1820s through the 1850s, like the theological and public education movements to which it was tied, vividly reflects the grassroots passions and the top-down strictures that had become apparent in political and social discourse.

Lowell Mason (1792–1872), a bank clerk turned hymnist, joined with the foremost purveyor of European classical artistic standards in America in 1822 to publish the *Boston Handel and Haydn Society Collection of Church Music,* launching a new era of sacred-music enterprise. The book and its successors made both Mason and the Society wealthy and became the prototype for countless other songbooks both sacred and pedagogical.

If Mason helped shape a taste for high-church hymnody modeled on British hymnists and German oratorio, the blind poet Fanny Crosby (1820–1915) more than any other author fused the spirit of camp-meeting hymnody and revivalism with popular melody. As a girl she sang popular songs, accompanying herself on guitar; as an adult she was credited with writing more than nine thousand hymns, spurring publishers to issue inexpensive hymnbooks for Sunday schools and revivalist meetings and providing a model for gospel hymnody, most notably that of Dwight Moody (1837–1899) and Ira David Sankey (1840–1908) after the Civil War.

"Camptown Races" sheet music cover, c. 1850. Foster's songs were initially written to be performed in minstrel shows, which were an extremely popular form of entertainment in the mid-nineteenth century. BROWN UNIVERSITY LIBRARY

The lyrics of popular secular songs constitute a significant printed literature. By 1870 the number of songs registered for copyright each year approached the number of books. The songs' musical styles throughout the century contrast classical (often Italianate and opera-influenced) style with ethnic or national elements but the textual influences are far wider. The musicologist Jon Finson distinguishes among several strains: early songs of romance, still bearing British genteel traits; the plethora of lyrics on loss and death in mid-century; and the growing fascination with transportation and communications after the Civil War. Throughout the century songs articulated varying views of ethnicity (representations of American Indians and Western European immigrants) and race (stereotypes became more hard-edged during Reconstruction). Dale Cockrell has shown that the origins of the racial characterizations lie in the antebellum urban literature (both printed and performed) about social class struggles, popularized particularly through the rise of blackface minstrelsy.

One songwriter who stood at the juncture of these themes—romance, loss, technology, ethnic representation, and class—was Stephen Foster, who was the first American songwriter to rely on public sales of his songs for his livelihood. His first published song (at the age of eighteen) was "Open Thy Lattice Love" (1844) on a poem by the American poet and journalist George Pope Morris (1802–1864), a quintessential idealization of the distant object of desire, unapproachable except through music. Foster's first hit, "Oh! Susanna" (1847), with his own lyrics, contrasts the dangerously destructive power of electricity (the telegraph) and steam (riverboats and railroad engines) with white Americans' preoccupations with love, entertainment, and travel. Foster sharpened the irony by putting a banjo on his singer's knee and setting his words to a polka, the latest social-dance fashion just arrived from Europe.

Foster grew up in Scots-Irish genteel society in Pittsburgh, the urban industrial north. His representation of the South and southerners was entirely imagined, distilled from stories in nationally distributed domestic magazines to which his mother subscribed. Foster also drew on the first-person accounts of the bonded African American servants and laborers around the Foster household, of his mother, who grew up on a plantation in Maryland, and his father and next-older brother, both of whom participated in commercial trade along the Mississippi River to New Orleans. Foster wrote only two dozen songs about the South, all for minstrel performers, and it is largely those songs that sustained him financially, even though he wrote more than 280 songs, hymns, piano pieces, dances, and arrangements before his death in 1864.

His lyrics and music of love and loss, such as "Jeanie with the Light Brown Hair," "Gentle Annie," and "Beautiful Dreamer," which continue to epitomize antebellum sentimentality for the general public in the twenty-first century, were relative financial failures during Foster's lifetime. Public sales depended on mass media, yet Foster declined to promote himself or his music. Radio and television revived his sentimental songs in the twentieth century, but during his lifetime it was the theater—and in particular the minstrel stage—that brought his songs before the public.

THEATER

As popular culture developed in the United States, the theater held a central role as the forum through which ideas, phrases, iconic characters, and music were introduced. Nearly all theater involved music, from the single violin in traveling tent shows to the pit orchestras that offered preshow selections, entr'acte music, and scene music underscoring action, songs, and ballets during productions at the largest urban theaters.

Following the practice in productions of Shakespeare, many of the plays presented on American stages included songs, usually interpolated to suit the mood, but sometimes freshly composed for the occasion by the theater musicians. The newly written songs often distilled the essence of a character, as for example the "Hot Corn Girl" from the play of the same name (1853), a tearfully emotional depiction of the starving urchin that became iconic for the urban social welfare movement.

Even the strictly dramatic theaters had musical directors. Wallack's Theatre in New York, for example, engaged the city's foremost theater conductors, who hired the musicians, led the pit orchestra during performances, and chose or wrote the music for each production.

Americans created theatrical works across a full range of genres from plays with inserted incidental music and songs to grand opera—with completely original libretti and music. The plays were easier to create and cheaper to produce; they were thus the most ubiquitous. Among composers, John Hill Hewitt (1801–1890) perhaps best represents the full array in his eight works for the stage written between 1838 and 1879, ranging from plays to operettas. The editors of his collected works note that "he considered himself an artistic *littérateur* as well as composer [and] wrote his own lyrics and dialogue"(p. xviii).

The musical practices of underscoring dramatic scenes—an essential part of film and television in the twentieth century—were well established by the 1820s. Romance dramas adapted from novels were popular throughout the period. Many were staged as melodramas, plays in which music served both aesthetic and psychological functions in telling the story. Melodramas of Alexandre Dumas's novel *The Count of Monte Cristo* (1844–1845) appeared in New York as early as 1848 and became central to the careers of such notable actors as Charles Fechter (during the 1860s and 1870s) and James O'Neill (1880s on). Besides the usual theatrical overtures and entr'actes, the music for melodramas consisted of "melos," brief formulaic pieces timed to accompany the action of the script: sudden entrances, duels, poignant and untexted moments, and such cues as "hurry music" that accompanied chase scenes.

Theater and music helped shape public notions of ethnic difference. Melodramas on Indian themes appeared even before 1820. The musicologist Michael Pisani has identified at least thirty-five "Indian" plays with music that were performed between 1830 and 1850—and that was before the vogue generated by Henry Wadsworth Longfellow's *The Song of Hiawatha* (1855). Through these dramatic representations, American culture formed a sort of musical portraiture of Indians and developed notions of nationalism and exoticism.

Antebellum minstrelsy was arguably the most widespread genre of musical theater. It began as performed discourse over class issues, employing ethnic difference to heighten the contrasts. As the music historians Jon Finson and Dale Cockrell describe it, minstrelsy arose from both European and African carnival and "misrule" ritual that involved masking. George Washington Dixon (c. 1801–1861) used the blackface urban dandy character "Zip Coon" with silk hat, watch fob, and effete prose, to comment on social injustice in Boston and New York. Thomas Dartmouth "Daddy" Rice (1808–1860) portrayed the broken-down laborer in tatters, "Jim Crow." Through the 1840s minstrel performers such as George Christy (1827–1868) increasingly were known as "Ethiopian delineators" of stereotyped African American caricatures, and newspapers and magazines carried on a debate over the authenticity of their representations. The minstrel music and lyrics contained nothing from African American culture, beyond the instruments themselves. Not until Foster merged the sentimental parlor song with plantation themes in such songs as "Nelly Was a Lady" (1849), "Old Folks at Home" (1851), and "My Old Kentucky Home" (1852) did a new sympathetic and compassionate portrayal of slaves evolve, usually as the last segment of the minstrel show. These were the songs taken up by abolitionists, and they became mainstays of sympathetic black characters in the theater. As Frederick Douglass (1818–1895) told an abolitionist gathering in 1855,

> It would seem almost absurd to say it, considering the use that has been made of them, that we have allies in the Ethiopian songs . . . "Old Kentucky Home," and "Uncle Ned," can make the heart sad as well as merry, and can call forth a tear as well as a smile. They awaken the sympathies for the slave, in which anti-slavery principles take root, grow and flourish. (P. 329)

It was not until after the war that audiences reinterpreted such antebellum songs as representing a mythical, rural past, a nostalgic utopia.

The literary work by far the most influential on American musical theater of the time was Harriet Beecher Stowe's novel *Uncle Tom's Cabin*. Within months of its publication in book form (1852) stage versions were produced in New England and soon thereafter in towns and by touring companies throughout the northern states. Many composers wrote songs for the "Tom shows," ranging from minstrel-inspired stereotypes in the wild Topsy dances to angelic evocations of Little Eva. As in melodrama, music was deemed essential to the pathos of the stage productions.

Opera, the most complex combination of music and theater, developed from the ballad operas popular in the British colonies. Immigrant composers and playwrights from England and Ireland supplied the earliest works. One of the first by an American-born author and composer was *The Saw Mill* (first staged in New York City, 1824) by Micah Hawkins (1777–1825), on a theme of the American frontier (then upstate New York).

Italian opera—sometimes in English versions—was in vogue from Boston to Philadelphia from the 1820s onward. Classic European myths found in opera entered American literature and were reinforced in the public imagination. For instance, the Englishman Rophino Lacy (1795–1867) in 1830 adapted the music, libretto, and significant details of Gioacchino Rossini's opera *La Cenerentola* (1817) for London audiences. His version, *Cinderella,* was imported to the United States in 1831. The music (not all by Rossini) and such elements as a glass slipper in place of the magic bracelet remained staples of the opera stage into the 1870s.

The vogue for opera prompted American authors to try their hand. William Henry Fry (1813–1864), who covered the arts for his father's *Philadelphia National Gazette,* wrote what is acknowledged to be America's first grand opera, *Leonora* (Philadelphia, 1845). The libretto was by his brother, Joseph Reese Fry (1811–1865), who had cut his teeth on arranging English versions of Italian opera. Both words and music were considered by critics to be noble attempts at high American art, but in the end the Frys produced unsatisfying imitations of their European models.

The selection of American literary sources by immigrant composers changed the native composers' viewpoint. Luigi Arditi's (1822–1903) *La Spia* (premiered New York, 1856), based on James Fenimore Cooper's novel *The Spy* (1821), was the most successful. American composers eventually caught the idea. At least three operas from this period were based on the writings of Washington Irving (1783–1859). Two composers found appeal in the way Irving combined European literary style with subjects from the American rural frontier: the libretto of James Gaspard Maeder's *The Peri; or, The Enchanted Fountain* (1852) adapts Irving's *A History of Columbus;* and George Bristow's *Rip Van Winkle* (1855) elaborates the short story of the same title. Charles Edward Horne was alone in looking to Irving as a source for an exotic, rather than an American, theme: his *Ahmed al Kamel* (1846) is based on Irving's *Tales of the Alhambra.*

Bristow's opera, the first "grand opera" based on an American literary source, was received by even the harshest critics as a breakthrough. John Sullivan Dwight (1813–1893) of Boston, allied with the transcendentalists and spokesman for the highest standards of Germanic art, responded approvingly, "If we are ever to have any national operas, they must be based upon our own language; the unison of intelligible, vigorous and attractive plays with kindred music" (quoted in Kirk, p. 93).

The wide performance of European opera and the nascent American efforts in this genre inspired parody. Francis James Child (1825–1896), the Harvard graduate who documented the traditional oral ballads of the British isles ("the Child ballads"), revealed his equal familiarity with grand opera in his 1862 spoof *Il Pesceballo,* a pasticcio of opera airs to a libretto (in Italian) telling the old comic ballad of "one fishball."

The theatrical genre of burlesque, in which the nuances of intricate wordplay depended upon the audience's familiarity with popular literary and theatrical works and conventions, capitalized with particular glee on the minstrel and Indian themes. John Brougham's (1814–1880) *Po-Ca-Hon-Tas; or, The Gentle Savage* (1855), with music adapted in burlesque fashion by Maeder, is a prominent example. It burlesques and freely pirates contemporary works in all forms of popular theater from opera to minstrelsy.

Music from the full range of theatrical genres was also performed in the home. Sheet-music publications of opera arias and piano arrangements of operatic melodies were legion. Playwrights also turned out amateur or "parlor" dramas as popular entertainment for middle-class Americans from the time of the Civil War. The most prolific pen belonged to Alfred B. Sedgwick, whose "musical dualities" (two roles), "sketches," and "parlor operas" entail witty wordplay and story ideas and music clearly borrowed from European operettas and operas popular in the United States.

INSTRUMENTAL MUSIC

The antebellum period saw American art-music practices grow to become established on a wide scale, fueled by literary, social, and theological movements. The historian Richard Hooker has identified literary aesthetic rules that underlay musical practices in the eastern seaboard cities after 1820, noting that writers for nationally distributed music journals created a sort of "musical anxiety" about the absence of an authentically American music.

Among the first composers of symphonic works in America was Anthony Philip Heinrich (1781–1861),

A family singing at a piano. Engraving by Capewell and Kimmel, c. 1850. The piano was a fixture in any home that could afford one during the nineteenth century. It provided entertainment for the family and guests, and learning to play was considered a mark of refinement for girls and young women. MARY EVANS PICTURE LIBRARY

the self-styled "Beethoven of America," many of whose symphonies are on Indian themes. He encountered Native Americans while living in a log cabin in Kentucky beginning in 1817. The score of his first symphony (1831, revised 1855) contains a note crediting John McIntosh's *Origin of the North American Indians* for

the epic tales that form the symphony's program. The magazine *Criterion* (23 May 1856) compared him to the artist George Catlin, painting on "the music staff instead of the canvas, and composing laments, symphonies, dirges, and war-songs, on the most intensely Indian subjects" (quoted in Maust, p. 309).

The Indian theme remained a source of distinctly American character for symphonic composers well into the twentieth century. The theme was given new breath by Henry Wadsworth Longfellow's epic poem *The Song of Hiawatha* when it appeared in 1855. The theater composer Robert Stoepel, who also wrote evocative music for the concert hall, composed his "Hiawatha: An Indian Symphony" in 1859.

American audiences approached the performances of even the most abstract concert music through a context shaped largely by their experience of America's authors. Notions of social class and dress, family and gender roles, ethnicity and identity, and national culture that were articulated and debated in American literature were also the frameworks through which even purely instrumental music was understood and reviewed in public discourse. Music and literature were intimately bound up with one another throughout this formative period for American culture.

See also Satire, Burlesque, and Parody; *The Song of Hiawatha;* Theater

BIBLIOGRAPHY
Primary Works

Cockrell, Dale, ed. *Pasticcio and Temperance Plays in America: Il Pesceballo (1862) and Ten Nights in a Bar-Room (1890).* Vol. 8 of *Nineteenth-Century American Musical Theater.* New York: Garland, 1994.

Douglass, Frederick. "The Anti-Slavery Movement, Lecture Delivered before the Rochester [New York] Ladies' Anti-Slavery Society, March 19, 1855." In *Frederick Douglass: Selected Speeches and Writings,* edited by Philip S. Foner and Yuval Taylor, pp. 311–331. Chicago: Lawrence Hill Books, 1999.

Fechter, Charles. *Later Melodrama in America: Monte Cristo.* Edited by Anne Dhu McLucas. Vol. 4 of *Nineteenth-Century American Musical Theater.* New York: Garland, 1994.

Hewitt, John Hill. *The Collected Works of John Hill Hewitt.* Edited by N. Lee Orr and Lynn Wood Bertrand. Vol. 6 of *Nineteenth-Century American Musical Theater.* New York: Garland, 1994.

Rossini, Gioacchino. *Italian Opera in English: Cinderella (1831): Adapted by M. Rophino Lacy from Gioacchino Rossini's "La Cenerentola."* Edited by John Graziano. Vol. 3 of *Nineteenth-Century American Musical Theater.* New York: Garland, 1994.

Sedgwick, Alfred B. *The Collected Works of Alfred B. Sedgwick.* Edited by Michael Meckna. Vol. 7 of *Nineteenth-Century American Musical Theater.* New York: Garland, 1994.

Secondary Works

Atkinson, Colin B. "Changing Attitudes to Death: Nineteenth-Century Parlour Songs as Consolation Literature." *Canadian Review of American Studies* 23, no. 2 (1993): 79–100.

Austin, William W. *"Susanna," "Jeanie," and "The Old Folks at Home": The Songs of Stephen C. Foster from His Time to Ours.* 2nd ed. Urbana: University of Illinois Press, 1987.

Brooks, William. "*Pocahontas:* Her Life and Times." *American Music* 2, no. 4 (1984): 19–48.

Cockrell, Dale. *Demons of Disorder: Early Blackface Musicians and Their World.* Cambridge, U.K.: Cambridge University Press, 1997.

Finson, Jon W. *The Voices That Are Gone: Themes in Nineteenth-Century American Popular Song.* New York: Oxford University Press, 1994.

Hamm, Charles. *Yesterdays: Popular Song in America.* New York: Norton, 1979.

Hooker, Richard. "The Invention of American Musical Culture: Meaning, Criticism, and Musical Acculturation in Antebellum America." In *Keeping Score: Music, Disciplinarity, Culture,* edited by David Schwarz et al., pp. 107–126. Charlottesville: University Press of Virginia, 1997.

Kirk, Elise K. *American Opera.* Urbana: University of Illinois Press, 2001.

Maust, Wilbur R. "The American Indian in the Orchestral Music of Anthony Philip Heinrich." In *Music East and West: Essays in Honor of Walter Kaufmann,* edited by Thomas Noblitt, pp. 309–325. New York: Pendragon, 1981.

Picker, John M. "'Red War Is My Song': Whitman, Higginson, and Civil War Music." In *Walt Whitman and Modern Music: War, Desire, and the Trials of Nationhood,* edited by Lawrence Kramer, pp. 1–23. New York: Garland, 2000.

Pisani, Michael V. "'I'm an Indian Too': Creating Native American Identities in Nineteenth- and Early-Twentieth-Century Music." In *The Exotic in Western Music,* edited by Jonathan Bellman, pp. 218–257. Boston: Northeastern University Press, 1998.

Root, Deane L. *American Popular Stage Music 1860–1880.* Ann Arbor, Mich.: UMI Research Press, 1981.

Sullivan, Jack. *New World Symphonies: How American Culture Changed European Music.* New Haven, Conn.: Yale University Press, 1999.

Thomas, Jean Waters. "Music of the Great Sanitary Fairs: Culture and Charity in the American Civil War." Ph.D. diss., University of Pittsburgh, 1989.

Deane L. Root

NARRATIVE OF THE LIFE OF DAVID CROCKETT OF THE STATE OF TENNESSEE

Authored in 1834 by David Crockett (1786–1836), with some editorial assistance from his congressional colleague from Kentucky, Thomas Chilton, the *Narrative of the Life of David Crockett of the State of Tennessee* is one of the most significant documents of the American pioneer experience in the first half of the nineteenth century. It describes the author's life from his first memories in eastern Tennessee through his progressive moves westward, his participation in the Creek War, his hunting experiences, and his political service in the Tennessee House of Representatives and the U.S. Congress. The book closes with Crockett's reelection to his final term in Congress (1833–1835), shortly before his fateful journey to Texas and his death at the Alamo in 1836.

CULTURAL AND LITERARY SIGNIFICANCE

Crockett himself had only limited schooling, and the literary influences on his *Narrative* were probably few, possibly including Benjamin Franklin's autobiography (which had first appeared in English in 1793) and the comic political commentary of Seba Smith's fictional "Jack Downing" letters, published in the *Portland (Maine) Courier* in the early 1830s. However, the greatest immediate influence and inspiration was the 1833 biography of Crockett written anonymously by James Strange French (1807–1886), *Life and Adventures of Colonel David Crockett of West Tennessee* (later published as *Sketches and Eccentricities of Colonel David Crockett of West Tennessee*). In a preface to his own *Narrative,* Crockett takes offense at his characterization in the biography and explains that his autobiography will provide a more accurate picture of himself. However, he must have known French and actively provided information for the book, for *Life and Adventures* provides many accurate details of Crockett's life, which in many cases is seconded by Crockett's own account in style as well as in substance. In several cases, an understanding of anecdotes related in the *Narrative* requires a prior reading of *Life and Adventures.*

Crockett's *Narrative* was very popular throughout America and England and greatly extended his multifaceted reputation as a frontiersman, bear hunter, Indian fighter, and politician, a reputation that had been previously established by French's book and by James Kirke Paulding's 1831 play, *Lion of the West,* about an eccentric and outspoken character generally assumed to have been Crockett.

The *Narrative,* which remains still widely available, is a masterpiece of frontier literature. It is a rare account of the western experience, made even more significant by the lively style of the narration, the colorful use of language, and the comic perspective taken throughout much of the book. Comparable works of the era include Augustus Baldwin Longstreet's *Georgia Scenes* (1835) and Joseph G. Baldwin's *Flush Times in Alabama and Mississippi* (1853); however, these latter two works include separate stories largely based upon second-person observations of frontier life by educated authors rather than the first-person account provided by Crockett.

Davy Crockett. Engraving by Charles Gilbert Stuart after the painting by J. G. Chapman, 1839. THE LIBRARY OF CONGRESS

Crockett provides rare insights into the human experience on the frontier as he describes being hired out as a child to neighbors by his father for labor; his two-and-a-half-year odyssey after running away from home at age thirteen, including his virtual kidnapping and daring escape in deep snow; his frequent relocations to emerging western frontier lands; and his near-death experiences from malaria, combat with Indians, starvation, freezing, and drowning. He describes in some detail his experiences in the Creek War as well as his unorthodox political campaigning style and his experiences in Congress as an opponent of President Andrew Jackson.

Some critics complain that the book lacks traditional plot and theme development, too often intrudes on the narrative with partisan invective against Jackson, and contains events that seem tedious or commonplace. However, these apparent flaws also serve to provide the book with its appearance of authenticity. Many expressions found in the book appear to be original, or at least new in literature, giving the book a feeling of freshness and novelty for the time. For example, Crockett describes in detail an example of his dogs "barking up the wrong tree," an expression that dates back only to the time of the *Narrative*. Some other expressions such as "neck or nothing" (p. 198), "stand up to [the] rack, fodder or no fodder" (p. 61), and "too close for comfort" (p. 164) found early literary appearances in the *Narrative*, as did Crockett's motto: "Be always sure you're right—then go ahead!"

Crockett employed a spare, realistic prose style that anticipated the later realism movement in fiction. This style generally was uncommon in popular fiction of the period, but it is similar to that of first-person accounts of other frontier authors of the period—for example, Black Hawk's 1833 autobiography or Elias Darnell's 1813 account of the battle of the Raisin River (Michigan) of the War of 1812. However, Crockett's stories contain an element of humor not found in those other works. Crockett's gift for storytelling may have arisen from his early years growing up in his father's eastern Tennessee tavern. An oral reading of Crockett anecdotes reveals the *Narrative*'s debt to the storytelling tradition, with its directness and the lively immediacy of its prose.

The *Narrative* has often been characterized as containing extensive use of hyperbole, and the author's name has been firmly linked to the "tall tale" of American frontier tradition. Although the *Narrative* does contain effusive uses of language, Crockett in fact omitted many of the most extravagant "half horse, half alligator" anecdotes from French's *Life and Adventures*, in which he was presented as a figure known for startling bears to death, "grinning" raccoons out of trees (and in one case, mistakenly grinning the bark off a tree), and being offered a commission to mount the Alleghenies and wring the tail off Halley's Comet. In the preface to his book, Crockett lamented the "great injustice" done him by the author of the previous work (p. 3). Since Crockett several times in the *Narrative* mentions the possibility of his running for president of the United States, it is possible that he wished to present himself as a less-extravagant character than that portrayed by French.

Actually, the *Narrative* overall may be more notable for its directness, simplicity, and humorous understatement than for its use of hyperbole. For example, Crockett describes a time when he had fallen ill with malaria, alone on a trace on the Alabama frontier, and he was met by some Indians, who signed to him that he would soon die: "a thing," Crockett recounts, "I was confoundedly afraid of myself"

(p. 129). With the help of the Indians and a pioneer family, Crockett survives this ordeal; he recovers and finally returns home to his family, where he finds that he was reported to have died and been buried. Crockett comments, "I know'd this was a whapper of a lie, as soon as I heard it" (p. 132). Another example of comic understatement is found in Crockett's description of his first congressional defeat, by two votes: "I have always believed that many other things had been as fairly done as that same count" (p. 173).

Crockett also provided some stark realism in his recounting of events he witnessed during the Creek Indian War. These passages have been thought by some to represent Crockett's indifference to the plight of American Indians; however, according to accounts by contemporaries who knew Crockett, these stories were intended to demonstrate the brutal realities of war, and in fact much of the bitterness he expressed concerning the U.S. government's treatment of the Indians may have been deleted at the advice of his editors. This latter view is also supported by Crockett's strong opposition to the Jackson-supported legislation to remove Indians from eastern lands.

Crockett's *Narrative* developed themes that, in conjunction with the stories of, for example, Augustus Baldwin Longstreet, Joseph G. Baldwin, and Johnson Jones Hooper, provided a rich legacy of frontier humor, expanded upon years later by Bret Harte and Mark Twain. Crockett's bear-hunting stories anticipated Thomas Bangs Thorpe's celebrated short story "Big Bear of Arkansas" (1841) and Henry Clay Lewis's "The Indefatigable Bear Hunter" (1850). The latter story describes a frontier protagonist who presents an interesting parallel to Captain Ahab in Herman Melville's (1819–1891) 1851 novel, *Moby-Dick*, in that Lewis's protagonist loses a leg to an encounter with an enormous bear, falls into deep depression during recovery, and sets out on a mission, on his new wooden leg, to become America's greatest bear hunter. As such, Crockett's *Narrative* can be seen as a substantial component of an emerging and important new American literature.

AUTHENTICITY OF THE *NARRATIVE*

Scholars have debated whether in fact Crockett was the primary contributor to his autobiography. This debate has largely centered on the arguments that the manuscript was submitted to the publisher in the handwriting of Thomas Chilton and contained peculiarities of spelling and grammar not found in Crockett's letters to friends, family, and constituents. Crockett maintained, however, that Chilton had merely edited his original manuscript for spelling and grammar. Furthermore, many of the anecdotes, attitudes, expressions, and overall style found in the *Narrative* in fact do resemble language that can be found in Crockett letters and speeches in Congress. Crockett himself claimed primary authorship for the work (he apparently did not privately claim primary authorship for other works published in his name), and he kept his family informed of his progress during the writing of the book.

Much of the debate regarding the authenticity of the *Narrative* reflects the claims of a proposed literary-political conspiracy first put forth in 1927 by Vernon Louis Parrington in his influential Pulitzer Prize–winning work, *Main Currents in American Thought*. This theory was further developed in 1956 by James Shackford, Crockett's principal biographer, and it has been restated by more recent biographers until the early twenty-first century.

According to this theory, Crockett's fame was largely manufactured by an eastern Whig elite who wished to promote him as a frontier-character alternative to Andrew Jackson and the Democrats. Part of this promotion effort included the production of literary works, one of which was the *Narrative*. (French's earlier biography was also said to have been ghostwritten by the clerk of the U.S. House of Representatives, Mathew St. Clair Clarke.) Skeptics suggest that Crockett, supposedly an ignorant, simpleminded frontiersman, would have been incapable of writing such a work himself and that the writing must have undertaken by Thomas Chilton.

Little hard evidence is provided in support of this theory, however, which appears to rest mainly on the notion that if Crockett opposed the supposedly proletarian Jacksonian Democrats, he must have been somehow duped by wealthy eastern interests. However, poor and middle-class loyalties of the time were approximately equally divided between Democrat and Whig. And in fact, Crockett had reason to distrust Jackson and the Democrats, who opposed him on land reform, on internal improvements to his district, and on his support for the national Bank of the United States and whose Indian removal bill Crockett opposed, referring to it in the *Narrative* as a "wicked, unjust measure" (p. 206). Furthermore, Jackson Democrats had campaigned against Crockett since at least 1825.

It is clear that Thomas Chilton served as a kind of technical editor of the work and may in some cases have assisted in more significant matters of style and substance. It is also true that the Whigs welcomed an authentic frontier character who opposed Jackson, and Whigs did help sponsor a Crockett tour of the eastern states in 1834. In spite of these influences, however, there is little substantive reason to believe that the *Narrative* is not largely Crockett's own work.

PROTAGONIST AS FRONTIER HERO

In the *Narrative*, Crockett elaborated upon a uniquely American tradition of the frontier hero, which appealed to the public's interest in finding authentic American characters and its fascination with the western frontier. Life on the frontier was first related to eastern readers in first-person accounts and in John Filson's 1784 "autobiography" of Daniel Boone, whose rescue of his daughter from Indians inspired events related in James Fenimore Cooper's (1789–1951) *Last of the Mohicans* (1826). Frontier heroes as depicted in Cooper's Leatherstocking Tales, Crockett's *Narrative*, and Timothy Flint's 1833 biography of Boone inspired tales of colorful frontier characters drawn from this tradition in popular fictional dime novels produced throughout the nineteenth century. Frontier heroes and characters in the Crockett mold are also found in Robert Montgomery Bird's *Nick of the Woods* (1837) and James S. French's *Elkswatawa* (1836). In Herman Melville's *The Confidence-Man: His Masquerade* (1857), the frontiersman as hero, and antihero, is presented in a more literary context.

The *Narrative* also provided a direct influence on the Crockett almanacs, the first of which appeared during Crockett's lifetime in 1835 and which continued through at least forty-four issues until 1856. Although almanacs had been published in America since the seventeenth century, the Crockett almanacs focused on colorful tales of wild animals and hunting, often adding comic hyperbole in the tall tale tradition, for example, in comic encounters between "Davy" Crockett and the keelboat man Mike Fink. Through these almanacs and other elements of the frontier literary tradition, inspired in part by Crockett's *Narrative*, the frontier hero—in equal parts boastful, comically unsophisticated, honest, moral, and courageous—emerged as a significant figure in American literature and popular culture throughout the nineteenth and twentieth centuries and have continued to appear in western novels and films even into the twenty-first century.

See also Borders; Folklore; Humor; Tall Tales

BIBLIOGRAPHY

Primary Work

Crockett, David. *A Narrative of the Life of David Crockett of the State of Tennessee*. 1834. Knoxville: University of Tennessee Press, 1973. Facsimile edition, annotated and with an introduction by James A. Shackford and Stanley J. Folmsbee.

Secondary Works

Arpad, Joseph, ed. "Introduction." In *A Narrative of the Life of David Crockett*, by David Crockett. New Haven, Conn.: College and University Press, 1972.

Derr, Mark. *The Frontiersman: The Real Life and the Many Legends of Davy Crockett*. New York: Morrow, 1993.

Hauck, Richard Boyd. *Davy Crockett: A Handbook*. Lincoln: University of Nebraska Press, 1986.

Lofaro, Michael A., ed. *Davy Crockett: The Man, the Legend, the Legacy, 1786–1986*. Knoxville: University of Tennessee Press, 1985.

Parrington, Vernon Louis. *Main Currents in American Thought*. New York: Harcourt, Brace, 1927.

Scruggs, Thomas E. "Davy Crockett and the Thieves of Jericho: An Analysis of the Shackford-Parrington Conspiracy Theory." *Journal of the Early Republic* 19 (1999): 481–498.

Shackford, James Atkins. *David Crockett: The Man and the Legend*. 1956. Chapel Hill: University of North Carolina Press, 1986.

Thomas E. Scruggs

NARRATIVE OF THE LIFE OF FREDERICK DOUGLASS

The author of the most influential African American autobiography of his era rebelled against his enslavement in the South and rose through the ranks of the American antislavery movement in the North to become the most electrifying speaker and compelling writer produced by black America in the nineteenth century. With the publication of the *Narrative of the Life of Frederick Douglass, an American Slave, Written by Himself* in June 1845, Frederick Douglass (1818–1895) became an international sensation at the age of twenty-seven. Within five years of its publication, Douglass's *Narrative* had become a best-seller, with an estimated thirty thousand copies in print by 1850. The *Narrative*'s sales dwarfed the combined sales of such mid-nineteenth-century American literary classics as Herman Melville's *Moby-Dick* (1851), Henry David Thoreau's *Walden* (1854), and Walt Whitman's *Leaves of Grass* (1855) during the first five years of their publication. The success of the *Narrative* spurred its author's enlistment into the antislavery literary wars, where he became black America's most effective exponent. For a half century after the appearance of his *Narrative*, Douglass enjoyed fame and endured controversy as a newspaper editor, the author of three more autobiographies, a professional orator, a U.S. government official and diplomat, and a tireless civil rights agitator, all predicated on the inspiring self-image that he fashioned in the pages of his first and best-known book, the *Narrative of the Life of Frederick Douglass*. In the late twentieth century, Douglass's *Narrative* joined the canon of American literature, having been recognized as one of the most artful and influential autobiographies of the nineteenth century.

Frontispiece drawing of Frederick Douglass. From the first edition of *Narrative of the Life of Frederick Douglass*, 1845. SPECIAL COLLECTIONS LIBRARY, UNIVERSITY OF MICHIGAN

DOUGLASS'S ORIGINS IN SLAVERY

Frederick Douglass was born a slave on Maryland's Eastern Shore sometime in February 1818, according to his master's property book. Frederick's mother was Harriet Bailey, about whom he knew little other than that she enjoyed the rare distinction of being able to read. Douglass was never able to trace his paternity, though he speculated in his *Narrative* that Aaron Anthony, his master, had been his father. Growing up under the care of his grandmother, Betsy Bailey, Frederick had little chance to learn more about the world beyond the obscure backwater where he was born. But in 1826 he was selected by his master's son-in-law, Thomas Auld, to go to Baltimore, where Frederick spent five years as a servant in the home of Auld's brother, Hugh. Hugh Auld's wife Sophia treated the bright and engaging slave boy with unusual kindness, giving reading lessons to Frederick until her husband forbade them. Ignoring Hugh Auld's dictates, Frederick took his first steps toward freedom and an eventual literary career by teaching himself to read and write.

In 1833 a quarrel between the Auld brothers brought Frederick, now a self-willed teenager, back to his home in St. Michaels, Maryland, where Thomas Auld, who had inherited Frederick, took charge of him. Provoked by the youth's lack of respect, Thomas Auld hired him out to Edward Covey, a local farmer and well-known slave breaker, in January 1834. After eight months of unstinting labor and repeated whippings, the desperate sixteen-year-old fought back. His forcible resistance unnerved Covey, compelling him to back down. In his *Narrative,* Douglass portrayed his struggle with Covey as "the turning-point in my career as a slave. It rekindled the few expiring embers of freedom, and revived within me a sense of my own manhood. It recalled the departed self-confidence, and inspired me again with a determination to be free" (p. 69). Douglass's portrayal of his triumph over Covey has become one of the most celebrated scenes in all of African American literature.

In the spring of 1836, after Frederick tried and failed to escape from slavery, Thomas Auld sent him back to Baltimore to learn the caulking trade on the city's docks. Restless and resentful of Hugh Auld's supervision, Frederick enlisted the aid of his future spouse, Anna Murray, in a scheme by which he would masquerade as a free black merchant sailor and board a northbound train from Baltimore to Wilmington, Delaware. On 3 September 1838 the young man made his escape. Within a month of his arrival in the North, Frederick and Anna were married and living in New Bedford, Massachusetts, as Mr. and Mrs. Frederick Douglass, the newly adopted last name having been recommended by a friend in New Bedford's thriving African American community. The friend who recommended Douglass to the runaway slave had been reading Sir Walter Scott's *The Lady of the Lake.*

Less than three years later, officials of the American Anti-Slavery Society, impressed by Douglass's preaching to a black congregation in New Bedford, invited the eloquent young man to speak at an antislavery rally in Nantucket, Connecticut. There Douglass recalled his experience as a slave so powerfully and persuasively that William Lloyd Garrison (1805–1879), the leading antislavery activist in America, declared (as he stated in his preface to Douglass's *Narrative*) that "Patrick Henry, of revolutionary fame, never made a speech more eloquent in the cause of liberty, than the one [Garrison heard] from the lips of that hunted fugitive" (p. 24), Frederick Douglass. Immediately the New Bedford wharf worker found himself recruited into the ranks of the American Anti-Slavery's Society's corps of full-time lecturers.

DOUGLASS AND THE SLAVE NARRATIVE

The next three years on the antislavery platform gave Douglass, who never had a day of formal schooling in his life, the practical lessons in rhetoric and self-representation before an audience that were crucial to his decision in 1844 to undertake the writing of his own life story. The genre Douglass chose for his literary debut, the fugitive slave narrative, was well established in England and the United States, though not entirely reputable because of frequent allegations that such narratives were ghostwritten and exaggerated by white abolitionists. A half century earlier the life stories of African-born slaves such as James Gronniosaw and Olaudah Equiano had begun to appear in Great Britain. In addition to attracting substantial attention and sales abroad, *The Interesting Narrative of the Life of Olaudah Equiano, or Gustavus Vassa, the African* (1789) went through multiple reprint editions in the early United States, indicating a receptive audience for such writing in colonial North America and the early Republic. Not until the 1830s, however, did the antislavery movement in the United States seek purposefully to enlist the talents and energies of black American writers in a national movement to extirpate slavery from the so-called land of the free.

Increasingly aggressive in its attacks on slavery in the late 1830s, the American antislavery press decided to seek out narratives by fugitive slaves who could document convincingly what they had experienced or witnessed in the South. As Theodore Dwight (1796–1866), secretary of the American Anti-Slavery Society, observed in an 1837 letter, "The north is so blinded it will not *believe* what we [abolitionists] say about slavery," but "facts and testimony as to the actual condition of the Slaves," Dwight asserted, "would thrill the land with Horror" (Andrews, *To Tell a Free Story,* p. 62). One of the founding texts of the fugitive slave narrative, *A Narrative of the Adventures and Escape of Moses Roper, from American Slavery* (1837), shocked its readers with graphic depictions of slavery's atrocities as Roper had experienced them. Roper's suspenseful accounts of his numerous attempts to escape followed by his ultimately successful flight to England guaranteed wide sales in English and American editions. A year after Roper's story came out, the *Narrative of James Williams, an American Slave, Who Was for Several Years a Driver on a Cotton Plantation in Alabama* appeared in Boston and New York, transcribed by the renowned antislavery poet John Greenleaf Whittier (1807–1892) and published by the American Anti-Slavery Society. Williams's *Narrative,* however, came under fire from proslavery critics who claimed the text was riddled with errors and untraceable references. Apprehensive that such challenges could discredit the growing effort to mobilize the firsthand testimony of fugitive slaves against slavery, the American Anti-Slavery Society withdrew the *Narrative of James Williams* from circulation.

Aware of the potential of the slave narrative to combat proslavery propaganda, Douglass had several motives in contributing to this relatively new form of American autobiography. Having heard doubts expressed about whether someone as articulate and knowledgeable as he could have ever been held in bondage, Douglass decided that issuing his own autobiography, in which he documented as many of the facts of his life as he could, would help to silence his critics. Unlike many of his predecessors in the slave narrative, including James Williams (b. 1805), Douglass was determined to write his own story instead of asking a white person, even someone as respected as Whittier, to transcribe it from his dictation. Douglass knew that a subtitle, "Written by Himself," featured on the title page of his *Narrative* would testify convincingly to the intellectual capacity of black people, even those who had been enslaved, to compose and represent themselves in language on a par with any white American writer. Even the presence of his autograph under the likeness of himself on the frontispiece of his *Narrative* bore political significance. By demonstrating that a former slave could read, write, and represent himself through authorship, Douglass's *Narrative* shattered the contention of many who tried to justify slavery by claiming that African-descended people lacked the intellectual ability to function proficiently in the world of letters.

Although many African Americans published narratives of their enslavement and freedom after Douglass, the *Narrative of the Life of Frederick Douglass* is generally considered the epitome of the pre–Civil War fugitive slave narrative. Priced at fifty cents a copy (about $8.50 in the early twenty-first century), the *Narrative*'s first printing of five thousand sold out in four months. To satisfy demand, four additional reprintings of two thousand copies each were brought out within a year. Editions appeared in England and Ireland. In 1846 a Dutch translation and in 1848 a French translation of the *Narrative* helped spread Douglass's fame on the European Continent. Positive reviews comparing Douglass's style to that of classic British writers John Bunyan and Daniel Defoe spurred sales. So did complimentary notices in prominent newspapers by such noted American writers as the transcendentalist and feminist reformer Margaret Fuller (1810–1850), who stated in the *New York Tribune* (1845) that she had never read a narrative "more simple, true, coherent, and warm with genuine feeling." The *London Spectator* called the *Narrative* a "singular book," striking because its denunciation of slavery rested not on the institution's physical cruelties but on "the brutish degradation to which the mind of the slave is reduced" (29 November 1945).

The self-consciousness of the writing in the *Narrative* attests to Douglass's determination to make his story not merely an exposé of the evils of slavery but also an exploration of the mind of a slave aspiring to freedom. The key to the originality and import of Douglass's rendition of his life, in contrast to that of most other fugitive slave narrators, is his emphasis on the psychological and intellectual struggle that he waged against slavery from his early childhood on Maryland's Eastern Shore. The *Narrative* recounts Douglass's boyhood as a series of challenges to white authorities intent on preventing him from achieving knowledge of himself and his relationship to the outside world. Resistance to slavery takes the form of an early clandestine pursuit of literacy. Armed with the power to read and write, the young slave graduates to a culminating physical rebellion against the slave breaker, Edward Covey, who symbolizes the ultimate physical tyranny of slavery. Douglass's reputation as a fighter gives him a leadership role in his local slave community, which he uses to teach other slaves to read and then to engineer a runaway plot. The first attempt for freedom fails, but a second try proves successful, thereby reinforcing the image Douglass gives himself in the *Narrative* as a man of indomitable determination to be free.

In the last chapter of the *Narrative*, Douglass recounts his marriage, his integration into a new life of economic independence and self-sufficiency in the North, and his discovery of an intellectually and spiritually self-validating vocation as a speaker for the American Anti-Slavery Society. Although the *Narrative* ends modestly, with Douglass inviting others to assess the achievements of his relatively short career as an antislavery lecturer, the cumulative effect of reading Douglass's entire life is to see the *Narrative* as a great American success story. This, no doubt, was one reason for the favorable reception the *Narrative* enjoyed. While it indicted slavery in the South, it presented the escaped slave in the North as a productive, respectable, and progressive member of American society.

MAJOR THEMES OF THE *NARRATIVE*

Like most slave narrators, Douglass knew that the majority of his potential audience was whites in the North, most of them ignorant of slavery and few committed to its abolition. To convince his readers of the injustice of slavery, Douglass had to revise their notions of what slavery was actually like. To change white assumptions about slavery as an institution, Douglass

THE OPENING SENTENCES OF THE 1845 *NARRATIVE*

In these opening lines of his Narrative, *Douglass introduces himself as a seeker of liberating knowledge about himself from his early childhood.*

I was born in Tuckahoe, near Hillsborough, and about twelve miles from Easton, in Talbot county, Maryland. I have no accurate knowledge of my age, never having seen any authentic record containing it. By far the larger part of the slaves know as little of their ages as horses know of theirs, and it is the wish of most masters within my knowledge to keep their slaves thus ignorant. I do not remember to have ever met a slave who could tell of his birthday. They seldom come nearer to it than planting-time, harvest-time, cherry-time, spring-time, or fall-time. A want of information concerning my own was a source of unhappiness to me even during childhood. The white children could tell their ages. I could not tell why I ought to be deprived of the same privilege. I was not allowed to make any inquiries of my master concerning it. He deemed all such inquiries on the part of a slave improper and impertinent, and evidence of a restless spirit.

Douglass, *Narrative of the Life of Frederick Douglass*, p. 31.

attacked stereotypical white attitudes toward black people as subhuman, a race fit only for slavery. Although he included sympathetic and complimentary portraits of several fellow-slaves in the *Narrative*, Douglass's brief in favor of the full humanity and dignity of black people rested primarily on the way he represented himself. The *Narrative* says little about Douglass's family, friends, or mentors in slavery. The focus is predominantly on Douglass's radical individuality and the process by which he became the man who could no longer be enslaved. The key, therefore, to Douglass's protest against slavery in the *Narrative* is the manner in which the author portrays himself as an exemplary black individual, the antithesis of everything considered slavish. By fashioning his *Narrative* into the story of the evolution of his own sense of indomitable selfhood, Douglass aimed to do two things: denounce the

principle and practice of human bondage while proving simultaneously the capacity of black people, personified by himself, for freedom and citizenship.

Knowing that the main reason his story would be read was because it revealed slavery in the South to white readers in the North, Douglass focused a good deal of his *Narrative*'s attention on the nature of slavery itself, the major theme of the early chapters of the book. Douglass's purpose was to debunk myths of slavery that claimed it was both an economic necessity and a morally defensible institution. Instead of myths espoused by slaveholders and their defenders, Douglass offers facts based on his own personal experience. With as much specificity about names and dates as he could muster, Douglass details the daily lives of slaves on the plantations where he lived, noting memorable instances of physical cruelty, such as the murder of William Demby by the overseer Mr. Gore and the terrible whipping of Douglass's aunt, Hester Bailey, by Aaron Anthony, Douglass's master. Although such atrocities were widely publicized in slave narratives, Douglass's story is distinctive for downplaying cruelties suffered by the author himself. Instead of beatings, Douglass recalls various forms of deprivation, some physical, such as shortages of food and clothing, but more often emotional and psychological, including denial of access to his mother and the withholding of information about when he was born.

The *Narrative* begins tellingly with the author's admission that, unlike most autobiographers, he cannot give the reader his birthday because his master "deemed all such inquiries on the part of a slave improper and impertinent, and evidence of a restless spirit" (p. 31). Thus from the first paragraph of his story, Douglass puts his reader on notice that slavery failed in its attempt to deny him the individuality that a birthday commonly gives every man and woman. Ironically the effort to deny him a sense of self elicited from him a "restless spirit" (p. 31) that demanded to know what he, as a slave, had been denied. This restless, searching spirit of inquiry characterizes Douglass throughout his story, driving him to become the individual who ultimately would triumph over slavery and tell the story of that triumph to the nation.

The story of Douglass's youth is predicated on an intellectual quest—for knowledge and the means of gaining it, literacy—that anticipates his eventual physical quest from enslavement to freedom. As a boy Douglass learns the importance of knowledge to a slave when he overhears Hugh Auld chastise his wife Sophia for teaching a slave to read. Once his Baltimore master acknowledges the effect of reading on a slave—"It would forever unfit him to be a slave" (p. 49)—the slave boy undergoes a kind of epiphany, realizing that ignorance was the source of "the white man's power to enslave the black man. . . . From that moment, I understood the pathway from slavery to freedom" (p. 48). Literacy becomes the pathway from slavery to freedom.

By teaching himself to read, the slave boy not yet ten years old makes his first conscious act of rebellion against his master. In the process he begins to think for himself, the first stage in becoming an independent self. Once the slave boy makes his commitment to literacy, a second major theme moves to the center of the *Narrative,* the process by which the slave realizes and exercises his sense of individual selfhood.

Although laying claim to selfhood would seem the most natural of acts for any autobiographer, whose writing is expected to chronicle the growth of an individual self, an African American in Douglass's time, particularly one who had been born a slave, made an inevitably political statement when he or she undertook to write a personal narrative. Mid-nineteenth-century America still heard much debate over whether African Americans deserved even to be called people. The Constitution of the United States did not consider the millions of slaves living in the South to be people. U.S. law ruled that slaves were chattel, that is, that they were property, having no more right to their own persons than a horse or a table. Property, since it could not be human, could not lay claim to human rights or human dignity, for the fundamental basis of such dignity, the belief in the unique selfhood of every human being, had no application to slaves.

The aim of the *Narrative* was to demonstrate the unique selfhood of the author so as to lay the groundwork for his eventual claim to full manhood. The *Narrative* is structured by moments of intense revelation that dramatize Douglass's evolving sense of selfhood. Through the first half of his *Narrative,* Douglass stresses the interconnectedness of selfhood and literacy. Reading breeds thinking, which leads to brooding about the differences between the life he lives as a slave and the world of freedom he discovers by peering into newspapers and books. Reading teaches him what abolitionism is, spurring in the teenage slave not only his latent desire to be free but fantasies about how he might actually attain his liberty. But the more pronounced Douglass's consciousness of himself as unjustly enslaved grew, the more the authorities who claimed him as their property—Thomas Auld, especially—distrusted him and sought to quash his recalcitrance and incipient rebellion. In the famous tenth chapter of the *Narrative,* Douglass's developing sense of selfhood expresses itself in open, violent defiance of white power when he successfully throttles Edward Covey. This victory over the slave breaker is the "turning-point" in Douglass's life as a slave because it restored to him a liberating "sense of my own manhood" (p. 69).

The last chapters of Douglass's *Narrative* bring out the third major theme of the story, the kind of "manhood" Douglass sought and earned both in slavery and freedom. Knowing that plenty of white readers would be disturbed by the association of violence and black masculinity that emerges in the battle with Covey, Douglass is careful in the *Narrative* to point out that his sense of manhood depended not on beating his oppressor but on preventing that oppressor from beating him. Douglass recounts the events leading up to the fight with Covey so as to argue that he turned to violence only as a last resort, when every other means of defending himself against the tyrannical slave breaker had failed. For Douglass, reclaiming his manhood entails, almost literally in the fight with Covey, standing up for himself and demanding his human rights not to be abused physically and humiliated psychologically.

After the battle with Covey, Douglass shows that his revived sense of manhood found expression in community building, namely, the establishment of a clandestine Sabbath school in which the seventeen-year-old taught other slaves to read. His commitment to his fellow slaves impels him to include several in his first attempt to escape. After the plan is betrayed and he is separated from his friends, Douglass recalls suffering greatly from his isolation. This reinforces the impression he gives his reader that the kind of fulfillment he sought as a black man was communal, not merely personal.

Virtually everything Douglass writes about his final years in slavery and his early years of freedom testifies to his dedication to an ideal of black manhood that is firmly aligned with traditional middle-class American standards. Hiring his time in the shipbuilding trades of Baltimore, Douglass espouses the Protestant work ethic: "I bent myself to the work of making money" (p. 85), saving as much as he could for his eventual flight to freedom. The economic freedom and independence he demands of Hugh Auld are utterly consistent with what any white male workingman would have expected as his employment rights in mid-nineteenth-century America. After he escapes, Douglass's actions—marriage, employment, continued self-improvement, and community activism—underline his bid for respectability as a productive, contributing member of a free society.

The climactic scene of the *Narrative* places Douglass on a platform, for the first time speaking out in a public setting against slavery. This scene effectively melds the central themes of the *Narrative* into a final positive statement that prefigures Douglass's future greatness. The occasion is an antislavery rally in Nantucket, Connecticut, in August 1841; it is the first time Douglass speaks to whites about slavery in general and his personal enslavement in particular. As he approaches the podium, Douglass acknowledges a lingering shackle on his sense of self: "The truth was, I felt myself a slave, and the idea of speaking to white people weighed me down" (p. 92). The act of speaking proves liberating, however. Marshaling the power of language to attack slavery and to identify himself as a self-liberated free man, Douglass at the end of his autobiography lays claim to the intellectual and moral authority necessary to become a public man of words, the eventual author of the *Narrative* itself.

LEGACY OF THE *NARRATIVE*

In the history of African American literature, Douglass's importance and influence are virtually immeasurable. Many memorable slave narratives, including William Wells Brown's *Narrative of William W. Brown, an American Slave* (1847) and Harriet Jacobs's *Incidents in the Life of a Slave Girl* (1861), were inspired by Douglass's example. His *Narrative* gave the world the most compelling and sophisticated rendition of African American selfhood and manhood seen in literature up to that time. Douglass's artistry invested his model of selfhood with a moral and political significance that subsequent aspirants to the role of African American culture hero—from the conservative Booker T. Washington (1856–1915) to the radical W. E. B. Du Bois (1868–1963)—would seek to appropriate for their own autobiographical self-portraits. In twentieth-century African American literature, from Paul Laurence Dunbar's brooding poetic tribute "Douglass" (1903) to the idealistic characterization of Ned Douglass in Ernest J. Gaines's novel, *The Autobiography of Miss Jane Pittman* (1971), the criterion for African American heroism and mastery of words as a weapon in the struggle for self- and communal liberation remains the Frederick Douglass pictured in his *Narrative*.

See also Abolitionist Writing; Autobiography; Blacks; *Incidents in the Life of a Slave Girl;* Literacy; Manhood; Rhetoric; Slave Narratives; Slavery

BIBLIOGRAPHY

Primary Works

Douglass, Frederick. *The Frederick Douglass Papers.* Edited by John W. Blassingame. New Haven, Conn.: Yale University Press, 1979–.

Douglass, Frederick. *The Oxford Frederick Douglass Reader.* Edited and with an introduction by William L. Andrews. New York: Oxford University Press, 1996.

Secondary Works

Andrews, William L. *To Tell a Free Story: The First Century of Afro-American Autobiography, 1760–1865.* Urbana: University of Illinois Press, 1986.

Andrews, William L., ed. *Critical Essays on Frederick Douglass.* Boston: G. K. Hall, 1991.

Huggins, Nathan Irvin. *Slave and Citizen: The Life of Frederick Douglass.* Edited by Oscar Handlin. Boston: Little, Brown, 1980.

Martin, Waldo E., Jr. *The Mind of Frederick Douglass.* Chapel Hill: University of North Carolina Press, 1984.

McFeely, William S. *Frederick Douglass.* New York: Norton, 1991.

Preston, Dickson J. *Young Frederick Douglass: The Maryland Years.* Baltimore: Johns Hopkins University Press, 1980.

Sundquist, Eric J., ed. *Frederick Douglass: New Literary and Historical Essays.* Cambridge, U.K.: Cambridge University Press, 1990.

William L. Andrews

NATIVE AMERICAN LITERATURE

Nineteenth-century Native American literature is a literature of transition, the bridge between an oral tradition that flourished for centuries before the arrival of Europeans and the emergence of contemporary fiction in the 1960s, known as the Native American Renaissance. Unlike the preceding oral tradition, nineteenth-century Native American literature was increasingly text-based and composed in English, the result of missionary schools that taught Indians the skills believed necessary to assimilate into white society. Nineteenth-century Native American authors employed Euro-American literary genres like autobiography and the novel, often combining them with traditional narratives like the trickster tale or creation myth to create hybrid forms. Although the early texts exhibit the struggle of Indian authors to find a voice within American culture, they foreshadow elements of later Native American literature such as the refutation of stereotypical depictions of Indians all too common in American literature. Like their successors, nineteenth-century Indian authors were aware of the power of literature as a tool in changing the political and social status of their people.

The nineteenth century was a disruptive political era for Native Americans, defined by the Indian

Removal Act of 1830. A federal law authorized by President Andrew Jackson, the Removal Act ruled that Indians living east of the Mississippi River could be displaced to land west of the river. A contentious debate about the limits of federal and state jurisdiction over Indian tribal lands and peoples, coupled with a cultural belief in the essential incompatibility of Indian and white societies, led to a movement to relocate Indians to territory less populated by and less desirable to white Americans. The Removal Act was met with resistance by many tribes, most significantly by the Cherokee who inhabited Georgia. The Cherokee Nation had adapted to white society more successfully than other tribes, including creating its own written alphabet or syllabary, adopting a constitution similar to the U.S. Constitution, and establishing a bilingual newspaper. But gold was discovered on Cherokee land, precipitating their expulsion. The Cherokee fought back in a lawsuit before the U.S. Supreme Court in 1831 and again in 1832. The Court's initial decision declared the tribe a "domestic dependent nation," outside federal law and thus outside federal protection. The second decision was more favorable to the Cherokee but was ignored by both the federal government and the state of Georgia. Instead, in 1838 the Cherokee were forced by federal troops to depart on foot for the Indian Territory to the west; an estimated four thousand Indians died on what is now known as the Trail of Tears. All Native Americans felt the impact of the new reservation policies, which sought to isolate and contain Indians to make room for an expanding American nation.

At the same time that Native Americans were being excluded from the nation, white Americans began to look to them as the source of a unique national identity and literature, distinct from European traditions. Literature from the period depicting Indian characters was incredibly popular, and many works are still celebrated as classics, including James Fenimore Cooper's *The Last of the Mohicans* (1826), Catharine Maria Sedgwick's *Hope Leslie* (1827), and Henry Wadsworth Longfellow's *Song of Hiawatha* (1855), to name only a few. These texts employ the trope of the "disappearing Indian," which represents the deaths of Indians as natural, similar to the changing of the seasons or the setting of the sun, rather than the result of political exclusion or social discrimination. Thus the disappearance of Indians from the American social landscape was not only depicted within this body of writing but also implicitly approved of.

Early Native American authors wrote within a hostile political climate and in response to a dominant literary tradition that sentimentalized and condoned the death of Indians. But they found the means to engage with their detractors by authoring their own accounts of Indians that challenged stereotypical beliefs, demanded equal political rights, and proved that Indians were neither disappearing nor silent.

AUTOBIOGRAPHY

Autobiography was one of the primary genres that Native American authors borrowed from the Euro-American literary tradition and adapted to address their own concerns and experiences. Most nineteenth-century Native American autobiographies derive from a Christian practice of "testifying" to one's conversion and reflect the fact that the authors were educated in mission schools. Indian autobiographies exhibit the authors' awareness of themselves as speaking not simply as individuals but as representatives for their tribes and even for their race. The "double consciousness" (to borrow the term coined by W. E. B. Du Bois in 1903) these authors experience is evident in their negotiation of insider and outsider status. Sometimes they adopt the voice of an "authentic" Indian with a complete knowledge of tribal traditions and practices. But just as often they position themselves outside of Indian culture or belief systems, as members of a Christian, educated, and white society. The complex tensions that result from this bifurcated view give rise to some of the most interesting and important moments in the texts.

The first full-length Native American autobiography was written by William Apess (Pequot, 1798–1839), *A Son of the Forest: The Experience of William Apess, a Native of the Forest* (1829). In this text Apess depicts his escape from a dark and abusive childhood through conversion to Christianity and particularly his involvement with the Methodist Church. For Apess, Christianity provides access to a democratic ideal: "I felt convinced that Christ died for all mankind—that age, sect, color, country, or situation made no difference" (p. 19). But his experience as a minister continually reminds him that this ideal is not realized, as he suffers discrimination even within his own church. Apess refutes stereotypical ideas about Indians by documenting his achievements at practices valued within white society (including reading, writing, and preaching), but he does not simply endorse assimilation. Instead, Apess seeks a delicate balance between embracing Christianity and maintaining pride in his Indian identity: "Having been excluded from the pales of the church . . . [I] soon returned to my *first love*. I went then to my native tribe" (p. 46). Apess's career as a public speaker and author was increasingly political after the publication of his autobiography, culminating in his involvement in the Mashpee Revolt in 1833 and—as evident in his protest literature

Cherokee Phoenix. The 10 April 1828 edition of the bilingual Cherokee newspaper. THE
LIBRARY OF CONGRESS

discussed below—his stance on Indian-white relations grew to be militant and revolutionary.

Another important autobiography of the time was written by George Copway (Ojibwe, 1818–1869). Titled *The Life, History, and Travels of Kah-ge-ga-gah-bowh* (1847), it recounts Copway's life from childhood in Upper Canada (now Ontario) through his conversion to Christianity and involvement with a Methodist missionary society in the United States. His autobiography recounts these events within the framework of a spiritual narrative in which conversion marks the transition between his traditional, Indian identity and his new, Christian one. He romanticizes both his past and present selves: "I loved the woods, and the chase. I had the nature for it, and gloried in nothing else. The mind for letters was in me, *but was asleep,* till the dawn of Christianity arose, and awoke the slumbers of the soul into energy and action" (p. 69). But for Copway, the choice between them was clear; he viewed the assimilation to white society through Christianity and education as necessary for Indian survival. Copway's autobiography was a huge success, and he embarked upon a lecture tour that took him throughout the United States and Europe. He was lauded by American luminaries like Washington Irving and James Fenimore Cooper. But despite his continued literary career (he authored four more books, issued two revised and expanded editions of his *Life,* and started a short-lived newspaper called *Copway's American Indian*), Copway found himself exiled from his own people and white society, a product of both but welcomed by neither.

The autobiography of Black Hawk (Sauk, c.1767–1838) differs in significant ways from the Christian Indian model. Published in 1833 as *Life of Ma-ka-tai-me-she-kia-kaik or Black Hawk,* the authenticity of the narrative is often questioned. Unlike Apess and Copway, Hawk was illiterate and did not speak English. His narrative was mediated by Antoine Le Claire, a French-Canadian Potawatami who acted as Black Hawk's translator, and John B. Patterson, who edited the text. The extent to which Le Claire and Patterson shaped and perhaps composed the text has caused many to doubt its legitimacy as a Native American autobiography. The literary critic Arnold Krupat describes the autobiography an "original bicultural composite composition" (p. 30), combining Black Hawk's own voice with those of his translator and editor. The composite nature of the text is evident in discrepancies within the narrative; while Black Hawk resisted white domination throughout his life, particularly in the 1832 struggle known as the Black Hawk War, certain portions of his autobiography express

gratitude and friendship toward whites. Still other portions preserve Black Hawk's anger, as when he declares:

> I reflected upon the ingratitude of the whites, when I saw their fine houses, rich harvests, and every thing desirable around them; and recollected that all this land had been ours, for which me and my people has never received a dollar, and that the whites were not satisfied until they took our village and our grave-yards from us, and removed us across the Mississippi. (P. 79)

The value of Black Hawk's autobiography lies in these inconsistencies, which demonstrate the struggle Indian authors faced in gaining a voice within the conventions of American literature.

PROTEST LITERATURE

Understandably much early Native American literature was occupied with challenging the political status of Indian people. One of the first authors to engage in protest literature was Elias Boudinot (Cherokee, c. 1804–1839). Boudinot was born Gallegina (or Buck)

Black Hawk. Author of *Life of Ma-ka-tai-me-she-kia-kaik or Black Hawk,* 1833. THE LIBRARY OF CONGRESS

Watie but changed his name to honor the president of the American Bible Society. While name change was common within Cherokee culture, Boudinot's choice reflects his allegiance to both Christianity and white society. At the age of six, Boudinot was sent to a mission school where he was encouraged to leave behind his culture's "savage" traditions in favor of white "civilized" practices. Boudinot was a prize pupil and subsequently returned to his people as a missionary to share this knowledge. Boudinot became a spokesperson for the Cherokee Nation, delivering a speech titled "An Address to the Whites" throughout the United States in 1826 in an attempt to raise money for a Cherokee newspaper and school. In the speech Boudinot demonstrates the capacity of the Cherokee people to be "civilized" by lauding them for their achievements and implicitly distancing them from other Native American tribes. He appeals to his audience by claiming that these improvements are only possible with white assistance: "I ask you, shall red men live, or shall they be swept from the earth? With you and this public at large, the decision chiefly rests" (p. 79). Boudinot's efforts were successful in raising money to purchase a printing press, and he became the editor of the *Cherokee Phoenix*, a biweekly, bilingual newspaper. But the controversy sparked by the Removal Act of 1830 ended Boudinot's career, when he joined a minority group that advocated that the Cherokee voluntarily relocate to the Indian Territory. For this reason Boudinot was considered a traitor, and after the Trail of Tears, he was assassinated by members of a rival faction. His "Address to the Whites" advocates acculturation and compliance as key for the survival of the Cherokee, but his life story draws attention to the limitations of this viewpoint.

The Pequot autobiographical writer William Apess also engaged in protest literature, but unlike Boudinot, Apess's writing is characterized by an angry resistance to white society. In an essay titled "An Indian's Looking-Glass for the White Man" (1833), Apess makes a fiery challenge to the ideology of white supremacy by arguing that whites are "blacker" than any other race in terms of their sins: "Now suppose these skins were put together, and each skin had its national crimes written upon it—which skin do you think would have the greatest?" (p. 157). By inverting Euro-American assumptions associated with skin color, Apess rejects the inferiority of indigenous people and casts aspersions upon whites for centuries of discrimination and violence. In a speech titled "Eulogy on King Philip" (1836), Apess celebrates the life of King Philip, the seventeenth-century leader of a war against the New England colonists. Apess suggests that Philip was a superior military and political

---

"ADDRESS TO THE WHITES"

In Elias Boudinot's speech "Address to the Whites" (1826), he describes the accomplishments of the Cherokee people, proudly boasting of their civil society and religious devotion. He concludes the speech, however, by acknowledging that the survival of the Cherokee rests little with that people and instead is determined by white America. The Cherokee are threatened with the fate suffered by many other Native American tribes: extinction. But Boudinot pleads with his white audience, if the U.S. nation were to intervene on behalf of the Cherokee, his people could rise from the grave like a phoenix from the flame.

There is, in Indian history, something very melancholy, and which seems to establish a mournful precedent for the future events of the few sons of the forest, now scattered over this vast continent. We have seen every where the poor aborigines melt away before the white population. I merely state the fact, without at all referring to the cause. We have seen, I say, one family after another, one tribe after another, nation after nation, pass away; until only a few solitary creatures are left to tell the sad story of extinction.

Shall this precedent be followed? I ask you, shall red men live, or shall they be swept from the earth? With you and this public at large, the decision chiefly rests. Must they perish? Must they all, like the unfortunate Creeks, (victims of the unchristian policy of certain persons,) go down in sorrow to their grave?

They hang upon your mercy as to a garment. Will you push them from you, or will you save them? Let humanity answer.

Boudinot, *Cherokee Editor: The Writings of Elias Boudinot*, p. 79.

---

leader than either Alexander the Great or George Washington. Moreover Apess holds Euro-Americans responsible for the widespread destruction of Indian society: "But let us again review their weapons to civilize the nations of this soil. What were they? Rum and powder and ball, together with all the diseases, such as the smallpox and every other disease imaginable" (p. 286). Apess's explosive political rhetoric proves the image of the silent, "disappearing Indian" that dominated American literature to be false.

THE NOVEL

The first Native American novel was written by John Rollin Ridge, or Yellow Bird (Cherokee, 1827–1867). *The Life and Adventures of Joaquín Murieta*, published in 1854, recounts the story of a notorious Mexican bandit in California. Murieta was a folk hero whose story was popularized through oral legends and Mexican *corridos* (narrative folk songs) as well as in dime novels like Ridge's. Ridge was descended from a prominent Cherokee family; his father and grandfather both advocated the removal of the Cherokee to the Indian Territory and were assassinated shortly thereafter (along with Elias Boudinot, who was a cousin). Ridge subsequently grew up and was educated in white society. Ridge traveled to California during the early years of the gold rush, fleeing a murder charge after he killed a man he believed to have participated in his father's murder. Ridge began a career in journalism in San Francisco, and it was there he learned the legend of Joaquín Murieta. In his novel Ridge transforms Murieta into a Robin Hood character, driven to be an outlaw by the egregious mistreatment he receives from whites. Ridge valorizes Murieta's actions, even when he seeks violent vengeance, perhaps expressing his own frustrated desire for revenge. Ridge concluded his novel with the lofty sentiment that "there is nothing so dangerous in its consequences as *injustice to individuals*—whether it arise from prejudice of color or any other source" (p. 158). But in his journalism Ridge argued that giving up traditional indigenous practices and adopting white ways was the only means for the survival of Indians.

EARLY NATIVE AMERICAN WOMEN WRITERS

The first Native American novel written by a woman is *Wynema: A Child of the Forest* by S. Alice Callahan (Muscogee [Creek], 1868–1894), which was published in 1891. But long before Callahan's *Wynema*, other women authors were entering the literary profession. One of the earliest is Jane Johnston Schoolcraft (Ojibwe, 1800–1841). Schoolcraft was married to Henry Rowe Schoolcraft, a renowned ethnographer, with whom she helped publish the *Literary Voyager or Muzzeniegun,* a journal of poetry, essays, and history. Schoolcraft published numerous poems in this journal and earned a glowing reputation among literary critics. Schoolcraft's poems reflect her education in classical and European literature; she employs the conventional rhyme structure and meter common at the time. Certain poems, like "Lines Written under Affliction" (1827), echo the style of Felicia Hemans and Lydia Sigourney, the two most popular women poets of the century:

> Ah! Who, with a sensitive mind possest,
> Recalls the swift years that are gone,
> Without mingled emotions—both bitter & blest,
> At the good & the ill he has known.
>
> (P. 60)

Still other poems reflect upon Schoolcraft's heritage, such as "Otagamiad" (1827), which depicts her grandfather, Waub Ojeeg, the Ojibwe chief, as a warrior whose actions are determined by reason and necessity rather than vengeance:

> 'Tis warlike acts that make a nation friends
> 'Tis warlike acts that prop a falling throne
> And makes peace, glory, empire, all our own.
>
> (P. 61)

Despite Schoolcraft's accomplishments, she never published a book of poems, a testament to the difficulties that women writers—especially Indian women—faced in achieving literary legitimacy in the nineteenth century.

See also Cherokee Memorials; *Hope Leslie;* Indians; "An Indian's Looking-Glass for the White Man"; Indian Wars and Dispossession; Leatherstocking Tales; *Life and Adventures of Joaquín Murieta; The Song of Hiawatha;* Trail of Tears

BIBLIOGRAPHY

Primary Works

Apess, William. *On Our Own Ground: The Complete Writings of William Apess, a Pequot.* Edited by Barry O'Connell. Amherst: University of Massachusetts Press, 1992.

Black Hawk. *Life of Ma-ka-tai-me-she-kia-kaik or Black Hawk.* 1833. Reprinted as *Black Hawk's Autobiography,* edited by Roger L. Nichols. Ames: Iowa State University Press, 1999.

Boudinot, Elias. *Cherokee Editor: The Writings of Elias Boudinot.* Edited by Theda Perdue. Athens: University of Georgia Press, 1996.

Copway, George. *Life, Letters, and Speeches.* Edited by A. LaVonne Brown Ruoff and Donald B. Smith. Lincoln: University of Nebraska Press, 1997.

Schoolcraft, Jane Johnston. "Poems." In *Native American Women's Writing, c. 1800–1924: An Anthology,* edited by Karen L. Kilcup, pp. 57–70. Oxford: Blackwell, 2000.

Ridge, John Rollin [Yellow Bird]. *The Life and Adventures of Joaquín Murieta.* 1854. Norman: University of Oklahoma Press, 1955.

Secondary Works

Jaskoski, Helen, ed. *Early Native American Writing: New Critical Essays*. Cambridge, U.K.: Cambridge University Press, 1996.

Konkle, Maureen. *Writing Indian Nation: Native Intellectuals and the Politics of Historiography, 1827–1863*. Chapel Hill: University of North Carolina Press, 2004.

Krupat, Arnold. *For Those Who Come After: A Study of Native American Autobiography*. Berkeley: University of California Press, 1985.

Maddox, Lucy. *Removals: Nineteenth-Century American Literature and the Politics of Indian Affairs*. New York: Oxford University Press, 1991.

Peyer, Bernd C. *The Tutor'd Mind: Indian Missionary-Writers in Antebellum America*. Amherst: University of Massachusetts Press, 1997.

Ruoff, A. LaVonne Brown. *American Indian Literatures: An Introduction, Bibliographic Review, and Selected Bibliography*. New York: Modern Language Association of America, 1990.

Walker, Cheryl. *Indian Nation: Native American Literature and Nineteenth-Century Nationalisms*. Durham, N.C.: Duke University Press, 1997.

Wiget, Andrew, ed. *The Handbook of Native American Literature*. New York: Garland, 1996.

Desirée Henderson

NATIVE AMERICANS

See Indians

NATURE

In *Land of the Spotted Eagle* (1933), Luther Standing Bear recalls the middle decades of the nineteenth century, the time before his Lakota people were driven from their homeland in what is now South Dakota and Nebraska:

> Only to the white man was nature a "wilderness" and only to him was the land "infested" with "wild" animals and "savage" people. To us it was tame. Earth was bountiful and we were surrounded with the blessings of the Great Mystery. Not until the hairy man from the east came and with brutal frenzy heaped injustices upon us and the families we loved was it "wild" for us. (P. 38)

As Standing Bear suggests, there is no "nature." There is only the inhabited planet—the land—which must be overlaid with specific cultural meanings to become natural or wild. In the United States in the nineteenth century, nature meant different things to different people, depending on who they were and what relation

they bore to the powerful historical trends that were reshaping both the land and them, especially imperial expansion, industrialization, and urbanization.

INDIAN REMOVAL, ROMANTIC FICTION AND POETRY, AND NATIVE RESISTANCE

One of the most powerful uses of the word "nature" was to designate places and people not yet "civilized," not yet incorporated into the growing capitalist republic. During the decades after the Revolution, Euro-American settlers pushed across the Alleghany and Appalachian ranges onto land that would soon become the second and third tiers of states. As they did, they came into immediate conflict with the native peoples of the region. In addition to epidemic diseases, the settlers brought with them the well-tried strategy of negotiating piecemeal treaties with individual tribes, treaties that gradually squeezed the tribes onto smaller and smaller remnants of their former territories. One of the most powerful tribes was the Shawnee, led by the great orator Tecumseh (1768–1813). At an 1810 frontier meeting with William Henry Harrison (who was then governor of the Territory of Indiana), Tecumseh protested against American imperial expansion and articulated a radical vision of native resistance and communal ownership of nature:

> The way, the only way to stop this evil is for the red men to unite in claiming a common and equal right in the land, as it was at first, and should be now—for it was never divided, but belongs to all. No tribe has the right to sell, even to each other, much less to strangers. . . . Sell a country! Why not sell the air, the great sea, as well as the earth? (Turner, p. 246)

Tecumseh hoped to bring together the northern tribes and lead them in a war to defend their homelands against the advance of the whites. But his plans were defeated during the War of 1812: he allied his forces with the British and was killed defending the rear of a retreating British column. The defeat of the Shawnee cleared the way for settlers to move into what was then called the Northwest, the vast reach of fertile hills and prairies below the Great Lakes.

Two decades later President Andrew Jackson made systematic displacement of the remaining natives into federal policy with the Indian Removal Act of 1830. Jackson's annual addresses to Congress during the period are bluntly racist justifications of what we now call ethnic cleansing. He represents Native Americans as childlike primitives and argues that forcing tribes like the Cherokee to march the Trail of Tears to Oklahoma is a necessary part of America's mission to occupy and transform the wild continent: "What good man would prefer a country covered with forests and ranged by a few thousand savages to our extensive

Republic, studded with cities, towns, and prosperous farms . . . and filled with all the blessings of liberty, civilization and religion?" Like most others who came to believe in white America's "Manifest Destiny" to settle the continent from sea to sea, Jackson recognized only one kind of liberty, the liberty to engage in the violent conquest of territory and profit.

American's transformation of its natural environment and the displacement of Native Americans formed the most central subject matter for some of its first "indigenous" literary texts, the early national historical romances. Modeled after the Highland romances of the Scottish novelist Sir Walter Scott, these fictions set out to narrate a usable past for the new nation. James Fenimore Cooper's (1789–1851) *The Pioneers* (1823), for instance, tells the story of Judge Marmaduke Temple, who clears a vast estate and founds the village of Templeton in central New York State. Based on Cooper's family history, *The Pioneers* is a triumphal narrative of civilizing the wilderness, of hard work awakening the land from "the sleep of nature" so that it can "supply the wants of man" (1:233). At the same time, the text is marked by anxiety about the destruction of

nature, an anxiety that is voiced most consistently by frontiersman Natty Bumppo, or Leatherstocking. Natty objects sorrowfully when Templeton's villagers gather in a clearing to kill tens of thousands of passenger pigeons for sport: "This comes of settling a country!" he says. "Here have I known the pigeon to fly for forty long years, and, till you made your clearings, there was nobody to skeart or to hurt them." Natty goes on to compare the pigeons to the region's natives who, he implies, are being slaughtered just as mercilessly: "There's Mr. Oliver, as bad as the rest of them, firing into the flocks as if he was shooting down nothing but the Mingo warriors" (1:248). Instead of calling on the villagers to stop firing, Natty responds to their indiscriminate destruction by demonstrating the more selective violence of his long rifle. As if to suggest that genocide would be more acceptable if more accurate, Cooper has his hero shoot a single pigeon, dropping it from a great distance after it becomes separated from the flock.

Cooper developed his characterization of Natty further in subsequent romances, especially *The Last of the Mohicans* (1826), which is set during the French and Indian Wars of the mid-eighteenth century. Here Natty

The First Harvest in the Wilderness, **1855.** Painting by Asher Brown Durand. © BROOKLYN MUSEUM OF ART, NEW YORK, USA, GIFT OF THE BROOKLYN INSTITUTE OF ARTS AND SCIENCES/THE BRIDGEMAN ART LIBRARY

plays an important liminal role: he is a colonial mediator between the overcivilized English and the noble savages of the New World. Raised by the Delaware chief Chingachgook, Natty has absorbed Mohican nature lore, but his blood remains safely European. By the end of the novel, he has come to embody a fantasized American identity that symbolically resolves national anxiety about genocide. By incorporating token elements of native culture while replacing actual natives, he represents an American republic that has connected itself with nature, thereby revitalizing itself in relation to degenerate European monarchies.

Cooper faced stiff competition in the production of historical romances. Both Lydia Maria Child's (1802–1880) *Hobomok: A Tale of Early Times* (1824) and Catharine Maria Sedgwick's (1789–1867) *Hope Leslie; or, Early Times in the Massachusetts* (1827) take on the fraught subject of miscegenation, or interracial marriage between whites and natives. A liberal Unitarian and early abolitionist, Child allows her heroine, Mary Conant, who is overcome by grief at the drowning of an English suitor, to marry an exaggeratedly natural Wampanoag man, Hobomok. As in so many sentimental novels of the time, this transgressive marriage choice is simultaneously matter for moralistic punishment and a vicarious enactment of radical possibility. In the end, the plot enforces segregation of the biracial couple. Mary's suitor turns out not to have drowned as she had believed. He returns, and Hobomok quietly withdraws into the receding wilderness, leaving behind a couple whose white offspring will populate the wilderness his departure makes available.

In Sedgwick's *Hope Leslie,* however, it is a young man, Everell Fletcher, who must make a difficult marriage choice. The orphaned Hope Leslie, a passionate and independent girl, is his foster sister. Also living with his family is Hope's noble soulmate, Magawisca, the captured daughter of a Pequod warrior. She wears a naturalized costume—deerskin waistcoat, leggings, and moccasins, decorated with feathers and beads—that gives her "an air of wild and fantastic grace" (p. 23). And she speaks in elaborate figures meant to evoke the alleged natural poetry of native dialects: "My foot . . . is used to the wild-wood path. The deer tires not of his way on the mountain, nor the bird of its flight in the air" (p. 24). On visits to nature outside the bounds of the Puritan community, Magawisca teaches Hope the stories and lifeways of her people. Meanwhile, their friend Esther Downing, a pious Puritan girl, cultivates the silence, industry, and submissiveness expected of her. All three are potential love objects for Everell. His eventual marriage to Hope enacts the founding moment of the American nation and determines the future identity of its people. Like Cooper's Natty

Bumppo, Hope is an intermediate figure, one whose white body is racially acceptable, but whose absorption of native self-reliance and culture through Magawisca has fitted her for the rigors of life in the natural New World. The plot drives Hope and Everell inevitably together while allowing Magawisca to nobly sacrifice herself and her own desires to their future prosperity.

Just as the first fiction writers in the United States patterned their work after British models, so too did the first American Romantic poets. William Cullen Bryant (1794–1878), Henry Wadsworth Longfellow (1807–1882), and other "Fireside Poets" wrote verse that was firmly rooted in the English accentual-syllabic tradition but that took up materials native to the American landscape. Bryant was known as "the American Wordsworth," and in his ode "The Prairies" (1832), nature is represented as a "magnificent temple" where the historical drama of the rise and fall of nations plays itself out. The poem stages an imaginary invasion in which red-skinned invaders wipe out a preexisting race of Mound Builders. Bryant remarks philosophically:

> Thus change the forms of being. Thus arise
> Races of living things, glorious in strength,
> And perish, as the quickening breath of God
> Fills them, or is withdrawn.
>
> *(Pp. 187–188)*

Thus Bryant erases the violence of conquest and naturalizes genocide, suggesting that it is just one more of nature's cycles. He ends by comparing the noise of an "advancing multitude" of settlers to the "domestic hum" of the bee, an "adventurous colonist" who enlivens a wilderness made silent by the passing of the savage "red men" (p. 189).

As actual natives were driven farther and farther west, retrospective idealization of their culture became a staple of Fireside poetry, as in Longfellow's *The Song of Hiawatha* (1855), a cycle of Ojibwa stories adapted in verse. This long poem begins by calling together its audience in lines that clearly reflect the cultural work that nature and naturalized people were being made to perform:

> Ye who love the haunts of Nature
> . . . .
> Ye whose hearts are fresh and simple,
> Who have faith in God and Nature,
> Who believe that in all ages
> Every human heart is human,
> That in even savage bosoms
> There are longings, yearnings, strivings
> For the good they comprehend not,
> . . . .
> Listen to this simple story,
> To this Song of Hiawatha!
>
> *(P. 114)*

Like Hobomok, Hiawatha is a primitivist caricature, a "noble savage" who quests mightily to defend his people. But in the end he paddles his canoe placidly into the western wilderness to make room for white men who will learn natural piety from the traditional stories of his tribe. In other words, as readers in the rapidly modernizing United States became conscious of their increasing distance from the frontier, poetry about native subjects offered a nostalgic vision of nature as a wellspring of uncomplicated morality and faith.

Native Americans did not acquiesce silently to being both literally and figuratively exiled into nature. They were extremely inventive in their efforts to use both printed literature and oratory to escape from the wilderness. In the late 1820s, Cherokee spokespeople dispatched several "memorials" to Congress. These highly formal documents ventriloquize the republican discourse of the Declaration of Independence in order to argue that the Cherokee are a sovereign nation seated on ancestral lands. The Cherokee leader Sequoyah invented an eighty-six-character syllabary that allowed for publication of a bilingual newspaper, the *Cherokee Phoenix*. The *Phoenix* reported on the tribe's adoption of a constitution, the building of schools, and advances in agriculture. One of its editors, Elias Boudinot (c. 1802–1839), toured the country soliciting funds to pay for a new press. In a speech he delivered before hundreds of audiences, titled "An Address to the Whites" (1826), he resolutely distanced himself and his people from nature: "You here behold an Indian, my kindred are Indians, and my fathers sleeping in the wilderness grave—they too were Indians. But I am not as my fathers were— broader means and nobler influences have fallen upon me" (pp. 3–4). By demonstrating that he, as a representative Cherokee, had abandoned nature and become civilized, Boudinot hoped to convince his audience, and the nation at large, to negotiate with his people as equals.

William Apess (1798–1839) was less conciliatory. His fiery essay "An Indian's Looking-Glass for the White Man" (1833) remains one of the most forceful native indictments of American racism and imperial expansion. Apess reaches a rhetorical pinnacle discussing the prohibition of miscegenation, denouncing "the ill-fated laws made by man to hedge up the laws of God and nature" (p. 159). Ironically, his hortatory conclusion draws an implied analogy between the settlers' conquest of nature and the defeat of racism: he calls for the "tree of distinction" or prejudice to "be leveled to the earth"; should this be done, "then shall peace pervade the Union" (pp. 160–161). That peace did not come. The last significant battle in the East

came in 1832 when Illinois and Wisconsin militia attacked and defeated a band of Sauk and Fox Indians led by Black Hawk and drove the survivors into Iowa. By 1840 all of the significant eastern tribes had either been physically destroyed or removed beyond the Mississippi River, leaving room for Euro-American writers and readers to forge new imaginary relations with the land.

CAPITALISM, PASTORALISM, AND NEW ENGLAND TRANSCENDENTALISM

The Quaker poet and New York newspaper editor John Greenleaf Whittier (1807–1892) was widely admired for his pastoral accounts of the New England countryside such as *Snow-Bound* (1866), a nostalgic portrait of his family at home on his childhood farm. He saw a firm link between natural piety and political radicalism, and in "The Tent on the Beach" (1867) he described his conversion to abolitionism as the moment when he decided to make "his rustic reed of song / A weapon in the war with wrong" (p. 243). In the Northeast, where native removal had been completed half a century earlier, and where industrialization and urbanization were moving forward quickly, the mid-nineteenth century saw important new applications of the very old idea that nature is a simple, innocent refuge from a degenerate civilization. A generation of northeastern intellectuals, many of whom, like Whittier, were just one generation removed from the farm, came to see nature as an idealized alternative to brawling capitalist cities like Boston, New York, and Philadelphia, where poverty and class conflict had become defining features of everyday life. The most visible manifestation of this pastoralism was a broad utopian socialist movement, Associationism, whose participants built large cooperative agricultural communities. George Ripley (1802–1880), for instance, founded the Brook Farm Institute of Agriculture and Education in West Roxbury, Massachusetts, in 1841. In a letter to Ralph Waldo Emerson (1803–1882), Ripley described his hope that a collective life of direct engagement with nature through manual labor would produce "a society of liberal, intelligent, and cultivated persons, whose relations with each other would permit a more simple and wholesome life, than can now be led amidst the pressures of our competitive institutions" (Frothingham, p. 307). Dozens of such pastoralist communities were founded across the United States and tens of thousands participated in the movement, mounting a direct ideological challenge to capitalism at the moment of its birth.

Ripley's close friend Emerson published an individualist's version of this challenge in an influential

THE SPIRITUALIZATION OF WILDERNESS

John Greenleaf Whittier's 1867 poem "The Worship of Nature" gives an absolute statement of the nineteenth-century idea that nature is a sacred and pristine space, a categorical opposite to the mundane, grubby landscape of society. The poem sets up an elaborate metaphorical comparison between an idealized forest grove and a cathedral, suggesting that a feminized Nature, rather than an anthropomorphic God, is the most reliable source of grace. Human beings seem to be absent from this place of worship, although implied personifications of natural phenomena provide ghostly images of devout nature worshippers. Then, people arrive with a vengeance in the poem's final line, the tone shifts to one of outrage, and "man" is dismissed as a sacrilegious philistine, incapable of understanding the immanent divinity of nature. On one hand, the poem expresses the abolitionist Whittier's desire for redemption in the wake of the horrifically bloody Civil War. On the other, it also reflects a clear trend among radicals who appealed to an idealized nature as a source of humane values: the contrast between their exaggerated vision of nature's purity and their century's cruel social history could inspire demoralization and finally detachment.

The harp at Nature's advent strung
    Has never ceased to play;
The song the stars of morning sung
    Has never died away.
And prayer is made, and praise is given,
    By all things near and far;
The ocean looketh up to heaven,
    And mirrors every star.
Its waves are kneeling on the strand,
    As kneels the human knee,
Their white locks bowing to the sand,
    The priesthood of the sea!
They pour their glittering treasures forth,
    Their gifts of pearl they bring,
And all the listening hills of earth
    Take up the song they sing.
The green earth sends its incense up
    From many a mountain shrine;
From folded leaf and dewy cup
    She pours her sacred wine.

The mists above the morning rills
    Rise white as wings of prayer;
The altar-curtains of the hills
    Are sunset's purple air.
The winds with hymns of praise are loud,
    Or low with sobs of pain, —
The thunder-organ of the cloud,
    The dropping tears of rain.
With drooping head and branches crossed
    The twilight forest grieves,
Or speaks with tongues of Pentecost
    From all its sunlit leaves.
The blue sky is the temple's arch,
    Its transept earth and air,
The music of its starry march
    The chorus of a prayer.
So Nature keeps the reverent frame
    With which her years began,
And all her signs and voices shame
    The prayerless heart of man.

Whittier, *Complete Poetical Works*, p. 261.

little book, *Nature* (1836), the central manifesto of what has since been dubbed New England transcendentalism. Emerson describes a pantheist divinity immanent in nature and announces that all people potentially can make direct contact with it. Doing so elevates us, for nature's "floods of life stream around and through us, and invite us by the powers they supply, to action proportioned to nature" (p. 7). Emerson calls on his readers to transform themselves spiritually through contact with the eternal truths of nature and thereby to transform the social world: "As fast as you conform your life to the pure idea in your mind, that will unfold its great proportions. A correspondent revolution in things will attend the influx of the spirit" (p. 48). *Nature* is structured in a somewhat mechanical, rationalist fashion that contrasts with its ideas, but Emerson also experiments with an accretive, sinuous style that he saw as natural; he would make his later essays grow like vines. Moreover, his natural idealism provided his readers, many of whom were elite liberals, with a secular warrant for participation in a wide range of reform projects directed at the growing urban working class, such as temperance and debt-relief campaigns, as well as prison and asylum reform.

It also laid the groundwork for more radical ways of thinking about nature's transformative power.

Henry David Thoreau's (1817–1862) *Walden; or, Life in the Woods* (1854) enacts and extends Emerson's ideas, telling the story of two years Thoreau spent living in a small cabin he built on the shores of a pond outside Concord, Massachusetts. *Walden* begins by detailing the mechanical "lives of quiet desperation" that townspeople endure (p. 8). Sullied by the curse of trade and trapped by the unnatural logic of the marketplace, "the laboring man has not leisure for a true integrity day by day" (p. 6). Thoreau acts out an organic alternative to town life: he sheds artificial needs and communes with nature, giving himself time to appreciate life's "finer fruits" (p. 6). He arrives in the end at an optimistic conviction that a "beautiful and winged" future lies waiting to spring forth from the "the dead dry life of society" (p. 333). *Walden* also experiments with the naturalization of literary form, collapsing two years of experience into one and organizing it according to the cycle of the seasons, thus offering the transition from inert winter to glorious spring as a metaphor for individual and social rebirth. Because it so insistently represents nature as a sacred space threatened by a degenerate society, *Walden* also includes some of the first proto-environmentalist discourse in American literature: Thoreau complains that "the wood-cutters, and the railroad, and I myself have profaned Walden" (p. 197). In essays like "Walking," he argues that "in wildness is the preservation of the world" (*Collected Essays*, p. 239). And in his natural history manuscript *Wild Fruits* (unpublished until 2000), he calls for the protection of large tracts of wilderness to be held by society as a "common possession forever" (p. 236). Protecting nature was not only an environmental issue for Thoreau but a social one, too. For like Whittier, he saw wild nature as the moral touchstone that inspired his own radicalism, including his commitment to the abolition of slavery and his staunch opposition to American imperial adventures in Mexico.

Nature operates as a utopian alternative to brutal modernity in many other important transcendentalist texts. Margaret Fuller's (1810–1850) travel narrative, *Summer on the Lakes, in 1843* (1844), represents the West as a potential feminist republic where nature "did not say, Fight or starve; nor even, Work or cease to exist; but, merely showing that the apple was a finer fruit than the wild crab, gave both room to grow in the garden" (p. 26). Caroline Kirkland (1801–1864) describes the western territories as a classless society in her memoir *A New Home—Who'll Follow?* (1839). In her village "home on the outskirts of civilization" people live "in complete equality" and all "rise with

the sun or before him—to breakfast with the chickens." For Kirkland, "this primitive arrangement" serves as an important reminder to those "who are apt occasionally to forget, when speaking of a particular class, that 'those creatures' are partakers with themselves of a common nature" (p. 4). Similarly, in Nathaniel Hawthorne's (1804–1864) *The Scarlet Letter* (1850), it is only in the forest that Hester Prynne is free to respond naturally to her own physical and emotional impulses. Exiled there by the sexist Puritan theocracy, she is transformed into a wise woman, "self-ordained a Sister of Mercy," for whom the symbolic *A* has come to mean "Able" (p. 259). In the forest, she decides that "the world's law was no law for her mind" (p. 259), and she immerses herself in the revolutionary spirit of times when "the human intellect, newly emancipated" concludes that "the whole system of society is to be torn down, and built up anew" (p. 260). Likewise, Emily Dickinson's (1830–1886) pastoral lyrics represent nature as a sacred retreat from the pressures of oppressive social institutions:

> Some keep the Sabbath going to Church—
> I keep it, staying at Home—
> With a Bobolink for a Chorister—
> And an Orchard, for a Dome—
>
> *(1:260)*

Dickinson's poems are wild hymns, cracking the metronomic meter of Protestant church songs and celebrating a redeeming communion with an often feminized natural world.

The transcendentalist vision of nature was by no means universally accepted. For America's most intensively oppressed people, wilderness often seemed to be anything but a safe space. In much African American literature of the mid-nineteenth century, nature is represented as a terrifying wasteland populated by slave hunters and their dogs. Escaped slaves must pass through this anarchic, isolating landscape on their way to the North, where a truer freedom is protected by law and the organized black community. In *Narrative of the Life of Frederick Douglass, an American Slave* (1845), nature stands as a terrorizing obstacle to escape from the South. Imagining the road north, Douglass (1818–1895) envisions a wilderness of the worst sort: "after swimming rivers, encountering wild beasts, sleeping in the woods, suffering hunger and nakedness,—we were overtaken by our pursuers, and, in our resistance, we were shot dead upon the spot!" (p. 74). In Douglass's novella *The Heroic Slave* (1853), however, nature is a more ambiguous space. The hero, Madison Washington, first articulates his desire for freedom in a "dark pine forest" near "a sparkling brook" (p. 177). But after his escape, he spends five purgatorial years as a refugee in "dismal swamps," wandering "at night with the wolf and the bear" until an apocalyptic forest fire drives him out, forcing him to make his way north to Canada (p. 193). Similarly, in Harriet Jacobs's (1813–1897) *Incidents in the Life of a Slave Girl* (1861), Linda Brent is forced to hide in "Snaky Swamp," passing a "wretched night" tortured by insects and paralyzed by fear. Even so, she remarks that the swamp's "venomous snakes were less dreadful to my imagination than the white men in that community called civilized" (pp. 112–113).

A second alternative to the transcendentalist spiritualization of nature appears, paradoxically, in the work of the most wholly city-based writers of the period. A powerful ideological current among the developing working class focused on "free soil" as a solution to urban poverty. Radical figures like the newspaper editor George Henry Evans and the labor leader Stephen Simpson called on the federal government to distribute western homesteads to relieve chronic unemployment. Their crusade centered on the claim that access to productive soil was a natural right, commensurate with the rights to life, liberty, and the pursuit of happiness that were enshrined in the Declaration of Independence. Nature was not an otherworldly retreat or alternative moral order but a material necessity, the ground of a productive and independent livelihood. Herman Melville's (1819–1891) powerful indictment of labor relations under capitalism, "Bartleby, the Scrivener" (1853), stages the consequences of workers' alienation from the physical earth. The protagonist is a tortured copyist imprisoned in a Wall Street workspace that is "deficient in what landscape painters call 'life'" (p. 636). Bartleby declares a solitary strike against this oppressively unnatural world. In the end, he finds peace by dying in a prison, the Tombs, next to an emblematic patch of grass, "a soft imprisoned turf" that has grown "by some strange magic" in the "heart of the eternal pyramids" (p. 671).

Similarly, in Walt Whitman's (1819–1892) *Leaves of Grass* (1855), nature is the physical ground of all human life, whether economic, spiritual, or political. Beginning from the egalitarian principle that "every atom belonging to me as good belongs to you" (p. 27), Whitman offers a utopian alternative to the shallow utilitarianism and turgid piety of his contemporaries: "That I eat and drink is spectacle enough for the great authors and schools, / A morning-glory at my window satisfies me more than the metaphysics of books" (p. 52). Whitman celebrates the irreducible physicality and naturalness of all things, including people, in breathless catalogs. His secular, democratic scriptures radically transvalue the mundane world of nineteenth-century capitalism, compelling us to see the natural beauty of the world's body and our own, showing us that "a leaf of grass is no less than the journeywork of the stars" (p. 57).

Unstable and multivalent though it was, the idea of "nature" was absolutely central to the history and culture of the nineteenth-century United States. It authorized westward expansion by marking the unsettled continent as raw wilderness awaiting cultivation. Native Americans were represented as occupants of the unimproved state of nature, as primitive savages requiring civilization or displacement. They contested this designation, harnessing the power of print to argue that they were just as civilized, perhaps more so, than their hypocritical adversaries. Once the dislocation of the eastern tribes was complete, native culture was revalued, becoming the subject of compensatory nostalgia for a natural life on the land. Then, as capitalism radically transformed both social hierarchies and the physical environment, this pastoral vision of harmony with nature became a complex moral touchstone for America's most powerful critics, the New England transcendentalists. The value of nature was challenged by the African Americans and women who were the subjects of the period's struggles for human equality; nevertheless, nature did much to inspire truly radical criticism of the young nation's most fundamental contradictions and discords.

See also Leatherstocking Tales; *Nature;* Romanticism; Transcendentalism; Wilderness

BIBLIOGRAPHY
Primary Works
Apess, William. *On Our Own Ground: The Complete Writings of William Apess, a Pequot.* Edited by Barry O'Connell. Amherst: University of Massachusetts Press, 1992.

Boudinot, Elias. *An Address to the Whites: Delivered in the First Presbyterian Church, on the 26th of May, 1826.* Philadelphia: W. F. Geddes, 1826.

Bryant, William Cullen. *Poetical Works of William Cullen Bryant.* New York: Appleton, 1878.

Child, Lydia Maria. *Hobomok: A Tale of Early Times.* 1824. Reprinted in *Hobomok and Other Writings on Indians,* edited by Carolyn Karcher. New Brunswick, N.J.: Rutgers University Press, 1986.

Cooper, James Fenimore. *The Leatherstocking Tales.* 2 vols. New York: Library of America, 1985.

Dickinson, Emily. *The Poems of Emily Dickinson.* 3 vols. Edited by R. W. Franklin. Cambridge, Mass.: Belknap Press of Harvard University Press, 1998. Variorum edition.

Douglass, Frederick. *The Heroic Slave*. In *Autographs for Freedom,* edited by Julia Griffiths. Boston: J. P. Jewett, 1853.

Douglass, Frederick. *Narrative of the Life of Frederick Douglass, an American Slave*. 1845. Reprinted in *Autobiographies,* edited by Henry Louis Gates Jr. New York: Library of America, 1994.

Emerson, Ralph Waldo. *Essays and Lectures*. New York: Library of America, 1983.

Frothingham, Octavius Brooks. *George Ripley*. Boston: Houghton, Mifflin and Co., 1882.

Fuller, Margaret. *Summer on the Lakes, in 1843*. 1844. Edited by Susan Belasco Smith. Urbana: University of Illinois Press, 1991.

Hawthorne, Nathaniel. *Collected Novels*. New York: Library of America, 1983.

Jackson, Andrew. "President Jackson's Message to Congress 'On Indian Removal,' December 6, 1830; Records of the United States Senate, 1789–1990." Record Group 46, National Archives, Washington, D.C.

Jacobs, Harriet. *Incidents in the Life of a Slave Girl*. 1861. Edited by Jean Fagan Yellin. Cambridge, Mass.: Harvard University Press, 1987.

Kirkland, Caroline. *A New Home—Who'll Follow? or, Glimpses of Western Life*. 1839. New Brunswick, N.J.: Rutgers University Press, 1990.

Longfellow, Henry Wadsworth. *The Complete Poetical Works of Henry Wadsworth Longfellow*. Boston: Houghton Mifflin, 1975.

Melville, Herman. "Bartleby, the Scrivener." 1853. In *Pierre, Israel Potter, The Confidence-Man, Tales, and Billy Budd*. New York: Library of America, 1984.

Sedgwick, Catharine Maria. *Hope Leslie; or, Early Times in the Massachusetts*. 1827. Edited by Mary Kelley. New Brunswick, N.J.: Rutgers University Press, 1987.

Standing Bear, Luther. *Land of the Spotted Eagle*. New York: Houghton Mifflin, 1933.

Thoreau, Henry David. *Collected Essays and Poems*. Edited by Elizabeth Hall Witherell. New York: Library of America, 2001.

Thoreau, Henry David. *Walden; or, Life in the Woods*. 1854. Edited by J. Lyndon Shanley. Princeton, N.J.: Princeton University Press, 1971.

Thoreau, Henry David. *Wild Fruits: Thoreau's Rediscovered Last Manuscript*. Edited by Bradley P. Dean. New York: Norton, 2000.

Turner, Frederick, III, ed. *The Portable North American Indian Reader*. New York: Penguin, 1987.

Whitman, Walt. *Complete Poetry and Collected Prose*. New York: Library of America, 1982.

Whittier, John Greenleaf. *Complete Poetical Works of John Greenleaf Whittier*. Boston: Houghton, Mifflin and Co., 1894.

Secondary Works

Buell, Lawrence. *The Environmental Imagination: Thoreau, Nature Writing, and the Formation of American Culture*. Cambridge, Mass.: Belknap Press of Harvard University Press, 1995.

Drinnon, Richard. *Facing West: The Metaphysics of Indian-Hating and Empire-Building*. Minneapolis: University of Minnesota Press, 1980.

Jehlen, Myra. *American Incarnation: The Individual, the Nation, and the Continent*. Cambridge, Mass.: Harvard University Press, 1986.

Kolodny, Annette. *The Lay of the Land: Metaphor as Experience and History in American Life and Letters*. Chapel Hill: University of North Carolina Press, 1975.

Marx, Leo. *The Machine in the Garden: Technology and the Pastoral Ideal in America*. New York: Oxford University Press, 1964.

McKusick, James C. *Green Writing: Romanticism and Ecology*. New York: St. Martin's Press, 2000.

Merchant, Carolyn. *Ecological Revolutions: Nature, Gender, and Science in New England*. Chapel Hill: University of North Carolina Press, 1989.

Miller, Angela L. *The Empire of the Eye: Landscape Representation and American Cultural Politics, 1825–1875*. Ithaca, N.Y.: Cornell University Press, 1993.

Nash, Roderick. *Wilderness and the American Mind*. New Haven, Conn.: Yale University Press, 1967.

Pratt, Mary Louise. *Imperial Eyes: Travel Writing and Transculturation*. London: Routledge, 1992.

Rosenthal, Bernard. *City of Nature: Journeys to Nature in the Age of American Romanticism*. Newark: University of Delaware Press, 1980.

Shi, David. *The Simple Life: Plain Living and High Thinking in American Culture*. New York: Oxford University Press, 1985.

Slotkin, Richard. *Regeneration through Violence: The Mythology of the American Frontier, 1600–1860*. Middletown, Conn.: Wesleyan University Press, 1973.

Smith, Henry Nash. *Virgin Land: The American West as Symbol and Myth*. Cambridge, Mass.: Harvard University Press, 1950.

Worster, Donald. *Nature's Economy: A History of Ecological Ideas*. Cambridge, U.K, and New York: Cambridge University Press, 1985.

Lance Newman

NATURE

Nature (1836) by Ralph Waldo Emerson (1803–1882) is the key statement of the principles informing New England transcendentalism. The transcendentalist movement was a highly diverse phenomenon whose representatives addressed themselves in many voices and from many different perspectives to every important concern agitating New England life and thought in the decades preceding the Civil War. In view of this diversity, it may seem hazardous to claim one text as central to the movement. *Nature* owes its pivotal position to Emerson's searching exploration and provocative expression of the philosophical principles that most vitally affected transcendentalist thought—whether that thought addressed itself to religious, literary, social, or political questions. Not surprisingly, *Nature* has often been called the "manifesto" of transcendentalism.

Nature is also the fundamental statement of Emerson's own philosophy. Although his first book, it was not a beginner's immature endeavor. It reflected years of intellectual questioning and assiduous attempts to accommodate complex, sometimes conflicting philosophical positions. *Nature* shows all the marks of a work still in progress, but it is for that reason all the more true to Emerson's intentions. Although Emerson wrote many works after *Nature*, the principles it explored and the mode of thinking it performed made it his defining achievement. In *Nature*, moreover, Emerson first demonstrated his profound engagement with the most challenging ideas of the age, the ideas advanced by German and English philosophy and literature. While transcendentalism is traceable to important native roots, Emerson's *Nature* also involved it in the speculative ferment of international Romanticism.

IDEALISM

Nature exemplifies Emerson's commitment to philosophical idealism. The book espouses the fundamental idealist tenets that Spirit or Mind (or Soul, Idea, Thought) has primacy both ontologically—only Spirit has real existence and everything outside it is merely phenomenal—and epistemologically: knowledge arises not from the senses (as empiricism supposed) but from the laws of the mind and from the mind's imposing its laws and structures upon the indeterminate data provided by the senses. Like Romantic—or, more strictly, Kantian and post-Kantian—idealism in general, Emerson's idealism privileges epistemology over ontology in the sense that it identifies true being with knowing. The world, our selves, and Spirit achieve reality through knowledge. The only world we have

is the world as we conceive it to be, the world congruent with our idea of it; our only real self is the self we are conscious of; and Spirit is not absolute object but absolute subject, pure thought thinking itself and realizing itself in our own thinking. According to *Nature*, knowing is being: the human "feels by knowledge the privilege to BE!" and our partaking of Spirit, our "apprehend[ing] the absolute," makes us feel that "for the first time, *we exist*" (*Collected Works* [henceforth *CW*] 1:25, 35). The famous "transparent eye-ball" passage also identifies real being with true seeing, with sharing transcendent insight, an experience eclipsing the "mean egotism" that constitutes nonbeing ("I am nothing"): "I become a transparent eye-ball. . . . I see all. The currents of the Universal Being circulate through me; I am part or particle of God" (*CW* 1:10).

Three related points need emphasizing. First, Emerson uses the term "nature" in a dual sense: in the "common sense," as referring to the natural world, and in the philosophical sense, as referring, in language ultimately derived from Johann Gottlieb Fichte, to "the NOT ME," that is, everything that is not my own mind, thus "both nature and art, all other men and my own body" (*CW* 1:8). To facilitate future reference to this distinction, this essay shall, when necessary to avoid confusion, refer to the natural world as Nature-A and to the not-me in its historical and cultural aspects as Nature-B. Second, although Spirit transcends time and space, which, Emerson says, "are relations of matter" (*CW* 1:35), the self-expression of Spirit of necessity takes place in time and space, and thus becomes part of the phenomenal world, as either Nature-A or Nature-B. Third, in line with Romantic thinking, Emerson conceives of Spirit as inexhaustibly creative and thus, in its self-expression, as ever new and infinitely progressive. The human mind thinking originally rather than conventionally or traditionally is the means through which Spirit expresses itself anew. Each such expression is a partial self-realization of Spirit and thus enhances its self-knowledge. Spirit, in other words, needs the human thinker as much for its self-realization as the human thinker needs Spirit for inspiration, for original thought. In a dramatic rhetorical gesture, Emerson allows Spirit itself to acknowledge its dependence on "the human form." Spirit says: "From such as this, have I drawn joy and knowledge. In such as this, have I found and beheld myself. I will speak to it. It can speak again. It can yield me thought already formed and alive" (*CW* 1:28). The human who transcends past expressions of Spirit, which constitute our historical or cultural heritage (Nature-B), and shows her or his unique individuality by expressing original thought, is the means through which

Emerson the mystic, or the "transparent eye-ball." Caricature by the transcendentalist poet and painter Christopher Cranch. BY PERMISSION OF THE HOUGHTON LIBRARY, HARVARD UNIVERSITY, bMS Am1506

Spirit expresses and realizes itself now. Such a human, Emerson says in his essay "Intellect" (1841), "respects the highest law of his being" (*CW* 2:202).

THE PROBLEM OF THE AGE

Emerson's commitment to idealism inspires the complaint that opens *Nature:* "Our age is retrospective. It builds the sepulchres of the fathers. It writes biographies, histories, and criticism," wasting its intellectual substance honoring and studying past expressions of Spirit (*CW* 1:7). All such expressions are limited and defective because in the act of expressing itself the pure idea becomes subject to time and space, the compromises of culture, the idiosyncrasies of fashion, linguistic inadequacies and stylistic conventions, failures in skill and flaws in temperament. "Why," then, "should we grope among the dry bones of the past?" (*CW* 1:7). Indeed, as explained in his 1837 Cambridge address "The American Scholar," "When [Man Thinking] can read God directly, the hour is too precious to be wasted in other men's transcripts of their readings" (*CW* 1:57). Not even Homer or Shakespeare can compensate for the loss of "an original relation to the universe" (*CW* 1:14, 7).

Emerson never objected to truly creative reinterpretations of the past, to past philosophy or literature being born anew through one's rethinking and mentally rewriting it. In such encounters, the mind of the present, far from being dominated by the past, actually puts the past in its debt; in his lecture on "Art," Emerson thinks Shakespeare indebted to Johann Wolfgang von Goethe and Samuel Taylor Coleridge "for the wisdom they detect in his Hamlet and Anthony" (*Early Lectures* 2:48). Emerson himself often creatively adapted past figures to the needs of his own thinking, as in his chapters on Plato, Montaigne, or Shakespeare in *Representative Men* (1850), to say nothing of the Jesus of the Divinity School "Address" (1838). What Emerson condemned, in the opening of *Nature* and elsewhere, was the mind of the present succumbing to the burden of history, to a sense of historical belatedness that devalues the present, discourages originality, and casts doubt on the individual's potential as "a newborn bard" of the Spirit (*CW* 1:90). He wanted his age to escape from spiritually impoverishing retrospection and be reawakened to a sense of its own responsibility to Spirit. A means to this end is men and women being reconnected with their own direct experience of Spirit-in-nature. Emerson, therefore, invokes the natural world, Nature-A, as an antidote to the world of tradition and culture, Nature-B. Like Spirit, Nature-A is always now: "The sun shines to-day also" (*CW* 1:7). As an American of his generation, Emerson also regarded appreciation of Nature-A

as a safeguard against deflection from a national cultural vocation by the example of a strongly European Nature-B. Nature-A was a great national asset, defining a new Eden. Emerson's introduction and chapter 1 ("Nature") stress, therefore, the need to be sensitive to the miracle that is Nature-A, a miracle that should lose none of its enchantment by its pervasiveness. Indeed, "The invariable mark of wisdom is to see the miraculous in the common" (*CW* 1:44). The content and quality of such seeing, however, depend not upon nature but upon the self because "what we are, that only can we see" (*CW* 1:45).

THE EDUCATION OF THE SELF

Chapters 2 through 5 demonstrate the human's advancing to deeper spiritual self-awareness. The starting point of this process is the individual's encounter with Nature-A. Unlike the human mind, which is Spirit as consciousness, Nature-A is Spirit as negation of consciousness: it is "a remoter and inferior incarnation of God, a projection of God in the unconscious" (*CW* 1:38). Confrontation with "unconscious" Nature-A evokes responses that enable humans increasingly to recognize the deeper spiritual dimension of their being and thus their distinctness from nature. They become aware of "the eternal distinction between the soul and the world" (*CW* 1:38). The most immediate encounter takes place on the level of "Commodity" (chapter 2), where the mind discovers its ability to make nature serve the needs of the body. The mind exploits and imposes structures upon nature that ensure and enhance physical survival, which is an obvious prerequisite for the flourishing of the individual's spirit.

One aspect of this flourishing is the human spirit's discovering in itself a yearning for beauty (chapter 3). Emerson asserts that "the desire of beauty" is "an ultimate end" of the soul and that "no reason can be asked or given why the soul seeks beauty." Beauty is simply, like truth and goodness, a postulate of Spirit that needs to be made real and concrete in individual experience (*CW* 1:17).

Emerson divides his chapter into three numbered sections. The first may be labeled "natural beauty." Nature-A as such is aesthetically neutral. It provides material whose "beauty" depends upon whether or not it is perceived as beautiful, and thus on an act of the mind. The mind could not possibly identify beauty in nature unless it brought to its perception a mental category called "beauty." Nature provides the opportunity to bring this category into play, thus actualizing it in experience. The second section may be called "moral beauty" because Emerson devotes it to the

From Plato onward, the pursuit of knowledge has been associated with ways of looking. Plato's "Ideas" imply vision: Greek idea *(from* idein, *"to see"; also, "to see mentally") means "that which is seen," "appearance," "form," and, as a product of mental perception, "notion," "idea." A vivid sense of the visual implication of* idea *still surfaces in Goethe's statement that, if the* Urpflanze *("archplant") was an idea, it was an idea he could "see with his eyes" (16:867–868). The term "theory" (*theōria*) was equally vision-rooted: it meant "a looking at," "a viewing," "a beholding," and hence, as in Plato and his successors, "contemplation," "speculation."* Theōria *also referred to the "contemplative life" (*bios theōrētikos*) and, in early Christian thought, to the contemplation of God. The phrase "eye of the mind" and its variants, which Plato used repeatedly to designate a suprasensory mode of perception, occur in such diverse ancient authors as Aristotle, Cicero, Ovid, St. Paul, and Marcus Aurelius. Given the enormous influence of Plato and the writers just mentioned, one is not surprised to find the image of the mind's eye reappearing in, for example, Chaucer and Sir Philip Sidney, Shakespeare and Goethe, Johann Gottlieb Fichte and Emerson ("the eye of Reason," as in the excerpt below). From its opening sentence to its final words,* Nature *invokes the sense of sight and shows the mind reaching for suprasensory vision—for insight through the mind's eye, for a higher theory and a transcendent idea. This privileging of suprasensory vision expresses Emerson's Romantic and transcendentalist rejection of eighteenth-century sensationalism and his conviction that the dominance of sense perception precluded higher vision and deeper insight. Like Coleridge and Wordsworth, he knew that seeing into the essence of things required emancipation from what the former called the "despotism of the eye" (*Biographia Literaria *1:107) and the latter the "tyranny" of "the bodily eye . . . / The most despotic of our senses" (the 1850* Prelude *12:135, 128–129). As Emerson himself points out in chapter 6 of* Nature *("Idealism"), excerpted below, only by negating "this despotism of the senses" can one attain true insight.*

From Sight to Insight

To the senses and the unrenewed understanding, belongs a sort of instinctive belief in the absolute existence of nature. In their view, man and nature are indissolubly joined. Things are ultimates, and they never look beyond their sphere. The presence of Reason mars this faith. The first effort of thought tends to relax this despotism of the senses, which binds us to nature as if we were a part of it, and shows us nature aloof, and, as it were, afloat. Until this higher agency intervened, the animal eye sees, with wonderful accuracy, sharp outlines and colored surfaces. When the eye of Reason opens, to outline and surface are at once added, grace and expression. These proceed from imagination and affection, and abate somewhat of the angular distinctness of objects. If the Reason be stimulated to more earnest vision, outlines and surfaces become transparent, and are no longer seen; causes and spirits are seen through them. The best, the happiest moments of life, are these delicious awakenings of the higher powers, and the reverential withdrawing of nature before its God.

Emerson, *Collected Works* 1:30.

---

beauty inherent in and demonstrated by virtuous or heroic action. Obviously, moral beauty involves a far greater contribution of Spirit, and therefore it ranks higher than the natural beauty of section 1. As action, moral beauty enters upon the world of time and space and thus (as Nature-B) is accessible to human perception. The moral beauty that such action radiates profoundly affects the world. It hallows battlefields and other places that have witnessed noble endeavors. It enables men and women to see beauty even in the scaffold if sanctified by martyrdom such as that of a Sir Henry Vane or a William Russell. The third section can be called "intellectual beauty" because it concerns the beauty of thought itself, the beauty of ideas. The principal way in which beautiful ideas express themselves is through works of art. The idea has primacy: without it the artist could not create a work of art because he or she would have nothing to imprint upon the material provided by Nature-A. The beauty of art is superior to the beauty of Nature-A (section 1) because it involves a far greater contribution of Spirit: art involves a more profound transforming of nature, a fuller fusion of Spirit and matter, than is required for the mere perception of natural beauty. By becoming part of Nature-B, works of art, moreover, make the beauty of ideas accessible to everyone.

In *Nature*'s progress toward its ultimate goal of gaining a deeper insight into Spirit, the fourth chapter, "Language," follows the chapter on "Beauty" because language is a more inwardly based, a more subtle and ethereal—in a word, a more spirit-imbued—instrument of spiritual self-expression. Put differently, "Beauty" is more heavily dependent on nature.

This is obvious with natural beauty, but also the greatness or heroism revealing moral beauty is firmly embedded in the world of time and space, in a historical context (e.g., the Spartan hero Leonidas at Thermopylae). Similarly, the works of art expressing intellectual beauty (architecture, sculpture, painting) are bound to matter and locale in a way that language is not. Language's higher level of transcendence of nature and its more intimate involvement in Spirit make it essential to human, and thus spiritual, self-definition to a degree that art is not.

Like "Beauty," "Language" is divided into three sections. In the first section, Emerson credits nature with providing our vocabulary. Words are simply "signs of natural facts." But as the term "sign" indicates, natural facts become words for us only through our mind's endowing them with meaning. This role of mind is all the more evident because the real focus of section 1 is on metaphor, which consists in turning words as signs of natural facts into words expressing "moral or intellectual fact[s]" (*CW* 1:18). Accentuating the contribution of mind, this process correspondingly attenuates the contribution of nature, as is also evident in section 2, whose subject is symbol. Emerson's claim that "every natural fact is a symbol of some spiritual fact" (*CW* 1:18) involves three levels: (1) it starts with the natural fact or object, which, though necessary, is merely inceptive; (2) the mind endows the object, as symbol, with meaning; and (3) since symbol suggests or hints at the spiritual fact but cannot encompass it, the mind recognizes symbol's inferiority to what it symbolizes. Through symbol, the finite mind reaches for insight into the spiritual dimension of reality. Through symbol, language not only transcends nature but also reaches beyond itself for something it cannot ultimately grasp. This inadequacy of language will help explain Emerson's attitude in the chapter "Spirit" and the ultimate "incompleteness" or open-endedness of *Nature* itself.

The third section of "Language" vindicates the claim in section 2 that "particular natural facts" correspond symbolically to "particular spiritual facts" (*CW* 1:17). The finite mind can establish such correspondences—can find an appropriate natural object to symbolize a specific thought—because Nature-A in its totality is a symbol of Spirit. The fact that the natural world is Spirit's own symbolic language makes possible and authorizes using part of that world when attempting to give voice to what is inevitably (given the finiteness of the individual mind) but a very limited and transient revelation of Spirit. But the objects of nature, which constitute Spirit's universal language, also have meanings beyond the ones consciously given them in the act of appropriating them symbolically.

At present, our limited insight into Spirit precludes our fully understanding the book of nature, but we do know that nature, as symbol of Spirit, also symbolizes the human mind and that, consequently, the laws of nature can be shown to illustrate moral laws. Emerson often uses "moral" and "ethical" in the broad sense of anything having reference to human character and practical wisdom. A statement like "The last ounce broke the camel's back" demonstrates a law of nature, but it also implies a moral truth, thus extending the statement's spiritual significance. Indeed, the laws of nature "have a much more extensive and universal sense when applied to human life" (*CW* 1:22).

Chapter 5 is called "Discipline," by which Emerson means the education of the self through confrontation with nature. The use of nature as discipline "includes the preceding uses" of the world (commodity, beauty, language) "as parts of itself" (*CW* 1:23). In "Discipline," Emerson invokes the most significant distinction in his age's idealist epistemology, the distinction between "the understanding" and "the reason." Ultimately traceable to Immanuel Kant's distinction between *Verstand* (understanding) and *Vernunft* (reason), the terms reached Emerson primarily as reinterpreted by Coleridge. In "Language" Emerson calls reason the "universal soul" and says that "intellectually [epistemologically] considered" we call reason that which "considered in relation to nature, we call Spirit" (*CW* 1:18–19). Not surprisingly, in "Discipline" reason is by far the higher faculty. The understanding derives "intellectual truths" from its confrontations with the data provided by the senses, which it subjects to analysis, reflection, and discursive reasoning. "Every property of matter is a school for the understanding," which "adds, divides, combines, measures." The understanding, in sum, "form[s] the Hand of the mind" and teaches "common sense" (*CW* 1:23–24).

Whereas the understanding provides the mind with both insight into and practical guidance concerning nature and the world, reason focuses upon the mind itself; "reason transfers all these lessons [of the understanding] into its own world of thought." Reason is able to do so because it perceives "the analogy that marries Matter and Mind" (*CW* 1:23). This perception of analogy is rooted in reason's grasping the unity underlying all seeming variety: "So intimate is this Unity, that, it is easily seen, it lies under the undermost garment of nature, and betrays its source in universal Spirit. For, it pervades Thought also" (*CW* 1:27–28). Spirit is the One pervading all, and the best evidence of this truth is that "all things are moral" (*CW* 1:25)—that the moral sense without which humanness is inconceivable finds in nature an inexhaustible source of moral lessons. Emerson followed

Kant in repeatedly stressing the primacy of ethics among human concerns. He held that "the moral is prior in God's order to the intellectual" (*Letters* 1:450). In "Discipline," Spirit is recognized primarily through human reason's discovering the inescapably moral character of its encounters with nature. For a geologist, a rock may hold "intellectual" (scientific) interest. Far more important to Emerson is the moral implication of the question: "Who can guess how much firmness the sea-beaten rock has taught the fisherman?" (*CW* 1:27). The geologist may learn scientific facts (at the level of the understanding). The fisherman may learn firmness, endurance, courage, and similar virtues—in other words, qualities of the soul.

SPIRIT

Emerson devotes three chapters of *Nature* to attempts to elucidate the ultimate reality, Spirit itself. In chapter 6, "Idealism," he establishes once and for all the ontological absoluteness of Spirit and the merely phenomenal existence of nature. Emerson's idealism does not deny the existence of matter. What it does assert is "the total disparity between the evidence of our own being, and the evidence of the world's being. The one is perfect; the other, incapable of any assurance" (*CW* 1:37). Our own being inheres in the mind's reason-based self-reflexivity; the world, by contrast, exists only as the content of the mind's sense-based representations. The only world we have is a phenomenal world, a world perceived by humans, and because a non-perceived world is not accessible to us, we are unable to determine the validity of our perceived world. In his fundamental philosophical statement on the Spirit-nature distinction, Emerson says that our mind's progress inevitably leads us "to regard nature as a phenomenon, not a substance; to attribute necessary existence to spirit; to esteem nature as an accident and an effect" (*CW* 1:30). He here invokes an ancient dichotomy much debated throughout the history of philosophy: substance versus accident. Spirit is substance, Latin *substantia*, Greek *ousia*, "being," "essence." Nature is accident, Latin *accidens*, Greek *to sumbebēkos*, "contingency," in philosophical usage designating that which is dependent on substance but cannot encompass it. For Emerson, nature is conceivable only in relation to Spirit, but it does not encompass Spirit's essence, both of which points are reconfirmed by his calling nature "an effect." Unlike nature, Spirit is "necessary," in the philosophical sense of being noncontingent, unconditioned, essential.

Emerson points out, however, that the inescapably phenomenal existence of our world in no way precludes "the stability of nature" based on "the permanence of natural laws" (*CW* 1:29–30). Nature is universal lawfulness because it reflects Spirit. Emerson agrees with Kant that the "serene order" (*CW* 1:39) of nature derives from the mind inescapably imposing its rules upon nature in the act of structuring and interpreting the content of sensation. Avoiding the complexity of Kant's argument, Emerson simply considers it a given that the laws of nature are but the mind's ideas objectified: "A law determines all phenomena" but "that law, when in the mind, is an idea" (*CW* 1:33–34). The mind, consequently, also derives self-knowledge from the study of nature, its objectified self. As stated in "The American Scholar," "the ancient precept, 'Know thyself,' and the modern precept, 'study nature,' become at last one maxim" (*CW* 1:55).

Emerson illustrates the superiority of mind to nature in several ways. He avers, for instance, that in all scenes of life the perceiver occupies a position of absolute centrality in that he or she unavoidably constitutes a center of awareness to which nature and other humans appear as merely spectacle. Similarly, the poet makes nature "revolve around the axis of his primary thought." Through imagination, which Emerson defines as "the use which the Reason makes of the material world," the poet demonstrates the secondary status of nature by making it vehicular to thought, whose primacy consists in its identity with "the Reason" (*CW* 1:31). Emerson also reminds readers that the superiority of mind to matter is an essential tenet of metaphysics and of religion and ethics. But "even in physics, the material is ever degraded before the spiritual" (*CW* 1:34). This claim holds not only for those advancing "a theory of nature" (*CW* 1:8) but also for the empiricist, who cannot subject nature to an experiment unless that experiment be mentally conceived beforehand, thus again showing the constructive initiative of mind and the "passivity" of nature.

Having established the primacy of Spirit, Emerson confronts in the next chapter ("Spirit") the question that the whole of *Nature* has been leading to: What is Spirit? Spirit is "ineffable essence," essence that "refuses to be recorded in propositions." Consequently, Emerson's idealist theory is unable to answer the question. Even though we can think Spirit, we cannot know Spirit because our language has no grip on it. Therefore, concerning Spirit, "he that thinks most, will say least" (*CW* 1:37). Emerson's inability to answer the question inheres in Spirit, as absolute "substance," being beyond the definitional reach of any of its predicates. Because nature, the medium necessary for the expression of these predicates, is but "an accident," none of the predicates provided by such chapters as "Beauty," "Language," and "Discipline" can do justice to Spirit: each of them is too deeply involved in "accidental" nature. Even the chapter "Idealism,"

AMERICAN HISTORY THROUGH LITERATURE, 1820–1870   *801*

which clearly sets off Spirit from nature, cannot truly define the former: by defining Spirit as distinctness from nature, it makes the identity of Spirit conditional upon the nature of nature, thereby denying that identity its transcendent absoluteness. Spirit, in sum, defies conceptualization.

Emerson's failure to define Spirit and his admission that his philosophical idealism was merely "a useful introductory hypothesis" (*CW* 1:38) were expressions of his dynamic conception of truth. He would have violated his deepest convictions as a Romantic and a transcendentalist had he pretended to give final answers to the questions raised in *Nature* or subjected his thoughts to rigid systematization. For Emerson, truth resides in one's striving to attain it, not in any final conclusion. He, therefore, concludes his book with a chapter in which nothing is concluded, a chapter whose very title, "Prospects," counters the opening sentence ("Our age is retrospective") and promises an escape from the intellectual stagnation there implied. In sometimes rhapsodic language, Emerson urges embracing the challenge of "undiscovered regions of thought" and having boundless faith in the promise of humanity: "Infancy is the perpetual Messiah" (*CW* 1:41–42). This message was singularly relevant to Emerson's young country, whose greatness, he was convinced, was contingent upon its orientation to the future, its attempts to realize the ideals informing the human spirit. Americans were called upon to serve humankind by exploring, in the words of "The American Scholar," "the unsearched might of man" (*CW* 1:69).

See also "The American Scholar"; "Experience"; Nature; "The Poet"; Romanticism; "Self-Reliance"; Transcendentalism

BIBLIOGRAPHY

Primary Works

Coleridge, Samuel Taylor. *Biographia Literaria; or, Biographical Sketches of My Literary Life and Opinions.* 1817. 2 vols. Edited by James Engell and W. Jackson Bate. Princeton, N.J.: Princeton University Press, 1983.

Emerson, Ralph Waldo. *The Collected Works of Ralph Waldo Emerson.* 6 vols. Edited by Alfred R. Ferguson et al. Cambridge, Mass.: Belknap Press of Harvard University Press, 1971–. When complete, this will be the standard edition, replacing *The Complete Works.*

Emerson, Ralph Waldo. *The Complete Works of Ralph Waldo Emerson.* 12 vols. Edited by Edward Waldo Emerson. Boston: Houghton Mifflin, 1903–1904.

Emerson, Ralph Waldo. *The Early Lectures of Ralph Waldo Emerson.* 3 vols. Edited by Stephen E. Whicher, Robert E. Spiller, and Wallace E. Williams. Cambridge, Mass.: Harvard University Press, 1959–1972.

Emerson, Ralph Waldo. *The Later Lectures of Ralph Waldo Emerson, 1843–1871.* 2 vols. Edited by Ronald A. Bosco and Joel Myerson. Athens: University of Georgia Press, 2001.

Emerson, Ralph Waldo. *The Letters of Ralph Waldo Emerson.* 10 vols. Edited by Ralph L. Rusk and Eleanor M. Tilton. New York: Columbia University Press, 1939, 1990–1995.

Emerson, Ralph Waldo. *Nature.* Boston: J. Munroe, 1836.

Goethe, Johann Wolfgang von. *Gedenkausgabe der Werke, Briefe und Gespräche.* 27 vols. Edited by Ernst Beutler. Zurich: Artemis Verlag, 1948–1971.

Wordsworth, William. *The Prelude, 1799, 1805, 1850.* Edited by Jonathan Wordsworth, M. H. Abrams, and Stephen Gill. New York: Norton, 1979.

Secondary Works

Berthoff, Warner. Introduction to *Nature,* by Ralph Waldo Emerson. San Francisco: Chandler, 1968.

Buell, Lawrence. *Emerson.* Cambridge, Mass.: Belknap Press of Harvard University Press, 2003.

Cameron, Kenneth Walter. *Young Emerson's Transcendental Vision: An Exposition of His World View with an Analysis of the Structure, Backgrounds, and Meaning of Nature.* 1836. Hartford, Conn.: Transcendental Books, 1971.

Richardson, Robert D., Jr. *Emerson: The Mind on Fire.* Berkeley: University of California Press, 1995.

Rusk, Ralph L. *The Life of Ralph Waldo Emerson.* New York: Scribners, 1949.

Wood, Barry. "The Growth of the Soul: Coleridge's Dialectical Method and the Strategy of Emerson's *Nature.*" *PMLA* 91 (May 1976): 385–397.

Gustaaf Van Cromphout

NAUTICAL LITERATURE

The United States in the first half of the nineteenth century was a country that looked to the sea. The largest towns were seaports. These acted as the economic engines of the country, controlling exports, distributing imports, and accumulating and investing capital. This is the context in which the American novel developed. It comes as no surprise, therefore, that James Fenimore Cooper, for instance, most celebrated for his tales of frontier life, also wrote over a dozen works of nautical fiction. What is surprising is just how effectively such nautical novels tackled questions about the emerging nation.

JAMES FENIMORE COOPER

There have always been sea stories, but Cooper (1789–1851) invented the sea novel, a work in which, in the words of Thomas Philbrick, "the principal characters and action are defined by the oceanic environment that surrounds them" (Introduction, p. ix). Cooper's first work, *Precaution* (1820), was a novel of manners, but in his first sea novel, *The Pilot* (1823), he starts to say something really significant about American life. The "Pilot" commands a frigate off the coast of England; his mission is to capture prominent Englishmen in order to force a modification of the British policy of impressment. What is striking in Cooper's novel is the sense of the Pilot as an American hero, a romantic individual outside any conventional social order. This connects with motifs repeatedly evident in American nautical novels: a sense of landlessness, of having no roots, which develops into an impression of the vastness of the sea and the isolation of the mariner. With its English setting, however, *The Pilot* seems to be still caught up in the past; it is as if the United States at this point is still defining itself in relation to Britain.

If *The Pilot* hints at the difficulties involved in forging a new identity, it is in *The Red Rover* (1827) that Cooper really explores the problem. The hero, a pirate, has rejected the past and become an outlaw. But a sense of American identity here involves far more than just an endorsement of rebelliousness. The Rover is happiest in command of his ship, where he feels liberated; the ship is free and represents freedom. In a similar way, his crew delight in the challenge of the voyage. The complication is that the Rover displays a callous disregard for life, imposing extreme forms of physical abuse upon his crew. The novel allows its readers to appreciate that, as against a simple idea of freedom, the reality of the United States is a set of contradictions; that is to say, the country's democratic ideal is at odds with the way in which it actually conducts itself. One way in which this is apparent in Cooper's novels is in his references to race; he returns repeatedly to the paradox of the existence of slavery in a country committed to liberty.

The setting of a ship provides an ideal stage for posing such dilemmas. It is an environment where a body of men have come together for their mutual advantage; men from different backgrounds must work together as they venture forth to places that are still waiting to be fully explored. But the structured regime of the ship, and the possibility of the abuse of power, raises questions about how authority is exercised in a democracy. Within this framework, Cooper confronts a range of issues, and issues that changed during his lifetime. By the time of *Afloat and Ashore* (1844) both Cooper and the United States had moved on. The novel has two main characters: Miles, who chooses a career at sea, and Rupert, who enters a lawyer's office. Cooper's focus here is on competing images of the nation's identity: the risk-taking existence of a sailor and the more cautious life that has evolved on the shore. But this is only one aspect of Cooper's grasp of the divisions in American society in the years before the Civil War. Slavery is again an issue in *Afloat and Ashore*, as is class. The sailor Smudge is a character who oversteps the mark; Miles is a gentle person, but in his position of authority he does not hesitate to hang Smudge. This and other events in the novel repeatedly demonstrate that it is clearly impossible to reconcile the variety of America with a unified vision of America.

The Capture. Illustration by F. O. C. Darley from *Afloat and Ashore*, 1844, by James Fenimore Cooper. The hero of the novel, Miles Wallingford, is attacked by Indians while serving aboard a ship anchored off the west coast of what is now British Columbia, Canada.

ADVENTURES AT SEA

Nautical novels look at the society Americans have created, but they also look to the future. A repeated impression of venturing into the unknown, and at the same time a sense of establishing an American empire, is most obvious in land-based narratives of the first half of the nineteenth century, where the travelers take possession of the American continent. A similar impression is evident in nonfictional nautical texts of the era, such as Owen Chase's *Narrative of the Most Extra-Ordinary and Distressing Shipwreck of the Whale-Ship "Essex"* (1821), Charles Stewart's *A Visit to the South Seas* (1831), Edmund Fanning's *Voyages round the World* (1833), and Francis A. Olmsted's *Incidents of a Whaling Voyage* (1841). Of particular interest is Charles Wilkes's five-volume *Narrative of the United States Exploring Expedition* (1845). The motivation in the voyages described by these texts might ultimately be economic but also present in all these narratives is what Bert Bender describes as "the essential motive for all literary voyages: the desire for renewal, discovery, light" (p. 4). Such qualities are especially prominent in Richard Henry Dana's *Two Years before the Mast* (1840); by the end of his tale, Dana is glad to leave the sea, but before this his experience is one that brings an idea of freedom, a sense of space, and a spirit of adventure.

Inevitably, however, darker notes intrude in such sagas; Dana's work also conveys, for example, the autocratic, bullying regime on the ship. In Edgar Allan Poe's *The Narrative of Arthur Gordon Pym of Nantucket* (1838) the immediate impression is of an adventure story set aboard a merchant ship sailing to the South Seas, but the work quickly becomes a disturbing fantasy in which Poe confronts the tensions that characterized his native South. What consistently informs such works is the consciousness of a gap between the original, innocent and inspiring conception of the United States and how the country has actually developed. For example, Cooper's final nautical novel, *The Sea Lions* (1848), constructs a sense of the world spinning out of control, a feeling prompted by the author's unease with what he sees as the downward-leveling tendencies of democracy.

HERMAN MELVILLE

Herman Melville (1819–1891) is a preeminent figure in the tradition of American nautical literature. In the five works that precede *Moby-Dick* (1851) the protagonists are all wanderers on the ocean. *Typee* (1846), *Omoo* (1847), and *Mardi* (1849) are suffused with a tantalizing sense of venturing into the unknown. This is particularly true in *Mardi,* in which the narrator abandons his ship, establishes a relationship with a young woman, and then, when she is kidnapped, embarks upon a kind of allegorical exploration of the world. *Redburn* (1849) is much more straightforward as an account of a young man's first sea voyage on a trader bound for Liverpool, his experiences onboard and in England, and his return to the United States. *White-Jacket* (1850), set on a man-of-war, is based on Melville's experience of service on the *United States* in 1844 and focuses on the degrading conditions on the *Neversink*. The narrator is the maker and wearer of the white jacket that throughout the journey causes him grief.

Melville writes in a tradition of nautical fiction, but he is clearly a writer in a different league: his works always move beyond our framework of expectations. *White-Jacket,* for example, is a powerful indictment of conditions and leadership in the U.S. Navy. As such, it poses the kinds of questions about the abuse of power that are aired repeatedly in nautical novels. By focusing on a brutal regime Melville, like Dana (Dana encouraged Melville to develop his experiences on the *United States* into a work of fiction), constructs an implicit analysis of the condition of the United States at a crucial stage in its expansion and development. The text operates powerfully at this level. The regime on the *Neversink* is oppressive, with extreme punishments for minor misdeeds. And perhaps even more disconcerting is the general air of indifference in relation to the sailors' lives. The most appalling example is the unnecessary amputation of the leg of a sailor by the ship's doctor, an act of brutality that results in the man's death. As always in nautical fiction, abuse of the body undermines any pretence of a reasonable social order. More specifically in an American context, the impression of the ordinary seaman as disposable is obviously incompatible with the notion of a society that has broken away from the European social model.

As powerful as Melville's critique is, however, this is not the most striking feature of the work. What is most likely to challenge the reader's expectations is the significance of White Jacket himself. Dressed so distinctively, he appears to be a symbolic figure, but it is difficult to be sure what effect is intended. In a puzzling way, White Jacket actually seems superfluous to the critique of the navy that the work offers. As such, he becomes a wild card, a figure that unsettles the narrative. His presence is consistent, however, with a more general impression that many of the incidents and details in *White-Jacket* cannot be accommodated within any coherent or convincing overall interpretation of the text. Rather than explain White Jacket, therefore, it seems more reasonable to suggest that the character evades comprehension.

Whereas *White-Jacket* is often strange, *Moby-Dick* (1851) is much stranger, and even more baffling. It was written at a significant moment, when whaling was still the United States's leading industry. Yet even as the novel was being written, the United States was turning its back on the sea, with the land as the new and only frontier that really mattered. A great deal of criticism of Melville's works since the late twentieth century has focused on just how sharp his analysis is of the economic, social, and cultural conditions of the country, at a time when the agricultural economy was being overtaken by an industrial economy. Whaling was part of the new industrial order of the United States, but, with an imminent collapse of the demand for whale oil, it was on the verge of becoming an activity associated with the past. When *Moby-Dick* is seen in this context, it becomes possible to account for the novel's baffling nature. As the maritime frontier lost its central role in the American imagination, the nautical story seemingly began to lose its commanding capacity to make sense of the country; inexplicable elements started to intrude into the story. Indeed, it is as if Melville uses the form of the novel to exploit a sense of the vastness and mysteriousness of the ocean in a way that subverts all attempts at explanation. The novel repeatedly sets the unpredictability of the sea, the voyage, and life in general against the human impulse to assume command, to explain and to understand. This irresolvable tension is anticipated in *White-Jacket:* it offers a damning and coherent critique of the U.S. Navy, but at the same time there is a sense of much that is elusive in the text.

The classic American nautical novel was never just a story about the sea and sailors. It was, unavoidably, a story about the whole structure of a trading nation and the social and cultural order that evolves in such a society. In the United States of 1820–1870, a series of books attempt to make sense of the nation through an examination of the maritime activity that was so central in determining the character of that nation. But in Melville, as the maritime frontier loses its central role in the American economy and imagination, the form of the nautical tale is stretched to its limits in trying to sustain its traditional role. After *Moby-Dick* the nautical novel was no longer a distinctive feature of American literary culture; consequently, Melville's masterwork stands as the final extravagant, even self-parodying, flourish of the genre.

See also Maritime Commerce; *Moby-Dick; Two Years before the Mast*

BIBLIOGRAPHY

Primary Works

Cooper, James Fenimore. *Afloat and Ashore*. London: Bentley, 1844.

Cooper, James Fenimore. *Sea Tales*. New York: Library of America, 1991. Includes *The Pilot* (1823) and *The Red Rover* (1827).

Dana, Richard Henry, Jr. *Two Years before the Mast and Other Voyages*. 1840. New York: Library of America, 2005.

Melville, Herman. *Moby-Dick*. 1851. Oxford: Oxford University Press, 1988.

Melville, Herman. *White-Jacket; or, The World in a Man-of-War*. 1850. Oxford: Oxford University Press, 1990.

Poe, Edgar Allan. *The Narrative of Arthur Gordon Pym of Nantucket*. 1838. New York: Penguin, 1999.

Secondary Works

Bender, Bert. *Sea-Brothers: The Tradition of American Sea Fiction from "Moby-Dick" to the Present*. Philadelphia: University of Pennsylvania Press, 1988.

Kopley, Richard, ed. *Poe's "Pym": Critical Explorations*. Durham, N.C.: Duke University Press, 1992.

Labaree, Benjamin W., et al. *America and the Sea: A Maritime History*. Mystic, Conn.: Mystic Seaport, 1998.

Philbrick, Thomas. Introduction to *The Wing-and-Wing; or, Le Feu-follet*, by James Fenimore Cooper, pp. ix–xv. New York: Henry Holt, 1998.

Philbrick, Thomas. *James Fenimore Cooper and the Development of American Sea Fiction*. Cambridge, Mass.: Harvard University Press, 1961.

Selby, Nick, ed. *Herman Melville, "Moby Dick."* New York: Columbia University Press, 1999.

Sundquist, Eric J. "Exploration and Empire." In *The Cambridge History of American Literature*, vol. 2, *Prose Writing 1820–1865*, edited by Sacvan Bercovitch, pp. 127–174. New York: Cambridge University Press, 1995.

John Peck

A NEW HOME—WHO'LL FOLLOW?

A New Home—Who'll Follow? or, Glimpses of Western Life (1839) presents the experiences of a woman settler in eastern Michigan, then the western frontier of the United States. Its author, Caroline M. Kirkland (1801–1864), was an educator from Geneva, New York, who relocated to Detroit in 1835 so her husband, William, could head the Detroit Female Seminary. In 1837 William purchased land to found a village, and the Kirklands moved farther west.

Initially lacking such basics as roads and a store, life in Pinckney, as the village was named, was harsh. For a cultivated woman like Kirkland the hardships also included proximity to—and interdependence

Pioneer Life in Missouri in 1820. Woodcut illustration by E. C. Hussey Co. after a drawing by D. H. Huyett depicting living conditions for midwestern settlers in the early nineteenth century. Mary Clavers's adjustment to such conditions after leaving a more ordered and privileged existence in the East is the subject of *A New Home.* © CORBIS

with—unrefined and minimally educated lower-class families for whom settling the West meant realizing the promise of Jacksonian democracy that white Americans could enjoy land ownership, economic betterment, and full citizenship. High-spirited and witty, Kirkland did not anguish over her circumstances, although she never liked them. Her greatest pleasure was apparently to write about what she recognized as a many-faceted situation in which no participant could be fully satisfied. *A New Home* is an entertaining, sometimes rueful, always variegated account of the emergence of the village of Montacute (as Kirkland calls Pinckney) in which Kirkland's fictional narrator, Mary Clavers, details her experiences and observations. Inflected by Clavers's persisting sense of gentility but also her deepening sympathy for many of her rougher-edged neighbors, its freewheeling satire targets the crudeness of Clavers's poorer neighbors' homes, behavior, and expressions as well as excesses of gentility to which Clavers and others of her class cleave.

THE SKETCH FORM AND THE MANY-SIDEDNESS OF *A NEW HOME*

The complexity of *A New Home* has presented difficulties for commentators who have wanted to classify it within a single category, be it cultural-political (Whiggishly elitist? Mildly democratic?) or generic (Autobiography? Travel literature? Fiction?). Reflecting on the generic backbone of the book, the sketch, helps one approach this intricacy. The sketch—a seemingly casual prose form often devoted to appearing to capture, or "sketch," what the sketcher sees or experiences, often as he or she travels—became very popular in the early nineteenth century. Sketches often blurred boundaries between fiction and nonfiction; many also appealed to readers' growing interest in ways of life different from their own. Many sketches mixed descriptions of sometimes remote places, people, and activities with thoughts and reflections more akin to those of the readers. The form's openness to rendering locales and domestic life contributed to its appeal for women writers.

A New Home uses many of the sketch's conventions. Its linked sketches are sometimes almost ethnographic in the detail with which they evoke frontier life, and the book is directed to East Coast readers, whose outlook its narrator shares. Like many sketchers, Mary Clavers constantly addresses her readers. (This may also reflect the book's origins—one story is that the New York literary man Nathaniel P. Willis read some of Kirkland's entertaining letters and asked her to write a book about life in the West—but it also bespeaks Clavers's/Kirkland's abiding identification with genteel culture.) While many sketches seem offhand and unassuming, however, *A New Home* accentuates its status as estimable literature. It distinguished itself from two popular forms of writing about the West produced mainly by men: rosy, romantic depictions of western life like Charles Fenno Hoffman's (1806–1884) *A Winter in the West* (1835) and emigrants' guides whose enthusiastic descriptions of obstacle-free land were designed to entice (male) purchasers. Its abundant quotations from European and British literature align it with belletristic writing, as does Clavers's declared model, the British writer Mary Russell Mitford's celebrated linked sketches, *Our Village* (1824–1832), which conveyed the look and feel of life in an actual English village to which Mitford gave the name Three Cross Roads.

Like Mitford's unnamed female sketcher, Mary Clavers describes life on the ground. She details the rough, marshy terrain, crude log cabins, and in many cases rugged settlers she encounters as she traverses her village-in-the-making and the area around it. She also takes in the gradual realization of the plan drawn by Mr. Clavers and his land agent as an actual village with flour mill, schoolhouse, store, and some frame houses and eventually a debating society, women's sewing circle, and court sittings presided over by a "Justas of the Piece." She is even more attuned to a subject that literature was just beginning to represent, the emergence of the village as a process. In her depiction, that process entails conflicts, cultural clashes, and often vexed adjustments between the "Wolverines" (the earlier settlers) and middle-class later arrivals like the Claverses. (Kirkland refers rarely to Native Americans and does not acknowledge that the "wilderness" was actually their homeland, although she would in later writing about Michigan.) The representation of interpersonal and cultural life in Montacute is especially complex. Kirkland's representation endorses the efforts of Clavers and her kind to preserve control as they establish a modus operandi with the older settlers, but the narrative also stresses the disparateness of the viewpoints of the two classes

of settlers as well as reflecting some modifications in Clavers's own outlook.

Many of the early sketches focus on Clavers's introduction to the wilderness and Wolverines, satirically contrasting her literature-nourished anticipation of a garden-like landscape and frontier with the difficult terrain of "bogs," "mudholes," and log-covered paths she actually encounters. When it comes to humans' behavior and domestic arrangements, though, her gentility may seem unquestioned. As Lori Merish and other commentators suggest, her descriptions of people and culture affirm the identification with possessions and order that accompanied the antebellum rise of a substantial middle class and of commodity culture. In effect, the bourgeois sense of order involved the internalization of a system of classification for domestic life that dictated which possessions one should group together and which one should keep separate, what space should be on display and what space should be kept private. This sense suffuses the offended propriety of Clavers's satiric account of a morning spent visiting two women in a "log house" while her husband inspects his newly purchased land. The text highlights her repelled depiction of "two large beds not partitioned off . . . but curtained in with cotton sheets pinned to the unhewn rafters" and the visible hodgepodge of the cabin's inhabitants' "go-to-meeting hats and bonnets, frocks and pantaloons" (p. 13). Also affirmed are her mockery of log walls "garnished" in poor taste with garish circus posters and the affront to her concepts of hygiene and decorum of a "strip of dingy listing [wood] . . . nailed in such a way as to afford support for a few iron spoons, and small comb, and sundry other articles grouped with the like good taste" (p. 13).

Even here, though, Clavers also mocks her own assumed superiority by reporting on her distress when her husband makes her depart without giving her time to eat the meal the unappealing residents offer her. Increasingly, moreover, her genteel disdain is crosscut (though never annulled) by her recognition that her own refinement is an obstacle to a life in which hazardous transportation, spartan domestic life, and debilitating ague (marsh malaria) are commonplace—a life in which she must depend on her Wolverine neighbors' expertise, labor, and goodwill. As the narrative accentuates the process of her adjustment to the frontier, it features her self-satire alongside her affirmation of her initial values. Thus in explaining that she has learned to work around the democratic expectations of the women who assist her in domestic work—and expect to take dinner with the Clavers family—she italicizes the local term "*wearing round*" (p. 52), meaning "manipulate," in describing her

The following excerpt is from the penultimate chapter of A New Home. *Addressing her East Coast readers, Mary Clavers summarizes some of the difficulties she has experienced living in close proximity with her rough pioneer neighbors, expressing scorn for what she regards as their presumptuousness. Yet she also mocks her readers' unreflecting expectations about their right to a fairly privileged way of life. (She also recommends a year on the Michigan frontier as a cure for ennui or dissipation.) Clavers's characteristic self-deprecation about her writing is part of the satire of* A New Home. *She, or Kirkland, may well be modest about her literary efforts, but she is also suggesting that decorous writing would be an inappropriate medium for representing life on the frontier.*

I have in the course of these detached and desultory chapters, hinted at various deficiencies and peculiarities, which strike, with rather unpleasant force, the new resident in the back-woods; but it would require volumes to enumerate all the cases in which the fastidiousness, the taste, the pride, the self-esteem of the refined child of civilization, must be wounded by a familiar intercourse with the persons among whom he will find himself thrown, in the ordinary course of rural life. He is continually reminded in how great a variety of particulars his necessities, his materials for comfort, and his sources of pain, are precisely those of the humblest of his neighbours. The humblest, did I say? He will find that he has no humble neighbors. He will very soon discover, that in his new sphere, no act of kindness, no offer of aid, will be considered as any thing short of insult, if the least suspicion of *condescension* peep out. Equality, perfect and practical, is the *sine qua non*, and any appearance of a desire to avoid this rather trying fraternization is invariably met by a fierce and indignant resistance. The spirit in which was conceived the motto of the French revolution, "La fraternite ou la mort," exists in full force among us, though modified as to results. . . .

This same republican spirit is evinced rather amusingly, in the reluctance to admire, or even to approve, any thing like luxury or convenience which is not in common use among the settlers. Your carpets are spoken of as "*one* way to hide dirt;" your mahogany tables as "dreadful plaguy to scour;" your kitchen conveniences as "lumberin' up the house for nothing;" and so on to the end of the chapter. One lady informed me, that if she had such a pantry full of "dishes," under which general term is included every variety of china, glass and earthenware, she should set up store, and "sell them off pretty quick," for she wold not "be plagued with them." Another, giving a slighting glance at a French mirror of rather unusual dimensions, larger by two-thirds, I verily believe, than any she had ever seen, remarked, "that it would be quite a nice glass, if the frame was done over." . . .

The doll of Fortune, who may cast a languid eye on this homely page, from the luxurious depths of a velvet-cushioned library chair, can scarce be expected to conceive how natural it may be, for those who possess nothing beyond the absolute requisites of existence, to look with a certain degree of envy on the extra comforts which seem to cluster round the path of another; and to feel as if a little might well be spared, where so much would still be left. To the tenant of a log-cabin whose family, whatever be its numbers, must burrow in a single room, while a bed or two, a chest, a table, and a wretched handful of cooking utensils, form the chief materials of comfort, an ordinary house, small and plain it may be, yet amply supplied, looks like the very home of luxury. The woman who owns but a suit a-piece for herself and her children, considers the possession of an abundant though simple and inexpensive wardrobe, as needless extravagance; and we must scarcely blame her too severely, if she should be disposed to condemn as penurious, any reluctance to supply her pressing need, though she may have no shadow of claim on us beyond that which arises from her being a daughter of Eve. We look at the matter from opposite points of view. *Her* light shows her very plainly, as she thinks, what is *our* Christian duty; we must take care that ours does not exhibit too exclusively her envy and her impertinence.

Kirkland, *A New Home, Who'll Follow?* pp. 182–185.

deflections of such expectations. The emphasized phrase relishes her skill at maneuvering the neighbors she has hired, but it also accentuates how calculating she is in playing on their culture to preserve class-based distinctions they abhor. She also calls attention to a salutary weakening of her sense of decorum as she learns to savor activities whose mundaneness and improvisational character she would initially have scorned: "Is one of your guests dependent upon a barber? Mr. Jenkins can shave. Does your husband . . . demolish his boot upon a *grub*? Mr. Jenkins is great at a *rifacciamento*. Does Billy lose his cap in the pond? Mr. Jenkins makes caps *comme il y en a peu*. Does your bellows get the asthma? Mr. Jenkins is a famous Francis Flute" (pp. 146–147). Although Mr. Jenkins's versatility is cast as a spectacle whose enjoyment unites Clavers and her reader, her appreciation for the Wolverines' idiom ("grub" is a vernacular term for root) as well as their skills bespeaks her deepening respect for them.

As Clavers becomes increasingly familiar with her Wolverine neighbors' material circumstances, her satire of them is crosscut by economic analysis and empathic imagining of the conditions of their lives. She exposes the riches of those who profit from speculation in land and currency, casting these activities as aspects of unchecked capitalism, itself an economic order in which the gains of a few depend on the losses of many. She mobilizes empathy so as to "unroof" the "humble log-huts of Michigan" and imagine farm families left without flour for bread when "splendid looking bank notes"—"their hard-earned all"—prove "valueless" (p. 126). Though she preserves an often-voiced disdain for the pride that informs Wolverines' sense of entitlement to the property of better-off neighbors, she gains the ability to imagine their outlook as well as expressing her own: to a "woman who owns but a suit a-piece for herself and her children," she explains, what is for a Mary Clavers merely an "abundant though simple and inexpensive wardrobe" appears "needless extravagance." Increasingly she also trains her satiric lens on her eastern readers. Typifying many easterners as "spoiled child[ren] of refined civilization" (p. 185) who could not endure frontier hardships, she suggests that their unalloyed elitism relies on a physical segregation of the poor with which the frontier is doing away. Likewise, taken as a whole, her shift from easy scorn to complicated cultural commentary, from flaunted censure of log-cabin tenants to compassionate, though grudging, tolerance, conveys a warning about the nation's future. It nudges readers to reflect that their own privilege, like hers, is contingent—dependent on economic, cultural, and topographic arrangements whose impermanence the frontier casts in high relief because the nation's future is unfolding there.

KIRKLAND'S LATER LIFE AND WORK

A New Home was received enthusiastically, but most readers were apparently inattentive to its urgings for self-examination about their own attitudes.

Edgar Allan Poe (1809–1849) articulated easterners' assumption that life on the frontier was fully different from their own, proclaiming the nation's "indebted[ness] to [Kirkland] for our acquaintance with the home and home-life of the backwoodsman." Those who did recognize themselves were Kirkland's Michigan neighbors, many of whom were openly resentful. Their reactions mortified and alarmed her, and although she continued to write, she was more cautious. *Forest Life* (1842) tailors the sketch to travelogue mode, describing people and places Clavers encounters on trips away from Montacute and satirizing fairly conventional targets, like swindlers and meddlesome old maids.

By 1843, weary of frontier hardships and realizing that their western ventures would not improve their finances, the Kirklands removed to New York City. There both taught and wrote; they were readily accepted into the city's lively literary circles. In 1846, however, William drowned while boarding a steamboat, and Caroline was forced to support herself and four children. She taught on and off until her death and also worked as a literary professional. From 1847 to 1851 she edited the well-respected *Union Magazine* (*Sartain's Union Magazine* after 1848). She persuaded the magazine to support a trip to Europe in exchange for columns about her travel observations; she penned many essays for *Sartain's* and other magazines on such subjects as corsets (which she opposed), the need for prison reform and temperance, women writers, the excesses of the urban rich, and the importance of stable homes. She also produced another volume of western tales, *Western Clearings* (1846), several anthologies, and *Memoirs of Washington* (1845), a book for young people whose outspoken support of abolition almost cost her her publisher. A staunch supporter of the Union, she took a leading role in the U.S. Sanitary Commission, forerunner of the Red Cross, after the Civil War began.

Kirkland died unexpectedly in April 1864, a day after opening a fair to raise money for the Sanitary Commission. Literary notables like Nathaniel P. Willis and William Cullen Bryant attended her funeral. Although appreciation for her writing waned during the postbellum era, interest in *A New Home* revived once American literature emerged as an academic discipline in the 1920s. With sociocultural aspects of American literature and American women pioneers subjects of intensive scholarly interest, a growing body of commentary has been taking the measure of the book's unusual mixture of tones and its combination of elitism, empathy, and incisive cultural and economic analysis.

See also Democracy; Dialect; Exploration and Discovery; English Literature; Health and Medicine; Humor; Individualism and Community; Labor; Manifest Destiny; Travel Writing; Wilderness

BIBLIOGRAPHY

Primary Works

Kirkland, Caroline M. *Forest Life.* 2 vols. New York: Francis, 1842.

Kirkland, Caroline M. *A New Home, Who'll Follow? or, Glimpses of Western Life.* 1839. Edited by Sandra A. Zagarell. New Brunswick, N.J., and London: Rutgers University Press, 1990.

Poe, Edgar Allan. "The Literati of New York City." *Godey's Lady's Book,* August 1846, pp. 55–65.

Secondary Works

Floyd, Janet. *Writing the Pioneer Woman.* Columbia and London: University of Missouri Press, 2002.

Gebhard, Caroline. "Caroline M. Kirkland's Satire of Frontier Democracy in *A New Home—Who'll Follow?*" In *Women, America, and Movement: Narratives of Relocation.* Edited by Susan L. Roberson, pp.157–175. Columbia and London: University of Missouri Press, 1998.

Georgi-Findlay, Brigitte. *The Frontiers of Women's Writing: Women's Narratives and the Rhetoric of Westward Expansion.* Tucson: University of Arizona Press, 1996.

Ketley, Dawn E. "Unsettling the Frontier: Gender and Racial Identity in Caroline Kirkland's *A New Home, Who'll Follow?* and *Forest Life.*" *Legacy: A Journal of American Women Writers* 12, no. 1 (1995): 17–37.

Kolodny, Annette. *The Land before Her: Fantasy and Experience of the American Frontiers, 1630–1860.* Chapel Hill: University of North Carolina Press, 1984.

Leverenz. David. *Manhood and the American Renaissance.* Ithaca, N.Y.: Cornell University Press, 1989.

Merish, Lori. *Sentimental Materialism: Gender, Commodity Culture, and Nineteenth-Century American Literature.* Durham, N.C.: Duke University Press, 2000.

Osborne, William S. *Caroline M. Kirkland.* New York: Twayne, 1972.

Zagarell, Sandra A. "'America' as Community in Three Antebellum Village Sketches." In *The (Other) American Tradition: Nineteenth-Century American Women Writers,* edited by Joyce Warren, pp. 143–165. New Brunswick, N.J., and London: Rutgers University Press, 1993.

Sandra A. Zagarell

NEW ORLEANS

According to many literary histories, New Orleans became significant after the end of Reconstruction with the publication of George Washington Cable's nationally popular short stories and novels. Cable's works of fiction, especially *The Grandissimes* (1880), introduced the national reading public to the peculiar cultural geography of New Orleans, the ethnic clashes of "Creoles" and "Americans," and the legacies of slavery and racial mixture in the city. A number of studies have traced the "myth of New Orleans" in literature from Cable forward. However, looking back to the middle decades of the nineteenth century demonstrates the city's unique role in the literary imagination of the United States.

URBANIZATION AND CULTURAL DIVERSITY

New Orleans was diverse from the beginning. In the half century preceding Louisiana's statehood in 1812, the territory had transferred from French to Spanish back to French and finally to American rule with the Louisiana Purchase in 1803. The French-speaking or "Creole" population, comprised primarily of descendants of the colonial period and refugees from the Haitian Revolution, dominated in the city during the early two decades of the nineteenth century. The bulk of the refugees made it to New Orleans in 1809 indirectly from their first resettlement in Cuba. This group consisted in almost equal numbers of whites, slaves, and free people of color. Slavery was officially outlawed throughout the French colonies in 1794, although Napoleon reinstated slavery later. This led to renewed fighting in Haiti and its subsequent declaration of a free independent state. The free people of color émigrés also had free status in New Orleans. However, after the arrival of the steamboat in 1812 and the expansion of the cotton and sugar economies of the old Southwest, migrants from English-speaking states flooded the city in response to its new commercial potential. Indeed, by 1850 New Orleans was, after New York City, America's second-busiest port and financial center. In the early part of the century New Orleans was little more than a grid of seven streets by twelve. However, by 1870, despite the shortage of habitable land, New Orleans had snaked along the Mississippi River to absorb the nearby plantations and towns.

The population of New Orleans population grew from about 20,000 in 1810 to approximately 180,000 in 1850, absorbing waves of immigration from the Caribbean and Europe and a steady stream of English speakers from other states. Approximately 350,000 immigrants entered New Orleans between 1847 and 1857, fleeing famine in Ireland and political repression

Canal Street, New Orleans, c. 1862. GETTY IMAGES

following the 1848 revolutions in Germany and France. Travelers to New Orleans often remarked on its cultural diversity, likening the levee to the tower of Babel and comparing the gaggle of different languages to the noise of frogs in a swamp. Reflecting this polyglot culture, newspapers catering to French and German speakers especially thrived during the antebellum period. Readers of these periodicals enjoyed serialized fiction that adapted European literary styles to an American context. The work of Charles Testut (1819–1892)—including two volumes of poetry, *Echos* (1849) and *Fleurs d'eté* (1851); a work of critical studies of other francophone writers, *Portraits littéraires* (1850); and an unpublished antislavery novel, "Le vieux Salomon" (1858)—bridges racial concerns and cultural groups. Likewise the Baron Ludwig von Reizenstein (1826–1885) published *Die Geheimnisse von New Orleans* (The mysteries of New Orleans) in 1854 and 1855 in the German-language newspaper *Louisiana Staats-Zeitung*. This antislavery novel followed the tradition of contemporary European urban mysteries in which the city itself seemed to be a central character.

Although linguistic diversity was a hallmark of antebellum New Orleans, perhaps the most distinguishing of its features among cities in the United States was its large mixed-race free population. Numbering almost twenty thousand at its peak in 1840, this group of free people of color, or *gens de couleur libre* as they were called, had its roots in the colonial period, when French and Spanish colonials manumitted their children by slave women. Natural increase and the influx of free people of color from Haiti in 1809 reinforced this group formally separated from slaves and whites by laws carefully circumscribing their marriage. Nevertheless, a tradition of interracial liaisons persisted, supported by informal institutions, such as the quadroon ball, social occasions for white men and free women of color, and *plaçage,* a practice by which a white man literally "placed" a woman of color under his protection; in many such cases the man would provide a home for the woman and their children.

Many historians have described the mid-nineteenth century in New Orleans as a period of "Americanization," a process in which English replaced French as the language of state and French and Spanish racial customs, characterized by the acknowledgment of racial mixture, faded before an Anglo-American black-white binary. During the antebellum period a sense of a fading Creole dominance and an Anglo-American ascendancy colored New Orleans politics. From 1836 until 1852 the city was split into three different municipalities, roughly corresponding to ethnic distinctions between French and English speakers. During the schism, Charles Gayarré (1805–1895), the preeminent historian of nineteenth-century Louisiana and a state senator, created an ideology of place that would assert Creole priority in Louisiana. His writing effected an ethnic reconciliation with English-speaking Americans and established "whiteness" as the ideology through which this reconciliation would take place. Gayarré's efforts culminated in a four-volume *History of Louisiana* (1854), offered in French and English and cast in the mold of Walter Scott's romantic nationalism. In Gayarré's account, French and Spanish colonials melded, albeit violently at times, to form a poetic race of "Creoles," and Creoles and "Americans" combined to embody the true Louisianian, while Native Americans disappeared without protest and Africans continued to provide menial and hard labor. During the 1850s Gayarré's historical account accompanied laws curtailing the rights of people of African descent and granting liberties to those who could establish a white identity.

SLAVERY AND RACE

New Orleans was simultaneously a place of great wealth and opportunity and a site of immense suffering and despair. Nothing demonstrates this paradox as much as the context of slavery. New Orleans depended heavily on the slave economy—on sugar and cotton, the agricultural products of the slave system, and also on the buying and selling of human property itself. The prominence of slavery in the economy of the city shaped its intellectual climate. The leading agricultural journal of the period, *De Bow's Review,* a clearinghouse for technical knowledge about slave agriculture and racial knowledge about enslaved Africans, was published in New Orleans between 1846 and 1869. The proslavery physician Samuel Cartwright lectured regularly in the city on slave "diseases" such as drapetomania, the "runaway disease," and dysaethesia aethiopica, causing mischievous behavior, conditions he observed on Louisiana's plantations. Josiah Nott,

a resident of nearby Mobile, Alabama, and author with George Gliddon of the lengthy ethnology *Types of Mankind* (1854), lectured frequently in New Orleans as well on topics such as "mulatto degeneracy" and polygenesis, a theory of the separate origins of the various human races.

Even though New Orleans was a key center for proslavery writings, it also played a significant role in African American thought. The terminus for the dreaded trip "down the river" for countless enslaved people, the slave market of New Orleans determined slave prices and reconfigured slave communities whenever individuals were sold or families were split apart. One's value and the fate of one's familial ties were often a matter of one's performance. Solomon Northup (b. 1808), whose narrative *Twelve Years a Slave* (1853) tells of his capture as a free man in New York and subsequent sale to the Deep South, recalls slaves being made to strut about and secure a high value for themselves in order to secure an owner. Northup and other enslaved people parlayed their slave-market experiences in New Orleans into episodes of literal self-making that are the hallmark of the slave-narrative genre.

The context of slavery in New Orleans and southern Louisiana also provided a rich legacy of slave rebellion and resistance. Inspired by the slave uprisings eventually culminating in Haitian independence, enslaved people in Pointe Coupee Parish planned a large-scale but abortive revolt in 1795. Fueled by the influx of refugees from the Haitian Revolution in 1809–1810, fears of rebellion continued throughout the first half of the century. Despite increasingly harsh restrictions on the mobility of black people, New Orleans and its environs provided an opportunity for escaped slaves to lose themselves in anonymity. Indeed, the swamps of the region sheltered extended maroon communities (runaway slave communities operating relatively autonomously) of former slaves and their Native American allies. Imaginative writers responded to this context of resistance. In "Le Mulâtre" (The mulatto), written in 1837, the first known short story by an African American, Victor Séjour (1817–1874), a New Orleans free man of color who achieved fame as a dramatist in France, illustrated the injustices of slavery with an Oedipal character that murders his white father/owner and escapes punishment to join a community of maroons with the revolutionary slogan "Afrique et liberté." Set in St. Marc, Haiti, the birthplace of Séjour's father, the story was published in *Revue des colonies,* a Parisian journal edited by the Martiniquan Cyril Bissette.

An indispensable node in the interstate slave trade and a site of seemingly indiscriminate cultural and racial mixture, New Orleans also provided abolitionist writers with a vision of the evils of slavery and a picture of the moral depths to which the country might sink if not checked. The symbolic significance of New Orleans during the years leading up to the Civil War is exemplified in Harriet Beecher Stowe's (1811–1896) *Uncle Tom's Cabin,* published serially in the *National Era* in 1851–1852. Articulating a moral judgment on slavery and the environment that would support it, the character of Ophelia, a New England spinster, pronounces New Orleans to be "old and heathenish." This moral atmosphere is contagious, endangering transplants to the region, such as the villainous slaveholder Simon Legree, who becomes irredeemably evil.

One of the most important figures in the sentimental antislavery literature was the tragic mixed-race character who appeared to be white but who had black ancestry and thus suffered under slavery and other race-based social ills. In the context of slavery, the mixed-race woman, or "fancy girl," commanded large sums of money because the distance between her apparent and "actual" identity heightened the slave master's sexual desire. In the context of antislavery literature, the mixed-race character commanded increased sympathy from a primarily white reading audience who could see its own features in her white visage. Gustave de Beaumont (1802–1866), the traveling partner of Alexis de Tocqueville, published *Marie; ou, L'esclavage aux États-Unis* in Paris in 1835 using the title character, a mixed-race woman from a New Orleans family, as a vehicle for demonstrating the injustices of racial hierarchy in the United States. Likewise, the dramatist Dion Boucicault's (1820–1890) *The Octoroon; or, Life in Louisiana,* a wildly popular drama of slavery in Louisiana and an ill-fated romance between a near-white enslaved woman and her white suitor, was staged in 1859 in New York and London.

While important symbolically in the debate over slavery and race and an irresistible subject for antislavery moralists, the francophone mixed-race population of New Orleans managed to form its own literary tradition during the antebellum period. Writing in the progressive tradition of French Romanticism and in some cases living in exile in France, free people of color of New Orleans drew inspiration from radical French activists such as Victor Hugo and Alphonse de Lamartine. In 1845 Armand Lanusse (1812–1867), a teacher, edited *Les Cenelles,* an anthology of poetry by free men of color which is often cited as the first African American poetry anthology. Although *Les Cenelles* has drawn criticism for its specific failure to condemn slavery, its themes of exile and return, denied birthright, and the melancholy caused by caste

distinction align it closely with the politically progressive Romantic literature of France.

RECONSTRUCTION AND BEYOND

New Orleans played as strategic a role in the political economy of Reconstruction America as it did in the moral economy of antislavery literature. Captured by Union troops in May 1862, southeastern Louisiana, including New Orleans, had perhaps one of the longest reconstructions in the South and thus became a testing ground for Reconstruction policies. Abraham Lincoln hoped that the relatively strong Union sentiment in the city would make Louisiana a prime candidate for readmittance to the Union under his 10 Percent Plan, whereby 10 percent of the Confederate population would swear oaths of allegiance to the United States. The conservative 1864 state constitution produced under this plan provoked opposition from Radical Republicans locally and nationally. At the forefront of the new campaign for racial equality and political reform, free people of color published the official newspaper of the Republican Party, the *New Orleans Tribune* (1864–1870). The *Tribune* and its predecessor, *L'Union de la Nouvelle Orleans* (1862–1864), offered news in French and English as well as poetry and serialized fiction. Although the political climate of New Orleans was extremely volatile, the proximity in the city of former Confederates and former slaves, an educated group of activists of color, Union occupiers, and carpetbagger politicians, provided an opportunity for some to imagine racial, cultural, and sectional reconciliation. Lydia Maria Child (1802–1880) dramatized this potential in her *Romance of the Republic* (1867), a novel that used the setting and cast of characters available in New Orleans to speculate about the ways in which a stronger United States could emerge from the ashes of the Civil War.

In the decades that ensued, New Orleans—in reality and in literature—witnessed heated and often violent debate over controversial issues ranging from federal jurisdiction to race relations. Struggles for black social equality and white supremacy originating in New Orleans played themselves out on a local and national scene, resulting most significantly in the compromise ending Reconstruction in 1876 and *Plessy v. Ferguson* in 1896, which declared segregation to be constitutional. Against this backdrop, late-nineteenth-century "local color" writers such as Cable, Grace King, Alice Dunbar-Nelson, and others entertained national audiences with exotic characters and local dialect. However, this seemingly benign body of literature extends the legacy of a volatile century of Americanization, offering readers and scholars a window onto the fraught issues of racial, cultural, and national identity.

See also Abolitionist Writing; Civil War; Ethnology; Foreigners; Immigration; Miscegenation; Proslavery Writing; Slave Narratives; Slave Rebellions; Slavery; *Uncle Tom's Cabin*

BIBLIOGRAPHY

Primary Works

Beaumont, Gustave de. *Marie; ou, L'esclavage aux États-Unis, tableau de moeurs américaines* [Marie; or, slavery in the United States: A novel of Jacksonian America]. 1835. Translated by Barbara Chapman. Stanford, Calif.: Stanford University Press, 1958.

Bouciault, Dion. *The Octoroon.* 1866. Cambridge, U.K.: Chadwyck-Healey, 1996.

Cable, George Washington. *The Grandissimes: A Story of Creole Life.* New York: Scribners, 1880.

Child, Lydia Maria. *A Romance of the Republic.* Boston: Ticknor and Fields, 1867.

Gayarré, Charles. *History of Louisiana.* New York: Redfield, 1854; W. J. Widdleton, 1866.

Lanusse, Armand. *Les Cenelles: A Collection of Poems of Creole Writers of the Early Nineteenth Century.* Translated by Regine Latortue and Gleason Rex Adams. Boston: G. K. Hall, 1979.

Nott, Josiah, and George Glidden. *Types of Mankind; or, Ethnological Researches, Based upon the Ancient Monuments, Paintings, Sculptures, and Crania of Races.* 1854. Philadelphia: J. B. Lippincott; London: Trubner, 1865.

Northup, Solomon. *Twelve Years a Slave.* London: Auburn, Derby, and Miller, 1853.

Reizenstein, Baron Ludwig von. *The Mysteries of New Orleans.* Translated and edited by Steven Rowan. Baltimore: Johns Hopkins University Press, 2002.

Séjour, Victor. "Le Mûlatre." In *The Multilingual Anthology of American Literature: A Reader of Original Texts with English Translations,* edited by Marc Shell and Werner Sollors. New York: New York University Press, 2000.

Stowe, Harriet Beecher. *Uncle Tom's Cabin; or, Life among the Lowly.* 1851–1852. Oxford and New York: Oxford University Press, 1998.

Secondary Works

Bell, Caryn Cossé. *Revolution, Romanticism, and the Afro-Creole Protest Tradition in Louisiana, 1718–1868.* Baton Rouge: Louisiana State University, 1997.

Bryan, Violet Harrington. *The Myth of New Orleans in Literature: Dialogues of Race and Gender.* Knoxville: University of Tennessee Press, 1993.

Hall, Gwendolyn Midlo. *Africans in Colonial Louisiana: The Development of Afro-Creole Culture in the Eighteenth Century.* Baton Rouge: Louisiana State University Press, 1992.

Hirsch, Arnold, and Joseph Logsdon. *Creole New Orleans: Race and Americanization.* Baton Rouge: Louisiana State University Press, 1992.

Johnson, Walter. *Soul by Soul: Life inside the Antebellum Slave Market.* Cambridge, Mass.: Harvard University Press, 1999.

Reinders, Robert. *The End of an Era: New Orleans 1850–1860.* New Orleans: Pelican Press, 1964.

Roach, Joseph. *Cities of the Dead: Circum-Atlantic Performance.* New York: Columbia University Press, 1996.

Rowan, Steve. "Introduction." In *The Mysteries of New Orleans,* by Baron Ludwig von Reizenstein, edited by Steven Rowan, pp. xiii–xxxiii. Baltimore: Johns Hopkins University Press, 2002.

Ryan, Mary. *Civic Wars: Democracy and Public Life in the American City during the Nineteenth Century.* Berkeley: University of California Press, 1997.

Shirley E. Thompson

NEW YORK

In the period from 1820 to 1870 New York City consolidated its status not only as the United States' largest city but also as the nation's economic and cultural capital. The literature of New York during this period reflected the city's diversity of voices, its complex balance of commerce and culture, and its increasing prominence as the cosmopolitan center of American literary life. Many of the most important American writers of the nineteenth century, including Washington Irving, James Fenimore Cooper, Edgar Allan Poe, Herman Melville, and Walt Whitman, spent a significant part of their careers in New York City. They joined a host of other writers associated with New York City, ranging from serious-minded reformers such as Margaret Fuller (1810–1850) and Lydia Maria Child (1802–1880) to the alternately urbane and sentimental sketcher and poet Nathaniel Parker Willis (1806–1850) to sensational writers of city-life exposés such as George G. Foster and "Ned Buntline" (Edward Zane Carroll Judson), all of whose work reflected the dynamic political, social, and cultural transformations taking place within the city during this period.

May Day in New York. Cartoon from *Harper's New Monthly Magazine,* May 1856, commenting on the transitory nature of life in the city, where the first day of May was traditionally regarded as moving day. GRADUATE LIBRARY, UNIVERSITY OF MICHIGAN

THE 1820S AND 1830S: PROGRESS AND NOSTALGIA

In 1820 New York City was a regional center ready to explode into national dominance. The Erie Canal, funded in 1817 and completed in 1825, made the city the most important domestic and international trade hub, for the first time linking the expanding interior of the United States to the Atlantic trade. Growing at an unprecedented rate, New York City's population tripled from 1825 to 1850, reaching over half a million people. During this period, real estate development spread north up Manhattan Island, moving from the irregular village-like streets of downtown up to the rationalized grid set out in the Commissioner's Plan of 1811, which was designed to maximize property values and trade. From the 1820s onward much of the population influx came from foreign immigration, most notably from Ireland and Germany. By 1850 foreign-born whites constituted almost half of New York City's population. Amidst these many changes, observers often identified the first day in May as the archetypal moment of New York City life. "May Day" or "Moving Day," as it was called, was traditionally when residential lease contracts ended and the city

streets turned to chaos, filling with carts transporting all the worldly goods of both rich and poor New Yorkers; "May Day" was a symbolic moment resonant of the bustling, transitory nature of city life in the period.

Given the disruptive effect of these transformations in New York, it is perhaps not surprising that the literature of the city in the 1820s and 1830s was nostalgic, drawing upon older English literary models and often taking the city and the region's past as its subject. Washington Irving (1783–1859) had the first American transatlantic literary success with *The Sketch Book* (1819–1820). Written in England, this work joined descriptions of English travel with sentimental sketches and, most famously, included the stories "Rip Van Winkle" and "The Legend of Sleepy Hollow," folklore tales that drew upon New York State's colonial Dutch heritage. Before the international success of *The Sketch Book*, Irving was well known as a regional author for his satirical sketches of New York types in *Salmagundi* (1807; written with his brother William Irving [1766–1821] and James Kirke Paulding [1778–1860]) and for a comic history of the city from the perspective of an "antiquarian" of Dutch descent, Diedrich Knicker-bocker, in *A History of New York* (1809). Irving returned to New York after his time in England and continued a long career as an author, adding trave-logues, histories and biographies to the sketches that made him famous. "Knickerbocker" became a name applied to other New York writers of this generation, including Paulding and Fitz-Greene Halleck (1790–1867), who had success with his Byronic poem of Federalist New York, *Fanny* (1819), but would leave writing to work as the assistant to John Jacob Astor (1763–1848), the wealthiest man in the city. William Cullen Bryant (1794–1878) is often associated with this group despite being a New England émigré. Like Halleck, Bryant also abandoned early poetic success for a career in law and journalism, holding the position of editor of the New York *Evening Post*. Even the most successful Knickerbocker authors often characterized authorship as a leisure pursuit rather than a vocation. In some ways, this reflected the economic realities of the American literary marketplace, but it was also a pose that recalled the eighteenth-century English ideals of the gentleman-author.

Despite being a New York author of the same gen-eration, James Fenimore Cooper (1789–1851) was not associated with the Knickerbockers. The son of the founder of Cooperstown, in upstate New York, Cooper became the first successful U.S. novelist through his application of Sir Walter Scott's model of the historical novel to the setting of his father's fron-tier in his Leatherstocking novels: *The Pioneers* (1823), *The Last of the Mohicans* (1826), *The Prairie* (1827), *The Pathfinder* (1840), and *The Deerslayer* (1841). Cooper wrote other types of novels through-out his career but experienced little critical or com-mercial success with them. Notable amongst his other works was the comedy of manners, *Home as Found* (1838), which savagely attacked the pretensions and provincialism of New York society from the perspec-tive of an American family returning from Europe; this unmistakably autobiographical frame did little to endear Cooper to his fellow New Yorkers and American readers more generally. Although very different from Irving and the Knickerbockers in style and literary format, Cooper's most popular work was also shaped by a cultural nostalgia that seemed at odds with the dynamic city in which he wrote.

THE 1840S: INDUSTRIALIZATION AND CLASS CONFLICT

During the 1840s canal transportation gave way to the railroad, leading to yet further penetration of trade throughout the nation. Meanwhile, industrialized modes of production began to take hold. Responding

to these shifts, New York City continued to grow and consolidate its power as the nation's financial and transportation hub in the decade. This had its effect as well on the business of literature in the city. At this time New York publishing houses such as Harper & Brothers began to conceive of a truly national audi-ence for their authors. In the 1840s the Harpers' pub-lishing house, a multistory and largely mechanized factory downtown, was reflective of the city's broader turn to industrialization after the construction of the Croton Waterworks (1842) which brought new sup-plies of water to Manhattan and helped power the steam engines that drove New York's 550 percent growth in industrial investment from 1840 to 1860. The increasing mechanization of printing helped fuel the proliferation of newspapers and magazines throughout the nation but nowhere as much as in New York City, where as many as three hundred dif-ferent journals were published between 1820 and 1850. Newspapers and magazines were no longer merely local. Bundled for distant sellers and trans-ported by rail free of postal charges, New York papers could be sold throughout the nation. During the 1840s, New York newspaper, magazine, and book publishing became an industry.

As a result of its new importance to the business of American literary publication, New York attracted a variety of authors from around the nation. The south-erner Edgar Allan Poe (1809–1849) published his second book of poetry in New York City in 1831 after being expelled from West Point. He returned to New York in 1837–1838 (when he published his only novel, *The Narrative of Arthur Gordon Pym*) and again in 1844–1847, earning a livelihood writing stories and poetry for newspapers and magazines and briefly becoming the sole editor and proprietor of the *Broadway Journal* before it failed. In 1846 Poe brought special attention to the city's authors with his series of profiles, "The Literati of New York City" in *Godey's Lady's Book*. The series was curtailed after Poe's blunt assessments were met with threats of legal action, but despite the often-personal insults offered, Poe stressed the prominence of New York writers in American let-ters as a whole. Nathaniel Parker Willis, another émigré from New England, came to New York in 1831 and became a national celebrity for his work as editor and writer for newspapers and magazines, including the *Evening Mirror* and the *Home Journal*. Later, Willis's sister, Sara Payson Willis Parton ("Fanny Fern," 1811–1872) also achieved celebrity and wealth as a colum-nist for New York City newspapers in the 1850s and as a novelist of an autobiographical story of her struggles, *Ruth Hall* (1855). Even Henry David Thoreau (1817–1862), famous for his nature writings and association with Concord, Massachusetts, came to New York to pursue a literary career. Although his tenure was brief, it indicated the allure of the professional opportunities that New York offered to writers from all over the country in this period.

New York's astounding population growth, economic successes, and turn toward industrialized production reshaped the social landscape of city life, revealing dramatic differences between the wealthy and poor that challenged long-held assumptions about American democracy. The city's poor lived and worked in the older but increasingly industrialized downtown area, most famously in the Five Points neighborhood, which was notorious for its prostitutes, bars, and gambling dens. The city's wealthy (often called the "upper ten" for the wealthiest ten thousand people) lived uptown in new homes built to their specifications and attended exclusive institutions like the opulent Grace Church and the Astor Place Opera House, which sought to bring foreign-language opera to those willing to pay the high subscription rate.

Exploring the inherent drama of these evident social extremes, literary depictions of city life fascinated New Yorkers and the nation as a whole. Lydia Maria Child (1802–1880), a controversial figure due to her endorsement of abolitionism in the 1830s, regained a national audience as editor of New York's *National Anti-Slavery Standard* for her series of sketches, "Letters from New-York" (1841–1843). In these "letters" to an unnamed friend, Child responded to the city's poverty and crime (visiting the city's new prison and asylum on Blackwell's Island) and its beauty (rhapsodizing over new fountains making use of water brought into the city by the Croton Waterworks). Margaret Fuller, a feminist and transcendentalist, moved from Boston to New York in 1844 to work for Horace Greeley's *New York Tribune.* Fuller used her position as a columnist on the arts to present an idealist, reformist perspective on a variety of city subjects, including the treatment of the poor and criminals. She also offered suggestions for how the city's newly wealthy might best contribute to the benefit of their fellow citizens. Her position was most notable in U.S. literary history, however, as the first full-time book reviewer for a daily newspaper in the United States, reflecting the new importance that literature played in people's day-to-day life. Another employee of Greeley's *Tribune,* George G. Foster (d. 1856), reached a wide audience with sketches of distinctive and seedy elements of city life, including the series "New York in Slices" (1848) and "New York by Gas-Light" (1849). In a city expanding beyond anyone's comprehension, Fuller's reformism and Foster's sensationalistic promise of an insider's view of adulterers, prostitutes, and con men offered the seemingly contradictory pleasures of reformist idealism and prurient voyeurism for the *Tribune's* readers.

Despite the dramatic economic disparity between New York's wealthy and poor, the city's cultural life was remarkably rich in the 1840s, with entertainment options readily available to individuals from all walks of life. What one read, what theater one attended, where one shopped: these all became important indices of identity in the city. Working-class New Yorkers, members of what was called "the Bowery Republic," so named by historians for their egalitarian political beliefs and association with downtown's Bowery Street, had their own fashions, cultural venues, and institutions—from cheap theaters with raucous "pit" seating to the often-brawling fire companies. Working-class New Yorkers also had their own literature, from the easily affordable "penny" newspapers, to "dime" novels that often cast workers as heroes, to plays that catered to their interests and sensibilities. Wealthy New Yorkers, by contrast, could be found promenading on Broadway, a street known for its elaborate commercial display, including Alexander Turney Stewart's "Marble Palace," a five-story precursor to the department store, built in 1844.

In 1849 the Astor Place Riots pitted the two worlds of New York City against each other in a surprisingly violent encounter based upon what started as a trivial feud between two actors. The riots revealed the deep social tensions and conflicts between the divided classes. Populist support for the American actor Edwin Forrest (1806–1872) by the Bowery Republic met up against the support on the part of the upper ten for the English actor Charles Macready (1793–1873), so that city police and state militia were posted inside and outside the Opera House. The popular protest became so heated that it ended in the state militia firing on the crowd outside the Opera House and killing more than twenty people. The Astor Place Riots have been called an important moment in the development of a distinction between "high" and "low" culture in American life. While this claim may be subject to debate, there is little question that the riots signaled the central place that cultural experience played in the conflicts of class and politics in nineteenth-century American life.

New York City writers participated on both sides of the Astor Place Riots, reflecting the complex place of authors within the class divides of the nineteenth century. Edward Zane Carroll Judson ("Ned Buntline," 1823–1886), one of the nineteenth century's most prolific and popular authors, wrote sensational novels such as *The Mysteries and Miseries of*

Birds-eye view of lower Manhattan looking south, c. 1849. Lithograph by C. Bachman. THE LIBRARY OF CONGRESS

New York (1848). Perhaps best known for his role in mythologizing "Buffalo Bill" Cody in dime novels of the West of the 1860s and 1870s, Judson was sentenced to a year in prison for his role in inciting the popular crowd to violence during the Astor Place Riots. On the other side, signers to a petition in support of Macready included Washington Irving and Herman Melville (1819–1891). Melville was born in New York City and returned to the city after the success of his early South Pacific travelogues, *Typee* (1846) and *Omoo* (1847), to pursue a career as an author. Although he moved to the Berkshires during the writing of his most famous work, *Moby-Dick* (1851), Melville often came back to New York to write, continued to work with New York publishers, and often took up New York as a location for his fiction, including his short story "Bartleby, the Scrivener: A Tale of Wall Street" (1853), which presents the seemingly irreconcilable conflict between Christian values of brotherhood and the competitive and hierarchical "common sense" values of business in the mercantile world of the city.

THE 1850S AND 1860S: IMPENDING CRISIS AND THE SEARCH FOR UNITY

Perhaps the quintessential New York City writer was the poet Walt Whitman (1819–1892), who came to national attention in the 1850s and 1860s with the appearance of multiple, extensively revised editions of his poetry collection, *Leaves of Grass.* Born in Long Island and raised in Brooklyn, Whitman moved to New York City in 1841 and entered the city's life and literature through newspapers and magazines. A literary jack-of-all-trades in his early career, Whitman covered the news of city police and coroner's offices, political meetings, opera performances, and art exhibits for newspapers. He also published poetry and fiction, including a sensational temperance novel, *Franklin Evans* (1842). In the 1850s, Whitman experienced a professional crisis linked to the political crisis of the impending sectional division of the Civil War. Whitman had been a committed member of the Democratic Party, personally invested in its populist politics and professionally involved as a writer and editor for newspapers allied with and financially supported by the

EXCERPT FROM "CROSSING BROOKLYN FERRY" BY WALT WHITMAN

This stanza from Whitman's poem is meant to highlight the way common elements of city life were a part of the poet's idealist project. It also serves as an example of Whitman's focus on city life.

What is it then between us?
What is the count of the scores or hundreds of
        years between us?
Whatever it is, it avails not—distance avails not,
        and place avails not,
I too lived, Brooklyn of ample hills was mine,
I too walk'd the streets of Manhattan island, and
        bathed in the waters around it,
I too felt the curious abrupt questionings stir
        within me,
In the day among crowds of people sometimes
        they came upon me,
In my walks home late at night or as I lay in my
        bed they came upon me,
I too had been struck from the float forever held
        in solution,
I too had receiv'd identity by my body,
That I was I knew was of my body, and what I
        should be I knew I should be of my body.

Whitman, "Crossing Brooklyn Ferry," in *The Complete
Poems*, pp. 192–193.

party. Over the course of the 1850s, however, Whitman became increasingly uncomfortable with the Democratic Party's support of slavery.

The first edition of his lifelong poetic project, *Leaves of Grass* (1855), was an attempt to create a poetic persona who could embody and reconcile the many differences—political, racial, class, and moral— that threatened national unity. In the poem "Song of Myself," Whitman turned often to images of the city life and its inhabitants, from the "jour printer" to the "machinist" to the "prostitute," to imagine a national union that would forestall the predicted political crisis. In "Crossing Brooklyn Ferry" (1856), Whitman took the common urban experience of the commuter ferry and transformed it into a meditation upon the universal bonds of corporeality and consciousness. In the overtly homosexual poems of "Calamus" of the 1860

edition of *Leaves of Grass,* Whitman wrote of Manhattan as a "city of orgies," described male lovers holding hands and kissing amid crowded scenes of city life, and imagined an utopian "new city of Friends," "invincible to the attacks / of the whole of the rest of the earth" (p. 164), casting the liberated experience of urban homosexuals as an answer to the imminent crisis of national disunion.

Whitman was not the only New Yorker seeking to ease the sense of impending crisis within the nation and city. Identifying city life itself as the greatest problem, many New Yorkers called for the development of a park within the city to offset the unremitting sprawl of urban development.

After much debate and political wrangling in the 1850s, land was acquired and in 1856 the Greensward Plan of Frederick Law Olmsted (1822–1903) and Calvert Vaux (1824–1895) was approved for Central Park. Olmsted, who went on to become North America's most influential landscape designer, had earlier pursued a career as author—writing a series of investigative travelogues about the South—and editor of the influential *Putnam's Magazine,* which published the work of Melville, Thoreau, Bryant, and Henry James, among others. Olmsted and Vaux's plan for Central Park was characterized by the aesthetic values of the picturesque, transforming the space from a mixture of farmland, scattered small communities, and undeveloped tracts into a carefully planned "natural" landscape of rolling green fields, lakes, and wooded areas. In addition to its aesthetic appeal, Central Park was intended to offer public health benefits, functioning as the city's "lungs" and helping to forestall the spread of disease as well having the social benefits of providing cultural and recreational resources for the masses and thus functioning as a safety valve for class conflict in the increasingly divided city.

Central Park, however beneficial, unfortunately did not solve New York City's social problems. Construction of the park was suspended during the Civil War, and it was ironically during this time that social division came to a head in the city, with the 1863 Draft Riots. New York's poor and working class, largely affiliated with the Democratic Party by longstanding tradition, were not supportive of the war effort, in part due to a belief that freed slaves would become their economic competitors. Although the possession of slaves in New York State had been wholly outlawed by 1827, New York City had a relatively small African American population, largely because of its prejudicial climate.

When Abraham Lincoln instituted the Union draft, with a provision that allowed the wealthy to purchase the services of a replacement, workers' protests turned violent. In July 1863 the protests spiraled into looting and violence against African Americans over the course of four days. City police and state militia could not stop the rioting and the Union Army was called in. This amounted to a military occupation of New York City. Melville's poetry cycle narrating the course of the Civil War, *Battle-Pieces* (1866), included a poem entitled "The House-Top: A Night Piece" that described the riot, and saw the army's presence as

> The grimy slur on the Republic's faith implied
> Which holds that Man is naturally good,
> And—more—is Nature's Roman, never to be
>   scourged.
>
> *(P. 87)*

Like Melville, many writers and other New Yorkers during the Civil War and its immediate aftermath came to question the optimism they had earlier expressed about the American nation and their great city.

CONCLUSION

The end of the war saw the extension of New York City's antebellum economic, social, and cultural trends across the nation, with the United States as a whole experiencing population growth and urbanization, the march of industrialism and the spread of a commercialized industry of the arts and entertainment. New York City retained its position as the dominant center of United States trade and financial power and solidified its position as cultural capital. For example, in 1870 the wealthiest New Yorkers helped to establish the Metropolitan Museum of Art in Central Park, creating the first American home for important European art. In the midst of northern postwar growth, New York City became the undisputed center of what Mark Twain mockingly called in 1874 "the Gilded Age," an era in which the national prosperity cast a superficial layer over moral hypocrisy and a range of injustices. In the decades to follow, a new generation of writers associated with the literary movement of realism, including such figures as William Dean Howells, Edith Wharton, Theodore Dreiser, and Stephen Crane, would explore the new, but not wholly new, social extremes of New York City life.

See also "Bartleby, the Scrivener"; "Crossing Brooklyn Ferry"; English Literature; Immigration; Knickerbocker Writers; Labor; Landscape Architecture; Leatherstocking Tales; *Leaves of Grass;* Political Parties; Sensational Fiction; Technology; Urbanization

BIBLIOGRAPHY
Primary Works

Child, Lydia Maria. *Letters from New-York.* 1843. Edited by Bruce Mills. Athens: University of Georgia Press, 1998.

Foster, George. *New York by Gaslight and Other Urban Sketches.* Edited by Stuart M. Blumin. Berkeley: University of California Press, 1990.

Fuller, Margaret. *Margaret Fuller, Critic: Writings from the New-York Tribune, 1844–1846.* Edited by Judith Mattson Bean and Joel Myerson. New York: Columbia University Press, 2000.

Melville, Herman. "Bartleby, the Scrivener." 1853. In *The Piazza Tales and Other Prose Pieces, 1839–1860,* pp. 13–45. Chicago: Northwestern University Press–Newberry Library, 1987.

Melville, Herman. *Battle-Pieces and Aspects of the War.* 1866. New York: Da Capo, 1995.

Whitman, Walt. *The Complete Poems.* Edited by Francis Murphy. New York: Penguin, 1977.

Secondary Works

Bender, Thomas. *New York Intellect: A History of Intellectual Life in New York City, from 1750 to the Beginnings of Our Own Time.* New York: Knopf, 1987.

Blackmar, Elizabeth. *Manhattan for Rent, 1785–1850.* Ithaca, N.Y.: Cornell University Press, 1989.

Burrows, Edwin G., and Mike Wallace. *Gotham: A History of New York City to 1898.* New York: Oxford University Press, 1999.

Miller, Perry. *The Raven and the Whale: Poe, Melville, and the New York Literary Scene.* Baltimore: Johns Hopkins University Press, 1997.

Reynolds, David S. *Walt Whitman's America: A Cultural Biography.* New York: Knopf, 1995.

Rosenzweig, Roy, and Elizabeth Blackmar. *The Park and the People: A History of Central Park.* Ithaca, N.Y.: Cornell University Press, 1992.

Wilentz, Sean. *Chants Democratic: New York City and the Rise of the American Working Class, 1788–1850.* New York: Oxford University Press, 1984.

John Evelev

ORAL TRADITION

Between 1820 and 1870 the United States was home to a rich oral culture, enhanced rather than eclipsed by the rising dominance of print culture. Older oral traditions of narrative, proverb, and song continued to circulate orally and were further disseminated in print forms. Jacksonian politics promoted vernacular forms of classical oratory; the belles lettres art of conversation flourished in a new female tradition that was noted as characteristically American by visitors such as Alexis de Tocqueville; and both these rhetorics were extended through expanded public schooling, a proliferation of rhetoric texts, conduct literature, and journalism. Large popular audiences enthusiastically received anthologies of speeches and sermons and some eventually came to accept women's public speaking on religious, political, reform, and cultural topics.

NEW-WORLD DEVELOPMENTS

The period generated new oral forms, such as the lecture, and institutions, such as the lyceum and the female literary associations that laid the ground for the later women's club movement. It also generated dialect fiction and poetry, forerunners to the regional traditions that would flourish in the second half of the century. Ethnic oral traditions, particularly those of Native Americans and African Americans, gained increasing publicity outside of the folk group of origin, and transcriptions of these traditions appeared, varied in their authenticity. Literature circulated oral culture, promoted it, and drew on its forms and subject matter as resources for literary art. Literary texts represented features of contemporary oral culture, debated aspects of it, influenced it. These texts were in turn influenced by oral culture.

Despite long-standing argument that the United States had no characteristic, unique oral traditions, and despite ongoing debate over both foundational terms of the classification "oral traditions," as well as over a methodology for approaching them, the contours of academic study of American oral traditions have remained remarkably stable across the past century. Scholars have debated questions of the origins of oral traditions in the United States (American or European and African?), of whether there is a single American tradition or multiple ones, and of whether the differences or the continuities between literary and oral traditions should be emphasized; they have addressed problems of defining genres, of the authenticity of translation and transcription, of aesthetic status, and the relations between oral and literary traditions. Yet what has constituted oral tradition for literary study has remained relatively undisputed. Literary histories and anthologies that attend to oral tradition between 1820 and 1870 tend to focus on Native American myth, legend, and oratory; African American spirituals and oratory; Anglo tall tales, especially Southwestern humor; and folk songs (mostly about men's work and politics). Women's expressive culture has been, arguably, the most neglected aspect in the study of historical oral traditions. While scholarly understanding of the "oral" character of traditions shifted from an emphasis on origins to the mode of transmission, and "traditions" came to be understood as signifying less the surviving relics of a receding past and more the

Illustration from *Godey's Lady's Book,* October 1862. The title of this picture is *Plotting Mischief;* the attitudes of the group suggest rapt attention to a storyteller. GRADUATE LIBRARY, UNIVERSITY OF MICHHIGAN

performances of living traditions with differing functions within specific contexts, a male-centered perspective has continued to limit the understanding of oral culture and its relations with literature.

The narrow map that academic study would draw after 1870 of the largely oral culture flourishing in the early national period would likely have surprised contemporaries. Samuel Knapp's (1783–1838) *Lectures on American Literature* (1820) voiced the assumption shared by contemporaries that oral forms of expression were a significant part of the literary field. Knapp discussed colonial hero legends about both women and men, songs of whaling and war, and Indian laments and oratory, and he mentioned novels, poetry, and plays. Rhetorical culture held an important place in Knapp's mapping of literature, not only the oratory that American men practiced in the pulpit, bar, and legislature, but also the social eloquence of the American fireside and drawing room, where both women and men combined learning with a new, more natural style of expression. The American mother, in Knapp's view, was responsible for laying in the nursery and domestic circle the foundations of a national art of speaking. Other commentators located any claim to unique American literary achievement in ethnic oral traditions, without resolving the challenges posed to notions of nationalism and a national culture by the forced displacement of the indigenous peoples and the forced immigration of slaves.

The anonymous author of "The Language and Literature of America" (*North American Review,* September 1815) claimed that everyone found the oral literature of the aborigines original and that it most properly constituted the literature of the country. The specimens of Indian oratory and legends that circulated in journalism, anthologies, school texts, and the collections of Indian agent and scholar Henry Rowe Schoolcraft (1793–1864) gave evidence of indigenous traditions and art, lending support to the *North American Review* and countering the opposing contention that Indians, as savages, had no valuable literary tradition. The abolitionist Theodore Parker (1810–1860), however, thought slaves' narratives marked the first original American expressive form, and another anonymous commentator, in *Putnam's Monthly* (January 1855), argued that the poetry of Negro minstrelsy should be given pride of place in American literature after authentic oral tradition was sorted from the impostures of white composing, a project begun with the publication by William Francis Allen, Lucy McKim Garrison, and Charles Pickard Ware of spirituals in *Slave Songs of the United States* (1867). Antiquarian interest in the traditionary lore of the colonizer groups, especially the English and Scottish, prompted collections such as John Fanning Watson's (1780–1860) popular *Historic Tales of Olden Time* from New York and Pennsylvania (1832, 1833) while, as the pursuit of literature turned professional, writers including Washington Irving, John Greenleaf Whittier, and Nathaniel Hawthorne capitalized on oral traditions with retellings of legends from European and settler sources.

SCHOLARLY PERSPECTIVES

By the 1880s, oral culture was displaced from literature in the instituting of American literature as an academic field and, further, was narrowed into "oral traditions" on one hand and oratory on the other as oral culture was progressively divided between the emerging fields of folklore and rhetoric. Charles Richardson's *American Literature* (2 vols., c. 1886–1888) equated literature with Anglo belles lettres writing, pointedly denying literary status to Native American oratory and poetry and ignoring other oral culture aside from Anglo men's oratorical forms. Concurrently, William Wells Newell, editor of the *Journal of American Folk-lore*, announced in his first issue a new folklore study whose focus would be on "oral tradition. . . . understood as the complement of literature" and whose aim would be to preserve traditional ballads, tales, proverbs, superstitions, jests, riddles, dialects, and such in four departments: the relics of Anglo Americans, Southern Negroes, Indians, and other European American groups (*Journal of American Folk-lore* 1 [1888]: 3–7).

Subsequently, scholarship has debated the boundaries and relations between the two fields, especially the hierarchy of values that privileges what is defined as literature and its study over oral traditions and folklorisitics. Tensions also emerged within folklore studies between those that followed the narrowly aesthetic system of Richardson's *American Literature* and others that, like the *Cambridge History of American Literature* (4 vols., 1917–1921), promoted a more comprehensive historical construction that included some mention of oral tradition. Yet the developing fields of literature, folklore, and rhetoric all came to agree that the oral

culture selected as the subject of their anthologies would be overwhelmingly male in provenance and values. "Fairy tales, beast fables, jests, by scores. . .on the lips of mothers and nurses" (*Journal of American Folk-lore* 1 [1888]: 4) in the early nineteenth century, like the other expressive art that flourished in women's oral culture, seldom attracted the attention of collectors and commentators. Instead, they were assimilated into men's oral traditions, as if indistinguishable, or were attributed to male sources and collectors, as in the case of Jane Johnston Schoolcraft's (1800–1841) transcriptions of Ojibwa legends, which appeared in works by her husband, Henry Rowe Schoolcraft. The *Cambridge History* was more concerned with explaining away the value of popular songs emanating from women's culture, as in the case of "Mary Had a Little Lamb," attributed to the editor of *Godey's Lady's Book*, Sarah Hale, than to understand such songs' long-lived centrality in oral tradition, and it construed the intersection of rhetorical and literary culture exclusively in terms of men's oratorical and sermonic practice. Increasing professionalization discouraged folklorists' collection of women's oral traditions. The reduction of nineteenth-century American literature in the modernist canon to a handful of men and Emily Dickinson (1830–1886) fed a similarly narrow reconstruction of oral traditions in literary history.

A CANON OF ORAL TRADITIONS

The work of scholars John Lomax and Constance Rourke, both informed by the now discredited frontier thesis of American history (that is, the notion that the confrontation of savagery and civilization at the edge of western settlement shaped a uniquely democratic and individualistic American culture), especially influenced the construction of oral traditions that most obtains in current literary history and anthologies. Although Lomax, as the pioneer collector of American folksongs, preserved and discussed a rich range of songs from the nineteenth century, literary history reflects more the focus of his first book, *Cowboy Songs and Frontier Ballads* (1910) and the typology he sketched in the *Journal of American Folklore* (1915) that equates American folksongs largely with men's work and African American tradition—the songs of miners, lumbermen, sailors, soldiers, railroaders, cowboys, and fieldworkers; only his category of outcasts imagines any place for women's songs. Rourke, a historian and American studies pioneer, in *The Roots of American Culture* points to some of the exclusions in such a scheme—the expressive traditions of women's domestic work and social rituals (weaving, spinning, corn husking) and those of marginalized groups in which women predominated, such as the Shakers—but it was her thesis of American humor that more than any other theory has given shape to what literary history takes as "oral traditions."

In *American Humor* (1931), Rourke, assuming German philosopher Johann Herder's (1744–1803) premise that any national aesthetic literature stems from powerful folk origins, underwrote the notion of a unique, valuable culture in the United States by elaborating a folk tradition of humor underlying the modernist canon of high American literature that scholarship was then consolidating, a folk tradition that alienated women as subjects, she observed, and as origins and disseminators. Later critics fixed on the three character types from popular theater and print sources that Rourke argued likely evolved from oral traditions (a mix of English regional dramatic types, Indian legends, Gaelic anecdotes, the era's proliferation of oratory, Southern lawyers' storytelling combats, and minstrel shows) and which, she claimed, represented the comic spirit of American culture in the early national period: the Yankee, the backwoodsman (including the boatman), and, especially, the Negro.

MODERNIST CRITICISM

Rourke influenced critics who had the most impact on the writing of literary history and the making of anthologies. Her study buttressed, for example, F. O. Matthiessen's Renaissance thesis of American literature (*American Renaissance,* 1941), Richard Volney Chase's romance thesis of narrative fiction (*The American Novel and its Tradition,* 1957), and Daniel Hoffman's method of myth criticism that seeks folk traditions behind canonical writers (*Form and Fable in American Fiction,* 1961). While critics note that the tall tale tradition is overstudied, literary history and anthologies, backed by such criticism and by Rourke's thesis and viewing history through a lens distorted by the extraordinary status accorded later writers such as Mark Twain and William Faulkner, continue to overrepresent the significance of the form, its mode of humor, and protagonists (Davy Crockett, Mike Fink), along with the writers later grouped as Southwestern humorists (Augustus Baldwin Longstreet [1790–1870], Johnson Jones Hooper [1815–1862], George Washington Harris [1814–1869]) and the Big Bear school following from Thomas Bangs Thorpe (1815–1878) with its hunting fables that pit men against nature writ large. None of these featured centrally in the oral culture of the period or in contemporary analyses of it.

Literary history's investigation of the relations between oral culture and literature generally has tended toward the assumption shared by Rourke and her followers that oral traditions are most interesting and valuable as a background or foundation of literary art, or as Daniel Barnes put it, as matter an author uses to create literature. The operation of this assumption in literature studies and often in folklore studies as well, although it has generated no established methodology for studying the two fields together, has focused a large body of criticism that teaches more about nineteenth-century canonical men's appropriations—or approximations—of oral motifs than it does about historical oral traditions. In addition to extending the links that Rourke observed between her construction of oral tradition (particularly the frontier matter) and the writing of canonical male writers (and, incidentally, Dickinson), critics have worked to identify and interpret oral materials in these texts.

Studies have discussed in particular Washington Irving's and Edgar Allan Poe's reworking of legendary tales of the supernatural or macabre, about the knowledge and use of the oral traditions of Indian tribes and Anglo frontier traditions in James Fenimore Cooper's Leatherstocking romances, Henry Wadsworth Longfellow's poetry, and Henry David Thoreau's prose, and about the retellings of New England legends by John Greenleaf Whittier and Nathaniel Hawthorne, especially the latter's address of witchcraft and other superstitions. Melville's work, particularly *Moby-Dick,* (1851) has been mined for evidence of his use of sea chanties, legends, songs, and proverbs, in addition to frontier matter, and Ralph Waldo Emerson's work excavated for his use of folk expressions and proverbs. Otherwise, folk material, including dialect tales and poetry, has largely been positioned as a feature of regional literature, which repeatedly was rated as lesser than canonized masterwork. While there has been decreasing interest in claiming the oratory of some figures, such as Daniel Webster (1782–1852), as literature, more claims are being made for other figures, such as Abraham Lincoln (1809–1865) and Frederick Douglass (1818–1895), and inquiry continues into ways that the conventions of oral traditions, such as oratory and storytelling, inform the writings of canonical male writers.

No equivalent body of criticism addresses the question of whether women's writing, too, might open a window on contemporary oral tradition, although that writing offers parallel opportunities, including the fictional use of ghosts and other supernatural motifs in Harriet Beecher Stowe's *Uncle Tom's Cabin* (1851–1852); Alice Cary's "Ghost Story

Number II" (1855), which rehearses neighborhood legends in a conversational narrative frame attentive to various modes of storytelling; and Harriet Farley's *Happy Nights at Hazel Nook; or, Cottage Stories* (1854), which presents tales of fairies, wizards, and ghosts told in a family writing club; Lydia Maria Child's version of Native American and European legends in her short fiction; Harriet Jacobs's *Incidents in the Life of a Slave Girl* (1861), with its invocation of slaves' songs and legends; and Margaret Fuller's reworking of proverbs and legends, including the Ojibwa tale of Muckwa or the Bear in *Summer on the Lakes, in 1843* (1844), a book that advocates the systematic compilation of Indian lore by a native collector so that the textual representation of native tradition might indicate the philosophy, symbol system, and values of indigenous peoples.

RECENT PERSPECTIVES

Scholarly anthologies now include work songs in the African American tradition that serve as women's expressive tradition and lullabies in Native American traditions, but neither form in Anglo traditions. As an understanding of literature as social practice gains currency, and theories of rhetorical and folk culture begin to account for women's conversational and oratorical forms of expression, inquiry is opening into the ways that literature informs women's speaking in the era, including African American activists and speaker-writers Maria Stewart and Frances Harper, and the ways that conversational traditions enter women's writing, notably Fuller's essays, the fiction of Stowe and Catharine Maria Sedgwick, and the poetry of Frances Osgood. While the texts are lacking that would illustrate reasons for the historical reputation of some women speakers, such as Lucy Terry, and the expressive innovations of others, such as Harper's recitation of poetry of her own composing in her reform lectures, reconstructed versions of the performances of other women, such as Sojourner Truth, are becoming available in literary anthologies. Women's fiction also affords a range of views on features of contemporary oral culture that were debated, including the promotion of women's rights speakers in Mary S. Gove Nichols's *Mary Lyndon* (1855) and Laura J. Curtis Bullard's *Christine* (1856), as well as the satire of oral institutions and dialects in Caroline Matilda Kirkland's *A New Home* (1839) and in Frances Whitcher's *Widow Bedott Papers* (1856).

Folklorists' repeated call for greater voice in the discussion of relations between written and oral traditions has gone largely unheeded in literary history, and with the shift in folklore study from an item-centered approach, focusing on texts and motifs, to emphasis on performance, contexts, and function of oral traditions, folkloristics shows less interest in nineteenth-century literature and more in ethnic traditions, especially in ethnopoetics, which works to understand oral traditions from a perspective and values closer to those of originary speech communities than to the Romantic and modernist definitions of literature and its aesthetic value that have informed American literary studies. Emphasis on context as well as performance has stressed the need to understand how the situatedness of oral traditions affects both their form and significance, and this emphasis informs arguments for more holistic study than literary history, ethnopoetics, or anthropological approaches have yet provided (Elliot, Prahlad), yet has not provoked much attention to issues of gender. The long-standing androcentrism in the study of Native American and African American lore, for example in the recovery and history of trickster figures—the figures in both traditions that have commanded the most critical attention—needs correcting, as Andrew Wiget (in Ruoff, p. 89) and Henry Louis Gates Jr. (p. 54) note. Yet the work of that project is just beginning, with scholars such as Paula Gunn Allen providing models for ways women's expressive culture might be viewed as equally important in the Native American oral traditions circulating through the nineteenth century. While the new scholarship brings problems of its own, it does promise a more balanced, comprehensive, and historical sense of the multiplicity of the era's oral traditions.

See also "The Celebrated Jumping Frog of Calaveras County"; Dialect; Folklore; Humor; Oratory; Rhetoric

BIBLIOGRAPHY

Primary Works

Baym, Nina, ed. *The Norton Anthology of American Literature.* 6th ed. Vols. B and C. New York and London: Norton, 2003.

Brooks, Cleanth, R. W. B. Lewis, and Robert Penn Warren, compilers. *American Literature: The Makers and the Making.* Vol. 1. New York: St Martin's Press, 1973.

Gates, Henry Louis, Jr. and Nellie Y. McKay, eds. *The Norton Anthology of African American Literature.* New York and London: Norton, 1996.

Lauter, Paul, ed. *The Heath Anthology of American Literature.* 2nd ed. Vol. 1. Lexington, Mass.: Heath, 1994.

Secondary Works

Paula Gunn Allen. *The Sacred Hoop: Recovering the Feminine in American Indian Traditions.* Boston: Beacon Press, 1986.

Barnes, Daniel R. "Toward the Establishment of Principles for the Study of Folklore and Literature." *Southern Folklore Quarterly* 43 (1979): 5–16.

Bercovitch, Sacvan, ed. *The Cambridge History of American Literature.* Vol. 2. Cambridge, U.K., and New York: Cambridge University Press, 1995.

Chase, Richard Volney. *The American Novel and Its Tradition.* Garden City, N.Y.: Doubleday, 1957.

Dundes, Alan. "The American Concept of Folklore." *Journal of the Folklore Institute* 3 (1966): 226–249.

Elliott, Michael A. "Coyote Comes to the *Norton:* Indigenous Oral Narrative and American Literary History." *American Literature* 75 (2003): 723–749.

"Folklore in Literature: A Symposium." *Journal of American Folklore* 70 (1957): 1–24.

Gates, Henry Louis, Jr. *The Signifying Monkey: A Theory of Afro-American Literary Criticism.* New York: Oxford University Press, 1988.

Handbook of American Folklore. Edited by Richard M. Dorson. Introduction by W. Edson Richmond. Bloomington: Indiana University Press, 1983.

Hegeman, Susan. "Native American 'Texts' and the Problem of Authenticity." *American Quarterly* 41 (1989): 265–283.

Hoffman, Daniel. *Form and Fable in American Fiction.* New York: Oxford University Press, 1961.

Knapp, Samuel Lorenzo. *Lectures on American Literature. 1829. Facsimile reproduction as American Cultural History 1607–1829.* Gainesville, Florida: Scholars' Facsimiles and Reprints, 1961.

Matthiessen, F. O. *American Renaissance: Art and Expression in the Age of Emerson and Whitman.* London and New York: Oxford University Press, 1941.

Prahlad, Sw. Anand. "Guess Who's Coming to Dinner: Folklore, Folkloristics, and African American Literary Criticism." *African American Review* 33 (1999): 565–575.

Rourke, Constance. *American Humor: A Study of the National Character.* 1931. Garden City, N.Y.: Doubleday/Anchor, 1953.

Ruoff, A. La Vonne Brown, and Jerry W. Ward Jr., eds. *Redefining American Literary History.* New York: Modern Language Association of America, 1990.

Spiller, Robert E., Willard Thorpe, Thomas Herbert Johnson, Henry Seidel Canby, and Richard M. Ludwig, eds. *Literary History of the United States.* 3 vols. New York: Macmillan, 1948.

Trent, William Peterfield, John Erskine, Stuart P. Sherman, and Carl Van Doren, eds. *The Cambridge History of American Literature.* 4 vols. New York: G. P. Putnam's Sons, 1917–1921.

Charlene Avallone

ORATORY

The art of public speaking has deep roots, theoretical and practical, in human history, but it is no exaggeration to claim that antebellum America marks a particularly fruitful period in the history of oratory. Already in the late eighteenth century, the tumultuous events of British America leading to the Revolutionary War led likewise to what Jay Fliegelman calls an "elocutionary revolution." The new eloquence of the new American nation was grounded in the persuasive performances of public speakers, and the performances became so persuasive that the period between 1820 and 1870 constituted a "golden age of American oratory," as the writer Edward G. Parker described it in his 1857 study by that name. Given the political, social, and cultural stakes of the expanding nation, it is not surprising that eloquence engaged some of the most talented men and women of the period. In state and national legislatures, at political rallies and Fourth of July celebrations, in the pulpits and camp meetings from Boston to the Mississippi, at antislavery meetings and women's rights conventions, and in the lecture halls and lyceums of cities and towns across the country, speakers rose, each of them trying to make the occasion of his or her own performance a memorable act of moral persuasion.

Many eminent orators learned their trade in the colleges of their youth. From the middle of the eighteenth century, American colleges like Yale, Harvard, and William and Mary encouraged students to give public declamations every week, and by the beginning of the nineteenth century they were offering courses in rhetoric and elocution. Textbooks such as Hugh Blair's *Lectures on Rhetoric and Belles Lettres* (1783), Caleb Bingham's *The Columbian Orator* (1797), and John Quincy Adams's *Lectures on Rhetoric and Oratory* (1810) combined theory and practice for the generation that came to maturity between 1820 and 1850. In addition, undergraduates often were members of literary and debating societies, which sponsored a wide range of weekly debates on cultural and political topics. Indeed, by 1800 the literary societies were so important at Yale College that entering students were automatically assigned to either the Linonia or the Brothers in Unity.

The education system of eighteenth-century British America emphasized classical languages and rhetoric, and it had as a primary goal the preparation of young men for the ministry. By the early nineteenth century, however, the college-bred man could expect to find more opportunities for public address than the pulpit would provide. Forensic, celebratory, and political speaking created a host of arenas in which the public address flourished. In all of these forums, the goal of oratory was more than simple instruction or entertainment, though it certainly kept those classical goals in mind. In addition, the American orator of the nineteenth century had to meet and persuade his or her audience of their common good, and in order to do so he or she could not stand above his listeners nor apart from them. Thus speakers in the period began to adopt a less-formal style, eschewing the grandiloquence of an Edward Everett and embracing the simple, direct eloquence of orators like John Adams, from the generation of the Founding Fathers, and Abraham Lincoln, from the generation of the Civil War. The effect of this stylistic shift was to emphasize the democratic influence of oratory in nineteenth-century American culture, which Jay Fliegelman describes as already vital to the late-eighteenth-century Republic: "True oratory represented and reiterated shared beliefs in an effort to maintain a shared cultural world, one that provided a circumscribed scene for human action and created consensus by calling forth the universal nature of man, whose moral dictates would then ensure that sociability would rule individual behavior" (p. 45).

Perhaps the most important literary innovation of the oratorical culture, the popular lecture, also came closest to this ideal version of "true oratory." The popular lecture developed out of the lyceum movement, which was begun in 1826 by Josiah Holbrook (1788–1854). The lyceum was a remarkable institution for popular education in communities of all kinds, and it spread throughout New England and into the upper Atlantic states, the Midwest, and the South. In the first decade, lyceums featured local lecturers, especially the clergy and self-proclaimed experts in applied sciences. By the mid-1840s, according to the historian Donald M. Scott, there were nearly four thousand communities with a lyceum or similar institution for sponsoring public lectures, especially in the winter months. Celebrities like Ralph Waldo Emerson, Oliver Wendell Holmes, Frederick Douglass, Bayard Taylor, Sylvester Graham, and Wendell Phillips could be seen regularly in New England and as far west as St. Louis, Missouri, or Davenport, Iowa. The topics were encyclopedic, ranging broadly over health, contemporary social life, social reform, travel, history, literature, aes-

Like the Gettysburg Address, delivered at the dedication of the cemetery at Gettysburg on 19 November 1863, President Lincoln's speech at his second inaugural (4 March 1865) was marked by its forceful brevity. In four paragraphs, Lincoln noted the hopeful conclusion of the war, reminded his listeners of the history of American slavery leading up to the war, and then concluded with these famous words:

With malice toward none; with charity for all; with firmness in the right, as God gives us to see the right, let us strive on to finish the work we are in; to bind up the nation's wounds; to care for him who shall have borne the battle, and for his widow, and his orphan—to do all which may achieve and cherish a just, and a lasting peace, among ourselves, and with all nations.

Lincoln, "Second Inaugural Address," in *Speeches and Writings: 1859–1865*, p. 687.

thetics, natural history, and philosophy. Like "true oratory," the public lecture was supposed "to incorporate the public, to embrace all members of the community, whatever their occupation, social standing, or political and religious affiliation. Useful to all and offensive to none, the lecture was an oratorical form deliberately and carefully separated from all partisan and sectarian discourse" (Scott, p. 793). Moreover, the lyceum circuit gave many intellectuals and writers a career and a decent living. By the 1850s the lecture system, run by a host of booking agents and bureaus, had created at least the myth of a "shared cultural world" in which successful lecturers like Emerson and Taylor kept divisive issues at bay and formed a common, public discourse in the neutral space of the lecture hall.

PULPIT ELOQUENCE

If the public lecture was to become the most innovative new literary form of oratory in antebellum America, it had its roots in the preaching of American ministers. As Lawrence Buell has argued, the change from strict Congregationalism to the more liberal doctrines of Unitarianism was accompanied by a liberalizing of religious writing: "During the nineteenth century the idea of the sermon as a means of expounding and enforcing doctrine tended to give way to the idea of the sermon as an inspirational oration. Much more was made of imagination and creativity in

> *In a host of lectures and essays, Emerson created the figure of the heroic orator, an extreme figure who perches on the very edge of the fight and calls upon humanity to follow him. The figure of eloquence is a fabulous, idealized character, but Emerson suggests that it serves an important function for both the orator and the culture. Standing at the border between speech and action, public and private, past and present, the figure of eloquence embodies the virtues he called forth at Harvard University, 31 August 1837.*
>
> ---
>
> He learns that he who has mastered any law in his private thoughts, is master to that extent of all men whose language he speaks, and of all into whose language his own can be translated. The poet in utter solitude remembering his spontaneous thoughts and recording them, is found to have recorded that which men in crowded cities find true for them also. The orator distrusts at first the fitness of his frank confessions,—his want of knowledge of the persons he addresses,—until he finds that he is the complement of his hearers;—that they drink his words because he fulfills for them their own nature; the deeper he dives into his privatest secretest presentiment,—to his wonder he finds, this is the most acceptable, most public, and universally true.
>
> Ralph Waldo Emerson, "The American Scholar," in *Nature, Addresses, and Lectures* (New York: AMS Press, 1979), p. 63.

preaching than had been the case before" (*Literary Transcendentalism,* p. 105). The earliest proponent of this shift, both in doctrine and in sermon style, was William Ellery Channing (1780–1842), who preached at the Federal Street Church in Boston from 1803 to 1842. Channing's sermon "On Unitarian Christianity" (delivered in Baltimore on 5 May 1819) articulated the central beliefs of Unitarians before a large audience of ministers and established Channing's reputation as the premier Unitarian in the country. In addition, Channing's liberal theology inspired the younger New England intellectuals and artists who would found the transcendentalist movement in the 1830s and 1840s. In sermons and speeches, his style was plain and direct, but he refused to pander to audiences.

Theodore Parker (1810–1860) was the heir apparent to Channing's Unitarianism, carrying the liberalization yet further. Inspired both by Channing and by Ralph Waldo Emerson's (1803–1882) 15 July 1838 address to the graduating seniors at Harvard Divinity School, Parker dedicated himself to writing sermons that would tell the truth as directly as Emerson and Channing had done. That truth led Parker to deliver the sermon "The Transient and Permanent in Christianity" on 19 May 1841, in which he argued that "oneness with God" was more important than any system of doctrines and rituals. From 1841 to his death, Parker was one of the most controversial and liberal preachers in New England. His theology and preaching style broke radically with the conventions of nineteenth-century American Protestantism, and his sermons often became indistinguishable from lectures. He was polemical and rationalistic, but he could also give way to flights of poetic sensibility and figurative excess.

A third great pulpit orator of the period was Henry Ward Beecher (1813–1887), who further liberalized Christian doctrine and blurred the boundary between sacred and secular speech. Beecher spoke most prominently from the pulpit of Plymouth Church in Brooklyn, New York, attracting huge crowds because of his dynamic style. His sermons joined liberal religion and such social reform issues as antislavery, women's rights, and temperance. He lectured widely on women's rights throughout his career, and he was a celebrity speaker, invited by President Lincoln to deliver the celebratory oration "Raising the Flag over Fort Sumter" on 14 April 1865. In a deep historical irony, Beecher delivered the oration on the day President Lincoln was assassinated. Rather than bespeaking reconciliation, Beecher's rhetoric was as divisive as the shot from John Wilkes Booth's pistol.

"A FRUITFUL NURSERY OF ORATORS"

The ideal of the sermon, lecture, or speech as a way of embodying a shared cultural world, uniting speaker and audience, is immediately challenged by the historical context of the golden age of oratory. The antebellum period was, according to the poet Walt Whitman (1819–1892) in his *Specimen Days,* characterized by "convulsiveness," not by the high-minded abstraction of the Fourth of July speech or the commencement address. In his 1846 lecture "Eloquence," Emerson asserted that "the resistance to slavery in this country has been a fruitful nursery of orators. The natural connection by which it drew to itself a train of moral reforms, and the slight yet sufficient party organization it offered, reinforced the city with new blood from the woods and mountains" (*Collected Works* 7:95). Both Whitman and Emerson point to the true occasions of true oratory in division, conflict, and passionate disagreement. Although Emerson tells only half the story, he accurately points to African American slavery as the nursery of great orators, for great orators appeared on both sides of the slavery debate.

The most fruitful of nurseries, at least in numbers, was the political. The three most famous political orators of the century were U.S. senators during the period from 1830 to 1850: John Calhoun of South Carolina, Henry Clay of Kentucky, and Daniel Webster of Massachusetts. Calhoun (1782–1850) is best known as the orator of nullification, state's rights, and proslavery, and his speeches were marked by their close reasoning and deliberative style. Clay (1777– 1852), the least educated of the great triumvirate, became celebrated as a forensic speaker, was elected Speaker of the House of Representatives in 1810, and became a figure of moderation, the "Great Pacificator," in the slavery debates of the Senate, especially in the bills that are known as the Compromise of 1850. His style was direct, emotional, and spontaneous, but he prepared thoroughly for his speeches. From all accounts his voice was impressively varied in tone, register, and rhythm. Without doubt the most prolific and celebrated of the three great political orators, Daniel Webster (1782–1852) excelled in forensic speaking, winning fame for arguing such important cases as *McCulloch v. Maryland* before the Supreme Court in 1819, which furthered the scope of federal power in relation to the states. Webster was equally famous for his ceremonial addresses, such as the Plymouth oration of 22 December 1820, the Bunker Hill Monument address delivered on 17 June 1825, and his "Eulogy on Adams and Jefferson" delivered on 2 August 1826. In the last of these three speeches, Webster famously re-created a speech by Adams concerning the Declaration of Independence, adopting the elder statesman's direct and forthright style: "Sink or swim, live or die, survive or perish, I give my hand and my heart to this vote. . . . Why put off longer the Declaration of Independence? That measure will strengthen us. It will give us character abroad. . . . But while I do live, let me have country, or at least the hope of a country, and that a free country. . . . Independence now, and Independence for Ever!" (quoted in Duffy and Ryan, pp. 420–421).

Webster's fame as a U.S. senator stems from slavery and states' rights debates on the Senate floor. Perhaps the most famous is the Webster-Hayne debate of 1830. Senator Robert Y. Hayne of South Carolina defended his state's right to ignore the federal tariff and, in response to Webster's answer, attacked the Massachusetts senator for inconsistency. Webster's reply stretched over two days and thirty thousand words, and it was circulated as a pamphlet after Webster revised it. The most famous line comes from the peroration: "Liberty and Union, now and forever, one and inseparable!" Three years later Webster debated Calhoun concerning President Andrew Jackson's force bill, which threatened South Carolina with invasion by armed federal troops. Webster carried the day and the vote, extending the power of the federal government. Finally, in the debates over the Compromise of 1850, Webster delivered a series of speeches supporting Clay's moderate view and combating Calhoun's states' rights position. The speech of 7 March 1850 became infamous for its careful legalisms and parsing of history. Though Webster's rhetorical and legislative compromises, including his support of the Fugitive Slave Law, led to his vilification by such liberal admirers as Emerson and Henry David Thoreau, he remained a political force in Massachusetts and the country until his death in 1852.

The debate over African American slavery and the future of the Union became the most important social issue of the day and provided a host of orators, not confined to the political arena, with a subject for speech. Three of the most famous orators of the period are associated with the antislavery movement: William Lloyd Garrison, Wendell Phillips, and Frederick Douglass.

Garrison (1805–1879) was the very embodiment of the antebellum abolitionist. He edited and published the abolitionist newspaper *The Liberator* from 1831 until the ratification of the Thirteenth Amendment in December 1865. While writing and publishing the inflammatory prose of abolitionism, however, Garrison also took to the lecture platform in Great Britain and in the United States. Moreover, he refused to ally himself and the movement with any political party, even refusing to vote. His rallying cry was "No Union with slaveholders," and he welcomed the secession of the Southern states in 1861. For Garrison, the page and the platform were interchangeable: he routinely printed his own and others' speeches in *The Liberator,* and the newspaper records nearly a thousand of his own speeches during the convulsive years leading up to the Civil War. Consistently combative and pious, Garrison proclaimed from the outset that he would be "harsh as truth, and uncompromising as justice," for he did not wish "to think, or speak, or write with moderation." In his antislavery lectures, Garrison would often introduce himself as "the peace-disturber Garrison—the fanatic Garrison—the madman Garrison," prompting delightful laughter in his audience at the sight of the innocuous, balding young man before them. In the autumn of 1865 Garrison conducted his own five-week lecture tour of the North and Midwest, traveling as far as Chicago and delivering "The Past, Present, and Future of Our Country"

Reformer Wendell Phillips Addresses an 11 April 1851 antislavery meeting to protest the case of Thomas Sims, a fugitive slave being tried in Boston. From *Gleason's Pictorial*, 3 May 1851. SPECIAL COLLECTIONS LIBRARY, UNIVERSITY OF MICHIGAN

to receptive audiences. But the tour convinced him that he was no lecturer, and so his career as a public speaker ended with *The Liberator*.

Wendell Phillips (1811–1884), born to a storied Boston family, distinguished himself as a public speaker at Harvard College and Harvard Law School and became the most famous extemporaneous abolitionist speaker of the antebellum period. By 1838 he was no longer a practicing attorney, devoting himself to the antislavery movement and making a living on the lyceum circuit. At the height of his fame he earned as much as $250 for delivering the popular lecture "The Lost Arts," which he could vary at will and which he delivered over a thousand times in his career. Consulting his own commonplace book (a personal journal containing newspaper clippings, quotation, and scraps) before the performance, Phillips would speak for over an hour without notes, and the audience would be certain to hear an impassioned, eloquent voice. Like

Garrison, Phillips was most renowned and effective as an agitator. His most famous antislavery speech, "The Murder of Lovejoy," narrated the career and death of the abolitionist Elijah Lovejoy, killed by a mob in Alton, Illinois. Phillips first delivered the Lovejoy speech at Faneuil Hall in Boston on 8 December 1837 to a crowd of five thousand listeners. The power of his eloquence galvanized the antislavery movement in Boston and established him as the voice of the movement. Until the disbanding of the American Anti-Slavery Society in 1870, when the Fifteenth Amendment was adopted, Phillips continued to speak on behalf of free speech, freedom of the press, and universal male suffrage. During the Civil War he agitated for female suffrage as well, but after 1866 he moderated his public statements in hopes of achieving suffrage for blacks.

Even in his final public address, "The Scholar in the Republic," Phillips maintained the independent, radical stance of the social reformer. Speaking at the centennial gathering of Phi Beta Kappa at Harvard University on 30 June 1881, Phillips urged the scholars to become agitators, for "the agitator must stand outside of organizations, with no bread to earn, no candidate to elect, no party to save, no object but truth,—to tear a question open and riddle it with light" (Warren, p. 2). In Phillips's narrative of American history, the abolitionists' "crusade against slavery" became an overarching reform movement, gathering the issues of free speech, universal suffrage, labor reform, women's rights, and states' rights into a single moral struggle. And Phillips sarcastically contrasted the courage of the moral reformer to the moral cowardice and silence of such speakers as Edward Everett, former president of Harvard University, who delivered his popular lecture "The Character of Washington" throughout the years of greatest agitation: "Everett carried Washington through thirty States, remembering to forget the brave words the wise Virginian had left on record warning his countrymen of this evil" (Warren, p. 6).

The abolitionist movement provided a further opportunity for new oratory by bringing black abolitionist speakers before white audiences. Charles Lenox Remond, William Wells Brown, Sojourner Truth, Frances Ellen Watkins Harper, and Frederick Douglass are only the most famous of the host of black orators in the antebellum period. Without doubt the most eloquent of them all was Frederick Douglass (1818–1895). Born a slave on the Eastern Shore of Maryland, Douglass escaped in 1838 and became a Garrisonian abolitionist in 1841. From 1841 to 1845 he was a paid lecturer for the Massachusetts Anti-Slavery Society, and after his *Narrative of the Life of Frederick Douglass, an American Slave, Written by Himself* was published in 1845, he conducted a successful two-year lecture tour of Great Britain and Ireland. In 1847 his British friends purchased his freedom for 150 pounds, and Douglass returned to the United States. By 1849 Douglass's sense of independence brought him to break with Garrisonian abolitionists and begin a long and successful career as a newspaper editor and journalist. At the same time, he became more and more famous and skillful as a social reformer and orator. Like Phillips, he spoke for women's rights, freedom of speech, civil rights for blacks, and universal suffrage as well as such issues as temperance, peace, and abolition of capital punishment. His most famous speeches include "What, to the Slave, Is the Fourth of July?" (delivered at the Independence Day celebrations in Rochester, New York, in 1852), "The Claims of the Negro Ethnologically Considered" (delivered at Western Reserve College in 1854), and "The Dred Scott Decision" (1857).

MOTHER TONGUES

Early in the period, women were largely excluded from public platforms, just as they were largely excluded from the possibilities of a college education or a public career. The Scottish-born reformer Frances Wright (1795–1852) is generally considered the first woman to deliver a public address in the United States, speaking on women's rights in New Harmony, Indiana, in 1828. Other early speakers were Sarah Grimké (1792–1873) and Angelina Grimké (1805–1879), who wrote and spoke for the American Anti-Slavery Society and on behalf of women's rights. Two other intellectual women associated with public speech and the transcendentalist movement were Elizabeth Peabody (1804–1894) and Margaret Fuller (1810–1850), who held "conversation" classes in Boston from 1839 to 1844, providing women with a forum for speaking and listening to one another in order to cultivate self-culture among the thinking women of metropolitan New England. The effects of Fuller's conversational style can be seen in both the style and the content of her important feminist work *Woman in the Nineteenth Century* (1845).

By mid-century the restrictions on women's speech were loosening, especially within the reform movements themselves. Three of the most important women orators in the period began within the abolitionist movement and moved toward issues of women's rights, especially female suffrage. Elizabeth Cady Stanton (1815–1902), Lucy Stone (1818–1893), and Susan B. Anthony (1820–1906) devoted their lives to lecturing, writing, and lobbying for women's right to vote. Anthony in particular was acquainted with the premier abolitionists of the day, and she was closely associated with Stanton for much of her life. Both women worked for antislavery organizations, and in their collaboration both were effective public speakers on behalf of women. The same connection between women's rights and antislavery runs through Stone's career. After becoming the first woman from Massachusetts to earn a bachelors degree (Oberlin College, 1847), Stone worked as a lecturer for the American Anti-Slavery Society. In 1869 Stone and Henry Ward Beecher split from Stanton and Anthony, with the result being two different national suffrage associations. The three women differed in their politics and strategies, but they appeared together as witnesses before the Senate Committee on Woman Suffrage on 20 February 1892, speaking eloquently to the lawmakers on behalf of truly universal suffrage.

ORATORY AND LITERARY CULTURE

The most important literary figure on the lyceum circuit was without doubt Ralph Waldo Emerson, and the lecture itself had a deep effect upon Emerson's literary style. Beginning as a Unitarian preacher and maintaining his position as a supply preacher throughout his life, Emerson was one of the most successful American speakers on the circuit. Beginning in the winter of 1835–1836, Emerson offered "courses" of lectures, writing a new series of six to ten addresses for each new season. He could vary the number and order of the lectures for any given lyceum, but unlike Phillips he did not employ the extemporaneous method of speaking. Perhaps as a result of speaking from a written text, the lectures became the source for Emerson's essays, though the process was by no means simple or linear. Instead the essays emerged from much revision, involving reorganization, addition of material from Emerson's voluminous journals, and rewriting of individual sentences to create the dense, surprising, and axiomatic style of Emersonian prose. Emerson's career paralleled the development of the lyceum into the popular lecture circuit of the 1850s, 1860s, and 1870s, and the circuit benefited as much from him as he did from it. In the 1850s, in particular, Emerson used the lecture platform to make telling speeches on the antislavery movement and to combat the compromising positions of Daniel Webster, who had been a personal hero of the younger writer. Despite these political and social interventions, however, Emerson maintained a distant, independent stance, one that exemplified the role of the public intellectual in the antebellum period.

Other prominent literary figures attempted to mount the platform and speak to their fellow citizens, but none was as successful as Emerson. The poets Henry Wadsworth Longfellow and James Russell Lowell gave academic lectures at Harvard University, and Lowell lectured on the lyceum circuit, as did Oliver Wendell Holmes and John Greenleaf Whittier. The relationship between the platform and the page, however, was strained for all these figures. The case is different for Henry David Thoreau (1817–1862), who was, like Emerson, on the board of the Concord Lyceum and delivered lectures in his hometown and surroundings. The prose of *Walden* (1854), dense and repeatedly revised over a seven-year period, clearly bears the marks of its origins in lectures delivered in 1848–1849. Though he grew to despise the popular lecture as a compromise, Thoreau still rose to speak when events called to him. On 4 July 1854, for instance, on the heels of the arrest of the fugitive slave Anthony Burns in Boston, he delivered "Slavery in Massachusetts," a fiery performance. Five years later he spoke in Concord and Boston in defense of John Brown, whose raid on the federal armory at Harpers Ferry, Virginia, signaled the coming convulsiveness of the Civil War. Meanwhile Thoreau continued to address audiences in lectures such as "Walking," "Wild Apples," "Cape Cod," and "The Maine Woods," and in the twentieth century these became some of his most influential writings.

The popular lecture exercised less influence on the literary culture of the South, though there were winter lecture series in the major cities of the region throughout the period. The most accomplished man of letters in the antebellum South, William Gilmore Simms (1806–1870), delivered public lectures and patriotic addresses through the 1840s and 1850s. But Simms's career as a lecturer was more telling in its failures than its successes. In the winter of 1856 Simms traveled to New York City to begin a lecture tour of the northern states, planning to speak on behalf of the much-maligned southern institutions. The lectures addressed the sectional conflict, mounting to a fever pitch after the passage of the Kansas-Nebraska Act of 1854 and Preston Brooks's caning of Senator Charles Sumner on the floor of the U.S. Senate. Over the space of two days, Sumner had given an inflammatory speech, "The Crime against Kansas," attacking Senator Butler of South Carolina and comparing the state to an imbecilic whore. Brooks, a congressman from South Carolina and a kinsman of Senator Butler, took it upon himself to answer Sumner's words with deeds. Simms sought to inject himself into the public debate, but the northern audiences were unwilling to listen to him. After delivering his lectures in Buffalo, Rochester, and New York City (150 persons attended the last performance), he canceled the tour and returned to South Carolina. In the early months of 1857 he toured the South, delivering a series of three lectures called "Our Social Moral," in which he excoriated the abolitionists, the northern politicians like Sumner, and the servile northern press, and accurately predicting a violent end to the conflict.

After the Civil War the lyceum circuit continued to hold an important position in American culture, and there was a proliferation of speakers' bureaus and agents. The popular lecture spread across the country, and oratory continued to flow from pulpits, platforms, and legislative halls. Still, the quality of the popular lecture changed in postbellum America. In the years leading to the Civil War, the lecture had created a kind of mythic moment of neutral investigation—high-minded, somewhat abstract perhaps, but earnest and eloquent. After the war, the popular and successful lecturers were entertainers and storytellers like Bret Harte and Mark Twain. The political arena produced no speakers on the order of Calhoun, Clay, or Webster.

Henry Ward Beecher was the most influential preacher of the postbellum period, but even his reputation was marred by scandal. By 1870 the "golden age of oratory" was nearing its end. By the time Phillips gave his speech at Harvard in 1881, the figure of the orator as "the Scholar in the Republic" had nearly disappeared.

See also Abolitionist Writing; "The American Scholar"; Education; Feminism; Lyceums; Proslavery Writing; Reform; Rhetoric; Suffrage; Unitarians; *Walden*

BIBLIOGRAPHY

Primary Works

Douglass, Frederick. *The Frederick Douglass Papers. Series One: Speeches, Debates, and Interviews.* Edited by John W. Blassingame. New Haven, Conn.: Yale University Press, 1979–1992.

Emerson, Ralph Waldo. *The Collected Works of Ralph Waldo Emerson.* Edited by Robert E. Spiller and Alfred R. Ferguson. Cambridge, Mass.: Belknap Press of Harvard University Press, 1971–.

Emerson, Ralph Waldo. *The Complete Sermons of Ralph Waldo Emerson.* Edited by Albert J. von Frank. Columbia: University of Missouri Press, 1989–1992.

Lincoln, Abraham. *Speeches and Writings: 1859–1865.* New York: Library of America, 1989.

Parker, Edward G. *The Golden Age of American Oratory.* Boston: Whittemore, Wiles, and Hall, 1857.

Phillips, Wendell. *Speeches, Lectures, and Letters.* Boston: Lee and Shephard, 1894.

Webster, Daniel. *The Papers of Daniel Webster.* Edited by Charles M. Wiltse. *Series 4: Speeches and Formal Papers.* 2 vols. Hanover, N.H.: University Press of New England, 1974–1979.

Secondary Works

Bode, Carl. *The American Lyceum: Town Meeting of the Mind.* New York: Oxford University Press, 1956.

Brigance, William Norwood, ed. *History and Criticism of American Public Address.* 2 vols. New York: Russell and Russell, 1960.

Buell, Lawrence. *Emerson.* Cambridge, Mass.: Harvard University Press, 2003.

Buell, Lawrence. *Literary Transcendentalism.* Ithaca, N.Y.: Cornell University Press, 1973.

Buell, Lawrence. *New England Literary Culture: From Revolution through Renaissance.* Cambridge, U.K., and New York: Cambridge University Press, 1986.

Duffy, Bernard K., and Halford R. Ryan, eds. *American Orators before 1900.* New York: Greenwood Press, 1987.

Fliegelman, Jay. *Declaring Independence: Jefferson, Natural Language, and the Culture of Performance.* Stanford, Calif.: Stanford University Press, 1993.

Foner, Philip S., and Robert James Branham, eds. *Lift Every Voice: African American Oratory, 1787–1900.* Tuscaloosa: University of Alabama Press, 1998.

Scott, Donald M. "The Popular Lecture and the Creation of a Public in Mid-Nineteenth-Century America." *Journal of American History* 66 (March 1980): 791–809.

Warren, James Perrin. *Culture of Eloquence: Oratory and Reform in Antebellum America.* University Park: Pennsylvania State University Press, 1999.

James Perrin Warren

THE OREGON TRAIL

"Last spring, 1846, was a busy season in the city of St. Louis. Not only were emigrants from every part of the country preparing for the journey to Oregon and California, but an unusual number of traders were making ready their wagons and outfits for Santa Fé. . . . Steamboats were leaving the levee and passing up the Missouri, crowded with passengers on their way to the frontier" (p. 13). Ever since it was first published— serially in *Knickerbocker* in 1847 and then as a book in 1849—Francis Parkman's *The California and Oregon Trail* (all subsequent editions would bear the title *The Oregon Trail*), more than any other literary text, perhaps, captured the sense of wonder, hope, and excitement that has been at the heart of the popular mythology of the American frontier. A record of a hazardous journey up the Oregon Trail into the haunts and hunting grounds of the Pawnee and Sioux tribes, it has become a symbol of the nation's collective nostalgia for a landscape, an ecology, and an era in America's turbulent ethnic history that were quickly fading even as Parkman was putting them on his literary canvas.

WILDERNESS VERSUS CIVILIZATION

Francis Parkman (1823–1893) enjoyed a reputation as one of the greatest American historians of the nineteenth century, based principally on his monumental study of the struggle between France and England for control of North America, the seven-volume historical epic *France and England in North America* (1865–1892). Yet curiously, Parkman liked to refer to his classic in narrative historiography as "the history of the American forest," and, what is perhaps even more remarkable, his principal mentor was not a fellow historian but a Romantic novelist—James Fenimore Cooper (1789–1851). As writers of Romantic fiction and Romantic history respectively, Cooper and Parkman

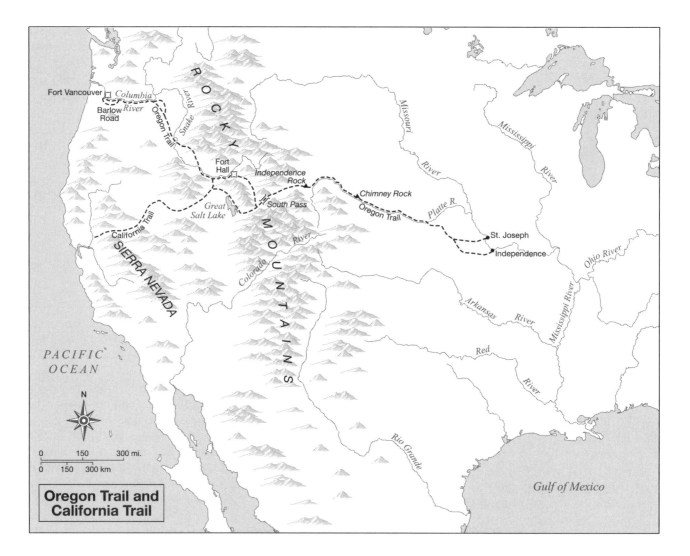

Oregon Trail and California Trail

were primarily concerned with the representation of the pristine American wilderness as the breathtaking backdrop for their explorations of the tension between the rival forces of nature and civilization. Like Cooper before him, Parkman used the wilderness in the first instance to create a mood of historical urgency and to add local color to his story. But he went beyond Cooper in that he consistently depicted environmental wildness as an ecological conditioner of civilized man. For Parkman, the natural wilderness was a storehouse of ecological and ethnohistorical metaphors of conflict (beauty versus ugliness, growth versus decay, creativity versus destructiveness), which mirrored similar clashes in the history of the civilized world.

Once described by the historian Frederick Jackson Turner as the epic chronicler of the American "primeval wilderness" (p. 451), Parkman's class standing, training, and disposition cannot by any stretch of the imagination be described as "wild," let alone "primeval." He was born in 1823 into an old, Boston

Brahmin family. He described his boyhood as "neither healthful nor buoyant" (Hubbell, p. 29): he grew up in the protective and socially privileged surroundings of the family's elegant and spacious mansion on Boston's Bowdoin Square, reaping all the benefits of his father's extensive library. An avid reader, he early on developed a passion for the American forest, "whose features . . . possessed his waking and sleeping dreams, filling him with cravings impossible to satisfy" (*Letters* 1:177). In 1840 he entered Harvard, where he studied language, literature, ethnology, and history, with a particular emphasis on the Romantic themes of such historians and novelists as Chateaubriand (1768–1848), Jules Michelet (1798–1874), Sir Walter Scott (1771–1832), and James Fenimore Cooper.

After completing his B.A., Parkman went on to study law, but he much preferred doing research for a historical account of "the Old French War." Because ethnography was still an infant science in the 1840s, he quickly realized that it would be impossible to write

***The Oregon Trail,* 1869.** Painting by Albert Bierstadt. © BUTLER INSTITUTE OF AMERICAN ART, YOUNGSTOWN, OH/THE BRIDGEMAN ART LIBRARY

such an epic narrative without first gaining "an inside view of Indian life" (quoted in Woodward, p. xxvii). To this purpose he initially inspected historical sites in the Old Northwest. Disappointed with the descendants of the once-powerful Six Nations Indians that he encountered at the ancient Onondaga stronghold, he began to prepare for an extensive journey to the far western frontier.

LIFE AMONG THE INDIANS

Parkman was just twenty-three when he and his cousin and companion, Quincy Adams Shaw, set out on their wilderness mission in March 1846. Neither was particularly qualified for the adventure, and both had only romantic notions at best about the rugged western prairie and the tribes that roamed there. But Parkman was determined to study American Indians in their natural habitat, and he very much owed his survival to that dogged determination (and to the help and wisdom of their guide, Henry Chatillon, a seasoned mountain man, whose marriage to the daughter of a deceased Sioux chief stood them in good stead). First making their way from the east across the Allegheny Mountains to Pittsburgh, then by river steamer down the Ohio River and up the Mississippi to St. Louis,

Parkman and his companions joined a medley of emigrants heading for California and Oregon as they "jumped off" from Westport (the present-day Kansas City) onto the western prairie. They traveled in a northwestern direction toward the Platte, then up that river to Fort Laramie, in what is now southeastern Wyoming. There Parkman spent some time observing the social dynamic of Indians, fur traders, and emigrants. Always eager for the authentic wilderness experience, Parkman decided to join a band of Sioux (or "Dahcotahs," as he called them) who were bent on wreaking bloody revenge on their enemies in the west, the Snakes, or Shoshones. To his disappointment, tensions between the Sioux and the Shoshones had subsided by the time he reached the Sioux camp. He stayed with the band anyway, riding with them into the "Black Hills" (in fact, the Laramie Mountains, not the Black Hills of South Dakota) and beyond, into the Medicine Bow Mountains. The appearance of buffalo in the area turned the warriors into hunters, which gave Parkman a taste of life in a Sioux hunting camp. After rejoining Shaw at Fort Laramie, Parkman traveled south, toward Pueblo and Bent's Fort, on the Arkansas River in present-day Colorado. From there he traveled east along the Santa Fe Trail, till he got back to Westport, Missouri, in late September.

Parkman worked his extensive field notes and diary (first published in 1947) into *The Oregon Trail*, producing one of the most vibrant and detailed narratives of the exploration of the American frontier wilderness. While it certainly gives us an insight into the daily dynamics of Indian life and culture, however, few historians would now reiterate without reservation the conventional claim that *The Oregon Trail* is one of the great historical records of our national past. Nor is Parkman's text the romantic eulogy for a relatively untouched ecosystem that it was long claimed to be. In fact, *The Oregon Trail* treats both Indian culture and the wilderness landscape as expendable obstructions to progress and civilization.

Parkman depicts the western wilderness from the outset as brutal, inhospitable, and even aggressive—fiercely resisting penetration by explorers and treacherously conspiring against peaceable emigrants. Thus, describing his journey by steamboat up the Missouri from St. Louis, Parkman observes that luckily the river was high in March, for when he descended the river on his return in the fall, it had fallen so low that "all the secrets of its treacherous shallows were exposed to view. It was frightful to see the dead and broken trees, thick-set as military abattis, firmly imbedded in the sand, and all pointing down stream, ready to impale any unhappy steamboat that at high water should pass over them" (*Oregon Trail*, p. 10). Even if travelers managed laboriously to make their way up the perilous river, all that awaited them was an endless, gloomy, and barren prairie. "Should any one of my readers ever be impelled to visit the prairies," Parkman muses somberly, "I can assure him that he need not think to enter at once upon the paradise of his imagination. A dreary preliminary . . . awaits him before he finds himself fairly upon the verge of the 'great American desert,'—those barren wastes, the haunts of the buffalo and the Indian, where the very shadow of civilization lies a hundred leagues behind him" (p. 34). Emigrants would frequently find that their wagons became stuck in the mud or their axletrees broke on the uneven trails. For weeks on end they had to subsist on whatever food they had brought, all the while beset by snakes and wolves. The days were excessively hot and oppressive, and they would be tormented by stinging insects, almost daily drenched in terrific thunderstorms and pelted by hailstones. The wagon trail across the prairie was marked by "abundant and melancholy traces" of the emigrants' progress (p. 49): shallow graves, some torn up by wolves, and the "shattered wrecks" of tables, desks, and chests (p. 72)—often ancient family heirlooms of European origin discarded from family wagons during the arduous trek across the desert plains.

Parkman's rendering of Indians and Indian culture is as sobering as his depiction of the prairie wilderness. Although Parkman was known to have had "Injuns on the brain" from an early age, he completely rejected the notion of the Noble Savage. The Indian warrior was to him essentially a crude barbarian, an anachronistic throwback to the primeval world. Thus, he described his Oglala hosts as "thorough savages. Neither their manners nor their ideas were in the slightest degree modified by contact with civilization. . . . Their religion, superstitions, and prejudices were the same handed down to them from immemorial time. . . . They were living representations of the 'stone age'" (p. 149). Yet despite his unsympathetic and unsentimental depiction of the Indian race, his "field trip" afforded him firsthand knowledge of Indian life, culture, and customs. Parkman shared their food and living conditions and rode their horses; he was able to gather details about their hunting practices and teepee building, their social life, gender relations, and intertribal feuds. Parkman probably knew more about woodland and Plains Indians than any other historian of his generation.

Perhaps it was because Parkman knew their way of life so intimately that there is such an overwhelming sense of *doom* in his account of Indian life in the western wilderness. Less a eulogy than a requiem for the open frontier and the nomadic life of the Plains Indians, *The Oregon Trail* was inspired and shaped by the author's awareness that he was traveling through a natural environment that was rapidly vanishing. Thus, living among the Oglala, he at one point observes that

> great changes are at hand in that region. With the stream of emigration to Oregon and California, the buffalo will dwindle away, and the large wandering communities who depend on them for support must be broken and scattered. The Indians will soon be abashed by whiskey and overawed by military posts; so that within a few years the traveller may pass in tolerable security through their country. Its danger and its charm will have disappeared together. (P. 149)

In the final analysis, Parkman was fascinated by the denizens of the western wilderness *because* they were on the verge of extinction.

Although an early work in a long and prolific career, *The Oregon Trail* already reveals Parkman's ambivalence toward both the wilderness and modern civilization—an ambivalence he very much shares with his great inspiration, James Fenimore Cooper, whose Leatherstocking Tales (1823–1841), notably *The Last of the Mohicans* (1826), reflect a similar patrician stance toward the vanishing Indians and their disappearing habitat—a habitat that is simultaneously romanticized and dreaded, mythologized and mourned, not for having escaped the destructive thrust of progress and civilization but for having fatally fallen under civilization's ever-lengthening shadow. In both Cooper and Parkman this ambivalence finds expression in a rudimentary form of ecological concern: most clearly in his novel *The Pioneers* (1823), Cooper describes the white man's wasting of game and wildlife; in *The Oregon Trail*, Parkman is concerned that hunters are shooting the buffalo bulls rather than the cows, for, in contrast to the cows, "thousands of [the bulls] might be slaughtered without causing any detriment to the species" (p. 258).

HISTORY OF THE CONSPIRACY OF PONTIAC

After *The Oregon Trail* Parkman was ready to undertake a more formidable task, the reconstruction of the rise and fall of Pontiac—the war chief of the Ottawa tribe—focusing on the episode known as the "Conspiracy of Pontiac." Parkman's letters and journals of the time reveal that above all he wanted to re-create the past and recapture the days of Indian frontier and woodland life in the pages of history. More than affording him "better opportunities than any other portion of American history for portraying forest life and the Indian character," however, the *History of the Conspiracy of Pontiac* (1851) allowed Parkman "to portray the American forest and the American Indian at the period when both received their final doom" (Turner, p. 452).

An exponent of the Great Man theory of history, Parkman's historical personalities tend to loom larger than life in his narratives, and the figure of Pontiac is no exception. In fact, in Parkman's work Pontiac is the epitome of the statuesque Indian warrior. Modern historiography does not share Parkman's method of arranging the results of historical and ethnological research into a single narrative of historical drama surrounding the rise and fall of a tragic hero; nor does it share Parkman's conclusion that the actions of Chief Pontiac constituted a "conspiracy" (we would characterize Pontiac's "conspiracy" as a war for Indian self-determination). But always lurking in Parkman's pristine wilderness is his villain archetype, the treacherous Indian barbarian. Ultimately, despite his nostalgic mythologization of the American Indian, Parkman could never descend from his Brahmin pedestal and in his life and writings always looked down on races and classes other than his own. If Parkman respected the Indian, it was because the Indian represented for him a figure of brute strength, courage, and endurance, a worthy foe of the patrician European soldier-explorer, who inevitably wins the battle and conquers the land.

CLASS BIAS

What is true for Pontiac is also true for Parkman's non-Indian foes in his magnum opus, *France and England in North America*. Prominent French figures such as Robert La Salle, Louis de Buade, comte de Frontenac, and Louis de Montcalm are first set up as formidable enemies, ultimately to be overcome by superior British patrician leaders such as Jeffrey Amherst and James Wolfe. To Parkman, the ultimate success of the British represented the victory of progress over reaction. For although he believed in a representative government, Parkman believed with even more conviction that leadership should lie with a natural aristocracy. The future of America was safe only in the hands of men of "birth and breeding," to cite his favorite phrase. Not surprisingly, he was strongly opposed to universal male suffrage and women's suffrage, pacifism, and philanthropy, and despised or at least resented Indians, Roman Catholics, the uneducated classes, poor immigrants, and blacks. Although he did not use the term Manifest Destiny, Parkman believed in a version of Social Darwinism that very much embraced that concept. The Indians were obliterated, in Parkman's way of thinking, because they stood in the path of progress. Progress "doomed" the Indians as well as the wilderness culture they inhabited; and likewise progress doomed the old French regime in Canada. It is not a coincidence that both *The History of the Conspiracy of Pontiac* and *Montcalm and Wolfe* (1884), the culminating volume of *France and England in North America,* end in the historic year of 1763, when the power of Anglo-America dealt a decisive blow to both the Indian tribes and old French Canada: "Could the French have maintained their ground," he writes, "the ruin of the Indian tribes could have been postponed; but the victory of Quebec was the signal of their swift decline. Thenceforth they were destined to melt and vanish before the advancing waves of Anglo-American power, which now rolled westward unchecked and unopposed" (Preface, *Conspiracy of Pontiac*).

Parkman considered *Montcalm and Wolfe* to be his masterpiece, a view generally shared by readers and critics. The book is the most consummate illustration of both Parkman's central theme (the ethno- or eco-history of the rise of British North America) and his style (the historical wilderness narrative, or forest epic). But the groundwork for the success in his mature years had been laid in his first publication, *The Oregon Trail.* It was there that Parkman first displayed his unique talent for writing history as literature. Combining rigorous scholarship with the art of history, he managed to bring the past to life in ways that more conventional historians can only dream of.

See also Borders; Exploration and Discovery; History; Travel Writing

BIBLIOGRAPHY

Primary Works

Parkman, Francis. *The Conspiracy of Pontiac*. 1851. New York: Library of America, 1991.

Parkman, Francis. *The Letters of Francis Parkman*. 2 vols. Edited by Wilbur R. Jacobs. Norman: University of Oklahoma Press, 1960.

Parkman, Francis. *The Oregon Trail*. 1849. New York: New American Library, 1950.

Secondary Works

Hubbell, John T. "Francis Parkman, Historian." *Midwestern Quarterly* 8, no. 1 (October 1966): 29–39.

Jacobs, Wilbur R. "Francis Parkman's Oration 'Romance in America.'" *American Historical Review* 18 (April 1963): 692–698.

Turner, Frederick Jackson. "Francis Parkman and His Work." *Dial* 300, no. 25 (16 December 1898): 451–453.

Woodward, C. Vann. "Foreword." In *Montcalm and Wolfe: The French and Indian War,* by Francis Parkman. New York: Da Capo Press, 1995.

Wil Verhoeven

ORIENTALISM

Although there has never been a political area called the Orient, the words "Orient" and "Orientalism" have become common usage because the Orient has been a long-standing Western invention: it is an imaginative geography but one with enormous consequences. Orientalism in the mid-nineteenth century was a nexus of political, ideological, racial, cultural, and aesthetic investments in the various parts of the world that denoted the "Orient" in the U.S. cultural imagination: Asia and the Near East, including Egypt and the Holy Lands. It is best approached in Edward Said's sense of Orientalism as being both a means of Euro-American self-definition and a method for having authority over the Orient, although in the nineteenth-century United States it also served to mark the nation as important in relation to European colonizing powers, a new empire ready to lead the world.

Although the particularities of this use of the Orient varied with the kind of discourse—political writing, travel writing, novels—the idea of these Orients as being storehouses of knowledge, embodying the past and needing regeneration in the present, remained remarkably consistent. As revealed in a special *Knickerbocker* article of June 1853 devoted to describing the scenes evoked by the word "Orientalism," in the American mind it meant a combination of luxury, indolence, and unreality:

> We frame to ourselves a deep azure sky, and a languid alluring atmosphere; associate luxurious ease with the coffee-rooms and flower-gardens of the Seraglio at Constantinople; . . . We see grave and revered turbans sitting cross-legged on Persian carpets in baths and harems, . . . we then bespread over all a sort of Arabian night-spell. (Pp. 479–480)

The stimulus for U.S. interest in Egypt was the military forays of the French and the British. The French Egyptologist Jean-François Champollion's deciphering of the hieroglyphs in 1822 created intense scholarly and political excitement which affected popular culture as well. P. T. Barnum acquired two mummies in 1826, and in 1832 Colonel Mendes Cohen of Baltimore returned from Egypt with 680 artifacts to establish the first private Egyptian collection in the United States.

By the early nineteenth century the United States, like Europe, would also be affected by what Raymond Schwab has called "the Oriental Renaissance" generated by the arrival of Sanskrit texts in Europe in the late eighteenth century. Interest in Asia is evident in the fact that in 1817, Thomas Moore's long poem *Lalla Rookh,* set in India, sold more copies than any other book published that year in the United States. For American readers, Oriental literatures were not simply exotic, trivial entertainment but literatures that warranted commentary and critique. Between June and November 1840, for instance, the *Southern Literary Messenger* published three papers on Arabian literature.

VISIONS OF EMPIRE AND CONTACT WITH THE ORIENT

In addition to the popularity of Orientalist works, the Orient was also brought closer because of increasing commercial interests both in the Near East and in Asia. Oriental trade was important, both in itself and as a sign of national power. By the 1830s trade with the Barbary States of North Africa became well established, and in 1832 alone, forty-six U.S. ships had landed at Smyrna and fourteen in Constantinople. More than trade with the Near East, trade with Asia was vigorously sought after. The leader in this trade, it was presumed, would lead the world. For many other thinkers, Asian trade exemplified the idea of civilization coming full circle. It was popularly held that empires had started in the Far East, moved to Europe, and were heading to the New World. Jefferson had been fascinated with the idea of "the North American road to India" since 1787, an idea taken up again in the early nineteenth century by Senator Thomas Hart Benton of Missouri, who cast his arguments about trade in terms of the human race and civilization moving west and the return of republican ideals to Asia.

With the introduction of steam packets in the 1830s, tourists from the United States started to choose Oriental destinations, the most popular of which were Egypt and the Holy Lands. U.S. appetite for Oriental travel is evidenced by the fact that by the winter of 1838–1839, Egypt had more travelers from the United States than of any other nationality but the British. The American Oriental Society in its first number lists thirty-four travel works about Asia, the Near East, and Middle East, all published between 1823 and 1843.

Most popular travel writers focused on the picturesqueness and exoticism of the "backward" Eastern races. Nathaniel Parker Willis's *Pencillings by the Way,* an account of a cruise on the eastern Mediterranean in 1833, no doubt fascinated readers with its raptures over Mediterranean sunsets, twilights, and veiled women. Similarly John Lloyd Stephens, author of *Incidents of Travel in Egypt, Arabia, Petraea, and the Holy Land* (1837) and *Incidents of Travel in Greece, Turkey, Russia, and Poland* (1838) had royalties reaching an unheard-of $25,000. Travel writing continued to enjoy popularity in the mid-nineteenth century with George William Curtis's *Nile Notes of a Howadji* (1851) and *The Howadji in Syria* (1852), the first an account of a journey along the Nile and the second a description of travels across Cairo, the Arabian deserts, Jerusalem, and finally, Damascus.

The most prolific of Oriental travel writers was Bayard Taylor (1825–1878). Taylor recorded his two-and-a-half years of travel in three volumes: *A Journey to Central Africa* (1854), *The Lands of the Saracen* (1856), and *A Visit to India, China, and Japan in the Year 1853* (1855). In addition Taylor wrote *Japan in Our Day* (1872) and *Travels in Arabia* (1872). Although Taylor had a flair for the dramatic, and his appearance on the lyceum circuit clad in Arab clothes and scimitar is reported to have made women swoon, many of his works deal with historical material rather than exotic Orient. Much of Taylor's *A Visit to India, China, and Japan,* for instance, corrects misconceptions about "ignorant" natives created by previous Orientalist writers, recounts the complex diplomatic maneuvers of the American commodore Matthew Perry in his gunboat diplomacy mission to facilitate the first Western trade treaty with Japan, and satirizes the imperial presumptions of his countrymen.

Missionary activity overseas began with the formation of the American Board of Commissioners for Foreign Missions (ABCFM) in 1810; shortly thereafter the board began work in the Near East and Asia. The formation of the ABCFM was quickly followed by clergy journeying to the region. By 1818 the board was running eleven schools in India alone, instructing an estimated six hundred students. The board reported, "In these schools, we seem to see a thousand Hindoo hands at work . . . in undermining the fabric of Hindoo idolatry" (ABCFM, p. 211). The ABCFM similarly saw the Near East as an area for cultural conversion. Many countries had strict laws forbidding attempts at converting Muslims, but missionaries regarded the Oriental churches as equally fit objects of concern, particularly because of the interracial contact there. The ABCFM established missions in Beirut through a system of schools and was instructing six hundred children by 1827. Missionary and imperial enterprises were also often related. For instance, in 1835 Eli Smith, a missionary in Syria, requested official action from the United States, adding that Syrians should be taught "that we are a powerful nation. And there is no other way to teach them this but to make them *feel* it" (Field, p. 210).

The establishment of missionary activity in Oriental countries also facilitated the formation of the American Oriental Society in 1843. This was clearly a scholastic society, but missionary and scholarly activities were connected. In the first address to the society, the president made repeated mention of the exemplary work of American missionaries abroad and compared them with their European counterparts. Yet the ambitious scholarly programs of the society also expanded the cultural horizons of the United States. Essays ranged from discussions of Eastern religions to economies and medicine. In May 1844, for instance, Edward E. Salisbury gave a talk at the annual meeting of the society titled "Memoir on the History of Buddhism."

LITERARY REPRESENTATIONS OF THE NEAR EAST

Despite imperial politics, literary representations of the Orient varied according to the region in question. The predominant genre of Near East Orientalist literature was satire, the object of which was both archaeological and missionary imperialism. The adventurer in the Orient was admirable and ludicrous, sincere but misguided in his role as discoverer. The same terms applied to missionary women. Writers thus produced missionary-colonial novels in which American men boldly ventured forth as archaeologists; American women were most often the conveyers of the gospel, converting Near Eastern women and steadying men in their purpose. Unlike Near Eastern women who were frivolous, indolent and oppressed, missionary women were independent and intelligent.

But while writers relied on the formulaic missionary-conversion plot, they also caricatured the ideological presumptions of American or Western heroes embodying imperial nationhood. Popular works in the genre were Henry Brent's "The Mysterious Pyramid" (1850), Maturin Murray Ballou's *The Turkish Slave* (1850), and John De Forest's *Irene the Missionary* (1879). It is significant that the immensely popular women's writer and author of *The Lamplighter,* Maria Susanna Cummins, also wrote a missionary novel, *El Fureidís,* in 1860. William Ware wrote *Zenobia* (1837), the story of a Palmyrean queen who challenges the power of the Roman Empire, emphasizing the difference between Eastern and Western leaders as that between heart and head. Significantly, Nathaniel Hawthorne's *Blithedale Romance* features a character named Zenobia. Near East Orientalist writing finds its most self-conscious expression and critique of archaeological imperialism in the tales of Edgar Allan Poe (1809–1849) and Harriet Prescott Spofford (1835–1921) and in Herman Melville's (1819–1891) *Clarel.*

Poe, Spofford, and Melville are the most important writers of Near East Orientalism. The comic and parodic critique of Orientalist power gives way here to a demonstration of the tragic consequences of mastery and control. The works critique the idea of the Near East as new frontier, and instead of confirming an imperial order, they close with chaos. Poe constantly parodied the culture's colonial use of the Orient, most notably in "The Thousand-and-Second Tale of Scheherazade." A more farcical subversion of Western cultural imperialism occurs in "Some Words with a Mummy," where a mummy comes to life and delivers a harangue on the inferiority of contemporary American civilization. "A Tale of Ragged Mountains" critiques British colonialism in India. In "Ligeia," signifiers of the Orient and U.S. southern womanhood intersect to generate an epistemological crisis about nationalism and empire. Ligeia and Rowena are more than abstractions of womanhood. Ligeia clearly represents Near East "Oriental" knowledge, control over which was a defining feature of U.S. nationhood in the early and mid-nineteenth century.

Like Poe, Spofford in "Desert Sands" (1863) dramatizes the dangers of imperialistic appropriation of the Orient. The story recounts the frantic efforts of the artist narrator, Sydney, to produce his masterpiece painting by capturing Arab lands on his canvas; it ends with the masterpiece completed but the artist struck blind. Writing contemporaneously with Spofford, Melville further complicates the idea of the Near East as the new frontier by dramatizing the resistance of the Near East to the hermeneutic mappings of the American hero. In 1856 Melville published a humorous piece called "I and My Chimney" in which he satirized the vogue for Egyptology popularized by travel writing. In autumn 1856 Melville traveled to Europe and then on to Greece, Turkey, Egypt, Italy and Palestine, all of which he documented in his journals. In his long prose poem *Clarel,* Melville fictionalized the doubts and hesitancies of the American hero seeking religious regeneration through a pilgrimage to the Holy Lands. Through Clarel, a young theological student, Melville eroticizes the relationship between the United States and the Near East and demonstrates how the racial-cultural difference of the Near East cannot be simplified by creating mind/body dichotomies. Instead Melville's poem questions the ideological oppositions between the United States and the Near East through the circulation of homoerotic desire.

LITERARY REPRESENTATIONS OF ASIA

Like the Near East, Asia was fodder for the literary imagination. For example, sixteen-year-old Lucretia Maria Davidson wrote *Amir Khan and Other Poems,* posthumously published in 1829. In 1821, Ralph Waldo Emerson (1803–1882) wrote a long poem called "Indian Superstition" for the Harvard College Exhibition. This fascination with the Far East culminated in the 1850s and 1860s in the works of writers such as Emerson, Walt Whitman, Henry David Thoreau, Henry Wadsworth Longfellow, James Russell Lowell, and Bret Harte.

The cultural representation of Asia was highly contradictory. Asia was revered as the land of scriptures and literatures, the birthplace of civilization; yet in order to be accommodated within the vision of empire in which civilization was seen as moving west, culminating in the New World, it had to be seen as either degraded present or transhistorical past. The acquisition of goods from India could be seen as the rightful fulfillment of Columbus's original dream or as a redemptive journey of the newest empire to the old. In either case, the present-day reality of colonial India had to be excluded, a feature evident in Thoreau's, Emerson's, and Whitman's highly contradictory sacralization of India as absolute spiritual past.

The politics of Asian Orientalism thus contributed to features that are commonly associated with transcendentalism—mysticism, spirituality, and a transcending of this world. Such a discourse was not divorced from history; it was in fact historically informed, being a product of the periods of colonization and slavery, even though it was ahistorically framed in its insistence on getting beyond history. In James Russell Lowell's (1819–1891) "Dara" (1850), Persia is an old, uninspiring empire, described in images of rot and sexual impotence. It is a "decaying empire," "wilted by harem-heats." Lowell's poem "An Oriental Apologue" (1849) similarly dramatizes the theme of the old, irrational Orient in need of youth and change. On the other hand, Thoreau in *Walden* (1854) recalls having spent many blissful moments immersed in the *Bhagavad Gita* and imagines Walden Pond, the metaphoric source of his knowledge, to have been fed by the Ganges.

Of all the transcendentalists, Emerson read Orientalist texts most extensively and used the Orient to stand for an absolute spiritual past against which a unified New World nationhood, as the latest seat of the westward Anglo-Saxon movement of civilization, could be formulated. This idea of Asia as unified "spiritual" territory was a political necessity for Emerson because it allowed him to deflect the idea of a fragmented nationhood. Emerson called his wife, Lydia, "Asia," and many of Emerson's essays rest upon binary distinctions between male and female, West and East, activity and passivity, dynamism and fate. In 1847 Emerson wrote, "Orientalism is Fatalism, resignation: Occidentalism is Freedom & Will," and "We occidentals are educated to wish to be first" (*Journals*, p. 90). Such ideas were crystallized in "Brahma," the most overtly Oriental of Emerson's poems, yet one in which the unity of India also stands for the unity of the nation.

Like Emerson, Walt Whitman (1819–1892) was fascinated with the Oriental cultures the country was increasingly coming in contact with. Asia and, in particular, India appealed to Whitman's imagination both as a symbol of the farthest reaches of empire and as maternal space through which the New World could be seen as youthful and dynamic; in turn, Whitman's loving persona could imperialistically embrace the world. We must not be duped into thinking that it was simply a "mystical" Asia that the transcendentalists repeatedly used—even though, as Malcolm Cowley argued, Whitman's poems were a cross between the *New York Herald* and the *Bhagavad Gita*—because the sites of Whitman's poems of the Orient were often concrete historical-material situations such as the parade on Broadway and the installation of the Atlantic cables. Whitman was in fact an omnivorous reader and an obsessive recorder of details about Asia. In a lengthy journal entry on China in June 1857, for instance, Whitman noted details about Chinese forms of worship, Chinese tea, the physiognomy of the people, the manner of executions, and the status of the United States in China.

Whitman uses a poetic persona representing the nation as a strong, earthy male with a desire to embrace all. The Asian Orient in relation to this persona appears most regularly as mother, thus reinforcing the idea of Asia as past. In "A Broadway Pageant," the march on Broadway is figured as a march of the westward movement of civilization in which Japan is past and the United States is "Libertad." The Orient, as India, is associated with maternal images. It is the birthplace of civilization, the early nurturer or "nest" of languages, and like a good mother it bequeaths culture to the world. Whitman's poetry consciously creates the spiritual Orient based on the exclusion of contemporary colonialism, a process most evident in "Passage to India," which romanticizes colonialism yet, in recording the trajectory of foreign conquerors in India, forgets to mention the British. Transcendentalists attempted to valorize India as past while excluding its brutal colonization and, consequently, the humanity of its people. Thus Orientalism in the mid-nineteenth century was an intensely political domain, a signifier of U.S. imperial power and a screen onto which writers projected racial anxieties about the nation.

See also Americans Abroad; Chinese; Ethnology; Exploration and Discovery; Foreigners; Manifest Destiny; Satire, Burlesque, and Parody; Tourism; Transcendentalism; Travel Writing

BIBLIOGRAPHY
Primary Works

ABCFM. *First Annual Reports of the American Board of Commissioners for Foreign Missions.* Crocker and Brewster, 1834.

Cummins, Maria Susanna. *El Fureidîs.* Boston: Ticknor and Fields, 1860.

Davidson, Lucretia Maria. *Amir Khan and Other Poems.* Edited by Samuel F. B. Morse. New York: G. and C. and H. Carvill, 1829.

Emerson, Ralph Waldo. *The Complete Works of Ralph Waldo Emerson.* 12 vols. Edited by Edward Waldo Emerson. Boston: Houghton Mifflin, 1903–1904.

Emerson, Ralph Waldo. *The Journals and Miscellaneous Notebooks of Ralph Waldo Emerson,* vol. 10, 1847–1848. Edited by William H. Gilman et al. Cambridge, Mass.: Belknap Press of Harvard University Press, 1973.

Lowell, James Russell. "Dara." *Graham's* (July 1850).

Lowell, James Russell. "An Oriental Apologue" *National Anti-Slavery Standard* (12 April 1849).

Melville, Herman. *Clarel: A Poem and Pilgrimmage in the Holy Lands.* Edited by Walter E. Bezanson. New York: Hendricks House, 1960.

Poe, Edgar Allan. *The Short Fiction of Edgar Allan Poe.* Edited by Stuart Levine and Susan Levine. Urbana: University of Illinois Press, 1976.

Spofford, Harriet Prescott. *The Amber Gods and Other Stories.* 1863. Reprint, New York: Books for Libraries Press, 1969.

Taylor, Bayard. *A Visit to India, China, and Japan in the Year 1853.* 1855. Reprint, New York: Putnam, 1862.

Ware, William. *Zenobia; or, The Fall of Palmyra.* New York: C. S. Francis, 1837.

Whitman, Walt. *Leaves of Grass.* 1855. Edited by Sculley Bradley and Harold W. Blodgett. New York: Norton, 1973.

Secondary Works

Field, James A. *America and the Mediterranean World; 1776–1882.* Princeton, N.J.: Princeton University Press, 1969.

Finkelstein, Dorothee Metlitsky. *Melville's Orienda.* New Haven, Conn.: Yale University Press, 1961.

Finnie, David H. *Pioneers East: The Early American Experience in the Middle East.* Cambridge, Mass.: Harvard University Press, 1967.

Horsman, Reginald. *Race and Manifest Destiny: The Origins of Racial Anglo-Saxonism.* Cambridge, Mass.: Harvard University Press, 1981.

Irwin, John T. *American Hieroglyphics: The Symbol of the Egyptian Hieroglyphics in the American Renaissance.* New Haven, Conn.: Yale University Press, 1980.

Isaani, Mukhtar Ali. *The Oriental Tale in America through 1865: A Study in American Fiction.* Ph.D. diss., Princeton University, 1962.

Luedtke, Luther S. *Nathaniel Hawthorne and the Romance of the Orient.* Bloomington: Indiana University Press, 1989.

Said, Edward W. *Orientalism.* New York: Random House, Vintage, 1978.

Schueller, Malini. *U.S. Orientalisms: Race, Nation, and Gender in Literature, 1790–1890.* Ann Arbor: University of Michigan Press, 1998.

Schwab, Raymond. *The Oriental Renaissance: Europe's Rediscovery of India and the East, 1680–1880.* Translated by Gene Patterson-Black and Victor Reinking. New York: Columbia University Press, 1984.

Sha'ban, Fuad. *Islam and Arabs in Early American Thought: The Roots of Orientalism in America.* Durham, N.C.: Acorn Press, 1991.

Van Alstyne, R. W. *The Rising American Empire.* Chicago: Quadrangle Press, 1960.

Malini Johar Schueller

OUR NIG

Forgotten or ignored by all but a handful of bibliographers—one of whom dismissed it as a text written by a white man—Harriet E. Adams Wilson's *Our Nig; or, Sketches from the Life of a Free Black* (1859) languished before its rediscovery by Henry Louis Gates Jr. and republication in 1983. Gates proved that Wilson authored the book and was a free African American. In part through the assertion that *Our Nig* was the first novel by an African American woman, he also actively advocated for its inclusion in the emerging canon of early African American literature.

While subsequent historians like Barbara White, P. Gabrielle Foreman, and Reginald H. Pitts have uncovered evidence that the book is exceedingly autobiographical, *Our Nig* has remained a key text in African American studies because of its own fascinating story of a young, poor, nominally free black child's coming of age in the racist North, because of its place vis-à-vis the slave narratives of the period (as well as its place among texts by women), and because of the compelling story of its author.

The book's stated purposes were much more modest—or, at least, much more personalized. Still, the book's broader attempts to assert both the need and the rights of free black children in the North may well have shaped both the book's plot and initial reception more than those stated purposes; such factors certainly shaped the book's play with genre and theme and so, too, the character of its modern reception.

PURPOSES AND PLOT

After offering the claim (standard to antebellum autobiography) that "abler pens" might improve upon "these crude narrations," Wilson directly sets out the book's purpose in her preface. "Deserted by kindred, disabled by failing health," she has been forced "to some experiment"—writing the book—to aid "in maintaining myself and child" (p. i). That child, George Mason Wilson, was seven when *Our Nig* was published. Throughout his youth, he and his mother were on and off the "Poor List" in Wilson's home of Milford, New Hampshire. Eventually, Wilson was forced to leave her child, first in the care of the Hillsborough County Poor Farm and later with a private family (probably Joshua and Irene Fisher Hutchinson), while she attempted to gain funds to care for him.

Wilson's call for aid—a call echoed by the three letters vouching for her character and circumstances that form the book's appendix—was based on sentiment but also on a sense of exchange: Wilson was trading her story for funds. The story Wilson tells, though, complicates both sentimental assumptions and the idea of exchange; the radicality of her critique, embodied in the novel's plot—as well as its complex positioning vis-à-vis genre and theme (described below)—may have put off the very readers she hoped would aid her.

Set in antebellum New England, the book centers on the title character Frado, "Our Nig," who is the daughter of a poverty-stricken white woman, Mag Smith, whose sexual and moral "fall" has left her an outcast, and a "kind-hearted African," Jim, who is willing to support her (pp. 7, 9). However, when Jim dies of consumption after the couple has two children, Mag abandons the six-year-old Frado, leaving her with the Bellmonts, a white family ruled by the "she-devil" Mrs. Bellmont. While husband John Bellmont and some of the Bellmont children are sympathetic to Frado's plight, Mrs. Bellmont and daughter Mary quickly turn the "our" in the book's title phrase into a term of complete ownership.

As the Bellmonts' "nig," Frado is subjected to increasing toil punctuated with beatings from Mrs. Bellmont; in essence, though she is technically, as the book's subtitle notes, a free black, she is enslaved. While the more kindly members of the Bellmont family (including the ineffectual Mr. Bellmont and his sister, Aunt Abby) make limited efforts to ease Frado's burden, their sympathy only causes Mrs. Bellmont's abuse to worsen. Frado struggles to come to terms with a world governed not by morality and law but by Mrs. Bellmont's whims: when the Bellmonts' son James tells her "you won't be whipped" if you "try to be a good girl," Frado can only cry, "If I do, I get whipped" (pp. 50–51). Frado is also deeply troubled that God made her black and Mrs. Bellmont white. Why, she wants to know, would a moral God not "make us *both* white?" And although James is unable to answer these "knotty queries," when he falls ill later in the book, it is his piety and kindness that draw Frado closer to Christianity (p. 51). But such ties remain limited; when Mrs. Bellmont tells Frado that "if she did not stop trying to be religious, she would whip her to death," Mr. Bellmont can only tell Frado, sadly, that she should attempt to avoid beatings because "you cannot endure beating as you once could" (p. 104).

In the book's turning point, Frado stands up for herself for the first time. As Mrs. Bellmont readies to beat her with a stick, Frado shouts, "Stop. . . . ! strike me, and I'll never work a mite more for you" and stands "like one who feels the stirring of free and independent thoughts" (p. 105). Mrs. Bellmont backs down.

The book's brief final chapters address Frado's life after leaving the Bellmonts—ongoing poverty, damaged health, and a failed marriage: "Watched by kidnappers, maltreated by professed abolitionists, who didn't want slaves at the South, nor niggers in their own houses, North. Faugh! To lodge one; to eat with one; to admit one through the front door; to sit next one; awful!" (p. 129). And while the book's end offers some poetic justice—Mrs. Bellmont is reported to have "an agony in death unspeakable"—the narrative leaves Frado "still an invalid" asking "for your sympathy, gentle reader" (p. 130).

PUBLICATION AND RECEPTION

The first edition of *Our Nig* was printed by George C. Rand and Avery, a Boston firm, and copyrighted by Wilson on 18 August 1859. The book was inexpensively produced, probably in a small run, and the title page assertion that the book was "printed" rather than "published" by Rand suggests that the book may have been self-published or, at least, subsidized.

Rand had strong ties to abolitionism: among other jobs, he printed the two-volume first edition of Harriet Beecher Stowe's (1811–1896) *Uncle Tom's Cabin* for John P. Jewett in 1852 and was friendly with the family of the abolitionist William Lloyd Garrison (1805–1879). Still, he seems to have made no effort to introduce the book to Boston's large and diverse abolitionist community. No contemporary reviews survive. Ownership patterns of extant copies as well as evidence that Wilson may have been, for a time, a sort of traveling saleswoman for hair products suggest that Wilson was primarily, if not solely, responsible for the book's distribution. Most copies trace to areas in New Hampshire and Massachusetts with which Wilson was familiar. Only one extant copy traces to a prominent abolitionist—William Lloyd Garrison Jr.— but researchers have not yet been able to determine if the book was consciously neglected by abolitionists or was simply not noticed. Similarly, while Wilson was, for a time, geographically positioned to place the book within Boston's noted black community—and even seems to call for such in her prefatory appeal "to my colored brethren universally for patronage"— researchers have found no evidence to explain its complete absence from that community's record.

The archival work of Foreman and Pitts proves that Wilson died on 28 June 1900 and is buried in the Mount Wollaston Cemetery in Quincy, Massachusetts. Despite having lived long after her book's publication, she does not seem to have attempted to further its reputation. Although the book may have begun as a venture of hope, it must have soon turned into a painful reminder of the tragedies racial, class, and gender discrimination could cause: her young son, George Mason Wilson, died on 15 February 1860. Foreman and Pitts have proven in their landmark research that Wilson turned to spiritualism in the latter half of the nineteenth century. This suggests that she needed to set aside and rewrite some of the most painful autobiographical pieces of the book. She asserted that through spiritualism "her father came and gave all the facts of his life and acquaintance with her mother, manifesting the tenderest interest in her" (Foreman and Pitts, p. xli). Through spiritualism, she regained the "kind-hearted African," whom she lost so early in life—and whose loss set in motion the tragic events of her childhood captured in her depiction of Frado.

If Wilson was not to rescue her book from obscurity, few nineteenth-century Americans would. Even Frederick Douglass (1818–1895) busily revised his once-small *Narrative* into much larger texts that focused more and more on what happened after slavery, and Frank J. Webb (1828–1894), author of one of the earliest African American novels, *The Garies and Their Friends* (1857), consistently asserted that his post–Civil War work was much better and much more important. White abolitionists from William Lloyd Garrison to Parker Pillsbury were intent on remembering themselves as the champions of a race, and their late-nineteenth-century histories of the movement gloss over the immense factionalism in the movement and say next to nothing of the extreme racial and gender prejudice that often fractured it. Literary criticism in its modern configuration simply did not exist; historians of American literature were much more interested in white male narratives that spoke to "American" values. Wilson's text was, in essence, lost.

Gates purchased a copy of the book from a rare book dealer in 1981 and was able to authenticate the book's authorship before reintroducing the book to the public and beginning the second phase of the book's reception. Gates's reintroduction of the book differed in almost every way from the book's original publication. Released by a major publisher, called "a black literary landmark" by the *New York Times,* emblazoned with laudatory quotations from major contemporary African American authors including Alice Walker and Ralph Ellison, and immediately celebrated by literary critics, the 1983 edition set off a flurry of scholarship as well as inclusion of excerpts from the book in several major anthologies. A third edition—with updated apparatus that linked the text to Gates's more recent discovery of an early black novel in manuscript, Hannah Crafts's *The Bondwoman's Narrative*—was issued in 2002. A fourth edition, with considerable new biographical information by Foreman and Pitts, came out in early 2005.

FICTION, AUTOBIOGRAPHY, AND HARRIET WILSON

While literary historians have spent great energy filling in the details of Harriet Wilson's biography, the status of *Our Nig* as a novel has also been actively discussed. It could be argued that the immense emphasis placed on establishing the book as fiction came in part from earlier recovery efforts in African American literary study. Both William Wells Brown's novel *Clotel; or, The President's Daughter* (1853) and Frank J. Webb's novel *The Garies and Their Friends* were republished in the late 1960s, and both were pointed to as important—albeit sometimes uneasy—ancestors of the then-flowering Black Arts movement. The recovery of Harriet Wilson—in both her story's form and in her story's reception (indeed, in her very biography)—clearly spoke to the struggle for artistic forebears. Furthermore, the very term "novel" suggested a level of critical literacy and artistry that went beyond many of the immense number of slave narratives that remain understudied. Beyond such contextual factors, there are many features of Wilson's text that are, indeed, fully in line with novelistic technique, including its third-person narrator, its characterization, its epigraphs, and its thematic concerns.

It has become more and more clear that the events of Frado's life run painfully parallel with those of Harriet Wilson's. Foreman and Pitts have, in Wilson's likely parents (African American Joshua Green and white Margaret Smith), found real-life figures that echo Jim and Mag Smith in almost every way. Barbara White has painstakingly detailed how fully and exactly the Bellmont family corresponds to the family of Nehemiah Hayward Jr. (1778–1849) and Rebecca Hutchinson Hayward (1780–1850). Gates and White have proven how the book's calls for aid were based on the facts of Harriet Wilson's life, and Foreman and Pitts have established exceedingly likely candidates for the authors of the appendix's letters in Calvin Dascomb Sr. (who signed himself "C. D. S."), Jane Chapman Demond ("Allida"), and Laura Wright Hutchinson ("Margaretta Thorn"). In addition to providing a fuller sense of the correspondence between Wilson's text and her life, the work of these scholars raises difficult questions for students of the antebellum North and of organized abolitionism. Rebecca Hutchinson Hayward, for example, as White has skillfully documented, was close kin to the Hutchinson Family Singers, perhaps the most famous abolitionist entertainers of their day. Milford, New Hampshire, too, as shown by Foreman, Pitts, and R. J. Ellis, was, although small, a kind of abolitionist hub for the surrounding area. That Harriet Wilson was raised around—and so mistreated within—such a strongly abolitionist community reminds readers of the pervasive cultural factors that led to her book's neglect.

In the end, the point may not be whether Harriet Wilson's book is a novel or an autobiography. Rather, it may be that, in the face of the difficulties in Wilson's life, *Our Nig* so effectively and richly dances between the two—and dances among a range of other genres—in its definition and treatment of themes key to Wilson's socioeconomic, racial, and gendered position in the antebellum North.

GENRE(S), THEMES, AND CONTEXTS

Our Nig, then, is at once participant in several genres and fully a member of none. If it is a novel, it is a heavily autobiographical one; if an autobiography, one structured and styled as a novel. It certainly tells a story of a kind of slavery from the point of view of the enslaved—and so is a "slave's narrative"—but the location and character of that slavery are far different from what readers would expect. It has many of the trappings of an antebellum sentimental novel but often exposes both sentimentality's failings and potential for hypocrisy. In "talking back" to all of these genres and their inherent themes, Wilson attempts to make space for voices like her own, for persons like herself; whether consciously or not, Wilson's book demonstrates the ways antebellum American literature actively and passively excluded the stories of free blacks in the North.

Our Nig's similarities to the slave narrative are perhaps most obvious; Wilson's extended subtitle—"Sketches from the Life of a Free Black, in a Two-Story White House, North, Showing that Slavery's Shadows Fall Even There"—calls readers' attention to such similarities immediately. As in most slave narratives, Wilson's virtual enslavement is clearly race-based, is repeatedly punctuated with brutality, and damages her spirit as much as her body. Like Frederick Douglass in his battle with the "slave-breaker" Covey, she finally reaches a moment where she knows she must resist. That resistance is both the turning point of the narrative and the signal of her eventual escape from the evil Mrs. Bellmont. Beyond these similarities in content

and structure, both the text's pairing with authenticating documents and its bifurcation of its audience along racial lines also echo slave narratives of the period.

But Wilson's story takes place in the North—the idealized end of many slave narratives—and her title page reminds readers of this, too. Rather than an evil southern planter, her chief tormentor is a northern churchgoing mother. When Wilson finally marries, it is to a free black who "had never seen the South" but created fictional "illiterate harangues" that served as "humbugs for hungry abolitionists" (p. 128). In a text full of wordplay (as the subtitle asserts, there are two very different "stories" of slavery told in the North; the white house is, indeed, an embodiment of whiteness as well as reminding readers of the White House, and so forth), Wilson may even play with pieces of the most famous slave narratives. Wilson, for example, would have known of Frederick Douglass and his *Narrative*—and perhaps of his master's assertion that "if you give a nigger an inch, he will take an ell" (p. 33); the "ell" that Wilson gains, her room in the farmhouse's ell above the kitchen (referred to in the text as the "L chamber"), symbolizes how boxed in and distanced from the domestic hearth free blacks in the North were. And, of course, in painful irony, in buying a book called *Our Nig,* readers were in one way purchasing a life—the life of "Our Nig."

The novel's critique of domestic ideology is even more stinging, in part because Wilson's torment takes place in a home that is ruled by a woman and a mother. As in many examples of sentimental fiction, the main character is a young girl in need, and the plot follows her trials and eventual triumph in a kind of bildungsroman. Often, indeed, the triumph is a direct result of the young heroine learning to deal with her trials sentimentally—that is, with benevolent fellow feeling centered on Christian principles. That sense of benevolent empathy and sympathy, embodied in both tears and deeds, calls on characters and readers to consider larger social ends (the version of abolitionism in books like *Uncle Tom's Cabin* [1851–1852] or the antipoverty stance suggested by Maria Susanna Cummins's *The Lamplighter* [1854]).

Our Nig certainly has all of these features except the unified triumph that often ends such novels. But this lack of a clear triumph figures twofold in examining the book. First, any triumph in *Our Nig* is dependent upon readers: only if those around Wilson buy her book and offer support for her eminently sentimental goals—only if prospective book buyers put domestic ideology into action—will she be reunited with her child and triumph. Second, though, the lack of a clear victory at the end of the book points to the ways in

The excerpts below, drawn from chapters 3 and 10, illustrate the level of brutality suffered by Frado, the protagonist of Our Nig, *and the moment when she takes a stand against that brutality.*

Frado was called early in the morning by her new mistress. Her first work was to feed the hens. She was shown how it was *always* to be done, and in no other way; any departure from this rule to be punished by a whipping. She was then accompanied by Jack to drive the cows to pasture, so she might learn the way. Upon her return she was allowed to eat her breakfast, consisting of a bowl of skimmed milk, with brown bread crusts, which she was told to eat, standing, by the kitchen table, and must not be over ten minutes about it. Meanwhile the family were taking their morning meal in the dining-room. This over, she was placed on a cricket to wash the common dishes; she was to be in waiting always to bring wood and chips, to run hither and thither from room to room.

A large amount of dish-washing for small hands followed dinner. Then the same after tea and going after the cows finished her first day's work. It was a new discipline to the child. She found some attractions about the place, and she retired to rest at night more willing to remain. The same routine followed day after day, with slight variation; adding a little more work, and spicing the toil with "words that burn," and frequent blows on her head. These were great annoyances to Frado, and had she known where her mother was, she would have gone at once to her. She was often greatly wearied, and silently wept over her sad fate. At first she wept aloud, which Mrs. Bellmont noticed by applying a rawhide, always at hand in the kitchen. It was a symptom of discontent and complaining which must be "nipped in the bud," she said.

Mr. Bellmont found himself unable to do what James or Jack could accomplish for her. He talked with her seriously, told her he had seen her many times punished undeservedly; he did not wish to have her saucy or disrespectful, but when she was *sure* she did not deserve a whipping, to avoid it if she could. "You are looking sick," he added, "you cannot endure beating as you once could."

It was not long before an opportunity offered of profiting by his advice. She was sent for wood, and not returning as soon as Mrs. B. calculated, she followed her, and, snatching from the pile a stick, raised it over her.

"Stop!" shouted Frado, "strike me, and I'll never work a mite more for you;" and throwing down what she had gathered, stood like one who feels the stirring of free and independent thoughts.

By this unexpected demonstration, her mistress, in amazement, dropped her weapon, desisting from her purpose of chastisement. Frado walked towards the house, her mistress following with the wood she herself was sent after. She did not know, before, that she had a power to ward off assaults. Her triumph in seeing her enter the door with *her* burden, repaid her for much of her former suffering.

It was characteristic of Mrs. B. never to rise in her majesty, unless she was sure she should be victorious.

This affair never met with an "after clap," like many others.

Wilson, *Our Nig*, pp. 29–30, 104–105.

which those who surround Frado are antisentimental specifically because of her racial difference. Benevolent fellow feeling, it seems, only extends to certain fellows; the idea that Christian principles allow transcendent sympathy is literally beaten out of Frado by the church-going Mrs. Bellmont. The marriage and child that often end sentimental fiction are exploded by the lies of her husband—lies that emphasize that much of the seeming sentiment among abolitionist audiences may actually be nothing more than a prurient interest in titillating stories. Beyond general themes, Wilson may also play consciously with readers' expectations of individual words here: Mrs. Bellmont, often referred to as "Mrs. B."—may, for example, call to mind another famous Mrs. B. who opens her home to a young female slave and who rules that home through domestic ideology, *Uncle Tom's Cabin*'s Mrs. Bird, who takes in the fugitive Eliza and convinces her reluctant senator husband to allow it. Wilson's Mrs. B., of course, takes the desperate youth in, but to enslave her rather than to aid her. The sentimental aspects of *Our Nig* seem to consciously call attention to the fact that the book is not—and is blocked from being—fully sentimental because of the pervasive racism in the North.

Because Frado is not technically a slave, Foreman and Pitts also place *Our Nig* in dialogue with captivity narratives; Ellis has called attention to *Our Nig*'s conversation with narratives of New England rural life; and Elizabeth J. West considers how *Our Nig* rewrites key features of nineteenth-century conversion narratives. These elaborations and connections further suggest the richness of this text. More than a century after its original publication—and after its probable failure at its central task of supporting Harriet Wilson's young son—*Our Nig* reminds readers of the need for sentiment, the distance over which slavery's shadows still fall, and the need to conceive of genres and approaches that feature voices still often unheard.

See also Abolitionist Writing; Autobiography; Blacks; Domestic Fiction; Literary Marketplace; Religion; Slave Narratives; Slavery; Spiritualism

BIBLIOGRAPHY

Primary Works

Wilson, Harriet E. *Our Nig; or, Sketches from the Life of a Free Black*. Boston: Printed by Geo. C. Rand and Avery, 1859. In-text quotations are from this edition.

Wilson, Harriet E. *Our Nig: or, Sketches from the Life of a Free Black*. Edited by P. Gabrielle Foreman and Reginald H. Pitts. New York: Penguin, 2005.

Wilson, Harriet E. *Our Nig; or, Sketches from the Life of a Free Black*. Edited by Henry Louis Gates Jr. New York: Vintage, 1983, 2002. Includes a facsimile of the original text.

Secondary Works

Ellis, R. J. *Harriet Wilson's "Our Nig": A Cultural Biography of a "Two-Story" African American Novel*. Amsterdam: Rodolpi, 2003.

Ernest, John. "Economies of Identity: Harriet Wilson's *Our Nig*." *PMLA* 109, no. 3 (1994): 424–438.

Foreman, P. Gabrielle. "The Spoken and the Silenced in *Incidents in the Life of a Slave Girl* and *Our Nig*." *Callaloo* 13, no. 2 (1990): 313–324.

Foreman, P. Gabrielle, and Reginald H. Pitts. "Introduction," "Chronologies," and "Notes." In *Our Nig; or, Sketches from the Life of a Free Black*, by Harriet Wilson. New York: Penguin, 2005.

Gardner, Eric. "'This Attempt of their Sister': *Our Nig* from Printer to Readers." *New England Quarterly* 66, no. 2 (1993): 226–246.

Gates, Henry Louis, Jr. "Introduction," "Chronology," "Notes," and "Afterword." In *Our Nig*, by Harriet Wilson. New York: Vintage, 1983.

Gates, Henry Louis, Jr. "Parallel Discursive Universes: Fictions of the Self in Harriet E. Wilson's *Our Nig*." In his *Figures in Black: Words, Signs, and the "Racial" Self*, pp. 125–149. New York: Oxford University Press, 1987.

Gates, Henry Louis, Jr. "Preface," "Introduction," "Chronology," "Notes," and "Afterword." In *Our Nig*, by Harriet Wilson. New York: Vintage, 2002.

Stern, Julia. "Excavating Genre in *Our Nig*." *American Literature* 67, no. 3 (1995): 439–466.

West, Elizabeth J. "Reworking the Conversion Narrative: Race and Christianity in *Our Nig*." *MELUS* 24, no. 2 (1999): 3–27.

White, Barbara. "'Our Nig' and the She-Devil: New Information about Harriet Wilson and the 'Bellmont' Family." *American Literature* 65, no. 1 (1993): 19–52. This article is also included in the 2002 edition of *Our Nig*.

Eric Gardner

"OUT OF THE CRADLE ENDLESSLY ROCKING"

For many readers, "Out of the Cradle Endlessly Rocking" is Walt Whitman's most moving poem. "Song of Myself" has the copious breadth of epic in a democratic world, "When Lilacs Last in the Dooryard Bloom'd" registers the somber meaning of Abraham Lincoln's death, and the *Drum Taps* poems catch the reality of war in impressionistic snapshots. But in "Out of the Cradle," Whitman (1819–1892) dramatizes the bare fact of mortality and achieves the profound expressiveness of high art. From its first utterance, when in late 1859 Whitman read the poem to his bohemian friends at Pfaff's saloon in the Greenwich Village neighborhood of New York City, to the famed evening at Edith Wharton's home, "The Mount," when Henry James (1811–1882) read "Out of the Cradle" (and other Whitman poems) in a voice that "filled the hushed room like an organ adagio," to the scene in the film *Doc Hollywood* (1991) in which the aging physician regales dinner guests with an inebriated rendition of the poem, "Out of the Cradle" has stood as Whitman's signal feat of lyricism. It is a tour de force of poetic talent and worldly vision.

The poem entered *Leaves of Grass* in the third edition (1860) under the title "A Word out of the Sea." Along with other compositions from the same period,

"Out of the Cradle" marked a new disposition for Whitman. These works impart despair and doubt instead of boisterous affirmation of nature and humanity. Critics speculate on whether the change was due to a failed love affair, to turmoil over Whitman's homoerotic feelings, to the course of the nation toward civil war, or to the insufficient adulation prompted by the first editions of *Leaves of Grass*. But whatever the reason, the shift is marked. In "I Sit and Look Out," Whitman remarks "upon all the sorrows of the world, and upon all oppression and shame," but has no reply: "all the meanness and agony without end I sitting look out upon, / See, hear, and am silent" (pp. 328–329). In "As I Ebb'd with the Ocean of Life," the desolation turns upon the poet himself:

> As I wend to the shores I know not,
> As I list to the dirge, the voices of men and
>   women wreck'd . . .
> I too but signify at the utmost a little wash'd up
>   drift,
> A few sands and dead leaves to gather.
>
> *(Pp. 319–320)*

The bardic expansiveness of 1855 has contracted, and defeatist wisdom takes its place.

"Out of the Cradle" shares in the pessimism but without the self-recrimination and bitterness. Despite its obsession with death and loss, at the time of its publication it inspired as much acclaim as it did censure. When Henry Clapp (1814–1875) heard Whitman recite it in Pfaff's saloon, he decided to publish it (under the title "A Child's Reminiscence") in the 1859 Christmas number of the literary periodical he edited, the *Saturday Press*. When the poem was attacked in the *Cincinnati Commercial* as "lines of stupid and meaningless twaddle" by "that unclean cub of the wilderness, Walt Whitman," Clapp defended the poem in a subsequent number of the *Press* and proceeded to print several of the new poems that would end up in the 1860 edition of *Leaves of Grass*. Indeed, Clapp's efforts probably inspired Thayer & Eldridge, Boston publishers, to propose the new edition in a letter dated 10 February 1860.

The opening lines of the poem quickly show why "Out of the Cradle" has proven so affecting. The first verse paragraph runs for twenty-two lines, a single sentence with twenty prepositional phrases, the grammatical subject ("I") buried in the twentieth line, and the epic verb "sing" placed as the very last word. (All citations here are from the final version of the poem.) To sustain the sentence through so many meandering phrases—"Down from the shower'd halo, / Up from the mystic play of shadows twining and twisting as they were alive" (p. 343), and so forth—Whitman fills it with musical cadences and sounds as well as effusive parallelisms. For instance, the opening line, "Out of the cradle endlessly rocking," balances two dactyls and two trochees, and after the "I" come two portentous qualifiers, "chanter of pains and joys, uniter of here and hereafter" (p. 344). Whitman also implants tantalizing hints in the opening that will be explained only at the end: "From the memories of the bird that chanted to me," "From the word stronger and more delicious than any" (pp. 343–344).

The vatic power of the opening mirrors the depth of theme. The poet recalls a scene from his youth, when all summer long he observed two birds with their nest and eggs until one disappeared, igniting in the child an apprehension of death and awakening his poetic self. Once the preamble sets the scene, the poem shifts into a fanciful narrative set among the briars on the seashore of Long Island. "Two feather'd guests from Alabama" have flown north for the summer to mate, while Whitman, "a curious boy," watches them unobtrusively and translates their mockingbird calls into operatic speech (p. 344). (The bird's words appear in italics in the poem.)

> Shine! Shine! Shine!
> Pour down your warmth, great sun!
> While we bask, we two together.
> Two together!
>
> *(Pp. 344–345)*

But then, Whitman continues, the "she-bird" disappears. The "he-bird" flies back and forth, calling to the air, but the nest remains empty. The young boy listens carefully to "the lone singer wonderful causing tears" (p. 345), blending with the shadows to heed his grief. He registers the bird's cries as a set of apostrophes to nature pleading for the return of his beloved. To the moon he asks, "*What is that dusky spot in your brown yellow? / O it is the shape, the shape of my mate!*" To the night: "*O night! do I not see my love fluttering out among the breakers?*" (p. 346). And to the land:

> *Land! Land! O land!*
> *Whichever way I turn, O I think you could give me*
>   *my mate back again if you only would,*
> *For I am almost sure I see her dimly whichever way*
>   *I look.*
>
> *(P. 347)*

The expression is overwrought, like the Italian opera that Whitman savored in the 1840s (and which Clapp in his defense of Whitman claimed was "the method in the construction of his songs"). But it bears a psychological truth about the habits of grief. The loss of his love leads the bird to confront a controlling presence, a being to which he might address his pain and plight. His suffering craves articulation and it needs a communicant.

To what other shall he deliver his sorrow than the natural world that enclosed their days together and now seems everywhere a reminder of the she-bird's absence? Sing to it he must, even as he acknowledges his songs as "*reckless despairing carols*" (p. 347). If nature does not respond, he continues, perhaps he should temper his voice:

> But soft! sink low!
> Soft! let me just murmur,
> And do you wait a moment you husky-nois'd sea,
> For somewhere I believe I heard my mate responding to me,
> So faint, I must be still, be still to listen.
>
> *(Pp. 347–348)*

Then again, maybe his lost mate is still living, but is just as distraught and must be guided back home: "*Do not be decoy'd elsewhere, / That is the whistle of the wind, it is not my voice*" (p. 348). With his love removed, nature becomes the reflection of his moods, sometimes appearing a benign power, sometimes an antagonist. These are the contortions of grief, but they cannot dispel the bare fact of loss and the ineffectuality of song: "*And I singing uselessly, uselessly all the night*" (p. 348).

The song climaxes in a monotonous outcry—"*Loved! loved! loved! loved! loved!*" (p. 348)—beyond which there is nothing more to say. But for the eavesdropping boy, the episode is a transformative experience. The bird's notes echo, the stars continue to shine and the winds to blow, but the boy is forever changed. Explaining the import of that change constitutes the remaining fifty-four lines of the poem, Whitman's most intense rumination upon the origin of his poetic identity.

The pathos of the he-bird, the breakup of this fantasized family, and the beauty and sublimity of the summer shore together affect Whitman in understandably emotional ways. The boy feels "ecstatic" as he sounds the bird's lament, much as an ancient bard does as the muse overtakes him. But something deeper happens as well, touching his ego and directing his fate.

> Demon or bird! (said the boy's soul,)
> Is it indeed toward your mate you sing? or is it really to me?
> For I, that was a child, my tongue's use sleeping, now I have heard you,
> Now in a moment I know what I am for, I awake,
> And already a thousand singers, a thousand songs, clearer, louder and more sorrowful than yours,
> A thousand warbling echoes have started to life within me, never to die.
>
> *(P. 348)*

With adult-like decisiveness—"I know what I am for"—he leaves behind the inquisitive childhood of that fateful summer and becomes a mortal spirit dedicated to song. Realizing his "destiny," as he puts it in the next verse paragraph, Whitman now judges the bird a "messenger" bringing him a cosmic truth that would "Never again leave me to be the peaceful child I was" (p. 350). He has grown into an "outsetting bard" (p. 350) immersed in the music he heard and inspired to create it anew. This is the birth of the poetic genius, dramatized as Whitman's entry into a procession of singers—the bird, the boy, the mature poet—joined in a chorus of "cries of unsatisfied love" (p. 350).

That formulation is crucial: "unsatisfied love." Simple love may lead to joyful song, but it will not carry others into the realm of primal inspiration. This is why Whitman needs a further "clew" to apprehend why the poetic impulse conquered his youthful self and why he requests it from a larger representative of nature than the he-bird.

> A word then, (for I will conquer it,)
> The word final, superior to all,
> Subtle, sent up—what is it?—I listen;
> Are you whispering it, and have been all the time, you sea-waves?
>
> *(P. 350)*

Now initiated into the course of love and grief, Whitman may speak directly to nature, and the sea will readily respond.

> Whereto answering, the sea,
> Delaying not, hurrying not,
> Whisper'd me through the night, and very plainly before daybreak,
> Lisp'd to me the low and delicious word death.
>
> *(P. 350)*

Love and death are the ingredients of inspired song. There on the moonlit beach that summer, Whitman witnessed the fundamental rhythms of life, and each thing he saw and heard became a stirring augury whose fundamental meaning was death. The birds' routine actions each day excited his curiosity, but only with the death of one of them did his passion intensify and spread into a soul-shaking intimation of an abiding reality. In the final image, the boy sits in the shallows as the water rises to his feet and creeps up to his ears, "Hissing melodious" a monotone phrase parallel to the earlier "Loved!": "Death, death, death, death, death" (pp. 350–351).

Whitman calls "death" the "word of the sweetest song and all songs" (p. 351), and he claims never to have forgotten the sea's lesson. The Thanatos theme marks "Out of the Cradle Endlessly Rocking" as a universalized elegy, a fanciful drama in which Whitman recognizes the fact of mortality. Additionally, the proposition that death is the origin of song (that is, of poetry) marks "Out of the Cradle Endlessly Rocking" as a metaphysical lyric broaching the wellsprings of art. The poignant combination of heightened lyricism and boyhood drama have provoked readers to interpret the poem in light of Whitman's biography, his psyche, his poetics, and his spiritual beliefs. That many have produced important insights into the poet's corpus and outlook testifies to the centrality and fullness of "Out of the Cradle." The note accompanying "Out of the Cradle" in the *Saturday Press* has proven true: "The piece will bear reading many times—perhaps, indeed, only comes forth, as from recesses, by many repetitions."

See also "Crossing Brooklyn Ferry"; Death; *Leaves of Grass;* Lyric Poetry; "When Lilacs Last in the Dooryard Bloom'd"

BIBLIOGRAPHY

Primary Work

Whitman, Walt. "Out of the Cradle Endlessly Rocking." In *Leaves of Grass: A Textual Variorum of the Printed Poems,* 3 vols., edited by Sculley Bradley, Harold W. Blodgett, Arthur Golden, and William White. New York: New York University Press, 1980.

Secondary Works

Lewis, R. W. B., ed. *The Presence of Walt Whitman.* New York: Columbia University Press, 1962.

Miller, Edwin Haviland. *Walt Whitman's Poetry: A Psychological Journey.* New York: New York University Press, 1968.

Whicher, Stephen. "Whitman's Awakening to Death." *Studies in Romanticism* 1 (1960): 173–186.

Zweig, Paul. *Walt Whitman: The Making of the Poet.* New York: Basic Books, 1984.

Mark Bauerlein

PERIODICALS

Periodicals offered an important venue for authors in the nineteenth century. The lack of any international copyright agreement guaranteed a mass influx of reprinted novels from abroad, so many American authors eventually came to rely on payments from magazines—meager as they were in this period—to augment their limited book-publishing income. While many works in periodicals were published anonymously, by the 1860s more and more editors were including, even trumpeting, the names of their contributors, and so magazines also emerged as a valuable marketing tool for authors and publishers. Most magazines were originally published on the East Coast and served primarily regional markets, but, as time passed, prominent periodicals appeared in the South and in the West, and improvements in transportation and technology laid the groundwork for truly national magazines to emerge.

THE TURBULENT TWENTIES

Magazine readers in the 1820s had a multitude of options to choose from, provided they never grew too attached to any particular publication. Magazines during these early years were most often sold by subscription with rates ranging from one to five dollars a year. Readers seldom had the opportunity to renew their subscriptions more than once. Nearly one hundred titles premiered during this decade, but far fewer emerged from it. So many periodicals triumphantly announced their appearances in breathless prospectuses, only to close shop shortly afterward, that some announcements took the form of apologies, attempting to account for why the public might possibly be interested in yet another journal. In their rush to reach their readers, the editors of the *Atlantic Magazine* of New York (1824–1825)—not to be confused with the later and infinitely more successful *Atlantic Monthly* of Boston—were forced to apologize for the quality of their contents, as well; inside of the front cover, they included this note: "The contents of the first number of this Magazine have been hastily collected, and rapidly printed, as the publishers were determined to comply with the promise of their prospectus . . . . It cannot, therefore, be considered a fair specimen of the quality or quantity of the matter, to which its pages are devoted." While unusual for its candor, this assessment of quality could describe many a new enterprise during these years.

Such was the gold rush mentality that seemed to grip publishers in the major publishing centers of New York, Philadelphia, and, trailing, Boston, early in the first quarter of the nineteenth century. It is true that some titles begun prior to the 1820s had managed to last—most notably the *North American Review,* which began publication in Boston in 1815 and survived into the twentieth century, and the *Port Folio,* which was produced in Philadelphia and ran from 1801 to 1827. Others would manage respectable runs of seven or eight years, but these rare successes seemed primarily to spur others to the attempt, not to provide models for how a magazine could make a go of it.

In an effort to attract readers and to ensure survival, editors often offered an eclectic variety of original stories, poems, and reviews, with a more than liberal helping of reprinted articles from popular British magazines. As the editors of the short-lived *Cincinnati Literary Gazette* (1824–1825) humbly put it,

> As it is our aim in this paper to be *useful* rather than original . . . we shall not hesitate to select from worthy sources, such sentiments as may accord with our own, particularly when the thoughts happen to be expressed in better language than our compositions may at all times exhibit. (P. 13)

Even those magazines most devoted to the cause of forwarding the development of an American literature were not exempt from the necessity of providing foreign material. One such magazine, among the few to survive its first year and recognized by later critics as one of the rare gems to emerge from this tumultuous period, was the all-inclusively titled *The New-York Mirror, and Ladies' Literary Gazette; Being a Repository of Miscellaneous Literary Productions, in Prose and Verse* (1823–1842). Its first editors, Samuel Woodworth (1785–1842) and George Pope Morris (1802–1864), note in the premier issue,

> The character of this work is intended to be, *literally and emphatically,* AMERICAN. Not that interesting articles of foreign origin will be wholly excluded; for that would be neither just nor politic. But all the *images* reflected from our *Mirror* . . . shall be in accordance with our national habits, patriotism, and modes of thinking. (P. 1)

Such an emphasis on nationalism was not uncommon in these magazines, with editors offering varying explanations both for their inclusion of so much foreign material and for the painfully short life spans of so many periodicals seeking to foster American literature.

Despite their "polite" gesture to the public's taste for republished works, Woodworth and Morris truly strove to offer a diverse selection of material in the *New-York Mirror,* as this early list of departments indicates: "Original Moral Tales," "Reviews," "Original Essays," "Female Character," "American Biography," "Problems—in the arts and sciences," "Literary Intelligence," "The Drama," "The Toilet— or a description of the newest fashions, foreign or domestic," "The Forum—or a brief sketch of the debates of that institution," "Desultory Selections— with original remarks," "Anecdotes," "Passing Events of the Week," and "Poetry—original and selected" (p. 1). Many other magazines followed this model, attempting to appeal to as broad an audience as possible. In keeping with this idea, several editors announced that they would studiously avoid matters of religious or political argument, leaving that field open to the many newspapers that were also circulating during this period.

OBSTACLES TO SUCCESS

In addition to competition from numerous newspapers and other periodicals, magazines were vulnerable to any number of disruptions. *The Minerva,* a New York publication that began in 1822 and managed to last until 1825, was forced to delay the release of its second number due to the illness of the printer. In 1827 the editor of *The Ariel* (1827–1832) was forced to plead with potential subscribers to stop sending requests for subscriptions without first paying the postage on their letters, so he could make the magazine "even moderately profitable" ("To the Public," p. 32). The vagaries of the postal system, which lacked uniform standards from town to town, were a considerable source of trouble. In 1844 Nathaniel Parker Willis (1806–1867) joined forces with Morris to produce the *New Mirror* (1843–1844), only to be stymied by the irregular system of mailing rates. When Willis learned that the rates varied from two to fifteen cents an issue, in some places nearly doubling the cost of a subscription, he howled at the injustice in his magazine before, a few months later, he announced the creation of the *Evening Mirror,* a daily newspaper that could ship at the more reasonable newspaper postage. Rates for newspapers were dramatically cheaper, and magazine subscribers paid the higher price for shipping until 1852, when the law was changed to both lower the rate for magazines and allow publishers to pay the cost and roll it into the standard subscription fee.

Even more insidious were episodes of deliberate tampering. Elihu Embree (1782–1820), the courageous editor and publisher of *The Emancipator* (1820), an early antislavery magazine produced in Jonesborough, Tennessee, vented his frustration with the postal service in the pages of his magazine: "POSTMASTERS: *The Emancipator* has been pillaged by some of those through whose hands it has to pass to subscribers, at a rate which reflects disgrace on human nature, when we compare it with the solemn obligation of the oaths they have taken, and the trust reposed in them" (p. 64). For Embree, who estimated in the third number that 2,600 copies would be sufficient to supply his entire subscription list, losses like these were no small matter. The editor even asked those who had decided not to continue subscribing to return their early numbers so that he could send them to new subscribers. Regardless of these obstacles, editors were often forced to expend space in their pages begging subscribers to send payment as soon as possible. Even larger publications publicly denounced the hundreds who had failed to send the money they owed. While publishers liked to brag that no expense was spared in producing their periodical, the fact was that, in light of the obstacles to success, thrift was an overriding concern.

NEW YORK GIANTS: *THE KNICKERBOCKER,* *PUTNAM'S,* AND *HARPER'S*

While New York had long been home to numerous—if short-lived—periodicals, scholars agree that the appearance of *The Knickerbocker* (1833–1862, and then surviving until 1865 as the *Knickerbocker Monthly*) marked a significant step forward in terms of quality and influence. Lewis Gaylord Clark (1808–1873), who served as editor from 1834 until 1860, secured a stable of contributors that was the envy of its rivals. Contributors included Washington Irving, Henry Wadsworth Longfellow, Nathaniel Hawthorne, James Fenimore Cooper, and Oliver Wendell Holmes. While its title clearly pointed to its regional roots, Clark did not hesitate to include the work of prominent New Englanders, as well as occasional pieces from other regions. His "Editor's Table" set a standard for both humor and comments on current events: for example, Clark quickly made known his opinions regarding the ongoing debate over international copyright, publishing a letter Cooper had written to his publishers in 1826 addressing the issue. So popular were his columns that Clark published them in a separate volume, *Knick-Knacks from an Editor's Table* in 1852. While not a tremendous financial success, *The Knickerbocker* stands out for the quality of the work it published.

Putnam's Monthly Magazine (1853–1857; 1868–1870) debuted in January 1853 with a great deal of optimism and national pride. In contrast with many of its contemporaries, particularly the periodical phenomenon known as *Harper's New Monthly Magazine* (which launched in 1850 and, after becoming *Harper's Monthly* in 1900, has continued into the twenty-first century), the magazine refused to reprint British articles. Like *The Knickerbocker,* the magazine boasted an initial list of contributors that included many of the most prominent authors of New York and New England. During its relatively short life span, it would publish some of Herman Melville's most important short fiction, including "Bartleby, the Scrivener" (1853) and "Benito Cereno," (1855), aiding the author's transition into a magazine writer, and works by James Russell Lowell and Henry David Thoreau. The publisher during the first two years, George Palmer Putnam (1814–1872), assembled a trio of experienced writers and journalists to edit the magazine: Charles Frederick Briggs, George William Curtis, and Parke Godwin. Twenty thousand copies of the first issue were printed, and, at least in the short term, this optimism was rewarded: during the first year, the number grew to thirty-five thousand. While its literary quality was and still is evident, the magazine also spoke to contemporary issues such as slavery and women's rights. In 1855, his publishing house

Harper's New Monthly Magazine, October 1850. First page of an article concerning the English poet William Wordsworth. GRADUATE LIBRARY, UNIVERSITY OF MICHIGAN

struggling, Putnam sold the magazine to Dix, Edwards, and Co., a firm that ran into trouble of its own and, despite adding illustrations and portraits to the pages, was forced to cease publication. The magazine reemerged after the Civil War, but its circulation was small, and it never achieved its former prominence. In 1870 it merged with *Scribner's Monthly* (1870–1881).

Harper's New Monthly Magazine was the juggernaut of American magazines during this period. Eschewing the proclaimed nationalist motives of many of its rivals, it openly embraced reprinting British authors. In its first number, the publishers promised to provide their readers the serial tales of authors like Charles Dickens and Edward Bulwer-Lytton.

With 144 pages in the first issue and a rate of only three dollars a year, the magazine quickly became popular, printing fifty thousand copies in its first year. Designed to help forward the cause of the Harper brothers' publishing house, the only advertisements it carried during its first thirty-two years were for Harpers books. To follow this success, the publishers introduced *Harper's Weekly* (1857–1976), a "family newspaper" that featured many illustrations and articles on current affairs. It rose to particular prominence during the Civil War; its reporting and pictures helped it to sustain a subscription list of over 100,000 throughout the conflict. Both of the *Harper's* magazines pointed the way toward truly national publications.

PHILADELPHIA AND GEORGE REX GRAHAM

Philadelphia produced a relatively high volume of magazines, several of which enjoyed long runs. One of the most prominent of these was *Casket* (1826–1840), primarily a collection of reprinted articles from other magazines. Its importance to later literary scholars can be traced to the day that George Rex Graham (1813–1894) purchased it in 1839. Graham combined it with another Philadelphia magazine, *Burton's Gentleman's Magazine* (1837–1840) and, in 1840, produced *Graham's Magazine* (1840–1858). At the time of Graham's purchase of *Burton's Gentleman's Magazine*, Edgar Allan Poe (1809–1849) was the editor, and he became literary editor for *Graham's* in 1841. He would go on to be a frequent contributor to the magazine during his time there, and his famous story "The Masque of the Red Death" appeared in the May 1842 issue. During its first two years in existence, Graham claimed to have grown his subscription list from 5,500 to 40,000. Even allowing for exaggeration, these are impressive figures. In addition to Poe, the magazine's contributors included figures such as Lowell, Cooper, and Longfellow. In 1848 Graham was forced to sell the magazine, but it survived his absence, and he was able to take the helm again in 1850. His timing was unfortunate, for *Harper's* debuted in that year, and *Graham's* could not compete. He sold it again in 1853, and, in later years, the editor and publisher would claim that his criticism of the immensely popular *Uncle Tom's Cabin* (1852) hastened the demise of the magazine. After the sale the magazine continued its decline for a few more years finally disappearing.

BOSTON VOICES

Although it never matched the sheer volume of magazines appearing and disappearing in New York and Philadelphia, Boston was also an important publishing center during this period. The popular *Juvenile*

Miscellany and *Merry's Museum* were produced there, as was William Lloyd Garrison's (1805–1879) influential *The Liberator,* an abolitionist magazine that ran from 1831 until the end of the Civil War. In 1840 *The Dial: A Magazine for Literature, Philosophy, and Religion* (1840–1844) appeared as the literary emissary for the transcendentalist movement. Although Margaret Fuller (1810–1850) was its primary editor in the beginning, Amos Bronson Alcott, Henry David Thoreau, and especially Ralph Waldo Emerson were influential in setting the course for the quarterly magazine, and Emerson would eventually serve as editor in 1842. Its circulation was quite small, but the magazine was read and reviewed carefully (if not always kindly) by those attempting to understand this new way of thinking. In contrast to its philosophical predecessor, no Boston periodical did more to influence literary opinions and fashions than the *Atlantic Monthly* (1857–present). Edited first by James Russell Lowell between 1857 and 1861 and then by James T. Fields from 1861 to 1871, the magazine set the standard for what was considered "literature" in American culture. While no Boston magazine of this period ever seriously challenged the popularity of *Harper's* or *Godey's Lady's Book,* these examples demonstrate that several made lasting contributions disproportionate to the number of copies sold.

REGIONAL MAGAZINES

Even in the first quarter of the nineteenth century, magazines were being published outside of the three major eastern cities. In the south, Charleston was an early contender for prominence, producing at least six titles from 1820 to 1835. None of these could compete in terms of importance with two magazines that would emerge from Richmond and New Orleans, respectively: the *Southern Literary Messenger* (1834–1864) and *The Commercial Review of the South and West* (1846–1870). James Heath (1792–1862), the editor of the *Messenger* during its first year, threw down the gauntlet before his fellow southerners in the first number:

> Hundreds of similar publications thrive and prosper north of the Potomac, sustained as they are by the liberal hand of patronage. *Shall not one be supported in the whole south?* This is a question of great importance;—and one which ought to be answered with sober earnestness by all who set any value upon public character, or who are in the least degree jealous of that individual honor and dignity which is in some measure connected with the dignity of the state. Are we to be doomed forever to a kind of vassalage to our northern neighbors— a dependence for our literary food upon our brethren, whose superiority in all the great points

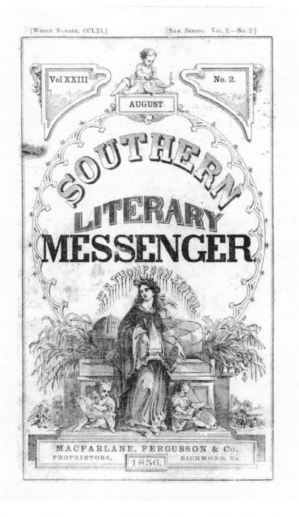

Cover of the August 1856 edition of the *Southern Literary Messenger.* CLEMENTS LIBRARY, UNIVERSITY OF MICHIGAN

of character,—in valor—eloquence and patriotism, we are no wise disposed to admit? ("Southern Literature," p. 1)

As this statement suggests, the magazine was avowedly sectional in content and outlook, although it did quote approvingly northern well-wishers, including among others Cooper and John Quincy Adams, and in its second number bragged of "the friendly and liberal support received from various gentlemen residing in the states north of the Potomac" (p. 33). Nevertheless, it included articles such as "Letters from New England. By a Virginian," acquainting readers with that strange and mysterious territory, "Yankee-land."

In 1835 Poe began a brief tenure as editor that lasted until 1837. While he wrote some fiction and poetry for the magazine during this period, and reprinted material he had first published elsewhere, his

writing in the *Messenger* that drew the most attention was his literary criticism. In sharp language, Poe tackled northern and southern writers alike. The gratitude, curiosity, and even-handed—if occasionally harsh—criticism directed toward the North that were evident throughout the pages of the early volumes faded as the years progressed. By the 1850s the magazine was growing increasingly political and publishing a great deal of material in defense of slavery. In 1861 the editor at the time, George William Bagby (1828–1883), wrote a call for secession that drove off most northern readers (Mott 1:654). The magazine struggled to survive during the Civil War, repeatedly raising prices and diminishing quality, and it finally ceased publication in 1864.

The Commercial Review of the South and West, began, like the *Messenger,* with a lament regarding the state of southern publishing. The editor, James D. B. De Bow (1820–1867), noted in the first issue, "In the higher departments little has yet been accomplished among us" (p. 3). To avoid the fate of other periodicals, De Bow set out to produce a magazine that would speak to the "practical wants of every-day life" (p. 4), and he also set forth a strictly regional focus. In keeping with such a mission, literature played only a minor role in the magazine (which in 1847 changed its title to *De Bow's Commercial Review of the South and West*), during its early years.

Despite the sectional ambitions and character set forth in the first number, De Bow also promised to steer clear of party movements and adopt "an active *neutrality*" (p. 6). As one might suspect, this became a difficult position to maintain as time went on, and by 1849 De Bow was already looking ahead to sectional conflict, if only in an economic sense. By the 1850s De Bow was actively discussing secession and publishing numerous proslavery articles. In 1853 the name of the magazine was shortened to *De Bow's Review* even as the scope of its interests and audience narrowed. The scholar Frank Luther Mott describes it during this period as "almost a textbook on the southern view of the slavery question" (2:344). Given De Bow's views, it is not surprising that the editor went on to work for the Confederacy, and, as the war progressed, the magazine was suspended. It reappeared in 1866 following a presidential pardon for its editor, and it managed to survive a few years longer, although it never regained its early stature. De Bow died in 1870, and the magazine disappeared a few months later.

Between 1820 and 1844 fewer than ten purely literary magazines were published in the West, a region that was generally considered during this time to extend as far as Ohio and Kentucky. With an undeveloped postal system and limited transportation options, these were almost exclusively small and regional publications. The center for many of these was Cincinnati. In 1836 the *Western Literary Journal, and Monthly Review* debuted at a modest subscription price of three dollars a year. In its first number, the editor W. D. Gallagher (1808–1894) bravely observed,

> The materials are in existence in the Mississippi Valley, for a fictitious literature at once attractive, wholesome, and unhackneyed. . . . With adventures interesting and hazardous, exploits daring and astonishing, characters original and unique, and states of human existence novel and peculiar,— what may not the fertile and ingenious literateur produce? (P. 66)

Gallagher's tone in this inaugural issue echoes that of his southern counterparts, but, with fewer than a thousand subscribers, his optimism appears to have been misplaced, and after six months the publishers were forced to sell the magazine.

In 1844 another magazine took the field in Cincinnati, with the less-than-original title *Western Literary Journal and Monthly Review* (1844–1845). In familiar rhetoric, the editors, E. Z. C. Judson and L. A. Hine, called upon their readers to show sectional loyalty, beseeching "the citizens of the west, to support a work which they should call their own, because devoted to their own interests, and filled with the productions of their own pens" (p. 51). In its first issue, the lead article offered a gloomy history of the failure of western periodicals, the author offering four reasons for the sad record. While others had often ascribed the lack of a vibrant literary press to the demands on time and energy that accompanied settling a new territory, this author offered far more prosaic rationales. These were a predilection in the newspapers for eastern and British publications, the failure of prominent western authors to provide material for the fledgling works, the failure of subscribers to live up to their commitments in paying their bills, and a lack of skilled and efficient publishers. Even with such an apparently clear understanding of the difficulties, the short lifespan of the magazine reveals that it was no more successful than its similarly titled forebear.

As the years passed, western magazines continued to appear and disappear with some regularity, even as the nation continued to expand. By the 1860s several periodicals were appearing in San Francisco. *The Californian* (1864–1868), edited by Charles Henry Webb (1834–1905), published the work of two local writers who would soon rise to more national prominence: Bret Harte (1836–1902) and Mark Twain (Samuel Langhorne Clemens, 1835–1910). When the magazine folded, another, the *Overland Monthly* (1868–1875), rose to take its place. With Harte as its principal editor, it garnered praise from a number of its eastern counterparts: readers were now paying attention to what was being published across the country, and, when Harte's story "The Luck of Roaring Camp" appeared in the second number, his national reputation was made—that is, when his identity was revealed, as contributors to the magazine were at this time still anonymous (Mott 3:404). Although Twain published several travel pieces in the magazine, including "A Californian Abroad—A Mediaeval Romance," it was his eventual rival Harte who was the prominent western writer at this time. Twain's rise would coincide with both his move east and the emergence of truly national periodicals.

"TO THE LADIES"

Women were already an important audience for American magazines in the 1820s, and their influence grew during the next fifty years. In addition to magazines like the *New-York Mirror* and *The Euterpeiad* (Boston, 1820–1821), which also called themselves "Ladies' Gazettes," a number of periodicals geared specifically toward women and families appeared. One important early title is the *Ladies' Magazine* (1828–1836), later titled *American Ladies' Magazine* (1834–1836) when it was discovered that it shared its title with a British counterpart. The editor, Sarah J. Hale (1788–1879), combined a fervent belief in education with conservative moral values. At the same time, however, she was a powerful voice in support of female participation in professional writing. In the pages of her magazine, one could find articles advising mothers to prevent their daughters from becoming close friends with other girls—such friendships proving "frequently injurious to their moral characters" (Phelps, p. 15)— alongside "Female Biography," celebrating "those who have been eminent for domestic virtues and benevolence, as well as those who have exhibited brilliant talents and literary excellence" (Hale, p. 41). Hale boasted of the quality and prestige of her female contributors, who included the popular authors Catharine Maria Sedgwick, Lydia H. Sigourney, and Lydia Maria Child.

Hale's influence grew when she joined forces with the Philadelphia publisher Louis Antoine Godey (1804–1878). He had published the *Lady's Book* for nine years (1830–1839), and in 1837 he purchased the *Ladies' Magazine* and hired Hale to edit his magazine. She would continue to edit the magazine, which went through a variety of name changes beginning in 1840 all revolving around the central title *Godey's Lady's Book*, until 1877. At its peak, the magazine boasted 150,000 subscribers. While the magazine continued to feature didactic essays alongside sentimental stories and poetry, Hale also continued to push for the inclusion of female voices. The January 1840 number included only female contributors, and, Hale commented in February, "The Ladies must be heard, and they always claim precedence" ("Publisher's Notices," p. 96). Men did eventually appear between the covers of this popular magazine, and contributors included William Gilmore Simms and the prolific magazine-writer and editor Nathaniel Parker Willis, as well as Emerson, Hawthorne, and Poe.

Other prominent female authors edited publications during this period. Child founded and edited the popular *Juvenile Miscellany,* a magazine designed for young readers, from 1826 to 1834, and Louisa May Alcott (1832–1888) served as editor for the long-running children's magazine *Merry's Museum* (1841–1872) for three years, from 1867 to 1870. Margaret Fuller edited the transcendentalist organ *The Dial.* Patricia Okker states that, throughout the nineteenth century, more than six hundred women served as editors at various times for various publications. While many magazines were written "to the ladies," often women were doing the editing as well as the reading.

ANONYMITY AND COMPENSATION IN MAGAZINES

The first issue of the *Atlantic Magazine* in 1824 began with a "Conversation between the Publishers and the Editor." During the course of the discussion, the two parties consider the problem of finding able contributors:

> *Ed.:* . . . We can find contributors enough, if they are paid; but where can we get the right sort? . . . And how pay a decent compensation for the labours of those whom we find worthy?
>
> *Pub.:* . . . Those who are able and willing to assist us, must accept their honorarium for the principle of the thing, until their exertions will permit us to make it respectable. And as to false delicacy, we will obviate its scruples, by forwarding every contributor's dues to any address given in his communication.
>
> *Ed.: Lucri bonus est odor ex re qualibet.* I do not think any body will be deterred from sending us a communication, by the fear of being tendered a pecuniary reward. But most of those gentlemen on whom we might rely for regular and interesting papers, are engaged in professional pursuits. We can only expect the occasional effusion of a leisure hour, or the hasty and incondite product of often interrupted efforts.
>
> *(P. 3)*

As this passage suggests, in the 1820s, payments to contributors were both irregular and not quite enough to allow one to make a "respectable" living off of them. There was no class of "professional" magazine writers, only "gentlemen" who tossed off the occasional piece as a recreation or distraction. This prominent perception of authorship, combined with the inadequate pay, contributed to the penchant for anonymity among American writers and editors: it was as unseemly for one to take public credit for one's work as it was to accept modest financial compensation for it. Authors might share the news of their literary success with their family or friends, but they shared their identity in print far less often. One was supposed to write for the magazines for recreation, not for wages and recognition.

As the century went on, these conditions changed considerably. Mott has pinpointed the early 1840s as the period when magazine writing began becoming a truly professional pursuit. Writers like Willis and Poe were appearing in numerous periodicals, and more and more magazines began offering remuneration to contributors. In particular, *Graham's Magazine* and *Godey's* offered rates considered "liberal." Graham offered up to sixty dollars for a five-thousand-word article (Mott 1:506). Such compensation was not the case for every magazine. Walt Whitman (1819–1892) lamented in 1846, "Most of our authors are frittering away their brains for an occasional five dollar bill from the magazine publishers" (p. 252). Harriet Beecher Stowe's *Uncle Tom's Cabin,* first serialized in the *National Era* (1847–1860) beginning in 1851 and running over the course of forty issues, earned the author a mere four hundred dollars (Mott 2:22). Authors with established reputations could expect something approaching fair compensation, but, with the rare exceptions, writing for magazines remained a difficult means of making a living for most. Still, in a sign of how things were changing, in 1868 Stowe wrote a series of articles giving advice to women looking to enter the literary profession by writing for the magazines, a prospect that editors of the 1820s may never have imagined.

Magazines and the reputations of their writers became more closely intertwined in the 1860s as the tradition of anonymous publication came to an end. Authorial attribution was occasionally given for some articles and reviews, and the sharp-eyed reader might scan the list of contributors to their favorite periodical and assign names to works, but there was no systematic policy. In 1868 the stalwart *North American Review* changed its policy and began publishing names, and other magazines soon followed suit. In 1870, when *The Galaxy* (1866–1878) signed a contract with Mark Twain, its editors trumpeted the news on the front covers. The careers of authors and the success of magazines grew more closely intertwined as a result.

AFTER THE WAR: THE RISE OF NATIONAL MAGAZINES

Many literary periodicals struggled during the Civil War, but, as the war drew to a close, the nation was poised for a period of remarkable publishing expansion. In 1865 there were roughly seven hundred periodicals published in the United States; by the end of the decade, that number had nearly doubled. The end of the war marked an end—at least on paper—of the sectional conflict that had divided Northern and Southern readerships, and the number of railroad lines that had sprung up for military and industrial purposes brought more and more of the West in reach. Both of these developments greatly expanded the potential market for magazines. Improvements in technology also allowed for more numbers to be printed more quickly and inexpensively, and the increase in advertising in magazines offered another revenue stream to keep the publications afloat. When *Scribner's Monthly* (later *The Century*) debuted in 1870, it already had forty thousand subscribers. A new age in American magazines was about to begin.

See also Book and Periodical Illustration; Civil War; *The Dial;* Editors; *Godey's Lady's Book; Harper's New Monthly Magazine;* Literary Marketplace; Publishers; Religious Magazines

BIBLIOGRAPHY
Primary Works
Cincinnati Literary Gazette 1 (1824): 13.

"Conversation between the Publishers and the Editor." *Atlantic Magazine* 1 (1824): 1–3.

De Bow, James D. B. "The Commercial Review" *Commercial Review of the South and West* 1 (1846): 2–6.

Embree, Elihu. "Postmasters." *Emancipator* 1 (1820): 64.

Gallagher, W. D. "Editor's Budget." *Western Literary Journal, and Monthly Review* 1 (1836): 65–67.

Hale, Sarah J. "Female Biography." *Ladies' Magazine* 7 (1834): 41.

Hale, Sarah J. "Publisher's Notices." *Godey's Lady's Book* 20 (1840): 96.

Heath, James. "Southern Literature." *Southern Literary Messenger* 1, no. 1 (1834): 1–3.

Heath, James. "To the Public, and Especially the People of the Southern States." *Southern Literary Messenge* 1, no. 2 (1834): 33.

Judson, E. Z. C., and L. A. Hine. "Editor's Table." *Western Literary Journal and Monthly Review* 1 (1844): 51.

"Note." *Atlantic Magazine* 1 (1824): n.p.

Phelps, A. H. L. "Intimate Friends." *Ladies' Magazine* 7 (1834): 15–19.

Putnam, George Haven. *George Palmer Putnam: A Memoir.* New York and London: G. P. Putnam's Sons, 1912.

"To The Public." *Ariel* 1, no. 4 (1827): 32.

Twain, Mark. *Contributions to* The Galaxy*: 1868–1871 by Mark Twain.* Edited by Bruce R. McElderry Jr. Gainesville, Fla.: Scholars' Facsimiles and Reprints, 1961.

Whitman, Walt. *The Journalism.* Edited by Herbert Bergman, Douglas A. Noverr, and Edward J. Recchia. Vol. 1. New York: Peter Lang, 1998.

Woodworth, Samuel, and George P. Morris. "Prospectus." *New-York Mirror, and Ladies' Literary Gazette; Being a Repository of Miscellaneous Literary Productions, in Prose and Verse* 1 (1823): 1.

Secondary Works
Austin, James C. *Fields of the Atlantic Monthly: Letters to an Editor, 1861–1870.* San Marino, Calif.: Huntington Library, 1953.

Exman, Eugene. *The Brothers Harper.* New York: Harper and Row, 1965.

Greenspan, Ezra. *George Palmer Putnam: Representative American Publisher.* University Park: Pennsylvania State University Press, 2000.

John, Arthur. *The Best Years of the* Century: *Richard Watson Gilder,* Scribner's Monthly, *and the* Century Magazine, *1870–1909.* Urbana: University of Illinois Press, 1981.

Mott, Frank Luther. *History of American Magazines.* 5 vols. Cambridge, Mass.: Harvard University Press, 1938.

Myerson, Joel. *The New England Transcendentalists and* The Dial: *A History of the Magazine and Its Contributors.* Rutherford, N.J.: Fairleigh Dickinson University Press, 1980.

Okker, Patricia. *Our Sister Editors: Sarah J. Hale and the Tradition of Nineteenth-Century American Women Editors.* Athens: University of Georgia Press, 1995.

Price, Kenneth M., and Susan Belasco Smith, eds. *Periodical Literature in Nineteenth-Century America.* Charlottesville: University Press of Virginia, 1995.

Sedgwick, Ellery. *The* Atlantic Monthly, *1857–1909: Yankee Humanism at High Tide and Ebb.* Amherst: University of Massachusetts Press, 1994.

Tebbel, John William, and Mary Ellen Zuckerman. *The Magazine in America: 1741–1990.* New York: Oxford University Press, 1991.

Martin T. Buinicki

PHILADELPHIA

Struggling to avoid being eclipsed by the economic upstart New York, Philadelphians entered the second quarter of nineteenth century with a self-conscious appreciation of their own sophistication mixed with anxiety over losing their supremacy. Since the mid-eighteenth-century, Philadelphia—measured by the breadth and value of its international markets, its infrastructure and cosmopolitan population, and the number and variety of its civic institutions—ranked just behind London as the second most dynamic city in the powerful British Empire. Those who experienced Philadelphia between 1820 and 1870 witnessed an acceleration of that dynamic.

But sophistication and acceleration proved insufficient. New York soon overtook Philadelphia in population and wealth. However, Philadelphia retained some unique attributes that earned it a distinctive niche in American economy and culture.

THE MODERNIZING CITY

In 1845, when William Henry Fry (1813–1864) unveiled his grand opera *Leonora,* Philadelphia was reminded that though it might no longer be the biggest and the richest, it was often still a city of innovation. Fry's opera—the first created by an American composer—was performed, with a sixty-piece orchestra, at the Chestnut Street Theatre. More than a decade later the work was translated into Italian and performed in New York.

Philadelphia was already sensitive to its own history. The Germantown bank cashier John Fanning Watson, a self-styled historian, had published in 1830 his *Annals of Philadelphia.* In this volume Watson was a trailblazer in using first-person interviews to capture how eighteenth-century Philadelphians viewed their world and their story. Watson had much to celebrate: the 1820s had brought the refurbishing of the Philadelphia State House, where the Declaration of Independence was signed. Now enshrined in a spiffed-up park, the statehouse reminded Philadelphians that they were part of the founding of the great experiment that was America. That same decade had seen the establishment of two other institutions devoted to promoting the city's image: the Historical Society of Pennsylvania and the Franklin Institute—the former for "elucidating the natural, civil and literary" history of Pennsylvania and the latter to "promote the mechanick" arts by sponsoring scientific education for those involved in manufacturing. Over the succeeding decades dozens of such organizations sprang up, aimed at celebrating, educating, protecting, or reforming the citizenry or to encourage Philadelphia's economic innovation. The city was poised to dazzle residents and tourists alike.

Philadelphians were justly proud of their social and economic innovation. In the 1830s a parade of foreign observers stopped in to view Eastern State Penitentiary, the new prison system housed in the stately building designed by the distinguished architect John Haviland (1792–1852). Haviland, who had earned his reputation by creating the Philadelphia Arcade, another shrine—this one to the city's burgeoning businesses—had also designed the city's innovative Pennsylvania Institute for the Deaf and Dumb. Eastern State provided state-of-the-art housing for local criminals; the arcade was the city's most modern conglomeration of shops and stores; and the Institute for the Deaf and Dumb reflected the growing sense of public responsibility for needy citizens.

Tourists were well-rewarded for their visits. The Frenchman Alexis de Tocqueville's *Observations on the Penitentiary System in the United States, and Its Application in France* were published by Philadelphia's Carey, Lea, and Blanchard in 1833. Two years later the same firm published the diary of the British actress Fanny Kemble, who found Philadelphia equally fascinating. (The publisher Henry Carey was the successor to his father's firm, Matthew Carey and Company, which dominated the U.S. publishing industry of the 1820s. Another Carey son, Edward, partnered with Abraham Hart in 1829 to form Carey and Hart, which also joined the ranks of the best-known publishing houses in the United States.) Transformed by the 1830s from a seaport city to a seat of urban industry, Philadelphia had an up-and-coming middle class, newly moneyed and anxious to take its place among the ranks of consumerism. Weathering two economic downturns in 1837 and 1843, it could still dream, and its dreams could still draw praise.

Having been the nation's innovator in developing a public water delivery system—designed by Benjamin Henry Latrobe in 1800—the city leaders took the bold step of buying up private riverside property in the 1840s in order to protect the purity of the water supply. So began Fairmount Park, which remains one of the world's largest contiguous city parks. Indoor plumbing, domestic gas service, and public street lighting followed close behind. With advances in lithography (pioneered in the 1820s by Cephas G. Childs, then later expanded by the partnership of George Lehman and Peter S. Duval), this urban development was well-documented in pictures as well as words. And one of America's first daguerreotypes immortalized the early years of Central High School, an institution that has retained its reputation as one of the nation's premier public schools.

By 1854, when the city and the surrounding county were consolidated into one municipality, the region encompassed a population that had almost doubled over the previous decade. Not only bigger—grown from one square mile to more than one hundred square miles—the city was also increasingly cosmopolitan, embracing (if sometimes contentiously) multiple nationalities, religions, and races. Elizabeth M. Geffen records that in 1850 the visiting Hungarian countess Theresa Pulszky saw "the stamp of wealth and commerce wherever we cast our glance on the buildings and inhabitants," while a British visitor of the same time found "something more than usually wonderful in the growth of Philadelphia" (p. 314).

Much of Philadelphia had been born out of Benjamin Franklin's (1706–1790) boundless energy and initiative, and his legacy stretched far beyond his death. So while New York outstripped it in size, Philadelphians more than kept pace in imagination.

THE WORLD OF MODERN PUBLISHING

Part of Philadelphia's "something wonderful" was a vigorous publishing industry. In fact Philadelphia entrepreneurs were leaders in the new profession of "publisher"—a career developing in the early nineteenth century from the marriage of what the historian Rosalind Remer calls "printers and men of capital." The 1830s modern publisher was, in many cases, a printer who had developed new strategies for enhancing his income. The first step was often for a skilled printer to team up with a savvy businessman who had access to ready funds. Hence many a mid-nineteenth-century publishing firm had two or more names—the craftsman plus the backers who had the ear of Philadelphia's powerful banking and insurance industry. In the early national period the First Bank of the United States and the Bank of Pennsylvania had dominated the American economy. Then the Second Bank of the United States, occupying the impressive Greek revival structure built for it by William Strickland in the 1820s, meant that Philadelphia was the seat of a deep well of capital from which to draw. The city also was home to an extensive community of wealthy individuals, whose informal investment network kept much of Philadelphia's business afloat.

Sometimes book producers sought to raise the visibility of their wares by relocating from the periphery to the commercial centers of the city. Other schemes for expansion were more aggressive. The bookseller William Woodward hired ministers to carry religious books to sell as they fanned out into the hinterland.

After 1834, when Philadelphia instituted public education administered by local school boards, schoolbooks became another valuable staple. The textbook firm of McCarty and Davis introduced both traveling salesmen and the branch store to expand their publishing empire as far afield as Tennessee, Louisiana, and Missouri. McCarty and Davis next secured their market by producing inexpensive almanacs, do-it-yourself legal works, and novels. Their mission was assisted by the tumbling costs of production and materials beginning in the 1820s, culminating in the transition from rag paper to wood-pulp sheets by the end of the 1850s.

Philadelphia still holds the distinction of having the oldest continuously operating lending library in the English-speaking world: the Library Company of Philadelphia. An important aspect of Benjamin Franklin's legacy, the library helped to sustain the stream of publishing by encouraging a reading public and building rich and international collections for its upper-class members. But Library Company members were only one element of the reading public. School texts, such as *The Arithmetical Expositor*, authored by Enoch Lewis in 1824 and reissued several times in succeeding decades, produced steady profits for the publisher Kimber and Sharpless. Lindley Murray's *English Grammar*, which first appeared in 1800, brought more than six decades of profits for Philadelphia book trade. And Jacob Snider's 1833 edition of the Bible, printed in embossed letters for students at the new Pennsylvania Institution for the Instruction of the Blind, reinforced the city's sense of nurturing innovation.

Popular periodicals also enlivened readers' days. Zachariah Poulson took over John Dunlap and David C. Claypoole's *American Daily Advertiser* in 1800, publishing it until 1839, when it was overshadowed by the more aggressive *Public Ledger*, founded in 1836. Philadelphia's first "penny paper"—a modern news sheet that took full advantage of inexpensive production techniques—the *Ledger* initiated the policy of hiring teams of reporters and home delivery boys to ensure that their customers got the hottest news—and they got it right at their own front doors. The *Ledger* soon had the largest circulation in Pennsylvania.

Godey's Lady's Book outpaced the *Ledger*, garnering a readership that stretched across the North and the South and by the 1850s claimed some 150,000 subscriptions for its monthly offerings. In a career that began in 1830 and ran for more than six decades (to 1898), *Godey's Lady's Book* both created and responded to the new woman who eagerly awaited its features of fashion, fiction, and music. Lavishly illustrated and richly focused on romantic images of domesticity and

The destruction of Pennsylvania Hall, Philadelphia, 17 May 1838. Undated lithograph by J. T. Bowen. The headquarters of the Philadelphia Female Anti-Slavery Society were burned by an angry mob. THE LIBRARY OF CONGRESS

motherhood, *Godey's* was perhaps the supreme symbol of modern publishing possibilities and the sophisticated urban audience.

The city's publishing enterprise also spawned some surprising offspring. Mathias Baldwin (1795–1866), who began as a manufacturer of bookbinders' tools in Philadelphia in the 1820s, had turned his metalworking know-how to more ambitious directions by the 1830s: he began producing steam-driven locomotives. By the time of his death in 1866, his factory at Broad and Spring Garden Streets had employed hundreds of immigrant workers to build more than one thousand of these machines, which he sold all over the world. In turn his factory had given rise to Midvale Steel, which turned out metal parts to supply the Baldwin Locomotive Works, beginning in 1867.

THE CITY OF REFORM

Partly resulting from the enduring influence of its Quaker founders, antebellum Philadelphia was host to two unique realities: a vigorous energy for social reform and a large and flourishing African American population. Often these two realities fed off each other. Since the eighteenth century, a number of Philadelphia Quakers had been active in antislavery agitation. As abolitionist ferment increased during the 1830s—sometimes intertwining with the women's rights movement—Philadelphians, especially Philadelphia Quakers, joined forces with African Americans in other cities like Boston and New York in pursuit of racial justice. Their various activities have left much evidence in the form of paper and ink. In 1838, for example, the five-year-old Philadelphia Female Anti-Slavery Society (PFASS, an interracial organization) built its own meeting place—Pennsylvania Hall—only to have it destroyed by a white mob that resented their cross-racial socializing. J. T. Bowen's lithograph immortalized the event.

Not all abolitionists were as wedded to racial equality as was the PFASS, but the debate about how to end slavery and the fate of freed people helped enliven Quaker periodicals such as the *Friend*, which began publishing in 1827. The *Friends Intelligencer*, by William Moore, joined the conversation in 1844, as the voice of the schismatic Hicksite Quakers tended to embrace a more radical antislavery strategy than did their more conservative Orthodox rivals. And the mathematics text writer Enoch Lewis took advantage of his captive school audience to insert short notes promoting racial justice and antimilitarism.

Travelers—black and white—found Philadelphia to be a crucial stop on any American tour, and inevitably they reported on the city's race relations and black enterprises. Tocqueville remarked upon the psychological freedom of the city's black population and upon the anxiety it caused many white residents. The Philadelphia experience figured prominently in the narrative of fugitive slaves, such as Ellen and William Craft, who fled to the city from Georgia in 1848 and documented their story in the memoir *Running a Thousand Miles for Freedom* (1860). Henry "Box" Brown's daring escape from Richmond, Virginia, by means of having himself nailed into a 2-foot-by-2-foot crate and shipped as "dry goods," ended with his being uncrated in Philadelphia and being immortalized in an image created by Peter Kramer and then lithographed by Louis Napoleon Rosenthal. The black historian William Wells Brown complained of Philadelphia's "colorphobia" (Weigley, p. 363), but when Martin Delany, the era's premier black political commentator, recounted his Philadelphia experience in his 1859 novel *Blake; or, The Huts of Africa*, he praised the array of organizations resulting from black enterprise. Little wonder that when Frank J. Webb wrote *The Garies and Their Friends,* America's second novel by a black author (published in New York in 1857), he set the story in Philadelphia's upper-class black community.

Philadelphia's black leaders early enjoined the city's literary discourse with their own set of concerns. As early as the 1790s yellow fever epidemic, black spokesmen developed a protest voice that swelled over the decades to include the wealthy sailmaker James Forten's *Series of Letters by a Man of Color,* published in pamphlet form in 1813, then republished in the nation's first black newspaper, *Freedom's Journal,* in 1827. Forten's son-in-law, Robert Purvis, took up the cause in 1837, authoring an "Appeal of Forty Thousand Citizens, Threatened with Disfranchisement, to the People of Pennsylvania," which also appeared in a black newssheet, the *Colored American.* Such abolitionist literature, which poured forth from black Philadelphians, was often published by sympathetic local Quaker printers, culminating in the 1872 publication of *The Underground Rail Road,* penned by the black Underground Railroad organizer William Still and published by the abolitionist Quaker firm of Porter and Coates. Perhaps the most enduring legacy

of black Philadelphia, however, is the *Christian Recorder,* founded in 1852 by the city's Mother Bethel AME (African Methodist Episcopal) Church. The only African American news sheet to publish continuously through the Civil War, the *Christian Recorder* stood, for many decades, as an authoritative voice of black Philadelphia and indeed of black America.

The Philadelphia that lost its supremacy never regained its first-place status. Nevertheless, creating its own niche in publishing, reform, finance, and industry, it remained an important stop on the American tourist trail. With its cosmopolitan population, reform initiatives, and innovative manufacturing strategies, it remained a major port and manufacturing center in the decades following the Civil War.

See also Abolitionist Writing; Banking, Finance, Panics, and Depressions; Blacks; Foreigners; Literary Marketplace; New York; Publishers; Quakers; Slave Narratives; Tourism

BIBLIOGRAPHY

Primary Work

Watson, John F. *Annals of Philadelphia and Pennsylvania: In the Olden Time; Being a Collection of Memoirs, Anecdotes, and Incidents of the City and Its Inhabitants, and of the Earliest Settlements of the Inland Part of Pennsylvania.* 1830. Philadelphia: The Author, 1844.

Secondary Works

Geffen, Elizabeth M. "Industrial Development and Social Crisis, 1841–1854." In *Philadelphia: A Three-Hundred-Year History,* edited by Russell Weigley, pp. 307–362. New York: Norton, 1982.

Hamm, Thomas D. *The Transformation of American Quakerism: Orthodox Friends, 1800–1907.* Bloomington: Indiana University Press, 1988.

Lapsansky, Emma J. "Building Democratic Communities, 1800–1850." In *Pennsylvania: A History of the Commonwealth,* edited by Randall M. Miller and William Pencak, pp. 153–202. University Park: Pennsylvania State University Press, 2002.

Lapsansky, Phillip. "Graphic Discord: Abolitionist and Antiabolitionist Images." In *The Abolitionist Sisterhood: Women's Political Culture in Antebellum America,* edited by Jean Fagan Yellin and John C. Van Horne, pp. 201–230. Ithaca, N.Y.: Cornell University Press, 1994.

Lehuu, Isabelle. *Carnival on the Page: Popular Print Media in Antebellum America.* Chapel Hill: University of North Carolina Press, 2000.

Remer, Rosalind. *Printers and Men of Capital: Philadelphia Book Publishers in the New Republic.* Philadelphia: University of Pennsylvania Press, 1996.

Wainwright, Nicholas B. "The Age of Nicholas Biddle, 1825–1841." In *Philadelphia: A Three-Hundred-Year History,* edited by Russell Weigley, pp. 258–306. New York: Norton, 1982.

Wainwright, Nicholas B. *Philadelphia in the Romantic Age of Lithography.* Philadelphia: Historical Society of Pennsylvania, 1958.

Weigley, Russell. "The Border City in Civil War, 1854–1865." In *Philadelphia: A Three-Hundred-Year History,* edited by Russell Weigley, pp. 363–416. New York: Norton, 1982.

Wolf, Edwin, and Marie Elena Korey. *Quarter of a Millennium: The Library Company of Philadelphia, 1731–1981; A Selection of Books, Manuscripts, Maps, Prints, Drawings, and Paintings.* Philadelphia: Library Company, 1981.

Zboray, Ronald J. *A Fictive People: Antebellum Economic Development and the American Reading Public.* New York: Oxford University Press, 1993.

Emma J. Lapsansky-Werner

PHILOSOPHY

American philosophy in the early nineteenth century was an enterprise shaped by beliefs in common sense, moral feeling, and self-culture. In addition to being decisively influenced by democratic values, however, philosophy in antebellum America was also divided by controversies about the roles science and faith would play in constituting knowledge. Scientific empiricism, Protestant theology, and Romantic literary theory contended with one another for the philosophical high ground in the colleges, churches, intellectual societies, and debate clubs of 1830s and 1840s. In this period of intellectual generalism, almost all philosophical debates were by nature interdisciplinary affairs. As a result, early American philosophy sometimes seems like an incoherent negotiation between irreconcilable ideas. Further complicating matters, philosophy was often voiced in the common tongue of the ordinary, self-taught citizen instead of the recondite language of the elite professor or minister. Ralph Waldo Emerson's (1803–1882) assertion in "The American Scholar" (1837) that the creative mind of the self-taught individual would matter much more than the trained thinking of highly educated bookworms in the creation of a more intellectual American culture suggests not only Emerson's radical individualism but also something of the reality on the ground. With an ear listening, then, to the philosophy of the street and of the classroom; an eye focused on the philosophical

debates among religious reformers and political activists; and a mind attuned to the Scottish, English, and German thinkers who most influenced their American counterparts, this essay explores three central features of the philosophical landscape of antebellum America: (1) the role of Lockean empiricism and Scottish common sense realism in American debates about science and faith; (2) the significance of international Romanticism to New England transcendentalism and New England transcendentalism to modern and contemporary American and international philosophy; and (3) the impact of the problem of slavery and the cause of abolitionism on antebellum American philosophy.

ORIGINS OF AMERICAN PHILOSOPHY

Like all things American, philosophy went through a creative process of democratization in the nineteenth-century United States. Readers in the antebellum literary marketplace wanted their philosophy to be useful in helping them to manage themselves and to cultivate self-trust in the emerging marketplace culture. This need for democracy and practicality in part accounts for the popularity among Americans of ideas adapted from the Scottish Enlightenment. While ordinary Americans did not read the works of Scottish common sense philosophers such as Francis Hutcheson (1694–1746) and Thomas Reid (1710–1796), these philosophers contributed profoundly to the developing American moral philosophy by charting a middle way between the Calvinist legacy of the Anglo-American, puritanical past and the eighteenth-century taste for scientific empiricism.

Reacting against Calvinistic beliefs in predetermined fate and innate human depravity at the time of the Puritan Revolution in England, John Locke (1632–1704)—the most important influence on both Scottish common sense and early American philosophy—conceives of the human mind as a blank slate on which impressions are written by experiences. According to Lockean psychology, human beings have no ideas that are innately their own. Sense impressions mark the mind, which in turn forms these impressions into simple but accurate ideas. Humans are consequently free agents who have a large say in how their understanding of the world is composed: they are neither predetermined nor depraved. But, according to Locke, the mind needs a rigorous education into an empirical method. Without such education, the mind tends to combine simple ideas into complex ones. Complex ideas, in turn, engage the memory and the imagination, which often cloud subsequent perception and comprehension. Thus, to retain a clear sense of things, the world must be grasped through a strictly empirical method.

Only when addressing the miracles of the Bible does Locke equivocate about empiricism. But where Locke seeks to retain a place in empirical philosophy for religious faith, David Hume (1711–1776) takes empiricism to a logical and skeptical extreme. Many philosophers in the eighteenth and nineteenth centuries felt that Lockean psychology and Humean skepticism worked together. To defenders of religious faith, the empiricism of Locke and Hume rendered problematic the notion that ideas of good and bad are derived from objective, universal moral laws. They seemed to suggest that all knowledge is based in sense, and what is sensed about God or anything else is both subjective and probabilistic—anything but objective and absolute.

In response to such doubts about the moral design of the universe, Francis Hutcheson—a Scotsman who more fully theorized ideas already proposed by the third Earl of Shaftesbury, Antony Ashley Cooper, in England—postulated that moral absolutes could be found within the self as a faculty of human sense. Hutcheson's idea is not that human beings have god-like intelligence, but, as Barbara Packer suggests, that "the same deity who has endowed us with bodily senses acute enough to preserve our lives has also instilled in us a moral sense whose operation . . . is as ineluctable as gravity" (p. 342). More than a feeling in the work of most common sense thinkers, the moral sense is a kind of mental function, which as Thomas Reid clarified, comes to human beings through intuitions or "immediate beliefs." In other words, according to Scottish common sense realism, the knowledge of right and wrong, of good and bad, is a part of human existence. The only thing needed to make use of common sense is an education into the higher, sociable impulses, which these thinkers variously called "benevolence," "gregariousness," or "sympathy."

Among professional philosophers in America influenced by common sense theorists, James McCosh (1811–1894)—who was appointed president of The College of New Jersey, later Princeton University, in 1868 and wrote the influential history *The Scottish Philosophy* (1875)—was probably most important. But across the wider culture in the nineteenth century, the idea that there exists a moral sense—like the senses of taste, touch, sight, hearing, and smell—endowed by a benevolent creator in humankind was widely accepted. Some have argued that Thomas Jefferson's Declaration of Independence (1776) and his confidence in the ability of ordinary people to govern themselves owes nearly as much to a Scottish faith in human nature as to

a Lockean political calculus. A dyed-in-the-wool empiricist, Jefferson takes it as a universal that "Reason and free inquiry are the only effectual agents against error" (p. 211). But he also admits in an 1814 letter to a friend that "I sincerely . . . believe with you in the general existence of a moral instinct" (p. 543). Even slaves—whom Jefferson otherwise demeans through purportedly empirical observation in *Notes on the State of Virginia* (1787)—have a fully formed moral sense in his account.

The Protestant Unitarians who held office at Harvard College in the early nineteenth century also combined a Lockean pedagogy demanding strenuous efforts at self-culture through memorization and drills with a generally sunny belief in the innate goodness of individuals and a benevolent God. In the 1830s and 1840s Emerson and other transcendentalists would repudiate the empiricism of Harvard Unitarians while retaining their prevailing healthy-minded faith that human beings can know themselves, nature, and the ways of God. And although Herman Melville (1819–1891), who had a very stern vision of nature and God, would scoff in his darkly metaphysical fiction at the childishness and ignorance about evil he attributed to the evasive northern intellectual culture, other genteel cultural leaders besides Emerson—including Harriet Beecher Stowe and Frederick Douglass—readily deployed Scottish philosophical ideals and metaphysics as part of their literary and philosophical arsenal against slavery. Indeed, a majority of the antebellum public intellectuals who are still read today subscribed to a democratically republican belief that everyone has access to the laws of the conscience and, thus, to universal moral truth.

All of this suggests that common sense philosophy had its greatest significance in antebellum America in the way it informed popular understandings of democratic ethics and cultural pedagogy. In the emerging marketplace society, where social mobility and capitalistic competition destroyed aristocratic forms of social cohesion, moral ideas derived from common sense philosophy helped to assure individuals and communities that they still lived in a morally accountable universe. As Thomas Augst in particular has shown, in the lyceums and lecture halls, debate societies and libraries where people spent their leisure hours, common sense moral philosophy helped to shape an emerging cultural pedagogy about the ethical and spiritual care of the self. By writing letters to family members, reflecting on their lives in their journals, reading useful literature, participating in polite conversation, and listening to oratorical performance, ordinary antebellum citizens sought to develop "character," to account for their actions, and to socialize themselves into democracy. Moral philosophy, thus, was a widespread social practice of literate citizenship; it had civic appeal in early America.

TRANSCENDENTALISM

Transcendentalism grew up as a generational movement in the 1830s and 1840s. Many of the transcendentalists were Harvard-educated divinity students who fought against the religious historicism and empiricism of their Unitarian predecessors. Influenced by international and especially German Romanticism, they championed individual intuition and spiritual self-trust over Christian dogma and religious institutionalism. Becoming a kind of antiestablishment avant-garde, the transcendentalists—including Emerson, Henry David Thoreau (1817–1862), Margaret Fuller (1810–1850), Amos Bronson Alcott (1799–1888), Theodore Parker (1810–1860), and others—were not philosophers in any strict sense of the vocation. However, they wove together theology, philosophy, literature, pedagogy, and political activism with genuine originality in their essays and treatises.

As the evangelical revivalism of the Second Great Awakening inspired an array of iconoclastic spiritual movements across the northeastern United States, transcendentalism emerged as the most philosophically subtle and intellectually cosmopolitan of these. The transcendentalists essentially fashioned a more Romantic Unitarian theology. While validating the Unitarian impulses toward self-culture, self-trust, and the humanization of Christ, the transcendentalists tended to repudiate the Unitarian appeal to "facts" to buttress their form of liberal Christianity. Christianity for the transcendentalists would not be sustained through Lockean powers of observation or exacting scholarship about the miracles of the Gospels. Instead, the way to universal godly truth for transcendentalists was through the portal of the inviolate self. Self-reliance—cultivated through intuitive experiences of solitary, often emotional revelation to the divinity within the self—became the guiding Romantic and spiritual ethos of transcendentalism. In addition, since the transcendentalists, as Lawrence Buell and others have shown, conceived of self-reliance as a process that involved freeing themselves from provincial intellectual entanglements as much as anything else, they helped to bring into being a more cosmopolitan philosophical culture in the United States. At a most basic level, the transcendentalists read fewer British and Scottish philosophical sources and more German ones.

In the 1820s and 1830s German philosophy arrived in the United States indirectly, through the works of translators and interpreters including Samuel Taylor Coleridge, Madame de Staël, and Thomas Carlyle. James Marsh (1794–1842), the leading figure among Vermont transcendentalists and the president of the University of Vermont, published the first American edition of Coleridge's *Aids to Reflections* in 1829. Marsh's edition of Coleridge, perhaps more than any other single text, helped to spark American transcendentalism. For Marsh, Emerson, and many others, Coleridge's engagement with German philosophy offered a way to diffuse the Enlightenment-era rage for empiricism by retheorizing the mind so as to elevate individual intuition as a means for discovering truth. Coleridge freely (and often inaccurately) adapted the terminology of Immanuel Kant (1724–1804) to his own purposes. What Coleridge gained from a creative reading of Kant was the idea that knowledge is immanent in experience and not simply derived from it. Coleridge and Marsh were both philosophically and religiously conservative, whereas Emerson and many other Boston transcendentalists were radically progressive or anarchic. Whatever their persuasion, however, the transcendentalists were fascinated by the distinction Coleridge made between "understanding"—the faculty of mind that derives knowledge from sense perceptions and methodical rationation—and "reason"—the higher faculty of mind that enables people to apprehend divinity and universal law through revelation.

As Emerson argues in *Nature* (1836), his provocative, essayistic reckoning with philosophical idealism, this specific distinction between understanding and reason enables transcendentalists to account for nature and the mind "by other principles than those of carpentry and chemistry" (p. 508). Emerson's claim is that, in moments of insight, "spirit does not act upon us from without . . . but . . . through ourselves" (pp. 508–509), bringing about "delicious awakenings of the higher powers, and the reverential withdrawing of nature before its God" (p. 503). Emerson also draws inspiration from Carlyle's heated, mystic responses to German philosophy, and both Emerson and Walt Whitman (1819–1892) endorse Carlyle's sense—inspired by J. G. Fichte and Johann Wolfgang von Goethe—of the poet's heroic, philosophic role: to perceive and seize the Universal idea and clothe it in an inspiring and accessible language.

Although professional philosophers often discount Emerson's writing for its lack of logic and consistency, its refusal to engage in reasoned argument, its aphorisms and flighty idiosyncrasies, Emerson's influence has nevertheless been profound on a range of important modern and contemporary philosophers, including William James, Frederich Nietzsche, Stanley

Cavell, and Richard Rorty. Many literary critics interested in philosophy have found in Emerson's thought the origins of American pragmatism, and philosophers from around the globe who value the active mind more than systemic philosophical exposition continue to respond enthusiastically to the two sides of Emerson that Buell identifies: the democratic idealist and the anarchic provocateur. In addition, Thoreau's philosophy of civil disobedience, which hangs on a transcendental understanding of self-reliance, helped to inspire the movements of peaceful revolution set in motion by Mohandas Gandhi and Martin Luther King Jr. Futhermore, Whitman's radically cosmic belief in the unique grandeur of every self and every mind—his Romantic vision of a universal oversoul connecting slave, whore, president, and preacher all alike through a daily sharing in the erotics of experience, as expressed in *Leaves of Grass* (1855)—amounts to the first philosophically significant statement of tolerance and multicultural acceptance in American letters.

This is not to say that the transcendentalists dominated academic philosophical debate in the United States of their day; they did not because they were not academics. More formally trained, establishment figures of Unitarian theology and philosophy like Harvard's Francis Bowen (1811–1890) sought to stem the revolution in American ideas that the transcendentalists helped to initiate. According to one widely respected history of American philosophy, Harvard establishmentarians like Bowen "consistently outmaneuvered the Transcendentalists philosophically" (Kuklick, p. 10). Still, while Bowen and his circle have been largely forgotten, Emerson and his peers discovered and inspired an American philosophical movement that was more dynamic, democratic, and cosmopolitan than anything that came before it.

ABOLITIONISM, LITERATURE, AND MODERN CONSCIOUSNESS

In the broadest sense, many American abolitionists argued that common sense made it transcendentally apparent that slavery—whether conceived of as a sin against a Christian God, a violation of nature, or some combination of the two—was immoral. Harriet Beecher Stowe (1811–1896), for instance, felt that slavery violated the common sense that every woman in the Republic could derive from her experience of sympathetic, maternal feelings. In *Uncle Tom's Cabin* (1852), the most influential antislavery novel ever written, Stowe repudiates reason as an unreliable male faculty for assessing moral truths—reason enables marketplace sophistries that allow the selling of humanity as chattel—in order to champion the

bedrock truth value of women's tears and affections. Organizing her entire antislavery philosophy around the relationship between mother and child, Stowe, like other philosophers of the domestic hearth, including her sister Catharine Beecher, genders common sense. She elevates women above men as intuitive philosophers and conceives of slavery as a patriarchal institution that the mothers of America needed to repudiate for the sake of children and motherhood itself. Frederick Douglass (1818–1895), by contrast, rationalizes his rage at being denied his right to manhood into an emphatically virile antislavery philosophy. The philosophy of masculine emancipation he elaborates in *Narrative of the Life of Frederick Douglass, an American Slave* (1845) still has considerable influence in the African American protest tradition. Gender differences aside, however, both Stowe and Douglass draw from a Lockean emphasis on the importance of personal liberty combined with universalized appeals to familial affection and human rights in their antislavery writings. Both also suggest the central role literary culture played in popularizing philosophical ideas during the period and in linking philosophy to activist politics and the ethics of social life.

Douglass's *Narrative* is not often thought of as a landmark philosophical work, because philosophy is not often conceived of as an expressive, autobiographical project among Europeans, as it frequently has been among African Americans. Arguing that literacy is the pathway from slavery to modern democratic consciousness, Douglass shows his mastery of republican political discourse; he crafts an intellectually balanced, concise, straight-talking style that embodies his claim to reason and the rights of humankind. Yet, Douglass's narrative, as Paul Gilroy suggests, is more significant from the perspective of philosophy because it uses the philosophical methods and the ideals of the Enlightenment to subvert the "scientific racism" afflicting works by thinkers as various as Hume, Jefferson, Kant, and G. W. F. Hegel (1770–1831).

In particular, Douglass's *Narrative* shows that he was conversant with the German idealist tradition out of which Hegel's thinking emerged. Like Hegel, Douglass conceives of the Ideal as something that can be expressed only through a historical process of progressive development. Both also work dialectically, by setting up dichotomies and then attempting to resolve them through philosophical or narrative exposition. In *The Phenomenology of Mind* (1807), Hegel presents an allegory of lordship and bondage. In the *Narrative*, Douglass uses more immediate language and imagery to deconstruct the dichotomies of nineteenth-century American society—white/black, free/slave, literate/

illiterate, mind/body—in order to advance human history. Like Hegel, Douglass also asserts that there comes a time when one must fight in a life-and-death struggle in order to claim a fully modern consciousness. But here too Douglass ultimately theorizes a more cosmopolitan understanding of modern consciousness than does Hegel; Douglass himself, through his struggle with a white slave breaker, gains the empowered, autonomous sense of "the consciousness that exists for itself" (Hegel, p. 234) that is reserved for the white European in Hegel's account. "It was a glorious resurrection" (p. 113), Douglass states of his experience putting down the slave breaker, thereby writing himself into modern history in a way Hegel would have deemed impossible for a black man. Whereas Hegel arrives at a theory of power, Douglass conceives of a philosophy of emancipation.

CONCLUSION

Herman Melville in "Benito Cereno" (1855) presents a more strictly Hegelian allegory of lordship and bondage, in that no one escapes the encounter between slave and master without disillusioning self-consciousness, except for the naive New Englander, Amasa Delano, a believer in common sense and beneficent nature. Delano's worldview, which fuses anti-intellectual parochialism and an arrogant sense of Manifest Destiny, is based according to Melville on the fundamental misconception of the Scottish Enlightenment: that the senses are reliable and human perception is direct and comprehensive. In Melville's modern world, none of this is true. Melville's descent into skepticism suggests how common sense philosophy met its demise as the antebellum aura of confidence, faith, and certainty wore off after the Civil War. In the new, post–Civil War era of intellectual specialization, as industrialization increasingly alienated human beings from the products of their labor, and urbanization separated them from nature, the certainty of common sense gave way to philosophic uncertainty, doubt, and provisionalism. Although William James and most other pragmatists attempted to resist the pull of amorality, determinism, and pessimism in post-Darwinian philosophical conversations, this pull was very real, as the realist and naturalist fiction of the late nineteenth century suggests.

A forward-looking belief system shaped by notions about the common sense and the potential to experience divinity found within everyone, American philosophy was forged in the first half of the nineteenth century as a more accessible and practical response to European philosophies. Debated, democratized, and deified, philosophy found its largely optimistic American temper in the efforts of several generations of thinkers

to modernize religion, humanize science, and repudiate slavery. While Darwinian science and the social fragmentation and modernization of the Gilded Age would challenge that temper, American pragmatists like William James, John Dewey, and Jane Addams sought to adapt the foundational healthy-mindedness they inherited as cultural baggage from the earlier era to the less confident, more complicated, social, cultural, and intellectual contexts in which they thought and wrote.

See also "The American Scholar"; "Benito Cereno"; German Scholarship; *Narrative of the Life of Frederick Douglass; Nature;* Romanticism; Transcendentalism

BIBLIOGRAPHY

Primary Works

Douglass, Frederick. *Narrative of the Life of Frederick Douglass, an American Slave.* 1845. New York: Penguin, 1986.

Emerson, Ralph Waldo. *Nature.* 1836. In *The Norton Anthology of American Literature,* 6th ed., edited by Nina Baym, et al., pp. 486–514. New York: Norton, 2003.

Hegel, G. W. F. *The Phenomenology of Mind.* 1807. Translated by J. B. Baillie. London: Allen and Unwin, 1964.

Jefferson, Thomas. *The Portable Thomas Jefferson.* 1975. Edited by Merrill D. Peterson. New York: Viking Penguin, 1977.

Secondary Works

Augst, Thomas. *The Clerk's Tale: Young Men and Moral Life in Nineteenth-Century America.* Chicago: University of Chicago Press, 2003.

Buell, Lawrence. *Emerson.* Cambridge, Mass.: Harvard University Press, 2003.

Camfield, Gregg. *Sentimental Twain: Samuel Clemens in the Maze of Moral Philosophy.* Philadelphia: University of Pennsylvania Press, 1994.

Fox, Richard Wightman, and James T. Kloppenberg, eds. *A Companion to American Thought.* Cambridge, Mass.: Blackwell, 1995.

Gilroy, Paul. *The Black Atlantic: Modernity and Double Consciousness.* Cambridge, Mass.: Harvard University Press, 1993.

Kloppenberg, James. *Uncertain Victory: Social Democracy and Progressivism in European and American Thought, 1870–1920.* New York: Oxford University Press, 1986.

Kuklick, Bruce. *The Rise of American Philosophy: Cambridge, Massachusetts, 1860–1930.* New Haven, Conn.: Yale University Press, 1977.

Menand, Louis. *The Metaphysical Club.* New York: Farrar, Straus and Giroux, 2001.

Packer, Barbara L. "The Transcendentalists." In *The Cambridge History of American Literature,* vol. 2, *Prose Writing 1820–1865,* edited by Sacvan Bercovitch, pp. 329–604. New York: Cambridge University Press, 1995.

William M. Morgan

"THE PHILOSOPHY OF COMPOSITION"

In spring of 1846, Edgar Allan Poe (1809–1849) moved from New York City to his country cottage in Fordham where he wrote "The Philosophy of Composition," an essay that promises to recount the method he used to write his famous poem "The Raven" (1845). In the essay Poe challenges those who suggest that writing is a mysterious process prompted solely by the imagination. Although the it offers a number of precepts for good writing, at the end of the essay, Poe undercuts his step-by-step instructions by insisting that all writing should have an "under-current" of meaning. Because he never demonstrates how to create that "under-current," Poe's essay never completely reveals the process that makes his work so powerful.

THE IMPACT OF "THE RAVEN"

At dawn on the full-moon morning of 19 July 1845 explosions at a saltpeter storehouse in lower Manhattan caused a widespread fire, rivaling the disastrous New York fire of 1835; hundreds of buildings went up in flames and many people died. Quite coincidentally, or maybe not so coincidentally, this was the day Edgar Allan Poe would give his recitation of "The Raven" at the home of Anna Lynch (1815–1891), the well-known literary salon hostess. Ms. Lynch described Poe's performance that night as "electrifying" in a letter to the poet Sarah Helen Whitman (1803–1878), who later had a short-lived relationship with Poe. Granted, Poe was known for his intent performances, but his reading "The Raven" on a night of full moon and devastation must have enhanced the drama and haunting effect of his poem.

Poe's poem had dazzled many readers, and numerous printings of "The Raven" appeared in magazines and newspapers around the country and abroad after its initial appearance in *The New York Evening Mirror* on 29 January 1845 (in which it was printed as an "advance of publication" copy that would appear in the *American Review* the next month). On 19 November 1845, almost a year after its initial appearance in the *Mirror,* "The Raven" was published

Edgar Allan Poe. GETTY IMAGES

by Wiley and Putnam in a collection using the famous poem in its title, *The Raven and Other Poems.* Two days later, the book was reviewed in the *Mirror* by the poet and editor George Pope Morris (1802–1864), a friend of Poe's. Morris described Poe's poetry this way: "Tall shadows and a sighing silence seem to close around us as we read. We feel dream land to be more real and more touching than the actual life we have left" (Thomas and Jackson, p. 592). A month later, Thomas Dunn English (1819– 1902), a poet, physician, editor, politician, and sometime friend of Poe's, wrote a review in the New York monthly magazine the *Aristidean* and described Poe's poetics in the following terms: "much of the effect depends upon the mode of construction, and the peculiar arrangement of words and incidents" (Thomas and Jackson, p. 599). Poe would later use these two approaches to his poetry—concern with effect and construction—to chart the process he used in composing "The Raven" and to suggest that "no one point in its composition is referable either to accident or intuition" (p. 195).

But this dissertation would come much after Poe had enjoyed the fame his "raven" had brought him.

With this newfound popularity and his position as owner and editor of *The Broadway Journal,* Poe was finally able to live in a fashionable neighborhood near Washington Square Park at 85 Amity Street. In this neighborhood and in his role as editor, Poe came into contact with prominent writers and artists of his time and because of the appeal of "The Raven," his fame as a poet grew at home and abroad. This idyllic time, however, was short-lived. On 3 January 1846 *The Broadway Journal* folded, and by the end of February Poe was forced to move his family from 85 Amity. In addition, his wife's poor health and her displeasure with the gossip about Poe's "affairs" and his "pending institutionalization" to cure his "insanity" prompted Poe's move from the city to the country in Fordham (Thomas and Jackson, pp. 623–624).

Shortly after this move, Poe wrote "The Philosophy of Composition," partly to build on the popularity that "The Raven" had afforded him and partly to counter the negative criticism written about his poetry and the numerous parodies of "The Raven" that had appeared in the press. Having earned the reputation of the "tomahawk critic" for his harsh analyses of other poets' works, Poe's poetry received similarly harsh appraisals; though praised by many, his poetry was also called "childish," "puerile," and "absurd" (Thomas and Jackson, p. 627). One of Poe's answers to such criticism was "The Philosophy of Composition," an essay that purports to detail the method he used to write poetry, a method that proceeds with "the precision and rigid consequence of a mathematical problem" (p. 195).

AN EXPLICATION OF "THE PHILOSOPHY OF COMPOSITION"

Poe's essay opens with an intimate tone; the first few words bring the reader into his study, as he points to "a note now lying before me" (p. 193). Referring to this note from the famous British novelist Charles Dickens is a purposeful pose on Poe's part to grant his treatise credibility. The basic premise of his dissertation seems to derive from two of England's most prominent authors—Dickens and William Godwin, a philosopher and novelist and the father of Mary Shelley. In his letter to Poe, Dickens remarked that Godwin wrote the second volume of his popular novel, *Caleb Williams* (1794), first and then "cast about him for some mode of accounting for what had been done" (p. 193). Although Poe believed that Godwin did not "precisely" follow the method Dickens suggested, Poe, nonetheless, asserts that the overall approach of keeping the end "constantly in view" is essential to effective composition (p. 193). He appears to base his philosophy of composition on this revelation from Dickens about Godwin's writing process.

Poe's ostensible purpose in publishing "The Philosophy of Composition" is simple: to demonstrate his ability to describe a step-by-step process that leads to a successful poem or narrative. No other author, Poe observes, had had either the desire or ability to do so. Unlike other poets and novelists who resist "letting the public take a peep behind the scenes," Poe promises to reveal all (p. 194).

To be successful, Poe advises, a writer must choose a desired effect before putting pen to paper, he must consider originality at all times, and, of course, he should have the dénouement always in mind. To create a desired effect a writer must determine which combination of tone and incident best provokes this effect (ordinary incident and peculiar tone, peculiar incident and ordinary tone, peculiar tone and peculiar incident). He then must decide upon a suitable length, one that sustains "unity of impression" (p. 196). The length should be directly proportional to the merit of the subject, or, in Poe's words, "the extent of a poem may be made to bear mathematical relation to its merit" (pp. 196–197). The length, however, should be sufficient enough to induce an effect, or, in Poe's words, "a certain degree of duration is absolutely requisite for the production of any effect at all" (p. 197). However, no "literary work" should require more than "one sitting"; otherwise, Poe argues, "the vastly important artistic element, totality, or unity, of effect" is lost (p. 196).

After determining length, the author must choose a theme that is "*universally* appreciable" and induces pleasure (p. 197). Then the writer must decide what form is appropriate to that purpose: poetry, Poe asserts, should elevate the soul and effect "Beauty" while prose should impress the intellect and effect "Truth" and/or impress the heart and effect "Passion." Poe reminds the reader that "Truth" demands precision and "Passion" requires "*homeliness*" (p. 198). Having set these parameters for writing in general, Poe turns to the specific requirements needed to create an effective poem. He allows that poetry can embrace both "Truth" and "Passion" but not at the expense of "Beauty"; "the true artist will always contrive, first, to tone them into proper subservience to the predominant aim, and, secondly, to enveil them, as far as possible, in that Beauty which is the atmosphere and the essence of the poem" (p. 197).

In using his experience of writing "The Raven" as a concrete example of how to write a poem, Poe, again, defers to "experience" rather than "inspiration" as the arbiter of the best choice of tone for poetry: "all experience [he writes] has shown that this tone is one of *sadness*" (p. 198). He continues by posing a rhetorical question: "Of all melancholy topics, what, according to the *universal* understanding of mankind, is the *most* melancholy?" (p. 201). Poe provides a simple, clear answer: "the death, then, of a beautiful woman is, unquestionably, the most poetical topic in the world" (p. 201). Such clarity on Poe's part may be why critics and poets so often quote this part of his advice.

After determining length and tone, Poe advises the poet to choose a mechanism, a pivot, around which the poem would be constructed. For "The Raven," Poe chose the refrain, ostensibly because "its employment sufficed to assure me of its intrinsic value" (p. 199). Poe improved the shape of the refrain by insisting on monotone "both in sound and thought" (p. 199). After making this choice, Poe lists the considerations that led him to choose the word "nevermore" for "The Raven." Most important, Poe concludes that he made his choice by imagining the last refrain of the poem: "I first established in mind the climax, or concluding query—that to which 'Nevermore' should be in the last place an answer—that in reply to which this word 'Nevermore' should involve the utmost conceivable amount of sorrow and despair" (p. 202). At this juncture, about halfway through his essay, Poe returns to the initial premise of keeping the ending "always in view," reminding his readers that "the poem may be said to have its beginning—at the end, where all works of art should begin" (p. 202).

Once the pivot is established the poet would then choose an appropriate locale and characters to reinforce the desired tone and effect. Complementary versification is essential. Yet Poe insists that originality in versification is not a matter of intuition but rather a matter of "negation"; such negation presumes a thorough knowledge of prosody and poetic precedent. Poe asserts that his "Raven" exhibits originality of versification only because of the way he combined individual lines of ordinary rhythm and meter: "nothing even remotely approaching this combination has ever been attempted" (p. 204). As Thomas O. Mabbott points out, this claim is suspect, and he suggests that Poe borrowed heavily from Elizabeth Barrett's "Lady Geraldine's Courtship" (1844), especially its "stanzaic form" (p. 356).

The rest of "The Philosophy of Composition" outlines the decisions Poe made in constructing "The Raven," purportedly revealing the linear progression of thought that produced his poem while citing complete stanzas as examples. In fact, the essay ends with the last stanza of "The Raven": "And my soul *from out that shadow* that lies floating on the floor / Shall be lifted—nevermore" (p. 208). Yet just before this dramatic ending is a paragraph that effectively undoes most of Poe's insistence that poetry can be written with "the precision and rigid consequence of a mathematical problem" (p. 195).

In this important paragraph Poe reveals that even if a poet diligently follows all of the suggestions he poses, an "under-current, however indefinite, of meaning" must be imbedded in the poem (p. 207). That "under-current," Poe claims, creates the "*richness*" so necessary to any poem of merit (p. 207). Poe also takes aim here at the "Frogpondians," Poe's disdainful nickname for the New England transcendentalists including, for example, Ralph Waldo Emerson and Henry David Thoreau. Poe's strong rejection of pedantic poetry is evident when he asserts that "excess" of meaning "turns poetry into prose" (pp. 207–208). For Poe the most important element of poetry is the "suggestiveness" that underlies a poem's effect. Even though Poe asserts that didacticism turns poetry into prose, he writes that the very suggestiveness of "The Raven" "disposes the mind to seek a moral in all that has been previously narrated" (p. 208). This is a curious contradiction that does not square with Poe's overall disdain for poetry that has a "moral" agenda. Following this conclusion is another questionable assertion. Poe claims that the phrase found in the last stanza of "The Raven," "from out *my heart*," is the "first metaphorical expression in the poem" (p. 208). This claim is simply not true. What about "Night's Plutonian shore," or "fiery eyes now burned into my bosom's core," or "perfumed from an unseen censer / Swung by seraphim whose foot-falls tinkled on the tufted floor"? These two contradictions lead the reader to question Poe's claim that he will reveal the "wheels and pinions" of his writing process (p. 195).

CRITICAL RESPONSE

In his introduction to "The Raven," Mabbott says quite simply that "The Philosophy of Composition" "includes a partly fictional account of the planning of 'The Raven'" (Poe, "The Raven," p. 353) and reminds readers that Poe "admitted freely that his 'Philosophy of Composition' . . . was not expected to be taken as literal truth" (p. 359). Some critics have suggested that Poe's essay is a purposeful hoax while others make a less strident assessment, as G. R. Thompson does when he characterizes the essay as "possibly half tongue-in-cheek" (p. xl). Daniel Hoffman argues that in "The Philosophy of Composition," Poe reveals "the method of his art [that] enables the madness of his matter to be spoken" (p. 92). Hoffman also points out that Poe must have taken pleasure in having

George Graham publish his essay after rejecting "The Raven" years earlier. As Hoffman succinctly puts it, Poe made Graham "eat raven" (p. 80). Dennis Pahl argues that "The Philosophy of Composition" not only "ends up reproducing many of the poem's features—becoming as it were seduced by the very rhetoric it is supposed to analyze" (p. 10) but also ultimately "engages in violating boundaries, in questioning assertions of mastery, in what might be called in other words, 'writing in the feminine'" (p. 20). No one has suggested that the essay is simply a recipe for good writing, yet many have excerpted particular ideas as nodal points of Poe's literary sensibility, especially the following: the death of a beautiful woman as "the most poetical topic in the world," the need for an "under-current" of meaning in all artworks, and the importance of "unity of effect."

INTERPRETATION

Clues to whether or not Poe actually revealed his writing method in "The Philosophy of Composition" can be found in the essay itself. Poe often advises the writer to do what is ordinarily done; for example, when he explains how he chose the refrain as the pivot of "The Raven," he says he chose it above all other devices because "no one had been so universally applied as that of the *refrain*" (p. 199). He further advises a writer to rely on themes that are "universally appreciable" and tones that allow for "universal understanding" (p. 201)—as if universality is most important, as if it is best to please the mob. Yet, considering that "The Raven" accomplished its goal of pleasing both "the popular and the critical taste," it is no wonder that Poe chose this poem as the concrete example for explicating his "*modus operandi*" (p. 195). But anyone who knows Poe's work knows a concern for universality would not be utmost in his mind at all times. Granted, he did wish his poetry and fiction to be read and, more importantly, to sell, but his aesthetic principles went far beyond a mere desire to please the populace and earn a living.

Poe wanted to be remembered as a poet even though most of his career was spent as a critic and magazine writer. In 1848, a year before his death, Poe dedicated his prose poem *Eureka,* the work he considered the culmination of his writing career, "to those who feel rather than to those who think—to the dreamers and those who put faith in dreams as in the only realities" (Poe, *Eureka,* p. 5). In *Eureka,* Poe defines intuition as "*the conviction arising from those inductions or deductions of which the processes are so shadowy as to escape our consciousness, elude our reason, or defy our capacity of expression*" (p. 22). This assertion counters his claim in "The Philosophy of

Composition" that writers who claim "ecstatic intuition" as the means of production are deluding themselves and others (p. 194). Yet Poe valued most an "under-current" of meaning in a poem or narrative, and Poe's pupil can nowhere find the rule for creating this "suggestiveness" in Poe's "Philosophy." Such "suggestiveness" more often than not is created by a process akin to the definition of intuition found in *Eureka.* Those who follow the steps outlined in "The Philosophy of Composition" would be remiss were they to think that that would be all they need to do to create an "art product." Poems or narratives produced in this way, Poe claims, would "repel the artistical eye" because they lack "adaptation" and "suggestiveness," the two aspects of writing that cannot be taught (p. 207).

Careful readers of Poe's essay would be confounded by what they find in the penultimate paragraph. Here Poe states, "Holding these opinions, I added the two concluding stanzas of the poem—their suggestiveness being thus made to pervade all the narrative which has preceded them" (p. 208). Should not those two last stanzas have been conceived first, according to what Poe says in his introduction? How could he "add" these two stanzas to make the rest resonate with "suggestiveness," when Poe ostensibly holds to the rule of having "the end always in view"? Like the Prefect in Poe's short story "The Purloined Letter," do readers overlook what is "in plain view"? Do they overlook evidence "by dint of [its] being excessively obvious"? (Poe, "The Purloined Letter," p. 990).

This glaring but subtle contradiction makes the reader question Poe's "sincerity" and purpose in writing "The Philosophy of Composition." Other hints throughout are not quite so obvious but persistent nonetheless. For example, Poe's insistence on "universality" as a primary consideration for many compositional decisions is suspect. Finally, his direct statement that "from out my heart" is "the first metaphorical expression in the poem" is outright dissembling (p. 208). Poe's essay holds the clues to its project: to purport to reveal all the "*modus operandi*" while withholding the essential components that transform technical prowess into art. Nonetheless, Poe's "Philosophy of Composition" illuminates many of the principles that make Poe's writing so engaging: unity of effect, adaptation of complexity, suggestiveness, careful attention to form as a reflection of content, and a fascination with death and perversity.

See also "The Fall of the House of Usher"; Literary Criticism; "The Poet"; "The Raven"

BIBLIOGRAPHY

Primary Works

Poe, Edgar Allan. *Eureka.* 1848. Edited by Stuart Levine and Susan Levine. Urbana: University of Illinois Press, 2004.

Poe, Edgar Allan. "The Philosophy of Composition." 1846. In *The Complete Works of Edgar Allan Poe,* vol. 14, edited by James E. Harrison, pp. 193–208. New York: AMS Press, 1979.

Poe, Edgar Allan. "The Purloined Letter." 1844. In *Tales and Sketches,* vol. 2, *1843–1849,* edited Thomas Ollive Mabbott, pp. 972–997. Urbana: University of Illinois Press, 2000.

Poe, Edgar Allan. "The Raven." 1845. In *Edgar Allan Poe: Complete Poems,* edited by Thomas Ollive Mabbott, pp. 353–364. Urbana: University of Illinois Press, 2000.

Secondary Works

Pahl, Dennis. "De-Composing Poe's 'Philosophy.'" *Texas Studies in Literature and Language,* vol. 38, no. 1 (1996): 1–25.

Person, Leland S. "Poe's Composition of Philosophy: Reading and Writing 'The Raven.'" *Arizona Quarterly* 46, no. 3 (1990): 1–15.

Hoffman, Daniel. *Poe Poe Poe Poe Poe Poe Poe.* 1972. Baton Rouge: Louisiana State University Press, 1998. See pp. 80–93.

Thomas, Dwight, and David K. Jackson. *The Poe Log: A Documentary Life of Edgar Allan Poe, 1809–1849.* Boston: G. K. Hall, 1987.

Thompson, G. R. "Edgar A. Poe: An American Life." In *The Selected Writings of Edgar Allan Poe,* pp. xiii–lii. New York: Norton, 2004.

Barbara Cantalupo

PHOTOGRAPHY

Photography was the most popular cultural phenomenon in nineteenth-century America. Americans had an exuberant love affair with the photograph, and its popularity surpassed that of all print media by the Civil War. The advertiser Frederick R. Barnard is famous for saying that "One picture is worth ten thousand words" (*Printers' Ink,* 10 March 1927, p. 114). But he was only giving authorship to a quip that many Americans were already repeating in 1839, when photography was invented.

While the Frenchman Louis Daguerre (1789–1851) is credited with inventing photography, it was in America that the medium gained its greatest popularity (followed by France, the two countries with the largest middle-class populations and democratic ideologies). By 1850 a photographer was available for hire in every county in every state and territory to satisfy the insatiable demand. In Manhattan there was a daguerreian studio on every street corner, where customers could go to have their portraits taken. The desire for photographs penetrated all regions of the country. And it was a profession that was easy to enter. Much like Nathaniel Hawthorne's Holgrave, the fictional daguerreotypist from *The House of the Seven Gables* (1851), early photographers came to their trade from other professions and typically abandoned it after a few years. Daguerreotypists needed no background in art, and they could learn the procedure by reading "how-to" pamphlets such as Francois Fauvel-Gouraud's *Description of the Daguerrotype Process* (1840), the first published instructions on the daguerreotype written in the United States. With comparatively modest investment, an enterprising man or woman could buy a camera and supplies, rent a room with a skylight or travel in a covered wagon, and open for business. A successful daguerreotypist made as much money as highly skilled artisans, and given the extremely short apprenticeship period of a few weeks, one could painlessly leave the profession for the next new thing.

The demand for photographs stemmed from a number of factors. It corresponded with the rise of the middle classes (especially in America and France), who wanted portraits of themselves but could not afford expensive paintings. By 1850, after improvements in lenses and reduction of exposure times, every American in possession of pocket change could have his or her portrait taken—and over 90 percent of all photographs were portraits. Portraits tapped into the desire for self-transformation among the emerging middle classes. As Americans rose and fell in social status, they wanted visible and tangible records of themselves at fixed intervals: markers for remembering the past and foretelling the future. In an important sense, Americans created pictures of themselves and then sought to become those pictures.

Photography also offered a way to replace an obsolete way of life with an alternate vision of America. The emergence and popularity of photography coincided with chronic social change and a radical transformation of the cultural landscape. Railroads and steamboats had transplanted enormous numbers of people to distant places and had irrevocably changed the faces of cities and towns. A widespread depression began with the panic of 1837, continued almost unheeded into the mid-1840s, and was followed by another "hidden" depression. The result was a further erosion of old communities and ways of life. In the face of such disintegration, photography, much like print culture,

Daguerreotype by Southworth & Hawes, Boston, c. 1850. THE GRANGER COLLECTION, NEW YORK

offered a way to recapture lost, "real" communities by imagining new ones. It helped people answer the question "Who am I?" on a national scale.

The daguerreotype was like print culture in another way as well: it "read" like a book. The daguerreotype image was contained inside a leather case with a velvet backing; one opened the case like a book and therein discovered a new world and another reality. It was thus no coincidence that books were the most common prop in daguerreotype portraiture, and many portraits feature the sitters reading, as though drawn into another world. Like the many histories of the new nation—whether in the form of fiction or nonfiction—daguerreotypes provided Americans with new visions of themselves and of their country.

By the end of the 1850s, cartes de visite, or visiting cards, had replaced daguerreotypes in popularity and represented the precursor to the modern wallet-size snapshot. Unlike daguerreotypes, which were one-of-a-kind, "precious" metal objects, cartes de visite were infinitely reproducible prints on paper. They were distributed as calling cards, purchased as souvenirs, and could be produced en masse quite cheaply. Hundreds of thousands of copies of portraits of famous men and women could be made in short order. The night before Abraham Lincoln's famous Cooper Union address of 27 February 1860, which helped put him in the White House, Mathew Brady (c. 1823–1896) photographed him and sold over one hundred thousand carte de visite copies. Following the attack on Fort Sumter, a thousand carte de visite copies were sold each day of the Union commander Major Robert Anderson. Through this wet-plate collodion process, Americans collected portraits of themselves and their families and friends as well as of the rich and famous and housed them in photo albums in their parlors. It was a way to identify themselves with famous people they had never met and to become a visible part of a larger collective identity created by portraits.

It was not until George Eastman's (1854–1932) Kodak camera, which allowed Americans to take their own snapshots, that the snapshot finally replaced cartes de visite in popularity. First introduced in 1888, the camera sold for $25 and came with a roll of paper negative film that allowed one hundred exposures. Kodak's slogan, "You press the button, we do the rest," famously summed up a system of creating portraits that remains for the most part the practice today.

WRITERS AND PHOTOGRAPHY

Like photographers, writers sought to represent reality and help create what Benedict Anderson calls "imagined communities" (p. 1), defined around beliefs in the new nation. Reformers in particular were especially influenced by photographs. In fact, based on the abundance of extant imagery, abolitionists probably had their pictures taken with greater frequency, and distributed them more effectively, than other groups (Stauffer, *Black Hearts,* p. 50). Their desire to transform themselves and their world fueled their interest in images, which helped to make visible the contrast between their dreams of reform and the sinful present. They believed that remaking themselves through pictures was a step toward achieving their new world. Frederick Douglass (1818–1895) in particular wrote more eloquently on the photograph than virtually any other American before the Civil War. He sat for his "likeness" whenever he could and had his portrait taken at least as many times as Walt Whitman, the poetic reformer who is legendary for visually creating and re-creating himself.

Douglass believed that "true" art could transcend racial barriers. A good part of his fame rested on his public-speaking and writing talents. But he also relied heavily on portrait photography and the picture-making process in general to create an authentic and intelligent black persona. He knew that his fame and influence could spread more quickly through his portraits than through his voice, and he continually sought to control how he appeared in his portraits.

For Douglass, the truthfulness of the daguerreotype prevented the distortions and exaggerations that came from the hands of whites. He wrote two separate speeches on "pictures" in which he celebrated photography and praised Daguerre as "the great discoverer of modern times, to whom coming generations will award special homage" ("Pictures"). Because of Daguerre's invention, he said, "we have pictures, true pictures, of every object which can interest us":

> Men of all conditions and classes can now see themselves as others see them and as they will be seen by those [who] shall come after them. What was once the special and exclusive luxury of the rich and great—is now the privilege of all. The humblest servant girl may now possess a picture of herself such as the wealth of kings could not purchase fifty years ago. ("Pictures")

The photograph—and accurate renditions or sympathetic engravings of it—became his medium of choice for representing himself visually. For Douglass, Daguerre had turned the world into a gallery of "true pictures," elevating ex-slaves and servants to the level of kings.

Yet the democratizing aspect of photography was only one reason why he thought photographs contributed to the cause of abolition and equal rights. He well knew that most Americans, including slaveholders and proslavery sympathizers, were in love with the photograph. The other reason was that photography inspired the picture-making process in general, and in his mind all humans sought accurate representations of both material reality and of an unseen spiritual world. This affinity for pictures was what distinguished humans from animals: "Man is the only picture-making animal in the world. He alone of all the inhabitants of earth has the capacity and passion for pictures" ("Pictures"). Emphasizing the humanity of all humans was central to Douglass's reform vision, as all but the most radical of Americans defended inequality and racial hierarchies on the grounds that black slaves and their descendants were fundamentally different from other humans.

Douglass attacked these racist arguments by championing the "truthfulness" of the photograph and stressing the picture-making proclivity of all humans. By doing so he emphasized humanity's common origins and the faculty of imagination over reason. The "full identity of man with nature," he said, "is our chief distinction from all other beings on earth and the source of our greatest achievements." While "dogs and elephants are said to possess" the capacity for reason, only humans seek to re-create nature and portray both the "inside soul" and the "outside world" through such "artificial means" as the photograph. Making pictures requires imagination, and Douglass quoted the transcendentalist Ralph Waldo Emerson to argue that the realm of the "imagination" is the "peculiar possession and glory of man." The power of the imagination is "a sublime, prophetic, and all-creative power." Imagination could be used to create a public persona in the form of a photograph or engraving. It could also be used to usher in a new world of equality, without slavery and racism. The power of the imagination links humans to "the Eternal sources of life and creation." It allows them to appreciate pictures as accurate representations of some greater reality, and it helps them to realize their sublime ideals in an imperfect world. As Douglass aptly put it: "Poets, prophets, and reformers are all picture makers—and this ability is the secret of their power and of their achievements. They see what ought to be by the reflection of what is, and endeavor to remove the contradiction" ("Pictures"). In the speech "Pictures and Progress," he even went so far as to suggest that "the moral and social influence of pictures" is more important in shaping national culture than "the making of its laws" (p. 456).

In their fiction, Douglass and other abolitionist writers tapped into Americans' love affair with daguerreotypes in order to inspire empathic awareness between readers and African Americans. In *The Heroic Slave* (1853), Douglass's only work of fiction and the first published African American novella, the black hero, Madison Washington, is "daguerreotyped on" the "memory" of his friend and white protagonist, Mr. Listwell (p. 45). Similarly Harriet Beecher Stowe (1811–1896) "daguerreotype[s]" her hero Uncle Tom "for our readers" in *Uncle Tom's Cabin* (1852; p. 68). Daguerreotyping a black character was a common trope in abolitionist narration. It conveyed more than physical description or even photographic memory, for a daguerreotype was thought to penetrate the perceiver's soul as well as his mind. Americans saw God's work in the daguerreotype. It was more than a mere picture; rather, it contained part of the body and soul of the subject. Daguerreotyping a black character for white viewers (or readers) was a way for authors to break down racial barriers and achieve spiritual connectedness, and equality, between blacks and whites.

Like Douglass, Walt Whitman (1819–1892) was enormously influenced by photography. In fact one might say that his lifelong project, *Leaves of Grass,* which he revised and expanded twelve times over during his career, depended upon the daguerreotype for its conception. In one of Whitman's self-reviews of the first (1855) edition of *Leaves of Grass* he describes the purpose of having his half-length portrait on the frontispiece rather than his name: "Its author," he notes, "is Walt Whitman and his book is a reproduction of the author":

> His name is not on the frontispiece, but his portrait, half-length, is. The contents of the book form a daguerreotype of his inner being, and the title page bears a representation of its physical tabernacle. (*Brooklyn Eagle*)

The poetry itself, in other words, is Whitman's effort to daguerreotype his soul and render the frontispiece engraving a daguerreotype that displays both body and soul.

In two poems, "My Picture-Gallery" (1880) and "Pictures," which was not published during his life, Whitman characterizes the very dwelling of his mind as a "picture-gallery," a camera obscura by which consciousness is made possible (pp. 401, 642). Whitman's faith in the democracy of photographs resembles his democratic poetic vision: there is enough room in his little house for all states, countries, and peoples. There is evidence as well that photography influenced particular poems in *Leaves of Grass* and especially the Civil War poems first collected in *Drum-Taps* (1865). Like most Americans, Whitman "saw" the Civil War chiefly through photographic reproductions, and poems like "Cavalry Crossing a Ford" probably derived from a photographic image rather than from an event Whitman actually witnessed.

Holgrave, the daguerreotypist in Nathaniel Hawthorne's (1804–1864) *The House of the Seven Gables,* is a radical social leveler who embraces self-sovereignty and equality for everyone. He associates with the "strangest companions imaginable": reformers, temperance lecturers, "cross-looking philanthropists," and outright abolitionists, some of whom "acknowledged no law" (p. 79). Holgrave has a "law of his own" (p. 80); he relies on the sacred sovereignty of the self and uses his daguerreotype art to "bring out the secret character" of his subjects "with a truth that no painter would ever venture upon, even could he detect it" (p. 85). He lacks "reverence for what [is] fixed"(p. 157) and displays an "effervescence of youth and passion" (p. 161): "The true vale of his character lay in that deep consciousness of inward strength, which made all his past vicissitudes seem merely like a change of garments" (p. 160).

But Hawthorne, unlike his protagonist, was not a democratic reformer and embraced neither progress nor the perfectionist vision of Whitman, Douglass, and Stowe. The "truth" of the inner, secret self that the daguerreotype illuminates was, for Hawthorne, dark-souled, drenched in sin, and thus could not be relied on. By the end of the novel Holgrave "progresses" by abandoning daguerreotypy, conforming to tradition and the authority of law and social superiors: "The happy man inevitably confines himself within ancient limits," the narrator concludes (p. 267). He marries Phoebe and lives respectably and conservatively.

Herman Melville (1819–1891) was another "dark romantic" who had little faith in progress, whether of a technology like photography or of a world without sin or slavery. Predictably, he loathed the new medium of photography. He rarely had his photograph taken, and in his novel *Pierre; or, The Ambiguities* (1852), the narrator laments the democratization of portraits that comes from the proliferation of daguerreotypists: "instead of, as in old times, immortalizing a genius, a portrait now only dayalized a dunce" (p. 254). Almost without exception, those writers who embraced the social virtues of photography also believed in progress and the possibility of perfection, and those writers who condemned the photograph were skeptical of such visions.

Ironically, however, the photograph helped to destroy such faith in progress. While the Crimean War was the first war to be photographed, the American Civil War was the first to depict images of dead soldiers. Such truthfulness exposed the costs of romantic visions and proved too realistic for Americans. In this sense Hawthorne was prophetic when he said in *The House of the Seven Gables* that photography brings "out the secret character" of its subjects "with a truth that no painter would ever venture upon, even could he detect it" (p. 85). Americans were not ready for the "truth" and reality of civil war. Alexander Gardner and George Barnard published beautiful "art books" of the Civil War in 1866. But few people purchased them. And Mathew Brady, the most successful photographer before the war, who became rich and famous from his art, went bankrupt after the war, largely because of the lack of demand for war photographs, on which he had staked everything. Photography was too real for romantic and sentimental sensibilities; it shattered the illusions of a world without sin and contributed to the rise of literary realism.

See also Abolitionist Writing; Art; Civil War;
The House of the Seven Gables; Leaves of Grass;
Technology

BIBLIOGRAPHY

Primary Works
Brooklyn Eagle, 15 September 1855.

Douglass, Frederick. *The Heroic Slave.* 1853. In Ronald T. Takaki, *Violence in the Black Imagination: Essays and Documents.* New York: Oxford University Press, 1993.

Douglass, Frederick. "Pictures." Holograph. n.d. [c. late 1864]. Frederick Douglass Papers, Library of Congress, and on microfilm.

Douglass, Frederick. "Pictures and Progress." 3 December 1861. In *The Frederick Douglass Papers,* series 1, vol. 3, edited by John W. Blassingame. New Haven, Conn.: Yale University Press, 1985.

Fauvel-Gouraud, Francois. *Description of the Daguerreotype Process. . . .* 1840. In *The Daguerreotype Process: Three Treatises, 1840–1849,* edited by Robert A. Sobieszek. New York: Arno Press, 1973.

Goldberg, Vicki, ed. *Photography in Print: Writings from 1816 to the Present.* Albuquerque: University of New Mexico Press, 1981.

Hawthorne, Nathaniel. *The House of the Seven Gables.* 1851. New York: Signet Classic, 1961.

Melville, Herman. *Pierre; or, The Ambiguities.* 1852. Edited by Harrison Hayford, Hershel Parker, and G. Thomas Tanselle. Evanston, Ill.: Northwestern University Press, 1971.

Raab, Jane M., ed. *Literature & Photography: Interactions, 1840–1990.* Albuquerque: University of New Mexico Press, 1995.

Stowe, Harriet Beecher. *Uncle Tom's Cabin; or, Life among the Lowly.* 1852. New York: Penguin, 1986.

Trachtenberg, Alan, ed. *Classic Essays on Photography.* New Haven, Conn.: Leete's Island, 1980.

Whitman, Walt. *Leaves of Grass.* Edited by Sculley Bradley and Harold W. Blodgett. New York: Norton, 1973.

Secondary Works
Anderson, Benedict. *Imagined Communities.* Rev. ed. New York: Verso, 1991.

Banta, Melissa. *A Curious & Ingenious Art: Reflections on Daguerreotypes at Harvard.* Iowa City: University of Iowa Press, 2000.

Folsom, Ed. *Walt Whitman's Native Representations.* New York: Cambridge University Press, 1994.

Orvell, Miles. *The Real Thing: Imitation and Authenticity in American Culture, 1880–1940.* Chapel Hill: University of North Carolina Press, 1989.

Reynolds, David S. *Walt Whitman's America: A Cultural Biography.* New York: Knopf, 1995.

Sandweiss, Martha A., ed. *Photography in Nineteenth-Century America.* New York: H. N. Abrams, 1991.

Sobieszek, Robert A., and Odette M. Appel. *The Daguerreotypes of Southworth & Hawes.* New York: Dover, 1976.

Stauffer, John. *The Black Hearts of Men: Radical Abolitionists and the Transformation of Race.* Cambridge, Mass.: Harvard University Press, 2002.

Stauffer, John. "Daguerreotyping the National Soul: The Portraits of Southworth and Hawes, 1843–1860." *Prospects* 22 (1997): 69–107.

Taft, Robert. *Photography and the American Scene: A Social History, 1839–1889.* New York: Macmillan, 1938.

Trachtenberg, Alan. *Reading American Photographs: Images as History, Mathew Brady to Walker Evans.* New York: Hill and Wang, 1989.

John Stauffer

PICTORIAL WEEKLIES

In the United States, the "weekly" was a paper that even in its earliest forms mixed dry news stories with more sensational ones. In *American Journalism,* Frank Luther Mott describes how the Boston *News-Letter,* established in 1704 by John Campbell, combined news from London with reports of sermons, deaths, abductions, and pirates (pp. 11–12). During the nineteenth century, especially between the 1830s and 1870s, the weekly news format was used in smaller towns and by religious and political organizations. The weekly format was also used throughout the nineteenth century for illustrated story papers, or pictorial weeklies. Some later nineteenth-century weeklies, such as the *New National Era,* an African American weekly edited by Frederick Douglass (1818– 1895) that ran from 1869 to 1875 and was published in Washington, D.C., focused on the political aims of a specific group. The *New National Era* drew from national, religious, and educational news to promote the paper's aim of full civil rights and recognition for African American citizens. Others, like the penny dailies that became popular in the 1830s, mixed news with fiction, gossip, and advertising. They provided cheap reading material for readers across a wide spectrum of age groups and classes.

These illustrated papers specialized in fiction that focused on the grisly and sensational, and serialized stories of suspense and adventure encouraged readers to buy and share the papers each week. New York was the publishing center for many such papers, although Boston and Philadelphia also had their share. The weeklies reported and illustrated sensational news stories, focusing especially on murder and scandal. In the twenty-first century tabloids such as the *National Enquirer* serve similar functions, providing entertainment and occasionally breaking a news story that must then be followed by a more traditional news source. Along with the sensational quality of the material included in the fiction and news of these stories, the illustrations added a significant level of interest. Large engravings attracted readers; they depicted train robberies, racist scenes of Native Americans, and "bodice ripping" images. The sensational images provided the necessary newsstand titillation to coax readers to purchase the entire paper.

Alexis de Tocqueville wrote in *Democracy in America* (1840) that "newspapers make associations, and associations make newspapers" (2:120). Pictorial weeklies associated fiction with news, used news of the Mexican-American war and the California gold rush to craft sensational stories, and drew together readers from working, middle, and upper classes. The papers created reading communities interested in the next episode of a suspenseful serial and used advertising to construct consumers who associated the products with the reading material. Advertisers learned from the powerful illustrations and incorporated illustrations and elements of the daily-life features that were part of the weeklies' stories into the advertising copy. The weeklies' format placed stories and illustrations between advertisements and news, so that readers could immerse themselves in sensational episodes but were also forced to notice the news, human-interest features, and ads surrounding the story on the page. The content of the weeklies informed regionalist writing, dime novels, and the development of realism. An examination of the history and culture surrounding the weeklies provides insights into this popular form's influence on many other aspects of nineteenth-century culture, particularly women's roles in the publishing communities.

WOMEN WRITERS

Louisa May Alcott (1832–1888), best known for her domestic fiction, such as *Little Women* (1868–1869), *An Old Fashioned Girl* (1870), and *Eight Cousins* (1875), was a frequent contributor to pictorial weeklies during the 1860s and 1870s. Her gothic thriller "Behind a Mask" tells the story of Jean Muir, a woman bent on profiting from revenge and deceit. Appearing as a serialized piece for the *Flag of Our Union* in October and November of 1866, it was published under Alcott's pen name A. M. Barnard. Alcott commented on her enjoyment of the sensation story:

> I think my natural ambition is for the lurid style. I indulge in gorgeous fancies and wish that I dared inscribe them upon my pages and set them before the public. . . . How should I dare to interfere with the proper grayness of old Concord? The dear old town has never known a startling hue since the redcoats were there. (Stern, p. xxvi).

In *Little Women,* Jo March contributes to fictitious pictorial weeklies with names like the *Blarneystone Banner* and the *Weekly Volcano,* which are modeled on the kinds of pictorial weeklies Alcott knew from experience. Elliott, Thomes, and Talbot was a publishing firm associated with the *Flag of Our Union,* which possibly served as the model for the *Blarneystone Banner.* William Henry Thomes partnered with James R. Elliott, who had also published the *True Flag.* Newton Talbot, their third partner, helped Thomes and Elliott set up a firm in Boston that produced sensational illustrated materials. The *Flag of Our Union* also published Alcott's "The Abbot's Ghost," a tale about devastating gambling, tragic injury, and mercenary marriages that reveals her wide reading in the English gothic

This lead story from an 1854 edition of the Flag of Our Union, *titled "The Royal Yacht; or, Logan the Warlock" (subtitled "A Revolutionary Romance of Sea and Land Adventure") combines history with fiction; it has dialog and graphic descriptions of violence, all characteristics of fiction published in pictorial weeklies.*

Long since, the summer of 1778 had opened in sunshine and warmth on the American colonies. The British had been moving from post to post, and the Americans had been hanging upon their course and worrying them exceedingly. Yet the cause of freedom in America looked dark and dubious. The onset of the patriots upon their enemy in Rhode Island utterly failed, and their French ally, the Count d'Estaing, was driven with his fleet to seek shelter in the harbor of Boston. On the western frontier a frightful war was carried on by the Indians and British against the peaceful inhabitants, and in this the tories had the leading hand. The terrible massacre of Wyoming shed a dark cloud over the people of the border, and it was the more dreadful from the fact that the bloody butchery was the result of the treachery of tories. One other thing tended to darken the dawn of independence, and that was the frequent dissatisfaction that was manifested among the American soldiers. They had suffered all kinds of privations and hardships, and some of them began to be disheartened. But the cause of freedom was

yet might, and the hearth-stones of Columbia had stout defenders. . . .

"She's a beauty, and no mistake," said Andrew Elliott, addressing young Edgerly. Elliott was the oldest man of the party, having seen some forty years of life, and he was a fair specimen of a Yankee sailor—rather short of stature, but with breadth and thickness of shoulder enough to make it up.

"Ay, Elliott," returned the young man, while his eye sparkled. "She is a beauty. It cost money to put such a craft as that upon the water."

"I guess it did," said another of the party, a man whose name was Caleb Wales, who possessed a frame of extraordinary muscular power, and a face of extraordinary shrewdness. He was a native of Connecticut, and an original genius in his way. "I guess it did," he repeated, with more emphasis. "By the great end of all creation, Ned Edgerly, she's in a very dangerous place."

This last sentence was spoken very slowly, and with a strange tone and manner.

Cobb, *The Royal Yacht*, pp. 9, 10.

tradition and the ways gothic devices lent themselves to the suspense and horror that sold the weeklies. Some of Alcott's sensational stories, like "V. V.; or, Plots and Counterplots," which appeared in the *Flag of Our Union* in 1865, contain significant political and cultural commentary embedded in the suspenseful serial form. "V. V." explores issues of identity—in this case, the branding of initials—to comment on the lasting horrors and inescapable legacies of slavery. Alcott's active participation in the culture of the weeklies offers just one example of a mainstream author who participated privately and profitably in a venue not publicly regarded as appropriate for women.

Many women besides Alcott wrote for the pictorial weeklies. E. D. E. N. Southworth (1819–1899) wrote for the *New York Ledger*, edited by Robert Bonner (1824–1899). The *Ledger* succeeded in part through innovative use of advertising. Bonner sometimes would take out entire columns in daily papers like the *New York Herald* and encourage readers to buy

the *Ledger* in order to read the sensation story. Southworth's novel *The Hidden Hand* was serialized in the *Ledger* in 1859. *The Hidden Hand* features Capitola, a young woman who dresses as a boy, fights duels, and survives dangerous adventures. Bonner's weekly also published the work of Fanny Fern (Sara Payson Willis Parton, 1811–1872). Women who wrote for the weeklies did not focus on domestic angels but wrote about passionate humans who struggled with greed, sought revenge, and pursued sexual gratification. The weeklies and women's magazines—such as the *Ladies' Companion* and *Peterson's Magazine*—that supported many women writers combined local and national news, patterns for fashions, and hair-raising adventures. The weeklies read by women, like *Peterson's*, also provided material for dime novels. Ann Sophia Stephens's *Malaeska: The Indian Wife of the White Hunter*, which was initially serialized in the *Ladies' Companion* in 1839, was published by Erastus Beadle as the first the dime novel in 1860.

"The Dead Alive," which appeared in Frank Leslie's Illustrated Newspaper *in January 1866, is representative of the sensational, dramatic stories that appeared alongside news and illustrations in this pictorial weekly. It suggests the mutability and tenuousness of identity and the drama of sudden changes in fortune. It is unsigned, but the afterword reads, "Reader, this story is true. But its names and dates and places are all false."*

When Maria Graham married Walter Forsythe, everybody said there was little love, save love of lucre, in the match.

Miss Graham was poor and ambitious. Her father had brought her up expensively, and died a bankrupt. She had need of luxury, but was forced to live as a dependent in the house of a distant relative. Walter Forsythe was rich and solitary. Not one of his blood lived to claim tithe of his heart or purse. He had recieved a military education; but inheriting a large fortune from the last of his house, and longing to travel through other lands, he left the army—the less reluctantly that the days were days of peace and idlesse for them of the sword—and went abroad for seven years.

When he returned he met Miss Graham, and, after a brief courtship, wedded her. Then once more he sailed for foreign shores, this time with his proud and beautiful bride.

What manner of life those two led in the brilliant route of the Old World its skills not knowing. But Forsythe, in the second year of his absence, expresses his intention of becoming a subject of France, and, withdrawing his fortune from his native land, invested it in that of his adoption. Another year, and Walter Forsythe was Monsieur Forsythe de Claireau, Claireau being the title of an estate he had purchased in the South of France. Three more years and the "dogs of war" were again let loose on olden battlefields, and Christian and Turk fought side by side, for the first time, on Crimean plains. Forsythe remembered his vocation, and became le Capitain de Claireau, aide-de-camp, voluntaire.

Three "stricken fields" he saw, and on each he left a trail of blood.

Then came Inkerman, and Madame de Claireau was a widow. A widow, without even the sorrowful comfort of seeing her hero husband in death, or weeping over his laurelled grave. Captain Forsythe was torn to pieces by a shell—so said the bulletin—with many others, and their indistinguishable remains committed to the common fosse, with hasty ceremonial. So, Maria Forsythe was a widow, still young, beautiful, childless and sole mistress of a noble fortune.

Frank Leslie's Illustrated Newspaper, 20 January 1866, p. 278.

Pictorial weeklies as well as other kinds of periodicals developed forms of popular literature that in turn supported the growing number of women who wrote professionally. Women contributed regularly to the weeklies, and some women worked on the editing end. Mrs. Frank Leslie (formerly Miriam Florence Squier, 1846–1914), who was an actress and worked as an editor for Frank Leslie before and after she married him, took over his empire after his death. Her life offers one example of how the periodical weeklies, as well as other periodical forms, provided women with opportunities to participate in literary and journalistic publishing cultures.

POLITICAL AND SOCIAL INFLUENCE

In addition to offering publishing venues to women writers and editors, the mixture of articles, fiction, engravings, and advertisements in the pictorial weekly also reflected the complex mixture of fiction and fact that shaped cultural attitudes toward nineteenth-century political issues—abolition, immigration, expansion, citizenship laws, and suffrage. George Lippard (1822–1854), who worked out of Philadelphia, produced the *Quaker City Weekly,* a pictorial paper that placed short stories and serialized novels alongside national and international news. Shelley Streeby has written about how this form "allowed Lippard, for one, to forge a closer connection between his writing and his numerous political and social projects, between his novels and the communities he helped to construct" (p. 187). The weekly form, especially weeklies that combine news, fiction, and advertising, provide fruitful fields of inquiry for understanding how this regularly produced form challenged and reinforced boundaries of class, race, and gender.

ILLUSTRATIONS

Between the 1830s and 1870s a number of technological advances dramatically changed the illustrations included in the weeklies. In the papers of the 1830s steel plates and woodcuts were used to produce illustrations that began as rough sketches approved by the editor. When final sketches were ready, skilled engravers worked painstakingly to reproduce the lines and dramatic energy of the artwork. Developments in photography made it possible to place photographs onto woodblocks directly and to reproduce lines and textures more exactly. While this made it possible to include more detailed illustrations in the weeklies, some critics, including the wood engraver William Linton (1812–1897), argued that the more precise engravings were static and lifeless and that the art of engraving had become merely a technical skill. Some smaller publishers clung to the older techniques, while others embraced the new developments since they allowed more illustrations to be produced with ease and speed. Gerry Beegan explains that Linton encouraged apprentices to remain familiar with the older forms of engraving and spent time in America teaching women wood-engraving techniques (p. 273). More scholarship about women's roles as engravers is certainly warranted, and further study about the connections between women's art and writing should produce interesting lines of inquiry about the pictorial weekly as a form shaped by women.

One of the most powerful influences on the pictorial weekly form in the United States was Frank Leslie (1821–1880). He worked on weeklies such as *Gleason's Pictorial and Drawing-Room Companion* and was the producer of many pictorial papers, including *Frank Leslie's Illustrated Weekly, Frank Leslie's Lady's Magazine,* and *Frank Leslie's Illustrated Newspaper.* He solicited contributions from writers like Alcott who devoted most of their time to more "respectable" venues, and he helped them to make money by publishing anonymously or pseudonymously in the weeklies. A gifted engraver who used his understanding of engraving technologies to improve the speed of his production process, Leslie's illustrations gave the pictorials he worked on immediate appeal. He carefully selected staff members who understood the significance of the illustrations and could produce images that would provide the necessary dramatic interest to sell papers. In some cases, double-page illustrations dominated the text of the paper, drawing attention to murders, scalpings, and seductions that made up only a small part of the episodes.

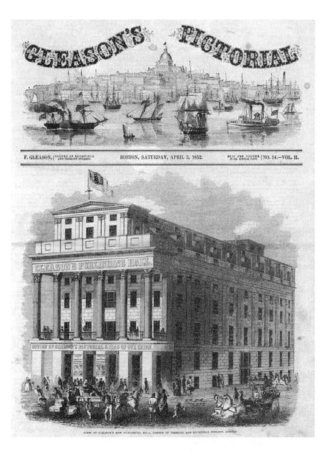

Cover of *Gleason's Pictorial,* 2 April 1852, showing Gleason's Publishing Hall in Boston. © CORBIS

PICTORIAL PAPERS FOR CHILDREN

Leslie's empire also produced a number of pictorial papers for children, including *Frank Leslie's Boy's and Girl's Weekly* beginning in 1867. Although not all pictorial weeklies were designed for children, many children read these pictorials avidly, enjoying the stories of sudden fame and fortune, suspense, murder, and intrigue that filled their pages. Edward J. Jennerich writes that in *Frank Leslie's Boy's and Girl's Weekly* the sensationalism was tempered: "maidens were pursued, but they were not caught and defiled by dastardly villains; chivalry and manly behavior were not dead in its pages" (p. 164). This softening of the violence suggests how Leslie's understanding of the readership and the market helped him to build a successful empire.

The readers of these papers were literate members of the working class, but others read them as well, including members of the middle and upper classes and writers fascinated by the gothic, sensational aspects of these papers. Articles in children's magazines criticized the pictorial weeklies for their addictive qualities, for their tendency to develop a taste for the sensational. On the other hand, magazines such as the very didactic weekly *Youth's Companion* drew from what was popular in the pictorial weeklies and included dramatic engravings of fights with animals and travel adventures. Mary Mapes Dodge's (1830–1905) monthly magazine for children, *St. Nicholas,* included many illustrations but carefully avoided anything that hinted of the sensational weekly. Michael S. Joseph notes that in her editorial criticisms of illustrations for Mark Twain's serialization of *Tom Sawyer Abroad* (which began in November 1893), Dodge insisted that the bare feet be covered, since it was possible that they were too "vulgar." Both children and adults enjoyed the illustrations in weeklies designed for children, and children also enjoyed the illustrations in comic weeklies such as *Puck* and *Judge* that began in the 1870s and 1880s and ran into the twentieth century. Illustrations in the comic weeklies took up double-page spreads and made use of color, drawing in readers with both size and subject matter.

Clearly the illustrated format of these papers had an important effect on magazines published for both adults and children. There are direct relationships between the tabloid press of the twenty-first century and the exciting stories of danger illustrated in the nineteenth-century weeklies. To argue, as some do, that present-day "news" has suddenly descended into the realm of the sensational is to neglect important aspects of journalistic history. Sensational tales and images have played significant roles in defining citizenship and in creating reading communities that relied on the regularity of the weeklies to reinforce political and cultural belief systems. The pictorial weeklies reveal that U.S. readers have long been fascinated by the murderous, the erotic, and the sensational. The fictional and pictorial elements are interwoven with political and cultural issues, showing how periodical forms intervened in constructions of attitudes about Americanness, class, gender, and race in the nineteenth century.

See also Art; Book and Periodical Illustration; Dime Novels; Female Authorship; Gothic Fiction; Literary Marketplace; Periodicals; Sensational Fiction

BIBLIOGRAPHY
Primary Works
Cobb, Sylvanus. *The Royal Yacht; or, Logan the Warlock.* New York: S. French, 185?.

Linton, William. *Wood-Engraving: A Manual of Instruction.* G. Bell and Sons, 1884.

Tocqueville, Alexis de. *Democracy in America.* Vol. 2. 1840. New York: Vintage, 1945.

Secondary Works
Beegan, Gerry. "The Mechanization of the Image: Facsimile, Photography, and Fragmentation in Nineteenth-Century Wood Engraving." *Journal of Design History* 8, no. 4 (1995): 257–274.

Jennerich, Edward J. "Frank Leslie's Boy's and Girl's Weekly." In *Children's Periodicals of the United States,* edited by R. Gordon Kelly, pp. 161–165. Westport, Conn.: Greenwood Press, 1984.

Joseph, Michael S. "Illustrating *St. Nicholas* and the Influence of Mary Mapes Dodge." In *St. Nicholas and Mary Mapes Dodge: The Legacy of a Children's Magazine Editor, 1873–1905,* edited by Susan R. Gannon, Suzanne Rahn, and Ruth Anne Thompson. Jefferson, N.C.: MacFarland, 2004.

Mott, Frank Luther. *American Journalism.* Rev. ed. New York: Macmillan, 1950.

Mott, Frank Luther. *A History of American Magazines.* Vol. 2, *1850–1865.* Cambridge, Mass.: Harvard University Press, 1957.

Stern, Madeleine. "Introduction." In *Behind a Mask: The Unknown Thrillers of Louisa May Alcott,* edited by Madeleine Stern. New York: William Morrow, 1975.

Streeby, Shelley. "Opening Up the Story Paper: George Lippard and the Construction of Class." *boundary 2* 24 (spring 1997): 177–203.

Lorinda B. Cohoon

THE PIONEERS

See Leatherstocking Tales

"PLYMOUTH ROCK ORATION"

The citizens of Massachusetts in 1820 knew themselves to be the fortunate heirs of history. They had survived interminable battles with indigenous peoples, fought for and won independence, and helped establish the foundations of republican government. Recent years, however, had been less than kind: a constitutional crisis had rocked those foundations, financial panic threatened to undermine the economic vitality of the region, and the shadows of slavery were darkening the national landscape. Now was the ideal time, then, to remind Bay Staters of their storied past and to brighten the prospects ahead. The bicentennial celebration of the Pilgrims' landing at Plymouth Rock would serve these purposes well, and no one was better suited to provide its keynote address than Daniel Webster.

THE ORATION IN CONTEXT

Born in New Hampshire of modest circumstances, Daniel Webster (1782–1852) moved to Boston in 1816, where he launched a public career of remarkable success in law, politics, and civic leadership. In an era known as the "golden age of oratory," Webster stood without peer as a spokesman for American nationalism. A Federalist by party affiliation, he provided eloquent testimony to America's unique station in the world; an adopted son of Massachusetts, he was especially proud of the Bay State's distinctive place in the annals of freedom. Webster was therefore the logical choice to speak before a crowd of fifteen hundred assembled in Plymouth's First Parish Church on 22 December 1820 for a public anniversary celebration of the Pilgrims' landing. So electrifying was the effect that one observer feared that "blood might gush from my temples" (Peterson, p. 107). Upon reading the address afterward, John Adams declared that it "ought to be read at the end of every century, and read at the end of every year, for ever and ever" (Peterson, p. 107). In the early twenty-first century the "Plymouth Rock Oration" remains, as Merrill Peterson has written, "a literary classic, long celebrated for its soul-stirring passages, recited by generations of schoolboys, and cherished as a primer of New England principle" (p. 107).

How to account for the power of Webster's words? The occasion itself was scarcely novel: Plymouth Rock celebrations dated back to 1769. The oration's general themes—courage, freedom, endurance, pride, hope—were certainly familiar to generations of New Englanders as the stuff of civic ceremony. Perhaps it is enough to say that Webster lent to these commonplaces a singular force of imagery and expression and gave to them a degree of artistry seldom accorded public declamations. Underwriting all of this was an unshakable conviction that the Pilgrim past, the Massachusetts present, and the American future were united in a single destiny. The rhetorical work of the speech is thus devoted to strengthening that conviction in its listeners, to assure them that they were actors in a sacred myth of human progress. A brief review of the oration will illustrate Webster's rendition of this story.

TIME AND PLACE IN THE TEXT

The address is organized, as tradition dictates, with reference to past, present, and future. At the same time Webster is careful to not to allow these temporal planes to remain mere abstractions. Rather, he stresses the immediate and concrete experience of occupying a place sanctified by the presence of New England's forefathers. "There is," he announces,

> a local feeling connected with this occasion, too strong to be resisted; a sort of genius of the place, which inspires and awes us. We feel that we are on the spot where the first scene of our country was laid; where the hearths and altars of New England were first placed; where Christianity, and civilization, and letters made their first lodgement, in a vast extent of country, covered with a wilderness, and peopled by roving barbarians. (P. 67)

This conjunction of place and origins is key to the overall meaning and force of the speech: it gives to lived experience a ground, source, and direction that will superintend the unfolding message. Webster says, in effect, that here is not just any place or any people coughed up on foreign shores: this is, rather, sacred ground to which the present generation owes obeisance. The identification of the present with the past is further cemented by the duty not only to acknowledge but also to be emotionally invested in a collective legacy. Thus "we have come to this Rock," Webster notes, "to record here our homage for our Pilgrim Fathers; our sympathy in their sufferings; our gratitude for their labors; our admiration of their virtues; our veneration for their piety; and our attachment to those principles of civil and religious liberty" (p. 66).

The present generation is thus tied to the past as in a covenant. Chief among the principles that command mutual assent, Webster observes, are those relating to free and equal access to property under a republican form of government. Here the speaker's Federalist sentiments are revealed; but more broadly

In the oration, Webster addresses the question of slavery by folding it within the foundational myth already established.

It is not fit that the land of the Pilgrims should bear the shame longer. I hear the sound of the hammer, I see the smoke of the furnaces where manacles and fetters are still forged for human limbs. I see the visages of those who by stealth and at midnight labor in this work of hell, foul and dark, as may become the artificers of such instruments of torture. Let that spot be purified, or let it cease to be of New England.

Webster, *The Speeches of Daniel Webster*, p. 113.

understood, Webster's point is that property under such conditions represents a kind of shared investment in the land that will stabilize and give permanence to the collective trust. "There is a natural influence belonging to property," Webster argues,

> whether it exists in many hands or few; and it is on the rights of property that both despotism and unrestrained popular violence ordinarily commence their attacks. Our ancestors began their system of government here under a condition of comparative equality in regard to wealth, and their early laws were of a nature to favor and continue this equality. (P. 100)

The generic expectations associated with ceremonial speaking do not typically include explicit reference to political issues. Webster, however, seizes on this conspicuous occasion to address the volatile question of slavery in a fashion that manages at once to attack the benighted system of slavery and to make such an attack consistent with the hallowed principles of New England's legacy. Such a legacy, Webster understood, could not be limited to the past alone. Indeed the full rhetorical force of his oration cannot be realized until its message is extended to future generations. Looking now ahead to those who will come after the efforts of this day, Webster assures his audience that

> when, from the long distance of a hundred years, they shall look back upon us, they shall know, at least, that we possessed affections, which, running backward and warming with gratitude for what our ancestors have done for our happiness, run forward also to our posterity, and meet them with cordial salutation, ere yet they have arrived on the shore of being. (P. 118)

Webster's "Plymouth Rock Oration" stands as a classic example of nationalist rhetoric, in which local pride of place and time animates a universal vision of America's unique past, present, and future. The story it tells has been told many times since but never more eloquently.

See also Oratory; Puritanism; Rhetoric

BIBLIOGRAPHY
Primary Work
Webster, Daniel. *The Speeches of Daniel Webster.* Edited by B. F. Tefft. New York: Lincoln Centenary, 1907.

Secondary Works
Browne, Stephen H. "Reading Public Memory in Daniel Webster's Plymouth Rock Oration." *Western Journal of Communication* 57 (1993): 464–477.

Erickson, Paul D. "Daniel Webster's Myth of the Puritans." *New England Quarterly* 57 (1984): 44–64.

Peterson, Merrill. *The Great Triumvirate: Webster, Clay, and Calhoun.* New York: Oxford University Press, 1987.

Stephen Howard Browne

POEMS OF EMILY DICKINSON

The most persistent image of Emily Dickinson (1830–1886) is that of the recluse, a woman whose creative endeavors were so hidden that even her sister Lavinia was taken aback by the amount of poems (currently estimated at 1,789) discovered shortly after her death. Like most myths, that of Dickinson as a recluse lacks subtlety but still has some truth to it. Biographical evidence shows that Dickinson stopped attending church and other public events in her twenties; after two enforced stays in Cambridge, Massachusetts, for eye treatment (in 1864 and 1865), she never again left the family house on Main Street, Amherst, and became extremely selective about receiving visitors. And her obituary (by her sister-in-law Susan Dickinson, thought to have known her better than most) acknowledged this domesticity as a willed arrangement, rather than something enforced by her father, caused by romantic disappointment, or resulting from mental distress—the three most common and erroneous explanations for her gradual withdrawal from civic life.

Such intense privacy makes Emily Dickinson's relation to history an oblique one: three other factors obscure it even further. First, Dickinson wrote lyrics, and though her earliest editors are often criticized for organizing her poems according to imposed categories (life, love, nature, and time and eternity), Dickinson often took as her subject areas of experience (is there more "than Love and Death?" she asked in L873; citations prefaced by "L" are to letter numbers in *The Letters of Emily Dickinson*) that she deemed to be essential, universal, and not culture dependent. Second, it is not always easy to reconstruct even the basic sense (who is speaking, what is being said) of some of Dickinson's best poems: there is a great deal of grammatical irregularity; standard punctuation is largely replaced by the dash; nouns and verbs are sometimes used interchangeably; normal syntax is often disrupted; and in addition to verbal play and innovation there are references to events that seem to derive from Dickinson's private history—events that are difficult and occasionally impossible to recover. Third, only ten of Dickinson's lyrics were printed, anonymously, in her lifetime, and there is no clear evidence that any appeared with her consent: unpublished poems intervene less directly in nineteenth-century concerns such as the abolition of slavery or the future of Native Americans than do, say, topical novels on these themes such as (respectively) Harriet Beecher Stowe's *Uncle Tom's Cabin* (1852) or Helen Hunt Jackson's *Ramona* (1884).

Viewing history through the lens of Emily Dickinson entails a shift of focus: instead of systematic commentary on catastrophic events such as the Civil War, for example, one sees that she composed hundreds of poems from 1862 to 1865, more than at any other period in her life. Such a sustained and massive loss of life (in one battle, 23,000 men died) clearly affected her, but otherwise the war was treated in a variety of ways: directly and specifically in a few poems (P518 "When I was small, a Woman died" and P524 "It feels a shame to be Alive," both from 1863; citations prefaced by "P" are to poem numbers in *The Poems of Emily Dickinson*), but also more obliquely in phrases such as "Uniforms of snow" (P138) and "Bodiless Campaign" (P629). At still another remove is her contesting what is meant by terms such as "Liberty" (P524 again), "Defeat," and "Victory" (P704). Dickinson's characteristic procedure in such lyrics is to privatize, redirecting attention to inner conflicts (between faith and skepticism, for instance) or contrasting acts of military bravery with less visible struggles for meaning in the face of loss and death (as in P1325, "I never hear that one is dead"), in order to assert that individual lives were often wracked by pressures that were equally dramatic and worth recording.

Dickinson's fractured grammar and obscurity can also be read (though not solely) in ways that are inflected by developments in nineteenth-century America. If grammar derives from a belief in an ordered and rational universe, then it follows that its dislocation may be attributed in part to a breakdown of those certainties—either passively (through a weakening of faith in the ideology of American progress occasioned by the Civil War, for example) or actively (as a desire to produce new forms of writing that are appropriate to an American identity that was still very much in the process of definition).

Even Dickinson's celebrated isolation can be linked to nineteenth-century experiments in alternative lifestyles: Dickinson too wrote about herself, about nature, and about God (or his absence), but unlike Henry David Thoreau (in *Walden*, 1854) or Nathaniel Hawthorne (in *The Blithedale Romance*, 1852), she did so without publicity. Indeed, with Dickinson we need to adjust our equation of publication with the circulation of printed texts. Martha Nell Smith was the first to argue that Dickinson's habits of enclosing manuscript poems in letters, and sometimes *as* letters, to family,

friends, neighbors, and strangers is significant: that five to six hundred poems were distributed this way reveals a profoundly social aspect to her aesthetic practice. And Dickinson did not confine herself to poetry. Those letters that survived number over a thousand, and her correspondents were often nationally eminent (including the newspaper owner and editor Samuel Bowles; the novelist Helen Hunt Jackson; Otis Lord, judge of the Massachusetts Supreme Judicial Court; and Thomas Wentworth Higginson, a New England abolitionist and man of letters).

DISTINCTIVE ELEMENTS OF THE WRITING

A number of features in Dickinson's work are unusual by the standards of poetry written in her day—among them the primacy given to the dash and the habit of capitalizing nouns. She might have learned the latter in part at school: capitalizing nouns was a feature of the German she studied. But it also serves to suggest that a word is being deployed in a figurative or symbolic way or in ways that may include an everyday meaning but that gesture simultaneously in other directions. The dash is more complicated: letter and journal writers in the nineteenth century commonly used it instead of formal punctuation, and some authors (Sarah Fielding among them) wrote in the expectation that professionals would replace their dashes with more exact punctuation at a later stage in the process of editing and typesetting. But interpretations of the dash are mediated by aspects of Dickinson's biography. Some scholars feel that because Dickinson did not publish she did not have to be careful about her punctuation; others argue that Dickinson refused publication on the grounds that her use of the dash—a free and improvisational form of phrasing—would be compromised by inflexible standards in the publishing industry. Still others say that because the dashes in Dickinson's handwritten originals vary in length and angle, they are equivalent to elocutionary accents that direct how her work is to be read (with a falling dash suggesting pathos or sadness, for instance).

A noticeable feature in some poems is the powerful first line: P764, "My Life had stood – a loaded Gun"; P479, "Because I could not stop for Death"; and P591, "I heard a Fly buzz – when I died" are among the best known. Some seem directly challenging: P260, "I'm Nobody! Who are you?" and P401, "Dare you see a Soul at the 'White Heat'?" for instance. At one level, such openings can be understood as a rhetorical technique, designed to capture attention. But there are equally startling lines in other poems that do not appear only at the start, and there is evidence for supposing that they reflect a belief in how language—and not just poetry—works. A common denominator in some of Dickinson's most positive instances of reading or listening is a rendering of the experience in physical or elemental language—a propensity she shared with Susan Dickinson, who wrote of a variant of P124 "Safe in their Alabaster Chambers" that it was "remarkable as the chain lightening . . . I always go to the fire and get warm after thinking of it, but I never can again" (note to L238). As Alfred Habegger points out, Susan's image of the lightning was repeated in P348, where the speaker longs for "the Art to stun myself / With Bolts - of Melody!" And note what seems close to admiration in the following (P477):

> He fumbles at your Soul
> As Players at the Keys
> Before they drop full Music on –
> He stuns you by degrees –
> Prepares your brittle nature
> For the Etherial Blow
> By fainter Hammers – further heard –
> Then nearer – Then so slow
> Your Breath has time to straighten
> Your Brain – to bubble Cool –
> Deals – One – imperial – Thunderbolt –
> That scalps your naked Soul –
>
> When Winds hold Forests in their Paws –
> The Universe – is still –

The poem not only reports an experience; it seeks to reenact it through forceful, even violent, imagery, and through a perfect control of rhythm—which is why there are four dashes in line 11, preceded by mid-line dashes in lines 7, 8, and 10, delaying the movement of the verse at the same time as there is a delay in the process being described. (This is even more successfully realized in a later copy, P477B, where there are three dashes in line 8, followed by mid-line dashes in lines 9, 10, and 11.) This is a poetic, then—a statement of how language of any kind, successfully delivered, works on the reader. The scalping of the soul, and the references to shifting temperatures, tally with a statement attributed to Dickinson by her friend and correspondent Thomas Wentworth Higginson: "If I read a book [and] it makes my whole body so cold no fire can ever warm me I know that is poetry. If I feel physically as if the top of my head were taken off, I know that is poetry" (L342a).

RELIGIOUS INFLUENCES

Though what is being described here can be almost anything—sexual, literary, religious, even natural (dictionary definitions of "thunderbolt" include both lightning and the act of vehement censure or ecclesiastical denunciation)—it was certainly not unusual for nineteenth-century sermons to be composed, and responded to, in similar ways. In *The New England Mind,* Perry Miller likened one strain of preaching to "holy violence in the pulpit" (p. 301) and quoted a comparison between the start of a sermon and the opening bars of a piece of music. The speaker of P477 meshes both sets of metaphor: the "Hammers" in line 7 may take up the image of piano music established by the reference to "Keys" in the first stanza, but they are also tools capable of dealing a blow to the body (and of opening it up).

Dickinson seems to have learned a great deal from pulpit effectiveness: Charles Wadsworth (1814–1882), a Dickinson correspondent and celebrated preacher, made a lasting impression for this reason. Richard Sewall notes that "He fumbles at your Soul" might have been about Wadsworth, who twice visited the poet, but goes on to point out that Dickinson "had heard other great preachers and had been 'scalped' by them" (Sewall 2:450–451). Edwards Amasa Park (1808–1900), perhaps the leading theologian of his day, was one of them. In a letter to her brother Austin, Dickinson enthused about a sermon on Judas delivered by Park at Amherst's First Church on 20 November 1853: "I never heard anything like it, and dont expect to again, till we stand at the great white throne. . . . And when it was all over, and that wonderful man sat down, people stared at each other, and looked as wan and wild, as if they had seen a spirit" (L142). Park is useful because many of his directions on verbal usage are similar to Dickinson's description of the unnamed event in P477: if a sermon were to "merely charm the ear like a placid song," he argued, "it is not the identical essence which is likened to the fire and the hammer" (p. 95). The idea that successful oratory and writing somehow bypass the rational brain—but not the imagination or the affections—in order to strike home links Dickinson's view of language to nineteenth-century linguistic theories, especially those of Horace Bushnell and Park himself, who was associated with a theology of the feelings (the phrase derives from his lecture to a convention of Congregational ministers in Boston on 30 May 1850) that rejected a rational, scientific, approach to religious discourse—and especially to the Bible. Dickinson clearly agreed: in "The Bible is an antique Volume" (P1577), her speaker says that the best interpreter is the "warbling Teller"—the one who "captivates" through the spell of musical and poetic language. And Wadsworth wrote, "We are . . . killing the bird of heaven, that we may measure the tension of its muscle, and detect the secret of its fine mechanism" (p. 7). In P905, one of Dickinson's lyric selves adopted the image:

> Split the Lark – and you'll find the Music –
> Bulb after Bulb, in Silver rolled –

Silhouette of the Dickinson family visiting Emily (second from right) at Mount Holyoke Female Seminary, 1848. Dickinson attended the seminary for one year but was unable to profess the Christian sentiments taught there.
THE GRANGER COLLECTION, NEW YORK

Scantily dealt to the Summer Morning
Saved for your Ear, when Lutes be old –

Loose the Flood – you shall find it patent –
Gush after Gush, reserved for you –
Scarlet Experiment! Sceptic Thomas!
Now, do you doubt that your Bird was true?

Drawing attention to similarities between Wadsworth and Dickinson is not meant as a rehearsal of biographical speculations or—more properly—as an attribution of influence: it is simply a way of drawing attention to the fact that even the most apparently private of her poems may relate in significant ways to nineteenth-century codes, ideas or values that a reader in the twenty-first century may not always be aware of. Her use of meter and rhyme are a case in point. Dickinson's most common stanza is a four-line unit rhyming *abcb* and alternating between four and three beats, a quatrain that she inherited from the kinds of hymns featured in Isaac Watts's *Hymns and Spiritual Songs* (1707–1709). The significance of such borrowing has repeatedly been understood as embodying her opposition to religious or patriarchal orthodoxy. Certainly, it *may* represent a rejection of communal certainties, but it may also represent exactly the opposite—an alignment with a tradition of belief and a desire to continue that tradition in vibrant ways. By extension, modern readers often and mistakenly assume that hymn forms were static and limited; however, there were multiple combinations of meter and stanza, and about half of the rhymes in Watts are false. To interpret Dickinson's own looseness in rhyming as an implicit critique of the norms and values of established Christianity, as these are embodied in hymn forms, would therefore seem historically naive.

SCIENCE, RELIGION, AND CULTURE

The social aspects of Dickinson's writing emerge from beneath its surfaces in the contexts of the words that she chose, for her vocabulary is saturated with terms derived from the cultural, ethnic, political, religious, and scientific issues of her day. For example, a contemporary reader of Dickinson's poems on butterflies and bees is easily lulled into seeing such scenes as sites of refuge. But nature in the nineteenth century was no longer an arena for pastoral retreat: Charles Darwin wrote about the same topics, as did scientists more local to Amherst—most important, Edward Hitchcock (1793–1864), professor of chemistry and natural history at Amherst College, and for ten years its president. Observing the life of plants and insects was one way in which nineteenth-century individuals attempted to fathom meaning or design in the lives of the world's species—explorations that were often seen as having implications for issues of race, class and forms of social behavior, organization and purpose. Even the title of Darwin's 1862 *On the Various Contrivances by Which British and Foreign Orchids Are Fertilized by Insects, and on the Good Effects of Intercrossing* can be viewed as having implications beyond its immediate subject matter—implications that also provide interesting contexts for Dickinson's many poems about flowers and their unregulated relations with bees.

Dickinson mentions Darwin twice in her letters, but he is not referred to by name in the poems. To Mrs. Elizabeth Holland, she regrets not having had a chance to part with her in private, then moves to a more abstract meditation on departures in general (acute loss or absence being a familiar preoccupation): "Why the Thief ingredient accompanies all Sweetness Darwin does not tell us" (L359). Whether the target here is Darwin in person or Darwin as a representative of science as a whole is unclear, but the message seems fairly unambiguous: even the most assured or arrogant of knowledge systems cannot penetrate all of the mysteries of human existence. And in a later letter, Dickinson reports to Otis Lord that "Mrs Dr Stearns called to know if we did not think it very shocking for [Benjamin F.] Butler to 'liken himself to his Redeemer,' but we thought Darwin had thrown 'the Redeemer' away" (L750). Again, it is not obvious from this remark that Dickinson had read Darwin—who did not actually discuss Christ in *On the Origin of the Species* (1859). Instead, she appears to be relying on conservative formulations of his ideas: this is the man who knows everything and nothing, she seems to suggest in her first remark. That Darwin is dismissed for having discarded the redeemer relates to his argument that human beings had a common and remote ancestry with primates, which undermined the scriptural plot of humans having descended from a single set of parents, who had then sinned, necessitating the intervention of a savior whose death redeemed their sins and allowed for the possibility of eternal life for their descendents.

In the nineteenth century, then, nature was a site about which there were competing claims of ownership and definition. Dickinson's birth and first years in Amherst coincided with the publication in London of Sir Charles Lyell's three-volume *Principles of Geology* (1830, 1832, and 1833), which refuted the traditional Christian view of the earth's formation as a fairly recent and divinely ordained phenomenon. Lyell further negated the idea of a single catastrophic flood that had covered the earth—thus calling into question yet another key element in the scriptural explanation of the world's formation. But many American Christians had already begun to move away from a belief in the literalness of the Bible, and just as many—including Lyell himself—had few problems in adjusting their faith to accommodate apparent advances in scientific thinking. Emily Dickinson's textbook on geology at Amherst Academy was Edward Hitchcock's *Elementary Geology* (1843): in early 1877, she recalled that when "Flowers annually died and I was a child, I used to read Dr Hitchcock's Book on the Flowers of North America. This comforted their Absence—assuring me they lived" (L488). Certainly there is no obvious conflict between scientific observation and the idea of an afterlife here (though "when a child" might signify a distance which is not solely temporal, but also intellectual), and in many of her poems Dickinson used the return of flowers in the spring as an emblem of resurrection. "My Cocoon tightens – Colors teaze" (P1107) is one of several that appears to draw on Hitchcock's writings: an illustration from his *Religious Lectures on Peculiar Phenomena in the Four Seasons* (1850) shows a butterfly emerging from precisely such a cocoon.

Dickinson heard Hitchcock at Mount Holyoke Female Seminary. At Mount Holyoke too she was classified as a "no-hoper" (unable or unwilling publicly to profess an experience of conversion). Perhaps because of that, it is often supposed that Dickinson's sympathies would lie more with science than religion, and though it is possible to find poems and letters that support this view, just as many contradict it. "Too much of Proof affronts Belief," she had a speaker proclaim in P1240: at one level, what she means is that a search for evidence of God's existence is at odds with, and beneath the dignity of, religious explanations of the world and its creation; at another, belief would not mean anything if it were not for uncertainty and doubt. In 1873 Dickinson complained "Science will not trust us with another World," continuing, "Guess I and the Bible will move to some old fashioned spot where we'll feel at Home" (L395). The poem P1641 *G* offers another example:

Though the great waters sleep
That they are still the deep
We cannot doubt.
No vacillating God
Ignited this abode
To put it out.

This is an elegy: four of its (slightly different) seven versions were sent, respectively, to Susan Dickinson (*D:* in a letter on the death of Samuel Bowles); to Dickinson's aunt Catherine Sweetser (*E:* in a letter on the deaths of her father and nephew); to Benjamin Kimball, Otis Lord's executor (*F:* in a letter on Lord's death); and to Abigail Cooper (*G:* perhaps on the death of Edward Tuckerman). "Though the great waters sleep" is therefore a good example of how Dickinson wrote poetry designed to transcend the specific circumstances of its occasion. enfolded physically in a letter to separate recipients, and semantically in the recent emotional history of each, its private relevance is nevertheless a profound and compassionate legerdemain capable of almost endless repetition.

Death, the poem may be construed as saying, obliterates the physical evidence of life represented by a human presence and therefore tests belief in the continuing existence of that person in a nonmaterial form. But our temporary absence from the world at night and in sleep (a conventional metaphor for death) does not prevent us from returning to fuller consciousness when awake: this is an emblem for the hope that death is a similarly illusive and nonpermanent removal. Of course, it is nature rather than human nature that the poet describes, and draws inferences from, here: a calm sea may appear motionless, but its power is simply invisible, and capable quickly of being roused again. In the context of scientific debates about the world's formation in fire or water, it is interesting that Dickinson situates her observations about "great waters" next to an emphatic reassertion of the world's creation by God—in fire. The balance is structurally and ideologically neat: what matters is not whether the world was created in one or the other but that it was *created* and that human beings express their intuition of this momentous truth in dramatic language. Whatever the poem's meaning, its vocabulary shows Dickinson mining a variety of descriptive systems for poetic materials: what attracts is not so much their accuracy as their figurative power. But there is a warning in the poem too. Evidence of a flood may no longer exist, but God's absolute power still remains latent in the ocean depths, and it would be wrong to grow too complacent.

Dickinson's interest in nature can be explained both personally and in relation to her cultural and religious heritage. Her education placed a heavy emphasis on the natural sciences. Though her interest in birds was not always accurate (real birds do not unroll their feathers, unlike the one in P359), she was known among her friends for her detailed knowledge of flora around Amherst, had her own conservatory (from 1855 onward), and compiled an impressive herbarium that survives to this day (it comprises 66 folios, with at least 450 entries). She sent flowers as gifts to friends, sometimes accompanied by poems, which tells us once again how she

took an active but withdrawn part in a local, informal, economy of exchange. Many of her poems are about flowers: understanding them is helped to some extent by familiarity with the language of flowers that nineteenth-century men and women shared, where individual plants were associated with specific human emotions. Though flowers were important elements in middle-class American culture (they were objects of display, indicators of taste), they were also convenient subjects for a consciousness attuned to the frailty, transience, and dignity of human lives.

POLITICS

If the nineteenth century was, in the words of one historian, the age of association, when men and women formed societies against alcoholism, the disenfranchisement of women, illiteracy, slavery, poverty, and prostitution, Emily Dickinson's life and writing were again atypical: "The Soul selects her own Society," she wrote in P409. The words "abolition" and "suffrage" do not appear in her correspondence, and the single deployment of the former in a poem occurs in the context of a typically aristocratic dismissal of the world: "The Soul's Superior instants," we are told, "Occur to Her – Alone" (P630). After declining an appeal for some poems for charity, Dickinson told her young cousins, Miss P (thought to have been Elizabeth Stuart Phelps, editor of the *Woman's Journal*) "did not write to me again—she might have been offended, or perhaps is extricating humanity from some hopeless ditch" (L380). By extension, there are no references to some of the major events of her time: no Seneca Falls women's convention and its Declaration of Sentiments; no references to labor disputes at the factories of Lowell, Massachusetts; no contemplation of death through overcrowding or poor sanitation and hygiene; no attention to ethnic or religious injustices.

Until the late twentieth century, discussions of Dickinson's politics tended toward the supposition of liberal alignment. The long-held view was that Dickinson's life and language embodied ideals of individualism that linked her implicitly with forms of social nonconformity. But some commentators, most notably Betsy Erkkila, have begun to complicate this picture, arguing that the same circumstances of biography and writing provide evidence of sympathies that are rather less than egalitarian. For example, in "I Came to buy a smile – today," Dickinson's speaker makes an offer that she claims would "be 'a Bargain' for a *Jew!*" (P258). And in "The Day came slow – till Five o'clock" (P572), another speaker describes an orchard that "sparkled like a Jew." Dickinson does not distance herself in any obvious way from the anti-Semitic stereotype of the miserly in one poem, or from the acquisitive in the other. But both works were enclosed privately in letters to friends, which suggests a lack of self-consciousness about their deployment—a confidence that such remarks constituted acceptable humor for people from the same ethnic and class background.

Consider the following: "I have just seen a funeral procession go by of a negro baby, so if my ideas are rather dark you need not marvel" (L9) or, likewise,

> We have a new Black Man and are looking for a Philanthropist to direct him, because every time he presents himself, I run, and when the Head of the Nation shies, it confuses the Foot –
>
> When you read in the "Massachusetts items" that he has eaten us up, a memorial merriment will invest these preliminaries. (L721)

These quotations seem undeniably racist: in the last, the man is identified by his color only; Dickinson associates him with the lowest part of the body and herself with the higher mind; and she jokes about him being a cannibal. The laborer is referred to as a "Foot," and such a term derives from a long tradition in conservative thinking whereby parts of the human body were used to illustrate and justify hierarchical relations in society. The head thinks, the foot carries: each has its own function, designed by nature (which is designed in its turn by God). By extension, because the parts of the body were fixed, they supported the argument that the members of the body politic ought similarly to remain in the class to which they were born.

Quotations such as this are nevertheless misleading, for by removing statements from their epistolary and biographical contexts one exaggerates not so much their significance as their *proportion*. What we have here are comments interspersed among approximately one thousand letters and scattered over more than thirty years of writing. The attitudes expressed are unpleasant, but not everyone who repeats stereotypes to close friends would endorse or otherwise promote these seriously. And jokes about Jews or African Americans (or elsewhere about the Irish) do not add up in Dickinson to a program—a coherent and publicly argued political agenda.

If Dickinson occasionally attempted humor at the expense of other races and classes, she was nonetheless equally ironic toward the opponents of progressivism. In 1860 she wrote of the Bell-Everett party that were "they cats I would pull their tails" (L225). She was writing about the candidates for president and vice president of the short-lived Constitutional Union Party, an essentially conservative group willing to compromise on the issue of slavery, and with whom her father was so closely allied that he was nominated

for lieutenant governor of Massachusetts on their ticket. To the same cousins, Louise and Frances, who had read her derision of the charity-minded "Miss P," Dickinson sent a generous message encouraging them to contact Margaret Maher, the Dickinson family servant, whose brother had died in a mining accident: "she does not know I ask it—I think it would help her begin, that bleeding beginning that every mourner knows" (L670). Two years later, in the incomplete fair copy of a letter to Otis Lord, Dickinson reported "Sue sent me a lovely Banquet of Fruit, which I sent to a dying Irish Girl in our neighborhood—That was my Thanksgiving. Those that die seem near me because I lose my own" (L790). Finally, a touching letter from 1880 tells of an "Indian woman with gay Baskets and a dazzling Baby" (L653) whom Dickinson invites into the back garden. This incident, and its extended, fond, recollection, does not fit straightforwardly into any thesis of ethnocentricity prompted by Dickinson's celebrated concern with "whiteness" in her poems, letters, and dress. With Dickinson, we need to be careful: three or four letters or poems will often suggest a rule that a fifth will utterly contradict. And we need to avoid thinking that a statement made in the nineteenth century can easily be equated with a political position in the twenty-first—or indeed that the political views of an individual must add up to a consistent and willed alignment.

As a middle-class woman of European descent, Dickinson was both disenfranchised and privileged: hers was a political identity that is not easily calibrated within conflicts among other forces. Perhaps that it why Dickinson's personae are often assigned the role of the spectator rather than that of the participant. The letter writer who watches from the woods as her father leads a march to celebrate the coming of the railroad to Amherst (L127), for instance, seems very like the lyric speaker who says of the train progressing across New England that she likes "to see it lap the Miles" (P383). Dickinson fails to mention the passengers on those trains, who were not only locals like her brother, coming back from teaching the children of Irish immigrants in Cambridge, Massachusetts, but eventually the Irish immigrants themselves, and other non-Americans, moving west in search of work and land. The forces of industrial technology, of immigration, and of class change can be observed, it seemed, but not checked or controlled, and this tells us a great deal about Dickinson's sense of her own social position: she has the power to witness but not to influence or change.

PUBLICATION HISTORY AND RECEPTION

After Emily Dickinson's death, Lavinia destroyed her sister's correspondence (according to Dickinson's wishes and the practice of the day) and then found close to a thousand manuscript poems in a bedroom chest of drawers. About eight hundred of these were gathered in forty fascicles—manuscript books assembled (for the most part between 1859 and 1865) by the poet from folded sheets of stationery that she sewed together and into which she copied approximately nineteen to twenty poems.

The posthumous appearance of Dickinson's work, with no directions as to its future organization or distribution (if any), has had multiple consequences. To begin with, no single, authoritative, edition of the complete poems appeared until 1955, and because Dickinson did not date her poems or give them titles, they were arranged and numbered by Thomas H. Johnson in a chronological order based on *estimated* dates (derived from changes to the handwriting, and with precedence given to the latest composition, in the case of there being more extant version of a poem). Though Johnson's reconstruction was, and is, a superb scholarly achievement, it was not unproblematic: handwriting changes did occur from year to year, and even within a single year, but are harder to detect in 1863, when Dickinson wrote a poem a day. More seriously, Johnson disarranged the internal order of the fascicles: that twenty poems appeared sequentially in a manuscript book did not mean that they followed each other in 1955. Some scholars believe that these volumes are more than archival, that they have thematic or imagistic connections to each other. And some pursue the idea that the fascicles as a whole constitute a linked narrative—though it is not quite clear if they tell a story of doubt and Christian affirmation, or of secret love, birth, and marriage.

Finally, several of Dickinson's latest interpreters have pointed to a discrepancy between handwritten poems and their printed equivalents. For instance, the first four lines of P1096 (as it is numbered in the latest, and best, of the editions) correspond to six rows of handwriting in Dickinson's second fair copy (version B; the first copy is lost):

A narrow Fellow in
the Grass
Occasionally rides –
You may have met Him –
did you not
His notice sudden is –

and seven rows of handwriting in the third (version C):

A narrow Fellow
in the Grass
Occasionally rides –
You may have
met him?
Did you not
His notice instant is –

The differences between the autographs might appear fairly minor—but the sequence from "You may have" to "not" breaks in different places, and according to manuscript critics, this shows Dickinson varying her lineation visually in order to achieve different effects. Standard printed editions render such experimentation undetectable.

The argument has an additional emotional force for two reasons. First, editions of Dickinson's work that followed her death, in 1890, 1891, and 1896, were amended by Mabel Loomis Todd and Thomas Wentworth Higginson: capitals were discarded; dashes supplemented with or replaced by conventional punctuation; meter, word choice, and rhyme were tidied; and titles were added. (Public interest and critical queries about her "errant form" suggests that such emendations—however distorting, egregious, and unsanctioned—may have been a necessary stage in preparing a nineteenth-century readership for her unconventional voice). Second, "A narrow fellow in the grass" was one of the ten poems published in Dickinson's lifetime: the sequence under discussion ("You . . . not") was printed as one line but followed by a question mark (a mistake repeated by the poet's niece in her premature *Complete Poems* of 1924). Shortly afterward, Dickinson complained to Higginson: "Lest you meet my Snake and suppose I deceive it was robbed of me—defeated too of the third line by the punctuation. The third and fourth were one" (L316). For many readers (especially those who read P519, "This is my letter to the World," as autobiography), this explains why Dickinson did not publish. Because the literary market refused her formal innovations, she left her materials to a more flexible posterity.

Fascinatingly, Dickinson refers to "You . . . not" as the "third" line, whereas the cumulative evidence of her manuscripts suggests that her handwriting would have taken up more space (and in the extant copies, this line occupies two and three rows). Granted, Dickinson's comments to Higginson refer to the published version of the poem, but even so it is interesting that she does not contest the *lineation;* rather, she contests a specific change to the *punctuation* at a particular point that robbed her of a meaningful connection between the lines. In addition, note that Dickinson begins certain rows in upper, and others in lower case: if she were truly experimenting with *graphic* alternatives to line and stanza, it would seem inconsistent to continue with the convention whereby the start of a *metrically* defined line was signaled by a capital. All of this suggests that the lineation in her manuscripts is not literal: in this case, Dickinson thought of the two rows of handwriting (in version B) and the three rows (in C) as the same *metrical* line of poetry.

Often overlooked in Dickinson's remarks to Higginson is her concern with deceit: having previously informed him of an aversion to publication, she now hastens to let him know that the poem appeared without permission. That desire to protect her privacy and reputation brings us back full circle to the Dickinson myth, but in fact it relates to changes in the status of the nineteenth-century writer. Washington Irving and Henry James (both writing about Shakespeare's birthplace) have amusing things to say about the public fascination with the author's private life. Dickinson was caught up in this cult of personality: she recommended biographies of her favorite novelists (Emily Brontë and George Eliot among them), had portraits of authors on her bedroom wall, and read about them in newspapers. But as a writer, she shunned attention that she could not control, celebrated being "Nobody" (P260) in an age when increasing value was attached to being somebody, and disparaged the publicity and fame associated with a media that, because of advances in the technologies of printing, communication, and transport, had a growing influence in literary culture. "The only news I know," she claimed in P820, "Is Bulletins all Day / From Immortality." Still, it remains for us to check her sources.

See also Individualism and Community; Death; Ethnology; Letters; Lyric Poetry; Nature; Political Parties; Religion; Science

BIBLIOGRAPHY

Primary Works

Dickinson, Emily. *The Letters of Emily Dickinson*. 3 vols. Edited by Thomas H. Johnson and Theodora Ward. Cambridge, Mass.: Belknap Press of Harvard University Press, 1958. Citation by letter number, prefixed by "L."

Dickinson, Emily. *The Poems of Emily Dickinson*. 3 vols. Edited by R. W. Franklin. Cambridge, Mass.: Belknap Press of Harvard University Press, 1998. Citation by poem number, prefixed by "P."

Wadsworth, Charles. *Sermons by Charles Wadsworth, D. D.* New York: Eagle Book and Job Printing Department, 1905.

Secondary Works

Errkila, Betsy. "Dickinson and Class." *American Literary History* 4, no. 1 (1992): 1–27.

Habegger, Alfred. *My Wars Are Laid Away in Books: The Life of Emily Dickinson*. New York: Random House, 2001.

Juhasz, Suzanne. "Materiality and the Poet." In *The Emily Dickinson Handbook*, edited by Gudrun Grabher, Roland Hagenbüchle, and Cristanne Miller, pp. 427–439. Amherst: University of Massachusetts Press, 1998.

Leyda, Jay. *The Years and Hours of Emily Dickinson*. 2 vols. New Haven, Conn.: Yale University Press, 1960.

Miller, Cristanne. *Emily Dickinson: A Poet's Grammar*. Cambridge, Mass.: Harvard University Press, 1987.

Miller, Perry. *The New England Mind*. 1939. Cambridge, Mass.: Belknap Press of Harvard University Press, 1963.

Park, Edwards Amasa. *Memorial Collection of Sermons*. Boston and Chicago: Pilgrim Press, 1902.

Sewall, Richard B. *The Life of Emily Dickinson*. 2 vols. New York: Farrar, Straus and Giroux, 1974.

Smith, Martha Nell. *Rowing in Eden: Rereading Emily Dickinson*. Austin: University of Texas Press, 1992.

St. Armand, Barton Levi. *Emily Dickinson and Her Culture: The Soul's Society*. Cambridge, U.K.: Cambridge University Press, 1984.

Wolosky, Shira. *Emily Dickinson: A Voice of War*. New Haven, Conn.: Yale University Press, 1984.

Domhnall Mitchell

"THE POET"

Poets and poetry were always of central importance to Ralph Waldo Emerson (1803–1882), as evidenced not only by the large quantity of his published and unpublished verse but also by the way in which he defined his vocation. As he wrote to his wife in 1842, "I am in all my theory, ethics, & politics a poet" (*Letters* 3:18). Even this remark suggests, however, that what he meant by "poet" exceeds what the term ordinarily denotes. This surplus defines his essay "The Poet," driving its discussion well beyond the bounds of poetry itself, which signifies to Emerson less a set of literary practices than a particular way of being in the world. One of Emerson's best-known, most-reprinted essays, "The Poet" (1844) is often invoked as a key statement of that loose American Romantic movement known as transcendentalism, as a landmark document for American poetry and criticism, and as a useful window on Emerson's own ideas and style. He worked on this essay slowly and repeatedly, even into the month it first appeared in *Essays: Second Series* (1844). By this time, the forty-one-year-old author had already solidified his place as one of the young nation's leading cultural voices. "The Poet" is well known for its grand declarations but like most of Emerson's writing is not reducible to easy formulas, for it includes an element of rhetorical extravagance that makes his work both a delight and a stumbling block for readers.

The essay begins with a literary focus, as Emerson tries to position the reader against "esteemed umpires

Ralph Waldo Emerson, c. late 1830s. © BETTMANN/CORBIS

of taste" who shrink poetry to little more than an effete, leisure pursuit comparable to a garden party. While he suggests that such poetry is good merely "for amusement or for show," perhaps worst of all it is so "civil and conformed" as to keep both writers and their readers "at a safe distance from their experience" (*Collected Works* 3:3, 6). In contrast to this inauthentic poetry, and to the malaise of which it is a symptom, Emerson points to a "true poetry" that is an essential philosophical, quasi-religious pursuit in which all of humanity has an urgent and fundamental stake. The rest of the essay is an exposition of this true poetry and its importance, a discussion that ripples outward in widening circles. Emerson's exposition is relatively clear and voices what may be familiar Romantic preoccupations, but readers in the twenty-first century may find it excessive or even strange.

THE POET OF THE SOUL

Emerson's underlying claim is that experience has a spiritual dimension that poetry can reveal. "Spiritual," however, is an elusive term in Emerson because his thinking combines eclectic elements of a deep Protestant inwardness with versions of Platonic and Neoplatonic idealism and post-Kantian epistemology, among other things. In his 1836 book *Nature,* which made

Emerson the unofficial spokesperson for transcendentalism, he had asserted that only an "unrenewed understanding" could believe the materialist idea that "things are ultimates"; on the contrary, "natural facts" are really "symbols of . . . spiritual facts," and "the whole of nature is a metaphor of the human mind" (*Collected Works* 1:30, 17, 21).

His discussion of spirituality in "The Poet" similarly refers to the "essential dependence of the material world on thought and volition," an imbroglio of mind and matter that makes nature a mirror in which people glimpse their own power (*Collected Works* 3:3). The poet is specially equipped as the "interpreter" of this metaphysical and moral lesson, expressing what is most central to people as persons, not only their share in the beauty reflected in nature but also their share in the creative power that made it. In one of the essay's more memorable passages, he says that "we are not pans and barrows, nor even porters" who carry around a portion of the divine "fire"; instead, the "hidden truth" is that people are "children of the fire, made of it, and only the same divinity transmuted, and at two or three removes" (*Collected Works* 3:3–4). It is the ultimate empowering message: the world should not be seen as a set of binding facts but as a malleable, ongoing creation in which all can potentially play a part.

This aspect of "The Poet" exemplifies the American transcendentalism that it helped to create. As described, for example, in O. B. Frothingham's classic early analysis of the movement, its hallmarks include both a theoretical assertion of "the immanence of divinity in instinct," which transfers "supernatural attributes to human nature," and a practical assertion of the "inalienable worth of man" and a keen sense of "the unmet capacities" of humankind (pp. 136, 143, 153). The poet, says Emerson, helps people outgrow the status of "minors, who have not yet come into possession of their own" (*Collected Works* 3:4). Emerson tries to reveal to a world of exiled princes their unsuspected transcendental heritage. In addition to aligning human creativity with universal creative power, he extends this birthright to everyone—the poet is "representative" (*Collected Works* 3:4).

This premise of unclaimed power leads Emerson to provide two seemingly conflicting descriptions of poets and poetry in the essay. One portrait is consistently ecstatic and relies on idealist and mythical associations to elevate the poet to extravagant heights. The poet is cast as a "sovereign," an "emperor," even a "liberating god" (*Collected Works* 3:5). Yet in other descriptions, Emerson presents an oppositional figure without public power, an outcast who "is isolated among his contemporaries, by truth and by his art"

CREATIVE POWER AND "ORGANIC FORM"

Emerson's emphasis on organic form entailed a freedom for poets to resist the normative constraints of received literary form in order for the poem to take the shape of the unique intuition that occasions it, and it is through intuition that consciousness taps the universal creative power. He often uses nature as a model for human creativity.

Come see the north wind's masonry.
Out of an unseen quarry evermore
Furnished with tile, the fierce artificer
Curves his white bastions with projected roof
Round every windward stake, or tree, or door.
Speeding, the myriad-handed, his wild work
So fanciful, so savage, nought cares he
For number of proportion.

Emerson, "The Snow-Storm," lines 10–17, in *Collected Poems*, p. 34.

(*Collected Works* 3:4), and he ends the essay by exhorting the American poet to turn his or her back on the world and its affairs. This alienation was a recurrent Emersonian theme, versified, for example, in his poem "Woodnotes I": "hard / Is the fortune of the bard"; "With none has he to do, / And none seek him"; a "Planter of celestial plants, / What he knows nobody wants" (*Collected Poems*, p. 35). The two contrasting descriptions are complementary, however. Insisting on the poet's higher truth and status comes in response to the lessening importance of poetry in an increasingly industrial age, and it is part polemic and part compensation. The alienated poet stands aside from the marketplace of commodities and defends alternative, humanizing values.

EMERSON'S ROMANTIC HERITAGE

Emerson's rendition of the poet's powers and vocation lie squarely in the Romantic mainstream. He echoes Percy Bysshe Shelley's assertion in "A Defence of Poetry" (1821) that because the true poet is "the hierophant of an unapprehended inspiration," poets are the "unacknowledged legislators of the world" (pp. 35–36). He follows Samuel Taylor Coleridge and William Wordsworth in distinguishing between the metaphysically potent "Imagination" and the mundane "fancy." There are also Blakean moments in which he defines

one's inability to grasp his or her own profound power as a spiritual blindness that threatens to confine one in a blank Ulro: "If any phenomenon remains brute and dark," Emerson says, "it is because the corresponding faculty in the observer is not yet active" (*Collected Works* 3:9). The poet's task is to awaken the sleepers who do not see that all of creation, down to the most quotidian, participates in beauty and divinity.

"The Poet" is most indebted to Wordsworth, however. Emerson's philosophical version of spirituality, the foundation for what he calls poetry's "metre-making argument," is a close cousin to the "high argument" that Wordsworth had offered in his 1814 preface to "The Excursion":

how exquisitely the individual Mind
. . . .
. . . to the external World
Is fitted:—and how exquisitely, too—
. . . .
The external world is fitted to the Mind
And the creation . . .
. . . which they when blended might
Accomplish:—this is our high argument.

(P. 590)

Wordsworth also considered nature the touchstone and clearly saw the poet and society as estranged. The opening of Emerson's "The Poet" echoes closely Wordsworth's impatience in his famous *Preface to Lyrical Ballads* with those "who talk of Poetry as of a matter of amusement and idle pleasure; who will converse with us gravely about a *taste* for poetry" the way they would "a taste for rope-dancing, or Frontiniac or Sherry" (p. 737). Emerson, though in some ways disappointed by Wordsworth, often expressed the highest praise for him, especially his clear allegiance to a poetic vocation that was at odds with dominant cultural values.

The social and political implications of such ideas about poetry were clear to Emerson, and in this, too, he shows his Romantic pedigree. Wordsworth, William Blake, and their contemporaries had assumed that the American and French Revolutions had initiated a march toward universal justice and happiness. Like his transatlantic predecessors, Emerson saw the poet's oppositional function as part of a wider social critique and saw poetry as a potential aid to renovating both the individual consciousness and an American nation steeped in the "cant of materialism" (*Collected Works* 3:17). Frothingham recognized that the transcendentalist is "by nature a reformer," a fact underestimated by many subsequent critics (p. 153). Emerson turns the bookish idea that poets are divine messengers into the electric statement that everyone, however latently, shares in world-shaping insight and power. This is a democratizing idea that he advances in several ways in

DEFINING THE POET

Emerson defined the poet as one who understands the symbolic nature of reality but always extended this gift to humanity as a whole as its essential, defining characteristic.

The schools of poets, and philosophers, are not more intoxicated with their symbols, than the populace with theirs. . . . Some stars, lilies, leopards, a crescent, a lion, an eagle, or other figure, which came into credit God knows how, on an old rag of bunting, blowing in the wind, on a fort, at the ends of the earth, shall make the blood tingle. . . . The people fancy they hate poetry, and they are all poets and mystics!

Emerson, "The Poet," in *Collected Works* 3:10.

the essay: through his opening analogy between effete classes and inauthenticity in poetry and in life; with the idea of the poet as representative human; and in his promotion, later on, of the nobility of the common classes and their experience. His essay "The American Scholar" (1837) is more direct on this last point, invoking Goethe, Wordsworth, and others as the vanguard of a new day in which

> the same movement which effected the elevation of what was called the lowest class in the state, assumed in literature a very marked and as benign an aspect. Instead of the sublime and beautiful; the near, the low, the common, was explored and poetized. . . . The literature of the poor, the feelings of the child, the philosophy of the street, the meaning of household life, are the topics of the time. It is a great stride. (*Collected Works* 1:67–68)

Raymond Williams notes that modern readers, schooled in what he calls the "dissociation" of literature and politics, may fail to appreciate the continuous or "interlocking" nature of Romantic aesthetic and social concerns (p. 30). In "The Poet," Emerson declares: "Words and deeds are quite indifferent modes of the divine energy. Words are also actions, and actions are a kind of words" (*Collected Works* 3:6). Emerson's poetic and social commitments, including his eventually impassioned involvement in abolition, were of a piece with his Romantic sense of renovation and democratization.

"THE POET" AND AMERICAN LITERARY INDEPENDENCE

Emerson gives this Romantic sense of liberation an American twist and literary focus in "The Poet" that helped to charter a distinctively American poetry. He exhorts writers to focus on the common realities of the American experience, which he catalogs as "our logrolling, our stumps and their politics, our fisheries, our Negroes, and Indians, our boasts, and our repudiations, the wrath of rogues, and the pusillanimity of honest men, the northern trade, the southern planting, the western clearing, Oregon, and Texas" (*Collected Works* 3:22). These are elements of American life that his audience would not have expected, or necessarily wanted, to see as a literary subject, but he elevates their dignity by putting them in a literary frame, asserting that they appear "flat and dull" only to "dull people." For Emerson, history begins with what one takes hold of in the present, and American life, he says, rests "on the same foundations of wonder as the town of Troy, and the temple of Delphos, and are as swiftly passing away" (*Collected Works* 3:21–22). Yet he also despairs of the current state of American letters, famously lamenting, "We have yet had no genius in America, with tyrannous eye, which knew the value of our incomparable materials" (*Collected Works* 3:21–22).

This nativism was meant to break American writers and readers from their ingrained habit of deferring to English and European culture as their yardstick; it was also meant to encourage them to make and appreciate art derived from their own unprecedented circumstances. In the 1840s, despite a decades-old promotion of literary nationalism, cultural deference to England was still the rule, and a relative lack of interest in American writers remained. As Emerson complained to Thomas Carlyle, almost every English book ends up reproduced cheaply in some fashion in America and sold by the hundreds in American streets. Even American writers, who had trouble making a living as literary professionals, focused largely on English or European settings and themes as their proper subjects. His words were a strong tonic for a nascent American literature and helped the country take another decisive step forward in its postcolonial cultural independence from England.

Emerson's essay helped break American poetry away from its transatlantic inheritance in matters of form and style as well as setting and content. Wordsworth's famous *Preface* had opposed the strictures of neoclassical aesthetics by insisting that poetry should use something like "the real language of men" instead of highly stylized diction and severely fixed forms (like heroic couplets), and like other Romantics he favored organic metaphors to describe the creative

EMERSON'S CALL FOR AN AMERICAN BARD

In an era in which America chronically looked to Britain and Europe as the proper sources for literary culture, Emerson's essay threw down the gauntlet to American writers and readers, challenging them recognize the American scene as a unique and rich source of poetic material. His call for an American bard fired the imagination especially of Walt Whitman.

I look in vain for the poet whom I describe. We do not, with sufficient plainness, or sufficient profoundness, address ourselves to life, nor dare we chaunt our own times and social circumstance. . . . America is a poem in our eyes; its ample geography dazzles the imagination, and it will not wait long for metres.

Emerson, "The Poet," in *Collected Works* 3:21–22.

process (p. 739). Emerson, however, pushes these renovations a step further. Just as he thought the material world should be reenvisioned as the malleable, changeable form taken by the creative imagination, he thought the form of a given poem should conform to the particular intuition it embodied. In "The Poet" he turns a cold shoulder to those mired in the "study of rules and particulars," preferring the true poet whose "expression is organic" (*Collected Works* 3:3, 14). Emerson called for a poetry that springs from "a thought so passionate and alive, that, like the spirit of a plant or an animal, it has an architecture of its own, and adorns nature with a new thing" (*Collected Works* 3:6). This idea is typically referred to as Emerson's poetics of organic form, so named after a similar distinction made by Coleridge. Emerson elaborates this organicism vividly in his own poems, for example "The Problem," "The Snow-Storm," "Merlin," and "Uriel." As a stylistic corollary, he dismisses the "trivial harp" of conventional poetry and asks the poet to

smite the chords rudely and hard,
As with hammer or with mace:
That they may render back
Artful thunder, which conveys
Secrets of the solar track.

(Collected Poems, p. 91)

EMERSON'S POETIC LEGACY

Despite such radical pronouncements, Emerson's own verse form was usually fairly conventional, though not always, especially in his unpublished manuscript verse. His poetics was in many ways the opposite of that espoused by his American contemporary Edgar Allan Poe (1809–1849), whose 1846 "The Philosophy of Composition" presented a more mechanical approach to creativity, based less on intuition than on self-consciously methodical contrivance. Poe thought the "so called poetry of the so called transcendentalists" to be flat and prosaic (p. 32); Emerson thought Poe's approach yielded poetry that earned him the name "the jingle-man" (Howells, p. 58). Many later American poets, unlike Poe, took Emerson as their guide, and the demands made in "The Poet"—a poetry of local materials and organic form—are his primary legacy to American poetry. They simultaneously defied much of the poetry produced in both England and America up to that point; declared, in an era of expanding material wealth and national power, that the poetic imagination should be considered central to human activity; and gave future American poets a new starting point for thinking about their vocation and craft. Most often mentioned as the poet who answered Emerson's call for a peculiarly American genius is Walt Whitman (1819–1892), who seemed self-consciously to enact the Emersonian script, especially in his poetry's democratic cataloging of Americana contained in his poetry and its free-verse forms and colloquial style. His organically titled 1855 *Leaves of Grass,* especially its preface, often reads like a translation of "The Poet" and "The American Scholar," and Whitman termed Emerson his "dear Master" and "original true Captain" (p. 1336). An Emersonian sensibility surfaces also in Emily Dickinson's verse experiments and in a variety of later poets like Robert Frost, Wallace Stevens, Hart Crane, Robinson Jeffers, Charles Olson, William Carlos Williams, and John Ashbery.

While his insistence on organic form and local materials was crucial to American poetic history, a subtler and less-remarked claim that Emerson makes in "The Poet" was equally important, and it also helps counterbalance the idealist and mystical extremes for which the essay is typically remembered. Emerson's poetics has often been described, because of this essay and others like it, as a form of divination, a theory of creativity based upon "the fusion of the human soul with the Divine," as one influential study put it in 1951 (Hopkins, p. 17). Yet while he seems to promote the dream of a perfect language and to gesture beyond human experience to a transcendental realm that the true poet unlocks, ultimately Emerson places the power and liberating function of poetry on a much less

THE EMERSONIAN INFLUENCE

Emerson insisted on the "transitive" and symbolic nature of language as the source of poetry's ability to liberate its readers; this idea also liberated American poetry and, along with his corollary emphasis on "organic form," was a potent influence on twentieth-century poets.

For all symbols are fluxional; all language is vehicular and transitive, and is good, as ferries and horses are, for conveyance, not as farms and houses are, for homestead. Mysticism consists in the mistake of an accidental and individual symbol for an universal one.

Emerson, "The Poet," in *Collected Works* 3:20.

Platonic foundation. Later poets also imbibed from him the notion that the strength of poetic language rests not simply upon its symbolic and metaphoric function but also on what he called the "accidency and fugacity of the symbol" (*Collected Works* 3:12), which entails a restless imperfection that is built into language itself. This issue is perhaps best approached through another of Emerson's apparently contradictory descriptions of poets and poetry in this essay.

On one hand, Emerson paradoxically links the creativity and authority of the poet to passive inspiration. He describes the true poet's task as overhearing in nature a divine conversation that can then be reported to everyone else, and he uses the phrase "abandonment to the nature of things" to describe a receptive self-surrender that is needed. The poet, in this view, is no artisan who succeeds by virtue of "industry and skill in metre" but a seer who lets the "ethereal tides . . . roll and circulate through him" (*Collected Works* 3:6, 16). He compares the poet's dependence on his unwilled intuitions to a lost traveler on horseback who must throw the reins on the neck of his horse and trust it to find the right path (*Collected Works* 3:6, 15–16, 3). This kind of description is one reason why "The Poet" is often cited as evidence of Emerson's mystical or Platonic definition of the poet and poetry.

Yet alongside this emphasis on passive inspiration is the more skeptical idea that the poet and language always fail as messengers of divinity. Emerson acknowledges that poems are always "a corrupt version."

"We lose," he says, "ever and anon a word, or a verse, and substitute something of our own, and thus miswrite the poem." People's "transcripts" of divine truth are always "imperfect" (*Collected Works* 3:15, 6). Words, he says in *Nature*, are only "finite organs" that "break, chop, and impoverish" truth (*Collected Works* 1:28). This second, more skeptical emphasis lies at the heart of the essay, for it links Emerson's insistence on the malleable nature of the world to his ideas about language. In "The Poet" Emerson takes great pains to portray the world as a "flowing or metamorphosis" and the poet as the person adept in the "manifold meaning of every sensuous fact" and in the symbolic resources of language. Poetry is a better guide to life than mysticism or religious doctrine, which attempt to "nail" language to a single transcendent truth that words can supposedly reveal. But for Emerson, all truths eventually become a "prison"; symbols are necessarily "fluxional," partial, and temporary. Literature, therefore, is most useful for "stimulating us through its tropes," not for offering final revelations (*Collected Works* 3:4–5, 18–20). Poetry helps people skate more successfully on the surfaces of experience, an ability he calls (in the essay "Experience" [1844]) "the true art of life" (*Collected Works* 3:35). This is a side of Emerson that appeals to neo-pragmatist readers.

Failure to be the perfect Platonic poet, whose word encompasses the ideal, turns out not to be a failure at all. Emerson ultimately anchors the poet's power in the ability to ride upon the "fugacity of the symbol" toward successive redescriptions of experience that disclose new angles of vision. This is another important Emersonian legacy to American poetry, echoed for example in Frost's "Education by Poetry" and Stevens's *The Necessary Angel*. The poet's ability to free people from their received and habitual ways of seeing is perhaps the best context for understanding Emerson's description of poets as "liberating gods" and agents of "liberation" and "emancipation." This claim need not be taken solely in aesthetic terms because dislodging received truths is also the essence of reform. A malleable world is a reformable world.

EXTRAVAGANCE: EMERSON'S RHETORIC AND STYLE

The contradiction between the passive, divinely inspired seer and the maker who shapes a contingent, protean language is not resolved in this essay, nor elsewhere in Emerson for that matter. The issue of passivity is especially interesting because in other texts, and even in his own habits of composition, he makes clear that writing requires strenuous effort and a "multitude of trials and a thousand rejections" (*Early Lectures* 1:317–318). It is important to consider why such discrepancies would be allowed to stand. In fact the polarities often found in Emerson's essays are rhetorically strategic, and the extravagant transcendental claims he makes in "The Poet" should be understood in this light.

One limited context to keep in mind is how the essay functions within the book that contains it. "The Poet" is a companion piece to the essay immediately following in *Essays: Second Series*, "Experience," another key Emerson text. Published (like "The Poet") shortly after the tragic death of his seven-year-old son Waldo, "Experience" is considered Emerson's great ode to dejection, a reference to Romantic writing that expresses spiritual exhaustion in the face of a world grown hostile, empty, and flat. In that essay readers glimpse a darker Emerson who asks, "Where do we find ourselves?" and who gives the discouraging answer that "we glide through nature" feeling homeless, "ghost-like," and enslaved to "the lords of life" (*Collected Works* 3:27, 25, 23). The underlying theme of "The Poet," on the other hand, is liberation and power, and its controlling tone is one of exhortation. It offers a contrasting declaration of human power and transcendence that one critic aptly refers to as an "almost manic optimism" (Rossi, p. 132). These two essays should be seen as halves of a single temperament and single purpose, each an exaggerated Emersonian mood that attempts to highlight a side of the human situation.

But perhaps the larger and more important context for readers is that exhortation and exaggeration are stylistic and rhetorical elements common in Emerson's writing overall. Readers who are tone deaf to Emerson's extravagance are likely to turn some of his statements against him as evidence of philosophical or ideological naïveté, or worse. The history of Emerson criticism is marked by what Michael Lopez calls an "anti-Emerson" tradition that has been fueled in part by such misunderstandings. Emerson states in "The Poet" that the poet's goal is "announcement and affirming," and his essay "Art" (1841) says the artist's is to "exhilarate, . . . awakening in the beholder the . . . sense of universal relation and power" (*Collected Works* 3:8; 2:215). These are Emerson's goals in "The Poet." He does not rely on naturalistic descriptions of poets and poetry to achieve them, however. Instead, he uses provocative overstatement, presenting idealized poets, poetry, and poetic authority to awaken in his audience a sense of their dormant powers. Emerson says that any "strong performance" requires "a little fanaticism," and certainly his essays are performances (*Emerson in Concord*, p. 95). "The Poet" provides a good example of an essay in which Emerson uses his stylistic and rhetorical tools to follow the counsel he gave in "The American Scholar": "The office of the scholar is to cheer, to raise, and to guide" (*Collected Works* 1:62).

See also "The American Scholar"; Literary Criticism; "The Philosophy of Composition"; Romanticism; Transcendentalism

BIBLIOGRAPHY

Primary Works

Emerson, Edward Waldo. *Emerson in Concord: A Memoir.* Boston: Houghton Mifflin, 1889.

Emerson, Ralph Waldo. *Collected Poems and Translations.* Edited by Harold Bloom and Paul Kane. New York: Library of America, 1994.

Emerson, Ralph Waldo. *The Collected Works of Ralph Waldo Emerson.* 6 vols. Edited by Robert Ernest Spiller, Alfred Riggs Ferguson, Joseph Slater, and Jean Ferguson Carr. Cambridge, Mass.: Harvard University Press, 1971–.

Emerson, Ralph Waldo. *Early Lectures of Ralph Waldo Emerson.* 3 vols. Edited by Stephen Whicher, Robert Spiller, and Wallace Williams. Cambridge, Mass.: Harvard University Press, 1959–1972.

Emerson, Ralph Waldo. *The Letters of Ralph Waldo Emerson.* 10 vols. Edited by Ralph L. Rusk and Eleanor M. Tilton. New York: Columbia University Press, 1939, 1990–1995.

Emerson, Ralph Waldo. *The Poetry Notebooks of Ralph Waldo Emerson.* Edited by Ralph H. Orth, Albert J. von Frank, Linda Allardt, and David W. Hill. Columbia: University of Missouri Press, 1986.

Howells, William Dean. *Literary Friends and Acquaintances.* 1900. Edited by William F. Hiatt and Edwin H. Cady. Bloomington: Indiana University Press, 1968.

Poe, Edgar Allan. "The Philosophy of Composition." 1846. In *Literary Criticism of Edgar Allan Poe*, edited by Robert L. Hough, pp. 20–32. Lincoln: University of Nebraska Press, 1965.

Shelley, Percy Bysshe. "A Defence of Poetry." 1821. In *Shelley's Critical Prose*, edited by Bruce R. McElderry Jr., pp. 3–36. Lincoln: University of Nebraska Press, 1967.

Whitman, Walt. *Complete Poetry and Collected Prose.* New York: Library of America, 1982.

Wordsworth, William. *Wordsworth: Poetical Works.* Edited by Thomas Hutchinson, revised by Ernest de Selincourt. New York: Oxford University Press, 1975.

Secondary Works

Blasing, Mutlu K. *American Poetry: The Rhetoric of Its Forms.* New Haven, Conn.: Yale University Press, 1987.

Ellison, Julie K. *Emerson's Romantic Style.* Princeton, N.J.: Princeton University Press, 1984.

Fredman, Stephen. *The Grounding of American Poetry: Charles Olson and the Emersonian Tradition.* New York: Cambridge University Press, 1993.

Frothingham, Octavius Brooks. *Transcendentalism in New England: A History.* 1876. Gloucester, Mass.: Peter Smith, 1965.

Gelpi, Albert. *The Tenth Muse: The Psyche of the American Poet*. Cambridge, Mass.: Harvard University Press, 1975.

Gougeon, Len. *Virtue's Hero: Emerson, Antislavery, and Reform*. Athens: University of Georgia Press, 1990.

Hopkins, Vivian Constance. *Spires of Form: A Study of Emerson's Aesthetic Theory*. Cambridge, Mass.: Harvard University Press, 1951.

Levin, Jonathan. *The Poetics of Transition: Emerson, Pragmatism, and American Literary Modernism*. Durham, N.C.: Duke University Press, 1999.

Lopez, Michael. *Emerson and Power: Creative Antagonism in the Nineteenth Century*. DeKalb: Northern Illinois University Press, 1996.

Loving, Jerome. *Whitman, Emerson, and the American Muse*. Chapel Hill: University of North Carolina Press, 1982.

Packer, Barbara L. *Emerson's Fall: A New Interpretation of the Major Essays*. New York: Continuum, 1982.

Pearce, Roy Harvey. *The Continuity of American Poetry*. Princeton, N.J.: Princeton University Press, 1961.

Poirier, Richard. *Poetry and Pragmatism*. Cambridge, Mass.: Harvard University Press, 1992.

Poirier, Richard. *The Renewal of Literature: Emersonian Reflections*. New York: Random House, 1987.

Porter, David. *Emerson and Literary Change*. Cambridge, Mass.: Harvard University Press, 1978.

Rossi, William. "Emerson, Nature, and Natural Science." In *A Historical Guide to Ralph Waldo Emerson*, edited by Joel Myerson, pp. 101–150. New York: Oxford University Press, 2000.

Von Frank, Albert J. *The Trials of Anthony Burns: Freedom and Slavery in Emerson's Boston*. Cambridge, Mass.: Harvard University Press, 1998.

Waggoner, Hyatt H. *Emerson as Poet*. Princeton, N.J.: Princeton University Press, 1974.

Williams, Raymond. *Culture and Society, 1780–1950*. New York: Harper and Row, 1966.

Yoder, R. A. *Emerson and the Orphic Poet in America*. Berkeley: University of California Press, 1978.

Joseph M. Thomas

POLITICAL PARTIES

By 1820 American politics had entered "The Era of Good Feelings," a time when divisive party politics seemed a thing of the past. From 1808 to 1824 the Democratic-Republican Party of Thomas Jefferson, James Madison, and James Monroe swept aside the Federalist Party of George Washington and John Adams in a series of lopsided electoral triumphs, concluding with Monroe's 231-1 victory in the electoral college in 1820. Such harmony soon ended. In the election of 1824 four Democratic-Republican candidates received electoral votes, with none achieving the constitutionally required majority. The contest was thrown into the House of Representatives, which elected John Quincy Adams (1767–1848) despite the fact that he finished second to Andrew Jackson (1767–1845) in the electoral college. The era of good feelings was over and a long period of party division and realignment had begun. Between 1820 and 1870 four different parties held the White House; a major second party (the Whigs) was born, matured, and died; several short-lived minority parties were formed; and the Republican Party was founded and developed into the chief rival of the Democrats. The era ended with the now-familiar two-party system firmly in place, shaping American politics and elections for the century ahead.

Most antebellum American authors grew up in a period of political disarray that made party affiliations fleeting and party labels imprecise indicators of actual ideology. These years were among the most politically unstable in America's history, with party alignments shifting rapidly, old parties splitting into competing factions, new parties arising almost overnight, and other parties coming to great power only to crumble in the next election or two. Local politics often trumped national issues, further complicating the picture in such rapidly changing states as New York, Pennsylvania, Massachusetts, Michigan, Wisconsin, Texas, and Illinois. Westward expansion, European immigration, and a rapidly expanding franchise created an electorate with unpredictable values and desires. Between 1824 and 1828 the popular vote for president more than tripled; it doubled again by 1840. Only 350,000 people voted for president in 1824; almost 6.5 million voted in 1872. This was, as many historians have noted, the "golden age" of democracy, when forces came into play that empowered individuals politically as never before. Mass demonstrations, torchlight parades, and party platforms, slogans, and symbols all developed during this period, creating the trappings of the modern American political campaign. At the same time, however, many Americans opposed the rising tide of democracy and formed parties designed to restrict voting rights and keep political power from the masses, particularly women, African Americans, recent immigrants, and Roman Catholics. As debate over the extension of slavery into the western territories increased, parties fractured along sectional lines that in 1860 led to a second presidential election with four candidates winning electoral votes. It took the Civil War to consolidate the

U.S. presidencies/vice presidencies and party affiliations, 1817–1877

Year(s)	President/Vice President	Political party
1817–1825	James Monroe/Daniel Tompkins	Democratic-Republican
1825–1829	John Quincy Adams/John C. Calhoun	Democratic Republican
1829–1837	Andrew Jackson/John C. Calhoun and Martin Van Buren	Democrat
1837–1841	Martin Van Buren/Richard Johnson	Democrat
1841	William H. Harrison/John Tyler	Whig
1841–1845	John Tyler	Whig
1845–1849	James K. Polk/George Dallas	Democrat
1849–1850	Zachary Taylor/Millard Fillmore	Whig
1850–1853	Millard Fillmore	Whig
1853–1857	Franklin Pierce/William King	Democrat
1857–1861	James Buchanan/John Breckinridge	Democrat
1861–1865	Abraham Lincoln/Hannibal Hamlin and Andrew Johnson	Republican
1865–1869	Andrew Johnson	Democrat
1869–1877	Ulysses S. Grant/Schuyler Colfax	Republican

country into the largely Republican Northeast and Midwest and the Democratic "Solid South," a regional divide that lasted until 1964.

THE FOUR MAJOR PARTIES

Historians have identified four major parties during this period: Democrats, Whigs, Americans (or "Know-Nothings"), and Republicans. In addition, a number of minor parties fielded presidential candidates: the National Republican Party of John Quincy Adams and Henry Clay from 1828 to 1836, the Anti-Masonic Party in 1832 and 1836, the Liberty Party from 1840 to 1848, and the Free-Soil Party from 1848 to 1856. Most minor parties originated in a faction within a previous party, but some were cobbled together from various patriotic associations and local political groups. The basic issues that divided them were the extent of federal power over the states, the extension of slavery into new states and territories, and ethnocultural issues such as immigration and the rise of Roman Catholic political power. The major parties contained members with divergent views on these issues, making the parties highly unstable coalitions of competing interests. The minor parties, however, represented narrow ideological or sectional interests that limited their appeal and led either to their demise, as with the National Republicans, or their absorption into one of the major parties. As they disintegrated, the Anti-Masons gravitated toward the Know-Nothings and Whigs, while the antislavery Liberty and Free-Soil Parties coalesced into the Republican Party.

The Democratic Party grew out of the 1824 election that split the Democratic-Republican Party into the Adams and Jackson wings. After the House of Representatives elected Adams, he formed the National Republicans to counter Jackson's Democrats. In 1828 Jackson soundly defeated Adams, ushering in an era when Democrats won six of the next eight presidential elections and controlled nearly every congressional session until 1859. As the self-styled "party of the common man," the Democratic Party exercised great strength in the South, on the frontier, and among working-class citizens in cities. As the latter group became increasingly immigrant, Irish, and Roman Catholic, Democrats found themselves representing constituencies that helped them in the populous Northeast but alienated them from the Protestant South. The party remained unified around the slavery issue, however, for both northern workers and southern farmers felt threatened by the prospect of free African American labor. This coalition held until the annexation of Texas as a slave state (1845), the Mexican-American War (1846–1848), and the Wilmot Proviso (1846) to exclude slavery from territories acquired in the war split the party into the antislavery Barnburners and the proslavery Hunkers. Many Barnburners supported the Free-Soil ticket of Martin Van Buren in 1848, which received 10 percent of the popular vote. By the 1850s a rising tide of antislavery sentiment fueled by the Fugitive Slave Law (1850) and the *Dred Scott* decision (1856) combined with anti-Catholic sentiment to drive many former Democrats out of the party, either toward Free-Soilers or Know-Nothings. By 1860 the Democratic coalition was as shattered as it had been in 1824, and when it fielded two presidential candidates—Stephen A. Douglas from the North and John C. Breckinridge from the South—it virtually assured the election of Abraham Lincoln.

The Whig Party arose from the ashes of Adams's National Republican party in the late 1820s and adopted its official name in 1834. For the next twenty years it constituted the primary opposition to the Jacksonian Democrats. It was a major national party and from 1836 on fielded presidential candidates who rivaled the Democrats for broad support. Whigs won narrow victories in the presidential elections of 1840 and 1848 with the war heroes William Henry Harrison (1773–1841) and Zachary Taylor (1784–1850) and also won short-lived majorities in the Senate. They defined themselves largely by their opposition to Jackson and his policy of a strong executive but had difficulty maintaining party cohesion. John Tyler (1790–1862), Harrison's vice president, assumed the presidency when the old general died after one month in office and was read out of the party when, like a Jacksonian Democrat, he vetoed bills to establish a national bank. Fundamentally conservative, Whigs included an unholy coalition of states' righters, New England Congregationalists, wealthy merchants, small businessmen, high-tariff protectionists, western frontiersman, and temperance advocates. Despite their two presidential victories, the Whigs enjoyed only one congressional majority (1841–1843) and, like the Democrats, split over slavery. Many "Conscience Whigs" defected to Van Buren's Free-Soil ticket in 1848, whereas proslavery "Cotton Whigs" supported Taylor. Senator Daniel Webster (1782–1852) of Massachusetts, along with Senator Henry Clay (1777–1852) of Kentucky, repeatedly compromised with the "slave power" in order to maintain the Union. But when they supported the Compromise of 1850 that forced northerners to return fugitive slaves to their masters, Whigs lost their last shred of antislavery support. They nominated another war hero, Winfield Scott (1786–1866), for president in 1852, but he lost badly in the electoral college to the Democrat Franklin Pierce (1804–1869), and the party disappeared from the national scene by 1855.

The American Party was popularly known as the "Know-Nothings" because their members, when asked about their party affiliation, were supposed to say "I know nothing." This response reveals the party's origins in a mix of secret, nativist, Protestant societies during the 1830s, including the Anti-Masonic Party of the early 1830s and the American Republican Party that allied with the Whigs in 1844. In the late 1840s these movements united under the American Party banner and advocated severe restrictions on Catholics and immigrants, such as a twenty-one-year naturalization period. As the Whigs disintegrated during the 1850s the Know-Nothings gained strength among southern Whigs, poorer classes who felt threatened by immigration, and Protestants fearful of Roman Catholic political power. From 1855 to 1859 the party elected several U.S. senators, and in 1854 it won 347 out of 350 seats in the Massachusetts legislature. In 1856 Millard Fillmore ran for president on the American Party ticket and won eight electoral votes and over 20 percent of the popular vote. Like the Whigs and the Democrats, the Know-Nothings split

An Available Candidate. This cartoon concerning the presidential election of 1848 criticizes the lack of credentials of Whig candidate Zachary Taylor, whose career up to that point had been confined to the military sphere. THE LIBRARY OF CONGRESS

over slavery, primarily the Kansas-Nebraska Act of 1854 that allowed voters in the territories to determine whether to legalize slavery. Although they did not last long on the political scene, the Know-Nothings offered a home for several strongly held and often reactionary minority positions, won numerous local and state elections, delayed the formation of the Republican Party, and helped bring about the dissolution of the Whigs.

The Republican Party developed from the growing opposition to slavery evident in the major parties and the unwillingness of Democrats or Whigs to take a firm stand on controversial issues. In 1856, spurred by the fighting over slavery in "Bleeding Kansas," a coalition of Free-Soilers, Conscience Whigs, Barnburner Democrats, and northern Know-Nothings nominated John C. Frémont (1813–1890) for president on the Republican ticket. He won an astonishing 114 electoral votes to Democrat James Buchanan's

(1791–1868) 174, demonstrating that a major party had arisen to challenge Democratic hegemony. The vacillations of Pierce and Buchanan on the slavery issue and the rising crisis of sectionalism split the Democrats in the 1860 election and paved the way for Lincoln, who won a four-way race for president with 40 percent of the popular vote but a clear majority in the electoral college. With a series of overwhelming victories in the House and Senate as well as the Executive Office, Republicans consolidated their power during and after the Civil War to become the majority party for the next fifty years.

AUTHORSHIP AND PARTY POLITICS

The rapid shifts of party and doctrine during this period make it difficult to align American writers consistently with any single party. Few major writers could be called "party men," and in many cases their party allegiances can only be surmised. Some, like James Fenimore Cooper (1789–1851), managed to alienate politicians of all stripes while others, like Washington Irving (1783–1859), ingratiated themselves with several parties. Under the prevailing "spoils system"—"to the victor belong the spoils"—parties who won power typically fired the appointees of the previous administration and replaced them with loyalists from their own party. Authors with friends in high places could win a coveted political appointment that allowed free time for writing, foreign travel, and sometimes significant remuneration. Because it was difficult to make a living on authorship alone, writers eagerly sought these appointments. Irving, for example, was a man of fundamentally conservative temper, an old-line Federalist by birth who remained unsympathetic to Jacksonian democracy. But he proved adept at negotiating the ideological shifts of his era and served as a secretary to the British legation under Jackson and as minister to Spain under Tyler, a position he resigned when the Democrats resumed power in 1845. Cooper, less politically agile than Irving, enjoyed a nonsalaried position as U.S. consul to Lyons, France, under the Adams administration. When he returned to America in 1833, he wrote such scathing political critiques of his bumptious, democratic countrymen that he antagonized both Whigs and Democrats and never served in government again.

Among the period's leading writers Nathaniel Hawthorne (1804–1864) was one of the more politically successful. He remained a Democratic loyalist his entire life, and although it paid off in government appointments, it eventually damaged his reputation. He worked in the Boston Custom House from 1839 to 1841 during Van Buren's administration and in the Salem Custom House from 1846 to 1849 during James

K. Polk's (1795–1849) presidency. When the Whig Millard Fillmore (1800–1874) succeeded Polk, Hawthorne was summarily dismissed. He recounts this experience memorably in his "The Custom-House" introduction to *The Scarlet Letter* (1850), offering an insider's view of the ups and downs of the spoils system. In 1852 Hawthorne wrote a campaign biography for the proslavery Democrat Franklin Pierce, and when Pierce won he appointed his old college chum to a consulship in Liverpool, a position that paid especially well. After seven years abroad Hawthorne returned to Massachusetts, finally financially secure. In 1863, during the Union's darkest days, Hawthorne dedicated his last published work, *Our Old Home,* to his patron Pierce. For Hawthorne it was a simple act of personal friendship. But many northerners, among them some of Hawthorne's greatest admirers, considered "Copperhead Democrats" like Pierce—Democrats who advocated compromise with the South—little more than traitors. Ralph Waldo Emerson (1803–1882) removed the dedication from his copy, and Harriet Beecher Stowe (1811–1896) could hardly believe Hawthorne had written it. This incident, along with an unflattering essay on Lincoln that Hawthorne had published a year earlier in the *Atlantic Monthly,* revealed his low opinion of the Republican Party and his refusal to commit to any extreme position, in this case abolition. For Hawthorne the parties changed faster than the man and left him isolated with an outmoded and discredited political ideology.

Herman Melville (1819–1891) was also an ardent Jacksonian Democrat, but unlike his friend Hawthorne he managed to keep his one political appointment for nineteen years. He tried several times to win a consulship, but he lacked the party credentials to succeed. His first and only government appointment came in 1866, when the pro-Union Democrat Andrew Johnson (1808–1875) was president and the highly partisan "Radical Republicans" dominated Congress. Melville became a deputy customs inspector in the New York Custom House, a modest, low-paying job he maintained through five Republican presidents and the first year of one Democratic president. He retired, relatively unscarred by public office, in December 1885.

Walt Whitman (1819–1892), whose enthusiasm for democracy knew no bounds, embraced politics as eagerly as he did America itself. As a journalist and newspaper editor, his early prose writings supported the Mexican-American War and other mainstream Democratic issues. With the ascent of the Free-Soil Party, however, he found a more hospitable home for his increasingly strong antislavery views, and by the time of the Civil War he was a strong supporter of Abraham Lincoln (1809–1865) and the

Republican Party. In 1865 he was appointed to a clerkship in the Bureau of Indian Affairs for the considerable salary of $1,200 a year, certainly more than he ever made from his poetry. Unfortunately, the new secretary of the interior found an annotated copy of the 1860 *Leaves of Grass* in Whitman's desk and fired the poet for writing indecent literature. With the support of his friends, Whitman managed to stay on the federal payroll until 1873, when ill health, not party politics, led him to retire.

Many lesser-known writers engaged in party politics with varying degrees of success. When the Maryland novelist John Pendleton Kennedy (1795–1870), a friend of Edgar Allan Poe (1809–1849), found that the Democrats had become too populist under Jackson, he joined the Whigs and served several terms in Congress. Millard Fillmore appointed him interim secretary of the navy in 1852. Kennedy's friend William Wirt (1772–1834), a Maryland lawyer and noted essayist, served twelve years as U.S. attorney general (1817–1829) and ran for president on the Anti-Masonic ticket in 1832. Edward Zane Carroll Judson (1823–1886), best known as the dime novelist Ned Buntline, was an early activist in the American Party and even served time in jail for his rowdy political activities. In contrast, many well-known writers stayed aloof from party affairs, even when they had strong political principles of their own. Emerson and Henry David Thoreau (1817–1862) felt strongly about the Mexican-American War, slavery, and American cultural nationalism but seldom identified with any one party. Poe repeatedly satirized Andrew Jackson and condemned the "mob," a popular term for the working class, yet focused his attention on poetry, criticism, editing, and fiction. In the turbulent world of antebellum America, political parties remained unstable and often short-lived. Yet out of this period emerged a strong two-party system that has exercised a generally moderating influence over the electorate and given the United States a political stability many once thought it would never attain.

See also Democracy

BIBLIOGRAPHY
Primary Works
Cooper, James Fenimore. *The American Democrat; or, Hints on the Social and Civic Relations of the United States of America.* With an introduction by H. L. Mencken, and an introductory note by Robert E. Spiller. New York: Vintage, 1956.

Hawthorne, Nathaniel. *Novels.* New York: Library of America, 1983. Particularly relevant are "The Custom-House, Introductory to 'The Scarlet Letter,'" pp. 121–157;

The House of the Seven Gables, pp. 347–627; and *The Blithedale Romance,* pp. 629–848.

Whitman, Walt. *Complete Poetry and Collected Prose.* New York: Library of America, 1982. Particularly relevant is *Democratic Vistas,* pp. 929–994.

Secondary Works
Bernhard, Winfred E. A., ed. *Political Parties in American History.* New York: Putnam, 1973–1974.

Holt, Michael F. *Political Parties and American Political Development from the Age of Jackson to the Age of Lincoln.* Baton Rouge: Louisiana State University Press, 1992.

Keyssar, Alexander. *The Right to Vote: The Contested History of Democracy in the United States.* New York: Basic Books, 2000.

Maisel, L. Sandy, ed. *Political Parties & Elections in the United States: An Encyclopedia.* New York: Garland, 1991.

Mellow, James R. *Nathaniel Hawthorne in His Times.* Boston: Houghton Mifflin, 1980.

Polakoff, Keith Ian. *Political Parties in American History.* New York: Wiley, 1981.

Roberts, Robert North, and Scott John Hammond. *Encyclopedia of Presidential Campaigns, Slogans, Issues, and Platforms.* Westport, Conn.: Greenwood Press, 2004.

Schlesinger, Arthur M., Jr. *History of U.S. Political Parties.* New York: Chelsea House, 1973.

Waples, Dorothy. *The Whig Myth of James Fenimore Cooper.* New Haven, Conn.: Yale University Press, 1938.

Dennis Berthold

POPULAR POETRY

The 1820–1870 period was early recognized as a remarkable time for American poetry production and consumption. Widespread 1890s nostalgia rightly heralded the culturally prominent role the genre had assumed. Poets during the earlier era wrote best-selling and profitable books, filled editorial posts at newspapers and magazines, and were in demand as commemorative voices at public occasions. Readers clipped verses from periodicals, memorized favorite lines, and turned to poets' lives for entertainment or moral edification. Russel Nye has argued that early-nineteenth-century readers were aware of the distinction between "'great' or 'high' poetry; and poetry that might guide, teach, and elevate the majority of people without being 'great'": "The nineteenth-century

"THERE IS NO DEATH"

The reach of this poem by J. L. McCreery is captured in Burton Egbert Stevenson's claim that "there is no poem in the language which has been spoken so often above an open grave, none which has brought so much consolation to stricken hearts" (p. 15).

There is no death! The stars go down
    To rise upon some fairer shore;
And bright in Heaven's jeweled crown
    They shine for evermore.
There is no death! The dust we tread
    Shall change beneath the summer showers
To golden grain or mellowed fruit,
    Or rainbow-tinted flowers.
The granite rocks disorganize,
    And feed the hungry moss they bear;
The forest leaves drink daily life
    From out the viewless air.
There is no death! The leaves may fall,
    And flowers may fade and pass away;
They only wait through wintry hours
    The coming of the May.
There is no death! An angel form
    Walks o'er the earth with silent tread;
He bears our best-loved things away,
    And then we call them 'dead.'

He leaves our hearts all desolate;
    He plucks our fairest, sweetest flowers;
Transplanted into bliss, they now
    Adorn immortal bowers.
The bird-like voice, whose joyous tones
    Made glad these scenes of sin and strife,
Sings now an everlasting song
    Around the tree of life.
Where'er he sees a smile too bright,
    Or heart too pure for taint and vice,
He bears it to that world of light,
    To dwell in Paradise.
Born unto that undying life,
    They leave us but to come again;
With joy we welcome them the same—
    Except their sin and pain.
And ever near us, though unseen,
    The dear immortal spirits tread;
For all the boundless universe
    Is life—there are no dead.

McCreery, "There Is No Death," p. 13.

reader who was moved by Lydia Sigourney knew quite well that he was not reading Milton" (pp. 93–94). The period is remarkable in part, however, because of the extent to which poets of both orders mixed company. The *Library of Poetry and Song* (1870), edited by William Cullen Bryant (1794–1878), in setting out to capture "the best Poems of the English language," included those "of merit though not of fame" *and* those "which, though less perfect than others in form, have, by some power of touching the heart, gained and maintained a sure place in the popular esteem" (p. iii). Not only could "best" poems be popular poems; "popular esteem" was a legitimate factor in determining which poems were among the "best." The second and third poems of an 1890s *Saturday Evening Post* series ("The Best Poems of the World"), apparently meant to complement each

other, were Bryant's well-known and much lauded "Thanatopsis" (1817) and the popular graveyard favorite by J. L. McCreery (1835– 1906), "There Is No Death" (1863). Readers apparently did not need critically distinct classes of poems separated for them.

POPULAR POETS, POPULAR TOPICS

The early figure of the popular poet was Lydia Sigourney (1791–1865). Known as the "American Felicia Hemans" and the "Sweet Singer of Hartford," Sigourney published fifty-six volumes of poetry, starting with *Moral Pieces in Prose and Verse* (1815), and was a ubiquitous presence in the day's periodicals. Others of early note included Fitz-Greene Halleck, Richard Henry Dana Sr., and Nathaniel Parker Willis; later ones included Josiah Gilbert Holland and the sisters Alice Cary and Phoebe Cary. But the dominant figures of this era undoubtedly were the "Fireside Poets": William Cullen Bryant, Oliver Wendell Holmes (1809–1894), Henry Wadsworth Longfellow (1807–1882), James Russell Lowell (1819–1891), and John Greenleaf Whittier (1807–1892). Their poetry, like much of this period's verse, largely has been characterized as sentimental and accessible, concerned with morality, and conventional in form and style.

Female poets were classed as most able to produce poetry of sentiment and moral purity. Both male and female poets, however, responded to and helped create public demands for such poetry by writing inspirational nature verses, narrative poems of stirring national events, and sentimental poems of domestic concern. And an ability to write all of these types certainly aided a poet's appeal. In Rufus Wilmot Griswold's *Readings in American Poetry: For the Use of Schools* (1843), Sigourney represented a range of short popular modes with "The Western Emigrant," "Indian Names," "Winter," and "Death of an Infant." And Longfellow, whose long narrative poems were dominant best-sellers, achieved significant success first as a lyric poet. Nineteenth-century readers not only chanted and lampooned rhythmic lines from *The Song of Hiawatha* (1855); they also learned his "A Psalm of Life," which famously begins, "Tell me not, in mournful numbers, / Life is but an empty dream!—" (p. 20) and admonishes in closing,

> Let us, then, be up and doing,
> With a heart for any fate!
> Still achieving, still pursuing,
> Learn to labor, and to wait.
>
> *(P. 22)*

Single-poem successes perhaps display best the qualities of sentiment and moral order often associated with the era's poetry. The British poet Martin Tupper's (1810–1889) admonishment "Never give up! it is wiser and better / Always to hope than once to despair" joined optimism with heightened sentiment in a poem purportedly "placed in each patient's room" in "an American lunatic asylum" (Hart, p. 132). And "There Is No Death," a popular favorite by J. L. McCreery, pictured a "boundless universe" of "life," where angels take away "our best-loved things" and fill the world again with the "unseen" (p. 13).

Longfellow's "The Day Is Done," in requesting a "simple and heartfelt lay" to "soothe this restless feeling, / And banish the thoughts of day," rejects the "grand old masters" and the "bards sublime." Instead, the verse asks,

> Read from some humbler poet,
> Whose songs gushed from his heart,

> As showers from the clouds of summer,
> Or tears from the eyelids start;
>
> *(P. 222)*

Poems like those by Tupper and McCreery (and Longfellow himself) fulfilled the larger public's similar demands for affect and sentiment.

The idea that poetry was socially and morally beneficial contributed to its distribution and preservation. American poetry anthologists of the 1820s and 1830s selected poetry in large part for its morality; later anthologists like Griswold typified the belief "that American poetry should be represented by specimens of the utmost moral purity, that poetry's function is inspirational" (Golding, pp. 6, 14). Such qualities helped the genre gain a dominant classroom presence. Schoolroom assignments furthered the popularity of Alfred, Lord Tennyson's *Idylls of the King*. Classroom reliance on memorization and recitation help explain how. Textbooks like Joseph Alden's (1807–1885) *Studies in Bryant* (1876) illustrate the process of classroom canonization. Alden follows Bryant's popular "To a Waterfowl," for example, with seventy-one questions and answers designed to help students dissect the poem. And Whittier's own 1866 *Snow-Bound* group, trapped by a blizzard, entertained itself when it "stammered from our school-book lore / 'The Chief of Gambia's golden shore.'" Attaining a place in schoolbooks allowed a poet to become part of the nation's conscience and consciousness.

Still, the belief that much popular poetry during this period was simply inoffensive—conforming to standard and accepted formal requirements of meter and rhyme and proffering generally held political and social beliefs—belies the variety of voices, themes, and forms that successfully found an audience. In fact, the entire class of women's poetry, long characterized as highly conventional, has been increasingly recognized by Paula Bennett and others for its political concerns and voices of protest. Nineteenth-century readers were hardly a singular group, moreover. Whittier's *Snow-Bound*, a fireside scene of New England domesticity, was popular, but so, too, was Lowell's *The Biglow Papers*, which argued strongly against the Mexican-American War in comic dialect verse (first in serial form in 1846, then as a book in 1848). Furthermore, in responding to Whittier's *Snow-Bound* invitation to

> Sit with me by the homestead hearth,
> And stretch the hands of memory forth
> To warm them at the wood-fire's blaze!
>
> *(P. 406)*

"worldling" readers not only forgot "city ways" for a time. They embraced, as postbellum readers, a poem by a famously abolitionist author who mixed his tranquil domestic portrait with reminders of those abolitionist views.

Poems of every kind succeeded during this period. Popular poems included panegyrics to national landmarks (John G. C. Brainard on "The Falls of Niagara"), long occasional poems (John Godfrey Saxe's 1846 "Progress"), and elegies (Fitz-Greene Halleck's "On the Death of Joseph Rodman Drake"). Too, whereas regional and national topics proved popular, British poets like George Gordon, Lord Byron, Tennyson, and Elizabeth Barrett Browning also had sizable American audiences—Tennyson apparently gained a larger and broader audience in the United States than in England, in part because of the publication of cheap editions of his poems. When critics lamented poetry's decline in the late nineteenth century, they did not only cite the succession of deaths of the Fireside Poets from 1878 to 1894. They often included British poets in that list as well. Even the success of one category like narrative verse illustrates the variety available. Longfellow reigned as the era's most popular poet in part through his long narrative poems, *Evangeline* (1847), *The Song of Hiawatha* (1855), and *The Courtship of Miles Standish* (1858). Much different in tone and focus was Edgar Allan Poe's (1809–1849) "The Raven" (1845), which became a classroom standard. Whittier's *Snow-Bound,* which related his family's entrapment during a winter blizzard, offered not simply narrative but an "idyl," a portrait of bygone rural home life with meditations on the function of memory. And William Allen Butler's (1825–1902) "Nothing to Wear" (1857), a long poem that gained notoriety beyond its author's name, tells the story of "Miss Flora M'Flimsey" in a sharp social satire that criticizes wealthy and fashionable women who claim "nothing to wear" because they lack "Brussels point lace," "camels'-hair shawls," "real ermine tippets," "a new Russian sable," an Indian shawl, and "the choicest assortment of French sleeves and collars" (p. 751).

POPULAR POETRY'S REACH

Although best-selling novels easily outperformed best-selling poetry volumes, book sales numbers indicate the popular audience poetry enjoyed. Josiah Gilbert Holland's (1819–1881) long narrative poem *Bitter-Sweet* (1858) proved immensely popular, and his *Kathrina: Her Life and Mine* (1867), another long narrative poem, "was reprinted fifty times in nine years" (Nye, p. 106). Lowell's *The Vision of Sir Launfal* (1848) also sold well—"nearly 175,000 copies during the decade after publication" (Radway and Frank, p. 304). By far the single most successful author, however, was Longfellow. His *The Song of*

Hiawatha, The Courtship of Miles Standish, and *Evangeline* all were best-sellers. *Hiawatha* in particular attracted attention: four thousand copies sold in advance of publication and "fifty thousand in five months" (Mott, p. 107). Money earned also makes the point. Whittier earned more than $100,000 from *Snow-Bound.* And the popularity of the genre at large seems proved further by the impressive payments poets received from places like the young *Atlantic Monthly.*

But tracking poetry's popularity depends on viewing it in all its forms of distribution. William Charvat rightly questions "the value of a statistical approach to the subject" (p. 33). Poetry's fragmented and diffuse means of production and reception affected standard indicators of popularity such as book sales numbers. Poetry was printed in periodicals, performed at public ceremonies, and collected in anthologies. And such venues offered countless ways by which poetry could be recorded, received, and re-performed. Periodicals offered poems not only through original publication and reprints; reviews regularly featured the liberal quotation of poems, offering multiple ways by which people could clip or transcribe favorite poems for scrapbooks. And poetry's significant ceremonial role not only offered an outlet for original compositions, commissioned for the occasion; it offered the expectation of poetry recitation so that some poems gained popularity in part from their suitability for public performance. Poetry also had tremendous circulation through collections and anthologies. Successful volumes like the 1870 Bryant-edited *Library of Poetry and Song* claimed sales of between 70,000 and 80,000, and Rufus Wilmot Griswold's popular anthology sold 300,000 copies, according to Frank Luther Mott. A proliferation of smaller collections offered their own gatherings of the day's verse. According to Bryant, "the same household contains several of these publications" (p. 1). The existence of all these modes of distribution suggests that poems and poets could achieve a degree of popularity not signaled by the sales numbers of single titles or even collected volumes.

The presence of popular poets, as much as popular poetry, means there were authors who attracted attention as personalities beyond the numbers generated by sales of their individual titles. The early- to mid-century sensation Nathaniel Parker Willis (1806–1867) suggests the keen interest in poets as people. An 1854 *United States Magazine and Democratic Review* article dismissed the urbane poet as a creature "produced" by "modern Frankenstein" "by making his skeleton out of a satin corset, with *Eau de Cologne* for blood, a nervous system of silk, a ball of almond soap for a heart, and a bottle of hair-dye or cosmetic for a moral centre." But Willis, whose popularity played out during his lifetime, was highly read during the period when his antics surrounded his publishing. His writings and personality were emphasized in periodicals like the *New York Mirror*, which he helped edit during the 1830s and 1840s, and the *Southern Literary Messenger*. In the *Southern Literary Messenger* in the 1830s and 1840s, Willis's sketches from Europe depicted a sophisticated urban life; the periodical defended his reputedly wanton work habits as a Yale student; and his published poems carried intrigue—one because an editor mistakenly thought he had commemorated Benedict Arnold. Later, the society poet's decreased fame served as a touchstone for the famous *Saturday Evening Post* article that bemoaned the "twilight" of the genre: an informal survey revealed, to the expressed shock of the surveyor, that "to three or four Nathaniel Parker Willis was merely a name, to the majority he was not even that" (McKinney, p. 426).

The American Fireside Poets and their British contemporaries attracted most attention, however—their lithographed faces reproduced in periodicals and the lines of their poems quoted in essays and popular novels. In 1869, for example, *Appletons' Journal* closed the calendar year by bestowing on its readers an elaborately illustrated 18 December cover featuring Bryant, "The Poet of Our Woods," and a more simple 25 December cover of Longfellow that linked to an article on "The Home of Longfellow"—the only two of that year's twenty-seven illustrated covers that were of actual people. How even the most prominent poets reached widespread recognition varied significantly, however. Although Longfellow's popularity is proved easily by his book sales numbers, Bryant illustrates the accumulated reputation of a lyric poet. He met with early critical acclaim, but his popular recognition mounted with widespread quotation of lines from "Thanatopsis," with repeated mention of him as America's nature poet, and with his classroom presence ("Thanatopsis" leads Griswold's 1843 *Readings in American Poetry: For the Use of Schools*). A late-nineteenth-century textbook on Bryant, Longfellow, Whittier, and Holmes says of Bryant's poems: "Take one, and read it until by very force of habit you learn to love it" (Cody, p. 67). The higher sales numbers achieved by his collected works (and his translations of the *Iliad* and the *Odyssey*) near the end of his life no doubt speaks of the diffuse distribution of lyric poets. It also suggests, perhaps, the extent to which he had become a larger public "habit." The work of making and keeping these poets popular often was the product of more than an immediate popular reception, and it continued even after their deaths.

BEYOND "THE AUTHOR"

Plenty of poetry circulated separately from authors' names, however. In the early part of the nineteenth century, writers regularly were published anonymously. As a result, in George B. Cheever's *The American Common-Place Book of Poetry* (1831), for one example, the editor not only includes anonymous texts alongside popular poets like Sigourney, Willis, Bryant, and Dana but also lists numerous texts under place of periodical publication rather than author. Moreover, in the case of the most famous "single poems," poems could be spread and distributed under multiple authors' names. Authorship disputes arose about McCreery's "There Is No Death," Sarah Josepha Hale's "Mary's Lamb," and J. W. Watson's "The Beautiful Snow." Watson's 1858 poem apparently was "ascribed to seven other poets" (Nye, p. 126). The prevalence of one-hit wonders thus further suggests why book sales numbers alone fail to signify poetry's reach.

In fact, single-poem successes, realized by a poem's frequent reprinting, recitation, or absorption into the popular music tradition, highlight the extent to which one measures popularity on the basis of critical comments and tales, rather than numbers, of demand and success. To claim that Sarah Josepha Hale's "Mary's Lamb" (1830), George Pope Morris's "Woodman, Spare That Tree!" (1830), and Major Henry Livingston Jr.'s "Visit from St. Nicholas" (1823; the scholar Donald W. Foster reattributes the authorship of this poem, long credited to Clement Clarke Moore) were popular poems from this era hardly demands proof for the simple fact that one can readily recognize their popularity. To note that Daniel Decatur Emmett's "Dixie" (1859) and Julia Ward Howe's "The Battle Hymn of the Republic" (1862) were poems spread widely as part of a popular song tradition seems proof enough. "Who is there that has not sung or read or heard 'The Old Oaken Bucket?'" asks George M. Young (p. 661) in an 1892 article about the 1817 poem by Samuel Woodworth, which recounts "How dear to this heart are the scenes of my childhood, / When fond recollection presents them to view!" (p. 658). Anecdotal accounts also shored up the reputations of authors with impressive sales figures: Longfellow's "Psalm of Life" (1838) purportedly prompted a "laborer" fan to seek his handshake and kept another "from suicide. I found it on a scrap of newspaper, in the hands of two Irish women, soiled and worn" (quoted in Cody, pp. 108–109). The storied benefits of poetry not only marked but also supported poems' popularity, and tales of effect repeatedly were conjoined with the poems themselves.

LOOKING BACK

At the close of the nineteenth century, the *Saturday Evening Post* offered its readers "The Best Poems in the World," an elaborately illustrated series that paired poems with anecdotes and biographical sketches. The forthcoming poems, the 28 May 1898 introduction explained

> will be selected, not from the standpoint of the ultra-literary man or woman, but for their appeal to lovers of sentiment. They will be poems of the emotions, those that appeal to the heart, poems that tell a story, those that are filled with human interest. They belong to what may be called the "Pocket-Book School of Poetry"—those poems that one cuts from a newspaper and carries in the pocket-book till they are worn through at the creases. (P. 8)

Post editors included lullabies of unknown origin, eighteenth-century patriotic lyrics, and recent poets like James Whitcomb Riley. But the series, despite a wide-ranging timeline, also solidified a critically prominent idea with its generous sampling of an earlier generation of American and British poets: that a culture of American poetry, better and better-loved, had only recently passed. The poems, it appeared, had been made popular by a particular poetry culture that appeared to be passing too. With that nostalgia, an earlier culture of American poetry since has been remembered as popular by, if nothing else, comparison. And whereas the demise of the genre was exaggerated, nineteenth-century poetry certainly deserves recognition for its cultural centrality, its wide and varied distribution, and its socially fostered consumption.

See also Death; Education; English Literature; Fireside Poets; Literary Marketplace; Lyric Poetry; Reform; Sentimentalism

BIBLIOGRAPHY

Primary Works

"The Best Poems in the World." *Saturday Evening Post,* 28 May 1898, p. 8.

Bryant, William Cullen. "Publishers' Preface." In *New Library of Poetry and Song,* edited by William Cullen Bryant, pp. iii–v. New York: J. B. Ford, 1876.

Butler, William Allen. "Nothing to Wear: An Episode of City Life." *Harper's New Monthly Magazine* (November 1857): 746–753.

Cody, Sherwin. *Four American Poets: William Cullen Bryant, Henry Wadsworth Longfellow, John Greenleaf Whittier, Oliver Wendell Holmes: A Book for Young Americans.* 1899. Folcroft, Pa.: Folcroft Library Editions, 1977.

Longfellow, Henry Wadsworth. *The Works of Henry Wadsworth Longfellow.* Vol. 1. Boston and New York: Houghton, Mifflin and Co. 1886.

McCreery, J. L. "There Is No Death." *Saturday Evening Post,* 4 June 1898, p. 13.

McKinney, M. S. "In the Twilight of Poetry." *Saturday Evening Post,* 31 December 1898, p. 426.

"Nathaniel Parker Willis." *United States Magazine and Democratic Review* (June 1854): 340–344.

Whittier, John Greenleaf. *Snow-Bound: A Winter Idyl.* 1866. In *The Complete Poetical Works of John Greenleaf Whittier,* pp. 399–406. Cambridge, Mass.: Riverside Press, 1927.

Woodworth, Samuel. "The Bucket." *New England Magazine,* January 1892, pp. 658–660.

Young, George M. "The Author of 'The Old Oaken Bucket.'" *New England Magazine,* January 1892, pp. 661–662.

Secondary Works

Bennett, Paula Bernat. *Poets in the Public Sphere: The Emancipatory Project of American Women's Poetry, 1800–1900.* Princeton, N.J.: Princeton University Press, 2003.

Charvat, William. *Literary Publishing in America: 1790–1850.* Philadelphia: University of Pennsylvania Press, 1959.

Foster, Donald W. "Yes, Virginia, There *Was* a Santa Claus." In his *Author Unknown: On the Trail of Anonymous,* pp. 221–275. New York: Henry Holt, 2000.

Golding, Alan. *From Outlaw to Classic: Canons in American Poetry.* Madison: University of Wisconsin Press, 1995.

Hart, James David. *The Popular Book: A History of America's Literary Taste.* 1950. Berkeley: University of California Press, 1963.

Mott, Frank Luther. *Golden Multitudes: The Story of Best Sellers in the United States.* New York: Macmillan, 1947.

Nye, Russel. *The Unembarrassed Muse: The Popular Arts in America.* New York: Dial Press, 1970.

Radway, Janice, and Perry Frank. "Verse and Popular Poetry." In *Handbook of American Popular Literature,* edited by M. Thomas Inge, pp. 299–322. Westport, Conn.: Greenwood Press, 1988,

Stevenson, Burton Egbert. *Famous Single Poems and the Controversies Which Have Raged around Them.* New York: Harcourt Brace, 1923.

Ingrid Satelmajer

POPULAR SCIENCE

For much of the nineteenth century the popular idea of science in general was based upon the notion of "vitalism," the belief that no living phenomenon could be defined or described by purely physical and chemical principles. Some unknown force, distinct from any other natural force, conditioned every action, whether it was magnetic, electric, or some other phenomenon of unseen waves.

Scientists at the time were fascinated by invisible fluids and forces in everything from miraculous gases to Isaac Newton's gravity and Benjamin Franklin's electricity. It was Franz Anton Mesmer (1734–1815) who named this force "animal magnetism" and described it as an extremely subtle universal fluid that permeated all things, ebbing and flowing in a kind of magnetic tidal manner. Whoever could control this fluid as it entered the human body could control illness and heal various diseases.

Mesmer's invisible fluid incorporated both religious and scientific visions because his theory straddled both worlds, the spiritual and the physical, and accounted for the mysteries within them. While science soon discredited his explanation, his sense of a single animating force permeated Romantic theory, although one is hard pressed to suggest which came first: Mesmer or Romanticism. The concept of nature as one organic whole that was ultimately harmonious and unified served as the very foundation of Romantic poetry.

The vision of animal magnetism permeated most of the popular science, or what has come to be called the "pseudosciences," of the nineteenth century. These included phrenology, mesmerism, phrenomagnetism, and others, each of which slowly shifted the focus of scientific investigations from the theological conception of the soul to the more psychological conception of the mind.

The agenda for popular science included healing and curing in everything from water cures to the creation of the graham cracker for better digestion. Immediate remedies were sought by the public at large, so much so that the most popular lecturers and performers on the lyceum circuit from the 1830s to the 1850s were those popularizers of scientific wonders that included mesmerists, phrenologists, self-promoting showmen, con artists hawking the latest elixir and miracle drug, and various faith healers.

Popular science also embodied the seemingly miraculous triumph of technology. Transatlantic steamships first appeared in 1838. Samuel Morse (1791–1872) invented the first electric telegraph in 1837. Peter Cooper built the first steam locomotive in the United States in 1829. By 1830 one-third of the factories in Pennsylvania and a quarter of those in Massachusetts were run by steam engines. Gas street lighting first appeared in Baltimore in 1816, reaching Boston in 1822 and New York in 1823. The public's fascination with such inventions was endless and increased its belief in ultimate progress and material advancement.

The popular notion of the scientist and his work began with the image of the physician as amateur that gradually changed into the scientist as professional. Popular science involved observation, description, classification, and categorization and very rarely involved theory. By the 1840s the word "scientist"

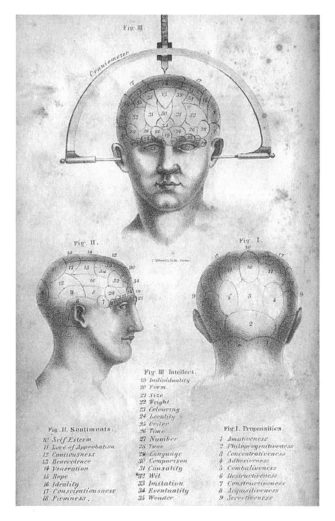

Frontispiece to *An Examination of Phrenology,* 1837, by Thomas Sewall. Phrenology, which purported to explain human behavior through analysis of the contours of the skull, exerted a great influence on the popular imagination during the nineteenth century. BROWN UNIVERSITY LIBRARY

had replaced "natural philosopher" or "philosopher" in popular use.

EXAMPLES AND METHODS

The idea of a universal, electrically charged fluid that influences all of human psychology underscored the theory of animal magnetism, the most popular "scientific" notion from Europe that took America by storm. Though all of the popular pseudosciences in America originated in Europe, it was in the United States that business-minded performers succeeded in terms of promotions, exhibitions, and lectures.

At his salon in Paris, Mesmer held séances in which patients would hold hands and press their knees together—so that the universal fluid could more easily pass from one to the other—while sitting around an oval tub filled with water and iron filings. From this they would extract long rods and apply them to the afflicted parts of their bodies while Mesmer walked among them, accompanied by a piano or harmonica. Thus began the mesmeric process, which eventually grew into the hypnotizing of individuals by putting them into a trancelike state. The mesmerized individual became a medium, speaking freely about his or her illnesses and troubles or, in some rare cases, prophesying future events or possible cures.

Charles Poyen St. Sauveur's (dates unknown) arrival in Boston from France in March 1836 provides the link between European mesmerism and the American fascination with it. The self-proclaimed professor of animal magnetism, who likened himself to Galileo, Christopher Columbus, and Christ, would mesmerize individuals and try to heal whatever ailments were bothering them. He mesmerized Phineas Parkhurst Quimby (1802–1866), who went on to devote his life to mental healing; he also mesmerized and cured Mary Baker Eddy, the founder of the Christian Science movement.

Other famous American mesmerists included the clairvoyant-medium Andrew Jackson Davis (1826–1910), who, after several sessions in which he was mesmerized, produced his monumental *The Principles of Nature: Her Divine Revelations, and a Voice to Mankind* in 1847. The tome sold nine hundred copies in a single week and went through four editions in a year. J. Stanley Grimes (1807–1903), a professor of chemistry at Emma Willard's school in New York City, adapted phrenology to mesmerism and later discovered the technique of posthypnotic suggestion. La Roy Sunderland (1802–1885), who began his career as a revivalist preacher, created what he called "pathetism," based upon electrical poles in the body that Mesmer had described.

In 1832 Johann Gaspar Spurzheim (1786–1832) came to New York City to offer a series of lectures on phrenology, a theory developed by his mentor Franz Joseph Gall (1758–1828) concerning the materialistic and physiological incarnation of animal magnetism that attributed certain emotions and conditions to specific organs in and areas of the brain. The phrenologist "read" a person's psychology by tracing the bumps on the head, each one in terms of its size and placement indicating the amount or absence of one emotional attribute or another. Orson Fowler (1809–1887), an eager publicist for phrenology, opened his Phrenological Cabinet in New York, which, with its skulls, plaster casts, and skeletons, became a famous tourist site. His brother Lorenzo (1811–1896) examined Walt Whitman's skull in 1849, and Whitman published his chart at least four times in his career. The publishing house of Fowler and Wells, known for its publications on phrenology and other pseudoscientific, self-help marvels, distributed the first edition of *Leaves of Grass* in 1855 and published another edition in 1860. Lorenzo even "read" Andrew Jackson's head in the White House.

Many of these popular pseudosciences were so creatively devised and transformed, often merging with one another (as in the case of "phrenomagnetism"), that they not only lent credence to transcendentalism and liberal Christianity but also eventually helped produce such lasting faith-healing denominations as Christian Science. While the "scientific" bases of these sciences were eventually discredited, many of them continued to play a popular role in the gradual progression of "moral philosophy" to "psychology" in the nineteenth century.

The scientific community was also torn between the works of the Swiss zoologist Louis Agassiz (1807–1873) and that of Alexander von Humboldt (1769–1859), whose 1845 book *Kosmos* by 1851 had sold eighty thousand copies. While Agassiz believed that all of nature was progressive, he also thought that each species was created in great numbers in particular regions, that when a catastrophe wiped out a species, the creator started all over again from scratch, and that special autonomous creations occurred at different times. Humboldt, on the other hand, viewed nature as a network of individual facts that could be collected and measured and that together revealed the sum total of all possible connections. Each viewed nature as developmental and progressive, but Humboldt's theories had more in common with the evolutionist ideas advanced by Charles Darwin (1809–1882) than they did with the natural theology favored by Agassiz.

PHRENOLOGICAL DESCRIPTION OF W. (AGE 29 OCCUPATION PRINTER) WHITMAN

The following is an excerpt from Lorenzo N. Fowler's phrenological analysis of Walt Whitman from 16 July 1849. The description of Whitman's character, based on the size and placement of bumps on his head, is followed by a chart giving number ratings to Whitman's "mental apparatus," "intellectual faculties," "self esteem," and "marvellousness" (the latter for which he received a "3").

You are very sympathetic and easily moved by suffering, and take much interest in those movements that are of a reformatory and philanthropic character. You are not any too fond of property but value it as a *means*—are not a penny-man, and despise narrowminded penuriousness—You have taste and considerable imagination but it does not blind you to fact or reality. You can adapt yourself to time place and company but you do not try to act out another's character but are yourself at all times.

You have both reason and perception, and hence can reason well. You have a strong desire to see everything and your knowledge is practical and *available*. You have a good mechanical eye and can judge well of and recollect forms and proportions well. You have a good sense of order either *mentally* or *physically*. By practice might make a good accountant. You can locate well and have a taste for geography. You are a great reader and have a good memory of facts and events much better than their *time*. You can compare, illustrate, discriminate, and criticise with much ability. You have a good command of language especially if excited.

The full text of Fowler's analysis, including Whitman's phrenological chart, is available at www.whitmanarchive.org.

POPULAR SCIENCE IN LITERATURE

Ralph Waldo Emerson (1803–1882), Henry David Thoreau (1817–1862), and Walt Whitman (1819–1892), the most notably optimistic Romantics of what has been called the American Renaissance, fully accepted the concept of nature as an organic and harmonious whole, the idea generated by popular science's notion of a universal fluid, which existed inside and outside the human body.

In essays such as "Circles," "Self-Reliance," and "The Poet," and in poems such as "The Rhodora," "Brahma," and "Each and All," as well as in *Nature*, Emerson expressed the complete unity between mind and matter, the ultimate identity that lies at the core of a harmonious universe. This was something to be celebrated and cherished, as much for the individual's powers of intuition and divine consciousness as for the beauty and bounty of the natural world. Mesmer's invisible fluid became Emerson's "transparent eyeball," through which and in which man could see into the life of things, both into his own soul and nature's. Nature became the utmost symbol of the spirit.

Emerson admired William Paley's (1743–1805) *Natural Theology* (1800), which attempted to connect the emerging naturalistic sciences with religious belief in a creator. The natural world revealed and indicated the creator as a watch revealed its maker. The correspondences between the natural sciences and moral value and the idea of science as moral investigation dovetailed perfectly with Emerson's vision of the organic growth in nature that paralleled the organic growth of the soul, as he made clear in four lectures he gave in 1833 and 1834, which included as reference points the theories of Carolus Linnaeus, Johannes Kepler, Humboldt, Galileo, and Newton.

Henry David Thoreau decided to live life deliberately in his homemade cabin in the woods of Concord, Massachusetts, to test Emerson's theories in his highly observant, minimalist manner, which famously included his recipe for bread, made without yeast, sal-soda, or other acid or alkali, following the idea of Sylvester Graham. This experience culminated in *Walden* (1854), the record of his two years in the woods, condensed into one year. For Thoreau, every natural fact expressed or contained an ultimate transcendent message of spiritual renewal and human hope. The pond at Walden, trees, stars, and sunlight each shimmered incandescently with the vision that man and his world were ultimately identical, instinctually linked and harmonious. Spring for him became the final declaration of regeneration and eternal rebirth.

While Thoreau was fascinated by the emerging science of botany and prided himself on his meticulous use of botanical categories and the names of insects, fish, birds and flowers, he finally decided that science was incompatible with poetic perception. For him, all naturalist observations were subjective. It was the relation between the self and nature that prompted his interest in the processes of nature, in seeds and the change of seasons that reflected human aspirations

and development. In this he was more in tune with
von Humboldt's teleological notions of nature as a
web of interconnected facts that revealed a cosmic
whole, a kind of protoecological holism, which suggests
Darwin's later theories.

Walt Whitman's *Leaves of Grass* (1855), with its celebration of sex and the body, of the natural world and its
intimate connection with the human spirit (both were
inseparable from one another), caused a sensation when
it first appeared. Its long sinewy lines, what Whitman
called his "negligent lists," broke every conventional
attribute of mid-nineteenth-century poetry and shocked
many readers. Emerson, at first, was delighted and
wrote, "I greet you at the beginning of a great career"
(Kaplan, p. 17). And Whitman later admitted that
"I was simmering, simmering, simmering . . . Emerson
brought me to a boil" (Waggoner, p. 154).

Whitman delighted in the possibility of developing the mental faculties through exercise as described
by Orson Fowler's lecture on perfectability in 1846.
He was also taken with Fowler's description of "ama-
tiveness," a phrenological category that Spurzheim
had added to Gall's theories, which identified the
intense friendship that was possible between members
of the same sex, and he treated sex in a frank and
healthy manner, as seen in "I Sing the Body Electric."
This theme also permeated most of Whitman's
work, as well as his idea, in such poems as "Song of
the Universal," "Song of the Open Road," "Song of
the Broad Ax," and "Crossing Brooklyn Ferry," that

the physical creation ultimately revealed a divine plan.
Another of Whitman's interests, one in water-cure
therapies, turned up in "Song of Myself," where he
described the poet as filtering the blood of his readers.

Writers such as Edgar Allan Poe (1809–1849),
Nathaniel Hawthorne (1804–1864), Herman Melville
(1819–1891), and Emily Dickinson (1830–1886),
however, had grave doubts about such popular ideas,
although Poe was examined by Lorenzo Fowler and
relied upon phrenological approaches in his introductions to "The Imp of the Perverse" (1850) and "The
Murders in the Rue Morgue" (1841), as well as in his
description of Roderick Usher's temples in "The Fall
of the House of Usher" (1839). Both Poe and
Hawthorne, however, viewed scientists as villains who
often exploited their powers, particularly as men over
women, and committed grave crimes against humanity. Evil scientists populated the popular fiction and
the "penny-dreadful" popular press of the day; in such
tales, poems, and novels as Poe's "The Facts in the
Case of M. Valdemar" (1845), "The Fall of the House
of Usher," and "Sonnet to Science" (1829) and
Hawthorne's "The Birth-mark" (1843), "Rappaccini's
Daughter" (1844), "Ethan Brand" (1850), *The Scarlet
Letter* (1850), and *The Blithedale Romance* (1852),
the demonic scientist-mesmerist reached his full
potential.

In "The Facts in the Case of M. Valdemar," a dying
man is placed in a magnetic sleep, but when he awakens
months later, he dissolves into liquid putrescence.
Roderick Usher is cursed with a kind of magnetic vision
that can see into the horrible life of things and feel the
oppressive sentience of even the stones in his house and
that eventually results in his death. In "Sonnet to
Science," Poe attacks science as a "vulture" who "preyest
thou thus upon the poet's heart" and "whose wings are
dull realities" (p. 9). His detective stories that feature
Auguste Dupin also make use of phrenology's conception that certain parts of the brain drive humans to
commit crimes or that phrenology can be used to analyze meticulously the criminal mind itself.

Hawthorne's relationship to mesmerism is particularly interesting because while he morally and philosophically despised it, he recognized its psychological
powers and evil potential to dominate and control. His
formula in writing the American romance was even
constructed around the mesmeric trance: he would
seduce his readers by focusing on strange objects, such
as the scarlet letter, a minister's black veil, and a marble
faun, spinning haunted tales about them.

Hawthorne's villains, however, remained the cold,
unfeeling scientists who experimented on others,
worked their spells upon them, and commanded them

to do their bidding. Ethan Brand commits suicide, recognizing how he has sinned by prying into others' minds with his dark arts. Rappaccini imprisons his daughter Beatrice in a poisonous garden to see how she will develop when isolated from all others, and his designs are undone by a fellow scientist, the envious Baglioni. Aylmer in "The Birth-mark," by trying to eradicate the mark from his wife's face to make her physically perfect, murders her. The two arch villains in *The Scarlet Letter* and *The Blithedale Romance* are the scientist-physician Chillingworth, who seeks revenge against his wife's lover by using his wiles and potions, and Westervelt ("western world" in German), the master mesmerist who imprisons the innocent Priscilla in his hypnotic spells and exhibits her on stage for public performances. Only the winsome Holgrave in *The House of the Seven Gables* (1851) manages to curb his mesmeric talents in order to win young Phoebe Pyncheon's true love.

Melville and Dickinson were very much aware of popular science and its misuses. Melville had read Darwin's *Journal of Researches* (first published in London in 1839) as well as essays in and introductions to astronomy, physiognomy, botany, and mineralogy. In *Moby-Dick* (1851) he described the whale from a distinctly phrenological point of view. He also suspected, however, that such scientists and physicians were con artists, a point of view that is particularly evident in his novel *The Confidence-Man* (1857), in which the title character adopts as one of his many disguises the snuff-colored surtout of an herb doctor. Here the "confidence man" is a peddler of panaceas who tries to persuade possible customers to purchase such dubious remedies as the Omni-Balsamic Reinvigorator, the Samaritan Pain Dissuader, and a liniment that will cure bone injuries and diseases. In the novel's characters of Mark Winsome and his disciple Egbert, Melville also skewers Emerson's and Thoreau's beliefs in the benign necessities of a persistently trustworthy universe.

Dickinson relied on scientific and medical images and metaphors as ways to explain the unexplainable, particularly in such poems as "There's a certain Slant of Light," in which the strange light gives us "Heavenly Hurt," after which

> We can find no scar,
> But internal difference,
> Where the Meanings, are—
>
> *(P. 36)*

She enjoyed Edward Hitchcock's (1793–1864) science lectures at Amherst but could not believe in the religious orthodoxy within which he practiced his scientific investigations.

SOCIAL RESPONSES TO POPULAR SCIENCE

The high point of popular science and the pseudosciences it embodied probably occurred on 12 February 1850, when the noted Universalist minister John Bovee Dods (1795–1872) gave a series of lectures on what he called "electrical psychology" in the Hall of Representatives in Washington, D.C. (which included seven U.S. senators). Dods described phrenology and mesmerism as the most relevant sciences of human psychology and attempted to show that the connection that existed between the body and the soul was electromagnetic.

At all times Dods made it clear that these new sciences did not in any way undercut orthodox religion. In fact they helped underwrite it because spiritual activity in the brain generated electrical impulses that in turn caused the human body to act. All disease, he maintained (as had Mesmer before him), clearly indicated an imbalance in the electrical forces that ebbed and flowed within the body. The idea that the soul ultimately ruled and used the body remained the most important overriding idea through the rest of the nineteenth century in both medical and scientific thought.

Of course many of these pseudosciences were thoroughly denounced, particularly when mesmeric trances were used to contact the dead in what became known after 1848 as spiritualism. Robert Collyer, for instance, found the New York City of 1838 full of "humbugs . . . and so much quackery abounds, where any one who has the impudence may leave his foreplane, or lapstone, or latherbrush, and become a physician" (p. 4). Collyer himself must have ultimately appreciated such impudence since, after attending lectures on phrenology, he went on to imitate them, setting up his own traveling skulls, charts, and lectures, "rising out of the dense obscurity that had always enshrouded him, and claiming to be the greatest, the most learned phrenologist of his day" (p. 17). Collyer eventually appeared in Hawthorne's 1843 story "The Hall of Fantasy," wherein the narrator and his guide meet many characters who have been magnetized by Collyer.

In the 1830s it was common for practicing scientists to give public lectures on the lyceum circuit, but by the 1860s, most of them denounced the profit-minded popularizers that had taken over the marketplace. By 1870 over four hundred American scientists were listed in an international directory of scientists.

All of this was set within the context of religious revivalism and the founding of several utopian communities. People were eager to believe in gold tablets sent by angels, lost Indian tribes, prophetic voices, personal conversions, ultimate salvation, and prophetic mesmerists. For instance, between 1825 and 1835 there were 1,343 religious revivals alone in New York State, and whereas fifteen experimental communities were founded in the 1820s, sixty were founded in the 1840s. After 1815 and particularly during the presidency of Andrew Jackson, cultural nationalism and optimism thrived and contributed to the popular faith in science, health, and social reforms.

Until the publication of Charles Darwin's *On the Origin of Species* in 1859, religion and science remained flip sides of the same coin, each proclaiming the miraculous and intricate revelations of God's works in the universe. To know and understand God's works was to promote his word. It was popularly assumed that men preparing for the ministry became scientists because Protestantism for centuries had encouraged scientific research. For instance Benjamin Silliman (1779–1864), the first professor of chemistry appointed at Yale University (in 1802), was himself a religiously orthodox believer, and Edward Hitchcock, who claimed in 1845 that "a true naturalist cannot be a bad man" (Burnham, p. 69) and went on to become the most famous geologist in America, began his professional life in 1821 as an orthodox minister in the Congregationalist church in Conway, Massachusetts. He, in fact, met Silliman at the Yale Divinity School and was persuaded by him to become the second science professor ever appointed by Amherst College.

Before Darwin's book radically changed the focus of American science, men like Timothy Walker, author of the article "Defence of Mechanical Philosophy" in the June 1829 issue of the *Edinburgh Review,* could easily defend the relationship between science and religion. Mechanistic theories like gravity did not utterly destroy humanity's spiritual nature but only added to our knowledge of the universe as a whole. Mechanical devices, in fact, liberated the mind by liberating men and women from physical labor. Perfection, of course, was impossible, but human progress depended upon the machine and our necessary use of it.

In 1859 Darwin changed all that. The process of natural selection, which seemed to operate on its own with no need of some divine intelligence behind it, revealed a sequence of cause and effect, of development and decay, that required no first cause. What came to be known in social theory as "the survival of the fittest" seemed to be brutally enacted in the Civil War and became the guiding scientific principle, however embattled and assaulted by both scientists and traditional religious believers, for the rest of the century.

As the century evolved, American scientists became more professional, and, as they were hired by colleges and universities, they grew apart from the more popular perceptions of science. Scientists began to specialize, as scientific thinking became a distinct category of its own, divorced from both philosophy and religion. While the public perception of science focused on technological marvels and various mesmerists and mediums, scientists joined university faculties. By the end of the 1830s, one-third to one-half of all college faculties were occupied by professors in mathematics, physics, chemistry, and geology. At Brown University in 1850, for instance, four of the seven full-time faculty members were scientists, and at Harvard between 1845 and 1869 the percentage of scientists on the faculty rose from 33 percent to 56 percent.

Silliman had founded the *American Journal of Science and Arts* in 1818, and it flourished throughout the entire century, but the first meeting of the American Association for the Advancement of Science did not meet until 20 September 1848, at the University of Pennsylvania. By that time specialization was fairly well established in higher education, while in that same year, spiritualism burst upon the popular scene, linking mesmerism to mediums who, entranced, could summon up and talk with the dead. The split between popular science and professional scientists could not have been greater.

See also Ethnology; Health and Medicine; Mental Health; Psychology; Science; Spiritualism

BIBLIOGRAPHY

Primary Sources

Collyer, Robert H. *Lights and Shadows of American Life.* Boston: Redding, 1838.

Dickinson, Emily. *Complete Poems.* Edited by Thomas H. Johnson. Boston: Little, Brown, 1960.

Emerson, Ralph Waldo. *Nature.* Boston: J. Munroe, 1836.

Emerson, Ralph Waldo. *Selections from Ralph Waldo Emerson.* Edited by Stephen E. Whicher. Boston: Houghton Mifflin, 1960.

Hawthorne, Nathaniel. *The Blithedale Romance.* 1852. New York: Modern Library, 2001.

Hawthorne, Nathaniel. *The House of the Seven Gables.* 1851. New York: Norton, 1967.

Hawthorne, Nathaniel. *The Novels and Tales of Nathaniel Hawthorne.* Edited by Norman Holmes Pearson. New York: Modern Library, 1937.

Hawthorne, Nathaniel. *The Scarlet Letter.* 1850. Boston: Bedford Books, St. Martin's Press, 1991.

Hawthorne, Nathaniel. *Selected Tales and Sketches.* Edited by Hyatt H. Waggoner. New York: Holt, Rinehart and Winston, 1966.

Melville, Herman. *The Confidence-Man: His Masquerade.* 1857. New York: Norton, 1971.

Melville, Herman. *Moby-Dick.* 1851. New York: Norton, 2002.

Poe, Edgar Allan. *Selected Writings.* Edited by Edward H. Davidson. Boston: Houghton Mifflin, 1956.

Thoreau, Henry David. *Walden.* 1854. Boston: Houghton Mifflin, 1995.

Whitman, Walt. *Whitman: Leaves of Grass and Selected Prose.* New York: Holt, Rinehart, and Winston, 1966.

Secondary Sources

Burnham, John C., ed. *Science in America: Historical Selections.* New York: Holt, Rinehart, and Winston, 1971.

Coale, Samuel Chase. *Mesmerism and Hawthorne: Mediums of American Romance.* Tuscaloosa: University of Alabama Press, 1998.

Daniels, George H. *American Science in the Age of Jackson.* New York: Columbia University Press, 1968.

Davies, John D. *Phrenology: Fad and Science: A Nineteenth-Century American Crusade.* Hamden, Conn.: Archon, 1971.

Kaplan, Justin. *Walt Whitman: A Life.* New York: Simon and Schuster, 1980.

Lebeaux, Richard. *Thoreau's Seasons.* Amherst: University of Massachusetts Press, 1984.

Pick, Daniel. *Svengali's Web: The Alien Enchanter in Modern Culture.* New Haven, Conn.: Yale University Press, 2000.

Reed, Edward S. *From Soul to Mind: The Emergence of Psychology, from Erasmus Darwin to William James.* New Haven, Conn.: Yale University Press, 1997.

Reingold, Nathan, ed. *The Sciences in the American Context: New Perspectives.* Washington, D.C.: Smithsonian Institution Press, 1979.

Reynolds, David S. *Beneath the American Renaissance: The Subversive Imagination in the Age of Emerson and Melville.* New York: Knopf, 1988.

Reynolds, David S. *Walt Whitman's America: A Cultural Biography.* New York: Knopf, 1995.

Schofield, Edmund A., and Robert C. Baron, ed. *Thoreau's World and Ours: A Natural Legacy.* Golden, Colo.: North American Press, 1993.

Trimpi, Helen P. *Melville's Confidence Men and American Politics in the 1850s.* Hamden, Conn.: Archon, 1987.

Waggoner, Hyatt H. *American Poets: From the Puritans to the Present.* Boston: Houghton Mifflin, 1968.

Samuel Chase Coale

PORNOGRAPHY

The term "pornography" did not appear in the English language before 1857 and did not enter American usage until the late nineteenth century. Until then, Americans referred to objectionable literature as "blasphemous," "obscene," or "indecent." Prior to 1820 the slow growth of literacy and the high expense of books erotic or otherwise generally limited circulation. In 1821, however, in the first recorded American prosecution of literary indecency, Massachusetts jailed Peter Holmes and Stillman Howe for selling John Cleland's *Memoirs of a Woman of Pleasure* (also known as *Fanny Hill,* 1748), a book previously owned by only affluent Americans such as Benjamin Franklin and William Byrd. Isaiah Thomas, the distinguished printer, ran off a few pages of *Fanny Hill* sometime between 1786 and 1814 but did not complete the project. Other printers, however, soon used new steam presses (1814) to pirate bawdy imports such as Cleland's novels and Laurence Sterne's *Tristram Shandy.*

EARLY OPPOSITION

Unlike Massachusetts, most states remained unconcerned about erotica. On his 1831–1832 visit, Alexis de Tocqueville observed that the United States had few laws against "licentious books" because lack of demand meant that no Americans wanted to write them (1:265). As if to contradict de Tocqueville, *McDowall's Journal,* issued by the Reverend John McDowall in 1833, inveighed against the proliferation of erotica in New York City, whose population had risen sharply since the completion of the Erie Canal in 1825. In 1834 McDowall assembled an exhibit of "indecent" books, pamphlets, papers, prints, and playing cards for fellow ministers. Twelve years later Henry Ward Beecher (1813–1887) complained that tasteless literature was by then epidemic (p. 211). The increase was associated not only with the rampant prostitution in American cities but also with the tumultuous politics of the Jacksonian era and the growth of a large workforce created by industrialization.

Historians have observed that obscenity often drives democratic movements as aggrieved groups level charges of misconduct at aristocrats or politicians. During the 1830s and 1840s radical American journalists used sexual invective to call for social and political reform in cities such as Boston, New York, and Philadelphia. Like other professionals, such journalists were drawn to a subculture called "the sporting life," the term applied to a volatile stratum of restless young males who worked in the cities' factories and businesses by day and roistered by night. The sporting life also flourished in the seedy sectors of riverboat towns in Ohio and West Virginia. Those western frontiers also generated bawdy works such *Davy Crockett's Almanac of Wild Sports of the West, and Life in the Backwoods* (1835), but sporting-life literature was more closely associated with the eastern seaboard. Here, for the first time, domestic sexual expression began to compete with classic European erotica.

THE SPORTING PRESS

Out of the masculine realm of prizefights, billiard rooms, poker dens, cockfight arenas, racetracks, music halls, saloons, and bordellos sprang the sporting press: cheap newspapers that were at first little more than catalogs of amusements. Presses on Ann and Nassau Streets in New York, in a district known at the time for its whorehouses, increasingly became partisan, as Jacksonian Democratic editors savaged Whig politicians. *The Whip, The Flash, The Weekly Rake,* and *The Libertine* often caught their political opponents patronizing brothels and bawdy music halls and charged them with hypocrisy and immorality. Some publishers blackmailed their targets by threatening to run exposés unless they were paid not to, but others seemed sincere in their outrage and identified themselves as crusaders determined to crush corruption.

Sporting papers led to penny papers, sensational novels, and the new writing class that produced them. The most famous penny newspapers, Benjamin Day's (1810–1889) *New York Sun* (1833) and James Gordon Bennett's (1795–1872) *New York Herald* (1835), attacked the sporting papers on "moral" grounds that scarcely disguised eagerness to destroy their rivals. In turn, the penny newspapers slightly sanitized the sexual scandal that was the sporting papers' stock-in-trade by transforming it into crime reporting, a species of salacious subliterature. Just as important, sporting papers extruded sensational novelists. Conservatives denounced as depraved George Lippard's (1822–1854) *The Quaker City; or, The Monks of Monk Hall: A Romance of Philadelphia Life, Mystery, and Crime* (1846). A radical newspaper editor, labor organizer, feminist, and reformer, Lippard wrote *The Quaker City* as a tale of seduction, revenge, forgery, drugs, and murder based on actual Philadelphia events. Its immense popularity triggered imitators of the "city mystery," most of them more sexually candid than Lippard, and influenced writers including Mark Twain (Samuel Langhorne Clemens, 1835–1910) and Walt Whitman (1819–1892); the latter, a newspaper editor himself, often printed scandal and actually tried to write a "city mystery" called "Proud Antoinette" in the late 1850s. Edgar Allan Poe (1809–1849) based his "The Mystery of Marie Roget" (1842) on an abortion scandal of 1841.

The most prolific author of city mysteries was George Thompson (1823–c. 1873). Also editor of *The Broadway Belle* (1855–1858), a sporting paper, Thompson wrote magazine serials, pamphlets, and novels (perhaps as many as sixty), often under the pen name of "Greenhorn." Of several publishers who printed Thompson's fiction, George Ackerman (sometimes spelled Akarman or Akerman) is representative. Ackerman operated a press at 167 William Street in New York. Here he issued sensational works under his own name, and "fancy" or "rich" titles (that is, erotic) under the imprint of "James Ramerio." In the first category was *Flora Montgomery, the Factory Girl: Tale of the Lowell Factories. Being a Recital of the Adventures of a Libidinous Millionaire, Whose Wealth Was Used as a Means of Triumphing Over Virtue* (1856), by "Sparks." Henry Spencer Ashbee, the great English bibliographer of erotic texts, points out that there is nothing "libidinous" in this story of social justice wrought by Flora, who, after having been duped into a sham marriage, leads a strike that ruins the factory owner who seduced her. By contrast, "James Ramerio" published Thompson's much racier *Venus in Boston* (1849) and a tabloid, *Venus's Miscellany* (1856–c. 1857), whose stories of wives seeking illicit pleasures, augmented by engravings of embracing couples, led to Ackerman's arrest.

THE FIRST AMERICAN PORNOGRAPHIC NOVELS

David Reynolds has argued that *Venus in Boston* is the first truly pornographic American novel. As Ashbee notes, however, its tales of "low-life"—abduction, attempted rape, confidence swindles, and murder—qualify only as "semi-erotica." Two other contenders for "first" are more plausible. Appearing also in 1849, *Madge Bufford: A Lively Letter to a Lonely Lover. What Uncle Bob taught her; and how she profited by his instruction with men and women black and white, with diversions among the quadrupeds. Showing that Yankee gals, grope, gape, gallop—give and take the salacious sweet as sensually as their smutty sisters over the sea* contains prurient descriptions of intercourse, sodomy, voyeurism, and miscegenation. The second candidate, also published in 1849, is *D'Amour La Rose: or, The Adventures of a Gentleman in Search of Pleasure,* whose equally anonymous American author (the legend "translated from the French" is fraudulent) set his story in Europe; here a rich rakehell deflowers women in castles, clubs, and brothels.

Deciding which was the first domestic pornographic novel is less important than observing that erotic fiction had entered a new phase as immigration, education, science (and pseudoscience), and feminism fostered greater awareness of the body and sexuality. From the Midwest came calls for female "dress reform," an attempt to replace shroud-like attire with pantaloons and bloomers. Faddists such as Sylvester Graham (1794–1851) and John Harvey Kellogg (1852–1943) crusaded against masturbation and intercourse, prescribing vegetarian diets, celibacy, and enemas as curbs to sensual appetites. At the other extreme, members of communitarian movements as diverse as the Oneida Community (1848) and the Brotherhood of the New Life (1861) engaged in physical unions justified by spiritual desire. After Robert Owen (1771–1858) purchased the Harmony Community (Indiana), a colony that originally endorsed celibacy, his son Robert Dale Owen (1801–1877) became the first to advocate birth control in America (in *Moral Physiology* [1830]). Doctrines of "free love" that would reach an apogee in the 1870s attracted feminists such as Victoria Woodhull (1838–1927) and freethinkers such as Ezra Hervey Heywood (1829–1893) because of their advocacy of birth control and the right of women to choose their partners. Their publications on such subjects were routinely suppressed as obscene. Thompson's *Fanny Greeley; or, Confessions of a Free-Love Sister Written by Herself* (c. 1865) charged freethinkers with promoting extramarital sex; its title probably twitted rival editor Horace Greeley (1811–1872) as well.

Because such trends seemed to undermine social order, moralists attempted to impose control over what they thought of as the easily inflamed passions of women, immigrants, and the urban poor. The outlawing of "low" fiction, ostensibly a matter of setting standards of taste, aimed to preserve fragile class and gender boundaries. Conservatives worried especially about the effects of romances written for women and about the curiosity stimulated by marriage manuals and physiology texts. In 1850 Dr. Frederick Hollick published his *Marriage Guide*, the first of an astonishing five hundred editions. It focused on female masturbation, which had been one of the major motifs, according to Peter Wagner, of erotica in the eighteenth century. Hollick's book was followed by Seth Pancoast's *The Ladies' Medical Guide and Marriage Friend* (1859), which expanded on the female orgasm but warned against lesbianism, and by Harmon Knox Root's *The Lover's Marriage Lighthouse* (1858), which cautioned against the use of dildoes, an indication that they were common. Images of female sexual appetites, at once frightening and titillating to Civil War soldiers separated from wives, informed steadily more explicit male-oriented pornography. Scenes of homosexuality

appeared only occasionally in texts otherwise aimed at heterosexual audiences; the market for exclusively homosexual erotic genres was small, uncertain, and dangerous, as reaction to Whitman's hardly pornographic *Leaves of Grass* (1855) would soon demonstrate.

THE CIVIL WAR AS EROTIC STIMULUS

By the late 1850s the reformer William Sanger (d. 1894) pointed out that newsboys around hotels, steamboat docks, and railway stations in New York sold "lecherous" publications surreptitiously but freely. Books and sexual appliances were available by mail from cities as large as New Orleans and towns as small as Georgetown, Ohio. The Civil War dramatically increased the number of dealers in both North and South, and advertisements quickly found their way into the trenches on both sides.

Typical was a notice in the September 1863 issue of *Ormsby's New York Mail Bag: A Journal of Wit, Humor, and Romance* (86 Nassau Street, New York City), which offered *Ovid's Art of Love;* "Gay & Witty Novels" such as *Confessions of a Voluptuous Young Lady of High Rank, Bertha; or, The Adventures of a Spring Mattress, The Private Looking Glass; or, Secrets of Nature, The Amours of a Quaker, The Intrigues and Amours of Aaron Burr,* and *Confessions of a Boarding School Miss;* as well as another manual by the prolific Dr. Hollick, *The Male Generative Organs in Health and Disease* (1853). Aside from the Hollick text, only one of these titles, *The Intrigues and Amours of Aaron Burr* (n.d.), was by an American, a proportion similar to that in the booklists of other dealers. A few ambitious American original erotic novels did appear, with titles such as *The Life and Amours of the Beautiful, Gay and Dashing Kate Percival, The Belle of the Delaware, Written by Herself, Voluptuous, Exciting, Amorous and Delighting* (1864) and *Amours of an American Adventurer in the New World and the Old* (1865), but most American erotic fiction was short, as was evident from the catalog of "Cupid's Own Library" (the first in the series was a twenty-nine-page illustrated pamphlet called *Amours of a Modest Man* [1864], by "A. Bachelor").

Postwar traffic in trashy books attracted the notice of increasingly alarmed authorities. In 1865 a federal mail statute prohibited the shipment across state lines of obscene materials, but the law seemed directed as much at birth control information as at erotic fiction. In 1868 conservatives and progressives formed the American Railway Literary Union, modeled on the Pure Literature Society of England, to persuade newsdealers along transportation routes not to handle books that were "unseemly" or "questionable," categories that often included dime novels of thrilling adventure and romance (pp. 3–4). Although the latter types managed to survive the efforts to censor them, campaigns against truly explicit fiction became more draconian and drove genuine pornography underground for the remainder of the century.

See also Literary Marketplace; Publishers; Sensational Fiction; Sexuality and the Body; Taste; Urbanization

BIBLIOGRAPHY
Primary Works
The American Railway Literary Union, for the United States and the Dominion of Canada. *To Publishers, Railway and Steamboat Managers, Newsdealers, the Public Generally.* New York: ARLU, 1868.

Ashbee, Henry Spencer [Pisanus Fraxi]. *Index Librorum Prohibitorum; Centuria Librorum Absconditorum; Catena Librorum Tacendorum, Being Notes Bio-Biblio-Iconographical and Critical on Curious, Uncommon and Erotic Books.* 3 vols. London: Privately Printed, 1877, 1879, 1885. Reprinted as *Bibliography of Forbidden Books.* 3 vols. New York: Jack Brussel, 1962.

Beecher, Henry Ward. *Letters to Young Men, on Various Important Subjects.* New York: Saxton and Miles, 1846.

Sanger, William W. *The History of Prostitution: Its Extent, Causes and Effects Throughout the World.* 1858. New York: Eugenics Publishing Company, 1937.

Thompson, George. *Venus in Boston and Other Tales of Nineteenth-Century City Life.* Edited by David S. Reynolds and Kimberly R. Gladman. Amherst: University of Massachusetts Press, 2002.

Tocqueville, Alexis de. *Democracy in America.* 2 vols. Translated by Henry Reeve and revised by Francis Bowen and Phillips Bradley. New York: Knopf, 1945.

Secondary Works
Boyer, Paul S. *Urban Masses and Moral Order in America, 1820–1920.* Cambridge, Mass.: Harvard University Press, 1978.

Burnham, John C. *Bad Habits: Drinking, Smoking, Taking Drugs, Gambling, Sexual Misbehavior, and Swearing in American History.* New York: New York University Press, 1993.

Gilfoyle, Timothy J. *City of Eros: New York City, Prostitution, and the Commercialization of Sex, 1790–1920.* New York: Norton, 1992.

Horowitz, Helen Lefkowitz. *Rereading Sex: Battles Over Sexual Knowledge and Suppression in Nineteenth-Century America.* New York: Knopf, 2002.

Hunt, Lynn, ed. *The Invention of Pornography: Obscenity and the Origins of Modernity, 1500–1800.* New York: Zone Books, 1993.

Kendrick, Walter. *The Secret Museum: Pornography in Modern Culture.* New York: Viking, 1987.

Lowry, Thomas P. *The Story the Soldiers Wouldn't Tell: Sex in the Civil War.* Mechanicsburg, Pa.: Stackpole Books, 1994.

Mendes, Peter. *Clandestine Erotic Fiction in English, 1800–1930: A Bibliographical Study.* Aldershot, U.K.: Scolar Press; Brookfield, Vt.: Ashgate, 1993.

Reynolds, David S. *Beneath the American Renaissance: The Subversive Imagination in the Age of Emerson and Melville.* New York: Knopf, 1988.

Reynolds, David S. *Walt Whitman's America: A Cultural Biography.* New York: Knopf, 1995.

Rose, David. "Prostitution and the Sporting Life." *Upper Ohio Valley Historical Review* 16 (1987): 7–31.

Rugoff, Milton. *Prudery and Passion: Sexuality in Victorian America.* New York: Putnam, 1971.

Sante, Luc. *Low Life: Lures and Snares of Old New York.* New York: Farrar, Straus and Giroux, 1991.

Slade, Joseph W. *Pornography and Sexual Representation: A Reference Guide.* 3 vols. Westport, Conn.: Greenwood Press, 2001.

Wagner, Peter. Wagner, Peter. *Eros Revived: Erotica of the Enlightenment in England and America.* London: Secker and Warburg, 1988.

Joseph W. Slade III

PRESBYTERIANS

American Presbyterians are related to other Calvinistic denominations in the Reformed heritage such as the Puritans, the Congregationalists, the French Huguenots, and the Dutch Reformed Church. These groups protested, hence the term Protestant, some of the doctrines of the Roman Catholic Church, beginning in the sixteenth century; this period of Christian Church history became known as the Reformation. Presbyterians had a congregation in Jamestown Colony, Virginia, as early as 1611, predating the 1620 founding of Plymouth Colony by the English Separatists ("Pilgrims") and the 1630 founding of the Massachusetts Bay Colony by the English Puritans. While the Puritans and Congregationalists dominated New England and Virginia largely embraced the Church of England, the Presbyterians prospered primarily in the middle colonies of New York, New Jersey, Pennsylvania, Maryland, and Delaware. Later, Scotch-Irish immigrants took Presbyterianism into the southern colonies.

At the Continental Congress in Philadelphia in 1776, twelve of the fifty-six members who signed the Declaration of Independence were Presbyterians, not counting Benjamin Franklin (1706–1790), who was

IMPORTANT DATES FOR AMERICAN PRESBYTERIANS

1517: Martin Luther breaks with Rome and launches the Protestant Reformation.

1536: John Calvin arrives in Geneva, Switzerland, where he develops Presbyterian Church government.

1559: John Knox returns to Scotland from study in Europe.

1560: The Scottish Parliament banishes Roman Catholicism and establishes Presbyterian as the national religion.

1683: The Reverend Francis Makemie, an Ulster Scot, arrives in America.

1701: Connecticut Presbyterians establish Yale College.

1704–1706: Makemie organizes congregations into a presbytery.

1746: Presbyterians establish the College of New Jersey (now Princeton University).

1861: Southern Presbyterians form the Presbyterian Church in the Confederate States of America at the outbreak of the Civil War.

1983: The southern and northern branches reunite as the Presbyterian Church (USA).

raised in the Presbyterian Church but who later became a deist. In brief, deists believed that the world was created by a deity that no longer concerns itself with the ongoing affairs of its creation. John Witherspoon, a Presbyterian minister and president of the College of New Jersey (now Princeton University), was the only clergyman to sign the Declaration of Independence. Thus Presbyterians have figured prominently in American history since the earliest days of the Republic.

EARLY HISTORY OF THE DENOMINATION

Presbyterians look to John Calvin (1509–1564) as their spiritual founder. The French lawyer followed the lead of Martin Luther (1483–1546) in converting from Roman Catholicism to the Protestant movement. Relocating to Geneva, Calvin shaped a denomination with innovations in worship, theology, and governance. The lineage of Presbyterians extends to Scotland's John Knox (c. 1513–1572), a student of Calvin in Geneva. Although Lutheran teachings existed in Scotland before Knox returned from Geneva, he attacked Roman Catholicism so enthusiastically that the Scottish parliament abolished Roman Catholicism and installed the Presbyterian Church as the state religion in 1560. While the English Protestants dispensed with some of Roman Catholicism's theological precepts, they retained many of the liturgical practices, so the gulf between the independent-minded Presbyterian congregations and the hierarchical English church widened.

Many Presbyterians came to America directly from Scotland and Northern Ireland (the Ulster Scots). Arriving in America from Ireland in 1683, the Reverend Francis Makemie (1658–c. 1707 or 1708), an Ulster Scot, became known as the "Father of American Presbyterians" because of his energetic preaching among the congregations dispersed along the east coast. About 1704–1706 (the date is uncertain) he organized several congregations into a presbytery; following Makemie's death, four presbyteries or representative assemblies reorganized into a synod. A presbyter, from the Greek, is an elder; Presbyterian congregations typically have a session of ruling elders and a diaconate consisting of individuals with the title of deacons (although some churches have experimented with a unicameral board of directors). Ministers are often referred to as teaching elders. These terms reflect the denomination's traditional desire for governance through democratic principles rather than episcopal authority (such as is held by a bishop). The U.S. Congress's two chambers, the Senate and the House of Representatives, mirror the upper and lower houses of the Presbyterians. When the Presbyterian General Assembly convenes, individual congregations send delegates, and every delegate has an opportunity to participate in the democratic process of selecting leaders.

SOME HISTORICAL AND LITERARY CONNECTIONS

Eight presidents of the United States were Presbyterians: Andrew Jackson, James Knox Polk, James Buchanan, Grover Cleveland, Benjamin Harrison, Woodrow Wilson, Dwight D. Eisenhower, and Ronald Reagan. Six vice presidents were Presbyterians: Aaron Burr, Daniel D. Tompkins, John C. Calhoun, John C. Breckenridge, William A. Wheeler, and Henry A. Wallace.

Presbyterians influenced literary and popular culture, ranging from the merely tangential to the important. Charles Scribner (1821–1871), born in Switzerland, established his publishing firm in New York City in 1846 for the purpose of making available books on Presbyterian theology. Washington Irving (1783–1859), an American author of the first rank, was the son of a Scottish immigrant who inculcated him with solid Presbyterian doctrines. The Romantic novelist and short story writer Edgar Allan Poe (1809–1849), known for his legendary bouts with alcoholism, was buried in the yard of Baltimore's Westminster Presbyterian Church. Harriet Beecher Stowe (1811–1896) was the daughter of Lyman Beecher, sister of Edward Beecher, and wife of Calvin Stowe, all Presbyterian ministers. Prompted by her strong religious upbringing and sense of social justice, she penned *Uncle Tom's Cabin*, published serially in 1851 and 1852, bringing the degradations of slavery to the fore and swaying public opinion in the years preceding the Civil War.

Presbyterians influenced the education of children in the nineteenth century. In 1836 William Holmes McGuffey (1800–1873), a professor of moral philosophy, produced the first of his famous *Readers*, encouraging virtuous acts among young people. In 1859 Anna Bartlett Warner (1827–1915) and her sister Susan Warner (1819–1885), Presbyterian authors of popular sentimental works, published the novel *Say and Seal* (1860), containing the song "Jesus Loves Me," sung by generations of children. Presbyterians in America also have a long history of promoting higher education. Yale College was founded by Connecticut Presbyterians in 1701 (and settled in New Haven in 1716). In 1746 Presbyterians founded the College of New Jersey, now known as Princeton University, as an alternative to Yale College. From those early years Presbyterians have continued their commitment and maintain a covenant relationship with more than seventy schools, colleges, and universities.

"DECENTLY AND IN ORDER"

Presbyterians tell jokes on themselves that indicate how the general public often perceives the denomination. One old joke holds that "the Methodists shout, 'Fire, fire,' the Baptists cry, 'Water, water,' but the Presbyterians insist on 'Order, order.'" Another long-standing joke from the pulpit mentions in passing "John the Baptist . . . Jesus the Presbyterian." Self-deprecatingly referring to themselves as "God's frozen chosen," Presbyterians acknowledge their stereotyped image as unemotional, orderly, systematic, and hard-working (the so-called Protestant work ethic). Presbyterian congregations

---

In chapter 17 of Harriet Beecher Stowe's novel Uncle Tom's Cabin *(published in book form in 1852), a free black man, George Harris, age twenty-five, is attempting to elude armed white men who would prevent him, his wife, and his child from escaping to Canada. Stowe's authorial voice intrudes on a tense, confrontational scene to offer a reasoned argument reflecting her Presbyterian beliefs.*

If it had been only a Hungarian youth, now bravely defending in some mountain fastness the retreat of fugitives from Austria into America, this would have been sublime heroism; but as it was a youth of African descent, defending the retreat of fugitives through America and into Canada, of course we are too well instructed and patriotic to see any heroism in it; and if any of our readers do, they must do it on their own private responsibility. When despairing Hungarian fugitives make their way, against all the search warrants and authorities of their lawful government, to America, press and political cabinet ring with applause and welcome. When despairing African fugitives do the same thing,—it is—what *is* it?

Stowe, *Uncle Tom's Cabin,* p. 299.

---

seldom act impulsively on important matters, preferring instead to form a committee, to conduct a survey, to engage in prayerful consideration, or to discuss issues in a deliberative manner in their various governmental bodies, the general assembly, the synod, the presbytery, the session, and the diaconate, and in congregational meetings. A phrase often mentioned in these deliberations is "decently and in order."

Mark Twain (1835–1910), who was raised as a Presbyterian, frequently made comic use of the reputation of Presbyterians. In chapter 21 of *The Adventures of Tom Sawyer* (1876), one of the girls in Tom's school recites in a declamation contest a dark and dreary Romantic story. Mark Twain says, "This nightmare occupied some ten pages of manuscript and wound up with a sermon so destructive of all hope to non-Presbyterians that it took the first prize" (p. 173). When he received an honorary doctorate from Oxford University in 1907, Twain appeared at one of the ceremonies inappropriately attired in a tuxedo instead of his scarlet academic gown. He said, "I looked as out of place as a Presbyterian in hell" (Paine, p. 1395). Mark Twain was playing on the central—but often misunderstood—doctrine for Presbyterians: predestination.

Double predestination, as it has come to be known, recognizes that God will choose some to be among the elect while others will not be chosen. God calls human beings to be among the elect regardless of their qualifications or achievements. The elect do not earn this distinction through good works but through God's grace or undeserved love. To some this doctrine appears to deny an individual's free will. How can one act morally and ethically if God chooses who will be among the elect who enter heaven? Predestination does not absolve individuals of their responsibility to "do justice, and to love kindness, and to walk humbly" with God (Micah 6:8). Presbyterians view predestination as an acknowledgment of God's authority and his unqualified mastery over the plan for all creation. That human beings cannot know or even understand the plan affirms the mystery of God's limitless sovereignty. When Presbyterians become too smug in thinking that they are among God's elect, they are supposed to remember that Jesus Christ, the revealed embodiment of God, represents mercy, forgiveness, humility, and kindness.

PRESBYTERIANS AND TRANSCENDENTALISTS

Presbyterians often speak of the via media, the middle way. They prefer the happy medium, the reasonable, the golden mean. Presbyterians shun appeals to the emotions from the pulpit; the flamboyant, the ostentatious, and the loud are anathematic to the Presbyterian tradition. Similarly, Presbyterians prefer to act as an informed group, following the collective wisdom of the congregation. Following the desires of one's own heart conflicts with the idea of glorifying God. Presbyterians found themselves positioned between the rationalists of the eighteenth century and the transcendentalists of the first half of the nineteenth century. The rationalists rejected spiritual revelation, basing belief upon the exercise of reason and logical thinking. The transcendentalists believed that knowledge derived from intuition, not objective experience. Drawing upon the best features of both movements, Presbyterians sought the via media.

According to the theologian Erskine Clarke, "Members of Reformed communities, believing their calling and election to be sure, have had a strong tendency not to be preoccupied with introspection, with worrying over the state of their soul—or much less discovering their 'true self'—but rather with action that will be to the glory of God" (p. 16). Although Presbyterians refer to God as a Transcendent Being, they are far afield of the transcendentalists, the philosophical Romanticism that influenced writers in New England in the 1840s. George Ripley, Ralph Waldo Emerson, Amos Bronson Alcott, Margaret Fuller, Nathaniel Hawthorne, Henry David Thoreau, and others met frequently in Boston and Concord to discuss the idea that some force in human nature transcends human experience. An individual's relationship to God could be established directly without the need for the trappings of orthodox religion. While not a denomination— they had no ministers, churches, liturgies, and the like—the transcendentalists sought communion with what Emerson called the "Over-Soul." The movement was a reaction against Puritanism, which was also closely associated with New England. The transcendentalists informally sponsored Brook Farm, a utopian community in Massachusetts from 1841 until 1846. There they could discuss their epistemology. Presbyterianism, rationalism, and transcendentalism were not opposing movements, but they were different in their approach to religious philosophy. Reformed churches in general held that God is reasonable, therefore Nature must be orderly. Rationalists thought that Nature is orderly, therefore God must be reasonable. Emerson's *Nature* (1836) abstractly discusses the "advantages which our senses owe to Nature" (p. 1076). Emersonian views would not be compatible with Presbyterian reliance on critical and analytic thinking, logic, and deliberation as a means to acquire truth. But the transcendentalists believed that systematic thinking was not as important as instinct, imagination, and feelings; for them, the inner spiritual life of the individual and the full, free development of each individual's human personality were paramount.

Seeking the via media, Presbyterianism tries to balance critical and analytic thinking with creativity and intuition. Logical thinking and artistic endeavors can be complementary, not mutually exclusive. Presbyterians believe that a person can remain a self-realized individual while functioning as a contributing member of the congregation. Because Presbyterian doctrine asks its members not to be concerned with personal moods and feelings, they are expected to direct their thoughts to doing good deeds that serve the community and, ultimately, God.

See also Calvinism; Catholics; Protestantism; Religion; Transcendentalism

BIBLIOGRAPHY

Primary Works

Emerson, Ralph Waldo. *Nature*. 1836. In *The Norton Anthology of American Literature*, 5th ed., vol. 1, edited by Nina Baym et al. New York: Norton, 1998.

Stowe, Harriet Beecher. *Uncle Tom's Cabin*. 1852. New York: Penguin, 1986.

Twain, Mark. *The Adventures of Tom Sawyer*. Hartford, Conn.: American Publishing Company, 1876.

Secondary Works

Clarke, Erskine. *Our Southern Zion: A History of Calvinism in the South Carolina Low Country, 1690–1990*. Tuscaloosa: University of Alabama Press, 1996.

Lingle, Walter L., and John W. Kuykendall. *Presbyterians: Their History and Beliefs*. 4th rev. ed. Atlanta: John Knox Press, 1978.

Loetscher, Lefferts A. *A Brief History of the Presbyterians*. 4th ed., with a new chapter by George Laird Hunt. Philadelphia: Westminster Press, 1983.

Paine, Albert Bigelow. *Mark Twain: A Biography*. New York: Harper & Brothers, 1912.

Smylie, James H. *A Brief History of the Presbyterians*. Louisville, Ky.: Geneva Press, 1996.

Spence, Hartzell. *The Story of America's Religions*. New York: Holt, Rinehart and Winston, 1960.

Philip W. Leon

PROSLAVERY WRITING

In the antebellum period the American South produced a wave of literature defending slavery in the region. Virtually all fiction and nonfiction published in the South, from poetry and novels to political science texts and sociological treatises, took up proslavery as a central theme. Proslavery also appeared prominently in works focused on seemingly unrelated topics such as biological science, biblical history, and travel. Northern writers also produced important proslavery writing, but proslavery absorbed the antebellum South's intellectual energies, dividing the nation's culture with immediate, violent, and enduring consequences. In 1831, with a simultaneity not noted at the time, the coincident inception of William Lloyd Garrison's (1805–1879) *Liberator,* which initiated the abolitionist movement, and the insurrection of Nat Turner (1800–1831) ignited an ideological conflagration. After 1831 southern proslavery polemics glorified the region. Southern identity, southern unity, southern belligerence, the sectional crisis, secession, and Civil War followed, with proslavery authors of every genre cheering each step.

The year 1831 marked not only a sea change in the volume and influence of proslavery writing but also the coalescence of a new proslavery ideology. History textbooks often argue that the South defended slavery as a "necessary evil" before 1831 and then began to defend it as a "positive good" in response to abolitionist assaults. Historians no longer accept this simple formula. Southerners typically defended slavery only as it was practiced in the southern states, not arguing that slavery would last forever or that slavery was a feature of an ideal society. Yet historians do agree that the arguments the South produced after 1831 differed significantly from those of the revolutionary and early national periods. New writers with new social and moral outlooks defended the morality of slavery in ever-greater numbers. Proslavery ideology became more self-conscious, thoroughly articulated, and central to white southerners' identity. The rapid growth and territorial spread of both the slave/cotton economy and southern religious revivalism between 1787 and 1831 had changed the region's culture. Antebellum proslavery had little defensiveness and was characterized by moral and intellectual certitude.

Southern writers led the antebellum shift toward an uncompromising defense of slaveholding. After 1831 southerners drove dissenters on the issue of the morality of slaveholding out of the region. Southerners might continue to disagree among themselves about the exact future of slavery, the region's politics, and the characteristics that made the South distinctively wonderful, but public dissent on the superiority of the South was rare and violently punished.

RELIGIOUS DEFENSES OF SLAVERY

Religious publications sold more copies than any other form of proslavery writing. The three major protestant evangelical denominations—Baptists, Methodists, and Presbyterians—accounted for more than 90 percent of southern churchgoers. Their ministers ran southern educational institutions, included a higher percentage of slaveholders than any other profession, and controlled an impressive religious press. The *Methodist Christian Advocate* had the highest circulation of any newspaper in the world in 1830.

Ministers, including the Baptist Richard Furman (1755–1825), who was instrumental in founding George Washington, Furman, and Mercer Universities, led the first wave of antebellum proslavery writing in the wake of the Denmark Vesey slave-revolt conspiracy in Charleston in 1822. Furman's "Exposition of the Views of the Baptists, Relative to the Coloured Population of the United States" (1823) trumpeted the numerous scriptural passages taken to favor slaveholders that would be repeated ad nauseam after 1831. The abolitionist movement launched that year sprang from radical northern churches. Southern ministers thus felt well positioned to answer the abolitionists' religiously based charges that slaveholding was a sin. Southern writers sought divine sanction for slaveholding by quoting select scriptural passages—a development that encouraged a culture of simple biblical literalism in the region. The refrain of the regional war of words had other dramatic and long-lasting historical effects. The Presbyterian (1837, 1857, 1861), Methodist (1844), and Baptist (1845) denominations split into northern and southern wings over the issue of southern demands that slaveholders receive moral vindication and that abolitionists be purged as biblical heretics and dangerous social subversives. Southern ministers then controlled new independent regional denominations, newspapers, and periodicals that they used to promote their proslavery biblical argument.

Of course, long-standing biblical arguments in defense of slavery were well known or available. Antebellum ministers North and South, like the earliest American proslavery publicists in the Puritan New England of the 1600s, were familiar with racist and biblical justifications for slaveholding common in Western culture. Racist religious ideologies based on scripture were used to justify enslavement of Africans before slavery was instituted in America. No society in history, however, produced nearly the volume of religious proslavery writings that the antebellum South did.

The Virginia Baptist minister Thornton Stringfellow (1788–1869) wrote the best-selling proslavery tract of the era and was probably the most widely distributed antebellum southern writer of any kind. In his *Brief Examination of Scripture Testimony on the Institution of Slavery* (1841) Stringfellow gave the authoritative catalog of scriptural proslavery references that would be emphasized by antebellum southern evangelicals throughout the Civil War. Other proslavery ministers constantly pointed out that the God of the Old Testament had sanctioned slaveholding. After all, his prophets, patriarchs, and chosen people held slaves: God chose Abraham and blessed him while he held slaves, two of the Ten Commandments affirmed the master-slave relationship, and Leviticus 25 gave license to the holding of foreigners in perpetual bondage. Like all subsequent biblical proslavery writers, Stringfellow gave greatest emphasis to Paul's letters (the slaves for this reason labeled the period of their enslavement "Paul's Time"). Paul's letters acknowledged that slavery was consistent with Christianity (Ephesians 6), thus creating a New Testament link to the innumerable Old Testament passages. Proslavery ministers reasoned that although

he preached in a slaveholding society, Jesus never condemned slavery. In Luke 7, after curing the Centurion's servant, Jesus commended the Centurion, who, southern ministers pointed out, was a slaveholder. In the economic boom and spread of evangelical profession in the antebellum South, ministers thought they again saw the Savior commending and blessing righteous men who held slaves.

The South saw massive territorial and economic growth starting with the invention of the cotton gin in 1793; similarly, the relatively unchurched South witnessed a wave of conversions, starting with the Great Revival of 1801, which turned the region into the Bible belt. Southerners believed the tremendous economic boom and the spread of evangelical profession in the region were linked. In line with the Protestant work ethic, God had rewarded his righteous followers. When Paul spoke of "believing masters" in Timothy 4, Bible belt masters saw a reflection of themselves in scripture. The most popular biblical passage among antebellum southerners was also from Paul's Letters. In his letter to Philemon, Paul sent a runaway slave, Onesimus, back to his master. Southern proslavery ministers saw biblical justification not only for the morality of slavery but also for the southern position on the Fugitive Slave Law and the Constitution in this endlessly cited passage.

Like political lessons found in the Bible, biblical myths not in the literal word of scripture also played an important role in southern views of race and territorial expansion. The most infamous of such myths were those surrounding Genesis 9, in which Noah curses his son Ham for mocking Noah's drunkenness. The curse falls on Ham's son Canaan, who will be the "lowest of slaves" to Ham's brothers, Shem and Japheth. Noah prophesies that Japheth will prosper, and white southerners, indeed all antebellum white Americans, especially appropriated Noah's prophecy that God would "make space for Japheth, and let him live in the tents of Shem; and let Canaan be his slave." Southerners (and northerners) saw Genesis 9 as foreshadowing a sacred history of the United States: antebellum white Americans (Japheth) had enslaved Africans (Ham) and made space for themselves by occupying the tents of Native Americans (Shem). Southern novelists like William Gilmore Simms (1806–1870) employed this racist myth and routinely referred to blacks as "Children of Ham," as did northern authors such as Harriet Beecher Stowe (1811–1896).

THE DIVERSITY OF PROSLAVERY WRITING

Although religious morality dominated proslavery writing the topic flourished in an eclectic range and fusion of literary genres and ideological strategies.

The market for proslavery argumentation provided the impetus for expansion of regional publications and emergence of new cultural forms, such as the plantation novel. Diverse journals, including the *Southern Presbyterian Review* (1847–1885), *Southern Literary Messenger* (1834–1864), and the commercial forum "DeBow's Review" (1846–1869), published leading religious proslavery authors alongside literary, political, and academic polemics. The Methodist minister Augustus Baldwin Longstreet (1790–1870) embodied the wide range of regional writing involving proslavery. He wrote important biblical proslavery books and articles, edited the newspaper *The State Rights Sentinel*, was president of Emory College, and authored the famous sketch *Georgia Scenes* (1835) that marked the advent of the Southwest Humor literary genre. Like Joseph Glover Baldwin's *The Flush Times of Alabama and Mississippi* (1853), which expanded southwest humor, and John Pendleton Kennedy's *Swallow Barn* (1832), which established the plantation novel, Longstreet's informal sketches of southern life shared the purpose of religious proslavery. They celebrated the South's distinct and superior culture and assumed that a society built on slavery and white supremacy was desirable. Southern travel writing, such as William Alexander Caruthers's *The Kentuckian in New York* (1834), and genteel novels of manners, such as E. D. E. N. Southworth's *Shannondale* (1851), made the superiority of southern life and the alien and degenerate nature of the North more explicit. Caruthers also participated with important proslavery authors, such as Nathaniel Beverley Tucker, in developing the same themes in southern historical romances, derivative of Sir Walter Scott and James Fenimore Cooper. The South's most prolific author, William Gilmore Simms, produced nearly every variety of fiction and nonfiction that celebrated the southern way of life. Simms contributed polemics to intellectual and political defenses of slavery such as James Henry Hammond's influential compilation *The Pro-Slavery Argument* (1852).

ACADEMIC DEFENSES OF SLAVERY

Hammond, who was governor of and senator from South Carolina as well as a journalist, and Simms were among the elite intellectuals who produced academic defenses of slavery and often collaborated with each other. Academic writers, like ministers, argued that the South had superior social organization and unity compared to the North, which southern writers associated with dangerous social experimentation. Proslavery academic writers of all genres labeled the North as a land of "isms and schisms." Abolitionism joined Mormonism, Catholicism, vegetarianism,

William Gilmore Simms.

socialism, women's rights, and transcendentalism on the southern list of radical ideologies that flourished only in the North. Prominent among the influential academic defenders of slavery was the economist Thomas R. Dew (1802–1846), who pioneered the academic defense of slavery in his 1832 *Review of the Debate in the Virginia Legislature, 1831–1832*. The legislature had debated ending slavery after the Nat Turner revolt and rejected the idea. Dew used emerging laissez-faire economic doctrine from England to argue that slavery was a natural product of market forces and could not, and should not, be regulated or abolished by government policy. Dew influenced most subsequent proslavery writers, especially ministers, and melded Christianity and capitalism in his ideology.

In contrast to Dew's conflation of slavery and capitalism, the innovative sociologists Henry Hughes and George Fitzhugh argued in the 1850s for the superiority of a slave society to a capitalist one. Authors of proslavery novels and poems in the 1850s also employed the sociological critique of free labor in the North and England. Other academic fields produced influential proslavery writing that developed distinct variations on the argument that the South had the only proper social organization. The agriculturist Edmund Ruffin (1794–1865), the philosopher Albert Taylor Bledsoe (1809–1877), and the biologist Josiah Nott (1804–1873) championed the South in their respective fields. Nott's biological theories created controversy in southern letters because he rejected biblical accounts of human origins and argued that blacks were a separate and inferior creation. His rejection of the Bible, rather than his white supremacy, troubled fellow proslavery writers. Many of these same intellectuals' works, in addition to those of religious proslavery authors like Stringfellow, were reprinted at the end of the 1850s in the massive and famous compilation E. N. Elliott's *Cotton Is King* (1860).

During the 1850s less academic but equally didactic defenses of slavery sprang from southern reactions to Stowe's *Uncle Tom's Cabin* (1852). Numerous hackneyed proslavery novels attempted to counter *Uncle Tom*. E. W. Warren's *Nellie Norton* (1864) focused on the biblical and moral defense of slavery, and Mary H. Eastman's *Aunt Phillis's Cabin* (1852) adopted a southern version of Stowe's romanticism that followed the "plantation myth" of happy slaves protected by patriarchal masters living by a superior, bygone rural ethic. While these southern novels of the 1850s met little literary or popular success, poetry, like that of Congressman William J. Grayson (1788–1863) of South Carolina, achieved more acclaim inside the South. Grayson's "The Hireling and the Slave" (1854) defended slavery and answered Stowe in the style of Alexander Pope.

Mary H. Eastman was not the only southern woman to take up pen to answer Stowe and defend slavery. Louisa S. McCord, in an impressive body of polemical academic articles, answered Stowe by defending slavery as an expression of free-market economics, drawing heavily on Thomas Dew, and by dismissing women's rights. She was one of the only antebellum women to write extensively about political economy.

PROSLAVERY AS AN INTELLECTUAL MOVEMENT

Given the range of proslavery publications, historians disagree sharply on the intellectual underpinnings of proslavery writings and on the nature of southern society revealed in them. Analysis of the southern political economy is at the root of long-standing historiographical debates. It also divides many proslavery writings. Most southern ministers and political economists, especially those in commercial centers, defended slavery as a progressive expression of free-market forces, property rights, liberal individualism, and the Protestant

work ethic. This camp made fewer distinctions between the North and South, factory and plantation, the modern and the traditional. They were very willing to admit that slavery would and even should pass away in the future. However, a smaller but influential group of intellectuals, politicians, scientists—especially biologists, ethnologists, and sociologists—and conservative ministers, especially Old School Presbyterians like the South's leading theologian, James Henley Thornwell (1812–1862), defended slavery as an older, superior, and permanent patriarchal relationship serving as a bulwark against the evils of the emerging market system. Historians choose to emphasize either the "free-market" or "patriarchal" (often "paternalist") proslavery writings in order to support their divergent analyses of the Old South.

Historians agree that racist assumptions were at the heart of every form of proslavery writing. The progressive "free-market" proslavery apologists argued that blacks were morally unfit for freedom and that they had failed (or would fail) in the competitive atmosphere of the American work ethic. Slavery, supposedly, constituted a "Christian School" that was uplifting blacks via the moral lessons of hard work. The conservative, "paternalist" brand of proslavery assumed that blacks—via biology, culture, or divine ordinance—were a permanent class of inferiors unfit for independence. Historians also agree that proslavery ideology set the stage for secession and sustained the Confederate war effort. The boom in proslavery literature, by definition, did not survive the Civil War, but the arguments and themes developed in it had transformed the South and reappeared in pro-segregation writing and the literature of the Lost Cause, which celebrated the righteousness of the Confederate cause for decades after the Civil War in publications nearly as various and voluminous as the proslavery genre. The proslavery themes of racial subjugation and of moral and cultural superiority of the Bible belt survived in a world without slavery and forged a legacy that southern authors wrestled with in the twentieth century.

See also Abolitionist Writing; *The Confessions of Nat Turner;* Ethnology; Female Authorship; Humor; Religion; The Romance; Slave Rebellions; *Sociology for the South; Swallow Barn*

BIBLIOGRAPHY
Primary Works
Barnes, Albert. *An Inquiry into the Scriptural Views of Slavery.* 1846. New York: Negro Universities Press, 1969.

Blanchard, Jonathan, and N. L. Rice. *A Debate on Slavery.* Cincinnati, Ohio: W. H. Moore & Co., 1846.

Bledsoe, Albert T. *Essay on Liberty and Slavery*. Philadelphia: J. B. Lippincott & Co., 1856.

Brownlow, Taylor G., and A. Pryne. *Ought American Slavery To Be Perpetuated? A Debate*. Philadelphia: J. B. Lippincott & Co, 1858.

Dew, Thomas Roderick. *Review of the Debate in the Virginia Legislature of 1831 and 1832*. Westport, Conn.: Negro Universities Press, 1970.

Elliott, E. N., ed. *Cotton Is King and Pro-Slavery Arguments: Comprising the Writings of Hammond, Harper, Christy, Stringfellow, Hodge, Bledsoe, and Cartwright, on this Important Subject*. Augusta, Ga.: Pritchard, Abbott & Loomis, 1860.

Fuller, Richard, and Francis Wayland. *Domestic Slavery Considered as a Scriptural Institution*. New York: L. Colby, 1845.

Ker, Leander. *Slavery Consistent with Christianity*. Baltimore: Sherwood & Co., 1840.

McCaine, Alexander. *Slavery Defended from Scripture*. Baltimore: Wm. Woody, 1842.

McTyrie, H. N., C. F. Sturgis, and A. T. Holmes. *Duties to Servants: Three Premium Essays*. Charleston, S.C.: Southern Baptist Convention, 1851.

Priest, Josiah. *Bible Defence of Slavery*. Glasgow Ky.: Walker and Richard, 1852.

Pro-Slavery Argument: As Maintained by the Most Distinguished Writers of the Southern States, Containing the Several Essays, on the Subject, of Chancellor Harper, Governor Hammond, Dr. Simms, and Professor Dew. Charleston, S.C.: Walker, Richards & Co., 1852.

Ross, Frederick. *Slavery Ordained of God*. Philadelphia: J. B. Lippincott & Co., 1857.

Smith, William A. *Lectures on the Philosophy and Practice of Slavery*. Nashville, Tenn.: Stevenson and Evans, 1856.

Smyth, Thomas. *The Unity of the Human Races Proved to be the Doctrine of Scripture, Reason, and Science*. New York: G. P. Putman, 1850.

Stearns, Edward J. *Notes on "Uncle Tom's Cabin": Being a Logical Answer to Its Allegations and Inferences against Slavery as an Institution*. Philadelphia: Lippincott, Grambo & Co., 1853.

Thornwell, James Henley. *Rights and Duties of Masters*. Charleston, S.C.: Press of Walker and James, 1850.

Warren, E. W. *Nellie Norton; or, Southern Slavery and the Bible. A Scriptural Refutation of the Principal Arguments upon which the Abolitionists Rely. A Vindication of Southern Slavery from the Old and New Testaments*. Macon, Ga.: Burke, Boykin, & Company, 1864.

Wilson, Joseph. *The Mutual Relations of Masters and Slaves as Taught in the Bible*. Augusta, Ga.: Steam Press of the Chronicle and Sentinel, 1861.

Secondary Works

Ambrose, Douglas. *Henry Hughes and Proslavery Thought in the Old South*. Baton Rouge: Louisiana State University Press, 1996.

Bailey, David T. *Shadow on the Church: Southwestern Evangelical Religion and the Issue of Slavery, 1783–1860*. Ithaca, N.Y.: Cornell University Press, 1985.

Daly, John Patrick. *When Slavery Was Called Freedom: Evangelicalism, Proslavery, and the Causes of the Civil War*. Lexington: University Press of Kentucky, 2002.

Davis, David Brion. *The Problem of Slavery in Western Culture*. Ithaca, N.Y.: Cornell University Press, 1966.

Farmer, James Oscar. *The Metaphysical Confederacy: James Henley Thornwell and the Synthesis of Southern Values*. Macon, Ga.: Mercer University Press, 1985.

Faust, Drew Gilpin. *A Sacred Circle: The Dilemma of the Intellectual in the Old South, 1840–1860*. Baltimore: Johns Hopkins University Press, 1977.

Faust, Drew Gilpin, ed. *The Ideology of Slavery: Proslavery Thought in the Antebellum South, 1830–1860*. Baton Rogue: Louisiana State University Press, 1981.

Finkelman, Paul, ed. *Proslavery Thought, Ideology, and Politics*. New York: Garland, 1989.

Fought, Leigh. *Southern Womanhood and Slavery: A Biography of Louisa S. McCord, 1810–1879*. Columbia: University Press of Missouri, 2003.

Fredrickson, George M. *The Black Image in the White Mind: The Debate on Afro-American Character and Destiny, 1817–1914*. New York: Harper and Row, 1971.

Genovese, Eugene D. *The Political Economy of Slavery: Studies in the Economy & Society of the Slave South*. New York: Pantheon, 1965.

Genovese, Eugene D. *The Slaveholders' Dilemma: Freedom and Progress in Southern Conservative Thought, 1820–1860*. Columbia: University of South Carolina Press, 1992.

Goen, C. C. *Broken Churches, Broken Nation: Denominational Schisms and the Coming of the American Civil War*. Macon, Ga.: Mercer University Press: 1985.

Haynes, Stephen R. *Noah's Curse: The Biblical Justification of American Slavery*. Oxford and New York: Oxford University Press, 2002.

Hill, Samuel. *South and the North in American Religion*. Athens: University of Georgia Press, 1980.

Jenkins, William Sumner. *Pro-Slavery Thought in the Old South*. Chapel Hill: University of North Carolina Press, 1935.

O'Brien, Michael. *Rethinking the South: Essays in Intellectual History*. Baltimore: Johns Hopkins University Press, 1988.

Paskoff, Paul, ed. *The Cause of the South: Selections from "DeBow's Review," 1846–1867*. Baton Rouge: Louisiana State University Press, 1982.

Rubin, Louis D., Jr. *The Edge of the Swamp: A Study in the Literature and Society of the Old South.* Baton Rouge: Louisiana State University Press, 1989.

Smith, H. Shelton. *In His Image But . . . : Racism in Southern Religion, 1780–1910.* Durham, N.C.: Duke University Press, 1972.

Snay, Mitchell. *Gospel of Disunion: Religion and Separatism in the Antebellum South.* Cambridge, U.K., and New York: Cambridge University Press, 1993.

Tise, Larry E. *Proslavery: A History of the Defense of Slavery in America, 1701–1840.* Athens: University of Georgia Press, 1987.

John Patrick Daly

PROTESTANTISM

In the summer of 1820, an impressive group of Protestant clergymen, educators, and business professionals gathered in western Massachusetts to lay the cornerstone for the first building of Amherst College. As a trustee of the fledgling institution, the grandfather of Emily Dickinson was among those in the group, but pride of place fell to the great maker of dictionaries, Noah Webster (1758–1843), whose task that day was to dedicate the college to the glory of God and the pursuit of a grand Protestant cultural enterprise.

In his oration, Webster tied the founding of the college to the hastening of the kingdom of God. In educating young men "for the gospel ministry," Amherst would be seconding "the efforts of the apostles themselves, in extending and establishing the Redeemer's empire—the empire of truth." It would raise "the human race from ignorance and debasement" and "teach them the way to happiness and glory." In the end, nothing short of the perfection of the kingdom of God was to be expected from Amherst College, the American republic, and the Protestant enterprise they together promoted. If the college did its work well, it would "convert swords into plowshares and spears into pruning hooks" and even "dispeople the state prison and the penitentiary!" (pp. 7–8, 11).

Within the brief compass of his speech, Webster outlined what the historian Mark A. Noll has identified as the unique synthesis of evangelical faith, republican political ideology, and commonsense moral reasoning that dominated American life from the beginning of the nineteenth century to the end of the Civil War. The expansive power of evangelical Protestantism formed the central religious reality of America in that period, and, as Noll argues, no other era in the nation's history saw such a dramatic increase in religious affiliation or such a pervasive influence of religion on the national culture.

The Protestant vision grounded nineteenth-century American culture in its explicitly Christian past but at the same time opened up possibilities for the nation's secular future; it inspired many immigrants and settlers with an expansive vision of American possibilities while it consigned others, particularly Catholics, to second-class status; and it provided powerful underpinnings for the supporters of slavery even as it supplied slavery's opponents with telling arguments and stirring claims against the institution.

PROTESTANT BEGINNINGS

The story of Protestantism in nineteenth-century America begins with events that unfolded three centuries earlier. The first recorded use of the term "Protestant" in English dates to 1539, when it was applied specifically to those German princes and their subjects who protested the Roman Catholic Church's efforts to silence Martin Luther and bring an end to the Reformation.

Initially, the word "Protestant" applied only to Lutherans in Germany, whereas the Swiss and French followers of John Calvin called themselves "Reformed." By the early seventeenth century, however, the term had come to be applied to all Western Christians who repudiated papal authority and Catholic doctrine. For a complex set of reasons, it was to be Protestants who undertook the colonization of North America in earnest, as Dutch Calvinists settled along the Hudson River, Anglicans moved to the mid-Atlantic coast, and Puritans followed two decades later to Massachusetts Bay.

The Massachusetts Bay Colony would have an enduring significance out of all proportion to its initial size and stature. Many of the most dynamic Protestant influences in American life stemmed from the belief system and cultural practices of this group of several hundred settlers. Long after most Americans had let go of the bracing theology of the Puritans, they continued to embrace a form of the Puritan vision of American destiny.

The first governor of the Massachusetts colony, John Winthrop (1588–1649), famously outlined that vision in a sermon written before or during the 1630 voyage that brought his group to the New World. Winthrop titled his sermon "A Model of Christian Charity" and in it elaborated the covenantal understanding at the heart of Puritan theology. For these Calvinists, the covenant was a legal agreement between

By the early nineteenth century, a surprising intellectual synthesis, distinctly different from the reigning intellectual constructs in comparable Western societies, had come to prevail throughout the United States. It was a surprise both because little in colonial history before the mid-eighteenth century anticipated its formation and because it came into being only as an indirect result of the American Revolution, the era's greatest intellectual as well as political event. The formation of this synthesis, in turn, explains much about what followed in the history of American thought from the early nineteenth century. Along with more distinctly religious factors, the plausibility, flexibility, and popularity of this synthesis at all social levels was a key to the remarkable Christianization that occurred in the United States, both North and South, during the period 1790–1865. . . .

The synthesis was a compound of evangelical Protestant religion, republican political ideology, and commonsense moral reasoning. Through the time of the Civil War, that synthesis defined the boundaries for a vast quantity of American thought, while also providing an ethical framework, a moral compass, and a vocabulary of suasion for much of the nation's public life. It set, quite naturally, the boundaries within which formal theological effort took place. Since the Civil War, the synthesis has declined in importance for both formal thought and public life, though not without leaving an enduring stamp upon the mental habits of some religious communities and episodic marks upon the public discourse.

Noll, *America's God: From Jonathan Edwards to Abraham Lincoln*, p. 9.

tatives, they would be carving out of the wilderness the kingdom of God.

Although it was only one among the many voices clamoring to be heard in the colonies, Puritanism would come to direct the cultural conversation of America in a number of surprising ways. Early on, for example, it developed an interpretive discipline that involved an exceptionally close reading of personal experience and natural phenomena, as these Protestants scoured their souls and searched their world for signs of God's coming kingdom. Even when Puritanism eventually fell out of favor, the interpretive habits it had inspired continued to thrive in new and different forms, whether in the prose of Henry David Thoreau (1817–1862) or the poetry of Emily Dickinson (1830–1886) and Robert Frost, in the fiction of Nathaniel Hawthorne (1804–1864), Herman Melville (1819–1891), and William Faulkner, or in the late-twentieth and early-twenty-first-century essays of Barry Lopez and Wendell Berry. Over several centuries, the Puritan practice of closely reading nature and experience consistently demonstrated a remarkable tenacity. Like other elements of the Puritan vision, it was compelling enough in its content and flexible enough in its form to adapt to changing cultural tastes.

Later scholars, however, intensely debated the nature and extent of that Puritan cultural influence. Some argued that the claims made on behalf of Puritanism by Perry Miller, Sacvan Bercovitch, and others obscured the vital contributions of other religious traditions to American literature and culture. At the same time, other observers questioned the very notion of American exceptionalism that lies behind the argument of Protestant influence. Spanish Catholics were here long before the English arrived, this line of reasoning goes, and native peoples lived on the land for thousands of years before the first European settlers set foot on North American soil. Since Roman Catholics and Anabaptists, freethinkers and tribal worshippers all played crucial roles in American religious history, on what grounds do we single out the efforts of a small band of Protestants from northwestern Europe?

In the end, such questions can be answered only by carefully charting influence in the many instances where it can be traced. As a case in point, seventeenth-century New England churches stressed individual experience in a manner that was to shape the larger culture profoundly. The Puritans conceived of the church as a gathering of freely consenting individuals. They made it a requirement that to become a member of the church, each man and woman had to undergo a

God and his chosen people: "We have entered into Covenant with Him for this Work, we have taken out a Commission, the Lord hath given us leave to draw our own Articles." If the Puritan colonists kept the terms of the covenant, God would make them "a praise and glory," and all other plantations in the New World would declare, "Make [us] like that of New England." This small band of emigrants at the edge of the known world would become "a City upon a Hill," with "the eyes of all people" upon them (p. 10). By settling in New England, these Protestants would not be pursuing their own destiny, but, as God's represen-

harrowing conversion, which involved turning away from sin and breaking with the past. If you were a Puritan, in other words, you could not receive your faith from your parents but had to achieve it on your own. Whereas for centuries birth had determined membership in the Roman Catholic Church and many early Protestant denominations, in New England conversion and consent were required before a church could be called into being.

The Puritan practice of establishing "gathered churches" led to the creation of what the sociologist Robert Bellah, the philosopher Charles Taylor, and others have called an American cultural tradition of "leaving home." Like their Puritan ancestors struggling to establish their own distinct relationship with God, countless later Americans would take it as a given that they had to make their own way in the world, free of the determining influence of parents and past. Thus we find established in American culture a paradoxical tradition of leaving tradition behind, or, to put it another way, our social expectation is for individuals to grow and prosper without paying heed to social expectations. In America, Jews and Christians, Muslims and pagans all adopt this tradition of abandoning tradition, and had it not been for the seeds sown by the early Protestant settlers, it is hard to imagine that such a tradition would have taken root so deeply in the soil of American culture.

ROMANTIC ADAPTATIONS

By the early decades of the nineteenth century, Puritanism had played itself out as an active force in American life, yet the Protestant cultural legacy remained a potent presence in the culture. That legacy adapted quickly to the vagaries of life in a religiously diverse republic and prospered following the removal of the last vestiges of state support, when Connecticut disestablished the Congregational Church in 1818 and Massachusetts followed suit in 1833. On the competitive field created by the constitutional freedom of religion, antebellum Protestantism consolidated its position as a dominant religious force, continuing to shape American culture, and with mixed results wrestling with growing religious diversity and the destructive reality of slavery.

Just months before Massachusetts brought an end to state-sanctioned religion, a drama of lasting importance in the history of Protestantism and American literature unfolded in a Boston church. The main player in this drama was Ralph Waldo Emerson (1803–1882), who was reluctantly voted out of office by the proprietors of the Second Church in late October 1832. They dismissed Emerson in response to a sermon he had preached several weeks earlier, in which he had explained why he would no longer administer the sacrament of the Lord's Supper.

For his sermon on that sacrament, Emerson had preached from Romans 14:17: "For the kingdom of God is not meat and drink; but righteousness, and peace, and joy in the Holy Ghost." He took this injunction literally, as a command from Jesus to forgo any outward signs of faith or practice. The Catholic Church had celebrated seven sacraments while most Protestant denominations had reduced that number to two, baptism and communion. Emerson saw no need for any because the form of the sacrament throttled freedom of the spirit. "Freedom is the essence of Christianity," he told his parishioners. "Its institutions should be as flexible as the wants of men. The form out of which the life and suitableness have departed should be as worthless in its eyes as the dead leaves that are falling around us" (*Essays,* p. 1139).

In spurning both the authority of the scriptures and the sanction of the sacraments, Emerson was seeking to sustain the Protestant cultural project without the support of the theology that had given birth to it. In doing so, he was in turn appropriating for American culture an effort that had been under way for several decades in the Protestant cultures of Germany and England. There, a series of Romantic philosophers, poets, and critics had sought, in the words of M. H. Abrams, "to save traditional concepts, schemes, and values which had been based on the relation of the Creator to his creature and creation" by recasting them within a secular framework of "the human mind or consciousness and its transactions with nature" (p. 13).

In recasting the Protestant creeds within a secular framework, Emerson sought to adapt to his own purposes key elements of the Protestant vision, including the millennial fervor of his Puritan ancestors, as well as their emphasis on free consent and the virtue of "leaving home." In all the major writers who had roots in New England between 1820 and 1870, the tension between the Christian past and the secular Protestant present was palpable. It manifested itself in the powerful psychology of Melville's *Moby-Dick* (1851) and "Bartleby, the Scrivener" (1853); it pervaded the tortured examination of the human soul in many of Hawthorne's short stories and in *The Scarlet Letter* (1850); it provided the pith and substance of Dickinson's poetic explorations of belief, suffering, and the silence of God; and it animated Thoreau's vision of a spiritually vital individualism.

At the same time, this cultural Protestantism had darker consequences in the nineteenth century because it fueled a strong anti-Catholic nativism. From the beginning of the American experiment, genuine religion had meant the Protestant faith. Roman Catholicism could be tolerated at the edges of the culture, but few in the colonial era or in the early decades of the Republic considered it a dynamic system of belief destined to play an ever larger role in American life. In 1790 there were but sixty-five Catholic churches in the United States, out of a total of almost five thousand Christian churches, and Catholicism had little impact on cultural or political affairs.

In the following decades, the situation changed dramatically, as immigration swelled the ranks of the Catholic Church in America. Even as evangelical Protestantism consolidated its hold on antebellum culture, the number of Roman Catholic churches grew at a markedly faster rate than that of Protestant ones in those years. On the eve of the war, there were 2,550 Catholic churches in the United States, and Catholicism was becoming at last a player on the cultural stage.

As the influence of the Catholic Church grew, so did the Protestant animus against it. Prejudice against Catholicism was to be found at every level of the culture, as is evidenced by an exchange of letters between Emerson, the American educator Charles Eliot Norton (1827–1908), and the English poet Arthur Hugh Clough (1819–1861). They wrote to one another about the conversion to Catholicism in 1858 of Anna Barker Ward, the wife of one of Emerson's literary associates, Samuel Ward. These three fretted over the prospect of her "Babylonish Captivity" and "grieved" that she had allied herself with a faith that "makes such carnage of social relations." The problem with this "perversion," Clough wrote, was that it seemed "so irrevocable a change" (p. 556). For the disease of this dogmatic faith, Emerson prescribed the "electuary"—the sweet, healing paste—of "house, children, & husband" (*Letters* 5:169). He told Samuel Ward, who had not joined his wife in the move to the Catholic Church, that Anna would eventually be cured of her spiritual disease, construing her conversion, and the whole of the Catholic Church, as a lamentable sickness from which one could only hope to recover.

Emerson's use of the metaphor of illness is in keeping with many antebellum Romantic characterizations of Catholicism. Fueled by Protestant millennialism in general and by the New World covenantal vision of the Puritans in particular, the romantics saw Catholicism as a remnant of the precritical history of humanity. Like an embarrassing adolescence, it was something to be blushed at and outgrown. Thoreau neatly captured this Romantic perception of Catholic belief in his depiction of Alek Therien, a French Canadian neighbor at Walden Pond. The intellectual

and spiritual elements in Therien "were slumbering as in an infant." He had been taught in that "innocent and ineffectual way in which the Catholic priests teach the aborigines." When those priests train a student, "the pupil is never educated to the degree of consciousness, but only to the degree of trust and reverence, and a child is not made a man, but kept a child" (p. 439). To be Catholic was to be like nature—dumb and in desperate need of the poet's consciousness and speech. "Nature is hard to be overcome, but she must be overcome" (p. 498), Thoreau concluded in *Walden* (1854). That was also the case for Roman Catholicism according to many cultural Protestants in the nineteenth century.

The attitudes of Emerson, Thoreau, and others need to be set within the broader context of nineteenth-century cultural history. The literary historian Jenny Franchot has argued that the anti-Catholicism of Protestant liberals of that time can be traced to the Puritan narrative of providential history, in which two monumental events, the Reformation and the Puritan settling of America, had unfolded just centuries earlier. According to Franchot, for the writers of the antebellum era Protestant America was allied with divine history, and reform was a matter of destiny. In such a context, a Catholic resurgence could only represent a reversal of history, a return to bondage, and a loss of the freedom of Protestant individualism.

While the growth of Catholicism struck fear in the hearts of the cultural elites, it also generated powerful responses at the popular level. From 1830 to 1860, what had been a trickle of anti-Catholic literature swelled into a torrent, as diatribes came cascading down from Protestant pulpits and flowed from the pages of popular tracts and novels. Especially popular were the fictional "memoirs" of people who had escaped the clutches of Catholicism. Where the seventeenth-century Puritans had written accounts of their captivity at the hands of Native Americans, antebellum Protestant writers wrote racy stories about captive abuse within the walls of the Catholic Church.

The most famous of these narratives, Maria Monk's *Awful Disclosures of the Hotel Dieu Nunnery,* appeared in 1836. This fiction parading as fact told of a prostitute who sought sanctuary in a convent, only to discover within its walls terror and sadism worse than anything she had known on the streets. The pages of Monk's "memoir" were filled with stories of brutal nuns and rapacious priests in the convent-turned-brothel, where ostensibly celibate men of God had their way with defenseless young nuns and murdered the children unfortunate enough to be born of the violent unions.

We can see the intensity of Protestant fear in the fact that Monk's narrative sold three hundred thousand copies in the twenty-five years between its publication and the outbreak of the Civil War. Aside from the Bible, it was outsold by only one book in that period, Harriet Beecher Stowe's fictional polemic against slavery, *Uncle Tom's Cabin* (1852).

SCRIPTURE, SLAVERY, AND THE PROTESTANT SYNTHESIS

The fact that Monk's captivity narrative and Stowe's abolitionist novel were the two best-selling books in the mid-nineteenth century shows that the Protestant influence was as divided as it was dynamic. For as powerfully as Monk's book reinforced stereotypes meant to keep Roman Catholicism at the cultural margins, with even greater force did *Uncle Tom's Cabin* crystallize religious and moral opposition to slavery in the decade leading up to the war. When Abraham Lincoln (1809–1865) was grappling with the question of emancipation in 1862, he borrowed from the Library of Congress Stowe's *A Key to Uncle Tom's Cabin* (1853), which documented the abuses she had exposed in her novel. When he greeted her later that year at the White House, Lincoln is reported to have said, "So you're the little woman who wrote the book that made this great war."

Through his use of hyperbole and humor, Lincoln was in fact making a serious point. It had taken a work of fiction to galvanize the nation to settle by force a conflict it had been unable to resolve through the play of ideas or the art of political compromise.

Leading up to the war, Protestant beliefs and practices played a crucial role on both sides of the battle over slavery. Many claimed scriptural support for slavery. They took encouragement from the Bible's ethical silence about the practice in the ancient world and strenuously defended it on the principle of obedience and submission to authority. Some sincerely believed in a biblical sanction for slavery, whereas others cynically employed the scriptures to support the practice even as they denied the Bible's authority over every other facet of their lives.

Although the Bible was often used to justify slavery, in many other cases a Protestant interpretation of the scriptures drove men and women to oppose it with action or to endure it with hope. With difficulty, many antebellum Protestants sought to combine their commitment to scriptural authority and their intuitive sense that slavery was either an injustice to be tempered or an abomination to be destroyed. Their struggle was complicated by the considerable skill with which the defenders of slavery linked a literal reading of the Bible—which acknowledged the scriptures' tacit acceptance of slavery—to the idea of biblical authority itself.

Other Protestants sought to avoid this impasse by stressing the difference between the letter of the Bible and its spirit. Even if the Old and the New Testaments had condoned the practice in their day, this line of reasoning held, the spiritual intentions of the scriptures were unmistakably opposed to its continuance. In the conclusion to *Uncle Tom's Cabin,* Stowe gave powerful voice to this feeling-based interpretation of the spirit of the Bible. Nothing could be written or conceived, she said, "that equals the frightful reality of scenes daily and hourly acting on our shores, beneath the shadow of American law, and the shadow of the cross of Christ" (p. 514). The only important question for the Protestant believer is not interpretive consistency or theological rigor but one's own sympathies: "Are they in harmony with the sympathies of Christ? or are they swayed and perverted by the sophistries of worldly policy?" (p. 515). Only if their sympathies are aright and they act upon them boldly may the people of the North and South together forsake their "injustice and cruelty" and thus mercifully avoid "the wrath of Almighty God" (p. 519).

Others in the Protestant tradition went beyond Stowe's sympathetic evangelical piety and embraced more radical positions, both in their attitude toward the Christian tradition and in their willingness to use violence to bring slavery to an end. This group included such well-known figures as Thoreau, Emerson, and John Brown, as well as a number of largely forgotten individuals, such as James McCune Smith and Gerrit Smith. According to the literary historian John Stauffer, these Protestants had an understanding of God that could not be separated from their understanding of themselves as moral warriors, from the vision they shared of America's millennial future, or from their passionate desire to eliminate social and racial barriers. They did not necessarily need the Bible to validate what their God-given moral sense had already convinced them to believe and to do.

For these Protestants, moral consistency on the issue of slavery often overrode any concerns about theological orthodoxy or biblical fidelity. On the eve of the Civil War, Gerrit Smith (1797–1874) gave voice to this passion for ethical rigor, as he explained why the Congregational minister George Cheever, like many other evangelical Protestants, was mistaken in his efforts to prove that the Bible condemned slavery: "Dr. Cheever sees no hope for freedom, if the Bible shall be given to the side of slavery. But I see no hope for the Bible if it shall be proved to be for slavery." Human nature provides the charter for human rights, "and [man's] rights are the rights of his nature—no more nor less—every book to the contrary notwithstanding" (quoted in Noll, pp. 387–388).

Fighting was to break out at Fort Sumter only months after this exchange between Cheever and Smith, and by the end of the war the era of Protestant hegemony had effectively come to a close. When Noah Webster dedicated the cornerstone at Amherst College in 1820, as a Protestant man, he stood in all his singularity as a representative of the larger nation and its ideals. By 1865 Webster would have become but one voice within a cacophonous conversation among Protestants of many different persuasions; and those Protestants in turn would now be jostling for space alongside newly emerging groups with decidedly different religious, intellectual, and political convictions. Although Protestantism would continue to exert a powerful influence on American culture, it has never since occupied the dominant position that belonged to it in the early and middle decades of the nineteenth century.

See also The Bible; Calvinism; Catholics; Proslavery Writing; Puritanism; Religion; Religious Magazines; *Uncle Tom's Cabin*

BIBLIOGRAPHY
Primary Works

Clough, Arthur Hugh. *Correspondence*. Vol. 2. Edited by Frederick L. Mulhauser. Oxford: Clarendon Press, 1957.

Emerson, Ralph Waldo. *Essays and Lectures*. Edited by Joel Porte. New York: Library of America, 1983.

Emerson, Ralph Waldo. *The Letters of Ralph Waldo Emerson*. 10 vols. Edited by Ralph L. Rusk (vols. 1–6) and Eleanor M. Tilton (vols. 7–10). New York: Columbia University Press, 1939–1995.

Monk, Maria. *Awful Disclosures of the Hotel Dieu Nunnery of Montreal*. New York: Hoisington & Trow, 1836.

Stowe, Harriet Beecher. *Three Novels: Uncle Tom's Cabin, The Minister's Wooing, Oldtown Folks*. New York: Library of America, 1982.

Thoreau, Henry David. *Walden; or, Life in the Woods*. 1854. In *A Week on the Concord and Merrimack Rivers; Walden; or, Life in the Woods; The Maine Woods; Cape Cod*. Edited by Robert F. Sayre. New York: Library of America, 1985.

Webster, Noah. *A Plea for a Miserable World*. Boston: Ezra Lincoln, 1820.

Winthrop, John. *The Journal of John Winthrop, 1630–1649*. Edited by Richard S. Dunn and Laetitia Yeandle. Abridged ed. Cambridge, Mass.: Belknap Press of Harvard University Press, 1996.

Secondary Works

Abrams, M. H. *Natural Supernaturalism: Tradition and Revolution in Romantic Literature*. New York: Norton, 1971.

Bellah, Robert, et al. *Habits of the Heart: Individualism and Commitment in American Life*. Berkeley: University of California Press, 1985.

Bercovitch, Sacvan. *The Puritan Origins of the American Self*. New Haven, Conn.: Yale University Press, 1975.

Franchot, Jenny. *Roads to Rome: The Antebellum Protestant Encounter with Catholicism*. Berkeley: University of California Press, 1994.

Miller, Perry. *Nature's Nation*. Cambridge, Mass.: Belknap Press of Harvard University Press, 1967.

Morgan, Edmund S. *Visible Saints: The History of a Puritan Idea*. 1963. Ithaca, N.Y.: Cornell University Press, 1965.

Noll, Mark A. *America's God: From Jonathan Edwards to Abraham Lincoln*. New York: Oxford University Press, 2002.

Stauffer, John. *The Black Hearts of Men: Radical Abolitionists and the Transformation of Race*. Cambridge, Mass.: Harvard University Press, 2002.

Taylor, Charles. *Sources of the Self: The Making of the Modern Identity*. Cambridge, Mass.: Harvard University Press, 1989.

Roger Lundin

PSYCHOLOGY

The relationship between psychology and literature may seem intuitively obvious given the ways that fictional narratives can create the impression that one has direct access to a character's thoughts and deepest feelings. This is the case with some of the earliest American novels, for example, *The Coquette* (1797) by Hannah Foster (1759–1840) and *Wieland* (1798) by Charles Brockden Brown (1771–1810), both of which present their stories largely in the form of emotional and dramatically revealing letters to intimates. Similarly, early American autobiographers derived authority from the appearance of candor when disclosing life experiences and lessons learned. While fictional and nonfictional works that convey states of mind may appear straightforward, the mental and emotional processes of both narrators and characters were derived from complex amalgams of beliefs about human psychology that differ markedly from current theories.

Psychological thinkers of the early nineteenth century, like their forebears, based their ideas on universal assumptions about human motivations and behaviors, and these assumptions would greatly affect the literature of the United States. For example, Ralph Waldo

Emerson (1803–1882) and James Fenimore Cooper (1789–1851) set forth ideas and depictions of strong-willed characters responding forcefully to their physical and intellectual environments, while Harriet Beecher Stowe (1811–1896) and Frederick Douglass (1818–1895) advanced visions of social change largely organized around accepted attitudes about social bonds. Writers also would depict unusual mental processes, as in the case of tales by Nathaniel Hawthorne (1804–1864) and Edgar Allan Poe (1809–1849). In addition, the question of how audiences respond to literature constituted a matter of concern common to writers and those psychologists who discussed aesthetics. Perhaps the most important connection between psychological theory and antebellum literature and culture may be found in the affiliation between the republican ideology of the American Revolution and certain psychological doctrines that had been produced by eighteenth-century European thinkers. Although early- and mid-nineteenth-century writers did not unthinkingly reflect the ideas of European and American psychological theorists, their ideas shaped literary treatments of mental processes and social relations.

EARLY NINETEENTH-CENTURY PSYCHOLOGY AND ITS BACKGROUND

The field of psychology during the years 1820–1870 resembles only slightly the academic discipline that is now familiar. For example, the scientific outlook underlying Charles Darwin's *On the Origin of Species* (1859) did not begin to have an impact on American psychologists until after the Civil War. Moreover, the use of empirical methodologies, most notably the physiological experimentation developed in German universities, was not systematically cultivated in the United States until the 1880s. In addition, the concept of unconscious motivations or drives associated with Sigmund Freud played no major role in conventional psychological models until the spread of psychoanalytic theory early in the twentieth century. Instead of relying on theories shaped by scientific methods or clinical practices, psychology as it was taught to students and disseminated throughout American culture before the Civil War largely reflected its historical foundation as a branch of philosophy.

The basic structure of the mind as outlined during this era can be traced back to Aristotle (384–322 B.C.E.) and his *On the Soul* (*De Anima*), the earliest systematic treatment of individual psychology as a unified discipline. What one customarily calls human thought, according to Aristotle, is based on a hierarchy of sensory and mental functions such as memory, imagination, and desire. This categorizing of mental functions into discrete units would ultimately serve as the basis

Edgar Allan Poe, whose tales of ratiocination and disordered thinking featured close attention to psychological states, also discussed aesthetics in psychological terms. In this excerpt from "The Poetic Principle," Poe adapts contemporary, moralistic faculty psychological theory, with its three-part division of the mind, to his idea of beauty.

Dividing the world of mind into its three most immediately obvious distinctions, we have the Pure Intellect, Taste, and the Moral Sense. I place Taste in the middle, because it is just this position, which, in the mind, it occupies. It holds intimate relations with either extreme; but from the Moral Sense is separated by so faint a difference that Aristotle has not hesitated to place some of its operations among the virtues themselves. Nevertheless, we find the *offices* of the trio marked with a sufficient distinction. Just as the Intellect concerns itself with Truth, so Taste informs us of the Beautiful while the Moral Sense is regardful of Duty. Of this latter, while Conscience teaches the obligation, and Reason the expediency, Taste contents herself with displaying the charms:—waging war upon Vice solely on the ground of her deformity—her disproportion—her animosity to the fitting, to the appropriate, to the harmonious—in a word, to Beauty.

Poe, "The Poetic Principle," p. 76.

for the development of philosophical approaches to psychology before the dominance of scientific methodologies. Thus, by the eighteenth century German theorists, such as Christian von Wolff, who were occupied with descriptions of mental functions had settled on what would be termed "faculty psychology," an approach further elaborated by eighteenth- and nineteenth-century Scottish common sense philosophers. While the division of the mind by philosophers into separate mental functions or faculties may seem in retrospect mechanistic, it does represent an effort to adopt a systematic approach to the field characteristic of later scientific thinking. What most clearly distinguishes pre-twentieth-century thinking about psychology from later methods is the attempt to fuse empirical observation with a moralistic sensibility.

American psychologists customarily followed the lead of Scottish common sense philosophers, and this influence may be found in the normative, moralistic tone of much nineteenth-century American psychological writing as well as the assumption of a tripartite division of the mind, in which the will properly predominates over the intellect and emotions. The common sense school of philosophy, associated with Thomas Reid, James Beattie, and other contemporary Scottish thinkers, influenced Americans in three interrelated manners: it furnished a conceptual foundation for American politics; it generated a series of deeply influential textbooks on the art of rhetoric; and it provided the most important systematic basis for thinking about psychology in the United States before the publication of William James's *The Principles of Psychology* in 1890.

The common sense argument that humans normally possess mental faculties or senses in common was understood by Americans during the time of the American Revolution as a philosophical foundation for the republican form of government. Thus, Thomas Paine, at the suggestion of Benjamin Rush, the founding figure of American psychiatry, would name his call for a government based on republican principles *Common Sense* (1776). The idea that no particular class of people, such as hereditary nobility, had a greater capacity to discern the truth than the general population is likewise reflected in other founding documents, such as the Declaration of Independence and *The Federalist Papers.*

People are equipped to follow arguments and thereby discern truth for themselves, according to common sense theory. This principle, along with associated political practices and the long history of discourse about rhetoric dating back to early Greek philosophy, helped spur the growth of persuasive discourse or rhetoric as an academic discipline within the United States. Again, Scottish common sense thinkers figured largely in the development of systematic approaches to rhetoric that would prove influential. George Campbell's *The Philosophy of Rhetoric* (1776) was routinely studied by American college students until 1870, and Hugh Blair's *Lectures on Rhetoric and Belles-Lettres* (1783) was used widely through the end of the nineteenth century. The notion that rhetorical skill was an important component of higher education now seems dated, but it reflects an antebellum sensibility that valued persuasive discourse as an essential feature of government. A potential weaknesses of this approach to government was dramatized by James Fenimore Cooper (1789–1851) in *The Last of the Mohicans* (1826), which repeatedly presents scenes in which Native Americans, depicted as democratic but easily manipulated by appeals to emotions, fall under the spell of a skillful, manipulative, and unprincipled speaker. Obviously the effective rhetorician needed to understand not only logical argumentation but also human psychology. For Cooper the ideal citizen was one to whom base appeals to self-interest or sensual pleasure would not usurp the decision-making authority properly the province of the suitably developed will.

The structures inherent to the human mind were important to common sense thinkers such as Dugald Stewart, whose *Elements of the Philosophy of the Human Mind* (published in three volumes from 1792 to 1827) as well as *Outlines of Moral Philosophy* (1793) were included in the Yale curriculum. The major American writers of college and high school textbooks on psychology followed the lead of Scottish writers in elaborating systematic approaches to the topic. For example, three basic texts of Thomas C. Upham (1799–1872)—*Elements of Mental Philosophy* (1832), *A Philosophical and Practical Treatise on the Will* (1841), and *Abridgment of Mental Philosophy* (1863)—remained in print even after the Civil War. Like Upham's, other texts, such as *Elements of Moral Science* (1835) and *Elements of Intellectual Philosophy* (1854) by Francis Wayland (1796–1865) and *Empirical Psychology* (1854) by Laurens Perseus Hickok (1798–1888) presented to American students a common sense framework for comprehending psychology. Their approach to psychology divided the mind into three components: the intellect (which included interactions with surroundings, such as sensations or perception, as well as internal processes, such as dreaming, memory, and association), sensibilities (emotions, desires, and the moral senses), and the will (incorporating all aspects of volition, decisions intended to lead to action).

While unconscious motivation was beyond the ordinary scope of rationalist psychology, attempts were made to account for unwilled thought through analysis of "the association of ideas," a phrase coined by John Locke in 1700 to describe the formation of complex ideas from simple sensations as well as to account for sequences of mental activities. This latter point would be especially significant to those interested in literary theory, such as the poet and editor William Cullen Bryant (1794–1878), who relied on association theory in "Lectures on Poetry" (1825–1826) to promote a nationalist aesthetics in which symbols of the nation or the home, for example, were presumed to elicit common emotional responses from readers. None of this was at odds with common sense thinking, as Upham, himself a published poet, would attempt to account for artistic creativity as a combination of ideas, willed thought, and sensory input. From Upham's common sense perspective, however, rational thought had priority over emotional states, and the will properly guided both intellectual and emotional functions. Disorders of this hierarchy or of association, what would

> *Early nineteenth-century psychologists viewed art from a moralistic perspective, yet a positive regard for the literary imagination prevailed. In this passage from a psychology textbook, Thomas C. Upham praises the imaginative faculty for its varied effects.*
>
> ---
>
> Many an hour it has beguiled by the new situations it has depicted, and the new views of human nature it has disclosed; many a pang of the heart it has subdued, either by introducing us to greater woes which others have suffered, or by intoxicating the memory with its luxuriousness and lulling it into a forgetfulness of ourselves; many a good resolution it has cherished and subtended, as it were, a new and wider horizon around the intellectual being, has filled the soul with higher conceptions, and inspired it with higher hopes. . . . The soul enters with joy into those new and lofty creations which it is the prerogative of the imagination to form; and they seem to it a congenial residence.
>
> Thomas C. Upham, *Abridgment of Mental Philosophy* (New York: Harper & Brothers, 1886), pp. 228–229.

be termed abnormal psychology, stimulated more limited interest, although Upham's *Outlines of Imperfect and Disordered Mental Action* (1840) and Isaac Ray's *A Treatise on the Medical Jurisprudence of Insanity* (1838) went through multiple editions.

NORMATIVE PSYCHOLOGY, FAMILY, AND SOCIETY IN LITERATURE

The Protestant religious allegiances of Scottish common sense philosophers and their followers in the United States dovetailed with the psychological emphasis on normal mental functions to produce a unified system of metaphysical and social values that promoted conventional social forms. Thus, for example, one may find across a wide spectrum of literature unquestioningly positive treatments of domestic values. This emphasis on the family by common sense thinkers interestingly coincided with that of advocates of separate spheres for the genders, which at its inception represented a challenge to patriarchal domination of the family. The agreement on this particular point by conservative psychologists with those promoting social change on behalf of women led to literary depictions of families that, at least on the surface, appeared to be similar from writers occupying a range of

opinions, from the staunchly abolitionist Harriet Beecher Stowe to such less bluntly political writers as Louisa May Alcott (1832–1888), Nathaniel Hawthorne (1804–1864), and the Fireside Poets.

One poem that illustrates the conventional values of the era is "The Village Blacksmith" (1841) by Henry Wadsworth Longfellow (1807–1882). In this poem Longfellow contemplates a scene that even in his day would appear to eulogize a simpler, pre-industrial time. The blacksmith, his regular labor interrupted by Sunday in church, where his daughter sings, grows tearful at the reminder of her mother, "Singing in Paradise" (p. 376). The sequential evocation of family, religion, and work within the poem leads to the concluding praise of the blacksmith:

> For the lesson thou hast taught!
> Thus at the flaming forge of life
> Our fortunes must be wrought.
>
> *(P. 377)*

The image of the blacksmith's labor as a metaphor for the willed shaping of one's own life develops out of his normative emotional attachments to family, church, and community. This didactic poem, often republished for children, moreover displays how domestic bonds helped ground even the ostensibly masculine realm of willed action.

One may find such allegiances also pervading the work of a writer who is famed for his critique of conventional moral strictures in *The Scarlet Letter* (1850), Nathaniel Hawthorne. While Hawthorne does plainly note with disapproval Puritan rigidity, this novel dramatizes the relationship between familial and social discord. From the perspective of psychologists contemporary to Hawthorne, the site where the individual learns social attachment is the family and the interpersonal force that binds people together in society is an attenuated version of familial love. Moral philosophers like Adam Smith (*The Theory of Moral Sentiments*, 1759) and Thomas Brown (*Lectures on the Philosophy of the Human Mind*, 1822) debated the nature of this social force, often called "benevolence" or "sympathy," the latter term repeatedly used by Hawthorne as he charts the changing distances between characters and society in his novel, which features a ruptured family unit within a society in which sympathy struggles against Puritan rigidity.

Hawthorne's classic novel may be understood to reflect the tenuous nature of social cohesion in the United States during the years before the Civil War, while similar values are asserted by Louisa May Alcott during the postwar years in *Little Women* (1868–1869). In Alcott's novel the relations between children and mother are central, and the concluding gesture toward the widening of such bonds when Jo March establishes a school suggests that a widening sphere of familial union may compensate for the trauma of the Civil War.

PSYCHOLOGY AND THE SOCIAL CRITICISM OF SENTIMENTALISTS AND TRANSCENDENTALISTS

Writers of sentimental novels largely accepted the centrality of the family, and within the family the bond between mother and child was treated as most important. Stowe's immensely popular *Uncle Tom's Cabin* (1852) epitomizes the regard of sentimental novelists for the family: she dramatized the effects on the family of slavery, an institution that profoundly undermined slave families while harming slave-owning families within the novel as well. Although the ethical argument against slavery was grounded within her defense of the family, Stowe departed from mainstream psychological thinking when positing emotional responses as the primary index of ethical behavior and the good. According to common sense theory, the intellect properly has priority over the emotions, yet in *Uncle Tom's Cabin* the reader is repeatedly asked to look not toward rational argument but toward those empathic feelings that would lead one to oppose slavery and, more conventionally, to adopt a Christian outlook.

Other works that promoted abolitionism followed similar strategies, such as *Incidents in the Life of a Slave Girl* (1861) by Harriet Jacobs (1813–1897), which tells a complex story of the effects of slavery on relations between parents and children. Along similar lines, the *Narrative of the Life of Frederick Douglass, an American Slave* (1845) made a point of arguing that any diminished family feelings among slaves was the result of slavery, thus tacitly displaying the fact that for Americans of that era family attachments were a crucial index of normal psychology. Douglass, moreover, presented a narrator who embodied the mainstream psychological virtue of the dominance of the will over other functions, and thus his narrative persona appeared to be aligned with other exemplary American figures, such as Benjamin Franklin.

A different sort of social and literary critique was developed by transcendentalist writers, most prominently Ralph Waldo Emerson and Henry David Thoreau (1817–1862). Emerson famously regarded traditional authority with skepticism, but unlike Stowe, for whom a correlation of biblical and emotional imperatives held sway, Emerson would argue for a source of authority derived from less tangible sources. In one sense, the introspective approach of his early essays resembles that of common sense thinkers, for whom introspection was vital. Yet the critical differ-

ence is articulated by Thoreau when he appealed to readers of "Resistance to Civil Government" (1849) to embrace social reform: "They who know of no purer sources of truth, who have traced up its stream no higher, stand, and wisely stand, by the Bible and the Constitution, and drink at it there with reverence and humility; but they who behold where it comes trickling into this lake or that pool, gird up their loins once more, and continue their pilgrimage toward its fountain-head" (p. 244). For Thoreau, as well as for Common Sense thinkers, truth is a universal phenomenon, but Thoreau's prioritizing of inspiration over sacred texts represents a substantial departure from the norm. Moreover, in *Walden* (1854), his sustained account of transcendentalist introspection, Thoreau integrated into his discussion unorthodox states of mind and emotion that beforehand would mainly have been found in literary accounts of disordered psychology.

DISORDERED PSYCHOLOGY AND LITERATURE

While some emotional disorders were described by psychology texts, the imaginative literature of the period generated some of the most striking descriptions of unusual, bizarre, or simply unhappy mental states, no doubt because of their dramatic possibilities. Most extravagant in this regard is *The Quaker City; or, The Monks of Monk Hall* (1845) by George Lippard (1822–1854), which parades before the reader an array of crazed behaviors, all with the purported goal of enhancing contemporary morality. One of Lippard's closest literary precursor is Charles Brockden Brown, whose *Wieland* tells a story of command hallucinations leading to murder. Unlike Lippard's novel, however, *Wieland* does more than depict madness: its ambiguities also create a state of mental uncertainty within the reader, whose attempts to comprehend narrative events correspond to those of fictional characters trying to grasp the unknown. In this respect, *Wieland* resembles later depictions of mental disorder by Poe and Hawthorne.

Hawthorne's stories, whether dealing with history or his own era, frequently depicted a range of mental disorders, such as the convulsive mass laughter of "My Kinsman, Major Molineux" or the husband's coldness in "Wakefield." Many of his stories revolve around problems of obsession or delusion. In the case of "The Birth-mark," for example, the scientist's obsessiveness destroys, while in "Ethan Brand" obsessive guilt triggers the plot. In all these stories as well as in Hawthorne's novels, disruptions to normal social attachments can either lead to or result from emotional disorder. Thus in "Young Goodman Brown," the protagonist's hallucinatory experiences can seem like both cause and effect of his remoteness from his family. Moreover, mental disorder furnished Hawthorne with the occasion for experimentation with narrative voice and form, as the reader is often led to a condition of doubt. It is no surprise that the master of the psychological novel, Henry James, would devote a full-length study to Hawthorne.

Like Hawthorne, Poe presents enigmatic pieces of information suggesting a state of mind while involving the reader in the attempt to decipher their significance. "The Fall of the House of Usher" is Poe's classic account of a disordered state leading to destruction, yet even in his mysteries Poe also describes mental operations with care. The unfolding of the mystery of "The Purloined Letter" thus involves an extensive record of intellectual detective work that finally does not fully account for the inspiration that leads to the solution. This suggests that while many writers displayed acuity when describing unconventional mental states, they could not draw from a commensurate development among psychologists. Thus the most famous madman of nineteenth-century literature, Captain Ahab of Herman Melville's (1819–1991) *Moby-Dick* (1851) is repeatedly diagnosed by the narrator as a "monomaniac," a label that has limited value in explaining behavior.

See also Curricula; Fireside Poets; German Scholarship; Gothic Fiction; Philosophy; Protestantism; Rhetoric; Sensational Fiction; Slave Narratives; Transcendentalism

BIBLIOGRAPHY
Primary Works
Longfellow, Henry Wadsworth. "The Village Blacksmith." 1841. In *American Poetry: The Nineteenth Century; Freneau to Whitman,* edited by John Hollander, pp. 375–377. New York: Library of America, 1993.

Poe, Edgar Allan. "The Poetic Principle." In *Essays and Reviews.* New York: Library of America, 1984.

Thoreau, Henry David. *Walden and Resistance to Civil Government.* 2nd ed. Edited by William Rossi. New York: Norton, 1992.

Secondary Works
Alkana, Joseph. *The Social Self: Hawthorne, Howells, William James, and Nineteenth-Century Psychology.* Lexington: University Press of Kentucky, 1997.

Boudreau, Kristin. *Sympathy in American Literature: American Sentiments from Jefferson to the Jameses.* Gainesville: University Press of Florida, 2002.

Fiering, Norman S. "Irresistible Compassion: An Aspect of Eighteenth-Century Sympathy and Humanitarianism."
Journal of the History of Ideas 37 (April–June 1976): 195–218.

Howe, Daniel Walker. *The Unitarian Conscience: Harvard Moral Philosophy, 1805–1861.* 1970. Middletown, Conn.: Wesleyan University Press, 1988.

Martin, Terence. *The Instructed Vision: Scottish Common Sense Philosophy and the Origins of American Fiction.* Bloomington: Indiana University Press, 1961.

Tompkins, Jane. *Sensational Designs: The Cultural Work of American Fiction 1790–1860.* New York: Oxford University Press, 1985.

Joseph Alkana

PUBLISHERS

Prior to 1820 in America, books, magazines, and other printed material typically were produced and sold locally by individual printers, binders, and booksellers, all working independently. Mechanical limitations, difficult transportation conditions, and the financial instability of the young nation made the business of publishing an unprofessional and unprofitable affair in early America. Only with improvements in transportation, such as the opening of the Erie Canal (1825), and the invention of new technologies—including stereotyping (1813), the steam press (1833), and advanced cutting, folding, and binding machines and materials—did businesses akin to the modern professional publishing house begin to emerge in American society.

In the years between 1820 and 1870 American publishers with such now-familiar names as Harper, Putnam, Little, and Brown consolidated the operations of printing, binding, distributing, and selling books to become successful businessmen, prominent figures in the development of a national literature, and literary tastemakers for much of the world. For each of these successful publishers, many more who once left their imprints on major American literary works, including James Fenimore Cooper's *Last of the Mohicans* (1825), Ralph Waldo Emerson's *Essays* (1841), and Harriet Beecher Stowe's *Uncle Tom's Cabin* (1852), have since been forgotten. Between 1820 and 1870, some of the nineteenth century's most prominent publishing firms, such as Carey and Lea, Ticknor and Fields, Phillips, Sampson, and Company, and John P. Jewett, variously fell to national financial crises, intense competition, overexpansion, or mergers with other firms.

The rise and fall of different publishing houses as well as geographical advantages and disadvantages led to competition among New York, Philadelphia, and

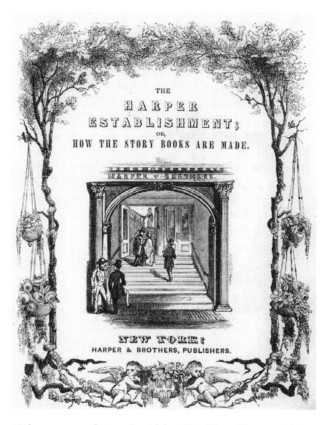

Title page of Jacob Abbott's *The Harper Establishment; or, How the Story Books Are Made,* **1855.**
THE LIBRARY OF CONGRESS

Boston to become the publishing capital of the United States. From the start of the century until the 1820s, Philadelphia initially was ascendant, due to its status as the nation's largest city and its proximity to major shipping routes to the South and near West. Transportation via the Hudson River and the Erie Canal, a surge in population, and the increasing concentration of businesses in Manhattan allowed New York City to overtake Philadelphia as the center of American publishing by mid-century. Publishers in Boston began the nineteenth century producing books primarily for a New England audience, largely as a result of the city's lack of major waterways into the interior. In 1840s Boston the construction of new railroad lines and the concentration of prominent writers in the area briefly returned some of the prominence in publishing that the city had enjoyed during the colonial period. Yet by 1850 the unparalleled success of Harper & Brothers and the continuing migration of businesses to Manhattan brought New York the national dominance in publishing that it maintains to the early twenty-first century.

Relations between authors and publishers during this time often were strained. American publishers regularly pirated the works of British and European authors in their bid to profit from a large domestic audience eager for the latest foreign fiction. While copyright law did more to protect American authors against such unauthorized reprinting, it was not extended to recognize the foreign copyrights of imported works. Initially, American publishers established what was known as a "courtesy of the trade"— a concession to the firm that was the first to reprint a foreign work in the United States. The immense profits reaped from such reprints, particularly from the novels of Sir Walter Scott (1771–1832), soon proved irresistible to competitors who began publishing their own editions of popular imported literature. The resulting competition to capture the market for new works published abroad became so intense that publishers often went to extraordinary lengths to obtain the first copy of an imported work. Some New York and Philadelphia publishers were known to meet ships even before they docked to rush the copy of a valuable work to their compositors and to run their presses overnight in hopes of producing the first American edition. Others are said to have gone so far as to dispatch typesetters abroad to compose reprint plates shipboard as they sailed to the United States.

Such practices did much to frustrate the efforts of American authors to gain a wider audience for their writings. Unwilling to assume the financial risk of publishing works by untested authors, American publishers largely dedicated their presses to reprinting literature that already had proven popular abroad. From 1820 into the 1850s, when American writers did convince publishers to put out their works, they typically were asked to finance the venture themselves, with the publishers only providing their printing and distribution services for hire. Not all authors suffered under such practices, however. Washington Irving (1783–1859) and James Fenimore Cooper (1789–1851), rare examples of successful early American authors, gained significantly from this arrangement, keeping up to 40 percent of profits for themselves. Innovating on this practice in the 1840s, Henry Wadsworth Longfellow (1807–1882), Herman Melville (1819–1891), and other enterprising writers began purchasing the stereotype plates for their works and offering them to publishers for lease or for royalties from each copy printed from them; some gained, while others lost substantial sums from their outlays in purchasing the costly plates. By the 1850s as American literature had gained increasing respect domestically and abroad, authors and publishers began establishing agreements in which the publisher assumed the initial expenses of publication and distribution and the author and publisher divided the eventual profits. While profits were not always shared in equal proportions, this arrangement allowed many authors who had been successful writing for popular periodicals yet could not afford to publish their own books or buy their own plates to enter the marketplace alongside established authors.

While American publishers and authors alike faced imposing odds against their success in the early nineteenth century, they gained rapidly and significantly as both professions expanded and stabilized. In 1820, $2.5 million worth of books were produced and sold in the United States. Between 1830 and 1842 publishers printed and distributed an average of only one hundred books per year; by 1850 they were capable of publishing $12.5 million worth of thousands of copies of books in a year (Tebbel 1:221). While the Civil War interrupted these steady gains by driving publishers in North and South alike out of business and limiting the production capacities of those who persisted, the profession quickly reestablished its prominence and profitability through further technological innovation and continuing competition. By 1870 the major American book publishers were thoroughly professionalized, well established, and poised to continue business into the twentieth century.

PHILADELPHIA PUBLISHERS

In the early nineteenth century, Philadelphia was the center of publishing in America, largely due to the efforts of an Irish immigrant named Mathew Carey (1760–1839), who began business there in 1785 as a printer, bookseller, and promoter of the printing arts. From his start publishing newspapers, Carey developed a substantial list of titles and a wide distribution of his publications. By the beginning of the nineteenth century, Carey had become the most successful printer in America and had done much to establish Philadelphia as the center of American publishing. In 1822 Carey turned the business over to his son, Henry Charles Carey (1793–1879). Shortly thereafter Henry brought his brother-in-law, Isaac Lea (1792–1886), into the family business as a junior partner and changed the firm's name to M. Carey and Sons, the first of several name changes and reorganizations common to nineteenth-century publishing firms. In their new partnership, Carey and Lea became the leading pirates of imported literature in the 1820s. At the same time, they were among the first publishers to promote works by American authors, among them Irving's *Tales of a Traveller* (1824) and Cooper's *Last of the Mohicans* (1826). In the late 1820s Carey established two magazines, the *Atlantic Souvenir* and the

American Quarterly Review, to feature new work by American writers; both ultimately proved short-lived at the firm as a result of too expensive production and distribution costs.

In 1828 Edward Carey left Carey and Lea to open Carey and Hart in partnership with the Philadelphia stationer Abraham Hart; the split was amicable and the firm operated immediately next door to Carey and Lea. Among Carey and Hart's most successful publications were the *Poets and Poetry of Europe* (1845), edited by Longfellow, and *Poets and Poetry of America* (1842), *Female Poets of America* (1849), and *Prose Writers of America* (1847), each edited by Rufus Wilmot Griswold, Edgar Allan Poe's (1809–1849) literary executor. Between 1835 and 1847 Carey and Hart also published two popular gift books, *The Gift* and *The Diadem,* each featuring substantial illustrations and new writings by significant and emerging English and American writers. With the arrival of William A. Blanchard as a third partner to Carey and Lea in 1833, the new firm of Carey, Lea and Blanchard initiated the first publication of Jane Austen's novels in the United States, meeting with significant success. While Carey, Lea and Blanchard suffered during the national banking crisis of 1833–1834, the firm survived to compete with rising New York publishers for national dominance. After Carey's retirement in 1838, Lea and Blanchard focused on medical publishing while losing ground to New York, subsequently continuing in this specialty through 1870 and into the late twentieth century. Last called Lea and Febiger, it was finally absorbed by a firm descended from another significant nineteenth-century Philadelphia publisher, J. B. Lippincott and Company.

Joshua Ballinger Lippincott (1813–1886) started in the book trade working as a young clerk in a Philadelphia bookstore in the 1820s. He quickly rose to take over ownership of the store, and by 1850 Lippincott had become a successful publisher of religious and general literature. Capitalizing on the financial difficulties of smaller rivals, Lippincott incorporated several firms into his own to become the largest publisher in Philadelphia in the 1850s. Successful titles published by Lippincott and Company include Noah Webster's *Blue-Back Speller,* acquired by the firm in 1858; its *Dictionary of American Authors* (1870); and *Lippincott's Magazine,* an illustrated general-interest periodical that was popular during the last quarter of the nineteenth century. Among the firm's innovations was the introduction of a line of photo albums to its catalog in 1860. Capitalizing on the growing popularity of cartes de visite, an early type of photographic print used for portraits, Lippincott sold albums ranging from simple and affordable to extravagantly detailed and priced. Such diversification enabled the firm to survive the Civil War and continue its publication of medical literature, gift books, and household editions of British authors beyond the nineteenth century.

BOSTON PUBLISHERS

The seeds of the so-called flowering of New England literary and intellectual culture in the antebellum period were sown in the region's most prominent publishing houses. Between 1832 and 1865, the imprint of the Boston publishers Ticknor and Fields appeared on the works of many of England's and America's major authors, including Longfellow, Oliver Wendell Holmes, John Greenleaf Whittier, Henry David Thoreau, Nathaniel Hawthorne, Ralph Waldo Emerson, Harriet Beecher Stowe, Alfred, Lord Tennyson, Robert Browning, William Makepeace Thackeray, and Charles Dickens. From its beginnings in the Old Corner Bookstore, at the corner of Washington and School Streets in the 1820s, the firm grew steadily under the direction of William Davis Ticknor (1810–1864) and James Thomas Fields (1817–1881). Ticknor's early focus on medical texts gradually expanded under the influence of Fields, who began working in the bookstore as a clerk and became a partner in 1843. Fields, a writer in his own right, frequently socialized with Boston's emerging intellectual elite, as the Old Corner Bookstore became a prominent literary gathering place modeled on the salons that Fields enjoyed during business trips to Europe.

Ticknor and Fields became known for its comparatively generous terms for paying authors, attracting, among others, Nathaniel Hawthorne (1804–1864) and a manuscript he had been keeping to himself in Salem after the publication of his *Mosses from an Old Manse,* published by the New York firm of Wiley and Putnam in 1846. A visit from Fields prompted Hawthorne to share his initial draft of *The Scarlet Letter* with the publisher. With Fields's encouragement, Hawthorne expanded what was originally a short story into what became an instant best-seller in 1850. In the 1850s Fields became a master promoter of the firm's authors, advertising its latest works nationwide, providing booksellers with color posters for their windows, and strategically placing favorable reviews of Ticknor and Fields's newest publications. In 1865 after the death of Ticknor, Fields sold the Old Corner Bookstore to the publisher E. P. Dutton and Company, while Ticknor and Fields, as the firm continued to be known, remained a thriving publishing house. Its prominence won Ticknor and Fields the right to serve as Dickens's exclusive American publisher in 1867. A year later the firm became Fields,

Photograph of (from left) James T. Fields, Nathaniel Hawthorne, and William Davis Ticknor. Ticknor and Fields published many of the nineteeth century's most prominent American and English authors. © BETTMANN/CORBIS

Osgood and Company, and in 1871 Fields retired to lecture and write his memoirs of a literary life.

During the same period, the Cambridge booksellers Charles Coffin Little (1799–1869) and James Brown (1800–1855) joined forces to form the publishing house of Charles C. Little and Company. Among their most prominent publications were Jared Sparks's editions of the writings of Franklin and Washington and George Bancroft's *History of the United States* (1834). Renamed Little, Brown and Company in 1847, the publishing house specialized in law books, English and other European reprints, and Latin books "for the gentleman's library." With the success of their affordable collections of English poetry, Little and Brown expanded their list to publish Daniel Webster's (1782–1852) speeches and writings and the letters of John Adams (1735–1826) and Abigail Adams (1744–1818). Their most successful venture was John Bartlett's (1820–1905) *Familiar Quotations,* first published in 1859 and revised and expanded nine times during Bartlett's life. While Brown died suddenly in 1855 and Little in 1869, after having become a Cambridge selectman, a state legislator, a bank president, and a director on several boards, the firm carried on in the late nineteenth century under Bartlett's direction, expanding its list of general publications.

The publishing house of Phillips, Sampson and Company, a Boston contemporary of Little, Brown and Ticknor and Fields, holds a significant place in American literary history as the original publisher of Emerson's *English Traits* (1856) and *Representative Men* (1850), the *Atlantic Monthly* magazine, and the lavishly illustrated Boston editions of works by Shakespeare, Milton, Byron, and other prominent British authors. Yet unlike Little, Brown, the firm did not survive the financial panic of 1857 and the deaths of its founders, Moses Dresser Phillips and Charles Sampson, in 1859.

Similarly, the firm founded by John P. Jewett (1814–1884), a bookseller, binder, and publisher of schoolbooks, also met with failure during the panic of 1857 following the incredible success of its first major publication, Harriet Beecher Stowe's (1811–1896) *Uncle Tom's Cabin* in 1852. Sympathetic to the cause of abolition, Jewett had followed Stowe's narrative as it appeared serially in the *National Era* (1847–1860) and offered to publish it in book form for either shared costs and profits or a flat 10 percent royalty. In choosing the 10 percent option, Stowe eventually lost millions, while Jewett initially feared that he had made a serious mistake as the novel grew in length to require its publication in two volumes. On 20 March 1852 Jewett published the novel two months before its conclusion in the *National Era,* selling the two volumes at a price of $2.50. Within days, the original printing of ten thousand copies had sold out; to meet demand, Jewett had to operate his presses continuously. After a year, 305,000 copies had been sold (Tebbel 1:427). Jewett followed up this incredible success by acquiring the rights to another popular serial novel, Maria Susanna Cummins's (1827–1866) *The Lamplighter* (1854). While its numbers did not match Stowe's, its profits allowed Jewett to open a Cleveland branch and to expand his list to temperance tracts, theology, and an edition of Margaret Fuller's (1810–1850) *Woman in the Nineteenth Century* (1845). With the firm's collapse in 1857, Jewett abandoned bookselling and publishing in favor of selling household goods and negotiating patents. Upon moving to New York in 1866, he returned to his career as a bookseller but did not resume his work as a publisher.

NEW YORK PUBLISHERS

In New York ready access to shipping routes for the import and export of goods allowed numerous publishing houses to flourish between 1820 and 1870.

One such firm was John Wiley and Sons, founded as a printing house and bookshop in the early nineteenth century by Charles Wiley (1810–1878). Wiley's bookstore, known as The Den, became a popular gathering place for writers and intellectuals, including Cooper, J. K. Paulding, Samuel F. B. Morse, William Cullen Bryant, and Richard Henry Dana Sr. In 1826 John Wiley took over the business upon the death of his father, and in 1833 he formed a partnership with George Palmer Putnam (1814–1872), an apprentice bookseller. As Wiley and Putnam, the firm began publishing its series the Library of Choice Reading, a popular collection of select literature, in 1840. Its success inspired the companion series, the Library of American Books, edited by Evert Augustus Duyckinck (1816–1878), the prominent activist for a national literature who befriended a young Melville and acquired his first novel, *Typee,* for publication in 1846. The latter series also included Poe's *Tales* (1845) and Hawthorne's collection of stories, *Mosses from an Old Manse* (1846). While Putnam focused on developing the firm's collection of American and British titles, Wiley pursued the publication of scientific and technical works. This division of labor and interests ultimately resulted in Putnam's departure to found his own firm in 1847.

Putnam began publishing on his own by gaining the reprint rights to Irving's works in 1847. From this profitable start, his firm, G. P. Putnam, expanded to publish Poe's *Narrative of Arthur Gordon Pym* (1847) and his quasi-scientific treatise *Eureka* (1848) and works by James Russell Lowell, Cooper, Thomas Carlyle, Leigh Hunt, and Samuel Taylor Coleridge. One of Putnam's greatest successes was Susan Warner's (1819–1885) *The Wide, Wide World* (1850), which Putnam published after its rejection by the rival firm of Harper & Brothers; in two years, thirteen editions of the immensely popular novel had been printed. In 1853 the firm launched *Putnam's Monthly Magazine.* Even as a venue for some of the century's most writers, including Hawthorne, Holmes, Longfellow, Lowell, Francis Parkman, and Whittier, the magazine operated for only four years, in each of which it failed to produce a profit for the firm. As with many publishers, Putnam foundered during the panic of 1857 and suspended publication during the Civil War but resumed business in 1866 as G. P. Putnam and Son.

The New York publisher Daniel Appleton (1785–1849) came to publishing from a somewhat unusual background; rather than apprenticing as a bookseller or printer, Appleton began work as a dry-goods seller in Massachusetts before moving to New York to sell books. In 1831 he published his first book, initially specializing in religious texts and eventually expanding into profitable British reprints. In the 1840s the firm enlarged its list to include Spanish-language books for the South American trade, which it dominated into the twentieth century, and profitable travel guides for American tourists venturing abroad. With Appleton's death in 1856, three of his sons took the helm and began the firm's largest publishing venture, the *New American Cyclopedia*. By the end of the century, over three million volumes of the *Cyclopedia* were sold door-to-door and by subscription. Between 1820 and 1870 Appleton published many school textbooks, the poetry of William Cullen Bryant (1794–1878), and more than forty novels by Mary Jane Holmes (1825–1907), who became the century's second-most financially successful female writer (second to Harriet Beecher Stowe). During the Civil War the strength of Appleton's *Cyclopedia* kept the publisher profitable and ensured its success through the end of the century.

The publishing house that came to dominate publishing in New York and, thereby, America began business as J. & J. Harper in 1817. James (1795–1869) and John Harper (1797–1875) were brothers who came to be considered as New York's finest printers for their advanced stereotyping equipment. In 1823 and 1825 two younger brothers joined the business and transitioned the family from printing to a full-fledged publishing operation. During the 1820s the Harpers published the first clothbound books in America, and in 1830 they launched the first series, or "libraries," of popular literature for mass audiences. In 1833, the year that the firm first came to be known as Harper & Brothers, the brothers installed a powerful steam press that replaced the horse-driven presses that were the industry standard to that point. Such technological advances resulted in the firm's popular abridged edition of Webster's *Dictionary* (1843) and the highly successful *Harper's Illuminated and New Pictorial Bible* (1844), which was printed using a new electrotyping process and was praised as the finest American printing achieved to its date. By the end of the 1840s Harper & Brothers had won claim to the title of the largest publishing house in America, operating nineteen power presses and countless hand presses to produce nearly two million volumes per year. The 1850s saw the firm's publication of Herman Melville's *Moby-Dick* (1851) and the launch of its two magazines, *Harper's New Monthly Magazine* (1850) and *Harper's Weekly* (1857), which enjoyed a success uncommon among publishers' magazines. In 1853 a major fire destroyed the Harpers' printing operation; they replaced it in 1855 with two fireproof plants built with innovative construction techniques that made them tourist attractions at the time. During the Civil

War the brothers initiated *Harper's Pictorial History of the Great Rebellion*, which began publication in 1862 and ended a successful run in 1868. Their magazines, widely read for their illustrated and timely coverage of the war, carried the firm through the conflict; its dominance in the nineteenth century ensured its longevity into the early twenty-first century.

REGIONAL PUBLISHERS

Beyond New York, Philadelphia, and Boston, smaller publishing houses provided the South and the expanding West with books and other printed matter beyond those publications imported from the Northeast. In North Carolina the firm of E. J. Hale and Son became one of the largest publishers in the South. Among its accomplishments was the *Observer*, a newspaper founded in 1850. Hale's *Observer* enjoyed the widest circulation of any newspaper in North Carolina, and by the 1860s it had become one of the leading newspapers in the Confederacy. In South Carolina, the publishing house of Russell and Jones produced a collection of southern poetry between 1846 and 1855 and several works by William Gilmore Simms (1806–1870). Further south, in New Orleans, a New York émigré named Benjamin Levy (1786–1860) became the first major Jewish printer and publisher in the United States, issuing law books, business and political titles, some literature, almanacs, and city directories. During the Civil War, numerous Southern publishers worked to fill the void left by books no longer imported from the North and England. Richmond, Charleston, and New Orleans emerged as centers of publishing activity, yet Southern publishers struggled without adequate paper supplies or stereotyping and electrotyping equipment. As the war progressed, many publishers attempting to continue operations in the South were reduced to using wallpaper and other available materials to print newspapers and bind books.

By the 1830s Cincinnati had become the center of the western book trade and fourth to the three eastern publishing cities in the number of volumes produced each year. Among the nearly two million books published in Cincinnati by the 1840s were the *Eclectic Series* and the successful textbooks *McGuffey's Readers*, published by the firm of Truman and Smith. Other prominent publishers included J. A. and U. P. James, George Conclin, Applegate and Company, and H. W. Derby and Company. By the 1870s western competition intensified as Chicago became the major regional rail hub. This reduced the numbers of significant Cincinnati publishing houses.

An early Chicago publisher, S. C. Griggs (1819–1897), began business as a bookseller in 1848, following the model of his eastern counterparts. His firm evolved into S. C. Griggs and Company, a successful publisher of schoolbooks and medical and theological texts and a major distributor of eastern books to the western United States. In 1856 William H. Rand (1828– 1915) relocated from Boston to Chicago to work as a printer. In 1858 he joined with Andrew McNally (1836–1904) to form a publishing house that they soon consolidated with the Chicago newspaper, the *Press and Tribune*. After the Civil War they reformed as Rand McNally and Company and began publishing books in the 1870s.

See also Banking, Finance, Panics, and Depressions; Boston; Civil War; English Literature; Gift Books and Annuals; Literary Marketplace; Literary Nationalism; New York; Periodicals; Philadelphia; Technology

BIBLIOGRAPHY

Secondary Works

Charvat, William. *Literary Publishing in America, 1790–1850*. 1959. Amherst: University of Massachusetts Press, 1993.

Comparato, Frank E. *Books for the Millions: A History of the Men Whose Methods and Machines Packaged the Printed Word*. Harrisburg, Pa.: Stackpole, 1971.

Exman, Eugene. *The Brothers Harper: A Unique Publishing Partnership and its Impact upon the Cultural Life of America from 1817 to 1853*. New York: Harper and Row, 1965.

Greenspan, Ezra. *George Palmer Putnam: Representative American Publisher*. University Park: Pennsylvania State University Press, 2000.

Kaser, David. *Messrs. Carey and Lea of Philadelphia: A Study in the History of the Booktrade*. Philadelphia: University of Pennsylvania Press, 1957.

Lehmann-Haupt, Hellmut, in collaboration with Lawrence C. Wroth and Rollo G. Silver. *The Book in America: A History of Making and Selling Books in the United States*. 2nd ed. New York: R. R. Bowker, 1951.

McGill, Meredith L. *American Literature and the Culture of Reprinting, 1834–1853*. Philadelphia: University of Pennsylvania Press, 2003.

Madison, Charles Allan. *Book Publishing in America*. New York: McGraw-Hill, 1966.

Moore, John Hammond. *Wiley, One Hundred and Seventy Five Years of Publishing*. New York: Wiley, 1982.

One Hundred and Fifty Years of Publishing, 1785–1935. Philadelphia: Lea and Febiger, 1935.

Overton, Grant Martin. *The First Hundred Years of the House of Appleton, 1825–1925*. New York: D. Appleton, 1925.

Rostenberg, Leona, and Madeleine B. Stern. *From Revolution to Revolution: Perspectives on Publishing and Bookselling, 1501–2001*. New Castle, Del.: Oak Knoll, 2002.

Stern, Madeline B. *Books and Book People in 19th-Century America*. New York: Bowker, 1978.

Tebbel, John William. *A History of Book Publishing in the United States*. 4 vols. New York: R. R. Bowker, 1972–1981.

Tryon, Warren S. *Parnassus Corner: A Life of James T. Fields, Publisher to the Victorians*. Boston: Houghton Mifflin, 1963.

Winship, Michael. *American Literary Publishing in the Mid-Nineteenth Century: The Business of Ticknor and Fields*. Cambridge, U.K., and New York: Cambridge University Press, 1995.

Marcy J. Dinius

PURITANISM

The influence of American Puritanism is pervasive in the literature of the nineteenth century. The uniquely American Puritan vision of the seventeenth century arose from the English Puritanism that engendered it. Indeed many first-generation American Puritans, such as John Cotton (1584–1652) and John Winthrop (1588–1649), were emigrants from England who sought religious freedom in the New World. First-, second-, and third-generation American Puritans developed and refined a special vision of Calvinist theology that has continued to influence American self-definition into the present. When Ronald Reagan argued in his 1980 presidential campaign that the United States had lost much of its former glory and should return to its position of past leadership in the world, he quoted John Winthrop's sermon "A Model of Christian Charity" (1630), delivered 350 years earlier during the sea voyage that ended in establishment of the Massachusetts Bay Colony:

> He shall make us a praise and glory, that men shall say of succeeding plantations: "The Lord make it like that of New England." For we must consider that we shall be as a city upon a hill, the eyes of all people are upon us. So that if we shall deal falsely with our God in this work we have under-taken, and so cause Him to withdraw His present help from us, we shall be made a story and a by-word through the world: we shall open the mouths of enemies to speak evil of the ways of God and all professors for God's sake; we shall shame the faces of many of God's worthy servants, and cause their prayers to be turned into curses upon us, till we be consumed out of the good land whither we are going. (P. 23)

This declaration succinctly articulates what has come to be known as American exceptionalism. At the root of American society and culture lie a vision of uniqueness and a sense of mission. In the introduction to her *American Exceptionalism*, Deborah L. Madsen states,

> Exceptionalism describes the perception of Massachusetts Bay colonists that as Puritans they were charged with a special spiritual and political destiny: to create in the New World a church and a society that would provide the model for all the nations of Europe as they struggled to reform themselves (a redeemer nation). . . . Thus America and Americans are special, exceptional, because they are charged with saving the world from itself and, at the same time, America and Americans must sustain a high level of spiritual, political and moral commitment to this exceptional destiny—America must be as "a city upon a hill" exposed to the eyes of the world. (Pp. 1–2)

This Puritan notion of election, divine sanction, and high purpose has pervaded American identity, politics, and culture ever since, although it has evolved over several centuries from a specifically religious vision into a much more secular one: rather than exemplifying a pure church America's mission became exemplifying a free, egalitarian, democratic society.

NATHANIEL HAWTHORNE

In the mid-nineteenth century Nathaniel Hawthorne (1804–1864) brought widespread attention to America's Puritan past by setting many of his works in seventeenth-century New England and by demonstrating the continuities of the seventeenth century with the nineteenth. *The House of the Seven Gables* (1851) is perhaps his most obvious illustration of these continuities, in which the "sins of the fathers" are visited upon succeeding generations of "children." Many of Hawthorne's plots center upon problems of doctrine and conscience that he detected in his wide reading about his own ancestors' past. "Young Goodman Brown" (1835), an allegory treating illusion and reality, resembles John Bunyan's *Pilgrim's Progress* (1678), complete with a journey motif, a spiritual burden that must be resolved, and an assessment of human character in relation to Puritan doctrine. "The Minister's Black Veil" (1836) also shows how character assessment is not always what it seems to be, and "The Maypole of Merry Mount" (1836) and "Endicott and the Red Cross" (1838) both reexamine historical incidents in the light of Hawthorne's humanistic understanding of Puritanism. His masterwork, *The Scarlet Letter* (1850), chronicles the story of Hester Prynne, an adulteress who mothers an illegitimate child, Pearl. The Puritans in *The Scarlet Letter*, described as dour,

severe, unpleasant people, act as a foil to the vibrant humanity of Hester and Pearl, whose life together as outcasts from the Puritan community assumes center stage for most of the novel. Indeed, it is their relationship and Hester's heroic overcoming of her punishment that gives readers an inaccurate portrait of seventeenth-century Puritanism as it conflicts with human love.

Even in works not set in early America, such as *The Marble Faun* (1860), which takes place in Rome, Hawthorne returns to such biblical themes as the Fall of Man and the effects of guilt. In "Rappaccini's Daughter" (1844), another narrative set in Italy, the blatantly obvious Garden of Eden is peopled by characters who may be identified as God, Man, and Satan. Thus Hawthorne's writing develops out of the materials of early American Puritanism, and though his narratives often disfigure the historical moments they purport to portray, his influence in spreading the gospel of early American Puritanism is undeniable. Moreover, his pervasive use of allegorical techniques and other rhetorical strategies learned from his ancestral Puritans extends their influence into succeeding centuries.

MANIFEST DESTINY

Another prominent nineteenth-century American theme closely associated with the "city upon a hill" and American exceptionalism is the idea of Manifest Destiny. In 1845 a journalist named John O'Sullivan (1813–1895) first used the term in an editorial for the *United States Magazine and Democratic Review*, in which he advocates the annexation of Texas, declaring that it is America's "manifest destiny to overspread the continent allotted by Providence for the free development of our yearly multiplying millions" (p. 5). It has been an important by-word of American development and progress ever since. Manifest Destiny was easy to understand as God's divine intention for America to expand westward, sanctioning the removal of Indians from their lands and the war with Mexico that resulted in America's acquisition of Texas and much of what is now New Mexico and southern California. The ideology of Manifest Destiny inherited by nineteenth-century writers from the canonical literature of the preceding centuries, captured the imagination of Americans as their frontiers expanded westward, from the Lewis and Clark expedition of 1804–1806 to the linking of east and west in the transcontinental railroad in 1869.

Walt Whitman (1819–1892) was only one of many American writers who embraced the idea of divine progress in the expansion of the United States. Herman Melville (1819–1891) and Richard Henry Dana Jr.

(1815–1882) were both experienced seamen who had seen the world, particularly the Far East and the islands of the Pacific, and whose writings are sprinkled with allusions to the power of ocean commerce to unite the world. Melville had been raised in the Calvinistic Dutch Reformed Church in upstate New York, and his works are filled with the rhetoric of Calvinism. In *Moby-Dick* (1851), for example, Father Mapple's sermon in the Whaleman's Chapel on that wayward biblical prophet Jonah, who attempted to run and hide from God's bidding, serves as a warning to the doomed sailors of the *Pequod* that Providence must be obeyed in all things and that individual destiny is predetermined. Captain Ahab's destiny is "fated," just as in *Billy Budd* (1924) the hapless young sailor is condemned by Captain Vere's peremptory judgment: "Fated boy . . . , what have you done!" (p. 99). Calvinism is everywhere and unavoidable in Melville's writings.

Contemporaries of Hawthorne and Melville were saturated with Puritan and Calvinistic doctrine, as churchgoing was regular and sermons were long. The Great Awakening , variously dated between 1730 and 1760, and the Second Great Awakening of the 1820s and 1830s insured that several generations of American churchgoers knew the meaning of God's wrath and could understand a jeremiad. Ralph Waldo Emerson (1803–1882), trained at Harvard to become a Unitarian minister, and Henry David Thoreau (1817–1862), also trained at Harvard in the early nineteenth century, both inherited the sins of the fathers from seventeenth-century Puritanism. Emerson's "Concord Hymn" (1837), celebrating the commencement of the American Revolutionary War on 19 April 1775, echoes American exceptionalism when his "shot heard round the world" gives global significance to the events in ways that the colonial militia could not have conceived in their simple determination to separate from Britain's domination. Emerson's *Nature* (1836) echoes the epistemology of Jonathan Edwards in such works as *A History of the Work of Redemption* (1774). Thoreau's *Walden* (1854), incorrectly perceived to be a manifesto for the green movement and mistakenly associated with his essay "Civil Disobedience" (1849) as an antiauthoritarian credo, is in fact a carefully written, rigorously revised examination of the cycles of nature with exact correspondences drawn between nature's ways and those of human beings, when they are not living what Thoreau famously calls "lives of quiet desperation." It is a testament of renewal and has all the hallmarks of a Puritan conversion experience, right down to the "before" and "after" structure that Thoreau intended for the piece to represent. More significantly Emersonian self-reliance may be traced to its roots in the Protestant-Puritan emphasis on the individual if not on self-determination.

American Puritanism, as interpreted by nineteenth-century ministers, did not always stress conformity and consensus. Rather it represented for the post-Revolution citizens of the new nation the strength to challenge authority and an often lawless individualism that expressed itself in the numerous reform movements found in the antebellum United States. Chief among these, of course, was the abolitionist crusade led by William Lloyd Garrison, Lydia Maria Child, Frederick Douglass, and Wendell Phillips. However, Garrison (1805–1879) got his start as a temperance crusader; and in antebellum slave narratives, biblical fundamentalism and a belief in divine intervention in human affairs are hallmarks of plot and theme. Utopian communities such as Brook Farm, in West Roxbury, Massachusetts, where Hawthorne spent much of 1841 and about which he wrote *The Blithedale Romance* (1852), were direct descendants of Plymouth Plantation and other New England Puritan communities of the seventeenth century. But it was the abolitionist movement and Harriet Beecher Stowe's *Uncle Tom's Cabin; or, Life among the Lowly* (1852) that best illustrate the continuity of the ideology and literature of the nineteenth century with early American Puritanism.

ABOLITIONISM

In January 1831 the abolitionist crusade caught fire in the rhetoric of William Lloyd Garrison's *The Liberator*, which continued weekly publication for thirty-four years, until the passage in December 1865 of the Thirteenth Amendment to the Constitution, by which slavery in the United States was abolished forever. Garrison was raised around Calvinist Puritans in Boston, and while he remained generally anti-institutional and anti-Constitutional throughout his career as a reformer and abolitionist, his moral perspective was deeply influenced by the Declaration of Independence, with its emphasis on individualism, and by the ancient doctrine of the Golden Rule. Like the New Testament Jesus, Garrison called not simply for the abolition of slavery but for total social equality for all minorities, and he eschewed pomp and circumstance even when his cause, the abolition of slavery, was triumphant. From the beginning he was determined and intolerant. "I am in earnest—I will not equivocate—I will not excuse—I will not retreat a single inch—AND I WILL BE HEARD," he declared in the first issue of *The Liberator* on 1 January 1831 (quoted in Mott, p. 278).

Even more deeply rooted in specific Puritan doctrines was the abolitionist and reformer John Brown (1800–1859). Brown was the son of an extremely pious, fundamentalist Calvinist Christian, Owen Brown, who was a humble shoemaker and farmer but whose calling in life was to oppose slavery, which he

Harriet Beecher Stowe's Uncle Tom's Cabin *(1852), through its apocalyptic cautionings that culminate in a severe warning on the last page, reflects the Puritanism of the likes of Jonathan Edwards:*

This is an age of the world when nations are trembling and convulsed. A mighty influence is abroad, surging and heaving the world, as with an earthquake. And is America safe? Every nation that carries in its bosom great and unredressed injustice has in it the elements of this last convulsion.

For what is this mighty influence thus rousing in all nations and languages those groanings that cannot be uttered, for man's freedom and equality?

O, Church of Christ, read the signs of the times! Is not this power the spirit of HIM whose kingdom is yet to come, and whose will to be done on earth as it is in heaven?

But who may abide the day of his appearing? "for that day shall burn as an oven: and he shall appear as a swift witness against those that oppress the hireling in his wages, the widow and the fatherless,

and that *turn aside the stranger in his right:* and he shall break in pieces the oppressor."

Are not these dread words for a nation bearing in her bosom so mighty an injustice? Christians! every time that you pray that the kingdom of Christ may come, can you forget that prophecy associates, in dread fellowship, the *day of vengeance* with the year of his redeemed?

A day of grace is yet held out to us. Both North and South have been guilty before God; and the *Christian church* has a heavy account to answer. Not by combining together, to protect injustice and cruelty, and making a common capital of sin, is this Union to be saved,—but by repentance, justice and mercy; for, not surer is the eternal law by which the millstone sinks in the ocean, than that stronger law, by which injustice and cruelty shall bring on nations the wrath of Almighty God!

Stowe, *Uncle Tom's Cabin*, p. 519.

---

saw as a sin against God. John quickly absorbed his father's intolerant fundamentalism and hatred of slavery. As David S. Reynolds observes,

> Intense Calvinism and a republican belief in human rights would combine uniquely in John Brown. He never surrendered the Calvinistic doctrines—predestination, total depravity, God's sovereignty, and so forth—he had learned from his parents. Their religion was not the modified Calvinism of nineteenth-century preachers like Charles Grandison Finney. . . . Instead, it harked back to the orthodox Calvinism of Puritan times. (P. 25)

The Unitarian minister Thomas Wentworth Higginson (1823–1911) observed that

> John Brown is almost the only radical abolitionist I have ever known who was not more or less radical in religious matters also. His theology was Puritan, like his practice; and accustomed as we are now to see Puritan doctrines and Puritan virtues separately exhibited, it seems quite strange to behold them combined in one person again. (Reynolds, p. 27)

Both Brown, who was always dirt poor, and Wendell Phillips (1811–1884), a devout Calvinist and a Harvard-educated Boston Brahmin, stressed their divine callings as emissaries of God in the crusade against slavery.

Where Phillips remained primarily in New England and depended on his superior oratorical skills to convert audiences to the antislavery cause, Brown modeled himself on the archetypal Puritan Oliver Cromwell, whose regime in England (1648–1660) provides English history with the only instance of regicide. In 1648 in Westminster Hall, London, Cromwell's Puritans beheaded King Charles I. For Brown this represented divine sanction for a righteous religious cause even though Cromwell's regime ultimately failed and monarchy was restored in 1660 by Charles II. What emerges from Brown's puritanical denunciation of slavery as a sin against God and humanity, and his murder of proslavery advocates in Kansas and Virginia, is the way that abolitionism, which he also represented, came to be perceived nationwide. In a country beset by sectional division and endless debates about slavery, Garrison's abolitionism and Brown's militant terrorism came to be associated with New England Puritanism's perverse influence in antebellum America. Reynolds says,

In 1863 the Democratic congressman Samuel Cox typically blamed the Civil War on disruptive New England reform movements that he said were rooted in Puritanism. He insisted that fanatical Abolitionism caused the war, and, in his words, "Abolition is the offspring of Puritanism. . . . Puritanism is a reptile which has been boring into the mound, which is the Constitution, and this civil war comes like a devouring sea!" (P. 16)

Southern war songs such as "The Southern Cross" (1861) contain the same sentiment:

> How peaceful and blest was America's soil,
> 'Till betrayed by the guile of the Puritan demon,
> Which lurks under virtue, and springs from its coil,
> To fasten its fangs in the life blood of freemen.
> (Reynolds, p. 16)

Reynolds goes on to say,

> What linked Puritanism with Northern reform [and abolitionism] was its powerful heritage of antinomianism—the breaking of human law in the name of God. Antinomian rebels from Anne Hutchinson onward put divine grace above social codes. In the nineteenth century this spirit fostered a law-flouting individualism that appeared variously in militant Abolitionism, Transcendentalist self-reliance, and the "individual sovereignty" championed by anarchists. (Pp. 16–17)

Thoreau's "Civil Disobedience," Emerson's "Divinity School Address" (1838), Benjamin Franklin's *Autobiography* (1791), and Martin Luther King Jr.'s civil rights movement of the 1960s all sanction obedience to individual conscience over slavish allegiance to immoral human laws. Although the theocracy of seventeenth-century New England was perhaps America's most intolerant society, its legacy to the United States was individualism based on a personal encounter with God in conversion that could not be rescinded by any state or governmental authority.

HARRIET BEECHER STOWE

Equally linked to the Puritan past was Harriet Beecher Stowe (1811–1896), the daughter of Lyman Beecher, a stern Calvinist who was president of Lane Theological Seminary in Cincinnati, Ohio, just across the Ohio River from Kentucky and one of the stops on the Underground Railroad. All six of her brothers were ministers, and she married Calvin Stowe, a minister and professor of biblical literature. Her masterwork, *Uncle Tom's Cabin*, sold more than 300,000 copies in its first year, and by the eve of the Civil War it had sold more than four million copies in the United States alone; thus one in every three persons in the United States in 1860 owned a copy of *Uncle Tom's Cabin*. Its Puritan roots run deep. In chapter 9, Mary Bird, a Bible reading fundamentalist Christian, confronts her U.S. senator husband about his recent vote in favor of the Fugitive Slave Law of 1850. The strength of her argument is entirely biblical. Characterization, plot structure, episodic allegories such as Eva's baptismal rescue from the Mississippi River by Tom and Eliza's crossing the "Jordan" (Ohio) River from slavery to freedom, all are present in this book-length Puritan sermon against slavery.

The rhetoric of New England Puritanism is present throughout Stowe's critique, and its popularity and influence in political and social affairs attest to the significant cultural work that texts often can do. Abraham Lincoln allegedly greeted her at the White House with the remark: "So you are the little lady who started this great big war." Lincoln also observed near the war's end, "I am only an instrument. The Abolitionists and the Union Army have done it all." Because Stowe's work and that of most abolitionists are so immersed in Puritan theology and the sense of a divine mission against slavery, it is clear that the seventeenth-century New England Puritans had a powerful influence not only on the literature of the nineteenth century, but also on its ideology in politics and social policy. The turbulent nineteenth century saw the newly minted United States, just a few decades old, desperately seeking an identity for itself. For all its carnage, the Civil War and the crusade against slavery assisted mightily in this quest, supported by the ideology of New England Puritanism, in all of its contemporary manifestations, from Emersonian self-reliance to John Brown's militant terrorism to Harriet Beecher Stowe's apocalyptic visions for America's future.

See also The Blithedale Romance; Calvinism; "Hawthorne and His Mosses"; The Liberator; Manifest Destiny; Moby-Dick; Protestantism; Religion; The Scarlet Letter; "Self-Reliance"; Transcendentalism; Uncle Tom's Cabin; Unitarianism

BIBLIOGRAPHY
Primary Works
Melville, Herman. *Billy Budd, Sailor (An Inside Narrative)*. 1924. Edited with an introduction by Harrison Hayford and Merton M. Sealts Jr. Chicago: University of Chicago Press, 1962.

O'Sullivan, John. "Annexation." *United States Magazine and Democratic Review* 17, nos. 85–86 (July–August 1845): 5–10.

Stowe, Harriet Beecher. *Uncle Tom's Cabin; or, Life among the Lowly*. 1852. In *Three Novels*, edited by Kathryn Kish Sklar. New York: Library of America, 1982.

Winthrop, John. "A Model of Christian Charity." 1630. In *Pragmatism and Religion,* edited by Stuart Rosenbaum. Urbana, Ill.: University of Illinois Press, 2003.

Secondary Works

Bercovitch, Sacvan. *The Puritan Origins of the American Self.* New Haven, Conn.: Yale University Press, 1975.

Elliott, Emory, ed. *Puritan Influences in American Literature.* Urbana: University of Illinois Press, 1979.

Heimert, Alan. *Religion and the American Mind from the Great Awakening to the Revolution.* Cambridge, Mass.: Harvard University Press, 1966.

Lowance, Mason. *The Language of Canaan: Metaphor and Symbol in New England from the Puritans to the Transcendentalists.* Cambridge, Mass.: Harvard University Press, 1980.

Madsen, Deborah L. *American Exceptionalism.* Jackson: University Press of Mississippi, 1998.

Mott, Frank Luther. "The *Liberator.*" In his *A History of American Magazines,* vol. 2, 1850–1865, pp. 275–296. Cambridge, Mass.: Harvard University Press, 1938.

Reynolds, David S. *John Brown, Abolitionist: The Man Who Killed Slavery, Sparked the Civil War, and Seeded Civil Rights.* New York: Knopf, 2005.

Mason I. Lowance Jr.

QUAKERS

The nineteenth century witnessed significant changes within the Religious Society of Friends (Quakers). Quakerism had arisen amid the tumult and experimentation of the English Revolution of the mid-seventeenth century. One of many radical religious groups of that era, Friends had proclaimed God's availability to each individual through the Inward Christ or the Inner Light, rendering creeds, outward sacraments, and clerical hierarchy unnecessary. Quakers worshiped by gathering in silence until the spirit inspired someone to speak. To the scandal of many in that day, women as well as men felt led to preach in Quaker worship. Early Quaker spirituality embraced both the inward and the outward life: inner purification led to a powerful sense of union with God and with one another, and the victory of good over evil in the soul energized Friends to seek to transform human society. Quaker social ethics emphasized equality, simplicity, integrity, and peace. When decades of persecution persuaded Friends that the rest of the world was not going to join their program, they withdrew into a quieter, settled life of spiritual discipline, tending toward separation from the larger society. William Penn's Holy Experiment in colonial Pennsylvania, however, kept alive the Quaker ideal of a humane political and social order until Friends withdrew from the legislature in the 1750s, when the English crown insisted on a militia. The American Revolution, during which Friends as pacifists maintained neutrality and suffered for it from both sides, pushed Quakers even further into a sectarian existence.

QUAKERS, 1820–1870: THEOLOGICAL DIRECTIONS

By 1820 new winds were blowing. Westward migration to Ohio and Indiana produced new social settings and structures, and the "hedge" that had separated "God's peculiar people" from "the world's people" was successively lowered. Some Quakers began to find common ground with other religious groups on matters of philanthropy or social reform, such as abolition. The evangelical movement was at the forefront of many progressive social issues at that time, and evangelical theology began to influence some Quaker thought.

The attraction to the evangelical movement was also a conscious move away from Quaker traditions of the eighteenth century. Quaker thought in that era is often described as "quietist." The turning inward of Quakers as a group paralleled an inward turning of each individual. Quietist thought built on the earlier Quaker understanding of the Inner Light and held that the only trustworthy religious experience was an inward, direct dependence upon God for guidance. Quietism was suspicious of all human initiative.

Elias Hicks (1748–1830) can represent the quietist position for the nineteenth century, though he himself did not use this term. In his understanding, in order to allow the Inward Christ to work in the soul, the self must abstain from all willing and acting. The animated devotion of evangelicals looked to him like emotional self-indulgence. The appropriate goal of the religious life was instead to lose the self in union with God, to experience annihilation, to become nothing. Evangelicals would find his description of God too impersonal, but to Hicks this did not matter because the aim was selflessness, a state in which there was practically speaking no self left that could be in relationship with a personal God. His views may remind others of the exalted but austere ideals of medieval mystics such as Meister Eckehart or Sufi mystics such as Ibn al-'Arabi.

Hicks was a radical on the issue of slavery. When others suggested that slaves should be purchased from their keepers in order to be set free, he replied that slave owners had no right to additional payment. Not only should they be denied such funds, but they should also be required to set their slaves free and then compensate

The abolitionist and poet John Greenleaf Whittier was the best-known Quaker literary figure of the era. Critics of a later generation regarded as a drawback precisely what was attractive to the audience of Whittier's day: a romantic appreciation of nature, a nostalgia that more recent tastes would consider sentimentality, and the subservience of his poetic craft to his moral passions (especially antislavery). In the early twenty-first century, it is Whittier's religious poetry that remains known in some circles: numerous poems of his are found in hymnals of many denominations. There is a mix of appropriateness and irony in this: his justly revered "Dear Lord and Father of Mankind," found in many hymnals of the evangelical tradition, is drawn from a larger poem, "The Brewing of the Soma," which is sharply critical of the emotional extremes of the evangelical revivals of that era. The verses used as a hymn reflect the gentle quietist element of his Quakerism, as do these lines from "The Meeting."

And so I find it well to come
For deeper rest to this still room,
For here the habit of the soul
Feels less the outer world's control;
The strength of mutual purpose pleads
More earnestly our common needs;
And from the silence multiplied
By these still forms on either side,
The world that time and sense have known
Falls off and leaves us God alone.

Whittier, *The Complete Poetical Works of John Greenleaf Whittier*, p. 446.

them for previous services rendered. Hicks promoted a boycott of slave-produced goods. Yet his radical ethic was also separatist: he did not believe that Quakers should cooperate with other antislavery activists. Such social promiscuity could endanger the purity of God's peculiar people. Some antislavery speakers, for example, were professional clergy, so to work with them could be seen as tacit approval of clergy. Hicks was reluctant to compromise on any issue.

Other Friends found the quietist impulse in Quakerism too confining. The sectarian strain prevented collaboration with other sincere Christians on the pressing social issues of the day. Quietism was inadequate to the needs of the times. Additionally, the lofty severity of quietist inwardness felt like a denial of human emotion as a divinely given gift. Evangelical

piety focused on love, centered in the love of God. The divinity of Jesus demonstrated God's love, and the humanity of Jesus affirmed the human qualities of the individual believer. To evangelicals, the suffering of Christ awakened in the faithful a sympathy that extended to others who are suffering. This sympathy motivated evangelicals to participate in efforts to relieve human suffering, such as the antislavery movement or prison reform.

Among North American Friends, quietists and evangelicals vied for political power within Quakerism, resulting in a schism in 1827–1828, first in Philadelphia and then spreading throughout North American Quakerism. The evangelicals called themselves Orthodox Friends. Their counterparts were the Hicksites, who came to include both quietists and liberals. Liberals valued reason over emotion and questioned the infallibility of the Bible. The progressive mood of the era fostered a desire for freedom from what liberals perceived as narrow dogma. Some quietists, fearing the heresy that they found inherent in liberalism, chose the Orthodox camp over the Hicksite. By mid-century this resulted in further division among the Orthodox, resulting in three major factions: the evangelical Gurneyite Friends who took their name from Joseph John Gurney (1788–1847); the quietist Wilburites whose name derived from John Wilbur (1774–1856); and the increasingly liberal Hicksites named after Elias Hicks. Later, the evangelical revivals of the late 1860s and beyond brought changes to the evangelical Quaker worship, which came to resemble mainstream Protestant worship with hymns, a planned sermon, and a paid pastor. But before those innovations, the divisions among Quakers must have seemed insignificant or imperceptible to the wider world. While it is true that other Protestant denominations in the United States were likewise dividing along the same lines regarding the evangelical movement, both Quaker parties continued to hold on to common Quaker traditions that were not matters of doctrine. Both parties continued the same pattern of worship in silence. Both groups allowed women to preach. Both sides followed the same pattern of plain dress. Both continued opposition to slavery and war.

QUAKERS AND SOCIAL REFORM MOVEMENTS

Quakers in the nineteenth century were perhaps best known for their antislavery work, and among Quaker abolitionists perhaps the best known was Levi Coffin (1798–1877). He had migrated from North Carolina to Indiana, as did many southern Friends, to leave behind the land where slavery was legal and to take up life in territories where it was prohibited. He became a

Dear Lord and Father of mankind,
Forgive our foolish ways!
Reclothe us in our rightful mind,
In purer lives Thy service find,
In deeper reverence, praise.

In simple trust like theirs who heard,
Beside the Syrian sea,
The gracious calling of the Lord,
Let us, like them, without a word,
Rise up and follow Thee.

O Sabbath rest by Galilee!
O calm of hills above,
Where Jesus knelt to share with Thee
The silence of eternity,
Interpreted by love!

With that deep hush subduing all
Our words and works that drown
The tender whisper of Thy call,
As noiseless let Thy blessing fall
As fell Thy manna down.

Drop Thy still dews of quietness,
Till all our strivings cease;
Take from our souls the strain and stress,
And let our ordered lives confess
The beauty of Thy peace.

Breathe through the heats of our desire
Thy coolness and Thy balm;
Let sense be dumb, let flesh retire;
Speak through the earthquake, wind, and fire,
O still, small voice of calm!

Whittier, *The Complete Poetical Works of John Greenleaf Whittier*, p. 450.

the Quaker commitment to equality led to careful reflection on Quaker devotion to moral integrity, when the traditional Quaker practice of honesty could threaten the lives and liberty of the escapees.

Levi Coffin's *Reminiscences* (1876) relates many tales of his work with the Underground Railroad and reveal his considerable skills as a raconteur. Among his stories is an account of his houseguest Eliza Harris, the historical figure who inspired her namesake in Harriet Beecher Stowe's *Uncle Tom's Cabin* (1852) Eliza Harris, escaping from Kentucky, crossed the Ohio River near Ripley on drifting broken ice with her child in her arm. Readers of *Uncle Tom's Cabin* from Levi Coffin's day to the early twenty-first century have speculated that Simeon and Rachel Halliday are Levi and Catherine Coffin in thin disguise. After some twenty years in Newport (now Fountain City), Indiana, where they assisted thousands of refugees from slavery, the Coffins moved to Cincinnati, where they continued in the Underground Railroad. Coffin also became a leader in the free-labor movement. Another form of protest against slavery, this movement bought and sold only goods produced without the exploitation of slaves. After the Civil War, Coffin worked with freed slaves in Arkansas. He traveled to England, where he raised $100,000 to support the work with freedmen.

Other Friends recognized for their antislavery work in this period include the abolitionist Thomas Garrett (1789–1871) and the Grimké sisters Sarah (1792–1873) and Angelina (1805–1879). Some used journalism to promote antislavery work, as did John Greenleaf Whittier (1807–1892), who worked for several newspapers; Benjamin Lundy (1789–1839) in his newspaper the *Genius of Universal Emancipation*; and Elisha Bates (1781–1861), whose *Moral Advocate* also protested against capital punishment and war and promoted temperance and prison reform.

American Quakers engaged in prison reform also included Stephen Grellet (1773–1855)—who made his home in New York but reported to the tsar, the pope, the sultan, and various European monarchs on the sorry conditions of their prisons—and Charles (1823–1916) and Rhoda (1826–1909) Coffin, relatives of Levi. Elizabeth Comstock (1815–1891) promoted prison reform and also worked in the Underground Railroad before the Civil War and with freedman's concerns thereafter as well as temperance and women's equality. Elizabeth Howland (1827–1929) shared these last three concerns.

If a single person can represent the breadth of Quaker commitment to social reform in the nineteenth century, Lucretia Coffin Mott (1793–1880, also related to Levi through common Nantucket

leader in the Underground Railroad, the clandestine movement of escaped slaves on their way to Canada. Coffin's activities were controversial among some Quakers. In earlier days Friends had broken the law— for example, to continue to hold Quaker worship when it was illegal in England—but they had done so publicly, despite the threat of persecution. Now their defiance of the law endangered not themselves but those whom they were attempting to help, so Coffin and others were comfortable acting in secret so as not to endanger the safety of the refugees. Fidelity to

A Dream Caused by Perusal of Mrs. H. Beecher Stowe's Popular Work Uncle Tom's Cabin, 1853. Lithograph by Colin Milne. Milne's anti-abolition cartoon highlights the role of nineteenth-century Quakers in the abolitionist movement: the figure at the center of his nightmarish vision of the world presented in *Uncle Tom's Cabin* is a black man dressed as a Quaker. THE LIBRARY OF CONGRESS

Quaker ancestry) may be the best candidate. A liberal Friend committed to freedom and progress, she acquired her antislavery views early in life. In 1830 she and her husband, James, befriended the renowned abolitionist William Lloyd Garrison. They supported the Anti-Slavery Society in America, though only James could join because women were not admitted into membership. In response, Lucretia Mott and other Quaker women, along with free blacks, formed the Philadelphia Female Anti-Slavery Society.

Mott was not satisfied to call for the end of slavery in the South: she also protested the racism of the North. She defied the segregationist customs of her day, offering hospitality to African Americans in her home and preaching in black churches. Lucretia and James Mott were appointed delegates to the first World Anti-Slavery Convention in London in 1840, but as a woman she was not seated as a delegate but

only invited to sit politely in the ladies' gallery. Quite a stir followed as she and others held for the recognition of women as official delegates. At that conference she befriended the young Elizabeth Cady Stanton. Upon their return to the United States, they committed themselves to laboring for women's rights. The outcome of their (and others') resolve was the conference at Seneca Falls, New York, in 1848 and its famous Declaration of Sentiments, which led the way to the women's suffrage movement. Mott also worked with peace societies, the Nonresistance Society, anti-Sabbath groups, Native American concerns, and on education, including women's medical education. Bold and unshakable in her ethical passions, Mott was nearly pushed out of Quakerism by more conservative voices. She stood her ground, and by her later years Hicksite Friends considered her as their spiritual leader.

QUAKERS IN LITERATURE

Portraits of Quakers in American literature from 1820 to 1870 range from the unsympathetic to the idealized. Nathaniel Hawthorne (1804–1864) was not especially appreciative of seventeenth-century Quakers, but then his literary works do not reveal much appreciation for any religion in that era. In "The Gentle Boy," from *Twice-Told Tales,* Hawthorne describes early Quakerism as "unbridled fanaticism" (1:104) and an "enthusiasm heightened almost to madness" that "abstractly considered, well deserved the moderate chastisement of the rod" (1:86). Yet the Quakers in this tale are chiefly a vehicle for comparison with the cold brutality of the Puritans who persecuted and martyred them. Quakers appear as victims of persecution in *The Scarlet Letter* (chapter 6), and in "Young Goodman Brown" the devil informs the protagonist that Brown's grandfather, who persecuted Quakers, was the devil's partner in so doing. In "Main Street" the narrator suggests a more positive regard, noting that the itinerant Quaker preachers in Salem had "the gift of a new idea" (3:461).

Herman Melville's (1819–1891) *Moby-Dick* includes Quakers, since Nantucket was a whaling as well as a Quaker community. Peleg and Bildad, the ship owners, seem more like caricatures, the former being the Quaker by culture who wears a plain coat but has no real use for religion and the latter a pious but hypocritical tightwad who will not pay Ishmael a decent wage if he can get away with it. Both of them Melville calls "fighting Quakers" (p. 71) who profess pacifism against humans but have no quarrel with the brutal killing of the noble monsters of the deep. Starbuck, the virtuous but cautious first mate, also a Quaker, is courageous enough to face any natural danger and to stand up to Ahab, only to give in ultimately. He ponders but then resists the urge to save the crew by killing Ahab. Melville's point may be that Starbuck's weakness is that, in spite of knowing good from evil, he cannot summon the strength to act decisively. Near the end Starbuck questions the justice of it all if his life of devotion leads only to a watery grave.

Ralph Waldo Emerson (1803–1882) held a genuine appreciation for Quakers, including Lucretia Mott, whom he knew personally. He wrote that much of the best thought of his day had been anticipated by early Friends. In his essay "Natural Religion," Emerson praised Friends for their likeness to the earliest Christians' ideals: "The sect of Quakers in their best representatives appear to me to come nearer to the sublime history and genius of Christ than any other of the sects. They have kept the traditions perhaps for a longer time, kept the early purity" (p. 57).

Walt Whitman (1819–1892), reminiscing some sixty years later, wrote of hearing the resonant preaching of Elias Hicks, whom he admired for his attacks on evangelical doctrines. Whitman appreciated the inwardness of Hicks's thought, which would submit to no outward creed, scripture, or theology of blood atonement. Hicks would have been surprised by some of Whitman's praise: "Always E[lias] H[icks] gives the service of pointing to the fountain of all naked theology, all religion, . . . namely yourself and your inherent relations. . . . This he incessantly labors to kindle, nourish, educate, bring forward and strengthen. He is the most democratic of the religionists" (2:627).

Harriet Beecher Stowe (1811–1896) has numerous Quaker characters in *Uncle Tom's Cabin,* some (as mentioned above) perhaps inspired by Levi and Catherine Coffin. Through them she pictured a religious life without ostentatious self-righteousness or racial bigotry. Her Quakers are idealized, as were Whitman's memories of Elias Hicks, but genuine Quakers would have recognized the ideas as their own.

The only Quaker of literary renown in this period was the poet John Greenleaf Whittier (1807–1892). He was an ardent abolitionist and a friend of William Lloyd Garrison, with whom he faced mob violence from opponents of abolition. Later the two came to differ over the issue of political involvement, when Whittier became an enthusiastic supporter of the antislavery Liberty Party. Whittier once aspired to a life in politics and was elected to the state legislature in Massachusetts, but frail health and his outspoken abolitionist views put an end to his hopes for election to Congress. He worked as an editor for abolitionist newspapers and composed antislavery poems, such a "The Christian Slave," "The Hunters of Men," and "Ichabod," and lived on the edge of poverty until the publication of *Snow-Bound* (1866) and "The Tent on the Beach" (1868) brought him popular fame. These collections of poetry captured the spirit of the age and spoke to the inner needs of a society struggling to recover from the trauma of a civil war. Late in his life he achieved such popularity that his birthday was a school holiday in his native Massachusetts. Whittier was a friend of the poets James Russell Lowell, Henry Wadsworth Longfellow, Oliver Wendell Holmes, and Ralph Waldo Emerson. In his poetry, as in his life, Whittier sought to integrate the inward life of quiet receptivity to the divine presence with a devoted effort to better human society. In this he reflected the ideals of Quakerism.

See also Abolitionist Writing; The Bible; Evangelicals; Feminism; *Moby-Dick;* Reform; Religion; Slavery; Transcendentalism; *Uncle Tom's Cabin;* Underground Railroad

BIBLIOGRAPHY
Primary Works

Coffin, Levi. *Reminiscences of Levi Coffin*. Cincinnati: Robert Clark, 1876.

Emerson, Ralph Waldo. *Uncollected Lectures by Ralph Waldo Emerson; Reports of Lectures on American Life and Natural Religion, Reprinted from the Commonwealth*. Edited by Clarence L. F. Gohdes. New York: W. E. Rudge, 1932.

Hawthorne, Nathaniel. *Complete Works of Nathaniel Hawthorne*. 13 vols. Boston and New York: Houghton Mifflin, 1882–1883.

Melville, Herman. *Moby-Dick; or, The Whale*. 1851. New York: Norton, 1967.

Mott, Lucretia. *Lucretia Mott: Her Complete Speeches and Sermons*. Edited by Dana Greene. New York: Edward Mellen Press, 1980.

Whitman, Walt. *Walt Whitman: Prose Works 1892*. 2 vols. Edited by Floyd Stovall. New York: New York University Press, 1964.

Whittier, John Greenleaf. *The Complete Poetical Works of John Greenleaf Whittier*. Edited by Horace E. Scudder. Boston and New York: Houghton Mifflin, 1894.

Secondary Works

Bacon, Margaret Hope. *Valiant Friend: The Life of Lucretia Mott*. New York: Walker, 1980.

Barbour, Hugh, and J. William Frost. *The Quakers*. Richmond, Ind.: Friends United Press, 1994.

Hamm, Thomas D. *The Transformation of American Quakerism: Orthodox Friends, 1800–1907*. Bloomington: Indiana University Press, 1988.

Ingle, H. Larry. *Quakers in Conflict: The Hicksite Reformation*. Knoxville: University of Tennessee Press, 1986.

Jones, Rufus M. *Later Periods of Quakerism*. 2 vols. London: Macmillan, 1921.

Michael L. Birkel